## Prefectures of Japan

1 Hokkaido
2 Aomori
3 Iwate
4 Miyagi
5 Akita
6 Yamagata
7 Fukushima
8 Ibaraki
9 Tochigi
10 Gunma
11 Saitama
12 Chiba
13 Tokyo
14 Kanagawa
15 Niigata
16 Toyama
17 Ishikawa
18 Fukui
19 Yamanashi
20 Nagano
21 Gifu
22 Shizuoka
23 Aichi
24 Mie
25 Shiga
26 Kyoto
27 Osaka
28 Hyogo
29 Nara
30 Wakayama
31 Tottori
32 Shimane
33 Okayama
34 Hiroshima
35 Yamaguchi
36 Tokushima
37 Kagawa
38 Ehime
39 Kochi
40 Fukuoka
41 Saga
42 Nagasaki
43 Kumamoto
44 Oita
45 Miyazaki
46 Kagoshima
47 Okinawa

*Hokkaido*
**Sapporo**
*Tohoku*
**Sendai**
*Chubu*
**Tokyo**
**Yokohama**
*Kanto*
*Chugoku*
**Kyoto**
**Nagoya**
**Kobe**
**Osaka**
**Hiroshima**
*Kansai (Kinki)*
**Fukuoka**
*Shikoku*
*Kyushu*

0 100 200km

Design and cartography: Ralph Lützeler

# The Demographic Challenge: A Handbook about Japan

# The Demographic Challenge: A Handbook about Japan

*Edited by*

Florian Coulmas, Harald Conrad,
Annette Schad-Seifert and Gabriele Vogt

BRILL

LEIDEN • BOSTON
2008

This book is printed on acid-free paper.

Library of Congress Cataloging-in-Publication Data

The demographic challenge : a handbook about Japan / edited by Florian Coulmas…[et al.].
p. cm.
Includes index.
ISBN 978-90-04-15477-3 (hardback : alk. paper) 1. Population aging—Japan. 2. Japan—Population. 3. Demographic transition—Japan. 4. Population aging—Government policy—Japan. I. Coulmas, Florian.
HQ1064.J3D45 2008
304.6'20952—dc22

2008006516

ISBN 978 90 04 15477 3



PRINTED IN THE NETHERLANDS

To Marga Dinkel,
as a token of our appreciation for
twenty years of unflagging service to
Japanese Studies

# CONTENTS

Acknowledgements ..... xiii
General Introduction ..... xv

PART I

FUNDAMENTALS OF JAPANESE DEMOGRAPHICS

Introduction ..... 3
CASE IN POINT: THE LAST JAPANESE
1. Japan's Population Growth during the Past 100 Years ..... 5
   Makoto Atoh
2. Fertility and Mortality ..... 25
   Hans Dieter Ölschleger
3. Statistical Foundations of Population Projections ..... 41
   Ryuichi Kaneko
4. Regional Demographics ..... 61
   Ralph Lützeler
5. Demographic Comparisons with Other Countries with the Emphasis on the More Developed Regions ..... 81
   Shigemi Kono
6. History of Demography in Japan ..... 97
   Matthias Koch

PART II

SOCIAL ASPECTS OF DEMOGRAPHIC CHANGE

Introduction ..... 121
CASE IN POINT: PARENTAL LEAVE: WOMEN AND MEN
7. Social Ageing and the Sociology of Ageing ..... 125
   Sepp Linhart
8. Changing Social Concepts of Age: Towards the Active Senior Citizen ..... 145
   Takeo Ogawa

9. Ageing Society and the Transformation of Work in the Post-Fordist Economy ..................................................... 163
Chikako Usui
10. Engaging the Generations: Age-Integrated Facilities ......... 179
Leng Leng Thang
11. Social Change and Caregiving of the Elderly .................... 201
Susan Orpett Long
12. Income Inequality in the Ageing Society ............................ 217
Sawako Shirahase
13. Changes in Family Structure ............................................. 235
Toshiko Himeoka

Case in Point: Time Spent with Children

14. Changing Family Life Cycle and Partnership Transition—Gender Roles and Marriage Patterns ............. 255
James M. Raymo and Miho Iwasawa
15. Child Care in a Low Birth Society .................................... 277
Akiko S. Oishi
16. Transcultural Society .......................................................... 293
Stephen Murphy-Shigematsu and David Blake Willis

PART III

Cultural Aspects of Demographic Change

Introduction .......................................................................... 319
17. Traditional Concepts and Images of Old Age in Japan .... 323
Susanne Formanek
18. Notions of Life, Old Age and Death in Ageing Japan ...... 345
Mayumi Sekizawa
19. Population Decline, Municipal Amalgamation, and the Politics of Folk Performance Preservation in Northeast Japan .............................................................................. 361
Christopher S. Thompson
20. Ancestors, Burial Rites, and Rural Depopulation in Japan 387
John W. Traphagan
21. Religion in Post-World War II Japan and Social Ageing ... 397
Kenji Ishii
22. Coming of Age: The Courts and Equality Rights in Japan's Ageing Society ........................................................ 417
Craig Martin

23. Coming to Terms with Age: Some Linguistic Consequences of Population Ageing ..... 455
Peter Backhaus
24. Population Ageing and Language Change ..... 473
Fumio Inoue
25. Age and Ageing in Contemporary Japanese Literature ..... 491
Lisette Gebhardt
26. Media Use in the Ageing Society ..... 513
Nobuko Shiraishi
27. Gendered Age ..... 531
Sumiko Iwao
Case in Point: A Pet Culture in the Making
28. Education in the Aged Society: The Demographic Challenge to Japanese Education ..... 547
Roger Goodman
29. Ageing Japan and the Transmission of Traditional Skills and Know-How ..... 561
Takanori Shintani
30. Age-specific Technology: A Demographic Challenge for Design ..... 571
Fumihiko Satofuka
31. Ageing Tourists, Ageing Destinations: Tourism and Demographic Change in Japan ..... 579
Carolin Funck
32. Pastimes ..... 599
John Clammer
33. Sports and Demographic Change in Japan ..... 613
Wolfram Manzenreiter

PART IV

Political Aspects of Demographic Change

Introduction ..... 635
34. Demographics and the State ..... 639
Leonard Schoppa
35. Politics of Old-Age Policy-Making ..... 653
John Creighton Campbell
36. Political Parties in an Ageing Society ..... 667
Paul Talcott

37. Civil Society Roles in Elderly Care: A Non-profit Organization Census ........... 689
David M. Potter
38. Neighbourhood Associations and the Demographic Challenge ........... 707
Robert Pekkanen and Yutaka Tsujinaka
39. "Induced" Voluntarism: A New Role for Schools? ........... 721
Akihiro Ogawa
CASE IN POINT: AGE STRUCTURE OF VOLUNTEERS
40. Educational Policy: Framework and Challenges ........... 733
Susanne Kreitz-Sandberg
41. Family Policy: Framework and Challenges ........... 749
Liv Coleman
42. Immigration Policy: Framework and Challenges ........... 765
Glenda S. Roberts
43. Infrastructural Policy: Framework and Challenges ........... 781
Thomas Feldhoff
44. Postal Privatization and its Implications for the Ageing Society ........... 799
Patricia L. Maclachlan

PART V

ECONOMIC AND SOCIAL SECURITY ASPECTS OF DEMOGRAPHIC CHANGE

Introduction ........... 817
CASE IN POINT: "SILVER" CUSTOMERS: JAPAN'S CENTENARIANS 1963–2005
45. Population Ageing and Economic Growth: The Role of Two Demographic Dividends in Japan ........... 821
Naohiro Ogawa
46. Macroeconomic Impact and Public Finance Perspectives of the Ageing Society ........... 841
Akihiro Kawase and Seiritsu Ogura
47. The Impact of the Ageing Society on Regional Economies ........... 861
Volker Elis
48. A Survey of Household Saving Behaviour ........... 879
Charles Yuji Horioka

49. The Ageing Society and Economic Inequality .................. 899
Fumio Ohtake
50. Poverty Among the Elderly .................................................. 921
Hisashi Fukawa
51. Economic Factors in the Declining Birth Rate .................. 933
Naohiro Yashiro
52. Labour Market and Labour Market Policies for the Ageing Society .................................................................... 947
Hendrik Meyer-Ohle
53. Gender Dimensions of the Ageing Workforce .................... 963
Karen A. Shire
54. Human Resource Management Practices and the Ageing Workforce .............................................................. 979
Harald Conrad
55. The Impact of the Ageing Society on Consumer Behaviour and Consumer Markets .................................... 999
Hidehiko Sekizawa
Case in Point: A Ward that Takes Pride in Being Traffic Safe for the Elderly
56. The Ageing Society and Reactions of the Automobile Industry – a Case Study
Andreas Moerke ............................................................... 1017
57. Ageing and the Social Security System ........................... 1033
Ito Peng
58. Providing Care for the Ageing Society ............................ 1049
Naoki Ikegami
59. Guardianship for Adults ................................................... 1065
Makoto Arai
60. The Public Health-Care System – a Financial Perspective ...................................................................... 1077
Tetsuo Fukawa
61. The Public Pension System and the Ageing Society ........ 1097
Takashi Oshio
62. The Search for More Equitable Pensions Between Generations ..................................................................... 1115
Noriyuki Takayama
63. The Restructuring of the Corporate Pension System ...... 1135
Tomoyuki Kubo

List of contributors ........................................................ 1151
Index of authors cited ........................................................ 1155
Index of subjects ........................................................ 1169

## ACKNOWLEDGEMENTS

This *Handbook* is the result of collective labour and has benefited from the hard work of many. First of all, we would like to express our gratitude to the large number of colleagues who have contributed to this volume. In spite of their tight schedules and numerous obligations they agreed to cooperate in this endeavour responding with alacrity and professionalism to all the requests that have been made of them in the process of editing their papers and joining them together to form a book. This book draws on the expertise of scholars in various fields and covers a wide canvas, because the subject matter it is concerned with has many aspects that interact with each other. With their contributions the authors have turned this *Handbook* into a comprehensive picture of the multifaceted process of demographic change in contemporary Japan.

In planning this volume we have relied on the generous advice and recommendations of many of the authors with whom we had stimulating discussions and an extensive correspondence. Two of them are deserving of special thanks, as they supported this project with constructive criticism and helpful suggestions from the very beginning, Makoto Atoh and John Campbell.

We would also like to acknowledge that the National Institute of Population and Social Security Research has been an invaluable source of information as well as encouragement for this project.

On the technical side we were assisted by Stanislaw Eberlein who with expert knowledge and great care compiled the index and helped with editing and proofreading, as did Tessa Carroll and Julia Lange. A couple of the chapters were skillfully translated from Japanese and German, respectively by Melek Ortabasi and Charles De Wolf. Anita Roodnat-Opdam, our desk editor, and Ingeborg van der Laan, Brill's social sciences editor, were patient and a pleasure to work with. Our profound thanks are due to all of them.

F.C., H.C., A.S., G.V.

## ACKNOWLEDGEMENTS

# GENERAL INTRODUCTION

Social ageing is one of the great challenges confronting Japan today. It is a challenge not just because of Japan's high life expectancy, or because of the low birth rate. Japan shares these demographic characteristics in some measure with other ageing societies, notably in Europe. Rather it is a challenge because Japan's demographic transition—the concurrent decline of mortality and fertility—occurred at a faster pace than elsewhere. Consequently, a need arose for accelerated adjustments in the formation and reproduction of Japanese institutional dynamics in all arenas of public and private life. The economy, the social system, public administration, health care and social security, government and politics, education, family structure, living arrangements, ethical principles and cultural production are all affected in one way or another by the demographic shifts that have led within a couple of generations' time from rapid population increase to depopulation. Japan's population started shrinking in 2005, and all projections point toward continuing decline until mid-century at least.

In Japan as in other advanced countries this happens as a result and concomitant of a very high standard of living, in the absence of famine, war or epidemics, and at a time of rapid technological innovation. Evidently, in advanced industrial societies the price of affluence seems to be dwindling birth rates and the resultant population ageing, but none of the social or economic sciences by themselves offer a theoretical foundation sufficiently broad to account for this development. Interdisciplinary cooperation is essential.

This *Handbook* offers documentation and analysis of the impact of population developments on present-day Japan in its full breadth and multifacettedness as well as of the various ways in which the Japanese as a nation respond to the challenges of population ageing. Over the past several decades a great deal has been uncovered about the causes and consequences of demographic change. Much of the knowledge that has been gained is confined to specialist circles not readily available to outsiders. By adopting an issue-centred approach, this *Handbook* is intended to stimulate discussion across disciplinary boundaries. It provides an up-to-date representation of knowledge on ageing and fertility decline in Japan. There are universal trends in population development, but these trends are subject to modulation by the contingencies of state formation, economic advancement and cultural tradition. It is through comparisons and in-depth studies of individual countries that it becomes possible to distinguish the universal from the particular. As the first non-Western country to industrialise and to go through the demographic transition, Japan continues to be a case of particular interest. This *Handbook* thus serves a double purpose. (1) It presents relevant issues—e.g., age, gender, fertility, family size, care for the elderly, decline of the labour force—in the light of a variety of theories and methods, thus contributing to cross-fertilising discussions. (2) It provides an exhaustive description of Japan's demographic change and its implications in a way that reveals both the commonalities Japan shares with other advanced industrialised countries and the differences that set it apart.

Ever since the Meiji period (1868–1912), Japan has been leading East Asia in industrial, economic and social development. It has also been ahead of other countries in the region with regard to population ageing and although in recent years fertility has declined in the Chinese polities and South Korea even more rapidly, Japan promises to be the oldest country for decades to come. Not only that, in terms of healthy life expectancy gains and total fertility rate decline Japan is at the forefront of population developments throughout the world. This implies among other things that it is more urgent for Japan than for most countries to find solutions for the ensuing problems and that Japan has to develop its own answers to meet the social and economic challenges of ageing rather than follow tested models of other countries. In many ways, Japan is charting out unknown territory of the hyperaged society and as a pioneer thus becomes a reference point for others headed in the same direction. This is not to say that Japan anticipates the problems of other countries or that the solutions developed in Japan can be adopted one-to-one by other countries. Yet, the various experiences of Japan's demographic challenges afford a valuable datum plane for others, especially because Japan must be expected to stay ahead of worldwide trends for some time.

## The Multidimensionality of Demographic Change

As is apparent from the wide range of topics discussed in the *Handbook*, few arenas of the Japanese polity remain untouched by the changes that are caused by and come along with Japan's transformation into a hyperaged society. Thanks to extensive media coverage as well as an abundance of polls and scientific research the Japanese are keenly aware of population issues many of them being immediately affected in one way or another. While not all of the adjustments Japan is currently undergoing can be attributed to population dynamics, it is clear that, in combination, fertility decline, life expectancy gains and depopulation are powerful forces affecting Japan as a society and, in the long run, as a nation and its position in the world. Drawing on the expertise of specialists in various disciplines, this book presents a comprehensive view of Japan's demographic challenge. It reflects our conviction that the significance of many of the changes that happen in one arena can be better appreciated if they are put into perspective with those in others. Interconnections are many and sometimes quite unexpected. For example, effects of below-replacement-level birth rates range from tax yield and the public pension system to family size and intergenerational relations, socialisation patterns, the education system, ethical maxims and legal norms. The shrinking labour force poses problems for personnel management, but also for immigration policy, social cohesion and equality rights. Fiscal sustainability of social services is a political issue which, however, has economic ramifications. Living arrangements affect social network formation but also relate to cultural issues such as filial piety. Caring for the elderly is a social responsibility concerning the division of labour between the sexes and generations. At the same time, it is a political question in as much as decisions must be taken about funding the costs of providing care. The increases in the share of national income that goes toward funding pensions, medical care and other welfare expenses is an important economic variable. The status, prestige and treatment of the elderly are grounded in the social structure, but have cultural characteristics, too. Population ageing causes gradual changes of conceptions of age with many social implications which are in turn reflected in language and literature.

This *Handbook* offers the opportunity to consider the changes associated with demographic ageing from a variety of viewpoints and to uncover the interconnectedness of social, economic, political and cultural occurrences that relate to Japan's changing population structure. While our emphasis is on empirical issues, discussions of how the society reacts to population developments conceptually, ideologically, by formulating policies and developing new legal norms also have a place in the *Handbook*. Since social ageing on the scale witnessed in contemporary

Japan is unprecedented, it presents a challenge not only to society, but also to our understanding of how humanity shapes its own progress. New ideas, hypotheses and theories are called for and research into entirely new fields. With this in mind, the contributors to the *Handbook* have been chosen among Japanese and international scholars to strike a balance between the descriptive and theoretical demands of coming to grips with the phenomenon of population ageing.

## Structure of the Handbook

Research on population ageing is diverse, because ageing concerns the whole human being, both as an individual endowed with a mind and a body and as part of a collective of economic and political actors engaging in social interactions and negotiating cultural patterns of their everyday life and their conceptual universe. To do justice to this complexity, we have partitioned the *Handbook* into five parts dealing, respectively, with demographic fundamentals, social aspects, cultural aspects, political aspects, economic aspects and social security aspects of the demographic challenge, in this order. Each part begins with a short introduction of its own, setting out the boundaries of the field and the principal concern it has with population issues.

Part I offers an introduction to major population issues to the non-specialist. Japan's population dynamics are situated in time and space and in comparison with other developed countries. Basic theoretical concepts of demographic research, notably fertility and mortality, and the statistical foundations of population projections are examined, the history and present state of population studies in Japan are described. Part II addresses issues of conceptualising ageing and age, both in scholarly and popular discourse. The major social dimensions of demographic change, notably family and gender issues as well as social and economic inequality are also addressed, as are the social transformation of work and migration. Part III details the cultural responses to ageing and low fertility examining cultural institutions, on one hand, and cultural activities and productions, on the other. Part IV deals with the question of how political actors address Japan's population ageing. The structures of the policy-making process and specific challenges in certain policy areas are of equal interest. Part V focuses on macro- and microeconomic implications, business and management aspects and the impact of ageing on the social security system.

This *Handbook* is about Japan, the country that has attracted more scientific observation than any other outside the Western world. Our invitations went to scholars with recognized expertise. The diversity of authors of the 63 chapters reflects this wide-ranging interest, 19 women and 48 men, 31 Japanese and 36 from 6 other nations, 39 living in Japan and 28 abroad. The view from within and the view from outside are both represented. We thus hope to make the *Handbook* serviceable to an international readership seeking information about specific aspects of Japan's demographic change or an all-embracing picture.

F.C., H.C., A.S., G.V., Tokyo, December 2007

PART ONE

# FUNDAMENTALS OF JAPANESE DEMOGRAPHICS

# INTRODUCTION

Interest in populations is probably as old as government, but the scientific study of demographic events is of relatively recent origin. It was first developed in Europe. For a number of historical reasons, especially Japan's rapid industrialisation as of the mid nineteenth century, the ensuing population growth, and the advent of the hyperaged society in recent years, the Japanese population has become the object of intensive research. This part of the *Handbook* offers an introduction to the Japanese population and the foundations of Japanese demographics with basic information on the present state of knowledge. The six chapters of this introductory part address the most fundamental demographic issues without presupposing much technical expertise.

First, Atoh provides an overview of Japan's modern population history since the beginning of the twentieth century demonstrating how the population grew and how its structure changed. In the next chapter Ölschleger explains the vital events that are of greatest significance to demographic research, births and deaths, and discusses the notions of fertility and mortality as well as the techniques of gathering and measuring quantitative data about theses population variables. Clearly defined notions of demographic events and knowledge of past developments are essential for a proper understanding of the present population situation. However, to the extent that population statistics are sought for purposes of state, such as, policy planning, taxation, healthcare, education, etc., demographic research is also expected to elucidate future trends. The methods employed to produce population projections are outlined in Kaneko's chapter which, using the 2006 projection prepared by the National Institute of Population and Social Security Research as an example, furthermore explains the function of population projections, what they are and aren't. Populations have a temporal extension from past to future and a spatial one across a defined territory, both requiring specific theories and methods of investigation. The distribution and movement of people across the Japanese territory is the subject matter of Lützeler's chapter. It sketches out the most notable regional differences in fertility and mortality patterns and shows how population events such as overcrowding and depopulation can be studied. As pointed out above, certain aspects of Japanese population events, especially ageing and fertility decline have attracted much attention. In order properly to appreciate these trends, international comparisons are indispensable. Kono thus puts Japan's demographic situation in perspective, comparing it with other highly developed regions of the world and pointing out some of the implications of comparisons of this sort with regard to future developments. While Japan was a latecomer to the scientific study of population the demand for reliable statistics for official purposes arose as suddenly as the Meiji government embarked on a modernization course. To round off this section of the *Handbook*, Koch provides a brief history of demography in Japan demonstrating how closely the interest in population studies is linked to the requirements of the modern state.

F.C.

Case in point: The last Japanese

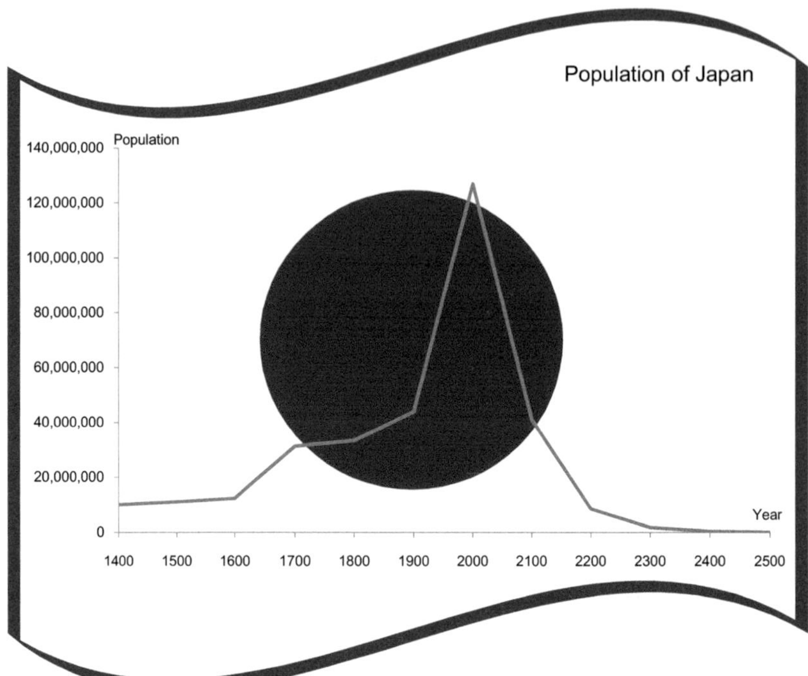


| Year | Population |
|---|---|
| 1400 | 10,000,000 |
| 1500 | 11,000,000 |
| 1600 | 12,270,000 |
| 1700 | 31,280,000 |
| 1800 | 33,300,000 |
| 1900 | 43,847,000 |
| 2000 | 126,926,000 |
| 2100 | 41,094,970 |
| 2200 | 8,520,301 |
| 2300 | 1,765,454 |
| 2400 | 365,757 |
| 2500 | 75,777 |
| 2600 | 15,700 |
| 2700 | 3,253 |
| 2800 | 674 |
| 2900 | 140 |
| 3000 | 29 |
| 3100 | 6 |
| 3200 | 1 |
| 3300 | 0 |

If present trends continue, the Japanese population will be decimated to a third of its 2005 level just a hundred years later. It will take a bit more time for the last Japanese to take her leave from this world, but the impending changes of population size and structure will soon require adjustments as the median age of the shrinking electorate rises unabatedly.

Source: Asahi Shinbun January 3rd, 2006 and
National Institute of Population and Social Security Research

CHAPTER ONE

# JAPAN'S POPULATION GROWTH DURING THE PAST 100 YEARS

Makoto Atoh

## 1. Introduction

Japan's population has changed dramatically as of the last quarter of the nineteenth century when a centralized (Meiji) government was established and economic development and the modernization process started, through the short-term turbulent period of World War II in the mid-twentieth century, to the beginning of the twenty-first century. This population change during the past 135 years can be described generally as demographic transition. The Japanese population, starting from the stage of its stagnation due to both high birth and high death rates in the pre-modern (Tokugawa) period, continued to increase during the stage of high birth and low death rates, and finally ceased to increase due to both low birth and low death rates. It can also be described economically as the process in which Japanese people have come to enjoy an affluent life because economic growth has on average outpaced population growth.

In this chapter, the period of population change during the past 135 years is divided into four demographically distinctive eras, which will be discussed consecutively in the following sections. They are: (1) the period between 1870 and 1945, here called the first stage of demographic transition, (2) the period between 1945 and around 1960, the second stage of demographic transition, (3) the period between around 1960 and the mid-1970s, the era of 'population bonus' (see below p. 13), and (4) the period after the mid-1970s, the era of declining fertility to below replacement level.

## 2. The First Stage of Demographic Transition

According to the population data available at the Meiji Restoration in 1868, after the beginning of the modernization process,[1] the Japanese population increased by 39.62 million in 72 years, from 34.81 million in 1872 to 74.43 million in 1944, giving an average annual rate of population growth (RPG) of 1.1 per cent. But looking at this trend in detail, it is seen that the RPG was about 0.5 per cent around 1870, increased thereafter, and reached about 1.5 per cent in the first half of the 1930s (KSJK 2007).

The gradually accelerating population growth between 1870 and 1920 is estimated to have been brought about by both a gradual increase in the crude birth rate (CBR) and a gradual decrease in the crude death rate (CDR) (Okazaki 1986). On the other hand, the similar population growth for the period between 1920 and 1945 was caused by the fact that the CDR declined more conspicuously than the CBR, which also started to decrease in this period.

### (1) *Declining trend in mortality*

Let us examine the long-term trend in mortality decline between 1870 and 1940. According to Okazaki's estimation, the CDR declined from 27 per thousand to 17 per thousand during this 70–year period, and life expectancy at birth increased from 32 years to 47 years for men and from 35 years to 50 years for women (Okazaki 1986; Mizushima 1962). The improvement of the survival rate was mainly caused by the increase in the survival rate for infants and children. The infant mortality rate declined from about 250 to 90 per 1,000 births during the same period.[2] An analytical study which decomposed the gain in life expectancy at birth into the contributions of the decline in age-specific

---

[1] The Meiji Government enacted in 1871 the *koseki* [Family Registration System]—law, by which every person was counted and registered under *honseki* [one's legal domicile under his or her family name], and released population data based on this law in 1872. Since then, population data based on *honseki*, adjusted by the registration of births and deaths every year, was released every year up to 1920, when the first modern population census was undertaken. Since 1920, the census has been consecutively carried out every five years except 1945 up to 2005.

[2] The most recent effort to estimate mortality trends between 1872 and 1925 reveals that mortality declined modestly up to around 1900 but increased until 1920 (Takase 1991).

death rates between 1891–98 and 1947 showed that the proportion of the gain in life expectancy at birth due to the decline in mortality for children under five was 68 per cent for men and 60 per cent for women (KSJK 2007).

Since the main causes of deaths in prewar years were infectious diseases, the gain in life expectancy at birth was by and large brought about by the decline in infant and child mortality due to infectious diseases, such as pneumonia, bronchitis and diarrhoea. On the other hand, mortality due to tuberculosis is estimated to have risen somewhat among young people in accordance with the increase in people living in densely inhabited cities that accompanied the process of industrialization and urbanization.[3] It should be noted, however, that, in contrast to other developed countries and currently developing countries, strokes were among the top three causes of death even in this period when infectious diseases dominated mortality in Japan (KSJK 2007).

Although the background factors to the prewar decline in mortality have not been fully explored, it was probably caused by a combination of factors, such as the improvement of nutrition, the development of public health, and the prevalence of better hygiene and health behaviour, which were related to economic development and the government's efforts (Takase 1991; Itoh 1998).

### (2) *Changes in fertility and families*

What are the causes of the probable rise in fertility in the period between 1870 and 1920? Fertility in the currently developing countries has very often increased temporarily because the period of post-partum amenorrhoea shrank owing to the replacement of lactation with bottled milk in their modernization process (Bongaarts and Potter 1983), but there seems to have been little change in lactation customs in prewar Japan. One important factor is the presumed rise in fertility due to the gradual improvement of under-enumeration that was brought about by the more strict application of the registration of births and deaths by the government after legally banning *mabiki* [infanticide]. Other factors

---

[3] In pre-industrial Japan, mortality in urban areas was usually higher than in rural areas because of the difference in population density (Hayami 1997). Such regional patterns in mortality lasted up until the late 1930s, when urban mortality became lower than rural mortality thanks to the improvement of public health in urban areas (Takahashi 1993).

are the rise in fecundity due to the improvement of nutrition, and the decrease in induced abortion (*datai*) owing to the enactment of a law penalizing it in 1880.

On the other hand, it is statistically confirmed that fertility declined gradually between 1920 and 1940 mainly because of the postponement of marriage. According to decomposition analysis, about 60 to 70 per cent of the decline in the total fertility rate (TFR) is explained by the decline in the proportion of women in the reproductive ages who were married and the rest by the decline in marital fertility (Otani 1993). The singulate mean age at marriage (SMAM) increased from 24.9 to 27.6 years for men and from 21.1 to 23.6 years for women between 1920 and 1940[4] (Atoh 1982). This general trend of rising marriage age is thought to have been brought about by the industrialization and urbanization of Japanese society. In this period, the proportion of workers engaged in the secondary and tertiary industries increased from 46.2 per cent to 55.7 per cent, and that of residents living in urban areas increased from 18.0 per cent to 37.7 per cent (KSJK 2007). In contrast with the changes in nuptiality, marital fertility remained relatively stable more or less at the level of natural fertility (Atoh 1982). Although the idea and the practice of family limitation may have started to spread among some social strata in this period, it is clear that the TFR declined from 5.1 to 4.1 between 1925 and 1940 mainly due to the postponement of marriage. We could call the fertility decline in prewar years "Malthusian transition".

According to the tables compiled from the 1950 population census of the number of children ever born by ever-married women's age groups, completed fertility remained relatively stable at around 5 births per ever-married woman from the pre-1890 birth cohorts to the 1901–05 birth cohorts (Atoh 1981). The distribution of ever-married women by parity showed that there was great variance, as shown in the fact that about 10 per cent of ever-married women were childless and just under 50 per cent of them had six or more births. Even if there was little change in the number of children ever born per completed family, its

[4] Since the date of marriage registration used to be later than the beginning of de facto marriage in prewar years and the difference between the two tended to shrink, prewar trends in the mean age at first marriage based on vital statistics do not reflect real trends (Okazaki 1950). SMAM is calculated based on the data on the proportions by age of the population who had never married (reflecting de facto marriage), which can be derived from population censuses since 1920.

average number of living children should have increased in accordance with the increase in the survival rate of children.[5] The increase of the average number of children must also have contributed to the scant enlargement of the average household size, from 5.0 to 5.1 persons, recorded between 1920 and 1940 (KSJK 2007).

## 3. The Second Stage of Demographic Transition: the Fifteen Years After World War II

World War II interrupted Japanese economic development. While economic production was decimated from its prewar level by the war, Japan resumed development efforts under the General Headquarters (GHQ) of the Occupied Army and recovered the prewar level of economic production by the mid-1950s. Politically, the new Constitution was enacted, according to which, people had sovereignty to govern and the principle of gender equality and the freedom to express opinions and beliefs of individuals were secured. The new Civil Code also abolished the *i.e.* (patriarchal family) system, and the nuclear family became its model. In addition, the dissolution of the *zaibatsu* [dominant giant financial and industrial corporate groups], heavy taxation for people with large assets and properties, agricultural reform, and three Acts concerning workers' rights, all of which were ordered by GHQ, contributed to the equalization of assets and income among the Japanese people. This great transformation of political, economic and social structures seems to have liberated among the masses aspirations for upward mobility that had been suppressed by the inflexibly unequal social structure in prewar years, and to have contributed to rapid economic growth thereafter.

Demographically, the fifteen years just after World War II were an important turning-point in modern Japan, despite being a relatively short period. This is because Japan substantively completed both fertility transition and epidemiological transition in this period, decelerated its population increase and started population ageing.

[5] While, for the 1890 female birth cohort, 3.0 out of 5 children reached 20 years old, 3.7 came to survive up to this age for the birth cohort of the 1930s (Nanjo and Yoshinaga 2002).

### (1) *The completion of fertility transition*

World War II had a direct and short-term effect on population in Japan: in 1945, when the war ended, population fell for the first time in modern Japan, because of the decrease in births as well as the critical increase in deaths of newborn babies. In 1947 to 1949, however, the TFR jumped up to around 4.4, higher than the lowest level recorded in prewar years, and the annual number of births was recorded as 2.7 million each year. This post-war baby-boom was caused by the recovery of marriage and childbearing when a large number of young and middle-aged men were repatriated from abroad. But just after the baby-boom, both the TFR and the annual number of births decreased precipitously, reaching 2.0 and 1.6 million respectively in 1957.

The post-war dramatic fertility decline in the 1950s can be seen as the second stage of fertility transition, which began around 1920. As previously described, the first stage of fertility transition was gradual mainly because of the postponement of marriage, but the change in the second stage was rapid, mainly due to the decline in marital fertility through the spread of fertility control behaviour among married couples (Muramatsu 1994). The average number of children ever born for completed families decreased rapidly from around 5.0 for the female pre-1905 birth cohort to 2.3 for the 1925–29 birth cohorts (Atoh 1981). In contrast with "Malthusian transition" in the first stage, therefore, fertility transition in this second stage could be called "neo-Malthusian transition".

How could such rapid fertility transition be possible in this period? From the viewpoint of proximate determinants of fertility, the substantive liberalization of induced abortion through the enactment of the Eugenics Protection Law in 1948 and its several subsequent revisions were critical (Muramatsu 1994). Before contraceptive behaviour became widespread, the control of unwanted births was made possible by abortion, and for a short while family limitation prevailed among married couples. At the same time contraception started to spread, thanks to the cooperative efforts of various NGOs, large firms, local communities and the government, and it is estimated that the effect of regulating fertility by contraception surpassed that of induced abortion by around 1960 (Aoki 1967; Tsuya 1994). Although the contraceptive usage rate increased from about 40 per cent around 1960 to about 60 per cent among married couples around 1970, it has remained more or less at the same level up to now. This is because a fertility control pattern where contraceptive failure was backed up by induced abortion to achieve desired fertility was consolidated in this period among married couples (Atoh 1982).

But why did family limitation spread so fast in this period? There seem to be at least two main reasons. First, the process of modernization—including industrialization, urbanization, the establishment of compulsory primary education, and the decline in infant and child mortality—may have nurtured the motives for family limitation already in prewar years. Since the government in the prewar years regarded children as precious human resources for families as well as the nation, however, abortion was illegal, and birth control movements were suppressed. Therefore, the availability of effective measures of fertility control was strictly limited, and family limitation among married couples could not acquire societal legitimacy. The liberalization of induced abortion and birth control movements supported by the government made family limitation legitimate among married couples and provided people with effective methods for it.[6]

Second, the social and economic system changed dramatically after the war. The Japanese people faced starvation just after the war and they continued to feel relative deprivation because they experienced lower levels of living than in the prewar period, at least up to the mid-1950s, due to the collapse of the economic system. Such economic hardship possibly became an additional factor in family limitation. Also, the democratization policies promoted by GHQ, as mentioned above, were conducive to supporting the motivation to improve levels of living among farmers and workers. Furthermore, the collapse of the power structure and the moral code respected in prewar Japan temporarily gave birth to social *anomie*, in which the pursuit of explicitly individual desires was socially accepted, leading to birth control by the wide use of induced abortion (Atoh 2000).

In this period, mortality declined rapidly together with fertility, and Japan completed all at once the second stage of "epidemiologic transition" (Omran 1982) and entered its third stage, characterized by the dominance of chronic and degenerative diseases. This is mainly because

[6] In European regional studies on historical fertility transition, Coale concluded that there should be three conditions for fertility transition: (1) birth control among married couples is not against the moral code; (2) low fertility is economically advantageous for families; and (3) effective birth control methods are available (Coale 1973).

the wider use of such new drugs as antibiotics dramatically reduced infant and child mortality, which was mainly due to such diseases as pneumonia and diarrhoea, as well as youth mortality, which was mainly due to tuberculosis. Life expectancy at birth in Japan reached 65 years for males and 70 years for females in 1960 and caught up with the lowest levels of the contemporary developed countries (KSJK 2007). The gain in life expectancy made it possible to secure 2.0 children at the age of 20 and 1.9 children at the age of 50 if married couples had born 2.2 children on average (Nanjo and Yoshinaga 2002), something which might itself have contributed to the prevalence of family limitation.

### (2) *The end of fertility transition and the beginning of population ageing*

With fertility having reached replacement level at the end of the 1950s, the Japanese population began to head towards zero population growth. The annual rate of population growth decreased from over 2 per cent in the baby boom period to just less than 1 per cent in 1956. But it remained around 1 per cent thereafter and began to decline continuously only after 1976. This is due to "population momentum" (Keyfitz 1971), in which a population has a disproportionately large size of female population of reproductive age for a few decades after the end of fertility transition.

The baby boom cohort, about 8 million born in 1947–49, later called *dankai no sedai* [the mass generation], has affected and will continue to affect Japanese society in no small way at each distinctive stage of their life course.[7] In particular, they gave birth to another baby boom cohort, about 8 million, in the first half of the 1970s when their female cohort reached their mid-20s; this was called *dankai junia* [the junior mass generation]. While the Japanese population was very young in 1950, with its median age as 22.3 and the proportion of the elderly population aged 65 or over as 4.9 per cent (KSJK 2007), it started ageing from the bottom of the age pyramid just after the rapid fertility transition.

[7] The novelist Sakaiya Taichi wrote a best-seller omnibus novel called *Dankai no Sedai*, in which the baby boomers experienced various hardships in their life course because of their large cohort size (Sakaiya 1976). This phrase is used very commonly in Japan even today.

## 4. The Era of Population Bonus and High Economic Growth Rates

The period of just less than two decades in Japan between the end of fertility transition and the beginning of the period of fertility decline below replacement level is characterized by the contrast of the great transformation of its economy with the stability of its population dynamics.

### (1) *Rapid economic growth and changing Japanese society*

In the 1950s and 1960s, the Japanese economy, measured by GDP, expanded by about 10 per cent per year on average, and its per capita income increased by 4.2 times between 1955 and 1975 (Hashimoto 2000). Of course, such rapid economic growth was caused by many factors, but from a demographic point of view, there is a commonly held view that the phenomenon that has recently been called "population bonus" or "demographic dividends" was conducive to economic development (UNFPA 1998; Lee et al. 2000). This describes the situation where the proportion of children in the population was reduced and that of the working-age population increased because of the achievement of fertility transition in the 1950s. The proportion of the population of working age, which had remained around 60 per cent up to the mid-1950s, rose to 68 per cent in 1965 and remained at levels of just under 70 per cent until 2000 (KSJK 2007). The increase in the working-age population kept labour costs relatively low and made the burden of supporting children smaller, which contributed to the increase in saving and investment, which in turn promoted rapid economic development.

In the two decades between 1955 and 1975, the secondary and tertiary industries developed rapidly, and the ratio of the output from the primary industries to the total economic output was reduced dramatically. The proportion of workers employed in the primary sector declined from 41 per cent to only 14 per cent, and in contrast, the proportions in the secondary and, particularly, the tertiary industries increased in this period (KSJK 2007). Rapid industrialization was accompanied by changing employment status of workers. The proportion of the self-employed and family workers decreased, and instead, that of employees increased from 46 per cent to 69 per cent between 1955 and 1975. Japanese society thus came to be called *sararīman shakai* "employee-centered society" during this period.

Many young people who graduated from compulsory schools or high schools migrated to seek higher education or jobs in this period, moving from rural areas to urban areas, particularly to the three largest metropolitan regions of Tokyo, Osaka and Nagoya. The ratio of inter-prefecture migrants to the total population reached a peak of about 4 per cent in the early 1970s, and the proportion of the total population living in *shi-bu* [cities] and in the three largest metropolitan regions increased between 1955 and 1975, from 56 per cent to 76 per cent and from 36 per cent to 44 per cent respectively. In addition, the richer the average household economy became, the more young people were enrolled into schools of higher education. In these two decades the high-school enrolment rate increased from 56 per cent to 91 per cent for males and from 47 per cent to 93 per cent for females, and the college enrolment rate from 15 per cent to 44 per cent for males and from 5 per cent to 33 per cent for females (KSJK 2007).

### (2) *Family nucleation and the stability of marriage and fertility behaviour*

With the emergence of an affluent, industrialized, urbanized, highly-educated and employee-centered society, how did marriage and fertility behaviour and families change? While those young people who left their parents' homes and migrated to urban areas to seek jobs or higher education at first lived in company dormitories or single rooms in apartments, they eventually got married and established their own households in urban areas. According to a series of nationally representative sample surveys, the ratio of newly-wed couples living together with their parents declined from about 60 per cent in the latter half of the 1940s to about 30 per cent in the first half of the 1970s (Atoh 1996). While the ratio of three-generation family households continued to decrease, that of nuclear-family households and single households increased from 63 per cent to 77 per cent between 1955 and 1975 (KSJK 2007).

On the other hand, from the viewpoint of women's life course, the percentage of employed women leaving their jobs when they got married was recorded as about 75 per cent in the 1960s (Ogawa 1996). The number and the proportion of women of reproductive age (15–49 years old) who were full-time housewives reached their peak in 1975, at 11million and 37 per cent (Atoh 2000). Women who married employed men were expected to give up their jobs and devote their time and energy to housework and child care. Wives of employed husbands worked only to make up for an insufficient household budget. The emergence of large numbers of *sengyō shufu* [full-time housewives] who were not involved in economic activity meant that of a historically new social group. We can say that "the modern family" (Shorter 1977), characterized by the breadwinner-homemaker-system, became prevalent in Japan in this period.

In contrast to the changing structure of the family, its demographic dynamics remained relatively stable in this period. Age at first marriage remained at around the same levels, about 27 years old for males and about 24.5 years old for females. Although Japanese marriage ages were some of the highest among the developed countries in this period, marriage was still universal in the sense that the proportions of the population that had ever been married at the ages of 30 and 50 were recorded in 1975 as 78 per cent and 98 per cent for men, and 90 per cent and 96 per cent for women respectively (KSJK 2007). Also, the relatively small variance in marriage age in this period meant that the social norm regarding marriageable ages (*kekkon tekireiki*) strongly regulated marriage behaviour. Married couples ended up having 2.2 children on average, and the proportion having two or three children was about 80 per cent, while the proportion with four or more children was only about 4 per cent (KJK 1983). Premarital sex was almost taboo, sexual activity among people in their late teens was rare, and cohabitation and extra-marital births were exceptional. In other words, "the trinity of marriage, sexual acts and procreation (Atoh 2000)" dominated Japanese society by this period. Furthermore, the divorce rate was still at a very low level, though it started to rise from the bottom of 0.8 per thousand population in around 1960. Based on the stability of marriage and child-bearing behaviour, fertility was also stable: the total fertility rate maintained levels close to replacement level, 2.0 to 2.1, between 1957 and 1973, except in 1966.[8] The cohort completed fertility was also about 2.0 for the 1932 to 1954 female birth cohorts who were in their twenties in this period (KSJK 2007).

[8] The TFR suddenly dropped from 2.14 in 1965 to 1.58 in 1966 and recovered to 2.23 in 1967. The year 1966 was a *hinoeuma* year according to the old Japanese 60–year calendar. People tried to avoid having children in this year because of the superstition dating from the Edo era that girls born in a *hinoeuma* year eat their husbands when they grow up.

## 5. The Era of Declining Fertility Below Replacement Level—Towards a Hyper-Aged and Depopulating Society

### (1) *The advent of an affluent society and fertility decline below replacement level*

The period after the mid-1970s up to now is, in contrast with the previous period, one when marriage and fertility has changed dramatically while the economy has matured and continued to expand at a moderate growth rate. The TFR, which had remained around the replacement level for just less than two decades, suddenly dropped below it in 1974 and continuously declined after that, reaching 1.25 in 2005 (KRTJ 2006). Although almost all the European countries have recently seen below-replacement fertility, Southern and Eastern European countries whose TFR is below 1.30 are sometimes called the lowest-low fertility countries (Kohler et al. 2002). It can be said that Japan became one of these countries in the 2000s. The annual number of births began to decrease from just more than 2 million in the first half of the 1970s and reached just more than 1 million in 2005.

The main demographic cause of this phenomenal fertility decline is the postponement of marriage and childbearing. During the 35 years between 1975 and 2005, the proportion of the population who had never married increased dramatically among people of reproductive age, from 21 per cent to 60 per cent for women aged 25 to 29 and from 8 per cent to 33 per cent for those aged 30 to 34 (STK 2006). Between 1975 and 2004, the mean age at first marriage rose from 24.7 to 28.0 years old for women, and the mean age at first birth increased from 25.7 to 29.1 (KRTJ 2006). In Western European countries too, there have continuously been postponement of marriage and childbearing and a rise in the proportion of single people since around the 1960s. But among those countries that have maintained relatively higher fertility today, cohabitation and extra-marital fertility have increased, which have compensated for the decline in marital fertility and have been conducive to the "catch-up" phenomenon among women in their 30s (Lesthaeghe et al. 2001).[9] In contrast, such a catch-up phenomenon is very weak in Japan because of the drastic rise in celibacy among

[9] For European countries whose TFR is between 1.6 and 2.0, such as the Nordic countries and English-speaking and French-speaking countries, the proportion of extra-marital births was about 30 to 60 per cent in 2004 (Council of Europe 2004).

women in their 30s as well as the very low prevalence of cohabitation and out-of-wedlock births.[10] Although marriage behaviour has changed dramatically since the mid-1970s, there was scant evidence showing changes in the intended and ideal number of children, around 2.2 and 2.6 on average respectively, as well as completed fertility among married couples, around 2.2 children ever born, up to the end of the1980s (KJK 1993). But there are some studies revealing that fertility among married women for the 1960 female birth cohort and thereafter has been decreasing from the levels of the older cohorts (Kaneko 2004; Iwasawa 2002).

With the dramatic postponement of marriage, sexual behaviour became more prevalent among single youth: the proportion of single women having experienced sexual intercourse by the age of 20 reached about 50 per cent by the mid-1990s (Wagatsuma 1998). This resulted in an increase in premarital pregnancies, leading to increases in both induced abortion among women under 20 and *dekichattakon* ("shotgun marriages").[11] The divorce rate has also increased dramatically, particularly in the early 1980s and 1990s, reaching 2.3 per thousand in 2002, comparable to the levels of Western European countries (KSJK 2007).

As described above, the period of declining fertility below replacement level is at the same time one when sexual activity, marriage and divorce have changed dramatically. What are the background factors?

First, the advent of an affluent society brought about by long-term economic growth caused the breakdown of existing social norms and gave birth to consumerism and individuation. Whereas, in the period of the developing economy, the security of adequate jobs and income was linked with conforming to broad social norms, in the period of the fully developed economy, the freedom of young people to choose their own life course expanded without any great social sanctions, and social norms relating to premarital sex, appropriate marriageable age and divorce were steadily relaxed (Atoh 1997). Various choices for consumption, such as travel, local or abroad, cars, audio-visual equipment and

---

[10] In Japan, the proportion of extra-marital births was 2 per cent in 2004 and, according to a nationally representative survey, the proportion of single women aged 18–34 currently cohabiting with partners is around 2.4 per cent (KSJK 2004).

[11] Recently, shotgun marriages, defined as those where married women gave birth to their first child within nine months of getting married, account for about one in four marriages (Yamada 2004).

software, and the internet, came to be easily available to many young people, and this may have contributed to the postponement of family formation. Youth phenomena such as "parasite singles", "freeters" and "NEETs" in contemporary Japan are unthinkable without the affluence of their parents' household economies.[12]

Second, women's emancipation (their higher educational attainment, increasing employment and shrinking gender wage differentials), brought about partly by affluence but mainly by the rising demand for gender equality among women and the industrial transformation to the service economy, made it easier for them to continue and enjoy life as a single. It also raised the relative demerit of married life with children in the form of increasing opportunity cost. Views supporting "the modern family", characterized by the breadwinner-homemaker gender division, have gradually weakened since the mid-1970s, although about half of the adult population still supports them in the 2000s (Atoh 1997). The government has strengthened policy measures aiming to balance work and child care, but the proportion of women in full-time employment who continue to work after their first birth is still limited to only about 30 per cent even in the 2000s (KRTJ 2004). In addition, the fact that disproportionately more women with university degrees remain unmarried than those with lower educational levels may reflect the fact that the former face difficulties in reconciling their careers with their family lives (Atoh 1994).

### (2) *The coming of a hyper-aged and depopulating society*

After around 1960 Japan entered the third stage of epidemiological transition, which was characterized by the dominance of chronic and degenerative diseases, such as cardio- and cerebro-vascular diseases and cancer. Life expectancy at birth continued to rise and reached one of the highest levels in the world for both sexes in the 1980s. The annual gains in longevity had gradually declined, but with about 0.3 years annual gain

[12] "Parasite singles" are defined by Yamada Mashahiro as single people who live in their parents' homes even after they have graduated from highschool (Yamada 1999). "Freeters" are defined as those young people who work only as part-time or temporary workers. NEETs are defined as those young people who are "Not in Education, Employment or Training". It is said that all these categories of young people, which of course overlap, have increased recently, particularly in the 1990s when the Japanese economy was in a slump (Kosugi 2005).

on average for both sexes since 1970, life expectancy at birth reached 78.6 years for men and 85.6 years for women in 2004. The main ages at which mortality decline contributed to the lengthening of longevity shifted gradually from young to old: for women, the extent to which mortality decline for those aged 65 or over contributed to the gains in life expectancy at birth changed from 36 per cent in the latter half of the 1960s to 78 per cent in the latter half of the 1990s (KSJK 2007). This is because the ages at which people got chronic and degenerative diseases, the major causes of death, gradually became older;[13] this was responsible for the rapid increase of the old-old population, who were much more exposed to the risk of long-term care than others.

Thanks to both the loss of population momentum and continuously declining fertility below replacement level, the annual rate of population growth in Japan dropped below 1 per cent in the mid-1970s, continued to decline, and was finally recorded as negative in 2004–2006. According to the medium variant population projections released in 2006 by the National Institute of Population and Social Security Research, the total Japanese population of 128 million around 2005 will fall to 95 million by 2050 and may be close to one third after 100 years (KSJK 2006). The percentage of people aged 65 or over will rise from 20 per cent in 2005 to 40 per cent in 2050 and the median age of the Japanese population will increase from 43 in 2005 to 57 in 2050.

Hyper-ageing and continuous population decline will have various effects on the Japanese economy and society. In terms of the macro-economy, they will bring about a shrinking labour supply, a decline in saving and investment, and the shrinkage of the domestic market, which in turn will cause economic stagnation and may even cause a decline in per-capita income (Ōbuchi 1997; IMF 2004). Japanese private companies will need to change their management strategy from one stressing the level of total sales to one stressing the level of profits (Matsutani et al. 2002), and also to transform the so-called "Japanese employment system" characterized by life-time employment and a seniority-based wage and promotion system, which is unfit for an ageing employee-composition.

[13] This trend of delayed degenerative diseases is more or less universal, and some have called it the fourth stage of epidemiological transition (Olshansky 1986).

The social security system has to be transformed so as to cut benefits and raise contributions, because the demand for income security, medical and long-term care services will continue to rise with the increase in elderly people, while the working-age population supporting them will decrease continuously. Ensuring sufficient personnel for the provision of care will be also a big issue. In addition, the recent population changes in Japan have already jeopardized the survival of local communities in remote areas, but the hyper-ageing and rapid population decline we are facing in the near future will exacerbate this situation (Yoshida 2005). They will also make the maintenance of national or local culture more difficult and may have tacit but definite impacts even on national security and the international influence of Japan (Kobayashi and Komine 2004).

### (3) *Policy responses to hyper-ageing and depopulating Japan*

Various policy responses have already been proposed, discussed, and implemented for tackling these social and economic issues caused by population change in Japan (Atoh 2002). Among them are the expansion of the employment of women and elderly people, the streamlining of the social security system, the promotion of the activities of NPOs and volunteers, the improvement of healthy life expectancy, and the reorganization of local governments and their revitalization of local economies through decentralization policies. In the business world, the Japanese employment system has been reexamined and a performance-based wage system is at least partially replacing the seniority-based wage system (Ōbuchi 2005; Nagase 2005).

In addition to these social and economic responses for adapting to the changing demographic situation, there have been policy efforts to affect population dynamics *per se* directly or indirectly. One is the so-called *shōshika taisaku* [policy responses to deal with declining fertility], which have been implemented by the government since 1990, when the TFR of the previous year was revealed to be the lowest ever recorded in Japan (Atoh 2005). Since then, the government has put emphasis on policies for reconciling work and child care, including the enactment of one-year parental leave with income compensation and the expansion of child-care services, in accordance with increasing women's employment. Since fertility continued to decline, however, the policies were expanded in the 2000s to include measures to support child care by non-working mothers and the improvement of child allowances. Also in 2004, two important laws were enacted: the Basic Law on Measures for the Society with Declining Birth Rate and the Law Promoting Measures for Supporting Nurturing the Next Generation (Naikakufu 2005). It remains to be seen whether stronger concrete measures will be implemented under these laws and whether they will affect the direction of fertility change in the near future.

The other policy option to affect population dynamics is to open the country more widely to foreign workers or permanent immigrants. The Japanese government has maintained the immigration policy decided in 1989 to the effect that Japan accepts technical and professional workers but not unskilled workers, except those of Japanese descent, mainly from the Latin American countries, particularly Brazil (Suzuki 2006).

Mainly because of this policy, the proportion of the population that is foreign was in 2004 still only 1.5 per cent, or, including illegal immigrants (estimated to be about 200,000) 1.7 per cent, which is one of the lowest levels among the developed countries (OECD 2005). Of course, how many immigrants Japan will accept in the future is decided mainly by government policy. Judging from the long-term prospects of the Japanese population, national or local, however, the Japanese economy seems to be destined to accept many more foreign workers in various sectors, particularly for "3D (difficult, dirty and dangerous) jobs". As a result, Japanese society will move much more towards a multi-ethnic or multi-cultural society in this century.

## References


Aoki, Hisao (1967): Kazoku keikaku no shusshō yokusei kōka [The effect of family planning on fertility control]. In: *Jinkō Mondai Kenkyū* 100, pp. 76–82.

Atoh, Makoto (1981): Waga kuni shusshōritsu no shakaiteki kettei-yōin [Social determinants of fertility in Japan]. In: *Jinkō Mondai Kenkyū* 157, pp. 1–27.

—— (1982): Kindai ni okeru kazoku—keisei katei no hensen [Changes in family formation process in modern Japan]. In: *Kazokushi Kenkyū* 5. Ōtsuki Shoten, pp. 216–237.

—— (1994): The recent fertility decline in Japan: Changes in women's role and status and their policy implications. In: Population Problems Research Council of the Mainichi Newspapers (ed.) *The Population and Society of Postwar Japan based on Half a Century of Surveys on Family Planning*. Tokyo: Mainichi Newspapers, pp. 49–72.

—— (1996): The direction of family change in terms of the parents-child relationship: family nucleation or individuation? In: Population Problems Research Council of the Mainichi Newspapers (ed.) *Report of the 23rd National Survey on Family Planning*. Tokyo: Mainichi Newspapers, pp. 91–114.

—— (1997): Nihon no chō-shōsanka-genshō to kachikan-hendō-kasetsu [Declining fertility below replacement level in Japan and value-change hypotheses]. In: *Jinkō Mondai Kenkyū* 53, 1, pp. 3–20.

—— (2000): *Gendai Jinkōgaku* [Contemporary demography]. Tokyo: Nihon Hyōronsha.
—— (2002): Population policies and the coming of a hyper-aged and depopulating society: The case of Japan. In: *Population Bulletin of the United Nations: Policy Responses to Population Decline and Aging*. New York: United Nations, pp. 191–207.
—— (2005): Shōshika to kazoku seisaku [Below-replacement fertility and family policies]. In: Hiroshi Ōbuchi and Makoto Atoh (eds.), *Shōshika no Seisakugaku* [Policy studies of below replacement fertility]. Tokyo: Hara Shobō, pp. 33–58.
Bongaarts, John and Robert C. Potter (1983): *Fertility, Biology and Behavior: An Analysis of the Proximate Determinants*. New York: Academic Press.
Coale, Ansley (1973): The demographic transition. In: *Proceedings of International Population Conference*, Liege 1973, Vol. 1, IUSSP. Liege, pp. 53–72.
Council of Europe (2004): *Recent Demographic Developments in Europe, 2004*. Strasbourg: Council of Europe.
Hashimoto, Jūro 2000: *Gendai Nihon Keizaishi* [The economic history of contemporary Japan]. Tokyo: Iwanami Shoten.
Hayami, Toru (1994): *Rekishi Jinkōgaku no Sekai* [The world of historical demography]. Tokyo: Iwanami Shoten.
IMF (2004): *World Economic Outlook 2004: The Global Demographic Transition*. Washinton, DC: IMF.
Itoh, Shigeru (1998): Senzen Nihon ni okeru nyūji-shibō-mondai to sono taisaku [Issues and policies related to infant mortality in prewar Japan]. In: *Shakai Keizai Shigaku*. 63, 6, pp. 1–28.
Iwasawa, Miho (2002): Kinnen no kikan-TFR-hendō ni okeru kekkon-kōdo oyobi fūfu no shusshōkōdō no henka no kiyo ni tsuite [On the contribution of changes in marriage behaviour and fertility behaviour among married couples to the recent change in the period TFR]. In: *Jinkō Mondai Kenkyū*, 58, 3, pp. 15–44.
Kaneko, Ryūichi (2004): Shōshika no jinkōgakuteki mekanizumu [Demographic mechanism of declining fertility below replacement level]. In: Hiroshi Ōbuchi and Shigesato Takahashi (eds.) *Shōsika no Jinkōgaku* [Demography of below-replacement fertility]. Tokyo: Hara Shobō, 2004, pp. 15–36.
Keyfitz, Nathan (1971): On the momentum of population growth. In: *Demography*. 8, 1, pp. 71–80.
Kobayashi Yotarō and Komine Tatsuo, (2004): *Jinkō-genshō to sōgō-kokuryoku* [Population decline and national power]. Tokyo: Nihon Keizai Shinbunsha.
Kohler, Hans-Peter *et al.* (2002): The emergence of lowest-low fertility in Europe during the 1990s. In: *Population and Development Review* 19, 4, pp. 641–684.
Kokuritsu Shakaihoshō Jinkō Mondai Kenkyūjo (KSJK) (National Institute of Population and Social Security Research) (2006): *Nihon no Shōrai-suikei Jinkō: 2006-nen 12-gatsu suikei* [Population projections for Japan as of December 2006]. Tokyo: KSJK.
—— (KSJK) (National Institute of Population and Social Security Research) (2007): *Jinkō Tōkei Shiryōshū* (Latest demographic statistics). Tokyo: KSJK.
*Kōsei-shō Jinkōmondai Kenkyūjo* (KJK) (Institute of Population Problems) (1983): *Dai-8-ji Shussanryoku Chōsa dai-1 Hōkoku: Nihonjin no Kekkon to Shussan* [First report of the eighth national fertility survey: Marriage and childbearing of the Japanese]. Tokyo: KJK.
—— (KJK) (Institute of Population Problems) (1993): *Dai-9-kai Shussōdōkō Kihonchōsa: Nihonjin no Kekkon to Shussan* [First Report of the 9th Basic Survey of Fertility Trend.: Marriage and Fertility among Japanese People]. Tokyo: KJK.
Kōseirōdōshō Tōkeijyōhōbu (KRTJ) (Statistical and Information Division, Ministry of Health, Labour and Welfare) (2004): Shusshōzengo no shūgyō henka ni kansuru tōkei: 21-seiki shusshōji jūdan-chōsa [Statistics on change in mother's employment status before and after childbirth: Panel survey on babies born in the Year 2000].
—— (KRTJ) (Statistical and Information Division, Ministry of Health, Labour and Welfare) (2006): *2005nen Jinkō dōtai Tōkei geppō nenkei no Gaikyō* [Summary of vital statistics in 2005].

Kosugi, Reiko (2005): *Furītā to nīto* [Freeters and NEETs]. Tokyo: Keisō-Shobō.

Lee, Ronald et al. (2000): Introduction. In C. Y. Cyrus Chu *et al.* (eds.), *Population and Economic Change in East Asia: A Supplement to Population and Development Review* 26, pp. 1–8.

Lesthaeghe, Ron *et al.* (2001): *Postponement and Recuperation: Recent Fertility Trends and Forecasts in Six Western European Countries*, paper presented at the IUSSP Seminar on International Perspectives on Low Fertility: Trends, Theories and Policies, Tokyo, Japan, 21–23 March 2001.

Matsutani, Akihito and Fujimasa Iwao (2002). *Jinkō-genshō-ka no shakai sekkei* [Social planning under population decline]. Tokyo: Chūō-Kōron.

Mizushima, Haruo (1962): *Nihon no dai-1-kai kara dai-4-kai seimeihyō no kaitei* [Revisions of the first to the fourth official life tables in Japan]. In: *Minzoku Eisei* 28–1, pp. 64–74.

Muramatsu, Minoru (1994): Fertility control in the postwar years. An overview. In: Population Problems Research Council (ed.), *Population and Society of Postwar Japan based on Half a Century of Surveys on Family Planning*. Mainichi Newspapers, pp. 73–96.

Nagase, Nobuko (2005): Shōsika to rodōshijō no henbō [Below-replacement fertility and changing labour market]. In: Hiroshi Ōbuchi and Hiroyuki Kanekiyo (eds.) *Shōshika no shakaikeizaigaku* [Socieconomics of below-replacement fertility]. Tokyo: Hara-Shobō, pp. 25–60.

*Naikakufu* (Cabinet Office) (2005): *Shōsika-shakai Hakusho*: [White Paper on Low-Fertility Society 2005]. Tokyo: Naikakufu.

Nanjo, Zenji and Kazuhiko Yoshinaga (2002): *Nihon no sedai seimeihyō-1891–2000nen no kikan. Seimeihyō ni motozuku* [Generational life tables for Japan based on period life tables 1891–2000]. Tokyo: Nihon University Population Institute.

OECD (2005): *Trends in International Migration—Annual Report 2004 Edition*. Paris: OECD.

Ōbuchi, Hiroshi (2005): Jinkō-seisi-shakai no jizokukanōsei (The sustainability of a society with a stationary population). In: Hiroshi Ōbuchi and Hiroyuki Kanekiyo (eds.) *Shōshika no shakaikeizaigaku* [Socioeconomics of below-replacement fertility]. Tokyo: Hara Shobō, pp. 153–178.

—— (1997): *Shōshika-jidai no Nihon Keizai* [The Japanese economy in the age of below-replacement fertility]. Tokyo: Nihon Hōsokyōkai Shuppan.

Ogawa, Naohiro (1996): Single Japanese women's attitudes toward marriage and their career plans. In: Population Problems Research Council of the Mainichi Newspapers (ed.), *Report of the 23rd National Survey on Family Planning*. Tokyo: Mainichi Newspapers, pp. 145–170.

Okazaki, Ayanori (1950): *Nihonjinkō no jisshōteki kenkyū* [Statistical studies of Japanese population]. Tokyo: Hokuryukan.

Okazaki, Yōichi (1986): *Meiji-Taishōki ni okeru Nihojinkō to sono dōtai* [Japanese population and its vital rates in the Meiji and Taishō periods]. In: *Jinkō Mondai Kenkyū*, 178. pp. 1–7.

Olshansky, Jay S. and Brian Ault (1986): The fourth stage of the epidemiological transition: The age of delayed degenerative diseases. In: *The Milbank Memorial Fund Quarterly* 64,3, pp. 355–391.

Omran, Abdel R. (1982): Epidemiologic transition. In: John A. Ross (ed.), *International Encyclopedia of Population*. New York: Free Press, pp. 172–183.

Ōtani, Kenji (1993): *Gendai Nihon shusshōryoku bunseki* [Analysis of Fertility in contemporary Japan]. Kyoto: Kansaigakuin Daigaku Shuppanbu.

Sakaiya, Taichi (1976): *Dankai no Sedai* [The Mass Generation]. Tokyo: Bungei-Shunjūsha.

Shorter, Edward (1977): *The Making of the Modern Family*. New York: Basic Books.

Sōmushō Tōkei Kyoku (STK) (Statistics Bureau, Ministry of General Affairs (2006): *2005nen Kokusei Chōsa Chūshutsu Sokuhō Shūkei Kekka* (Interim report of the 2005 population census based on its sampling).

Suzuki, Eriko (2006): Nihon no gaikokujin rōdōsha ukeire seisaku [Japan's immigration policies for foreign labour]. In: Ryōsei Yoshida and Shigemi Kono (eds.): *Kokusai jinkōidō no shinjidai* [A new age of international migration]. Tokyo: Hara-Shobō, pp. 187–216.

Takahashi, Shinichi (1993): Meijiki no shibō no chiiki patān [Regional mortality pattern in the Meiji era). In: *Kokumin Keizai Zasshi*, 168, 2, pp. 13–30.

Takase, Masato (1991): *1890-nen~1920-nen no waga kuni no jinkōdōtai to jinkō seitai* [Vital rates and population dynamics between 1890 and 1920]. In: *Jinkōgaku Kenkyū* 14, pp. 21–34.

Tsuya, Noriko (1994): Proximate determinants of fertility decline in postwar Japan. In: Population Problems Research Council (ed.), *The Population and Society of Postwar Japan based on half a century of surveys on family planning*. Tokyo: Mainichi Newspapers, pp. 97–132.

UNFPA (1998): *The State of World Population 1998—The New Generations*. New York: UNFPA.

Wagatsuma, Takashi (1998): Sexual activities of single women and changing practice of contraception and abortion. In: Population Problems Research Council of the Mainichi Newspapers (ed.), *Report of the 24th National Survey on Family Planning*, Mainichi Newspapers, pp. 109–126.

Yamada, Masahiro (1999): *Parasaito shinguru no jidai* [The age of 'parasite singles']. Tokyo: Chikuma-Shobō.

—— (2004): Ninshin-senkōgata kekkon to sono shūhen [Shotgun marriages and their social context]. In: Population Problems Research Council of the Mainichi Newspapers (ed.): *Changing Family Norms among Japanese Women in an Era of Lowest-low Fertility*. Mainichi Newspapers, pp. 181–194.

Yoshida, Yoshio (2005) Shōshika ni tomonau chiikishakai no shomondai [Issues of local communities brought about by below-replacement fertility]. In: Hiroshi Ōbuchi and Hiroyuki Kanekiyo (eds.) *Shōshika no shakaikeizaigaku* [Socieconomics of below-replacement fertility]. Tokyo: Hara-Shobō, pp. 133–152.

CHAPTER TWO

# FERTILITY AND MORTALITY

Hans Dieter Ölschleger

## 1. Introductory Remarks

There are good reasons to study fertility and mortality in the social sciences, and especially so if the region of study is Japan. Changes in the size and composition of given populations are caused by three factors: fertility, mortality, and migration across borders. The last factor has not played a significant role in Japan, at least since the end of the Pacific War although there is now a growing awareness of the possible role that migration might play in reducing problems caused by a declining and aged population. Therefore, it may safely be assumed that changes in the rates of fertility and mortality are responsible for the quite dramatic demographic changes in Japan. Thus, the most pressing problems faced in Japanese society today—rapid ageing of society, lack of manpower for the economy, to name only two—can be attributed to the demographic processes of declining fertility and mortality.

The size and structure of populations are never static. This was true in the case of pre-modern Japan, too. As far as the scant data allow us to say, pre-modern Japan was characterized by regional differences in fertility and mortality which reflected differences in ecology, mediated by economy, as well as social and historical conditions (see, for example, Hayami 2001). But the demographic processes take on a hitherto unseen speed and complexity by the onset of modernization, the Meiji Restoration in 1868. This limits the period under scrutiny in this chapter to less than 140 years. Unfortunately, the first decades of the Meiji Period (1868–1912) are characterized by a lack of data with which to adequately reconstruct and interpret the demographic processes. The situation slowly improved with the establishment of a functioning nationwide bureaucracy and the need for population data as a requirement for modernization. The first census meeting Western scientific standards was conducted in 1920; population figures before that date are merely educated guesses.[1] Therefore, the main emphasis of this description is on the years after 1920.

## 2. The Demographic Transition

Changes in birth and death rates during the process of changes commonly classed under the general term of "modernization" seem to follow a common pattern. Observed regularities of this population change during the last two centuries in societies of northwestern Europe, and later in North America, formed the foundation of the model of the "demographic transition" in the late 1920s (Thompson 1929). Refined by later authors (see Bähr 2004: 219), this model is an idealized typical picture of population changes in modernizing societies, a generalization which in its pure form does not describe each single case in question accurately.

The demographic transition of industrialized societies is subdivided into four (Montgomery n.d. Internet) or, more commonly, five stages (see, for example, Marschalck 1979).[2] The first stage (pre-transformative) is characterized by high birth and death rates in near balance, resulting in extremely slow population growth (less than 0.05 per cent) that is periodically counterchecked by population decrease resulting from natural disasters, famines and so on. This situation seems to have existed in all premodern societies until it began to change slowly in the eighteenth century. In the second (early transformative) and third (middle transformative) stages (in the aforementioned four-stage model, the early and middle transformative phases are one stage), the death rate declines, whereas the birth rate remains stable or even increases slightly only later showing the first signs of decrease. The growing gap between birth and death rates results in a population increase that might sometimes be called a "population explosion." The rate of population increase begins to slow significantly during stage four (late transformative): the birth rate declines rapidly, whereas death rates change only slowly. The last (post-transformative) phase is again characterized by a balance of birth and death rates, but on a much lower level than

[1] See for example, Hayami 2001: 5–6, 65.

[2] The following description is based on demographic development in modern industrialized societies. As Montgomery (n.d. Internet) remarks: "Whether or not it applies to less developed societies today remains to be seen."

during the pre-transformative phase (5–15 per thousand, as compared to 30–50 per thousand).

These developments are accompanied by changes in the age structure of the population. During the first phase, a declining death rate results in more children surviving the first years of their life, and thus in the younger age-groups occupying a growing ratio of the whole population. This, in turn, results in an increase in population growth, as reproduction is still characterized by the high birth rates of the early phases of demographic transition.

Figure 1 shows the development of the crude birth and death rates between 1873 and 2005 in Japan, spanning the time of the demographic transition. As has already been mentioned, this model does not describe each individual case accurately, and this is true in the case of Japan. First of all, the data before 1920 are based on sometimes widely diverging estimates, as the first population census in Japan was not been conducted until 1920. As Lützeler (2004: 25–27) notes in summarizing the ongoing debate on the population dynamics of Japanese society before 1920, the opponents of the applicability of the demographic transition model to the Japanese case point to the fact that fertility increased during the first decades of modernization. Nevertheless, in Lützeler's (2004: 27) opinion, the fact that "a long-term decline in mortality and fertility [happened] as a result of the modernization process" makes the model still productive.

In the following paragraphs, the changes in mortality and fertility will be described in more detail, starting with mortality, since, as the model of the demographic transition postulates, the process starts with a decline in the death rate of a given population.

## 3. Mortality

The level of mortality is one of the most fundamental factors of the living conditions of every society, and, as we have seen above in the discussion of the demographic transition, changes in mortality precede changes in fertility. A prolongation of the average life expectancy at birth is an early consequence of developments such as modernizing efforts in public and private hygiene and developments in the medical sciences. Of special importance, and therefore a focus of social policy, is the extension of that phase of human life which is not impaired by illness and/or psychological and emotional disturbances (Hauser 1991: 71).

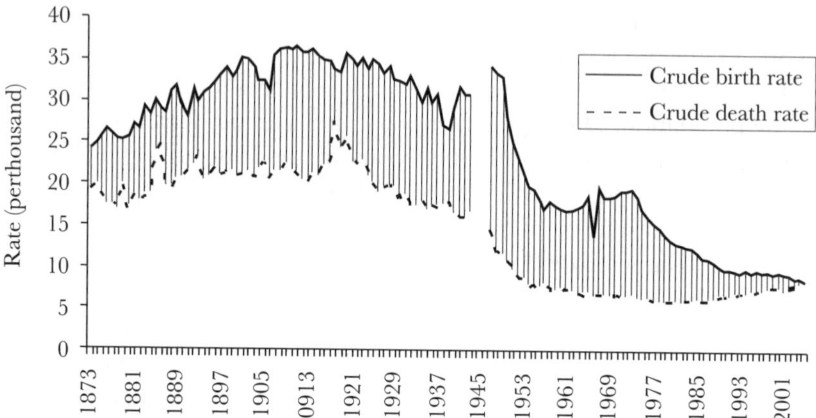


Source: Ohbuchi 1976: 330–331, Kōseishō Daijin Kanbō Tōkai Jōhōbu (several years); Kokuritsu Shakai Hoshō Jinkō Mondai Kenkyūsho 2006b.
Note: The data for the years before 1920 is based on modern estimates.
Acknowledgement: This graph has been prepared by Dr. Ralph Lützeler as a result of nearly 20 years of research on demographic developments in Japanese society.

Figure 1. Birth and death rate trends, Japan 1873–2005.

### 3.1. *Life expectancy*

In 2004, life expectancy in Japan was 78.64 years for men, and 85.59 years for women. The average life expectancy for women is the longest in the world, while for men, Japan shares first place with Iceland and San Marino. Less than 60 years ago, in the immediate post-war years, the average male life expectancy was 50.06 years and the average female life expectancy was 53.96, which amounted to nearly 15.4 years less than in most other industrialized countries. Table 1 shows the development of the average male and female life expectancy in Japan between 1921 and 2050 (projected). Varying estimates of the average life expectancy in Japan for still earlier periods are given by several Japanese authors and have been compiled by Mosk (1983: 146); these figures range from 35.76 (m) and 37.89 (f) for the year 1875, to 42.80 (m) and 44.30 (f) in 1890.

Table 1. Life expectancy at birth and at the ages of 15 and 65.

| | At birth | | | At age 15 | | At age 65 | |
|---|---|---|---|---|---|---|---|
| Year | Male | Female | Difference | Male | Female | Male | Female |
| 1921–25 | 42.06 | 43.20 | 1.14 | 42.31 | 43.12 | 9.31 | 11.10 |
| 1926–30 | 44.82 | 46.54 | 1.72 | 43.58 | 45.11 | 9.64 | 11.58 |
| 1935–36 | 46.92 | 49.63 | 2.71 | 43.85 | 46.33 | 9.89 | 11.88 |
| 1947 | 50.06 | 53.96 | 3.90 | 44.93 | 48.81 | 10.16 | 12.22 |
| 1950–52 | 59.57 | 62.97 | 3.40 | 50.95 | 54.10 | 11.35 | 13.36 |
| 1955 | 63.60 | 67.75 | 4.15 | 53.09 | 56.96 | 11.82 | 14.13 |
| 1960 | 65.32 | 70.19 | 4.87 | 53.74 | 58.17 | 11.62 | 14.10 |
| 1965 | 67.74 | 72.92 | 5.18 | 54.93 | 59.71 | 11.88 | 14.56 |
| 1970 | 69.31 | 74.66 | 5.35 | 55.97 | 60.99 | 12.50 | 15.34 |
| 1975 | 71.73 | 76.89 | 5.16 | 58.03 | 62.94 | 13.72 | 16.56 |
| 1980 | 73.35 | 78.76 | 5.41 | 59.35 | 64.58 | 14.56 | 17.68 |
| 1985 | 74.78 | 80.48 | 5.70 | 60.54 | 66.13 | 15.52 | 18.94 |
| 1990 | 75.92 | 81.90 | 5.98 | 61.58 | 67.46 | 16.22 | 20.03 |
| 1995 | 76.38 | 82.85 | 6.47 | 62.00 | 68.39 | 16.48 | 20.94 |
| 2000 | 77.72 | 84.60 | 6.88 | 63.19 | 70.01 | 17.54 | 22.42 |
| 2001 | 78.07 | 84.93 | 6.86 | 63.51 | 70.33 | 17.78 | 22.68 |
| 2002 | 78.32 | 85.23 | 6.91 | 63.75 | 70.63 | 17.96 | 22.96 |
| 2003 | 78.36 | 85.33 | 6.97 | 63.76 | 70.73 | 18.02 | 23.04 |
| 2004 | 78.64 | 85.59 | 6.95 | 64.04 | 70.94 | 18.21 | 23.28 |
| 2005 | 78.11 | 85.20 | 7.10 | 63.53 | 70.58 | [18.72] | 22.87 |
| 2025 | 79.76 | 87.52 | 7.75 | 65.08 | 72.79 | 18.88 | 24.75 |
| 2050 | 80.95 | 89.22 | 8.27 | 66.20 | 74.43 | 19.73 | 26.16 |

Source: Kokuritsu Shakai Hoshō Jinkō Mondai Kenkyūsho 2006b: Table 5–13.

The overall length of life as based on mortality data does not show the number of years an individual is able to live a life in full health without being dependent on care by either family members or paid carers. WHO specialists have therefore developed an indicator summarizing these "healthy" years. The so-called Disability Adjusted Life Expectancy (DALE) has been calculated for the first time for babies born in 1999. Here, too, the Japanese have the longest life expectancy, 74.5 years on average, with females predicted to live an average healthy life of 77.2 years, and males 71.9 years (World Health Organization 2000; for more detailed information, see Mathers *et al.* 2000 Internet; for data on Japan, see Mathers *et al.* 2000: 50 Internet).

There are at least two different phases to this rapid increase in average life expectancy. During the first two decades after the end of the Pacific War, the gain in years was mainly due to the decline in mortality of infants, children and young adults, as infectious diseases, among them tuberculosis, were no longer the main causes of death (see below). After

1970, the older age-groups contributed more years to the increase in life expectancy (see Lützeler 2004: 29).

### 3.2. *The crude death rate and the main causes of death*

In 1921, the crude death rate[3] (CDR) in Japan stood at 22.7; in 1947, the first year after the end of the Pacific War for which reliable data are available, the rate had dropped to 14.6, and in 1951 the level of 9.9 was reached. In 1979 and again in 1982, the death rate hit its lowest point ever at 6.0, then started rising slowly again (Kokuritsu Shakai Hoshō Jinkō Mondai Kenkyūsho 2006b: table 3–1; see also Figure 1). According to the latest population projections, the CDR will continue to increase to reach 10.0 again in 2011 and 16.2 in the year 2050. Apparently in contradiction to the increase in average life expectancy, this development is the result of the rapid ageing of the population of Japan and of the increase in the ratio of the senior population.[4] This development is interesting from two different perspectives. First, the case of Japan has shown that the influence of modernization, for example, phenomena such as economic growth, urbanization, internal migration, and rising standards of living, shows the same result in the reduction of the crude death rate in non-Western societies. Therefore, the model of the demographic transition model described above may be considered appropriate, despite its obvious flaws. Second, the development in Japan proceeded at a much faster rate than in Western industrializing societies several decades earlier, thereby showing the differing influence of external factors, such as the adoption of hygienic standards and Western medicine, on the reduction of the death rate in Japan.

### 3.3. *Changes in mortality and the epidemiological transition*

Observing the changes in the main causes of death over time, we see a development following the model of the so-called *epidemiological transition*. This term was coined to denote the overall process of alterations in the pattern of mortality occurring during the process of modernization of a society. The model, developed by Abdel R. Omran (1971;

---

[3] Crude death rate: the number of deaths in a year per 1,000 population; see http://new.hst.org.za/indic/indic.php/4/.

[4] See for these data the projections by the Kokuritsu Shakai Hoshō Jinkō Mondai Kenkyūsho at http://www.ipss.go.jp/pp-newest/e/ppfj02/suikei_g_e.html (found 31/08/06).

see also Lützeler 2004: 30 and Caldwell 2001), initially postulated a unidirectional shift in the main causes of death, from infectious and deficiency diseases to chronic noncommunicable diseases: "During the transition, a long-term shift occurs in mortality and disease patterns whereby pandemics of infection are gradually displaced by degenerative and man-made diseases as the chief form of morbidity and primary cause of death" (Omran 1971: 512). This shift was described as passing through three major stages, namely, the Age of Pestilence and Famine, the Age of Receding Pandemics and the Age of Degenerative and Man-Made Diseases. Later research has shown that this description painted a simplistic picture, and that the epidemiological transition is far more complex and dynamic as a result of a variety of factors, including economic, technological, environmental, and attitudinal developments during the process of modernization. Old diseases disappear and re-appear after some time, and new ones enter the scene, for example, AIDS (Wahdan 1996: 1; Gribble and Preston 1993).

Nevertheless, the model of the epidemiological transition as such seems to be valid, although the number of phases has grown to four: (1) recurring epidemic diseases and famines are followed by (2) a phase of retreating infectious diseases finally also leading to a decline in mortality from chronic infections, (3) a phase of the preponderance of chronic degenerative disease, and finally (4) the gradually later occurrence of these chronic degenerative diseases. Phase 1 is characterized by high mortality; phase (2) as a period of transition shows a decrease in death rates; and finally, phases (3) and (4) show low mortality rates and still rising average life expectancy (Picheral 1989: 134–138).

Table 2. Ranking of main causes of death, 1900–2004.

| | Ranking of cause of death | | |
|---|---|---|---|
| Year | 1 | 2 | 3 |
| 1900 | Pneumonia and bronchitis | Tuberculosis | Cerebrovascular diseases |
| 1910 | Pneumonia and bronchitis | Tuberculosis | Gastroenteritis |
| 1920 | Pneumonia and bronchitis | Gastroenteritis | Tuberculosis |
| 1930 | Gastroenteritis | Pneumonia and bronchitis | Tuberculosis |

Table 2 (*cont.*)

| Year | Ranking of cause of death | | |
|---|---|---|---|
| | 1 | 2 | 3 |
| 1940 | Tuberculosis | Pneumonia and bronchitis | Cerebrovascular diseases |
| 1950 | Tuberculosis | Cerebrovascular diseases | Pneumonia and bronchitis |
| 1960 | Cerebrovascular diseases | Malignant neoplasms | Heart diseases |
| 1965 | Cerebrovascular diseases | Malignant neoplasms | Heart diseases |
| 1970 | Cerebrovascular diseases | Malignant neoplasms | Heart diseases |
| 1975 | Cerebrovascular diseases | Malignant neoplasms | Heart diseases |
| 1980 | Cerebrovascular diseases | Malignant neoplasms | Heart diseases |
| 1985 | Malignant neoplasms | Heart diseases | Cerebrovascular diseases |
| 1990 | Malignant neoplasms | Heart diseases | Cerebrovascular diseases |
| 1995 | Malignant neoplasms | Cerebrovascular diseases | Heart diseases |
| 2000 | Malignant neoplasms | Heart diseases | Cerebrovascular diseases |
| 2004 | Malignant neoplasms | Heart diseases | Cerebrovascular diseases |

Source: Kōseishō Daijin Kanbō Tōkai Jōhōbu (several years).

As the data in Table 2 show, Japan reached phase (3) during the 1950s, when tuberculosis ceased to be the main cause of death, a development brought about by the advent of Streptomycin in 1951 (see Lützeler: 1994: 42). The reasons for the spectacular fall in death rates in Japan can be summarized as follows—and here we see at least some of the more general reasons found in modernizing societies as a whole, although it is impossible to estimate the exact contribution of each of these factors in relation to the others (see Hauser 1991: 75–76):

- the increase in economic productivity led to a rise in the general standard of living and better nutrition;
- improvements in public hygiene and the creation of sanitary conditions meeting modern standards helped to control infectious diseases;
- private hygiene likewise changed for the better as a result of better living conditions and the spread of public education;
- medical progress (for example, the aforementioned adoption of Streptomycin) reduced mortality and contributed to an increase in average life expectancy.

In Japan, as well as in other East Asian countries such as China, strokes were a dominant cause of death for several decades, but in the 1970s, stroke mortality began to decline and continued to do so at least until the early 1990s. In a comparative study, Sarti *et al.* (2000: 1588) find Japan one of a small number of countries "that have been the most successful in reducing previously very high mortality from stroke."

The latest available information on the dominant causes of death is given in Table 3.

Table 3. Estimated deaths per 100,000 population by cause, 2002, crude rate and age-standardized rate.[1]

| Cause | Crude rate | Age-standardized rate |
|---|---|---|
| All causes | 763.4 | 364.3 |
| Infectious and parasitic diseases | 16.5 | 8.2 |
| Tuberculosis | 3.5 | 1.5 |
| HIV/AIDS | 0.0 | 0.0 |
| Hepatitis B | 1.0 | 0.6 |
| Hepatitis C | 3.5 | 1.8 |
| Respiratory infections | 72.4 | 28.7 |
| Maternal conditions | 0.1 | 0.1 |
| Perinatal conditions | 0.2 | 0.5 |
| Nutritional deficiencies | 1.8 | 0.8 |
| Malignant neoplasms | 241.7 | 119.2 |
| Other neoplasms | 7.5 | 3.7 |
| Diabetes mellitus | 10.1 | 4.8 |
| Endocrine disorders | 5.5 | 2.7 |
| Neuropsychiatric conditions | 11.3 | 5.8 |
| Cardiovascular diseases | 244.4 | 106.4 |
| Respiratory diseases | 38.0 | 16.0 |
| Digestive diseases | 30.9 | 15.1 |
| Genitourinary diseases | 18.8 | 7.7 |
| Skin diseases | 0.7 | 0.3 |
| Musculoskeletal diseases | 3.5 | 1.8 |
| Congenital anomalies | 2.2 | 3.2 |
| Unintentional injuries | 32.5 | 20.1 |
| Intentional injuries | 25.2 | 19.3 |

Source: WHOSIS (WHO Statistical Information System): *Core Health Indicators*. http://www3.who.int/whosis/core/core_select.cfm (found 20/08/06).

[1] "Age-standardized death rates are calculated by applying age-specific death rates for the Member State to a global standard population" (from the Note Sheet to this table). Calculating age-standardized death rates aims to eliminate the effects of differences in the age structures of different populations.

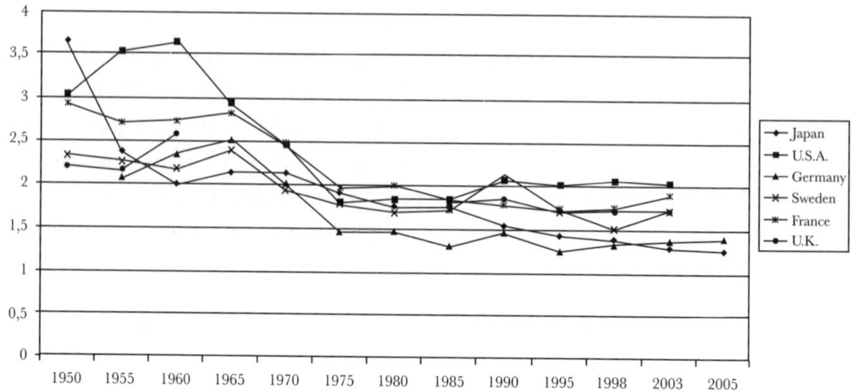


Source: Based on United Nations, Department of Economic and Social Affairs, Statistical Division 2001; additional data from Martin *et al.* 2005 (U.S.A.), Statistics Bureau 2006 (Japan), Statistisches Bundesamt 2006 Internet (Germany), and Population Reference Bureau 2005 Internet (others).

Figure 2. Total fertility rate in selected industrialized countries, 1950–2005.

## 4. Fertility

The analysis of fertility is far more complex than that of mortality, in so far as the reasons for changes in fertility behaviour are found on the microsociological level of individual behaviour, whereas biological constraints play a minor role.

As we have already seen in Table 1, fertility rates started decreasing some decades after the death rates, and it is not before the end of the 1940s that the dramatic decline in fertility rates can be observed as the most conspicuous demographic development in Japan. At the beginning of the twentieth century, the crude birth rate (CBR), the number of births per 1,000 population, stood at 32.4 and remained at around that level, with slight variations between 36.2 (1920) and 29.4 (1941, during the war), until 1947. In 1950, the CBR dropped to 28.1, and five years later, to 19.4. In 1991, for the first time the CBR fell below the 10.0 level (see also Figure 1).

More convincing than the crude birth rate, which is an age-dependent measure, is the total fertility rate (TFR).[5] After the short baby boom in

[5] The total fertility rate is an age-standardized measure of fertility behavior. It is defined as the average number of children born to a woman during her reproductive

the years immediately following the end of the Pacific War,[6] the total fertility rate was more than halved, from 4.54 to 2.04 children, during the decade between 1947 and 1957 alone. The case of Japan may be considered unique in a certain way, as fertility fell to a level near the point necessary for replacement with an unprecedented speed, never to recover again.[7] Between 1957 and 1974, the total fertility rate remained fairly constant, oscillating between 1.96 in 1961 and its highest level of 2.23 in 1967.[8] Then things changed and the total fertility rate fell to 1.91 in 1975, and from that year it continued to plunge downwards. In 1989, the term "1.57 shock" was coined as the TFR reached the level of 1.57, and in 1990, the Japanese government decided to react to this development, which was observed with growing concern by the public, the media and politicians alike. The first measures to combat further population decline wereplanned by the government at this time (Atoh 2000: 6). In 2005, the total fertility rate stood at 1.25, the lowest ever.

The development that began in the mid-1970s in Japan was not unique in the world. Changes in the processes of marriage and family formation could be observed in Western industrialized nations from the 1960s onwards. These changes were of such a profound nature as to merit the designation of "Second Demographic Transition" (cf.

years (15 to 49) if the current age-specific fertility rates persist through her life. To replace the population, a TFR of 2.1 is necessary (replacement rate). In the absence of migration a population remains stable under this condition; otherwise the population will increase (TFR > 2.1) or decrease (TFR < 2.1) (see United Nations, Department of Economic and Social Affairs 1958).

6 Actually, the total fertility rate for the years 1947 and 1948 (4.54 and 4.40 respectively) did not reach the level of the years before the war (4.72 in 1930). The growing birth numbers of these years constitute a baby boom only in as much as the total fertility rate had decreased during the war years until it had dropped to 3.74 in 1939; for these data, see Kokuritsu Shakai Hoshō Jinkō Mondai Kenkyūsho 2006b: Table 4.3.

7 Japan was the first country in East Asia to enter modernization and the subsequent population changes, but in the meantime the other societies in Asia have pursued the same course: "Asia's fertility decline over the past three decades has been of truly historical significance on a planetary scale" (Yeoh *et al.* 2003: iii).

8 There is only one exception, the year of 1966 with a total fertility rate as low as 1.58. The reason for this seems to be purely cultural: according to the Sino-Japanese calendar, this was a year of the firehorse (*hinoeuma*) and according to superstition, women born in such a year, which comes round every 60 years, are strong-willed and difficult to control, and are therefore supposed to be bad wives. Parents try to avoid having children in such years (see Aymanns 1980).

Van de Kaa 1998: 11, 2002). The characteristics of the European situation are:

1. a fertility rate significantly below societal reproduction;
2. an increase in the mean ages at first marriage and at first birth;
3. an increase in divorce rates;
4. an increase in the ratio of the population living in single households;
5. an increase in unwedded cohabitation;
6. growing importance of low-dose contraceptive pills.

With the exception of the last two points, these phenomena can also be observed in Japan, that is, low total fertility, higher mean ages at first marriage and first birth, higher divorce rates, and a growing ratio of women not married during their reproductive period (for Japan, see Ölschleger 2002: 258–264; and, for a more comparative approach, see Lützeler 2002).

Over varying periods of time, differing demographic mechanisms behind this fertility decline can be identified:

- The reduction in births of third or fourth children was the major factor behind the decrease between 1951 and 1973; in other words, the decrease in the birth rate was caused by a change in marital fertility.
- At the beginning of the 1980s, a decline in first marriages can be seen as responsible; or rather, later marriage and a gradual rise in the proportion of those who never married caused the decline in fertility beginning in 1980. The ratio of children born out of wedlock fluctuated around the 1per cent level and can be ignored as far as our argument is concerned (see Ueno 1998: Figure 12). Thus, when more women decided not to marry, the fertility rate automatically dropped.
- The rise in the number of childless couples began to play a significant role in the decline in fertility since the beginning of the 1990s, while the falling probability of ever marrying at all dropped to second place as a contributory factor (Ogawa 2000: 183).

One important factor behind the rapid decline in marital fertility was related to government policy concerning birth control: a pronatalist stance during the years before the Pacific War was followed by radical liberalization of abortion as a means of birth control in the Eugenic Protection Law of 1948.[9] This change of official policy was made necessary by the baby boom in the years following the disastrous end of the Pacific War and the repatriation of several millions of soldiers and civilians to the Japanese islands, leading to a fear of overpopulation, a fear which was aggravated by the low standard of living due to the consequences of the war. Thus, abortion became the most important means of reducing the marital fertility mentioned above. As Taeuber (1958: 383) observes, abortion was later practised more by young, urban, upper-class families, that is, families freed from economic pressures, thereby making possible rapid upward social mobility.

Concerning the reasons for the drop in the fertility rate, several authors point to far-reaching changes in values and attitudes with respect to the family and marriage, and especially to the changing role of women.[10] Between 1955 and 1975 the modern nuclear family was the nearly universal form of the family in Japan, and the rate of marriage approached the level of 97 per cent, thereby resembling the situation in the Western industrialized countries during the 1950s and 1960s. Moreover, marriage and family were inseparable from children, a connection still observed in Japan today (see above). Industrialization and concomitant social changes were responsible for this uniformity (see Ochiai 1997: Chapter 5). Then the process of social individualization reached women too, and they started looking for their own ways of self-fulfilment: growing numbers of women decided to postpone marriage or not to marry at all in pursuit of their own career. Combining work and family means a double burden for the wife in the majority of cases, as Japanese husbands are of no great help in household tasks. This seems to be, in a nutshell, the explanation for the dramatic decrease in the birth rate in Japanese society.

---

[9] The Eugenic Protection Law replaced the National Eugenic Law of 1940 and its main object was the protection of the lives of mother and child as well as the prevention of the birth of handicapped children. In 1949, the law was revised for the first time, introducing an economic hardship clause, whereby abortion would be legal if the birth would be harmful to the mother for economic reasons. Since the last revision in 1996, the law has been called the Motherhood Protection Law of Japan; see, for example, Hardacre 1997: *passim*, and Norgren 2001. On the role of abortion as a means of birth control and the popular attitudes towards abortion see Mainichi Shinbunsha Jinkō Mondai Chōsakai 2000.

[10] Compare for this Atoh 1997 and Ölschleger 2002; see also Kokuritsu Shakai Hoshō Jinkō Mondai Kenkyūsho 2006b Internet for the latest results of a nationwide opinion poll on marriage and births.

## 5. Conclusion

This short—perhaps in some respects too short—overview of the development of fertility and mortality in Japan since the beginning of modernization has shown us a society passing through different stages of a demographic transition comparable to the same process in Western industrialized societies. There are peculiarities to this transition which can be explained by the fact that Japan was a latecomer to industrialization and modernization, and that several important factors in the development were exogenous, for example, medical innovations. This, of course, makes the case of Japan especially interesting in research on newly industrializing societies of the so-called Third World. Nevertheless, the case of Japan seems to corroborate the model of the demographic transition as developed in northwestern Europe.

## References

Atō, Makoto (1997): Nihon no chōshōsanka genshō to kachikan hendō kasetsu. In: *Jinkō mondai kenkyū* 53, 1, pp. 3–20.

Atoh, Makoto (2000): Very Low Fertility in Japan and Value Change Hypothesis. In: *Review of Population and Social Policy* 10, pp. 1–21.

Aymanns, Gerhard (1980): The Unanimous Society. Remarks on the Generative Behavior of the Japanese Society in an Extraordinary Year. In: *GeoJournal* 4, 3, pp. 215–230.

Bähr, Jürgen (2004): *Bevölkerungsgeographie.* 4th edition. Stuttgart: Eugen Ulmer.

Caldwell, John C. (2001): Population Health in Transition. In: *Bulletin of the World Health Organization* 79, 2, pp. 159–170.

Gribble, James N. and Samuel H. Preston (eds.) (1993): *The Epidemiological Transition: Policy and Planning Implications for Developing Countries.* Washington, DC: National Academy Press.

Hardacre, Helen (1997): *Marketing the Menacing Fetus in Japan.* Berkeley: University of California Press.

Hauser, Jürg A. (1991): *Bevölkerungs- und Umweltprobleme der Dritten Welt.* Vol. 2. Bern and Stuttgart: Haupt (= UTB für Wissenschaft: Uni-Taschenbücher; 1569).

Hayami, Akira (2001): *The Historical Demography of Pre-Modern Japan.* [Tōkyō:] University of Tokyo Press.

Kokuritsu Shakai Hoshō Jinkō Mondai Kenkyūsho (2006a): *Dai 13-kai shusshō dōkō kihon chōsa: kekkon to shussan ni kansuru zenkoku chōsa.* Tōkyō: Kokuritsu Shakai Hoshō Jinkō Mondai Kenkyūsho. http://www.ipss.go.jp/ps-doukou/j/doukou13_s/Nfs-13doukou_s.pdf (found 30/07/06 22.16).

—— (2006b): *Ippan jinkō tōkei—jinkō tōkei shiryōshū (2006 nenban).* Tōkyō: Kokuritsu Shakai Hoshō Jinkō Mondai Kenkyūsho. http://www.ipss.go.jp/index.html (found 18/08/0621.45).

Kōseishō Daijin Kanbō Tōkai Jōhōbu (several years): Jinkō dōtai tōkei / Vital Statistics of Japan. Tōkyō: Kōsei Tōkei Kyōkai.

Lützeler, Ralph (1994): *Räumliche Unterschiede der Sterblichkeit in Japan. Sterblichkeit als Indikator regionaler Lebensbedingungen.* Bonn: Dümmler (= Bonner Geographische Abhandlungen; 89).

—— (2002): The "Second Fertility Transition" in Comparative Perspective: The Impact of Female Employment, Care Services, and Familism. In: Axel Klein, Ralph Lützeler, and Hans Dieter Ölschleger (eds.): *Modernization in Progress: Demographic Development and Value Change in Contemporary Europe and East Asia.* Bonn: Bier'sche Verlagsanstalt (= JapanArchiv; 4), pp. 47–80.

—— (2004). Demography. In: Josef Kreiner, Ulrich Möhwald, and Hans Dieter Ölschleger (eds.): *Modern Japanese Society.* Leiden: Brill (= Hand Book of Oriental Studies. Section V: Japan; 9), pp. 15–61.

Mainichi Shinbunsha Jinkō Mondai Chōsakai (2000): *Nihon no jinkō—sengo 50 nen no kiseki* [The population of Japan—loci of 50 post-war years]. Tôkyô: Mainichi Shinbunsha Jinkō Mondai Chōsakai.

Marschalck, Peter (1979). Zur Theorie des demographischen Übergangs. In: Bundesministerium für Jugend, Familie und Gesundheit (ed.): *Ursachen des Geburtenrückgangs. Aussagen, Theorien und Forschungsansätze zum generativen Verhalten.* Stuttgart: Kohlhammer (= Schriftenreihe des Bundesministeriums für Jugend, Familie und Gesundheit; 63), pp. 43–60

Martin, Joyce A., Brady E. Hamilton, Paul D. Sutton, Stephanie J. Ventura, Fay Menacker, and Martha L. Munson (2005): *Births: Final Data for 2003.* Washington, DC: U.S. Department of Health and Human Services (= National Vital Statistics Report; 54,5).

Mathers, Colin D., Ritu Sadana, Joshua A. Salomon, Christopher J.L. Murray, and Alan D. Lopez (2000): *Estimates of DALE for 191 Countries: Methods and Results.* Geneva: World Health Organization (= Global Programme on Evidence for Health Policy Working Paper; 16). http://www.who.int/health-systems-performance/docs/articles/paper16.pdf (found 30/08/06 20.17).

Montgomery, Keith (.n.d.): *The Demographic Transition.* http://www.uwmc.uwc.edu/geography/Demotrans/demtran.htm (found 19/08/06 20:45).

Mosk, Carl (1983): *Patriarchy and Fertility: Japan and Sweden, 1880–1960.* New York: Academic Press (= Population and Social Structure: Advances in Historical Demography Series).

Norgren, Tiana (2001): *Abortion Before Birth Control: The Politics of Reproduction in Postwar Japan.* Princeton: Princeton University Press.

Ochiai, Emiko (1997): *The Japanese Family System in Transition: A Sociological Analysis of Family Change in Postwar Japan.* Tokyo: LTCB International Library Foundation.

Ohbuchi, Hiroshi (1976): Demographic Transition in the Process of Japanese Industrialization. In: Hugh Patrick (ed.): *Japanese Industrialization and Its Social Consequences.* Berkeley: University of California Press, pp. 329–361.

Ölschleger, Hans Dieter (2002): Fertility and Marriage in Japan: On the Relationship Between Value Change and Demographic Behavior. In: Axel Klein, Ralph Lützeler, and Hans Dieter Ölschleger (eds.): *Modernization in Progress: Demographic Development and Value Change in Contemporary Europe and East Asia.* Bonn: Bier'sche Verlagsanstalt (= JapanArchiv; 4), pp. 257–283.

Ogawa, Naohiro (2000): Josei no kyaria shikō no shinten to shussan no taimingu henka [The progress of women's careers and the timing of births]. In: Mainichi Shinbunsha Jinkô Mondai Chôsakai (Hg.) (2000): *Nihon no jinkô—sengo 50 nen no kiseki* [The population of Japan—loci of 50 post-war years]. Tōkyō: Mainichi Shinbunsha Jinkō Mondai Chōsakai, pp. 179–210.

—— (2003): Japan's Changing Fertility Mechanisms and Its Policy Responses. In: *Journal of Population Research* 20, 1, pp. 89–106.

Omran, Abdel R. (1971): The Epidemiologic Transition: A Theory of the Epidemiology of Population Changes. In: *The Milbank Memorial Fund Quarterly* 49, 4, pp. 509–538.

Picheral, Henri (1989): Géographie de la transition épidémiologique. In: *Annales de Géographie* 546, pp. 129–151.

Population reference Bureau (2005): *2005 World Population Data Sheet.* Washington, DC: Population Reference Bureau. http://www.prb.org/pdfr05/05WorldDataSheet_Eng.pdf (found 2/08/0615:00).

Sarti, Cinzia, Daiva Rastenyte, Zygimantas Cepaitis, and Jaakko Tuomilehto (2000): International Trends in Mortality From Stroke, 1968 to 1994. In: *Stroke* 31, 7, pp. 1588–1601.

Statistics Bureau, Ministry of Internal Affairs and Communication (2006): *Statistical Handbook of Japan 2006.* Tōkyō: Ministry of Internal Affairs and Communications.

Statistisches Bundesamt (2006): *Pressemitteilung: Geburtenentwicklung in Deutschland im langfristigen Vergleich.* Wiesbaden: Statistisches Bundesamt. http://www.destatis.de/presse/deutsch/pm2006/p1220023.htm (found 14/06/06 12:45).

Taeuber, Irene B. (1958): *The Population of Japan.* Princeton: Princeton University Press.

Thompson, Warren S. (1929): Population. In: *American Journal of Sociology* 34, pp. 959–975.

Ueno, Chizuko (1998): The Declining Birth Rate: Whose Problem? In: *Review of Population and Social Policy* 7, pp. 103–128.

United Nations, Department of Economic and Social Affairs (1958): *Multilingual Demographic Dictionary, English Section.* New York: United Nations, Department of Economic and Social Affairs (= Population Studies; 29).

United Nations, Department of Economic and Social Affairs, Statistical Division (2001): *Demographic Yearbook/Annuaire démographique.* Vol. 51/1999. New York: United Nations, Department of Economic and Social Affairs, Statistical Division.

Van de Kaa, Dirk J. (1998): *Postmodern Fertility Preferences: From Changing Value Orientation to New Behaviour.* Canberra: Australian National University, Research School of Social Sciences, Demography and Sociology Program (= Working Papers in Demography; 74).

Van de Kaa, (2002): *The Idea of a Second Demographic Transition in Industrialized Countries.* Paper presented at the Sixth Welfare Policy Seminar of the National Institute of Population and Social Security, Tokyo, Japan, 29 January 2002. http://www.ipss.go.jp/webj-ad/WebJournal.files/population/2003_4/Kaa.pdf (found 18/08/06 16.00).

Wahdan, M.H. (1996): The Epidemiological Transition. In: *Eastern Mediterranean Health Journal* 2, 1, pp. 8–20.

Wilmoth, John R. (1998): Is the Pace of Japanese Mortality Decline Converging Toward International Trends? In: *Population and Development Review* 24, 3, pp. 593–600.

World Health Organization (WHO) (2000): *Press Release: WHO Issues New Healthy Life Expectancy Rankings: Japan Number One in New 'Healthy Life' System.* Washington, DC, and Geneva: World Health Organization.

Yeoh, Brenda S.A., Wolfgang Lutz, Vipan Prachuabmoh, and Evi Nurvidya Arifin (2003): Editorial: Fertility Decline in Asia: Trends, Implications and Futures. In: *Journal of Population Research* 20, 1, pp. iii–viii.

CHAPTER THREE

# STATISTICAL FOUNDATIONS OF POPULATION PROJECTIONS

Ryuichi Kaneko

## 1. Introduction

In December 2006, the National Institute of Population and Social Security Research in Tokyo announced a new population projection for Japan. This projection provides a sketch of expected demographic changes over a 50 year period up to 2055, with ancillary calculations of the total population up to 2105. The projection indicates that Japan's population will fall to less than 90 million by 2055; this is a decline of 37.8 million or 30 per cent from the starting population (roughly 127.8 million in 2005). Besides, there will be an exchange of 10.7 million between the age groups under 65 and 65 and over, resulting in a proportion of the elderly as high as 40.5 per cent. This projection suggests that the future of the country will see substantial population decline and unprecedented ageing.

Nowadays, people have come to understand that the future economy and society depend on demographic changes and, moreover, that demographic trends are shakier than previously believed. Population projections indicate future population changes. However, in many countries the inaccuracy of these projections is subject to serious criticism. How reliable are population projections? How should we use the results? What is the process of population projection in the first place? The answers to these questions are more complicated than people usually expect.

Broadly speaking, population projection is the numerical simulation of change in population size and composition in the future, based on current data and specific assumptions on the components of population change. Population projection is often conducted for the purpose of the assessment of policy or marketing planning. For example, social security systems such as retirement (pension) plans and medical insurance are deeply influenced by the size and the structure of the population supporting them. Similarly, the expected size and composition of the labour force, the market, the rate of technological innovation, and expected changes in cultural standards are also dependent on the basic structure of the population. Therefore, quantitative predictions on the size and structure of the future population are required in order to prepare for the impact of demographic change on economy and society. In this connection, the term "population projection" is often used in the sense of official population projections conducted by governments or public agencies that are directly or indirectly responsible for policy planning.

Global population projections by region and country are periodically provided by the United Nations Population Division, the World Bank, and certain other organizations. Until 1978, the UN published a revision of *World Population Prospects* every five years, now it does so approximately every two. The World Bank has been publishing an annual projection in the *World Development Report* since 1978. Projections published by the International Institute for Applied Systems Analysis (IIASA) and those from the U.S. Census Bureau are widely acknowledged among the other projections for the world. Most countries have government agencies charged with producing their own domestic population projections. In Japan, the National Institute of Population and Social Security Research provides official population projections every five years, which consist of projections of national and regional populations and number of households.

Populations in most nations of the developed world are expected to undergo two major shifts within the first half of the current century: the onset of long lasting population decline and a structural transformation called population ageing. These changes will have a profound impact on the societies in which they occur. At no time in the past has there been so much demand for detailed information on future populations as there is today. On the other hand, unprecedented new trends of low fertility far below replacement level and unpredicted life expectancy gains are spreading over the developed world and even to some developing countries. Both changes, sometimes summarily called the "Second Demographic Transition", are quite different from the conditions population scientists had to deal with in the past. As a consequence, the methods of population projection are being put to the test.

## 2. Population Projection as Prediction

Population projection is often called population forecasting, which implies unconditional predictions about the future population. For obvious reasons, governments seek exact information on the numerical strength of the future population. However, from a scientific point of view, exact predictions about social phenomena cannot be expected. For one thing, the complexity of social reality is such that it defies "forecasting" with certainty. Furthermore, when properly used, predictions that affect policy will often alter the future that they describe. Therefore, current population projections can not be "forecasts" in the sense of precognition, or prophecy. They should rather be strictly regarded as conditional predictions of the future population based on certain assumptions as premises. In other words, population projection must be understood as translating assumptions about changes in vital components into propositions about the size and composition of the future population by means of demographic models of population dynamics. Therefore, accuracy, plausibility, usefulness, and all other values of a projection depend on how we arrive at the premises from which we proceed. If these premises can be regarded as a forecast, the projection derived from them will be a forecast as well, but at the present state of the art this is highly unlikely. Notice in this connection, that "population forecast" is an informal term for "population projection" indicating the intent rather than a full-fledged prediction.

If the present state of our knowledge in this regard seems inadequate, it should be noted that "conditional predictions may seem a weak tool, but in fact can be very powerful (Cohen 1995)" as long as they are properly utilized based on the understanding of their true nature. For example, it is difficult to figure out what proportion of the elderly will co-occur with certain levels of the total fertility rate and life expectancy (say 1.5 and 80, respectively). Population projections have played an indispensable role for social and economic planning in contemporary society. In the academic domain, they are a driving force of collecting and processing data and developing efficient demographic techniques for more "accurate forecasting," much like alchemy or perpetual motion did in the early development of science.

## 3. Historical Overview of Population Projection Techniques

It is said that population projections were first conducted by the Political Arithmeticians of the 17th century, i.e. Thomas Browne (1605–82), James Harrington (1611–77), John Graunt (1620–1674), William Petty (1623–87), Sébastien le Prestre de Vauban (1633–1707), among others (Waterlar 2006). The future population was projected by extrapolation based on a mathematical function applied to past developments of the total population. This kind of projection was utilized until the mid 20th century. For instance, Thomas Malthus, observing on the basis of data from colonial America that human populations free from environmental constraints would double every 25 years, famously employed an exponential model for predicting population growth, which he contrasted with a linear model of the increase in food resources in the early 19th century. Raymond Pearl and Lowell Reed, who had begun studying the logistic function in the early 20th century, used it to project the United States population (Pearl and Reed 1920). Around the same time, demographers started to look at the population structure as well as the total population. For instance, during this period R. R. Sharpe and A. J. Lotka (1911) formulated the Stable Population Theory (in which the reproductive process is structured by age composition), one of the seminal works in the field of population studies.

In the meantime, *the cohort component method* was introduced by the English economist E. Cannan in 1895, and further developed by demographers in several other countries, such as Tarasov in the Soviet Union, G. A. H. Wiebols in the Netherlands, J. G. K. Wicksell in Sweden, C. Gini in Italy, and the Statistisches Reichsamt in Germany. This method was also influentially utilized by Whelpton, who applied it to the U.S. population in the 1930's. Starting in 1928 in a series of population projections, he introduced many practical techniques which are currently incorporated in the method, (Thompson and Whelpton 1933, Whelpton 1936). In the 1940's, Leslie formulated the cohort component method in mathematical terms with matrices (Leslie 1945). Frank Notestein, a contemporary authority in the field of population studies, conducted world population projections with the cohort component method (Notenstein 1943) while Alfred Sauvy assessed the risk of French population decline with its help (Sauvy 1932, 1937). One of the background factors causing the method's rapid diffusion was the dynamic population fluctuation seen in some European countries before World War II induced by unexpected fertility declines. Population projections by extrapolating total population trends as a mathematical function were increasingly recognized as producing unrealistic estimates.

World War II and the many socio-economic changes accompanying it had a tremendous impact on the population processes in the affected countries. In fact, birth decline during the war and the subsequent baby boom brought about massive population fluctuations which provided a first major test for the modern techniques of population projection. For example, in 1947, Whelpton foresaw that the US fertility would go down based on population projection, following exhaustive analysis of data including those from other countries (Whelpton et al. 1947). However, the massive and long lasting baby boom that took place in the United States had been completely underestimated by Whelpton's projection. This case is a typical indication of the unreliability inherent in even carefully worked-out population projections. In spite of this pronounced difficulty, the importance of population for economic, social and political purposes was increasingly recognized by governments and official agencies. Various international organizations also started to conduct population projections on a regular basis. The United Nations in 1951, INED in 1953 (Bourgeois-Pichat 1953), OEEC (OECD today) in 1956, and the World Bank in 1978 started to publish their own periodic projections.

As computers advanced, techniques involving massive numerical calculation such as the systems analysis model developed. The most influential was the Club of Rome study, "The Limits to Growth" (Meadows, et al. 1972), in which various paths of the world population growth with capital investment, resource consumption, and environmental change were simulated, demonstrating the large impact of population growth on the world development.

An extension of the cohort component method for multiregional settings was the natural direction of further development. In the mid 1960's, Rogers introduced the "multiregional population projection", generalizing demographic techniques such as the life table and the stable population model to multiregional settings (Rogers 1966, 1975). This approach was subsequently extended to multistate demography incorporating many other properties of individuals such as marital status (Schoen and Land 1979), and being formulated in terms of the probability theory or the event history techniques (Tuma and Hannan 1984, Hoem 1982). These efforts provided the basis for population projection with multiple statuses other than just age and sex, including household projection. Such projections of multistate populations are not yet commonly used in official surveys for they depend on data for transition probabilities between every combination of statuses sorted in the form of a transition matrix.

Since the latest trends of below-replacement fertility and declining old age mortality in advanced countries have not been predicted yet, a new paradigm is sought for projections of population changes in the 21st century. The most noteworthy development of population projection in recent years is the probabilistic approach to the uncertainties in the demographic movements discussed below.

## 4. Methodology

The future population may be projected by fitting a specific mathematical function (e.g. an exponential or logistic curve) to the total population size. In the past, this was commonly done.[1] However, this kind of extrapolation is rarely performed today. For one thing, the procedure does not take into account the dependence of population growth on age composition. Two populations of identical size may have quite different propensities for growth due to differences in their age structures. It is intuitively clear that a population with more people of reproductive age will tend to grow more rapidly than a population with more people past reproductive age. Second, the results of such mathematical extrapolation are crude; they do not provide a classification of the projected population even by age and sex. Obtaining information on the age composition of future populations is often one of the essential purposes of population projection; the target of state measures, or of marketing for that matter, is often limited to a subpopulation specified by age. A structured population projection (in any sense) requires more sophisticated methods.

For age structured populations, there is an approach called the *cohort component method*. In this method, future population size and age-sex composition are projected by updating the sizes of each age-sex cohort group repeatedly for each year with assumptions on the three

[1] Population at time $t$, denoted by $P(t)$, is expressed like $P(t) = P_0 e^{rt}$, if it grows exponentially and like $P(t) = K/(1 = Ce^{-rt})$, $C = (K - P_0)/$if it goes along with the logistic function, where $P_0$, $r$, and $K$ are constants that stand for the initial population size, the growth rate and the asymptote of logistic population respectively.

elemental components, fertility, mortality and migration. Here is a brief example of the procedure. From the already existing population, the future population in each age bracket is calculated by subtracting the number of deaths along with losses into the next bracket due to ageing, and by adding the net number of international migration. The newly born population will be derived by calculating the number of live births according to the female population of reproductive age, taking international migration into account. The sex ratio at birth, which is usually assumed constant at around 105 male to 100 female due to biological design, is used to divide the number of births into sex categories. Repeating this accounting procedure gives a series of projected future populations with an age-sex structure.

Considering population changes by age cohort inevitably leads to incorporating the components of population change since the factors work differently in different age groups, as illustrated above. The cohort component method is a translation of age schedules of fertility, mortality and migration into a prediction of an age-sex structured future population.

The cohort component method has long been the de facto standard employed by most public agencies responsible for official demographic forecasts. While in the wake of advances in statistical technology various projection methods have been proposed, the cohort component method is the basis of all advanced approaches. Mathematical models of population dynamics, such as the stable population model including the extended version (Arthur and Vaupel 1984, Preston and Coale 1982), provide the theoretical basis for the procedure demonstrating the mechanism through which vital and migratory events compose a structured population with asymptotic dynamics.

One of the biggest challenges for population projection is its uncertainty. Even though population movements are regarded as relatively stable compared to other social phenomena, any degree of uncertainty is problematic for future social planning. This is especially the case when the profile of people's life course is rapidly changing.

In most official population projections, uncertainty is handled by giving possible population ranges with multiple projections, called variants, on the basis of alternative sets of assumptions, called scenarios. For example, in recent official projections in Japan, three variants from three scenarios of future fertility levels, i.e. medium, high and low, have delimited the possible range of population developments. However, reflecting life expectancy gains in recent times faster than expected, the latest projection also includes three additional scenarios for mortality trends. As a result, nine projection variants (3 × 3) are presented.

Nowadays, numerous variants derived from a combination of multiple assumptions of components are quite common. In the 2002 projection of Australia, 24 variants are presented, combining 3 fertility, 2 mortality and 4 international migration scenarios (3 × 2 × 4). On the basis of a 3 × 3 × 3 combination, the US Census bureau presents 10 variants in the 1994 projection, while the United Kingdom Government Actuary's Department (GAD) provides 19 variants from a combination of 5 × 4 × 4 in the 2006 projection.

The drawback of the scenario approach lies in the fact that the different variants produced by automatically combining component scenarios do not have to be equally plausible. A combination of extreme scenarios is often totally implausible. Another way of dealing with the uncertainty of population projections is by means of probabilistic projections, where instead of preparing multiple scenarios, vital events are given a distribution probability index.

Such an index may be derived from a time series analysis of measured trends or from expert opinion. Probabilistic projection is a solution to the combination problem of the scenario approach. However, it should be noted that the probability distribution of a projected population and its indices is not tantamount to the probability of their realization because the parameter distribution of vital events does not represent the probabilities of their realization. In addition, each of the above-mentioned ways of determining the probability distributions employed in probabilistic projections has its own shortcomings. The variability derived from time series analysis depends on the length and quality of time series data. It ignores all regularities of vital events not apparent in the data. On the other hand, utilizing expert opinions bears the risk of subjectivity caused by the choice of experts and the wording of questionnaires.

## 5. Models for Vital and Migratory Events

An essential aspect of population projection is to establish assumptions on future occurrences of the vital and migratory events. The nature of these assumptions typically depends on the purpose of the projection. The basic techniques for describing and predicting those life course events are life tables and event history models. The life table is a nonparametric statistical tool used to describe the mortality state of a cohort along with life course progression. It is usually applied to hypothetical cohorts and provides the survival ratio from one age group to the next in a given period. For the other components (fertility and migration), various techniques are employed to represent life patterns, ranging from empirical models to purely mathematical ones. However, the event history technique provides the basis for all models.

In the latest official projection of Japan, the Lee-Carter method was employed for mortality projection. This is an extrapolation technique based on the life table (age-specific mortality rate). For fertility projection, the Generalized Log-gamma model (the extension of the Coale-McNeil model) was employed. The future international net migration rate was assumed to be constant at current levels, although for the immediate future recent trends of non-Japanese movements were extrapolated.

The basic strategy for developing demographic projections for vital events should be to decompose the phenomena by means of quantities and parameters into three types, i.e. the conservative, the trend-based and the random. Conservative quantities tend to be constant over time. For example, the regularity seen in mortality age patterns, identified as "the law of mortality", is a key feature of mortality models. It is on this regularity that relational models of mortality such as the Lee-Carter model and the Brass logit system are based. Trend-based parameters play a major role in prediction. For example, in the Lee-Carter model, the parameter representing the relative mortality level (originally denoted as *kt*), tends to change linearly which enables us to extrapolate for the purpose of prediction. Random factors are residuals that encode random fluctuation.

The future course of the trend-based parameter values representing vital and migratory behaviour is the most important part of population projection. Linear models and time-series extrapolation predict the trend-based parameters fairly accurately for the proximate years, but in the long run they often lead to unrealistic results because the decomposition is imperfect. It is then useful to consult expert judgments based on knowledge from beyond the scope of the model, including observations of other advanced societies. In this regard, Japan is facing a challenge because its population exhibits the lowest fertility and the highest life expectancy in the world. There is no model society for Japan to refer to; it will have to develop its own projections and

Table 1. Projected future population: 2005-2105.

| Year | F-Med | F-High M-Med | F-Low | F-Med M-High | F-Med M-Low |
|---|---|---|---|---|---|
| 2005 | 127,768 | 127,768 | 127,768 | 127,768 | 127,768 |
| 2010 | 127,176 | 127,463 | 126,829 | 126,998 | 127,352 |
| 2015 | 125,430 | 126,232 | 124,508 | 125,044 | 125,811 |
| 2020 | 122,735 | 124,234 | 121,224 | 122,121 | 123,335 |
| 2025 | 119,270 | 121,567 | 117,190 | 118,430 | 120,100 |
| 2030 | 115,224 | 118,347 | 112,578 | 114,163 | 116,273 |
| 2035 | 110,679 | 114,636 | 107,448 | 109,412 | 111,936 |
| 2040 | 105,695 | 110,529 | 101,834 | 104,259 | 107,127 |
| 2045 | 100,443 | 106,225 | 95,918 | 98,886 | 102,004 |
| 2050 | 95,152 | 101,947 | 89,966 | 93,508 | 96,803 |
| 2055 | 89,930 | 97,775 | 84,106 | 88,193 | 91,669 |
| 2060 | 84,592 | 93,489 | 78,154 | 82,770 | 86,412 |
| 2070 | 73,488 | 84,448 | 65,881 | 71,706 | 75,294 |
| 2080 | 63,387 | 76,356 | 54,721 | 61,844 | 64,954 |
| 2090 | 54,925 | 69,776 | 45,407 | 53,570 | 56,297 |
| 2100 | 47,712 | 64,074 | 37,697 | 46,538 | 48,906 |
| 2105 | 44,592 | 61,489 | 34,518 | 43,512 | 45,689 |

F-Med: Fertility medium assumption, F-High: Fertility high assumption, F-Low: Fertility low assumption.

M-Med: Mortality medium assumption, M-High: Mortality high assumption, M-Low: Mortality low assumption.

National Institute of Population and Social Security Research, *Population Projections for Japan (Projection as of December 2006)*.

explanations of demographic behaviour for the foreseeable future of prolonged demographic transition.

## 6. New Population Projection for Japan

Based on the results of the 2005 population census and the newly obtained vital statistics, the National Institute of Population and Social Security Research announced a new population projection for Japan in December 2006. The details of this projection are explained in the remainder of this chapter.

The projection covers the total resident population of Japan which is also the target population of the Census. The projection starts from the population at the time of the 2005 Census, and covers the period up to 2055, enumerating the population as of October 1 each year. It also includes calculations of the population up to 2105 in order to

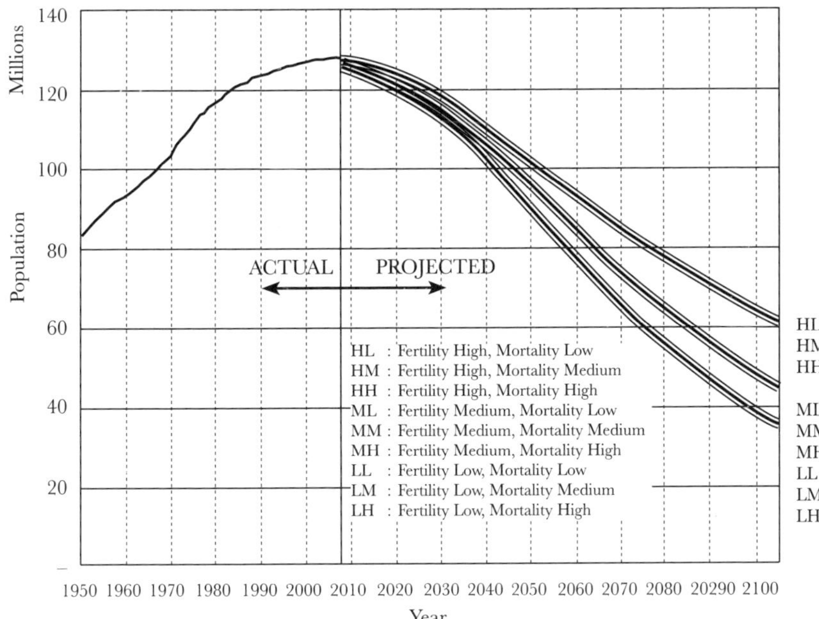


National Institute of Population and Social Security Research, *Population Projections for Japan (Projection as of December 2006)*

Figure 1. Actual and projected population of Japan 1950–2105: Nine variants.

examine the long-term demographic development assuming constant vital rates at the level of 2055.

The population (segmented by sex and single year of age) is projected through the cohort component method with assumptions on vital events and international migration based on past statistical trends. Because of the uncertainty of birth and death in future movements, three assumptions are made for each factor to produce a range of forecasts for the future population by means of the nine variants, i.e. 3 × 3.

The assumed total fertility rate in 2055 is 1.26 for the medium fertility variant, 1.55 for the high variant, and 1.06 for the low variant. Life expectancy at birth in 2055 is 90.34 years, and 83.67 years respectively for female and male for the medium mortality variant, 89.17 years and 85.41 years for the high variant, and 91.51 years and 84.93 years for the low variant.

When the results of the medium fertility variant are combined with the medium mortality level, the total population is projected to fall from 127.8 million in 2005 to 89.9 million in 2055 (Table 1, Figure 1). This is a loss of 37.8 million, or 30% of the initial population. Initially, the decline takes place slowly, but after 2039 it accelerates to a pace of more than one million every year. The population changes that occur over the 50 year period are significantly unevenly distributed across age groups. The age group under 15 is reduced by 10.1 million and that of the working age group 15 to 64 by 38.5 million, while the group of the elderly aged 65 and over increases by 10.7 million. The uneven changes within the three age groups result in an age structure that is very different from the starting population. In 2050, the proportion of children under 15 will be down to 8.4 per cent from 13.8 per cent in 2005. The working age group 15 to 64 will be reduced to 51.1 per cent from 66.1 per cent in 2005. And the proportion of the elderly will grow from 20.2 per cent in 2005 to 40.5 per cent 50 years later (Table 2, Figure 2).

The amount of population loss over 50 years ranges from 28.2 million in the high fertility with low mortality-variant to 45.4 million in the low fertility with high-mortality-variant. The proportion of the elderly ranges from 36.3 per cent in the high fertility with high mortality-variant to 44.4 per cent in the low fertility with low mortality-variant. The ancillary calculation of the population in 2105 with vital rates assumed constant at the 2055 level is 44.6 million or 35 per cent of the initial population in the medium fertility with medium mortality-variant. The assumption of low fertility combined with high mortality results in a total population of 33.6 million or 26 of the starting population, while the result of the high fertility with low mortality-variant is 62.7 million or 49 per cent of the 2005 population size.

## 7. Assumptions about Fertility Rates

Fertility assumptions underlying the projection were made on the basis of the cohort-fertility method. That is, the level of completed fertility and the birth timing of each female birth cohort including cohorts whose birth process is not yet completed are statistically projected to future female birth cohorts. Future age-specific and total fertility rates can be obtained by converting the cohort rate into annual data. The age-specific fertility rate of a cohort was statistically estimated and/or assumed on the basis of birth order, using models of lifetime birth probability, timing and other traits. The lifetime birth process is statistically estimated from actual figures of the birth process for cohorts that have completed a substantial part of the birth process. For younger cohorts

Table 2. Projected future population and proportion by age group: 2005–2105: Fertility Medium (Mortality Medium) variant.

| Year | Population in 1,000 | | | | Proportion (%) | | |
|---|---|---|---|---|---|---|---|
| | Total | 0–14 | 15–64 | 65+ | 0–14 | 15–64 | 65+ |
| 2005 | 127,768 | 17,585 | 84,422 | 25,761 | 13.8 | 66.1 | 20.2 |
| 2010 | 127,176 | 16,479 | 81,285 | 29,412 | 13.0 | 63.9 | 23.1 |
| 2015 | 125,430 | 14,841 | 76,807 | 33,781 | 11.8 | 61.2 | 26.9 |
| 2020 | 122,735 | 13,201 | 73,635 | 35,899 | 10.8 | 60.0 | 29.2 |
| 2025 | 119,270 | 11,956 | 70,960 | 36,354 | 10.0 | 59.5 | 30.5 |
| 2030 | 115,224 | 11,150 | 67,404 | 36,670 | 9.7 | 58.5 | 31.8 |
| 2035 | 110,679 | 10,512 | 62,919 | 37,249 | 9.5 | 56.8 | 33.7 |
| 2040 | 105,695 | 9,833 | 57,335 | 38,527 | 9.3 | 54.2 | 36.5 |
| 2045 | 100,443 | 9,036 | 53,000 | 38,407 | 9.0 | 52.8 | 38.2 |
| 2050 | 95,152 | 8,214 | 49,297 | 37,641 | 8.6 | 51.8 | 39.6 |
| 2055 | 89,930 | 7,516 | 45,951 | 36,463 | 8.4 | 51.1 | 40.5 |
| 2060 | 84,592 | 6,987 | 42,778 | 34,827 | 8.3 | 50.6 | 41.2 |
| 2070 | 73,488 | 6,158 | 36,325 | 31,005 | 8.4 | 49.4 | 42.2 |
| 2080 | 63,387 | 5,304 | 31,505 | 26,578 | 8.4 | 49.7 | 41.9 |
| 2090 | 54,925 | 4,600 | 27,674 | 22,651 | 8.4 | 50.4 | 41.2 |
| 2100 | 47,712 | 4,093 | 24,144 | 19,475 | 8.6 | 50.6 | 40.8 |
| 2105 | 44,592 | 3,856 | 22,631 | 18,105 | 8.6 | 50.8 | 40.6 |

National Institute of Population and Social Security Research, *Population Projections for Japan (Projection as of December 2006)*, the fertility medium (mortality medium) variant.

for which no, or only scant actual figures were available, the cohort born in 1990 served as a reference cohort whose figures were examined in depth. The index was projected based on actual statistics for first marriage behaviour, reproductive behaviour of couples, as well as divorce, bereavement and remarriage. Finally, the cohort total fertility rate and the distribution by birth order were calculated as the result of that index. The details of the three assumptions are as follows.

The cohort age specific fertility rate fixed in the manner explained above is converted into the annual fertility rate. The annual fertility rate for the total resident population is obtained by combining the fertility rates of Japanese and non-Japanese women. With regard to total fertility, the same amount of change is assumed for both groups while the mean age at giving birth, its variance and the age pattern of both groups are held steady.

A note of caution is in order here, for the officially announced total fertility rate in Japan contains only Japanese women in the denominator of the formula, while in the numerator it includes births by non-Japanese women married to Japanese men. This results in an inflation of the fertility rate of Japanese women and in some variability in the nationality composition of the population. Annual total fertility rates comparable to the official value are therefore calculated on the basis of projection results instead of being set as an assumption.

The fertility assumptions for the variants are as follows. The following four parameters of the cohort fertility rate are assumed for each variant; (i) the mean age at first marriage for marriage timing, (ii) the proportion of never married for marriage prevalence, (iii) the completed number of births from married women for couples' fertility, and (iv) the coefficient of divorce, bereavement and remarriage for effects of those behaviours.

(i) The mean age at first marriage of females by cohort will advance from 24.9 for the cohort born in 1955 to 28.2 for the cohort born in 1990, eventually reaching 28.3 for the cohort born in 2005, which remains unchanged thereafter.
(ii) The proportion of never married increases from 5.8 per cent for the cohort born in 1955 to 23.5 per cent for the cohort born in 1990 and eventually reaches 23.6 per cent for the cohort born in 2005, which remains unchanged thereafter.
(iii) The completed number of births from married couples is affected by later marriage, later childbearing, and changes in the reproductive behaviour of couples. The coefficient showing changes in the reproductive behaviour of couples (marital fertility variation coefficient) uses couples with the wife being born between 1935 and 1954 as a benchmark (1.0). The value for the cohort born in 1990 is down to 0.906, declines further to 0.902 for the cohort born in 2005, and remains unchanged thereafter. The completed number of births from married couples is derived from this coefficient and change in first marriage behaviour shown in (i) and (ii) above as follows: The value of 2.19 for the cohorts born from 1953 to 1957 decreases to 1.70 for the cohort born in 1990, and to 1.69 for the cohort born in 2005, which will remain unchanged thereafter.
(iv) The coefficient of effect of divorce, bereavement and remarriage on couples' fertility was derived from the completed number of births by women's marital status including divorced, bereaved and remarried, and the trend of future structural changes in marital status. As a result, by taking the birth level of a couple of a first-married husband and a first-married wife that has completed the

birth process as a benchmark (1.0), the coefficient value decreases from 0.952 or 95.2 per cent for the cohort born in 1955 to 0.925 or 92.5 per cent for the cohort born in 1990, to remain unchanged thereafter.

On the basis of the results of (i) to (iv), the cohort total fertility of Japanese females decreases from the actual figure of 1.964 for the cohort born in 1955 to 1.202 for the cohort born in 1990, eventually reaches 1.198 for the cohort born in 2005 to remain unchanged thereafter.

In the other fertility scenarios, the values assumed for the parameters for the cohort born in 1990 (2005) are as follows: (i) 27.8 (27.8) years, (ii) 17.9 (17.1) per cent, (iii) 1.91 (1.91) per married women, (iv) 93.8 (93.8) per cent in the high variant, and (i) 28.7 (28.8) years, (ii) 27.0 (27.4) per cent, (iii) 1.52 (1.49) per married women, (iv) 91.8 (91.8) per cent in the low variant. This yields a total fertility rate of the cohort born in 1990 (2005) of 1.467 (1.478) in the high variant, 1.202 (1.198) in the medium variant, and 1.022 (0.999) in the low variant.

As noted above, these figures are for Japanese female cohorts. The period total fertility rates comparable to the official figures, which include births by foreign women married to Japanese men, are calculated from the projection results as 1.26, 1.55, and 1.06, respectively for the medium, high, and low variants.

## 8. Mortality Assumption for Future Life Table

The Lee-Carter model is adopted as a basis to construct future annual life tables. The procedure is, however, modified by introducing new features called the shifting logistic model (Bongaarts 2005) which describes improvements in the mortality rate as a shift of the ageing process toward old age. This modification reflects actual mortality trends in Japan, that is, continuing life expectancy gains. Combining the Lee-Carter model with the shifting logistic model seems to be a better way of accounting for this trend.

Because of the unpredicted life expectancy gains in recent years, a higher degree of uncertainty than before was assumed for the future mortality rate transition and the level reached. This was accomplished by making assumptions with a range. The high and low variants of mortality are derived from the boundaries of the 99 per cent confidence interval of the mortality level parameter of the Lee-Carter model (denoted *kt* in the original literature).

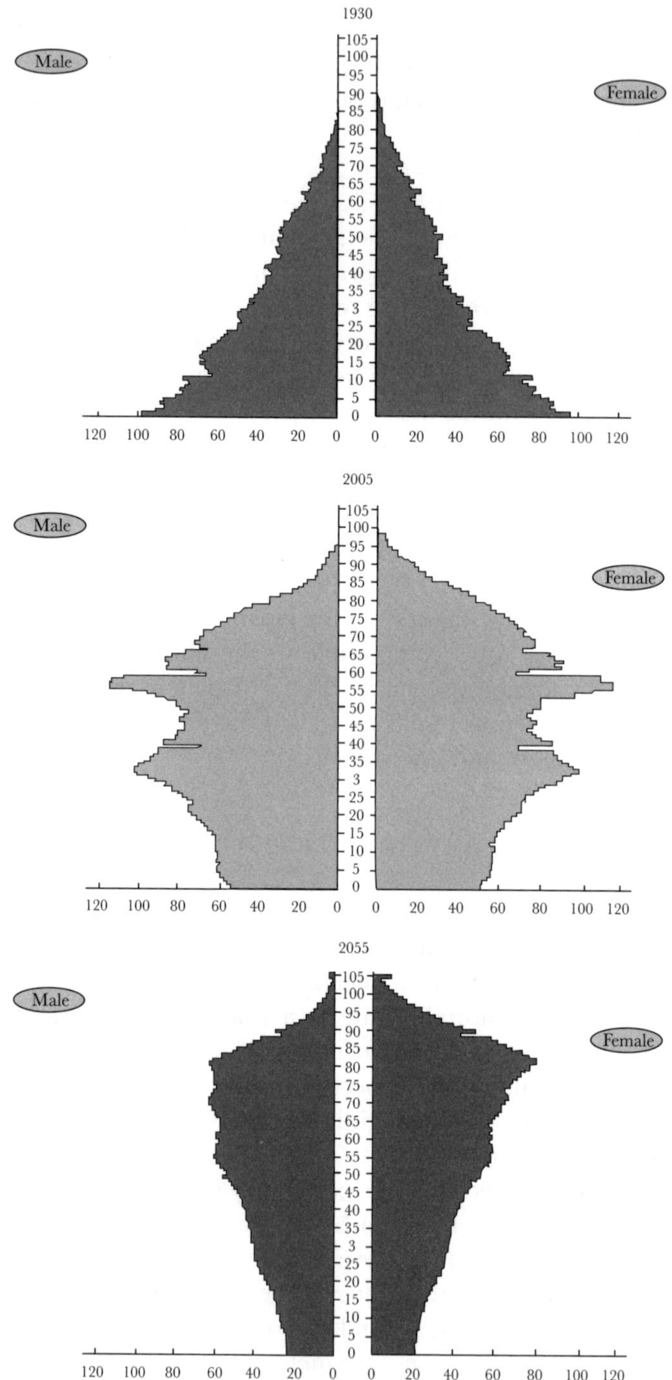


National Insitute of Population and Social Security Research, Population Projection Projections for Japan (Projection as of December 2006), the fertility medium (mortality medium) variant.

Figure 2. Transformation of the Japanese population pyramid: 1930–2055.

According to the standard future life tables or the medium variant assumption of mortality, life expectancy, which in 2005 was 78.53 years for males and 85.49 years for females, is expected to extend to 79.51 years for males and 86.41 years for females by 2010, to 81.88 years for males and 88.66 years for females by 2030, and to 83.67 years for males and 90.34 years for females in 2055.

The assumed mortality rate for the high mortality variant will be higher, and consequently life expectancy will be shorter than for the medium variant. According to this assumption, life expectancy in 2055 will be 82.41 years for males and 89.17 years for females. Similarly, in the low mortality assumption the mortality rate will be lower and therefore life expectancy will be longer than in the medium variant. Life expectancy by 2055, according to this assumption, will be 84.93 years for males and 91.51 years for females.

## 9. Assumption of International Migration Rate and Numbers

International migration varies largely according to advances in internationalization and fluctuations in the economy. It is also affected by immigration policies, economic and social conditions of other countries, and unforeseen events such as terrorism (e.g. the 9.11 attack in 2001) and epidemics (e.g. SARS in 2002–3). Statistics show that international migration trends for Japanese and non-Japanese residents differ. Therefore, separate assumptions were made for the net international migration rate of Japanese citizens on the one hand, and the net immigration rate of non-Japanese citizens on the other. As for the former, a fixed migration rate of Japanese citizens was assumed for the future based on the average annual net international migration rate 1995 to 2005 with smoothing the age pattern and excluding the years 2001 to 2004, which were affected by terrorist attacks and SARS.

As for the international migration of the non-Japanese population, the number for future net migrants by sex was calculated for the period from 2006 to 2025 by projecting the actual trend of net migrants from major sender countries. The figure was assumed as unchanged after 2026. Also, because the proportion of sex-specific non-Japanese entries by age has been relatively stable since 2000, the average value for 2000–2005 was adjusted and assumed as unchanged after 2006.

## 10. Conclusion

This chapter has explained the importance of population projections, outlined the basic methods that have been developed and discussed the results of the most recent projection prepared by the National Institute of Population and Social Security Research.

Technically, population projection is a numerical simulation. However, once a population projection is conducted officially and used for public planning, it accrues social significance. On account of recent unpredictable trends of fertility decline and prolongation of life expectancy, future population developments are increasingly uncertain today. Nevertheless, the latest population projection represents a consistent view on the nation's future, and its results provide a common yardstick of decision making, regardless of the decision makers' positive or negative outlook on the future. This is so because a population projection is, or should be, a neutral account prepared by up-to-date methods of the current demographic situation grounded in our knowledge of the events of human societies.

It is less important whether or to what extent the results of the population projection come true than how we adjust our future life courses to it. The future depicted in a population projection is not fixed but can, or ought to be changed, as the case may be.

## References

Arthur, W. B. and J. W. Vaupel (1984): Some General Relationships in Population Dynamics. In: *Population Index* 50, pp. 214–226.

Bongaarts, John (2005): Long-range Trends in Adult Mortality: Models and Projection Methods. In: *Demography* 42, 1, pp. 23–49.

Bourgeois-Pichat, Jean (1952): Essai sur la mortalité biologique de l'homme. In: *Population* 3 (juillet–septembre), pp. 381–394.

Cannan, E. (1895): The Probability of a Cessation of the Growth of Population in England and Wales during the Next Century. In: *The Economic Journal* 5(20), pp. 505–515.

Cohen, Joel. E. (1995): *How Many People Can the Earth Support?* New York and London: W. W. Norton & Company.

Funck, Hoem J. and Jensen U. (1982): Multistate Life Table Methodology: A Probabilistic Critique. In: Land, K. C. and A. Rogers (eds.): *Multidimensional Mathematical Demography*. New York: Academic Press, pp. 155–264.

Leslie, P. H. (1945): On the Use of Matrices in Certain Population Mathematics. In: *Biometrika* 33, pp. 183–212.

Meadows, D. H., et al. (1972): *The Limits to Growth: a Report for the Club of Rome's Project on the Predicament of Mankind*. New York: Universe Books.

National Institute of Population and Social Security Research (2006): *Population Projections for Japan: 2006–2055*, With Long-range Population Projections: 2056–2105. URL: http://www.ipss.go.jp/pp-newest/j/newest03/newest03.asp (found 8 March 2007).
Notenstein, Frank W. (1943): Some Implications of Population Change in Post-war Europe. In: *Proceedings of the American Philosophical Society* 87, 2, pp. 165–174.
Preston, Samuel. H. and Ansley. J. Coale (1982): Age Structure, Growth, Attrition and Accession: A New Synthesis. In: *Population Index* 48(2), pp. 217–259.
Rogers, A. (1966): Matrix Methods of Population Analysis. In: *Journal of the American Institute of Planners* XXXII(1), pp. 40–44.
——. (1975): *Introduction to Multiregional Mathematical Demography*. New York: John Wiley.
Pearl, R. and L. J. Reed (1920): On the Rate of Growth of the Population of the United States since 1790 and its Mathematical Representation. In: *Proceedings of the National Academy of Sciences* 6, pp. 275–288.
Sauvy, A. (1932): Calculs démographiques sur la population française jusqu'en 1980. In : *Journal de la Société statistique de Paris* 7–9, pp. 319–338.
——. (1937): Perspectives statistiques sur la population, l'enseignement et le chômage. In: *Journal de la Société statistique de Paris* 6, pp. 227–248.
Schoen, R. and K. C. Land (1979): A General Algorithm for Estimating a Markov-generated Increment-decrement Life Table with Applications to Marital Status Patterns. In: *Journal of the American Statistical Association* 74, pp. 761–779.
Sharpe, F. R. and A. J. Lotka (1911): A Problem of the Age Distribution. In: *Philosophical Magazine* 6(21), pp. 435–438.
Thompson, W. S. and P. K. Whelpton (1933): *Population Trends in the United States*. New York: McGraw-Hill.
Tuma, N. B. and M. T. Hannan (1984): *Social Dynamics: Models and Methods*. Stanford: Stanford University Press.
Wattelar, C. (2006): Demographic Projections: History of Methods and Current Methodology. In: Caselli, G., J. Vallin and G. Wunsch (eds.): *Demography: Analysis and Synthesis: A Treatise in Population Studies.* New York: Academic Press, Vol. 3, pp. 149–160.
Whelpton, P. K. (1928): Population of the United States, 1925 to 1975. In: *American Journal of Sociology* 34 (2), pp. 253–270.
——. (1936): An Empirical Method of Calculating Future Population. In: *Journal of the American Statistical Association* 31, pp. 457–473.
Whelpton, P. K., H. T. Eldridge and J. S. Siegel (eds.) (1947): *Forecasts of the Population of the United States 1945–1975*. Washington D.C.: U.S. Census Bureau.

CHAPTER FOUR

# REGIONAL DEMOGRAPHICS

Ralph Lützeler

The distribution of people across the Japanese territory is highly uneven. According to the latest census figures of 2005, total population density amounted to 343 persons per square kilometre (Sōmushō Tōkeikyoku 2006a, Internet), thus comparable with the density figures of Belgium or the Netherlands. Broken down by prefectures, population density ranges from 72 in Hokkaido to 5,751 persons per square kilometre in Tokyo Prefecture (see Figure 1). The highest densities can be found in a 1,000km stretch connecting the capital region with the old industrial area of north Kyushu. Apart from this "Pacific Belt", in which most economic activities are located, there are only two other areas with higher-than-average densities: the island prefecture of Okinawa in the far south, and northeastern Miyagi Prefecture; the latter incorporates Sendai, the central city of the Tohoku Region. The northernmost part of Japan as well as some remote prefectures of the southwest, on the other hand, are only sparsely settled.

It has to be admitted though, that conventional density figures such as those presented above are somewhat misleading, since the mountainous surface structure of Japan means that almost all settlements are restricted to a much smaller part of the land. Steep slopes with a gradient of 15 degrees or more occupy 47.9 per cent of the territory. When the population is related to the remaining land, this results in a real density of more than 650 persons per square kilometre. The actual spatial concentration of population in Japan, however, is even higher than it would be if natural limitations were the only factor. In 2005, 46 per cent of all inhabitants of Japan (about 58.8 million people) lived on 8.8 per cent of the territory, that is, the area occupied by the three large metropolitan regions of Tokyo, Nagoya and Osaka (own calculations, based on Sōmushō Tōkeikyoku 2006a, Internet).[1] A

[1] This area includes the prefectures of Saitama, Chiba, Tokyo, Kanagawa, Aichi, Kyoto, Osaka and Hyogo.

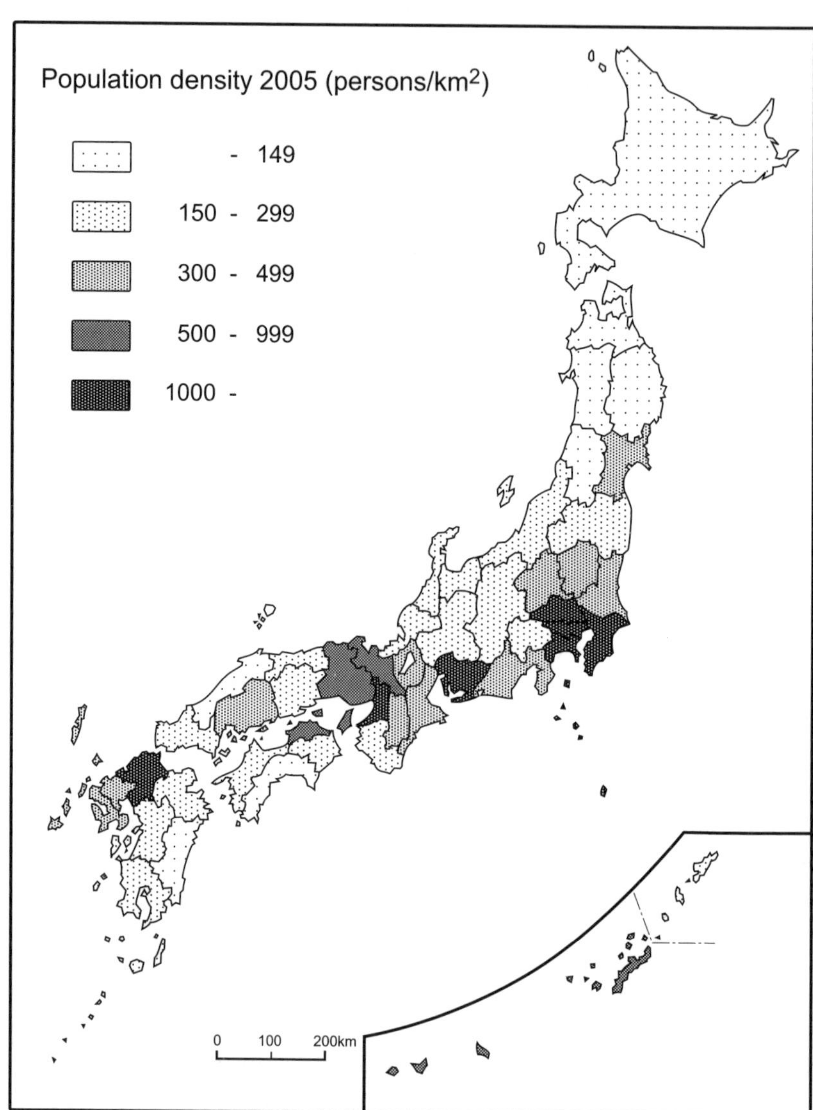


Source: Sōmushō Tōkeikyoku 2006a, Internet.

Figure 1. The distribution of population by prefecture, 2005.

major reason for this extreme population concentration can be found in the highly centralist character of the Japanese state, leading to a hypergrowth of the capital region in particular. In the four prefectures of Tokyo, Kanagawa, Saitama and Chiba alone, which form the Tokyo Metropolitan Region (3.5 per cent of the total Japanese landmass), live 34.5 million people or 27 per cent of the entire population (Sōmushō Tōkeikyoku 2006a, Internet). In Japan this development has become widely known by the term "Tokyo one-point concentration" [*Tōkyō ikkyoku shūchū*]. Cramped housing conditions, a chaotic spatial mixture of different urban functions, urban sprawl connected with daily commuter streams of immense proportions, and lack of public green space because of extremely high land prices are the negative effects of such concentration. It has also been argued that a major disaster such as a devastating earthquake in the Tokyo Region would be a serious threat to the functioning of the Japanese state or even to the world economy, since almost all corporation headquarters or political bodies of the country would be struck simultaneously (Flüchter 1997: 11–12).

Urban overcrowding [*kamitsu*] contrasts with rural depopulation [*kaso*]. In 2000, 7.3 per cent of the total population (9,310 million people) lived on 51.7 per cent of the Japanese territory that was officially acknowledged as depopulated or underpopulated [*kaso chiiki*], resulting in a population density figure of 48 per square kilometre. These areas, which are mostly situated in mountainous regions or on remote islands, are recognized in a special law aiming at their revitalization. According to this law, a municipality is classified as depopulated if it met the following criteria: (1) net population losses of at least 25 per cent between 1960 and 1995; (2) a proportion of aged persons of 65 years or older of 24 per cent or higher and/or a proportion of the young adult population (15–30 years of age) lower than 15 per cent in 1995; and (3) the index of financial potential, which measures the balance of municipal revenues to expenditures, being constantly below 0.42 between 1996 and 1998. However, the actual situation is much worse: in 2000 the index of financial potential for all *kaso chiiki* stood at 0.21, while the percentages of aged people and young adults reached 28.1 and 13.9 respectively (SJGKT 2005, Internet: 2). As a result, these regions also suffer from social deprivation of their inhabitants. The highest rates of households receiving public livelihood assistance and of suicide deaths in Japan are recorded here (Lützeler 1998: 288).

The evolution of this unbalanced population distribution is closely connected to the process of modern industrialization. While during the Edo Period (1603–1868) the size of population in a given area depended more or less on local rice yields, the opening up of Japan to the West following the Meiji Restoration (1868) and the increased importance of export trade put the Pacific Coast at an advantage over the Japan Sea Coast, since the former offered more and better natural harbours and was closer to international shipping routes in general. The different fate of the two coastal areas can best be illustrated by a comparison of population development in the former castle towns of Kanazawa (Ishikawa Prefecture) and Nagoya (Aichi Prefecture). While in 1872 both cities had about 100,000 inhabitants, by 1920 population numbers had risen sixfold to 610,000 in Nagoya, favourably situated between the capital of Tokyo and the rising commercial city of Osaka, whereas increase had been sluggish in the portless city of Kanazawa, reaching no more than 130,000 residents (Yazaki 1968: 420–421). With the onset of high-speed economic growth in the 1950s, further population increases in the Tokyo, Nagoya and Osaka areas led to the formation of vast urban agglomerations incorporating surrounding prefectures that became suburban hinterlands (see Figure 2). Population gains were also marked in Okinawa Prefecture and in those prefectures which include the regional capital cities [*chihō chūsū toshi*] of Sapporo (Hokkaido), Sendai (Miyagi), Hiroshima and Fukuoka, functioning as quasi-capitals of the outer regions of Hokkaido, Tohoku, Chugoku-Shikoku and Kyushu, respectively. Most rural parts of the Tohoku and Chugoku regions, of Shikoku and Kyushu, by contrast, had fewer inhabitants in 2005 than in 1955.

Since in the Japanese case the volume of international migration flows has been extremely low, regional population change during the last half-century can be interpreted as the almost exclusive result of internal migration flows on the one hand and the balance of births and deaths on the other.[2] Internal migration in particular had a major impact in bringing about the current regional pattern of population distribution outlined above (see Table 1). During the heyday of post-war economic growth, the five years from 1960 to 1965, only the three major metropolitan regions and surrounding prefectures gained from migration, while nearly all rural prefectures lost. The volume of migration

[2] In no year since 1960 have net migration figures ever exceeded 100,000 international migrants. With rising numbers of "newcomer foreigners", the socio-demographic impact of immigration has nevertheless become more significant recently.

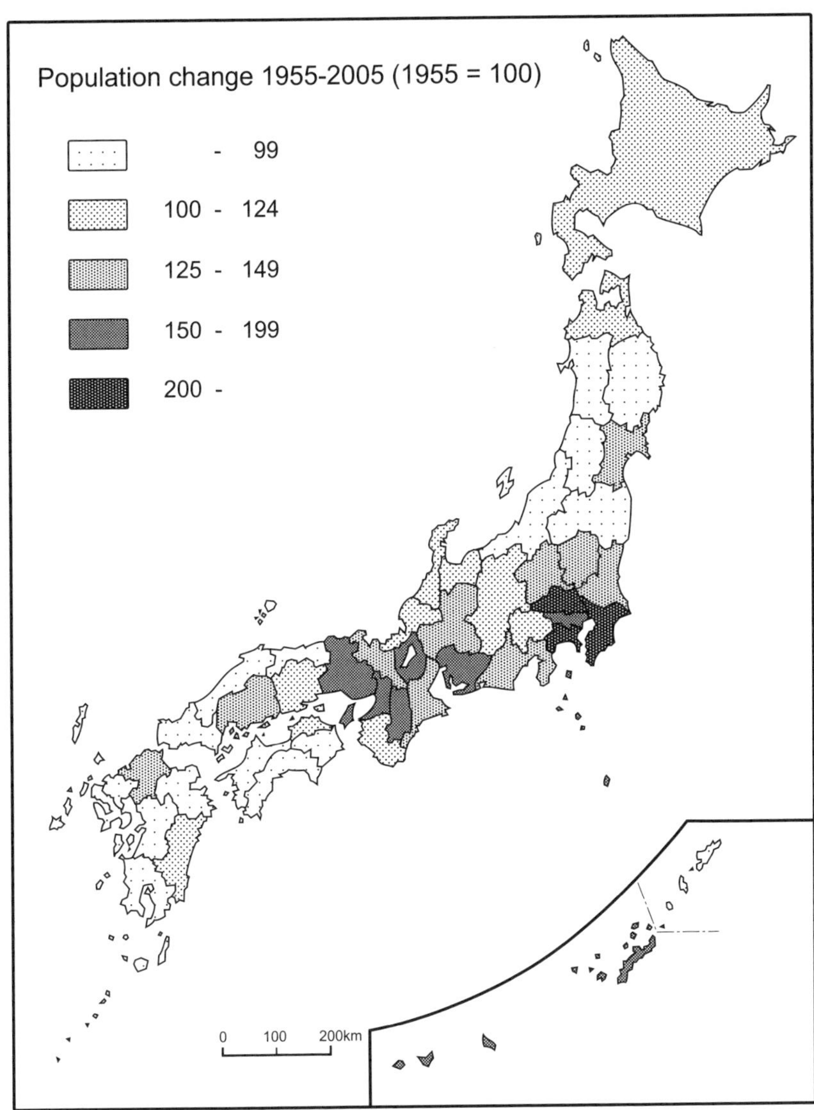


Source: Own calculations, based on Sōmushō Tōkeikyoku 2006a, Internet; KSHJMK 2006, Internet.

Figure 2. Population change by prefecture, 1955–2005.

was extremely high, ranging from a 20.6 per cent population increase from migration alone in Kanagawa Prefecture, including the city of Yokohama, to a loss of 12 per cent in Nagasaki Prefecture. Out-migration was particularly intense from south-western Japan, while in the northeast a considerable proportion of the population still resorted to seasonal out-migration [*dekasegi*] instead, thus slowing down the process of depopulation there to some extent (Fujita 1981: 245–247).

Table 1. Population change due to internal migration in the five prefectures with the highest increase and decrease rates respectively, intercensal periods 1960–1965, 1975–1980 and 2000–2005.

| | 1960–1965 | | 1975–1980 | | 2000–2005 | |
|---|---|---|---|---|---|---|
| Rank | Prefecture | Rate (%) | Prefecture | Rate (%) | Prefecture | Rate (%) |
| 1 | Kanagawa | 20.6 | Chiba | 8.1 | Tokyo | 3.0 |
| 2 | Saitama | 17.3 | Nara | 7.8 | Kanagawa | 1.5 |
| 3 | Osaka | 12.9 | Saitama | 6.0 | Chiba | 0.8 |
| 4 | Chiba | 11.5 | Shiga | 4.7 | Shiga | 0.7 |
| 5 | Aichi | 7.1 | Ibaraki | 4.6 | Okinawa | 0.7 |
| 43 | Miyazaki | –9.5 | Wakayama | –1.5 | Wakayama | –1.6 |
| 44 | Kagoshima | –9.7 | Hyogo | –1.6 | Nara | –1.7 |
| 45 | Shimane | –10.0 | Nagasaki | –2.6 | Akita | –1.7 |
| 46 | Saga | –11.5 | Osaka | –2.9 | Aomori | –1.8 |
| 47 | Nagasaki | –12.0 | Tokyo | –5.0 | Nagasaki | –2.0 |

Source: KSHJMK 2003a: 182; own calculations, based on KSHJMK 2004, 2005, 2006, Internet; Sōmushō Tōkeikyoku 2006b: table 5.

Post-war trends in internal migration were influenced by two main factors. The first was the demographic or "cohort size" factor, which means that larger cohorts naturally produce a larger migration potential when they become adults and enter the labour market. In Japan a large excess of births from around 1925 to 1950 produced overpopulation in the underdeveloped rural areas that was eventually solved by massive out-migration of most young people except for the inheriting eldest son and his spouse. The second was the economic factor, regulating migration via changes in the supply of urban jobs. During the period of high economic growth (1956–1973), both factors produced a strong effect on migration. While population pressure was high in the countryside, the urban economy flourished, so that large rural-urban migration flows were the natural outcome. In the early 1970s, by contrast, both factors lost their momentum, which led to a slump in migration rates at that time.[3] Due to an increasing scarcity of building land and rising real estate prices, the urban core prefectures of Tokyo and Osaka even suffered from migration losses. At the same time modest return migration flows back into rural prefectures became discernible, then much commented on as "U-turn-migration", which was thought to mark the beginning of a more decentralized population development (see, for instance, Wiltshire 1979). This expectation, however, turned out to be false. Although the volume of internal migration has declined even more, Table 1 reveals that during the period from 2000 to 2005 the highest migration surplus was again recorded in the urban core prefecture of Tokyo, while rural prefectures lost people.

Although the notion is generally correct that post-war migration was mainly directed toward the three major metropolitan regions, a closer look reveals important differences between these areas (see Figure 3). It was only during the period of high-speed economic growth that all regions recorded a remarkable influx of population. Following the oil crisis and the decrease of the demographic migration potential in the early 1970s, migration flows generally subsided but did so especially with regard to the Nagoya and Osaka (Kansai) areas, where out-migration came to exceed in-migration, thus showing a trend toward counterurbanization then common in many Western countries as well (Ishikawa 1994: 58–60). The Tokyo area, by contrast, continued to grow through migration, albeit slowly. During the 1980s trends diverged even more, with Tokyo experiencing a second immigration boom, while the other conurbations stagnated at best. As the focal point of government-related institutions and the most prestigious universities in Japan, as well as due to its new role as a world financial centre alongside New York and London, the Tokyo area managed to retain its attraction for migrants (Flüchter 1990: 117–124; 1995: 34). After the collapse of the so-called bubble economy in the early 1990s, the capital region too suffered temporarily from net migration losses. Absurdly high land and housing prices and a loss of jobs, especially in manufacturing, were seen as the main factors for this unprecedented situation (Kokudochō 1996: 6–11). Since then, however, shrinking real estate prices combined with

[3] According to calculations made by Ōe (1995: 9–13), the demographic factor explained 45 to 55 per cent of net migration change in the Tokyo region from the late 1950s to the early 1970s, but the impact of this factor fell to only 10 per cent in 1980.

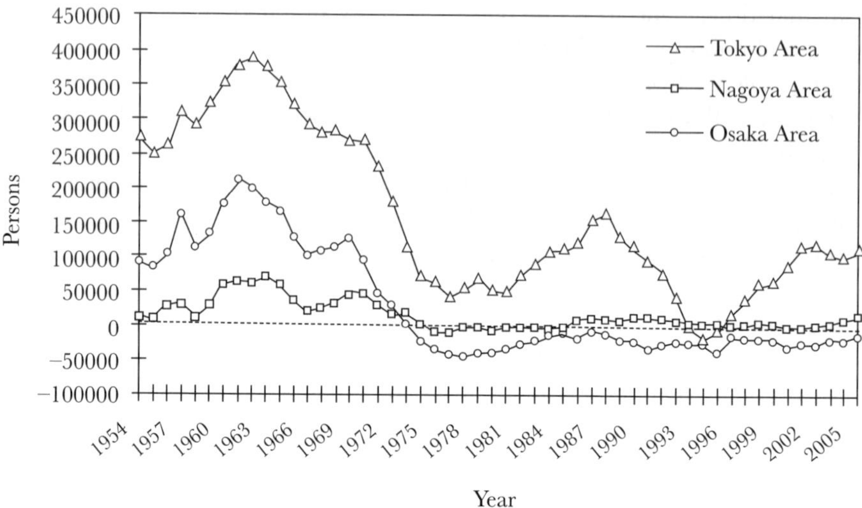


Note: In this case "Metropolitan Regions" include the prefectures of Saitama, Chiba, Tokyo and Kanagawa (Tokyo Area); Gifu, Aichi and Mie (Nagoya Area); Kyoto, Osaka, Hyogo and Nara (Osaka Area).
Source: Lützeler 2004: 46; Sōmushō Tōkeikyoku 2006b: appendix 1.

Figure 3. Changes in net migration, metropolitan regions 1954–2005.

a higher supply of new attractive high-rise apartment blocks in the central wards have led more and more people to stay in Tokyo instead of moving to the suburban fringe (Hohn 2002; Lützeler 2005), hence the current recovery of net migration rates in the Tokyo Metropolitan Region. It is as yet not clear whether such a "return to the city core" [*toshin kaiki*] at the expense of suburban prefectures will also happen in the Osaka and Nagoya areas.

Migration over long distances is usually highly age-selective. In Japan, too, migration was dominated by young adults who left their rural homes and poured into the cities in search of better employment or education. Most stayed in the urban areas where they married and founded a family. As a result, from the early 1960s onwards the highest birth surpluses were consistently recorded in urban prefectures, thus adding to population increases there (see Table 2). Conversely, those prefectures which already suffered most heavily from migration losses also show the lowest natural increase rates—even turning to death surpluses recently—due to their lack of people of a reproductive age. These age-selective effects of population migration are thus more impor-

Table 2. Population change due to natural increases (birth surpluses) in the five prefectures with the highest and lowest increase rates, intercensal periods 1960–1965, 1975–1980 and 2000–2005.

| Rank | 1960–1965 | | 1975–1980 | | 2000–2005 | |
|---|---|---|---|---|---|---|
| | Prefecture | Rate (%) | Prefecture | Rate (%) | Prefecture | Rate (%) |
| 1 | Okinawa | 9.7 | Okinawa | 7.6 | Okinawa | 3.0 |
| 2 | Kanagawa | 8.1 | Saitama | 6.4 | Aichi | 1.6 |
| 3 | Osaka | 8.0 | Kanagawa | 6.1 | Kanagawa | 1.5 |
| 4 | Tokyo | 7.4 | Chiba | 6.0 | Shiga | 1.5 |
| 5 | Aichi | 6.9 | Aichi | 5.7 | Saitama | 1.4 |
| 43 | Tottori | 3.1 | Wakayama | 2.9 | Tokushima | −1.0 |
| 44 | Kagawa | 2.9 | Kagoshima | 2.7 | Yamaguchi | −1.1 |
| 45 | Tokushima | 2.8 | Tokushima | 2.6 | Shimane | −1.3 |
| 46 | Kochi | 2.4 | Shimane | 2.2 | Kochi | −1.4 |
| 47 | Shimane | 2.4 | Kochi | 2.0 | Akita | −1.8 |

Source: KSHJMK 2003a: 181; own calculations, based on KSHJMK 2004, 2005, 2006, Internet; KRDKTJ 2006, Internet: table 3–1.

tant with regard to natural increase rates than regional differences in fertility or mortality levels. The only exception is the island prefecture of Okinawa, where both total fertility rates and female life expectancy are far above the national average (see also Figure 6), leading to high birth surpluses in spite of slight migration losses.

There is another side-effect of internal migration that has major repercussions on regional development: due to the massive out-migration of young people during the era of rapid economic growth, demographic ageing in Japan is much more prevalent in the rural areas. In 2005, the rural southwestern prefecture of Shimane had a proportion of 27.1 per cent of the population aged 65 years or over, while in suburban Saitama Prefecture, part of the Tokyo conurbation, no more than 16.4 per cent of the population fell into this category. This figure was only surpassed by the prefecture of Okinawa (16.1 per cent) due to its high birth rates (Sōmushō Tōkeikyoku 2006a, Internet). The massive outflow of young and economically active persons also had the effect of weakening the social, economic and financial bases of the municipalities and prefectures concerned. It is here where the problem of *kaso chiiki* or depopulated regions discussed above emerged. As rural-urban population shifts have almost subsided, however, in the long run ageing will become a problem of the urban agglomerations as well. In absolute numbers, urban regions are already burdened with

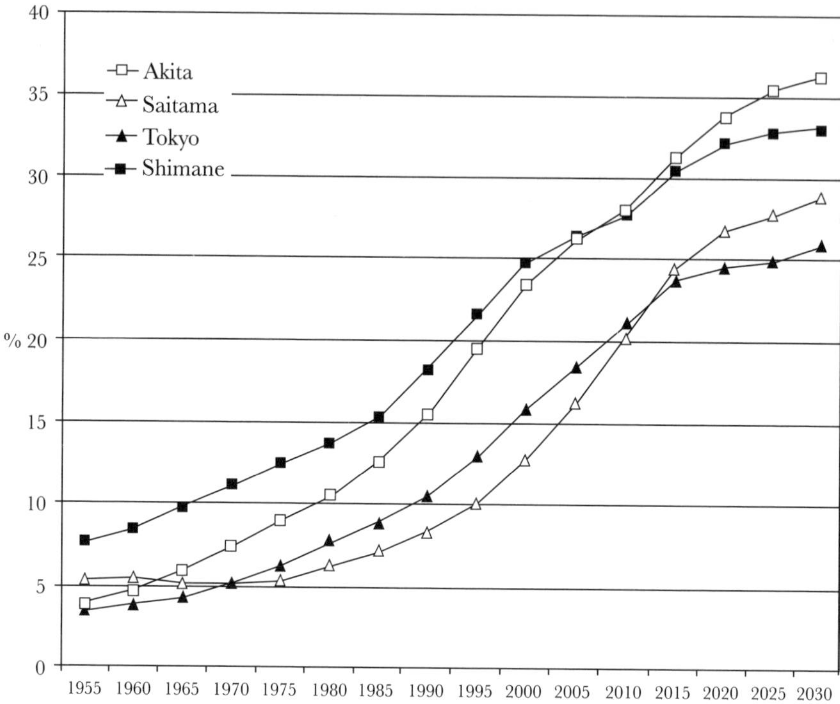


Note: Data from 2005 onward are based on projections.
Source: KSHJMK 2002: 19; 2003a: 195–196.

Figure 4. Proportion of the elderly (65 years of age or older), selected prefectures 1955–2030.

the larger share of the elderly. Since most cities will need their financial resources for further consolidating their general infrastructure (especially traffic, sewerage and housing), these areas might be equally unable to cope with the problem by themselves (Lützeler 2002a). From Figure 4 it can be seen that suburban prefectures such as Saitama in particular will experience large increases in the proportion of the aged (see also KSHJMK 2002: 18), while the growth rate in core urban prefectures such as Tokyo is expected to be more moderate, owing to the return-to-the-city drift of young and middle-aged adults mentioned above. The figure also illuminates the fact that the southwest-northeast gradient in ageing rates that has emerged during the 1950s as a consequence of earlier and more massive out-migration from the southwest had disappeared at the time of writing, in 2006.

Due to smaller age cohorts, it can be expected that in the future internal migration will become less important with regard to regional population trends. However, the indirect consequence of past migrations, that is, a young population producing birth surpluses, will ensure continued growth in the metropolitan regions for at least another one to two decades, while the population of most rural regions will continue its downward trend due to their high proportions of elderly people. In addition, international migration, too, might become a factor, since almost all foreign immigrants choose urban areas as their destination. In 2005, 1,261,165 people holding a foreign passport, or 62.7 per cent of all foreign citizens permanently residing in Japan, lived in one of the three large metropolitan regions (own calculations, based on Nyūkan Kyōkai 2006: 48). According to the prefectural population projection results released by the National Institute of Population and Social Security Research in March 2002 (KSHJMK 2002: 7), 45 out of 47 prefectures will have smaller populations in 2030 than in 2005. Overall, however, population losses will be higher in rural than in urban prefectures, thus aggravating the imbalances of population distribution in Japan (see Figure 5). The population of Okinawa Prefecture is expected to rise, mostly because of above-average total fertility rates, while Shiga Prefecture will profit from suburbanization and corresponding high birth surpluses.

It is expected that in the not-so-distant future population decrease will occur even in some of the larger cities of Japan. This should, on the one hand, alleviate the problem of urban overcrowding in the municipalities concerned, but on the other hand, it could put heavy strains on the local economy as well as on municipal financial budgets, since the proportion of the economically active population in particular is likely to fall. Based on the population projection figures for municipalities released by the National Institute of Population and Social Security Research in December 2003 (KSHJMK 2003b: kekkahyō 1), it becomes clear that 33 out of 41 municipalities with 300,000 to 500,000 residents in 2000 will have smaller populations in 2030, the most severe case being the western port city of Nagasaki, which is expected to shrink from 423,000 to 300,000 inhabitants by 2030. Among the eleven cities with 500,000 to 1.000,000 residents in 2000, six are likely to show population losses, while there are still seven out of 13 cities of over one million inhabitants—Tokyo among them—which will continue to grow slightly. By contrast, Nagoya, Osaka and the old industrial city of Kitakyushu

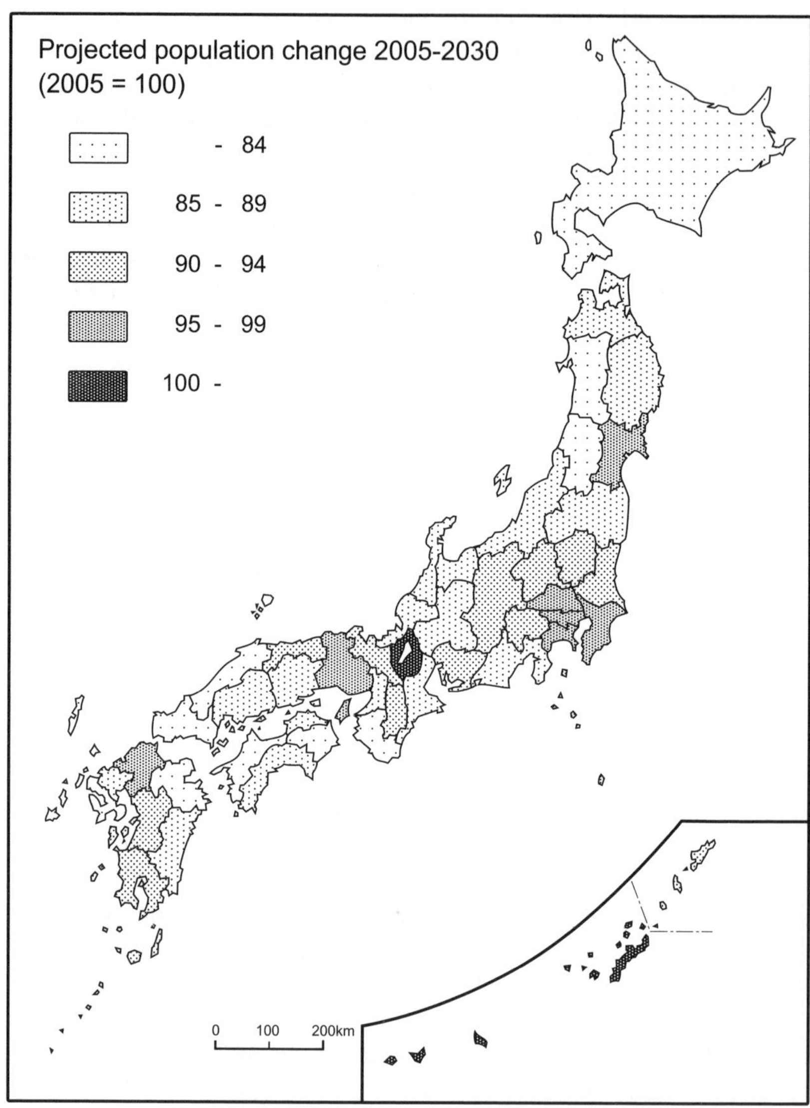


Source: Own calculations, based on KSHJMK 2002: 7; Sōmushō Tōkeikyoku 2006a, Internet.

Figure 5. Projected population change by prefecture, 2005–2030.

are expected to shrink considerably to 80 to 90 per cent of the 2000 population level.

Since it is assumed that differences in age structure among prefectures will level out somewhat during the next decades, and with internal migration flows decreasing almost every year, age-standardized mortality and fertility levels will become more important factors with regard to future population distribution trends. Turning to fertility first, Figure 6 shows the current interprefectural pattern of the total fertility rate (TFR) measuring the average number of children a woman gives birth to during her reproductive life. It becomes obvious that, although rates are somewhat higher in rural than in urban regions, fertility is below replacement level in all prefectures, including Okinawa, which shows the highest rate (1.72 in 2005). This means that in the long run all prefectures will need to attract migrants to prevent population losses.

In order to detect possible determinants of the regional fertility pattern, a decomposition of the TFR into the effects of the proportion of married women and those of the numbers of children ever born to married women (marital fertility) is appropriate. The first factor is of particular importance, since statistics show that the recent fertility decline in Japan leading to one of the lowest TFRs in the world is almost exclusively the outcome of marriage behaviour changes (see, for instance, Atoh 2000: 110–112). At the regional scale, low proportions of married women are found in the urban agglomerations of Tokyo, Osaka and Fukuoka, but also on the island of Hokkaido, with its regional metropolis of Sapporo, as well as in Okinawa. While this result is mostly consistent with the common sense assumption of high celibacy rates in urbanized regions, it is more surprising to see that there are significant differences inside rural Japan. Generally speaking, a dichotomous northeast-southwest pattern prevails, with higher rates in the northeast (Lützeler 2002b: 72). This pattern dates back to the Edo Period and can be linked to regional family type differences. According to Hayami and Kurosu (2001: 305–311), in the poor north-eastern regions the eldest son in a stem family household, which was the dominant household type there, married very early in order to make longer use of the working capacity of his even younger wife, who became a member of her husband's family.[4] By contrast, in the central

[4] Following the results of several village studies, during the Edo Period age at first marriage in the north-eastern Tohoku region was around 19 to 22 years for men and 13 to 17 years for women (Hayami and Kurosu 2001: 305–306).

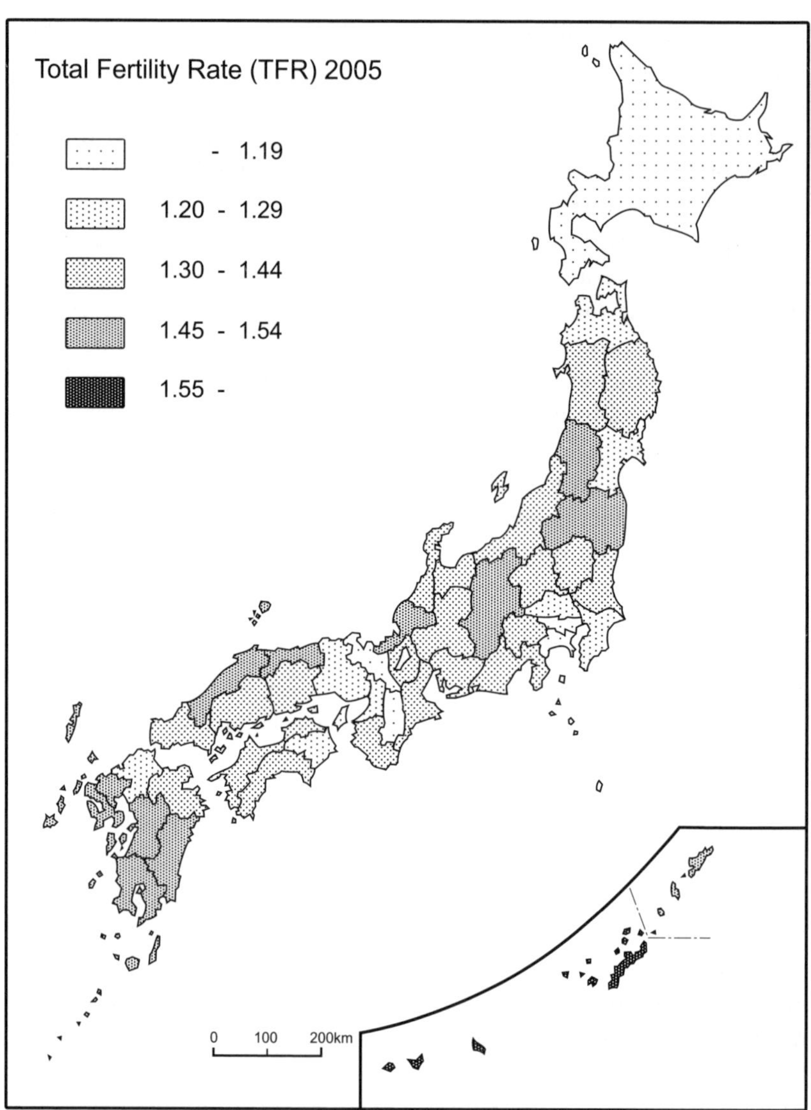


Source: KRDKTJ 2006, Internet.

Figure 6. Total fertility rate (TFR) by prefecture, 2005.

and south-western parts of Japan, where nuclear households were more common and urbanization more advanced, it was customary to work away from home for several years before marriage. It is interesting to see that, in spite of the dramatic socio-economic changes that have occurred since then, this regional marriage behaviour pattern has not yet vanished completely.

While differences between south-western and north-eastern Japan have persisted, during recent decades a tendency toward later marriage and more people remaining single has nonetheless spread throughout the whole of Japan. It started in the urban agglomerations of Tokyo and Osaka during the period from 1975 to 1980, then spread to neighbouring prefectures, the urbanized prefecture of Hokkaido and the Nagoya area. During the late 1980s, marriage behaviour change had spread across almost all of central Japan and, pushing forward along the main communication routes, had reached the regional capital areas around Sendai, Niigata, Hiroshima and Fukuoka. By the beginning of the 1990s, change had finally reached even the remoter parts of the country (Lützeler 2002b: 74). Female participation rates in university education or gainful employment first increased in metropolitan areas like Tokyo or Osaka Prefecture, and can be identified as the main contributor to marriage rate decline there. The underlying reason is that Japanese women who plan to have a career often see no choice but to abandon their desire to marry and have children, since conventional gender role division is still widely taken for granted (Atoh 1992: 57). Likewise, more critical views on marriage might have evolved independently in urbanized regions before they spread to other prefectures. According to results presented by Ogawa and Retherford (1993: 730–731), the approval of attitudes favouring a single life is higher in Japanese cities, even after controlling for such factors as occupation or formal education level. It confirms the overall finding by Retherford, Ogawa and Matsukura (2001) that rising employment opportunities and a gradual weakening of familistic attitudes are responsible for changing marriage behaviour in Japan, the former being more important than the latter.

Contrary to the proportion of people getting married, neither the volume nor the regional pattern of marital fertility has changed much during recent decades. Again, the lowest rates are recorded in urbanized areas, but only a few marked differences appear between rural prefectures (Lützeler 2000: 90). To be sure, marital fertility is quite high in Okinawa, possibly related to the fact that the custom of son adoption that was very wide-spread in the rest of the country had never taken root there, thus encouraging parents to carry on having children until the birth of a male successor (Nishioka 1994). Apart from this, however, there are only weak correlations between fertility and regional characteristics. Since marriage in Japan is still inextricably linked with having children, neither high educational attainment nor other social attributes of married women are of high relevance with regard to their number of births (Lützeler 2000: 96–97).

It is well known that since the early 1980s the population of Japan shows the highest life expectancy of all major societies in the world. In 2000, average life expectancy stood at 77.7 years in males and 84.6 years in females. Broken down by prefectures, male life expectancy ranged from 75.7 years in Aomori to 78.9 years in Nagano; female life expectancy varied between 83.7 years in Aomori and 86.0 years in Okinawa (KSHJMK 2006, Internet).[5] Overall, life expectancies are lower in north-eastern Japan as well as in parts of the Kansai area and northern Kyushu and higher in the rural areas of central Japan and in Okinawa. It has often been argued that unfavourable nutritional habits are in part responsible for higher mortality rates in the northeast. Deaths from stroke or gastric cancer in particular have been attributed to traditional features of the north-eastern diet: an excessive consumption of salted food, such as pickled vegetables and soy sauce, and a low intake of food rich in minerals. Furthermore, the very low temperatures found in wooden Japanese homes during the winter season have been identified as a risk factor promoting high blood pressure, which in turn could lead to strokes. In Hokkaido, on the other hand, stroke mortality rates are quite low, which is generally explained by better insulation of houses on this northerly island (Wynder and Hirayama 1977; Kagami 2004: 63–67). Apart from diet and housing conditions, a higher-than-average proportion of socially disadvantaged groups such as day labourers [*hiyatoi*] or *burakumin*,[6] who suffer from discrimination, might explain

[5] In 2005, average life expectancy in Japan had further increased to 78.6 years in males and 85.5 years in females (KRDKTJ 2007, Internet). However, still no prefectural figures had been published for this year at the time of writing.

[6] *Burakumin* are the descendants of people who were engaged in despised occupations such as public executioners, tanners or jugglers during the Edo Period. Although the premodern class system was officially abolished by the Meiji government, discrimination against these groups has prevailed to this day. The number of *burakumin* is believed to be close to three million people. Several case studies have found very low life expectancies in *burakumin* communities, which has been explained by the adverse material and psychological living conditions of many *burakumin* (see Lützeler 1995: 48).

why life expectancies are low in some prefectures of south-western Japan. Finally, the fact that the population of north-eastern Aomori Prefecture shows by far the lowest life expectancy in Japan might be interpreted as the result of unhealthy dietary habits overlapping with problematic social conditions, in this case a high percentage of seasonal out-migrants (Lützeler 1994).

## References

Atoh, Makoto (1992): Nihon ni okeru shusshōritsu no dōkō to yōin [Birth rate trends and their causes in Japan]. In: Kōno, Shigemi and Minoru Okada (eds.): *Tei-shusshōryoku o meguru shomondai* [Problems concerning low fertility]. Tokyo: Taimeidō, pp. 48–68.

—— (2000): *Gendai jinkōgaku. Shōshi kōrei shakai no kiso chishiki* [Demography of today. Basic knowledge about aged societies with few children]. Tokyo: Nihon Hyōronsha.

Flüchter, Winfried (1990): *Hochschulstandorte und Bildungsverhalten unter Aspekten der Raumordnung in Japan*. Paderborn: Schöningh (= Bochumer Geographische Arbeiten; 52).

—— (1995): Japan. Raum- und Ressourcen-Probleme unter Aspekten von Geopolitik, Anpassungsmaßnahmen und Landesentwicklung. In: *Japanstudien. Jahrbuch des Deutschen Instituts für Japanstudien der Philipp-Franz-von-Siebold-Stiftung* 6 (1994), pp. 17–45.

—— (1997): *Tōkyō quo vadis? Chancen und Grenzen (?) metropolitanen Wachstums*. Duisburg: Institut für Ostasienwissenschaften, Universität Duisburg (= Duisburger Arbeitspapiere Ostasienwissenschaften; 15).

Fujita, Yoshihisa (1981): *Nihon no sanson* [The mountain villages of Japan]. Kyoto: Chijin Shobō.

Hayami, Akira and Satomi Kurosu (2001): Regional Diversity in Demographic and Family Patterns in Preindustrial Japan. In: *The Journal of Japanese Studies* 27, 2, pp. 295–321.

Hohn, Uta (2002): Renaissance innerstädtischen Wohnens in Tōkyō. Trend zur Reurbanisierung. In: *Geographische Rundschau* 54, 6, pp. 4–11.

Ishikawa, Yoshitaka (1994): *Jinkō idō no keiryō chirigaku* [Quantitative geography of population migration]. Tokyo: Kokon Shoin.

Kagami, Masahiro (2004): *Byōki no chiikisa o yomu. Chirigaku kara no apurōchi* [Interpreting regional differences of diseases. A geographical approach]. Tokyo: Kokon Shoin.

Kokudochō (1996): *Kokudo repōto '96. Kokudo kōzō no hensen to arata-na kokudojiku* [National Land Report '96. Changes in the territorial structure and the new territorial axes]. Tokyo: Ōkurashō Insatsukyoku.

KRDKTJ (Kōsei Rōdōshō Daijin Kanbō Tōkei Jōhōbu) (2006): *Heisei 17-nen jinkō dōtai tōkei (kakutei-sū) no gaikyō* [Outline of vital statistics for the year 2005 (confirmed figures)]. http://www.mhlw.go.jp/toukei/saikin/hw/jinkou/kakutei05/index.htm (found 22/03/07).

—— (2007): *Dai 20-kai seimeihyō* (kanzen seimeihyō) [The 20th life table (complete life table)]. http://www.mhlw.go.jp/toukei/saikin/hw/life/20th/index.html (found 22/03/07).

KSHJMK (Kokuritsu Shakai Hoshō Jinkō Mondai Kenkyūsho) (2002): *Todōfuken no shōrai suikei jinkō (Heisei 14-nen 3-gatsu suikei)—Heisei 12 (2000)-nen–Heisei 42 (2030)-nen* [Prefectural population projections for the period 2000–2030 (estimated in March 2002)]. Tokyo: Kokuritsu Shakai Hoshō Jinkō Mondai Kenkyūsho.

—— (2003a, 2004, 2005, 2006): *Jinkō no dōkō—Nihon to sekai. Jinkō tōkei shiryōshū* [Population trends—Japan and the world. A collection of population statistics]. Tokyo: Kōsei Tōkei Kyōkai [data related to the 2004, 2005 and 2006 editions were taken from the internet: http://www.ipss.go.jp/site-ad/index_Japanese/population.html (found 23/05/06)].

—— (2003b): *Nihon no shikuchōson-betsu shōrai suikei jinkō (Heisei 15-nen 12-gatsu suikei)—Heisei 12 (2000)–42 (2030)-nen* [Population projections for Japanese municipalities for the period 2000–2030 (estimated in December 2003)]. Tokyo: Kokuritsu Shakai Hoshō Jinkō Mondai Kenkyūsho.

Lützeler, Ralph (1994): *Räumliche Unterschiede der Sterblichkeit in Japan. Sterblichkeit als Indikator regionaler Lebensbedingungen.* Bonn: Dümmlers (= Bonner Geographische Abhandlungen; 89).

—— (1995): The Regional Structure of Social Problems in Japan. In: *Geographical Review of Japan* 68 (Ser. B), 1, pp. 46–62.

—— (1998): Regionale Wirtschaftsstruktur und Raumordnungspolitik. In: Deutsches Institut für Japanstudien (ed.): *Die Wirtschaft Japans. Strukturen zwischen Kontinuität und Wandel.* Berlin, etc.: Springer, pp. 269–292.

—— (2000): Zur regionalen Dimension von Geburtenrückgang und abnehmender Heiratsneigung in Japan. In: Manthey, Barbara *et al.* (eds.): *JapanWelten. Aspekte der deutschsprachigen Japanforschung. Festschrift für Josef Kreiner zu seinem sechzigsten Geburtstag von seinen Schülern und Mitarbeitern.* Bonn: Bier'sche Verlagsanstalt, pp. 83–101 (= Japan Archiv; 3).

—— (2002a): Demographic and Regional Aspects of Aging and Long-term Care in Japan. In: Conrad, Harald and Ralph Lützeler (eds.): *Aging and Social Policy—A German-Japanese Comparison.* Munich: iudicium, pp. 275–298 (= Monographien aus dem Deutschen Institut für Japanstudien; 26).

—— (2002b): The "Second Fertility Transition" in Comparative Perspective: The Impact of Female Employment, Care Services, and Familism. In: Klein, Axel, Ralph Lützeler and Hans Dieter Ölschleger (eds.): *Modernization in Progress. Demographic Development and Value Change in Contemporary Europe and East Asia.* Bonn: Bier'sche Verlagsanstalt, pp. 47–80 (= JapanArchiv; 4).

—— (2004): Demography. In: Kreiner, Josef, Ulrich Möhwald and Hans Dieter Ölschleger (eds.): *Modern Japanese Society.* Leiden and Boston: Brill, pp. 15–61 (= Handbook of Oriental Studies/Handbuch der Orientalistik; Section 5, Japan, vol. 9).

—— (2005): *Städtische Segregation in Japan. Aktuelle sozialräumliche Tendenzen in der* global city *Tōkyō im Lichte der neuen Debatte über eine zunehmende Polarisierung städtischer Gesellschaften.* Bonn: Philosophische Fakultät der Universität Bonn [unpublished habilitation thesis].

Nishioka, Hachiro (1994): Effects of the Family Formation Norms on Demographic Behaviors. Case of Okinawa in Japan. In: *Jinkō Mondai Kenkyū* (Journal of Population Problems) 50, 2, pp. 52–60.

Nyūkan Kyōkai (2006): *Heisei 18-nenban zairyū gaikokujin tōkei* (Statistics on the foreigners registered in Japan 2006). Tokyo: Nyūkan Kyōkai.

Ōe, Moriyuki (1995): Kokunai jinkō bunpu hendō no kōhōto bunseki—Tōkyō-ken e no jinkō shūchū purosesu to shōrai tenbō (Cohort analysis of population distribution change in Japan—processes of population concentration to the Tokyo Region and its future). In: *Jinkō Mondai Kenkyū* (Journal of Population Problems) 51, 3, pp. 1–19.

Ogawa, Naohiro and Robert D. Retherford (1993): The Resumption of Fertility Decline in Japan; 1973–92. In: *Population and Development Review* 19, 4, pp. 703–741.

Retherford, Robert D., Naohiro Ogawa and Rikiya Matsukura (2001): Late Marriage and Less Marriage in Japan. In: *Population and Development Review* 27, 1, pp. 65–102.

SJGKT (Sōmushō Jichi Gyōseikyoku Kaso Taisakushitsu) (2005): *Heisei 16-nenban kaso taisaku no genkyō ni tsuite (gaiyōhan)* [About the present state of depopulation countermeasures, 2004 edition (summary version)]. http://www.soumu.go.jp/c-gyousei/2001/kaso/pdf/note.pdf (found 02/06/06).

Sōmushō Tōkeikyoku (2006a): *Heisei 17-nen kokusei chōsa. Dai-ichiji kihon shūkei kekka* [2005 population census of Japan. Results of first basic complete tabulation]. http://www.stat.go.jp/data/kokusei/2005/kihon1/index.htm (found 22/03/07).

—— (2006b): *Jūmin kihon daichō jinkō idō hōkoku nenpō. Heisei 17-nen* (Annual report on the internal migration in Japan derived from the basic resident registers 2005). Tokyo: Nihon Tōkei Kyōkai.

Wiltshire, Richard (1979): Research on Reverse Migration in Japan: (II) Personnel Transfers. In: *The Science Reports of the Tohoku University, 7th Series (Geography)* 29, pp. 135–142.

Wynder, Ernst L. and Takeshi Hirayama (1977): Comparative Epidemiology of Cancers of the United States and Japan. In: *Preventive Medicine* 6, pp. 567–594.

Yazaki, Takeo (1968): *Social Change and the City in Japan. From Earliest Times through the Industrial Revolution*. Tokyo: Japan Publications [translation of the original version *Nihon toshi no hatten katei* (publ. 1962) by David L. Swain].

CHAPTER FIVE

# DEMOGRAPHIC COMPARISONS WITH OTHER COUNTRIES WITH THE EMPHASIS ON THE MORE DEVELOPED REGIONS

Shigemi Kono

## 1. Recent Demographic Situations in the More Developed Regions

Despite their obvious differences in history, culture, religion and other aspects, there is a considerable extent of convergence among the more developed countries in respect of demography. Here, the "more developed countries" (or simply "developed countries") are those included in the "more developed regions", designated as such according to the nomenclature of the United Nations Population Division (2005). According to this designation, these "more developed regions" comprise all regions of Europe, North America, Australia and New Zealand, and Japan. On the other hand, the "less developed countries" or simply "developing countries" are those belonging to the "less developed regions", and these comprise all regions of Africa; Asia (excluding Japan); Latin America and the Caribbean; and Melanesia, Micronesia and Polynesia. In this broad categorization, there are some anomalies in classifying specific countries. For example, countries such as the Republic of Korea, Israel, and Singapore, which are by any standard fully-fledged developed countries, are here labelled as "less developed", while others, such as Albania, Bulgaria, and Macedonia, whose per capita incomes are far below the above-mentioned "less developed" countries, are formally included in the more developed regions.

Hence the countries in the more developed regions are in practical terms the Western nations of Europe and North America, and Japan is the only country from the non-Western world to be included. The more developed countries are noted for their very low birth rates, high life expectancies, incipient or foreseeable population decline, and rapid population ageing. In addition, except for some eastern European and southern European countries, most of the developed countries have now become migrant-receiving countries. Before World War II, the migrant-receiving countries were limited to the former colonies of Canada, United States, Australia, and New Zealand, which might be called Neo Europe, but recently the tide has shifted. Italy, Spain, and Greece in southern Europe were once well-known for sending migrants overseas until recent years, but they have now shifted to become migrant-receiving countries.

## 2. Population Decline and Population Size

Table 1 presents a synopsis of the demographic situation of the world as a whole and of five selected countries from the more developed regions, together with the two demographic giants of China and India. The world population has expanded from 2,519,500,000 in 1950 to 6,464,800,000 in 2005, increasing by 2.5 times. But the more developed countries have grown rather modestly, from 812,800,000 in 1950 to 1,211,300,000 in 2005, increasing by only 1.5 times. During the same period, the population of Japan has increased by 1.5 times, that of the United States by 1.9 times, and those of Germany, France, and the United Kingdom by 1.2 times, 1.4 times, and 1.2 times respectively. However, the population of the less developed regions has expanded by 3.1 times overall, including that of China by 2.4 times and that of India by 3.1 times. Generally speaking, the less developed countries have tended to grow much more rapidly than the developed countries.

The relatively slow growth in the more developed countries is conceivably attributable to the continuation of extraordinarily low birth rates in recent years, but at the same time, it can also be explained by the relatively slow increases in life expectancy in the more developed countries, which have become less dramatic than those in the less developed countries. In the less developed countries, life expectancies were quite low at the initial point of observation immediately after World War II, so they had the potential to increase more rapidly and substantially than the developed countries, given even small improvements in standards of living, nutrition, and public health. On the other hand, life expectancies in the more developed countries had already attained relatively high levels immediately after World War II. Therefore the chances of gaining further increases would be smaller than those in the less developed countries. Furthermore, their crude death rates, which are directly related to the natural growth of a population, have

Table 1. A Synopsis of Demographic Indicators for the World and Select Countries: c. 2005.

| Indicator | World | Japan | U.S.A. | Germany | France | U.K. | China | India |
|---|---|---|---|---|---|---|---|---|
| Population (million) | | | | | | | | |
| 1950 | 2,519.5 | 83.6 | 157.8 | 68.4 | 41.8 | 49.8 | 554.8 | 357.6 |
| 2005 | 6,464.8 | 127.8 | 298.2 | 82.7 | 59.7 | 59.7 | 1,315.8 | 1,103.4 |
| 2050 | 9,075.9 | 112.2 | 395.0 | 78.8 | 63.1 | 67.1 | 1,329.3 | 1,592.7 |
| Annual growth rate (%) | | | | | | | | |
| 2000–05 | 1.21 | 0.17 | 0.97 | 0.08 | 0.41 | 0.34 | 0.65 | 1.55 |
| Total fertility rate, 2004 | 2.60 | 1.29 | 2.04 | 1.37 | 1.90 | 1.74 | 1.72 | 2.85 |
| Life exp. for both sexes (years) | 65.4 | 81.9 | 77.3 | 78.6 | 79.4 | 78.3 | 71.5 | 63.1 |
| Age composition (%) | | | | | | | | |
| Under 15 | 28.1 | 14.0 | 20.7 | 14.3 | 18.2 | 17.9 | 21.4 | 32.1 |
| 15–64 | 64.5 | 66.3 | 67.0 | 66.9 | 65.2 | 66.1 | 71.0 | 62.6 |
| 65+ | 7.4 | 19.7 | 12.3 | 18.8 | 16.6 | 16.0 | 7.6 | 5.3 |
| Old age dependency ratio | 11 | 30 | 18 | 28 | 25 | 24 | 11 | 8 |
| Pop. density | 48 | 339 | 31 | 232 | 110 | 246 | 137 | 336 |
| GDP (U.S. trillion $) | 44.384 | 4.506 | 12.455 | 2.782 | 2.110 | 2.193 | 2.229 | 785 |
| GDP per capita (U.S. $) | 6.987 | 38.980 | 43.740 | 34.580 | 34.810 | 37.600 | 1.740 | 720 |

Note: Unless otherwise indicated, the year referred to is 2005.
Source: United Nations. 2005. *World Population Prospects: The 2004 Revision*, Vol. I. Comprehensive Tables, New York; World Bank. 2006. *World Development Report 2006*, Washington, D.C.; United Nations Population Fund. 2006. *State of the World Population*, New York.

recently been rising, since their aged populations are rapidly expanding in terms of absolute numbers as well as a proportion of the total population, and aged populations are generally more vulnerable to mortality risks.

The population decline and shrinking population size in Japan and other more developed countries predicted to take place through the twenty-first century are challenges to their survival and economic growth. According to the United Nations population projections made in 2004, Japan's population is 128 million in 2006, ranking tenth in the world. But by the year 2050 the population will decline to 112 million and rank 16th in the world. This means that by the year 2050, Japan will be dwarfed by neighbouring Vietnam and the Philippines, which are at present considerably smaller in population. Moreover, according to the population projections prepared by the National Institute of Population and Social Security Research (2002), by the year 2100, Japan's population will shrink further down to only 64 million, just half of the present population size.

Table 2 shows the rise and fall of populations that are currently large. Among the developed countries, the United States has a population of 298 million, ranking third after China and India and attaining the 300 million mark in October 2006. Germany's population stands now at 83 million, ranking 14th, but by the year 2050 it will fall to 79 million, ranking 22nd. The United Kingdom's population at present is 60 million, ranking 21st, but in the year 2050 it will rise to 67 million, ranking 24th. The biggest country in terms of population size has always been China until now, but by 2050 it will become the second biggest, surpassed by India, whose population will be 1,593 million in the same year.

Population size still matters as a symbol of international political and military power as well as of economic strength. A country with a large population can have a large labour force and provide a sufficiently large domestic market that is less susceptible to volatile and fickle international economic and monetary changes.

## 3. Fertility

Fertility varies greatly among the countries of the world. Table 3 shows the ten countries with the highest total fertility rates and the ten countries with the lowest rates. This table simply shows how much human fertility differs among the countries of the world according to level of development and region. It is striking to note that, among the less developed countries, there are countries whose total fertility rate is even lower than low fertility countries in the more developed regions. As already mentioned, almost all the more developed countries have fertility rates below the replacement level. The replacement level of

Table 2. Countries and areas accounting for about 75 per cent of the world population, estimates and medium variant, 1950, 2005, and 2050.

| Rank | Country or area | Population in 1950 (millions) | Cumulated percentage | Rank | Country or area | Population in 2005 (millions) | Cumulated percentage | Rank | Country or area | Population in 2050 (millions) | Cumulated percentage |
|---|---|---|---|---|---|---|---|---|---|---|---|
| 1 | China | 555 | 22.0 | 1 | China | 1316 | 20.4 | 1 | India | 1593 | 17.5 |
| 2 | India | 358 | 36.2 | 2 | India | 1103 | 37.4 | 2 | China | 1392 | 32.9 |
| 3 | United States of America | 158 | 42.5 | 3 | United States of America | 298 | 42.0 | 3 | United States of America | 395 | 37.2 |
| 4 | Russian Federation | 103 | 46.6 | 4 | Indonesia | 223 | 45.5 | 4 | Pakistan | 305 | 40.6 |
| 5 | Japan | 84 | 49.9 | 5 | Brazil | 186 | 48.4 | 5 | Indonesia | 285 | 43.7 |
| 6 | Indonesia | 80 | 53.0 | 6 | Pakistan | 158 | 50.8 | 6 | Nigeria | 258 | 46.6 |
| 7 | Germany | 68 | 55.7 | 7 | Russian Federation | 143 | 53.0 | 7 | Brazil | 253 | 49.4 |
| 8 | Brazil | 54 | 57.9 | 8 | Bangladesh | 142 | 55.2 | 8 | Bangladesh | 243 | 52.0 |
| 9 | United Kingdom | 50 | 59.9 | 9 | Nigeria | 132 | 57.3 | 9 | Dem. Republic of the Congo | 177 | 54.0 |
| 10 | Italy | 47 | 61.7 | 10 | Japan | 128 | 59.2 | 10 | Ethiopia | 170 | 55.9 |
| 11 | France | 42 | 63.4 | 11 | Mexico | 107 | 60.9 | 11 | Mexico | 139 | 57.4 |
| 12 | Bangladesh | 42 | 65.0 | 12 | Viet Nam | 84 | 62.2 | 12 | Philippines | 127 | 58.8 |
| 13 | Ukraine | 37 | 66.5 | 13 | Philippines | 83 | 63.5 | 13 | Uganda | 127 | 60.2 |
| 14 | Pakistan | 37 | 68.0 | 14 | Germany | 83 | 64.8 | 14 | Egypt | 126 | 61.6 |
| 15 | Nigeria | 33 | 69.3 | 15 | Ethiopia | 77 | 66.0 | 15 | Viet Nam | 117 | 62.9 |
| 16 | Spain | 28 | 70.4 | 16 | Egypt | 74 | 67.1 | 16 | Japan | 112 | 64.1 |
| 17 | Mexico | 28 | 71.5 | 17 | Turkey | 73 | 68.2 | 17 | Russian Federation | 112 | 65.3 |
| 18 | Viet Nam | 27 | 72.6 | 18 | Iran (Islamic Republic of) | 70 | 69.3 | 18 | Iran (Islamic Republic of) | 102 | 66.5 |
| 19 | Poland | 25 | 73.6 | 19 | Thailand | 64 | 70.3 | 19 | Turkey | 101 | 67.6 |
| 20 | Egypt | 22 | 74.4 | 20 | France | 60 | 71.2 | 20 | Afghanistan | 97 | 68.7 |
| 21 | Turkey | 21 | 75.3 | 21 | United Kingdom | 60 | 72.2 | 21 | Kenya | 83 | 69.6 |
| | | | | 22 | Italy | 58 | 73.1 | 22 | Germany | 79 | 70.4 |
| | | | | 23 | Dem. Republic of the Congo | 58 | 73.9 | 23 | Thailand | 75 | 71.3 |
| | | | | 24 | Myanmar | 51 | 74.7 | 24 | United Kingdom | 67 | 72.0 |
| | | | | | | | | 25 | United Republic of Tanzania | 67 | 72.7 |
| | | | | | | | | 26 | Sudan | 67 | 73.5 |
| | | | | | | | | 27 | Colombia | 66 | 74.2 |
| | | | | | | | | 28 | Iraq | 64 | 74.9 |

Note: Countries are ranked by decreasing size of population.
Source: United Nations Department of Economic and Social Affairs/Population Division (2006): World Population Prospects: The 2004 Revision, Vol. III. Analytical Report. New York.

Table 3. The ten countries or areas with the highest total fertility rate and the ten countries and areas with the lowest total fertility rate, by level of development, 2000–2005.

| Rank | Less developed country or area | Total fertility (children per woman) | Rank | More developed country or area | Total fertility (children per woman) |
|---|---|---|---|---|---|
| A. *Highest* | | | | | |
| 1 | Niger | 7.91 | 1 | Albania | 2.29 |
| 2 | Democratic Republic of Timor-Leste | 7.79 | 2 | United States of America | 2.04 |
| 3 | Afghanistan | 7.48 | 3 | Iceland | 1.97 |
| 4 | Guinea-Bissau | 7.10 | 4 | New Zealand | 1.96 |
| 5 | Uganda | 7.10 | 5 | Ireland | 1.94 |
| 6 | Mali | 6.92 | 6 | France | 1.87 |
| 7 | Burundi | 6.80 | 7 | Norway | 1.79 |
| 8 | Liberia | 6.80 | 8 | Denmark | 1.75 |
| 9 | Angola | 6.75 | 9 | Australia | 1.75 |
| 10 | Democratic Republic of the Congo | 6.70 | 10 | Luxembourg | 1.73 |
| B. *Lowest* | | | | | |
| 1 | Macao, China SAR | 0.84 | 1 | Ukraine | 1.12 |
| 2 | Hong Kong, China SAR | 0.94 | 2 | Czech Republic | 1.17 |
| 3 | Republic of Korea | 1.23 | 3 | Slovakia | 1.20 |
| 4 | Armenia | 1.33 | 4 | Slovenia | 1.22 |
| 5 | Singapore | 1.35 | 5 | Republic of Moldova | 1.23 |
| 6 | Georgia | 1.48 | 6 | Bulgaria | 1.24 |
| 7 | Barbados | 1.50 | 7 | Belarus | 1.24 |
| 8 | Trinidad and Tobago | 1.61 | 8 | Greece | 1.25 |
| 9 | Cuba | 1.61 | 9 | Poland | 1.26 |
| 10 | Cyprus | 1.63 | 10 | Latvia | 1.26 |

Source: United Nations Department of Economic and Social Affairs/Population Division. 2006. *World Population Prospects: The 2004 Revision, Vol. III: Analytical Report.*

fertility means that fertility is at such a level that, given the mortality rates, the rate of population growth will ultimately become zero. If the lowest mortality as observed in present Japan is assumed for the calculation, then a total fertility rate of 2.07 is required to maintain a stable population in the future.

Perhaps the only exception among the developed countries in not having sub-replacement fertility is the United States. Japan has been among the lowest-low fertility countries, which include eastern European and southern European countries and East Asian countries such as the Republic of Korea, Taiwan, and Singapore. The term "low fertility" usually denotes sub-replacement fertility, while "lowest-low fertility" is conceived of as being lower than 1.3 in terms of the total fertility rate. It is indeed striking that, in 2004, the Republic of Korea had a total fertility rate of 1.08, Taiwan 1.12, and Singapore 1.24, while the city state of Hong Kong had a fertility rate of only 0.97. Low fertility rates accelerate population decline and ageing. However, the Japanese government's efforts in the fields of population and family policies to restore its fertility have been without success. Many other developed countries have had similar experiences, but there are success stories like France and some Nordic countries.

In the more developed countries, fertility decline generally started around 1965 when oral contraceptives were introduced to northwest Europe. After the 1970s, the fertility rates of most of the developed countries started to fall below replacement level. In the twenty-first century, sub-replacement fertility is spreading all over the world.

By 1975–1980, fertility in northwestern Europe, comprising the United Kingdom and Ireland plus the Nordic countries, and western Europe, including the Benelux countries, Austria, France, Germany, and Switzerland had already fallen to sub-replacement level. But since around 1980–85, fertility rates in countries with traditionally high rates, such as Italy, Spain, Portugal, and Greece in southern Europe, started declining rapidly. The causes of these declines have yet to be clearly identified, but the leading theory to explain the phenomenon is the Second Demographic Transition. This argues that there were fundamental transformations in the mode of industrial production and shifts of labour force activities from the secondary to tertiary sectors of industry with the advent of the post-industrial society, and that consequently, ideational changes have occurred that emphasize more self-actualization and freedom from traditional family constraints, particularly among women. Women's educational attainment has risen enormously, and their economic activities outside the home have subsequently soared. At present in Europe, however, the lowest-low fertility countries are not in northwestern Europe, but are located in southern and eastern Europe as well as the German-speaking nations in western Europe.

Map 1 represents the current situation of fertility in the European countries. This kind of map was originally prepared by a French demographer-historian, Emmanuel Todd (2006), who demonstrates that there is a great divide between two groups of countries in Europe with respect to their fertility levels. More up-to-date values of total fertility rates are presented in a similar map by the author of this chapter. Split by a great dividing line, a demographic *fosse magna*, northwestern Europe, including the United Kingdom, the Benelux countries, France,

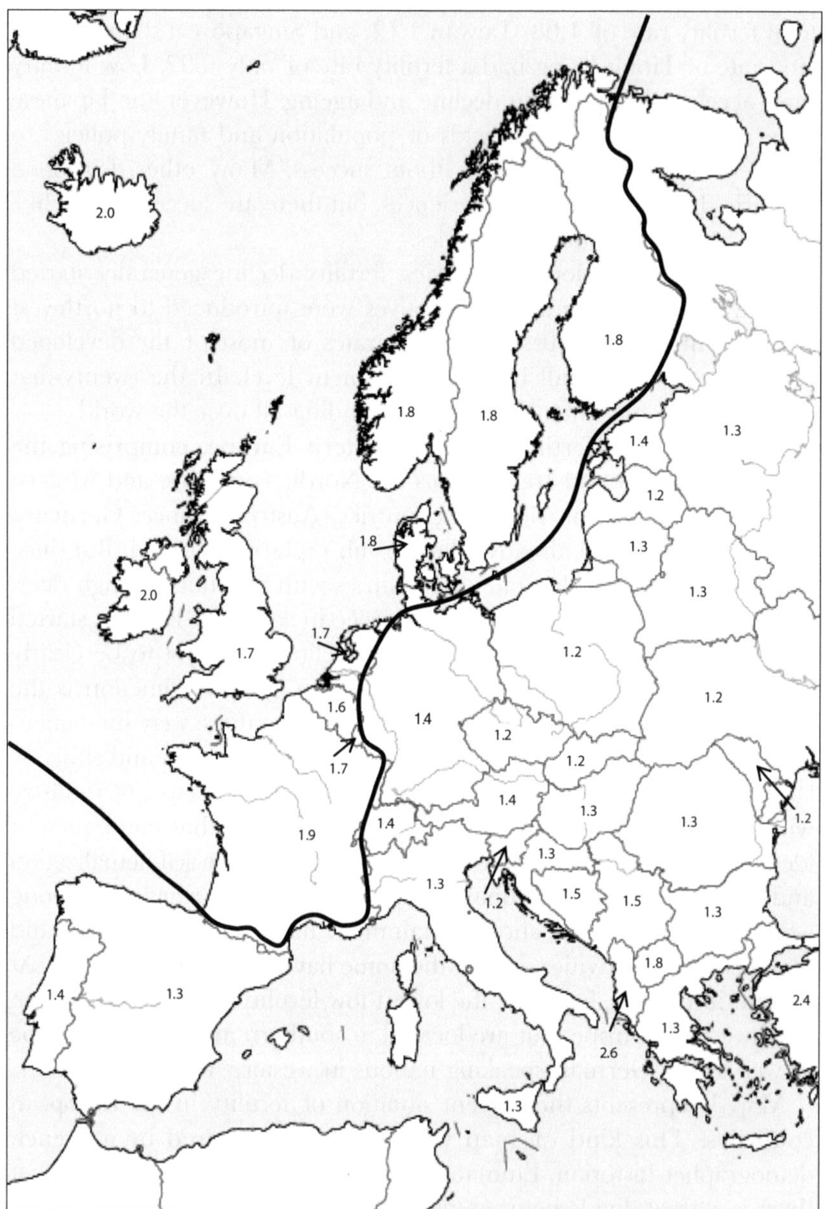


Sources: EUROSTAT.

Map 1. Total Fertility Rates of the European Countries with Dividing Line between "High" and "Low": 2004.

and the Nordic countries of Sweden, Norway, Denmark, Iceland, and Finland, represents a group of countries with relatively high fertility, although still slightly below the replacement level. The other group covers the remaining countries of western Europe, namely the German-speaking countries of Germany, Austria, and Switzerland, plus all the countries of southern Europe and eastern Europe, which show very, often extremely, low fertility. Note that, within northwestern Europe, the German-speaking countries are unique, exhibiting exceptionally low fertility since the 1960s.

Peter McDonald, a social demographer in Australia, argues that, if very high levels of gender equality are achieved in a society outside the family and are combined with very low levels of equality for women within the family as wives or mothers, the outcome for the society is very low fertility (McDonald 2000). The German-speaking and southern and eastern European countries, as well as East Asian ones, might have fallen into this trap. But, at the same time, the lowest-low fertility situations in the East Asian countries of Japan, the Republic of Korea, Taiwan, and Singapore, could also be partly explained by the extraordinarily fierce competition in examinations for entrance to high-ranking universities and consequently by the ridiculously high cost of sending children to prep schools and after-school cram sessions to prepare for these examinations.

## 4. Mortality

Every society appreciates and strives to have good health and longevity for its citizens. Advancement in life expectancies is a triumph for civilization and successful economic and social development. On the other hand, it also tends to accelerate population ageing and increase the numbers of patients with senile dementia and of bedridden elderly people.

As shown in Table 4, prepared by the United Nations, as in the case of fertility, there is still wide variation in life expectancies according to the level of development of the country concerned, and there are great variations between countries with the highest and lowest levels of development. While the eastern European countries, such as Russia and Ukraine, represent low life expectancies, substantially lower than some of the developing countries with high life expectancies, we can also note that there are indeed a number of countries with extremely low life

Table 4. The ten countries and areas with the highest life expectancy at birth and ten countries and areas with the lowest life expectancy at birth, by development region, 2000–2005.

| Rank | Country or area[a] | Life expectancy (years) | Rank | Country or area[a] | Life expectancy (years) |
|---|---|---|---|---|---|
| A. *More developed regions* | | | | | |
| Rank | Highest life expectancy at birth | | Rank | Lowest life expectancy at birth | |
| 1 | Japan | 81.9 | 1 | Russian Federation | 65.4 |
| 2 | Iceland | 80.6 | 2 | Ukraine | 66.1 |
| 3 | Switzerland | 80.4 | 3 | Republic of Moldova | 67.5 |
| 4 | Australia | 80.2 | 4 | Belarus | 68.1 |
| 5 | Sweden | 80.1 | 5 | Estonia | 71.2 |
| 6 | Italy | 80.0 | 6 | Romania | 71.3 |
| 7 | Canada | 79.9 | 7 | Latvia | 71.4 |
| 8 | Spain | 79.4 | 8 | Bulgaria | 72.1 |
| 9 | France | 79.4 | 9 | Lithuania | 72.2 |
| 10 | Norway | 79.3 | 10 | Hungary | 72.6 |
| B. *Less developed regions* | | | | | |
| Rank | Highest life expectancy at birth | | Rank | Lowest life expectancy at birth | |
| 1 | Hong Kong, China SAR | 81.5 | 1 | Swaziland | 32.9 |
| 2 | Macao, China SAR | 80.0 | 2 | Botswana | 36.6 |
| 3 | Israel | 79.6 | 3 | Lesotho | 36.7 |
| 4 | Martinique | 78.7 | 4 | Zimbabwe | 37.2 |
| 5 | Singapore | 78.6 | 5 | Zambia | 37.4 |
| 6 | Cyprus | 78.5 | 6 | Central African Republic | 39.4 |
| 7 | United States Virgin Islands | 78.5 | 7 | Malawi | 39.6 |
| 8 | Guadeloupe | 78.3 | 8 | Sierra Leone | 40.6 |
| 9 | Costa Rica | 78.1 | 9 | Angola | 40.7 |
| 10 | Chile | 77.9 | 10 | Mozambique | 41.9 |

[a] Countries or areas with 100,000 persons or more in 2000.
Source: United Nations Department of Economic and Social Affairs/Population Division (2006): *World Population Prospects: The 2004 Revision, Vol. III: Analytical Report.*

expectancies in the least developed regions. This is particularly the case among Sub-Saharan countries characterized by life expectancy levels in the thirties and forties, which are obviously affected by the spread of HIV epidemics in Sub-Saharan Africa. It should also be noted that rich developing countries or territories such as Hong Kong, Macao, or

Israel have life expectancies more than twice as high as those of the HIV-stricken countries.

Three factors have been important in the dramatic and unprecedented mortality declines of the past hundred years and in the still more dramatic declines in developing countries since World War II. These factors are income growth, improvements in medical science, and public health programmes combined with the spread of knowledge about health (World Bank 1993).

## 5. Population Structure and Population Ageing

Almost all the more developed countries have experienced population ageing. Population ageing is an inevitable outcome of population development, when industrialization, urbanization, and secularization progress. Rapid population ageing combined with population decline exerts great negative impacts on a country's economy and society, generating a loss of economic vitality, labour shortages, difficulties in sustaining decent social security systems, and decay in peripheral regions far from the central metropolitan districts. Positive aspects, however, include a reduction in heavy population density, alleviation of traffic jams, and less environmental damage.

Along with the declines in both fertility and mortality, there have been substantial changes in population structure. All the more developed countries have experienced population ageing, that is, an increase in the proportion (and sometimes in the absolute numbers) of the elderly population (usually classified as people of 65 years of age and over). But now increasingly, some of the less developed countries that have recently undergone rapid declines in fertility and mortality are facing rapid population ageing. In Table 1, it was noted that three European countries with large populations and Japan all have proportions of the total population aged 65 years and over of higher than 16 per cent. On the other hand, China and India, the two demographic giants of the world, have low percentages of elderly people, 7.6 and 5.3 per cent respectively, while the world average is only 7.4 per cent. Another interesting feature is the proportion of the population of working age (15 to 64). This proportion used to be very high, approaching 70 per cent in Japan, but has rapidly fallen. According to Table 1, in the three European countries, the proportion of the population of working age remains somewhere around 66–67 per cent, but in China it is 71 per cent, reminiscent of the highest Japanese proportion recorded in the 1990s. It is obvious, that the greater the proportion of the population aged 15–64, the better are the chances of having a relatively large labour force. Other things being equal, it is easier to have better economic development, since the dependent population is a smaller proportion of the total population. Hence a nation with a relatively small economic burden of supporting children and the elderly will naturally be in a better position to invest more capital resources in economic development rather than in supporting childrearing expenses or social security costs.

Table 5 shows countries in terms of median age, comparing the ten countries with the oldest populations with the ten countries with the youngest populations. Needless to say, in the year 2005, the oldest populations all belong to the more developed regions, while Japan shows the highest median age at 42.9 years. In contrast, all ten countries with the lowest median ages are in Sub-Saharan Africa, with median ages below 17 years. By the year 2050, both the more developed and less developed countries will undergo further ageing. According to Table 5, by the year 2050, the most aged countries or areas will be Macao (54.4 years), the Republic of Korea (53.9), and Martinique (53.0). Note that all three currently belong to the less developed regions. Obviously the most aged countries of the world in 2050 are those which currently and will continue to have very low fertility rates, combined with relatively high life expectancies, in the period 2005–2050.

## 6. International Migration

In the absence of any recent success in encouraging the recovery of fertility in some of the industrialized countries, many scholars and policy makers inevitably come to think of international migration as an alternative solution to prevent further population decline. In the case of Japan, the foreign population residing in Japan is still relatively small, amounting to 2.3 million, including undocumented migrants, which comes to only about 2 per cent of the total population.

There are three key magnet regions of migration in the world. One is the United States and Canada, receiving immigrants from Latin America, Asia, and Europe. Second is Europe, specifically northern, southern and western Europe. The third focus of migration is in the oil-producing countries of the Persian Gulf, namely Saudi Arabia,

Table 5. The ten countries and areas with the oldest populations and the ten countries and areas with the youngest populations, estimates and medium variant, 2005 and 2050.

| 2005 | | | 2050 | | |
|---|---|---|---|---|---|
| | Country or area[a] | Median age (years) | | Country or area[a] | Median age (years) |
| A. *Oldest population* | | | | | |
| 1 | Japan | 42.9 | 1 | Macao, China SAR | 54.4 |
| 2 | Italy | 42.3 | 2 | Republic of Korea | 53.9 |
| 3 | Germany | 42.1 | 3 | Martinique | 53.0 |
| 4 | Finland | 40.9 | 4 | Italy | 52.5 |
| 5 | Switzerland | 40.8 | 5 | Japan | 52.3 |
| 6 | Belgium | 40.6 | 6 | Singapore | 52.1 |
| 7 | Croatia | 40.6 | 7 | Slovenia | 51.9 |
| 8 | Austria | 40.6 | 8 | Ukraine | 51.9 |
| 9 | Bulgaria | 40.6 | 9 | Slovakia | 51.8 |
| 10 | Slovenia | 40.2 | 10 | Lithuania | 51.7 |
| B. *Youngest population* | | | | | |
| 1 | Uganda | 14.8 | 1 | Burundi | 20.3 |
| 2 | Niger | 15.5 | 2 | Uganda | 20.5 |
| 3 | Mali | 15.8 | 3 | Liberia | 20.9 |
| 4 | Guinea -Bissau | 16.2 | 4 | Chad | 21.0 |
| 5 | Burkina Faso | 16.2 | 5 | Niger | 21.5 |
| 6 | Dem. Republic of the Congo | 16.3 | 6 | Guinea-Bissau | 21.5 |
| 7 | Malawi | 16.3 | 7 | Equatorial Guinea | 21.8 |
| 8 | Chad | 16.3 | 8 | Congo | 21.9 |
| 9 | Congo | 16.3 | 9 | Dem. Republic of the Congo | 22.1 |
| 10 | Liberia | 16.3 | 10 | Angola | 22.9 |
| World | | 28.1 | World | | 37.8 |

[a] Countries or areas with 100,000 persons or more in 2000.
Source: United Nations Department of Economic and Social Affairs/Population Division (2006): *World Population Prospects: The 2004 Revision, United Nations, Vol. III. Analytical Report.* New York.

the Arab Emirates, Oman, Qatar, Kuwait and others. This last case of major migration streams is, however, considerably smaller in scale than the first two. In addition, there are relatively minor streams of migration, for example, towards Australia and New Zealand, Japan, and some of the developing countries.

European countries were predominantly migrant-sending countries in the eighteenth, nineteenth and the early twentieth centuries. But since around 1970, they have all become migrant-receiving countries. Recently the traditionally migrant-sending countries of Italy, Spain, and Greece have all switched to the opposite status, while the traditionally migrant-receiving countries of the United States, Canada, and Australia, which used to receive migrants from Europe, are now receiving more migrants from the developing countries of Latin America and Asia.

In the decade 1990–2000, the ten countries with the highest net migration are ranked in the following order: United States, with net immigration of 11,400,000; Russian Federation (4,158,000); Germany (3,822,000); Canada (1,375,000); Spain (1,176,000); Italy (1,173,000); United Kingdom (955,000); Australia (900,000); Greece (776,000); and France (643,000) (United Nations 2006b). All the major migrant-receiving countries are in the developed countries. On the other hand, the highest levels of net out-migration during the decade 1990–2000 are in the developing countries. These countries are, ranked in order: Mexico, China, Kazakhstan, India, Pakistan, Iran, Philippines, Indonesia, Somalia, and Egypt.

## 7. Conclusion

This chapter provides a rough outline of the past and current demographic situations of various countries with particular emphasis on the more developed regions. To an extent the world is becoming homogenous, that is to say, the glaring demographic disparities that once existed between the more developed and less developed regions are now being reduced: fertility, mortality, and age structure are converging among the regions and countries of the world. It is striking to observe that fertility has declined below replacement level, not only in the more developed countries, but also in many less developed countries of Asia and the Caribbean. Most countries are attaining ever higher life expectancies and at the same time are ageing rapidly. Nevertheless, there remain some marked differences between the more developed countries and the least developed countries of Africa and Asia.

The United Nations projections fit the convergence hypothesis, which argues that all demographic differences among the different countries will eventually disappear by the end of the twenty-first century. But it must be reiterated here that there will nevertheless be a gulf dividing the very rich countries and the very poor countries of the less developed regions. It is debatable, whether these very poor countries can reach the levels of sound health and high standards of living enjoyed by the people in the more developed countries today by the end of the twenty-first century.

## References

McDonald, Peter (2000): Gender equity in theories of fertility. In *Population and Development Review*, 26, 3, pp. 427–439.

National Institute of Population and Social Security Research, Japan (2002): *Population Projections for Japan: 2001–2050 (with Long-range Population Projections; 2051–2100)*, Research Series No.303, March 29.

Todd, Emmanuel (2006): An interview with E. Todd: Low fertility and immigration policies in the developed countries. In *Kan*, 26 (Summer) pp. 98–109. Tokyo: Fujiwara Shoten.

United Nations (2005): *World Population Prospects: The 2004 Revision, Vol. I: Comprehensive Tables*. New York: United Nations.

—— (2006a): *World Population Prospects: The 2004 Revision, Vol. III: Analytical Report.* New York: United Nations.

—— (2006b): *International Migration 2006.* Wall chart.

United Nations Population Fund (2006): *State of World Population 2006.* New York: UNFPA.

World Bank (1993): *World Development Report 1993: Investing in Health.* Oxford: Oxford University Press.

## CHAPTER SIX

# HISTORY OF DEMOGRAPHY IN JAPAN

Matthias Koch

## 1. Introduction

The purpose of this article is to give an introduction to and an overview of the development of demography in Japan. The population is the very foundation of a society, be it a premodern agrarian society with a feudal mode of production or a modern industrial society with a capitalist mode of production. Demography or population science is understood as the scientific study of human population, mainly focusing on size, distribution, composition, population dynamics, and the socio-economic determinants and consequences of population change. The specific factors of population change are births, deaths, migration, marriage, divorce and morbidity. The scope of demographic categories is subject to continuous debate, and conclusions depend on the focus of interest. The sheer number of demographic characteristics (for example, age, sex, place of birth, ethnicity, religion, citizenship, marital status, educational status, labour force status), and the interrelation of demographic factors indicate the interdisciplinary character of demography [*gakusaiteki na gakumon*].

The study of the interrelation of these demographic factors is the research focus of formal demography [*keishiki jinkōgaku*], also called "basic demography", "quantitative demography" or "pure demography" [*junsui jinkōgaku*]. Formal demography provides theoretically and methodologically sophisticated approaches to population problems and is therefore closely linked to statistical and mathematical sciences. Nevertheless, it is not always easy to draw a clear-cut line between basic demography and applied demography, that is, socio-economic demography, which in Japan is known as "substantive demography" [*jittai jinkōgaku*]. Basic demography serves the interests of formal demographic research, while applied demography serves the interests of policy makers, administrations, and private business. This idealized distinction between basic and applied demography often proves to be simplistic, because the subject matter and methodological specialties of both subfields overlap (Takeuchi et al. 1989: 757; Siegel and Swanson 2004: 1–2).

## 2. Demography and Modernisation

In Japan, the development of demography or population science [*jinkōgaku* or *jinkō tōkeigaku*] is intrinsically tied to the introduction of statistics in the Meiji period (1867–1912), the implementation of nationwide censuses on a regular basis during the late Taishō period (1912–1926), and the establishment of a think-tank on population studies during the undeclared war in China in the early Shōwa period (1926–1989). The study of population problems became an integral part of economics relatively early on, as well as of medical science through public health and disease surveillance questions in subpopulations such as the military and the expanding workforce in modern industries. The mainstream of demography as a scientific discipline was dominated by economists and medical scientists from the very beginning. The first Japanese translations of Western demographic classics by Johann Peter Süßmilch (1707–1767), John Graunt (1620–1674), William Petty (1623–1687), and Thomas Robert Malthus (1766–1834) were provided between the 1920s and 1940s by economists and economic historians such as Ōuchi Hyōe (1888–1980), Takano Iwasaburō (1871–1949), Morito Tatsuo (1888–1984), Taniguchi Yoshihiko (1891–1956), Kuruma Samezō (1893–1982), and Takuma Terao (1899–1984).

The term "demography" was coined by the Belgian statistician Achille Guillard (1799–1876) and used in 1855 in the title of his work *Éléments de statistique humaine, ou, Démographie comparée* [Elements of human statistics and comparative demography]. Minami Ryōzaburō was among the first in Japan to use the term *jinkōgaku* [study of the people] in 1943 in the title of his book *Jinkō genri no kenkyū: jinkōgaku kensetsu no ichi kōsō* [Studies on the principle of population: An idea aiming toward constructing demography]. Before the terms *jinkōgaku* and *jinkō tōkeigaku* came into use in the second half of the twentieth century to designate "demography", the term *minseigaku* [study of the people's strength] was an alternative term developed from the older term for "population census" [*kokusei chōsa*], which was previously referred to as *kuni no ikioi* ["momentum" or "trend of the country"] or *tami no ikioi* ["momentum" or "trend of the people"]. Nonetheless, in Japan, because of the international population debate and the influence of English, German, French and Italian literature from the first half of the twentieth century onwards, topics concerning the population were most commonly addressed as a set of more practical matters in the form of "population problems", [*jinkō mondai*].

The construction of demographic theory, demographic methodology, and demographic institutions was well under way in the first half of the twentieth century, but demography was not developed and established as an academic discipline in its own right until World War II. The prehistory of demography or population science in Japan shows that it developed in the wake of the nation's modernisation and the centralization of government administration, first and foremost as applied demography for the purpose of official statistics. Centralisation was an important way to meet the threats posed to Japan by the unequal treaties and foreign trade and culture and to regain full sovereignty. As a consequence, obstacles to centralisation were abolished one after another. Kido Takayoshi and Ōkubo Toshimichi were central figures in a series of policies which led in the first half of 1869 to the transfer of household registers and the population to the rule of the emperor [*hanseki hōkan*], and in July 1871 to the dissolution of the domains and the establishment of prefectures [*haihan chiken*]. This marked a decisive step toward centralisation and a trifold administrative segregation within the newly unified nation-state.

In the second half of the nineteenth century, the science of statistics was introduced into Japan first of all as official statistics or applied science for practical governmental and administrative purposes, whereas academic statistics as a mathematical science, in other words, the theoretical basis of the subject, only began to be developed after the establishment of the Imperial Universities. In the 1860s, the term *Statistik* was introduced into Japanese through the study of Western sciences by means of the Dutch language [*rangaku* or *yōgaku*]. A variety of words were in use, for example, *sutachisuchikku, keiseigaku, seihyōgaku*, and *hyōkigaku*, all conveying slightly different semantic connotations of governance through tabulation.

The term *Statistik* was originally coined by the German cameralist Gottfried Achenwall in the middle of the eighteenth century and derives from the Latin word *statisticum* [concerning the state] and *statisticum collegium* [council of state] with a Greek ending. It designated the comparative description of states through the collection, classification, and analysis of data, particularly about the most valuable resource of state power and wealth, that is, the people inhabiting a specific area.

To express the concept of "science(s) of state" and "political arithmetic" in Japanese, terms such as *kokuseigaku, kokujōgaku, kokumugaku, kokkagaku*, and *keikokugaku* were used from the Meiji period onwards. The two-character compound *tōkei*, a loanword from China that was later reinterpreted in its modern Japanese meaning, was used officially for the first time in the sense of "statistics" on 27 July 1871, in connection with the naming of a Department of Statistics in the Japanese Ministry of Finance [*Ōkurashō Tōkeishi*]; several weeks later, the name was changed to *Tōkeiryō*. Nevertheless, the Japanese word *tōkei* does not directly bear the meaning "state" like its Western counterparts *Statistik, statistics, statistique, statistica, estadistica* and so on. On the basis of the etymology, an uninformed Japanese reader of *tōkei* is likely to think of *gōkei* and *sōkei*, "total sum" and "total amount". However, the use of statistics later broadened beyond state or government control, to include such areas as public agencies and private businesses and finding its way into all fields of science (Nagayama 2005: 2–10; Sagaza 2005: 15–22; Jinkō Mondai Kenkyūjo 1989: 341–353).

## 3. Demography as a Scientific Field and Demographic Surveys as a Government Tool

At the end of the Bakumatsu period (1854–1867) and during the Meiji period, the introduction of applied statistics [*ōyō tōkei*] was of utmost importance, above all for the development of government statistics [*kanchō tōkei*] on the basis of which to make informed decisions. Thus, from the very beginning, the significance of statistics extended far beyond mere population counting and affected a wide range of questions concerning nation-state building and state governance. The introduction of descriptive statistics [*kijutsu tōkeigaku*] and inferential statistics [*suisoku tōkeigaku*] was later complemented by the import of innovations in the field of mathematical statistics [*sūri tōkeigaku*], and led to a domestically and internationally networked development of knowledge transfer and cultural exchange.

Sugi Kōji (1828–1917) was one of the first to realize the significance of statistics, and stressed the importance of censuses for the modernisation of Japan. Sugi is therefore considered one of the pioneers of modern statistics in Japan. He studied Dutch, French and Western sciences and later taught at the Shōgun's Western Learning Reseach and Teaching Institute [*Kaiseijo*] which became part of the University of Tokyo [*Tōkyō Daigaku*] after the Meiji Restoration. It was at the Kaiseijo that Sugi first read numerical data about the illiteracy rate in Bavaria in the Dutch newspaper *Rotterdamsche Courant*. These figures initially sparked his interest in the hitherto unknown science of statistics. Without teacher or textbook, Sugi had to rely on any source of information. One such source of information was Tsuda Mamichi, who belonged to the first generation of *ryūgakusei* [Japanese students studying abroad]. Like Nishi Amane, Enomoto Takeaki and others, Tsuda was sent to the Netherlands in 1862 to study law and political economy at Leiden University under Professor Simon Vissering. After his return to Japan, Tsuda published his lecture notes under the title of *Taisei kokuhōron* [On Western Law] in 1868 and thereby introduced German social statistics into Japan. In May 1869, this work served as the theoretical and conceptual basis for a population census in the Province of Suruga [*Suruga no Kuni Ninbetsu Shirabe*] under Sugi's guidance. Sugi was also influenced by Alexander von Oettingen's *Moralstatistik* [Moral Statistics], in which he coined the word, and established the concept, of *Sozialethik* [social ethics], and Max Haushofer's *Lehr- und Handbuch der Statistik in ihrer neuesten wissenschaftlichen Entwickelung* [Textbook and compendium of statistics in its latest scientific development].

On 18 October 1870, the Central Chamber [*Seiin*] of the Great Council of State [*Dajōkan*] proclaimed an order to compile the first modern statistics about farm, forest, marine, mining and industrial products drawn from prefectural reports, later called *Fuken Bussanhyō* [Tables about Products by Prefecture]. Since this date is considered to be the start of modern official statistics, today it is commemorated every year as Statistics Day [*Tōkei no Hi*] by central and local governments to promote the understanding of the population of the importance of statistics.

In 1871, the Dajōkan started to compile *Nihon Seihyō* [Japan Statistics], the predecessor of the post-war *Nihon Tōkei Nenkan* or *Japan Statistical Yearbook* (1949–). The first two editions of 1871 and 1872 covered the period before the introduction of the Gregorian calendar in January 1873 and accordingly were titled "Shinmi Statistical Tables" [*Shinmi Seihyō*] and "Jinshin Statistical Tables" [*Jinshin Seihyō*], using the appropriate year names according to the Japanese lunar calendar. Thereafter, the naming and dating of years changed to Japanese era names [*nengō*], a practice still in use today. The main purpose of these surveys was to collect data in order to better maintain public order and to implement the new systems of compulsory military conscription and compulsory education, but they were also used to guarantee the collection of taxes and to get a clearer picture of public health and other basic population issues.

In April 1871, the Dajōkan promulgated the Household Registration Law [*Koseki-hō*] which led to the introduction of the household registration system [*koseki seido*] and the suspension of the system of census registration based on religious faith investigation registers [*shūmon aratame chō*], which had been established in the second half of the seventeenth century to fight and eradicate Christianity. For the first time in the history of Japan, every person was listed and registered in a household register [*kosekibo*]. As of this time, all Japanese were required to have family names as well as given names.

In the course of the third reorganisation of the early Meiji government system [*Dajōkan seido*], in December 1871, the Dajōkan established a Statistics Division [*Seihyōka*] within the Seiin, which at that time was the highest policy-making body of the government. This Seihyōka was the earliest predecessor of today's National Statistics Center [*Dokuritsu Gyōsei Hōjin Tōkei Sentā*] of the Statistics Bureau [*Tōkeikyoku*], which is administered by the Ministry of Internal Affairs and Communications [*Sōmushō*]. Sugi Kōji was appointed its first head and served for more than nine years through several reorganisations.

The Meiji government introduced the household registration system, based on the Household Registration Law, and carried out the first nationwide census through registration on 29 January 1872; this date is still commemorated as Population Census Memorial Day [*Jinkō Chōsa Kinenbi*]. The 1872 population census was called the Jinshin Census [*Jinshin Koseki*], and 33,110,825 people were enumerated. An earlier countrywide population census carried out under Tokugawa Yoshimune in 1721 had not counted noblemen, warriors, outcasts, and their families. However, the 26 million people counted at the time testify to the fact that the population was stable for some 150 years. Huge land reclamations, soil improvements, and the introduction of new labour-saving agricultural tools balanced Malthusian positive checks on population growth, notably the Great Famines of the Edo Period, such as the Kyōhō Famine (1732–1733), the Tenmei Famine (1782–1787), the Hōreki Famine (1755–1756), and the Tenpō Famine (1833–1838). Between the *Jinshin Koseki* of 1872 and the end of the nineteenth century, the Japanese population was estimated annually on the basis of the permanent residential population by adding registered live births and new registrations and subtracting registered deaths and removals from the registers as well as the number of Japanese subjects living abroad (Sōmushō Tōkeikyoku 2005: 26–31 and 2004: 24–29).

In 1878, the predecessor of today's Japan Statistical Association (JSA) [*Nihon Tōkei Kyōkai*] was established under the name of the Tokyo Statistical Association (TSA) [*Tōkyō Tōkei Kyōkai*]. The JSA was founded as an affiliate organisation of the predecessor of today's Statistics Bureau [*Tōkeikyoku*], then called the Census Bureau [*Chōsakyoku*]. Around the end of the nineteenth century, the TSA introduced the punchcard system and Herman Hollerith's electrical tabulation system to Japan. After several years of further development, Kawaguchi Matsutarō presented the first punchcard system adapted for Japanese requirements. Shortly before the end of World War II, in 1944, the TSA merged with the Statistics Company (founded in 1876 as *Hyōkigaku Sha*, renamed twice as *Sutachisutikku Sha* in 1878 and as *Tōkeigaku Sha* in 1892) to form the Statistical Association of Greater Japan [*Dai Nippon Tōkei Kyōkai*]. The current name, JSA, was adopted two years after World War II. The staff of the JSA consisted in large part of former personnel from the Statistics Bureau.

In the 1870s and 1880s, a series of statistical surveys were conducted and their results published. On the last day of 1879, Sugi Kōji conducted a demographic sample survey in Yamanashi Prefecture, in which several questions were asked, such as name, address, sex, marital status, age, country of birth, religion, and profession. The survey report was published under the title "Population Survey of the Province of Kai" [*Kai no Kuni Genzai Ninbetsu Shirabe*] in 1882. This survey served as a test case for applied statistics and can be considered a pilot study for a nationwide population census.

In 1881, the predecessor of today's Statistics Bureau started to publish the *Statistical Abstracts* [*Tōkei Yōran*]. The Household Register Bureau of the Home Ministry (Naimushō Kosekikyoku) issued the *Japanese National Population Tables* [*Nihon Zenkoku Jinkōhyō*], and the Gunma Prefectural Government in Maebashi completed the *Statistical Tables for the Prefecture of Gunma* [*Gunma-ken Tōkeihyō*]. In the same year, on the recommendation of Sugi's successor, Ōkuma Shigenobu, the predecessor of today's Statistical Bureau, then called the Statistics Division of the Accounting Department [*Kaikeibu Tōkeika*], was reorganised and strengthened as the Statistical Institute [*Tōkeiin*] of the Great Council of State. In the following year, in March 1882, the Tōkeiin published the first edition of the *Statistical Yearbook* [*Tōkei Nenkan*].

Statistical divisions were chronically understaffed in the early period of government statistics. In the course of time, official statisticians became more experienced and submitted their results faster and at more regular intervals. As of 1880, private schools and national universities began to offer lectures on statistics. Senshū Gakkō (the predecessor of Senshū Daigaku), Tōkyō Senmon Gakkō (the predecessor of Waseda University) and the University of Tokyo [Tōkyō Daigaku] were among the first. In 1883, the Tokyo Statistical Association [*Tōkyō Tōkei Kyōkai*] and the Statistical Institute [*Tōkeiin*] jointly established the School of Statistics [*Kyōritsu Tōkei Gakkō*]. Three years later, the school became a part of the Tokyo Statistical Association. Like Sugi Kōji, scientists like Kure Ayatoshi, Yokoyama Masao, Matsuzaki Kuranosuke, and Takano Iwasaburō became experts in statistics. In the formation period of economics, statistics was taught by several foreign social scientists at the Imperial University of Tokyo [*Tōkyo Teikoku Daigaku*], for example, Karl Rathgen (1882–90) and Udo Eggert (1887–93).

In December 1885, with the establishment of the cabinet system, the Statistical Institute [*Tōkeiin*] became the Statistics Bureau, an external bureau of the Cabinet [*Naikaku Tōkeikyoku*]. In 1898, the Statistics Bureau began the compilation of *Nihon Teikoku jinkō tōkei*, an in-depth data book of population statistics of the Japanese Empire published in 1901. Preparations were then initiated for the first modern nationwide population census. The Law Governing the Population Census [*Kokusei Chōsa ni Kansuru Hōritsu*] was promulgated in 1902. In 1905, occupational categories for use in population censuses were proposed for the first time. Punchcard tabulation machines and sorters were further developed during World War I. In 1918, the Implementation Orders for the National Population Census [*Kokusei Chōsa Shikōrei*] were promulgated. In May 1918, the Temporary Bureau of the Population Census [*Rinji Kokusei Chōsakyoku*] and the Council for the National Population Census [*Kokusei Chōsa Hyōgikai*] were established within the Cabinet Office. The Statistics Bureau [*Tōkeikyoku*] and the Military Demand Bureau were [*Gunjukyoku*] merged by establishing the Census Office [*Kokuseiin*] within the Cabinet Office in May 1920. Eventually, on 1 October 1920, a full-scale population census [*daikibo chōsa*] was conducted. A total of 55,963,053 people were enumerated in 1920. During the modernisation and industrialisation period spanning nearly half a century from the early Meiji period to the late Taishō period, the Japanese population had thus increased by some 22,852,228 people. The only slowdown of population growth between 1872 and 1920 was caused by the outbreak of Spanish influenza, which took an unprecedented toll on the Japanese population between 1918 and 1920. Latest estimations of deaths due to the outbreak vary between 220,000 (Ikeda et al. 2005: 369–375) and 450,000 people (Hayami 2006: 427) for Japan proper. This was also the only period in U.S. history that the population declined.

When the census had been carried out, the Temporary Bureau of the Population Census was abolished, its staff taken over by the First Division of the Census Office [*Kokuseiin Daiichibu*]. In 1922, the Law Governing the Population Census was revised in order to stipulate an additional quinquennial interim population census, also called micro-census or simplified census [*kan'i chōsa*]. Large-scale population censuses and micro-censuses have been repeated decennially and quinquennially ever since, with the exception of 1945 when the country was in ruins. Subsequently, the Census Office was abolished and its First Division attached again to the Cabinet Office as the Statistics Bureau [*Tōkeikyoku*]. The Statistics Bureau implements the population census and oversees coordination between the prefectures, the municipalities, the supervisors, the enumerators and the households as the main unit of census-taking. As survey techniques improved, demand for information about the populace on the part of the government increased. This is evident when we compare post-World War II simplified censuses with interwar full-scale censuses, the former being almost as detailed as the latter. The first full-scale population census comprised 22 items, the first simplified census 17 items. The usefulness and universal applicability of statistics and the growing public and private demand for specific statistical data is reflected by the expanding range of statistical surveys. This is especially true in the case of designated statistical surveys [*shitei tōkei chōsa*] after World War II. From the promulgation of the Statistics Law [*Tōkei-hō*] (Law No. 18, 26 March 1947), which provides the main legal framework for the post-war population censuses [*kokusei chōsa*], to the beginning of the twenty-first century, a total of 55 "designated statistics" [*shitei tōkei*] were selected to be compiled or commissioned by Japanese ministries, for example, the business and enterprise census [*jigyōsho kigyō tōkei chōsa*], the census of manufacturers [*kōgyō tōkei chōsa*], the census of commerce [*shōgyō tōkei chōsa*], the labour force survey [*rōdōryoku chōsa* and the fishing industry census [*gyogyō sensasu*], to name only a few important early complete surveys [*zensū chōsa* or *shikkai chōsa*]. This development began in the 1920s and holds true for the interwar period, to an increasing degree for war-planning purposes in the 1930s. In 1924, the Ministry of Home Affairs enacted the first labour survey. In August 1925, the Statistics Bureau published the volume *Collection of Statistical Tables as Models* [*Mohan Tōkei Yushū*] (Jinkō Mondai Kenkyūjo 1989: 341–353; Okazaki 1987: 3–14; Nagayama 2005: 2–10; Sagaza 2005: 15–22).

## 4. The Foundation Institute for Research of Population Problems and the Institute of Population Problems

In the late Taishō (1912–1926) and early Shōwa periods (1926–1989), several authors addressed the study of population problems [*jinkō mondai*] as both quantitative population problems [*ryōteki jinkō mondai*] and qualitative population problems [*shitsuteki jinkō mondai*] in their historical, domestic and international context (unemployment, food shortages, overpopulation), for example, Kameda Toyojirō and Ōba Saneharu (1920), Inada Shūnosuke (1924), Yanaihara Tadao (1928), Minoguchi Tokijirō (1941), Ueda Teijirō (1943), and Ueda Masao (1949). In 1927, the first World Population Conference was held in Geneva. In the same year, population problems came onto the political agenda in Japan, when the Cabinet of Tanaka Giichi established the Population and Food Problems Investigation Committee [*Jinkō Shokuryō Mondai Chōsakai*]. The members were bureaucrats and scientists such as Hatoyama Ichirō, Nagai Hisomu, and Nagai Tōru. In February 1928, Nagai Tōru and Nitobe Inazō submitted a proposal to establish a facility to explore population problems. Four months later, as a result of the World Population Conference in Geneva, the International Union for the Scientific Investigation of Population Problems (IUSIPP) was launched in Paris. Its 35 founding members from twelve countries organized three research committees on Population and Food, on Differential Fertility, Fecundity and Sterility and on Statistics of Primitive Races. In Japan, the Population and Food Problems Investigation Committee concluded a report to the Cabinet of Hamaguchi Osachi, in which it recommended the establishment of a permanent research organisation on population problems. It finally ceased its activities in 1930.

The committee's recommendation was partly realized when the Foundation Institute for Research on Population Problems (FIRPP) [*Jinkō Mondai Kenkyūkai*] was established in October 1933 as an incorporated semi-governmental and semi-private association [*hankan hanmin*]. High-ranking civil servants acted as members of its board of directors, such as the Secretary of the Home Ministry [*Naimushō*], the Director of its Social Bureau [*Naimushō Shakaikyoku*], and the Director of the Cabinet Statistics Bureau [*Naikaku Tōkeikyoku*]. Academia was represented in the board of directors, for example by Nagai Tōru, Nasu Hiroshi, and Ueda Teijirō. Research fellows were Tachi Minoru, Masuda Shigeki, Odauchi Michitoshi, and Sōda Takeo. Fujiyama Raita, Kimura Masutarō, and Kodaira Gon'ichi dealt with food problems [*shokuryō mondai*]; Miyake Kiichi, Nagai Hisomu, and Toda Teizō with population quality [*jinkō shishitsu*]; and Yano Tsuneta, Shimomura Hiroshi, and Takagi Tomosaburō with population policy problems [*jinkō taisaku mondai*]. The FIRPP received government funding and was also supported financially by its first president, Count Yanagisawa Yasutoshi, and the life insurance company Daiichi Seimei Hoken Sōgo Kaisha. Thanks to his influence and efforts, Tokyo hosted the nineteenth session of the International Statistics Institute in 1930. The FIRPP hosted lectures and organized seminars, and in February 1935, it launched the academic quarterly *Jinkō Mondai* [Population Problems], dealing with topics such as censuses, surplus population, unemployment, migration, and eugenics. This periodical was printed by the Social Bureau of the Home Ministry, together with the Statistics Bureau a hotbed for population debates within the bureaucracy (Jinkō Mondai Kenkyūkai 1983: 2; Takazawa 1992: 103–120).

With the intensification of Japanese military activities in China in 1937, the FIRPP called for a meeting of the National Conference on Population Problems [*Jinkō Mondai Zenkoku Kyōgikai*] in order to respond to governmental requests for advice concerning population problems. In October 1938 and in December 1939, the FIRPP published two voluminous reports of the *Jinkō Mondai Zenkoku Kyōgikai*. The Home Ministry authorized Tachi Minoru, a FIRPP research fellow, to prepare for the establishment of an Institute of Population Problems that was finally launched in 1939. Through the establishment of a national institute, the Japanese government made a significant commitment to the study of demographic phenomena both inside and outside Japan, the more so as the quantity and quality of human resources for waging war became a concern of the political and military elite at the time.

In fact, the Ministry of Health and Welfare [*Kōseishō*] itself was a product of war planning, aiming to make the Japanese population fit to reach the ambitious war goals of the Japanese Army and to prepare the nation for the war effort. Whereas Prime Minister Prince Konoe

Fumimaro (first term of office June 1937 to January 1939) focused on social policy and the creation of a welfare state system, the Ministry of War [*Rikugunshō*] concentrated upon health and hygiene administration. Finally, both concerns were met by establishing the Ministry of Health and Welfare in January 1938, and Kido Kōichi was appointed its first minister to administer social welfare [*shakai fukushi*], social security [*shakai hoshō*], and public health [*kōshū eisei*] (Imperial Ordinance No. 7, 11 January 1938).

The Institute of Population Problems (IPP) [*Jinkō Mondai Kenkyūjo*] was set up under Ohara Naoshi, Minister of the Interior and simultaneously third Minister of Health and Welfare, on 25 August 1939 (Imperial Ordinance No. 603). At first, the IPP staff consisted of 27 researchers and three secretaries. For comparison, in fiscal year 2005–06, eight years after the merging of the IPP and the Social Development Research Institute (SDRI) [*Shakai Hoshō Kenkyūjo*], the staff of the IPP's organisational successor, the *Kokuritsu Shakai Hoshō Jinkō Mondai Kenkyūjo* (*Shajinken*) [National Institute of Population and Social Security Research, NIPSSR] numbered 54, among them 43 researchers. Okada Fumihide (1892–1989), formerly head of the Home Ministry's Bureau of Hygiene [*Naimushō Eiseikyoku*], the Bureau of Civil Engineering [*Naimushō Dobokukyoku*] and Vice-Minister of the Ministry of Health and Welfare [*Kōseishō*], became founding director-general of the IPP. In 1939 and 1940, a procreation campaign was launched at the homefront using the slogan "Give birth and multiply" [*Umeyo fuyaseyo*].

In April 1940, the IPP launched a new periodical: *Jinkō Mondai Kenkyū* [Journal of Population Problems]. In the editorial of the first issue, director-general Okada Fumihide stressed the importance of population studies under special circumstances, such as a liberation war to free Asia from Western colonialism and imperialism ("Asia for Asians") and establish a mutually beneficial order under Japanese leadership, later officially expressed by the ideological concept of a "Greater East Asia Co-Prosperity Sphere" [*Dai Tōa Kyōeiken*]:

> The present state of emergency of our country, which has been flying the flag for a new order in East Asia and is pushing forward with the Holy War for the prosperity of Asia, has brought about great changes with regard to demographic conditions and various social phenomena and has assigned population problems high importance.

Contributors to the first issue were Kitaoka Juitsu, Nakagawa Tomonaga, Tachi Minoru, Ueda Masao, and Okazaki Ayanori. Interestingly, Shimamura Toshihiko contributed a book review on *Living-space' and population problems* [*Seikatsu ryōiki to jinkō shomondai*] (1939) by René Robert Kuczynski (1876–1947), a leftist German-Jewish population researcher and economist who had to live in exile in Britain and was known in the 1930s particularly for the calculation of gross and net reproduction rates of the European, the North American and colonial populations.

The expertise of the IPP was in demand by the Japanese government. The Guidelines for Establishing Population Policy (GEPP) [*Jinkō Seisaku Kakuritsu Yōkō*], which were set by a cabinet decision in January 1941, were originally drafted by the IPP under the supervision of Kitaoka Juitsu, and the Planning Bureau [*Kikakuin*] completed them with the help of Tachi Minoru. Their main goal was to develop the above-mentioned Greater East Asia Co-Prosperity Sphere. A variety of population policy measures were formulated and implemented to encourage pregnancy and childbirth and to reduce infant and child mortality. The legal marriage age was lowered by three years to increase the number of children to five per married couple, and a target was set to increase the total "Japanese inland population" [*naichijin jinkō*] to one hundred million by 1960. (This goal was actually realized in 1967.) During times of international tension, the Japanese government issued many statements to the effect that marriage [*kekkon hōkoku*] and child care [*ikuji hōkoku*] were an obligation of the Japanese people towards the nation-state. In November 1940, more than 10,000 couples with more than 10 children were awarded a certificate of commendation by the Ministry of Health and Welfare.

The National Eugenics Law [*Kokumin Yūsei-hō*], which came into effect in 1941, called for multiplying the genetically fit population and permitting abortion only in cases of genetic defects. Unmarried women between the age of 14 and 24 were obliged to provide thirty days of labour per year by the Order of National Cooperation of Labour Service to the State [*Kokumin Kinrō Hōkoku Kyōryoku Rei*]. The Bureau of Population [*Jinkōkyoku*] of the Ministry of Health and Welfare was newly established by merging parts of the Bureau of Physical Strength [*Tairyokukyoku*], the Bureau of Hygiene [*Eiseikyoku*] and the Social Bureau [*Shakaikyoku*] in order to strengthen the medical administrative system for the protection of maternal and childhood health. A national system for supervising pregnancy and children's health was organized and complemented by a loan system for marriage funds and scholarships for students from households with a large number of children. A population survey was carried out in February 1944, according to which the population of Japan proper added up to a total of 73.46 million. After the war, the regular census due in 1945 did not take place (Jinkō Mondai Kenkyūkai 1983: 2–109; Takazawa 1992: 103–120; Jinkō Mondai Kenkyūjo 1989: 341–353).

## 5. Demographic Research after World War II

Koya Yoshio (1890–1974), a professor at Kanazawa Medical University [*Kanazawa Ika Daigaku*] and an expert in what was then called "racial hygiene" [*minzoku eiseigaku*], was a central figure in post-war population politics and the establishment of population studies as a scientific discipline. In October 1945, the government set up a New Committee of Population Measures [*Shin Jinkō Taisaku Iinkai*] under his chairmanship. Koya supervised tuberculosis surveys and became head of the National Institute of Public Health [*Kokuritsu Kōshū Eiseiin*] in 1946. The Ministry of Health and Welfare held a Round-Table Conference on Population Problems [*Jinkō Mondai Kondankai*] in order to revitalize discussions and research concerning population problems. The Jinkō Mondai Kenkyūkai set up a special committee for population policy which submitted a "Proposal concerning Basic Principles for a New Population Policy" [*Shin Jinkō Seisaku Kihon Hōshin ni kansuru Kengi*]. In general, the end of the war did not bring much change. Rather, there was much continuity in terms of institutions and personnel (*Jinkō Mondai Kenkyū*, Vol. 6, No. 2, pp. 20–21).

A population census was carried out in October 1947, based on the Statistics Law. Excluding the population of Okinawa Prefecture, 78,101,473 Japanese were enumerated. The official figure of the Japanese death toll of World War II was 3.1 million. The first baby boom occurred between 1947 and 1949, when an average of 2.7 million babies were born in three consecutive years. At the same time, the death rate fell and life expectancy rose markedly. With the establishment of the Prime Minister's Agency, the former Statistics Bureau of the Cabinet Office [*Naikaku Tōkeikyoku*] became the Statistics Bureau of the Prime Minister's Agency [*Sōrichō Tōkeikyoku*]. The International Union for the Scientific Investigation of Population Problems (IUSIPP), founded in 1928, was reconstituted in 1947 as the International Union for the Scientific Study in Population (IUSSP). The Union organized conferences and published scientific information; it developed from a union of national committees with political agendas in the pre-war period into a professional association for individuals interested and engaged in population studies.

On the academic side, demography still lacked the status of a scientific discipline in Japan when the Population Association of Japan (PAJ) [*Nihon Jinkō Gakkai*] was established in November 1948 by a diverse group of 56 founding members. The above-mentioned medical doctor and professor, Koya Yoshio, Mizushima Haruo, Morita Yūzō, and Tachi Minoru were appointed managing directors of the board [*jōmu riji*]. The majority of the early PAJ members were economists, statisticians, and medical scientists. The main purpose of the association was the comprehensive study of the Japanese population from the different perspectives of relevant disciplines. The PAJ holds annual meetings and organizes symposia.

Minami Ryōzaburō (1896–1985) has been called the "father of demography in Japan" (Okada and Ōbuchi 2004: ii), because he held the first lectures on demography in Japan, at Chuo University [*Chūō Daigaku*] in summer 1952, and because he authored many groundbreaking books, amongst them *Jinkō riron to jinkō mondai* [Population theory and population problems, 1935], *Jinkō riron to jinkō seisaku* [Population theory and population policy, 1940], *Jinkōgaku sōron: Jinkō genri no kenkyū* [An introduction to demography: Studies on the principle of population, 1960], *Jinkō shisōshi* [History of population thought, 1963] and *Jinkō seisaku: Jinkō seisakugaku e no michi* [Population policy: Towards population policy as a science, 1969]. Trained as an economist under the economic theorists Sōda Kiichirō (1881–1927) and Ōnishi Inosuke (1888–1922), his influence was much broader, contributing to the development of economics, political science, and sociology.

In collaboration with Tachi Minoru and others, Minami was instrumental in publishing the first Japanese "Population Encyclopedia" [*Jinkō Daijiten*] in 1957, a 940-page volume which achieved the highest international standards. A total of 108 authors contributed to this encyclopaedia, which took all aspects of population science inside and outside Japan into account. This was achieved mainly through the combined efforts of the Institute of Population Problems (IPP), the Population Association of Japan (PAJ), and members of study and research groups on population science, mostly university professors and researchers as well as heads of government departments and agencies related to population problems and statistics, such as the Statistics Bureau of the Prime Minister's Office [*Sōrifu Tōkeikyoku*]. In addition, there were not only contributions from prominent civil servants and statisticians of the Economic Planning Agency [*Keizai Kikakuchō*], the Ministry of Agriculture and Forestry [*Nōrinshō*] and the Foreign Ministry [*Gaimushō*], but also from bankers and newspaper publishers. The revised edition of the population encyclopaedia, published 45 years later under the title *Jinkō Daijiten* [*Encyclopedia of Population*] (Baifūkan, 2002), does not bring together authors from such a wide range of fields. A total of 133 specialists in the field of population science have contributed to this 999–page volume, which is not well-known outside Asia, because American and European demographers do not usually read Japanese.

In addition to the IPP, the Social Development Research Institute (SDRI) [*Shakai Hoshō Kenkyūjo*] was established in January 1965. It publishes two Japanese-language quarterly journals concerning social security in Japan and overseas. These are *The Quarterly of Social Security Research* [*Kikan Shakai Hoshō Kenkyū*], published since July 1965 and *The Review of Comparative Social Security Research* [*Kaigai Shakai Hoshō Kenkyū*], published since February 1968. Since March 1978, the PAJ has published the academic journal *Jinkōgaku Kenkyū* [The Journal of Population Studies]. The Ministry of Health and Welfare decided in 1996 to integrate the IPP and the SDRI to establish the National Institute of Population and Social Security Research (NIPSSR) [*Kokuritsu Shakai Hoshō Jinkō Mondai Kenkyūjo, Shajinken*] for synergetic reasons.

By the 1990s, demography had reached a certain stage of maturity. In fiscal year 2001, the Population Association of Japan conducted a survey about university education and training in demography [*jinkōgaku kyōiku*] at undergraduate [*gakubu kyōiku*] and graduate levels [*daigakuin kyōiku*]. According to this survey, "demography proper" [*jinkōgaku sono mono*] can be studied at undergraduate level at more than three dozen universities and at graduate level at more than a dozen universities. Among them are Aoyama Gakuin University, Asia University, Chuo University, Keio University, Kobe University, Komazawa University, Kyushu University, Meiji University, Nihon University, Nihon Women's University, Reitaku University, Seijo University, Shimane University, The University of Tokyo, and Waseda University (www.eco.shimane-u.ac.jp/~hirosima/paj/kki/kki.htm).

Historical demography can be divided roughly into the pre-Edo period and the early modern era, the Edo period. Research about the pre-Edo period is based on a limited number of genealogical tables [*kakeizu*] and death registers from Buddhist temples [*kakochō*] and was carried out, for example, by Inō Hidenori (1805–1877), Yokoyama

Yoshikiyo (1826–1879), and Sawada Goichi (1861–1931). The early modern period from the seventeenth to the nineteenth century is much better known, thanks to the availability of historical sources such as land registers [*tochi daichō* or *tochi tōkibo*], family or household registers [*kosekibo*], population registers [*ninbetsu aratame chō*] and religious faith investigation registers [*shūmon aratame chō*] (cf. for example, Honjō Eijirō 1930, 1941 and 1971, Takahashi Bonsen 1941, 1955, 1962 and 1975–76, Sekiyama Naotarō 1942, 1948 and 1958, Uchida Kan'ichi 1971, Nomura Kanetarō 1935, Kobayashi Kazumasa 1988, Suda Keizō 1978, 1985, 1989 and 1992, Kitō Hiroshi 1983, 2000 and 2002a, and, last but not least, Hayami Akira 1973, 1997, 2001 and 2006; Hayami is the organiser of the international EurAsia Project on Population and Family History). The third generation of historical demographers deals with teaching students and providing primary historical materials through modern research tools, and is at the same time engaged in modelling and theory construction. The influence of social and economic historians is still indispensable and felt strongly in historical demography (Kitō 2002b: 320–325).

## 6. Conclusion

Demography in Japan developed in the wake of the modernisation and industrialisation process from the beginning of the Meiji period, first of all as applied science, that is, official statistics, to meet the needs of practical governmental and administrative purposes. Japan became an "economically rich and militarily powerful country" [*fukoku kyōhei*], in other words, an industrial nation, by the end of World War I, and conducted its first large-scale population census in 1920. During the interwar period the complexity of population dynamics at home and abroad and persistent "population problems" [*jinkō mondai*]—(relative) overpopulation, unemployment and food shortages—led to the establishment of a proper Ministry of Health and Welfare-affiliated research entity, the Institute of Population Problems [*Jinkō Mondai Kenkyūjo*]. Thus population science arose and flourished in the war-like atmosphere of the historical circumstances on the eve of World War II. Scientists practised demography with a concern about the power and wealth of their nation in an internationally aggressive environment. After World War II, population specialists founded the Population Association of Japan [*Nihon Jinkō Gakkai*] in 1948 as a pressure group to further the institutionalisation of demography and finally provide it with the intellectual authority of an academic activity on the international level.

The specific strength of demography is at the same time its main weakness (Greenhalgh 1996; Hodgson 2001; Caldwell 2003). It seems that theoretical construction was and still is somewhat limited to mathematical models (Newell 1988; Hinde 1998; Siegel 2002; Siegel and Swanson 2004). On the one hand, the science of population study consists by and large of numerous methods, models, and techniques serving, among other things, as tools to estimate and project future demographic trends from sampled data and to quantify the impact of changing fertility and mortality rates, trying to meet the demands of applied demography. And demography has indeed achieved disciplinary independence through the development of technical skills and a prevailing positivist methodology. On the other hand, this produced an inclination to disregard everything that is difficult or impossible to measure. In the second half of the twentieth century, demography went on from the foundation stage of an incipient discipline and a subfield of established social sciences, medical sciences and mathematical sciences to develop into a self-contained discipline, while redefining a multi-science approach. Today, within and alongside formal demography or population science as mathematical demography, there are various demographies: economic demography, political demography, social demography or population sociology, population geography, biodemography, medical demography, historical demography and anthropological demography. Thus demography is likely to be deconstructed and reconstructed again and again. When thinking about the theory and practice of demography as it has developed and is further developing, it is of particular importance always to remember the "political embeddedness and social constructedness of knowledge" (Greenhalgh 1996: 33) while surveying the past, creating the present, and imagining the future.

## References

Caldwell, John C. (2003): History of demography. In: Paul Demeny and Geoffrey McNicoll (eds.): *Encyclopedia of population*. New York: Macmillan Reference USA, Vol. 1, pp. 216–221.

Greenhalgh, Susan (1996): The social construction of population science: An intellectual, institutional, and political history of twentieth-century demography. In: *Comparative Studies in Society and History* 12, 2, January 1996, pp. 26–66.

Hayami, Akira (1973): *Kinsei nōson no rekishi jinkōgaku kenkyū: Shinshū Suwa chihō no shūmon aratame chō bunseki* [Studies in historical demography on the farming village in early

modern history: An analysis of Shūmon Aratame Chō in the Shinshū-Suwa region]. Tōkyō: Tōyō Keizai Shinpōsha.
—— (1997): *Rekishi jinkōgaku no sekai* [An overview of historical demography]. (Iwanami Seminā Bukkusu; 65) Tōkyō: Iwanami Shoten.
—— (2001): *Rekishi jinkōgaku de mita Nihon* [Japan seen from the perspective of historical demography]. (Bunshun Shinsho; 200) Tōkyō: Bungei Shunjū.
—— (2006): *Nihon o osotta Supein infuruenza: Jinrui to uirusu no daiichiji sekai sensō* [Japan hit by the Spanish influenza pandemic: Mankind and the First World War of the virus]. Tōkyō: Fujiwara Shoten.
Hayami, Akira, Kitō Hiroshi and Tomobe Ken'ichi (ed.) (2001): *Rekishi jinkōgaku no furontia* [Frontiers of historical demography]. Tōkyō: Tōyō Keizai Shinpōsha.
Hinde, Andrew (1998): *Demographic methods*. London, New York, Sydney, Auckland: Arnold.
Hodgson, Dennis (2001): Demography: Twentieth-century History. In: Neil J. Smelser, Paul B. Baltes (editors-in-chief): *International Encyclopedia of the Social & Behavioral Sciences*. 26 Volumes. Amsterdam; New York: Elsevier Science Ltd., Vol. 5, pp. 3493–3498.
Honjō, Eijirō (1930): *Jinkō oyobi jinkō mondai* [Population and population problems]. Tōkyō: Nihon Hyōronsha.
—— (1941): *Nihon jinkōshi* [Population History of Japan]. Tōkyō: Nihon Hyōronsha.
—— (1971): *Kinsei jinkō mondai shiryō* [Historical documents about population problems during early-modern history]. Kyōto: Keizaishi Kenkyūkai; Seibundō Shuppan.
Ikeda, Kazuo, Fujitani Masakazu, Nadaoka Yōko, Kamiya Nobuyuki, Hirokado Masako and Yanagawa Yoshitoki (2005): *Nihon ni okeru Supein kaze no seimitsu bunseki* [Precise analysis of Spanish influenza in Japan]. In: Tōkyō-to Kenkō Anzen Kenkyū Sentā Kenkyū Nenpō = Annual Report of Tokyo Metropolitan Institute of Public Health, vol. 56, pp. 369–375.
Inada, Shūnosuke (1924): *Jinkō mondai* [Population problems]. Tōkyō: Yūhikaku.
Jinkō Mondai Kenkyūjo (ed.) (1989): *Jinkō Mondai Kenkyūjo sōritsu gojisshū nen kinenshi* [In commemoration of 50 years after the establishment of the Institute of Population Problems]. Tōkyō: Kōseishō Jinkō Mondai Kenkyūjo.
Jinkō Mondai Kenkyūkai (ed.) (1983): *Jinkō Mondai Kenkyūkai gojū nen ryakushi* [A short history of 50 years of the Foundation Institute for Research on Population Problems]. Tōkyō: Jinkō Mondai Kenkyūkai.
Kameda, Toyojirō and Ōba Saneharu (1920): *Jinkō mondai* [Population problems]. Tōkyō: Tōkasha.
Katō, Hisakazu (2001): *Jinkō keizaigaku nyūmon* [An introduction to population economics]. Tōkyō: Nihon Hyōronsha.
Kitō, Hiroshi (1983): *Nihon nisen nen no jinkōshi: Keizaigaku to rekishi jinruigaku kara saguru seikatsu to kōdō no dainamizumu* [2000 years of Japanese population history: Searching for the dynamism of life and behaviour from economics and historical anthropology]. (Nijūisseiki Toshokan; 6) Kyōto: PHP Kenkyūjo.
—— (2000): *Jinkō kara yomu Nihon no rekishi* [Decoding of Japanese history by population history]. (Kōdansha Gakujutsu Bunko; 1430) Tōkyō: Kōdansha.
—— (2002a): *Bunmei to shite no Edo shisutemu* [The Edo system as civilisation]. (Nihon no Rekishi; 19) Tōkyō: Kōdansha.
—— (2002b): Rekishi jinkōgaku. In: Nihon Jinkō Gakkai (ed.): *Jinkō daijiten* [Encyclopedia of population]. Tōkyō: Baifūkan, pp. 320–325.
Kobayashi, Kazumasa and Nanjō Zenji (1988): *Nihon no sedai seimeihyō: 1891–1986 nen kikan seimeihyō ni motozuku* [Generation life tables for Japan based on period life tables covering the years 1891–1986]. Tōkyō: Nihon Daigaku Jinkō Kenkyūjo.
Kondō, Norio (2005): Kokusei chōsa no rekishi [The history of the population census]. In: *Tōkei* (Tokushū: Tōkei to Rekishi) [Statistics. Special Issue: Statistics and History], No. 10, October, pp. 11–14.

Minami, Ryōzaburō (1935): *Jinkō riron to jinkō mondai* [Population theory and population problems].Tōkyō: Chikura Shobō.

—— (1940): *Jinkō riron to jinkō seisaku* [Population theory and population policy].Tōkyō: Chikura Shobō.

—— (1943): *Jinkō genri no kenkyū: jinkōgaku kensetsu no ichi kōsō* [Studies on the principles of population: An idea aiming toward constructing demography]. Tōkyō: Chikura Shobō.

—— et al. (eds.) (1957): *Jinkō daijiten* [Population encyclopedia]. Tōkyō: Heibonsha.

—— (1960): *Jinkōgaku sōron: Jinkō genri no kenkyū* [An introduction to demography: Studies on the principles of population.]. Tōkyō: Chikura Shobō.

—— (1963): *Jinkō shisōshi* [History of population thought]. Tōkyō: Chikura Shobō.

—— (1969): *Jinkō seisaku: Jinkō seisakugaku e no michi* [Population policy: Towards population policy as a science]. Tōkyō: Chikura Shobō.

Minoguchi, Tokijirō (1941): *Jinkō mondai* [Population problems]. (Seikatsu no Kagaku Shinsho; 5) Tōkyō: Hata Shoten.

Nagayama, Sadanori (2005): Nihon no tōkei no rekishi [History of Japanese Statistics]. In: *Tōkei* (Tokushū: Tōkei to Rekishi) [Statistics. Special Issue: Statistics and History] No. 10, October, pp. 2–10.

Nakamura, Takafusa (ed.) (1983): *Journal of the Japan Statistical Society. Special Issue on Japanese Statistics*. Tōkyō: Nihon Tōkei Gakkai, September 16th, 1983, pp. 123.

Newell, Colin (1988): *Methods and models in demography*. New York: The Guilford Press.

Nihon Jinkō Gakkai (ed.) (2002): *Jinkō daijiten* [Encyclopedia of population]. Tōkyō: Baifūkan.

Nomura, Kanetarō (1935): Tokugawa kōki ni okeru nōson jinkō no ichirei (gairon). Shimotsuke no kuni Tsuga-gun Kamiizumi-mura [An example of the rural population in the latter half of the Tokugawa period (an outline): the village Kamiizumi in the county Tsuga in the province of Shimotsuke]. In: *Mita Gakkai Zasshi* 29 (6), pp. 777–815.

Okada, Minoru and Ōbuchi Hiroshi (ed.) (2004): *Jinkōgaku no genjō to furontia* [Status quo and frontiers of demography]. (Shirīzu Jinkōgaku Kenkyū; 6) Tōkyō: Hara Shobō.

Okazaki, Yōichi (1987): Population statistics and employment structure. In: *Nihon Tōkei Gakkaishi* (Journal of the Japan Statistical Society), Special Issue, Volume 17, September 1987, pp. 3–14.

Sagaza, Haruo (2005): Jinkō tōkeigaku no rekishi [History of demography]. In: *Tōkei* (Tokushū: Tōkei to Rekishi) [Statistics. Special Issue: Statistics and History], October, pp. 15–22.

Sekiyama, Naotarō (1942): *Nihon jinkōshi* [Population history of Japan]. Tōkyō: Shikai Shobō.

—— (1948): *Kinsei Nihon jinkō no kenkyū* [Studies on the population history of early modern Japan]. Tōkyō: Ryū Ginsha.

—— (1958): *Kinsei Nihon no jinkō kōzō. Tokugawa jidai no jinkō chōsa to jinkō jōtai ni kansuru kenkyū* [Population structure of early modern Japan. Studies in population censuses and the demographic situation during the Tokogawa period]. Tōkyō: Yoshikawa Kōbunkan.

Siegel, Jacob S. (2002): *Applied demography: Applications to business, government, law, and public policy*. San Diego, San Francisco, New York, Boston, London, Sydney, Tokyo: Academic Press.

Siegel, Jacob S. and David A. Swanson (eds.) (2004): *The methods and materials of demography*. Second edition. San Diego, California; London: Elsevier Academic Press.

Sōmuchō Tōkeikyoku (ed.) (1992): *Tōkeikyoku Tōkei Sentā hyakunijū nen shi* [The National Statistics Centre of the Statistics Bureau: 120 years of history]. Tōkyō: Nihon Tōkei Kyōkai.

Sōmushō Tōkeikyoku (ed.) (2004): *Nihon Tōkei Nenkan, daigojūyon kai, Heisei 17 nen* [Japan Statistical Yearbook, 54th Edition, 2005)]. Tōkyō: Nihon Tōkei Kyōkai and Mainchi Shimbunsha.

—— (ed.) (2005): *Nihon Tōkei Nenkan, daigojūyon kai, Heisei 18 nen* [Japan Statistical Yearbook, 55th Edition, 2006)]. Tōkyō: Nihon Tōkei Kyōkai and Mainchi Shimbunsha.

Suda, Keizō (1978): *Zassōen: Hida no aru machii no kiroku* [Garden weeds: Chronicles of a residential doctor in Hida]. Takayama: Suda Byōin.

—— (1985): *Zassōen: Hida no aru machii no kiroku* [Garden weeds: Chronicles of a residential doctor in Hida]. Kokufuchō: Suda Byōin.

—— (1989): *Zassōen: Hida no aru machii no kiroku* [Garden weeds: Chronicles of a residential doctor in Hida]. Kokufuchō: Suda Byōin.

—— (1992): *Hida no hōsōshi: Bokumetsu sareta mono e no banka to shite* [History of smallpox in Hida: Elegy on the eradication of a disease]. Gifu: Kyōiku Shuppan Bunka Kyōkai.

Takahashi, Bonsen (1941): *Nihon jinkōshi no kenkyū. Daiichi* [Studies on population history. Volume 1]. Tōkyō: Sanyūsha.

—— (1955): *Nihon jinkōshi no kenkyū. Daini* [Studies on population history. Volume 2]. Tōkyō: Nihon Gakujutsu Shinkōkai.

—— (1962): *Nihon jinkōshi no kenkyū. Daisan* [Studies on population history. Volume 3]. Tōkyō: Nihon Gakujutsu Shinkōkai.

—— (1975–1976) (Hg.): *Nihon jinkō tōkeishi ronshū. Jō, Ge* [Collection of essays on the history of Japanese statistics. Volumes 1 and 2]. Tōkyō: Daitō Bunka Daigaku Tōyō Kenkyūjo.

Takazawa, Atsuo (1992): Senjika Nihon ni okeru Jinkō Mondai Kenkyūkai to Jinkō Mondai Kenkyūjo [The Foundation Institute for Research on Population Problems and the Institute of Population Problems during the war]. In: Senjika Nihon Shakai Kenkyūkai (ed.): *Senjika no Nihon: Shōwa zenki no rekishi shakaigaku* [Wartime Japan: Historical sociology in the early Shōwa period]. Kyōto: Kōrosha, pp. 103–120.

Takeuchi, Kei et al. (ed.) (1989): *Tōkeigaku jiten* [Dictionary of statistics]. Tōkyō: Tōyō Keizai Shinpōsha.

Uchida, Kan'ichi (1971): *Kinsei nōson no jinkō chiriteki kenkyū* [Studies in population geography of the early modern farming village]. Tōkyō: Teikoku Shoin.

Ueda, Masao (1949): *Jinkō mondai* [Population problems]. (Shakaika Bunko, B11) Tōkyō: Sanseidō Shuppan.

Ueda, Teijirō (1943): *Jinkō mondai* [Population problems]. Tōkyō: Nihon Hyōronsha.

Weinstein, Jay und Vijayan K. Pillai (2001): *Demography: The science of population.* Boston, London, Toronto, Sydney, Tokyo, Singapore: Allyn and Bacon.

Yanaihara, Tadao (1928): *Jinkō mondai* [Population problems]. Tōkyō: Iwanami Shoten.

Yaukey, David and Douglas L. Anderton (2001): *Demography: The study of human population.* Second edition. Prospect Heights, Illinois: Waveland Press.

# PART TWO

# SOCIAL ASPECTS OF DEMOGRAPHIC CHANGE

# INTRODUCTION

Japanese society experienced a long period of population growth and even population pressure with its high urban population density in the postwar decades. Since 2005, the Japanese population has started to decline, because of falling birth rates and a very low immigration rate. But the ageing of Japan's population was becoming evident already in the 1970s, brought about by a number of factors such as universal family planning and birth control, nuclearization of families, later marriages and the increased participation of women in the labour force, as well as one of the highest life expectancies in the world.

Discussions in academia and the public media since then reveal a high level of concern about the social implications of the growing percentage of elderly people aged 65 and over. Because the incidence of chronic disease and the need to be cared for increases with age, the growing burden in terms of care giving and retirement pensions has been seen as the main factor that will put the social contract between the generations under severe strain.

This aspect of the ageing society is one issue that is dealt with in this part of the handbook. The chapters by Linhart and Ogawa in particular describe the process of growing academic interest in both the ageing society and social ageing as shown in changing social concepts of age and elderly people. As ageing is mostly seen in terms of the growing burden that negatively affects the younger working population, Ogawa's chapter challenges the view that becoming old necessarily leads to a life style where one becomes passive, frail and dependent, recognizing instead the growing percentage of older people who stay healthy and socially active and the various positive challenges that this trend presents to society. The negative image of an ageing society is also addressed in Usui's chapter, when she questions the tendency to discuss and measure demographic changes in terms of an increased dependency ratio. She concludes that this logic is based on assumptions of social organization and life cycle that characterized the Fordist economy of the twentieth century. Post-Fordist economies, in contrast, have a different productive capacity, as Usui maintains, and if social policies utilize these capacities for the benefit of society, for example, by making better use of female labour, the problem of population ageing will become much less severe.

In her chapter, Thang reports from her field of empirical research on another attempt to counter the negative impacts of the ageing society. This comprises different kinds of generational interaction between elderly people and young children in age-integrated institutions. As the trend to fewer children and the nuclearization of families have led to a problem of age segregation among generations, the state and local communities have initiated programmes to support intergenerational contact between non-relatives, an initiative that has already brought many advantages for both the elderly and young children in these newly established institutions.

Despite these more optimistic trends and challenges, the problems of ageing in Japanese society today have to be clearly addressed, as in Long's and Shirahase's chapters. Social policy has already recognized that the lower probability of an elderly person residing with an adult child and the higher probability of participation of women in the labour force will make it less likely that the traditional task of family care giving by women will be maintained. Long describes the still growing necessity of extending the responsibility for care giving beyond the family circle, and sees a remarkable transformation of care-giving patterns taking place both in family homes and in professional care business institutions due to developments in social policy and technological advances.

The structural changes in private households resulting from demographic change are addressed in Shirahase's chapter. Many social scientists maintain that population ageing has brought an increase in economic inequality among elderly people. Shirahase explores this assumption by providing a detailed household analysis, and concludes that the growing percentage of people aged 65 and over does not in itself lead to any economic disadvantages, but rather that the social changes in household composition due to the demographic transformation have to be seen as the main factors in differences in living standards among elderly people.

The changing values that people hold about family and child bearing that lie behind the changes in fertility behaviour are another topic that is raised in this part of the handbook. The sharp reduction in fertility is directly linked with the reproductive behaviour of the younger generation, and many social scientists have pointed out that changes in the female life course, such as pursuing a professional career instead of marrying, can be assumed to be the main factor in the declining birth rate. This assumption places the problem of gender very much at the heart of social scientific research on demographic change. After Himeoka's chapter, which provides a general overview of the historical changes in family structure and female labour and describes how demographic changes have brought about different types of "modern family", the double chapter of Raymo and Iwasawa explores in detail the process of family and partnership formation over the last three decades. Women's growing social and economic opportunities, combined with limited opportunities to balance work and family and a gender-role division in family labour, have to be recognized as the main factors underlying the trend toward later and fewer marriages.

The institutional setting of child care has to be seen as another factor disadvantaging of working mothers, as is shown in Oishi's chapter. It is already 12 years since the government began implementing measures to increase the number of child-care facilities and to establish an environment that is supportive of working mothers, including projects called "Angel Plans". However, demand for institutional child care is still far from being satisfied, as the high number of children on waiting lists reveals.

If women and men are deciding to have fewer children, and measures to encourage people to have more babies remain ineffective, another solution to maintain the population is to allow more people to immigrate. Population decline and falling birth rates are affecting the rural areas particularly, and the economy is in great need of labour in the areas of manual work and nursing. Whether immigration is a viable solution to Japan's demographic imbalance is highly contested. However, immigration is clearly already taking place, and is one of the most obvious forces working towards the pluralization of Japanese society. As the double chapter of Murphy-Shigematsu and Blake Willis describes, this will inevitably involve the question of how migrant communities are to be integrated into mainstream society and how society is being transformed by the inflow of migrants.

In short, the chapters of this part of the handbook focus on the challenges of the ageing of society: to avoid societal cleavage—between generations, between the sexes, between parents and non-parents, between the local population and immigrant communities, and between the rural and urban populations.

A.S.

Case in point: Parental leave: Women and men

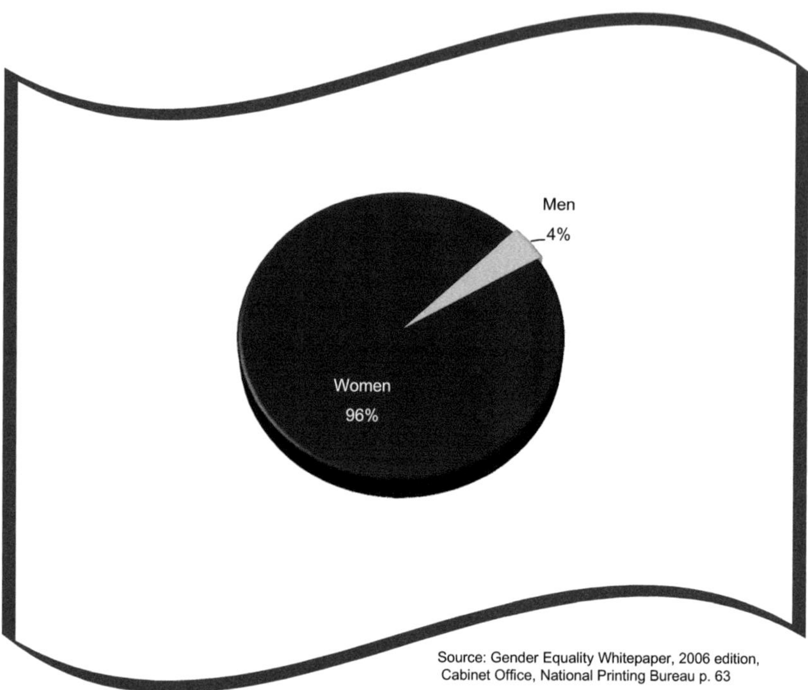


Source: Gender Equality Whitepaper, 2006 edition, Cabinet Office, National Printing Bureau p. 63

| Reasons for not taking parental leave: Men and women | Men | Women |
|---|---|---|
| My spouse or family are opposed. | 0.0 | 7.5 |
| My career will suffer. | 7.3 | 0.0 |
| I will lose the ability to react to changing working conditions. | 8.9 | 25.0 |
| I couldn't abandon my work. | 14.5 | 7.5 |
| My working environment is hostile to parental leave. | 15.3 | 20.0 |
| Economic constraints. | 29.0 | 32.5 |
| Too busy. | 42.7 | 35.0 |
| It will inconvenience my colleagues. | 41.1 | 57.5 |
| Somebody else is taking care of the children. | 57.3 | 12.5 |
| others | 10.5 | 22.5 |

Source: Cabinet Office (2006): Shōshika shakai hakusho, gyōsei, p. 73

CHAPTER SEVEN

# SOCIAL AGEING AND THE SOCIOLOGY OF AGEING

Sepp Linhart

## 1. Social Ageing

> Social aging, in contrast to biological aging and to psychological aging, refers to age-related changes in the individual or society as a whole that results (sic!) from forces arising from society and the individual's and/or group's response to those socially imposed forces. Although society may 'expect' an older person to behave in a certain way, this socially imposed expectation may be internalised or rejected. Social aging influences our role and status in society. This includes age-related problems such as multiple losses, retirement, and age discrimination (Detroit Eldernet n.d., Internet).

Of special importance seem to be the social definitions of old age which refer to chronological age and which do not take into account the actual state of physical or psychological ageing of an individual, although the subjective definition of one's own ageing is very likely to be heavily influenced by them.

In Japan, at a time when "life lasted only fifty years" (*jinsei wazuka gojūnen*), the age of 40 was considered to be the threshold of old age (*shorō*). The popular novel *Seken danna katagi* [The way of a gentlemen in this world] from 1774 tells us: "At the age of 46 he was already past the so-called beginning of old age" (NKD 11: 26). During the Edo period "a man of 40" (*shijū-otoko*) or "a woman of 40" (*shijū-onna*) were equivalent to people in early old age. *Shijū-sagari no irogoto*, a man still interested in making love after 40, *shijū Shimada*, a woman of 40 with a Shimada hairstyle like a younger woman, or *shijū-furisode*, a woman wearing a kimono with long sleeves at 40, are expressions that denoted improper behaviour of people aged 40 and over. Several expressions which deal with the decline of one's physical ability also take the age of 40 as reference. Expressions such as "the shoulder at 40" (*shijū-kata*), "the arm at 40" (*shijū-ude, shijū-kaina*) or the "darkness at 40" (*shijū no kime, shijū-kuragari*), which refer to declining sight or other bodily deficiencies, are typical examples (NKD 9: 514–518).

While these citations reveal that social age was related to chronological age, in traditional society, events in the life cycle of the individual were also very important indicators of social age. Men who did not marry, for whatever reason, remained in the young men's groups (*wakamonogumi*) as long as they stayed single. Without marriage a person could not achieve full adult status. As far as the social definition of old age is concerned, the transfer of one's status as household head to one's son was the event that defined the beginning of old age. There was no unified age limit at which a household head had to retire (*inkyo*), neither for artisans and merchants, nor for peasants, but it seems that rich merchants in Osaka preferred to retire relatively early, so that they could enjoy their retirement leisurely, devoting themselves to pastimes such as poetry or bonsai. As for farmers, those in Northeast Japan stayed in office until death, and *inkyo* was thus unknown there, while in Southwest Japan, *inkyo* was generally practised. The age for retirement was often linked to the decision that the successor had reached a good age for taking over the obligations of a household head. A special variant of *inkyo* available for wealthier farmers was the *inkyo bunke* [retirement branch house]: a household head retired from the main house, which he handed over to his oldest son, and founded a small branch house with only a few fields together with his youngest son, who was later to inherit this branch house. But more commonly the retired former household head and his wife lived with the new household head, either under the same roof or in a special small detached house for retirement (*inkyo hanare*), and the retired parents were cared for by the successor and his family. Little is known about the old age of childless people and people without any property, but it seems that they performed small services for the community and were in turn cared for by it.

In the new civil code of 1897, an age limit of 60 was instituted, at which a person was allowed to retire without giving special reasons such as illness for early retirement. The idea of *kanreki*, a kind of rebirth at 60, when the sexagenary year cycle which began with one's birth is completed, might lie behind the new importance given to age 60 as a watershed. Celebrations of this event, at which the 60-year-old person has to wear red clothes like a child, thus indicating that he/she is reborn, became popular during the Edo period. Consequently the concept of social old age was from then on clearly bound to chronological age: people over the age of 60 were considered to be elderly. However, 50 years later in the post-World War II modified civil code, the concept of household head was abolished. Since then the definition of old age has been closely linked to companies' retirement age. Until 1955, the majority of Japan's population was still working in the agricultural sector, but in the following years the agricultural population decreased very rapidly, and most of Japan's working population shifted from agricultural work to industrial or service industry occupations, thus turning the Japanese into salaried employees. As a result the occupational role and the company one worked for became the main factors in indicating a person's social status, and for the overwhelming majority of men, reaching the company's retirement age did come to mean one had attained old age. This was far from easily accepted, since many companies had regulations which forced their employees to retire at a rather early age, such as 50 or 55, a practice which prompted many individuals to look for new employment after their first retirement. Taking up a second or third job after the first retirement usually meant being paid less and having a lower status, and people sometimes took part-time jobs instead of full-time jobs. But, on the other hand, this practice of being re-employed after retirement made social ageing less abrupt. The so-called retirement shock (German: *Pensionsschock*) was certainly alleviated, especially when people were working fewer and fewer hours until they ceased working at all.

As for people's perceptions of when old age begins today, this transitional process of the *rite de passage* into old age, namely this process of retirement lasting several years, results in a broad range of answers to this question. The results from a number of national opinion polls taken between 1966 and 2004 on when old age (*rōnen*) begins show that, until the middle of the 1990s, "at 60", "at 65" and "at 70" were given as the three most frequent answers, but since then the three most frequent responses were "at 65", "at 70", and "at 75." This proves that the age at which people consider a person as being old is rising continuously. Similarly, if we look at the age of 70 and what percentage of the population links this age with the notion of being old, it is clear that, until 1980, the group that answered in this way comprised about 35 per cent of the population, whereas, since 1990, a growing proportion of 60 to 70 per cent states that old age starts at 70 (results of 14 opinion polls of a nationwide sample of people aged 20 and over in the Opinion Polls About Old People Database [OPAOP] of the Department for East Asian Studies of the University of Vienna). Since people tend to mention a higher age as the beginning of old age the older they themselves are, the general ageing of Japanese society might have influenced this change in perceptions.

## 2. The Sociology of Ageing/Old Age

Taking a look at the field of sociology that deals with social ageing, there are expressions such as the sociology of old age (*rōnen shakaigaku*), the sociology of old people (*rōjin shakaigaku*), the sociology of people of high age (*kōreisha shakaigaku*) and social gerontology (*shakai rōnengaku*). There are no significant differences between these sciences, but *rōjin shakaigaku* is used more commonly than the other terms. All but the last of these disciplines are sub-disciplines of sociology, and people specializing in it are sociologists who might also be experts in other fields of sociology, whereas social gerontology is a sub-discipline of gerontology, such as medical gerontology (*rōnen igaku*) or gerontological psychology (*rōnen shinrigaku*). The Japan Gerontological Society (Nihon Rōnen Gakkai), founded in 1959, comprises five academic societies: the Japan Geriatrics Society (Nihon Rōnen Igakkai, founded in 1959), the Japan Socio-Gerontological Society (Nihon Rōnen Shakaikagakkai, founded in 1959), the Japan Society for Biomedical Gerontology (Nihon Kisō Rōka Gakkai, founded in 1980), the Japanese Psychogeriatric Society (Nihon Rōnen Seishin Igakkai, founded in 1986), and the Japanese Society of Gerodontology (*Nihon Rōnen Shikai Gakkai*, founded in 1990). Thus, the Japan Socio-Gerontological Society and the Japan Geriatrics Society were the first academic societies devoted to the academic study of ageing.

However, academic engagement in questions of old age dates back much further. Mention should be made in particular of Hozumi Nobushige's *Inkyoron* (On Retirement), of which two very different editions have been published, in 1891 and in 1915, the latter being three times as long as the first one. In the first edition, Hozumi (1855–1926), who, together with his younger brother Yatsuka, belonged to the most important legal scholars of his time, criticised the traditional Japanese retirement system, and considered it only a matter of time until it would disappear. In contrast, in the second edition, he placed it together with the family system on which it was founded in opposition to the pension systems of Western countries which were slowly evolving at the time. However, Hozumi acknowledged the right of the individual to be cared for by the community or by the state, and is praised for this by social gerontologists to this day (Yuzawa 1977, Formanek 2003).

The legally imposed social changes after World War II, as expressed in a new constitution and a new civil code, which were based on the idea of individualism, led to a decline in old people's status in society.

Since, under the modified civil code, every child of a family had an equal right to inherit and the special position of the oldest son as the sole heir who had to care for the aged parents was abolished, in many cases, the responsibility for elderly parents that was now divided equally among the children caused a situation where care of the elderly was neglected. Despite the weakening function of the family system that had taken care of old people in the past, the social welfare system was not yet fully established; this aggravated the situation of many old people, who were thus neither supported by their heir's family nor received support from the state. It is understandable that this situation, which was not only discussed in the media but also in literary works such as *Iyagarase no nenrei* (The hateful age, 1947) by Niwa Fumio or in *Narayama bushi-kō* (English title: *The Ballad of Narayama*, 1956) by Fukazawa Shichirō, resulted in increased interest from sociologists in the place of old people in Japanese society, and the "problems of old people/old age" (*rōjin/rōgo mondai*) or the "period after having attained old age" (*rōgo*) became widely discussed social topics.

## 3. Pioneer Studies on the Ageing Society

The first book which dealt with the "problems of old age" in a comprehensive way was published by the Group for Investigating Life Science (Seikatsu Kagaku Chōsakai) in 1961 under the title *Rōgo mondai no kenkyū* [Study of the problems of old age]. Divided into six chapters with easily understandable titles (1. How to deal with the problems of old age; 2. Attitudes towards old people; 3. Old people in the family; 4. Work and occupations of old people; 5. Housing of old people; 6. The social welfare system and morals) and with relevant statistics and photographs appended, this book dealt with the most important fields of the sociology of ageing. Later, other fields were gradually added, such as leisure and social participation, care giving and care taking, and love and sex in old age. But given the fact, that, in 1960, only 5.71 per cent of the population were aged 65 and over, that is, the same rate as in 1884 or 1918, the six authors of *Study of the problems of old age* showed great foresight. They already understood the many new problems with which Japanese society would be confronted due to the rapid ageing of its population in the next decades. In fact, Japan grew older faster than most demographers had expected. While Japan's National Institute of Population Problems (Jinkō Mondai Kenkyūsho) had calculated in 1960 that, in 2005, 15 million Japanese or 14.9 per cent of the population would be aged 65 and over, there were in fact 27 million Japanese in that age group in 2005, comprising 21 per cent of the whole population. In other words, today one in five Japanese is aged 65 or over, and the percentage of old people in the Japanese population is still growing.

Among the authors of *Study of the problems of old age* was a young scholar of sociology who was soon to become an authority in the sociology of the elderly, Soeda Yoshiya (born 1934). Soeda edited a three-volume work *Kōza rōnen shakaigaku* (Lectures on the sociology of ageing) in 1981; published a volume on Japanese culture and the generation of the elderly (*Nihon bunka to rōnen sedai*, 1984); and worked as co-editor of many works on the elderly, the ageing society and social welfare for the aged. He made an important contribution to the field by being the first to touch on the subject of sex and old age, when he edited an issue of the journal *Gendai no esupuri* in 1978 with the special topic: Old age: sexual love, work, education (*Rōnen: Seiai, rōdō, gakushū*). In more recent years, Soeda, who always showed a liking for new, unexplored fields, has begun to publish on the sociology of dying.

There were some other pioneers active in the sociology of ageing somewhat earlier than Soeda, such as Kasahara Masanari (1913–?), who published *Rōjin shakaigaku* (Sociology of the elderly) in 1962 and *Rōjin shakaigaku yōron* (Essential theories about the sociology of the elderly) in 1968. As early as 1966, Daidō Yasujirō (1903–1987) wrote a book *Rōjin shakaigaku no tenkai* (The development of the sociology of the elderly), in which he presented mainly American theories and research results. The other pioneer figure, Nasu Sōichi (1914–1990), a pupil of the famous family sociologist Toda Teizō, applied methods from family sociology to the field, as did many others after him. His first book, one of the earliest in the sociology of ageing, was *Rōjin sedai ron* (Theories about the older generation, 1962), while his book *Rōjin fuyō no kenkyū* (Care of the elderly, 1970), co-edited with Yuzawa Yasuhiko, surveys the problems of old people in urban and rural Japan and compares them with the situation in other countries. Two years later there followed a widely read pocket book about enforced retirement practices in Japanese companies, which at that time used to send their employees into a pensioner's life at 55 (Nasu 1972); and in the same year a co-edited book about the elderly and their families (Nasu and Masuda 1972) was published. This book is the first volume of a series of essays on the elderly in Japan published under the title *Kōza Nihon no rōjin* [Lectures on the elderly in Japan]; the other two volumes deal with psychiatric problems and with social welfare for the aged. Nasu was also one of the two editors of the first comprehensive handbook of gerontology, which appeared in 1976 (Hasegawa and Nasu 1976).

With the beginning of the 1970s, the sociology of ageing was thus beginning to establish itself as an independent discipline in Japan. Of special importance for its further development were two quite different events: the opening of the Tokyo Metropolitan Institute for Gerontology (Tōkyō-to Rōjin Sōgō Kenkyūsho) in April 1972, and the publication of Ariyoshi Sawako's novel *Kōkotsu no hito* (Lit.: A man in ecstasy, English translation: *Twilight Years*) in June 1972, which became an immediate bestseller and shocked the Japanese audience.

The importance of the Tokyo Metropolitan Institute for Gerontology for the field is that it not only carried out medical research, but also at its beginning established a department for social research under the headship of Professor Nasu, who also served as the Institute's vice-president for ten years from its foundation to 1982. At that time the sociology of ageing was not yet established as a discipline at universities. In addition to Soeda Yoshiya, Nasu hired two young female researchers, Sodei Takako (born 1938) and Naoi Michiko (born 1944), who were later to become two of the best-known Japanese sociologists internationally, and who were also representative in their field as social gerontologists. Maeda Daisaku and Asano Hitoshi, who both worked at the Institute from the beginning, later became prominent professors of social welfare. The Institute conducted numerous highly relevant empirical surveys, whose findings were used in social welfare and social policies for the elderly, and at the same time produced important researchers in the sociology of ageing. An overview of the sociological research that was accomplished during the first 20 years of its existence is documented in the history of the institute's first two decades (Tokyo-to Rōjin Sōgō Kenkyūsho 1992: 101–113). From 1975 until 1994 the institute issued the journal *Shakai rōnengaku* (Social gerontology), of which 39 volumes were published. Another scientific journal in the field is still being issued by the aforementioned Japan Socio-Gerontological Society, published in 28 volumes since 1979 under the title *Rōnen shakaikagaku* with the English subtitle *Japanese Journal of Gerontology*. On the occasion of the 11th International Congress of Gerontology, which was held in Tokyo in 1978, Nasu edited a special volume in English, which gives a good overview of the state of gerontological research in Japan at the end of the 1970s (Nasu 1978).

During the 1980s, the mass media helped to highlight the problem of the ageing of Japanese society as an important topic (Linhart 1988). Since the 1980s, social ageing was no longer a theme that was exclusively treated by scholars of sociology and social work, something that can be seen in the publication of a five-volume series *Oi no hakken* (The discovery of ageing) from the famous publishing house Iwanami Shoten in 1986–1987. The main editors were prominent intellectuals, such as the theoretical economist Itō Mitsuharu, the Jungian psychiatrist Kawai Hayao, the sociologist Soeda Yoshiya, the philosopher and cultural critic Tsurumi Shunsuke, and the famous physician Hinohara Shigeaki (Itō *et al.* 1986/87).

But despite these achievements, the sociology of ageing remained a badly treated poor cousin within mainstream sociology. In a review of seven books on the sociology of ageing from the first half of the 1980s, Hiraoka (1986: 84–87) arrives at the conclusion that the sociological study of ageing should not only concentrate on problems of old age (*rōgo mondai*) and those of the family in particular, but should rather treat the topic of old age from a much wider perspective. Secondly, the aged society (*kōreika shakai*) should be given more weight in sociological studies. Thirdly, sociology should also try to make proposals to administrators and politicians based on their research findings. Fourthly, while comparative studies are very much needed, these studies should not only be confined to comparisons with highly developed countries such as the United Kingdom, the United States, and Sweden, but should also include other, less-developed countries. Fifthly, the importance of the earlier studies lies in their accumulation of empirical data, but too many studies resemble each other and do not refer to already existing studies. Finally, he mentions that in the sociology of ageing, empirical studies preceded theoretical considerations, and therefore the development of adequate theories taking into account what has already been done in other countries is an urgent task, in order to give future studies a more theoretical foundation.

Ten years later, in a volume devoted to the sociology of maturity and old age, which appeared as one volume of a 27-volume series on contemporary sociology in Japan, Soeda contributed a chapter which attempts to evaluate the sociology of the elderly in Japan (Soeda 1997). He starts with an analysis of Japan's most representative sociological journal, *Shakaigaku hyōron* (Japanese sociological review), and notes that, over a period of ten years, between 1986 and 1995, only three articles dealing with old age appeared among more than 200 articles, which for him clearly indicates that the sociology of ageing is only a second- or third-rate discipline within Japanese sociology. He then analyses the 142 papers published in *Shakai rōnengaku* (Social ageing) between 1986 and 1994, and arrives at the conclusion that most of these papers use excellent methods to arrive at trivial results, which might have been the reason that research results from the sociology of ageing remained ignored within general sociology. It is perhaps interesting to note that the Dial database of literature on the sociology of ageing (*Dial shakai rōnengaku bunken dēta bēsu*) lists one paper from *Shakaigaku hyōron* related to the sociology of ageing for the period 1981 to 1985, four for 1986 to 1990, none for 1991 to 1995, four for 1996 to 2000, and six for 2001 to 2005. These data give the impression that, perhaps due to Soeda's aforementioned criticism, papers in the field of the sociology of ageing have become more widely accepted since 1996.

## 4. Studies on Social Ageing Since 1980

Enumerating all the many books that have appeared over the last 25 years is an impossible task, and therefore only some of the particularly important ones will be mentioned here. In 1979, Sodei and Naoi edited a book about middle-aged and elderly women, written by six female scholars, who addressed the specific problems of women, which was still a novelty at that time. They also stressed that the study of middle-aged women is important in order to better understand women in old age (Sodei and Naoi 1979). This book was part of a multi-volume series which treated the middle-aged and the elderly simultaneously as one generation. Makino and Harada (1981) edited a volume based on a survey report *Kōreika shakai e no taiō* [Responding to an increasingly ageing society], and in the same year an 8-volume series on society with an ageing population began to be released. The editors were Miura Fumio, a key person in the field of social welfare, and other well-known sociologists and social critics, and the contents range from simple essays to excellent academic papers (Miura *et al.* 1981–85).

A very important book on social welfare for the elderly was edited by Yamashita and Ueda (1987), which attempts to link theory and data. Similarly, Kinoshita (1989), Satō *et al.* (1989), as well as Naoi and Hashimoto (1990) also deal with the welfare of the aged, but Kinoshita concentrates on care for old people. Matsumura (1990) has written an important study in which he shows how regional welfare in Hitachi city in Ibaraki prefecture affected the lives of the elderly, and how they emancipated themselves from being welfare recipients of social services to become elderly citizens for whom self-realization was meaningful. Another detailed research report by the Shakai Hoshō Kenkyūsho [Institute of Social Security Research] (1990) in Kakegawa city in Shizuoka challenges the myth that cohabitation of the elderly with one of their children is the ideal way to spend one's life in old age, by indicating the many problems involved. Another excellent study on regional welfare and the elderly was published by Kaneko Isamu (1993). Shimizu Hiroaki (1992), a scholar who is influenced by social anthropology, wrote a study on the regional characteristics of the family in an ageing society, and Arakaki *et al.* (1993) did research about the intergenerational relationships of the elderly in Okinawa, the Japanese prefecture with the highest life expectancy, which might also relate to the fact that the elderly seem to be especially well treated there, as one of the authors reports.

Hamaguchi and Sagaza (1990) concern themselves with the question of how life will look in an age of mass longevity (*taishū chōju jidai*), and point to the fact that lifestyle, sex, and leisure will gain much more importance for people. From the beginning of the 1990s onwards the concept "society of longevity" (*chōju shakai*) gradually replaced the older notion "ageing society" (*kōreika shakai*). Perhaps this reflects the insight of scholars that a new stage of societal development has finally been reached. In this context it has to be mentioned that, in 1989, a Centre for the Development of a Society of Longevity (*Chōju Shakai Kaihatsu Sentā*) was established and supported by the Ministry of Welfare and Labour. This Centre succeeded the *Rōjin Fukushi Kaihatsu Sentā* [Centre for the Development of Welfare for the Aged], and thus the less positive older name of the institution was replaced. It should also be mentioned that, during the period of the bubble economy, the renaming of old-fashioned concepts which were considered to bear negative connotations became very popular, and words such as "old" and "grey" for old people were also affected. The substitution of "silver" for "grey" is well known, but the Ministry of Welfare even held a contest to introduce new words for "middle age" and "old age" in 1985. In accordance with the public response it was decided that *jitsunen* was best suited to denote people between 50 and 69, while for those aged 70 and above, *jukunen* was selected. Both words mean "age of fruition." Concerning the society of longevity, the family sociologist

Aoi Kazuo (1920–) published a general introduction on the impacts that such a society would have on the family and the community (Aoi 1992), and a similar book was written by Kurata Washio and Asano Hitoshi (1993). In 1994 and 1995 Aoi edited two volumes on social participation by the elderly for the Centre for the Development of a Society of Longevity.

The other doyen of family sociology, Morioka Kiyomi, Japan's foremost expert on life course studies, edited a volume on the changing lifestyles of the elderly (Morioka and Nakabayashi 1994), while Kaneko Isamu (1995, 1998) wrote general introductions to the ageing society and Yamaguchi Tōru (1994) edited a study on the same subject based on the research of six sociologists. Maki (1994) was one of several researchers who dealt with the issue of work for the elderly.

One of the most severe problems in Japan's greying society is the high suicide rate among the elderly, especially among elderly women. About 30,000 suicides are committed in Japan every year, of which one third are committed by persons aged 65 and over. The most common method of killing oneself is hanging. In 1993 a suicide manual was published which is said to have sold more than one million copies. Interestingly, most Japanese old people commit suicide for physical reasons: when their bodies no longer function as they used to, many elderly people try to end their lives in order to avoid bothering their families with their bodily dysfunctions. Matsumoto Toshiaki (1995) wrote a lengthy study on suicide in old age, while Hamaguchi and Sagaza (1995) edited a book about ways of dying in a society of mass longevity. Related to these academic studies, a popular book written by Takeda Kyōko became a small bestseller in 1994. In her book, which bears the sensational title *Rōjo wa naze kazoku ni korosareru no ka?* [Why are old women killed by their families?] Takeda describes in detail numerous cases where old women were killed by their daughters-in-law, their husbands or their children, and aims to prevent such murders in the future. Yoshida Yoshishige had already dealt with the same problem in 1986 in the movie *Ningen no yakusoku* [A promise between people].

In 1997 Sagaza published an analysis of the 1995 population census data with relation to the ageing of society, a publication which provides basic data to all those doing research on ageing. The same authors co-edited the *Gendai eijingu jiten* [Dictionary of contemporary ageing] (Hamaguchi *et al.* 1996). Hamaguchi (1997), one of the most prolific writers on social ageing, also published an introductory book on ageing. Nishishita and Asano (1997) is a textbook for social workers, while Takahashi and Takahagi (1996) stress the importance of volunteers in an aged society.

One of the three pillars on which welfare for the aged in Japan rests is the local community, the other two being the family and the state. Therefore numerous studies have been written on community welfare for the aged, such as Kaneko (1997), Ogawa (1996), and Matsumura (1998). Among these, Komiya's (1999) study on the recovery of people with senile dementia, and Osada's (1999) book about the costs of medical care for old people are more specialized.

Yamashita Kesao (1998) attempted to relate Japan's post-war social change to the problems of the elderly, and Fujisaki Hiroko (1998) concerns herself with the elderly and their families as well as other social networks. A new theme was taken up by Tsuji Shōji (2000), who did research on the discrimination and stigmatization of the elderly.

In April 2000, a nursing care insurance system was introduced, which immediately prompted a number of studies about nursing care, too many to be enumerated here. Two broader studies of welfare for the elderly are Kyōgoku and Takegawa (2001) and Ichibangase and Kawabata (2001), while Aikawa (2000) concentrates on the situation of the elderly in rural villages.

Hashimoto and others (2002) carried out surveys on what kind of life people would choose in advanced age, while Sagaza Haruo (2002) edited a volume in which the living arrangements of old people in several Asian societies were compared. In 2003, Koyano Wataru and Andō Takatoshi edited a volume proposing a new social gerontology. A lengthy book by Amada Jōsuke, *"Oiotoroeyuku koto" no shakaigaku* [A sociology of ageing and decaying], was awarded the Prize for the Best Sociological Book Published in 2003, the third time that this prize was awarded.

## 5. Works by non-Japanese Authors on the Sociology of Ageing in Japan

In 1984 the author of this chapter compiled an annotated bibliography of Western-language materials about old age in Japan (Linhart and Wöss, 1984). Although he found 380 pieces—articles, essays, papers, some books, literary works dealing with old age—written on this theme, most of them were written by Japanese scholars, such as

Asano Hitoshi, Maeda Daisaku, Nasu Sōichi, Shimizu Yutaka, and Yashiro Naohiro. All of these authors except Yashiro were members of the Tokyo Metropolitan Institute of Gerontology, which shows that this institute not only promoted research on social ageing in Japan, but was also instrumental in internationalizing its research results.

The first well-informed articles about old age in Japan were written by David W. Plath (1972, 1973a, 1973b), a cultural anthropologist from the University of Illinois, who had apparently become aware of the enormous attention given to the elderly in Japan at that time. He later edited a volume, *Adult episodes in Japan*, which included chapters dealing with social ageing (Plath 1975), and published a monograph about attaining maturity in Japan, which deals with middle-age, but also partly with the coming old age (Plath 1980). Although Plath's work received much acclaim, the most influential work in a Western language was perhaps written by an American gerontologist, Erdman Palmore (1975), *The honorable elders. A cross-cultural analysis of aging in Japan*, which appeared ten years later in a revised edition (Palmore and Maeda 1985). Palmore used the Japanese example as a mirror for the American people, in order to demonstrate how well-treated the elderly were in Japan compared to those in the United States, a hypothesis which was soon severely criticised by Tobin (1987).

Other American scholars in this field are John Campbell (1992), who described how the Japanese government reacted to the rapid ageing of society by implementing a variety of policies for the aged. Kinoshita and Kiefer (1992) carried out a thorough study of a home for wealthy aged people near Hakone, while Margaret Lock (1993) compared the universal phenomenon of the menopause among women in Japan and in the United States, and tried to look at cultural variations of a biological phenomenon. Hashimoto (1996) compared the social contract between the generations in Japan and in the United States and came to the conclusion that a convergence of the two systems in the near future is not likely to occur. Another comparative study between Japan and the United States is concerned with the practices and policies of caring for the elderly (Long 2000). Susan Orpett Long (2005) published an important book about end-of-life decision-making. The anthropologist John W. Traphagan published a study based on fieldwork on the cultural construction of senility (2000), and another about the relation between religion and ageing (2004). Together with John Knight he also edited a volume on the significance of the demographic changes for the family (Traphagan and Knight 2003).

In Europe the Department for Japanese Studies of the University of Vienna conducted comprehensive research about the elderly in Japan during the 1970s and 80s. Linhart and Wöss (1984), Maderdonner (1987) and Kargl (1987) compiled basic data on Japan's ageing society, while Linhart (1983) did fieldwork about old people's clubs and universities which brought him to a very positive evaluation of these organizations. Getreuer-Kargl (1990, 1992) carried out an empirical study of expert views on how ageing would influence Japanese society, while Wöss researched the suddenly emerging phenomenon of Buddhist temples that catered to elderly people who were praying for a quick death (1993). Formanek and Linhart (1997) are mainly concerned with ageing in Japan, but also compare the developments there with other Asian countries, not only in the present but also in the past. The Department for East Asian Studies of the University of Vienna continues to work on a database that covers all questions from public opinion surveys on old age from the 1960s to date (OPAOP). The German Institute for Japanese Studies in Tokyo started research on Japan's ageing society in the 1990s. While Oberländer and Lützeler (1997) dealt with care of the elderly, Conrad and Lützeler (2002) edited a volume about Japanese social policy in comparison with Germany. The Handbook of Oriental Studies volume on *Modern Japanese society* contains an overview on old age by Oberländer (2004). In Sweden, Anbäcken (1997) has written a monograph about caring for the elderly in Japan.

Summing up, one can say that, among Western studies on old age in Japan, studies that deal with families' capacity to care for the elderly and studies on institutions for the aged are in the majority, while studies on old people's work or culture and leisure are not yet well developed. However, given the present broad interest in the ageing of Japanese society and social ageing, such studies are sure to appear before long.

## References

Aikawa, Yoshihiko (2000): *Nōson ni miru kōreisha kaigo* [Care for the elderly in rural villages]. Tokyo: Nōrinsuisanshō Nōgyō Sōgō Kenkyūsho.

Amada, Jōsuke (2003): *'Oiotoroeyuku koto' no shakaigaku* [A sociology of ageing and decaying]. Tokyo: Taga Shuppan.

Anbäcken, Els-Marie (1997): *Who cares? Culture, structure, and agency in caring for the elderly in Japan.* Stockholm: The Institute of Oriental Languages, Stockholm University.

Aoi, Kazuo (1992): *Chōju shakai ron* [On a society of longevity]. Tokyo: Ryūtsu Keizai Daigaku Shuppankai.

—— (1994): *Sedaikan koryū ni yoru kōreisha no shakai sanka sokushin ni kansuru kisōteki kenkyū—kōreika shakai no sedaikan kōryū.* [A basic study of the promotion of social participation by the elderly through intergenerational exchange—Intergenerational exchange in an ageing society]. Tokyo: Chōju Shakai Kaihatsu Sentā.

—— (1995): *Sedaikan koryū ni yoru kōreisha no shakai sanka sokushin ni kansuru kisōteki kenkyū—ronbun, shiryōshū* [A basic study of the promotion of social participation by the elderly through intergenerational exchange—Articles and materials]. Tokyo: Chōju Shakai Kaihatsu Sentā.

Arakaki, Toyoko, Tamaki Takao, Ōshiro Noritake and Hanashiro Rieko (1993): *Okinawa no kōreisha o meguru sedai kankei* [Generational relations pertaining to the elderly of Okinawa]. Tokyo: Taga Shuppan.

Campbell, John (1992): *How policies change: The Japanese government and the aging society.* Princeton, N. J.: Princeton University Press.

Chōju Shakai Kaihatsu Sentā [Centre for the Development of a Society of Longevity]: http://www.nenrin.or.jp/index.html (found 14/7/2006).

Conrad, Harald and Ralph Lützeler (eds.) (2002): *Aging and social policy. A German-Japanese comparison.* Munich: Iudicium.

Daidō, Yasujirō (1966): *Rōjin shakaigaku no tenkai* [The development of the sociology of the elderly]. Kyōto: Mineruva Shobō.

Detroit Eldernet (n.d.): *Understanding the aging process.* http://comnet.org/detroiteldernet/_private/answers/active/process.htm (found 9/6/2006).

Dial Shakai Rōnengaku Bunken Dēta Bēsu [Dial database of literature on the sociology of ageing]. http://www2.yume-net.ne.jp/dial/itiranhyou/list.asp (found 14/7/2006).

Formanek, Susanne (2003): Der Diskurs um Ausgedinge und Pension in Tokyo und Wien [The discourse on parent's estate and retirement pension in Tokyo and Vienna]. In: Linhart, Sepp (ed.): *Wien und Tokyo um die Wende vom 19. zum 20. Jahrhundert* [Vienna and Tokyo at the turn of the 19th to the 20th century]. Wien: Abteilung für Japanologie, Institut für Ostasienwissenschaften, Universität Wien [Japanese Studies Department, East Asian Institute, Vienna University], pp. 83–106.

Formanek, Susanne and Sepp Linhart (eds.) (1997): *Aging. Asian concepts and experiences. Past and present.* Wien: Verlag der Österreichischen Akademie der Wissenschaften.

Fujisaki, Hiroko (1998): *Kōreisha, kazoku, shakaiteki nettowāku* [The elderly, their families and their social networks]. Tokyo: Baifūkan.

Getreuer-Kargl, Ingrid (1990): *Ende der Dynamik? Eine Expertenbefragung zur Alterung der japanischen Gesellschaft* [The end of dynamics? A study of experts' opinions on Japan's ageing society]. Wien: Institut für Japanologie.

—— [Getoroiyā-Kāgeru, Inguriddo] (1992): *Kōreika shakai no katsuryoku. Nihon de no yūshikisha chōsa yori* [The dynamics of an ageing society. A study of experts' opinions on Japan's ageing society]. Tokyo: Shakai Hoken Fukushi Kyōkai.

Hamaguchi, Haruhiko (1997): *Eijingu to wa nani ka? Kōrei shakai no ikikata* [What is ageing? On living in an aged society]. Tokyo: Waseda Daigaku Shuppankai.

Hamaguchi, Haruhiko and Sagaza Haruo (eds.) (1990): *Taishū chōju shakai no ikikata* [Ways of living in an age of mass longevity]. Kyoto: Mineruva Shobō.

—— (eds.) (1995): *Taishu chōju jidai no shinikata* [Ways of dying in an age of mass longevity]. Kyoto: Mineruva Shobō.

Hamaguchi, Haruhiko *et al.* (1996): *Gendai eijingu jiten* [Dictionary of contemporary ageing]. Tokyo: Waseda Daigaku Shuppankai.

Hasegawa, Kazuo and Nasu Sōichi (eds.) (1976): *Handobukku rōnengaku* [Handbook of gerontology). Tokyo: Iwasaki Bijutsusha.

Hashimoto, Akiko (1996): *The gift of generations. Japanese and American perspectives on aging and the social contract.* Cambridge, New York, Melbourne: Cambridge University Press.

Hashimoto, Kazuyuki, Usui Takashi, Mikami Katsuya and Katano Masayoshi (2002): *Kōreika shakai to seikatsu sentaku* [Life choices in an ageing society]. Tokyo: Taga Shuppan.

Hiraoka, Kōichi (1986): Shakaigaku ni okeru rōnen kenkyū no dōkō to kadai [Recent trends and problems in the sociology of old age]. In: *Shakaigaku Hyōron* 37, 1, pp. 79–87.

Hozumi, Nobushige (1978): *Inkyoron* [On retirement]. Tokyo: Nihon Keizai Hyōronsha. [1. Edition 1915].

Ichibangase, Yasuko and Kawabata Osamu (eds.) (2001): *Kōreisha to fukushi bunka* [The elderly and the culture of welfare]. Tokyo: Akashi Shoten.

Itō, Mitsuharu, Kawai Hayao, Soeda Yoshiya, Tsurumi Shunsuke and Hinohara Shigeaki (eds.) (1986/87): *Oi no hakken* [The discovery of ageing]. 5 vols. Tokyo: Iwanami Shoten.

Kaneko, Isamu (1993): *Toshi kōrei shakai to chiiki fukushi* [Urban ageing society and regional welfare]. Kyoto: Mineruva Shobō.

—— (1995): *Kōreishakai. Nani ga dō kawaru ka* [The ageing society. How and what will change]. Tokyo: Kōdansha.

—— (1997): *Chiiki fukushi shakaigaku* [Sociology of community welfare]. Kyoto: Mineruva Shobō.

—— (1998): *Kōreishakai to anata* [The aged society and you]. Tokyo: Nihon Hōsō Shuppan Kyōkai.

Kargl, Ingrid (1987): *Old age in Japan. Long-term Statistics*. Wien: Institut für Japanologie.

Kasahara, Masanari (1962): *Rōjin shakaigaku* [Sociology of the elderly]. Tokyo: Surugadai Shuppan.

—— (1968): *Rōjin shakaigaku yōron* [Essential theories about the sociology of the elderly]. Tokyo: Surugadai Shuppan.

Kinoshita, Yasuhito (1989): *Rōjin kea no shakaigaku* [Sociology of care for the aged]. Tokyo: Igaku Shoin.

Kinoshita, Yasuhito and Christie W. Kiefer (1992): *Refuge of the honored: Social organization in a Japanese retirement community*. Berkeley: University of California Press.

Komiya, Emi (1999): *Chihōsei kōreisha kea. Gurūpu hōmu de tachinaoru hitobito* [Care of elderly people with senile dementia: people who recover in group homes]. Tokyo: Chūō Kōronsha.

Koyano, Wataru, and Andō Takatoshi (eds.) (2003): *Shin shakai rōnengaku. Shinia raifu no yukue* [A new social gerontology. Locating the senior's lives]. Tokyo: Wārudo Puraningu.

Kurata, Washio, and Asano Hitoshi (1993): *Chōju shakai no tenbō to kadai* [Prospects and issues for a society of longevity]. Kyoto: Mineruva Shobō.

Kyōgoku, Takanobu and Takegawa Shōgo (eds.) (2001): *Kōreisha shakai no fukushi sābisu* [Welfare services in an aged society]. Tokyo: Tōkyō Daigaku Shuppankai.

Linhart, Sepp (1974): Das Problem der älteren Menschen in der japanischen Gegenwartsliteratur—eine soziologische Betrachtung [The problem of elderly people in Japanese modern literature—a sociological perspective]. In: *Nachrichten der Gesellschaft für Natur- und Völkerkunde Ostasiens* [Bulletin of the Society for Science and Ethnology of East Asia] 115, pp. 35–44.

—— (1983): *Organisationsformen alter Menschen in Japan. Selbstverwirklichung durch Hobbies, Weiterbildung, Arbeit* [Forms of organization of elderly people in Japan. Self-realization through hobbies, continued education, work]. Wien: Institut für Japanologie.

—— (1988): Japan's post war history as the history of the elderly. In: *Fukuoka Unesco* 23, pp. 287–297.

Linhart, Sepp and Fleur Wöss (1984): *Old age in Japan. An annotated bibliography of Western-language materials*. Wien: Institut für Japanologie.

Lock, Margaret (1993): *Encounters with aging: mythologies of menopause in Japan and North America*. Berkeley: University of California Press.

Long, Susan Orpett (2000): *Caring for the elderly in Japan and the US. Practices and policies*. London and New York: Routledge.

Long, Susan Orpett (2005): *Final days—Japanese culture and choice at the end of life*. Honolulu: University of Hawai'i Press.
Maderdonner, Megumi (1987): *Old age in Japan. An annotated bibliography of Japanese books*. Wien: Institut für Japanologie.
Maki, Masahide (1994): *Kōreika shakai to rōdō mondai. Shokuba soshiki no kasseika no kenkyū* [Labour problems in an ageing society. A study of the revitalization of workplace organizations]. Tokyo: Tasseisha Kōseikaku.
Makino, Noboru and Harada, Akira (eds.) (1981): *Kōreika shakai e no taiō* [Responding to an ageing society]. Nihon Hōsō Shuppan Kyōkai.
Matsumoto, Toshiaki (1995): *Rōnenki no jisatsu ni kansuru jisshōteki kenkyū* [An empirical study of suicide in old age]. Tokyo: Taga Shuppan.
Matsumura, Naomichi (1990): *Chiiki fukushi seisaku to rōgo seikatsu* [Regional welfare policies and life in old age]. Tokyo: Keisō Shobō.
—— (1998): *Kōreisha fukushi no sōzō to chiiki fukushi kaihatsu* [The creation of welfare for the elderly and the development of community welfare]. Tokyo: Keisō Shobō.
Miura, Fumio *et al.* (eds.) (1981–85): *Kōreika shakai shiriizu* [Series on the society with an ageing population]. 8 vols. Tokyo: Chūō Hōki Shuppan.
Morioka, Kiyomi and Nakabayashi Itsuki (eds.) (1994): *Henyō suru kōreishazō—Daitoshi kōreisha no raifu sutairu* [The changing image of the elderly—The lifestyles of the elderly in a big city]. Tokyo: Nihon Hyōronsha.
Naoi, Michiko and Hashimoto Masaaki (eds.) (1990): *Rōjin fukushi ron* [On welfare for the elderly]. Tokyo: Seishin Shobō.
Nasu, Sōichi (1962): *Rōjin sedai ron. Rōjin fukushi no riron to genjō bunseki* [Theories about the older generation. Theories of social welfare for the elderly and an analysis of the present state]. Tokyo: Asahi Shobō.
—— (1972): *Teinen. 55-sai no shiren* [Retirement. The trial at age 55]. Tokyo: Nihon Keizai Shinbunsha.
Nasu, Sōichi (ed.) (1978): *Ageing in Japan*. Tokyo: Japan Institute for Gerontological Research and Development.
Nasu, Sōichi, and Masuda Kōkichi (eds.) (1972): *Rōjin to kazoku no shakaigaku* [The sociology of the elderly and their families]. Kōza Nihon no rōjin [Lectures on the elderly in Japan], 3. Tokyo: Kakiuchi Shuppan.
Nasu, Sōichi and Yuzawa Yasuhiko (eds.) (1970): *Rōjin fuyō no kenkyū. Rōjin kazoku no shakaigaku* [A study of care for the elderly. Sociology of the families of the elderly]. Tokyo: Kakiuchi Shuppan.
*Nihon Kokugo Daijiten* [Great Dictionary of the Japanese Language] (NKD) (1974): 20 vols. Shōgakkan.
Nishishita, Akitoshi, and Asano Hitoshi (eds.) (1997): *Kaiteiban. Rōjin fukushi ron* [Rev. Ed. Welfare for the elderly]. Tokyo: Kawashima Shoten.
Oberländer, Christian and Ralph Lützeler (eds.) (1997): *Altern und Pflegepolitik in Japan* [The elderly and care policies in Japan]. Berlin, Tokyo: Deutsches Institut für Japanstudien [German Institute for Japanese Studies] (= *Miscellanea* 15).
Oberländer, Christian (2004): Old age. In: Kreiner, Josef, Ulrich Möhwald, and Hans Dieter Ölschleger (eds.): *Modern Japanese society*. Leiden: Brill, pp. 109–139.
Ogasawara, Yūji (ed.) (1990–1992): *Rōjin mondai kenkyū kihon bunken shū* [Collection of basic works on the problems of the aged]. 29 vols. Tokyo: Ōsorasha.
Ogawa, Takeo (1996): *Chiiki no kōreika to fukushi. Kōreisha no komyuniti jōkyō* [The ageing of local communities and welfare. The community conditions of the elderly]. Tokyo: Tasseisha Kōseikaku.
Okamoto, Takiko, and Nakamura Ritsuko (eds.) (2006): *Sengo kōrei shakai kihon bunken shū* [A collection of basic post-war works on the ageing society]. Dai-ikki, 12 vols. Tokyo: Nihon Tosho Sentā.
OPAOP = Opinion Polls about Old People in Japan Database, Department for East Asian Studies, University of Vienna.

Osada, Hiroshi (1999): *Shōshi kōreika jidai no iryō to fukushi. Iryō, fukushi no keizaishakaigaku nyūmon* [Medical care and welfare in a period of few children and an ageing population. An introduction to the economic sociology of medical care and welfare]. Tokyo: Akashi Shoten.

Palmore, Erdman (1975): *The honorable elders. A cross-cultural analysis of aging in Japan.* Durham: Duke University Press.

Palmore, Erdman and Maeda Daisaku (1985): *The honorable elders revisited. A revised cross-cultural analysis of aging in Japan.* Durham: Duke University Press.

Plath, David W. (1972): Japan: the after years. In: Donald O. Cowgill, Donald O. and Lowell D. Holmes (eds.): *Aging and modernization.* New York: Appleton-Century-Crofts, pp. 133–150.

Plath, David W. (1973a): "Ecstasy years"—old age in Japan. In: *Pacific Affairs* 46, 3, pp. 421–429.

—— (1973b): Japanese psychology through Japanese literature. Cares of career, and careers of care taking. In: *The Journal of Nervous and Mental Disease* 157, 5, pp. 346–357.

—— (ed.) (1975): *Adult episodes in Japan.* Leiden: Brill, 164–174 (= International studies in sociology and social anthropology 20).

—— (1980): *Long engagements. Maturity in modern Japan.* Stanford: Stanford University Press.

Sagaza, Haruo (1997): *Jinkō kōreika to kōreisha—saishin kokusei chōsa kara miru kōreika shakai* [The ageing of the population and the elderly: The ageing society as seen from the latest National Census]. Tokyo: Ōkurashō Insatsukyoku.

—— (ed.) (2002): *Ajia ni okeru kōreisha no ribingu arenjimento ni kansuru bunken mokuroku oyobi kaidai: Nihon, Kankoku, Marēshia, Shingapōru, Taiwan o chūshin ni* [A bibliography with annotations about the living arrangements of the elderly in Asia, focusing on Japan, South Korea, Malaysia, Singapore, and Taiwan]. Tokyo: Waseda Daigaku Ningen Sōgō Kenkyū Sentā [Waseda University Advanced Research Center for Human Sciences].

Satō, Hiroki, Ōta Hiroko, Takegawa Shōgo, and Satō Naoto (eds.) (1989): *Futsū no shimin ga anshin dekiru rōgo seikatsu no tame ni* [For an old age in which ordinary citizens will feel at ease]. Tokyo: Gendai Sōgō Kenkyū Shūdan.

Seikatsu Kagaku Chōsakai (ed.) (1961): *Rōgo mondai no kenkyū* [Study of the problems of old age]. Tokyo: Seikatsu Kagaku Chōsakai.

Shadan Hōjin Nihon Rōnen Igakkai (The Japan Geriatrics Society) (ed.) (2002): *Nihon rōnen gakkai tō no kanren gakujutsu dantai* (Academic societies connected with The Japan Geriatrics Society). http://www.jpn-geriat-soc.or.jp/kanren/dantai.html (found 28/6/2006).

Shakai Hoshō Kenkyūsho (ed.) (1990): *Kōreika shakai e no seikatsu henyō* [Changes in living to cope with an ageing society]. Tokyo: Idemitsu Shoten.

Shimizu, Hiroaki (1992): *Kōreika shakai to kazoku kōzō no chiikisei* [Regionalism of family structure in an ageing society]. Tokyo: Jichōsha.

Sodei, Takako and Naoi Michiko (eds.) (1979): *Nihon no chūkōnen 2: Chūkōnen joseigaku* [Japan's middle aged and old aged 2: Women's studies on the middle-aged and the old-aged]. Tokyo: Kakiuchi Shuppan.

Soeda, Yoshiya (ed.) (1978): *Rōnen: Seiai, rōdō, gakushū* [Old age: sexual love, work, education]. = *Gendai no esupuri* No. 126. Tokyo: Shibundō.

—— (ed.) (1981): *Kōza rōnen shakaigaku* [Lectures on the sociology of ageing]. Tokyo: Kakiuchi Shuppan.

—— (ed.) (1984): *Nihon bunka to rōnen sedai* [Japanese culture and the generation of the elderly]. Tokyo: Chūō Hōki Shuppan.

—— (1997): Rōnen shakaigaku no tenbō to hihan [Criticism of and the outlook for the sociology of the elderly]. In: Inoue, Shun, Ueno Chizuko, Ōsawa Makō, Mita Munesuke and Yoshimi Shunya (eds.): *Gendai shakaigaku 13: Seijuku to oi no shakaigaku*

[Contemporary sociology 13: Sociology of maturity and of old age]. Tokyo: Iwanami Shoten, pp. 197–214.
Takahashi, Yūetsu and Takahagi Tateo (eds.) (1996): *Kōreika to borantia shakai* [Ageing and the volunteer society]. Tokyo: Kōbundō.
Takeda, Kyōko: *Rōjo wa naze kazoku ni korosareru no ka?* [Why are old women killed by their families?] Kyoto: Mineruva Shobō.
Tobin, Joseph Jay (1987): The American idealization of old age in Japan. In: *The Gerontologist* 27, pp. 53–58.
Tokyo-to Rōjin Sōgō Kenkyūsho (ed.) (1992): *Rōjinken 20-nen shi* [The history of the first 20 years of the Tokyo Metropolitan Institute for Gerontology]. Tokyo: Tokyo-to Rōjin Sōgō Kenkyūsho.
Traphagan, John W. (2000): *Taming oblivion. Aging bodies and the fear of senility in Japan.* Albany: State University of New York Press.
—— (2004): *The practice of concern: ritual, well-being, and aging in rural Japan.* Durham, North Carolina: Carolina Academic Press.
Traphagan, John W., and John Knight (2003): *Demographic change and the family in Japan's aging society.* Albany: State University of New York Press.
Tsuji, Shōji (2000): *Kōreisha raberingu no shakaigaku. Rōjin sabetsu no chōsa kenkyū* [The sociology of the labelling of the elderly: An empirical study of discrimination of the old people]. Tokyo: Tasseisha Kōseikaku.
Wöss, Fleur (1993): Pokkuri-temples and aging. Rituals for approaching death. In: Mullins, Mark R., Shimazono Susumu and Paul L. Swanson (eds.): *Religion and society in modern Japan. Selected readings.* Berkeley: Asian Humanities Press, pp. 191–202.
Yamaguchi, Tōru (ed.) (1994): *Kōreishakai e no taiō* [Responses to an aged society]. Tokyo: Kōbundō Shuppansha.
Yamashita, Kesao (1998): *Sengo no shakai hendō to kōreisha mondai* [Post-war social change and problems of the elderly]. Kyoto: Mineruva Shobō.
Yamashita, Kesao and Ueda Chiaki (eds.) (1987): *Gaisetsu rōjin fukushi* [An overview of welfare for the aged]. Kyoto: Mineruva Shobō.
Yuzawa, Yasuhiko (1977): Hozumi Nobushige ni okeru "Inkyoron" no hatten—Meiji 24nenban to Taishō 4nenban no hikaku shōkai [The development of Hozumi Nobushige's "On retirement". A comparative introduction to the 1891 and the 1915 editions]. In: *Shakai rōnengaku* (Social ageing) 6, pp. 92–98.

CHAPTER EIGHT

# CHANGING SOCIAL CONCEPTS OF AGE: TOWARDS THE ACTIVE SENIOR CITIZEN

Takeo Ogawa

## 1. Introduction

Japan is undergoing a continuous increase in the proportion of elderly people in its population. In times when most people were dying in their sixties, those who were over 70 years old would be considered as living unusually long, and would be respected as venerable elderly people. However, in a society in which most people reach the age of 80, those who are still in their sixties are regarded as ordinary people. Nevertheless, people are expected to retire at the age of 60 and leave their posts to make way for younger generations, even though they are capable of working longer. The question I am dealing with in this chapter is: how will older persons be treated in the new ageing society, in which there is a higher percentage of elderly persons in relation to the young and a smaller working population in relation to the dependent population?

Japanese society has already reached its historical peak in population growth, and, since 2005, the population has been decreasing. The total fertility rate hit an all-time low of 1.25 in 2005, and the proportion of the population aged 65 and over is continuously growing. The working population is decreasing in scale. Although elderly people have increased in number, the burden of the working population that supports them has become somewhat lighter, because the child population is decreasing. This is called the period of "population bonus," a term used by demographers to describe the situation in a country where fertility rates are low and the largest proportion of the population is aged between 25 and 40. According to the results of the Japanese census, the ratio of the dependent population to the working population had a downward tendency from 1950 until 1995, but changed to an upward tendency from 2000 onwards. At this point, Japan entered the phase of "population onus", which means an increase in the burden upon working generations with regard to social security, including pensions, medical treatment and welfare. How does the concept of elderly people change in such a social context?

## 2. Traditional Concepts of Japanese Elderly People

Until 1950, the Japanese population pyramid showed a high proportion of young people and a small proportion of aged people. Since there were relatively few elderly people, they were venerated in Japanese society, which valued ancestor worship and filial piety highly.

The Japanese sense of normative behaviour related to age was very strong. The traditional way of life was defined by age: school, initiation into adulthood, marriage, retirement, and so on. The local community and family life were maintained on the basis of age hierarchy, and the gerontocracy of political decision-making and the seniority-oriented order of social status were ever-present. The Japanese labour system also emphasized the seniority wage system.

The principles of obedience and respect for the elderly are strongly influenced by the spirit of Confucianism, which was a dominant ethical tradition in East Asia. Among the ethical precepts of Confucianism, filial piety is an important value, according to which children should obey their parents and take care of them in old age. Filial piety was positioned as a fundamental norm of social order and was generalized in the priority of seniority. Not only did the older parent have the highest status in the family, but also the oldest person had the highest rank and prestige in society in general.

There was one key difference in the status of an older person between Japan and other East Asian societies. In China or Korea, a senior person was always the head of a family. However, compared with these East Asian countries, it is conspicuous that Japanese society has developed the social norm of "disengagement from the position of household head", the so-called *inkyo*, which means retirement from active life and the ruling position in the patriarchal family system. On reaching the age of 60, or at the marriage of the eldest son, the head of the household passed on this role to his (or her) successor and turned from being the supporter to being the recipient of care. The Japanese system of retirement continued until after World War II. The old parents yielded most household rights to the first-born son, built a retirement room or a retirement house and moved into it. Although retired people in

Table 1. Japanese Age Norm.

| Age | Health & Social Services | | Education | Work | Responsibility |
|---|---|---|---|---|---|
| **3** | Dependents | Day Care | Kindergarten | | Child Welfare Act & Juvenile Act |
| **6** | | Child Centre | Elementary | | |
| **12** | | | Secondary | | |
| **15** | | | High | Start Work | |
| **18** | | | College & University | | Convictable |
| **20** | | | | | Voter, & Insured National Pension |
| **25** | National Health Insurance & Employee Insurance | | | | Candidature |
| **40** | | | | | Insured Public Long Term Care Insurance |
| **55** | | Senior Club | | | |
| **60** | Adjustment | | | Retirement | |
| **65** | New System | Pension | | Continuous Work | |
| **75** | | | | | |

Note: Compiled by Ogawa Takeo.

principle received support from their child's family, some of them still cultivated fields in order to support themselves.

The social norm of *inkyo* was applied to the retirement system in working and income. As an ideal concept of retirement, older people, who had carried out duties throughout their adulthood life, should be able to enjoy their old age and be supported by their offspring. The ideal concept could be realized if the community had enough resources to distribute among all generations. If the community was poor, older people had to decide to leave so that they stopped consuming scarce resources. Sometimes, this meant a tragedy.

The novelist Shichirō Fukazawa published *Narayama bushi-kō* [The Ballad of Narayama] in 1957, which was based on the legend of *Ubasute yama* [The mountain where old women were abandoned].

*Ubasute yama* is the story of elderly people who were abandoned by their families in the mountains because they had become unproductive and a burden on their families. However, the story refers to the wisdom of older people and admonishes against their maltreatment. Fukazawa described as a very impressive message the dignified behaviour of an abandoned elderly woman who passes into the next world. The film director Imamura Shōhei later produced a movie of the same title. The Japanese audience sympathized with the heroine, and felt gloomy about a society in which a person had to experience such a cruel fate. Perhaps the film stimulated Japanese anxieties about the ageing society and their own lives in old age.

Until around 1960, Japanese society maintained its rural characteristics, with the majority of Japanese living in rural areas and older people honoured as dignified people. Elderly people, who, in rural communities, had many descendants, were able to be respected by them as ancestors, even if they retired from farming. During the 1960s, many young people were mobilized in the labour force of the expanding industrial sector. Because the number of children was falling and the percentage of elderly people was still small, the burden of the supporting population was comparatively light. Since the Japanese economy was growing at an exceptionally high rate, every generation was able to share its fruits. The Confucian sense of filial piety still had a strong influence on the parent-child relationship, and gerontocracy was alive, not only in rural communities, but also in the growing companies of the business world.

## 3. The Concept of Seniority in the Era of High Economic Growth

During the period of high economic growth after 1960, Japan changed from a rural society to an urban one. As there were problems of overpopulation and unemployment in rural areas after World War II, many people, apart from first-born sons and first-born daughters, migrated from their home villages to countries abroad, to places of inland cultivation, or to industrialized cities. While the younger population migrated into urban areas in great numbers, the older parents were left behind in the rural areas. Japanese society mobilized its domestic rural population to work in the expanding industrial sector. This is different from industrializing societies such as Germany, where foreign workers were used to fill the lack of manpower in the industry.

In Japan, the baby-boomers who were born during the short period from 1947 to 1949 were the main population resources for industrialization and urbanization. In 1950, the Japanese national government quickly adopted a family planning policy in order to reduce the population pressure. When the national government promoted industrial development in urban settings, young baby-boomers between 15 and 24 moved from rural areas, such as Kyushu and Tohoku, to Tokyo during the decade from 1960 to 1970.

Domestic migration and social mobility in Japan's economic growth period caused social changes in many ways, such as the emergence of the nuclear family, the disintegration of the local community, economic privatization, and the development of mass culture. Sociological research has primarily focused its interest on the phenomenon of social mobility and how it has affected social stratification. While most sociological research paid attention to the urbanization of societies, the social effects of rural depopulation remained largely ignored.

The large-scale migration changed the situation of elderly people. On the one hand, older people in urban communities had to compete with younger generations. On the other hand, older people in rural areas were still engaged in the maintenance of their family properties, because their successors had moved away. Rural elderly people had predominance over their children in terms of social status, being the landowners and household managers. However, if their children worked in urban industries and earned a large amount of cash income, the status of older people in a family would fall. If social status is defined by economic income, elderly people will be relatively deprived of value.

From the perspective of the younger generations, older people were mainly seen as retirees or pensioners. A redistribution of national resources to older people, through pensions, medical insurance, and social service programmes, was established in 1963, when the national government enacted the Welfare Law for the Aged. This law has two characteristics. Firstly, it was a starting point for the development of many social service programmes. Secondly, it dealt with older people as being merely service recipients. Administrators were not interested in the active role of older people, but focused on their passive role as beneficiaries.

Japanese are bound by strong age norms. Children must enter school at the age of 6. Young men must enter the labour force by the age of 25. Men and women must be married by the age of 30. Employees must retire at the age of 60. Therefore, older people, even if they still want to be active, are of no use and have to face discrimination in the form of ageism (Table 1).

The social resentment towards older people is symbolized in a book called *Ijiwaru baasan* [Bullying Grandmother], which was published by Hasegawa Machiko as a comic (*manga*) in 1966. The heroine was described as an elderly trickster who behaved contrary to the expectations of the people around her. She was a cheerful person at first but gradually became alienated and liberated herself from ageism and established common sense. The comic was made into a television cartoon series, and became a hit. *Ijiwaru Baasan* was a symbolic character of rebellion against the accepted social order.

## 4. Focusing on Concepts of the Cared-for Elderly in an Ageing Society

In the 1970s, the majority of Japanese people were not yet aware of population ageing, although statistical data already showed ageing trends (Table 2).

When people live longer, the period during which they will probably need help from others also lengthens. Therefore the situation of long-term care became a focus of attention. Old people who need to be looked after in fact comprise only about 15 per cent of the whole

Table 2. Economic Growth and Population Ageing in Japan.

| | National Income (in trillions of Yen) | Population Age 65 plus Proportion (%) |
|---|---|---|
| 1970 | 61.0 | 7.1 |
| 1975 | 124.0 | 7.9 |
| 1980 | 199.6 | 9.1 |
| 1985 | 260.3 | 10.3 |
| 1990 | 348.3 | 12.1 |
| 1995 | 374.2 | 14.6 |
| 2000 | 378.4 | 17.4 |

Sources: Social Security Costs in Japan, FY2003; National Institute of Social Security Research; MHLW, and Population Census 1970–2000.

elderly population, but their specific needs and the actual conditions faced by caregivers affected the public greatly. Dementia patients in particular, who are still in physically good condition but suffer from memory loss, become a special problem in terms of care.

The novelist Ariyoshi Sawako published *Kōkotsu no hito* [The Twilight Years] in June 1972, whose Japanese title refers to "a senile person in a trance." It describes a caregiver, a daughter-in-law, struggling with the care of her father-in-law, who suffers from dementia. She runs into deep psychological conflicts about expectations, traditions and the realities of caretaking. Finally, she becomes aware of the nature of ageing, and becomes reconciled with taking care of a senile and incontinent old man, as the father-in-law becomes before he dies.

The book drew public attention to the problems of growing old and caring for the frail elderly. In this context the question of the universalism of social welfare was raised, and a change in public opinion took place, to the effect that social services should help not only elderly people who are poor and without relatives but anyone who wished to be looked after.

In the 1970s the capacity of Homes for the Aged (*yōgo rōjin hōmu*) was 60,000 beds, and that of Special (Nursing) Homes for the Aged (*tokubetsu yōgo rōjin hōmu*) was 11,000. Although the capacity of nursing homes amounted to 80,000 beds in 1980, the capacity of homes for the aged remained at 70,000 beds. Homes for the aged are facilities for poor and frail elderly people who have no relatives; whereas the nursing homes are institutions for elderly people who have to be looked after in everyday life but who have relatives and who may be financially well-off. It is significant that universal services for the elderly were developed at this time (Figure 1).

Various services came to be carried out from the perspective of considering elderly people to be in a weak position, not only for the frail elderly who have to be cared for, but also for older people who are still, for example, able to go to town by themselves. The assumption that elderly people should be helped because they are weak has become widely accepted in Japanese society. For example, "silver seats," reserved seats for elderly people, were adopted in the public transport system in 1974. Older people were considered by the public at that time to be passive, cared for, and retired. The process of ageing was seen as negative, unpleasant, and unwelcome.

The Japanese word *shirubā* from English "silver" is derived from the Japanese notion of an older person, because the hair of older people

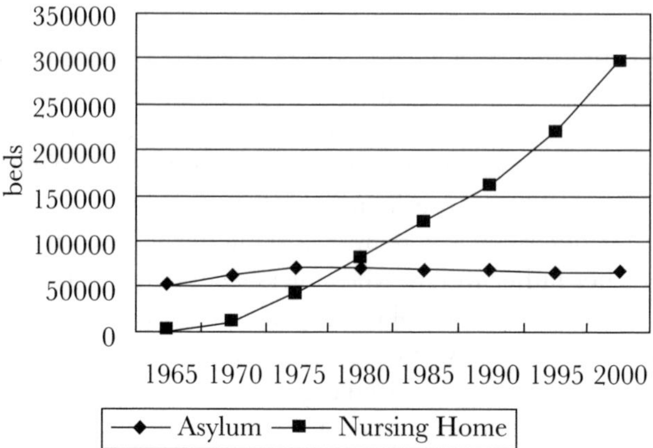


Notes: The term "Asylum" refers to "Homes for the Aged (General)" and the term "Nursing Home" refers to "Special Nursing Homes for the Aged."
Source: Survey Report on Social Welfare Institutions.

Figure 1. Institutions for the Elderly.

goes white. Following the initial concept of "silver seats", the so-called "silver services", which refers to social and health services for older people provided by private companies, and the "silver market", which refers to businesses that target senior consumers, became established. Now, the "silver industry" is a popular concept, not only in Japan, but also in East Asia, where private sector organisations, either for-profit or non-profit, are interested in the business opportunities provided by older people, and use the term "silver" as a romantic image of them.

In the universalistic view, it is important to treat everybody equally. However, older people were considered to be a special case, for whom different treatment was necessary.

## 5. Transformation to an Active Role for Older People

In the 1980s, more people became aware of population ageing, especially after the White Paper on Welfare "Towards a Soft Landing in the Ageing Society" (MHLW 1980) was published. Although a process of social breakdown was taking place, the Japanese government nonetheless emphasized the "Japanese-style welfare system," with its focus on family care. However, the Japanese family was changing from the traditional multi-generation family to the nuclear family, and the more people in need of care who would have to live without a family, the more expensive the social welfare costs would become. Because of the passive image of older people, care requirements that are typical for dementia patients were emphasized, and the idea that everyone would be suffering from dementia in later life activated the fears of many people. At that time, it was regarded as an ideal service for older people that everyone should be cared for everywhere and at any time. The universal care system for older people was promoted as being the best for society. However, this involved a concept of older people as passive. Elderly people were still only considered as recipients of social services.

On the other hand, as shifting from being dependent elderly people to active ones was encouraged, the Japanese government was looking for a new concept of the elderly. In 1980 the government proposed the new concept *jitsunen* [age of fruition] as an alternative word for *rōjin* [elderly people], or *kōreisha* [old person]. At the same time the Japanese advertising company Dentsū brought up the concept of *jukunen*, which means "age of maturity", with a similar meaning to *jitsunen*. In the process of renaming, the term "ageing society" was newly conceived as *chōju shakai*, which means "society of longevity", in the White Paper on Welfare in 1985; and in the same year, the Cabinet Office implemented measures under the title "Guidelines for the Society of Longevity." Thereafter, the word *chōju* (longevity) became widespread as a pleasant-sounding term. Centres for the Development of a Society of Longevity (*Chōju Shakai Kaihatsu Sentā*) were established in all prefectures to promote active lives for healthy older people. A festival for sports and culture for older people is held regularly; this is called *nenrinpikku*, which is a compound word made from *nenrin* [a growth (tree) ring, a symbol for older people] and "Olympics". However, these concepts, *jitsunen*, *jukunen*, and *chōju*, still refer to disengaged life after retirement and to people who are not interested in working activities, but only in leisure activities.

To emphasize a brighter image of ageing society, the word "gold" was used for the title of a new social policy, instead of "silver." At the end of 1989, the Japanese central government declared the "Ten-year Gold Plan for the Development of Health and Welfare Services for the Elderly." On the one hand, this was adopted as a symbolic measure for the ageing society; on the other hand, the consumption tax system was also introduced by the government in order to finance the rising costs caused by social ageing.

The implementation of public health and welfare services for the elderly was simultaneously restructured into a decentralized and community-based care system, which meant that older people were defined as people who should take responsibility for their own lives through the local government system.

In 1995, the Great Hanshin earthquake occurred, and many older people suffered severe injuries, and were therefore described in the mass media as *saigai jakusha* [people who are vulnerable to disasters]. In the 1980s and early 1990s, Japanese policy makers and journalists used the concept of longevity very frequently. Everyone was supposed to enjoy longevity, and society was also expected to be able to sustain healthy elderly people as a matter of principle. However, the Great Hanshin earthquake revealed that elderly people were the most vulnerable group in a crisis. As a consequence, the cheerful word "*chōju*" disappeared from public policies and the neutral concept of "aged society" (*kōrei shakai*) was again emphasized.

The Basic Law on Measures for the Ageing Society (*Kōrei Shakai Taisaku Kihon-hō*) was enacted in 1995, and the General Principles as Guidelines for Basic and Comprehensive Measures for the Aged Society (Kōrei Shakai Taisaku no Sōgōteki na Suishin) were implemented by the central government. These guidelines reflect a revision of the conventional stereotypes of the elderly so that older people are considered not only as being dependent people but also as productive ones.

As many elderly today are active, healthy, and financially secure, policies have to be developed that are based on the diversity of older people and are free from conventional stereotypes of the elderly as physically and financially impoverished. These transformations of the role of older people are now being implemented in national policies.

At last, the view that services for older people are not special services, but ordinary became widespread. Because of the normalization of social services, institutionalization and hospitalization was gradually destigmatized. As older people have become important as consumers, various service providers have offered social services for a variety of needs. Moreover, there was a change from the uniform public service provided by the national government to a range of services under municipal management. The decentralized variety of social services was rapidly promoted as older people are conceptualized not only as welfare service recipients but also as taxpayers and insurance holders.

Therefore, older people have become a target group for Japanese social policies. After 2000, the public long-term care insurance system was introduced into all local municipalities to be administered by them. New jobs were generated by the new system, for example, care workers, care managers, and lecturers in social welfare, and older people were treated as clients and consumers of these care services by them.

Those who need care services that are covered by the public long-term care insurance system comprise only about 15 per cent of older people. The rest enjoy healthy lives as today's aged people are comparatively well off. However, most Japanese do not consider old people from the perspective of the UN's principles for the aged, which are independence, participation, self-realization, care, and dignity. Until recently, only care was emphasized, but for healthy people the other principles are even more important than care. The WHO has also adopted the concept of active ageing as a policy framework. Despite these trends, Japanese older people have not been aware of their own situation (Figure 3).

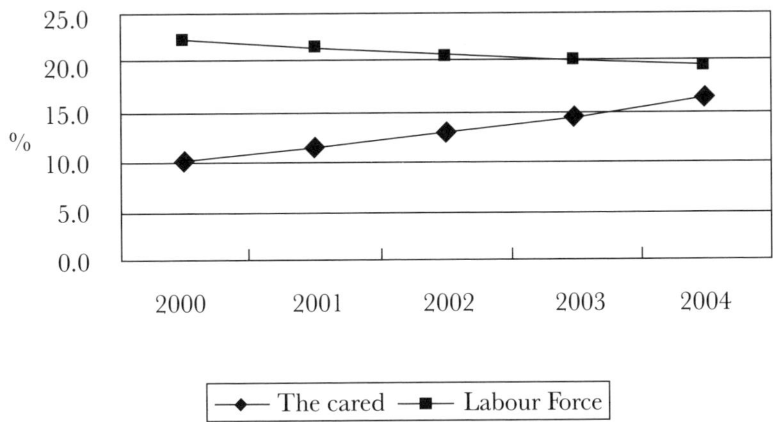


Notes: Compiled by Ogawa Takeo.
Sources: MHLW (2004): Kaigo hoken jigyō jōkyō hōkoku [Survey on long-term care insurance facilities]. MHLW (2004): 2004nen kōnenreisha shūgyō jittai chōsa [2004 General survey on working conditions of workers at advanced age]. Statistics Bureau (2004): Rōdōryoku chōsa nenpō [Annual report on Labour Force Survey].

Figure 2. Proportion of cared-for elderly and labour force in population aged 65 plus.

## 6. Shifting Concepts of the Active Senior in a Depopulating Society

Finally, the topics of low fertility and decreasing population impacted upon today's Japanese people, who started to feel anxious about their lives in old age (Figure 3).

As the Japanese population is ageing rapidly (the proportion of the population aged 65 and over will soon be the highest in the world), and the low fertility trend is set to continue, the society has entered the period of population onus (Figure 4). In particular, the working population will decrease significantly after 2007 because of the retirement of the baby-boomer generation. Governmental efforts to cope with these demographic changes are concentrating on the transformation of the social security system, which includes pensions, medical insurance, and public long-term care insurance. The public long-term care insurance system has already been modified and these changes were implemented in April 2006. The private sector is also making efforts to cope with the new phase of population development. For example, companies will start to re-employ workers aged 65 and over on a continuous basis. Older people will also have to adapt their way of life to meet the requirements of an ageing society. They are looking for financial planning, opportunities to work, a "prosumer" way of life, tax

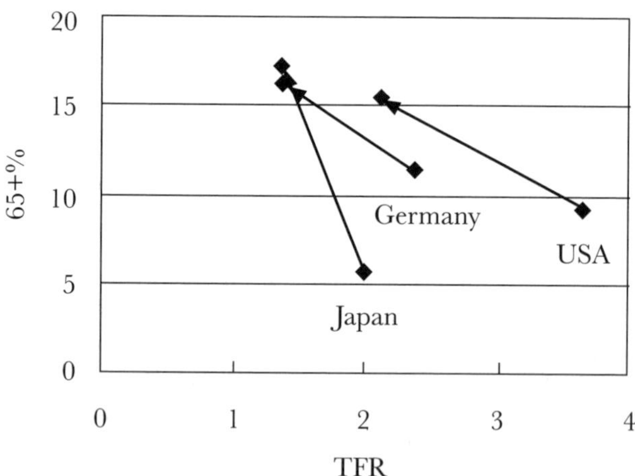


Source: UN (2005): Demographic Yearbook, and National Institute of Population and Social Security Research (2005): Latest Demographic Statistics.

Figure 3. Total Fertility Rates and 65+ Rates from 1960 to 2000.

reduction, paid/unpaid volunteer activities, and so on. "Prosumer" is a compound word made up of either "producer" or "professional" and the word "consumer", which was coined by the futurologist Alvin Toffler in his book *The Third Wave* in 1980. In this book, Toffler predicted a new lifestyle of the knowledge-oriented society. In modern society, the producer/professional and the consumer have been differentiated, but they will become integrated in post-modern society in order to reach a high degree of customization. Consumers will have to take part in the production process, especially in specifying design requirements, and in this sense, consumers would be called "prosumers."

The Japanese central government and some prefectures are introducing strategies for transforming over-differentiated social services into an all-inclusive system. Programmes encouraging older people to be more active are to be developed, and new "Principles of Measures for the Aged Society" were created in 2005 by the cabinet in order to emphasize the active ageing policy. These will be applied to the ageing baby-boomer cohort in particular. The Japanese concept for active ageing is *shōgai gen'eki*, which literally means "lifelong in active service." Its opposite meaning is *taieki*, which means "retirement from service."

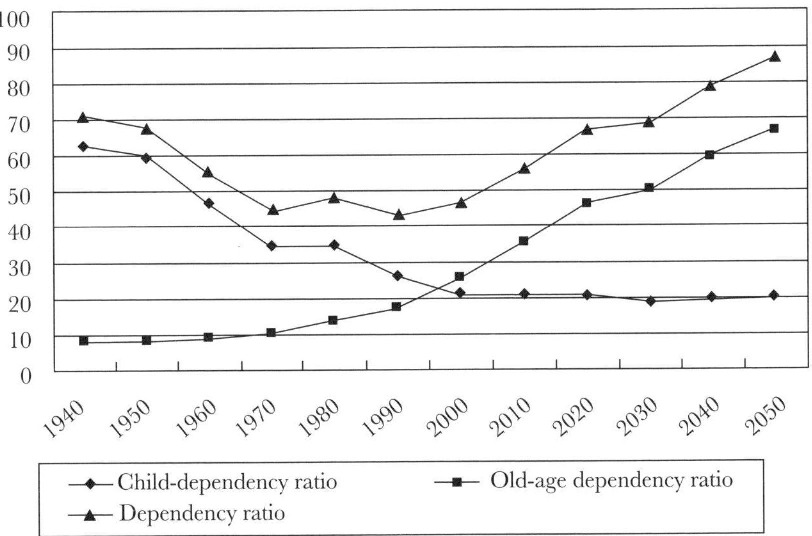


Figure 4. Japanese Population Bonus and Onus (%).

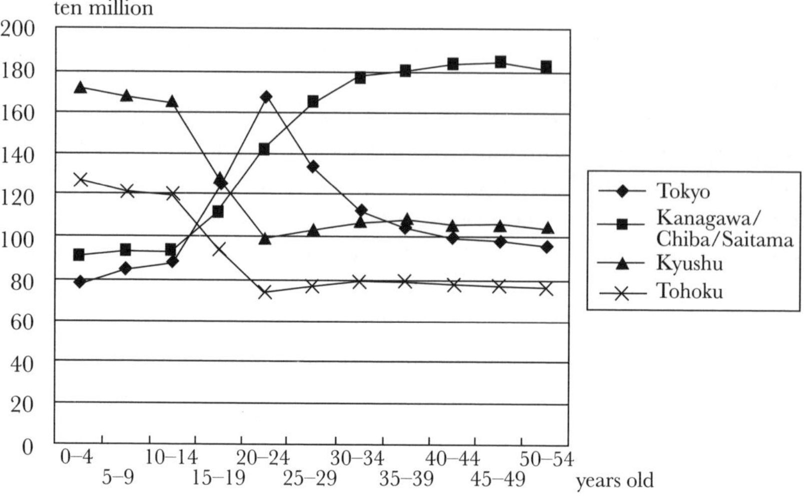


Source: Population Census 1950–2000.
Note: I have selected four areas and calculated the population of the 0–4 cohort at every census for the years 1950–2000.

Figure 5. Where did Baby-boomers live?

Baby-boomers who could not afford to live in Central Tokyo when they established their own families moved to suburban areas in prefectures in the vicinity of the city of Tokyo, such as Saitama, Chiba, and Kanagawa. When this generation reaches retirement age around 2007, the question is whether they will continue to live in these suburbs, return to their hometowns, move to downtown areas in Tokyo, migrate to resort areas in Japan, or go abroad (Figure 5).

Attention has been paid to the wealthy baby boomers, who will be able to receive a retirement allowance (a lump-sum payment) and comparatively high pensions. Perhaps some of them will enjoy their retirement life in the same ways as Western people in Europe and the United States, who go for holidays in resorts and pursue affluent leisure-time activities. In Japan, older people may appear to be the leisured classes. However, there is still a huge gap between rich older people and poor ones. Those who have no high pension or bank savings cannot enjoy such a luxurious way of life. They will have to continue to work for their living expenses. On the one hand, the Japanese government regulated the compulsory retirement age at 60 in 2005. On the other hand, the eligibility age for national pension payments will be gradually raised to 65 by 2025. This means that most retirees will have to consider being re-employed during the five years inbetween. Accordingly, the Amendment Act of Job Security for Older People (Kōnenreisha nado no Koyō no Antei ni Kansuru Hōritsu Kaisei) was published in 2004.

The concept of *shōgai gen'eki* has spread into the labour market and reflects the social background of older people who keep on working and believe that the value of life lies in working. These discourses are now discussed and adopted as social policies. For example, labour economist Seike Atsushi has proposed the "lifelong in active service" plan for employees and Japanese society. According to Seike, Japanese companies should employ labour on a continuous basis, including older people, because it will be a way of maintaining social productivity and reducing social costs (Seike 2001).

Manufacturing companies that wish to employ skilled workers after the retirement of the baby boomers are planning to raise their retirement age to 65 years, a plan that is also supported by the central government. Local municipalities are promoting the setting-up of new businesses by older people. In rural areas in particular, there are many cases of retirees who live as farmers after retiring from urban industries. Responding to Japan's low birth-rate and people's longevity, the business world is considering new employment strategies, such as the extension of the retirement age, continuous employment, re-employment, the abolition of mandatory retirement, work-sharing, and job re-design.

Job opportunities for older people are not limited to wage earning. Elderly people will be working in various organizations and forms, such as self-employment, contract agreements, membership systems for mutual help, cooperatives of companies, or SOHO, (Small Office and Home Office). In rural areas, there are many morning markets, street markets, and farmer's markets, at which older people are engaged in producing and selling products.

The opportunity to work in fields not suitable for profit companies is open to older people in order to develop the citizens' activities for the public benefit, such as health, medicine and welfare improvement, social education, community planning, culture, art and sport promotion, promotion of environmental preservation, disaster relief, local safety, the protection of human rights and peace promotion, international cooperation, joint participation of men and women, training for children, cyber-information, technology promotion, revitalization of the economy, occupational skills development and job opportunity expansion, consumer protection, or acting as intermediaries for NPOs (non-profit organizations).

The opportunities for older people to be active as volunteers are not limited to temporary activities but are also organized in regular NPO activities. A lot of new organizations which develop profit-making activities, such as community business, started as NPO activities. The medical doctor Hinohara Shigeaki, who became 88 years old in 2000, has coined the concept of *shin rōjin* [new elderly citizen], by presenting himself as a person who can contribute actively to society. He has earned a lot of admiration for his initiative, and a "New Elder Citizens' Movement" has now been founded as an organization for healthy people aged 75 and over. The images of older people who contribute to society in "lifelong active service" reflect new ways of life in a period when the population is shrinking. As the population trend shows a decrease in the birth rate, many elderly people will not be able to depend upon their children, and will therefore have to be able to live independently.

The White Paper on Welfare and Labour published in 2003 was on the topic "Vital Image of Older People and the Construction of New Relationships among Generations" (MHLW 2003a). The plan with which the government is aiming to implement programmes for social activities of older people in relation to and cooperation with other generations is shown in the title. With these programmes, the government aims to alleviate the burden for the young population. Another report, "Elderly Care in 2015: Aiming to Establish Adult Care in order to support Dignity for Older People", was published in 2003 (MHLW 2003b). In order to realize the concept of active ageing, the report emphasized that older people should make efforts to avoid becoming in need of nursing care, and that health and social service providers should advocate rehabilitation. Moreover, the report refers to the new long-term care system as a means for maintaining an autonomous life. Construction of small-scale and multifunctional service stations that support older people living independently in their own homes is mentioned. The report also mentioned caring for the elderly suffering from dementia and the maintenance of the quality of optional services. The views presented in the report are reflected in the public long-term care insurance programme revision of 2006.

Even if a person's health is damaged and he or she has become handicapped, it is desirable that their maximum capacity for living autonomously is utilized. Even when patients are mentally disordered while their physical functions remain intact, it is important to treat the person with dignity. In Japan, in this sense, an elderly person's "quality of active life" is considered, beyond economic independence and medical treatment. It is important for everyone to establish an active way of life. After all, how to develop a social system that includes active older people will be a challenge for Japan's political agenda in the future.

## References

MHLW (Ministry of Health, Labour and Welfare) (1980): Shōwa 55 nenpan. Kōsei Hakusho. Kōreika shakai e no nanchakuriku o mezashite [1980 White Paper on Welfare. Towards a Soft Landing in the Ageing Society]. Tokyo: Ministry of Health, Labour and Welfare.

—— (Ministry of Health, Labour and Welfare) (2003a): *Heisei 15 nenpan. Kōsei Rōdō Hakusho: Katsuryoku aru kōreishazō to sedaikan no aratana kankei no kōchiku* [2003 White Paper on Labour and Welfare. Vital Image of Older People and the Construction of New Relationships among Generations]. http://wwwhakusyo.mhlw.go.jp/wpdocs/hpax200301/body.html (found 25/11/2006).

—— (Ministry of Health, Labour and Welfare) (2003b): *2015nen no kōreisha kaigo: Kōreisha no songen o sasaeru kea no kakuritsu ni mukete, hōken* [Elderly Care in 2015: Aiming to Establish Adult Care in order to support Dignity for Older People]. http://www.mhlw.go.jp/topics/kaigo/kentou/15kourei/index.html (found 25/11/2006).

Seike, Atsushi (2001): *Shōgai gen'eki jidai no koyō seisaku* [Employment policy in an age of lifelong activity]. Tokyo: Nihon Hyōronsha.

CHAPTER NINE

# AGEING SOCIETY AND THE TRANSFORMATION OF WORK IN THE POST-FORDIST ECONOMY

Chikako Usui

## 1. Rapid Population Ageing

The Japanese population grew to 127.7 million in 2006 but is projected to decline to 105 million in 2050. Not only will Japan's population become smaller, it will also grow much older. The proportion of persons aged 65 and above will rise from 17.1 per cent in 2000 to 26.7 per cent in 2025, making Japan one of the "oldest" countries among industrialized nations (see Table 1). The trends of depopulation and ageing are the result of a sharp reduction in fertility, that is, women's reproductive choices. This places women at the center of Japan's so-called "demographic dilemma." If women choose to have even fewer children in the future, Japan's ageing dilemma will be further intensified.

The "aged dependency ratio" is a common measure for gauging the burden of the "dependent" population in an ageing society. It is a number of actively working population divided by the number of "aged dependents" in the population. In 2000 in Japan, there were 3.9 active workers supporting each person 65 years of age and older.

Table 1. People over Age 65 as a Percentage of Total Population.

| | 1985 | 1995 | 2000 | 2005 | 2025 | 2050 |
|---|---|---|---|---|---|---|
| Japan | 10.3 | 14.6 | 17.1 | 19.2 | 26.7 | 31.8 |
| Italy | 12.7 | 16.8 | 18.2 | 22.6 | 26.1 | 34.9 |
| Germany | 14.5 | 15.0 | 16.4 | 17.8 | 23.4 | 28.4 |
| France | 12.5 | 15.0 | 15.9 | 16.7 | 21.7 | 25.5 |
| U.K. | 15.1 | 15.9 | 16.0 | 16.4 | 21.2 | 24.9 |
| Sweden | 17.5 | n.a. | 17.0 | 16.6 | n.a. | 27.0 |
| United States | 11.8 | 12.5 | 12.5 | 12.6 | 18.8 | 21.7 |

Note: Projections for 2005, 2025 and 2050 are based on UN's medium-variant projections.
Source: United Nations (2000: 8, 112–143).

Table 2. Aged Dependency Ratio, Japan.

| Age | 2000 | 2010 | 2015 | 2025 |
|---|---|---|---|---|
| 0–14 | 14.6 | 13.4 | 12.8 | 11.6 |
| 15–64 | 68.1 | 64.1 | 61.2 | 59.7 |
| 65+ | 17.4 | 22.5 | 26.0 | 28.7 |
| (15–64)/(65+) | 3.92 | 2.84 | 2.36 | 2.06 |

Note: Author's own calculation.
Source: Proportion of cared elderly and labour force in population aged 65 plus.

By 2010, there will be fewer than three workers, and by the year 2025 the figure is predicted to drop to two active workers for every aged dependent member (see Table 2).

Although the aged dependency ratio has become conventional in describing economic burden in an ageing society, it is based on questionable assumptions. For example, the productivity and consumption patterns of different age groups are based on past patterns and assumed to be static. On average, people of working age (aged 15–64) are considered productive and consumption oriented, while the older population (aged 65 and over) is considered unproductive with relatively low incomes and low levels of consumption. In addition, policy-makers often focus exclusively on the denominator in the aged dependency ratio (i.e., older population) and look for solutions that reduce the burden of the "aged dependents." The aged population is viewed in isolation and presumed to provide little or no contribution to society, while the active population is assumed to have a static carrying capacity with little change in their production or consumption patterns.

In contrast, I make a different set of assumptions. First, demographics are an intrinsic part of social organization of society. Historically, demographic patterns have been altered by political, economic, and technological changes in society. Second, I focus on both the numerator and denominator of the dependency ratio because expansion of the *carrying capacity* of either group will decrease the level of dependency for the same proportion of elderly. Third, I contend that the role of public policy is to link the economic and technological changes to demographic changes in society. Fourth, productivity and consumption of any age group are more variable and dynamic than presently supposed. The logic that the working population will have to support the dependent population is based on assumptions of social organization and life cycle that characterized the Fordist economy of the 20th century. In the 21st century, industrialized countries are shifting to a new logic of the post-Fordist economy. It is more appropriate to address the issue of ageing societies in the context of the transformation in the *productive capacity* of the post-Fordist economy (Usui 2001).

## 2. Shift from a Fordist to a Post-Fordist Economy

Is population ageing a "dilemma"? The answer depends on economic conditions and the carrying capacity (productivity) of active workers, that is, on the economy's capacity to support its dependent members. Policy discussions often narrowly frame population ageing as exclusively a demographic issue (of fertility and immigration) and distract us from the fact that the economy and its carrying capacity determine, in large part, whether the ageing of the population will have dire long-term effects. The demographic ageing of a society's population should be viewed in the context of the economy's capacity to support that population. Most critical is the transition from a Fordist to a post-Fordist economy, along with issues of labour, social welfare, family, and education policies to support such a transition.

Sociologists use the "Fordist" and "post-Fordist" distinction to discuss the societal transformation of modern industrial economies. Sometimes the terms "old economy" and "new economy" are used in similar fashion. The term "Fordist" refers to an innovative industrial organization system associated with the Ford Motor Company of the early 20th century (Jaffee 2001; Myles 1990). Essentially, a Fordist economy is based on mass-production technology and consumption, with an exaggerated division of labour and products having a relatively long life cycle. Correspondingly, worker skills, once acquired, have a relatively long life cycle; the productivity level of workers remains relatively static throughout their working lives. The automotive, steel, and rubber industries are good examples of this model of industrial economy. "Retirement" is a socially constructed new life-course stage to manage the work force of a Fordist economy.

A post-Fordist economy is quite different. It is more oriented to the application of intensive information technology. The economy is geared to the flexible production of selective goods and consumption of variety of goods. Goods and services have relatively short production life cycles, requiring continuous innovation (Myles 1990). Automation based on the use of information technology eliminates routine, repetitive tasks that can be programmed so worker's skills must be constantly upgraded. Educational training is required at several career junctures and skills must be constantly upgraded. Workers must adjust to the flexible production system by seeking multiple careers over their life times. Payoffs to educational investment do not last for a lifetime but require continuous skill upgrades. The computer software, telecommunications, and information-based service industries represent the leading sectors of a post-Fordist economy. This model has diffused through the use of micro-electronic based machinery in manufacturing and service sectors including financial, educational and social services.

As production and consumption patterns are altered, the assumptions of the aged dependency ratio are no longer valid. This transformation is analogous to the shift in how many farmers it takes to feed a population (Myles 1990: 282). At the turn of the 20th century, it took more than one-third of the American labour force (37.6%) to supply the food necessary to feed the nation (Ford 1988: 40). However, with innovations in farm technology, improvements in crop yields, resistance to disease and pests, and better organization, the capacity of farmers to support the population increased geometrically in the 20th century so that less than 2 per cent of the American labour force is now in the agricultural sector.

The manufacturing sector of the economy has similarly used technology to raise productivity. Today, service industries are integrated to intensive use of information technology and thus mechanized and automated. The diffusion of information technology, propelled by globalization, has had similar effects in factories, offices and service organizations. Expansion in the manufacturing and service sectors created new job opportunities and absorbed workers no longer needed in the primary industries. Similarly, technological advancements in the manufacturing sector have increased worker productivity while reducing the number of workers needed. Analogously, future increases in worker productivity will support ever-increasing numbers of a "dependent" older population in a post-Fordist economy. It is not the ratio of the working or dependent population but the output of the economy that largely determines whether an ageing population becomes a problem (Schulz, Borowski and Crown 1991; Schulz 1995; Usui 2003; Campbell 2003: 14).

Further, the older population is in a position to consume more than is currently assumed. Post-material values such as quality of life become an important goal in the post-Fordist economy, creating new demand for more selective goods and services. The older population has more consumption capacity than previous generations. An increase in the older population creates demand for new industries in financial and business services, health and medical services, housing construction, telecommunications, recreational and educational services, and personal/domestic services. According to the World Health Organization, Japan is the healthiest nation with people living free from disability until age 75 (WHO 2000). Japan's healthy population promises a bright future that is often overlooked. The older population increases productivity and consumption as workers, volunteers, and consumers. Considering future advancements in health and medical technology, future extensions of life spans may not necessarily aggravate old-age dependency. It is more likely that older persons will live longer in good health, increasing the potential social and economic output and consumption of the society.

Japan's future lies not only in private sector flexibility to integrate changes in the economic and technological changes with demographic changes, but also in the ability of the government to promote such flexibility and integration. Japan's future hinges on whether new growth industries will emerge and raise economic productivity and whether labour-market fluidity will accommodate these new industries. Japan's dilemma has more to do with the restructuring of the economy and institutions to raise economic productivity than how to maintain the current aged dependency.

In the Fordist economy, education followed by a stable, life-long job characterized a typical male worker's career. In the post-Fordist economy, workers will be more differentiated in terms of their skills, sequential job careers, full- versus part-time work, and partial retirement (as opposed to complete, one-step retirement) and active ageing. The traditional male career patterns of the Fordist economy would be "feminized" in the post-Fordist economy, with more chaotic career transitions over one's life. The demarcation of the life cycle from the completion of education to the entry to the work force, as well as the exit from the work force to retirement, will be blurred and more irregular. In other words, "the traditional form of work, based on full-time employment, clear-cut occupational assignment, and a career pattern over the life cycle is being slowly but surely eroded away" (Castells 1996: 268).

Advanced industrial countries have all experienced a feminization of work in their transition to a post-Fordist economy, as indicated by the explosion of women's employment. Men's employment has, for the most part, declined and men's unemployment has become higher than women's unemployment. Women provide more appeal to employers because "there is a fit between women's working flexibility, in schedules, time, and entry and exit to and from the labour market, and the needs of the new economy" (Castells 1997: 173). The steady erosion of the traditional form of work is accompanied by, in particular, women's employment in full-time and part-time or temporary work in all post-Fordist service industries. Recent studies on the growth of women's employment in service sectors show that women are distributed across the entire skill structure. Their employment surged from the low end to the upper end of the service employment (from professional/technical, administrative/managerial to clerical positions) especially in business services to social/personal services. Of particular note is a dramatic increase in non-standard or part-time work (Castells 1996; 1997: 163–65). Employers prefer women to men not only for their cheaper labour but also for their relational skills necessary for managing people in these expanding sectors. In addition, women's work flexibility and disruptive career patterns fit well with the logic of the post-Fordist economy. What is important to note is the increasing employment of women that changes the character and capacity of the active labour force, which also expands their decision-making participation as consumers.

Japanese women are still under-employed compared to their counterparts in other advanced industrial countries despite their potential for making the productive ages more productive and offsetting the shrinking labour force. As mentioned, the post-Fordist economy is an information and service-oriented economy. With the "feminization" of job requirements in the post-Fordist economy, women can supply vital labour to the expanding service economy. With their increased educational attainment, female employment could potentially produce a qualitative rise in skilled labour contributing to increased carrying capacity of the economy. Increased labour force participation of women aged 15–64 would make the productive labour force (the numerator in the dependency ratio) more productive in a post-Fordist economy.

Is the transformation of work taking place in Japan? Although women's capability to combine family *and* work is the best hope for easing Japan's ageing dilemma, in reality women are still withholding their investment from having a family while keeping their job. Policy-makers therefore will have to reform existing employment structures and family policies in order to encourage the compatibility of motherhood and meaningful participation in work.

## 3. Women, Work, and Declining Fertility

The issue of demographic dilemma is intertwined with women's postponement of marriage, which contributed to a fertility rate of 1.29 babies per woman in 2006. Demographers estimate that by 2010 close to 20 per cent of men and 8 per cent of women aged 45–49 will be unmarried. Japan's fertility level remained at the replacement level, which is 2.08, until the mid-1970s, but fell to 1.81 in 1984, which, at that time, was similar to the level in the United States, the United Kingdom and France. It declined further to 1.42 in 1995, 1.36 in 2000 and 1.25 in 2005. In developed countries as a whole, the fertility level was 1.56 in 2004, and in Europe it was 1.38. Thus, most developed countries are facing a baby drought (the United States and New Zealand are the only exceptions with a fertility level of 2.0), but it is much more severe in Germany (1.32), Japan (1.29), Italy (1.21), Spain (1.12), and South Korea (1.17).

Despite women's potential to ease demographic challenges, their employment has not increased in the 1990s and early 21st century, which is due primarily to Japan's prolonged recession that began in the late-1990s. Other employment data reveal a mixed picture in relation to the transformation of work. What separates Japan from other major post-Fordist economies is that employment practices are still anchored by the traditional (patriarchal) division of labour, with women's employment concentrated in positions with no meaningful career prospect. Female labour force participation as a whole dropped from 50.2 per cent in 1994 to 48.5 per cent in 2006. In 2004, women's wages were on average 67.6 per cent of male wages, up from 62.0 per cent in 1994. Meanwhile, the concentration of women in the part-time work force increased and the wage gap between full-time and part-time work further widened. In 2006, the proportion of part-time workers (defined as those working fewer than 35 hours per week) grew to 33.0 per cent of total employed workers (male and female combined), up from 18.8 per cent in 1994. Women working part-time increased from 32.5 in 1994 to 40.6 per cent in 2005. Women's part-time wages fell to 68.4 per cent of their full-time wages, down from 70.6 in 1997 (MHLW 2005: 5–7; Kazuka 2000: 1).

Compared to full-time positions, part-time work is based on explicit contractual agreement, is free from compulsory overtime and is easier to combine with family obligations. However, once women leave full-time positions, reentry is difficult; mid-career hiring remains limited, and regular positions with flexible work schedules are still scarce. As women resort to part-time work or temporary work schedule, the vicious cycle of women's concentration in low-paying, low-status positions is perpetuated. *Neither women nor corporate personnel decision-makers want to invest in the other.*

Further, existing corporate and government policies remove women's stake in investing their future. It is common to attribute low levels of job mobility and high levels of non-regular positions among women to institutional barriers or discrimination in the labour market as well as to the lack of family-friendly policies and the low acceptance of women to continue working after giving child birth (Usui 2002: 474). In addition, lengthy commutes to work, demands of full-time work, family responsibilities, and Japan's tax system all constrain and direct married women's decisions and aspirations in their efforts to balance the needs of work and family. The tight institutional configuration of corporate work styles and family roles (including children's education and elder care) reinforced by cultural norms leads women to underinvest in their job mobility and withdraw from work or switch to part-time employment after marriage or childbirth. Thus, in spite of the high percentage of married women aged 25–34 willing to work, a smaller percentage of them actually do. For example, among women age 25–34, 72.9 per cent wish to work but 62.4 per cent actually do, according to the Ministry of Health, Labour and Welfare (2005). College-educated married women are less likely to be employed than women without college education because they tend to have husbands with high incomes. These patterns are pronounced among married women over age 40 (MHLW 2005: 15).

It bears repeating that it is the declining fertility that is driving Japan's ageing dilemma. While the age-specific fertility rate among married women is unchanged, women's postponement of marriage led to lower fertility. As in other advanced countries, today's young women are better educated than in the past, and have new opportunities for enrichment outside of marriage and thus women aged 25–29, the prime childbearing age group, are not marrying at the rate they used to. Birth outside of marriage remains extremely low relative to many other advanced countries where single (lone) motherhood continues to rise. In Japan, only one per cent of births occur outside of marriage, compared to 33 per cent in the United States, 38 per cent in the United Kingdom, 47 per cent in Denmark, and 55 per cent in Sweden (*The Economist* 18 April 2002; Ogura, 2003: 14).

Moreover, the choices of young women (and men) are influenced by their parents' willingness to house and support them well into adult life. The current generation of parents is the first generation willing and economically able to support their children in perpetually dependent adulthood. *Also, today's young women are the first to face downward mobility after marriage*. Thus, marriage offers fewer benefits, while society increasingly accepts their single lifestyle and sexual freedom. In 2002, 54 per cent of women aged 25–29 were single, compared to 18 per cent in 1970 (Ogura 2003: 14). In Tokyo, the bellwether of Japan, over 65 per cent of women aged 25–29 and 38 per cent of women aged 30–34 remained single. The average age of women at first marriage increased to 28.2 in 2006 (30.0 for men) from 24 in 1970. In Tokyo, it was 29.2. In short, marriage and family are no longer the locus of life-course attainment for women from their late 20s onward. In addition, there is a growing perception that marriage creates more burdens than satisfactions. According to a 1998 survey conducted by the Japanese Prime Minister's Office, 19.8 per cent of women say they derive satisfaction from child rearing, as opposed 49.8 per cent in the United States and 70.9 per cent in Britain (Yamanaka 1998, Internet; Horlacher 2002: 56).

The high costs of raising children create yet another pressure to postpone marriage. Japan, Italy, and Spain rank lowest in the provision of child allowance among industrially advanced countries (Sechiyama 2001: 41). High costs of housing and education are additional burdens on the income of young couples. Because of the competitive nature of the Japanese education system, the time, money, and emotional costs of bringing up a child also remain high. The Japanese corporate employment system that forces a work-driven life style on men also hinders a husband's participation in child rearing.

Although Japan's government policies for maternity and child-care leave are formally generous, legal enforcement is lacking and access to benefits is limited. Japanese maternity benefits, created in 1972, provide for 14 weeks with 60 per cent of wages paid during the leave (increased from non-paid leave in 1992, to 25 per cent in 1995, 40 per cent in 2001, and 60 per cent in 2003). In contrast, Germany pays maternity benefits for 14 weeks with 100 per cent of wages paid, France for 16–26 weeks with 100 per cent wages paid, and Italy for 20 weeks with 80 per cent wages paid. In the United States, the Family and Medical Leave Act of 1993 provides a total of 12 weeks of unpaid leave and it applies to companies with 50 or more workers (ILO 1998, Internet; The Clearinghouse on International Developments in Child, Youth and Family Policies at Columbia University, 2004). In addition, Japan provides Childbirth and Lump Sum Grant of $3,000 (366,000 yen) for each child, and in 1992, it introduced the Child-care Leave Law allowing leave for a female or male parent until a child reaches the age of one. This leave pays 40 per cent of wages (Nagase 2001: 18). However, only 8 per cent of women who gave birth took advantage of child-care leave between 1995 and 1997 (Nagase 2001). According to the Ministry of Health, Labour and Welfare (2005: 5), mothers who took maternity and child-care/family leave constituted only 0.2 per cent of the female work force in 2004. Why is there a gap between formal opportunity and women availing themselves of these benefits?

It is due to lack of enforcement of the law, differences between formal prescriptions and informal norms, and differences between formal opportunities for choices and lack of practically available alternatives. Researchers have long suggested the need for family-friendly policies that would make child rearing easier for working women and their families. This would allow married women to offset the future shrinking size of the active working population. Thus, the Japanese government enacted the Child-care and Family Leave Law in 1992 and worked out a plan that was called the "Basic Direction of Measures for the Support of Child Rearing in the Future." This so called Angel Plan to be realized in the years from 1995 to 1999 aimed to increase the number of child-care facilities and to improve the maternity benefit system. The New Angel Plan (2000–2004) set higher target values, and the revised New Angel Plan (2005–2009) further improves family-friendly policy features. Yet, women still have difficulties to receive these benefits due to weak legal enforcement and problems of accessibility and affordability of child-care benefits and services. For example, employers still discriminate against women who take maternity leave and child-care leave (*Asahi Shimbun* 9 June 2005). Employers may decide to move women to inconvenient job positions or company locations to encourage them to quit work upon marriage, pregnancy, or childbirth. If women voluntarily quit, they lose their entitlement to these benefits. The receipt of maternity benefits and the child-care leave requires the employer's consent, making it difficult for women to take them. Small firms are often excused from providing these benefits for female employees (Nagase 2001). The number of lawsuits over unfair treatment after becoming pregnant or giving birth has continuously increased in recent years (Gross and Weintraub 2004, Internet). The Equal Employment Opportunity Law (EEOL) (legislated in 1985) stipulates that employers not discriminate against women in job training, fringe benefits, mandatory retirement age, resignation, and dismissal. Also, the law "requests" that employers use their best efforts not to discriminate against women in recruiting and hiring, job assignment, and promotion. The EEOL does not sanction employers who violate the law because compliance with the law is voluntary, not mandatory. The Ministry of Health, Labour and Welfare administratively guides companies in upholding the law. The EEOL was revised in 1997 by widening the scope of discriminatory treatment prohibition, prevention of sexual harassment in the workplace, and abolishing overtime, holiday and late night work restrictions for women. In addition, sanctions by the Ministry against companies with violation of the Law were tightened.

Even if women stay on the job after giving birth with maternity leave benefits, it is not easy to take one-year child-care leave due to a strong negative perception in the work place that working mothers who take such leave are a nuisance. Silent pressure from employers and peers discourages women (and men) from taking it, and such pressure becomes even stronger with a second child. Moreover, there is still a shortage of child-care facilities that provide infant care, convenient locations, and extended hours of child care, especially in urban areas. Over 30,000 pre-schoolers were on the waiting list in major urban areas in 2003 and the costs of infant-care services are out of reach for average-income families (Ogawa 2003: 10). So, even if a woman takes a year of leave and wants to return to work, there are no child-care facilities where she can place her one-year-old child, which forces her to quit or retire.

Since 1997, women in non-standard work (such as part-time, contractual, or other temporary work) are legally entitled to these benefits as result of the revision of the Equal Employment Opportunity Law. However, to qualify, they must have stayed with the same employer longer than one year. Thus, employers terminate their contract and may re-hire them to avoid their obligation to honor these benefits. The Newspaper *Asahi Shimbun* (9 June 2005, Internet), for example featured these problems illustrating the ordeal of a 32 year old woman with her employer in getting 5 months child-care leave.

Japan is not unique in experiencing a precipitous fall in birth rates and women's postponement of marriage. No advanced country (with the exception of the U.S. and New Zealand) has been successful in restoring a replacement fertility level. However, there are differences in the level of fertility and speed of its fall among advanced nations. These variations are due to family policies and social organization of employment. That is, variations in fertility levels are related to variation in the burden of institutional and cultural embeddedness of women's role in attempting to balance both work and family careers. An empirical study of 14 European and Nordic countries based on Luxembourg Income Study 1985–87 found a clear connection between the two: the more generous the package of maternity leave policies and child-care services, the greater the level of maternal employment (Gornick, Meyers and Ross 1996, Internet).

With a birth rate around 1.7 in the 1980s, West European countries introduced family-friendly policies to ease women's role conflict. Countries with weak policies, such as Germany, Spain, and Italy, experienced acute falls in fertility. These countries are generous in maternity benefits (shown above) but provide little child-care services. Other countries—most notably France, Belgium, and the Netherlands—did not experience drastic declines in fertility. France (and Belgium) has generous maternity benefits and child-care services that benefit 95 per cent of its children age 3 to 5. Among Nordic countries, Sweden successfully maintains its fertility level at 1.6 with extensive family service programs.

Women in these countries are nested in their own dynamics that produced diverse integration of women in the labour market. Sweden's approach, for example, is based on a two-earner family model developed in the 1970s and 1980s. It maintains a high level of women's employment that is harmonized with gender-equal family policies. The labour market is highly professionalized with few low-paying, dead-end jobs (Esping-Andersen 1996). The Netherlands, with generous maternity leave but limited child care, developed highly paid part-time work. It reduced conflict between work and family and integrated women in the labour market by minimizing differences between part-time and full-time work. Disparities in wage and benefits between full- and part-time work narrowed, and by 1997, close to 40 per cent of female Dutch employment was accounted for by part-time work (Steffen 1998: 4, Internet).

Japan has developed its unique employment patterns and has always utilized women in non-standard work during the Fordist economy. The tax code and the cultural norms reinforced this labour market dualism involving a strict gender division of labour. However, it has become increasingly at odds with the changing reality. Japan, Italy, and Spain—countries with acute fertility decline are also those with emphasis on traditional gender division of labour, making only partial or ambiguous commitment to women and families—generous maternity leave benefits yet lacking extensive child-care services.

To date, Japanese public policies to slow demographic ageing are aimed at raising marital fertility (childbirth within marriage) and helping married women and their families balance work and family. Some prefectures have organized events for singles in the hope of promoting marriage. However, there are no public policies directly aimed at helping young men and women find future marriage candidates. Instead, existing family policies support the traditional type of families under the Fordist economy. They worked well, assuring improvement in the standard of living and stability and predictability of family life. However, these policies are unable to assist changing families. Women's productivity and existing social institutions are too disjointed to support the changing needs of families and the life-course regime of the post-Fordist economy.

## 4. Conclusion

Ageing should be viewed as an intrinsic part of the economy and society of any country. The issues of ageing are structurally embedded in economic, political, and social institutions. Population ageing should be seen in the context of the transition to a robustness of the economy and government social policy. An ageing population is a problem when the economy is weak and the policies uncoordinated. I make this case by suggesting an imminent move toward a post-Fordist information- and service-based economy. The transition requires collateral policies that restructure and reorient labour, welfare, family, and educational institutions. This transition requires insightful interpretation, policy, and masterful leadership.

Japanese policy makers have made progress in making it easier for married women to balance work and family needs, but this progress is slow. Not only government and corporate policies, but also company culture and practices, integrate women only as secondary workers based on the traditional division of gender roles, not as equal partners. Policies do not solve the fundamental tension between gender roles in employment and family commitment. Another reason that progress for women is slow is that Japan is a "network society" where men and women are embedded in institutional and cultural networks built on traditional boundaries between work and family careers. The degree and consequences of embeddedness vary among groups. Subordinate groups, like women, find that society mutes their criticism, limits their aspirations, and paralyzes their activities to combine employment mobility and child rearing. Japanese institutions do not provide women with motivation to invest in the labour force and family futures, nor provide them access to recruitment and training for responsible (career) jobs or to national policy-making.

Japanese policy makers have focused on the problems of marital fertility more than the issues of marriage postponement. Thus, a September 2002 advisory committee organized by the Ministry of Health, Labor and Welfare consisted almost entirely of married members with children. The lone unmarried female committee member noted that discussion was based on the traditional norms of gender division of labour, and did not touch on lack of interest in marriage or the role of single men in infertility (Sakai 2003: 53–55).

Japanese women rationally calculate their future success in work and family in their embeddedness in institutional and cultural norms (Brinton 1993). Government and corporate policies remove women's stake in a future of labour market mobility and family careers. Women's response is to withhold their investment in family and work. Women put off marriage and child rearing and either enter the auxiliary work force or withdraw from the full-time labour force upon childbirth—thus limiting their investment in the future. It is my contention that women are guided by their families and socialized by the experiences of their mothers, older sisters, and friends to recognize the costs and probability of satisfactory participation in work and family. Therefore, it is important to devise policies by reconceptualising the relationship between the changing economy and the needs of the family system.

## References

*Asahi Shimbun* (9 June 2005): *Umitai? Umenai? Dankai Junia* [Want to give birth? Cannot give birth? The junior babyboomer].

Brinton, Mary (1993): *Women and the Economic Miracle: Gender and Work in Postwar Japan*. Berkeley: University of California Press.

Campbell, John C. (2003): Population Aging: Hardly Japan's Biggest Problem. In: Woodrow Wilson Center for International Scholars *Asia Program Special Report* 107, pp. 10–15.

Castells, Manuel (1996): *The Information Age: Economy, Society, and Culture*, Volume 1: *The Rise of the Network Society*. Oxford and Malden, MA: Blackwell Publishers.

—— (1997): *The Information Age: Economy, Society, and Culture*, Volume 2: *The Power of Identity*. Oxford and Malden, MA: Blackwell Publishers.

Esping-Andersen, Gøsta (ed.) (1996): *Welfare States in Transition: National Adaptations in Global Economies*. Thousand Oaks, Calif.: Sage.

Ford, Ramona L. (1988): *Work, Organization, and Power*. Needham Heights, Mass.: Allyn and Bacon.

Gornick, Janet, Marcia Meyers and Katherin Ross (1996): *Public Policies and the Employment of Mothers: A Cross-national Study*. Luxembourg Income Study. Working Paper No. 140, (June 1996). http://www.lisproject.org/publications/liswps/140.pdf (found 25/8/2005).

Gross, Ames and Rachel Weintrub (2004): *2004 Human Resource Trends in Japan*. SHRM Global Forum. http://www.pacificbridge.com/Publications/JapanDec2004.htm (found 25/8/2005).

Horlacher, David E. (2002): *Aging in Japan: Causes and Consequences. Part I: Demographic Issues*. Laxenburg: International Institute for Applied Systems Analysis. http://www.iiasa.ac.at/Publications/Documents/IR-01-008.pdf#search=%22david%20horlacher%20aging%20in%20japan%20part%201%20demographic%22 (found 25/9/2006).

ILO (International Labour Organization) (1998): *More than 120 Nations Provide Paid Maternity Leave*. Press release as of February 16, 1998. http://www.ilo.org/public/english/bureau/inf/pr/1998/7.htm (found 25/9/2006).

Jaffee, David (2001): *Organization Theory*. New York: McGraw Hill.

Kazuka, Katsutoshi (2000): Legal Problems Concerning Part-time Work in Japan. In: *Japan Institute of Labor Bulletin* (Special Topic) 39 (September). http://www.jil.go.jp/bulletin/year/2000/vol39-09/06.htm (found 25/8/2005).

MHLW (Ministry of Health, Labor and Welfare) (2005): *Heisei 16 nenhan—Hataraku josei no jitsujō* [The real situation of working women, 2004]. http://www.mhlw.go.jp/houdou/2005/03/h0328-7.html

Myles, John (1990): States, Labor Markets, and Life Cycles. In: Friedland, Roger and A. F. Robertson (eds.): *Beyond the Marketplace: Rethinking Economy and Society*. Somerset N. J.: Aldine Transaction, pp. 271–298.

Nagase Nobuko (2001): Balancing Work and Family in Japan: Inertia and a Need for change. In: *Issues for the 21st Century Think Social Harmony*. Canada-Japan Social Policy Symposium. http://www.asiapacificresearch.ca/caprn/cjsp_project/japan.PDF.

NIPSSR (National Institute of Population and Social Security Research) (2002): *Population Projections for Japan*. Table 1: Projected future population and proportion by age group, 2000-2050: Medium variant. http://www.ipss.go.jp/index-e.html (found 24/9/2006).

Ogura, Chikako (2003): *Kekkon no jōken* [Terms of marriage]. Tokyo: Asahi Shimbunsha.

Omata, Noriko (2000): Recent Employment and Income Conditions in Japan. In: *Tokyo Mitsubishi Review* 5, No. 9 (September). http://www.btm.co.jp/html_e/databank/rev0009e.htm (found 24/3/2004).

Sakai, Junko (2003). *Makeinu no toboe* [Howl of the loser dogs]. Tokyo: Kodansha.

Schulz, James H. (1995): *Economics of Aging*. New York: Auburn House.

Schulz, James H., Alan Borowski and William H. Crown (1991): *Economics of Population Aging: The "Graying" of Australia, Japan, and the United States*. New York: Auburn House.

Sechiyama, Kaku (2001): Shifting Family Support from Wives to Children. In: *Japan Echo* 28, 1, pp. 35–42.

Steffen, Christian (1998): *The Dutch "Polder Model" – An Answer to the German Crisis?* http://tiss.zdv.uni-tuebingen.de/webroot/sp/spsba01_W98_1/germany10.htm (found 24/9/2006).

Takahashi, Hiroyuki (1998): Prospects for Personal Income Tax Reform in Japan. In: *Japan Economic Institute Report*, No. 24, (June 26). http://www.jei.org/Archive/JEIR98/9824f.html (found 14/4/2005).

The Clearinghouse on International Developments in Child, Youth and Family Policies at Columbia University (2004): *Table 1.11: Maternity and Parental Leaves, 1999–2002.* http://www.childpolicyintl.org/ (found 25/9/2006).

*The Economist* (18 April 2002): Survey Japan, Consensus and Contraction: Social Conventions and Demography Add to the Sclerosis. http://www.economist.com/surveys/printerFriendly.cfm?Story_ID=1076735 (found 24/9/2006).

United Nations (2000): *Replacement Migration. Is it a Solution to Declining and Ageing Populations?* New York: United Nations, Population Division. http://www.un.org/esa/population/publications/migration/migration.htm.

Usui, Chikako (2001): The Misplaced Problems of Aging Society: Crisis or Opportunity? In: *International House of Japan Bulletin* 21, 1 (Spring), pp. 42–55.

—— (2002): Women's roles. In: Allan Bird (ed.): *Encyclopedia of Japanese Business and Management.* London: Routledge, pp. 474–477.

—— (2003): Japan's Aging Dilemma? In: Woodrow Wilson Center for International Scholars *Asia Program Special Report* 107, pp. 16–22.

WHO (World Health Organization) (2000): *New Healthy Life Expectancy Rankings—Japan Number One in New 'Healthy Life' System.* Press Releases (4 June). http://www.who.int/inf-pr-2000/en/pr2000-life.html (found 24/9/2006).

Yamanaka Akiko (1998): *Changing roles of Japanese Women.* Paper Presented at WAPPP Weekly Study Group, November 18. http://www.ksg.harvard.edu/wappp/happen/yamanaka.html (found 15/6/2005).

CHAPTER TEN

# ENGAGING THE GENERATIONS: AGE-INTEGRATED FACILITIES

Leng Leng Thang

## 1. Introduction

In a super-ageing society prompted with concurrent decline of mortality and fertility, Japanese find themselves more likely to grow well beyond the age of their grandparents, but less likely to become grandparents as fertility rates of the younger generations declines. Even for those who eventually gain grandparenthood, greater mobility of the population, urbanization and nuclearization of families only diminish the opportunities to engage with the younger generations.

The demographic challenge confronting Japan, while affecting the economy, health care and social security on the macro level, also affects intimacy between the generations when it couples with social and cultural changes.

Although a survey has shown that older persons (age 65 and above) prefer to stay with their married children,[1] in reality, the proportion of three-generation households have fallen from 54.4 per cent in 1975 to 27.3 per cent in 1999. At the same time, households consisting of older persons only have increased from 15 per cent to 38.8 per cent in the same period (Naikakufu 2001: 62). Staying separately affects the frequency of contact between the older and younger generation. Older Japanese have lesser contact with their non co-residing children as compared to their U.S. and German counterparts. While older persons in the U.S. and Germany meet their non co-residing children in the frequency of almost everyday to at least once a week constitute the majority, at about 55 per cent and 60 per cent; the percentage is

[1] The survey on the perceptions of ageing problems among middle and older age cohorts shows that 52.5 per cent of persons age 65–76 years old and 62.1 per cent of persons above age 75 prefers to co-reside with their married children. Majority prefers to stay with their married son than daughter's family (cited in Naikakufu 2001: 13).

lower at about 30 per cent for older Japanese. More (close to 40 per cent) of older Japanese meet their children only a few times in a year (Naikakufu 2001: 27).

Outside of the family, there are few opportunities for older Japanese to engage with the younger generation. The survey on community participation among seniors conducted by the Office for Policy on the Elderly in 1998 shows that while 52.9 per cent of the young-old (age 65–74) responded that they do engage with the young either frequently or sometimes, among the old-old (above age 75), 67.4 per cent claimed that they have no or almost no contact with the young. Even among those who engage with the young, for both groups of older persons, more than 70 per cent of the engagement is with the adult young. In general, intergenerational contact among the old with school-age and pre-school children is infrequent and declines with age (Naikakufu 2001: 27–29; Sagaza 2001: 77).

One of the negative consequences of little contact between the generations is an increase in "ageist" attitudes among the younger generations. An overview of studies on the perception of high school and college students has concluded that the attitudes of Japanese youth towards older persons are characterized by negative attitudes (Koyano 1989). An international comparison of college students' perceptions of older persons among Japan, United States, Britain and Sweden has further shown that more young Japanese perceive older persons as grouchy and stubborn and fewer see them as kind and honest than do peers in the other three countries (Koyano 1993). Age-segregation and the consequent negative perception of ageing and old age, therefore, foretell concerns on different levels, from personal concerns about the children's attitudes toward their own ageing parents in the future, to wider social implications on the future survival of the ageing society.

An age-segregated society has negative consequences to the quality of life of all generations. Kaplan (1993: 71–2) summarises the negative consequences as a reduction in the extent and quality of both the children's and the elders' social support networks; an increase in feelings of loneliness and increased vulnerability to depression experienced by older persons; an increase in the younger generation's negative perceptions of, and informational inaccuracies about, the process of ageing; and, a decrease in people's familiarity with ageing as a natural process in the continuum of life. Mass media's negative portrayal of older persons further attributes to the negative perceptions of the old among the young (Koyano 1993, Sagaza 2001).

Moreover, the lack of grandparents to serve as moral guideposts and transmitters of desirable social values to the young is believed to have attributed to the growing problems among youth in Japanese society. As children in nuclear familes are often overprotected by their own parents, they tend to lack self-control, tolerance and the ability to communicate well (Sawano 2000: 57). The increase in deviant behaviours and violence among the children has caused great concern among educators, parents and social commentators who doubt if they can rely on these children to be responsible citizens who will support them in the future.

## 2. Initiatives to Link the Generations

Concerns arising from the trend towards age-segregation have led to active efforts in recent years by both the state and the community to re-engage the generations. Such efforts are typically termed *sedaikan kōryu katsudō* (intergenerational interaction activities) aimed to bring together older persons with children and youth to promote cooperation, interaction or exchange. They include funded and unfunded programmes that may run on a periodical, once-only or seasonal basis. Intergenerational programmes may be classified according to the direction of serving, i.e. older persons serving children/youth; children/youth serving older persons; community-based initiatives and age-integrated facilities (Thang 2002). The following gives a brief description of the different 'directions of serving' except for age-integrated facilities, which will be discussed in depth in the latter part of the chapter.

### 2.1. *Old-age groups related initiatives*

Intergenerational programmes initiated by older persons are common through organizations such as old-age clubs and senior volunteer groups. Such programmes are usually supported under ageing policy guidelines which promote 'active social participation' among older persons in the framework of *ikigai* (purpose of life) and in lifelong learning.

Most senior citizens clubs have intergenerational initiatives such as through traditional games crafts, food and cooking. One popular initiative among old-age clubs—especially those in the rural areas—is letting the young experience rice planting and other traditional crafts such as weaving and making bamboo craft (e.g. *taketonbo*). Older persons conducting 'local history' classes in local schools is also another popular activity often supported by local governments. Stories about local neighbourhood help in creating a sense of community between the generations and give older persons the opportunity to impart morale and civic lessons to the children.

The idea of narrative as an intergenerational activity leverages on the past life experiences of older persons as a community asset. A volunteer narrative group in Kobe formed primarily by seniors who are survivors of the 1995 Great Hanshin earthquake has evolved into an intergenerational initiative as they developed lessons for the children in their narrative sessions about the earthquake in schools. From the initial objective of the narrative as a way to preserve the collective memories of the disaster, the volunteers have turned to serve the schools by imparting moral and safety messages to children (Thang 2005).

However, it is more common for the senior volunteer groups to serve the young in ways such as conducting games and performances in children's homes, serving as mentors for school children in after-school centres and as museum and gallery guides for school groups. In Shizuoka prefecture, graduates from the silver college turned into part-time teachers in elementary and junior-high schools and teach subjects such as Japanese calligraphy, haiku poetry, home economics, physical education, as well as club activities such as arts and craft (Yamamoto 1997: 91).

Intergenerational activities initiated by older persons are growing as a result of the increasing number of older Japanese who are living longer and in good health. In addition, the phenomenon depicts the eagerness of the older generation in serving and interacting with the young beyond the family circle; although it also reflects lesser family commitments for older persons as low fertility means many would have lesser grandchildren to care for.

However, in comparison, intergenerational programmes initiated by the young, mainly the schools, kindergartens and nurseries; are by far the most common form of intergenerational activities. Compared with older persons, children and youth have more experiences interacting with the older generations (Naikakufu 2001: 30). This shows on the one hand, the norm of perceiving intergenerational programmes from the perspective of young serving the old; and on the other hand, the positive impact of state policies to promote intergenerational interaction, leading to a wide range of activities organized by the schools and preschools, as well as the increasing acceptance of age-integrated facilities among social and community services.

### 2.2. *Schools/preschools initiatives*

Intergenerational activities seem more common among younger children. The most common forms of intergenerational programmes are event-based ones such as concert performances at old-age homes and invitations to schools' sports days although some sustain regular interaction (*Higashi Shakai Fukushi Kyōkai Hoikubu Tsūshin* 1995). For example, a nursery in Arakawa Ward, Tokyo, has monthly-interaction among its three- to six-year-old children and elders in a special nursing home nearby. After a year of group interaction, the children pair up with the 'grandparent' of mutual choice and continue with more intimate dyad relations. Besides the monthly interaction, the two facilities invite each other to their various cultural and social events.

There are also emerging forms of innovative intergenerational programmes which have expanded intergenerational activities beyond games and interaction to achieve language learning objectives. For example, the Ohana English Preschool Minato Mirai in Yokohama, a privately owned child-care and education facility, has partnered with the Hawaii Intergenerational Network to allow for Hawaiian female senior volunteers to teach English and watch over the pre-school children in the Elders/Kids Play Club.[2]

Among school children, the opportunities to interact with older persons are enhanced by structured initiative such as the 'volunteer school' program (*borantia kyōryoku kō*) started in 1977 by the Ministry of Education with the aim of promoting volunteerism, understanding and awareness of social welfare among school children. This scheme funds selected schools with ¥100,000 annually for the period of their participation. In 1993, 60 per cent of the 4,600 participating schools across the nation were elementary schools whereas junior and senior high schools constituted 30 and 10 per cent respectively.

The majority of school children in such programmes visit old-age institutions or older persons living alone in the community. The forms of interaction with older persons include: letter correspondence; playing traditional games together; learning about traditional crafts and history from the elders; and helping with cleaning. Older persons are invited to attend sports days, musical concerts, Respect the Elderly Day, and 'culture festivals' at the schools. Sometimes the students have joint sports activities with older persons, such as gate ball and ground golf.

---

[2] See web site of the preschool for more information http://www.ohana-ep.jp

Some schools develop a 'foster grandchild system' in which children pair up with elders in a particular nursing home for frequent and intimate interactions. One elementary school in Higashiyama City (Tokyo metropolitan area) allows the children to bring the elders out shopping in their wheelchairs as the children reach sixth grade. Such consistent contact has encouraged the development of long-lasting relationships between them.

During the three-year 'volunteer school' period, one high school in Ibaraki Prefecture introduced new courses in the home economics curriculum: besides lessons such as sewing, cooking and child care, there were lessons that included practical activities in understanding social welfare for the students. Students in the cooking class also started a monthly meal service which they called 'the heart of grandchildren' service. The boxed lunches were wrapped with 'lunch mats' made by the sewing class, while students from the child-care class delivered the boxed lunches to the elders and ate with them (JARC 1994).

The programme has received positive feedback, and some students are said to have embarked on a career in welfare services influenced by their volunteer experience in school. However, as the scheme relies heavily on funding from the ministry, some activities initiated during the period suffered when they discontinued as a participating school of the scheme. While some schools were forced to cut back on costly projects, others managed by securing new funding from local administrative bodies to enable the activities to continue (Saito 1994: 177).

Besides the volunteer school program, since the late 1990s, within the broad framework of lifelong education for children, the concept of school-community partnership was introduced under various plans such as the Three-Year National Children Plan, 1999–2001, and the 'Comprehensive Learning Time' for all schools to be launched in 2002. These plans provide opportunities for students to do volunteer work and interact with the older generations who represent the community (Sagaza 2001: 35).

The opportunities to volunteer and interact with older persons are perceived as one important component of 'education of the heart,' a part of social education and lifelong education in schools. It is hoped that thoughtfulness and kindness cultivated through contact with older persons will help alleviate problems such as bullying and school phobia faced in the Japanese education system today (Kurauchi and Suzuki 1998).

The 'education of the heart' is further expanded since 2002 with five-year school week and weekly time for integrated learning (*sōgōteki gakushū*) where students are expected to gain more experience in activities relating to welfare and volunteering in the community during their Saturdays and integrated learning time. Such community activities will nevertheless provide opportunities for intergenerational contacts since older persons are usually identified as an essential presence in the community.

During the experimental integrated learning time for the fourth graders in an elementary school at Kodaira city (Tokyo metropolitan area), children were encouraged to propose their own projects and request help from their parents and neighbourhood to execute them. Among the various things they could do under the theme, 'Let's widen our world!' one group chose to interact with older persons from old-age home and in the community. The children initiated regular visits; besides the integrated study time, they also went during the weekends and after school. As one student expressed, 'When we make friends, we have to meet a few times to become close. Therefore we want to meet the elderly many times.' (Sagaza 2001: 145–6).

### 2.3. *Community initiatives*

Intergenerational activities initiated by community groups, such as neighbourhood associations, civic halls, local volunteer groups, self-governing bodies, charity organisations, private business groups and even community individuals are also increasingly widespread. Many are event-based which could be annual or periodic events, or just one-shot deals. They include three-generational sports meets and walkathons for multigenerations, three-generational festivals and events that promote cultural and religious themes (Kaplan 1996; National Federation of Civic Halls 2000). Some municipalities organise them on a regular basis. For example, Kamō Town in Kagoshima Prefecture has since 1992 designated the third Saturday of the month as the 'Intergenerational Interaction Day' on which all civic halls organise activities such as 'listening to the experience of the elders,' 'learning about local history,' sports, volunteering and crafts to enhance interactions across the generations (JARC 1994). Another important municipal effort is shown in the creation of space for the old and young to interact within the community, such as building 'elders' space' in children's playgrounds (Hyōgo Prefecture), setting up 'child-care space' in public places (Tochigi Prefecture), establishing a children's library in an old-age home (Saitama Prefecture) and within a special nursing home (Kumamoto Prefecture), and placing swings and slides in the open ground of an old-age home. In the recent years, with the flourishing of new NPOs (non-profit organizations), we are also witnessing new forms of intergenerational initiatives in the community catering to help not only the old and young, but also the middle generation in the think of childrearing. The Nikko ri-ta (Smiling) child-care salon established by the NPO called "Obāchan-chi" (Grandma's House) is one such attempt which provide a space for the young children, their parents as well as young and older adults in the community to gather. In 2005, the Obāchan-chi organized all generations' seminars on childrearing especially for parents. It also established a local support network for intergenerational child care.[3]

Multigenerational participation in community events often symbolizes efforts to (re-)unite the whole community and the multiple generations within it. Such efforts resonate in the larger on-going project of *furu-sato-zukuri* [hometown making]—efforts on the national and local levels to integrate present-day activities and interpretations with past events, and to set in motion the construction of an 'authentic' image (flavour) of the future (Robertson 1991: 14).

The state has played a significant role in promoting intergenerational activities, particularly in the context of ageing population. The above mentioned initiatives have shown the role of various policies and measures in promoting intergenerational interaction and age integrated attempts. To further promote intergenerational initiatives, the Ministry of Public Management, Home Affairs, Posts and Telecommunications has established the Intergenerational Exchange Award; in 1999, 33 organisations nationwide received the award for their active involvement in the area (Sawano 2000).

One illustration of strong state support is manifested in the 2001 White Paper on Ageing Society which emphasizes intergenerational interaction through the theme "towards cross-generational interactions". The front cover of the white paper further supports the theme with interesting illustrations of interactions between the young and the old.

---

[3] See website http://www.obachanchi.org

Among the academics, activists and agencies involved with intergenerational programmes, too, there have been regional efforts to set up mutual support groups to advance intergenerational initiatives. One of the most recent developments is the establishment of the Japan Intergenerational Unity Association (JIUA), a non-profit organization with "a mission to stimulate, nurture, and sustain intergenerational programming efforts in Japan" (JIUA 2004, Internet) as well as to promote a national agenda for an inclusive society. In August 2006, the JIUA organized a national forum on intergenerational programmes in Tokyo which included key international members of the intergenerational movement. The gathering hoped to advance intergenerational programmes in Japan and to strengthen linkages with international developments for all to benefit from best practices as well as to advance research with intergenerational focus.

Studies on re-engaging the generations in the Japan context have surfaced since the 1990s (e.g. JARC 1994, Aoi 1996, Kaplan et al. 1998; Hiroi 2000; Sagaza 2001; Thang 2001). Many publications document positive results arising from programmes and activities linking the old and the young. For instance, the JARC report[4] on a survey of intergenerational activities (1994) provides an example of intergenerational volunteer activities initiated by a home economics club in a high school in Toyama prefecture. Out of the 150 members in the club, 47 participated in the volunteer activities focussing on older persons who lived alone in the community. These students interacted with older persons through home visits, letter correspondence and telephone calls. Responses from the students reveal that although many lived with their grandparents, they often did not talk to them until they became volunteers. From the opportunities to interact with other older persons, they learnt about their lifes and thoughts, and this enabled them to understand and communicate better with their own grandparents. In a survey to understand the effect of intergenerational interaction on school-age children and youth, it is found that especially for elementary school children, the opportunities to interact with older persons "have promoted their understanding towards the older generation" (above 40 per cent) and "have been an enjoyable experience to them" (about

[4] The study represents one of the several research initiatives funded by Sōmucho to survey intergenerational initiatives across the country and develop some guidelines for planning and implementation.

30 per cent) (Naikakufu 2001: 31). In a society where nuclear household arrangement is the norm, the opportunities to engage across the generations in the community and school settings have increasingly become a necessity for the generations to benefit from each other.

This chapter explores Japan's attempt to deal with the dilemma of generational disengagement by examining how larger trends of an ageing society with fewer children has on the one hand, led to age-segregation, while on the other hand, promoted opportunities for re-engagement as young and aged facilities begin to co-locate. As low fertility resulted in an excess of classrooms in schools, we have witnessed more services for older persons set up in the school premises. Some facilities have also purpose-built to be age-integrated to allow for intergenerational interactions otherwise not common in nuclear households. The following section will focus on two case studies representing age-integrated facilities in the form of a purpose-built age-integrated setting and co-location with elementary school. They will be analyzed in the framework of its impact on both the older and younger generations. The chapter concludes with discussions on the potential of the roles of age-integrated facilities and other attempts to re-engage the generations in softening the impact of the great demographic challenge.

## 3. Age-Integrated Facilities in Japan

Age-integrated facilities, defined as facilities in which "children/youth and older adults receive ongoing services and/or programming at the same site concurrently, and where the participants interact through regularly scheduled planned intergenerational activities, as well as through spontaneous, informal encounters" (Goyer, cited in Hayer, 2003: 114), are regarded as a more effective model in engaging the generations as the co-existence of the services creates opportunities for more spontaneous interaction resembling intergenerational relations within the family and community. In Kaplan's (2001) framework of classifying intergenerational programmes according to the "depth of engagement scale",[5] age-integrated facility is regarded as the highest in the scale of

[5] Kaplan's depth of engagement scale is a 7-point scale. While point 1 refers to initiatives that provide no direct contact between age groups, the other end of the scale—point 7 represents intensive contact and ongoing opportunity for intimacy (Kaplan 2001: 13).

7, in which intergenerational engagement takes place as a function of the way community settings are planned and established. Such a site, community or society reflects values of intergenerational reciprocity and interdependence through social norms, institutional policies and priorities (Kaplan 2001).

The age-integrated facility is a relatively new alternative of engaging the generations in Japan. Services can become age-integrated either by moving into an existing facility or by constructing new projects with the goal of integrating services for different generations in mind. For the former, the most common combination is the setting up of day service centres or other old-age services in the empty classrooms of schools and nurseries. In the latter, where the facilities were purpose-built from the beginning to accommodate both generations, combinations range from the more usual day service for older persons and nursery co-location, to more uncommon ones such as a senior house combined with a dormitory for college students and a nursing home combined with a secondary school and nursery.[6] A 2002 figure further indicated that 562 nurseries are located in the same compound with elderly care facilities.[7]

In a national survey of interaction between the old and young in facilities/institutions in Japan, Hayashi (2000) found from the 370 responses (out of a random sample of 1000) that 21.9 per cent of the local administrative units, (cities, towns and villages) have age-integrated facilities, of which the most common forms of integration are:

- Day service centre with child-care centre (27 cases)
- Welfare centre for elderly with children's hall (21 cases)
- Welfare centre for elderly with child-care centre (20 cases)
- Special nursing home and other with child-care centre (19 cases)

Although the survey has not included the integration of old-age facilities with schools, Hayashi (2000: 92) notes that in the case of combination

[6] I identified 39 age-integrated facilities in Tokyo in 1996. They represent a good cross-section of various combinations - age-integrated facilities combining nursery, nursing home, day service centres (3); a nursing home with nursery and junior high school (1); nursing homes with nurseries (4); an old-age home with nursery (1); day service centres with nurseries (2), with children's after-school centres (2), or with elementary school (1); elder's rest centres with nursery (1), with children's after-school center (1), or with both a children's after-school centres and "silver pia" housing (1); an elder care house with university students' dormitory (1).

[7] Figure taken from an article on welfare based intergenerational practices (Kitamura 2003).

with schools, it usually comes in the form of day service centres in schools, primarily to occupy the empty classrooms available in schools. He comments on the unique case of a special nursing home combined with a secondary school and nursery situated in Shinagawa Ward (Tokyo) and reveals the reality of land squeeze as the main reason for building such age-integrated facilities. Positive benefits to the residents and users of these facilities thus serve as an added bonus to the practical advantages of age-integrated facilities.

As noted above, the emergence of age-integrated facilities reflects the consequences of an ageing society with fewer children. As a result of low fertility, in the last decade, the number of public elementary school students has decreased more than 20 per cent from 9.26 million in 1990 to 7.24 million in 2000 (Hani 2001). By 2005, there were a total of 125,405 classrooms in elementary and junior high schools nationwide that became vacant permanently because of changing demography.[8] To make full use of these vacant classrooms, the local government has opened these school premises to other social services, such as day care centres and centres for the elderly. The Takashima Number Sixth Elementary School in Itabashi Ward (Tokyo), for example, converted in 1996 the empty classrooms into a mini day service centre for the elderly in the community. To further promote intergenerational interaction in a casual setting, since 1999, the school has run an 'in touch lunch' programme (*fureai kyūshoku*) which enables older persons from the day service centres to attend school lunch with the children (Tokyo Volunteer and Action Center 2000: 52–3).

Such attempts match the needs for more old-age services prompted by the onset of ageing society. With the shortage of land in major metropolitan areas, many old-age services had to be established in the suburbs or the country, forcing older persons to move from the communities in which they have lived much of their lives. The setting up of day service centres or other old-age services inside the schools and nurseries thus offers an effective relief to the need of space for old-age services that are easily accessible by older persons in the community.

[8] Out of the 125 405 vacant classrooms in public schools, 836 have turned into social education facilities, which include life long learning centres for older persons, and 152 became social welfare facilities, which include facilities for elderly (Monbukagakusho 2002, Internet).

In fact, the co-locating of services for older persons in the school compound represents a major "breakthrough" in bureaucracy; schools come under the purview of the Ministry of Education, while elderly welfare belongs to the Ministry of Health and Welfare. Until the pressing need for increased elderly welfare was felt, transferring the "property" of one Ministry to another was almost impossible.[9] Nonetheless, the anticipated increase in old-age service centres targeted in the Gold Plan implies that the presence of older persons in the compound could become more common among schools in the near future. The presence of the 'community' in schools also has the potential to change the perception of school. Ideologically, the 'opening up' of schools to outsiders relates to the 'community school' movement started in the 1930s in the United States (Kurauchi and Suzuki 1998: 121); it is interesting to note the relevance of the idea in providing the conceptual framework to the pragmatic solutions on problems such as empty classrooms in schools due to the phenomenon of ageing.

In the case of purpose-built age-integrated facilities, the different services usually choose to coexist because of practical factors such as effective use of limited land and resources as well as the 'emotional' motivation of providing opportunities for intergenerational interaction. Kotoen in the following case description is often regarded as a model of such an age-integrated facility and has gained much attention as a result of the characteristic of offering multiple services for multiple generations under one-roof. It is heartening to note that following the successful model of Kotoen, more similar age-integrated complexes have emerged in Japan with the explicit objectives of enhancing intergenerational communication and interaction within the community.[10]

## 4. "Big Family" Kotoen

Kotoen, located in Edogawa Ward (Tokyo), is a pioneer age-integrated facility in Japan. The facility includes a special nursing home for the

---

[9] It was only in spring 1996 that the Ministry of Education announced for the first time that using empty classrooms for day activities by the elderly was acceptable (*Asahi Shimbun* 6 November 1996).

[10] For example, the "Akasaka Kodomo Chūkōsei Plaza" and "Sun Sun Akasaka" in Minato Ward (Tokyo) are newly integrated complexes for older persons (special nursing home and day services), children and youth activities established in 2003 and managed by the Social Welfare Foundation "Tokyo Seirōin" (see http://www.222.seirouin.or.jp).

aged, an old-age home, day care services for elderly, a nursery for children from 6 months to 6 years old, home nursing support centre, care management support, home help station and rehabilitation programmes.[11] On a typical day, there are more than 250 members in the facility, including 100 children from the nursery who come in the morning and stay till as late as 6:30 p.m. at the nursery; 50 ambulant older residents in the old-age home, 50 semi-ambulant or bed-ridden older residents in the special nursing home. In addition, 25 older persons from the community attend day care service on the weekdays with transport provided by the centre. The centre also offers short stay service for bedridden older persons, rehabilitation and bath services for older persons in the community as well as regular seminars for caregivers in the community. Its effort to reach out to the community through multi-services for different age groups represents a departure from the stereotypical image of old age institutions as a dull and isolated space to one that is filled with activities that engages the wider community.

Kotoen started as a *yōrōin* (old age asylum) in 1962 as a private NPO and changed its name to *yōgo rōjin hōmu*—old-age home[12] in accordance with the 1963 Welfare Law for the Aged (*Rōjin Fukushi-hō*). The nursery was initially built next to it in 1976 and became combined under one roof since 1987.

Since the co-existence of both populations, Kotoen has set up a committee called the *fureai sokushin iinkai* [committee to promote interactions] which meets monthly to discuss events and evaluate their intergenerational programmes. There are various programmes to promote interactions, including activities on a daily basis such as morning exercises, engaging older residents' help to dress the children and joint activities such as arts and crafts and story-telling. There are also monthly events such as the "open child-care program" where groups of older residents from the old-age home take turns spending a day with the children and annual events including the "beginning child-care" program where older

---

[11] I did fieldwork in Kotoen for ten months from 1995–1996, where I worked as a volunteer at the centre. Besides participant observation, interviews and surveys were conducted with various people related to the centre or involved in age-integrated facilities. I continue to keep abreast of developments in Kotoen after that, and did a brief follow-up in 2001. For a detailed ethnography of the facility, read Thang 2001.

[12] Under the 1963 Law, *yōrōin* was changed to a new name, *rōjin hōmu*, an attempt to reduce the stigmatization of institution for the aged. The Law also divides *rōjin hōmu* into three types, namely *yōgō rōjin hōmu* (home for the elders), *tokubetsu yōgō rōjin hōmu* (special care home for the elders), and *keihi rōjin hōmu* (low cost home for the elders).

residents are invited to help in babysitting the newly enrolled one-year-old toddlers. In addition, almost all cultural and annual events such as the nursery's graduation and opening ceremonies involve both the older persons and children. Besides the planned programmes, children are encouraged to visit the older residents whenever they feel like it. It is not uncommon to see nursery teachers bringing their little ones for a walk to greet the older residents. Besides preschoolers from the Kotoen nursery, children from nearby schools also visit Kotoen to interact with the older residents for handicraft sessions, or sometimes as volunteers to help clean the vicinity.

Kotoen maximizes its unique combination to re-engage the generations through active promotion of intergenerational interaction both in planned programmes and casual contacts. Through the conceptual framework of *daikazoku* [big family], it strives to achieve the goal of a 'happy home' (*ikka danran*) in daily interactions across the generations. The *daikazoku* concept is well accepted by the children, their parents and the elderly residents in the institution. The parents and children find the multigenerational presence enriching of their lives as members of a nuclear family. Some mothers have even established frequent contact with the elderly through their children. Children who have experienced frequent contacts with older persons feel closer with their own grandparents and are more readily to help the old and frail on the street. Older residents agree that the big family emphasis bring warmth and love to institutions for the aged that are usually stigmatised as a dumping ground for the family-less elderly. In an age-integrated setting, there is mutual learning where the older residents teach the children about traditional customs, folktales and handicraft, they also learn about contemporary youth culture, such as comic book characters and new vocabularies from the children. The children help promote interaction among the elderly too, as they become a subject for conversation among the residents. The presence of the children have been said to encourage some frail older persons to attend physiotherapy regularly in the hope to walk again and resume active interaction with the children.

The resonance of a family-like atmosphere is shown through the children's greeting of the residents as 'grandparents.' The older residents, too, are expected to perform their roles as 'grandparents' by playing with the 'grandchildren,' helping them to change their attire before and after their afternoon naps; telling them fables and tales, and making them gifts during traditional festive celebrations. Kotoen's commitment to the big family has gained the attention of the mass media; over the years, it has appeared in various international, national and regional TV programmes and news coverage.

## 5. Age-integrated Community in Kodaira Elementary School

The age-integrated setting in Kodaira elementary school evokes the practices of an open school concept where the community is integrated into a part of the school. As the mission of the Kodaira second elementary school shows, the school "aims to cultivate children with joint efforts of the school, family and the community" (*gakkō, katei, chiiki no renkei no naka kara yutakana kokoro o motsu jidō o ikusei shimasu*). The school has been active in community participation and has been a participant of the 'volunteer school' program. The setting up of a space for older persons from the community within the school premise is thus wholeheartedly welcomed by the school. Besides solving the problem of empty classrooms, it matches the need of an ageing society and the desire to foster community relations with the school. The initiative is also enhanced by funding available for schools to turn their empty classrooms into facilities for older persons.

In the Kodaira second elementary school, the classrooms are remodelled and the space is named "interaction room" (*kōryū shitsu*).[13] Set up in February 2001, it has the long term aim of developing the centre beyond its current focus of an activity centre for older persons, but also a place for older persons to feel at home within the community, i.e. as a focal point where older persons will converge and then move on from the centre to work elsewhere for part of the day.

The interaction room at Kodaira serves healthy older persons. In June 2001, it has 73 registered members, ranging from 60 to 91 years old. Men made up about 14 per cent of its membership (10 persons). The members visit the centre, which opens from ten o'clock in the morning to three o'clock in the afternoon, at an average of once a week, although a few drop in everyday. As older persons in good health may choose to continue working, they can only visit the centre during their day off. On an average day, about five to ten older persons will

---

[13] Fieldwork was conducted in Kodaira in June 2001. Besides participant observations, I interviewed the members from the city educational committee, the school principal Mr. Yamashita, teachers, older participants at the interaction centre, volunteers, parent volunteers and students.

be present for various activities run by the volunteers. Out of the 32 volunteers at the centre, five are designated as co-ordinators on different days of the week (the centre is open from Monday to Friday following the school schedule); there are also other specialized volunteers such as volunteers who teach dancing and pottery. Volunteers are in charge of preparing lunch for older persons using the kitchen situated within the centre, as well as the program of the day, which may be connected with community events. For example, dance lessons are incorporated as a weekly program to prepare the older persons for a dance item during the Christmas and New Year events.

The interaction room offers a play space for school children. During the recess time from 10:20 to 10:40 a.m., and 1:20 to 1:40 p.m., children stroll in to play the games available at the room; admire the handicraft on display and making small talks with older persons. During one morning break, I observed two ten year-old girls who came by to chat with a 77 year-old woman and they later played the traditional game of *kendama*[14] together. The girls were fascinated with the skill of the 'granny' and engaged with a lively interaction on playing games. As the older woman, who is staying alone mentioned, she enjoys going to the centre because of the lively atmosphere and the presence of other people's voices around. Besides informal chatting and games, the members from the interaction centre also visit the school children during their arts and craft lessons as 'instructors'. As one of the 'instructors', she is seen engaged with the volunteer in a discussion on teaching the children how to make paper baskets.

Close proximity to older persons enables the school to plan various programmes to enhance interaction between the generations. While the school taps on the resources of older persons in classes, such as arts and craft, social education, and history lessons, older persons are empowered with a sense of satisfaction and *ikigai* as they engage with the young as 'teachers'. For the increasing number of older persons who are living alone in the community, the interaction room helps solves their problem of loneliness and contribute to a sense of usefulness and connectedness with the community and the young.

[14] *Kendama* is a popular game with a wooden instrument.

## 6. The Potential of Age-Integrated Facilities in Japan

Whether conceptualized as a community or a big family, the case studies have shown that age-integrated facilities represent the ideal desired in a community or a family, where intergenerational engagements exist in harmony and provide mutually satisfying experiences to all generations. The different intergenerational programmes and models in Japan have impacted the younger generation in positive ways, including the fostering of more positive attitudes towards older persons; better communication with their own grandparents as a result of their engagement with older persons in the community and facility; promoting appreciation towards traditional arts/crafts and local history; cultivating of desirable values and social skills such as tolerance, cooperation and respect the differences of others. To the older generation, connecting with the young improve their self esteem, health and purpose of life; change their perceptions towards young people and empower them as volunteers serving the young. In an age where age-segregation is the norm, accelerated by consumer marketing and mass media, efforts to engage the generations has become more essential for the building of an inclusive society which will harness the potential and strength of all generations for mutual benefits and for the stability of the society.

However, although age-integrated facilities represent the ideal combination in social services for maximum opportunities of cross-age interaction, generations do not become integrated just by living in close proximity. From the family setting, we learn that even when an older person lives with his/her children and grandchildren, they may see little of each other if no effort is made to foster the sense of togetherness. Members in the family may take their own meals, watch television in their own room and provide very little time for each other. The success of age-integrated facilities thus depends not only on close proximity and spatial planning to encourage interaction, but also require programmes and activities with the purpose of integrating the generations. Not all service providers are enthusiastic about the additional responsibilities and may only engage in organized event-based activities such as festive celebration. A facility combing after-school care and day service for older persons (but run by two different organizations) claims that they only hold joint events twice a year: during the summer bon dancing and fire prevention drill. Parents could also hinder interaction if they withdraw their children due to fear that their children may contract disease from older persons, whom they perceive as sick and senile.

There is thus the need for support from the state on training and skills development in intergenerational programming to promote interaction meaningful and beneficial for all, instead of viewing age-integrated facilities simply as 'built together' due to 'limited land' (*Rōjin Hoken Fukushi Jānaru* 1993: 8).

Recent developments and emphasis on intergenerational interaction indicate that the state is proactive on ways to promote intergenerational interaction, including the setting up of more age-integrated facilities. Age-integrated facilities as a new model of care have received more acceptance and support compared to the 1980s when the plan was first conceptualized by Kotoen. The Director recalled the various barriers they faced when they submitted the proposal to the ward office; eventually they were forced to comply with the regulation of separating the services for different generations with a wall (which they constructed as removable and never put up) before the approval was obtained. The awkwardness of trying to place an age-integrated facility into the current age-segregated division of services implies the need for a cross-department and cross-agency administrative unit to address the new entity. An administrative unit from the lens of integrating services across the life course may advise age-integrated facilities on the sharing of utility spaces and thus generate cost savings, and further expand the potential of age-integrated facilities in addressing social problems. Hiroi (2000: 3) suggests that the goal of 'community support' in social security policy in Japan should be perceived independently and across the age-segregated emphasis. In addition, the division of elderly, children, disabled and other social welfare law system should also be revised, to either be replaced or to include in addition a "community care law" or "social service law" which provide a workable system for the integration of care.

It is heartening to learn that age-integrated facilities and other attempts to re-engage the generations are gaining recognition for the potential it has in addressing the needs of an ageing society with fewer children. Indeed, never before has Japan been confronted with such a record number of older persons and a record low number of births. Although a great dilemma to the society, the demographic challenge also signals an opportunity for Japan to embark on new strategies such as adopting the intergenerational perspective to achieve a society where all individuals can realize their full potential through mutual care and empowerment.

## References

Aoi, Kazuo (ed.) (1996): *Sedaikan kōryu no riron to jitsugen* [The Theories and Practices of Intergenerational Interaction). Tokyo: Chōju Shakai Kaihatsu Sentā (Centre for Exploring the Long-lived Society).

Hani, Yoko (2001): Empty classrooms renovated for public use. In: *The Japan Times Online* (11 March).

Hayashi, Hiroko (2000): Rōjin to kodomo tōgō kea ni kansuru jichitai no torikumi jōkyō chōsa [Survey of conditions among administrative units about integrated care for the old and young]. In: Hiroi, Yoshinori (ed.): *Rōjin to kodomo tōgō kea*. Tokyo: Chūō Hoki.

Hayer, Hayes (2003): An observational study in developing an intergenerational shared site program: Challenges and insights. In: *Journal of Intergenerational Relationships* 1, 1, pp. 113–132.

*Higashi Shakai Fukushi Kyōkai Hoikubu Tsūshin* [The East (Division) Social Welfare Association Child Care Department Correspondence] (1995): 20 October issue.

Hiroi, Yoshinori (ed.) (2000): *Rōjin to kodomo tōgō kea* [Integrated Care for the Old and the Young]. Tokyo: Chūō Hoki.

Japan Aging Research Center [JARC] (1994): *Sedaikan kōryu ni kansuru chōsa kenkyū hōkokusho* [Survey report on intergenerational interaction]. Tokyo: Japan Aging Research Center.

Japan Intergenerational Unity Association (JIUA) (2004): *About the Japan Intergenerational Unity Association.* http://www.jiua.org/eng/eabout.html (found 20 October 2006).

Kaplan, Matthew (1993): Recruiting senior adult volunteers for intergenerational programmes: working to create a "jump on the bandwagon" effect. In: *Journal of Applied Gerontology* 12, 1, pp. 71–82.

Kaplan, Matthew (1996): A look at intergenerational program initiatives in Japan: A preliminary comparison with the US. In: *Southwest Journal on Aging* 12, 1–2, pp. 73–9.

Kaplan, Matthew, Atusko Kusano, Ichiro Tsuji and Shigeru Hisamichi (1998): *Intergenerational Programs: Support for Children, Youth and Elders in Japan.* New York: SUNY Press.

Kaplan, Matthew (2001): *School-based Intergenerational Programs*. Hamburg: UNESCO Institute for Education. http://www.unesco.org/education/uie/pdf/schoolbasedip.pdf (found 22/11/2006).

Kitamura, Akiko (2003): *Fukushi seisaku ni okeru sedaikan kōryū* [The viewpoint of intergenerational interaction in welfare policies]. http://group.dai-ichi-life.co.jp/dlri/ldi/note/notes0311.pdf (found 22/11/2006).

Koyano, Wataru (1989): Japanese attitudes towards the elderly: A review of research findings. In: *Journal of Cross-cultural Gerontology* 4, pp. 335–345.

—— (1993): Age-old stereotypes. In: *Japan Views Quarterly* 2 (Winter), pp. 41–2.

Kurauchi, Shiro and Mari Suzuki (eds.) (1998): *Shōgai gakushū kiso* [The basics of lifelong learning]. Tokyo: Gakubunsha.

Miyagi Prefecture Federation of Old-age Clubs [1991]: *Chiiki ni ikitsuku shiruba bolantia* [Silver volunteers who liven up the community]. Tokyo: Toei Company Educational Filming Department.

National Federation of Civic Halls (2000): *Atarashii kōminkan katsudō no arikata ni kansuru chōsa kenkyū hōkokushō* [Report on survey of new activities at civic halls].

Robertson, Jennifer. 1991. *Native and Newcomer: Making and Remaking a Japanese City.* Berkeley: University of California Press.

*Rōjin Hoken Fukushi Jānaru* [Journal of Elderly Healthcare and Welfare] (1993): *Hitotsu yane no shita ni atsumareba* [As we gather under one roof], October issue, pp. 4–17.

Sagaza, Haruo (ed.) (2001): *Shōshi kōrei shakai to kodomotachi* [Ageing society with a declining birth rate and children]. Tokyo: Chūō Hōki.

Saito, Sadao (1994): Shakai fukushi bunya ni okeru sedaikan kōryu no genjō—fukushi kyōiku o tōshite [Present conditions of intergenerational interaction in social welfare sphere—through welfare education). In: Aoi, Kazuo (ed.): *Kōreika shakai no sedaikan kōryu* [Intergenerational Interaction in Ageing Society]. Tokyo: Chōju Shakai Kaihatsu Sentā, pp. 160–205.

Sawano, Yukiko (2000): Intergenerational exchange programme for lifelong learning: Japanese experiences. In: *Report of the 1st International Conference on Intergenerational Programmes, 13–14 October 1999. Netherlands*, pp. 56–61.

Monbukagakusho [Ministry of Education, Culture, Sports, Science and Technology] (2002): *Yoyū kyōshitsu, haikō shisetsu no yukō katsuyō* [Effective use of vacant classrooms and school facilities] http://www.mext.go.jp/a_menu/shotou/zyosei/yoyuu.htm (found 8/11/2006).

Naikakufu [Cabinet Office] (ed.) (2001): *Kōreishakai Hakusho* [White Paper on Ageing Society]. Tokyo: Gyōsei.

Thang, Leng Leng (2001): *Generations in Touch: Linking the Old and Young in a Tokyo Neighborhood*. Ithaca: Cornell University Press.

—— (2002): Touching of the hearts: an overview of programs to promote interaction between the generations in Japan. In: Goodman, Roger (ed.): *The Anthropology of Social Policy in Japan*. Cambridge: Cambridge University Press, pp. 156–176.

—— (2005): "A message on life to the young"—Perceiving a senior volunteer activity in Japan from an intergenerational perspective. In: *Journal of Intergenerational Relationships* 3, 4, pp. 7–22.

Tokyo Volunteer Action Center (2000): San nen kan no takara sagashi [Three years of treasure hunting] Volume 4. Tokyo: Tokyo Volunteer and Citizens Center.

Yamamoto, Yoshihiro (1997): *Shichōson ni okeru shōgai gakushū bolantia banku no katsuseika ni kansuru jisshōteki kenkyū* [Case research of the activation of lifelong learning volunteer bank in cities, wards, towns and villages]. Tokyo: National Education Research Center.

CHAPTER ELEVEN

# SOCIAL CHANGE AND CAREGIVING OF THE ELDERLY

Susan Orpett Long

## Introduction

In the year 2000, Japan established a new public programme, the Long Term Care Insurance System or *kaigo hoken seido*, to assist in caring for frail elderly people in the community and in residential institutions. As other chapters in this volume attest, this was a daring programme in many ways. It was a significant departure from previous policies on developing services for the elderly since funding depended on premiums paid by current and future beneficiaries. The system encouraged the development of private and non-governmental service organizations rather than relying on public administration to provide care services. It led to the expansion of new occupational categories such as care managers and home helpers, and to educational programmes to train and certify them.

The Long Term Care Insurance System was also a policy that voiced a radical departure from previous cultural assumptions about family care giving, a change considered long overdue by some in government and by ordinary people who felt overwhelmed by the demands of caring for elderly relatives. Today's elderly grew up in an era in which the head of household, normatively the eldest son, was expected to provide for all members of the household, including frail parents. Due to the gendered division of labour in the household, the daily tasks of hands-on assistance were the responsibility of the wife of the household head. However demographic and value changes in the second half of the 20th century meant that such care giving became less tenable, more burdensome, and less desirable. Increased life expectancies and declining birth rates meant that there were fewer potential caregivers relative to the number of people who needed care. Those who were expected to provide the day-to-day care, that is, daughters-in-law, were more likely to be employed outside of the household, and increased geographical mobility for employment took younger generations away from older family members who needed assistance. Changes in family law after World War II shifted inheritance from a single heir in the next generation to inheritance by a surviving spouse or shared equally by siblings. Without a single child identified as heir, expectations about responsibilities for elder care were altered as well. As longevity increased, more and more families tried to cope with these changes at an interpersonal level, drawing media and government attention to the question of how to provide elder care. The elderly, and then the ageing society more generally, came to be seen as a social problem.

In policy and in personal lives, the result has been to spread responsibilities for care giving to a variety of new caregivers within and beyond the family. This chapter describes the changes that have taken place in the environment of home care preceding and subsequent to the introduction of the public long-term care insurance programme. These changes have led to an early 21st century family care giving situation characterized by the breakdown of prior generational and gender roles and the commercialization of care as strangers become caregivers for pay.

## 1. Changes in Family Caregiving

Historically, the care of ill and frail members of society took place within the household. Although some institutions for the elderly existed, these were welfare facilities primarily for the poor and childless. Through the 20th century, the stigma of those associations remained a challenge for those who wish to utilize modern residential care facilities and for policy makers who saw the need to develop these institutions. The increased availability of professionally-staffed nursing homes and other residential options and the changes in attitude accompanying the payment of premiums for long term care are beginning to decrease that stigma.

Nonetheless, the vast majority of elder care continues to be home-based,[1] and it is this type of care that is the focus of this chapter. The assertion of continuity might lead to the overlooking of the significant changes that have taken place in who provides care, in the type of care given, and in the technology available. In the early 20th century,

[1] In 2001, less than 3 per cent of the population 65 and older was living in an elder care institution, excluding hospitals (calculated from Naikakufu 2004: 35).

the typical caregiving situation might be a daughter-in-law caring for her husband's parent due to serious illness. Infectious diseases such as tuberculosis were common causes of death before the introduction of sulfa and antibiotic drugs. The ill elderly person often required bed rest and total care, but the person either recovered or died in a matter of weeks or months. Co-residence of a single adult child (future heir) and spouse with the parental generation was assumed, so the daughter-in-law would already have well-established roles and relationships in the household. Her productive labour was likely to be as a farmer or shopkeeper in the household enterprise, and so providing care to an ailing family member did not mean the end of such work, since it was not physically separated from family care responsibilities. Assistance with eating and medication, preparation of special foods, assistance in toileting and bathing, laundry, and cleaning, though often unpleasant tasks, were extensions of her regular work as a housewife. She was the assumed, and often the only, caregiver.

The picture of a typical caregiving situation at the turn of the 21st century is quite different. Contemporary family care giving requires a different set of skills and often necessitates the sharing of responsibilities over longer periods of time than in the past. The control of many infectious diseases has led to an older population in which cancer, circulatory, heart, and lung diseases are common problems. With advances in medical knowledge and technology, people are living longer with chronic illnesses which limit their ability to function fully in daily activities. The need for care is now often measured in years and even decades.

At the same time, families can no longer assume that a daughter-in-law will be available to serve as the sole caregiver. Declining birth rates through the second half of the 20th century limit the possibilities demographically. Moreover, even when there is a daughter-in-law, she is likely to be contributing to the household income though paid employment,[2] and/or has responsibilities for caring for her own parents as well as her in-laws. Geographical mobility necessitated by employers and personal preferences of members of both the older and younger generations have also led to the nuclearisation of the family. Whereas as late as 1960, the great majority of those 65 years of age and older

[2] In 2005, 48.4 per cent of women aged 15 to 64 participated in the labour force (Statistics Bureau, 2006).

were living with an adult child, in 2003 only 24.1 per cent were in three-generation households and another 11.8 per cent lived with an unmarried child (Naikakufu 2005b). By the late 1990s, the proportion of older people responding to public opinion polls who wished to reside separately from their adult children was nearly equal to those who wanted to co-reside (Naikakufu 1994 and Sōmuchō 2000). Who will care for elderly parents in the future, and especially who will do the hands-on work of care giving, has become a topic of discussion and sometimes negotiation prior to marriage (Traphagan 2003; Jenicke 2003). That a daughter-in-law's care giving is not assumed and that the issue is discussed at all is a dramatic change from the early 20th century situation.

Although a daughter-in-law remains the preferred caregiver for many who grew up in the earlier period, the relationship of the family member to the person needing care has become much more varied due to these changes in longevity, fertility, residence, and employment patterns. By 2001, as shown in Table 1, the most common caregiver of a frail elderly person was the spouse (25.8 per cent of caregivers). Since co-residing with an adult child is now the exception, when an elderly person requires assistance with daily living, care giving is likely to fall on a spouse regardless of preparation or willingness. Because women generally outlive their husbands, and because care giving is generally associated with feminine roles, more wives than husbands provide care for a spouse. But the proportion of male caregivers has grown. Husbands now constitute over 8 per cent of caregivers nationally (Naikakufu 2004: 39). The reliance on a spouse as the most likely caregiver represents a generational shift in caregiving. It brings with it new challenges for physical strength, learning new skills later in life, and the need to redefine past roles and relationships.

Daughters-in-law still comprise over 22 per cent of caregivers of the elderly. It is still common in cases of co-residence. However women of both generations voice a preference to care for their own mothers and to be cared for by their own daughters, a relationship expected to be emotionally close and uncomplicated by concerns about unwanted judgment or unwanted dependency. Daughters were the main caregivers in 12 per cent of elder care situations nationally in 2001. Out of a sense of responsibility or because their wives refuse to do so, sons, some retired and some still employed, comprise nearly 8 per cent of caregivers (see Table 1). Although in some families, care giving tasks are shared by a husband and wife or among siblings, in general one

Table 1. Main Family Caregivers of Long Term Care Insurance Care Recipients, 2001.

| | |
|---|---|
| Husband | 8.2 |
| Wife | 17.6 |
| Son | 7.6 |
| Daughter | 12.3 |
| Daughter-in-law | 22.1 |
| Son-in-law | 0.5 |
| Other co-residing relative | 2.8 |
| Non-co-residing relative | 7.5 |
| Paid service providers | 9.3 |
| Other | 2.5 |
| Unknown | 9.6 |

Source: Naikakufu (2004: 39).

person is still considered the person responsible for the elderly relative. The increased array of caregivers means that more people are crossing generational and gender lines to take up new tasks and roles.

Moreover, care giving tasks themselves have changed. The work of assisting an elderly person with a chronic illness has expanded to include not only cooking, cleaning, and bathing, but also things like passive exercise of a stroke victim, feeding through nasogastric tubes, and giving injections. New concepts of proper care emphasize rehabilitation and mobility rather than bed rest. With financial assistance from the long term care insurance programme, the physical environment of the home may be modified to create "barrier-free" entrances and to install grab bars and railings. Wheel chairs and walkers are common furnishings in the homes of frail elderly people. Western-style toilets and portable toilets for those unable to get to the family toilet have generally replaced the older squat-style toilets, and hospital beds with adjustable positions frequently take the place of futon spread on *tatami* floors. The 21st century family caregiver is expected to utilize, as needed, disposable diapers and special cushions to prevent bedsores. Classes in elder care are offered by local government welfare offices and by private nursing homes. Some specialize in assisting older men to become caregivers for wives by teaching them cooking, bathing others, and other tasks that would previously have been done by the wives. Other classes advise people on how best to deal with problems presented by living with someone with Alzheimer's disease or stroke. Thus caregiving is not only for longer periods than in the past with a wider variety of family caregivers, but is also more complex.

Since the daughter-in-law is no longer the assumed caregiver, the question of motivation comes into play. The burdens of caregiving, both past and present, include the physical strain caused by assisting an older adult and the lack of sleep due to caregiving responsibilities Caregivers are also emotionally exhausted, especially when relatives have dementia and behavioural problems.[3] The mental strain is caused in part by the demands on them to provide good care both from their own sense of worth and from the watchful eyes of extended kin and neighbours. Daughters-in-law complain that siblings and their spouses criticize their care giving with little understanding of the difficulties of the job. Husbands may harp on their wives regarding their care of their parents but offer little or no assistance. The relative receiving the care may be demented or crabby, demanding much and offering little in the way of thanks. These burdens are part of the public discourse of ageing and care giving and thus offer little incentive for people to step up to assume these responsibilities. Thus, many family caregivers are assisting by default. They are the assumed caregiver or the co-residing family member, so they take up the tasks as necessary. But other caregivers are motivated by personal relationships, by a desire to "pay back" a parent or a spouse for past care, by a belief that family care is better than institutional care, or by a lack of satisfaction with the care provided by another relative. Some spouses, children, and daughters-in-law gain satisfaction from the caregiver role. Other times, care giving or even its potential, leads to tension, arguments, divorce, career changes, and/ or depression.

Thus in the early 21st century, family care giving has become an increasingly common but more diverse experience. The former expectations of generation and gender regarding who would be the main caregiver have been dramatically altered so that spouses, men, and daughters now frequently take on care giving tasks. Moreover the role itself has become more diversified, requiring more specialized knowledge and skills.

[3] For descriptions and research on caregiver burden in Japan, see Anbäcken (1997), Jenike (1997), Okamoto (1988), Sodei (1994), and Webb (2002). Generally, Japanese research on caregiver burden adapts standardized scales developed abroad, such as the Zarit scale, to measure feelings of burden, as in Arai *et al.* (2004).

## 2. The Incorporation of Non-Family Care Providers into Home Care

Related to the changes regarding family caregivers is the expansion of responsibility for home-based care beyond the family. Most broadly, this has come in the form of national policy decisions leading to increasing assumption of government responsibility for the welfare of its elderly citizens. As described elsewhere in this volume, government bureaucrats watched the rapid ageing of Japan and began studying ways to respond as early as the mid-1960s (Campbell 2000). In addition to the economic basis of concern was what Akiko Hashimoto (1996) has called "structured security". By this she means a protective approach to old age security that guarantees certainty and predictability. That the government would take the lead in providing this was little challenged. The questions were what was needed and how to fund it. The first major initiative concerning care of the frail elderly in particular was the 1990 Gold Plan that set standards and targets for the development of institutional and home-based services that would provide "care security". When these targets were deemed insufficient, they were revised upward in 1995. The policy of the Gold Plan and its revision established pilot and demonstration projects and began a surge of building residential facilities and establishing home care services, especially home helpers, visiting nurses, respite care, and day care. Educational programmes for care workers were developed. Many of these services were administered by local governments, but there was also political pressure in the 1990s to revamp the legal status of non-governmental organizations. The interest of some of them in providing services for the elderly in part helped in the passage of the 1998 NPO law. These local governmental and NPO services were extremely limited in quantity, and in many areas providers could offer assistance only to the frail elderly who were living alone or with an elderly spouse only. Those qualifying for day care might be able to attend only one day per week due to heavy demand. Considering further expansion of services through tax revenue to be unrealistic, the government turned to the insurance model of the Long Term Care Insurance System. Nonetheless, the Gold Plan interventions were important contributions to the process of de-stigmatizing nursing homes and service providers coming in to private homes.

By the time the long term care insurance system was operating in 2000, many, but not all, family caregivers welcomed the assistance. After decades of government-led programmes and the study of ways in which various other countries dealt with the challenges of mass longevity, the Long Term Care Insurance System was established based on universal access and shared costs. All Japanese citizens or long term residents aged 40 and over paid premiums, which were matched by local and national tax revenues to finance the system. People 65 and older or with certain "diseases of ageing" were eligible for various services depending on their ability to function in activities of daily living (ADL). Recipients were classified into care levels, each of which had a monetary value in services associated with it.

Even with a gradual start to the programme, this vast new initiative created a tremendous demand for elder care services. Service providers might be the local governments which had previously developed programmes under the Gold Plan. However, most growth in the new system was in the provision of services by private, for-profit corporations and by non-profit organizations. This led to a rash of new businesses and to the expansion of previously existing corporations into the elder care market, some of which have proven to be successful. Others have not stayed in business in the years since the beginning of the programme. Examples of the business opportunities greatly expanded by the introduction of the long term care system are: adult day services, home nursing (visiting nurses), institutionally-provided respite care (short stay service), home medical equipment suppliers, care management services, and home helpers, which are aides providing personal care assistance and in some cases where no one in the household is able, housekeeping assistance.

This has of course created a large job market for care workers. Local bureaucrats and physicians have roles to play in the process of certification. A new category of workers called "care managers" emerged to arrange for and coordinate services in line with eligibility and the client's and family's wishes. (Clients or family caregivers may serve as their own care managers, but the majority of participants utilize a paid manager.) Care managers often have a background in nursing, home care, or social work, but universities are increasingly offering social welfare majors which could lead to this career option. When the long term care system was introduced, care managers minimally needed at least five years of experience, special coursework, and to pass an examination.

Nurses' work options increased, not only with care management opportunities, but also with home nursing, which offers greater autonomy than hospital or clinic work. Home nurses may establish their own businesses or may work in the employment of for-profit agencies, government health or welfare departments, hospitals, nursing homes, or the local medical association. Rehabilitation workers, including physical therapists and occupational therapists, have become more common with the introduction of the public long-term care insurance because of greater demand and the response of educational institutions to that demand by creating new training programmes for these workers.

Home helpers, like nurses, may work for corporations, the local government, or non-profit agencies, but the job of home helper requires less education. However home helpers must take classes for several months and be certified through passing an examination. It was at first considered a job for middle-aged women re-entering the labour force, but reasonable pay, status resulting from certification, and the sense for some that they are doing something worthwhile has led to a great deal of interest in care work by men as well as women. Aides are employed in residential facilities and day care centres as well as in home care.

How has this changed home care? One change seems consistent with one of the goals of the long term care programme, that older people are able to obtain support to stay longer in their own homes with minimal or no family assistance because they have paid service providers to perform some caregiving tasks. As of 2001, the majority of long term care insurance recipients are co-residing with relatives.[4] However with the rapid growth of single person and couple households of elderly people, it is not surprising to find that 15.7 per cent of care recipients are living alone and 18 per cent are living only with a spouse (Naikakufu 2004: 37–38). Services are not sufficient to allow the most impaired people to continue to live independently, but among those at lower care levels, the paid service providers play an important role in maintaining greater independence from family, a goal valued by many older people who voice that they do not wish to become a burden on their children.

Once an elderly person has been certified as eligible for a certain level of care, the person and his or her family decides which if any

[4] The largest proportion, 32.5 per cent are residing in three-generation families with an adult child, and another 11 per cent are living with an unmarried child. In addition, some of the 22.4 per cent in "other types of households" are people living with an adult child and his or her spouse only, but the exact proportion is unclear from published statistics (Naikakufu 2004: 37–38).

services they wish to use within the allowance given for that care level.[5] For example, an 87-year old woman in a small town who had diabetes and was extremely frail was classified as Care Level 3 (a middle level of impairment). Through the insurance system, the family rented a walker and a wheel chair for her. They had done some minimal remodelling, including installing grab bars in the bath and toilet rooms. A care manager came once a month, as required by the system. However since the son was retired and willing to be the caregiver, the family decided not to use any additional services for which she would have been eligible, including day care, respite care, and personal care from a home helper. The son explained that his mother was hard of hearing and had difficulty seeing, and did not want to spend time with others at a day care centre. In another family in the same area, a frail and forgetful 91-year old woman was similarly classified at Care Level 3. Her daughter-in-law was the primary caregiver. This family made greater use of insurance programme services: a care manager, day care two days a week which the sociable mother-in-law enjoyed, and 60 days of respite care spread through the year. The family had also done some home remodelling and the daughter-in-law had attended caregiving classes. Others at the same care level could select other combinations of services. People at lower care levels would have a lower total of benefits, but might still, for example, utilize day care twice a week but not use respite care.

With a complicated schedule of services outside and inside the home, one way that the role of the family caregiver has changed is that the job now requires some familiarity with the system, judgment of the quality of services (since the care manager and other service providers can be changed at the individual's or family's request), and a great deal of coordination of caregiving tasks. Outside services also provide some relief to family caregivers both from the intensity of 24-hour responsibility and from specific tasks. For example, a typical day at a day care centre includes rehabilitation or light exercise, lunch, a craft activity, rest time, social time which might include music or games,

[5] In 2004, 15.7 per cent of the eligible population (primarily those 65 years old and older) were certified eligible for long term care services. Of those certified to receive benefits, 82.5 per cent actually utilized services (of these, 75.6 per cent used home-based services and 24.4 per cent were in residential facilities). From 2000, when the system was introduced, the number utilizing some home-based services has increased 94 per cent (Naikakufu 2005a).

and a bath. Bathing an adult with strength and mobility problems in most Japanese homes is extremely difficult. Family caregivers whose relatives attend day care several times a week are spared that task since it is done by aides in larger spaces with specialized equipment at the centre. Outside service providers may have knowledge that they can teach to family caregivers, for example, ways to respond to demented care recipients, or their work may provide assistance with some of the skilled or technical elements of contemporary care giving.

On the other hand, benefits to family caregivers are sometimes countered by new stressors. Frail participants may return from the stimulation of a day at the day care centre exhausted. Some are pleased to go and enjoy the time with the care workers and other older people in the community, but others complain they are bored with the activities and find it depressing to witness the severity of physical and mental problems of the other participants. Some family caregivers claim that regression in mobility occurs during respite care at nursing homes (although others find the rehabilitation there to be better than they can do at home) or complain that the care workers there allow the elderly person to become too dependent. Although home nurses dress wounds such as bedsores and change feeding tubes, the family caregiver often serves as an aide, heating water, fetching supplies, and so on. Aides wash hair, help with toileting, and provide companionship. Where there is no family caregiver able to do so, aides may also shop, do laundry, clean, and cook. Yet for some families there is still a reluctance to open their private home life to strangers, and some elderly people resent that they get this care from paid strangers rather than the expected family members.

Regardless of the assessment of whether long term care services reduce the family caregiver's feeling of burden (Arai *et al.* 2004; Kumamoto *et al.* 2006), there is no doubt that the incorporation of paid outsiders into shared responsibility is a dramatic departure from past approaches to family care giving.

## 3. Changing Meanings of Elder Care

These trends in who provides care suggest that the cultural meaning and styles of caregiving are also changing. Ethnographic interviews suggest that in the past, ideal caregiving was characterized by three factors beyond the accomplishments of the caregiving tasks themselves.

One was that the caregiver by physically present. This is consistent with the expectation that co-residence was the basis of caregiving, but as Caudill and Weinstein (1969) suggested for maternal care of infants, the caregiver was not only in the same house, but was ideally nearby at all times to be able to respond to the needs and wishes, spoken or unspoken, of the ill or frail relative. Another element of ideal care giving was the creation of the proper atmosphere for rest and healing. Terms such as calm and cheerful characterize such an atmosphere, in which conflict was to be avoided and unpleasant topics remain unacknowledged. Moreover, these things were a sole caregiver's responsibilities. For that person, the caregiver role was to be central to and defining of the individual's status and life style during the period of care giving. Following from the expectation of continuous presence with the care recipient, other responsibilities that would interfere with good care should be compromised or postponed, including outside employment. To juggle multiple responsibilities would lead to a loss of focus on the care recipient and disturb the calm atmosphere required for good care (Long 1997).

Such an ideal, of course, never assured its reality in practice. What has changed is that other types of care giving have become legitimate alternatives. Son and daughter caregivers might continue to work away from home, depending on home helpers to cover the care giving responsibilities during the day. Some family caregivers now consider it good care to confront a stroke victim who does not feel like exercising, or to insisting that a shy senior try the day care programme. These newer approaches are based on new ideals taught by class instructors, care managers, nurses, and physicians, and extensively covered in the media. Skilled care managers arrange for respite care to give stressed caregivers a break rather than focus solely on the wishes of the frail older person. The unpleasant topic of institutionalization can now be discussed more openly in at least some homes. Thus, a transformation of the meaning of caring for an elderly person results from a complex set of interrelated factors: new public policy, adjustments in who is providing care and the skills they bring to the job, and changing attitudes about the relationship between the individual and society.

The type of care giving that represented the ideal of the past continues to exist. But along side of it are a new variety of acceptable and even ideal approaches. In one home, the son and daughter-in-law had different images of good care for the impaired mother. To the son, what was most important was to demonstrate his support by doing as much as possible for her, even when she did not ask for assistance. He felt that his job was to be there and to respond to her needs. The daughter-in-law was a nurse who had been taught the importance of maintaining function by acting independently. Her approach was to care for her mother-in-law by allowing her to do as much as possible on her own. Although the daughter-in-law's approach is the one currently sanctioned by the experts from the medical and social service communities, in the early 21st century family caregivers choose from a range of caregiving styles the approaches and methods they think most appropriate for their situation.

Having multiple, culturally legitimate options for providing care, however, does not assure adjustment to the new realities. The elderly of today grew up in an era in which female, family care giving was presumed and problems not discussed outside the house. Some older people believe it is appropriate to become frail and dependent when they are in their 90s; others are ready to embrace newer models of remaining active and social despite physical or mental limitations. Yet it is not always about individual choice. New constraints and expectations result in quiet home-bodies sent to day care, and men in their 80s take classes on how to do household tasks formerly defined as feminine. Dependency on new technologies requires new skills and definitions of self. Relationships with children change with unwanted dependency on non-normative caregivers. Unhappy marriages are revealed to outsiders and acknowledged to oneself. These social adjustments are part of what it means to age and to care for others in the new "society of longevity."

For both caregiver and care recipient, the meaning of elder care in Japan is thus undergoing rapid change due to the demographic shifts and technological developments of the last century and the policies of the 21st century. Care giving requires more expertise and new skills. The primary family caregiver can no longer be assumed to be available to do the job, leading to greater variation in who in the family takes on the role of caregiver. Non-family members provide services both in and outside of the home. There is a new emphasis on rehabilitation and independence. Perhaps the most significant change is that care giving is no longer the responsibility of one person in the family, but rather is a balancing of responsibilities among government, paid care providers, family, and self.

## References

Anbäcken, Els-Marie (1997): *Who Cares? Culture, Structure, and Agency in Caring for the Elderly in Japan*. Stockholm: Stockholm East Asian Monographs, No. 9.

Arai, Yumiko, Keiko Kumamoto, Masakazu Washio, Teruko Ueda, Hiroko Miura and Kei Kudo (2004): Factors Related to Feelings of Burden among Caregivers Looking After Impaired Elderly in Japan under the Long-Term Care Insurance System. In: *Psychiatry and Clinical Neurosciences* 58, pp. 396–402.

Campbell, John C. (2000): Changing Meanings of Frail Old People and the Japanese Welfare State. In: Long, Susan Orpett (ed.): *Caring for the Elderly in Japan and the US: Practices and Policies*. London: Routledge, pp. 82–97.

Caudill, William and Helen Weinstein (1969): Maternal Care and Infant Behavior in Japan and America. In: *Psychiatry* 32, pp. 12–43.

Hashimoto, Akiko (1996): *The Gift of Generations: Japanese and American Perspectives on Aging and the Social Contract*. New York: Cambridge University Press.

Jenike, Brenda Robb (1997): Home-Based Health Care for the Elderly in Japan: A Silent System of Gender and Duty. In: Formanek, Susanne and Sepp Linhart (eds.): *Aging: Asian Concepts and Experiences, Past and Present*. Vienna: Verlag der Österreichischen Akademie der Wissenschaften, pp. 329–346.

—— (2003): Parent Care and Shifting Family Obligations in Urban Japan. In: Traphagan, John W. and John Knight (eds.): *Demographic Change and the Family in Japan's Aging Society*. Albany: State University of New York Press, pp. 177–202.

Kumamoto, Keigo, Yumiko Arai and Steven H. Zarit (2006): Use of Home Care Services Effectively Reduces Feelings of Burden among Family Caregivers of Disabled Elderly in Japan: Preliminary Results. In: *International Journal of Geriatric Psychiatry* 21, 2, pp. 163–170.

Long, Susan Orpett (1997): Risōteki na kaigo to wa? Amerika kara mita Nihon no rinen to genjitsu [What is ideal care giving? Japanese ideals and reality from an American's perspective]. In: *Hosupisu to zaitaku kea* [Hospice and home care] 5, 1, pp. 37–43.

Naikakufu [Cabinet Office] (1994): *Kōreisha hitorigurashi, fūfu setai ni kansuru ishiki chōsa kekka no yōyaku* [Summary of the results of the public opinion survey concerning the elderly living alone or in an elderly couple household]. http://www8.cao.go.jp/kourei/ishiki/h06_kiso/h06–gaiyo.html (found 22/01/2007).

—— (2004): *Kōrei shakai hakusho* [White Paper on the ageing society]. Tokyo: Gyōsei.

—— (2005a): Hyō 1–2–36, yokaigotō kōreisha no joken (Yokaigotō ninteisha-sū) [Table 1–2–36: The situation of elderly care recipients. (Numbers of people certified to receive care)]. In: *Heisei 17–nenpan kōrei shakai hakusho* [The 2005 annual report on the ageing society]. http://www8.cao.go.jp/kourei/whitepaper/w-2005/zenbun/html/H1232100.html (found 22/01/2007).

—— (2005b): Zu 1-2–1, setai kōzōbetsu ni mita 65–sai ijō no mono no iru setaisū oyobi kōsei wariai no suii [Figure 1–2–1: Changes in number and proportion of households containing persons 65 and older by household composition]. In: *Heisei 17-nenpan kōrei shakai hakusho* [The 2005 White Paper on the ageing society]. http://www8.cao.go.jp/kourei/whitepaper/w-2005/zenbun/html/H1211000.html (found 22/01/2007).

Okamoto, Hideaki. (1988): Zaitaku chihōsei rōjin no kaigosha no nayami [Problems of caregivers of demented elderly in the home]. In: *Rōnen shakai kagaku* [Social gerontology] 10, 1, pp. 75–90.

Sodei, Takako (1995): Care of the Elderly: A Woman's Issue. In: Fujimura-Fanselow, Kumiko and Atsuko Kameda (eds.): *Japanese Women: New Feminist Perspectives on the Past, Present, and Future*. New York: The Feminist Press at the City College of New York, pp. 247–254.

Sōmuchō (Management and Coordination Agency) (2000): *Heisei 11-nendo kōreisha hitorigurashi, fūfu setai ni kansuru ishiki chōsa kekka no yōyaku* [Summary of the results of the 1999 public opinion survey concerning the elderly living alone or in an elderly couple household]. http://www8.cao.go.jp/kourei/ishiki/h11_kiso/html/0-1.html (found 22/01/2007).

Statistics Bureau (Ministry of Internal Affairs and Communications) (2005): *Labor Force Survey: 2005 Yearly Average Results*. http://www.stat.go.jp/English/data/roudou/zuhyou/1542.xls (found 22/01/2007).

Traphagan, John W. (2003): Contesting Coresidence: Women, In-laws, and Health Care in Rural Japan. In: Traphagan, John W. and John Knight (eds.): *Demographic Change and the Family in Japan's Aging Society*. Albany: State University of New York Press, pp. 203–228.

Webb, Philippa (2002): Time to Share the Burden: Long Term Care Insurance and the Japanese Family. In: *Japanese Studies* 22, 2, pp. 113–129.

CHAPTER TWELVE

# INCOME INEQUALITY IN THE AGEING SOCIETY

Sawako Shirahase

## 1. Introduction

The total fertility rate hit an all time low of 1.26 in 2005. The downward trend has continued for decades in Japan since the rate fell below 2.00 in 1975. Since then, Japan's population is rapidly ageing. The share of persons aged 65 and over was 20.2 per cent in 2005 and it took only 24 years to increase the proportion of those aged 65 and over from 7 per cent to 14 per cent (National Institute of Population and Social Security Research 2006). The speed of population ageing accelerated during the 1990s when the long-term economic recession took place.

Figure 1 shows the ageing index computed by the ratio of the population aged 65 and over to that aged 0 to 14 years and a particularly high increase in the ageing index can be seen after 1990. Japan is character-

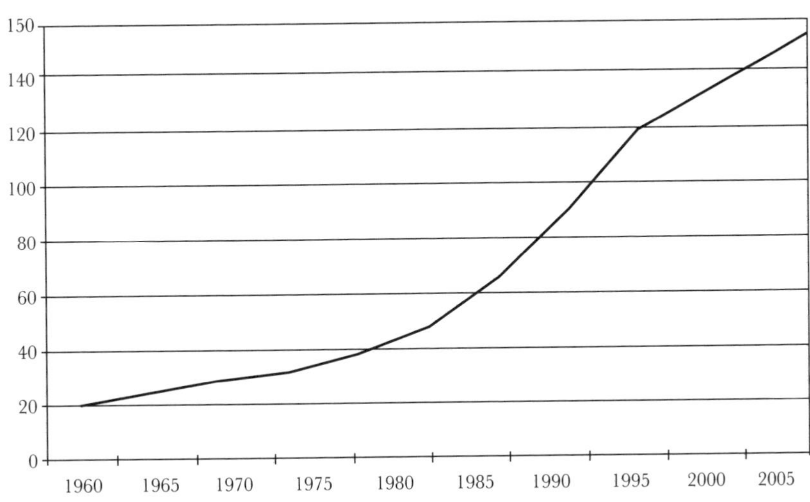


Source: National Institute of Population and Social Security Research (2007): Latest Demographic Statistics 2007.

Figure 1. Trend in ageing index since 1960.

ized by a fast speed of ageing and the continuous decline of the fertility rate. Rapid transformation of the demographic structure brought about generational imbalance between beneficiaries and contributors in the Japanese social security system. The burden of the working population to support the elderly increased in as much the proportion of the retired population grew. In fact, the younger generation displays doubts on the sustainability of Japan's social security system, and they feel that they can no longer rely on the benefits of a social security system for their well-being when they are aged (MHLW 2003).

The main purpose of this chapter is to discuss the impact of a rapid change in the demographic structure on income inequality. The economist Fumio Ohtake (2005) claims that most of the increase in income inequality after the 1980s in Japan can be explained by the ageing of population. He provides convincing evidence, but he does not offer sufficient explanation about the significance of the high extent of income inequality among the elderly. I therefore would like to explore income inequality among the elderly population from a sociological perspective. The ageing of population does not simply mean the increase in the number of persons aged 65 and over, but is accompanied by a change in the structure of households in which the elderly reside. The household is one of the key concepts in social stratification studies (Acker 1979, 1980; Goldthorpe 1980; Ōsawa 2002) and it is the basic unit in which the level of consumption is determined among individual members. In this chapter, I will focus on the household in which the elderly spend their daily life and examine the extent of income inequality by household type.

Traditionally, Japanese elderly used to satisfy their needs of livelihood security through sharing the household with their child's family, typically represented by the three-generation households. However by now, the number of three-generation households has declined, while the number of one-person households and couple-only households has increased. On the other hand, young people's marriage rate has dropped, and the number of adult unmarried children who stay in their parental home has increased. Such a change in the demographic behaviour of young people also leads to changes in the household structure. As a result, the number of nuclear households in which parents and their unmarried adult children co-reside has increased, while the number of three-generation households where a young household head is co-residing with parents and small children has declined. Further, following the increase in the divorce rate, the number of one-parent families with small children has increased even though its number is still relatively small. Thus, reflecting changes in people's lives, the composition of household structure has largely shifted, and I will examine whether the changes in income inequality are associated with those demographic changes.

## 2. Ageing of Population and Income Inequality

The proportion of persons aged 65 and over has increased from 5.7 per cent in 1960 to 20.2 per cent in 2005, and more than a fifth of the total population belongs to this age group now. As Figure 1 shows, the ratio of the persons aged 65 and over to that aged 0 to 14 years largely increased from 19.1 in 1960 to 146.5 in 2005. However, the ageing of population does not simply mean an increase in the proportion of the persons aged 65 and over, but the household structure also changes according to the transformation of the population structure. Under the Japanese-type welfare state where the family played an important role in providing welfare services to family members, the type of household had an important influence on the living conditions of the elderly.

Figure 2 presents the proportion of the households with elderly members, which continuously increased from 21.7 per cent in 1975

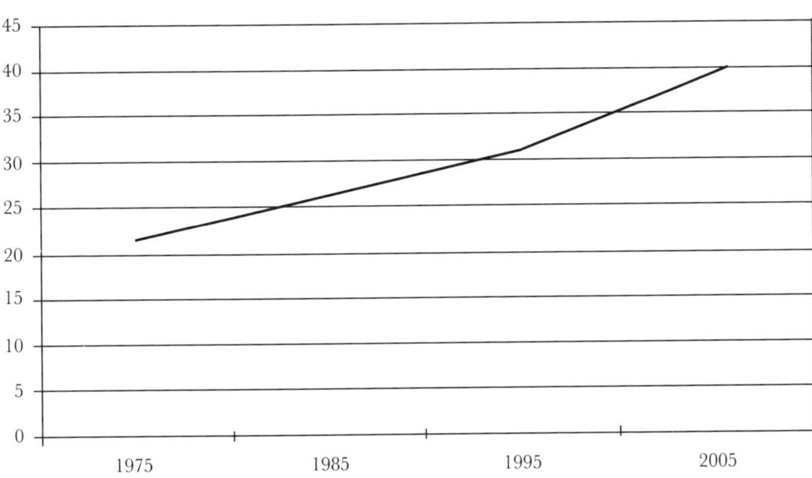


Source: National Institute of Population and Social Security Research (2007): *Latest Demographic Statistics 2007*.

Figure 2. Proportion of the households with the elderly (%).

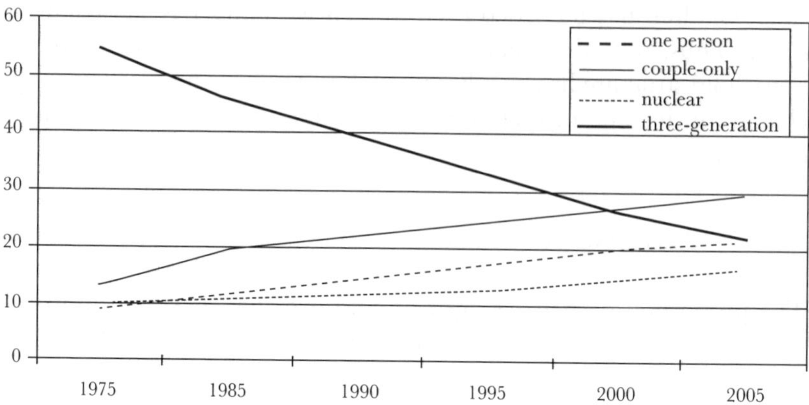


Source: National Institute of Population and Social Security Research (2007): *Latest Demographic Statistics 2007*.

Figure 3. Household type among those with the elderly aged 65 and over (%).

to 39.3 per cent in 2005 (MHLW 2004). Recently more than one third of total households include elderly. What kind of households do older persons live in? The types of households with elderly members are divided into five categories: (1) one-person household, (2) couple-only household, (3) nuclear household where only parents and their unmarried child(ren) co-reside, (4) three-generation household, and (5) other-type household.

Figure 3 shows the distributional change in the types of households with elderly members. The most obvious change in Figure 3 is the large decline of the share of three-generation households. On the other hand, the proportion of couple-only households and that of one-person households increased between 1975 and 2005 from 13.1 per cent to 29.2 per cent, and from 8.6 per cent to 22.0 per cent, respectively. It means that the cases where the elderly received support from the younger generation within the same household significantly declined. On the other hand, the elderly-only households consisting of one person living alone and couple-only households increased significantly from 15 per cent in 1975 to 44.0 per cent in 2005. What does such a change in the household structure mean for the living conditions of older persons? Let us examine the relationship between the household structure among the elderly and income inequality.

## 3. Did the Income Inequality Expand?

Japan is the first Asian society which achieved a mature level of industrialization (Vogel 1979; Ōkouchi *et al.* 1973). Due to its peculiar process of late but rapid industrialization (Dore 1973; Cole 1979), Japan's development took a different character than the countries in Europe and North America. At the same time, in Japan, a middle-class society has emerged and the homogeneity of the Japanese society has been emphasized in the 1970s and 1980s.

Murakami (1977, 1984) was the one who initiated the debate by designating Japan as a "new mass middle-class" (*shin chūkan taishū*) society. According to him, Japanese people shared increasingly similar life styles and attitudes, and therefore became very homogeneous. The intermediate stratum of Japanese society grew continuously and a class-less mass society emerged in Japan. On the contrary, Kishimoto (1977) insisted on the existence of social class in Japan. Tominaga (1979) joined this debate by proposing the notion of status inconsistency among education, income and occupational prestige, stating that status inconsistency contributes to the blurring of class boundaries. Status inconsistency means that different levels of social status coexist in one person (Imada and Hara 1979), such as a person with a high educational credential has a low level of income but identifies himself with the members of higher social class.

Sawyer (1976) has claimed that the extent of income inequality in Japan is one of the lowest among OECD countries, based on his cross-national study in the 1970s. His finding was welcomed by the advocates of the homogeneous mass middle-class society, and it confirmed the image according to which all Japanese people share the middle-class consciousness and similar life styles. However, after the bubble economy ended in the 1990s, people were increasingly suspicious about the claim of Japan being an equal society. Reflecting increased suspicion about equality, *Nihon no keizai kakusa* [Economic inequality in Japan], written by the economist Toshiaki Tachibanaki (1998) and *Fubyōdō shakai Nihon* [Unequal Society, Japan] written by the sociologist Toshiki Satō (2000), attracted attention. Tachibanaki's publication sent a shocking message stating that Japan's income distribution is as unequal as that of the United States. Satō (2000) claimed that Japan became a class society with limited intergenerational mobility into the upper white-collar class, and the new social trend that sons originating from higher white-collar class background disproportionately enjoy a high chance to inherit an upper white-collar status can be found.

After World War II, the extent of income inequality declined. However, it became larger in the 1950s and declined again in the era of high economic growth. Kanomata (1999), based on his analyses of the Social Stratification and Mobility (SSM) survey, agrees with the pattern of change in the extent of income inequality until the 1970 as mentioned above, but he states that income inequality became larger in the mid 1970s at the time when the first oil shock occurred. Satō (2000) claims that growing social mobility and income equality have continued until the beginning of the 1980s, followed by a reverse trend after which income inequality increased. He claims the V-shape pattern of change in the extent of income inequality since the high economic growth era.

Ishikawa (1991, 1994) and Tachibanaki and Yagi (1994) showed that Japan was not as equal in terms of income and capital distributions as many Japanese believed and denied that Japan was a homogeneous society. Hara and Seiyama (1999) and Ishida (2001) stated that the chances of intergenerational mobility have been more or less stable in post-war Japan. Ohtake and Saitō (1999) claimed that the recent expansion of income inequality can be largely explained by the ageing population and the increase of the number of dual-earner families (Ohtake 1994, 2000; Ohtake and Saitō 1998). Similarly, Nishizaki *et al.* (1998) showed that expansion of income inequality for the decade since 1984 was due to ageing population.

In my analyses, I will examine disposable income that is, subtracting the social insurance fees and tax from the total income. People do not live by themselves, but they share the basic consumption at the household level. However, there are one-person households and the households consisting of five members. It is possible to assume that the household income with larger number of household members is higher than the single person household. Therefore, I will take into account the difference in the number of household members and examine the economic well-being per person. If the extent of income inequality is represented by the gini coefficient[1] of the disposable income, it can be computed as follows.

[1] The Gini coefficient implies how large the gap between the hypothetical situation of the perfect equal distribution of income and the real distribution of income is. It ranges between 0 and 1. If the figure is close to 1, it means that the extent of income inequality is large, while if it is close to 0, the extent of income inequality is small.

$$Gini = \left(\frac{2}{\mu\, n^2}\cdot\sum_{k}^{n} k\, W_k\right) - \frac{n+1}{n} = \frac{2\,\mathrm{cov}\left(W_k, \frac{k}{n}\right)}{\mu} = \frac{\frac{2}{n}\sum_{k=1}^{n}(W_k - \mu).\left(\frac{k}{n} - \frac{1}{n^2}\sum_{k=1}^{n} k\right)}{\mu}$$

$W_k$ is the disposable income with the equivalent scale per person in the household $_k$, and $W_k$ can be calculated as $D_k/S_k^{\varepsilon}$. $D_k$ is the disposable income of the household $_k$, and $S_k$ is the number of household members in the household $_k$. ε is referred as an equivalence scale, and it is set to 0.5, following OECD studies in my analysis. $n$ is the total number of the households and $\mu$ is the mean disposable income of the total households. For instance, if ε is 1 (per capita), all the members of the household including a pre-school age child and a 70-year old elderly are treated equally and the economy by scale is regarded as none.

Figure 4 presents the trend in income inequality from the mid-1980s to the late 1990s, using the Comprehensive survey of living conditions

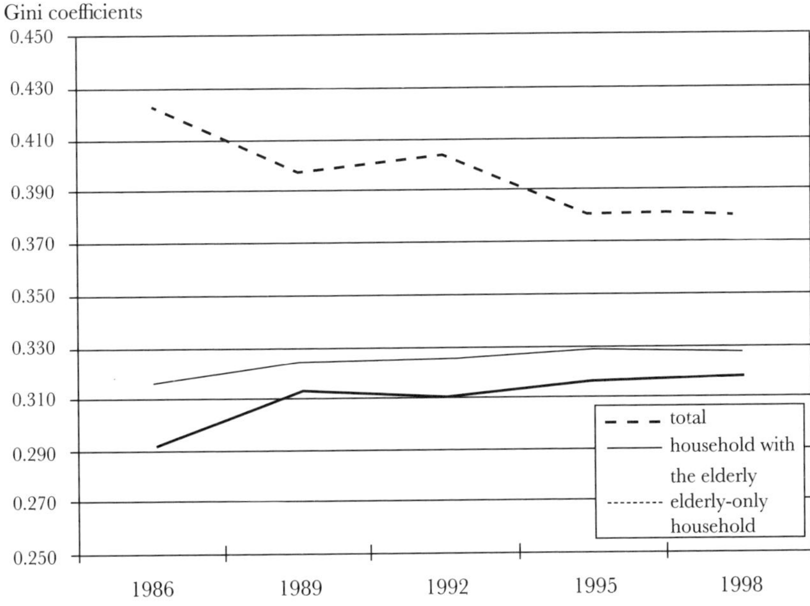


Source: MHLW (several years): *Kokumin seikatsu kiso chōsa* [Comprehensive survey of living conditions of the people on health and welfare].

Figure 4. Trend in gini coefficients by household type.

of the people on health and welfare (*Kokumin seikatsu kiso chōsa*).[2] Looking at gini coefficients for all households (the bold line), we saw that it increased from 0.293 in 1986 to 0.312 in 1989, and afterward it has been more or less stable during the 1990s. Figure 4 presents not only the gini coefficients for the total households but also those for the households with elderly members and those for the household consisting of only the elderly aged 65 and over. The gini coefficients of the households with elderly members are higher than the overall gini coefficients, and the extent of income inequality among the households with the elderly is higher than that among the entire households. The difference in the extent of income inequality between these two groups is becoming smaller, as the overall gini coefficients are becoming higher. Nevertheless, the extent of income inequality has been more or less stable among these two groups during the 1990s.

While the overall gini coefficients have been stable over the 1990s, the pattern of the trend in the extent of income inequality within different types of households differs. In fact, the elderly-only households consisting of the single person households and the couple-only households show different pattern of changing the extent of income inequality. The extent of income inequality improved from 0.423 in 1986 to 0.380 in 1998. On the other hand, Ohta (2004) claims that the substantial income inequality has increased using the panel survey whose respondents are in the 20s and 30s, and Higuchi (2004) similarly using the same panel data concluded that income inequality has expanded by the increase in the number of the homogamy of low-income and high-income couples.

Figure 5 presents the trend in the gini coefficients by the age of the household head since 1986. The most important finding is that there is a difference in the changing pattern in the gini coefficients among the relatively young head of the households and that among the elderly head of the households. Gini coefficients increased among the households whose heads are aged 20s and 30s. In particular, among the households whose heads are in the late 20s, the gini coefficients jumped from 0.228 in 1986 to 0.273 in 1998. Further, among the households whose heads

---

[2] My analyses in this paper, using the Comprehensive Survey of Living Conditions of the People on Health and Welfare, was supported by the research grant of Japan's Ministry of Health, Labour and Welfare. The title of the research grant was "The study of the new social security system corresponding to the changing families and working life in Japan," conducted from 2002 to 2005.

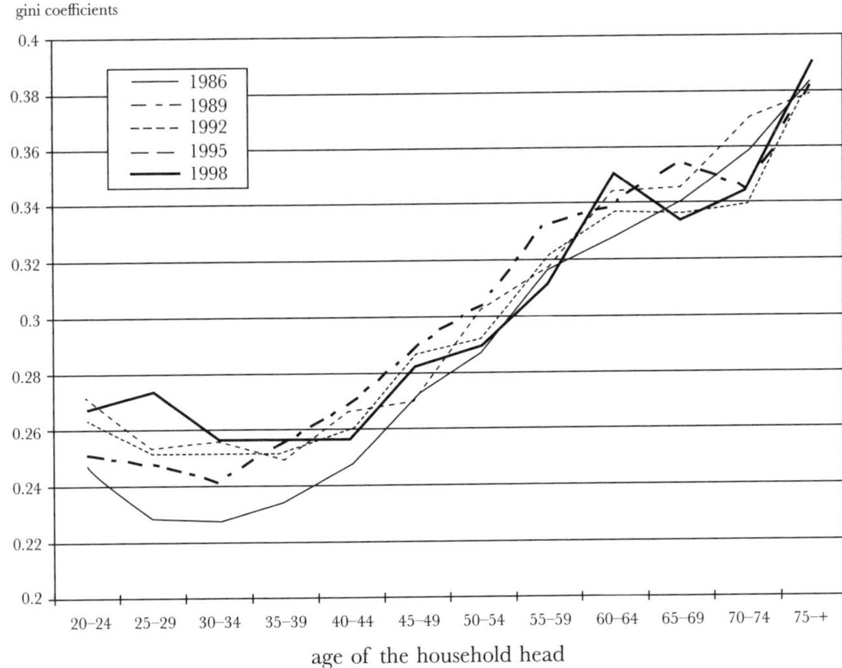


Source: MHLW (several years): *Kokumin seikatsu kiso chōsa* [Comprehensive survey of living conditions of the people on health and welfare].

Figure 5. Trend in gini coefficients by the age of household head.

are in the early 60s when many people enter the retired stage of their life course, the gini coefficient has recently become larger. One possible reason for the increase in the extent of income inequality among households whose heads are in the 20s and 30s and in the early 60s is probably due to the fact that the long-term economic recession directly hit the relatively vulnerable labour force, that is, relatively young people and old people who are about to enter the retired age.

On the other hand, the decline in the gini coefficients among the households of the head aged 65 and over, is largely due to improvement in the level of social security benefits including the increased level of public pension benefits. This result can be related to the criticism that Japan's social security is biased towards the elderly people, and does not fully take into account young families. Further, from Figure 5 it can be understood that the transition period to entering the retirement stage in the early 60s was not covered by the current social security system in Japan. However, it is not supposed that Japan's social security systems should easily shift their attention from the elderly to the younger people. While the extent of income inequality has decreased among the elderly, it is still true that the extent of income inequality among households with elderly members is relatively high compared with young and middle-aged households. In fact, the gini coefficient among the 25–29 age group is 0.273 in 1998 and that among the 65–69 age group is 0.334. The overall pattern of income inequality by age group remains the same. The extent of income inequality increases by age of the household head and it is highest among the elderly households. Therefore, one should not set in opposition young and old households in terms of social security and it cannot be easily concluded that the elderly people were no longer poor. It should not be underestimated that a substantially large extent of economic discrepancies can be seen at the later stage of life.

## 4. Income Inequality and the Households with the Elderly

Figure 6 presents the trend in gini coefficients by household type among households with elderly members. The household type which showed the highest gini coefficient is the male single household, that is, 0.495 in 1986. On the other hand, the household type in which the extent of income inequality is the lowest is the other-type household including three-generation households: its coefficient is 0.295 in 1986. The changing patterns in the extent of income inequality are not the same by household type. The gini coefficients among the male-single households have largely declined from 0.495 in 1986 to 0.395 in 1998. The female-single household does not show the same trend as their male counterparts: the gini coefficients increased from 0.336 in 1986 to 0.380 in 1992, and it declined to 0.365 in 1998. The couple-only household showed the same but a more gradual decline than the male-single household, and its coefficients declined from 0.406 in 1986 to 0.344 in 1998. However, the other-type households showed very little change, and its coefficient was 0.295 in 1986 and 0.303 in 1998. Thus, the overall trend in gini coefficients among all households with elderly members by household type is in the direction of declining inequality, and the extent of income inequality among different types of households is converging.

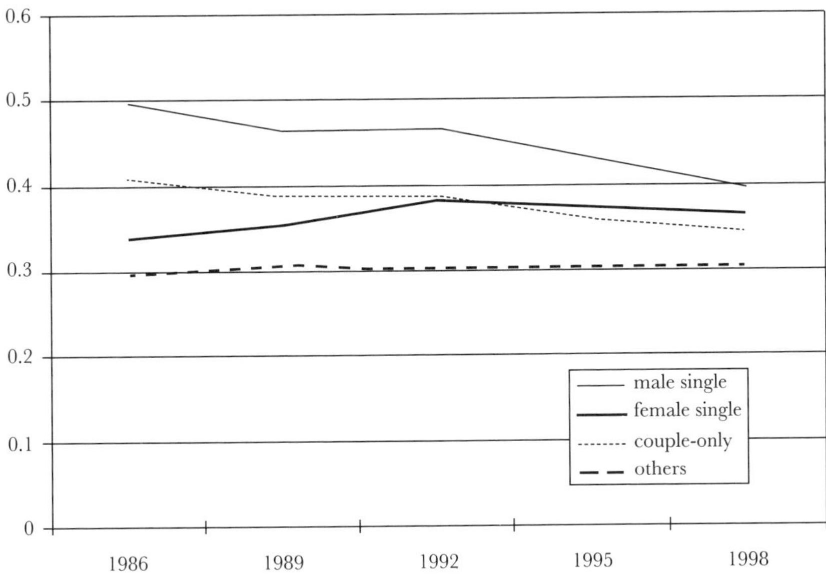


Source: MHLW (several years): *Kokumin seikatsu kiso chōsa* [Comprehensive survey of living conditions of the people on health and welfare].

Figure 6. Gini coefficients by the type of household with the elderly.

The next question is whether the economic well-being of the elderly who belong to different types of households is different. Table 1 shows the ratio of the median disposable income of the households with the elderly and the median disposable income of the elderly-only households to that of the households without the elderly. The ratio 100 means that there is no economic discrepancy compared with the household without the elderly.

Table 1. Ratio of mean disposable income by household type.

| | 1986 ratio | 1989 ratio | 1992 ratio | 1995 ratio | 1998 ratio |
|---|---|---|---|---|---|
| Household with the elderly | 104.40 | 101.28 | 102.66 | 104.91 | 106.14 |
| Elderly-only household | 53.02 | 59.50 | 59.85 | 63.82 | 64.75 |
| Household without elderly | 100.00 | 100.00 | 100.00 | 100.00 | 100.00 |

Source: MHLW (several years): *Kokumin seikatsu kiso chōsa* [Comprehensive survey of living conditions of the people on health and welfare].

Table 2. Ratio of mean disposable income by type of household with elderly members.

| | 1986 ratio | 1989 ratio | 1992 ratio | 1995 ratio | 1998 ratio |
|---|---|---|---|---|---|
| Male-single | 45.75 | 54.26 | 61.29 | 57.24 | 59.02 |
| Female-single | 35.57 | 44.39 | 37.85 | 40.13 | 41.11 |
| Couple-only | 64.63 | 69.99 | 69.34 | 71.49 | 71.15 |
| Other-type | 100.00 | 100.00 | 100.00 | 100.00 | 100.00 |

Source: MHLW (several years): *Kokumin seikatsu kiso chōsa* [Comprehensive survey of living conditions of the people on health and welfare].

The economic difference between the elderly-only households and the households without the elderly has narrowed, and the relative disadvantage of the elderly-only households was reduced: the ratio in 1986 was 53.0 and it became 64.8 in 1998. However, even in 1998 the median disposable income of the elderly-only household is about two thirds of that of the households without the elderly. On the other hand, the economic situation of the households where the elderly live with their young generation is relatively better-off, compared with the household without the elderly, and its advantage has increased recently since 1992. The economic well-being of the elderly who share their household with their offspring remains relatively advantageous.

Table 2 presents the relative difference in the median income by different type of household by further dividing the households with the elderly into four categories: (1) male-single household, (2) female-single household, (3) couple-only household, and (4) other-type household (where the elderly usually live with the younger generation). The relative disadvantage of the economic well-being among male-single household, female-single household, and couple-only household, compared with other-type household with the elderly was generally reduced. Even so, the economic well-being of the elderly living alone, particularly, female-single household, is still disadvantageous, compared with those living with the younger generation. In 1998, the median disposable income of the female-single household is 41.1, when the median disposable income of the other-type household is set at 100. In sum, the Japanese elderly are characterized by a large discrepancy in their level of economic well-being depending on what kind of household they belong to (Shirahase 2002).

Table 3. Income discrepancies by type of household with elderly members among industrial societies in mid 1990s (other-type = 100).

| | Japan ratio | U.S. ratio | U.K. ratio | Sweden ratio | Taiwan ratio |
|---|---|---|---|---|---|
| Male-single | 57.24 | 127.54 | 115.90 | 102.71 | 115.11 |
| Female-single | 40.13 | 99.43 | 106.10 | 101.97 | 85.87 |
| Couple-only | 71.49 | 116.74 | 95.96 | 87.19 | 91.67 |
| Other-type | 100.00 | 100.00 | 100.00 | 100.00 | 100.00 |

Source: MHLW (1995): *Kokumin seikatsu kiso chōsa* [Comprehensive survey of living conditions of the people on health and welfare]. Luxembourg Income Study for U.S., U.K., and Sweden in 1995.

As shown in Table 3, the relative disadvantage of economic well-being among Japanese female-only households is obvious, compared with those in other societies. The ratio of median disposable income of the female-single households to that of the other-type households is only 40.1 in 1995 in Japan. In contrast, the same ratios in the United States, United Kingdom, and Sweden are around 100, indicating no major difference in median income between the female-single households and the other-type households. Even in Taiwan where there is similar family structure to Japan, the ratio (85.9) is much larger than that of Japan. Large gaps in the economic well-being among the elderly by household type in Japan are partly derived from the Japanese-type welfare society where the family is expected to play an important role. The family has played a critical role in providing a basic livelihood security to their family members. Therefore, what kind of household type the elderly belong to is closely associated with the level of their economic well-being. On the other hand, in Europe and the United States, the elderly seldom share the same household with the younger generation, and the majority of them live alone or live with their spouse. The different types of households to which the elderly belong do not largely affect the extent of the economic well-being in Europe and the United States, as far as the results in Table 3 are concerned.

As I have already mentioned, in Japan, the number of three-generation households which provide the basic economic security to household members has declined, while the number of one-person household and couple-only household has increased. Reflecting these changes in the household structure among the elderly, we can no longer expect the family to perform the same social welfare function as before.

It is no doubt that a critical role in providing the basic livelihood security to the elderly will shift from the family to the state and that the social security system will gain more importance.

## 5. Discussion

According to my analyses of income inequality, it can be stated that income inequality among households composed of only the elderly is much higher than households which do not include elderly members in Japan because Japanese elderly live now in a variety of household types; 22.0 per cent live in single households, 29.2 per cent live in couple-only households, and 21.3 per cent of the elderly live in multi-generation households in 2005. Three-generation households used to be the typical living arrangement among the elderly in Japan, but its share has declined rapidly in the last ten years. In its place, one finds an increase in the households composed of single elderly people or of older couples. Nevertheless, the proportion of multi-generation households is still higher in Japan than in Europe and the United States. In fact, in Sweden, almost all elderly live either alone or with their spouse; similarly in Britain, less than 10 per cent of the elderly live with non-elderly family members.

Such a large difference in living arrangement between the Japanese elderly, and those in the European and American societies, appears to be directly responsible for larger income inequality among the elderly in Japan. In particular, living alone appears to have negative consequences for the economic well-being of the elderly, and the female-single household has the worst economic conditions in contemporary Japan. Since women tend to live longer than men and wives are generally younger than their husbands, elderly women face the risk of falling into the low-income groups after the death of their husbands. Indeed, the proportion of female-single households is gradually increasing in Japan, and the further improvement of the living conditions of these households will become a key policy issue. In contrast, in other societies, the degree of economic condition does not differ greatly by the type of household in which the elderly reside.

Smeeding and Saunders (1998) claim that co-residence with the younger generation can be a safety net for the elderly in Taiwan, and Japan appears to follow this pattern. Co-residence with non-elderly members leads to strengthening the economic level among the elderly, and in fact, the median disposable income of the households with the elderly is higher than that of the households without the elderly. This implies that the living arrangements have determinant consequences for the economic well-being of the elderly in Japanese society. One of the major reasons for a higher extent of income inequality among the elderly in Japan is due to a variety of living arrangements among the elderly.

We should no longer treat the elderly as one homogeneous group; a wide range in the level of economic well-being among the elderly should not be overlooked. The Japanese elderly as a whole are sometimes considered being in a favourable economic condition (Takayama and Arita 1996), but it does not necessarily mean that all the elderly are better off. Due to recent budget constrain by the Japanese government, the imbalance between the contributors (the younger generation) to the pension system and the beneficiaries (the older generation) of such a system is a major issue in reforming the social security system in Japan. Since we find that the elderly are by no means homogeneous in their level of economic well-being, the picture of the young versus the old generation is too simplistic. We then had better take into account the diversity in the economic situations among the elderly and consider the income redistribution within the older generation. In particular, the elderly who live alone face a high risk of falling into poverty in Japan. A policy specifically targeted at the economically disadvantaged elderly should therefore be seriously discussed.

## References

Acker, Joan (1973): Women and Social Stratification: A Case of Intellectual Sexism. In: *American Journal of Sociology* 78, pp. 936–45.

—— (1980): Women and Stratification: A Review of Recent Literature. In: *Contemporary Sociology* 9 (January), pp. 25–35.

Cole, Robert E. (1979): *Work, Mobility, and Participation: A Comparative Study of American and Japanese Industry*. Berkeley: University of California Press.

Dore, Ronald (1973): *British Factory—Japanese Factory*. Berkeley: University of California Press.

Goldthorpe, John H. (1983): Women and Class Analysis: In Defence of the Conventional View. In: *Sociology* 17 (November), pp. 465–88.

Hara, Junsuke and Kazuo Seiyama (1999): *Shakai kaisō yutakasa no naka no fubyōdō* [Social stratification: Inequality in the affluent society]. Tokyo: University of Tokyo Press.

Higuchi, Yoshio (2004): Defure ga kaeta josei no sentaku [Women's choices changed by the deflation]. In: Higuchi, Yoshio, Kiyoshi Ohta and Research Institute of Consumer Economics (eds.): *Joseitachi no Heisei fukyō*. Tokyo: Nihon Keizai Hyoron Sha, pp. 9–28.

Imada, Takatoshi and Junsuke Hara (1979): Shakaiteki chii no ikkansei to hi-ikkansei [Consistency and inconsistency of the social status]. In: Tominaga, Ken'ichi (ed.): *Nihon no kaisō kōzō*, pp. 161–197.

Ishida, Hiroshi (2001): Industrialization, Class Structure, and Social Mobility in Post War Japan. In: *British Journal of Sociology* 52, 4, pp. 579–604.

Ishikawa, Tsuneo (1991): *Shotoku to tomi* [Income and wealth]. Tokyo: Iwanami Shoten.

—— (ed.) (1994): *Nihon no shotoku to tomi no bunpai* [Income and wealth distribution in Japan]. Tokyo: University Tokyo Press.

Kanomata, Nobuo (1999): Shotoku kakusa to shotoku kettei no henka [Income discrepancies and the change in income determinants]. In: *Nihon Rōdō Kenkyū Zasshi* [Journal of Japan Labour Research] 472, pp. 17–25.

Kishimoto, Shigenobu (1985): *Chūryū no gensō* [The illusion of the middle class]. Tokyo: Kōdansha.

MHLW (Ministry of Health, Labour and Welfare) (2003): Report on the Attitudes Survey on the Social Security System in Japan, Preliminary Results. Tokyo: Ministry of Health, Labour and Welfare.

—— (Ministry of Health, Labour and Welfare) (several years): *Kokumin seikatsu kiso chōsa* [Comprehensive survey of living conditions of the people on health and welfare]. Tokyo: Ministry of Health, Labour and Welfare.

Murakami, Yasusuke (1977): Shin chūkan kaisō no genjitsusei [The reality of the new middle class]. In: *Asahi Shimbun*, 20 May 1977.

—— (1984): *Shin chūkan taishū no jidai* [The era of the new middle mass]. Tokyo: Chūō Kōron Sha.

Nishizaki, Fumihira, Yasushi Yamada and Hidehiro Ando (1998): *Nihon no shotoku kakusa* [Income discrepancies in Japan]. Tokyo: Keizai Kikakuchō Keizai Kenkyūjo.

Ohta, Kiyoshi (2004): Shotoku kakusa to kaisō no koteika [Income discrepancies and the strengthening structure of social stratification]. In: Higuchi, Yoshio, Kiyoshi Ohta and Research Institute of Consumer Economics (eds.): *Joseitachi no Heisei fukyō*. Tokyo: Nihon Keizai Hyoron Sha, pp. 191–201.

Ohtake, Fumio (1994): 1980 nendai no shotoku/shisan bunpai [Income and capital distribution in the 1980s]. In: *Quarterly Journal of Economic Theory* 45, 5, pp. 385–402.

—— (2000): 90 nendai no shotoku kakusa [Income discrepancies in the 1990s]. In: *Nihon Rōdō Kenkyū Zasshi* [Journal of Japan Labour Research] 480, pp. 2–11.

—— (2005): *Nihon no fubyōdō—Kakusa shakai no gensō to mirai* [Economic inequality in Japan: Illusion and future in a society of disparities]. Tokyo: Nihon Keizai Shinbun Sha.

Ohtake, Fumio and Makoto Saito (1998): Population Aging and Consumption Inequality in Japan. In: *Review of Income and Wealth* 44, 3, pp. 361–381.

Ohtake, Fumio and Saito Makoto (1999): Shotoku fubyōdō ka no haikei to sono seisakuteki gan'i [The background of the increase in the income inequality and its policy implication]. In: *Kikan Shakai Hoshō Kenkyū* [Quarterly Journal of Social Security] 35, 1, pp. 65–76.

Ōkouchi, Kazuo, Bernard Karsh and Solomon B. Levine (eds.) (1973): *Workers and Employers in Japan: The Japanese Employment Relations System*. Tokyo: University of Tokyo Press.

Ōsawa, Mari (2002): *Danjo kyōdō sankaku shakai o tsukuru* [Constructing the gender-equal society]. Tokyo: NHK Shuppan Kyōkai.

Satō, Toshiki (2000): *Fubyōdō shakai Nihon* [Unequal society Japan]. Tokyo: Chūō Kōron Sha.

Sawyer, Malcolm (1976): Income Distribution in OECD Countries. In: OECD Employment Outlook. Paris: OECD.

Shirahase, Sawako (2005): *Shōshi kōrei shakai no mienai kakusa—Jendaa, sedai, kaisō no yukue* [The unseen gaps in an ageing society: Locating gender, generation, and class in Japan]. Tokyo: University of Tokyo Press.

—— (ed.) (2006): *Henka suru shakai no fubyōdō* [Inequalities in a changing society]. Tokyo: University of Tokyo Press.

Smeeding, Timothy and Peter Saunders (1998): *How Do the Elderly in Taiwan Fare Cross-Nationally? Evidence from the Luxembourg Income Study (LIS) Project.* Luxembourg Income Study Working Paper No. 183. http://www.lisproject.org/publications/liswps/183.pdf (found 22 November 2006).

Tachibanaki, Toshiaki (1998): *Nihon no keizai kakusa* [Economic discrepancies in Japan]. Tokyo: Iwanami Shoten.

Tachibanaki, Toshiaki and Takumi Yagi (1991): *Shotoku bunpai no genjō to saikin no suii.* [The current situation of the income distribution and the future trend]. In: Ishikawa, Tsuneo (ed.): *Nihon no shotoku to tomi no bunpai.* Tokyo: Iwanami Shoten, pp. 159–170.

Tominaga, Kenichi (ed.) (1979): *Nihon no kaisō kōzō* [The structure of Japanese social stratification]. Tokyo: University of Tokyo Press.

Vogel, Ezra (1979): *Japan as Number One.* Cambridge: Harvard University Press.

CHAPTER THIRTEEN

# CHANGES IN FAMILY STRUCTURE

Toshiko Himeoka

## Introduction

The form, function and composition of the family have changed over time, as have the concept and its definition. In Japan, the development of the family since the Meiji period (1868–1912) can be divided into three stages. In the first stage, the public and private spheres were not yet separate; the family was a management body or cooperative living system that was also a place of production. Stage two is the closed-off "modern family," centred on the emotional relationships and gendered roles of its members. The third stage family is contemporary and progressive; its diversification and individualization will likely increase in the future. Traditional norms are weakening. Rather than the family regulating the life of the individual, the increasing tendency is for individuals to regulate the family life cycle.

However, these three categories are ultimately general tendencies to change. In reality, there have been periods when two different family types have coexisted. This is particularly the case for the pre-WW II period, when family structure differed greatly according to region, class, and profession of the head of household. Similarly, these changes did not happen all at once, but gradually. There are even ambiguous cases where one could say that two different stages existed simultaneously within the same family. This paper will examine transitions in the family from a sociological perspective, particularly with regard to changes in women's labour.

## 1. The *Ie* System and the "Modern Family"

No discussion of the family during Japan's modern period can fail to mention the *ie* (house/lineage) system, which expressed itself in the generational inheritance and continuation of a family name, estate, and/or business. The typical *ie* was to be found among the samurai class since the middle ages, but other classes too placed importance on the continuation of their houses (Ochiai 2000: 30). A civil law enacted in 1898, intended to restructure the *ie* system, institutionalized the *ie* as a group of family members governed by a head of household, thus extending the system to the entire population. Every family was required to have a head of household to whom was granted the authority to govern family affairs. Since succession to the head of household was through inheritance, one could change the head of household through the "retirement" of the senior generation, even if there were three generations of the same family present on the family register. Succession to head of household was limited to the eldest son, thus making illegal inheritance by the eldest daughter[1] or the youngest child, as had sometimes been the custom prior to the 1898 law. There were regions where inheritance by the eldest daughter was common, as well as households that sent their elder children into apprenticeship, passing the household on instead to the youngest—but after the law, only the eldest son could inherit the household.

The *ie* system was abolished in 1947 with the enforcement of the new constitution, which gave equal rights to husbands and wives. A law enacted the same year fundamentally prohibited more than three generations are recorded in the same family register. These changes in family law have been considered by sociologists as representing the modernization of the family, which they contrasted with the old, feudal and patriarchal *ie* system that had prevailed before the war. In short, the common idea was that the democratic "modern family" came into being only after the war.

This is true, of course, from the perspective of legal history. However, feminist scholars have strongly criticized this viewpoint since the 1980s, arguing that designating the year 1947 as being the starting point of the modern family neither reflects contemporary thought on the family nor its actual form at the time (Sechiyama 1996: 17–21). Clearly, feminist scholars have taken a different perspective on the patriarchal family system than have traditional sociologists of the family. For traditional sociologists, the patriarchal family was a family where the head of household governed the other family members; for feminists, it was a system in which men dominated women. Therefore, the patriarchal

[1] In cases where the eldest child was female, regardless of whether there were younger male siblings.

family was seen as a gendered group within which the husband had the upper hand. Through this characterization, feminists were eager to point out the continuity between pre-war and post-war families.

Based on the research of the Annales School and other Western social historians influential at the time, alternative concepts of the "modern family" emerged. A particular characteristic of the "modern family" was seen in its separation from the public sphere and withdrawal into the private sphere. Additionally, non-relatives were excluded from the family circle, which was defined by the strong emotional bonds among its members and the focus on children. The modern family is defined by a gendered division of labour whereby men work in the public sphere, while women remain in the private sphere (Ochiai 1989: 18). As will be discussed in more detail below, these characteristics already existed in families before the war (Koyama 1991: 8), and the discourse on the "modern family" thus became the basis for pointing out the continuity of this model with pre-war family structures. As a result, the viewpoint that the modern family is a synonym for the democratic family gradually receded into the background.

In the meantime, the discussion about the "modern family" has become a fixture in research about family history. There is now little room for doubt that the formation of the "modern family" had already begun before the war. However, this is not to declare that the importance of the *ie* system or its existence have been denied. Scholars are now examining the relationship between the *ie* system and the modern family during the pre-war period (Mitsunari 2005: 188–190). There are some feminist scholars, like Ueno, who lump the two together and maintain that the *ie* was in fact Japan's version of the "modern family" (Ueno 1994: 94). The more influential argument, however, is that the *ie* and the "modern family" coexisted, whether scholars treat the two as separate concepts (Ochiai 2000: 31), or whether they argue that the *ie* itself was a hybrid concept with "modern family" characteristics (Muta 1996: 12–23; Mitsunari 2005: 189).

According to the more influential viewpoint the *ie* already possessed "modern family" characteristics, and vice versa. Nevertheless, because the idea of lineage by primogeniture is unique to the *ie*, I agree with Ochiai, who maintains that the two are separate concepts.

The *ie* has unquestionably been a key concept in determining family structure in Japan. However, the three-stage history of the family described earlier makes no mention of the term. Certainly, the majority of Stage One families, who were "a management body or cooperative living system," could easily be grouped according to the norms of the *ie*, but during the pre-war period there were families that could be defined neither as *ie* nor as "modern family." Even if one defines *ie* and "modern family" as separate concepts, characteristics of both could coexist within one family. In other words, it is impossible to describe a linear trajectory from the *ie* to the "modern family." Instead of using the term *ie* to designate the Japanese family during a particular historical period, this chapter employs the term selectively to indicate *ie*-like characteristics.

## 2. Families as Management Bodies or Cooperative Living Systems

### 2.1. *Farming families*

The vast majority of families in Japan before WW II were engaged in farming. In the sixth year of the Meiji period (1873), no less than 88 per cent of the employed population was working in the agricultural, forestry and fishing professions. Thereafter, this percentage slowly began declining, but was still more than 75 per cent at the turn of the century. Heavy industry began to develop, and by 1940, when Japan became a manufacturing society, the rate had fallen to just over 50 per cent (Nagaoka 1988: 232).

Among farming families, there existed landowners, landed farmers, a combination of landed and tenant farmers, and tenant farmers. Passing on one's family inheritance, particularly farming land, to the next generation was of great importance to landowners and landed farmers. Even families who owned no land placed importance on staying in their birthplace and continuing to farm the plots of land their family had worked on for generations. Uprooting one's family from one's home village was considered a last resort, to be avoided at all costs. If a family could not support itself on the land and had to leave the village, it would usually end up living in an urban slum. In this connection, it is worth noting that from the Meiji period to the end of the Taishō period (1868–1926), the average woman would give birth to at least five children (Naikakufu 2004: 181). Given that the infant mortality rate at that time was holding around 15 per cent (MHLW 2006, Internet), one can speculate that four of these offspring reached adulthood. The eldest son would usually inherit the *ie* and form his own family, living together with his parents. If the family was wealthy, the second and third sons could form "branch families" and continue to pursue farming in the same village. In other cases, younger siblings would have to either move to the city or seek non-agricultural employment in the vicinity.

There were other reasons, too, why poor families did not have to leave their ancestral villages: many could depend on supplemental income from non-agricultural work such as *tatami* mat-making, sericulture, spinning, and weaving. Additionally, younger daughters and sons could be sent to neighbouring regions or cities to work as servants or apprentices: they would be expected to send part of their income home; at the same time, there was one less mouth to feed. Even landed farmers generally engaged in side businesses. Landowners, who were few in number, were the ones who hired these sons and daughters for farm work, and also participated in the management of non-agricultural industries such as weaving, etc. Thus farming households, where the home was also the place of production, were fully part of the public sphere. In addition, it was normal that all members of the household, with the exception of very young children, were engaged in some kind of productive labour. Even after the end of WW I in 1920, 70 per cent of women of working age who were part of farming households were employees or labourers. Unemployed dependents constituted only 20 per cent of the total (Tanimoto 2003: 146). Considering that there were women among this 20 per cent who supervised the servants and took care of their daily needs (such as cooking for them) or assisted in the management of the household in some other way, those who devoted their energies solely to their families must have been few indeed. In this connection, since farming in Japan has tended to be small-scale and therefore less dependent on hired labour, most of these female workers were in fact family employees.

In farming households, the father/head of household and sons of working age would do farm work, while the women, in addition to farm work, would engage in side businesses such as weaving, sericulture, and peddling wares. During the farmers' busiest seasons, women would perform a higher proportion of farm work, whereas in the off seasons, men too would engage in side businesses. While housework was "women's work," but responsibility for that work and the amount of time devoted to it was determined by how much the wife was needed for other kinds of labour. In most farming households, the mother of the head of household was responsible for most of the housework, while the wife (daughter-in-law) and her grown daughters would help.

In regions where side businesses such as weaving could be expected to produce high income, the wife would usually devote herself to this enterprise rather than the housework. In this case, her son(s) would help out with babysitting, while servants could be hired to do the cooking and cleaning. Thus, the farming family took a flexible approach toward employing the labour force available within the household, with the intent of reproducing itself. It is in this sense that the family was both a "management body" as well as a "cooperative working/consuming system."

### 2.2. *Independent, self-employed urban families*

In the cities, the number of independent family-owned businesses, particularly in the small shops and small-scale industry (including handicrafts), increased along with industrial development. Here too the home was a place of production, one in which the boundary between private and public was unclear. As in the farming household, the wife's position as family employee/worker was very important. In Kumamoto, where the statistics regarding family labour were recorded relatively accurately, the 1907–1908 numbers show that for every independent male, there were additional family members helping in the business (0.363 individuals in the service and transportation industries; 0.381 individuals in the mining and manufacturing industries) (Tanimoto 2003: 163). These statistics only count those family members (especially wives) who worked on a more or less full-time basis. If one were to include those who worked on a more part-time basis, these numbers would surely increase even more. There were also many women who took care of the daily needs of resident employees, even though they themselves did not work directly in the business. According to a 1941 survey, average working time of additional family members was 300 minutes per day, which is about half of men's working time. This seems short compared to that of farming wives (500 minutes per day), but on the other hand, these urban women spent about 100 more minutes a day on housework and sewing work than their rural peers (Tanimoto 2003: 167–168). One cause for this was the higher incidence of nuclear families in the urban environment. There was no mother-in-law present to take care of shopping and housework, and higher standards in this area meant that urban women had more to contend with. This kind of family could also be considered a "management body," and with the changing times, characteristics of the "modern family" became increasingly apparent.

### 2.3. *Lower class urban families*

In the cities, there were also those who worked as rickshaw pullers, porters, day labourers, plasterers, garbage men, and street merchants. In these families, both husband and wife, and anyone else in the family capable of making money, would work to earn the income necessary for that day's living expenses. After the turn of the century, the economic situation of this group had improved greatly. Even so, according to the "Survey on the Poor" conducted by the Ministry of the Interior's Regional Bureau in 1911 and 1912, 70 per cent of wives were engaged in some kind of employment. About half of this number was doing piecework at home, such as matchbox making, papering, tobacco-rolling, socks-mending, and so forth (Chimoto 1990: 218).

Japan was a latecomer to the heavy industrialization that was based on the female labour-intensive textile manufacturing industry, and so it was not until after the turn of the century that factory labour determined the composition of the urban family. Since the heads of households were usually second or third sons from farming villages, these families tended to be nuclear rather than extended three-generation families. During this period, a man's income from factory work did not differ much from the family income of the lower classes, so if an improvement in lifestyle was desired, the family would have to look to the wife's income (Chimoto 1990: 197). There were some who continued to work in the factory as they had done before they were married, but most married women had to find part time work that could be done at home, since this was more compatible with their housework and child-care responsibilities.

Factory workers and other members of the lower classes would reside in one or at the most two rooms in the row houses typical of the time. Walls were thin, so one could hardly call these living areas private, closed family space. Again, since most wives were engaged in piecework, the home still doubled as a place of production. As a result, these families did not live in a comfortable living space that was closed off from the public sphere. It was not an environment in which women could be devoted solely to housework and child care, so the "modern family" expectation that women create a nurturing home had not yet been established.

It was possible for these new urban families to formally remove themselves from the original family register and found a new "branch family" or *ie* by choosing a new head of household. However, among the lower classes, a contemporary report stated that "among every ten houses, there are only two or three legally wed couples," showing that many couples lived together without marrying (Yokoyama 1949: 57). Even if these families were legally registered as *ie*, they could hardly be considered as such since they had no family business or estate to pass down, nor ancestors to worship. Neither did they fill the requirements of the "modern family." These families can only be described as cooperative living systems that belonged to neither category.

## 3. The "Modern Family"

### 3.1. *The form of the "modern family"*

The prerequisite of the modern family is the separation of the public from the private, in other words, that the family exists separate from the workplace. In addition, there is a housewife who devotes herself entirely to housework and child care. It was expected that the housewife provides her husband with a sanctuary where he could rest mind and body, and her children a safe, loving place to grow up. This is not to say, of course, that members of the management body/cooperative living system family type did not feel affection for one other, but such emotional bonds was not deemed the main reason for the family's existence.

New views on the family appeared on the pages of general-interest magazines in the years after 1887, around the same time that "breaking away from Asia and joining Europe" (*datsu-A nyū-Ō*) became the slogan of the day. As their use of the Western neologism "home" (*katei*) indicated, these articles began to place great value on filial and marital affection within the family circle. By the turn of the century, the home was described as the exclusive province of women, and the term "housewife" (*shufu*) was in common use. Proclamations about women's duties and abilities as wives and mothers were widely published (Muta 1996: 54). Additionally, children were no longer viewed as part of the family labour force, but instead were to be educated and protected (Koyama 1999: 31). At around the same time, the so-called "good wife, wise mother" (*ryōsai kenbo*) ideology took hold, which was based on modern gender norms that stipulated, that "the woman's place was in the home." These ideas also became the basis of a national canon that authorized the standards for girls' education (Koyama 1991: 48).

These Westernized philosophies about the family, however, preceded their actual implementation, which did not start until after the Russo-Japanese War (1904–1905). The period from this victory up until WW I saw not only rapid industrialization, but also a jump in urban population growth, particularly in large cities such as Tokyo and Osaka. Along with the increase in factory workers, a new middle class established itself. Members of this social class included so-called "salary men" who performed clerical work and received a monthly salary, i.e. civil servants, bank employees, teachers, factory administrative staff, etc. It was they who, in accordance with their social status, formed new-style "modern families" (Koyama 1999: 37–38). It was after WW I that the middle class style "modern family" began to spread. One important factor in this expansion was that both white-collar and factory workers earned enough income to maintain the household and did not need to depend on their wives' secondary income. Accordingly, the number of wives who devoted themselves completely to housework and child care increased (Chimoto 1990: 214–218).

### 3.2. *The universalization of the "modern family"*

The "modern family" that emerged before WW II became the norm around 1955, and dominated throughout the period of high economic growth that continued until the oil shock of 1973. One could characterize this period as "the age of the housewife," since the concept came to define the life course of most women during these years.

The percentage of employed women continued to decrease after the war, but was still 56.7 per cent in 1955 (Sechiyama 1996: 190). At this time, there was still a high proportion of the Japanese population involved in agriculture and in small, self-owned businesses, so many women still worked as family employees. However, as people moved from the country to the cities, and the number of corporate employees continued to rise, the percentage of employed women declined. The low point was 45.7 per cent, in 1975, thereafter the number gradually started to increase (Sechiyama 1996: 190). During this period, women became housewives according to the definition of the word, devoting themselves to housework and child care. The house servant, an indispensable figure in the middle class household before the war, disappeared from the scene shortly after the war. In her stead came an array of home electrical appliances as the housewife took over the task of housecleaning herself. During this period of high economic growth, corporations instituted a

Figure 1. Private households by family type (Japan 1955–2000).

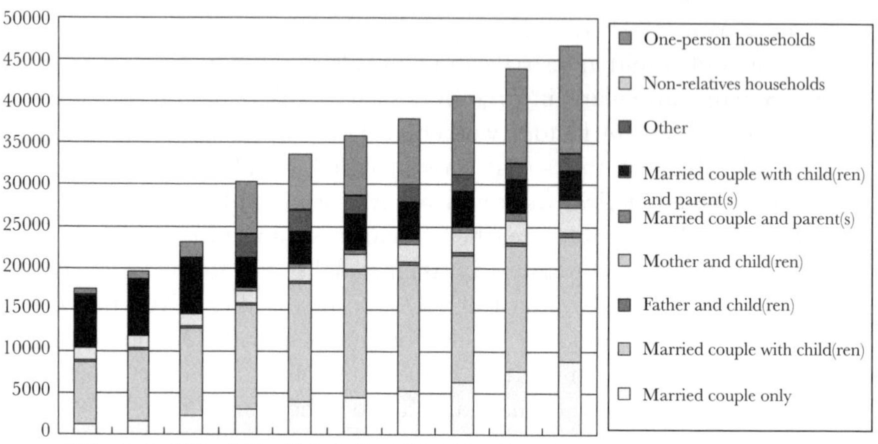


Note: The years 1955, 1960, 1965 include "Other" and "Married couple and parent(s)" under "Married couple with child(ren) and parent(s)."
Source: Statistics Bureau, Ministry of Internal Affairs and Communication (several years)

variety of welfare incentives to ensure the loyalty of the family man to the company and the "retirement" of women from employment at the time of marriage: lifetime employment, a pay scale tied to seniority, company housing, family allowances, etc.

A special characteristic of Japan's "modern family" is that it tends to comprise three generations rather than only two. Though the number of nuclear families continued to increase, Figure 1 shows that children who continued to live with their parents or other close relatives after marriage did not decrease significantly. In 1955, the percentage of parents who lived with their married children was close to 90 per cent (Ochiai 2004: 91); households comprised simply of husband and wife increased only after 1970. Until the 1960s, it was still taken for granted that the eldest son would live with one's parents after marriage. This was particularly true in rural areas, but even among urban dwellers, three-generation families were not at all rare. Even though the percentage of nuclear families increased in cities after the mid-sixties due to the influx of workers from the rural areas, most families of this generation had three or more children, thus allowing one sibling to remain in the countryside living with his parents. The number of children started decreasing after the baby boom ended in 1950 (3.65 children per family), until by 1960, there was an average of exactly two children per family (Naikakufu 2004: 181).

During the 1960s most young people preferred to live as a nuclear family, not with their parents. Two slogans that emerged during this decade, "Plus house, plus car, but minus grandma" (*ie tsuki, kā tsuki, baba nuki*) and "My home-ism," (*mai hōmu shugi*) certainly symbolize this desire. For young women who were not keen on living like their mothers, who had had to serve their in-laws in the name of the *ie*, the idea of marrying an urban "salary man" and keeping a loving home for him and his children seemed an attractive prospect. As Figure 2 shows, the dream of being a salary man's wife quickly became a reality, with the percentage of full-time housewives reaching its peak in the seventies.

"My homeism" and the idea of living in close harmony with one's spouse were also supported by the increase in love marriages. In 1949, love marriages accounted for only 22 per cent, while arranged marriages were at 56 per cent, but these numbers had reversed themselves by 1965, during the peak period of post-war economic growth (Yuzawa 1995: 16–17).

## 4. The Decline of the "Modern Family"

The "modern family" entered its golden age in the early 1970s; at the same time, the so-called "women's liberation movement" came onto

Figure 2. Proportion of full-time housewives in salary man households.

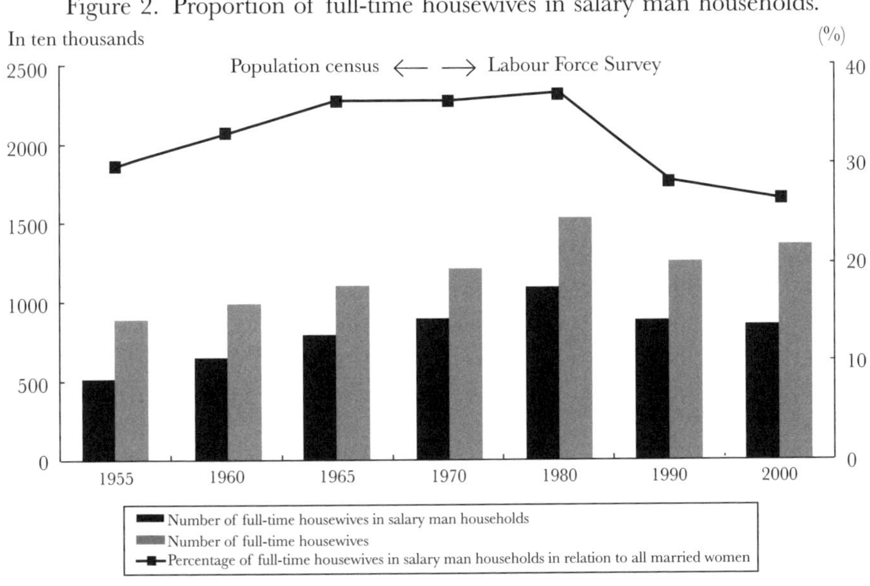


Source: Naikakufu (Cabinet Office) (2002: 5).

the scene in Europe, North America and Japan. Feminists involved in the movement began to publicly rethink their own identities as women, exposed hitherto taboo subjects such as sex, and even challenged the institutionalized concept of marriage. Questioning the restrictive ideas of femininity and sexuality that marriage had implied, they searched for a more assertive subjectivity outside this institutional framework. There is no doubt that the women's liberation movement had a very large impact, but the Japan's women's lib did not develop into a mass movement as it did in Europe and North America. There was no great decrease in common law marriages, nor was there any damage to the family as institution. Though the *ie* system existed only in name by this time, there was still a strong desire to ensure the continuance of one's house, and issues of inheritance and ancestor worship continued to hold sway. Unlike in Europe and North America, simply appealing to morality could not dispel these concerns.

On the other hand, the common view that marriage was a woman's path to happiness, and the strong pressure that decreed women should wed by age 25, survived only into the early 1970s. In fact, though 1972 and 1973 recorded the lowest average ages for marriage in a decade (23.8 years for women, 26.5 years for men), the average has been climbing since then. Nevertheless, family life was changing steadily due to the increase in love marriages, the spread of sexual activity before marriage, and so on. The English expression "new family" became popular at this time, signifying the trend in cultivating a friendly family circle, as opposed to the "husband leads, wife follows" ideology that had prevailed previously. The wife still did not work, and tended her family, but husband and wife had equal status. Together with their children, they strove to enjoy family life.

The family underwent great changes in the wake of the 1973 oil shock. To compensate for the labour shortage that resulted as migration to the cities from rural areas tapered down, housewives entered the labour market as part-time employees. Looking at the changes in employment of women with respect to marital status, we can see that the percentage of married women in the workforce increased from only 32.7 per cent in 1962 to 57.4 per cent in 1980. The latter number comes close to 70 per cent if widows and divorcées are included, a figure that has remained constant until the present day (Inoue and Ehara 1991: 89; Yuzawa 2005: 81). In other words, it is no longer the norm that a woman becomes a full-time housewife once married; instead, she takes on the housework as well as a part-time job. What

Figure 3. Changes in percentage of labour force participation for different age groups.

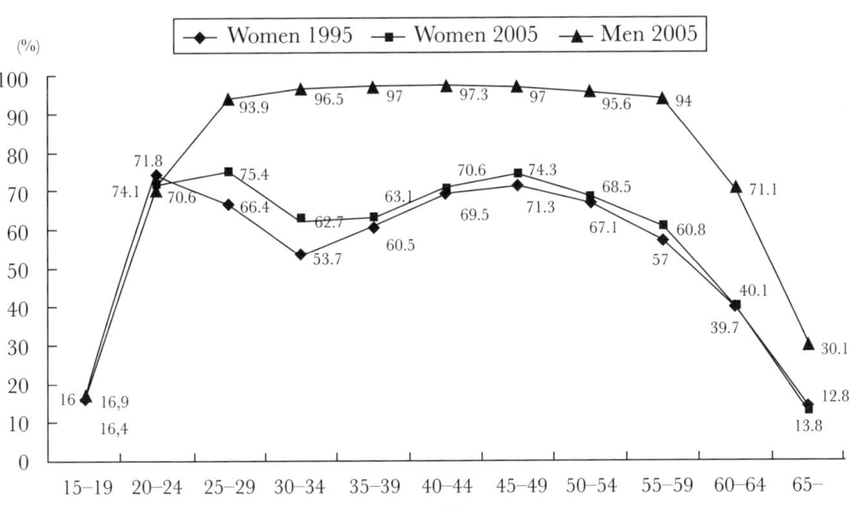


Source: Ministry of Public Management, Home Affairs, Posts and Telecommunication, Surveys on Labour Force, 1985–1992; 2003–2005.

is particular to Japan is that the average married woman's working career is described by the so-called "M-curve;" that is, she stays home until her children have reached a certain age before re-entering the workforce. The M-curve becomes generally flatter with each passing year, as does women's average marriage age, but the basic shape has remained the same (Figure 3).

Up until the economic "bubble" burst in the early 1990s, Japanese corporate management policies such as lifetime employment and seniority-based remuneration attracted attention all over the world. Men were transformed into corporate soldiers, leaving more and more of the household affairs and childrearing to women. The absence of fathers even led, in some cases, to the so-called "Mother-child co-dependency" phenomenon. Actually, most women, even housewives, became more and more involved in volunteerism and cultural study—not for the sake of their families, but for self-improvement. Furthermore, an Equal Employment Opportunity Law (*Danjo Koyō Kikai Kintō-hō*) was enacted in 1986, which had the purpose of ending discrimination against women in both employment and promotion matters. However, there were many obstacles to its implementation, since, among other issues, there was no penalty for breaking the law, its observance being left to the discretion of the companies themselves. Even so, at least the law had opened the way for women with the desire and the ability to work on an equal footing with men.

In the mid-eighties, the government attempted to implement a "Family Support Policy" that was intended to encourage women to take care of their children and ageing parents in the home. However, a higher spousal tax exemption and a progressive pension plan for full-time housewives as well as those who earned below a certain amount through part time work were not enough. The days when a bride was automatically expected to care for her husband's ageing parents were long past. Forced to recognize this, the government shortly launched an alternate plan for nursing assistance funded by public monies. At around the same time, in 1987, the long-standing preference for male children fell below 50 per cent for the first time, the reasons being that parents hoped for longer, closer relationships with their daughters, and that their own daughter would care for them in their old age. This tendency continues today (Yamada 2004: 152–153). It is no longer the norm to live with one's parents after marriage; this has become a personal choice. The *ie* consciousness that still remained in the 1970s has now vanished, and the age of the homogeneous "modern family" standard, too, is nearing its end.

## 5. Diversification and Democratization of the Family

The single most important characteristic of the Japanese family since 1990 has been the diversification of form and lifestyle. In 1997, the year the percentage of the population over 65 exceeded that of those under fifteen, Japan officially became an ageing society with a low birth rate. The composition of the household, too, was changing. By examining the numbers of types of households in 1970 and 2000, we can see that while single- and two-person (i.e. husband and wife) households are on the rise, the supposedly "normal" nuclear family composed of husband, wife and children, as well as multiple generation households are on the decline (Figures 4 and 5). The number of divorces has also increased rapidly, as shown when comparing the divorce rate (per 1000 population per year) of 1989 (1.29) with that of 2000 (2.10) (Naikakufu 2002: 190). One of the reasons for the low birth rate is also the higher age of men and women at their first marriage: between 1980 and 2000, the proportion of those in the 20 to 34 age group who were still unmar-

Figure 4. Private Households by Family Type (Japan 1970).

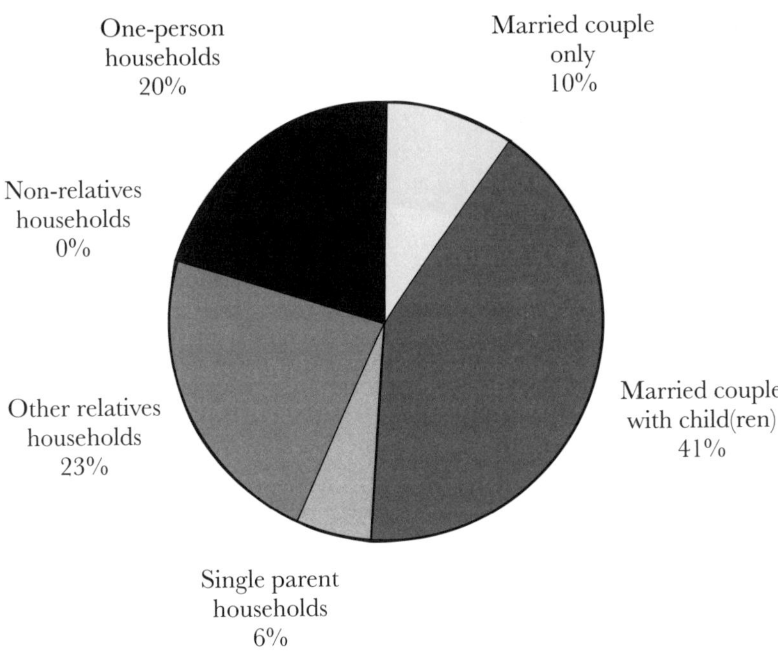


Source: Ministry of Internal Affairs and Communications, Statistics Bureau.

ried increased by roughly 22 per cent (in the case of women) and 16 per cent (in the case of men) (Naikakufu 2004: 17).

In modern Japanese society, there was a strong pattern of male-based succession. This traditional concept too is changing due to evolving ideas about the family and the increase in households without male offspring (a natural result of fewer children being born). It is true that the overwhelming majority of couples choose the husband's surname upon marriage (spouses may not have different surnames according to Japanese law), but it is no longer the case that the couple has more dealings with the husband's side of the family. Relations between married couples and the wife's side of the family are on the rise. Though somewhat outdated, the data shows an increase in couples living with the wife's parents (from 6.0 per cent in 1980 to 10.6 per cent in 1990), and a decrease in couples living with the husband's parents (from 34.8 per cent in 1980 to 28.2 per cent in 1990) (Ochiai 2004: 211). The

Figure 5. Private Households by Family Type (Japan 2000).

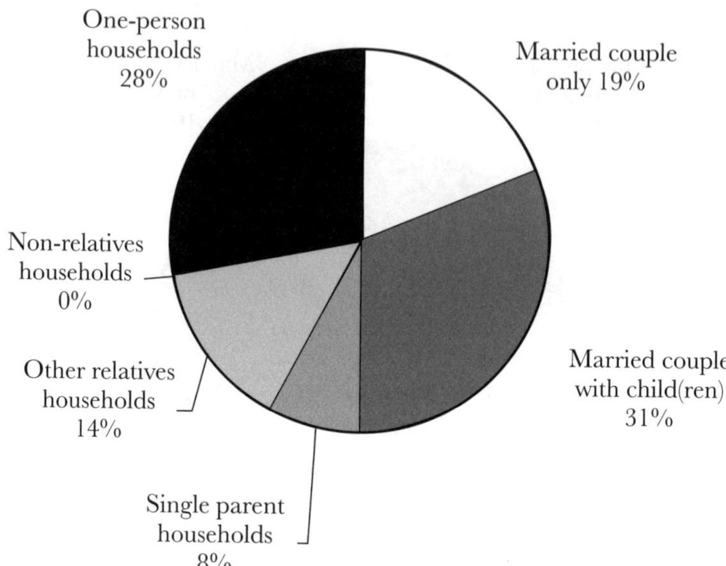


Source: Ministry of Internal Affairs and Communications, Statistics Bureau.

relationship between young wives and their own mothers has grown much stronger, especially in the areas of child rearing and nursing care. In families with both a daughter and a son, parents will seek to be equally involved with the families of both children, sometimes giving rise to competition with their in-laws. Because of this daily involvement on both sides of the family, one can say that there is no longer a bias toward the male line.

The family's diversification is linked to the increasing diversification of individuals' lifestyles. One manifestation of this is the increasing number of women who choose to develop a career. The 1997 revision of the Equal Employment Opportunity Law and the 1999 Basic Law for a Gender-equal Society (*Danjo Kyōdō Sankaku Shakai Kihon-hō*) as well as the switch from a seniority-based to a merit-based system, are allowing more and more women to display their abilities in the workplace. Despite this, corporations still operate on the assumption that their male employees have a wife at home to take care of the household. This, combined with the fact that many men do not help at all with the housework, makes it difficult for women to balance family and work. This situation is undoubtedly one of the causes of late marriage and the low birth rate, as well.

The increasingly unstable job market of the late 1990s has also added some unforeseen variables to the situation. Part-time, contract and temporary employment, which had previously been limited to women, have expanded to include men as well. Even permanent, regular employees have no guarantees for the future, since the uniquely Japanese principle of lifetime employment has now crumbled as well. Young people in non-regular employment, dubbed "freeters" and unemployed youth called NEET (not in employment, education or training), are regarded as a widespread social problem. Men and women who have grown up during a prosperous economic period are hesitating before marrying or bearing children, commitments that would certainly lower their standard of living. Married women continue to work in ever greater numbers, afraid of the financial risk to their families if they quit.

In the 1990s, as individual lifestyles have become more diverse, so too has happened with the nature and life cycle of the family. Unlike earlier periods where the image of the family was determined by the pervasive "modern family" model, one can no longer identify what a "typical" family looks like. The definition of marriage has also changed. That one must belong to a family is not self-evident, since more and more individuals are choosing to spend most if not all of their lives without a spouse and children. "Having a family is not a natural part of human life, but something you make with other people with whom you have an affinity, during a certain period in your life" (Meguro 1987: iv).

Traditionally, the family has been seen as a unified body, but today, the dominant view is rather that of an aggregation of individuals, bound together through their personal life cycles. Of course, it is a place where one has close, irreplaceable relationships with one's partner, children, and/or parents, but the interests of the family and various individuals sometimes come into conflict. In this case, the conflict has to be negotiated, a role that has typically been played by women. Since the husband had been absorbed with his work, the task of maintaining family "unity" naturally fell to his wife.

However, the idea that the family is always a unified body, at all times, is no longer current. Families and individuals are going their own ways. If the family is an aggregation of individual life courses, then intra-family conflicts will certainly increase—but women do not need to shoulder the responsibility of conflict mediation alone. Working out the differences between individuals within a family is an important issue for men and women alike, one they should solve together. Otherwise, the family may well fall apart. Both men and women need to take equal responsibility if the family is to continue as a place of close interpersonal relationships.

## References


Chimoto, Akiko (1990): Nihon ni okeru seibetsu yakuwari bungyō no keisei—Kakei chōsa o tooshite [The formation of gender role segregation in Japan—As seen in family statistics]. In: Ogino Miho *et al.* (eds.): *Seido toshite no 'onna'* [The 'women' as an institution]. Tokyo: Heibonsha, pp. 187–228.

Inoue, Teruko and Yumiko Ehara (eds.) (1991): *Josei no dēta bukku. Sei, karada kara seiji sanka made* [Women's data book—From sex and body to political participation]. Tokyo: Yūhikaku.

Koyama, Shizuko (1991): *Ryōsai kenbo to iu kihan* [Good wife and wise mother as a norm]. Tokyo: Keisō Shobō.

—— (1998): *Katei no seisei to josei no kokuminka* [The formation of the household and the nationalisation of the woman]. Tokyo: Keisō Shobō.

Meguro, Yoriko (1987): *Kōjinka suru kazoku* [The individualization of the family]. Tokyo: Keisō Shobō.

MHLW (Ministry of Health, Labour and Welfare) (2006): *Jinkō dōtai sōran no nenjisuii* [Annual changes of general population development]. http://www.mhlw.go.jp/toukei/saikin/hw/jinkou/geppo/nengai02/toukei1.html (found 12/11/2006).

Mitsunari, Miho (2005): *Jendā no hōshigaku—Kindai Doitsu no kazoku to sekushuaritī* [Legal history of gender—The family and sexuality in modern Germany]. Tokyo: Keisō Shobō.

Muta, Kazue (1996): *Senryaku toshite no kazoku—Kindai Nihon no kokumin kokka keisei to josei* [The family as strategy—The formation of the nation state in modern Japan and the women]. Tokyo: Shinyosha.

Nagaoka, Shinkichi (ed.) (1988): *Kindai Nihon no keizai—Gaisetsu to tōkei* [The economy of modern Japan—Surveys and statistics]. Kyoto: Minerva Shobō.

Naikakufu [Cabinet Office] (2004): *Shōshika shakai hakusho, Heisei 16nen ban* [2004 White Paper on the low fertility society]. Tokyo: Gyōsei.

—— (2002): *Heisei 13nendo. Kokumin seikatsu hakusho. Kazoku no kurashi to kōzō kaikaku* [2001 White Paper on the citizens' living. The life of the family and the structural reform]. http://www5.cao.go.jp/seikatsu/2002/0326wp-seikatsu-s.pdf (found 12/11/2006).

Ochiai, Emiko (1989): *Kindai kazoku to feminizumu* [The modern family and feminism]. Tokyo: Keisō Shobō.

—— (2000): *Kindai kazoku no magarikado* [The turning point of the modern family]. Tokyo: Kadokawa Shobō.

—— (2004): *21seiki kazoku he—Kazoku no sengo taisei no mikata, koekata* [Towards the family of the 21st century—Ways to look at and overcome the post war family system]. Tokyo: Yūhikaku.

Sechiyama, Kaku (1996): *Higashi Ajia no kafūchōsei—Jendā no hikaku shakaigaku* [Patriarchy in East Asia—Comparative sociology of gender]. Tokyo: Keisō Shobō.

Tanimoto, Masayuki (2003): Kindai Nihon no josei rōdō to "shō keiei" [Female labour and "petty" management in modern Japan]. In: Ujiie Mikito *et al.* (eds.): *Kindai Nihon kokka no seiritsu to jendā.* Tokyo: Kashiwa Shobō, pp. 144–187.

Ueno, Chizuko (1994): *Kindai kazoku no seiritsu to shuen* [The rise and fall of the modern family]. Tokyo: Iwanami Shoten.

Yamada Masahiro (2004): *Kibō kakusa shakai—'Makegumi' no kibōkan ga Nihon o hikisaku* [Expectation-gap society—The despair of the 'losers' is dividing Japan]. Tokyo: Chikuma Shobō.
Yokoyama, Gennosuke (1949): *Nihon no kasō shakai* [Japan's lower class society]. (First edition 1899).Tokyo: Iwanami Shoten.
Yuzawa, Yasuhiko (1995): *Zusetsu kazoku mondai no genzai* [Today's family problems in figures]. Tokyo: Nihon Hōsō Shuppankai.
—— (2005): *Meiji no kekkon Meiji no rikon—Kateinai jendā no genten* [Marriage and divorce in the Meiji era—The starting point of household's gender]. Tokyo: Kadokawa Shoten.

Case in point: Time spent with children (weekdays)

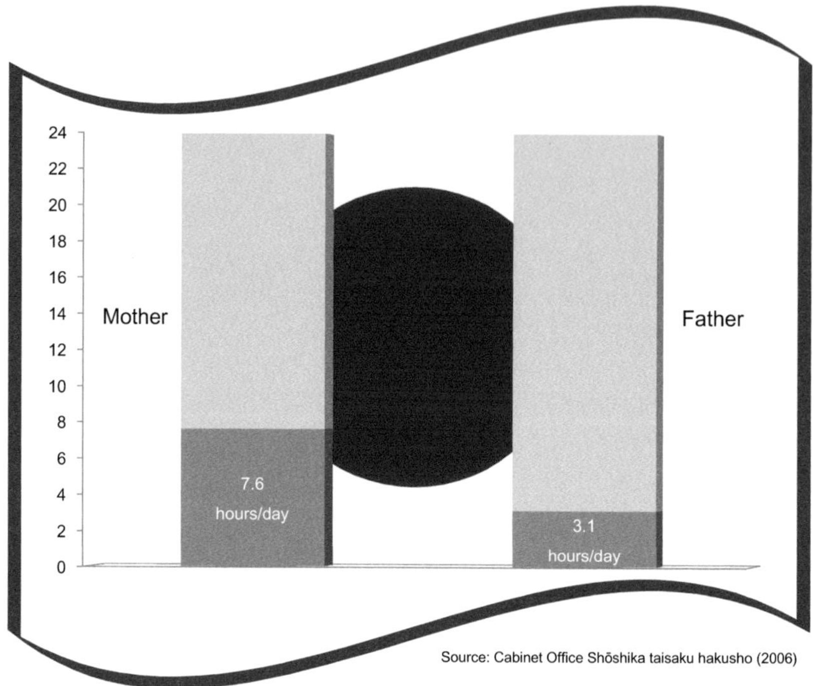


Source: Cabinet Office Shōshika taisaku hakusho (2006)

CHAPTER FOURTEEN

# CHANGING FAMILY LIFE CYCLE AND PARTNERSHIP TRANSITION—GENDER ROLES AND MARRIAGE PATTERNS

James M. Raymo and Miho Iwasawa

## 1. Introduction

The family formation process has changed dramatically in Japan over the past 20–30 years. Marriage is being delayed to progressively later ages, a growing proportion of Japanese men and women will likely never marry, the prevalence of premarital cohabitation has increased, and the likelihood of lifelong marriage has decreased substantially. Theoretical explanations for these dramatic changes in family behaviour have emphasized increasing economic independence for women, declining economic prospects for less educated men, changing attitudes toward marriage and family, extended coresidence with parents, and shifting marriage market composition. Although similar patterns of family change and associated explanations characterize most industrialized countries, distinctive features of the Japanese experience provide important insights into the mechanisms underlying observed change. For example, the decline in Japanese marriage rates has not only been particularly rapid, but has also been most pronounced among highly educated women. Interpretations of this distinctive pattern of change have emphasized the highly asymmetric division of domestic labour between husbands and wives and the associated difficulty that women face in balancing family and full-time work.

A similar emphasis on gender context has emerged in recent discussions of very low fertility in Europe. Substantial declines in marriage and fertility—often described as part of a "second demographic transition" (Lesthaeghe 1995; Van de Kaa 1987)—have occurred in all industrialized societies but have been most dramatic in societies characterized by "strong families" (Reher 1998) and relatively low gender equality. Attempts to understand the observed decline in the negative correlation between female labour force participation and fertility (Kögel 2004) have highlighted the potential importance of tension between growing economic opportunities for women in the labour market and limited change in men's and women's roles within the family (e.g., Blossfeld 1995; Chesnais 1996; Kohler, Billari and Ortega 2002; McDonald 2000a, 2000b). The basic argument is that women with access to sufficient resources will postpone (or avoid) marriage and childbearing in societies where family formation is relatively incompatible with other pursuits—especially paid employment.

Japan is clearly a society in which women encounter great difficulty in balancing full-time work with family responsibilities. Tension between work and family is reflected in the distinctive M-shape of the age-specific labour force participation rates of Japanese women and arises from the limited availability of flexible day care (Yu 2001), men's long work hours and relatively inflexible work schedules (Ogasawara 2001), husbands' very limited participation in housework and child care (Tsuya *et al.* 2005), a strong belief in the value of maternal care provision for preschool age children (Hirao 2001), and heavy parental involvement in children's education (Tsuya and Choe 2004). In this context, some scholars have argued that, as changes in social and economic opportunities for women outside of marriage reduce the economic necessity of marriage, women have become increasingly critical of the "Japanese wife's subordinated and highly domesticated position within the family" (Tsuya and Mason 1995: 162) and increasingly hesitant to enter a marriage in which they are expected to assume such a position.

This chapter consists of three sections. In the first section, we draw upon data from the Japanese census, Vital Statistics, National Fertility Surveys, and other sample surveys to summarize trends in the transition to marriage. We also discuss related trends in divorce and non-marital cohabitation and the dramatic increase in the heterogeneity of the family life course in Japan. In the second section, we summarize trends in attitudes toward marriage and family. We do not make any attempt to causally link changes in attitudes and changes in behaviour but highlight a growing ambivalence toward marriage and scepticism regarding the benefits of marriage. We also discuss gender differences in attitudes toward marriage and family life. In the third section, we provide a brief overview of posited explanations for these changes. In this section, we place particular emphasis on recent work by Raymo and colleagues (Raymo 2003a; Raymo and Iwasawa 2005; Raymo and Ono 2006) emphasizing how a focus on gender relationships within marriage may help to understand the distinctive patterns of change in Japanese family formation.

## 2. Trends in Family Formation

In this section, we provide a brief overview of changes in Japanese marital behaviour, with particular emphasis on trends after 1970. We describe trends in (a) age at marriage, (b) variance in age at marriage, (c) the proportion never marrying, (d) the process leading to marriage, including place of meeting and the role of cohabitation, (e) the link between marriage and childbearing, (f) the link between marriage and employment, and (g) the likelihood of marital dissolution. This descriptive overview is based upon the aggregate data contained in census and vital statistics publications as well as published tabulations of recent National Fertility Surveys.

### 2.1 *Age at marriage*

The first two columns of Table 1 show that, between 1950 and 2004, mean age at first marriage rose steadily by 3.7 years (from 25.9 to 29.6 ) for men and by 4.8 years (from 23.0 to 27.8 ) for women. The trend toward later marriage has been particularly pronounced since 1970 and Japan is currently one of the latest marrying societies in the world (NIPSSR 2006). Mean age at first marriage, however, is a conservative measure of changes in marriage timing in that it reflects only the behaviour of men and women who actually marry in a given year. The age-specific proportions never married presented in Table 2 provide an even more striking picture of the decline in marriage rates, particularly for women in their 20s and men in their late 20s and 30s. For example, whereas only one in seven women aged 25–29 in 1950 had yet to marry, over half of similarly aged women in 2000 had never married. Among men in this age group, the proportion yet to marry doubled from 35 per cent to 69 per cent. For men in their early thirties, the proportion never married increased more than five-fold, reaching two-fifths by 2000. As with mean age at marriage, the trend toward later marriage began to accelerate after 1970 and has been particularly pronounced since 1980.

Table 1. Mean and standard deviation of age at first marriage, 1950–2004.

| Year | Mean age at first marriage | | Standard deviation of age at first marriage (15–49) | |
|---|---|---|---|---|
| | Men | Women | Men | Women |
| 1950 | 25.9 | 23.0 | 3.7 | 3.5 |
| 1960 | 27.2 | 24.4 | 3.2 | 3.5 |
| 1970 | 26.9 | 24.2 | 3.6 | 3.5 |
| 1980 | 27.8 | 25.2 | 3.8 | 3.7 |
| 1990 | 28.4 | 25.9 | 4.7 | 4.0 |
| 2000 | 28.8 | 27.0 | 5.1 | 4.3 |
| 2004 | 29.6 | 27.8 | 5.3 | 4.6 |

Source: Vital Statistics of Japan, various years.

### 2.2 *Variance in age at marriage*

Until recently, norms about "appropriate" ages for marriage (*tekireiki*) have been strong and first marriage has tended to occur within a very narrow range of ages. Through 1980, over 60 per cent of women's first marriages took place between the ages of 20 and 25 while a slightly smaller proportion of men's marriages were concentrated between the ages of 22 and 27. By 2004, however, these percentages had declined by roughly half. This substantial increase in the variation of age at first marriage is depicted in the third and fourth columns of Table 1. The standard deviation of women's age at first marriage increased from 3.5 years in 1950 to 4.6 years in 2004. For men, the corresponding increase has been from 3.7 years to 5.3 years. Men and women are not only marrying later and less, but are also marrying across a wider range of ages.

### 2.3 *Proportion ever marrying*

Although mean age at first marriage has been relatively high throughout the post-war period, nearly all Japanese men and women have eventually married. Table 2 shows that the proportion never married at age 45–49 (a reasonable proxy for the proportion who never marry) remained stable at about 2–4 per cent through 1980. The proportion of women remaining unmarried has grown somewhat since 1980 while nonmarriage among men has increased rapidly. The large increase between 1980 and 2000 (from 3 per cent to 15 per cent) is presumably due, in part, to a male marriage squeeze brought about by gender differences in age at marriage and the rapid fertility decline that followed the brief baby boom of 1947–49 (Anzo 1985). The likelihood of significant further increase in non-marriage is suggested by the very high proportions of never married men and women in their late 30s in 2000. Indeed, official population projections are based on the assumption that the proportion of women who never marry will increase to 24 per cent for women born after 1990.[1]

## 2.4 *Marriage process*

Several recent studies have addressed dramatic changes in the marriage process. Perhaps most notable is the dramatic decline in the proportion

Table 2. Proportions Never Married by Sex and Age Group, 1950–2000.

| **Women** | | | | | | |
|---|---|---|---|---|---|---|
| Age | 1950 | 1960 | 1970 | 1980 | 1990 | 2000 |
| 15–19 | 0.97 | 0.99 | 0.98 | 0.99 | 0.98 | 0.99 |
| 20–24 | 0.55 | 0.68 | 0.72 | 0.78 | 0.85 | 0.88 |
| 25–29 | 0.15 | 0.22 | 0.18 | 0.24 | 0.40 | 0.54 |
| 30–34 | 0.06 | 0.09 | 0.07 | 0.09 | 0.14 | 0.27 |
| 35–39 | 0.03 | 0.06 | 0.06 | 0.06 | 0.08 | 0.14 |
| 40–44 | 0.02 | 0.03 | 0.05 | 0.04 | 0.06 | 0.09 |
| 45–49 | 0.02 | 0.02 | 0.04 | 0.04 | 0.05 | 0.06 |
| **Men** | | | | | | |
| Age | 1950 | 1960 | 1970 | 1980 | 1990 | 2000 |
| 15–19 | 1.00 | 1.00 | 0.99 | 1.00 | 0.99 | 1.00 |
| 20–24 | 0.83 | 0.92 | 0.90 | 0.92 | 0.92 | 0.93 |
| 25–29 | 0.35 | 0.46 | 0.47 | 0.55 | 0.64 | 0.69 |
| 30–34 | 0.08 | 0.10 | 0.12 | 0.22 | 0.33 | 0.43 |
| 35–39 | 0.03 | 0.04 | 0.05 | 0.09 | 0.19 | 0.26 |
| 40–44 | 0.02 | 0.02 | 0.03 | 0.07 | 0.12 | 0.18 |
| 45–49 | 0.02 | 0.01 | 0.02 | 0.03 | 0.07 | 0.15 |

Source: Latest Population Statistics (2006).

[1] This is the assumption used in making the medium-variant population projections. The proportion of women assumed to never marry is .13 in the high-fertility projection and .23 in the low-fertility projections (NIPSSR 2006: 6).

of *miai* (arranged) marriages from 54 per cent in the 1950s to about 7 per cent for marriages taking place after 1995 (Kaneko and Mita 2003). More recently, it appears that marriages among coworkers (*shokuba kekkon*) are also declining. According to a recent study by Iwasawa and Mita (2005), the decline in *shokuba kekkon* is a primary component of the overall decline in marriage rates since the 1970s. Perhaps reflecting the decline in these two formerly common and relatively institutionalized pathways to marriage, recent surveys indicate that a substantial proportion of unmarried men and women are postponing marriage because they have not met a suitable partner. Among women in the most recent National Fertility Survey in 2002, 30 per cent cohabited prior to marriage and 25 per cent were pregnant (NIPSSR 2004: 226). These figures suggest that, for a sizeable proportion of unmarried Japanese men and women, the transition to first marriage is influenced by the difficulty of meeting potential spouses.

Among those with a partner, the pathway to marriage is increasingly complex, with premarital cohabitation and premarital pregnancy emerging as important stages in the marriage process. These changes emerge clearly from tabulations of data from the 1st Survey of Population, Families, and Generations conducted in 2004 by the Mainichi Newspaper Population Research Council presented in Figure 1. The proportion of couples following the "standard" pathway to marriage—i.e., without cohabiting and prior to pregnancy—has declined from 79 per cent of marriages in the 1980s to slightly over half of marriages taking place between 2000–2004. Among those women in the most recent cohort, 29 per cent cohabited prior to marriage and 24 per cent were pregnant at the time of marriage. Studies of U.S. data documenting higher rates of marital dissolution among those who cohabited or were pregnant prior to marriage (e.g., Bumpass, Castro Martin and Sweet 1991) suggest that these changes may have implications for subsequent marital stability in Japan.

### 2.5 *Marital dissolution*

Japanese marriages are, in fact, increasingly likely to end in divorce. Using vital statistics tabulations, Raymo, Iwasawa, and Bumpass (2004) show that the proportion of marriages dissolving within ten years increased from 12 per cent for marriages taking place in 1980 to 17 per cent for marriages taking place in 1990. More striking, their synthetic

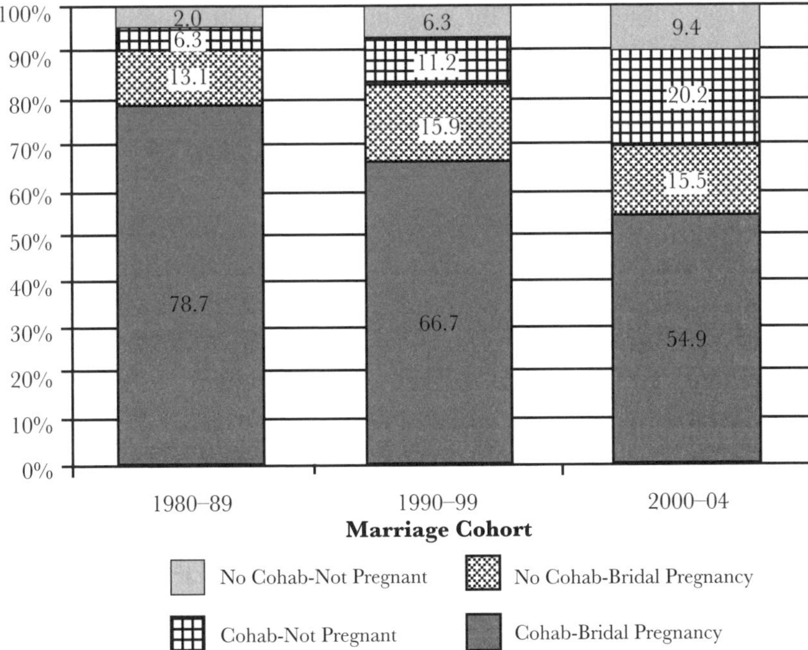


Source: Authors' tabulations of data from the 1st Survey of Population, Families, and Generations conducted in 2004 by the Mainichi Newspaper Population Research Council.

Figure 1. Marriages classified by cohort, cohabitation experience, and pregnancy status at marriage.

cohort estimate of the lifetime probability of marital dissolution based on duration-specific dissolution rates for 2002 is roughly one-third. Although lower than the corresponding figure for the U.S., this figure is similar to the level observed in most European countries.

### 2.6 *Marriage, childbearing, and employment*

Aspects of marriage that have changed relatively little include the strong link between marriage and childbearing and the relatively limited labour force attachment of married women in Japan. Although pregnancy appears to represent an increasingly important motivation for marriage, non-marital childbearing remains very uncommon in Japan. The proportion of births to unmarried mothers in 2004 was only 2 per cent in Japan, compared to 30 per cent in the U.S. (NIPSSR 2006). Although the interval between marriage and first birth has lengthened somewhat (Shintani 1998), the close link between marriage and childbirth is apparent in the consistently high proportion of couples having their first child within the first years of marriage, the relative rarity of childless marriages (Sasai 2004), and the stability of childbearing ideals and intentions since the mid-seventies (Moriizumi 2003).[2]

Unlike their counterparts in most western industrialized societies, whose labour supply profiles now resemble those of men, a large proportion of Japanese women continue to exit the labour force during their prime childrearing years (e.g., Brinton 2001). In 1995, for example, only 18 per cent of women with children under the age of three were in the labour force (Shirahase 2003). Career interruptions associated with marriage and childbearing have profound implications for women's earnings potential in Japan given that continuous job tenure and work experience are heavily rewarded in the labour market (e.g., Brinton and Ngo 1993), and that opportunities to re-enter the labour force are largely confined to low-paying jobs in small companies or part-time work (Houseman and Osawa 2003). When married women do return to the labour force, tax policies provide a strong incentive to work part-time and limit earnings in order to qualify for dependent status (Ogawa and Ermisch 1996). The difficulty of remaining in full-time employment may thus lead some economically independent women to postpone or avoid entering "the onerous status of the Japanese wife and mother" (Tsuya and Mason 1995: 156).

## 3. Attitudes toward Marriage and Family

Changes in marital behaviour have been accompanied by important changes in attitudes toward marriage and family. Particularly important are (a) scepticism about the benefits of marriage, (b) changes in attitudes about gender and appropriate roles for men and women, and (c) increasingly tolerant attitudes toward innovative family behaviours such as cohabitation and divorce. The data summarized here are taken primarily from published tabulations of recent National Fertility Surveys.

---

[2] Although childlessness is relatively rare among intact marriages, it is important to note that a substantial proportion (40 per cent) of recent divorces involves childless couples (NIPSSR 2006). Divorce, remarriage, and childbearing in higher order marriages are thus an important, but understudied, components of fertility behaviour in contemporary Japan.

### 3.1 *Attitudes toward marriage*

In contrast to the dramatic decline in marriage rates, the marriage intentions of young Japanese have remained relatively stable. The proportion of 18–34 year-old single men and women stating that they intend to marry at some point (*izure kekkon suru tsumori*) declined somewhat from about 95 per cent in 1982 to about 88 per cent in 2002 (Kaneko 2004a). Over the same period, the proportion indicating that they intend to never marry increased slightly but remains low at about 5 per cent (Kaneko 2004a). It is important to note, however, that survey questions about respondents' own marriage intentions likely understate the acceptance of non-marriage as a legitimate life choice. Rindfuss *et al.* (2004) show, for example, that one-third of Japanese adults know someone who has indicated an intention to never marry and that only a minority of respondents believes that marriage is necessary for men and women to live a full and satisfying life. Importantly, those who know someone who intends not to marry are much less likely to believe in the necessity of marriage (Rindfuss *et al.* 2004: 853).

Despite the relative stability of marriage intentions, it is clear that many unmarried Japanese are not particularly sanguine about the benefits of marriage. Data from the 12th National Fertility Survey (conducted in 2002) indicate that one-third of unmarried men and one-fourth of unmarried women felt that there are no advantages to marriage while 80 per cent of men and 90 per cent of women felt that single life possesses advantages not available from marriage (Kaneko 2004b). Both men and women consider personal freedom (*kōdō ya ikikata ga jiyū*) to be a particularly important advantage of remaining single. Survey data analyzed by Tsuya, Mason, and Bumpass (2004) also indicate that unmarried Japanese are substantially more pessimistic than their American counterparts about the economic benefits of marriage. The proportion believing that marriage would result in a lower standard of living was much higher in Japan (35 per cent) than in the U.S. (23 per cent) whereas the proportion believing that marriage would improve their standard of living was much higher in the U.S. (46 per cent vs. 24 per cent). This same study demonstrated that the perceived benefits of marriage in Japan are particularly low for women and for those coresiding with parents.

One important reason for these U.S.-Japan differences in perceptions of marriage may be the extremely high costs of educating children in contemporary Japan. The high cost of raising children is increasingly cited by both men and women as a primary reason for the well-documented gap between intended fertility and desired fertility (e.g., Moriizumi 2003). Between 1982 and 2002, the proportion of married women citing the high costs of raising children as an important reason for intending to have fewer than their desired number of children rose from 24 per cent to 63 per cent (Ikenoue and Mita 1998; Moriizumi 2003).[3] Given that marriage and childbearing remain closely linked, these shifting perceptions of the cost of children suggest that declining rates of marriage may reflect a decline in the desire for children. That is, causal relationships between marriage and fertility may go in both directions.

### 3.2 *Attitudes toward gender*

It is also possible that growing ambivalence towards marriage and relatively pessimistic views of the benefits of marriage may be linked to changing attitudes toward gender. Atoh (2001) examines long-term trends in several attitudinal measures to conclude that individualistic attitudes emphasized in discussions of the "second demographic transition" have changed very little while gender related attitudes have shifted significantly. For example, support for statements such as "women should marry" and "women should get married because a woman's happiness lies in marriage" has declined substantially in recent decades (Tsuya 1994; Tsuya and Mason 1995; Retherford, Ogawa and Sakamoto 1996). Between 1992 and 2002, the proportion agreeing (completely or somewhat) that "the husband should work while the wife takes care of the house" declined from 62 per cent to 40 per cent among unmarried men, from 50 per cent to 29 per cent among unmarried women, and from 39 per cent to 29 per cent among married women (Iwasawa 2004). At the same time, it is important to note that nearly three-fourths of all respondents to the 2002 National Fertility Survey agreed that it is best if mothers stay at home and not work while children are young (Iwasawa 2004).

Attitudes about married women's labour force participation across the life course also suggest that disapproval of work is increasingly confined to the period when children are very young. In the 1987 National

[3] Note that the wording of this question and the ordering of response categories changed slightly in the most recent survey.

Fertility Survey, only 19 per cent of 18–34 year old unmarried women stated that they hoped to continue working without interruption after marriage and childbirth, while 31 per cent preferred to return to work after raising children, and 34 per cent preferred to become full-time housewives. By 2002, however, 28 per cent stated that they hoped to continue working while only 19 per cent preferred to become full-time housewives. Although at a lower level, the proportion of unmarried men who hope that their wives will continue working after marriage has also increased substantially—from 11 per cent in 1987 to 19 per cent in 2002 (Kamano 2004). Importantly, the majority of women who would like to balance work and family expect to either exit the labour force temporarily before returning at a later age or to become full-time housewives. This gap between women's desired and expected life course suggests that many women who anticipate being unable to fulfil career aspirations may have a strong incentive to postpone marriage in order to remain involved in rewarding employment. In this context, it is also interesting to note that a substantial proportion of married women would like to work more than they are currently working and many of their husbands would also prefer them to work longer hours (Bumpass *et al.* 2006).

While attitudes toward gender and family have changed across the board, it is important to recognize that, in all cases, women's attitudes have changed to a greater extent than men's (Tsuya and Mason 1995). Women are increasingly less likely than men to support gender specialization within marriage, to feel that mother's work is detrimental to children, and to disapprove of divorce as a solution to an unsatisfactory marriage (Iwasawa 2004). Women are also more likely than men to consider the likelihood of coresidence with in-laws as a condition for choosing a spouse (Sasai 1999), suggesting a possible divergence in men's and women's attitudes toward intergenerational relations and care-provision. Taken as a whole, gender differences in the pace of attitudinal change suggest a divergence in what men and women expect from marriage (Tsuya and Mason 1995). It is not unreasonable to believe that these diverging attitudes toward marriage and family may play some part in explaining the observed decline in rates of marriage and increase in rates of divorce.

### 3.3 *Tolerance of innovative family behaviours*

Concurrent with changes in attitudes toward men's and women's roles, tolerance toward formerly deviant family behaviours has increased markedly. For example, data summarized by Atoh (2001) indicate that the proportion of 20–29 year old women agreeing that divorce is an acceptable solution to an unhappy marriage doubled from about 30 per cent in 1972 to about 65 per cent in 1992. Data describing long-term trends in family related attitudes are rare, but tabulations of National Fertility Survey data indicate some decline between 1992 and 2002 in disapproval of premarital sex and cohabitation as well as in the perceived importance of having children (Iwasawa 2004). Other sources of data also show relatively little normative disapproval of premarital sex and cohabitation (e.g., Rindfuss *et al.* 2004). In fact, one recent survey shows that a striking 52 per cent of 20–24 year old unmarried women would like to cohabit at some point (Iwasawa 2005). Non-marital childbearing is one family behaviour for which normative disapproval remains relatively strong but it is important to recognize that only 40 per cent of respondents explicitly disapprove (Rindfuss *et al.* 2004).

Attitudinal survey data also suggest that the links between love, sex, and marriage are not particularly strong in contemporary Japan. For example, among those surveyed in 1997, 64 per cent of unmarried men and 58 per cent of women (unmarried and married) agreed with the statement "Love and marriage are two different things" (*renai to kekkon ha betsu de aru*) (Iwasawa 1999: 90). A similarly weak link between love and marriage is suggested by the fact that one-third of the unmarried men and women currently involved in a relationship state that they do not necessarily intend to marry their current partner (Satō 1999: 36). Focusing on these large shifts in dating and premarital sexual behaviour, some scholars have suggested that changes in marriage timing reflect a decrease in the non-financial opportunity costs of remaining unmarried (e.g., Retherford, Ogawa and Matsukura 2001). In other words, the incentive to marry (early) has declined as companionship and sex have become increasingly available outside of marriage.[4]

As Rindfuss *et al.* (2004) note, behavioural change and attitudinal change reinforce each other. Attitudes become more tolerant as for-

[4] A similar argument is made by Oppenheimer (1988) in her theoritical framework for understanding changes in U.S. marriage timing.

merly deviant behaviours become more common and hence more visible. Exposure to those engaging in innovative family behaviours (e.g., family, friends, coworkers) fosters greater tolerance of those behaviours which, in turn, contributes to the "mainstreaming" of formerly deviant behaviours. For example, while non-marital childbearing remains very uncommon in Japan, it is not unreasonable to expect that rapid increase in exposure to single parent families formed via divorce will contribute to a reduction in normative barriers to single parent families formed via non-marital childbearing.

## 4. Marriage and Gender Context

### 4.1 *Women's economic independence*

Unlike the U.S. and other industrialized societies, where women's educational attainment is positively or insignificantly related to marriage (e.g., Blossfeld and Huinink 1991; Bracher and Santow 1998; Goldstein and Kenney 2001; Sweeney 2002; Thornton, Axinn and Teachman 1995), the trend toward later and less marriage in Japan has been most pronounced among highly educated women (Raymo 2003a). Similar cross-national differences have been observed with respect to other indicators of women's economic resources such as earnings and employment. Women's economic resources are positively or insignificantly associated with marriage in the U.S. (e.g., Sweeney 2002; Xie *et al.* 2003), Sweden (Ono 2003), and Australia (Santow and Bracher 1994), but negatively associated with marriage in Japan (Ono 2003). Italy is one of the few other industrialized countries in which an inverse relationship between women's educational attainment and marriage has been documented (Pinelli and DeRose 1995). Thus, it is only in Japan and other select countries that recent patterns of marriage are consistent with sociological and economic theories of marriage emphasizing concepts of specialization and exchange to suggest that women's economic independence should deter marriage (e.g., Becker 1991; Parsons 1949).

Sociologists have attributed these cross-national differences in the relationship between women's education and marriage to gender context, arguing that women's economic independence may be most relevant for understanding changing marriage behaviour in societies where gender-asymmetry in the division of domestic labour makes it difficult for women to balance work and family (e.g., Blossfeld 1995). Research on the U.S. suggests that although women continue to perform the majority of domestic work (Shelton and John 1996), the terms of marriage have shifted such that most families are no longer characterized by the gender-asymmetric division of labour upon which neoclassical economic and functionalist theories of marriage are predicated (Oppenheimer 1997). This view of the "shifting economic foundations of marriage" (Sweeney 2002) suggests that the association between women's educational attainment and marriage is most likely to be negative when relative improvements in women's economic opportunities are not accompanied by convergence in men's and women's economic roles within the family. In societies such as Japan, where gender specialization remains a basic feature of marriage (Tsuya *et al.* 2005; Tsuya and Mason 1995), marriage typically requires women to either reduce market employment or engage in a burdensome "second shift." As women's educational attainment and associated economic opportunities increase, both of these alternatives may become progressively less attractive (Ono 2003; Raymo 2003a; Tsuya and Mason 1995).

### 4.2 *Marriage market mismatches*

At the same time, however, recent research highlights a fundamental limitation with this conventional approach of interpreting relatively large declines in the marriage rates of highly educated women in relatively gender-inegalitarian societies as evidence of increasing economic independence. For example, Raymo and Iwasawa (2005) develop and test an alternative explanation for the inverse relationship between women's education and marriage that emphasizes shifting marriage market composition and stability in spouse selection criteria. They demonstrate that roughly half of the "excess" decline in marriage observed among female university graduates in Japan (typically interpreted as support for the economic independence hypothesis) is explained by changes in marriage market composition in conjunction with stable preferences for marriages in which the husband has at least as much education as the wife. Relative improvements in women's educational attainment have increased the representation of highly educated women in the marriage market, thus contributing to lower rates of marriage among these women and among less educated men. In fact, this shift in marriage market composition accounts for all of the change in the relative proportions of two-year college graduates and high school graduates ever married by a given age. The composition-independent propensity to marry among junior college graduates has actually increased relative to that of high school graduates (Raymo and Iwasawa 2005: 816).

It is important to keep in mind that these results do not imply that economic independence is unimportant for understanding the trend toward later marriage in societies such as Japan where asymmetric gender relations make it difficult for women to combine work and family. Indeed, Raymo and Iwasawa's (2005) findings are consistent with predictions of the economic independence hypothesis in that changes in the composition-independent propensity to marry account for roughly half of the differential decline in marriage of university graduates relative to high school graduates. At the same time, however, the strong marriage-inhibiting effect of shifts in marriage market composition points to the importance of women's continued economic dependence on men. The marriage-facilitating effect of women's economic resources discussed in studies of marriage in the U.S. (e.g., Oppenheimer 1988) thus appears to be less relevant in societies such as Japan where the highly asymmetric gender-division of work and family roles reinforces highly educated women's desire for status homogamous or status hypergamous marriages.

If these asymmetric spouse pairing preferences remain strong while the relative supply of highly educated men continues to decline, it is likely that increasing proportions of highly educated women (and less educated men) will marry at later ages or not at all. The plausibility of this scenario is suggested by evidence that highly educated women in the U.S. appear to prefer to remain single rather than marry a man with less education than themselves (Lichter, Anderson and Hayward 1995).[5] Although there is some evidence that the association between spouses' educational attainment in Japan has weakened over time (Raymo and Xie 2000; Suzuki 1991), this change has clearly not been sufficient to offset the large changes in marriage market composition. It is conceivable, however, that changes in men's contribution to housework and the implementation of policies designed to facilitate work-family balance may result in more symmetric spouse pairing preferences that offset declines in the relative supply of highly educated men. In the absence of such changes, however, continued improvements in women's economic opportunities may actually strengthen the role of men's economic

[5] See Lewis and Oppenheimer (2000), however, for evidence that women adjust their spouse selection criteria in response to limited mate availability.

resources as a spouse selection criterion (i.e., because the opportunity costs of career interruption would increase), thus exacerbating marriage market mismatches.

### 4.3 *Extended coresidence with parents*

Another explanation for delayed marriage popularized in the mass-media emphasizes the material benefits of extended coresidence with parents. Using catchy terms such as *dokushin kizoku* (aristocratic singles) and *parasaito shinguru* (parasite singles), this hypothesis suggests that young men and (especially) young women are increasingly taking advantage of free room and board to enjoy a relatively luxurious lifestyle while remaining in the parental home. Despite popular endorsement, most empirical studies have found little or no support for this hypothesis. Indeed, it appears that it is those who are the least likely to enjoy the material benefits of coresidence with parents are also the most likely to remain in the parental home while delaying marriage (Raymo 2003b).

A recent analysis based on more detailed information about coresident women's household contributions paints a more complicated picture, however. Raymo and Ono (2007) posit that the lack of empirical support for the extended coresidence hypothesis may reflect the implicit assumption in earlier studies that all women respond to the benefits of coresidence with parents in the same way. Contrary to this assumption, the evidence relevant to theoretical emphases on women's economic independence, the difficulty of work-family balance, and spouse pairing patterns summarized above suggests that the mechanisms through which extended coresidence influences marriage behaviour may depend fundamentally upon women's own socio-economic characteristics. Because the opportunity costs of gender specialization within marriage are proportional to women's own earning potential, the ability to invest in career development without the competing demands of domestic work may make extended coresidence with parents an attractive alternative to marriage for women with higher levels of human capital. In contrast, women with lower levels of human capital may view the economic benefits of extended coresidence with parents as an attractive alternative to early marriage given that the impact of recent increases in unemployment and contingent employment and reduced access to jobs likely to provide lifetime employment has been felt most strongly by the men they are most likely to marry (Genda and Kurosawa 2001; Kosugi 2001).

Consistent with this modified hypothesis emphasizing the importance of gender context, Raymo and Ono (2007) demonstrate that relationships between "the comforts of home" and later marriage depend fundamentally on coresident women's own socio-economic resources. More specifically, it appears that limited responsibility for domestic work is associated with later marriage for those women for whom entry into a typically gender-asymmetric marriage would entail the highest opportunity costs—i.e., the most highly educated women, those in professional and managerial occupations, and those with the highest earnings. However, they found little support for the hypothesis that lower living expenses slow the transition to marriage among coresident women whose potential spouses have the most tenuous economic prospects. Overall, these results are consistent with the studies summarized above in suggesting that the highly asymmetric division of labour within marriage and the associated difficulty women face in balancing work and family may indeed be an important part of an explanation for the observed inverse relationship between socio-economic status and marriage among Japanese women.

## 5. Discussion

As in other industrialized countries, patterns of family formation and dissolution have changed dramatically in Japan. Marriages are taking place at later ages, are increasingly likely to follow cohabitation and pregnancy, and are increasingly likely to end in divorce. In this chapter, we have described ways in which the Japanese experience provides important insights into contextual variation in the mechanisms central to theoretical explanations for the trend toward later and less marriage. We have placed particular emphasis on the combined effects of rapid expansion of social and economic opportunities for women and limited change in the division of labour within the home. The resulting difficulty that women face in balancing work and family provides a compelling explanation for the relatively sceptical attitudes toward marriage in Japan, for evidence that Japan is one of the few countries where educational attainment and other indicators of women's human capital are negatively associated with marriage, for evidence that gender convergence in educational attainment has contributed to marriage market mismatches detrimental to more highly educated women, and for evidence that the limited domestic responsibilities associated with coresidence in the parental home contribute to later marriage for women with the highest levels of human capital.

It is important to stress that our emphasis on gender-asymmetric work and family roles does not imply that Japanese women are rejecting a primarily domestic role for themselves. Rather it highlights the importance of Tsuya and Mason's (1995) call for greater attention to heterogeneity in young Japanese men's and women's attitudes toward marriage and family. Questions asking unmarried women about their ideal and expected life course suggest that there are some women who have no interest in sacrificing their careers for marriage and family, others who are eager to marry, have children, and become homemakers, and a majority who hope and expect to adjust their work commitment to meet family demands and responsibilities (e.g., Kamano 2004). These three groups correspond roughly to Hakim's (2000) work-centred, home-centred, and adaptive women, respectively. In the context of expanding social and economic opportunities for women and little change in the extreme difficulty that women face in balancing work and family, the trend toward later marriage likely reflects an increasing reluctance on the part of the women in the "adaptive" category "to enter marriage before enjoying a period of relative autonomy and freedom from domestic burdens during which they can seek higher education and work for pay" (Tsuya and Mason 1995: 162).

These interpretations of findings from our recent work point to the potential effectiveness of efforts to promote marriage and family formation through policies such as the "New Angel Plan" designed to facilitate work-family balance (e.g., stricter enforcement of maternity leave policies, increased access to child care). At the same time, it also suggests that the impact of policies designed to promote a family-friendly workplace may be limited to the extent that women with higher earnings potential postpone marriage based on a perception that their potential husbands will provide little domestic support.

## References

Anzo, Shinji (1985): Measurement of the Marriage Squeeze and its Application. In: *Jinkōgaku Kenkyū* [Journal of Population Studies] (May) 5, 8, pp. 1–10.

Atoh, Makoto (2001): Very Low Fertility in Japan and Value Change Hypotheses. In: *Review of Population and Social Security Policy* 10, pp. 1–21. http://www.ipss.go.jp/publication/e/R_S_P/No.10_P1.pdf (found 30/05/2006)

Becker, Gary S. (1991): *A Treatise on the Family.* Cambridge, MA: Harvard University Press.

Billari, Francesco C., Hans-Peter Kohler and Jose A. Ortega (2002): The Emergence of Lowest-Low Fertility in Europe during the 1990s. In: *Population and Development Review* 28, pp. 641–680.
Blossfeld, Hans-Peter (1995): Changes in the Process of Family Formation and Women's Growing Economic Independence: A Comparison of Nine Countries. In: Blossfeld, Hans-Peter (ed.): *The New Role of Women: Family Formation in Modern Societies*. Boulder, CO: Westview Press, pp. 3–32.
Blossfeld, Hans-Peter and Johannes Huinink (1991): Human Capital Investments or Norms of Role Transition? How Women's Schooling Affects the Process of Family Formation. In: *American Journal of Sociology* 97, pp. 143–168.
Bracher, Michael and Gigi Santow (1998): Economic Independence and Union Formation in Sweden. In: *Population Studies* 52, pp. 275–294.
Brinton, Mary C. (2001): Married Women's Labor in East Asian Economies. In: Brinton, Mary C. (ed.): *Women's Working Lives in East Asia*. Stanford, CA: Stanford University Press, pp. 1–37.
Brinton, Mary C. and Hang-Yue Ngo (1993): Age and Sex in the Occupational Structure: A United States-Japan Comparison. In: *Sociological Forum* 8, pp. 93–111.
Bumpass, Larry L., Teresa Castro Martin and James A. Sweet (1991): The Impact of Family Background and Early Marital Factors on Marital Disruption. In: *Journal of Family Issues* 12, pp. 22–42.
Bumpass, Larry L., Minja Kim Choe, Noriko O. Tsuya and Ronald Rindfuss (2006): *Role Overload: Preferences for Wife's Employment in Japan*. Paper presented at conference on: Fertility Decline, Women's Choices in the Life Course, and Balancing Work and Family Life: Japan, the USA, and other OECD Countries. Abe Fellowship Program CGP-SSRC Seminar Series. Chicago, IL (May 16–17).
Chesnais, Jean-Claude (1996): Fertility, Family, and Social Policy in Contemporary Western Europe. In: *Population and Development Review* 22, pp. 729–739.
Genda, Yuji and Masako Kurosawa (2001): Transition from School to Work in Japan. In: *Journal of the Japanese and International Economies* 15, pp. 465–488.
Goldstein, Joshua A. and Catherine T. Kenney (2001): Marriage Delayed or Marriage Foregone? New Cohort Forecasts of First Marriage for U.S. Women. In: *American Sociological Review* 66, pp. 506–519.
Hakim, Catherine (2000): *Work-Lifestyle Choices in the 21st Century*. Oxford, U.K.: Oxford University Press.
Hirao, Keiko (2001): Mothers as the Best Teachers: Japanese Motherhood and Early Childhood Education. In: Brinton, Mary C. (ed.): *Women's Working Lives in East Asia*. Stanford, CA: Stanford University Press, pp. 180–203.
Houseman, Susan and Machiko Osawa (2003): The Growth of Nonstandard Employment in Japan and the United States: A Comparison of Causes and Consequences. In: Houseman, Susan and Machiko Osawa (eds.): *Nonstandard Work in Developed Economies: Causes and Consequences*. Kalamazoo, MI: Upjohn Institute for Employment Research, pp. 175–211.
Ikenoue, Masako and Fusami Mita (1998): Kodomosū ni tsuite no kangaekata [Attitudes towards the number of children]. In: *Nihonjin no kekkon to shussan—Dai 11kai shusshō dōkō kihon chōsa* [Marriage and fertility in Japan—The eleventh national fertility survey]. Tokyo: National Institute of Population and Social Security Research, pp. 35–41.
Iwasawa, Miho (1999): Kekkon, kazoku ni kansuru ishiki [Attitudes about marriage and family] In: *Dokushinshanensō no kekkonkan to kodomokan—Dai 11kai shusshō dōkō kihon chōsa* [Attitudes toward marriage and the family among Japanese singles—The eleventh national fertility survey]. Tokyo: Kōsei Tōkei Kyōkai, pp. 90–96.
—— (2004): Kekkon, kazoku ni kansuru ishiki [Attitudes about marriage and family] In: *Dokushinshanensō no kekkonkan to kodomokan—Dai 12kai shusshō dōkō kihon chōsa* [Attitudes toward marriage and the family among Japanese singles—The twelfth national fertility survey]. Tokyo: Kōsei Tōkei Kyōkai, pp. 108–111.

—— (2005): Nihon ni okeru dōsei no genjō [Unmarried cohabitation in Japan]. In: Mainichi Shinbunsha Jinkō Mondai Chōsakai [Mainichi Newspaper Population Research Council] (ed.): *Chōshōshika jidai no kazoku ishiki* [English: *Family Attitudes in an Era of Lowest-Low Fertility*]. Tokyo: Mainichi Shinbunsha, pp. 71–106.

Iwasawa, Miho and Fusami Mita (2005): Shokuen kekkon no seisui to mikonka no shinten [Boom and bust in workplace marriages and the marriage decline in Japan]. In: *Nihon Rōdō Kenkyū Zasshi* 535, pp. 16–28.

Kamano, Saori (2004): Kibō suru raifu kōsu [Desired life course]. In: *Dokushinshanensō no kekkonkan to kodomokan—Dai 12kai shusshō dōkō kihon chōsa* [Attitudes toward marriage and the family among Japanese singles—The twelfth national fertility survey]. Tokyo: Kōsei Tōkei Kyōkai, pp. 78–84.

Kaneko, Ryūichi (2004a): Kekkon no iyoku [Desire to marry]. In: *Dokushinshanensō no kekkonkan to kodomokan—Dai 12kai shusshō dōkō kihon chōsa* [Attitudes toward marriage and the family among Japanese singles—The twelfth national fertility survey]. Tokyo: Kōsei Tōkei Kyōkai, pp. 13–29.

—— (2004b): Kekkon no riten, dokushin no riten [Advantages of marriage, advantages of single life]. In: *Dokushin shanensō no kekkonkan to kodomokan—Dai 12kai shusshō dōkō kihon chōsa* [Attitudes toward marriage and the family among Japanese singles—The twelfth national fertility survey]. Tokyo: Kōsei Tōkei Kyōkai, pp. 30–37.

Kaneko, Ryūichi and Fusami Mita (2003): Fusai no kekkon katei [The marriage process]. In: *Wagakuni fūfu no kekkon katei to shusshōryoku—Dai 12kai shusshō dōkō kihon chōsa* [Marriage process and fertility of Japanese married couples—The twelfth national fertility survey]. Tokyo: Kōsei Tōkei Kyōkai, pp. 12–36.

Kögel, Tomas (2004): Did the Association between Fertility and Female Employment within OECD Countries Really Change its Sign? In: *Journal of Population Economics* 17, pp. 45–65.

Kosugi, Reiko (2001): The Transition from School to Work in Japan: Understanding the Increase in Freeter and Jobless Youth. In: *Japan Labor Review* 1, 1, pp. 52–67.

Lesthaeghe, Ron (1995): The Second Demographic Transition—An Interpretation. In: Mason, Karen O. and An-Magrit Jensen (eds.): *Gender and Family Change in Industrial Countries*. Oxford, U.K.: Clarendon Press, pp. 17–62.

Lewis, Susan K. and Valerie K. Oppenheimer (2000): Educational Assortative Mating Across Marriage Markets: Non-Hispanic Whites in the United States. In: *Demography* 37, pp. 29–40.

Lichter, Daniel T., Robert N. Anderson and Mark D. Hayward (1995): Marriage Markets and Marital Choice. In: *Journal of Family Issues* 16, pp. 412–431.

McDonald, Peter (2000): Gender Equity in Theories of Fertility Transition. In: *Population and Development Review* 26, pp. 427–439.

Moriizumi, Rie (2003): Kodomosū ni tsuite no kangaekata [Attitudes towards the number of children]. In: *Wagakuni fūfu no kekkon katei to shusshōryoku—Dai 12kai shusshō dōkō kihon chōsa* [Marriage process and fertility of Japanese married couples—The twelfth national fertility survey]. Tokyo: Kōsei Tōkei Kyōkai, pp. 54–62.

—— (2004): Kibō kodomosū [Desired number of children]. In: *Dokushinshanensō no kekkonkan to kodomokan—Dai 12kai shusshō dōkō kihon chōsa* [Attitudes toward marriage and the family among Japanese singles—The twelfth national fertility survey]. Tokyo: Kōsei Tōkei Kyōkai, pp. 92–97.

NIPSSR (National Institute of Population and Social Security Research) (2004): *Dokushinshanensō no kekkonkan to kodomokan—Dai 12kai shusshō dōkō kihon chōsa* [Attitudes toward marriage and the family among Japanese singles—The twelfth national fertility survey]. Tokyo: Kōsei Tōkei Kyōkai.

—— (National Institute of Population and Social Security Research) (2006): *Latest Demographic Statistics*. Tokyo: Kōsei Tōkei Kyōkai.

Ogasawara, Yuko (2001): Women's Solidarity: Company Policies and Japanese Office Ladies. In: Brinton, Mary C. (ed.): *Women's Working Lives in East Asia*. Stanford, CA: Stanford University Press, pp. 151–179.

Ogawa, Naohiro and John F. Ermisch (1996): Family Structure, Home Time Demands, and the Employment Patterns of Japanese Married Women. In: *Journal of Labor Economics* 14, pp. 677–702.

Ono, Hiromi (2003): Women's Economic Standing, Marriage Timing, and Cross-National Contexts of Gender. In: *Journal of Marriage and Family* 65, pp. 275–286.

Oppenheimer, Valerie K. (1988): A Theory of Marriage Timing. In: *American Journal of Sociology* 94, pp. 563–591.

—— (1997): Women's Employment and the Gains to Marriage: The Specialization and Trading Model of Marriage. In: *Annual Review of Sociology* 23, pp. 431–453.

Parsons, Talcott (1949): The Social Structure of the Family. In: Anshen, Ruth N. (ed.): *The Family: Its Function and Destiny*. New York: Harper and Brothers, pp. 173–201.

Pinelli, Antonella and Alessandra De Rose (1995): Italy. In: Blossfeld, Hans-Peter (ed.): *The New Role of Women: Family Formation in Modern Societies*. Boulder, CO: Westview Press, pp. 174–190.

Qian, Zhenchao and Samuel Preston (1993): Changes in American Marriage: 1972–1987. In: *American Sociological Review* 58, pp. 482–495.

Raymo, James M. (2003a): Educational Attainment and the Transition to First Marriage among Japanese Women. In: *Demography* 40, pp. 83–103.

—— (2003b): Premarital Living Arrangements and the Transition to First Marriage in Japan. In: *Journal of Marriage and the Family* 65, pp. 302–315.

Raymo, James M. and Miho Iwasawa (2005): Marriage Market Mismatches in Japan: An Alternative View of the Relationship between Women's Education and Marriage. In: *American Sociological Review* 70, pp. 801–822.

Raymo, James M., Miho Iwasawa and Larry Bumpass (2004): Marital Dissolution in Japan: Recent Trends and Patterns. In: *Demographic Research* 11, pp. 395–419.

Raymo, James M. and Hiromi Ono (2007): Coresidence with Parents, Women's Economic Resources, and the Transition to Marriage in Japan. In: *Journal of Family Issues* 28, pp. 653–681.

Raymo, James M. and Yu Xie (2000): Temporal and Regional Variation in the Strength of Educational Homogamy (Comment on Smits, Ultee, and Lammers, ASR 1998). In: *American Sociological Review* 65, pp. 773–781.

Reher, David (1998): Family Ties in Western Europe: Persistent Contrasts. In: *Population and Development Review* 24, pp. 203–234.

Retherford, Robert D., Naohiro Ogawa and Satomi Sakamoto (1996): Values and Fertility Change in Japan. In: *Population Studies* 50, pp. 5–25.

Rindfuss, Ronald R., Minja Kim Choe, Larry L. Bumpass and Noriko O. Tsuya (2004): Social Networks and Family Change in Japan. In: *American Sociological Review* 69, pp. 838–861.

Sasai, Tsukasa (1999): Kekkon aite no jōken [Conditions for a marriage partner]. In: *Dokushinshanensō no kekkonkan to kodomokan—Dai 11kai shusshō dōkō kihon chōsa* [Attitudes toward marriage and the family among Japanese singles—The eleventh national fertility survey]. Tokyo: National Institute of Population and Social Security Research, pp. 64–68.

—— (2003): Fūfu no shusshōryoku [Married couple's fertility]. In: *Wagakuni fūfu no kekkon katei to shusshōryoku—Dai 12kai shusshō dōkō kihon chōsa* [Attitudes toward marriage and the family among Japanese singles—The twelfth national fertility survey]. Tokyo: Kōsei Tōkei Kyōkai, pp. 38–44.

Satō, Ryūzaburō (1999): Isei to no kōsai [Interactions with the opposite sex]. In: *Dokushinshanensō no kekkonkan to kodomokan—Dai 11kai shusshō dōkō kihon chōsa* [Attitudes toward marriage and the family among Japanese singles—The eleventh national fertility survey]. Tokyo: National Institute of Population and Social Security Research, pp. 32–40.

Shelton, Beth A. and Daphne John (1996): The Division of Household Labor. In: *Annual Review of Sociology* 22, pp. 299–322.

Shintani, Yuriko (1998): Kekkon, shussanki no josei no shūgyō to sono kitei yōin [Determinants of women's work during the marriage and childbearing years]. In: *Jinkō Mondai Kenkyū* [Journal of Population Problems] 54, 4, pp. 46–62.
Shirahase, Sawako (2003): *Wives' Economic Contribution to the Household Income in Japan with Cross-National Perspective*. Luxembourg Income Study Working Paper Series No. 349, http://www.lisproject.org/publications/liswps/349.pdf (found 30/05/2006).
Suzuki, Tohru (1991): Nihon no tsūkonken (2) shakaiteki tsūkonken [Social intermarriages in Japan]. In: *Jinkō Mondai Kenkyū* [Journal of Population Problems] 46, 4, pp. 14–31.
Sweeney, Megan M. (2002): Two Decades of Family Change: The Shifting Economic Foundations of Marriage. In: *American Sociological Review* 670, pp. 132–147.
Thornton, Arland D., William G. Axinn and Jay D. Teachman (1995): The Influence of School Enrollment and Accumulation on Cohabitation and Marriage in Early Adulthood. In: *American Sociological Review* 60, pp. 762–774.
Tsuya, Noriko O. (1994): Changing Attitudes toward Marriage and the Family in Japan. In: Cho, Lee-Jay and Moto Yada (eds.): *Tradition and Change in the Asian Family*. Honolulu: East-West Center, pp. 91–119.
Tsuya, Noriko O., Larry L. Bumpass, Minja Kim Choe and Ronald R. Rindfuss (2005): Is the Gender Division of Labour Changing in Japan? In: *Asian Population Studies* 1, pp. 47–67.
Tsuya, Noriko O. and Minja Kim Choe (2004): Investments in Children's Education, Desired Fertility, and Women's Employment. In: Tsuya, Noriko O. and Larry L. Bumpass (eds.): *Marriage, Work, and Family Life in Comparative Perspective: Japan, South Korea, and the United States*. Honolulu: East-West Center, pp. 76–94.
Tsuya, Noriko O. and Karen O. Mason (1995): Changing Gender Roles and Below Replacement Fertility in Japan. In: Mason, Karen O. and An-Magrit Jensen (eds.): *Gender and Family Change in Industrialized Countries*. Oxford: Clarendon Press, pp. 139–167.
Tsuya, Noriko O., Karen O. Mason and Larry L. Bumpass (2004): Views of Marriage among Never-Married Young Adults. In: Tsuya, Noriko O. and Larry L. Bumpass (eds.): *Marriage, Work, and Family Life in Comparative Perspective: Japan, South Korea, and the United States*. Honolulu: East-West Center, pp. 39–53.
Van de Kaa, Dirk (1987): Europe's Second Demographic Transition. In: *Population Bulletin* 42, pp. 1–57.
Xie, Yu, James M. Raymo, Kimberly Goyette and Arland Thornton (2003): Economic Potential and Entry into Marriage and Cohabitation. In: *Demography* 40, pp. 351–367.
Yu, Wei-hsin (2001): Family Demands, Gender Attitudes, and Married Women's Labor Force Participation: Comparing Japan and Taiwan. In: Brinton, Mary C. (ed.): *Women's Working Lives in East Asia*. Stanford: Stanford University Press, pp. 70–95.

CHAPTER FIFTEEN

# CHILD CARE IN A LOW BIRTH SOCIETY

Akiko S. Oishi

In this chapter, I present how children are cared for in modern Japan with paying attention to the institutional settings. The first part describes features of labour force participation of married women in Japan. The second part presents child-care arrangements of preschool children. The third part overviews child-care systems in Japan. The fourth part describes who bears the child-care costs. In the last part I discuss topics in child care and give some concluding remarks.

## 1. The Situation of Labour Force Participation of Mothers in Japan

The labour participation ratio of women by different age groups is still clearly M-shaped, with two peaks in the twenties' group and the forties' group, reflecting the fact that women tend to leave the labour market after giving birth and returning to employment after their children are grown up. The base of the "M" has become shallower in recent years, but this is largely due to increases in unmarried working women in their thirties. If we focus on married women in this age group, the ratio of working women was 49 per cent in 2003, almost the same level as thirty years before (Statistics Bureau 2003a). In fact, about 70 per cent of women who had been working a year prior to the first childbirth left the job in 2002 (MHLW 2004b).

The low labour participation rate of women at childbearing ages is attributable to several factors. First, there is a chronic shortage of licensed day-care centres for children and out-of-school hours care centres. As of April 2005, the number of children on waiting lists for day-care centres amounted to 23,338, many of them in large cities. Second, Japanese husbands tend to work long hours which makes it difficult for them to contribute to housework or childrearing. In fact, about three-fifths of Japanese men work over 43 hours, two-fifths work 49 hours or more, and one-fifth over 60 hours per week (OECD 2004).

Thus, compared to a typical Japanese woman who spends daily an average of 3.5 hours per day for housework and child care, a typical Japanese man spends only 38 minutes per day for housework and child care (Statistics Bureau 2006).

Third, there is a wide-spread belief that a mother's presence during the child's first three years is crucial to a "healthy" development of the child (the so-called 'three-year-old myth' [*sansaiji shinwa*]) (Ohinata 2000). Faced with pressure to be a good mother, even highly-educated women often give up their careers against their wishes. As a result, the vast majority of children under the age of three are cared for by their mothers.

## 2. Who Takes Care of Children?

Table 1 demonstrates the primary child-care arrangements in the daytime by age of the youngest child. In a word, the younger the child, the less likely it is to be in a day-care centre, and the more likely the mother is taking care of the child by herself. For instance, only 6.2 per cent of children under one year of age are in licensed day-care centres, while more than 30 per cent of children over three are in licensed centres.

Table 1. Primary childcare arrangements by age of the youngest child.

(%)

| | Total | Age of the youngest child | | | | | | |
|---|---|---|---|---|---|---|---|---|
| Type of arrangement | | 0 | 1 | 2 | 3 | 4 | 5 | 6 |
| Total | 100.0 | 100.0 | 100.0 | 100.0 | 100.0 | 100.0 | 100.0 | 100.0 |
| Parent | 55.3 | 88.2 | 75.5 | 69.5 | 50.8 | 32.0 | 27.9 | 25.9 |
| Grandparent | 8.7 | 10.2 | 12.0 | 10.2 | 8.1 | 6.6 | 6.2 | 6.8 |
| Licensed daycare centres | 24.7 | 6.2 | 18.1 | 24.8 | 31.5 | 32.7 | 30.6 | 32.2 |
| Non-licensed daycare centres | 2.3 | 0.9 | 2.8 | 4.0 | 2.5 | 2.0 | 1.5 | 1.0 |
| Kindergartens | 21.7 | — | — | — | 26.1 | 44.4 | 49.5 | 46.4 |
| Other arrangements | 1.3 | 1.6 | 1.6 | 1.7 | 1.0 | 1.1 | 1.2 | 1.3 |
| Unknown | 5.8 | 2.5 | 2.5 | 3.1 | 3.7 | 9.2 | 11.3 | 15.3 |

Source: MHLW (2004a).

Table 2. Primary childcare arrangements by mothers' working status.

(%)

| Type of arrangement | Total | Not working | Working |
|---|---|---|---|
| Parent | 55.3 | 73.3 | 26.3 |
| Grandparent | 8.7 | 5.0 | 14.7 |
| Licensed daycare centres | 24.7 | 8.3 | 51.6 |
| Non-licensed daycare centres | 2.3 | 1.2 | 4.1 |
| Kindergartens | 21.7 | 25.7 | 15.5 |
| Other arrangements | 1.4 | 1.2 | 1.5 |
| Unknown | 5.8 | 3.7 | 8.8 |
| Total | 100.0 | 100.0 | 100.0 |

Source: MHLW (2004a).

Table 2 outlines the primary child-care arrangements by mothers' working status. According to the results, 51.6 per cent of the working mothers are using licensed day-care centres for child care in the daytime, and only 4.1 per cent of them are using non-licensed day care. For households with working mothers, grandparents also play an important role as caregivers, especially when the child is under one year old. In contrast, 68.3 per cent of non-working mothers are taking care of their children by themselves. Kindergartens account for 21.7 per cent of child-care arrangement of all preschool children, but the ratio is lower for mothers with jobs (15.5 per cent).

Table 3 summarizes the economic situation of the households by type of child-care arrangements. Household income is the lowest for those using licensed day-care centres when adjusted by an equivalence scale. On the other hand, household income for those using non-licensed day-care centres or kindergartens tends to be higher not only in the absolute value but also in the relative value of income adjusted by an equivalence scale.

Turning to the incomes of mothers and fathers, it is clear that fathers using licensed day-care centres earn the least (4.07 million Yen per annum) on average, while fathers using kindergartens earn the most (6.05 million Yen per annum). Although the gap in fathers' earnings between the two types of households is nearly 2 million Yen, the difference in the total household income between the two is not so large due to mothers' contribution: mothers using licensed day-care centres earn 1.45 million Yen on average, while mothers using kindergartens earn 0.58 million. In fact, median income of mothers using kindergartens is zero, because most of them are not working.

Table 3. Household yearly income, by primary childcare arrangements.

| Type of Arrangement | | Household income | Household income, EQV adjusted | Father's income | Mother's income |
|---|---|---|---|---|---|
| | | million Yen | | | |
| Total | Median | 5.90 | 2.06 | 4.80 | 0.00 |
| | Average | 6.78 | 2.30 | 4.96 | 0.70 |
| | Std. Error | –4.62 | –1.43 | –3.24 | –1.53 |
| Parent | Median | 5.40 | 2.04 | 4.90 | 0.00 |
| | Average | 6.30 | 2.23 | 5.10 | 0.29 |
| | Std. Error | –4.37 | –1.26 | –2.82 | –0.97 |
| Grandparent | Median | 7.12 | 2.06 | 4.32 | 0.00 |
| | Average | 8.02 | 2.31 | 4.30 | 1.08 |
| | Std. Error | –5.25 | –1.41 | –2.71 | –1.63 |
| Licensed daycare centres | Median | 6.00 | 1.96 | 4.10 | 0.80 |
| | Average | 6.79 | 2.23 | 4.07 | 1.45 |
| | Std. Error | –4.54 | –1.56 | –3.04 | –1.90 |
| Non-licensed daycare centres | Median | 6.57 | 2.28 | 4.46 | 0.63 |
| | Average | 7.20 | 2.54 | 4.88 | 1.57 |
| | Std. Error | –5.09 | –1.61 | –3.74 | –2.50 |
| Kindergartens | Median | 6.42 | 2.27 | 5.73 | 0.00 |
| | Average | 7.36 | 2.52 | 6.05 | 0.58 |
| | Std. Error | –4.71 | –1.64 | –4.31 | –1.50 |

Note: "EQV adjusted income" = (average household income) / (EQV); where "EQV" = 1 + 0.7 * ([number of adults] – 1) + 0.5 * (number of children).
Source: Oishi (2002: 54).

To summarize, without licensed day-care services a significant number of mothers would have been unable to work and the income disparities among the childrearing households would have been wider. In that sense one can say that licensed day-care centres have some kind of inequality reducing effect. On the other hand, those who are unable to use licensed day care have to rely on care by non-licensed institutions that vary in price and quality or on care by relatives (mostly grandparents). Consequently, there arises an equity problem among parents with young children.

## 3. Child-Care Systems in Japan

Child care and educational institutions for pre-school age children in Japan can be classified into three types: (1) licensed day-care centres,

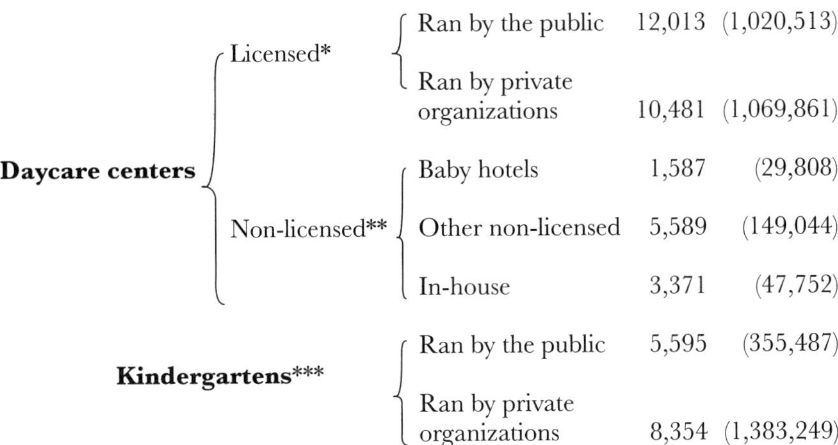

Daycare centers
Licensed*
Ran by the public 12,013 (1,020,513)
Ran by private organizations 10,481 (1,069,861)
Non-licensed**
Baby hotels 1,587 (29,808)
Other non-licensed 5,589 (149,044)
In-house 3,371 (47,752)
Kindergartens***
Ran by the public 5,595 (355,487)
Ran by private organizations 8,354 (1,383,249)


Notes: Figures in parentheses show the number of children enrolled. Surveyed dates: * October 1, 2004, ** March 31, 2005, *** May 1, 2005.
Source: Author's calculations based on Hoiku Kenkyūsho [Institute for Child Care Research ] (2006).

Figure 1. Number of childcare and educational institutions for pre-school children by type.

(2) non-licensed day-care centres and (3) kindergartens. The number of child care and educational institutions by type is summarized in Figure 1.

Day-care centres provide full-day centre-based care for 0–6 year old pre-school children regardless of licensed institution or not. Differences between licensed and non-licensed day-care centres lie in standards and availability of government subsidy. Licensed day-care centres, whether they are operated by public or private organizations, fulfil minimum standards set by the Ministry of Health, Labour and Welfare. A set of items that are specified as the minimum standard is mostly what Blau (2001) calls "structural quality." For example, these include the child-staff ratio and the space of the room available per child. In exchange for these regulations, a large share of running costs of licensed day-care centres is subsidized by central and local governments (see Figure 2).

As of October 2004, there are 22,494 licensed day-care centres in Japan. 2.09 million children, or 26 per cent of pre-school children in Japan, are enrolled in licensed day-care centres. More than half of the licensed day-care centres are under the direct management of local governments (public), while the rest is managed by private organizations,

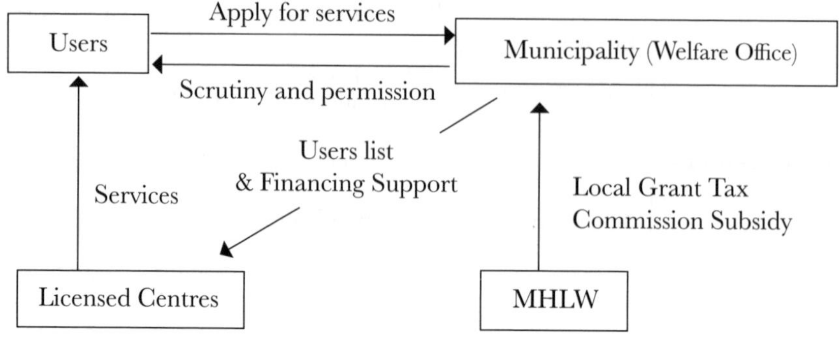


Source: Oishi (2003a: 32).

Figure 2. Mechanism of licensed daycare system.

mostly non-profit social welfare organizations.[1] Licensed day-care centres, regardless of public or private, are subject to regulations and have little freedom in management. For example, it is not licensed day-care centres but the municipality's local welfare office that decides who should be admitted to licensed day-care centres, or how much the users should be charged.[2] Usually, the admission criteria are based on needs for child care, such as household income, family structure, and mother's working status. Fee structure for licensed day-care services is uniform within municipality but differs by applicant's household income, age of the child, number of siblings and residing municipality.[3] Fees tend to be lower for older children, and if younger siblings are admitted to licensed day-care centres, they are given discounts up to 50 per cent according to their income level.[4]

In contrast, the majority of non-licensed day-care centres are operated either by private organizations or individuals. A third (31 per cent) of them are "in-house" or child-care facilities located within firms established by employers for employees with children, as represented

[1] As of October 2005, there are 920 licensed day-care centres run by corporations.

[2] With the Amendments to Child Welfare Law in 1997, potential users of licensed day-care centres are now able to choose their preferred day-care centres. In reality however, because demand for licensed day-care centres exceeds supply, users are sometimes not able to choose the centres.

[3] Oishi (2002) estimated the average users' fee to be about 22,000 Yen ($185 calculated at $1 = ¥119) per child per month.

[4] The rate of discount differs by municipality.

by in-hospital day-care centres for medical practitioners. About 15 per cent of the centres are so-called "baby hotels."[5] The rest are generally small-scale day-care centres operated by various organizations including not-for-profit and for-profit ones.

Because non-licensed day-care centres are not under the government's strict supervision on standards or financial support, the quality of child care in non-licensed centres is quite varied. With respect to the structural quality, the majority of non-licensed day-care centres do not fulfil the minimum standards set by the government, since many of them are much smaller in scale. With respect to the quality of child care for child development, some non-licensed day-care centres provide high-quality care services comparable to or even higher than that of licensed day-care centres, whereas others such as infant nurseries and the so-called "baby hotels" provide very low quality care. In terms of flexibility of services, non-licensed centres are said to be utilized at best. Because of time flexibility, some full-time working mothers prefer to choose non-licensed day-care centres. In response to the publication of a series of child deaths that occurred in baby hotels, all non-licensed centres, excluding in-house centres, are now required to notify the local authorities of their child-care services after the amendment to the Child Welfare Law which became effective in 2002.

Another major concern regarding non-licensed day-care centres is its fee. Because non-licensed day-care centres do not receive government financial support, user's fee can be quite expensive. But on the other hand those who apply for the service do not have to give proof about need of child care, lack of caregiver, household income or family structure. Therefore, even non-working mothers are able to utilize their services. Usually working mothers utilize non-licensed centres temporarily, while being on the waiting list to be admitted for licensed day-care centres. When the admission is given, parents will transfer children to the licensed day-care centre, usually at the beginning of the fiscal year in April.

Kindergartens are centre-based pre-schooling educational services for 3–6 year old children. Because kindergartens are considered as educational facilities, the Ministry of Education, Culture, Sports, Science and

[5] The so-called "baby hotels" are defined as child-care facilities that meet at least one of the following criteria: (1) facilities that provide child-care services during the night time, (2) facilities that provide child-care services over night, or (3) facilities of which more than half of the children are non-regular users.

Technology (MEXT) is in charge of running the kindergartens. Fees of public kindergartens are generally lower, between 6,000 to 7,000 Yen per month, while private kindergartens usually charge 20,000 to 30,000 Yen per month. Since kindergartens operate only for half a day, the majority of mothers whose children are in kindergarten are either not working or working in a part-time job.

## 4. Who is Bearing the Child-Care Costs?

The running costs of licensed day-care centres for FY2003 amounted to 1,528 billion Yen, or 0.31 per cent of the GDP. These expenditures are shared among central government, local government and users. Specifically, half of the costs (excluding nominal charge for users) have been covered by the national budget, 25 per cent by prefecture budget, and 25 per cent by municipality budget before 2004 when the "Trinity Reform" was put into effect (see Figure 3). The standard cost set by MHLW can be considered as the amount of cost necessary to provide the minimum standard licensed day-care.

To be emphasized, although the central government (MHLW) has set a standard expenditure criterion for licensed day-care centres, many municipalities have been infusing additional budget to lessen the burden of users and to subsidize labour costs of day-care centres in hiring temporary staffs and improving benefits of child minders. When additional

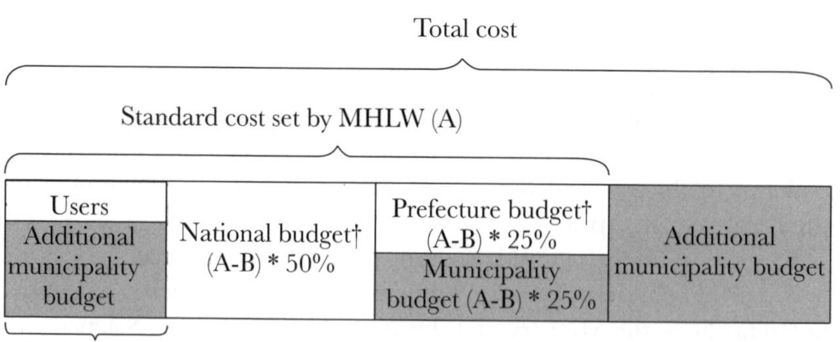


Note: † indicates the part which is borne by the municipality budget from 2004 because of the Trinity Reform.

Figure 3: Burden sharing of the running cost of licensed day-care centres.

subsidies from municipalities are considered, the total operating expenses for licensed day-care services could exceed 2 trillion Yen.[6]

In 2002, the central government initiated reform of central-local government fiscal relations, since low fiscal autonomy is thought to weaken the fiscal discipline of local government and to discourage efficient provision of local public services. The reform is called the "Trinity Reform," because it aims to implement the following three reforms as one package, namely, (1) the transfer of the tax base from the central to the local government, (2) reduction of specific purpose subsidy, and (3) reform of general purpose subsidy.

In the field of child-care services, starting in FY2004, specific purpose subsidies for expenses for public licensed day-care centres were abolished and incorporated into general revenue. The reduction in child-care subsidies amounts to a total of 181 billion Yen between FY2004 and FY2006. With delay in transfer of the tax base from the central government, some local governments are keen to privatize existing public licensed day-care centres. As of April 2005, 398 public centres were consigned to the private sector, and about 280 centres were privatized.

## 5. Capacity Concern

Urban residents in metropolitan areas of Japan are suffering from a chronic shortage of licensed day-care centres. Although the number of children admitted to licensed facilities has been rising significantly since 1995, the demand for licensed day care has been increasing at an even faster pace. As a result, the number of children on waiting lists hit a record high of 23,338 (43,434 by traditional definition) in April 2005, but there seems to be an even larger group of hidden demand for licensed day-care services if the waiting list were not so long. For example, Zhou and Oishi (2005) estimate the total number of children aged 0 to 2 in the status of underlying demand for licensed day-care services in the Tokyo Metropolitan Area to be 199,000 which is 111 per cent of the actual enrolment in 2002.

---

[6] Fukuda (2000) estimates that the total operating expenditures of licensed day-care centres in 1998 may be around 2 trillion yen, or 0.4 per cent of GDP in that year.

To meet the growing demand for child-care services, the government has launched the Angel Plans (1995–1999, 2000–2004) to increase the child-care capacity especially for 0–3 year old children. However, it is not easy to establish new day-care centres while running huge fiscal deficits in both the central and local governments. Thus, the government has been coping with the long waiting lists by deregulating the minimum standards of child-staff ratio for existing licensed day-care centres. For example, from April 1998, licensed day-care centres are required to admit 10 per cent more children than the capacity set by the standard, if there exists a waiting list in that locality.

Some local governments where shortage of child-care facilities is significant have established their own licensed day-care centre system. Local governments of cities such as Tokyo, Yokohama and Kawasaki certify some relatively high quality non-licensed day-care centres as local government licensed day-care centres, such as Tokyo-certified Day-care Centres and Yokohama Day-care Centres. The main characteristics of local government licensed day-care centres are as follows. First, although these centres do not reach standards set by the MHLW, they fulfil minimum standards set by the local governments and they are able to receive financial support from the local government.[7] Second, since these centres are not publicly operated, services can be purchased by anyone who wishes to use these centres. Thus, there are neither admission criteria nor approval from the municipality's local welfare office. Third, these centres can charge users freely within the maximum of government's fee criteria.[8] In 2006, the number of local government licensed day-care centres has reached 332 in Tokyo (as of August 1st), 131 in Yokohama (as of September 1st) and 37 in Kawasaki (as of May 1st), respectively.

In contrast to the over demand for child-care services, the number of children enrolled in kindergartens as well as the number of kinder-

[7] For example, some metropolitan governments such as Yokohama provide special license to some non-licensed day-care centres that do not fulfill minimum standard set by the central government but fulfills the standard set by Yokohama. The day-care centres licensed by Yokohama are able to receive financial support from the city government of Yokohama.

[8] The government's fee criteria set the maximum charge 80,000 yen per month for children below 3 years and 77,000 yen per month for children aged 3 years and older. Recall that the actual charges for users of licensed day-care centres are often heavily subsidized and thus below the criteria in most municipalities.

gartens itself is in decline since 1985. Because of the financial difficulty in running kindergartens in the period of declining births, some kindergartens are searching ways to combine both child-care service and educational service. In 2005, about 70 per cent of kindergartens extend opening hours beyond the usual closing time for users who wish to have their children cared for longer than the usual closing time. An increase in the number of kindergartens extending opening hours is partly due to the demand of mothers who are working on a part-time job, but more so due to the severe competition in the market for early-childhood education. The government considers an increase in the number of kindergartens that extend opening hours as one of the possible measures to alleviate undersupply of child-care services, and began subsidizing the kindergartens extending opening hours since 1997.

## 6. Quality Concern

In recent years, capacity concerns rather than quality concerns for child development are more stressed. Even when quality is highlighted, the context under which it is discussed is more of a flexibility and convenience for parents. As such, in discussing "quality" of child-care services, it is crucial to keep in mind whether the quality is discussed in terms of parent's need for more flexibility, or in terms of the children's developmental education.

### 6.1 *Flexibility of services*

One of the major quality related issues regarding day-care centres in Japan is the flexibility of child-care services. A large share of working mothers in large metropolitan areas is not able to utilize public-run licensed day-care centres, due to the inflexible nature of services. For example, many centres still close before seven o'clock in the evening when full-time working parents are hardly able to leave the office earlier than six o'clock and commuting time is usually more than an hour. In comparison, the child-care service provided by licensed day-care centres run by private non-profit social welfare organizations is much more flexible. Larger share of non-public licensed day-care centres are open longer hours. For example, about 70 per cent of non-public centres are open more than 11 hours, while only 26 per cent of public centres are open this long. Probably due to the higher flexibility of private centres,

Table 4. Comparison of licensed day-care centres by ownership.

| | Public | Private | Total |
|---|---|---|---|
| Number of institutions | 12,013 | 10,481 | 22,494 |
| Maximum number of children that can be enrolled (A) | 1,069,500 | 959,701 | 2,029,201 |
| Actual number of children enrolled (B) | 1,020,513 | 1,069,861 | 2,090,374 |
| (B)/(A) (%) | (95.4) | (111.5) | (103.0) |
| Number of centres open for more than 11 hours | 4,422 | 8,664 | 13,086 |
| (%) | (36.8) | (82.7) | (58.2) |
| Number of centres open on holidays | 64 | 554 | 618 |
| (%) | (0.5) | (5.3) | (2.7) |
| Number of centres providing temporary childcare services | 1,859 | 3,799 | 5,658 |
| (%) | (15.5) | (36.2) | (25.2) |
| Number of staffs | 195,426 | 209,486 | 404,912 |
| Number of regular staffs | 168,528 | 187,169 | 355,698 |
| (%) | 86 | 89 | 88 |
| Number of CMs | 142,470 | 155,235 | 297,705 |

Note: Figures are as of October 2004.
Source: MHLW (2004c).

the per cent of children enrolled is much higher in private centres than public centres. Table 4 illustrates that children in private centres are over-enrolled (111.5 per cent).

### 6.2 *Quality for child development*

In Japan, the study focusing on the quality of child care provided by day-care centres have only just begun and no reliable data is available. Generally, it was long believed that public day-care centres are the best in terms of both structural quality and quality of care for child development. However, recent study implies that this is not necessarily so. Based on the original survey on child-care suppliers and demanders, Noguchi and Shimizutani (2003) examined the quality of care in licensed day-care centres. They found that private licensed day-care centres are more likely to provide higher quality of services than public centres with respect to (1) quality of workers and (2) responsiveness to users' requests.

The data on the quality of care provided by non-licensed day-care centres are virtually nonexistent. According to a survey targeted at non-licensed day-care centres (excluding baby hotels), there is a large gap in the number of centre staffs as well as in the number of child minders per centre between licensed and non-licensed. For example, there are little more than 5 care staffs in non-licensed day-care centres, of which little less than 4 were child minders. On the contrary, numbers of staffs and child minders in licensed centres are about three times as higher. These gaps reflect the difference in the size of day-care centres. The number of children per child minder shows higher structural quality of licensed centres as well. There are about 9 children per child minder in non-licensed centres while the figure drops to 8 children per child minder for licensed centres as a whole (Oishi 2003a).

With an aim to improve the quality of care in social welfare institutions as part of a structural reform in the field of social welfare, the MHLW has established a committee in 1998 to discuss the method to evaluate the social welfare service by outside experts. The committee submitted a report on categories and standards of items to be evaluated in 2001. According to the report, the quality of day-care centres is evaluated from the following four categories: (1) promotion of child development, (2) support for parents, (3) coordination and cooperation with local residents and related organizations, and (4) management and operation. So far, the evaluation of day-care centres is carried out only for a trial basis and many local governments are not prepared for introducing the evaluation system.

## 7. Recent Topics on Child-Care Policy

### 7.1 *Authorized children's centres*

Due to changing and increasing demand for child care and early-education, there has been cross-ministry cooperation to start new facilities that have both features of day-care centres and kindergartens. The "authorized children's centres," starting in October 2006, share the features of municipality-certified day-care centres, such as Tokyo-certified Day-care Centres, in the following respects.

First, children who do not meet the current admission criteria for licensed day-care centres can apply to use if they wish to. Second, parents make a contract directly with the facility they want to put their children in. Third, the authorized children's centres are subject to the standards set by the local governments but do not have to fulfil the national minimum standards for licensed day-care centres. Forth, these centres can charge users freely according to the type of service they provide and subsidies they receive. Fifth, these centres are requested to play the role of community child-care support centres.

Since most of the municipalities plan to start their authorized children's centres in the next fiscal year (April 2007), whether the centres effectively reduce the number of children on the waiting list is uncertain.

### 7.2 *Out-of-school hours care*

In 2005, 63.2 per cent of mothers with 7–9 year old children are in labour force, an increase of 4.5 points since 1995. With more mothers resuming work when their children become school age, there is an increasing demand for out-of-school hours (OSH) care. As of May 2006, there are 15,858 OSH care clubs (*gakudō kurabu*) nationwide which provide care for 683,000 children. It is surprising that the number of children enrolled in OSH care more than doubled since 1998 when the amendment for OSH care to the Child Welfare Law became effective. Although most of OSH care clubs set no enrolment limits, some of them have, and there exist 11,360 children on the waiting list in 2005. Among those clubs with no enrolment limits, congestion has become a serious problem. The number of children per OSH care clubs has reached 43.1 in 2006, a 40 per cent increase since 1993. About 13 per cent of OSH care clubs enrol more than 70 children, of which 2.7 per cent enrol more than 100 children in 2006. Since nearly a half of OSH care clubs are utilizing school facilities such as vacant classrooms, children have to endure heavy crowding especially on rainy days.

Another problem associated with OSH care clubs is their quality. Unlike licensed day-care centres, there have been no minimum standards for OSH care clubs set by the government. Even at the municipal level, it was not until very recently that the development of guidelines for OSH care clubs had begun. Average child-staff ratio of OSH care clubs is 11.1 in 2003 (ZGHRK 2006), although the ratio is quite varied. In contrast to licensed day-care centres, most of the staffs at OSH care clubs are contingent workers with half of them earning less than 1.5 million Yen per annum, which resulted in a high turnover rate.[9]

[9] Half of OSH care staffs quit their jobs within three years.

To alleviate congestion in OSH care clubs, the government set forth the "After School Children's Plan" in October 2006. The main features of the Plan are, (1) set up a total of 20,000 OSH activities base in every school area, (2) abolish subsidies to the OSH care clubs which enrol more than 70 children from FY2010, (3) promote coordination with the MEXT's after school play and study activities.

## 8. Child Care in a Society with Fewer Children

It is a common understanding among researchers in Japan that the trade-off between work and family life is one of the main causes of declining fertility. Even a temporary withdrawal from the labour market around the birth of a child would result in depreciation of human capital and thus firms' reluctance to invest in female workers. Therefore, reconciliation policies such as expanding parental leave and increasing availability of child-care services can reduce the opportunity costs of women having a child and help to recover fertility rates.

Another reason for reconciliation policies is child well-being. Along with an increase in the income inequality since the 1980s, poverty rate for children has been on the rise. Abe (2005) reports that the poverty rate for children in Japan has reached to 14 per cent in 2001, which is still lower than the U.S. and Italy but higher than most European countries such as Germany and France. Oishi (2006a) states that children's probability of being in poverty is as high as the elderly aged 65 years and over. Oishi (2006b) finds that the relative risk of poverty for children whose mothers are non-working housewives are higher than children of working mothers. Given the increased precariousness in the labour market, parental employment is the best way to keep away from, and out of poverty.

Faced with the population decline starting in 2005, the need to extend capacity and quality of child care is apparent in order to achieve two goals of improved fertility and female labour participation. In June 2006 the Japanese government launched a new policy agenda for the declining fertility society (*atarashii shōshika taisaku*). Although the new agenda maintains the pro-reconciliation attitude, it puts more emphasis on cash benefits to young couples with small children. Furthermore, the agenda departs from traditional policies by asserting "family values" and "neighbourhood ties." Some researchers criticize that putting emphasis on family values might worsen the double-bind of women. The effect of the new agenda on the birth rates is still to be seen.

## References

Abe, Aya (2005): Kodomo no hinkon: kokusai hikaku no shiten kara [Children's poverty: from an international perspective]. In: National Institute of Population and Social Security Research (ed.): *Kosodate-setai no shakai hoshō* [Social policy for families with children]. University of Tokyo Press, pp. 119–142.

Blau, David M. (2001): *The Child Care Problem: An Economic Analysis*. New York: Russell Sage Foundation.

Fukuda, Motoo (2000): Hoiku sābisu no kyōkyū ni tsuite—Hiyōmen kara no kentō o chūshin ni [Study of child-care supply—A perspective of cost]. In: *Kikan Shakaihoshō Kenkyū* [Quarterly Journal of Social Security Research] 36, 1, pp. 90–101.

Hoiku Kenkyūsho [Institute for Child-Care Research] (2006): *Hoiku Hakusho* [White Paper on child care]. Tokyo: Chiisai Nakama Sha.

MHLW (Ministry of Health, Labour and Welfare) (2004a): Kokumin seikatsu kiso chōsa [Comprehensive survey of living conditions of the people on health and welfare]. Tokyo: Ministry of Health, Labour and Welfare.

—— (Ministry of Health, Labour and Welfare) (2004b): *Panel Study of Adults in the 21st Century*. Tokyo: Kōsei Tōkei Kyōkai.

—— (2004c): Shakai fukushi shisetsu chōsa hōkoku [Report on survey of social welfare institutions]. Tokyo: Kōsei Tōkei Kyōkai.

Noguchi, Haruko and Satoshi Shimizutani (2003): Quality of Child Care in Japan: Evidence from Micro-level Data. In: *ESRI Discussion Paper Series No. 54*. Economic and Social Research Institute, Cabinet Office.

OECD (2004): *Babies and Bosses: Reconciling Work and Family Life*, Vol. 2, Paris: OECD.

Ohinata, Masami (2000): *Boseiai shinwa no wana* [The trap of the myth of maternal love]. Tokyo: Nihon Hyōronsha.

Oishi, Akiko (2002): The Effect of Child-care Cost on Mother's Labor Force Participation. In: *Journal of Population and Social Security*, pp. 50–65.

—— (2003a): Child-care System in Japan. In: *Child Related Policies in Japan*. Tokyo: National Institute of Population and Social Security Research, pp. 34–43.

—— (2003b): Hahaoya no shugyō ni oyobosu hoiku hiyō no eikyō ni tsuite [The effect of child-care cost on mother's labour force participation]. In: *Kikan Shakaihoshō Kenkyū* [Quarterly Journal of Social Security Research] 39, 1, pp. 55–69.

—— (2006a): Shotoku kakusa no dōkō [Trends in Income Inequality]. In: Kemiei Kaizuka and Policy Research Institute, Ministry of Finance (eds.): *Wagakuni keizai kakusa no jittai to seisaku taiō* [Policy responses towards the income inequality in Japan]. Tokyo: Chūō Keizai, pp. 19–36.

—— (2006b): Shigoto to ikuji no ryōritsu o koete [Beyond reconciliation of work and family]. In: Takao Komine and Rengo-soken (eds.): *Jinkō genshō shōshika shakai ni okeru keizai rōdō shakai-hoshō seisaku no kadai* [Issues in the declining birth society: economy, labour and social security]. Tokyo: Akashi Shoten.

Statistics Bureau, Ministry of Internal Affairs and Communications (2003a): *Labour Force Survey*. Tokyo: Statistics Bureau.

—— (2006): *Survey on Time Use and Leisure Activities*. Tokyo: Statistics Bureau.

ZGHRK (Zenkoku Gakudō Hoiku Renraku Kyōgikai) (2006): *Gakudō Hoikusū chōsa* [Survey on the number of out-of-school hours care centres]. http://www2s.biglobe.ne.jp/~Gakudou/ (found 25/11/2006).

Zhou, Yanfei and Akiko Oishi (2005): Underlying Demand for Licensed Child-care Services in Urban Japan. In: *Asian Economic Journal* 19, 1, pp. 103–119.

CHAPTER SIXTEEN

# TRANSCULTURAL SOCIETY

Stephen Murphy-Shigematsu and David Blake Willis

At a recent gathering of our two families in Tokyo we marvelled at the diversity in the room. There was Cheena, a woman from Hokkaido, who had lived in Mexico and California. Her sister-in-law Ann, came from Kenya five years ago after marrying her brother Taiji, who was studying at the University of Nairobi and working for Mitsubishi. There was Toshiko, who grew up in Tokyo, married an American and lived in Massachusetts for fifty years before settling into a lifestyle of spring and fall in Japan and summer and winter in the U.S. Her son Stephen was born in Japan, grew up in the U.S. and returned to Tokyo to become a national university professor and a naturalized citizen. His children, Sho and Gen, are second-generation mixes of Japanese and Irish ancestry and bearers of multiple passports who attend local public schools. David's sons, Jeffrey and Luke, attended Japanese public elementary and junior high schools before moving to the U.S. for high school and college. Luke has returned to Japan and now works in Tokyo. Ironically, David, the one who is commonly identified by others as American, has spent more years in Japan than anyone else in the room.

Like our families, the people who comprise Japanese society are an increasingly diverse group who continually redefine what the boundaries are of the supposedly stable category of "Japanese." The identity assertions of these people reveal an expanding sense of what it means to be Japanese. They challenge stereotypes and create cognitive dissonance in the minds of many mainstream Japanese. This does not mean, however, that their identities are always validated by others. They often encounter doubters who claim that they cannot be Japanese if they have or don't have a certain appearance, speak Japanese imperfectly or speak English perfectly, act in a particular way, or have a name that doesn't sound typically Japanese. Still, their acts of self-definition create new meanings for what it is to be Japanese today.

Japan is undergoing a remarkable transformation that began in its cultural borderlands and is now spreading throughout the country. The number of those who hold passports other than Japanese has more than doubled since 1990 to over two million in June 2006. Sojourners, immigrants, and long-term residents who are "Others" are now integral parts of the fabric of Japanese society. More and more residents, with or without Japanese passports, neither "look Japanese" nor "act Japanese." Some have names that sound foreign and speak with impeccable English or equally fluent Japanese. More than 15,000 persons now naturalize each year and become part of Japan's citizenry. There are Japanese citizens who are Others (Ainu, Burakumin, Returnees are some examples), too, and Others who are Japanese citizens (such as Koreans who have naturalized). For all of these individuals, questions of identity and place are common, as their lives in the cultural borderlands and transnational crossroads of Japan reveal the dynamic contradictions, complex textures, and multiple levels of reality found in contemporary society.

New and complex contexts reveal a transcultural world overlooked in our preoccupation with conceptual dichotomies and dialectical oppositions. Rather than stable, bounded cultural wholes, transformations and innovative cultural formations are now occurring which create constellations of fluid and shifting social relationships (Crehan 2002). Instead of simply seeing those people who are different as separate ethnic communities, we now understand that the people on the margins bear tremendous significance for the mainstream. In a rapidly changing Japan, "the Japanese" themselves are being transformed as they confront a new range of diversity in their midst. The struggles of on-going multiculturalism in Japan can be seen in multiple and diverse narratives of personal and larger social change of Others who are both being changed by and who are changing Japan.

## 1. Globalization and Borderlands

This is an historic moment in Japanese history as globalization and changing demographics bring great changes to Japanese society. The Internal Affairs and Communications Ministry announced the first decline in the Japanese population in October 2005, as the population of 126.76 million decreased by 20,000 (Yoshida 2005). In December of the same year, the government declared that unless something is done soon, Japan's population would be cut in half in less than a century (*The New York Times* 2006). The rapidly ageing population and a postmodern economy, that has a range of labour requirements if it is to be maintained at or near present levels, have pushed the government and the media to undertake serious soul-searching (Arudou 2006; Hisane 2006). These discussions inevitably focus on foreigners and immigrant labour in Japanese society in ways that raise further questions about globalization and the cultural and psychological borderlands which accompany such changes.

Some, like the former head of the Tokyo Immigration Bureau and now president of the Japan Immigration Policy Institute, Sakanaka Hidenori, are pressing for a clear and measured response by the government to the problem of the declining Japanese population. Business also recognizes the need for importing labour, as seen in Keidanren's description of immigration as reinvigorating the Japanese economy. Leading opinion leaders have called for the country to attract talent through such measures as recruiting foreign students and granting automatic permanent residence to them upon graduating from Japanese universities.

This concern was stimulated by reports in January 2000 from the United Nations and the Japanese government which forcefully noted the impending need for large-scale immigration to maintain Japan's labour force. Immigration has become a prominent new theme for Japan as the demographics of the relentless graying of the population and low fertility reveal grave needs. These reports made it clear that 380,000–600,000 new immigrants would be needed yearly, resulting in a foreign population in Japanese society of over 10,000,000 within 13 years. Various scenarios painted almost unimaginable forecasts that there might eventually be anywhere from 14 to 33 million people of foreign origin in a society of 120 million people by the year 2050. If the state seeks to simply add new members and force them to assimilate, then an immigrant society which will "become Japanese" would appear to be the goal.

The government's once stubborn opposition to immigration is being replaced by a grudging resignation that immigrants will likely have to be admitted but should be kept at arms' length. The term *kyōsei shakai* [lit.: symbiotic society, i.e., a society in which people live together harmoniously] is now being used in the media and by the government, replacing the buzzword of the early 1990s, *kokusaika* [internationalization] (Kajita 2001). Like *kokusaika*, this new term was created by elites to describe Japan's relations with other nations. By the beginning of the 21st century *kyōsei shakai* began to be widely used domestically, echoing the policies of countries in Europe such as France, Germany, and Sweden, where the importation of labour had originally come with an expectation (and a hope) that the "foreigners" would eventually "go home."

However, immigration has been irreversible for these countries, as it will be for Japan. As Max Frisch so poignantly remarked on the guest-worker programme in Switzerland, "We asked for workers but human beings came" (Hollifield 2000: 149). Will "Other-blindness" lead to the kind of recent upheavals observed in France, America, and elsewhere? Human rights issues surrounding foreign workers are sure to grow in Japan, too, especially in terms of housing for migrants and schooling for children (Arita 2003, Internet), where discrimination is often said to be widespread.

Despite the obvious economic trajectory and needs, no consensus has even been reached on whether it is desirable or necessary for more workers to come to Japan and no clear decision has been reached to pursue the goal of replacement migration. Sakanaka, who has said in the past that Japan has failed to address immigrant issues, has stated that the situation has been posed as a choice of only two options. One is to offset a decline in the Japanese labour force with an influx of foreign labourers and maintain the current economic power. The other is to keep tight control on immigration, which means to accept a smaller Japan in terms of economic power. While the media frames this as a choice between "A Big Japan" vs. "A Small Japan," there appears to be a realization that at least some labour will have to be imported, given the pressing needs of service industries such as geriatric care, nursing, manufacturing, and even agriculture. There are other consequences as well. The depopulation of the countryside has meant not only a shortage of labour, for example, but of eligible brides for young farmers.

Therefore, the questions of which foreigners and how many will be allowed to enter the country loom large for Japanese society. While citizens and government ponder the questions, people from other countries continue to come. As Japan moves relentlessly from a mythically "homogeneous society" to one in which somewhere between 8–27 per cent of the population will be of foreign origin, the society faces a dramatic, threatening transition. The data speak of a new Japan in need of a new understanding. We see the importance of doing the inverse of the path-breaking work of Befu and Guichard-Anguis (2001) who have examined the global presence of the Japanese, by looking at the increasing presence of the global in Japan.

## 2. Transcultural Japan

What do we mean by transcultural in the Japanese context? We choose to use this word instead of multiculturalism, which has generated minefields of interpretation, denigration, and advocacy. The multicultural debate needs to be moved beyond a restrictive view of ethnic identity, typical examples of this discourse being found in the media and in numerous academic texts in English and Japanese about different ethnic communities in Japan. This view of rigid identities and indivisible ethnicities encounters numerous obstacles when faced with what is actually happening in individual lives and communities (Befu 2001; Goodman *et al.* 2003). Multiculturalism is thus not simply the old concept of culture multiplied by the number of ethnic groups, but a new and internally plural "praxis of culture" within oneself and others.

The word *transcultural* describes even more explicitly what is happening, as it indicates movement across time, space, and other cultural boundaries. This concept enables us to better understand the deeper workings of Japanese and other societies (Banks 2004, 2006); the 'tribalist' preoccupation with boundaries misses the interactions and lives across and on the borders of cultures. While boundaries are maintained in many ways, at the same time there are those individuals who cross these boundaries and who can move freely into different contexts, mobilizing identities and enacting them fluidly according to the circumstances.

A liberating theory of culture and multiculturalism is a theory about process and dialogue, not about reified tribes, nationalist religions, and communalist conformity. This processual approach, versus a materialist (identity as property) approach, is therefore something new in the debate about multiculturalism. Culture is not just something we have and are members of, but also something we make and shape. All identities are situational, and differences are relational rather than absolute. Cultures are multi-relational rather than one-dimensional.

There are commitments, too, that reach across national boundaries as bonds of exchange and meaning. Transnational flows across borders are especially important. Families, politics, religions, and other bonds, moral as well as social and economic, help us to understand the diasporic exchanges occurring, not only between cultures of place but cultures of era, gender, and class. There are cross-diasporic exchanges as well, such as between Brazilians and Chinese, that we are only now beginning to glimpse and understand.

Applying words like transcultural or multicultural to Japan is actually not new. Contrary to popular belief, Japanese history has been a multicultural and transcultural story, from the mass migrations in ancient times from the south and west that brought new and different peoples to these islands. Large numbers of people came to the archipelago from many places throughout medieval and colonial times, and the Japanese empire (1868–1945) itself was explicitly multiethnic. Nationality was granted to Koreans and Taiwanese, and people from Japan and its colonies moved in the millions: Japanese and Koreans to Manchuria, Okinawans to Nanyo and Taiwan, and large numbers of colonials coming to Japan to work, some as forced labourers. The multicultural empire and its emphasis on the unity of peoples in Asia under the Japanese flag included places like the colonies of Manchukuo and Nanyo which were depicted as multicultural paradises (Peattie 1992; Young 1999).

Inclusion, however, did not mean equality, and a sense of Japanese superiority was maintained in a severe division between inside and outside distinguishing those closer to the center of "civilization," and those further away, those who belonged and those who didn't (Doak 1997; Clammer 2001), ideas inherited from the Chinese. This layering has often been problematized, too, as we see in the pre-war racial or ethnic classifications of colonial Manchuria (Tamanoi 2000).

How Other cultures and their representatives are seen in Japan has been dramatically affected by this ebb and flow of looking inward or looking outward, of an open or a closed Japan. Others living in Japan after World War II, for instance, became invisible, with restrictions raising the bar too high for any significant immigration and state ideology stressing that homogeneity is one of the most positive Japanese characteristics (Tanaka 1995). Japan "became" a monoethnic nation, and the Japanese a singular ethnic group. This belief achieved the status of mythology and, though now challenged, our impression is that it continues to be widely shared, not just by scholars of Japan and the Japanese themselves, but also seemingly by virtually everyone else (Murphy-Shigematsu 1993; Befu 2001).

The new demographics are changing these "realities." The demands of the economy from the 1980s have forced the gates to open to Iranians, Bengalis, Thais, Filipinos, and Japanese-Brazilians who wanted to work in Japan, particularly in the 3K jobs that had become available—*kitanai* (dirty), *kitsui* (difficult), and *kiken* (dangerous). The numbers of these peoples remained relatively small, especially in relation to the older populations of *Zainichi* Koreans and Chinese, but the presence of non-Japanese in the society continues to raise questions of ethnicity, identity, and the Other. Not only have the numbers of people in Japan who can no longer be characterized as ethnically or culturally "pure" Japanese now become considerable, but the reality that the Japanese themselves are a mixing of multiple cultures and societies is now becoming more accepted.

Today, nearly two million foreign nationals reside in Japan, accounting officially for over 1.5 per cent of Japan's population. Coming from 188 countries, according to Justice Ministry statistics for 2005, their numbers are rising (see Figure 1 and Table 1). The overall gain during the last ten years is almost 50 per cent and nearly 40 per cent of those non-Japanese living in Japan are now permanent residents. The largest group continues to be Koreans (607,419), followed by Chinese (487,570), Brazilians (286,557), Filipinos (199,394), Peruvians (55,750), and Americans (48,844) (see Table 2 and Figure 2; Korean numbers have dropped, partly because of naturalization). Many of these people have lived so long in Japan that their dominant cultural background is more Japanese than anything else, while others are of Japanese ancestry, some of whom are actually returnees. Most Brazilians or Peruvians are *Nikkei*, people of Japanese ancestry. The large increases over time of some of these communities are noted in Table 3. Of the foreign residents, 129,873 are students.

Table 1. Foreign nationals in Japan (December 2004).

| | Number | Ratio |
|---|---|---|
| Total Japan | 1,973,747 | 1.55% |
| Korea (N, S) | 607,419 | 31% |
| China | 487,570 | 25% |
| Brazil | 286,557 | 15% |
| Philippines | 199,394 | 10% |
| Peru | 55,750 | 3% |
| USA | 48,844 | 2% |
| Other | 288,213 | 15% |

Source: MoJ (2005b).

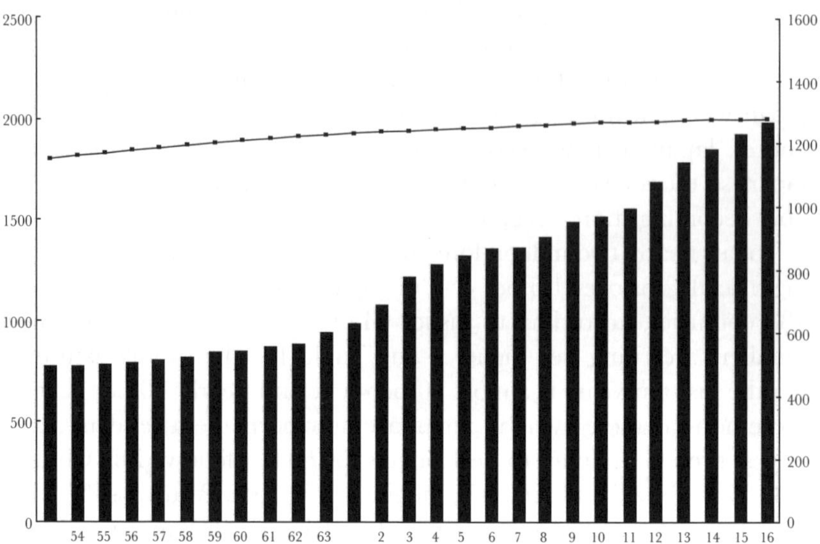


Note: Bars are the number of registered foreigners, read on the left scale, in units of 1000. The dotted line is the total Japanese population, measured on the right scale, in units of 100,000. The figure would be alarming for Japanese as of 2006 (Heisei 18) as it would show the dotted line dropping, as the bars would continue to rise and cross the line.
Source: MoJ (2005a).

Figure 1. Population increase of non-Japanese in Japan 1975–2004.

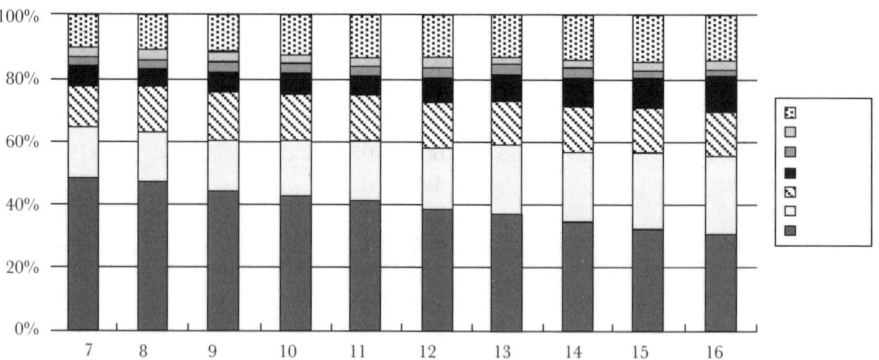


Note: From top to bottom: Other, USA, Peru, Philippines, Brazil, China, South and North Korea.
Source: MoJ (2005b).

Figure 2. Foreigners in Japan by nationality, percentage changes (1995–2004).

Table 2. Foreigners in Japan by Nationality (1995–2004).

| Nationality | (1995) | (1996) | (1997) | (1998) | (1999) | (2000) | (2001) | (2002) | (2003) | (2004) |
|---|---|---|---|---|---|---|---|---|---|---|
| TOTAL | 1,362,371 | 1,415,136 | 1,482,707 | 1,512,116 | 1,556,113 | 1,686,444 | 1,778,462 | 1,851,758 | 1,915,030 | 1,973,747 |
| Korea North/South | 666,376 | 657,159 | 645,373 | 638,828 | 636,548 | 635,269 | 632,405 | 625,422 | 613,791 | 607,419 |
| (%) | (48.9) | (46.4) | (43.5) | (42.2) | (40.9) | (37.7) | (35.6) | (33.8) | (32.1) | (30.8) |
| China | 222,991 | 234,264 | 252,164 | 272,230 | 294,201 | 335,575 | 381,225 | 424,282 | 462,396 | 487,570 |
| (%) | (16.4) | (16.6) | (17.0) | (18.0) | (18.9) | (19.9) | (21.4) | (22.9) | (24.1) | (24.7) |
| Brazil | 176,440 | 201,795 | 233,254 | 222,217 | 224,299 | 254,394 | 265,962 | 268,332 | 274,700 | 286,557 |
| (%) | (13.0) | (14.3) | (15.7) | (14.7) | (14.4) | (15.1) | (15.0) | (14.5) | (14.3) | (14.5) |
| Philippines | 74,297 | 84,509 | 93,265 | 105,308 | 115,685 | 144,871 | 156,667 | 169,359 | 185,237 | 199,394 |
| (%) | (5.5) | (6.0) | (6.3) | (7.0) | (7.4) | (8.6) | (8.8) | (9.1) | (9.7) | (10.1) |
| Peru | 36,269 | 37,099 | 40,394 | 41,317 | 42,773 | 46,171 | 50,052 | 51,772 | 53,649 | 55,750 |
| (%) | (2.7) | (2.6) | (2.7) | (2.7) | (2.7) | (2.7) | (2.8) | (2.8) | (2.8) | (2.8) |
| USA | 43,198 | 44,168 | 43,690 | 42,774 | 42,802 | 44,856 | 46,244 | 47,970 | 47,836 | 48,844 |
| (%) | (3.2) | (3.1) | (3.0) | (2.8) | (2.8) | (2.6) | (2.6) | (2.6) | (2.5) | (2.5) |
| Other | 142,800 | 156,142 | 174,567 | 189,442 | 199,805 | 225,308 | 245,907 | 264,621 | 277,421 | 288,213 |
| (%) | (10.5) | (11.0) | (11.8) | (12.6) | (12.9) | (13.4) | (13.8) | (14.3) | (14.5) | (14.6) |

Source: MoJ (2005a).

Considering other factors besides nationality, Lie (2001) estimated the population of "non-Japanese" in Japan to be 4–6 million, numbers in considerable variance with the official statistics indicated in Figure 1 and Tables 1, 2. Lie included the Ainu (25,000–300,000), Koreans (700,000–1 million), "foreigners" (150,000–200,000), Chinese (200,000), children of mixed ancestry (10,000–25,000), Okinawans (1.6 million), and Burakumin (2–3 million). Many in these groups are Japanese citizens, but Lie and some other scholars believe that they are considered different enough by many in Japanese society to the point of being culturally different and exotic, in the case of the Okinawans, or ineligible as marriage partners or workmates, in the case of the Burakumin.

More than 60 years after the end of the Pacific War, the American military, along with their dependents and civilian workers, are another group of residents totaling 104,500. They mostly live on bases, especially in Okinawa, and are short-termers, most gone in one to three years. There are also a large number of undocumented and "illegal" foreigners, officially 207,299, but perhaps numbering up to 400,000, mostly from other parts of Asia: Koreans 20.8%, Chinese 19.1%, Filipinos 14.8%, Thais 6.2%, Malaysians 3.6%, and others. Of these over-stayers, 67.3% came on short-term visas (MoJ 2006).

The Ministry of Justice has been on a campaign the last few years to tighten visa regulations, eliminating or at least strictly defining visas for short-term trainee internships of 3–4 years and visas for those of Japanese ancestry. Many workers have entered the country since the early 1990s through these routes. How far the Ministry of Justice will succeed in this is very much open to question as they are in direct opposition to other ministries and the business community, who favour loosened regulations in order to increase the supply of skilled and unskilled labour.

Regardless of how much and how quickly the numbers increase, what is especially revealing about the statistics is that they mean that more than 5 per cent non-Japanese now reside in Japan, roughly the same level of diversity as the United Kingdom had in the early 1990s. We would even venture that, more broadly defined, Others in Japan already comprise up to 10 per cent of the society of Japan. It hardly seems likely that a nation with this degree of diversity will be able to persist much longer in a portrayal of a society that is uniquely homogenous (*tan'itsu minzoku*) (Oguma 1998a, 1998b).

For many Others in Japan, the official position, that those who are non-Japanese are those with non-Japanese citizenship, belies the reality of identities and lived experiences. In reality, there are people who are not legally Japanese who regard themselves as Japanese and there are people who have Japanese citizenship but do not classify themselves as Japanese. The figures themselves mask the considerable numbers of people who are culturally or ethnically diverse or otherwise Othered, but who carry Japanese passports. Characterizing people like these as "insider minorities," Roth (2005) contrasts them with the more visible "outsider minorities" whose race, culture, or language distinguish them from mainstream Japanese (Guo 1999; Komai 1994, 1996). Among these several hundred thousand "insider minorities" are returnees—children, men, and women whose long experience overseas makes them outsiders—and naturalized citizens, mostly formerly Korean.

There are large numbers of people who are "different" in all parts of Japan now, and especially in the cities, as indicated in Tables 4, 5 for the most important urban areas. This is not the same Japan that many have imagined where all of the people are similar. These figures also reveal different patterns of diversity and multicultural communities in different cities. Tokyo is not the same as Osaka or Yokohama, while Kobe has yet another different mix of peoples (see Tables 3–7).

Along with the locations of jobs and the comfort factor of being near people who share a common language and culture is the continuing "Dejima mentality" of the Japanese foreigners being isolated in social enclaves like the small historical island of Dejima in Nagasaki

Table 3. Foreign nationals in Japan by prefecture (December 2004).

| | Number | Ratio |
|---|---|---|
| Total Japan | 1,973,747 | |
| Tokyo | 345,441 | 18% |
| Osaka | 212,590 | 11% |
| Aichi | 179,742 | 9% |
| Kanagawa | 147,646 | 7% |
| Saitama | 102,685 | 5% |
| Hyogo | 101,963 | 5% |
| Chiba | 95,268 | 5% |
| Shizuoka | 88,039 | 4% |
| Kyoto | 55,682 | 3% |
| Ibaragi | 51,123 | 3% |
| Other | 593,568 | 30% |

Source: MoJ (2005b).

Table 4. Foreign nationals in Tokyo (1 January 2006).

| | Number | Ratio |
|---|---|---|
| Total Tokyo | 364,653 | |
| Males | 172,827 | 47% |
| Females | 191,826 | 53% |
| Asia | 299,518 | 82% |
| Myanmar | 3,454 | 1% |
| Bangladesh | 3,166 | 1% |
| Sri Lanka | 1,373 | |
| China | 123,611 | 34% |
| India | 6,993 | 2% |
| Indonesia | 2,692 | 1% |
| Iran | 1,309 | |
| Korea (S, N) | 106,697 | 29% |
| Malaysia | 2,693 | 1% |
| Nepal | 2,404 | 1% |
| Pakistan | 1,519 | |
| Philippines | 31,077 | 9% |
| Singapore | 1,218 | |
| Thailand | 6,096 | 2% |
| Vietnam | 2,604 | 1% |
| Europe | 24,191 | 7% |
| France | 4,759 | 1% |
| Germany | 2,569 | 1% |
| Russia | 1,908 | 1% |
| UK | 7,696 | 2% |
| Africa | 2,983 | 1% |
| Ghana | 594 | |
| Nigeria | 687 | |
| Egypt | 228 | |
| North America | 23,374 | 6% |
| Canada | 3,621 | 1% |
| USA | 18,848 | 5% |
| South America | 9,014 | 2% |
| Brazil | 5,012 | |
| Peru | 2,414 | |
| Oceania | 5,325 | 1% |
| Australia | 4,174 | 1% |
| New Zealand | 1,017 | |
| Stateless/Other | 248 | |

Note: Data is for Tokyo Prefecture, including Tokyo City.
Source: Tokyo Metropolitan Government (2006).

Table 5. Foreign nationals in Osaka (December 2004).

| | Number | Ratio |
|---|---|---|
| Total Osaka | 213,124 | |
| Australia | 1,112 | 1% |
| Brazil | 4,871 | 2% |
| Canada | 1,053 | |
| China | 39,484 | 19% |
| Korea (N, S) | 144,994 | 68% |
| Peru | 1,224 | 1% |
| Philippines | 5,336 | 3% |
| Thailand | 1,448 | 1% |
| UK | 1,060 | |
| USA | 2,902 | 1% |
| Vietnam | 2,006 | 1% |

Note: Data is for Osaka Prefecture, including Osaka City.
Source: Osaka Prefectural Government (2006).

Table 6. Foreign nationals in Yokohama (March 2006).

| | Number | Ratio |
|---|---|---|
| Total Yokohama | 69,965 | |
| China | 24,289 | 35% |
| Korea (N, S) | 15,993 | 23% |
| Philippines | 6,900 | 10% |
| Brazil | 3,940 | 6% |
| USA | 2,744 | 4% |
| Peru | 1,804 | 3% |
| Vietnam | 1,354 | 2% |
| Thailand | 1,349 | 2% |
| UK | 1,174 | 2% |
| India | 1,036 | 1% |

Source: Yokohama City Government (2006).

Table 7. Foreign nationals in Kobe (January 2006).

| | Number | Ratio |
|---|---|---|
| Total Kobe | 44,553 | |
| Korea (N, S) | 23,102 | 52% |
| China | 12,481 | 28% |
| USA | 1,265 | 3% |
| Vietnam | 1,197 | 3% |
| India | 1,075 | 2% |
| Philippines | 813 | 2% |
| Brazil | 743 | 2% |
| UK | 460 | 1% |
| Australia | 280 | 1% |
| Canada | 253 | 1% |
| Thailand | 250 | 1% |
| Peru | 222 | |
| Germany | 210 | |
| Indonesia | 206 | |
| Others | 1,996 | 4% |

Source: Kobe City Government (2006).

Bay during the Tokugawa Era. This has, wittingly or unwittingly, meant that foreigners have clustered in certain areas in Japan, as Willis (2007) discusses, often around an international school. In spite of this clustering, at least in certain large urban areas, Japanese society has thus become heterogeneous and multi-ethnic. This has not, however, precluded a scattering of foreigners living throughout Japan. Many of these foreigners, especially Chinese and Koreans, are invisible, too, making blending in easier physically while they also bring new cultural diversity in other ways. One is no longer very far anymore, anywhere in Japan, from diversity.

An exhibition at the National Museum of Ethnology in the spring of 2004, *Taminzoku Nippon: Zainichi gaikokujin no kurashi* [Multiethnic Japan—Life and History of Immigrants] reflected this reality, emphasizing that Japan was gradually becoming a multiethnic society. Pointedly translating *zainichi* and *gaikokujin* as "immigrants" rather than with the nuances of living here temporarily or being long-term stayers (*zainichi*) or being outsiders (*gaikokujin* or *gaijin*), the exhibition made a political statement with which not all Japanese would find themselves in agreement.

## 3. Being Other in Japan

These are dissonant, contradictory times in Japan. Though historically antagonistic, Korea, at least South Korea, has recently become popular in some circles. A Korea boom that began with *Winter Sonata* (*Fuyu no sonata*), a syrupy melodrama from Korea, has extended to cuisine and pop stars and shows no signs of letting up. The other side of this story is of course the concerns of long-term Koreans in Japan regarding prejudice, discrimination, and their survival as an ethnic community.

The number of foreign students is greater than ever. Most of these students are Chinese, yet at the same time local police warnings are out all over Japan about the menace of foreign (Chinese) gangs. Young people aspire to hip-hop styles, buying their clothes from Africans dressed like Gangsta American Blacks in Osaka's Amerika-mura and Tokyo's Harajuku. The courts continue to make statements now and again about race and difference in Japan, the most recent being rulings in the spring and fall of 2006. These court decisions first went against and then in support of the claims of Steve McGowan, an African-American designer from Kyoto, who says that he and a South African friend were denied entry to an eyeglass shop because of their skin color (Johnston 2006).

Japan moves unsteadily forward, sometimes clinging to old ways, while at other times boldly engaging in new challenges. In terms of immigration, for example, she remains among the most restrictive societies, mired in the kind of contentious debate and inaction on long-term policies that is happening in many countries with regard to immigrants. But many of the more oppressive discriminatory rules and treatments have been removed, and there is a widespread awareness of the need for the protection of individual human rights against abuses by the society and the government.

The Japan that we knew no longer exists and signs of the new demographics are everywhere. Some of this society's diverse members are easily identifiable in faces and languages, whereas others are more invisible on the surface if not underneath. The stereotypical images of Others in Japan as either White Westerners or as victims of historical discrimination have given way to far more complex stories. Many Others in Japan today are themselves members of multiculturalized, Creolized families (Willis 2001a). So-called *kokusai kekkon* (international marriages) are numerous and growing, and only a minority are those stereotyped marriages of a Japanese woman and White Western man.

There are, in fact, far more Japanese men marrying Other women, mainly Koreans, Filipinas, Chinese, and other Asians.

## 4. The Other in Japan: Globalization and Changing Ethnoscapes

Japan has historically alternated between periods of celebration of a diverse, multicultural society and severe spells of xenophobia and persecution of the Other. Both forces, of open-ness and closed-ness, are of course present in any historical period. Leaders are re-introducing the idea of Japan as a multicultural society, but in ways that are more varied and contested than earlier imperial visions of a diverse nation (Tsuboi 2003). The existence of Others in Japanese society is gradually being recognized, with discrimination and exclusion occurring at the same time as inclusion and acceptance.

What multiculturalism or transculturalism mean in this society is thus represented in the way the question of difference is newly addressed. Categories over time change, and we may be on the edge of such an important change now. Diverse forms of citizenship are being proposed, with some people advocating a new, broader sense of citizenship in Japan with the push for rights for "denizens." The practices of democracy and citizenship in general show remarkable change, particularly at the local, community level where elections have seen former foreigners elected as officials and, in one case, a National Diet member (Brooke 2002; Morris-Suzuki 2002; Tarumoto 2003). Acknowledging that there are citizens who may have multiple identities, such as Korean-Japanese, Chinese-Japanese, or American-Japanese (Tai 2004) is a major step forward.

But many questions have yet to be answered about Others in Japan: What are their memberships and social networks, local, ethnic, national, and transnational? What do these networks mean for identity and how might they conflict? To what extent are the issues of culture, ethnicity, religion, values, and the presentation of cultural autonomy or identities central to their experiences? How is the pursuit of meaning, psychological and spiritual, as well as material, carried out by those who are not "mainstream" Japanese? How has social change, in Japanese society and elsewhere, had an impact on their lives and lifestyles?

Cultural differences are sometimes seen as either lasting and immutable or as giving way to a social homogenizing, assimilating process that is often defended as just and equitable. We see a greater complexity occurring that is multi-centered. While the privileging of pure cultural traits and assimilation, are of course occurring in the social landscapes of Japan, there is another view too, that of a mix, of a hybrid of possibilities, generating new differences in the process.

As Japan confronts the dilemmas brought on by the new demographics, she is moving in two seemingly contradictory directions at the same time. One the one hand, we see signs of increasing isolation in the sharpened discourse on crime and foreigners, the two commonly linked, with a particular reference to Chinese. There has been the appearance of virulent racism, not limited to Tokyo's Governor Ishihara Shintaro, who has made scurrilous, race-baiting remarks against foreigners in the society, targeting Chinese and Koreans (Shipper 2005). The UN Human Rights Commission Report of Japan (Diène 2006) has brought renewed attention to these issues of racial discrimination and xenophobia.

On the other hand, we can observe the opening of doors, symbolic and real, and an embracing of Others. NPOs and NGOs advocate for the rights of foreign workers. Trajectories, trends, and flows thus emerge in ways both positive and negative, for Others in Japan, for the Japanese themselves, and for the Japanese context. Citizens call for more flexible immigration and supportive policies for foreign labourers.

Former Prime Minister Koizumi demonstrated both sides of the discourse on April 7, 2006, when he ordered government officials to look into measures to help society accept foreign workers, saying that, "Whether we like it or not, there are many foreigners who want to come to Japan. We must think about how we can accept those who want to work or settle in Japanese society without friction." But then he added, "If we accept foreigners beyond a certain scale, there must be friction. We must think how to improve the environment and education system in order to let foreigners work comfortably as a steady labour power" (Nambu FWC 2006, Internet).

The challenge Japan faces is how to integrate those who it does allow to settle in the country. Minorities have either not had a voice or have had their voice softened to a whisper (Murphy-Shigematsu 2002). Others have had strong, vocal representation, such as Koreans and Burakumin, in areas where their numbers are greater but they have still been marginalized and ignored.

Education is a place where this challenge is seriously apparent, in the plight of the children of foreign workers, now over 20,000, many of whom do not attend school. There is no legal obligation for them to be in school, and bilingual or multicultural education programs are practically nonexistent. Moreover, many undocumented foreign workers are extremely vulnerable to human rights abuses as they are denied health and welfare benefits. Others, with working visas, avoid joining health and social welfare schemes because of the onerous premiums, which would detract from their overall wages.

We are looking for the meanings of globalization in Japan through these diverse communities and individuals. These are not harmonious, utopian communities by any means, as they are formed in contexts, both global and local, of unequal power relations. We see the multiple processes associated with globalization leading to a larger hybridization, to a global mélange of social, cultural, political, and economic forces and the emergence of what could be called trans-local Creole and Creolized cultures (Willis 2001b). Creolization, a powerful act of cultural creation, transmission, and mixing almost seen as taboo in earlier eras in Japan (and the West) can now be viewed as an important force in Japanese society.

Seeing Japan as increasingly diverse reveals new layers of meaning where Others encounter Japanese society. As Nederveen Pieterse (1995, 2004) has shown for other parts of the world, globalization does not mean homogenization; just the opposite is usually the case. Moving beyond static conceptions of ethnic groups and minority politics reveals border crossings, borderlands, and border zones. Boundaries have become more contingent and permeable, their meanings altered with the fluidity of politics and power. This has boundary fetishism made both more pronounced and less visible, more pronounced in the political landscape and less visible in the economy, society and daily life, which are increasingly globalized.

We are thus concerned with transnational spaces, with difference, and marginality (Iyotani 2001; Vertovec 2001; Yoshimi and Kang 2001). Likewise, society and change in Japan, especially in terms of cultural identities, cultural transformations, and globalization, are important themes for us. Moving beyond the grand meta-narratives of Japan as either homogeneous or multiethnic, we are interested in conveying the voices and experiences of people who reflect the complexity and breadth of Others in Japan who have been crossing borders in provocative, new, and imaginative ways.

## 5. Contested Terrain: Transnational Japan

Strange things are happening in Japan today. During the Fall Sumo Tournament of 2005 the Emperor's Cup was decided in a match between Asashōryū, a Mongolian, and Kotōōshū, a Bulgarian. At the same time, across the Pacific, at a talk given at Stanford University by the late former Prime Minister Hashimoto Ryūtarō, shortly before his untimely death, he sharply rebuked a questioner who spoke of "Japan's monoethnic society" by saying pointedly, "Japan is NOT a monoethnic society." Simultaneously, Aso Tarō, at the time one of Japan's leading aspirants to become the next Prime Minister, was telling an audience in Kyushu how lucky it was that Japan was one nation with one race, one language, and one culture. These words, of course, echo the controversial remarks made by former Prime Minister Nakasone and others back in the 1980s. Aso apparently had not checked the sumo ranks recently, as 12 of the top 42 sumo wrestlers in this *kokugi* (national sport) are foreign-born: seven Mongolians, two Russians, one Bulgarian, one Georgian, and one South Korean.

The shifts are dramatic and undeniable. Many outsiders are now becoming insiders in Japan. The managers of the winning teams in the Japan Series in 2005 and 2006 were widely admired Americans Bobby Valentine and Chris Hillman. Nissan was turned around by Carlos Ghosn, a CEO with a Lebanese-Brazilian-French background. And in an article titled "Japan's New Insider Speaks Up for the Outsiders," we learn of Tsurunen Marutei, a naturalized Japanese of Finnish origin and the first blue-eyed Japanese to sit in the Diet (Brooke 2002).

Less obvious but all the more real for being in people's everyday lives are those numerous "foreigners" integrated across the landscape, in factories, restaurants, universities, schools, and local governments. At the same time, Ainu, Okinawans, and Other "insider minorities" in Japan's midst are now more assertive and visible than ever before. To be different in Japan is now fashionable and not just outwardly with a change of hair color or clothing styles, but in terms of individual attitudes, approaches, and personal life directions. The heroes of anime and the objects of cool travel desires are now Others and their cultures, be they Vietnamese, Korean, or African-American (Carruthers 2004). Food, fashion, music, and dance are now being joined by vibrant new expressive cultures and an expansive new individuality and there is a de-emphasis on homogeneity, coherence, and timelessness in Japanese society today.

Multiculturalism in Japan has thus turned the spotlight onto culture itself in Japan, as Morris-Suzuki (1998) notes, forcing us to reconsider previous images of stability and harmony which the word culture seemed to imply and emphasizing the necessity of recognizing the multiple identities of individuals. The transnational cultures and peoples have done more than that, standing the stereotypes of cultural essentialism on their head, revealing streams of meaning that embrace networks of complexity in human relations.

Culture in Japan, as in many countries, has thus become an increasingly contested terrain as new and old immigrant cultures begin to permeate society and new hybrid forms and identities have emerged which synthesize multiple, older, and more traditional forms of culture. Japanese culture being transformed by the increasing inter-penetration by non-mainstream societies and cultures as society finds itself caught in the swirl of global cultural transition and deep transformations. The world is now in Japan, just as Japan is in the world. What Japan shares, or does not share, with other societies has important implications far beyond the borders of this island nation. How Japanese society has responded to these changes and challenges thus offers us new perspectives on the Other and how to respond, or not to respond, to difference in an age of globalization and the transformations of a transcultural/transnational world.

## References

Arita, Eriko (2003): Japanese Discrimination against Korean and Other Ethnic Schools. In: *Japan Focus*. http://www.japanfocus.org/products/details/2137 (found 21/05/2006).

Arudou, Debito (2006): The Coming Internationalization: Can Japan Assimilate Its Immigrants? In: *Japan Focus*. http://www.japanfocus.org/products/details/2078 (found 21/05/2006).

Banks, James A. (2006): *Race, Culture and Education: The Selected Works of James A. Banks*. London: Routledge.

—— (ed.) (2004): *Diversity and Citizenship Education*. San Francisco: Jossey-Bass.

Befu, Harumi (2001): *The Hegemony of Homogeneity: An Anthropological Analysis of Nihonjinron*. Melbourne: Trans Pacific Press.

Befu, Harumi and Sylvie Guichard-Anguis (eds.) (2001): *Globalizing Japan: Ethnography of the Japanese Presence in Asia, Europe, and America*. London: RoutledgeCurzon.

Brooke, James (2002): Yugawaramachi Journal; Japan's New Insider Speaks Up for the Outsiders. In: *The New York Times* (Online edition 8 March 2002). http://www.nytimes.com/2002/03/08/international/asia/08JAPA.html ex=1148961600&en=10e78deda51171a5&ei=5070 (found 28/05/2002).

Carruthers, Ashley (2004): Cute Logics of the Multicultural and the Consumption of the Vietnamese Exotic in Japan. In: *positions: east asia cultures critique* 12, 2, pp. 401–429.
Clammer, John (2001): *Japan and Its Others*. Melbourne: Trans Pacific Press.
Crehan, Kate (2002): *Gramsci, Culture and Anthropology*. London: Pluto Press.
Diène, Doudou (2006): *Racism, Racial Discrimination, Xenophobia and All Forms of Discrimination—Mission to Japan*. UN Commission on Human Rights. http:www.imadr.org/en/news/DieneReportJapan_E.pdf (found 21/05/2006).
Doak, Kevin M. (1997): What is a Nation and Who Belongs? National Narratives and the Ethnic Imagination in Twentieth-Century Japan. In: *American Historical Review*, 102, 2, pp. 283–309.
Goodman, Roger, Ceri Peach, Takenaka Ayumi and Paul White (eds.) (2003): *Global Japan: The Experience of Japan's New Immigrant and Overseas Communities*. London: Routledge Curzon.
Guo, Fang (1999): *Zainichi kakyō no aidentitī no henyō* [The changing identity of Chinese in Japan: Their multidimensional acculturations]. Tokyo: Toshindo.
Hisane, Masaki (2006): Japan Stares into a Demographic Abyss. In: *Japan Focus* (14 March 2006). http://www.japanfocus.org/products/details/1864 (found 21/05/2006).
Hollifield, James F. (2000): The Politics of International Migration. In: Brettel, Caroline and James F. Hollifield (eds.): *Migration Theory: Talking Across the Disciplines*. London: Routledge, pp. 000–000.
Iyotani, Toshio (2001): *Gurobarizeishon to imin* [Globalization and immigrants]. Tokyo: Yushindo.
Johnston, Eric (2006): On the Road to Apartheid? Japan and the Steve McGowan Case. In: *ZNet* (6 February 2006). http://www.zmag.org/content/showarticle.cfm?ItemID=9677 (found 21/05/2006).
Kajita, Takamichi (ed.) (2001): *Kokusaika to aidentitī* [Internationalization and identity]. Kyoto: Minerva.
Komai, Hiroshi (1994): *Imin shakai Nihon no kōsō* [Vision for a Japan as a country of immigrants]. Tokyo: Kokusai Shoin.
—— (ed.) (1996): *Nihon no esunikku shakai* [Japan's ethnic society]. Tokyo: Akashi Shoten.
Lie, John (2001): *Multiethnic Japan*. Cambridge, Mass.: Harvard University Press.
MoJ (Ministry of Justice) (2006a): *Heisei 16 nenmatsu genzai ni okeru gaikokujin tōrokusha tōkei ni tsuite* [Statistics of registered foreigners by end of year 2004]. http://www.moj.go.jp/PRESS/050617-1/050617-1.html (found 14/05/2006).
—— (2006b): *Kokuseki (shusshinchi) betsu gaikokujin tōrokushasū no suii* [Changes in number of registered foreigners by nationality (place of birth)]. http://www.moj.go.jp/PRESS/050617-1/050617-1.html (found 14/05/2006).
—— (2006c): *Honpō ni okeru fuhō-zanryūsha-sū ni tsuite* [Regarding the number of illegal overstayers in Japan]. http://www.moj.go.jp/PRESS/050328-1/050328-1.html (found 14/05/2006).
Morris-Suzuki, Tessa (1998): *Re-Inventing Japan: Time, Space, Nation*. Armonk, NY: M. E. Sharpe.
—— (2002): Immigration and Citizenship in Contemporary Japan. In: Maswood, Javed, Jeff Graham and Miyajima Hideaki (eds.): *Japan—Change and Continuity*, London: RoutledgeCurzon, pp. 163–178.
Murphy-Shigematsu, Stephen (1993): Multiethnic Japan and the Monoethnic Myth. In: *MELUS* 18, 4, pp. 63–80.
—— (2002): *Amerajian no kodomotachi: shirarezaru mainoritī mondai* [Amerasian children: an unknown minority problem]. Tokyo: Shūeisha Shinsho.
Nambu FWC (Nambu Foreign Worker Caucus) (2006): Japan Rethinks Immigration Policy. http://nambufwc.org/2006/05/05/japan-rethinks-immigration-policy/ (found 22/05/ 2006).

Nederveen Pieterse, Jan (1995): Globalization as Hybridization. In: Featherstone, Michael, Scott Lash and Roland Robertson (eds.): *Global Modernities*. London: Sage.

—— (2004): *Globalization & Culture: Global Mélange*. Lanham, MD: Rowman & Littlefield.

Oguma, Eiji (1998a): *Tan'itsu minzoku shinwa no kigen* [Origins of the myth of the homogeneous nation]. Tokyo: Shinyosha.

—— (1998b): *Nihonjin no kyōkai* [The boundaries of the Japanese]. Tokyo: Shinyōsha.

Osaka Prefectural Government (2006): *Ōsaka-fu no kokuseki (shusshinchi) betsu gaikokujin tōrokusha* [Registered foreigners in Osaka Prefecture by nationality (place of birth)]. http://www.pref.osaka.jp/kokusai/policy/16kokusekibetu.htm (found 14/05/2006)

Peattie, Mark R. (1992): *Nan'yō: The Rise and Fall of the Japanese in Micronesia, 1885–1945*. Honolulu: University of Hawaii Press.

Roth, Joshua Hotaka (2005): Political and Cultural Perspectives on Japan's Insider Minorities. In: *Japan Focus* (posted 10 April 2005). http://www.japanfocus.org/products/details/1723 (found 21/05/2006).

Shipper, Apichai W. (2005): Criminals or Victims: The Politics of Illegal Foreigners in Japan. In: *The Journal of Japanese Studies* 31, 2, pp. 299–327.

Tai, Eika (2004): Korean Japanese. In: *Critical Asian Studies*, 36, 3, pp. 355–382.

Tamanoi, Mariko Asano (2000): Knowledge, Power, and Racial Classifications: The 'Japanese' in 'Manchuria.' In: *The Journal of Asian Studies* 2 (May), pp. 248–276.

Tanaka, Hiroshi (1995): *Zainichi gaikokujin: Hō no kabe, kokoro no mizo* [Resident foreigners: The wall of law, the estrangement of the heart]. Tokyo: Iwanami Shoten.

Tarumoto, Hideki (2003): Multiculturalism in Japan: Citizenship Policy for Immigrants. In: *International Journal on Multicultural Societies (IJMS)* 5, 1, pp. 88–103.

*The New York Times* (30 June 2006): Japan Elderly Population Ration Now World's Highest, online edition. http://www.nytimes.com/reuters/world/international-japan-population.html (found 30/06/2006).

Tokyo Metropolitan Government (2006): *Dai nihyō, Kokuseki betsu gaikokujin tōroku jinkō* [Second sheet, Population of registered foreigners by nationality]. http://www.toukei.metro.tokyo.jp/gaikoku/2006/ga06010000.htm (found 16/03/2007)

Tsuboi, Hiroshi (2003): *Tabunka shakai e no michi* [The road to a multicultural society]. Tokyo: Akashi.

Vertovec, Stephen (2001): Transnationalism and Identity. In: *Journal of Ethnic and Migration Studies* 27, 4, pp. 573–582.

Willis, David B. (2001a): Pacific Creoles: The Power of Hybridity in Japanese-American Relations. In: Matsuda, Takeshi (ed.): *The Age of Creolization in the Pacific: In Search of Emerging Cultures and Shared Values in the Japan-America Borderlands*. Hiroshima: Keisuisha, pp. 169–214.

—— (2001b): Creole Times: Notes on Understanding Creolization for Transnational Japan-America. In: Matsuda, Takeshi (ed.): *The Age of Creolization in the Pacific: In Search of Emerging Cultures and Shared Values in the Japan-America Borderlands*. Hiroshima: Keisuisha, pp. 3–40.

—— (2008): Dejima: Creolization and Enclaves of Difference in Transnational Japan. In: Willis, David B. and Stephen Murphy-Shigematsu (eds.): *Transcultural Japan: At the Borderlands of Race, Gender, and Identity*. London: RoutledgeCurzon, pp. 239–263.

Yokohama City Government (2006): *Yokohama shi kubetsu gaikokujin tōrokusha jinkō* [Population of registered foreigners in Yokohama City listed by ward]. http://www.city.yokohama.jp/me/stat/jinko/non-jp/new-j.html (found 14/05/2006)

Yoshida, Reiji (2005): Japan's population declines by 19,000. In: *The Japan Times* (28 December 2005).

Yoshimi, Shunya and Kang Sang-jung (2001): *Gurobaru-ka no enkinho: Atarashii kōkyō-kūkan o motomete* [Perspectives on globalization: in search of a new public space], Tokyo: Iwanami.

Young, Louise (1999): *Japan's Total Empire: Manchuria and the Culture of Wartime Imperialism.* Berkeley: University of California Press.

# PART THREE

# CULTURAL ASPECTS OF DEMOGRAPHIC CHANGE

# INTRODUCTION

The cultural effects of demographic change are addressed in this part of the *Handbook*. They are diverse and complex, ranging over the entire lifespan from the construction of generations to the meaning of death and the afterlife. In obvious and subtle ways social ageing transforms the very definition of human life and its cultural interpretation. This part of the *Handbook* concerns (1) the construction of age, (2) ethical and legal challenges of population ageing, (3) the reflection in language, literature and media use of ageing, (4) knowledge transfer and technology in the ageing society, and (6) life expectancy gains and what to do with them.

Age is a cultural domain, because in all cultures chronological age is subject to cultural formation. Stereotypes about age and what separates the young from the old and the middle aged vary across cultures. The progression of individuals through the life cycle is structured, relying on the categories that index life from birth to death in characteristic patterns that distinguish cultures one from another. There is order in the temporal flow of the life course. Anthropologists have uncovered that order in studies of age cohorts, cultural variation in ageing, and cultural values associated with age stratification. In Meiji-Japan the saying, *jinsei wazuka gojūnen* 'life, a mere fifty years,' was still understood quite literally. The fact that, today, reaching twice that age is not rare drastically alters conceptions of life, intergenerational relations and life plans, but we are only beginning to understand how.

Cultural anthropology is interested in the institutions members of the community have to negotiate. Age is a significant social marker associated with such institutions and highlighted by rites of passage. As an aspect of its Confucian heritage, Japanese culture is particularly sensitive to age divisions of the life cycle. However, from an anthropological point of view, age grades have usually been considered as stable entities moving through time. Changes in a community's age structure have only recently attracted attention. How are the institutions in which age differences are salient criteria for interaction and allocation of responsibilities adjusting to social ageing? The importance of seniority in Japanese kinship and employment is well-known, but age differentiation and the effects of social ageing in other institutions and organisations are only incompletely understood.

Every culture, every society lives by the validity of its moral principles. Social ageing has a profound effect on values such as respect for the elderly and filial piety, among others. Demographics has much to offer regarding the difficult question of why certain values are effective in some periods of time but not in others, because collective beliefs and values reflect, however indirectly and with temporal delay, the life conditions of the society in question. Respect for the elderly is a Confucian tenet that few Japanese would call into question. Yet, as becomes apparent in several chapters of this part of the *Handbook*, in the ageing society it becomes more difficult for an increasing number of people to live according to it. Deconstructing the notion of ageing as progress towards human perfection, Formanek shows that as a cultural topic respect for the elderly has always been counterbalanced by negative notions of old age, while associations with decrepitude and senility have become more prominent in recent times. In the past, the veneration of old age used to find expression in the observance of rites, taking care of the family grave, and passing on the knowledge one had inherited from one's parents and grandparents to one's successor. In rural areas in particular, this process was linked to certain religious roles that elderly men were assigned. Folklore studies reviewed in detail by Sekizawa indicate that this process of cultural transmission is being weakened by depopulation and the resultant lack of household successors, and that as a consequence rural as well as urban communities are in the midst of searching for a new mode of situating individual lives between ancestors and descendants. In this connection Traphagan draws attention to a very special aspect of the changing demographic structure, the growing number of uncared-for gravesites and the implications for the relationship between the living and the dead. And Ishii diagnoses waning respect for religion as a by-product of demographic change, surprisingly as this may be to some, because the elderly are often expected to be more religious than the young. However, Japan's greying society is increasingly preoccupied with this-worldly concerns rather than with otherworldly orientations, a shift that also manifests itself in the legal domain. In response to demographic change, the elderly, women and foreigners are destined to play a more prominent role in Japanese society. Thus Martin argues in his chapter that, as a result of this social transformation, reliance on tacit principles of social harmony gives way to legally grounded protection against the discrimination of these groups.

Demography also affects cultural production – literature, art, film, theatre, mass media – on the side of both producers and consumers. While age and ageing have always been present in the arts, population ageing has added several new dimensions. Ageing itself is a topic calling for artistic expression, a development that is analysed at length by Gephardt for literature. Iwao addresses the issue of shifting gender roles and their reflection in TV dramas, while Shiraishi in a data-driven study considers the use of mass media in the ageing society. Symbolic expressions of age in language are constantly being renegotiated as language changes through time. Backhaus demonstrates that the ageing society requires some lexical adjustments, while Inoue argues that the linguistic changes in response to demographic ageing are harder to substantiate than might be expected.

The demographic challenges to Japan's educational system are both highly complex and a matter of concern, because the number of children is declining and the age structure of the teaching staff is changing dramatically. Goodman examines the implications of these developments from elementary school through university, whereas Shintani focuses on the effects of ageing and technological innovation on the transmission of practical skills and traditional knowledge. To suit society's needs, technical know-how must be transmitted from one generation to the next, but at the same time it must also adjust to demographic change. Elderly users have their own specific demands for technical devices, and their participation in society increasingly depends on the ability competently to handle such devices. This is the topic of Satofuka's chapter.

As an extension of the human body and mind technology is applied in many fields to alleviate the downside of old age which, however, makes itself felt ever later in life. This, too, is one of the consequences of population ageing. Gains in overall life expectancy are accompanied by advances in disability-free life expectancy. Healthy old men and women living away from their families have more time to spend for travel, pastime and sports, as detailed, respectively in the chapters by Funck, Clammer and Manzenreiter. From different points of view all three of them show how a new culture of leisure and wellbeing for the elderly is coming into existence as part of the demography-driven pluralisation of lifestyles.

In sum, the chapters in this part of the *Handbook* shed light on the re-formation of ideas, words, artefacts and interests, as Japanese culture adjusts to the challenges of the ageing society.

F.C.

CHAPTER SEVENTEEN

# TRADITIONAL CONCEPTS AND IMAGES OF OLD AGE IN JAPAN

Susanne Formanek

## 1. Introduction

Ever since Western societies have become aware of population ageing and its problems, scholars have turned to Japan in hopes of finding positive alternatives to contemporary Western "cults of youth". Back in the 1960s, Smith (1961) noted that in Japan painters, authors, actors and artisans—and to these one might add politicians as well—usually attain full competence only in their mid or late fifties, with many of them remaining active until their seventies or eighties and even beyond. Rohlen (1978) further elaborated on this idea, establishing that in the traditional arts—called *dō* or "Way" precisely because they must be followed over a long period by those seeking mastery in them—the old are considered to be the personifications of their art, and, in post-war Japan, are sometimes even officially recognized as "living national treasures". In analogy to this, Rohlen asserted, in Japan the elderly in general are venerated because they similarly have striven throughout a life-time properly to fulfil the roles life has assigned to them.

Phenomena such as these, however, do not necessarily have to do with particular respect for old age as such. According to Silverman and Maxwell (1983: 52), the status of the elderly strongly depends on their ability to control information. This is highest in so-called "closed societies" in which communication between subgroups is severely restricted. Japanese society, with its emphasis on in-groups based on regional or local origin, social strata, shared educational background and the like, is a particularly representative example of such a society. As far as the arts are concerned, the *ie*- or family-based structure of the various "schools", with their often secret transmission of relevant traditions, further reinforces this tendency. Last but not least, in the face of more and more thorough Westernization, reverence for the elderly in Japan today is almost certainly linked to a phenomenon characteristic for endangered ethnicities (Cool 1981): in the endeavour to preserve their identity, they accord a renewed or even unprecedented importance to the aged as preservers of the very traditions in peril of disappearing.

## 2. Hieratic Concepts of Old Age

Uniquely optimistic views of late life can, however, already be found in pre-modern Japan. For instance, in the epilogue of his *Hundred Views of Mount Fuji* (*Fugaku hyakkei*, 1834), at 74 years of age, the famous painter Katsushika Hokusai (1760–1849) noted:

> From the age of six, I delighted in drawing the shape of things. At 50, I had published a vast number of drawings. In the end, however, nothing I produced prior to the age of 70 is worth mentioning. Only at 73 was I finally able to recognize the rough structure of nature, the true shape of animals, birds, fish and insects. Thus, at the age of 80 I will have made further progress, at 90 I will gain insight into the fundamental enigma of things, and at the age of 100 I will certainly attain a most blissful state of mind. Once I am 110 years old, everything I draw will be filled with life, whether it is a simple dot or a mere line (Rinharuto 1986: 267).

This view of ageing as a never-ending progress towards human and/or artistic perfection, while by no means typical of traditional Japanese attitudes towards old age throughout, nonetheless draws on a number of sources infused by a "traditional respect for old age" in Japan. The most comprehensive—although somewhat superficial and also highly controversial—review of these is still to date the American social-gerontologist Erdman B. Palmore's widely known *Otoshiyori—The Honorable Elders* (1975). Among the main cultural-ideological currents singled out by Palmore as sources of persistently positive images of old age in Japan, Confucianism first deserves our attention. As is well-known, it emphasizes tradition and the value of history and the past, which is considered to enshrine the universal law which rules the world. Elderly people, with their long-standing acquaintance with the "Way", are therefore respected as teachers and advisors and their opinions held in high esteem. Confucian emphasis on vertical relationships of subservience of juniors to seniors obviously also serves the case of the elderly very well. What is more, the *Confucian Analects* record a portrayal of Confucius' personal development which, in its emphasis on steady self-improvement in the process of ageing, is an ancient forerunner of Hokusai's previously mentioned statement:

> Confucius said: 'When I was 15, I was firmly bent on learning; at the age of 30, I stood fast; at 40, I no longer harboured doubts (*madowazu*); at 50, the Law of Heaven was revealed to me (*tenmei o shiru*); at 60, my ears were opened wide (*mimi shitagau*) [i.e, he knew how to respect the deeper sense of what others had to say]; at 70, I was able to follow my heart's desires (*kokoro no hossuru tokoro*) without so much going beyond the proper limits (Linck-Kesting 1981: 385).

Confucius' saying was well-known in Japan, and honorific expressions for the older ages were directly modelled after it, in the form of compound nouns consisting of the relevant Chinese characters in their Sino-Japanese reading, i.e. *fuwaku*, *chimei*, *jijun* and *jūshin* respectively designating the ages of 40, 50, 60 and 70 (Formanek 1994: 93–94).

Still other propitious appellations adorned the older age levels. *Kakō* [literally: flowery armour], denoted the age of 61 (by Japanese, or 60 by Western reckoning), because the character *ka* contains six times the character for ten, plus one stroke, while *kō* or *kinoene* is the first year in the 60-years zodiac cycle, thus implying the return of the birth-year zodiac (*kanreki*); following a Chinese poem, *koki*, "precious rarity of old", was used for the age of 70; 77 was *kiju* [blissful age], since the character *ki* or *yorokobu* in its cursive form resembles a seven on top of ten (times) seven; 80 was *sanju* [umbrella age], because the abridged form of the character *san* or *kasa* resembles a ten beneath an eight; 88 was *beiju* [rice age], as the character for rice contains a ten enclosed by two eights. In this tradition, contemporary Japanese have not been slow in creating new names adapted to today's increased longevity, when people may reach *chaju* [tea age], meaning 108, since the character for tea has two tens = twenty on top of eight (times) ten plus eight. In 2002, entrepreneurial Japanese firms have started to address the needs of the *rokuju* [green age] cohort. Referring to the still active 66-years-plus seniors, the newly-coined term is an abbreviation of the homophonous *rokurokuju* (66); in addition, it suggests vitality and a new life-style of the third-agers appropriate to environment-keen 21st century (Gogen yurai jiten n.d., Internet).

The reaching of the respective age milestones traditionally was—and often still is today—solemnized by festivities in honor of the jubilee. Special celebrations, such as the *shōshikai* [assemblies in honour of age], were also held for the elderly in general. During the Heian period, only a handful of such *shōshikai* are recorded to have been celebrated among the nobility for aged peers (Formanek 1994: 183–187). During the Edo period, however, the custom spread to all strata of society

(Sugano 1993: 380); often backed by the authorities, it then took on a form presaging today's administration-sponsored gatherings on *keirō no hi* [Respect-for-the-Aged-Day, a national holiday held on the third Monday of September, see chapter 23].

Hieratic concepts of old age also resulted in the elderly being assigned auspicious social roles. For example, as *yowaibito* [men of age], they served as godfathers in the naming ceremonies and other rites of passage of young girls and boys (Formanek 1994: 322–323). As Ihara Saikaku reported in *Nippon eitaigura* (1688, *The Japanese Family Storehouse*), during the Edo period it was customary to ask "rice-age"-blessed seniors of 88 for *masukaki* [small bamboo sticks used to level the content of rice measures], in hopes of partaking of their good luck and longevity (NKBT 48: 36).

In Palmore's (1975) view, customs such as these are related to **the** religion of the Japanese, i.e. the ancestor cult, in the framework of which the fortunes of the living are believed to depend ultimately on the well-being of their forebears in the beyond. Within such a setting, the elderly as those closest to ascending to the deified status of ancestors, would presumably enjoy a similar veneration. Although it is questionable whether the ancestor cult as it has been practiced from the Meiji period onward already existed in the ancient period, the elderly were undeniably perceived as having a close affinity to the holy realms. In the ancient myths recorded in *Kojiki* (712, *Records of Ancient Matters*) and *Nihon shoki* (720, *Chronicles of Japan from the Earliest Times to A.D. 697*), the so-called Earthly Deities (*kunitsukami*)—as opposed to the Heavenly Deities residing in Takamagahara—often made their appearance in the human world in the shape of aged men and women. In the *Sarashina nikki* (1060, *The Sarashina Diary*), the authoress recounts how in the presence of a venerable old priestess she was suddenly overwhelmed by the feeling of having been blessed with the very appearance of *Amaterasu Ōmikami* herself (Formanek 1994: 453–462).

Shamanic roles of the elderly in early Japanese religion might have contributed to this. The ancient records know of at least one very important figure of the kind: Takeshiuchi no sukune, the Japanese Methuselah, said to have served five Tennō. Acting as an augur interpreting omens and predicting the future, he is also famous for having accompanied Jingū Kōgō on her Korean campaign and for helping her in giving birth to Ōjin Tennō. His effigy thus eventually came to adorn Meiji-period one-yen banknotes. Medieval records reckon his life-span to have lasted 360 years, at which time he ascended to heaven, leaving his sandals behind (Formanek 1994: 27–28).

This was a sign of his having become a *sennin* [Daoist immortal]. Although Daoism was never institutionalized in Japan, its promise of extreme longevity or even immortality exercised a considerable appeal on the Japanese. The means of attaining the blissful state of a *sennin* were varied. In any case, many years of practice were requisite, and, since the ability of prolonging life well beyond the normal measure formed part of the magic powers attributed to them, *sennin* were typically imagined as extremely old men. In accordance with the Daoist virtue of non-action, when these numinous beings made their appearance in the world of humans, it was generally in some remote place in the mountains, where they dwelt as if they had become one with nature itself (Formanek 1994: 488–490). Clad in leaves, covered with moss like old trees—as they were abundantly depicted on Edo-period *netsuke*—they represent an ideal of aged persons who, living in complete harmony with nature, no longer have to exert themselves in order to work wonders, just as Hokusai claimed.

Buddhism also added weight to this view. In the community of monks, seniors prevailed over juniors. Buddhist emphasis on repeated spiritual exercise and sutra recitation contributed to a view of old priests as particularly wise and holy men. The expression *dokuju no yowai tsumori* [aged in sutra recitation] became a stereotypical synonym for blissful late-life experiences in Buddhist hagiographies (Formanek 1994: 490–96). And in an almost unconscious syncretism with Daoism, mysterious, completely self-sufficient old men often appeared in a host of Buddhist legends as ephemeral incarnations of Buddhas, or their Japanese alter egos (*suijaku*), to reveal some transcendental truth (Yamaori 1984; Formanek 1994: 472–483).

All this culminated in the remarkable fact that, in Noh, the representative theatrical form of medieval Japan, figures of aged men and women play central roles. The play entitled *Okina* [an archaic term for "old man"], featuring two old men incarnating a Buddha and uttering auspicious words, is the most sacred play within the whole repertoire. In numerous other plays, old men, although of humble appearance, reveal themselves to be deities. According to the great Noh master Zeami, all roles in Noh can be reduced to three types, one of which is the old person (*rōtai*). For Zeami, this *rōtai* in fact represented all divine figures in Noh, precisely because the *rōtai* itself was a figure of "divinely serene appearance (*kamisabi kanzen naru yosooi*)" (NST 24: 112).

It is of course a highly idealized and stylized view of old age that is represented in these figures and one which is tightly bound to Buddhism and its strife for abnegation of the world. In Zeami's view, the key to the felicitous representation of elderly persons lay, not in reproducing the visible decay of old age, but rather in emulating the old person's attempts to look just like the young, while simultaneously being aware of, and resigned to, the impossibility of achieving this (Scheid 1997: 101–104). In other words, the serenity—and the holiness—of *okina* figures in Noh stem from their having accepted mortals' finitude. This image still persists today, as when, for example, in an essay dated 1993, we read about a famous author: "Some time before he died, his face became so wonderful one could not believe one's eyes. One fancied seeing an *okina* mask, so good-hearted and suave did he appear" (Yamaori 1994: 91).

Equally, the serene image of an old couple as it is depicted in the Noh play *Takasago* is still alive and well in today's Japanese minds and hearts. Dolls depicting the old couple as they quietly sweep the fallen needles under a double-stemmed pine tree (*aioi-matsu*) (a symbol of their having grown old together) still adorn marriage ceremonies, and songs from the play express the wish that the newly-wed may enjoy a similarly fulfilling and long-lasting conjugal life.

Lofty figures of single old women were also present in Noh, although they were less serene. Ono no Komachi, the famous 9th-century noble poetess, who presumably fell into deep poverty in old age, features prominently in a number of plays, dressed in rags, subsisting on alms, staying in a miserable hut or sleeping under the open sky. Her physical decay is equally depicted in sombre tones: wrinkles cover her face like waves, her back is utterly bent and she walks with difficulty, her skin is covered with dark spots as of spattered ink, and her once so beautiful black hair has turned white, thin and tousled so as unflatteringly to resemble some odd water plant. Nonetheless, she is treated with admiration, because old age and the decay of the personality that it implies have awakened her to the Buddhist aspiration of escaping the world; the fits of nostalgia for her splendid, mundane youth that overcome her from time to time make her final Buddhist insight all the more poignant. She thus becomes a Buddhist paradigm of the conditio humana itself (Formanek 2005a: 169–170).

## 3. Abandonment and Ostracism of the Aged

In tune with the simile of Ono no Komachi as a beggar roaming the countryside, a part of the divine nature of elderly figures in Noh plays stemmed from the concrete circumstance that the aged were, in actual fact, no longer considered as fully pertaining to the world of normal adults. Much has been written about the Obasuteyama [Granny-Abandoning-Mountain] motif and its implication of a custom of abandoning the elderly, especially since Fukazawa Shichirō's (1914–1987) modern depiction of it in *Narayama bushi-kō* (1956, *The Ballad of Narayama*), with its emphasis on the dire conditions in pre-modern villages when people could not afford to sustain those who were no longer able to work or otherwise contribute to the community's welfare. The version most widely known in ancient times—found, for instance, in the *Yamato monogatari* (ca. 950, *Tales of Yamato*)—recounted how a commoner's wife grew tired of her husband's aunt, an 80-year-old woman so bent by age that she looked "as if folded in two", and talked her husband into abandoning the old woman on a mountain. Seeing the moon rise above the same mountain that night, however, the husband is overwhelmed by feelings of guilt and hurries to bring the old lady back (Formanek 1994: 215–216).

This Obasuteyama version owed much of its enduring popularity to the fact that the mountain of the same name in Nagano was (or later became) a famous moon-viewing spot. Other tales focussed more closely on a presumed custom of abandoning the elderly. The *Makura no sōshi* (955–1000, *The Pillow Book of Sei Shonagon*) and later the *Konjaku monogatarishū* (*Tales of Times Now Past*) both told that, once upon a time, there had been a mandatory custom of ostracizing the aged. One particularly loving son, however, refused to follow the rule and hid his parents in the cellar. As it happened, at that time Japan was being defied by China to solve three riddles; no one was able to do so, except the old couple in hiding. Recognizing the value of the elders' experience and wisdom, people gave up their previous custom and instead turned to due reverence for the elderly (Formanek 1994: 215–221).

Although stories such as this reveal, to say the least, ambiguous attitudes towards old age and the elderly, they do not offer absolute proof that the aged were routinely abandoned. On the other hand, it is also a matter of historical fact that aged people might undergo ostracism under certain circumstances. This is negatively hinted at by an edict of 813, which banned "inhumane acts" such as "driving servants, who have served one faithfully for their whole lifetime, out of the house once they become ill, leaving them on the roads without anybody to care for them until they starve", and imposed a penalty of 100 club blows upon offenders (Yamamoto 1993: 27). A tale in the *Konjaku monogatarishū* recounts how an old nun, driven out of the house by her brother because of a sudden illness, and denied shelter wherever else she asked for it, finally betakes herself to the cemetery where she lays herself to her final rest (NKBT 26: 298–299). Actual instances of similar behaviour can be found as late as the early 16th century. The court nobleman Sanjōnishi Sanetaka (1455–1537), for example, noted in his diary that the illness of his old servant Ukyō no daibu had worsened and that he therefore had abandoned her near a temple; one month later, he reported that she had now indeed died; another four days later, he asserted having commissioned the copying of sutras for the repose of her soul (Yamamoto 1993: 22f.).

These practices, doubtless stemming from fear of pollution by death, seem to have been current mostly among the nobility. Ostracism of the aged among the commoner population followed different paths. As Tanaka (1997) has shown, senescence there obviously was regarded as polluting per se, so that the senile elderly were effectively driven out of the villages. Nonetheless, this did not necessarily mean that they were left to starve. As vagrants and mendicants, they could make a livelihood from the alms they received. On certain festive occasions, they were treated as *marebito* [ holy visitors] invited to the villages in hopes of receiving their blessing.

An image of the elderly as vagrants and mendicants can be traced throughout Nara and Heian period belles lettres (Formanek 1994: 228–235). In the *Man'yōshū* (ca. 760, *Ten Thousand Leaves*) poems, attributes of the wanderer such as the *haribukuro* [needle bag] or the *suribukuro* [pouch for utensils needed during a journey] were commonly used to evoke the old man (*okina*), the mentioning of which also prompted the epithet *kusatabimakura*, the grass on which the traveller rests his head as on a pillow for the night's sleep (NKBT 7: 297). *Konjaku monogatari-shū*, for instance, recounts the story of an old, feeble looking beggar, who, upon coming across a track carrying melons to the capital, asks the porters for one melon, lest he die of thirst. They deny his request, whereupon he proceeds to plant one melon seed. Out of this, in no time, there grows a whole field of ripe melons which he magnanimously distributes among all those present. When, after a while, the porters awaken from their bewilderment, they are forced to realise that the old man has disappeared without a trace, taking with him their whole load of melons (NKBT 26: 121–122). Incidentally, this legend can serve as a classic example for the anthropological thesis according to which the function of ascribing magic powers to certain persons lies in maintaining communal duties of sustaining them (Foner 1984: 157–191).

In direct continuation of these beliefs, we later find Buddhist legends with a similar structure: utterly decrepit, senile monks, who in day-to-day life are despised by everyone, suddenly become the mediums through which deities deign to reveal some transcendental truth. Usually, the old monk himself is later found to have disappeared (Formanek 1994: 474–475, 481). In other words, the divine character attributed to elderly, decrepit people in the early epochs of Japanese history often was a corollary of their utter liminality; their mental and physical decay caused them to be simultaneously despised and feared, and therefore to be pushed towards the fringes of society; this in turn was precisely what qualified them to act as recipients of the numinous. Plath (1980: 180) has suggested that such an attitude is still alive and well in modern Japan. In Ariyoshi Sawako's novel *Kōkotsu no hito* (1972, *The Twilight Years*), the heroine first strongly resents having to quit her job in order to care for her hopelessly senile father-in-law. However, she ends up feeling that she has become the servant of a deity and thus, in a kind of modern rationalization of an old behavioural pattern, she is able to find satisfaction in her new role.

## 4. A History of Negative Views of Old Age

As can already be read between the lines in the accounts given above, highly pessimistic views of both physical and mental decay in old age were current in Japan from ancient times onward, and authors did not refrain from showing their disgust and disdain (Skord 1989; Formanek 1994: 97–155). Sei Shōnagon, in the *Makura no shōshi*, noted among the category of things "of bad taste": "Rubbing one's hands by the fireplace to warm them up, sleeking them over and over again as if to smoothen them. Would young people ever do such a thing? Of course not, but the old do, all wrinkled as they are!" (NKBT 19: 69). Sei Shōnagon may have had her own good reasons for being acid-tongued vis-à-vis improper behaviour of elderly people confronting others with their all-too-ugly appearance. In an episode long famous even afterwards, her father, Kiyohara no Motosuke, had publicly disgraced himself when, on the occasion of a formal parade, he had lost his court hat, thereby revealing his bald head glittering in the evening sun, so that all present burst out in reverberating laughter (NKBT 26: 67–68).

The list of the mental deficiencies thought to accompany old age ranged from listlessness, forgetfulness and a general decline in the mental and artistic faculties, to a tendency towards melancholia, talkativeness as well as grouchiness. People thus felt that, as the common saying had it, "the older you grow, the greater the shame" (*inochi nagakereba haji ōshi*), and hoped to avoid that fate, as a famous *Kokinshū* poem formulated:

> Would that I'd heard/When old age was nearing,/I'd shut my door fast,/Pretend not to be there,/And never have had to meet it! (NKBT 8: 282, nº 895)

Negative views on old age did not cease to be widely current even in the Edo period, when Confucian precepts of respect for seniors had come to typify the standards of morality promoted by the authorities. One verse-lampoon, in particular, seems to have circulated widely. It can be found on a drawing by the famous Zen painter Sengai (1750–1837) as well as on a more plebeian woodblock print by Utagawa Kuniyoshi (1797–1861):

> Wrinkles cover the face, dark dots all over the skin, a crooked back, a bald head or hair white as snow. Hands in constant tremor, a staggering walk, fallen-out teeth, with ears half-deaf and eyes no longer able to see well. For everyday companions one is left with scarves and shawls, a walking stick and eyeglasses, hot-water bags and warming stones, a chamber pot and the guiding hand of a grandchild. Obtrusive, short-tempered, always complaining about one thing or another, entertaining jaundiced views, greedy and acquisitive, remembering only things long past. Anxiously worrying, witnessing old friends passing away one after the other, feeling lonesome and abandoned, and nonetheless talkatively meddling in everything. Telling the same old stories all over again and again, proudly praising their children and grandchildren, boasting themselves to be still going strong, no wonder that people detest them!

Matsuura Seizan (1760–1841) also received a copy of this text from a Confucian scholar friend, remarking that this was probably in order to show him his contempt (Nakamura and Nakano 1980: 233–235). For Confucianism did not think of the ageing process as bringing about an improvement of the personality in and of itself; life-long self-cultivation was required in order to avoid the pitfalls of old age. The book on morals *Chikubashō* (1383, "Writings on Hobby-horse Childhood Days") noted that "when people age without practicing any art, this results in their old age not being any worthier than that of any ragged old fox or badger"; "in order to avoid a despicable fate in old age, when one is commonly disliked by people, it is imperative that one exercise oneself in some art such as poetry, which might provide some consolation in old age and cause people to seek one's company, at least from time to time." People, however, must start early in this endeavour, because once they are 40 or 50 years old, they lack the necessary impetus to begin something new (Shinmura 1992: 148–150).

In the mind of a man deeply imbued with Confucian thought, such as Arai Hakuseki's (1657–1725) father, fear of senescence obviously prompted a whole programme of life-long self-cultivation. Witnessing the growing senility of a friend, the old man—so we are told in Hakuseki's memoirs *Oritaku shiba no ki* (*Told Round a Brushwood Fire*)—remarked:

> Senility occurs because when people get old, they forget the proper way of doing things. Isn't that a shame! Therefore, it is imperative to exercise oneself in the proper way of doing things for a whole life-time... I myself have from youth onwards restricted my actions to the minimum, living only by that which I could do myself without anybody's help, repeating the same actions day after day, always putting the same things in their own same place,... which is why today that I am old, things still go my own and the proper way" (NKBT 95: 164).

## 5. The Ideal of Disengagement and Leisurely Retirement

Buddhism also counted decay in old age among the four unavoidable grievances of human life: the *shōrōbyōshi* [birth, old age, illness and death], which awakened men to the holy truth of the impermanence of all earthly things and the necessity of seeking to escape from the cycle of rebirths. For laymen, care for what was ahead after death and reliance on the Buddha were requisite, at least in their declining years. The Kamakura-era regent Hōjō Shigetoki (1198–1261) thus wrote:

> According to their age, men should act in the following way: until the age of 20, one should dedicate oneself to the arts and acquire capacities in the ways of the world. During one's 30s, 40s and 50s one should protect one's lord, take care of the people, restrain oneself, gain insight into the principles that rule the world, exert oneself in the virtues of humanity and justice... and dedicate oneself to the way of politics... At the age of 60, however, it is imperative that one give up all earthly things, pray wholeheartedly for one's life to come and invoke Buddha's name... Never again should one turn one's heart to the things of this passing world,... put one's trust solely in Buddha's way and consider oneself as in fact no longer pertaining to this world (Scheid 1996: 33).

This ideal of reclusion infuses some of the most representative literary works of the Middle Ages, such, for example, as Kamo no Chōmei's

(1153–1216) *Hōjōki* (1212, *Notes from a Ten Feet Square Hut*). Having renounced the world in his advanced years and living as a recluse in the forests, the author regards his small hut as a privileged place where there is almost no possibility of transgressing Buddha's law (Scheid 1997: 98). During Antiquity and the Middle Ages, many nobles did indeed take holy orders in the second part of their lives. This, however, usually did not preclude their continuing to take active part in secular politics. Even once they had handed over rank and possessions to a successor this act could be "revoked by regret" (*kuigaeshi*) (Iinuma 1990: 169–170).

This was to change when the custom spread to the warrior class. By then, the successor had to be acknowledged by the feudal lord and, once installed, could not easily be removed afterwards. In his *Kagetsu sōshi* (1803, "Flower and Moon Miscellanies"), the late-Edo-period statesman Matsudaira Sadanobu (1758–1829), from old-age decline of the physical faculties, even derived a "natural law" of late-life disengagement:

> When in old age teeth have fallen out, digestion no longer functions as well as in youth, which is why one should eat only soft food.... And because one can no longer hear well, people say that one has turned far-eared (*mimi ga tōi*, i.e. hard of hearing), from which it follows that, at that time, one should keep away from things, withdraw without interfering any longer,...lest one be insulted and laughed at (Sugano 1993: 384).

In the early Edo period, emulating the lifestyle of noblemen, the upcoming merchant class also began to hand over their businesses to their successors in old age. Ihara Saikaku's novels, for instance, are replete with well-to-do merchants who followed the advice of "the god Daikoku, who...has declared that a man who cudgels his brains and tires his strength in youth will early taste the pleasures of old age" (NKBT 48: 131): they retired into *raku inkyo*, as was the consecrated term for late-life leisurely retirement. In *Seken munesan'yō* (1692, *This Scheming World*), Saikaku renders the life-course ideals of his times as a slightly secularized version of Hōjō Shigetoki's precepts:

> The proper way for a man to get along in the world should be this: in his youth until the age of twenty-five to be ever alert, in his manly prime up to thirty-five to earn a lot of money, in the prime of discretion in his fifties to pile up his fortune, and at last in his sixties...to turn over his business to his eldest son. Thereafter it is proper for him to retire from active affairs and devote the remainder of his days to visiting temples for the sake of his soul (NKBT 48: 221).

While concern with the afterlife in the later years continued to be part of the life project, secular leisure and/or cultural activities also infiltrated ideal old-age life-styles. *Nippon eitaigura* presents us with an example:

> In a mere forty years he made a hundred thousand *ryō*. All this was the result of taking millionaire pills in his younger days [i.e. exercising diligence and thrift]. Now that he was well past his seventieth year he judged that a little relaxation of the treatment would do no harm, and for the first time in his life he changed into a complete outfit of Hida homespun silk, and even cultivated a taste for the marine delicacies of Shiba. On his way back from regular morning worship at the Nishi Honganji temple in Tsukiji he dropped in at theatres in Kobiki-chō, and in the evenings he played Go at home with groups of friends. While snow fell outside he held social gatherings to mark the opening of the winter's first tea-jars, and as soon as the early daffodils were in bloom he set out tasteful flower arrangements in the impressionist manner. Exactly when he had learnt all these refinements is not clear—but money makes everything possible... There are people who draw no distinction between the beginning and the end,... but [he] had wisely set aside a portion for his declining days, and with this he thoroughly enjoyed himself (NKBT 48: 90).

By the end of the Edo period, retiring into *raku inkyo* in old age had become something most commoners aspired to as a kind of life-time achievement (Ujiie 2001). Ōta Motoko (1992) even speaks of a "discovery of old age" as a time of leisure that occurred at the beginning of the 19th century in Japan: Tamura Yoshishige (1790–1876), a well-to-do farmer of samurai origins, for example, retired in 1839, thinking that he had only one or two more years to live, which he wanted to dedicate to writing down the agricultural knowledge he had gained through his life-time experience. During the 37 subsequent years he thereafter spent in *inkyo*, he became the author, known even today, of agricultural and other writings. He is noteworthy because he also left "family rules" in which he emphasised that old age was to be spent in leisure, that is, without worrying about matters of household economy and income; for a smooth co-existence of the generations it was imperative that the retired farmer refrain from interfering in these matters and from retaining possessions of his own; instead, he should subsist on family meals, asking for pocket money when necessary (Ōta 1992: 169–174).

Smaller farmers shared the same ideal of *raku inkyo*, although not all succeeded in attaining it. Kobayashi Issa's *Chichi no shūen nikki* (1801, *Journal of My Father's Last Days*) is, among other things, an oppressively sombre document of such a failure. After the death of Issa's mother, his father, a moderately well-to-do farmer, had remarried; his second wife bore him a second son, and he sent Issa away to Edo. Many years later, when the by then aged father fell ill, he was brought to Issa to take care of him, as the father felt that he was being mistreated by the rest of his family. Issa reports his father as saying:

> In the year when you became fourteen, I sent you away to the capital to hard service as a menial, thinking, however, of having you come back within a few years. Then, I thought, I would hand over household and possessions to you, so that you would be able to secure a livelihood and I myself could spend my declining years in leisure—what a poor father you must think I am...But alas, people age, and weakening and illness are unavoidable. If you return home with lame legs and your back bent, they will treat you even worse than an animal (NKBT 58: 411, 416).

Just how deeply rooted the idea of old age as a time of idleness was can be gathered from what a major Meiji-period opponent of the custom had to say about it. In 1886, Shigeno Yasutsugu (1827–1912), a prestigious historian, published a vituperative lampoon against *inkyo* (Formanek 2003: 88–89). Conceding that it originally sprang from the laudable desire of elders to provide for their offspring and avoid earning themselves a reputation as avaricious despots forever unwilling to yield their share of authority and possessions, he stressed that, in recent times, negative side-effects of the custom had come to prevail over its advantages. *Inkyo* was the cause of a plethora of grievances in Japanese society at large. Since the hosts of idle retirees enjoyed indulging in a variety of pseudo-artistic leisure activities and striking a grand pose as masters in these arts, the fine arts themselves were insufficiently developed. Further, this *inkyo* attitude of merely dabbling in this or that had infected the younger generation, with the result that unambitious young people proliferated. Borrowing the expression used by Ihara Saikaku in his *Nippon eitaigura* stories to designate those who retired to a life as rentiers as early as aged 40 or even younger, Shigeno polemically called his contemporaries a feckless pack of *waka-inkyo* [preterm retirees]. Even politics were affected, he lamented: the Genrōin, analogous to European senates and staffed with experienced men well advanced in years, was a case in point. A crucial legislative organ, it was fated not to be taken seriously, since people were accustomed to view old age as a time of idleness spent with retiree businesses (*inkyo-yaku*): that is, inconsequential sinecures. Shigeno's article also bears witness to how quickly images and ideals of old age can change under the impact of a new era. "Even horses and oxen pull their loads as long and as well as they can. How much more should one expect of human beings, who never can be content with what they have achieved, as they bear responsibility not only for themselves, but also and even more importantly, for the nation and state", Shigeno stated. The abolition of *inkyo*, in his view, was thus a necessary contribution to the *fukoku kyōhei* policies of the Meiji government aiming at a rich and militarily strong Japan.

During the Edo period there had been a rush towards *inkyo* among the commoner population and high-class *bushi* such as the *daimyō*, lower-rank *samurai* regarded it as a shame when they had to retire on the grounds of serious illness or incapacitation. *Banzuke*-like ranking lists were regularly issued, recording champions in length of service and age (Formanek 2003: 96). In the course of the "samuraization" of Japanese society as it occurred from the Meiji period onward, the former ideal of leisurely retirement thus lost much of its appeal. Today's renewed interest in Edo-period *inkyo* on the part of publicists such as Nakae Katsumi (1999) stems precisely from their endeavours to offer models of meaningful third-age life-styles to former company employees confronted with the proverbial "retirement shock".

## 6. Filial Piety

Whether or not we agree with Tatsukawa (1996), for whom *inkyo* in the Edo period was of such an appeal that people had begun to value old age more than any other period over the life-course, a felicitous old age strongly depended on one's health status and the willingness and ability of one's offspring to care for one when need arose. In this context, the Confucian concept of filial piety gained new importance and significance. The famous Twenty-Four Chinese Paragons of Filial Piety (*nijūshikō*) had been widely diffused in Japan since Antiquity. From Kakkyo, who had decided to sacrifice his young son in order to be able to sustain his old mother, when luckily he found a golden pot that solved all his problems; to Mōsō, who thanks to Heaven's compassion was able to do the impossible and found the bamboo shoots his old mother was craving in the midst of winter when usually there are none; and Yōi, who was spared by a tiger moved by Yōi's pleading for his life not for his own sake, but in order not to deprive his aged mother of her caregiver; these stories had usually revolved around children devoted to their parents to the point of self-abandonment, Heaven intervening helpfully in recompense (Formanek 1994: 248–257).

During the Edo period, however, a considerable ageing of the population had taken place. In some villages, the segment over 60 years of age amounted to an incredible 15% (Matsumoto 1998). Under such circumstances, filial piety tended more and more to stress the care of incapacitated, bedridden parents. In 1801, the authorities issued the *Kōgiroku* ("Records of Filial Piety and Righteousness"), a collection of exemplary children's biographies. It is replete with examples such as that of Tōjūrō, a small farmer who lost his father when still very young. His mother afterwards suffered a stroke, so that his nursing duties, such as feeding her or carrying her around, left Tōjūrō no time to work outside. He thus came to subsist on his neighbours' charity, reserving all that he could afford for his mother, while he himself was clad in worn-out rags (Sugano 1999: 41–42). The image of the devoted son carrying his incapacitated parent around on his back was so familiar that it even gave rise to a form of beggary: so-called *oya-kōkō* mendicants roamed the streets of Edo with the paper-mâché effigy of an old person strapped to their backs, begging for alms "for the sake of filial piety" (Tatsukawa 1996: 44).

Manuals of advice on daily life routinely offered suggestions as to mutually beneficially behaviour on the part of both the dependent elderly and their caretakers. Kaibara Ekiken's views as expressed in his *Yōjōkun* (1713, *Rules of Health*) were subsequently popularized widely in works such as the *Kanai yōjinshū* (1730, "Collected Household Knowledge") or the *Minka yōjutsu* (1831, "Basics of Household Management"). On the one hand, they stressed that the elderly—perhaps because they knew that they were running out of time—tended to be greedy, short-tempered and cross, worrying about trifles and constantly interfering even in minor affairs. The elderly were warned not to indulge in "bad habits" such as these, lest they might earn their offspring a reputation of lacking in filial piety; instead, they should display decent restraint becoming to old age (*bansetsu*). On the other hand, the caretakers were enjoined to take all these age-related quirks into due consideration and therefore treat their elders in the same way as they would treat young children (Sugano 1993: 390–391).

Taking care of bedridden parents obviously exerted considerable strain on family relations, since there was no alternative to it whatsoever, neither from the viewpoint of the authorities, who adhered to a strict subsidiarity principle (Ōtake 1990), nor from that of family members. In the course of the Edo period, it had become a generally accepted tenet that the child who cared for the elderly parents would also be the one to inherit the lion's share of their possessions. A story in the *Kinsei kijinden* (1790, "Biographies of Outstanding Persons of Our Times") even reports of a man who forbade his wife to take care of his father: the old man, he thought, was in such a repulsive condition that no one save his own flesh and blood could nurse him without utter disgust (Tatsukawa 1996: 51).

## 7. Gender-Specific Views of Old Age

This is, however, what generally was the case between the old mother and the daughter-in-law. For a number of demographic reasons, old men in general could count on their younger wives to take care of them. By contrast, the old mother usually had to rely on her daughter-in-law, a mere stranger in the first place. This, in my view, was one of the roots of the proverbial *shūtome-yome*-conflict topos: the animosity between the mother-in-law and the daughter-in-law mention of which even today usually causes Japanese men to sigh as in the face of some terrible, but inevitable calamity. The strife between the two women is usually considered to concern the questions of "housewife's right" (*shufuken*). Traditionally, this was settled when the mother-in-law formally handed over the symbolic rice paddle (*shamoji watashi*), i.e. recognizing the daughter-in-law as the one responsible for household management. At least until that date, the mother-in-law might tyrannise her daughter-in-law (*yome ibiri*). This was understood as being a part of her efforts to train the new-comer to the ways of the family. However, male contemporaries also interpreted this hazing as showing the perversity of female character. As one author, although in another context, noted: "Generally, women are utterly egoistic and wicked beings, so that their greatest strength lies in domineering over subordinate women. The older they become, however, the less does their greed know any bounds" (Formanek 2005a: 385).

Extremely negative views of female old age such as this did not stem solely from intergenerational conflicts. Buddhism also added weight to them. From its inception in Japan, it stylised elderly women into greedy and forever mischievous beings, partly because, as mothers, they were distraught at their sons renouncing the world, and partly because they represented an older religion. In the Noh drama, this resulted in the circumstance that alongside the serene male old age as represented by the *okina*, female characters often were of the old-witch type, as in the case of the play *Yamanba*. These *uba* figures may, at some remote time, originally have represented old shamanesses serving the gods; in time, they came to be only feared as evil old witches (*onibaba*) (Yamaori 1994: 91). Related legends as well as fairy-tales such as *Shitakiri suzume* [The Tongue-Cut-Sparrow] contrasting a kind-hearted old man and a greedy, merciless old woman abounded (Hirota 1992); these lent themselves very well to being adapted to and rationalized in later Edo-period Kabuki plays and novels. In these works, figures of diabolical old hags regularly appeared. They were endowed with a life-history and displayed characteristics typical of despotic mothers and/or needy elderly women active as of midwives, pedlars, procuresses, or in other similarly disreputable trades. Throughout, these crones served as foils upon which to project the very real fears called forth by the authoritarianism and self-assertion actually displayed by older women—traits which ran counter to the ideal of a docile and subservient womanhood (Formanek 2005a). As a late descendant of the wicked crones of Edo-period popular culture, the heroine of late-1960s' *manga* series *Ijiwaru bāsan* [Cranky Grandma] displayed similar, albeit less gruesome characteristics: she was an ugly, temperamental and self-assertive old woman, not prepared to give in to the younger generation and always ready to oppose being pushed towards the fringes of society. Thus, she earned herself the horror of her contemporaries, as well as their sympathies (Formanek 2005b).

## 8. Conclusion

Cross-national surveys have repeatedly established the persistence of such negative views on old age well into the modern period. In questionnaires, the Japanese agreed with prejudiced statements such as "the majority of the elderly are senile", "set in ways", "grouchy" or "selfish" to a much higher percentage than, for example, Americans or British (Koyano 1997: 215–217).

Taken together with the traditional concepts outlined above, these findings strongly support Hashimoto Akiko's (1996) thesis on the specificity of the Japanese generation contract and suggest that it may have its roots in the Edo-period developments previously described. In Hashimoto's view, the persistently high co-residence rates and the major reliance on family care of the elderly are not the result of any particular respect for the aged in Japan; rather, the anticipation of unavoidable dependency and ultimate need of care causes Japanese parents consciously to socialize their children with a view to receiving this care by them in old age; the very same anticipation also creates a willingness on the part of the young to pay the price of old age at an early stage. Assistance for elderly parents is therefore given less out of real need than, rather, for their being ascribed the status of "aged person". Admitting to having grown old occurs, not necessarily because an advance age is a particularly blissful state, but because it makes it possible to demand the appropriate assistance.

Within this framework, when intergenerational conflicts occur, the elderly, rather than severing relations, resign themselves to being disliked by the other family members (Hashimoto 1996: 86). The title heroine of previously mentioned Hasegawa Machiko's *manga Ijiwaru bāsan* may serve as a particularly telling example. Only in recent years, since better living conditions have led to an increase in the years of active old age spent in good health, have things begun to change. From the 1980s, alternative models of old age have been provided by figures such as the 70-year-old heroine of a number of best-selling books by Tanabe Seiko. Refusing to co-reside with her son, she instead enjoys life, wandering from party to party dressed in a shocking pink coat and hat (Tsuji 1996: 205).

In the last analysis, then, what, if anything, contributes to the unique qualities characterising the historical experience of old age in Japan? Above all, it would seem to be the life-long awareness (nourished by a number of sources and developments) of the inescapability of old age. Further important factors include a concomitant concern with adjustment in due time to the limitations imposed by ageing upon the individual, along with the newly gained freedom and opportunities which it holds in store.

## References

Cool, Linda (1981): Ethnic Identity: A Source of Community Esteem for the Elderly. In: *Anthropological Quarterly* 54, pp. 179–189.

Foner, Nancy (1984): *Ages in Conflict. A Cross-cultural Perspective on Inequality between Old and Young.* New York: Columbia University Press.

Formanek, Susanne (1994): *Denn dem Alter kann keiner entfliehen. Altern und Alter im Japan der Nara- und Heian-Zeit.* Vienna: Verlag der Österreichischen Akademie der Wissenschaften.

—— (2003): Der Diskurs um Ausgedinge und Pensionssystem um die Jahrhundertwende in Tokyo und Wien. In: Sepp Linhart (ed.): *Wien und Tokyo um die Wende vom 19. zum 20. Jahrhundert*. Vienna: Abteilung für Japanologie am Institut für Ostasienwissenschaften der Universität Wien, pp. 83–106.

—— (2005a): *Die „böse Alte" in der japanischen Populärkultur der Edo-Zeit. Die Feindvalenz und ihr soziales Umfeld.* Vienna: Verlag der Österreichischen Akademie der Wissenschaften.

—— (2005b): Eine alte Frau sekkiert ihre Umwelt. Altersbilder im Japan der späten 1960er Jahre anhand Hasegawa Machikos Manga *Ijiwaru bāsan*. In: Roland Domenig, Susanne Formanek and Wolfram Manzenreiter (eds.): *Über Japan denken – Japan überdenken. Festschrift für Sepp Linhart zu seinem 60. Geburtstag von seinen Schülerinnen und Schülern*. Wien, Münster: LIT Verlag, pp. 93–126.

Gogen yurai jiten (n.d.): *Rokuju*. http://gogen-allguide.com/ro/rokujyu.html (found 29 August 2006).

Hashimoto, Akiko (1996): *The Gift of Generations. Japanese and American Perspectives on Aging and the Social Contract*. Cambridge: Cambridge University Press.

Hirota Masaki (1992): Otoko no oi to onna no oi [Male and female old age]. In: Nakamura Keiko, Miyata Noboru et al.: *Oi to "oi". Kakuri to saisei* [Ageing and growing. Isolation and renewal]. Tokyo: Fujiwara Shoten, pp. 324–341.

Iinuma Kenji (1990): Nihon chūsei no rōjin no jitsuzō [The real image of the elderly in the Japanese Middle Ages]. In: Toshitani Nobuyoshi, Ōtō Osamu and Shimizu Hiroaki (eds): *Oi no hikaku kazoku-shi* [A comparative family history of old age]. Tokyo: Sanseidō, pp. 159–176.

Koyano Wataru (1997): Myths and facts of aging in Japan. In: Susanne Formanek and Sepp Linhart (eds.): *Aging: Asian Concepts and Experiences Past and Present*. Vienna: Verlag der Österreichischen Akademie der Wissenschaften, pp. 213–226.

Linck-Kesting, Gudula (1981): Alt und Jung im vormodernen China. In: *Saeculum* 32, pp. 374–408.

Matsumoto Junko (1998): Kinsei shakai ni okeru jinkō "kōreika" to "en" [Population ageing in pre-modern Japan and the importance of social networks]. In: *Rekihaku* 91, pp. 16–19.

Nakae Katsumi (1999): *Edo no teinengo. "Go-inkyo" ni manabu gendaijin no chie* [After retirement in the Edo period. What people today can learn from their forebears in *inkyo*]. Tokyo: Kōbunsha.

Nakamura Yukihiko and Nakano Mitsutoshi (eds.) (1980): *Kasshi yawa zokuhen 5*. Tokyo: Heibonsha.

NKBT. *Nihon koten bungaku taikei*. Tokyo: Iwanami Shoten 1957–1969. 102 vols.

NST. *Nihon shisō taikei*. Tokyo: Iwanami Shoten 1970–1982. 67 vols.

Ōta Motoko (1992): Rōnenki no tanjō. 19seiki zenki nōson no "raku inkyo" o tegakari ni [The birth of old age. The custom of "leisurely retirement" in peasant villages at the beginning of the 19th century]. In: Nakamura Keiko, Miyata Noboru et al.: *Oi to "oi". Kakuri to saisei* [Ageing and growing. Isolation and renewal]. Tokyo: Fujiwara Shoten, pp. 153–200.

Ōtake Hideo (1990): Edo jidai no rōjinkan to rōgo mondai. Rōjin fuyō no mondai o shu to shite [Images and problems of old age in the Edo period. With special consideration of the problem of elderly sustenance]. In Toshitani Nobuyoshi, Ōtō Osamu and Shimizu Hiroaki (eds): *Oi no hikaku kazoku-shi* [A comparative family history of old age]. Tokyo: Sanseidō, pp. 177–204.

Palmore, Erdman B. (1975): *Otoshiyori – The Honorable Elders: Cross-Cultural Analysis of Aging in Japan*. Durham, N.C.: Duke University Press.

Plath, David (1980): *Long Engagements. Maturity in Modern Japan*. Stanford: Stanford University Press.

Rinharuto, Zeppu (= Sepp Linhart) (1986): Nihon shakai to oi. Enbō [Japanese society and old age: a view from afar]. In: Itō Mitsuharu *et al.* (eds.): *Oi no jinruishi* [A historical anthropology of ageing]. Tokyo: Iwanami shoten, pp. 257–280.

Rohlen, Thomas P. (1978): The promise of adulthood in Japanese spiritualism. In: Erik H. Erikson (ed.): *Adulthood*. New York, London: Norton, pp. 129–147.

Scheid, Bernhard (1996): *Im Innersten meines Herzens empfinde ich tiefe Scham. Das Alter im Schrifttum des japanischen Mittelalters*. Vienna: Verlag der Österreichischen Akademie der Wissenschaften.

—— (1997): "An old tree in bloom": Zeami and the ambivalent perspectives on old age. In: Susanne Formanek and Sepp Linhart (eds.): *Aging: Asian Concepts and Experiences Past and Present*. Vienna: Verlag der Österreichischen Akademie der Wissenschaften, pp. 97–106.

Shinmura Taku (1992): *Oi to mitori no shakaishi* [A social history of old age and sick-nursing]. Tokyo: Hōsei Daigaku Shuppankyoku (1991[1]).

Silverman, Philip, and Robert J. Maxwell (1983): The significance of information and power in the comparative study of the aged. In: Jay Sokolovsky (ed.), *Growing Old in Different Societies. Cross-Cultural Perspectives*. Belmont, California: Wadsworth Publishing, pp. 43–55.

Skord, Virginia (1989): "Withered blossoms": Aging in Japanese literature. In: Prisca von Dorotka Bagnell und Patricia Spencer Soper (eds.): *Perceptions of Aging in Literature: A Cross-Cultural Study*. New York: Greenwood Press, pp. 131–143.

Smith, Robert (1961): Japan, the later years of life and the concept of time. In: Robert W. Kleemeier (ed.), *Aging and Leisure: A Research Perspective into the Meaningful Use of Time*. New York: Oxford University Press, pp. 95–100.

Sugano Noriko (1993): Yōjō to kaigo [Nourishing the vital forces and nursing]. In: Hayashi Reiko (ed.): *Josei no kinsei* [Women's early modern period]. Tokyo: Chūō Kōronsha, pp. 371–403.

—— (1999): *Edo jidai no kōkōsha*. Kōgiroku *no sekai* [Filial children of the Edo period. The world of the *Kōgiroku*]. Tokyo: Yoshikawa Kōbunkan.

Tanaka Yoshiaki (1997): Kodai rōja no "sute" to "yashinai" [Abandonment of and care for the elderly in antiquity]. In: *Rekishi Hyōron* 565, pp. 2–16.

Tatsukawa Shōji (1996): *Edo oi no bunka* [Edo—A culture of old age]. Tokyo: Chikuma Shobō.

Tsuji, Yohko (1997): Continuities and changes in the conceptions of old age in Japan. In: Susanne Formanek and Sepp Linhart (eds.): *Aging: Asian Concepts and Experiences Past and Present*. Vienna: Verlag der Österreichischen Akademie der Wissenschaften, pp. 197–210.

Ujiie, Mikito (2001): *Edojin no oi* [Old age of Edo people]. Tokyo: PHP Kenkūjo.

Yamamoto Shigemi (1993): *Jinsei, makuhiki wa geijutsu de aru. Wa ga kokoro no Obasuteyama* [In life, it is the exit that matters. The "Granny-abandoning-mountain" within our hearts]. Tokyo: Kōdansha.

Yamaori Tetsuo (1984): *Kami kara okina e* [From gods to *okina*]. Tokyo: Seidosha.

—— (1994): Okina to ōna ["Old man" and "old woman"]. In: Furuhashi Nobutaka, Miura Sukeyuki and Mori Asao (eds.): *Jinsei to koi* [Human life and love]. Tokyo: Benseisha, pp. 91–108.

CHAPTER EIGHTEEN

# NOTIONS OF LIFE, OLD AGE AND DEATH IN AGEING JAPAN

Mayumi Sekizawa

## 1. Folklore Studies and Discussions of Old Age

In terms of discussions of old age in folklore studies to date, in the past there were, for example, the discussions of Yanagita (1931, 1946) and Orikuchi (1928), and in recent years, those of Miyata (1996), Yamaori (1984) and others. Yanagita discussed the elderly viewing them as an image or symbol of the ancestors, while Orikuchi's discussions focused on elderly men as represented in the performing arts, as in *Okina no Hassei* [The Emergence of an Old Man]. Yanagita and Orikuchi were seeking to gain a thorough understanding of things like the ancestors' spirits and the deities [*kami*] by looking at the elderly. Later, from the 1980s onwards, theories of old age and childhood were attempted by Noboru Miyata, Tetsuo Yamaori and others, drawing on the centre–margin theory of Victor Turner (1969). These positioned the elderly and children as marginal beings compared to adults, and highlighted the spirituality and sacred nature of these two groups. In this way, from the discussions of the elderly of Yanagita and Orikuchi to those of Miyata and Yamaori, the spirituality and sacred nature of children and the elderly have been noted, but in all of them, the view of the elderly as an image is dominant, and it is difficult to say that they are entirely based on data from direct observation of the elderly in real life.

## 2. Village Societies and the Role of Elderly People

There are many villages in the Kinki region, the neighbouring Wakasa and Banshū areas, and the Iseshima area where it is established that the elderly men of the village take on a set religious role, such as looking after the local tutelary deity, as their duty after retiring from village administration. In these villages, the traditional organization that oversees the rituals for the tutelary deity's shrine is called the *miyaza* [shrine worship association], and in the fields of history, folklore studies and the sociology of religion, research on these associations in terms of shrine ritual organizations has been carried out for a long time (see, for example, Higo 1938, 1941; Harada 1975, 1975; Sekizawa 2005). It has also been recognized that the structures called the *tōya* [household rotation] system and the age system are characteristic of the shrine worship associations. I have drawn attention to the fact that it is elderly people who are at the heart of the shrine worship associations, and have not only analyzed these associations in terms of the aforementioned shrine ritual organizations, but have also tried to combine this with analysis from the standpoint of individual elderly people (Sekizawa 2000).

I will introduce here two case studies as part of the results of this research: the group of elders of the shrine worship association known as the "group of ten elders" [*jū nin shū*] of Kitanaiki, Minakuchi-chō, Kōka City in Shiga prefecture; and the household head rotation [*tōya*] system of the deity of Ōyagyū in Nara City.

### *Case study 1: The "group of ten elders" of Kitanaiki, Minakuchi-chō, Kōka City in Shiga prefecture*

#### *The elders of the miyaza [shrine worship association]*

Kitanaiki is currently a community of 81 houses, and of those, 35 old established families play the main roles in running the village. It is the custom that the heads of these families retire from village administration in March of the year they reach 65 in the traditional *kazoedoshi* method of calculating age (see footnote 2). They then pass on the right to participate in village administration as family representative to the oldest son, in a handover known as *yakuhari*. When *yakuhari* takes place, the successor takes on the duties of attending the monthly assembly, called *sankai*, working in positions other than head of ward, participating in communal village work, and participating in the rituals of the Yōfuku temple (Jōdoshū sect) to which their families are affiliated, and of the tutelary deity's Kawata shrine. The seating order at meetings and the order of serving as head of ward are decided by age. In particular, it is the rule that someone who is older even by only one year takes the higher seat at meetings. Moreover, in cases where more than one person was born in the same year, rather than comparing their own dates of birth, the years of birth of their respective fathers are compared, and the one whose father was born earliest, even by only one year, takes the higher seat, in an age criterion system called *oya otona* [parent adult] unique to the village.

The group of elders called *jū nin shū* [group of ten elders] exists as an organization for these men after they have retired from village administration. It is customary to call the eldest among this group of ten elders by the particular name of *wanjō*. On the occasions of village religious services centring on the tutelary deity's Kawata shrine, which take place around 30 times a year, the youngest member of the group of ten elders acts as the messenger summoning the other members [*yobi-tsukai*], including the *wanjō*, to the service. Then the youngest member and the household head whose turn it is [*tōya*] carry out the preparation of the offerings of food and drink to the deity, the preparation of the food for the celebratory meal [*naorai*] that follows such rituals and the cleaning of the shrine compound. Then the elders' group participates in the religious service as representatives of the villagers.

It is clear that, in Kitanaiki, there is a system in which there is a shift from a secular role to a religious one at the age of 65, accompanying the shift in age. Until then, the heads of the old households take the main roles in village administration; after retiring from running village affairs at 65, they take on a religious role, as when they look after the temple and in rituals at the shrine.

Because the elders' group is a lifelong system, if it lacks one person, the next oldest one joins the group. Comparing the members of the groups in 1986 and 2005, we see that only three members are the same: Matsuzō Kurata, almost 100 years old; 91 year-old Senzō Kurata; and 84 year-old Ichinosuke Kurata. The other original seven have died, and new members have been added. The oldest member in 1986, Risaburō Miyamoto (90), was in poor health and was absent from the group's rituals, but the other nine members carried them out with Matsuzō Kurata playing the central role. However, today in 2005, the five oldest members, including Matsuzō Kurata, the oldest, are all in poor health and absent from the group rituals, and only the five younger ones are carrying out service at the shrine.

When someone joins the group of ten elders, even if he loses his health or becomes bedridden in due course, he is required to carry out his role of service to the shrine as long as he lives, and it is the rule that he cannot be excused.[1] In fact, the *wanjō* in March 1986, Risaburō

[1] If we look at the examples of shrine worship associations in various areas, we see that, because the role of belonging to an elders' group is lifelong, no matter how old the person becomes, as long as he has the support of his family, including his heir and the latter's spouse, he can take on the role. However, in cases where there is no heir, if his

Table 1. *Members of the "group of ten elders"*.

| In March 1986 | | In August 2005 | |
|---|---|---|---|
| Name | Year of birth (age in brackets) | Name | Year of birth (age in brackets) |
| Risaburō Miyamoto | 1896 (90) | Matsuzō Kurata | 1905 (100) |
| Matsuzō Kurata | 1905 (81) | Senzō Kurata | 1914 (91) |
| Yūkichi Kurata | 1909 (77) | Kurata Ichinosuke | 1921 (84) |
| Seibei Kurata | 1910 (76) | Kazuo Kurata | 1924 (81) |
| Seitarō Kurata | 1911 (75) | Heihachirō Kurata | 1925 (80) |
| Genzaburō Kurata | 1913 (73) | Sōichi Kurata | 1926 (79) |
| Yūji Kurata | 1913 (72) | Haruyuki Kurata | 1928 (77) |
| Senzō Kurata | 1914 (72) | Gisaburō Kurata | 1928 (77) |
| Sadakazu Kurata | 1918 (68) | Keitarō Kurata | 1928 (77) |
| Ichinosuke Kurata | 1921 (65) | Ryōichi Kurata | 1930 (75) |

Miyamoto, died three months later in June. Both private matters—his family and himself—and public ones—in his role as *wanjō*—are recorded in his 1984 diary, written in his declining years. In particular, he never failed to write about days when the rituals of the elders' group were held, even at times when he was unable to attend himself. One sees that, even as he declined physically, he took his responsibility as *wanjō* seriously until the end.

*The old age of Mr. Matsuzō Kurata*

The current *wanjō*, Matsuzō Kurata (100), began participating in running the village in 1945 at the age of 40, taking over the right from his father in the *yakuhari* process. Later, in 1967, he joined the elders' group at the age of 62, working as one of the younger members of the group. Because there were not as many elderly people at that time as there are today, he joined the elders' group three years before retiring

wife dies before him and he is living alone, in reality, carrying out the duties of being a member of the elders' group becomes difficult. In fact, Mr Hirata (born in 1931), who belonged to the group of ten elders of Hashimoto in Ryūō-cho, Gamō-gun in Shiga prefecture, used to live with his wife. In Hashimoto, the elders' group carries out rituals at the shrine of the tutelary deity on the 1st and 16th of each month. *Hakama* [formal pleated long overskirt] must be worn at these gatherings. After his wife died several years ago, he was unable to put on the *hakama*, so he asked the leader of the elders' group, the *ichibanjō*, to be excused from the group, and after consultation this was allowed as an exception. There had not been a case like this before, so Mr Hirata was the first person ever to have been excused from the group of ten elders.

from village administration. In 1970, he reached 65 and retired from village administration, passing on this duty to his son. After he retired from village administration, his son also became the main person running the family farm, so Matsuzō became absorbed in growing his beloved chrysanthemums, and widened his circle of friends who were also chrysanthemum enthusiasts. However, in his late 70s, he suffered from rheumatism and his fingers would not work properly, so he had to give up growing chrysanthemums. Just when he thought there was nothing else to enjoy in life, he was shown a report on a survey of folk customs by students at Tokyo Women's University, *Kōka Somanaka no Minzoku* [The Folk Customs of Somanaka, Kōka City] (1983), by a friend living in Somanaka, also within Minakuchi-chō. He thought to himself, "I could write something like that", and immediately began to write about the history and folk customs of Kitanaiki. And so, in 1984, at the age of 79, Matsuzō published *Furusato Kitanaiki* [Home Village Kitanaiki] (1985) at his own expense. In the book, he writes about his motivation for writing, and his feelings of responsibility to write about and pass on to young people the history of the village are well expressed: "People have asked me about these (the details and origins of the traditional events of the village), and thinking that I should try to respond, if I were up to the task and could contribute in my small way, I took up these topics and searched for materials on the history and folk customs of this village from ancient times to the present. [...] Moreover, so that everyone will understand properly what the "group of five people" and "group of ten people" in our village are, and what kind of things they do, I took up these topics too and have recorded something of them here."

Then, in 1986, when Matsuzō was 81, he became *wanjō*, following in the footsteps of Risaburō Miyamoto. That was the spur for him to publish a memoir, *Rōshō no Hana* [Flowers of an Old Pine, Pine means 'Matsu' in Japanese], again at his own expense, in 1991. After that, when he thought he had nothing more to write about, a friend suggested that he should write poetry: "You can write poems in your sleep". So Matsuzō, who had even entered verse competitions in his youth, began to write 31-syllable *tanka* poems on special *tanzaku* paper and to stick them in an album. He wrote about many things in this album under the title of "Ramblings of an old man": chrysanthemums, his late wife, visiting the shrine with the group of ten elders, visits from his friends, the television news, the seasons and other changes in nature, and so on. If one looks at these poems, it is clear that, for Matsuzō, writing poetry is not something done for someone else, but rather comes from the desire to write about himself, to express his own world—part of his self-expression. He continues to write poems today at the age of 100.

From the example of Matsuzō, perhaps we can make the following points about the relationship between the physical decline that accompanies ageing and the desire for spiritual fulfilment. First, spiritual fulfilment lies above all in interchange with friends who share the same hobbies and interests, and in self-expression and understanding other people. Then, when forms of self-expression that are realized physically, such as growing chrysanthemums, become impossible, one shifts to self-expression through language, such as recording history and writing poetry. It also seems that that becomes the last desire, even if one loses the ability to speak on one's sickbed, and that desire remains until the very end of life.

*Elderly people undergoing self-transformation*

What can be shown from observation of these elders involved in the shrine worship association are the following two points. First, the source of the authority of the eldest of the shrine worship association lies in three things: the accumulation of age and *toshidama*,[2] in other words, in the notion of respect for the ability to survive over a long lifetime; the achievement of service in worship of the deity and looking after the shrine; and knowing the history and origins of how things were in the past, in other words, being knowledgeable. Second, even though one may be an elder in the shrine worship association, in everyday

[2] There were two methods of calculating age in Japan: *kazoedoshi*, and completed years. Today, the completed number of years system is the one that is generally used. This method spread at the beginning of the Meiji period with physical examinations for conscription of men of 20 full years, a result, one might say, of modernization, and what it measures is the number of years lived since birth as the starting point. On the other hand, there is the traditional method of calculating age, in which a baby is not counted as zero years old when it is born, but as one year old, and adds a year at each subsequent New Year. By this calculation, someone born on 30 December would be counted as one year old, and then would immediately become two at New Year two days later. This method does not measure the length of time lived, as does the completed years system, but, according to Yanagita Kunio, it measures the age of souls. No baby is born without a soul. Then that soul at New Year receives *toshidama* given by that year's deity, in the concrete form of a round rice cake, and thereby another year's vitality is requested and conferred. It was thought that accumulating the vitality of the *toshidama* was to gain survival over a long life, something that was unusual (Yanagita 1940).

life, one is just an ordinary elderly person; however, that elderly person changes through his role in the shrine worship organization, undergoing self-transformation. He becomes possessed of a feeling of responsibility and, at the same time, of a personality appropriate to fulfilling that role. One can say that in the shrine worship association, there is a mechanism for self-development bringing honour to the elderly person. Self-transformation is naturally thought of as characteristic of the young, who are still growing up and flexible, but it is also the case that self-transformation is evident within the organization and system of the shrine worship association.

### *Case Study 2: Household head rotation [tōya] system of the deity of Ōyagyū in Nara City*

The farming village of Ōyagyū in Nara City is a community of about 100 houses. At the head of the tutelary deity's Yagyūyamaguchi shrine worship association that has been handed down from generation to generation is the oldest person, called *Ichirō*. A group of up to eight people including him is called the "group of eight people", and a group of up to 20 people including him is called the "group of 20 people". In particular, the group of eight people carries out the main role in shrine rituals. Around the time that someone joins the group of eight people, he takes his turn in assuming the duty as *tōya* to maintain and venerate the *Bunrei* [a localized spiritual representation] of Myōjin, the tutelary deity of the shrine, in his own home for a year.

The tatami-matted reception room at the home of the *tōya* where the deity is enshrined is cordoned off by a sacred straw rope [*shimenawa*], and it is forbidden for women to enter this room throughout the year. The *tōya* lives alone in the room where Myōjin is housed, and it is he who carries out the cleaning of the room. Although his clothes are washed by his wife or daughter-in-law, this is done separately from any women's clothing. As for food, any strong-smelling foods such as meat, spring onions, onions and garlic are strictly forbidden. Moreover, his family avoid eating these foods too. He is also required to avoid the pollution of death completely and to preserve his physical and spiritual purity: people who have been to the graveyard cannot enter the house; he does not visit the family graves, even at the festival of the dead [*bon*] in August and the autumn and spring equinoxes; he does not go to houses that are having funerals, nor does he send funeral offerings. In short, just as the *tōya* is called by the name of the deity,

Myōjin-san [Mr. Myōjin] by the villagers, restraint appropriate to the title is required.

The most important part of the *tōya*'s duties is above all to worship the deity properly. Every morning he makes offerings of sacred *sake* [rice wine], washed rice, water and salt, and offers up ritual Shinto prayers. Early in the morning of the first, eleventh and twenty-first of each month (all the dates with "one" in them), he puts on *hakama* [formal pleated long overskirt], a *haori* jacket and a black lacquer *eboshi* hat, and pays a visit to the Yagyūyamaguchi shrine, holding a leaf of the sacred *sakaki* tree between his teeth and taking a branch of *sakaki* and sacred *sake*. While the *tōya* is entrusted with Myōjin in his home, one of his tasks is also to be sure to pay his respects to the deities in the compound of the Yagyūyamaguchi shrine three times a month.

The *tōya* in 1996, Fukunishi Toshio, acted as *tōya* when he was 80. The *tōya* in 1997, Tadayoshi Mukai, acted as *tōya* when he was 81. The decision to take on the role of *tōya* at the advanced age of 80 in this way is not easy. One must decide whether to take it on after taking all the various factors into account, such as one's own state of health, the economic and moral support of one's family, and also the family's state of health. "When you are born in this village, you come to feel you want to help your father to be *tōya*." So say both the son of the third eldest of the group, Kentarō Ōishi (born in 1911), and the son of the fourth eldest, Yasuharu Tabata (born in 1913). Backed up by the unusual ability to survive over a long lifetime, the family's cooperation, and his own energy, a man is able to be entrusted with Myōjin for a year as representative of the village for the first time. For the men of the village, born in Ōyagyū and spending their lives alongside the shrine worship association, being able to be entrusted with Myōjin is considered the greatest fortune in life. In fact, both Mr. Fukunishi and Mr. Mukai, who have acted as *tōya* for Myōjin, talked about improvements in their health: Mr. Fukunishi says, "My chronic headaches got better", and Mr. Mukai says, "I felt livelier than before".

From such analysis of the structures and formalities of the shrine worship association, something that should be called an initiation into old age (a fixed test as a formality of joining the group of elders) becomes apparent. Acting as *tōya* for Myōjin in Ōyagyū when one is nearly 80 effects in a sense a transformation into a person fitting to the state of old age, through formally assuming the role of the shrine's deity at an advanced age and carrying out the responsibility of being the village's representative. Unlike economic and social roles, the religious role of acting as *tōya* for Myōjin is not something that a man can get someone else to stand in for him to fulfil. Rather, accomplishing the task is connected to a reinvigoration of one's own life force in old age.

The value of old age varies in different societies. If there are societies where the value of life falls gradually with age from an economic point of view, there are also societies, such as those discussed here, where the value of life is seen as increasing with age, as proof of vitality, and where the elderly are valued and are to be venerated.

## 3. Purpose in Life and Successors

### *Regional differences in village societies*

Japan's village societies are formed basically by organizing a number of households in some way and administering them together. It is clear that there are regional differences in the criteria for organizing the village societies formed by the households, or in how the villages are run. Specifically, two different types of organization are seen: same family system villages and age-grade system villages. We can see this from the tendency for village societies in northeastern Japan to be determined mainly by the qualification of belonging to a main or branch household, whereas in western Japan, the tendency is for them to be determined by individual circumstances, such as the ages of the village community members, rather than by that kind of genealogical family relationship (Emori 1970). The villages that have handed down from generation to generation the shrine worship associations described above are of the second type. It is a characteristic of these communities that the authority that determines village society is located in the individual's age rather than in the household, and the criterion of age is used in organizing that society. As well as being used in the shrine worship associations, it is also the criterion used for seating order at meetings and in relation to the communal use of graveyards.

### *Regional differences in having a purpose in life*

Now, let's look at the national survey carried out by the Rural Life Research Centre in 1982 on couples of various age groups, from their twenties to their sixties, engaged in farming: "Relation between leisure activities and feelings of fulfilment in life". When we look at the analysis of the survey, we see that, in the case of Shiga prefecture and the rest of the Kinki region, high proportions of people participate in "local events", "religious rituals", "festivals, *bon* dancing", "service to the community" and "local gatherings". In contrast, in the Tohoku region, such as Aomori and Yamagata prefectures, apart from individual hobbies, a high proportion of leisure time was spent in seeing people as individuals or family, for example, "seeing relatives" and "seeing people from the neighbourhood". And in the case of elderly people in their sixties, "religious rituals" and "seeing relatives" were the most popular leisure activities in western Japan and the Tohoku region respectively.

In the 1980s, Niigata prefecture attracted attention as an area with a high suicide rate among the elderly, and two motivations for elderly people committing suicide were written about in the Niigata Daily News Department's *Mura wa Kataru* [Villages Telling Stories] (1983) and Takashi Takabayashi's "Pathology of families where people commit suicide in old age" (1979). One motivation is that people cannot continue to work because of poor health. The other motivation is seen in cases where they want to have grandchildren but their sons cannot find wives, or where their children have moved to town and will not come back to the village so they have no successor, or conversely, where they have to leave the village and home where they are used to living in order to go and live with their sons' families in town: in short, when circumstances have become unsettled and uncertain and the succession of the family is in doubt. In fact, in cases where the son and his wife go to town to work during the winter, few elderly people commit suicide at this time, because they feel they have to look after the household. One old woman, who had lived to the advanced age of 104 and had become bedridden for the last year, said she wanted to die because she was a burden on her children, and she did indeed commit suicide by drowning herself in early spring. Apparently, this old woman used to say that the time she was saddest in her whole life was when the head of the main household died. From these words too, we can gather the feelings of this elderly woman, for whom the continuity of the family and the household was the priority. In contrast with the elders discussed above, who serve in the shrine worship associations in the Kinki region, adding this duty to their concern for themselves and their households, and for whom fulfilling a social role in the village gives them something to live for, in this case, one can say that concern is focused on the family and the household. The differences in the roles that elderly people are expected to assume gives rise to differences in their values and feelings of purpose in life, and it is predictable that there are regional differences here too.

### *Existence of household successors*

Although one can highlight the point that the different forms of village society determine elderly people's feelings of having a purpose in life in this way, if one analyzes these in terms of an ageing society, it is clear that there are problems that are common to all, regardless of regional differences among villages.

For example, in *Senzo no Hanashi* [About our Ancestors], Yanagita (1946) argues that it is the elderly who are in the position of linking the ancestors and successors of the household, likening them to a link in a chain. In fact, from the viewpoint of a foreign researcher carrying out a survey in villages in the Tohoku region, the practice of families, particularly elderly women, worshipping the memorial tablets in the *butsudan* [household Buddhist altar] or their ancestors' graves is analyzed as an act of purification of their own bodies and as giving meaning to their lives (Traphagan 2004). Undoubtedly, the relationship between elderly people and the memorial tablets in the household Buddhist altar and the ancestors' graves is still strong today.

The following is a case study of the S family, one of the old families of my hometown of Ichihana, Ichikai-machi, Haga-gun in Tochigi prefecture. The current head of the household and his wife have no children, so they adopted a child. In the mountains about 20 metres from their home is the S family graveyard, with more than ten gravestones, and on 13 August at *bon* [festival of the dead], they place flowers and water on each of the gravestones, light welcoming fires, and welcome back the spirits of their ancestors in a reception room at home. In the same way, it is customary to send off the ancestral spirits to the graveyard on 16 August. However, when the head of the household and his wife were over 70, they carried out repair work at the graveyard. One stone monument with the inscription "for the generations of ancestors" was built, and all the other gravestones were collected together there. Until then, the family members had been buried, but this was done so that from now on they could be cremated and all the remains placed in the one grave. The elderly couple say, "We can take care of the ancestors' graves while we are alive, but we decided to alter the family grave so that, when we die, we can be cremated and not be a nuisance to those coming after us, and also to make looking after the grave easier." In the old family of M household living in Kamimonoi, Ninomiya-machi, Haga-gun, Tochigi prefecture too, there are no successors. Since reaching his late seventies, the husband often says to his wife, "We couldn't find an adopted child, so I resigned myself to it, but I want someone to look after the family grave."

These are examples that clearly show that, when elderly people are faced with a crisis of succession of an old family because there is no heir, what they are worrying about to the last is looking after the ancestors' graves. And at the same time as expressing their wish that their ancestors' graves be looked after, this is also an expression of their anxiety about what will happen after they themselves die.

In the past there would be a successor, and it was possible to pass on what one oneself had inherited from one's own parents and grandparents, but today, in cases where there is no heir, the situation is such that people are reaching extreme old age without being able to pass this knowledge on to their successors, and the knowledge they have inherited ends up being lost. After the war, the shift towards high academic achievement advanced, and even the eldest sons left the villages and went off to the cities. But now that the parents, who had always thought of themselves as still young, have reached extreme old age, there is a phrase that expresses their impatience to entrust their knowledge to the next generation: "As far as children are concerned, it's best to have the dregs". In the old days there was the saying: "Children cement a marriage", but the new saying is a pun on that,[3] said half in jest, meaning that it is the children who are no good at studying that stay with their parents rather than going to the city.

## 4. Elderly People in the Cities

### *Rapid demographic shift*

The rapid population shift from rural communities to the big cities and changes in employment structures took place in the high growth period from 1955 to 1973. According to *Sūji de Miru Nihon no 100 Nen* (1981), the proportion of the working population employed in farming fell steeply

[3] The original Japanese saying is "Ko wa kasugai", and the new version is "Ko wa kasu gaī".

from 45.2 per cent in 1950 to 30.0 per cent in 1960, and to 17.9 per cent in 1970, and the depopulation of rural communities proceeded. In contrast, the population of the cities rose, from 20,020,000 in 1945 (28 per cent) to 75,430,000 in 1970, meaning that 72.1 per cent of the population had come to live in the cities.

In the 1960 national census, the number of people employed in the secondary sector exceeded that employed in the primary sector for the first time. Namiki (1960) observed that a "landslide shift" was taking place in rural communities at that time, with not only the second sons, but even the eldest sons who were the household successors, moving to the city. The certainty of a successor for a farming household had fallen from 100 per cent in 1955 to 57 per cent by 1967.

The policy adopted to deal with such a sudden increase in the population of the cities was the 1955 "10-year housing construction plan", and the body set up to accelerate the realization of this policy was the Japan Housing Corporation. At first, the Corporation had three main aims: the housing supply for workers; building fireproof mass housing; and the development of housing on a large scale based on wide area integrated plans for the outskirts of the big cities. Then in 1958, the *Shūkan Asahi* [Asahi Weekly] coined the term *danchizoku* [housing estate dwellers].

In the first half of the 1960s, housing estate construction on a large scale was carried out by the Japan Housing Corporation, private electric railway companies and real estate companies. Later, the period from 1965 to after 1975 was called "the age of regional development", when developments such as Tōkyu Tamadenen City, built by the Tōkyu electric railway company, and Tama New Town and Kōhoku New Town, built by housing corporations, were carried out. In this way rural communities on the outskirts of cities were turned into residential areas, with housing estates of flats and detached houses with gardens being built. As a consequence, the city 'salaryman' lifestyle, in which work and home are separated, took root, and the salaryman led a new way of family life there with his wife and children in a nuclear family. This gave rise to new values, such as having a home of one's own and respect for privacy.

### *The privatization of society*

And so now, the people who moved to the cities in the period of high growth are reaching retirement age. Many of the inhabitants of the new towns developed between 1965 and 1975 tend not to want to live with their children's families. These people, who have chosen freely throughout their lives—university, occupation and lifestyle after retiring—without being subject to the restrictions of the family or village society, have a variety of purposes in life and views on life and death. Moreover, the fact that they have done so of their own volition—privatizing themselves—rather than because of social obligation is evident as a characteristic of this group.

In the case of these elderly people in the cities too, one can say that they fall into the category of those who are unable to pass on their knowledge to a successor. What is more, there are no ancestors' graves that they have to look after. What they will be concerned about to the last when they have become old is something that needs to be observed in the future. However, what one can say now is that there are elderly people who cannot pass on their knowledge to successors, both in the countryside and in the cities. But, in contrast to the rural communities, where people who have a traditional outlook in which they feel that they must look after the household and the ancestors' graves are distressed, in the cities, there are extreme cases where many people think that the household and the family grave are limited to their own generation and that there is no need for a grave. Such people characteristically do not think much about passing on traditions and knowledge to the next generation. In this connection, the difference between rural communities and the cities is manifested in how they spend *bon* [festival of the dead] (Shintani 2004). In the rural communities, people must be at home during the *bon* period in order to clean the graves before *bon*, to welcome back the ancestors' spirits and send them off again, and to receive relatives. In the cities, on the other hand, because there are no graves and no ancestors to welcome back, many people use *bon* as a precious summer break to go abroad.

The issue of family succession arises both in the rural communities, where people are worrying about the lack of successors, and in the cities, where people have already become resigned to this. However, regardless of this issue, it may be said that, in the context of the advance of this kind of privatization, Japanese society today, which has arrived at the end of post-war economic growth, is without doubt right in the midst of confusion and searching concerning the forms in which the links of individual lives between ancestors and descendants will be perceived and expressed in the future and concerning elderly people's feelings of having a purpose in life and their views on life and death.

## References

Emori Itsuo (1966): Shakai kōzō—sonraku no shakai soshiki ni kansuru kenkyū no kaiko [Social structures—review of research on the organization of village society]. In Nihon Minzokugaku Kai ed. *Nihon Minzokugaku no Kaiko to Tenbō* [Retrospective and Prospects for Japanese Ethnology], pp. 127–167.

Harada Toshiaki (1975): *Mura no Saishi* [Village Rituals]. Tokyo: Chūōkōronsha.

—— (1976): *Mura Matsuri to Za* [Village Festivals and Associations]. Tokyo: Chūkōronsha

Higo Kazuo (1938): *Ōmi ni okeru Miyaza no Kenkyū* [Research on shrine worship associations in Ōmi]. In *Tōkyō Bunrika Daigaku Bunka Kiyō*, 16 [Tokyo University of Literature and Science Humanities Bulletin] 16.

—— (1941): *Miyaza no Kenkyū* [Research on Shrine Worship Associations]. Tokyo: Kohbundo.

Miyata Noboru (1996): *Rōjin to Kodomo no Minzokugaku* [Folklore Studies of the Elderly and Children]. Tokyo: Hakusuisha.

Namiki Shōkichi (1960): *Nōson wa Kawaru* [Rural Communities are Changing]. Tokyo: Iwanami Shinsho.

Nippō Hōdōbu [Niigata Daily News Department] (1983): *Mura wa Kataru* [Villages Telling Stories].

Orikuchi Shinobu (1928/1975): 'Okina no Hassei [The Emergence of an Old Man]'. In *Orikuchi Shinobu Zenshū 2* [Collected Works of Orikuchi Shinobu]. Tokyo: Chūōkōronsha.

Sekizawa Mayumi (2000): *Miyaza to Rōjin no Minzoku* [Folk Customs of Shrine Worship Associations and the Elderly]. Tokyo: Yoshikawa Kōbunkan.

—— (2005): *Miyaza to Bo sei no Rekishi Minzoku* [Historical Folk Customs of Shrine Worship Associations and Grave Systems]. Tokyo: Yoshikawa Kōbunkan.

Shintani Takanori (2004): *Kurashi no Naka no Minzokugaku 2—Ichi Nen* [Folklore Studies in the Context of Daily Life 2—One Year]. Tokyo: Yoshikawa Kōbunkan.

*Sūji de Miru Nihon no 100 Nen* [A Century of Japan in Figures] (1981). Tokyo: Kokuseisha.

Takabayashi Takashi (1979): Rōnen jisatsusha kazoku no byōri [Pathology of families where people commit suicide in old age]. In *Tōyō Daigaku Daigakuin Kiyō* [Tōyō University Graduate School Bulletin], 15, pp. 91–104.

Traphagan, John W. (2004): *The Practice of Concern: Ritual, Well-Being, and Aging in Rural Japan*. Durham, NC: Carolina Academic Press.

Turner, Victor W. (1969): *The Ritual Process: Structure and Anti-Structure*. Hawthorne, NY/Chicago: Aldine.

Yamaori Tetsuo (1984): *Kami kara Okina e* [From God to Aged Man]. Tokyo: Seidosha.

Yanagita Kunio (1931/1990): Meiji Taishō Shi Sesō Hen [Meiji and Taisho History: Social Conditions]. In *Yanagita Kunio Zenshū* 26 [Collected works of Yanagita Kunio 26] (1990). Chikuma Bunko.

—— (1940/1990): Tabemono to Shinzō [Food and the Heart]. In *Yanagita Kunio Zenshū* 17 [Collected works of Yanagita Kunio 17] (1990). Chikuma Bunko.

—— (1946/1990): Senzo no Hanashi [About our Ancestors]. In *Yanagita Kunio Zenshū* 13 [Collected works of Yanagita Kunio 13] (1990). Chikuma Bunko.

CHAPTER NINETEEN

# POPULATION DECLINE, MUNICIPAL AMALGAMATION, AND THE POLITICS OF FOLK PERFORMANCE PRESERVATION IN NORTHEAST JAPAN

Christopher S. Thompson

## Introduction

In rural Japan, post-war population decline is drastically changing the way local folk traditions are situated in community life. This chapter explores a relatively unknown consequence of the Great Heisei Era Amalgamation Initiative (Heisei [1989—present] Dai Gappei), instituted in 1999 as one of many state mandated decentralization policies designed to mediate the effects of the nation's declining total fertility rate currently at 1.26. This figure, an all time low, contrasts sharply a post-World War II peak of 4.54 in 1947, the largest number of births in a single year recorded in 1949 (2.7 million), and a rate sufficiently above 2.08 until the end of 1974—high enough to maintain existing population levels. Yet, during the ensuing decades, fertility numbers have dropped below 2.0, and have continued to shrink. At the same time, experts predict that by mid-century, over one-third of Japan's population will consist of seniors over the age of 65 (Miyazaki et al. 2006:14). In recent years, much speculation has centred on the possible negative social, economic, and political ramifications of this demographic shift, as well as the state implemented strategies intended to negotiate this change, especially at the district level and in neighbourhood life (Ikegami 2003). In this discussion, the possible repercussion on local cultural history and folk performance traditions, though particularly significant in provincial areas, is rarely addressed. For this reason, this chapter focuses specifically on how the Great Heisei Era Amalgamation Initiative may be affecting the future of potentially hundreds of historical folk performance traditions that survive at the local level, especially in rural areas of the nation's periphery.

In 21st century Japan, there remain many folk performing arts that are rooted deeply in the traditional culture of the region in which they exist. In Iwate prefecture, located in northeastern Honshu, one of these local traditions is *kagura*, or Shinto shamanic dance. The study of folk performance traditions such as *kagura* in northeast (Tohoku) Japan have been a mainstay of Japanese ethnology since the early 20th century. But surprisingly, little has been written about the present-day challenges faced by those who actively maintain these traditions in the communities where they persist. In the past two decades, Japan's fluctuating demographics and state mandated decentralization initiatives designed to help regulate population change have been recognized as major factors challenging the stability of community life and the preservation of local folk culture in Japan's rural townships (Thornbury 1997: 110–114; Tsubohari 1999: 1–16; Thompson 2006: 127–128). Despite this finding, not much is known about how specific state policies implemented to accommodate national population decline are affecting efforts to practice and preserve historical traditions at the community level. This chapter contributes toward filling this void by examining how Japan's most recent state imposed Cities, Towns, and Villages Amalgamation Law (*Shichōson Gappei Tokurei-hō*) enacted in 1999, known more colloquially as the Heisei Dai Gappei, is affecting the *kagura* tradition in Ishihatooka, a rural hamlet in the municipality of Tōwa-chō, located in south central Iwate prefecture.

The chapter begins with a historical overview of state mandated amalgamation initiatives during Japan's modern period (1868–present) to establish the connection between municipal consolidations, population decline, and funding for folk performance preservation in the nation's rural, regional areas. Next, Ishihatooka Kagura is situated within the heritage of its age-old tradition, and inside the boundaries of Towa-cho, itself a product of an earlier state mandated municipal merger in 1955. Following this discussion, I articulate a contemporary emic view of *kagura* in Ishihatooka, and describe the many challenges this troupe and its support community have faced as the Great Heisei Era Amalgamation Initiative has been implemented locally. Key here is an understanding of the troupe's relationship to its municipality that make it structurally and organizationally similar to a majority of local level grassroots folk traditions in Iwate and across the nation, but different from a more famous group in Take, a hamlet in the neighbouring town of Ōhasama, and others like it. This difference is examined further as I describe why a required merger of Towa-cho with three nearby towns impelled by the Cities, Towns, and Villages Amalgamation Law is sure to erode Ishihatooka Kagura as a historically hamlet-centred practice, changing it forever. Finally, I elucidate the many social, political, and economic obstacles that folk preservation groups like Ishihatooka Kagura are likely to encounter in the years to come as systemic symptoms of the Great Heisei Era Amalgamation Initiative in south central Iwate and other rural areas of regional Japan.

Research for this chapter was conducted during biannual visits to the Tohoku region from 2002–2006 utilizing an ethnographic approach. Data were collected from informant interviews, participant observation, focus group sessions, and through primary and secondary documents collected during fieldwork. I also consulted with *kagura* practitioners in the hamlets of Ishihatooka and Take, and support community members in each locale. In addition, the opinions of folk tradition specialists in south central Iwate, educators at the Towa-cho Board of Education, and bureaucrats in the Towa-cho Town Hall were actively solicited throughout the fieldwork period. All references to informant's names are pseudonyms.

## 1. State Mandated Amalgamations and Local Folk Preservation Funding

The connection between state sponsored municipal amalgamation initiatives and local level folk preservation funding in Japan is a product of developments during the nation's modern period (1868–present). Prompted by the state historically to bring about various kinds of structural and institutional changes from the top-down in response to fluctuating political, economic, or social circumstances in the nation as a whole, Japan has experienced three significant periods of state mandated consolidation activity during the last 118 years. The first, implemented from 1888–1889 during the Meiji period (1868–1912) abolished the feudal domain system and implemented the current prefectural organization scheme. Known as the Great Meiji Era Amalgamation Initiative (Meiji Dai Gappei), the purpose of this plan was to increase the scale and relevance of autonomous governing bodies (*jichitai*) that could more efficiently be controlled (and taxed) by the new Meiji government. Consequently, the approximately 71,314 "natural settlements" that existed within a structure of feudal domains recognized during the Edo period (1603–1868) were converted into just over 15,800 modern cities, towns, and villages (*shi, chō, son*) (Rausch 2006: 2–6). During the late Meiji, Showa, and Heisei periods, the state's ability to manage the size and number of these civic units has played a major financial role in enabling the nation to accommodate population change. Amalgamations continued when and where possible.

A second state amalgamation initiative was instituted between 1953 and 1956 during the Showa period (1926–1989) (Nakanishi 2000: 50). The Great Showa Era Amalgamation Initiative (Showa Dai Gappei) was undertaken for many strategic reasons designed to streamline state governance including the goal of establishing the foundation for a National Treasury Subsidy System through the collection of a Regional Support Tax (*Chihō Kōfu Zei*). The purpose of this strategy was to more efficiently redistribute the nation's tax income, a majority of which was (and still is) generated in the Tokyo-Osaka industrial corridor, to towns in less populated, peripheral regions that lacked locally generated revenue to fund basic city services tied to municipal operating budgets. The Showa Dai Gappei reduced the 9,868 townships (cities, towns, and villages) remaining from 1889 to approximately 4,668 civic units of 20,000 residents or less (and 435 cities larger than this size) and paved the way for the financial structure that made Regional Support Funds (*Chihō Kōfu Kin*) available to needy local governments by request from the state (Rausch 2006: 2–6; Thompson 2003: 95).

Interestingly, for poor depopulated regional municipalities, the funding necessary for folk performance preservation has been closely tied to Regional Support Funding and the state policies designed to address depopulation and dwindling fertility rates in Japan's regional areas. Since 1953, and as rural depopulation has progressed during the postwar period, a large proportion of regional municipalities (about 75%) have depended on Regional Support Funds for as much as 50 per cent of their total annual operating budgets (Aqua 1974, 15; Thompson 2003: 95). During a majority of this time, Regional Support Funds have been disbursed to qualifying municipalities in part based on a formula that considers local population size. Typically, a per-resident subsidy amount pre-determined by the state has been paid out directly to qualified municipalities each year to help balance local operating budgets (Thompson 2003: 95).

In the late 1990s, the subsidized value of one adult citizen in regional Japan was estimated at close to ¥1,000,000 (approximately €6,500)[1] a year (Thompson 2003: 95). Until April 1st, 2006, the most recent deadline for incremental local level compliance with the Great Heisei

[1] This figure is calculated based on an exchange rate of .006142 € to the Japanese yen.

Era Amalgamation Initiative, small townships received subsidy revenue based on population numbers they claimed at each triennial census. Even if residents moved away following a census, the subsidy amount dispersed locally was not adjusted until the next count. This practice often resulted in Regional Support Fund surpluses. Lacking few private sector funding options, it is no secret that bureaucrats in regional townships, particularly small depopulated municipalities with a primarily agricultural economic base typically strapped for cash, have over the past two decades increasingly depended on "soft" funds derived from this source to sponsor (in part or in full) local level community based enrichment activities including folk preservation efforts (Mabuchi 2001: 2; Thompson 2003: 89–93; Ōhashi Interview 2006).

During the past 20 years, another way for small depopulated communities to finance community based enrichment activities has been the implementation of creative, municipally initiated fund raising projects designed to generate supplementary income locally—a development strategy favoured by the state. Particularly since the late 1980s, even if such efforts didn't result directly in a balanced budget, municipalities that demonstrated an active agenda to generate their own budget subsidies have gotten preferential treatment from the state in receiving special dispensation funds (derived in part from the Regional Support Tax) designated for specialized local activities including folk tradition preservation (Thompson 2004a: 585). While municipal offerings associated with local schools, lifelong learning, and athletics often receive funding through the local board of education, grassroots level folk performance traditions without special credentials historically have not. Therefore, special dispensations funds designated for this purpose have been an important source of support for hamlet residents trying to keep their local traditions alive.

Especially in depopulated rural areas of regional Japan, surplus Regional Support Funds, locally initiated profit seeking projects, and special dispensation funds have been invaluable sources for financing local cultural preservation activity short of attracting special cultural preservation money usually reserved for the most skilful and prestigious troupes. Thus, in rural, regional Japan, state mandated amalgamations, local population figures, and funding for local enrichment activity such as folk performance preservation have been inextricably intertwined during a majority of the post-war period. More specifically, the Great Showa Era Amalgamation initiative resulted in Regional Support Funding that has been an important source of sustenance for folk performance troupes at the grassroots level in rural areas of regional Japan (Sasaki Interview 2006; Ōishi Interview 2006).

As indicated above, folk performance preservation hasn't always fit neatly into existing categories of state funded activity. As representatives of the state, local bureaucrats in such communities, often themselves folk practitioners or supporters of local traditions, have been instrumental in channelling available funds from town hall to local interests since the 1980s. Overall, the regional subsidy system has worked well for needy townships during the post-war period as long as population levels in the nation's urban areas produced sufficient amounts of surplus tax revenue. This system, however, has understandably been very costly for the state.

## 2. The Great Heisei Era Amalgamation Initiative: A Depopulation Response

In 1989, as the nation's fertility rate hit 1.57, the relationship between the local tax base, local population figures, and municipal treasuries became a major liability for both the state and small rural towns. In regional townships, fewer local births meant larger municipal deficits. It then became clear that Regional Support Funds alone could no longer be counted on to balance small town budgets. And with fewer citizens involved in the nation's economy, the state's national surplus tax income also began to shrink. It was at this time that Japan's public and private sectors awakened to the realization that drastic changes had to be made quickly in order to accommodate structurally and financially a country that had increasingly fewer children and a rising percentage of seniors that were sure to have a variety of age-related social and medical needs (Miyazaki *et al.* 2006: 14).

The nation's economic downturn in the early 1990s, coupled with the impending retirement of the Japanese baby boom generation needing access to the National Pension System (men and women in their 50s and 60s who make up 20% of the population) prompted the state to launch several aggressive measures designed to conserve and consolidate Regional Support subsidies dispersed to the local level (Miyazaki *et al.* 2006: 14). In regional Japan, quotas were established on subsidy amounts, and special dispensation funds were cut. The state also began discouraging unprofitable municipally initiated money making projects. State enforced administrative standardization requirements were also implemented, limiting the use of Regional Subsidy Funds for projects other than those explicitly approved in newly established guidelines. At the local level, no longer could state funding be used freely for folk preservation activity. While resourceful urban-based folk troupes found private sector sponsors for their craft, many preservation groups in depopulated, rural, regional areas and their municipal leaders were left to fend for themselves (Sasaki Interview 2006; Ōishi Interview 2006).

In 1995, The Decentralization Promotion Law (*Chihō Bunken Suishin-hō*) was passed, officially shifting the responsibility of finding funds to balance municipal budgets in regional municipalities from the state to the local level (Thompson 2006: 135–39). This policy in effect sealed the destiny of towns that could not balance their municipal budgets without subsidy help. The state's Heisei era amalgamation plan, implemented from April of 1999 to the present, requires all municipalities smaller than 30,000 residents that cannot balance their operating budgets alone (many of them located in the nation's rural areas) to merge with a neighbouring community or suffer even more subsidy cuts (Ikegami 2003: 9–23). This measure practically eliminated Regional Support Funding as a source for folk preservation support and made the application for increasingly smaller amounts of special dispensation money for this purpose much too competitive to count on regularly for most grassroots groups (Thompson 2006: 137–138). For many rural farm towns, the source of funding for folk performance preservation local bureaucrats had used for years systematically disappeared (Sasaki Interview 2006; Ōishi Interview 2006).

There are four reasons commonly cited by the state to justify the need for the Great Heisei Era Amalgamation Initiative implemented in 1999: (1) to promote further decentralization of government at all levels so that more local decisions can be made by those affected most, (2) to better cope with local level needs associated with the declining national birth rate and ageing population in Japan's municipalities with less than 30,000 residents, (3) to control state spending associated with disbursements to subsidize falling tax revenues resulting from population decline in Japan's smaller cities and towns (half of which are located in regional areas), and (4) to reduce the duplication of public sector programs and services at the local level so that redundant human and financial resources can be re-allocated to projects designed to address the upcoming needs in Japan's ageing society (Mabuchi 2001: 12; Rausch 2006: 4–6). But far from achieving these goals, in many of the smaller cities and towns in regional Japan, amalgamations have only created new uncertainties and concerns.

The latest compliance deadline on April 1, 2006 reduced the number of cities, towns, and villages from the 3,232 at the beginning of 1999, to a mere 1,820 in 2006 (NHK 2006a). In theory, all municipalities in Japan are now much more self-sufficient self-governing bodies. However, the Great Heisei Era Amalgamation Initiative is making folk performance preservation more difficult for amateur performers especially in depopulated communities because consolidations and subsidy cuts place hamlet level troupes already lacking in resources in competition with larger pools of practitioners for what are often diminishing amounts of the only available support funds, frequently coming solely from the public sector. As one scholar of regional Japan has observed, state mandated municipal amalgamations during the Heisei period have been, "easy on the powerful but severe on the weak" by forcing townships that without state subsidies could not otherwise afford to offer some of their city services and extra curricular programs to do without them or merge with a neighbouring municipality so they can (Rausch 2006: 142).

In many parts of regional Japan, the state's Heisei era consolidation initiative is also having a damaging affect on grassroots attempts to preserve and perpetuate even high profile folk traditions such as *kagura*. This is because, the 1999 Cities Towns, and Villages Amalgamation Law undermines the social and financial support structure that has enabled small rural towns and their locally based folk performance traditions to thrive during the post-war period, even in communities with few financial resources. The case of Ishihatooka Kagura, provides a revealing example of why many farm communities and their local level folk performance traditions—especially those located in low population, lower income areas of regional Japan—are particularly vulnerable to the Great Heisei Era Amalgamation Initiative.

## 3. Kagura in Northeast Japan and the Origin of the Ishihatooka Tradition

*Kagura*, which exists in many parts of Japan, has been an integral part of folk festivals in the Tohoku region for several hundred years. Thus, understandably, the way in which Ishihatooka Kagura is situated within the *kagura* tradition and its host community requires some explanation.

Often translated as, "entertainment of the *kami* [Shinto gods]", *kagura* has the distinction of being the nation's most ancient form of Shinto shamanic dance. Japan's origin myth known as *Iwato biraki*, or "[The] Opening [of] the Rock-Cave Door," first compiled in 712 CE, describes a magical rite, performed as a dance, by the goddess Ame-no-uzume and other deities, to coax the Sun Goddess, Amaterasu Ōmikami, out of the Heavenly Cave where she hid to avoid her prankster brother Susa-no-ō. This dance is universally regarded as the first *kagura* performance. Enticed by the music, the moment when Amaterasu Ōmikami stepped out of the cave, the light of life is said to have returned to the universe, darkened by her absence, symbolizing the birth of what was to become Japanese civilization. *Kagura* in any venue is considered to be a sacred rite intended to re-enact Ame-no-uzume's performance in part or in full. Doing so is thought to evoke the presence of *kami* necessary to reactivate the light of life, also thought of as the universal life force (Averbuck 1995: 10).

The *kagura* practiced in Iwate is a folk variety of the courtly version described above known as *sato* or "hometown" (folk) *kagura*. *Sato kagura* is usually associated with specific shrines (and sometimes temples) in small towns and villages in the nation's countryside. In the stages leading up to its present form, *sato kagura* incorporated a wide range of non-Shinto theologies, folk beliefs, rituals, and symbolism as the tradition spread from where it originated at Ise Shrine[2] (present day Mie prefecture) and Kasuga Shrine[3] (present day Nara prefecture) in central Japan to peripheral territories including the Tohoku region.

*Kagura* was introduced to the Tohoku by Buddhist monks known as *yamabushi* [mountain ascetics], who spent long periods cultivating their spiritual powers in the mountains along the way as they brought the tradition to the Northeast. For this reason, *sato kagura* in Iwate is sometimes referred to as *yamabushi* Kagura. *Sato kagura* performances in the *yamabushi* tradition have the aim of revitalizing the human spirit as well as being an expression of the universal life force known indigenously in Iwate as the *yamanokami* [mountain spirit] (Kojima and

---

[2] Ise Shrine is dedicated to the Sun Goddess Amaterasu Ōmikami.

[3] Kasuga Shrine is the shrine of the Fujiwara family that established the capital of Hiraizumi and ruled the in present day Iwate prefecture from 1089 to 1189. As a direct result (not discounting other influences from central Japan to this region prior to and after this period), many thoughts, beliefs, and practices from central Japan were disseminated to northeast Japan during this time.

Crane 1987: 389). The most well-known *yamabushi kagura* tradition in Iwate is Hayachine Kagura, made famous by the late Japanese folklore scholar Honda Yasuji, following his visit to the villages of Take and Ōtsugunai in 1931, located in the present day municipality of Ōhasama, where both styles continue to be performed (Honda 1960: 67; Thornbury 1997: 45).

Hayachine Kagura (based at Hayachine Shrine located at the foot of the sacred mountain that is its name sake in south central Iwate) can document an uninterrupted performance history back to the 8th year of Bunroku (1594) (Ichinokura *et al.* 1995: 33).[4] Ishihatooka Kagura, the focus of this chapter, traces its lineage to Hayachine Kagura practiced in Take hamlet, which, according to records kept by Komagata Shrine (located in Ishihatooka), was passed down to local farmers directly from performers in Take sometime toward the end of the Edo period (1603–1868). As a result, Ishihatooka residents have been performing seasonal rituals using the esteemed Take style of Hayachine Kagura annually since the 8th year of Tempō (1834) (see Figure 1).

Many Japanese scholars including Honda from early in the 20th century to the present, and Western scholars including Irit Averbuck (1995) and Barbara Thornbury (1997), have contributed greatly to our understanding of the rich and varied meanings represented symbolically in the performance of *yamabushi kagura*. However, the invisible cultural, sociopolitical, and economic dynamics that shape and mould this and other grassroots folk traditions in Japan are still not well documented or understood.

As established earlier in this chapter, the Great Heisei Era Amalgamation Initiative is focused specifically on Japan's declining population because of the close relationship between local population figures, the local economic base, and state subsidies that have padded the operating budgets of regional municipalities and rural agricultural hamlets like Take, Ōtsugunai, and Ishihatooka. Furthermore, these state subsidies have helped to fund grassroots level folk performance preservation in such locales during a majority of the post-war period. A closer look

[4] Hayachine Kagura cites as evidence an inscription inside one of a prized *shishi gashira* (lion heads) used in one of the most important dances in the tradition, the *yamanokami mai* (the mountain deity dance). However, a shrine document dating back to 1477 indicates that the tradition may date back to Hayachine Shrine to a time even earlier (Ichinokura et al. 1995:33).

Figure 1. Members of Ishihatooka Kagura performing a dance called the Iwato Biraki "Opening the Rock Cave Door" during a house performance in February 2004. Note: Photograph by Aoki Rikizō.

at the culture and organization of *sato kagura* at the local level shows us more clearly how.

## 4. The Culture and Organization of *Sato Kagura*

In Iwate prefecture, *sato kagura* is performed by trained local residents, interested persons from outside the community and/ or by Shinto and Buddhist priests, for a variety of secular and religious festivals as well as rituals, in venues ranging from private homes and rural village shrines, to tourist attractions and regional, national, and international cultural events. In a typical performance, one or more dancers perform in front of a ceremonial backdrop to the ear piercing jangle of *chappa* (miniature steel cymbals), and an unusual rhythmic drumbeat, complimented by a melody played on a flute. Performances re-enact religious myths, legends, and theology pertaining to *yamanokami* through specialized music, comedy, fun spirited acrobatics, and serious ritual veneration. At the hamlet level, *kagura* is performed at wedding receptions, age grade celebration (*toshi iwai*), in January and February for New Years, and for various auspicious occasions that correspond to the lunar calendar. Where it is performed regularly, *sato kagura* is well integrated into the social fabric of community life.

*Sato kagura* troupes were once supported solely by the shrine or temple parish socially and financially, but this is no longer feasible. Like a majority of traditional folk performance genres situated at the local level in rural areas, a *sato kagura* troupe is typically organized according to a structure that reflects the practices of the past, modified to accommodate the post-war legal and funding requirements of the present. Ishihatooka Kagura, like its parent troupe Hayachine Take Kagura, is set up according to a dual association model. Past, present, and future performers are members of the troupe's preservation association, or *hozonkai*. Troupe logistics and financial affairs are typically managed by a separate but related *kōenkai*, or support organization. Each division of the troupe has one designated leader and officers. Performers don't get paid, but on occasion receive stipends to covers basic personal costs. Costumes, equipment, and supplies are kept at a central location, and maintained by a designated team. For the most part, folk performance troupes such as Ishiihatooka Kagura are volunteer organizations that exist because those involved enjoy the activity and take pride in preserving a historical aspect of local culture. Most troupes are bare-bones operations that are easily capable of using-up all of the financial support they can attract (Nakamura Interview 2006).

During the post-war period, particularly since the Great Showa Era Amalgamation Initiative, the successful maintenance of a folk performance troupe in the agricultural municipalities of regional Japan has depended primarily on establishing a preservation association, forming a support association, and applying regularly through the local town hall for public sector support funds to pay for the basic expenses associated with troupe functions and activities. A majority of folk performance traditions including Ishihatooka Kagura in Iwate prefecture have followed this pattern (Thompson 2006: 139).

Well-known troupes such as Hayachine Take Kagura tap private sector resources for a majority of their financial support. While the *hozonkai* and its members can officially only be given token offerings out of propriety and respect, the *kōenkai* can receive incentives and sometimes even charge fees. For the last thirty or so years, this system facilitated the symbiosis of folk performance troupes at all ability and prestige levels (Sasaki Interview 2006).

## 5. The Political Economy of Ishihatooka Kagura

Ishihatooka Kagura is one of over 400 registered *sato kagura* troupes in Iwate prefecture (Iwate Prefecture 2006: 1–31). The troupe takes great pride in maintaining this classic tradition in Ishihatooka, a hamlet which boarders the southern boundary of Ōhasama, the home of its parent troupe. While not possessing nearly the fame or cultural stature of the troupe in Take, touted by prominent *kagura* scholars as a premium example of Japan's folk performance tradition, Ishihatooka Kagura has developed an excellent reputation regionally and nationally during the last twenty years as a high quality performance both in technique and repertoire.[5]

According to *sato kagura* aficionados, in the last decade, Ishihatooka Kagura has become even more famous in Iwate than the original

[5] Among practitioners of Hayachine Kagura, the Take Style is regarded as more physically demanding, rigorous, and therefore difficult than the Ōtsugunai style thought of as easier. Thus, an association to Take Kagura is considered slightly more prestigious than a tie to the Ōtsugunai style.

performance in Take village. This is because Ishihatooka performers are now in their prime. At a time when the Take Kagura troupe is in transition as veteran performers phase out and their younger understudies phase in, the Ishihatooka performers are widely thought to have at present matched and surpassed their legendary skills (Nakajima 2006). But as evidenced by a recent edition of the Hanamaki town newsletter that featured Hayachine Take Kagura, not Ishihatooka Kagura, as THE troupe that represents the best of Iwate's folk heritage, Take Kagura's illustrious history and reputation is firmly entrenched in the minds of prefectural residents as the best in the region (Hanamaki 2006: 1).

For Take Kagura, this kind of exposure translates into political and economic capital in south central Iwate in a way Ishihatooka Kagura and other troupes just can't compete against. The date and time of cultural events is determined based on the availability of Hayachine Take Kagura, often at the expense of other troupes. Members of Take Kagura have become minor celebrities influential in community governance and even local politics just because of the troupe's history and reputation. Take Kagura is always billed over all other folk performance troupes at commercial and cultural events as the main attraction, earning the highest amount of appearance money. The fame and prestige this troupe commands even when not at its best also results in endorsement deals that enables its preservation association to operate as an autonomous organization with an independent operating budget. Ōhasama (population 8,000), with a thriving wine industry, also has a socio-economic foundation that provides a stable environment in which the tradition (its performers and support community) can thrive.

On the other hand, Ishihatooka hamlet, located in the northern most section of Towa-cho (population 10,426 [see Table 1]), where depopulation, part time rice-farming and full-time employment in neighbouring cities is the norm, *kagura*, despite the troupe's celebrated lineage, has struggled for survival during the post-war period. Towa-cho, established in 1955 when the villages of Oyamada, Nakanai, and Taninai amalgamated into the township of Tsuchizawa as dictated by the Great Showa Era Amalgamation Initiative, once had over 16,000 residents. But during the last two decades, Towa-cho has been loosing as many as 300 residents a year due to deaths, relocations, and low fertility rates (Tōwa-chō Shiryōhen 1998: 2). This loss has taken a huge toll on the municipal treasury and as a result, funding for the town's supplementary activity offerings had suffered greatly.

Like many farming communities in the Tohoku and other parts of Japan, in Ishihatooka, over one-third of the 263 hamlet residents are

Table 1. Towa-cho Population (November 1, 2005).

| | |
|---|---|
| Males: | 5,022 |
| Females: | 5,404 |
| TOTAL: | 10,426 (Year-to-date [+7, −118].)*1 |
| Households: | 3,062 (Year-to-date [+2, −22].)*2 |

Note: *1: + indicates number of births;—indicated resident deaths and those who moved away. *2 + indicates number of new households;—indicates households that have legally terminated or have relocated out of town.
Source: The final Population-by-Age chart created for Ishihatooka hamlet by Tōwa-chō Town Hall (Tōwa-chō Kōhō 2005: 14).

senior citizens. Only 3 infants were born in Ishihatooka last year. Most local offspring graduate from junior high or high school and move away for education and work. As a result, there are few successors interested in taking over the many family farms (see Table 1), not to mention roles in the hamlet's *kagura* troupe. In the late 1980s, the demise of cultural traditions in Ishihatooka and Towa-cho seemed all but assured.

Despite the dismal 1980s, in the 1990s, Ishihatooka Kagura was able to mount a noteworthy comeback. The key to the troupe's rejuvenation has been in the creative use (up until the present) of Regional Support Funding and of special state dispensations secured for the cause by sympathetic bureaucrats in the Towa-cho Town Hall. Like many regional farm towns in the early 1990s, in a last resort attempt to address the long menu of social and economic symptoms of depopulation and low fertility causing local cultural decline, Towa-cho's town government decided to turn repopulation into a municipality-wide development project. This town hall initiated effort was aimed at combating the lack of young people, the increasing percentage of senior citizens, and the declining capacity of the municipal coffers to provide the kinds of services that support the culturally endowed farm town lifestyle that is a part of the local heritage. By using a series of self initiated economic development projects (*jisaku shuen jigyō*) in combination with standard Regional Support Funds and special grants, Towa-cho bureaucrats created a budget and a support structure aimed at stabilizing their municipal population and preserving their highly valued local culture that has enabled their folk traditions to survive—as long as state subsidies have continued.[6]

[6] Since 1990, the state's renewed emphasis on funding opportunities for local development projects in regional areas (the village revival movement [mura okoshi undō] and the hometown creation plan [furusato sōsei undō]) are well known (Thompson 2003: 92).

Since the mid 1994, the Towa-cho Town Hall's creative support of repopulation and the preservation of its local folk traditions have taken the form of both long and short term initiatives. Permanent policies include municipality-wide cash donations for bearing more than one child, reduced tuition for young families who use municipal day care facilities and participate in citizen enrichment opportunities (*shimin ikusei jigyō*) provided by the local board of education. The Towa-cho Town Hall even subsidized expensive annual health checks for resident children 12 years of age and under.

As initiatives subject to renewal more directly related to the folk preservation effort, the Towa-cho treasury also provided start up money to promote local folk preservation for children, youth, as well as adults, and financial support for necessary equipment, practice facilities, and transportation to performance events. Folk performance education has even been incorporated into the local public school curriculum at the elementary, junior high, and high school levels—and for the first time in some traditions, girls and women are being allowed to perform. Ishihatooka Kagura is a major beneficiary of these town hall based initiatives. In late 2005, over half of their troupe's expense budget of approximately ¥500,000 (approximately €3,250)[7] was covered by the initiative provided in their town (Nakamura interview 2006).

Many farm towns in regional Japan have designed similar municipally sponsored programs that have enabled their local folk traditions to survive. The result of Towa-cho's self-designed development project has been the creation of a township of some 10,500 residents that boasts 54 designated prefectural and national *bunkazai* (cultural treasures), 15 of them *mukei* (intangible—methods or practices recognized as valuable)—a majority of these being folk performance arts, one of them a troupe known formally as Hayachine Take Ryû (style) Ishihatooka Kagura. In no small part due to Towa-cho's municipal support mechanisms, Ishihatooka Kagura earned a prefectural intangible cultural asset endorsement in 1996 (Ōhashi 2006 interview). As of December 2005, the troupe that 20 years earlier had only 5 active members left had grown to 12 adult performers and 7 junior high understudies.

[7] This figure is calculated based on an exchange rate of .006142 € to the Japanese yen.

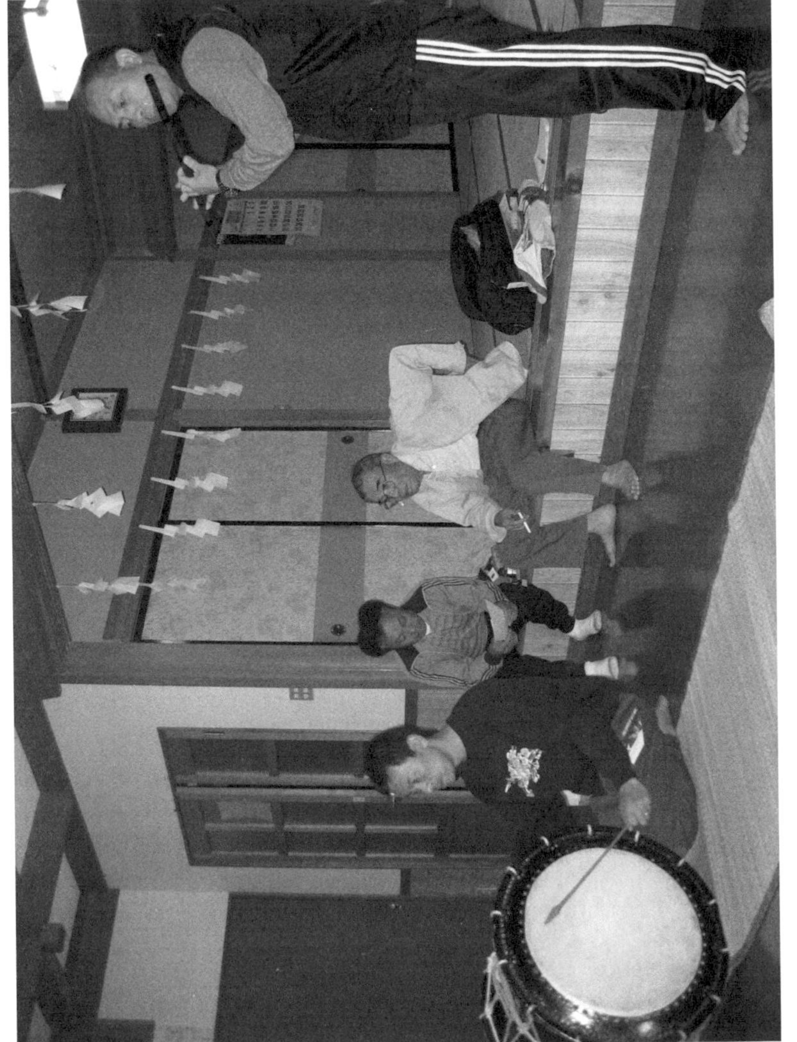

Figure 2. Members of the Ishihatooka Kagura adult troupe playing the *taiko* (drum) and *fue* (flute) to accompany practicing dancers at a practice in September 2005. Note: Photograph by the author.

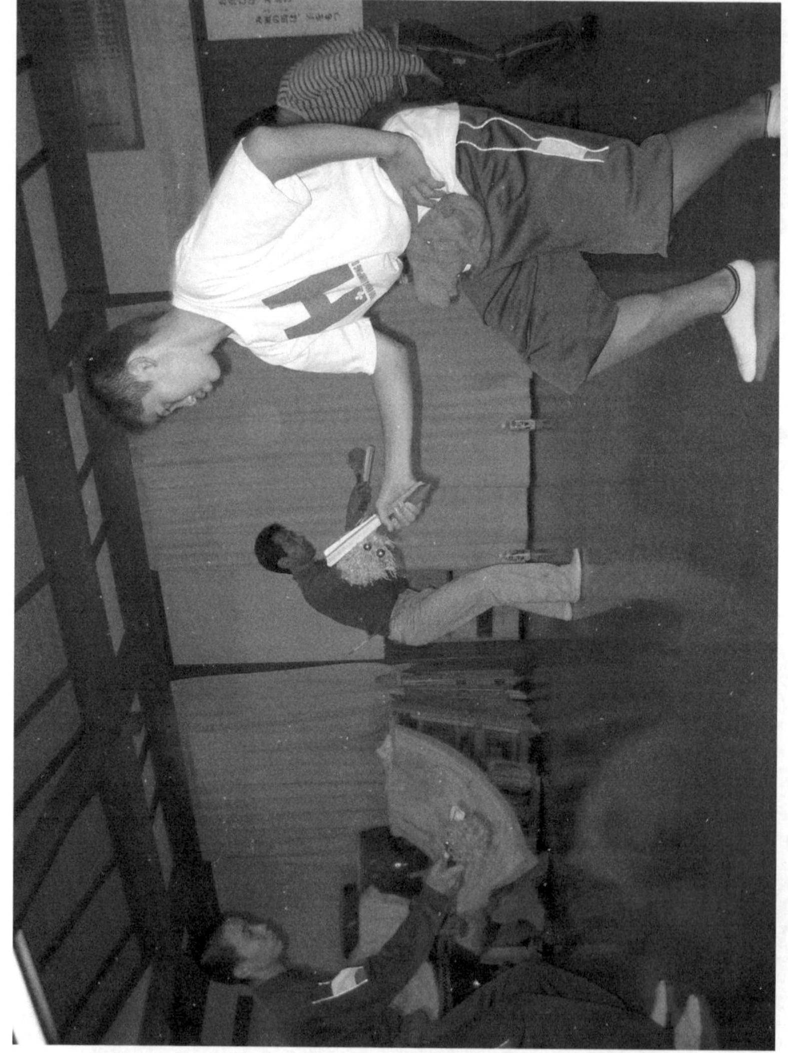

Figure 3. Members of the Ishihatooka Kagura junior high troupe practicing in September 2005.
Note: Photograph by the author.

## 6. The Amalgamation of Towa-cho

I have written elsewhere about the measures introduced by Towa-cho's past mayors Obara Hideo (1988–1999) and Odashima Mineo (1999–2006) to configure the municipal economy so it could support its many special projects with the help of Regional Support Funds and other state subsidies while proudly remaining independent as a township (Thompson 1998, 2000, 2003, 2006). Drilling a hot spring and building an accompanying resort in the middle of town, creating third sector companies to sell local farm products in Japan's major cities, building an antenna shop and restaurant serving Towa-cho dishes on the Ginza, and direct sales of locally produced rice were a few such ideas. The state used to encourage such measures, even if subsidy amounts could not be significantly reduced as a way to help towns like Towa-cho to cope with depopulation and fertility decline. But with the introduction of the Great Heisei Era Amalgamation Initiative, Towa-cho's predicament has changed.

Unable to find self-sustaining funds for the 40 per cent deficit in its operating budget by a state mandated deadline in April 2005, on January 1st, 2006, Towa-cho was officially amalgamated into its eastern neighbour, the city of Hanamaki (population 73,000). At the same time, Ishidoriya (population 16,000) and Ōhasama (population 8,000), both bordering Hanamaki's northern boundary, also joined the merger for similar reasons in a four-way consolidation that created a New Hanamaki (*Shin-shi* Hanamaki) with a population of 107,000 residents—well above the state's guidelines for minimum size.[8] But while this amalgamation took care of Towa-cho's immediate financial problems, it placed into jeopardy the community's beloved folk traditions. Towa-cho's post-amalgamation budget cannot operate at a loss. This invariably means that the special programs available to residents in pre-consolidation Towa-cho will likely have to be cut. For Ishihatooka Kagura and Towa-cho's other folk performance traditions, this is not good news.

## 7. Ishihatooka Kagura in the New Hanamaki

Exactly how the four-way consolidation will affect folk performance preservation in Ishihatooka and the other hamlets that have now been

[8] All population figures utilized in this paragraph are approximates.

absorbed into the New Hanamaki remains to be seen. The outcome will be telling. This is because all Iwate residents know that a majority of folk performance troupes in their prefecture and elsewhere in Japan share more in common with Ishihatooka than with Take Village (Hirano Interview 2006; Nakamura Interview 2006). For this reason, local level folk preservation and support association members all across the country are also watching.

In recent months, opinions regarding what will happen to Towa-cho and the town's array of intangible cultural treasures have been hotly contested among local residents in neighbourhood association gatherings, seasonal festival committees, and even at Sakura, the local pub. Following a monthly meeting of the Towa-cho Entertainment Culture Association (Tōwa-chō Geinō Bunka Kyōkai) one Saturday in late September 2005, a spontaneous debate on the topic erupted among several members who have stopped off at Sakura to unwind.

Ōhashi Yoshiko, a retired Ishihatooka resident and former Towa-cho Town Hall employee (a city government insider), contends that the amalgamation will change Towa-cho programs as residents now know them. No matter what promises may have been made to the consolidating towns before amalgamation, Ōhashi asserts that sooner or later, the mandate of the Heisei amalgamation plan to reduce costs will force Hanamaki to start making decisions that will require the highest degree of administrative efficiency and the least amount of financial output (Ōhashi 2006 Interview). The practical realism of Ōhashi's opinion is hard to ignore.

Interestingly, Nakamura Jirō, a middle-aged *kagura* leader in Ishihatooka, has a contrary opinion. Nakamura claims that this recent *gappei* will have no effect on his hamlet folk tradition. In a sense, this could be true too. The political boundaries of residential communities have changed dozens of times over the centuries in the Hayachine region, and *sato kagura* is yet to disappear. Many folk scholars suggest the current practice of the *deshi* [apprentice] *kagura* system is sufficient to perpetuate most of the mainline *sato kagura* traditions in Iwate. However, as noted earlier in this chapter, the politics inherent in these relationships can be tricky. And for *deshi kagura* to prosper, master troupes would need even more of the difficult-to-secure financial resources to cultivate their apprentice groups. Most grassroots level troupes, being more like Ishihatooka Kagura than *kagura* troupes in Take or Otsugunai (Thornbury 1997: 113–114), would not necessarily be able to generate enough of the required funding purely on their own.

In early October of 2005 Nakamura explained why he felt optimistic:

> Thanks to the support of our local superintendent of education, we (volunteers from Ishihattoka Kagura) now teach *kagura* at the community level and in our local schools. It's called faith heritage education (*kyōiku shinkō*), a policy that encourages school districts to incorporate the traditions of their communities into their school curriculum. It's a policy sanctioned by the board of education independent of town hall. It's been about 10 years since this policy was first implemented. Even school officials are finally coming to understand that culture is as important as test scores in nurturing a well-adjusted child—and that folk performance preservation can play an important role in this process. As long as we have access to our children, something will work out (Nakamura 2005 interview.)

Unfortunately, it is this very community support network and flexible thinking that Nakamura praises which is being threatened by the state's Heisei amalgamation plan. A talk with bureaucrats in the former Towa-cho Town Hall (now the Towa-cho Extension Office [Tōwa-chō Sōgō Shisho]) in February of 2006 revealed that large-scale administrative changes in the New Hanamaki are only one year away. A top priority in Towa-cho will be school consolidation—namely, the merger of the five existing Towa-cho elementary schools. Students currently attending Haruyama Elementary, where the Ishihatooka community sends their children to school, will be fused into the much larger Tsuchizawa Elementary, on the opposite side of town. Tsuchizawa has its own *kagura* and other historical folk performance traditions as do the Tase, Nakanai, and Narushima elementary schools that will also merge. Even if Ishihatooka Kagura is incorporated into the consolidated elementary school's Heritage Religion curriculum, in fairness to the other consolidating schools, it will not likely become a central part of it. As a result, Ishihatooka Kagura will most probably loose the special emphasis it currently receives at Haruyama Elementary School. (Hirano 2006 Interview).

Furthermore, a plan to homogenize all government programs and services in each of the four districts within the New Hanamaki is also scheduled for next fiscal year (Ōishi 2006; Sasaki 2006). This measure will eliminate all of the "pro-preservation" services that the administrators of the independent Towa-cho dutifully provided until the end of 2005, rendering the present system for supporting Ishihatooka Kagura and the township's other folk performance troupes obsolete. Unless Hanamaki City Hall initiates a new folk performance preservation initiative—at this point, a move thought to be highly unlikely—all Towa-cho troupes will have to compete for funding with Ishidoriya and Ōhasama against the existing Hanamaki groups.

## Conclusion

For Ishihatooka Kagura, the Great Heisei Era Amalgamation Initiative means a complete reconfiguration of the existing social, economic, and political mechanisms in Towa-cho that their folk performance tradition, preserved and perpetuated on a volunteer basis by local citizens at the community level, have depend on during the postwar period in order to survive (Tōwa-chō Kikaku Zaiseika 2002:3). By extension, this means that grassroots level folk performance traditions in similar rural, regional townships are vulnerable in the same way. The Ishihatooka example also exposes several systemic realities of the Heisei amalgamation plan at the local level that all folk performance preservationists everywhere in Japan must now confront.

First, the Great Heisei Era Amalgamation Initiative may affect grassroots level folk preservation groups such as Ishihatooka Kagura much more than is commonly understood. This is because typically, hometown folk performance troupes are situated within their municipalities in a way that the 1999 Cities, Towns, and Villages Amalgamation Law renders structurally and financially vulnerable. If community level folk performance troupes, particularly in the rural municipalities of regional Japan, hope to survive, they must implement strategies to resituate themselves locally in more secure ways.

Secondly, high profile preservation groups with political celebrity such as Hayachine Take Ryû Kagura will not be as seriously affected by the Great Heisei Era Amalgamation Initiative simply because their support structures are independent of local level funding. In short, folk performance traditions that already have secure access to external funding will survive *gappei* easily to the possible detriment of their not so famous counterparts.

Third, the Great Heisei Era Amalgamation Initiative may have a hegemonic influence on community affairs including folk performance preservation at the local level broader in scope than the political and economic impact that is initially apparent. In Hanamaki, consolidation even influenced the reinterpretation of educational policy designed to protect and preserve Ishihatooka's local folk heritage.

While further research is necessary to determine specifically how these dynamics play out in other communities across Japan, it is clear that the Cities, Towns, and Villages Law of 1999 will likely have the most serious impact on the future of grassroots level folk performance preservation in the poorest, least populated areas of regional Japan. For Japan's fertile folk performance heritage, this is indeed unfortunate because it is within these very peripheral areas, in the rural districts of places such as the six Tohoku prefectures (Aomori, Akita, Iwate, Yamagata, Miyagi, and Fukushima prefectures) where some of the most remarkable and intriguing grassroots level folk performance traditions Japan has to offer persist (Thornbury 1997: 113–114).

On December 20th, 2006, the National Institute of Population and Social Security Research announced that the nation's total fertility rate will fall even further to 1.21 by the year 2013. The Institute now estimates that Japan's population will decline from 127 million recorded in 2005 to 89 million by 2055. In locations such at Tokyo, fertility rates are already below 1.0. The fact that Japan's declining population and the falling birth rate are a major impediment to maintaining Japanese economic power, social security funds, and the public pension system is well known and widely accepted. But very little attention has been paid to how state measures to combat these problems are also changing life at the local level in undesirable ways. The case of Ishihatooka Kagura shows that without implementing any countermeasures, Japan's current demographic trends and state policies designed to counter them place the cultural history and folk performance traditions of the nation's most financially disadvantaged citizen at considerable risk.

Interestingly, despite the transformation that Ishihatooka Kagura has undergone from the Edo period to the present, in the hamlet, there remains a manifest assumption that the performance is unchanging and will endure. A historical process of reorientation, reintegration, and assimilation into a constantly changing world is at the core of the symbolic unity of Ishihatooka Kagura that keeps the tradition alive. In post consolidation Towa-cho, Ishihatooka Kagura will have to resituate itself again, in order to survive. This might seem a difficult proposition with no easy answers at present. But if the history of this troupe is any indication, the metaphysics of Ame-no-uzume, if not the mystical power of the great *yamabushi*, is bound to empower them to find yet another way.

Tōwa-chō, Ishihatooka Population-By-Age Chart

| Age | Male | Female | Total | Households |
|---|---|---|---|---|
| 0–4 | 7 | 3 | 10 | — |
| 5–9 | 5 | 3 | 8 | — |
| 10–14 | 9 | 3 | 12 | — |
| 15–19 | 8 | 2 | 10 | — |
| 20–24 | 8 | 6 | 14 | — |
| 25–29 | 2 | 3 | 5 | — |
| 30–34 | 6 | 6 | 12 | — |
| 35–39 | 0 | 3 | 3 | — |
| 40–44 | 9 | 4 | 13 | — |
| 45–49 | 7 | 6 | 13 | — |
| 50–54 | 9 | 7 | 16 | — |
| 55–59 | 1 | 0 | 1 | — |
| 60–64 | 6 | 5 | 11 | — |
| 65–69 | 0 | 2 | 2 | — |
| 70–74 | 12 | 8 | 20 | — |
| 75–79 | 9 | 19 | 28 | — |
| 80–84 | 9 | 10 | 19 | — |
| 85–89 | 4 | 5 | 9 | — |
| 90–94 | 2 | 3 | 5 | — |
| 95–99 | 0 | 0 | 0 | — |
| Grand Total: | 140 | 122 | 262 | 67 |

Table 2. The last population-by-age Chart created for Ishihatooka hamlet by Tōwa-chō Town Hall before amalgamation into Hanamaki which reflects figures up to August 31, 2005 (Tōwa-chō Town Hall 2005b:1; Tōwa-chō Town Hall 2005c:1).

## References

Aqua, Ronald (1974): *Local institutions and rural development in Japan*. Special series on rural local government. No. 8. Ithaca, N.Y.: Rural Development Committee, Center for International Studies, Cornell University.

Averbuch, Irit (1995): Performing Power: On the Nature of the Japanese Ritual Dance Performance of Yamabushi Kagura. In: *Journal of Ritual Studies* 10, 2, pp. 3–34.

Brown, L. Keith (1976): *Shinjo: The Chronicle of a Japanese Village*. Pittsburg: Center for International Studies and Department of Anthropology, University of Pittsburg.

Hanamaki City (ed.) (2006): *Kōho Hanamaki* [Hanamaki Newsletter]. Vol. 1, No. 1–15.

Hirano, S. (pseudonym) (2006): Interview by author. Tape recording. Towa-cho, Iwate prefecture, 21 March.

Honda, Yasuji (1960): *Zuroku Nihon no minzoku geinō*. Tokyo: Asahi Shimbun Sha. http:/www.bunka.pref.iwate.jp/dentou/kyodo/list/Kagura.html (found 6 June 2006).

Ichinokura, Shunichi, Yukio Kuronuma, Kazuo Fujiwara, and Takehito Kamiyama (1995): *Hayachine Kagura*. Morioka: Kawaguchi Shuppan.

Ikegami, Hiromichi (2003): *Shichōson gappei: Koredake no gimon* (City, town, and village amalgamations: All of these questions). Tokyo: Jijitai Kenkyūkai.

Iwate Prefecture (2006): Iwate dentō/kyōdō list.

Kelly, William (1990): Regional Japan: The Price of Prosperity and the Benefits of Dependency. In: *Daedalus* 119, pp. 209–227.

Kojima, Setsuko and Gene A. Crane (eds.) (1987): *Japanese-English Dictionary of Japanese Culture*. Union City: Heian.

Mabuchi, Masaru (2001): *Municipal Amalgamation in Japan*. World Bank Institute Working paper. Stock No. 37175. http://siteresources.worldbank.org/WBI/Resources/wbi37175.pdf (found 22 November 2006)

Miyazaki, Tetsuya (2006): What Can We Do About the Baby Bust? In: *Japan Echo* 33, 1, pp. 14–19.

Nakamura, J. (pseudonym) (2006): Interview by author. Tape recording. Towa-cho, Iwate prefecture, 25 March.

Nakanishi, Hiroyuki (2002): *Shichōson gappei: machi no shōrai wa jūmin ga kimeru* [Municipal Mergers: Residents to decide the future of our cities]. Tokyo: Jichitai Kenkyusha.

NHK (2006a): NHK 7 p.m. TV News. TV Japan 6 a.m. Eastern Standard Time. (Broadcasted 3 March 2006).

Ōhashi, Y. (pseudonym) (2006): Interview by author. Tape recording. Towa-cho, Iwate prefecture, 25 March.

Ōishi F. (pseudonym) (2006): Interview by author. Tape recording. Towa-cho, Iwate prefecture, 28 March.

Rausch, Anthony (2005): Municipal Mergers in Rural Japan: Easy on the Powerful, Severe on the Weak. In: *Electronic Journal of Contemporary Japanese Studies*. http://japanesestudies.org.uk/discussionspapers/2005/Rausch.html (found 6 June 2006).

—— (2006): The Heisei Dai Gappei: a case study for understanding the municipal mergers of the Heisei era. In: *Japan Forum* 18, 1, pp. 133–156.

Sasaki, A. (pseudonym) (2006): Interview by author. Tape recording. Towa-cho, Iwate prefecture, 21 March.

The Asahi Shimbun (2006): Japan Almanac 2006. Toppan Printing Co. Ltd. Tokyo.

Thompson, Christopher (2001): Cyber Chomin@Towa-cho: Reterritorializing Rurality in Regional Japan. In: *Pan Japan: The International Journal of the Japanese Diaspora* 2, 2, pp. 95–116.

—— (2002): Recruiting Cyber Townspeople: Local Government and the Internet in a Rural Japanese Township. In: *Technology in Society* 24, pp. 349–360.

—— (2003): Depopulation in Rural Japan: Population Politics in Tōwa-chō. In: Traphagan, John W. and John Knight (eds.): *Demographic Change and the Family in Japan's Aging Society*, pp. 89–106. Albany: SUNY Press.

—— (2004a): Host Produced Rural Tourism: Towa's Tokyo Antenna Shop. In: *Annals of Tourism Research* 31, 3, pp. 580–600.

—— (2004b): You are your House: The Construction and Continuity of Family and Identity Using Yagō in a Japanese Suburban Farming Community. In: *Social Science Japan Journal* 7, 1, pp. 61–81.

—— (2006): Preserving the Ochiai Deer Dance: Tradition and Continuity in a Tōhoku Hamlet. In: Thompson, Christopher and John W. Traphagan (eds.): *Wearing Cultural Styles in Japan: Concepts of Tradition and Modernity in Practice*, pp. 124–150. Albany: SUNY Press.

Thornbury, Barbara (1997): *The Folk Performing Arts: Traditional Culture in Contemporary Japan*. Albany: SUNY Press.

Tōwa-chō Dentō Bunka Kyōkai [Society for Traditional Culture of Tōwa] (2001): Tōwa no geijutsu bunka [The cultural arts of Tōwa]. Social Education Section, Board of Education, Towa-cho Town Hall. Tōwa: Kikuchi Insatsu.

Tōwa-chō Kikaku Zaiseika (2002): Hontō ni hitsuyō na no!? Shichōson gappei [Is consolidation really necessary?]. In: *Tōwa-chō Kōiki Hōkoku* No. 1 (March), pp. 1–4.

*Tōwa-chō Shiryōhen: Chōsei yōran* [Towa-cho Town Statistics Catalogue], p. 2.
Tōwa-chō Sōmu-ka [Towa-cho General Affairs Division] (2002): *Jinkō* [Population]. In: Tsubohari, Mamoru (1999): *Waga michinoku no dentō geinō: Hayachine kagura, shishi odori, onikembai* (Traditional folk performance in my Michinoku: Hayachine Kagura, Shishi Odori, Onikembai). Kinseisha: Tokyo.

CHAPTER TWENTY

# ANCESTORS, BURIAL RITES, AND RURAL DEPOPULATION IN JAPAN

John W. Traphagan

## 1. Introduction

This chapter explores the intersection of demographic change—specifically increased longevity, decreased fertility, and rural depopulation—and interactions between living and dead. I consider the influence of population decline on the care of deceased family members and argue that rural depopulation in Japan needs to be understood as having an influence not only on the living but also on the dead.

When one walks into city hall in many rural municipalities in Japan, it is not uncommon to find a chart on the wall, placed in a prominent area, that shows the current population of the town or city, with an indication of the increase or decrease since the previous month. Local newsletters that update townspeople on government activities often show births and deaths and contain a population count as well. These reminders that depopulation is a concern, however, are not necessary for most people living in rural Japan; one merely needs to walk along the main street in many towns to be aware of the population problems everyone is confronting. The only faces one is likely to see in any abundance are those of the elderly (cf. Traphagan 2000). Young adults are relatively few in number, as are children. Population, and particularly depopulation, is a central issue confronting rural Japan, particularly in an era where it is not uncommon to find villages and towns that have elder populations (defined as those 65 and above) comprising over 30% of the total population and children representing less than 15% (see Traphagan and Knight 2003, also Jussuame 1991).

A simple fact of life in rural Japan is that population is declining (see Traphagan and Knight 2003). In areas such as the Tōhoku region (see Figure 1), where research for this chapter was conducted, rural prefectures such as Akita and Iwate are losing population or, at best, remaining stable, while prefectures with urban centers like Sendai

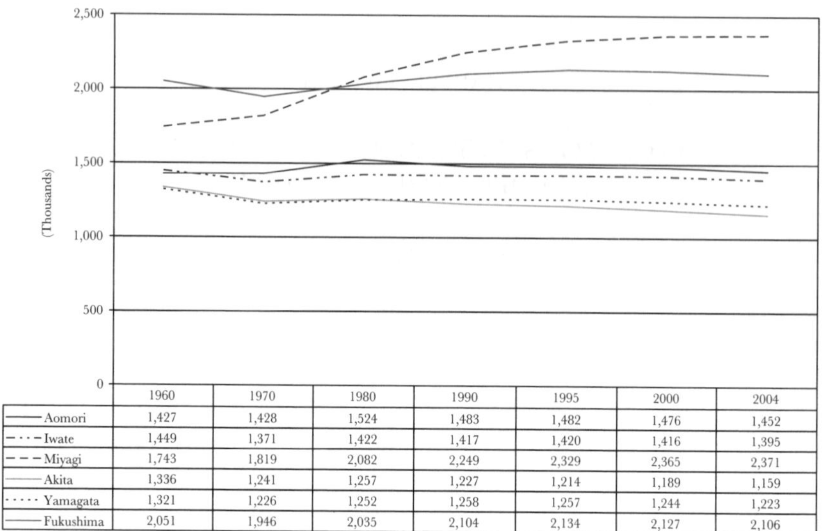


| | 1960 | 1970 | 1980 | 1990 | 1995 | 2000 | 2004 |
|---|---|---|---|---|---|---|---|
| Aomori | 1,427 | 1,428 | 1,524 | 1,483 | 1,482 | 1,476 | 1,452 |
| Iwate | 1,449 | 1,371 | 1,422 | 1,417 | 1,420 | 1,416 | 1,395 |
| Miyagi | 1,743 | 1,819 | 2,082 | 2,249 | 2,329 | 2,365 | 2,371 |
| Akita | 1,336 | 1,241 | 1,257 | 1,227 | 1,214 | 1,189 | 1,159 |
| Yamagata | 1,321 | 1,226 | 1,252 | 1,258 | 1,257 | 1,244 | 1,223 |
| Fukushima | 2,051 | 1,946 | 2,035 | 2,104 | 2,134 | 2,127 | 2,106 |

Source: National Population Census and the Annual Report on Current Population Estimates; as of October 1, 2004.

Figure 1. Population Change in Tohoku, 1960–2004.

in Miyagi Prefecture have experienced population growth as young people have been drained from the countryside (Traphagan 2000). As the elderly of these areas die off, the local population, like the population of Japan in general over the next 100 years, will decline precipitously. This process has already created a stress on institutions such as schools—for example, in one mountain area in the town of Tōno in Iwate Prefecture, an elementary school and middle school have been combined in the same building due to a lack of children and in the nearby town of Kanegasaki, one elementary school that was designed to hold 200 students holds 54 as of 2006 (see chapter 28).

One area that is often overlooked when considering the situation of the living in depopulating areas is that of the dead in those same areas. As I will discuss below, Japanese ritual practice surrounding the dead involves regular visits to the gravesite to clean the grave area and also to conduct rituals for the deceased. Along with depopulation, several problems arise in relation to these graves: What happens to the dead when no-one is left alive to care for them? How do rural temples (and other institutions) maintain themselves and care for the dead when faced with declining numbers of families in their associated parishes? In this chapter, I will discuss these issues as they have been playing out in the town of Kanegasaki, which is located in Iwate Prefecture in the northern part of Japan's main island of Honshū. I also will include some data collected during fieldwork in Akita Prefecture in the summer of 2000. I begin by discussing ancestor veneration in Japan, following which I will look at the problems that arise in continuing this care when populations are in decline.

## 2. Ancestor Veneration in Japan

Rituals associated with ancestors in Japan are performed at two primary locations. In terms of daily activity, ancestor rituals are performed in the home, normally at the Buddhist altar known as a *butsudan*, a piece of furniture on which tablets containing the posthumous names of deceased family members are displayed. Family members, and others who visit the household, may make offerings of rice, water, or gifts brought to the household as the need arises, but also typically on a schedule either every morning or evening (or both). As Robert J. Smith (1974) notes, there is considerable micro-variation in how and when rituals related to ancestors are performed among different households, even within the same hamlet or neighborhood, but virtually all households in which a member of the family has died perform some sort of regular ritual to venerate ancestors.

In addition to performing rituals at the family *butsudan* people perform rituals associated with ancestors at the family grave. In general, Japanese cremate the dead and place the ashes in a common grave with other members of the immediate family line.[1] Figure 2 shows an example of a typical family grave. At the center is a tall stone on which is carved the family name, beneath which is an altar at which one can perform rituals that typically involve incense burning and making offerings of food or drink.[2] At least one family member will visit the family grave on a minimum of three occasions throughout the year: the vernal equinox, the autumnal equinox, and the summer festival of the dead known as *obon*. However, it is not uncommon for people to visit the family grave at any time throughout the year, and family members returning to their

---

[1] Recent research by Kawano has shown that there is a small, but growing, interest in scattering of ashes among some Japanese. See Kawano (2004).

[2] For the purposes of this paper, a detailed discussion of ritual performance is not necessary. Those who are interested in details of ritual performance are referred to Traphagan (2004) or Kawano (2005).

natal homes for a visit during holidays will often visit the grave and conduct ancestor-related rituals as well.

Grave visits involve a combination of cleansing of the grave site and *omairi*, which can be understood as a form of prayer or, in the case of Buddhism, a remembering of one's ancestors, at the gravesite or family altar (Traphagan 2003, 2004). Depending upon the grave site, family members will bring implements for washing the grave area with water (many temples have buckets, ladles and water available at the entrance, but public cemeteries may not). Water is poured over the top of the stone and over other areas of the grave to remove dirt and the stone may be wiped down. Any debris, such as leaves, sticks, or remnants of offerings from previous visits, are removed from the grave and the area surrounding it. Following cleaning, family members will normally light incense and place their hands together in front of their faces and remain quiet for a few moments.[3] They also may make offerings of food for the deceased and place flowers in vases that are designed for the purpose and are part of the gravestone.[4] The entire process is normally relatively brief, lasting from 15 to 30 minutes, depending upon how much clean-up of the area is required, and it is not necessary that all family members visit the grave, as long as at least one person carries out the ritual at the appropriate times throughout the year.

This brief discussion of ritual practices related to the family graves in Japan serves only to point out the basic activities that are involved. The key point for most Japanese is that the rituals be performed on a regular basis and that the grave site be kept clean and orderly (Traphagan 2004). Performance of the rituals and maintenance of the grave site is part of a complex relationship that Japanese share with their ancestors, but the primary issue for our purposes here is that ritual performance and care of the grave is understood as a way in which to express concern or caring for lost loved-ones (Traphagan 2004). To leave the gravesite uncared for and the rituals unperformed is to show, at the least, a lack of respect for one's ancestors and more generally a lack of love, caring, or concern for those that gave one life in the first place.

[3] Persons conducting the ritual may request favors of the ancestors, report on family happenings to the ancestors, or simply bring a particular loved-one to mind. The content of the activity varies significantly from one person to another.

[4] The manner in which Japanese conceptualize the ancestors is more complex than can be dealt with in this chapter. See Traphagan (2004) or Plath (1964) for detailed discussions of ancestors.

Figure 2. Family grave located in Kanegasaki.

## 3. Lonely Ancestors

In general, Japanese tend to conceptualize ancestor veneration as being important for the living as much as it is for the dead. For example, in a focus group[5] conducted in Akita Prefecture, there was a general sense that people conducted ancestor rituals in order to maintain their personal well-being, but there is often a sense that the ancestors are involved in the world of the living. As one woman indicated:

> I ask the person who died, please help me or please protect me or my family, or when I am going to do something, please help my project do well, or when traveling [I ask for safe travel]. So when I pray, I am asking for help from the ancestors.

Another woman stated:

[5] The focus-group session was conducted with the aid of two graduate student assistants from the Department of Anthropology at the University of Pittsburgh: Blaine Connor and Jennifer McDowell.

> We do ancestor rituals when we come back from a journey or come back to the family; the first thing we need to do is visit the ancestors and grandparents. When I go back from Akita, I go to tell my ancestors the things that happened while I was there, to update them. The other thing we did in our family [when I was growing up] was that my grandfather did ancestor rituals every morning at the altar [*butsudan*]. He did this to show appreciation for our health our peace. It is good to appreciate our good family and good relationships and things like that.

The relationship between ancestors and living is reciprocal; while it is important for the living to stay in touch with the ancestors, the ancestors are also in need of attention from the living (Traphagan 2004). I have often asked what happens if there is no-one to do the ancestor rituals, to which several of my informants have indicated that they do not feel good, or that they feel sorry for the ancestors. There is clearly a personal aspect to ancestor rituals that motivates regular practice, but there is also concern about the ancestors themselves that needs to be taken into account and which has relevance for understanding issues related to grave sites and rural depopulation.

One of the more serious issues that may arise when no-one cares for ancestors is that they may become what are known as *muenbotoke* or unattached spirits. These unattached spirits are seen as lonely or, in some cases, potentially dangerous to the world of the living. Not all Japanese believe in the existence of *muenbotoke*, but it is not uncommon in rural areas, at least, for people to believe that *muenbotoke* are real. When, for example, I spoke to one woman in her fifties about the existence of *muenbotoke* she was convinced that they exist. Part of her conviction arose from her experiences in hearing the voices of dead people, which she explained as being a characteristic of her family since her mother and son also had these experiences. Although many people do not believe that *muenbotoke* exist, there is a general sense that the ancestors should be cared for and those who do believe that ancestors may become *muenbotoke* also believe that this will happen if the family gravesite is either not cared for or is not made at all:

> **Woman**: I don't think [my ancestors will become *muenbotoke*] because they already have *ohaka* and *butsudan*. Only people who have no-one to care for them become *muenbotoke*.
>
> **Man**: As long as there is a family, *butsudan*, and *ohaka* [grave], there is no worry that they will become *muenbotoke*.

> **Woman**: There are a lot of children that do not have anyone related and thus there are more and more *muenbotoke*, this is a big problem in Japan.

In some writing on Japanese ancestor veneration, *muenbotoke* are presented as being dangerous to the living. Earhart (1989: 47) describes a situation in a new religion, known as Gedatsu-kai, in which a priest links sickness in the family to neglect of the ancestors, and Guthrie (1988) looking at another new religion notes that neglect of the ancestors is viewed as having the potential to bring misfortune, illness, or accident upon the living (see also Traphagan 2003: 128). Nonetheless, in many cases there is a strong sense that it is the living who are most affected by the failure to carry out ancestor rituals:

> **Woman**: I myself have no children, so I have the possibility to become *muenbotoke*. But I feel o.k. because, well I feel guilty when I do not take care of *ohaka* or *butsudan*, but I feel it is o.k. for me to become a *muenbotoke*.
>
> **Man**: Why?
>
> **Woman**: Because, I'm dead! [laughter] It is o.k. for me, but I feel guilty for my ancestors if I don't do something for them, but for me it is o.k.
>
> **Other woman**: Death is just a part of nature, so I am o.k. with this too.
>
> **Man**: Then why do you feel guilty? If you are not taking care of your ancestors...A sense of obligation?
>
> **Woman**: Yes, it is a sense of obligation. My parents did it so I think it is important that I do it as well. My mother did it, so I feel I should do it if I am in that situation, but since I have no children, it is o.k. for me. I feel free and I don't expect that other persons should feel guilty about taking care of my *ohaka* and *butsudan*. So as long as I live, I will take care of my husband's *ohaka* or *butsudan*. I feel it is a duty to take care of this as long as I am alive.

## 4. Depopulation and Ancestor Veneration

How do these perspectives on caring for ancestors intersect with rural depopulation? Perhaps the most obvious manner in which they intersect is that the loss of population means that there may be no-one left to care for the dead. Indeed, this is a growing problem in rural Japan evident in numerous Buddhist temples, many of which are facing serious problems with maintaining the size of the temple parish (*danka*) as local populations shrink. While visiting one temple, which has a very small parish of only 15 families,[6] the priest was giving a tour of the temple to a group who had come to visit from another temple. The group consisted entirely of people in their sixties and above. As the head priest was talking about the main hall, one of the men in the group asked her about the size of the parish. When she told him, everyone was amazed at how small it is. Then the man talked about their own temple, at which he explained they are having big problems because of the decrease in the size of the parish (they have only 40 families). The priest from that temple agreed that it is a serious problem they are facing. This conversation arose spontaneously, an indication of the fact that it is on the minds of parishioners in rural areas.

In general, when faced with issues such as repairing temple buildings or graveyards, temple priests depend upon the parish to provide necessary funds. As a parish declines in size, the ability to carry out repairs diminishes. But other problems also exist in relation to the loss of parish size, or, if not decrease in size, decrease in active membership. This is evident at a temple known as Hōun-ji which is located in Kanegasaki. Hōun-ji is roughly 400 years old and is set against a large hill and has a graveyard that goes up the hill behind the temple; the graveyard and temple are surrounded by beautiful gardens that are cared for by the temple priest and his parents. There are between 500 and 600 hundred families in the temple parish. Unlike other temples in the area, the size of the parish has increased slightly because there has been an influx of people into the center of Kanegasaki in recent years. This is largely due to the presence of an industrial park, as well as the large number of houses that have been built around the main road, highway, and railroad lines that run through the center of town. However, the influx of people has not translated into a major rise in the size of the parish; as the head priest explained:

These new families either are not interested, have connections elsewhere, or do not have anyone who has died, thus they generally do not have strong connections to the temple.

[6] This particular temple is unusual in that it has always had a very small parish, from its beginnings approximately 1200 years ago. Thus, the current small size is not a result of depopulation.

Although loss of size of the parish is a concern for the future of Hōun-ji, the current issue they are facing centers on the fact that there are several families in which there are no remaining children nor relatives to care for the grave. The head priest described these abandoned graves as "*gomi*" or trash in that there is no-one to care for them and they are just scattered around without being cleaned or without anyone making offerings. As the priest at Hōun-ji explained:

> This is a growing problem. It's not that people have moved away, it's just that there isn't anyone to care for the grave. I wind up having to do it, but this isn't the same as having family care for the grave.

In other words, population loss as a result of a lack of children and the death of elders has left a significant number of unattended graves and, thus, concomitant unattended dead. The priest at Hōun-ji went on to explain that there are a growing number of *muenbotok* as a result of these problems; he does not view them as dangerous, but he does think that they are pitiful (*sabishii*).

The problems faced by temples like Hōun-ji are amplified when one considers temples located in remote areas such as mountain villages. In these cases, not only is there a problem with inadequate people to care for graves, but the parish size often is decreasing rapidly as the remaining elders die off and there are no remaining relatives to carry on the relationship with the temple. The long-term consequences for these temples can be extreme. In one case, the head priest told me that he believes that it is likely that in the future the temple will have to amalgamate with another temple in order to survive. Otherwise, there will simply not be enough people to maintain the temple structure, nor to care for the dead who inhabit the temple's graveyard.

## 5. Conclusion

In societies such as Japan, where an important task of the living is to make sure that dead family members are remembered and cared for, population decline represents a problem that crosses the lines of life and death. To be dead in Japan is not to be removed from the world of the living, thus when the living are no longer around it presents a problem that transcends obvious population issues such as falling school enrollments or a declining labor force. Japanese living in rural areas are confronted on a daily basis with a problematic equation; as the population of the living declines, the population of the dead increases. Although the need for specific ritual performance may end for particular deceased at either 33 or 50 years, depending upon the region of Japan, the ancestors, as a collective group of deceased, require perpetual ritual care in the form of regular offerings at the family altar and gravesite. The result of this equation is that at the least there are a growing number of uncared for gravesites that are unsightly. At worst, there are a growing number of unattached spirits who for some may represent dangerous entities, but for many represent sad figures who are doomed to an eternity of silent detachment from the world of the living and the loved ones no longer left behind to care for them.

## Acknowledgements

Research for this chapter was supported by a Franklin Research Grant from the American Philosophical Society and funds from the Mitsubishi Endowment for Japanese Studies in the Department of Asian Studies at the University of Texas at Austin.

## References

Earhart, H. Byron (1989): *Gedatsu-Kai and Religion in Contemporary Japan: Returning to the Center*. Bloomington: Indiana University Press.

Guthrie, Stewart (1988): *A Japanese New Religion: Risshō Kōsei-kai in a Mountain Hamlet.* Ann Arbor: Center for Japanese Studies, University of Michigan.

Jussaume, Raymond A. (1991): *Japanese Part-time Farming: Evolution and Impacts.* Ames: Iowa State University Press.

Kawano, Satsuki (2004): Scattering the Ashes of the Family Dead: Memorial Activity among the Bereaved in Contemporary Japan. In: *Ethnology* 43(3), pp. 233–48.

—— (2005): *Ritual Practice in Modern Japan: Ordering Place, People, and Action.* Honolulu: University of Hawaii Press.

Plath, David W. (1964): Where the Family of God Is the Family: The Role of the Dead in Japanese Households. In: *American Anthropologist* 66, pp. 300–317.

Smith, Robert J. (1974): *Ancestor Worship in Contemporary Japan*. Stanford: Stanford University Press.

Traphagan, John W. (2000): The Liminal Family: Return Migration and Intergenerational Conflict in Japan. In: *Journal of Anthropological Research* 56, pp. 365–385.

—— (2003): Older Women as Caregivers and Ancestral Protection in Rural Japan. *Ethnology* 42(2): 127–40.

—— (2004): *The Practice of Concern: Ritual, Well-Being, and Aging in Rural Japan.* Durham: Carolina Academic Press.

Traphagan, John W. and John Knight (2003): *Demographic Change and the Family in Japan's Aging Society.* Albany: State University of New York Press.

CHAPTER TWENTY-ONE

# RELIGION IN POST-WORLD WAR II JAPAN AND SOCIAL AGEING

Kenji Ishii

## 1. Japanese People's Changing Religiosity

After World War II, Japanese society greatly changed its social system, including its politics and economy. It was not only politics and the economy that changed: the Japanese people's way of life and religiosity were also transformed.

The Institute of Statistical Mathematics (Inter-University Research Institute Corporation) has carried out statistical surveys on the attitudes and feelings of Japanese people in daily life every five years since 1953, revealing the characteristics of Japanese people's viewpoints and attitudes in a quantitative way. In 2000, the Institute prepared a report summarizing half a century of the "Survey on the Japanese National Character" (Institute of Statistical Mathematics 2000). The opening article, "How have Japanese people's attitudes changed: 50 years of the survey on the Japanese national character", indicates how the consciousness of the Japanese people has changed greatly since the war. A shift to prioritizing personal life becomes consistently apparent, with the opinion "the most important thing is the family" showing the greatest increase. The article also notes that a shift can be seen in religious feelings and personal relations in recent years, areas that have until now been exceptional in remaining more or less stable in the "Survey on the Japanese National Character", in which changes in attitudes over the years have been the norm. The report observes a shift in recent years, noting that the numbers of people expressing the opinions "a religious mind is important", and "if you had to choose, would you say that you are someone who venerates your ancestors or not?" are gradually falling. The percentage agreeing that "a religious mind is important" fell by 12 percentage points (from 80 per cent to 68 per cent) in 15 years, and the proportion saying that they did venerate their ancestors also fell by 12 percentage points (from 72 per cent to 60 per cent) in 20 years.

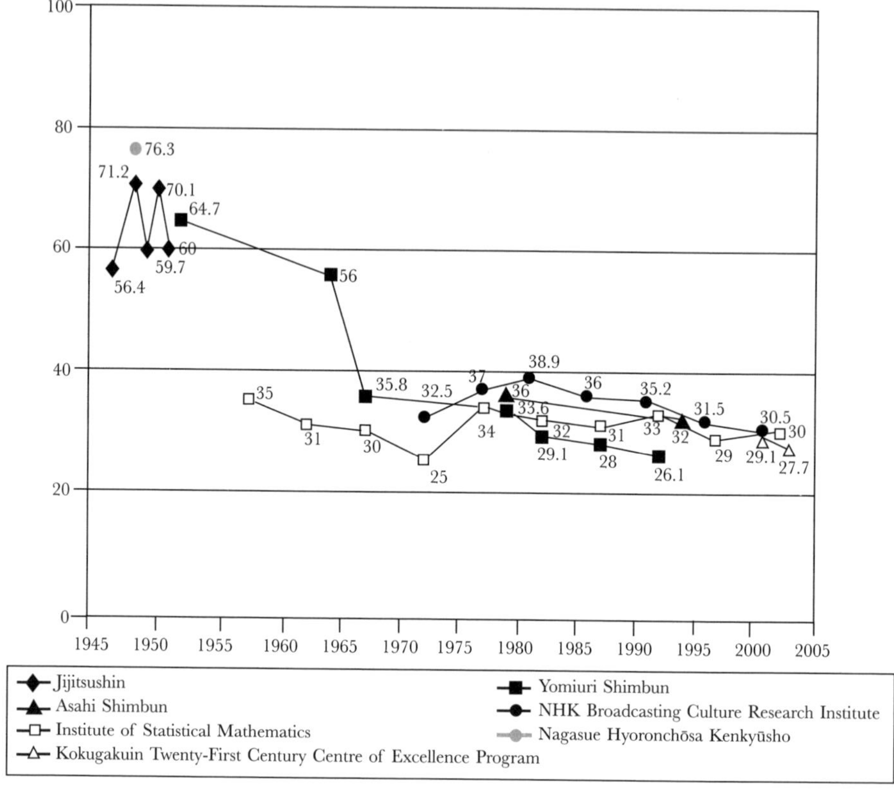


Figure 1. Changes in whether or not people have faith.

On the basis of other public opinion surveys, it is clear that the phrase "a shift in recent years" used in the Survey on the Japanese National Character is an extremely moderate one (Ishii 1997).

Since 1978, *Asahi Shimbun* has been carrying out regular public opinion surveys to find out about changes in Japanese attitudes and lifestyles. The 2003 survey marked the 25th anniversary, and it brought together a quarter-century of Japanese attitudes under the title "Japanese people's value systems: big changes in the last quarter-century".

In 1978, a combined total of 39 per cent of those surveyed said they were "interested in" or "quite interested in" religion and faith. This figure had fallen by 16 percentage points to 23 per cent 25 years later in 2003. The decrease was more noticeable among women than men. It was reported in the newspaper as "Large increase in those 'not interested in religion' to 77%" (Asahi Shimbun 2003).

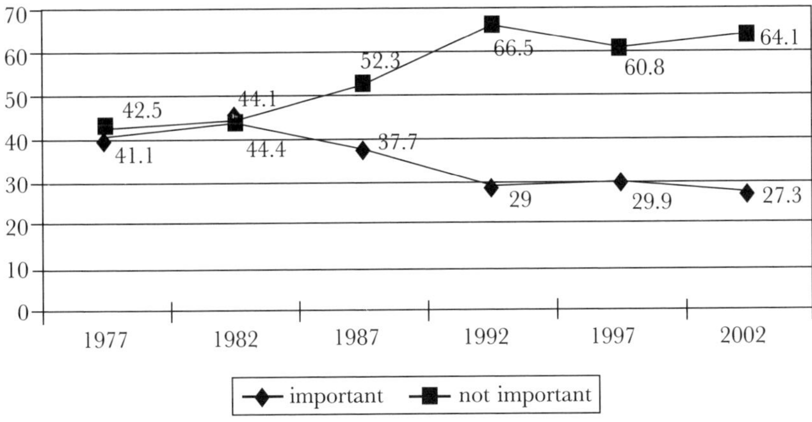


Source: Naikakufu Seisaku Tōkatsukan 2004.

Figure 2. Is religion important?

Figure 1 brings together the results of various post-war opinion polls relating to whether or not people have faith. It is clear that the proportion of Japanese people in the post-war period saying they have faith is gradually falling, and has currently fallen below 30 per cent.

I cited above the finding that the percentage of people agreeing that "a religious mind is important" fell by 12 percentage points in 15 years, and I will show that a dramatic change has taken place regarding this point. Until now, even if Japanese people did not have faith, it was thought that a high proportion considered religion important. Figure 2 illustrates the results of the World Youth Opinion Survey carried out every five years by the Cabinet Office (Cabinet Office 2004). Since the mid-1980s, the number of those responding that "religion is not important" has exceeded those answering that "religion is important." In the 2003 survey, the proportion that thought religion was "important" was 27.3 per cent, while those saying "not important" reached 64.1 per cent. This kind of trend is similar in other surveys. If people do not recognize religion as important, they are unlikely to have religious faith.

Table 1. Numbers of legally constituted religious bodies, religious teachers and officiants, and believers.

| | Religious bodies | Believers |
|---|---|---|
| Shinto | 84,996 | 107,559,322 |
| Buddhism | 78,469 | 93,986,387 |
| Christianity | 4,222 | 2,157,476 |
| various | 15,298 | 93,986,387 |
| Total | 182,985 | 213,826,700 |

Source: Agency of Cultural Affairs, "Religions Yearbook", Heisei 17 edition, 2005.

## 2. Is the Religious Population of Japan Really Two Hundred Million?

Now I will discuss the first point, "believers or members of a religious organization". First of all, I would like to point out that, for reasons of space, what follows is only a summary.

When discussing religious population, there is one particularly well-known figure: 200 million. The current Japanese population is around 120 million, so the religious population is 1.7 times that. This figure is sometimes used intentionally as a means to argue that cults are a threat, in claims such as "200 million people are believers of cults".

The reason that this paradoxical figure exceeding the total population is in general circulation is that it appears in the *Religions Yearbook* published annually by the Agency for Cultural Affairs. This absurd figure is released by a public body because it is based on self-reporting by religious organizations. It certainly does not mean that Japanese people are actively members of specific religious organizations, or even of several religious organizations.

The Minister of Education, Culture, Sports, Science and Technology confers religious organization status. However, freedom of belief and the separation of religion and politics are declared in the constitution, and so the state does not carry out public opinion surveys on religious groups. For that reason, the figures in the *Religions Yearbook* are self-reported figures from the religious corporations.

Table 1 shows that the total "number of believers in Japan" is 213,826,700. If you look at the breakdown of religions, the largest is Shinto, with 107,559,322. Next are Buddhist sects (93,986,387), followed by various other religions (10,123,515), and Christianity is the smallest (2,157,476). Incidentally, the status of the religious corporations is also based on self-reports by the religious organizations themselves. Even if they are new religions, groups that consider themselves as drawing on Buddhist traditions are classified as Buddhist sects.

### 3. Numbers of Believers in Religious Organizations

The number of believers given by the Association of Shinto Shrines is 96,622,992, which accounts for 45.2 per cent of the number of believers in Japan. This figure is the result of adding the number of worshippers at Ise Shrine to the total numbers of believers provided by each regional branch of the Association. In Shinto, there is a distinction between *ujiko* [people under the protection of the local deity] and *sūkeisha* [worshippers]. In its widest sense used, the category of *ujiko* refers to all the inhabitants of the shrine's parish. In this case, people are counted as believers irrespective of how they perceive their relationship to their local shrine. In a narrower sense, the category refers to those inhabitants of the local shrine's parish who join in shrine activities. The category of worshippers indicates those living outside the area covered by a particular shrine who have a special sense of reverence for it, or those who have a sense of reverence for a shrine that does not cover a particular district. The numbers of worshippers at the Grand Shrine of Ise are calculated from figures such as those for the distribution of amulets from Ise.

I will discuss Buddhism later under "household religion".

It is clear that the number of official believers in Christianity is close to reality. According to the most recent *Yearbook of Christianity 2006 edition* (Kirisutokyō Shimbun 2005), there are approximately 480,000 Catholics and approximately 610,000 Protestants in Japan. The figures in the *Yearbook of Christianity* also include sects such as Mormons and Seventh Day Adventists. The numbers of Catholics have increased in recent years, whereas those of Protestants have fallen.

The category "various religions" cited in the *Yearbook of Religions* refers to those other than Shinto, Buddhism and Christianity. One could think of these as the new religions, and the majority are believers in Tenrikyō.

The definition of believers used above is, apart from Christianity, different from the type where one goes to church regularly, follows doctrine, and carries out fixed observances

From the discussion above, it is clear that the figures from the public opinion surveys are closer to the actual numbers of believers. The

Table 2. Membership of religious organizations (per cent).

| | |
|---|---|
| Belong | 8.8 |
| Do not belong | 91.2 |

Note: Figures are out of 100.

Sub-question: *What kind of religious organization is this? Please choose as many as you wish from the alternatives.*

| | |
|---|---|
| Shinto organization | 0.4 |
| Traditional Buddhist organization | 1.6 |
| Christian organization | 1.1 |
| Sōka Gakkai | 3.7 |
| Risshō Kosei-kai | 0.3 |
| Tenrikyō | 0.4 |
| Shinnyo-en | 0.4 |
| Other religious groups | 0.6 |
| Don't know | 0.1 |

Source: Kokugakuin (2006).

answers given by the respondents are more precise for the purposes of understanding the overall picture.

The "Survey of Japanese Religiosity and Beliefs about Kami", conducted in 2003 by the Kokugakuin University Twenty-First Century Centre of Excellence Programme, followed a question on membership of religious organizations with one on the kind of religious organization. According to the survey, just 8.8 per cent of the respondents answered that they belonged to a specific religious organization (Kokugakuin 2006).

If the question is put in this way, even the figure for traditional Buddhism is only 1.6 per cent. This indicates that there is a large gap between Buddhism as "household Buddhism" and Buddhism as belonging to an organization.

## 4. Household Religion and Individual Religion

In Figure 1, the proportion of people in their late forties and early fifties answering that they have faith is extremely high, at around 60 per cent. What underlies this affirmative answer is Buddhism as household religion.

In the "Survey on the nation's customs" carried out by the Society for the Investigation of Superstitious Beliefs in 1950 (Meishin Chōsa

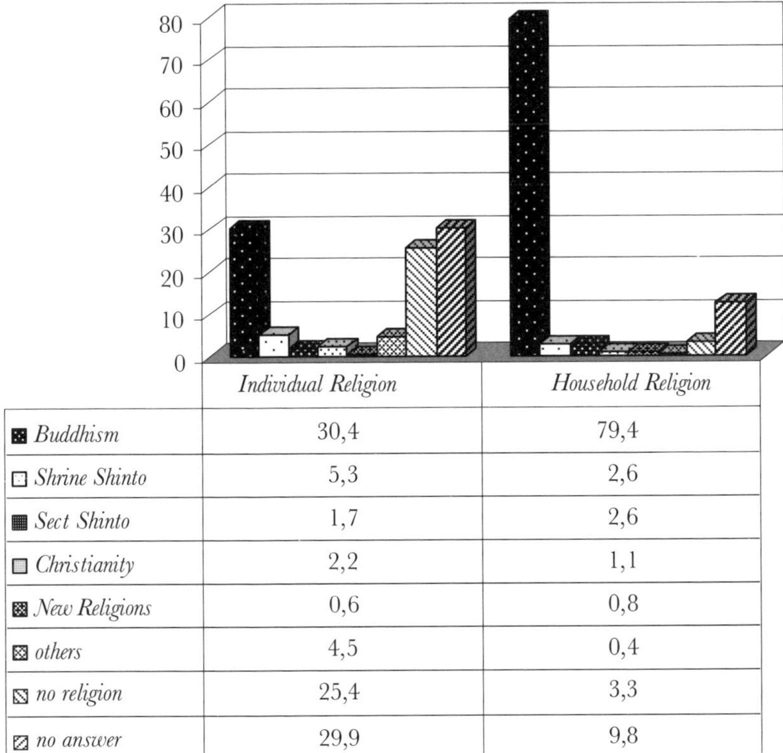


| | *Individual Religion* | *Household Religion* |
|---|---|---|
| *Buddhism* | 30,4 | 79,4 |
| *Shrine Shinto* | 5,3 | 2,6 |
| *Sect Shinto* | 1,7 | 2,6 |
| *Christianity* | 2,2 | 1,1 |
| *New Religions* | 0,6 | 0,8 |
| *others* | 4,5 | 0,4 |
| *no religion* | 25,4 | 3,3 |
| *no answer* | 29,9 | 9,8 |

Source: Meishin Chōsa Kyōgikai (1950).

Figure 3. Religious groups by category.

Kyōgikai 1952), "individual religion" and "household religion" were asked about separately (see Figure 3). According to this survey, the total for "household religion" was more than 84.5 per cent. Within that total, Buddhism exceeded other religions by far, at 79.4 per cent. However, when it came to "individual religion", the proportion of those saying they did not have faith increased greatly, and even Buddhism accounted for only 30 per cent of responses.

Even though the religion people believed in was Buddhism as household religion, it cannot necessarily be thought of as simply a matter of form with no content. This is because Japanese people had occasion to think about things like death, the afterlife and reincarnation, through funerals and memorial masses, or through praying in front of the Buddhist altar in their home, and accepted a popular Buddhist faith and a familiarity with the Buddhist world, whether or not this was orthodox Buddhism, through repeatedly meeting Buddhist priests.

Table 3. Is there a religion you believe in?

| | 2000 | 2001 | 2002 |
|---|---|---|---|
| Yes | 9.5 | 10.0 | 9.7 |
| I don't have a particular faith, but I do have a household religion | 25.0 | 24.9 | 19.5 |
| No | 64.6 | 63.4 | 70.0 |
| No response | 0.9 | 1.8 | 0.9 |

Note: Figures in per cent.
Source: *Japanese General Social Surveys* 2006.

As we saw in Figure 1, over 50 per cent of the people surveyed in 1940 answered that they had faith, and the proportion has fallen since then. One major reason for this is the decline of household religion. Buddhism as household religion had gradually come not to be considered as meaning that one had faith. The background to this is the breakdown of the Japanese family household system and changes in family structure after the war.

The Japanese General Social Surveys conducted since 2000 have included a question that explicitly refers to "household religion" in relation to whether or not people had faith (JGSS 2006).[1] The question and results are shown in Table 3. According to these results, no more than a tenth of respondents said they had faith, but far more people answered, "I don't particularly have faith, but I do have a household religion". Adding together the figures for these two answers gives a total of around 30 per cent, which corresponds to the proportion of people in other surveys who say they have faith. Moreover, the figure of 10 per cent saying that they have faith is almost the same as the percentage of those who declare that they actively belong to a religious organization.

If we consider that the rate/proportion answering "household religion" in the 1940s and 50s was relatively high, it is undeniable that the proportion of respondents to the JGSS saying they have a household

[1] The Japanese General Social Surveys (JGSS) Project is a Japanese version of the original General Social Survey (GSS) project carried out in the USA. Surveys have been conducted annually since 1999 by a project team from the Institute of Regional Studies at the Osaka University of Commerce and the Institute of Social Science at the University of Tokyo, and the data is supplied to data archives. Five reports have been published up to 2006, making public many results such as basic summary tables. Summaries and partial results are published on the website http://jgss.daishodai.ac.jp/japanese/frame/japanesetop.html

religion has fallen remarkably. It is the same in the case of Buddhism. In the case of Buddhist temples, "parishioners" again means believers attached to a temple, and refers to people who take responsibility for the maintenance of the temple, but the actual relationship between people and temples is not something that is really at the heart of conscious faith.

## 5. Faith no Longer Increases with Age

It is clear that there are great disparities in Japanese people's religiosity according to age. Figure 4 shows the results by age group of various public opinion surveys by the *Yomiuri Shimbun* about whether or not people have faith.

Looking at the form of the graph, it is clear that, although the trend changes depending on the year that the survey was carried out, overall the proportion of Japanese people saying that they have faith increases gradually with age. The proportion of those in their twenties who have faith is low, at between 10 and 20 per cent; after that, the proportion goes up with age.

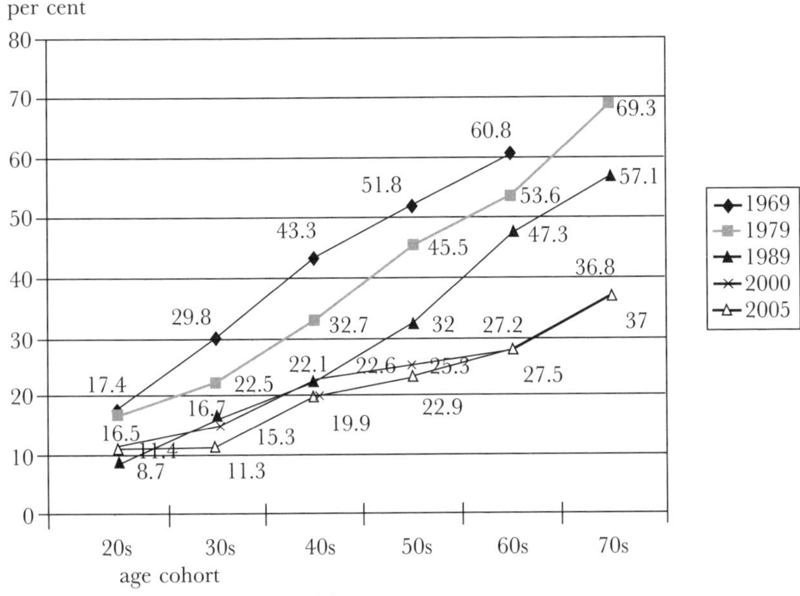


Source: Yomiuri Shimbunsha (2005).

Figure 4. Faith and age.

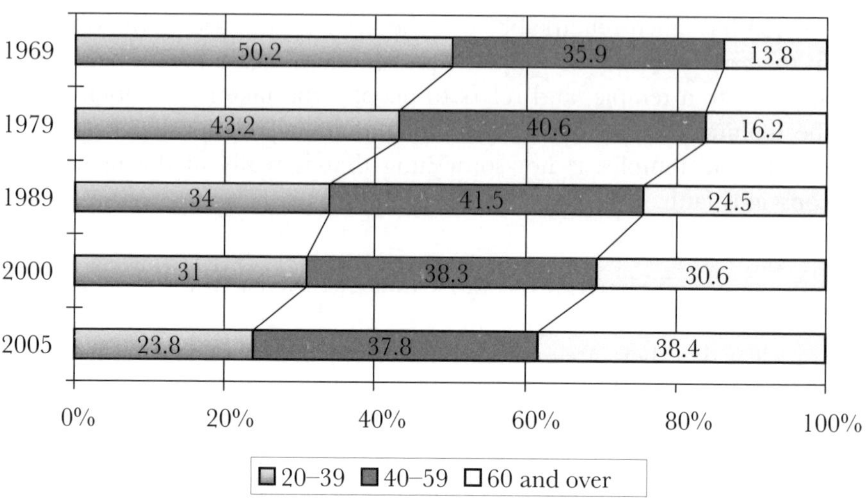


Source: Yomiuri Shimbunsha (2005).

Figure 5. Age groups of respondents.

As we saw in Figure 1 above, it is clear that Japanese people's faith has declined in the 60 years since the war. On the other hand, it is well known that Japan is a rapidly ageing society. Aren't these therefore contradictory facts? Today too, as people grow older, the proportion of those with faith increases, and if we take into account the fact that elderly people are increasing as a proportion of the respondents (see Figure 5), the overall proportion that does have faith should, if anything, increase. So why does it continue to fall in spite of that?

Data from each year the survey was carried out are shown in Figure 4. If these data are compared, the starting point is almost the same, but it is clear that the slope of the broken line has become less steep in the more recent surveys. In particular, there seems to be a large gap between the periods up until 1989 and since 2000. There is hardly any difference between the data from 2000 and 2005.

Let's compare the oldest data, from 1969, and the most recent, from 2005. The gap between the two years gradually widens, from only 6 percentage points for people in their twenties to 19 percentage points for people in their thirties, 23 points for those in their forties, 29 points for those in their fifties, and 33 percentage points for those in their sixties. The decline in faith amongst the elderly is the main factor pushing down faith in the total population.

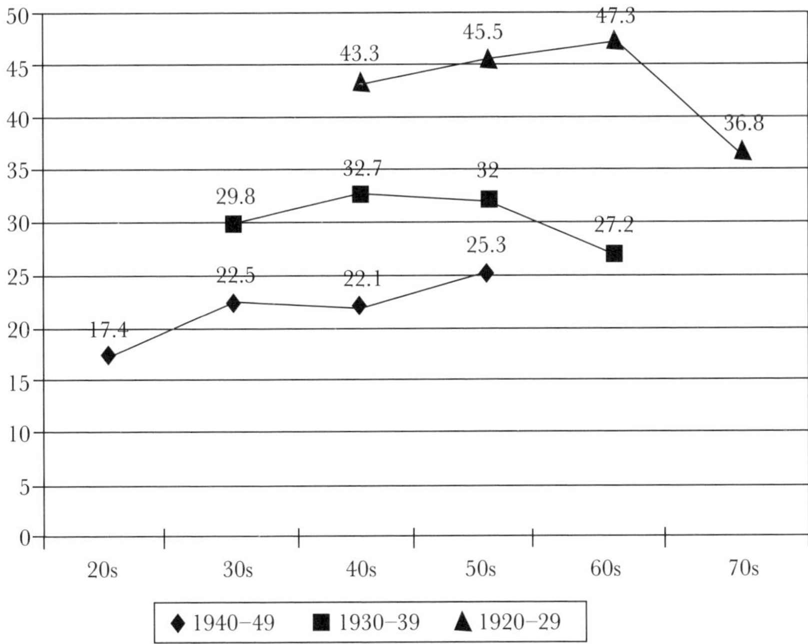


Source: Yomiuri Shimbunsha.

Figure 6. Whether or not one has faith, categorised by age.

In the 2000 and 2005 surveys, the proportion of people in their sixties and seventies who have faith is just under 40 per cent. This is a situation where we can no longer say that people are elderly so they must be interested in religion. This trend is not only apparent in the *Yomiuri Shimbun* surveys, but is the same in other data, such as the surveys carried out by the Kokugakuin University Twenty-First Century Centre of Excellence (COE) Programme and the NHK Culture Research Institute International Social Survey Programme (ISSP) surveys.

The decline in faith amongst the elderly is certainly very significant. Taking care of worship at the Buddhist and Shinto altars in the home used to be thought of as the task of the elderly, and they were the ones who had close links with shrines and temples. The decline in religious piety among the elderly has an impact on traditional religion above all.

## 6. Religiosity of the Baby-Boomers

Figure 6 shows how the respondents of certain generations have changed the proportion of those answering they had faith. Using only those surveys carried out over long periods that also published data by age group means that only data from the *Yomiuri Shimbun* surveys could be used.

In Figure 6, the highest figure is the proportion of respondents born 1920–29. The lowest is the age group born 1940–49, which includes the baby boomers born 1947–49.

It seems that the gap in the graph between the 1940–49 generation and the 1930–39 one is wider than that between the 1920–29 and 1930–39 generations. Although it is a stereotypical assumption, the cause of this gap must be the impact of post-war social changes in the areas of education, the economy, politics, and social life in general.

Moreover, if we look at the form of the graph, it is very interesting to note that the proportion of people with faith falls with age. In the age group born 1920–29, the percentage falls from 47.3 per cent for those in their sixties to 36.8 per cent for those in their seventies, and in the age group born 1930–39, it falls from 32.0 per cent for those in their sixties to 27.2 per cent for those in their seventies.

The baby boomers who were born and received their education after the war are recognized as having one particular characteristic as a group. Rebelling strongly against the values and structures of the pre-war generation, they were involved in mass conflicts such as the anti-US-Japan Security Treaty demonstrations, the student protests, and the anti-Vietnam war movement. To put it another way, they invented ways of life that had not existed before.

In terms of religious faith, the proportion who had faith in their twenties was low compared to other generations, but is slowly increasing. Whether it will decline in the future, following that of previous generations, or whether, on the other hand, after this generation who have lived their lives in a competitive society have stood back from being at the forefront of society, their interest in religious matters will grow, or whether they will return to more traditional religion, or whether this will be a religiosity with a strongly individualized trend is an extremely interesting question.

## 7. How are Religions and Religious Groups Perceived and Evaluated?

Even if people do not belong to religious groups and do not say that they have faith, recognition of religion as a social issue develops, and it is also possible to make value judgements. The question relevant to value judgements that is most widely asked is "Do you think religion is important?", the question which was introduced at the beginning.

The image that Japanese people have of religion today is generally "spiritual", "a matter of the heart", but the image varies greatly depending on the religious system, that is, Shinto, Buddhism, Christianity and the new religious groups. In contrast to Shinto and Buddhism, where responses are concentrated on "spirit, spirituality", "traditional events and ceremonial occasions", and "traditional culture", in Christianity, the description "mysterious" follows "spirit, spirituality" and "traditional events and ceremonial occasions".

The proportion of those choosing "traditional events and ceremonial occasions", and "traditional culture" was higher for Buddhism than for Shinto. On the other hand, the rates choosing "benefits" and "mysterious" was higher for Shinto. From the point of view of religious tradition, Shinto is the indigenous folk religion and Buddhism is an imported one. Nevertheless, it is likely that associating "traditional events and ceremonial occasions", and "traditional culture" with Buddhism is because Japanese people today have more occasions to have dealings with temples rather than with shrines. Likewise, there is a reason that Christianity is seen as "mysterious". Despite over a century of missionary work, Japanese people have little daily contact with Christianity, and, the answer "nothing in particular/unclear" was overwhelmingly dominant in the survey.

As far as we can see from looking at Japanese people's opinions via public opinion surveys, one can say that their value judgements regarding religious groups have gradually worsened or become more critical since the war.

If we compare the surveys relating to value judgements regarding religious groups carried out by the *Yomiuri Shimbun* in 1952, 1994 and 1999, Japanese people's attitudes towards religious groups become clear. Questionnaire statements with low levels of agreement in 1952 have uniformly gained high response rates in the surveys carried out in the Heisei period (1989 onwards). For example, the highest response rate in the 1952 survey was 16.9 per cent for "priests are getting too much

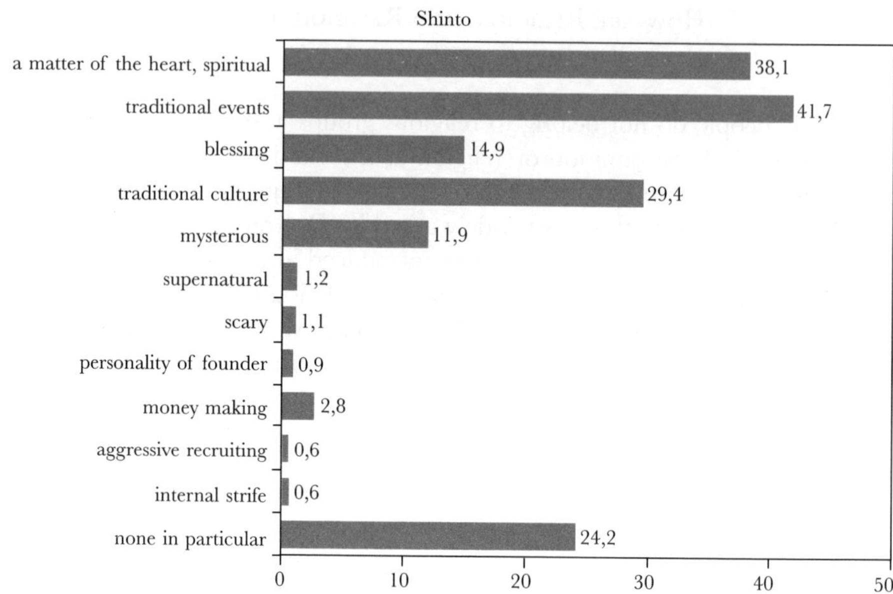


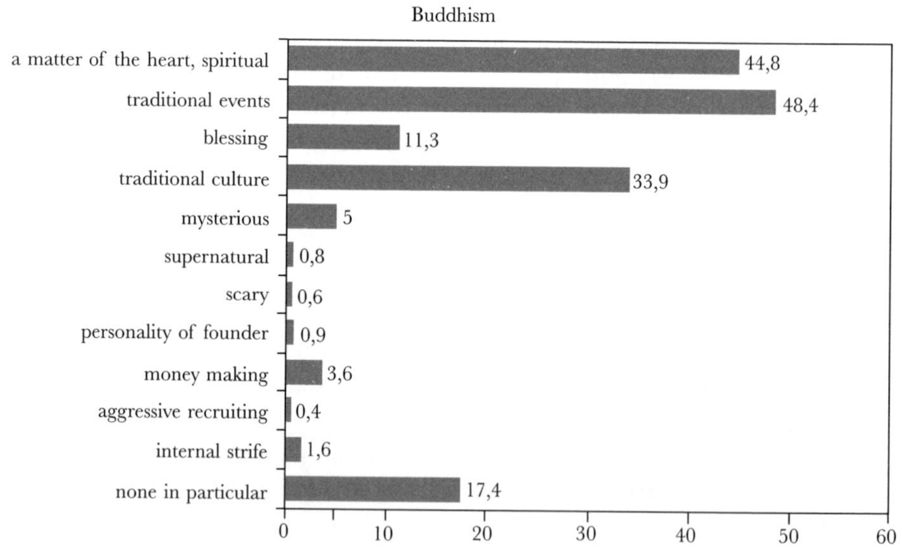


Source: ISSP "Religious attitudes" survey, 1998.

Figure 7. The image of religion categorised by religious organizations.

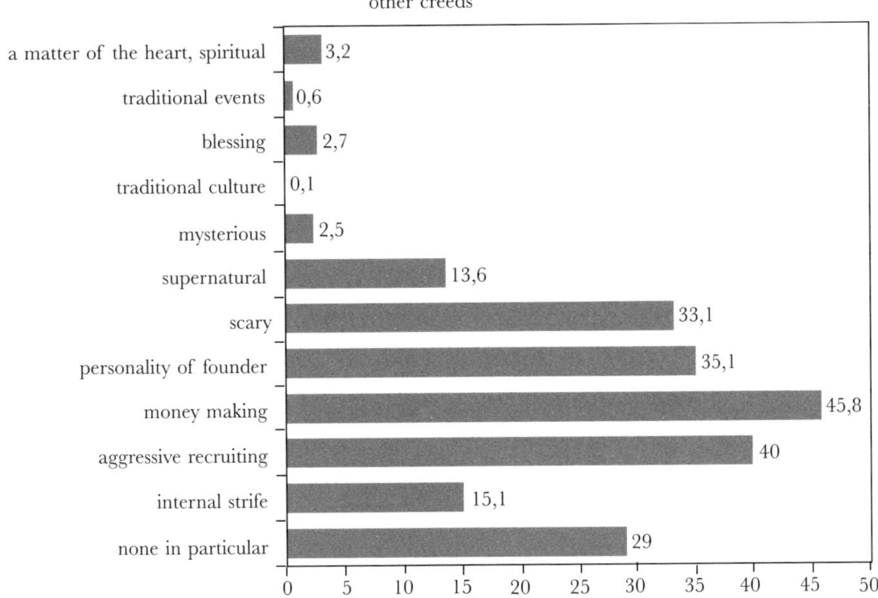
other creeds
a matter of the heart, spiritual
3,2
traditional events
0,6
blessing
2,7
traditional culture
0,1
mysterious
2,5
supernatural
13,6
scary
33,1
personality of founder
35,1
money making
45,8
aggressive recruiting
40
internal strife
15,1
none in particular
29
0 5 10 15 20 25 30 35 40 45 50

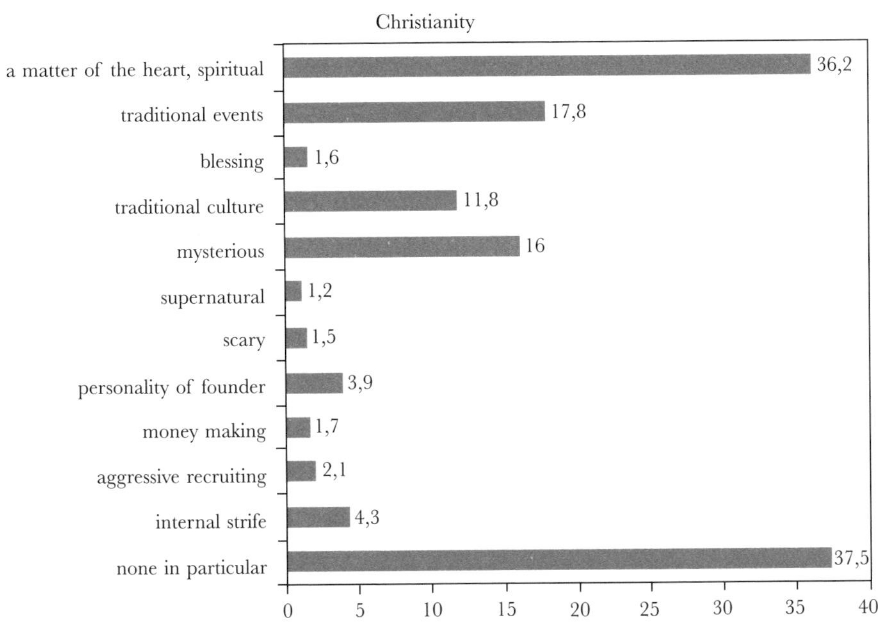
Christianity
a matter of the heart, spiritual
36,2
traditional events
17,8
blessing
1,6
traditional culture
11,8
mysterious
16
supernatural
1,2
scary
1,5
personality of founder
3,9
money making
1,7
aggressive recruiting
2,1
internal strife
4,3
none in particular
37,5
0 5 10 15 20 25 30 35 40

money (ask for too high fees)", but the response rate leapt to 47.4 per cent in 1994 agreeing that "they are keen on making money", and to 43.8 per cent in 1999 agreeing that "they collect large amounts of fees and alms". Although only four statements, in addition to the one mentioned above, were chosen by over 10 per cent of respondents in 1952: "they should teach doctrine aimed at people today" (15.6 per cent), "they should relate to life in society" (15.1 per cent), and "priests should follow their own teachings" (11.2 per cent), in the subsequent surveys, the agreement rate for all the statements exceeded 10 per cent.

Japanese people's opinions of religious groups have become remarkably low. This becomes very clear if we look at international comparisons. According to the ISSP survey[2] carried out in 1998, Japan occupies the lowest position of 35 countries (see Figure 8) (NHK Broadcasting Culture Research Institute 1999). Adding together those who said they had "complete confidence", "a great deal of confidence" and "some confidence" in religious institutions gave a total of only 27 per cent.

Now I will show other survey results comparing other national institutions from the same survey. The institution in which people had the most confidence was "courts and the legal system", with over 70 per cent saying they trusted them. The next was "schools and the educational system", at 55 per cent, and the lowest was "religion", which did not even reach 10 per cent.

## 8. Post-War Changes in Japanese People's Religious Attitudes and Religious Behaviour

We have looked at various attitudes and behaviours of Japanese people with regard to religion over the 60 years since the war, but I will now summarize the major trends in three points. The first is the decline of traditional religion. The rapid population shift to the cities that accompanied economic development after the war destroyed the basis of traditional religion. The real rate of religious observance and participation in events relating to traditional religion has fallen, and the

[2] The International Social Survey Programme (ISSP) is an ongoing programme of cross-national collaboration on social science surveys, led by the Centre for Survey Research and Methodology in Mannheim and the National Opinion Research Center at the University of Chicago. The NHK Broadcasting Culture Research Institute has been a member since 1992. Some of the surveys appear in a 1999 report by Noriko Onodera.

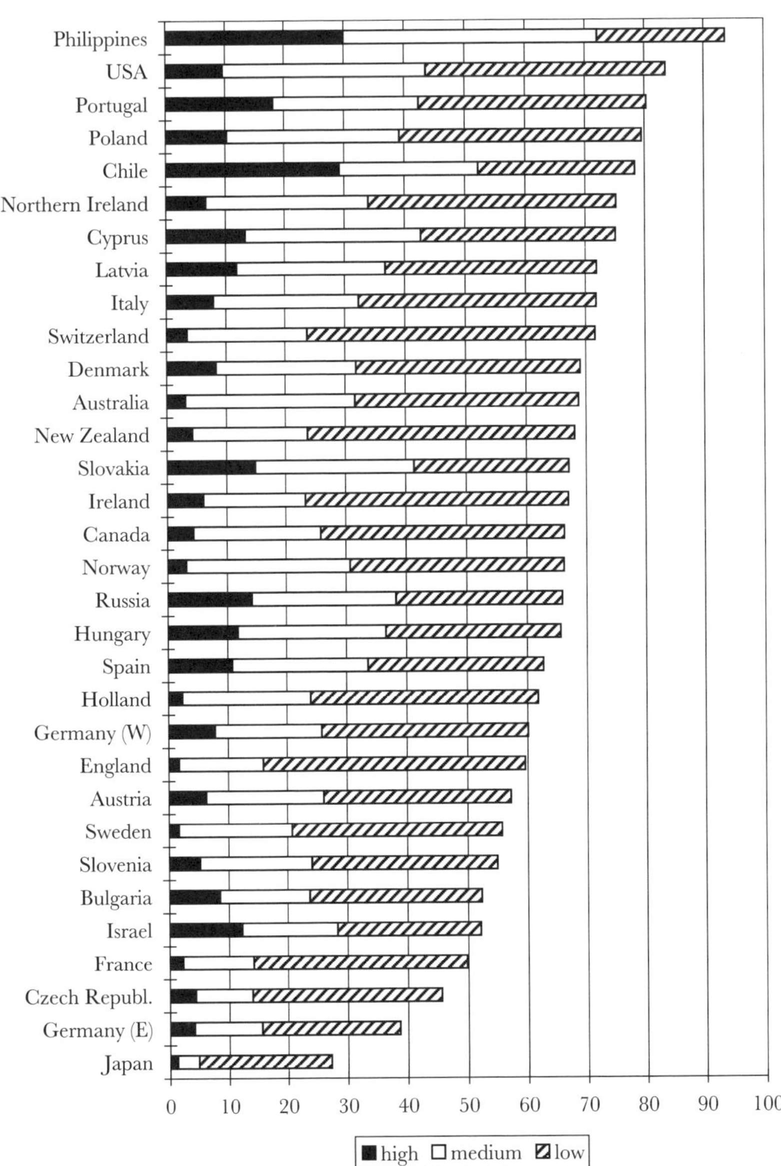


Source: ISSP "Religious attitudes" survey, 1998.

Figure 8. Confidence in religious organizations—International comparison.

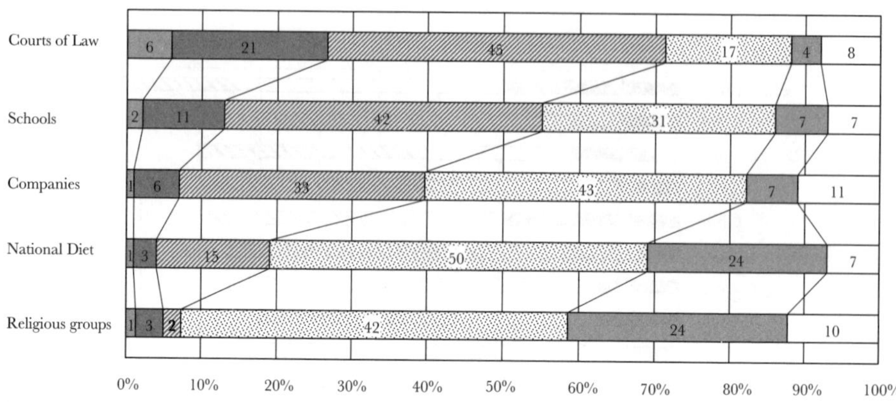


Source: ISSP "Religious attitudes" survey, 1998.

Figure 9. Degree of confidence in organizations and institutions.

rate of possession of household Shinto altars and household Buddhist altars has also declined. Veneration of ancestors and belief in tutelary deities, which used to exist strongly among Japanese people, has weakened. Only funeral services have narrowly survived, but even here the traditional Buddhist funeral is starting to change in the midst of postwar changes in family structure, in other words, the shift to the nuclear family and increase in the number of single-person households. The new religions expanded their influence in the high economic growth era of the 1960s in the search for new images of the family, but now they are losing support.

The second trend is the individualization of religion. Within the narrow personal relations of oneself and the family, there is a trend to ask for worldly benefits according to need, such as when taking examinations or in unlucky years, and to try to acquire religious knowledge and information. Or, one could say that there is a shift towards religious awareness and religious activities based on the individual, which are different from traditional forms. A tendency to seek individual spiritual comfort in things like healing and spirituality is widely seen. On the other hand, one can say that this also means the spread of a lack of interest in religion. The attitude that people only want to get involved in religion to the extent that it is related to themselves is one that means they have no interest in religion unless they have a need to do so.

The third trend is the increase in critical attitudes towards religious groups. Joining religious groups and organizations with memberships has not expanded. Christianity and the new religions have not done well in this respect. In 1995, when the sarin gas incident carried out by Aum Shinrikyō happened, the media and some researchers reported that many young people had joined cults and that such cults were increasing, but that is not the real situation. The majority of Japanese people clearly reject cults, even though they have no actual dealings with them.

Since the 1980s, a revival in religion on a worldwide scale has been in evidence. The revival of fundamentalism, the rise of religiosity linked to racism and nationalism, or new religions and religious movements that emphasize mystical spirituality can be cited. Nevertheless, it seems that in Japan today, people are almost indifferent to such manifestations of religious revival. The Yasukuni Shrine issue between Japan and China and Korea, which has become a long-standing problem, has been reacted to as a political issue rather than a religious one.

The detachment from traditional religion in daily life continues. Religiosity based on the individual lacks a group perspective. These religions are increasingly alienated from religious issues on both religious and political levels.

## References


Asahi Shimbun (8 January 1985): *Yon han seiki no nihonjin* [Japanese people over 25 years].

—— (2003): Seron chōsa shōhō. Dai 25 teiki ishiki chōsa [Public opinion survey full report no. 25 regular attitudes survey]. In *Asahi Kenkyū Ripōto* [Asahi Research Report] No. 160. Tokyo: Asahi Shimbun.

Ishii, Kenji (1997): *Dētabukku Gendai Nihonjin no Shūkyō* [Databook on Japanese people's religion today]. Tokyo: Shinyōsha.

JGSS (Japanese General Social Surveys) Project (2006): *Japanese General Social Surveys.* http://jgss.daishodai.ac.jp/japanese/frame/japanesetop.html (accessed 12 September 2006).

Kirisutokyō Nenkan Henshūbu [Editorial Committee of the Christian Yearbook] (2005): *Kirisutokyō Nenkan 2006 nenpan* [Yearbook of Christianity 2006 edition]. Tokyo: Kirisuto Shimbunsha.

Kokugakuin University Twenty-First Century Centre of Excellence Program (2006): *Research Report: Survey of Japanese Religiosity and Beliefs about Kami (2003), Survey of Japanese Participation in, Recognition of, and Value Judgments Regarding Japanese Religious Organizations (2004).* Tokyo: Kokugakuin University.

Meishin Chōsa Kyōgikai (1952): *Zokushin to Meishin* [Folk beliefs and superstitions]. Tokyo: Gihōdo.

Naikakufu Seisaku Tōkatsukan [Cabinet Office Policy Coordination Office] (2004): *Sekai no Shōnen to no Hikaku kara mita Nihon no Shōnen. Dai 7 kai Sekai Shōnen Ishiki Chōsa Hōkoku* [Japanese Youth In Comparison with Youth in the World. A Summary Report of The Seventh World Youth Survey]. Tokyo: Naikakufu.

Onodera, Noriko (1999): Seron chōsa ripōto: Nihonjin no shōkyō ishiki [Public opinion survey report: Japanese religious attitudes]. In *Hōsō Kenkyū to Chōsa* [NHK Monthly Report on Broadcast Research]. 49,5. Tokyo: Nihon Hōsō Shuppan Kyōkai.
Tōkei Sūri Kenkyūjo Kokumin Chōsa Iinkai [Institute of Statistical Mathematics National Survey Committee] (2000): *Tōkeiteki Nihonjin Kenkyū no Hanseiki* [Fifty years of statistical research on the Japanese people]. Tokyo: Tōkei Sūri Kenkyūjo.
Yomiuri Shimbunsha Yoron Chōsabu (2005): *Nihon no Yoron* [Japanese public opinion]. Tokyo: Hirofumidōkan.

CHAPTER TWENTY-TWO

# COMING OF AGE: THE COURTS AND EQUALITY RIGHTS IN JAPAN'S AGEING SOCIETY

Craig Martin

Japan has the most rapidly ageing society in the world. There are a range of important ramifications flowing from the demographic changes giving rise to that phenomenon. The other articles in this handbook examine many of the economic, financial, political, sociological, and health-care issues related to the demographic changes. In this article we turn to the legal issues, and examine an area of the law that is likely to become more significant in Japan's ageing society. Specifically, this article suggests that there is likely to be more discrimination and more litigation over discrimination as a result of the response to the demographic changes, and argues that the courts must change the manner in which they analyse such claims, if they are to make a meaningful and positive contribution to how Japan responds as a democratic society to the challenges of ageing.[1]

As a result of the ageing of society and Japan's response to those demographic changes, women, the elderly and foreigners will all begin to play more prominent roles in Japanese society. There will be increased reliance on all three groups to supplement the diminishing labour pool. The increased reliance on foreigners in employment will lead to increased numbers of foreigners resident in Japan. The elderly, apart from being looked to as a source of labour, will make greater claims

[1] One might ask "Why equality rights?" when there are so many other legal issues also implicated. Many of the policy decisions that the government will have to make in struggling with the various socio-economic issues will be implemented through the passage of new legislation, and indeed there has already been the enactment of new and amended laws to address issues of the ageing society, as noted below. Thus the legal framework of the country will be significantly affected by the demographic changes. But in looking at the legal issues raised by the ageing of society, it is perhaps more interesting to inquire into how the legal system itself will be affected, and particularly how the judiciary will respond. In other words, how fundamental principles of law may both impact the social tensions resulting from the demographic changes, and how the principles themselves may be affected by the process.

on resources, particularly in the form of social welfare and health care, as they constitute an ever larger proportion of the overall population. All three groups have been subjected to unequal treatment within Japanese society in the past, and the absence of statutory protections, together with deep-rooted attitudes and practices, make it likely that members of all three groups will continue to face discrimination. In the case of women, such discrimination will be primarily in the employment context, but with foreigners and the elderly it will be present in many areas, in both public and private relations. As foreigners and the elderly increase in size as a proportion of the population, and as all three groups play larger roles in society, the number of incidents of such discrimination will increase. There is also likely to be increased recourse to the courts to seek redress for such discrimination, and thus there is likely to be increasing numbers of claims of discrimination as one result of the ageing of society.

Since the adoption of the new Constitution in 1947, the courts have not developed a robust analytical model for adjudicating claims of discrimination. With the narrow exception of women's equality rights in the context of job security, the courts have not been assertive in enforcing the equality rights of minorities and the disadvantaged in society ("equality rights" meaning the right to be treated equally under the law, and not be discriminated against; what in American constitutional law is commonly referred to as equal protection). There are many factors that can be looked to in trying to explain why the Japanese courts have been so reluctant to enforce the constitutional right not to be discriminated against, ranging from the sociological and cultural to the political and institutional. One factor, however, and one that is purely legal and that perhaps has not been sufficiently explored, is the nature of the analytical framework that the courts employ in adjudicating discrimination cases.

The Supreme Court has failed to develop a legal test for the determination of discrimination cases that incorporates the fundamental ideas underlying the right to be treated equally, which would guide the reasoning of judges in a manner that would give full effect to the constitutional right. Rather, the Supreme Court has developed a legal test for analysing discrimination that focuses on the question of whether, in the circumstances of the case, the discrimination in question was "reasonable", which is to be determined by reference only to criteria internal to the policy or law in question. This so-called "reasonable discrimination" test not only lends itself to result-oriented decision making, but also creates confusion over what constitutes the essence of discrimination and the right to equality, and provides the lower courts with no assistance in terms of how to analyse issues of discrimination. Its application typically leads to a finding that the discrimination in question is "reasonable".

With increased claims of discrimination likely in the ageing society, however, this analytical approach to the right to be treated equally may come under increasing pressure. Recent cases before the Supreme Court suggest that the courts will continue to justify discrimination against minorities and the marginalized as being "reasonable". Doing so will lead to further unjust results and increasingly exacerbate the tensions caused by the ageing of society, and will be at odds with many of the policy objectives of the government in its attempts to meet the challenges of the demographic changes. Ultimately, it could undermine the credibility and legitimacy of the courts and the Constitution itself.

This article sets out to analyse the theoretical weaknesses of the "reasonable discrimination" test, and examines how it has been applied recently to deny the equality rights of minorities. It will explain why the model is inadequate to properly protect the fundamental right to equality under the law, and suggests that the weakness of the test is one reason the courts fail to properly enforce equality rights. From a normative perspective, it will argue that the judiciary ought to play a positive role in easing the tensions created by the ageing of Japanese society, by developing a new legal test for analysing discrimination that is more consistent with the fundamental idea of equality and the values of the Japanese Constitution.

## The Premise: Increased Claims of Discrimination

It is necessary to examine briefly the premise that the confluence of policy decisions, social pressures and market forces will lead to increased discrimination and the probability of increased equality rights litigation. This could itself be the subject of a long study, and we can only provide a brief overview of the basis for that inference here.

The most direct evidence relates to the area of employment, and the government's response to the declining labour force. The government has increasingly made it clear that it views increased employment of women, the elderly, and foreigners, in that order of preference, as being necessary to supplement the labour force, which is projected to diminish significantly over the fifty years commencing in 2007. There have been many and varied statements to this effect reflected in various white papers, cabinet reports, and other government policy planning documents.[2] The government has begun giving effect to these views in the form of new and revised laws to create an incentives structure that will encourage increased numbers of all three groups in the workforce. Thus the revised *Equal Employment Opportunity Law* (the "EEOL"),[3] a new *Basic Law for a Gender-equal Society*,[4] and the *Child Care and Family Care Leave Law*[5] are all aimed at encouraging increased employment of women. Similarly the *Basic Law on Measures for the Ageing Society*[6] was enacted in 1995, and the *Law Concerning the Stabilization of Employment of Older Persons*[7] (the "SEOP"), has been recently revised to encourage an increase in the employment of people post-retirement, and to encourage companies to either raise or abolish the age of mandatory retirement. Even the *Immigration Control and Refugee Recognition Law*[8] has been revised and new policies developed to give effect to the stated policy of more openly accepting highly-skilled foreign workers,[9] and to employ non-skilled workers through such devices as the so-called "trainee system".[10]

---

[2] Ministry of Justice, *Basic Plan for Immigration Control*, 3rd Edition, 2006, available on-line at http://www.moj.go.jp/ENGLISH/information/bpic3rd.html (last viewed 26 December 2006); Gender Equality Bureau Cabinet Office, *Steps Towards Gender Equality in Japan* (Government White Paper on Gender Equality, 2006); Report of the Prime Minister's Commission on Japan's Goals in the 21st Century, January 2000; Ministry of Health Labour and Welfare, *White Paper on the Labour Economy 2005*, summary available online at www.mhlw.go.jp/english/wp/l-economy/2005/index.html, full report at http://www.mhlw.go.jp/wp/hakusyo/roudou/05/index.html, (last viewed 6 January 2007).

[3] *Law on Securing etc. of Equal Opportunity and Treatment Between Men and Women in Employment* (Law No. 113 of 1972, as amended) [the "Equal Employment Opportunity Law", or "EEOL"). The EEOL was enacted in 1985 as an amendment to the 1972 *Working Women's Law*, so one should not be misled by the date. It was substantially amended again in 1997, and has been the subject of several less substantial amendments since then.

[4] *Basic Law for a Gender-equal Society* (Law No. 78 of 1999).

[5] *Law Concerning the Welfare of Workers Who Take Care of Children or Other Family Members Including Child-Care and Family-Care Leave* (Law No. 76 of 1991).

[6] *Basic Law on Measures for the Ageing Society* (Law No. 129 of 1995).

[7] *Law Concerning the Stabilization of Employment of Older Persons* (Law No. 68 of 1971).

[8] *Immigration Control and Refugee Recognition Law* (Law No. 135 of 1999).

[9] *Basic Plan for Immigration Control, supra*, note 2, at 1.

[10] See Sumi Shin, "Global Migration: The Impact of 'Newcomers' on Japanese Immigration and Labour Systems" (2001) 19 *Berkeley Journal of International Law* 265, at 315–320, on how the trainee and on-the-job training system has been developed and expanded to increase access to foreign unskilled labour.

There is considerable evidence that market forces will similarly lead to increased employment of women, the elderly, and foreigners. Indeed, the experience of the Japanese economy during the so-called bubble period of the 1980s, when the supply of labour was outstripped by demand, is instructive. That period was marked by increased employment of both women and foreigners. Following declines during the post-bubble recession, there have again been increases in the numbers of women in the workforce, as well as a continuing increase in immigration and employment of foreigners in recent years.[11]

Nonetheless, while both market forces and government policy suggest that there will be increased participation of these groups in the workforce as a result of the demographic changes, there is no reason to expect that discrimination against such groups will diminish. A great deal has been written on such discrimination in the past, and it need not be repeated here.[12] But in looking forward, it is significant that the government itself does not present a uniform or entirely consistent picture in its policy development. It continues to be ambivalent on

---

[11] The Japan Institute for Labour Policy and Training, "Labour Situation in Japan and Analysis: Detailed Exposition 2005/2006" 25 July 2005, available online at http://www.jil.go.jp/english/laborinfo/library/index.htm (last viewed 15 December 2006); *Basic Plan for Immigration Control, supra* note 2; *Steps Towards Gender Equality in Japan, supra* note 2; Yasuo Kuwahara, "Migrant Workers in the Post-War History of Japan" (2005) *Japan Labour Review*, Vol. 2 No. 4, at 29 *et seq.* Ogawa Makoto "Current Issues Concerning Foreign Workers in Japan" (2005) *Japan Labour Review* Vol. 2 No. 4 at 6 *et seq.* Junko Kumamoto-Healey, "Women in the Japanese Labour Market, 1947–2003" (2005) *International Labour Review* Vol. 144 No.4 at 451 *et seq.* Robbi Louise Miller "Women's Job Hunting in the 'Ice Age': Frozen Opportunities in Japan" (1998) 13 *Wisconsin Women's Law Journal* 223. Tadashi Hanami, "Equal Employment Revisited" *Japan Labour Bulletin*, Vol. 39 No. 1. January 1, 2000. (Note that in conformity with the style of this book, Japanese names in the footnotes are provided with last name last)

[12] Aside from the abundance of secondary source material available on the subject of discrimination in Japan, an outline of the issues can be found in the observations and country reports of the various committees related to the major international human rights conventions. See for example "Concluding Observations of the Committee on the Elimination of Racial Discrimination: Japan", April 27, 2001, UN Doc. CERD/C/304/Add.114 [hereinafter "CERD Report"]; "Report of the Special Rapporteur on Contemporary Forms of Racism, Racial Discrimination, Xenophobia and Related Intolerance, Doudou Diene: Mission to Japan", 24 January 2006, UN Doc E/CN.4/2006/16/Add.2 [hereafter CERD Rapporteur Report]; "Concluding Observations of the Human Rights Committee: Japan", 1998, UN Doc. CCPR/C/79/Add.102 [hereafter HRC Report]; "Concluding Observations of the Committee on Economic, Social and Cultural Rights: Japan." 24 September 2001, UN Doc. E/C.12/1/Add.67; and "Consideration of Reports Submitted by States Parties Under article 18 of the Convention on the Elimination of All Forms of Discrimination Against Women—Fifth Periodic Report of States Parties: Japan", 13 September 2002, UN Doc. CEDAW/C/JPN/5 [hereafter "CEDAW Report"].

immigration, notwithstanding the purportedly more open approach noted above. Many new policies, ostensibly motivated by security concerns, are inconsistent with the more "open" approach, and are likely to be a source of discrimination claims.[13] The government also shows no signs of changing some of its older policies towards foreigners that have caused friction in the past.[14] Similarly, while the government purports to make gender equality a significant priority, other policies work directly against the incentive structure being developed for that purpose, and the government has failed to take effective steps to address such issues as the increasing employment of women in part-time, dispatched, and non-management track employment.[15]

The private sector is equally unlikely, on its own, to alter the well-documented discriminatory practices in the area of employment. Women continue to be predominantly employed as part-time or dispatched employees, and even when full-time, continue to be employed primarily in the so-called "general" non-managerial track.[16] The labour-cost savings to companies from such practices, combined with

[13] For example, the government announced at the end of 2006 that it was considering increased registration requirements and tracking systems for foreigners so that the government can maintain up-to-date information on the whereabouts, employment status, and other aspects of a person's activities in Japan. "Panel Eyes Restrictions, Services for Foreigners", *Japan Times*, 27 December 2006.

[14] Examples would include the fingerprinting of foreign residents (which was discontinued in the 1990s but then re-introduced in 2007), the criminalization of the failure to carry foreign registration identity cards, refusal to extend social and health-care benefits to certain classes of foreign residents, and so forth. Again, there is abundant secondary source literature on the issue, but one can find the main issues documented in the HRC Report, CERD Rapporteur Report and the CERD Report, *supra* note 12.

[15] For example, the tax laws continue to create incentives for women to remain either unemployed or below a specified income level once married: Hiroaki Watanabe "Public Policy and Gender Discrimination in the Japanese Labor Market", submitted for the Hawaii International Conference on Social Sciences in 2003, unpublished, on file with the author. *Steps Towards Gender Equality in Japan, supra* note 2, at 10–11.

[16] The term "dispatched labour" refers to the practice of personnel agencies supplying companies with short-term employees, where the employment contract is between the individual and the personnel agency rather than with the company for which work is being done. The practice is governed by the *Worker Dispatch Law* of 1985, which was passed at the same time as the EEOL, and could be seen as providing corporations with a means of circumventing the strictures of the EEOL; see Daniel H. Foote, "Judicial Creation of Norms in Japanese Labor Law: Activism in the Service of—Stability?" (1996) 43 *U.C.L.A. Law Review* 635 at 674–675. See also, for discussion of legal issues with respect to part-time and temporary labourers in general, Katsutoshi Kezuka, "Legal Problems Concerning Part-Time Work in Japan" *Japan Labour Bulletin*, Vol. 39 No. 9, 1 September 2000.

deep-rooted attitudes towards gender roles, are such that without further regulation by the legislature or the courts, such practices are unlikely to change. In the case of foreigners, the increasing numbers of immigrants are already provoking exaggerated media accounts of foreigners engaging in crime and otherwise violating the norms of society, which can only encourage the type of prejudices that cause discrimination.[17] Similarly, as the percentage of society that is over age 65 rapidly increases, discrimination against the elderly can also be expected to increase. As discussed in more detail below, the increased health-care costs of the increasing numbers of elderly people in society is already giving rise to discrimination in the provision of health-care services to the elderly.

Elder abuse is already an area of increasing attention as a distinct legal issue in other jurisdictions, but has only recently been raised as an issue in Japan. The first study of the issue by the government, released in April 2004, found that authorities at all levels of government were doing little to address the problem,[18] and a new law for the prevention of elder abuse came into effect in 2006.[19] The new law primarily sets out procedures for local government authorities to follow in responding to reports of abuse, and it does not provide any sanctions for abuse itself. It remains to be seen how it will operate and how helpful it will be, but to the extent that the Japanese government may be said to have failed to provide adequate legislative protections against such abuse in the future, this too may raise equality rights issues.[20]

---

[17] For a discussion of media treatment of foreigner-related crime, see Kakumi Kobayashi, "Ishihara crime fight serving Big Brother, stoking xenophobia?", *Japan Times*, 28 August 2006.

[18] Survey released by the Ministry of Health, Labour and Welfare. See Ritsuko Inokuma, "Abuse of Elderly a Growing Problem in Japan", *Yomiuri Shinbum*, 8 May 2004, available online at www.medicalnewstoday.com/medicalnews/php?newsid=8076.

[19] *Law Related to the Prevention of Elder Abuse, the Support of Providers of Elder Care, and so forth*, (Law No. 24 of 2005).

[20] For an analysis of elder abuse in England, for example, see Michael D. Freeman, "The Abuse of the Elderly—Legal Responses in England" in John M. Eekelaar and David Pearl eds., *An Aging World: Dilemmas and Challenges for Law and Policy* (Oxford: Clarendon Press, 1989) at 741. The failure of the Japanese government to provide adequate legislative protection to women against domestic violence and sexual harassment is a consistent element of the criticism of the Japanese government on gender equality issues; see, for example, the CEDAW Report and the HCR Report, *supra* note 12.

Finally, there have been changes that will make litigation more likely. There has been a significant increase in the proliferation of advocacy groups and NGOs that are willing to assist minorities and the disadvantaged in prosecuting their claims in the courts. Thus, while in the past the long and expensive process of litigation was not a viable option for most foreigners, particularly unskilled labourers, it is now increasingly accessible.[21] Similarly, it has been argued that women are increasingly left with no option but to pursue litigation in the employment context, as the dispute resolution procedure under the EEOL, the law that was ostensibly enacted to protect women from discrimination in the workplace (as will be discussed in more detail below) has proven to be utterly inadequate as a mechanism for enforcing their rights.[22] The number of labour-related law suits more generally has also been increasing over the last ten years,[23] and there have been more high-profile cases of foreigners seeking legal remedies for discrimination in various spheres of activity.[24]

## Equality Rights in Japan—Overview of Sources

Equality rights in Japan have as their primary source article 14 of the Constitution, specifically article 14(1). It provides that:

> All of the people are equal under the law and there shall be no discrimination in political, economic or social relations because of race, creed, sex, social status or family origin.

The phrase "all of the people" is the accepted translation of *subete kokumin* in the context of article 14, and it has been interpreted to include

[21] Shin, *supra* note 10 at 268 *et seq*.

[22] Japanese Federation of Bar Associations, "Report of JFBA Regarding Second Periodic Report by the Government of Japan under article 16 and 17 of the International Covenant on Economic, Social, and Cultural Rights", 2 March 2001, [hereafter "JFBA Report"] at 23–24. See also Robert Larsen, "*Ryousai Kenbo* Revisited: The Future of Gender Equality in Japan After the 1997 Equal Employment Opportunity Law" (2001) 24 *Hastings International & Comparative Law Review* 189, at 216–219.

[23] See, for example, the "Number of Labour-Related Lawsuits Hits Record High 2,321" *Japan Labour Bulletin*, 1 May 2003.

[24] See, for example, action against an Osaka store owner for refusing to serve a black customer, *Japan Times* 19 October 2006 (the plaintiff was successful in winning damages on appeal, but the Osaka High Court refused to do so on the basis of discrimination. Decision not reported); and an application against the Otaru Municipal government for failure to enjoin a local *onsen* [hot spring] owner from excluding foreign customers, *Japan Times*, 19 March 2004.

foreigners.[25] A great deal has been written on how the terms "social status" and "family origin" are to be interpreted, and what concrete factors may fall within their scope, and also on the issue of whether the list of categories is exhaustive or illustrative.[26] However, for our purposes we may simply note that the Supreme Court has ruled on at least two occasions that the list is illustrative and not exhaustive.[27] It has also held that, while age is not the type of unchanging characteristic normally associated with social status for the purposes of the right, age is considered to fall within its scope.[28] Similarly, foreign nationality has been treated as being a prohibited ground of discrimination falling within the scope of "social status", even in the cases that have upheld the discrimination as having been reasonable.[29] Finally, article 98 of the Constitution provides that the Constitution is the supreme law of the land, and that any law, ordinance or other act of government contrary to the provisions of the Constitution are invalid, while article 81 provides that the Supreme Court is the court of last resort with the power to determine the constitutionality of any law, regulation, or official act of government. Thus, the courts have the authority, and arguably the duty, to enforce constitutional rights.

While the right to equality in article 14 strictly applies only to the relationship between the state and the individual, the Supreme Court has confirmed the practice of lower courts in employing the constitutional values of the equality right in Article 14 to inform and give substance to statutory provisions governing private relations. Thus, the broad and rather ambiguous provisions of the *Civil Code* that prohibit juristic acts that have as their object matters that are contrary to public policy or good morals, and that require the *Code* to be construed from the standpoint of the dignity of the individual and the essential equality

[25] Supreme Court Judgement, Grand Bench, 18 November 1964.

[26] A convenient overview of the leading academic interpretations of the prohibited grounds of discrimination in Japanese scholarship can be found in Hideki Shibutani, "Kenpō 2" [Constitution 2] (2000) 3 No. 234 *Hōgaku kyōshitsu* 113.

[27] Supreme Court Judgement, Grand Bench, April 4, 1973, (the *Patricide* case); Supreme Court Judgement, Grand Bench, 27 May 1964 (*Tateyama Mayor* case).

[28] *Teteyama Mayor* case, *supra* note 27, at para. 3.

[29] Supreme Court Judgement, 18 November 1964. Shigenori Matsui suggests that, at least from a process theory perspective, the support for this position flows more from the international legal obligations that inform the constitutional analysis, in accordance with article 98(2) of the Constitution, than from a proper interpretation of article 14 itself. See Shigenori Matsui, *Nihon Koku Kenpō* [Japanese Constitutional Law], 2nd ed. (Tokyo: Yuhikaku Publishing Co. Ltd., 2002), at 313.

of the sexes, have been interpreted in a manner that imported the equality values of article 14.[30]

There are no other overarching statutory protections against discrimination in private relations. There are provisions in statutes governing specific spheres of activity that provide some protection, but these tend to be narrow, limited, and of debatable effectiveness. For instance, in the area of employment, the *Labour Standards Law* provides that "employers are forbidden to engage in discriminatory treatment with respect to wages, working hours or other working conditions by reason of nationality, creed or social status of any worker."[31] While the clause "other working conditions" is open to interpretation, hiring, recruitment and termination are not covered. Gender is conspicuously absent, which is one reason that the early sex discrimination cases were advanced on the basis of the *Civil Code*.[32]

As referred to earlier, the EEOL was enacted in 1985 as a step towards the gradual strengthening of women's equality rights in the context of employment.[33] It prohibited discrimination in relation to termination and retirement, as well with respect to benefits, but it only imposed a duty on employers to "endeavour" to avoid discrimination in recruitment, hiring, promotion and transfers. No sanctions were provided for violations of the law, and the mediation process that was established could be vetoed by either party.[34] The amendments to the

---

[30] Article 90, and article 1–2, *Civil Code* (Law No. 9 of 1896, as amended). See Supreme Court Judgement, 24 March 1981 (the *Nissan Gender Discrimination Case*). English translation in Lawrence W. Beer and Hiroshi Itoh, *The Constitutional Law of Japan, 1970 through 1990*, (Seattle: University of Washington Press, 1996), at p. 179.

[31] *Labour Standards Law*, (Law No. 49 of 1947, as amended), article 3. There are similar provisions in the *Employment Security Law* (Law. No. 141 of 1947).

[32] Frank K. Upham, *Law and Social Change in Postwar Japan* (Cambridge, Mass.: Harvard University Press, 1987), at 130.

[33] See Takashi Araki, "Equal Employment and Harmonization of Work and Family Life: Japan's Soft Law Approach" (2000) 21 *Comparative Labour Law and Policy Journal* 451, as one example of the argument that the "gradualism" or "soft-law" approach represented by the EEOL was a deliberate strategy choice by policy makers, and preferable to more categorical legislative interventions.

[34] A great deal has been written on the EEOL. In English, an excellent analysis of the development and operation of the law can be found in Upham, *supra* note 32; see also, for a later analysis of the operation of the law, Kiyoko Kamio Knapp "Don't Awaken the Sleeping Child: Japan's Gender Equality Law and the Rhetoric of Gradualism" (1999) 8 *Columbia Journal of Gender & the Law* 143. For an analysis of the law subsequent to the 1997 amendments, see Jennifer S. Fan "From Office Ladies to Women Warriors?: The Effect of the EEOL on Japanese Women" (1999) 10 *U.C.L.A. Women's Law Journal* 103, and Larsen, *supra* note 22. See also the standard

law in 1997 and 2004 have strengthened the prohibitions on discrimination in the areas of recruitment, hiring and promotions, but again, the internal dispute resolution mechanism is non-binding, and there are no sanctions for violation of the law. It has been argued that the existence of a statutory dispute resolution mechanism will actually make courts reluctant to interfere, and that one of the objectives of the government in enacting the law was actually to take back bureaucratic and legislative control of the issue from the courts.[35]

With respect to the elderly, again in the area of employment, there have been amendments to the SEOP as recently as 2004 that are aimed at gradually increasing the protection against age-based discrimination in hiring and termination, and that create duties on employers to make efforts to retain employees beyond retirement age. Thus, setting a mandatory retirement age of below 60 is prohibited, and, pursuant to the 2004 amendments, employers have the duty to develop policies for the employment of employees up to 65 or to abolish retirement ages of less than 65. In the recruitment process companies are required to provide reasons where it is "unavoidable" that maximum ages are posted as conditions for positions. The *Employment Measures Law* similarly creates a duty on companies to "endeavour" to provide equal opportunity without reference to age in hiring.[36] Violations of these provisions are, however, subject only to administrative guidance.

The U.N. Committee on the Elimination of Racial Discrimination discussed this absence of general equality rights legislation in its report on Japan in 2001, and observed that the failure to enact legislation prohibiting racial discrimination was inconsistent with Japan's obligations under the *International Convention on the Elimination of all Forms of Racial Discrimination*.[37] The Ministry of Justice reported that it had drafted and submitted to the Diet a *Human Rights Protection Bill* in 2002, but the bill was not passed, and the Ministry of Justice reports that it is still "under review", notwithstanding that the Ministry views it as being "vital in

text on employment law, Kazuo Sugeno, *Japanese Employment and Labor Law*, trans. Leo Kanowitz, 5th Ed. (Durham, N.C.: Carolina Academic Press, 2002).

[35] Upham, *supra* note 32, at 163–164.

[36] *Employment Measures Law* (Law No. 103 of 2004). For a discussion of these provisions, see Masahiro Yano, "*Kōreishakai to Rōdōhō—teinennsei no hōkaishakuron to hōseisakuron*" [Ageing Society and Labour Law—Legal Interpretation and Legal Policy Debates on the Mandatory Retirement System] (2005) 73 Rūdaihōgaku 209.

[37] CERD Report, *supra* note 12, at paragraphs 10–12.

establishing a society based on respect for human rights".[38] It appears at this stage, however, that it is unlikely to be enacted any time soon. Indeed, the *Law on the Promotion of Measures for Human Rights Protection*,[39] enacted in 1996 as a step towards the establishment of a human rights regime, was repealed in 2002. No mention of the legislation has been made in the periodic reports of Japan to the U.N. Human Rights Committee.[40]

Some local governments have initiated the passage of human rights bi-laws or more narrow anti-discrimination ordinances, but local governments have limited powers in Japan. Moreover, these efforts have actually been the object of attack by conservatives, such that the first such prefectural ordinance had to be repealed.[41] Finally, under article 98(2) of the Constitution, the treaties to which Japan is a state party are incorporated into the law of Japan, and thus the equality provisions in the *International Covenant on Civil and Political Rights* (the "ICCPR"),[42] *International Covenant on Economic and Social Rights* ("ICESR"),[43] the *International Convention on the Elimination of All Forms of Racism* ("CERD"),[44] and the *Convention on the Elimination of Discrimination Against Women* ("CEDAW"),[45] to name the most important, theoretically provide protections in the public domain.[46]

---

[38] Ministry of Justice web-page entitled "Promotion of Measures for Human Rights", available at www.moj.go.jp/ENGLISH/issues/issues07.html (last viewed 9 January 2007).

[39] Law No. 120 of 2000, repealed 25 March 2002.

[40] Japanese 4th Periodic Report to the Human Rights Committee, October 1, 1997, UN Doc CCPR/C/115/Add.3, available online at http: www.unhchr.ch/tbs/doc.nsf/(Symbol)/CCPR.C.115.Add.3.En?Opendocument (last viewed December 26, 2006), also available at the website of the Ministry of Justice at http://www.mofa.go.jp/policy/human/civil_rep4/index.html (last viewed 26 December 2006). Japan also posted its 5th Periodic Report, dated December 2006, which was due to be filed in 2002, at http://www.mofa.go.jp/policy/human/civil_rep6.pdf (last viewed 26 December 2006).

[41] Debito Arudou, "How to Kill a Bill: Tottori's Human Rights Ordinance is a Case in Alarmism" *Japan Times*, 2 May 2006.

[42] *International Covenant on Civil and Political Rights*, 999 U.N.T.S. 171, entered into force 23 March 1976. Japan has been a state party since 21 June 1979.

[43] *International Covenant on Economic, Social and Cultural Rights*, 993 U.N.T.S. 3, entered into force on 2 January 1976. Japan has been a state party since 21 June 1979.

[44] *International Convention on the Elimination of all Forms of Racial Discrimination*, 660 U.N.T.S. 195, entered into force on 4 January 1969. Japan has been a state party since 15 December 1995.

[45] *Convention on the Elimination of all Forms of Discrimination Against Women*, 19 I.L.M. 33 (1980), entered into force 3 September 1981. Japan has been a state party since 1985.

[46] This proposition is not universally accepted, but is the dominant view of constitutional academics in Japan, has been endorsed by the Supreme Court, and is the

The courts of Japan, however, are reluctant to enforce provisions of such international treaties in individual litigation.[47]

## Equality Rights and Discrimination—The Legal Analysis

Given the lack of robust statutory protections against discrimination, the manner in which the courts interpret and enforce the constitutional right to equality becomes that much more important. Before launching into a critical examination of the Japanese judicial model for the analysis of discrimination, however, it is necessary to be clear about what we mean when we speak of equality rights and discrimination, and to say a few words about the theoretical perspective that informs the analysis in this article.

The right to be treated equally under the law and not to be discriminated against, as that right is enshrined in a number of modern constitutions and human rights instruments, means at the very minimum that the individual has a right to be treated by the state with equal respect and concern as compared to anyone else. At its foundation lies the Kantian concept of human dignity, in the objective sense of the inherent worth of every human being, and the notion that to treat someone as being intrinsically worth less than another is to do harm to their human dignity. Discrimination, defined broadly, is treating some differently than others, in the denial of benefits or imposition of burdens, in a manner that is unfair.[48]

---

position taken by the government in its reports to the Human Rights Committee. See Yuji Iwasawa, *International Law, Human Rights and Japanese Law* (Oxford: Clarendon Press, 1998) at 28–32, and Japan's 4th Periodic Report to the HRC, *supra* note 40, at paras 9–11. Also, it should be noted that the international human rights instruments provide much more limited protection against discrimination on the basis of age than many constitutions and national human rights acts.

[47] See, for example, JFBA Report, *supra* note 22, at 2. The government also noted in the 4th Periodic Report to the HRC, that in none of the decisions that considered the ICCPR was any law of Japan held to be inconsistent with the convention, 4th Periodic Report to the HRC, *supra* note 40, at paragraph 10.

[48] There is obviously a vast abundance of literature on the issue of equality rights and discrimination, not only in law but also in political philosophy, ethics, and a range of other disciplines. It is a complex theoretical field and the overview of a perspective provided here is the very barest thumbnail sketch. An excellent analysis of the recent literature for the purpose of examining equality rights in the Canadian context, which I have drawn on here, is Sophia R. Moreau, "The Wrongs of Unequal Treatment" (2004) 54 *University of Toronto Law Journal* 291. The perspective represented here is also informed by the writing of Ronald Dworkin, *Taking Rights Seriously*, (Cambridge, Mass.:

This leads to the question of what makes any particular differentiated treatment unfair, so as to constitute discrimination that violates the right to be treated equally. The fact that the distinction treats persons in a manner that suggests that they are less worthy of the state's respect and concern, and thus does harm to their dignity, would be one indicia that the treatment is unfair. Where the treatment is based on prejudice or a stereotype, there is a presumption of harm to the individual, in terms of treating them on the basis of generalizations that may be inaccurate and that define the individual according to another group's perceptions, all of which undermines the individual's autonomy. Similarly, where the treatment reflects and perpetuates excessive power imbalances, which again undermines the autonomy of a weaker group by limiting their access to social and political institutions and the policy making process, or other such social goods, this may be an indicia of unfairness. A further indicia is where the treatment is likely to undermine the subjective sense of dignity of the individual, or at least would do so to a reasonable person in the individual's position. When we speak of the subjective sense of dignity rather than the objective inherent worth of a human being discussed above, it is the individual's own sense of self-worth and self-esteem that is implicated.[49]

Such constitutions as those of Japan, Canada, and South Africa, as well as the European Convention on Human Rights, actually build into the equality rights provision the presumption that differentiated treatment on the basis of certain grounds will be *prima facie* unfair. The prohibited grounds of discrimination (or suspect categories, to use the American terminology) in those constitutions include such characteristics as sex, race, creed, religion, age, and social status. This reflects the conceptions discussed above regarding the harms that unfair discrimination is thought to cause. It suggests that to treat individuals differently on the basis of personal characteristics that are immutable, or at least deep-rooted and difficult to alter (such as religion), and which are related to one's sense of self and self-worth, will often be based on prejudice or stereotype, but in any event will be likely to cause harm to the person's dignity, both in the objective and subjective sense. The discrimination need not be invidious or intended in order to be a

Harvard University Press, 1977), and *Sovereign Virtue: The Theory and Practice of Equality* (Cambridge: Harvard University Press, 2000).

[49] Moreau, *supra* note 48.

violation of the right, and it may have rational policy objectives and yet still be unfair and thus a violation of the right.[50] The question of fairness, and thus the issue as to whether some treatment constitutes discrimination, is separate from the question as to whether it may still be justified for policy reasons that are consistent with the values of a democratic society.

Different analytical models and legal tests have been developed by the courts in different liberal democracies for giving substantive meaning to the right as articulated in constitutional documents, and thereby determining what constitutes discrimination in the concrete circumstances of a given case and when it can be justified. Certainly not all share the foregoing philosophical approach in all its particulars as a starting point; but if the right is to be taken seriously (to use Dworkin's language),[51] then the model must contain criteria for determining which grounds of discrimination are impermissible (where an explicit set of factors are not provided for, as in the U.S. 14th Amendment, or where the list is not exhaustive, as in the case of Canada, South Africa, and Japan), who is to be compared with whom for the purposes of assessing the discrimination, and what kinds of difference in treatment are inappropriate.[52]

---

[50] I am most influenced by the Canadian jurisprudence on this issue. The two cases that reflect the bookends of the development of the analytical approach of the Canadian courts are *Andrews* v. *Law Society of B.C.* [1989] 1 S.C.R. 143, and *Law* v. *Canada (Minister of Employment and Immigration)*, [1999] 1 S.C.R. 497. For examples of how the right to equality in the Constitution of South Africa is analyzed by its courts, see *Fourie* v. *Minister of Home Affairs*, Case 232/2003, 30 November 2004 (Supreme Court of Appeal of South Africa), available online at http://www.law.wits.ac.za/sca/files/2322003/2322003.pdf, and *Larbi-Odam* v. *Ministry of Education*, 1998 (1) SA 745 (Constitutional Court of South Africa), available online at http://www.constitutionalcourt.org.za/Archimages/1616.PDF. As will be discussed further later, article 14 of the Japanese Constitution is actually much closer in form and substance to equality rights provisions of the Canadian Charter, the South African Constitution, and the European Convention on Human Rights, than it is to the 14th Amendment of the U.S. Constitution. The Canadian jurisprudence is thus in many respects more useful for purposes of comparison. See Peter H. Hogg, *Constitutional Law of Canada*, 4th ed. (Toronto: Carswell, 1997), Chapter 52, for an overview of the judicial treatment of equality in Canada.

[51] Ronald Dworkin, "Taking Rights Seriously" in *Taking Rights Seriously*, *supra* note 48.

[52] Moreau makes the argument that, in most of the specific conceptions of treatment that constitutes discrimination that she considers, a comparison with others who may receive the benefit in question is not a necessary element of the analysis, although it may be helpful from an evidentiary perspective. Moreau, *supra* note 48. The courts in Canada and other jurisdictions, however, continue to rely on the notion of comparison with others as an essential element of the analysis of discrimination.

Moreover, on the separate question of justification, there have to be sufficiently objective criteria, applied within a model that is logically consistent with the ideas underpinning the right, for determining when the state may be justified in overriding the right. A simple balancing of the individual right against the broader benefit to the public welfare that may be gained in violating the right is simply not consistent with the notion of rights. The public welfare will always outweigh the individual's right, and the right becomes meaningless.[53] Finally, it has to be emphasized that these two distinct aspects of the analysis, and their very different inquiries, have to be kept clearly in mind, if not separated into separate stages, the first aspect being the determination of whether some difference in treatment constitutes discrimination in violation of the right, and the second aspect being the determination of whether such a violation may be justified on terms consistent with the values of the right.

Nor should this be understood to be some "western" notion of equality that is somehow foreign to Japanese legal thinking. Many of the doyens of Japanese constitutional law have remarked on the necessity to develop criteria for the interpretation of article 14 that are consistent with the values of a free and democratic society and which recognize the dignity of the human being.[54] The problem is primarily that the courts have failed to do so. The Human Rights Committee under the ICCPR has, as recently as 1998, in its observations on the periodic reports submitted by Japan, criticized the analytical model employed by courts in assessing discrimination as being inconsistent with Japan's obligations to enforce the right to equality under the ICCPR. In particular, it expressed concern over "the vagueness of the concept of 'reasonable discrimination', which, in the absence of objective criteria, is incompatible with article 26 of the Covenant", and about "the restrictions that can be placed on the rights guaranteed in the Covenant on the grounds of 'public welfare', a concept that is vague and open-ended and which may permit restrictions exceeding those permissible under the Covenant."[55] An examination of how the courts analyse discrimination

---

[53] Ronald Dworkin, "Taking Rights Seriously" in *Taking Rights Seriously*, *supra* note 48, at 194 and 197.

[54] Toshiyoshi Miyazawa, *Kenpō II* [Constitutional Law II] (Tokyo: 1971), at 289; Nobuyoshi Ashibe, *Kenpō hanrei wo yomu* [Reading Constitutional Cases] (Tokyo: Iwanami shoten, 1987) at 136–140; Kōji Satō, *Kenpō* [Constitutional law], 3rd ed. (Tokyo: Aobayashi shoin, 1995), at 477–483.

[55] HRC Report, *supra* note 12, at paragraphs 11 and 8.

illustrates the validity of these observations, although we will focus here primarily on the issue of "reasonable discrimination".

The Supreme Court established in the first equality cases that, notwithstanding the unqualified language of article 14, only discrimination that was "unreasonable" or that lacked "rationality" (*gōrisei*, which can be translated as either "reasonableness" or "rationalality") was prohibited by the Constitution. It did not elaborate criteria for determining what made any given discriminatory law or policy reasonable, but the subsequent jurisprudence reveals that it is simply to be assessed by reference to the objectives and means of the law or policy in question. It is instructive to begin our discussion with what is probably the most famous equality case in Japan, and one of a only a handful of decisions in which the Supreme Court has actually held a law to be unconstitutional. The so-called *Patricide* case of 1973 involved article 200 of the *Criminal Code*,[56] which provided for a harsher sentence for the murder of a lineal ascendant than the punishment for the murder of anyone else, as provided for in article 199 (death or life imprisonment, with less sentencing discretion, which ultimately meant the difference between a minimum of a 3 year sentence, and a conditional discharge).[57] The issue had come before the Supreme Court before, and the distinction made by the law had been upheld.[58] In the case that arrived before the court in 1973, however, the accused presented a tragic set of facts, having been the victim of a violent incestuous relationship with her father from the age of 14, and having borne five of his children before she finally killed him.

The majority of the court held that article 200 was unconstitutional on the grounds that the disparity between the two punishments (for murder of an ascendant and murder simpliciter) was too great, such that the harshness of the punishment for patricide was disproportionate to the legislative objective, and so made the discrimination itself "unreasonable". And that answered the question the court initially posed as being the issue in the case: "whether Article 200 of the *Criminal Code* violates [article 14]; and [this issue] is to be settled based on a determination of whether or not the discrimination has reasonable

[56] Law No. 45 of 1907, as amended. Article 200 has since been repealed, though this did not happen until 1995, more than 20 years after the decision of the court!

[57] *Patricide* case, *supra* note 30, translation available in Beer, *supra* note 30, at p. 143 *et seq*.

[58] Supreme Court Judgement, First Petty Bench, 24 May 1956.

grounds."[59] In trying to identify the legislative purpose, the court noted the ideological background of Confucian values regarding filial piety, and the extended family system that had been abolished immediately following the World War II. Ultimately, the court found that the legislative purpose was to maintain and protect the respect and gratitude that people ought to have for their ascendants. It held that it was not unreasonable for the law to treat the murderers of ascendants differently, but that the harshness of the punishment, as compared to that for other murders, was disproportionate. A strong concurring judgement written by Justice Tanaka dissented on this latter point, holding that the differential treatment was itself unconstitutional.[60]

At first blush this case is difficult to understand from a traditional perspective on equality rights. The primary reason is that the court never addresses the question of what, precisely, constitutes the discrimination in the case. It is assumed as given that article 200 is discriminatory, but the court never applies any criteria for assessing what harm is caused by the differentiated treatment or how it is unfair, or who the accused is to be compared with for the purposes of the equality analysis. Are we to understand that the accused claims that she, and all other murderers of ascendants, are being treated unfairly as compared to "regular" murderers? Are we comparing two groups of murderers for the purpose of assessing the unequal treatment? That, quite obviously, cannot be right.

The case can only be understood in terms of the legislative objective of holding out ascendants as deserving greater respect and concern than descendants within the family organization, rather than the differentiated treatment of different accused in murder cases based on their relationship with their victims. The law, as the court itself recognized, was attempting to foster and preserve a culture of enhanced respect for ascendants, and on its face meant that the killing of an ascendant was morally more pernicious than the killing of one's descendant.

We are all descendants at one stage of our lives, and most of us will be ascendants at a later stage, and many will be both simultaneously for part of their lives. Thus, it may not strike us that one's status as ascendant or descendant is the type of immutable characteristic upon which we would say that different treatment amounts to unjust discrimination.

---

[59] *Patricide* case, in Beer, *supra* note 30, at 144.
[60] Reasons of Justice Tanaka, in Beer, *supra* note 30, at 150 *et seq.*

Yet in a very real sense the law suggested that, in any given family relationship, the life of the parent was of greater worth than that of the children or grandchildren. The opinion of Justice Tanaka does not articulate the nature of the harm or the basis for comparison either, but he obviously had both in mind when he wrote that the creation of special protection for ascendants is "based on a kind of status morality" that is likely to be "repugnant to the fundamental idea of democracy based upon the dignity and equality of individuals."[61]

The discrimination, therefore, lies not in the difference in the treatment of a specific accused based on her relationship with her victim, but rather in the lesser protection (through lesser deterrence) provided to descendants under the law than to ascendants. Descendants were not being treated equally by the law in their capacity as potential victims, and the law signalled that they were worthy of less respect and concern than ascendants generally. The harm caused was to the dignity of the descendants, in both the objective and subjective sense of the word, in their relations within the family, rather than the penal sanction that was actually meted out to the rare accused in a patricide case.

Had the court more deliberately explored and clearly articulated the nature of the comparison, and thus what in precise terms constituted the discrimination, it might well have come to a different conclusion on the question of the validity of the legislative objective. It almost certainly would have led to different reasoning regarding the "reasonableness" of the discrimination. For once the essence of the discrimination and the harm it caused becomes clear, and the distinction that is really being impugned has been isolated, then it becomes equally clear that the extent of the relative harshness of the punishment is really beside the point. While the court's reasoning is cast in terms that resemble the standard "rational connection" and "proportionality analysis" within justification arguments, it does not make sense in the context of the actual discrimination at issue. *Any* harsher treatment of a convicted accused based on her status of being a descendant of the victim, designed to create greater deterrence against attacks on ascendants and to foster the notion that the lives of ascendants are worth more than those of descendants, would be illegitimate, and different levels of harshness of the punishment do not constitute greater or lesser degrees of discrimination.

[61] Ibid. at 152.

While the court ends up concluding that the provision is unconstitutional, it does so on the grounds that the discrimination is "unreasonable". The only criteria offered for that finding is that there is a lack of proportionality between the harshness of the means and the objective of the legislation. Yet, this should not be confused with a "less restrictive alternative" or "minimal impairment" type argument. For the court does not quibble with the means. The court does not suggest that the objective ought to be pursued through a different avenue that differentiates between ascendants and descendants to a lesser degree. It merely questions the harshness of the punishment and mistakenly calls that the means. Varying the harshness in no way alters the nature of the discrimination. Moreover, the Court suggests no specific criteria for assessing the "reasonableness" of the actual discrimination.[62]

This lack of criteria for determining what constitutes "reasonable discrimination" is perhaps the single most significant problem with the judicial model. Without external objective criteria the notion of "reasonable discrimination" simply relies on the court concluding that the government policy, taken on its own terms, has some rational basis, which, depending on the level of generality the argument is pitched at, is very easy to do.[63] Moreover, it collapses and conflates the two distinct aspects of rights analysis—the first being the nature of the distinction being made and whether it is unfair and causes harm so as to constitute discrimination, and the second being whether such discrimination (if such has been determined) can be justified. By collapsing the analysis and focusing primarily on the justification, without first analysing the nature of the discrimination and how it may violate

[62] Ashibe, in his analysis of the case, disagrees with the majority decision, but applauds what he suggests is a nuanced and sophisticated distinction between the legislative objective and the means of achieving it. But as argued here, the court was wrong in considering the difference in severity of punishment as being the means of achieving the objective that constituted the discriminatory treatment. Ashibe, *Kenpō hanrei wo yomu, supra* note 54, at 140–141.

[63] Hidenori Tomatsu has suggested that the Supreme Court has quite consciously limited itself to a "mild scrutiny" or rationality test with respect to equality, because the court recognizes that it would be difficult to obtain compliance from the executive and legislative branches of government. Hidenori Tomatsu, "Equal Protection of the Law" in *Japanese Constitutional Law*, Percey R. Luney, Jr. and Kazuyuki Takahashi, eds., (Tokyo: University of Tokyo press, 1993), at 202.

the right, the justification analysis itself cannot be handled with any substantive precision.[64]

## Recent and Future Application of the Reasonableness Test

The Supreme Court has never held another law to be unconstitutional on the grounds that it was discriminatory in violation of article 14,[65] and the vast majority of lower court decisions have followed the model of the Supreme Court in finding that discrimination is "reasonable" in the circumstances. Moreover, as we will see, the test has been applied by the courts in analysing discrimination in the private sphere, where the values underlying article 14 have informed the analysis, upholding discrimination by corporations and other entities on the grounds that it was "reasonable" in light of the circumstances and the entity's objectives. Before looking at cases in the private domain, however, we should address the most recent important decision of the Supreme Court on the issue of how the equality rights of foreigners are to be protected. It is, in my view, highly suggestive as to how the courts will deal with foreigners' rights in at least the short-to-medium term, and it is instructive as to how the legal test of "reasonable discrimination" continues to be applied generally.

---

[64] The inadequacy of the standard of review is recognized by Japanese constitutional scholars, although, in my view, Japanese scholarship would benefit from looking at jurisprudence from the Canadian and South African courts. There is a tendency among Japanese academics looking at this issue to focus exclusively on the U.S. experience, but the two-tier standard of review applied in 14th Amendment jurisprudence is not helpful, given the differences in the constitutional language. The 14th Amendment contains no criteria whatsoever for determining what types of unequal treatment is presumptively unfair discrimination, and thus the American courts have developed different categories of treatment, and different levels of review for suspect categories (such as race) and non-suspect categories. The Japanese "reasonable discrimination" test resembles the "rational basis" level of review, the least strict level of review, developed by the American courts for non-suspect categories. For examples of Japanese constitutional discussion of the standards, see Matsui, *supra* note 29, at 364 *et seq.*; Ashibe, *Kenpō hanrei wo yomu*, *supra* note 53, at 136 *et seq.*; Ashibe Nobuyoshi, *Kenpō* [Constitutional Law] 3rd ed. (Tokyo: Iwanami Shoten, 2002), at 125 *et seq.*

[65] The Supreme Court has twice held the disparity in the ratio of voters per candidate as between rural and urban federal political ridings to be unconstitutional under article 14, although it did not purport to find the election law itself unconstitutional in either case.

The *Tokyo Metropolitan Government* case of 26 January 2005, involved the claims of discrimination asserted by a Korean-Japanese woman who was a local public employee within the Tokyo Metropolitan Government. Her mother was Japanese and she had been born in Japan, and she had special-permanent resident status. She was a health-care professional already employed by the Tokyo government, and she sought to take the exams that qualified employees for promotion to managerial level. She was twice denied on the grounds that only Japanese nationals were entitled to take the exams (the first time she was denied there was in fact no such officially established policy; by the following year, when she was again denied, the policy had been formalized).[66] The employee sued the Tokyo government for violation of, among other things, article 3 of the *Labour Standards Law* and article 14 of the Constitution. The Tokyo High Court granted her partial relief, on the grounds that foreigners are protected by the rights of article 14, the policy of the Tokyo government was discriminatory, and the impugned policy was overly broad and not the least restrictive means of achieving its stated objectives.[67] The Supreme Court granted the appeal and overturned the decision of the Tokyo High Court.

It is apparent from the reasons of the Supreme Court that the Tokyo government had argued that the discriminatory policy was necessary because the government had developed an "integrated management appointment system", whereby all employees who were promoted to certain managerial rank would become eligible for managerial positions throughout the government apparatus. The Supreme Court accepted that, while the applicant had sought to take specialized exams related to her health profession, the whole system was predicated on the idea that once having passed the exams she would be eligible to work in a post with "public authority". The court re-affirmed previous interpretations of article 15 of the Constitution, which provides for the rights of suffrage and sovereignty of the people, as meaning that only Japanese

[66] The "policy" was never actually promulgated by ordinance or regulation duly passed by the Tokyo government, and, not having been prescribed by law, one would expect such a "policy" to be treated with heightened suspicion. For instance, under the test developed by the Canadian courts for determining whether an act of government that has been held to have infringed a fundamental right in the Charter of Rights and Freedoms, can nonetheless be justified in accordance with the values of a free and democratic society, the threshold question is whether the act in question was prescribed by law. Where it is not, the act cannot be justified.

[67] Tokyo High Court Judgement, 26 November 1997.

nationals could hold office as local government employees with "public authority". The integrated management system being such as it was, and given the necessity of restricting employees with public authority to Japanese nationals, the Court held that the Tokyo government's policy of excluding all foreign nationals from promotion to managerial status was reasonable.[68]

The article 15 sovereignty argument is highly questionable, but is beside the point for our purposes.[69] Assuming it to be correct, the reasoning of the court in finding that the Tokyo government policy was "reasonable" reflects the acute weakness of the test as a means of giving effect to the right to equality. The *ratio* of the case may be found in paragraph 4(2), in which the court held that:

> It follows that where an ordinary local public body establishes such an integrated management appointment system and then takes a measure to allow only Japanese employees to be promoted to managerial posts, the ordinary local public body is deemed to distinguish between employees who are Japanese nationals and those who are foreign residents based on reasonable grounds, so it is appropriate to construe such measure not to be a violation of Article 3 of the Labour Standards Law or Article 14 para 1 of the Constitution.[70]

The Court merely accepted that it is within the discretion of a local public body "to establish, based on its own judgment, an integrated management appointment system", and so there was no discussion whatsoever as to the importance or necessity of a comprehensive system that required that everyone promoted to management level would

[68] Judgement of the Supreme Court, 26 January 2005 (*Tokyo Metropolitan Government* case), at section 4. A court translation is available at http://courtdomino2.courts.go.jp/promjudg.nsf/766e4f1d46701bec49256b8700435d2e/064defe5111351 50492570310028d4fa?OpenDocument (last accessed 19 December 2006).

[69] Article 15 provides that: "The people have the inalienable right to choose their public officials and to dismiss them. (2) All public officials are servants of the whole community and not of any group thereof. (3) Universal adult suffrage is guaranteed with regard to election of public officials. (4) In all elections, secrecy of the ballot shall not be violated. A voter shall not be answerable, publicly or privately, for the choice he has made." It is very difficult to see how a plain reading of this provision can give rise to a principle that limits all exercise of "public authority" to Japanese nationals. Even if "the people" [*kokumin*] is interpreted here to mean "Japanese citizens", which would be to give the same word two very different meanings in two provisions of the same document, the provision still can only be read as limiting the right to *choose* public officials to Japanese citizens, rather than saying anything at all about the right to *serve* as a public official.

[70] Ibid., section 4(2).

be eligible for later appointment to positions of "public authority". Indeed the policy objective was never clearly articulated by the court. There was no analysis as to whether the policy of limiting promotion to Japanese nationals, or the feature of making all managers eligible for positions with "public authority", was rationally connected to the policy objectives. There was no analysis of whether the objectives could be achieved through means that would be less discriminatory. The Tokyo High Court, for instance, had reasoned that a narrower policy could be fashioned, whereby foreigners could be promoted to managerial rank but be restricted from transfer to positions wielding public authority. That argument was rejected in the majority decision of the Supreme Court without any analysis.

Indeed, the court did not discuss the nature of the discrimination or the harm that it might occasion in any sense whatsoever. There was no examination of what stereotypes might underlie the policy, the power imbalances it might perpetuate, or the extent to which it might deeply harm the dignity, both objective and subjective, of foreigners resident in Japan. Once again, as in the *Patricide* case, the issue of discrimination and the violation of the right are collapsed into and lost within the justification argument. The decision, boiled down to its essentials, was simply this: (1) only Japanese nationals may fulfil positions of public authority; (2) the integrated management system of the government operates on the basis that all those promoted to management rank may fill positions of public authority; (3) therefore the policy of excluding foreigners from promotion to management rank is reasonable.

Moreover, when one goes on to examine the concurring opinions of several of the other justices, there is even further reason to query how the court approaches the issue of equality rights. Justices Ueda, Kanatani, and Fujita, in three separate opinions, each addressed the question of whether the Constitution "guarantees foreign nationals the right to take office as government employees", as though this was indeed the operative constitutional question in the case. They completely fail to address the question that was in fact before the court, which is whether a public policy that treats foreigners differently by denying them promotion within the municipal government service constitutes discrimination on the basis of nationality, and unjustifiably violates the right to be treated equally under the law. Justice Fujita goes so far as to suggest that the right to equality is not an "inherent right" in any event, writing that "freedom of choice in employment, the principle of equality, etc. are rights to freedom, which are originally intended to only protect inherent rights and freedoms from restrictions, rather than creating rights and freedoms that are not inherent."[71] All three ultimately address the issue as one of government discretion, and whether the integrated management appointment system and the policy excluding foreigners "go beyond the bounds of legally acceptable personnel policy".[72]

Justice Fujita in a sense put his finger on the very crux of the issue of the policy objectives in his opinion. In discussing the Tokyo High Court's consideration of less restrictive means, Justice Fujita wrote that if such special personnel considerations were required of local government in developing their policies, it would harm the flexibility of the personnel management systems.[73] Thus, the issue for him was one of balancing the fundamental right to equality on the one hand, and mere administrative efficiency and convenience on the other.[74]

Turning to the private sector, we will see that while the test can be used to reach different results, it provides no real protection against discrimination here either. The values underlying the right to equality in article 14 have been used by the courts to inform equality rights issues in private litigation. It has done so most famously in the line of cases in which the courts greatly advanced the right of women not to be discriminated against with respect to termination and retirement in the employment context. As mentioned earlier, the courts did so using article14 as a basis upon which to interpret vague provisions of the *Civil Code*. Indeed, in the seminal case that began this judicial advance of women's rights, decided in 1966 and known as the *Sumitomo Cement*

---

[71] *Tokyo Metropolitan Government* case, *supra* note 68, opinion of Justice Fujita, section 2.

[72] Ibid., opinion of Justice Fujita, section 3; Opinion of Justice Kanatani, section 3; Opinion of Justice Ueda, section 3.

[73] Ibid., opinion of Justice Fujita, section 3.

[74] As discussed further below, there were are two strong dissents in the decision. For the purposes of comparison, it may be useful to examine the Canadian Supreme Court decision in *Lavoie* v. *Canada*, [2002] 1 S.C.R. 769, and that of the South African Constitutional Court in *Larbi-Odam* v. *Ministry of Education, supra* note 50, as the issue in both cases was the validity of government personnel policies which used nationality as one criterion for decision making with respect to advancement (*Lavoie*) and hiring (*Larbi-Odam*). Both courts found the policies to be discriminatory, although the Supreme Court of Canada in *Lavoie* found that the federal government promotion policy that contained a preference for Canadian nationals constituted an infringement of the fundamental right that was nonetheless justifiable in a free and democratic society. The case has been heavily criticized, but the approaches of both the majority and the dissents are very interesting to compare to that in the *Tokyo Metropolitan Government* case.

case,[75] the Tokyo District Court's reasoning on the issue of the reasonableness of the discrimination stands in stark contrast to the reasoning of the Supreme Court in the *Tokyo Metropolitan Government* case.

The company had argued that it was entirely reasonable to require women to retire earlier than men (upon marriage, to be more precise), because under the life-time employment and seniority-based pay system, women became less and less efficient in terms of the value of their labour relative to their cost to the company as time went on. This, of course, was because the system also entailed employing women in secretarial, clerical, and other forms of low-value employment, with no prospects for advancement, while men were employed in an upwardly mobile career path. But under the seniority-based pay system they all received salary increases in step, and women over time became more costly than they were worth, and so mandatory retirement upon marriage was a "rational" means of keeping the labour costs of female employees down.

The similarities in form between this argument and that of the Tokyo Metropolitan Government in respect of its integrated management appointment system are quite striking. So long as one accepted the personnel system created by the discriminator as being necessary and sacrosanct, then the discrimination in accordance with the terms and in furtherance of the objectives of that system could be argued to be "rational". But the Tokyo District Court would have none of Sumitomo Cement's argument. It held that, to the extent women were less efficient than men in the workplace, it was an inefficiency caused by the manner in which they were employed and by the seniority-based pay system itself. The inefficiency having been the result of the company's own policies, the company could not rely on such inefficiency as the basis for explaining the rationality of its discrimination.[76] The same argument could, of course, have applied with equal force in the *Tokyo Metropolitan Government* case.

Nonetheless, the court in the *Sumitomo Cement* case did repeat in its reasons that only "unreasonable discrimination" was prohibited, and it simply turned the company's reasonableness argument on its head.

[75] Tokyo District Court, 20 December 1966 (*Sumitomo Cement* case). For an excellent analysis of the so-called first phase of women's rights litigation over employment issues, see Upham, *supra* note 32, Chapter 4.

[76] *Sumitomo Cement* case, *supra*; see Upham, *supra* note 32, for discussion of the case, at pp. 131–133.

Indeed, in a very real sense, this case and those that followed it show just how malleable the "reasonableness" analysis is to manipulation and result-oriented reasoning in either direction. And what is most significant to note for our purposes, is that the "reasonable discrimination" analysis established by the Supreme Court in respect of article 14 cases, has been carried over to the private sector discrimination cases that were informed by the values of article 14. Thus, even most recently in the *Tokyo Metropolitan Government* case examined above, the Court held that the "reasonableness" of the discrimination meant that the policy violated neither the Constitution nor article 3 of the *Labour Standards Law*, thereby importing an "unreasonableness" requirement to proving discrimination where none is reflected in the language of the *Labour Standards Law*.[77] This reflects the extent to which the "reasonableness" test has come to permeate judicial thinking in respect of all discrimination, both public and private.

The extent to which the courts went well beyond both the statutory language and the contractual intent of the parties in protecting the rights of women in the first phase of women's rights litigation in the 1960s and 1970s does not mean that the courts will be inclined to protect women from discrimination in the era of the ageing society. An excellent analysis of the employment-related litigation for that period has proposed a more over-arching theory that places the *Sumitomo Cement* line of cases in perspective.[78] According to this theory, the courts were engaged in creating a coherent and internally consistent legal framework for the employment relationship in Japan, and one fundamental plank of that framework was job security in a life-time employment system. Thus, not only women were receiving the protection of the courts, but employees generally were protected from termination of all sorts. Thus the early women's rights cases, in which the primary issues were related to job security, can be seen as falling within this grander judicial project. The *quid pro quo* in this judicially created scheme, however, was that companies would be given very wide discretion in terms of how they managed their employees. Thus the courts deferred to corporate discretion and dismissed claims for damages where the issues involved

[77] *Tokyo Metropolitan Government* case, *supra* note 68, paragraph 4(2) and paragraph 4(3).

[78] Foote, *supra* note 16.

transfers, promotions, farming out employees to sister companies, and the like.[79]

It is, therefore, less than clear how the courts, and certainly how the Supreme Court, will respond to increasing litigation claims of women on the issues of indirect discrimination, discrimination in recruitment, hiring and promotion, and in respect of the very structure of personnel systems that tend to result in a disproportionate number of women in part-time employment and dispatched labour, with lower wages and less benefits.[80] The decisions of the lower courts to date have been mixed and no discernable trend has emerged.[81] What is certain, however, is that the courts will continue to employ the "reasonableness" analysis in such cases.

The judicial approach to equality rights will be even less promising for the elderly. It is true that age has been held to be a prohibited ground of discrimination within the scope of the term "social status", as mentioned earlier. But age is a difficult concept to deal with in the context of equality. Like the status of "ascendant" and "descendant" discussed earlier, we all go through the various stages of life, and so while we cannot change the characteristic of our age at any given stage in our life, it is not itself unchanging. Moreover, we all recognize that there is some relationship between ability, maturity and judgement, and age. The laws and policies of most countries reflect all sorts of age-based criteria for access to everything from driving licences to movie theatres. Thus discrimination based on age is often justifiable, even under the standards of the strictest constitutional scrutiny.[82] Unfortunately, how-

---

[79] Ibid.

[80] The journal *Juristo* published a series of articles on the state of the law with respect to indirect discrimination in November 2005. See Hiroya Nakakubo, Mami Nakano, and Shone Kinoshita, "*Kansetsu sabetsu*" [Indirect Discrimination] *Juristo* 1 November 2005, No. 1300, at 116. On discrimination with respect to wages and promotion, see Michiko Nakajima, "*Koyo ni okeru seisabetu—chinkin, shōshin, shōkakusabetsu no hanrei no chushin ni*" [Gender Discrimination in Employment—Focus on Cases Relating to Wages, Advancement and Promotion Discrimination] *Juristo*, 1 January 2003, No. 1237 at 89.

[81] Some see the 2002 Tokyo District Court Judgement, 20 February 2002, in which the court held that Nomura Securities' two-track personnel system was discriminatory and unlawful under the EEOL, as being a turning point. See Kumamoto-Healey, *supra* note 11 at 451. But it seems too early to tell in light of other decisions going the other way, for example, the Tokyo District Court Judgement, 5 November 2003, in which the dual-track system at Kanematsu was determined by the court to be "reasonable". See Nakajima, *supra* note 80, for further discussion of recent cases.

[82] The Canadian Supreme Court, for instance, found that mandatory retirement in the context of a university constituted a violation of the right to equality, but held it

ever, it means that under the "reasonable discrimination" test it will always be a matter of great ease to demonstrate some rational basis for discrimination against the elderly.

The courts have upheld mandatory retirement in several cases, and indeed the Supreme Court judgement that determined that age fell within the scope of "social status" as a prohibited ground of discrimination in article 14, was itself a mandatory retirement case in which the Court held that mandatory retirement at age 55 constituted reasonable discrimination.[83] The corporate practice of requiring employees to retire at 60 but then continuing to employ them for several more years at lower salaries and in positions of lower responsibility is very likely to give rise to claims of unfair treatment and age-based discrimination.[84] Such pressure will be exacerbated when recent revisions to the pension laws increasing the age of eligibility for state pensions to 65 become effective in 2013, as the elderly will suffer significant declines in income in the gap years between retirement from full-time employment, and the commencement of their national pension.[85]

Increased discrimination against the elderly will not only arise in the area of employment, and indeed perhaps the most dangerous discrimination will come in the area of health care.[86] The Japanese Federation of Bar Associations has reported that revisions in 1998 to the Medical Treatment Fee Reimbursement Scheme reduced the compensation hospitals and doctors would receive for patients over 70 years of age. Similarly, the revised scheme created a system whereby compensation to hospitals for inpatients diminishes over the duration of their stay, which typically means that elderly patients who require long-term care generate less revenue for hospitals. As a result of the incentive structure thus created, hospitals are increasingly unwilling to accept elderly patients requiring long-term care, and the discharge of elderly patients has been inappropriately accelerated.[87]

---

to be justified in accordance with the principles of a free and democratic society; see *McKinney* v. *University of Guelph*, [1990] 3 S.C.R. 229.

[83] *Tateyama Mayor* case, supra note 27; see also Supreme Court Judgement, 25 December 1968 (*Akita Bus* case).

[84] Hirotake Tamada et al. *Kōreishakai no hōritsu, keizai, shaki no kenkyū* [Legal, Economic, and Social Research on the Ageing Society], (Tokyo: Shinsansha, 1996) at 18–19.

[85] Yano, *supra* note 36, at 210. Tamada, *supra* note 84, at 18.

[86] See generally on health care and rights issues of the elderly in an ageing society, Bernard M. Dickens, "Medico-Legal Issues Concerning the Elderly—An Overview" in *An Aging World: Dilemmas and Challenges for Law and Social Policy, supra* note 20, at 487.

[87] JFBA Report, *supra* note 22, at p. 42.

The outlook for foreigners is the bleakest of all. Japanese constitutional scholars observe that, under the "reasonable discrimination" test, the courts have always found it remarkably easy to classify discriminatory treatment of foreigners as reasonable.[88] That is illustrated in the *Tokyo Metropolitan Government* case itself. Another recent example is a case in which the courts upheld the government's denial of pension and disability benefits to Taiwanese-Japanese who served with the Imperial Japanese Army, on the grounds that they were now foreigners. In the Supreme Court decision on this issue, the Court held that the discriminatory treatment was reasonable, based as it was on nationality, even though the claimants (or their family members) had been Japanese nationals when they served in the Japanese military, and had been stripped of their Japanese nationality by the Japanese government after the execution of the *San Francisco Peace Treaty*.[89] There is no analysis in the decision as to the fairness of the distinction, or the harm that it caused. Nor was there any examination of what the objective of the distinction is alleged to have been, or why it was either necessary or important, or whether it could have been achieved through some means that was less discriminatory.[90]

The courts have similarly upheld as reasonable the denial to foreigners of pension benefits,[91] and, more recently, of social security benefits.[92] The denial of coverage under the *Daily Life Security Law*[93] to foreigners who have neither permanent nor long-term resident status means that such foreigners may be refused treatment by health-care providers. Without the benefit of any analysis whatsoever, this too was held to be reasonable discrimination, and to have been within the sphere of legislative discretion in any event.[94]

---

[88] See for instance, Matsui, *supra* note 29, at 381.

[89] Supreme Court Judgement, 28 April 1992 (*Taiwanese Veterans* case), at paragraph 5.

[90] Ibid.

[91] Supreme Court Judgement, 2 November 1959 (the law in question has since been superseded).

[92] Tokyo High Court, 24 April 1997.

[93] Law No. 144 of 1950, as amended.

[94] Tokyo High Court Judgement, 24 April 1997, section 4(2) of reasons. For an overview of the legal treatment of foreigners with respect to social security and health-care benefits, see Kazuaki Tetsuya, *Gaikokujin to hō* [Foreigners and the Law], 3rd ed. (Tokyo: Yuhikaku, 2005) at 301–330.

## Why the Legal Test Matters

All of these cases illustrate how facile the "reasonable discrimination" test can be, when "reasonable" simply means that there is some rational connection between the apparent objective or purpose of the discriminatory policy, and the means chosen to achieve it. But they also raise questions about *why* the courts, and particularly the Supreme Court, have been so unwilling or unable to better protect the right to equality. For, given how malleable the "reasonable discrimination" test is, were the courts more predisposed to enforce the right not to be discriminated against, they could use the test to do so. This of course goes to the broader question of why the Supreme Court has been so timid in exercising its judicial review powers more generally, and much has been written on the issue, with explanations ranging from lack of real judicial independence, conservatism of the court, political weakness and a fear that the court's decisions might be ignored by the legislature and the executive, to broader sociological and cultural explanations.[95] One might be inclined to think that these are really the more important issues, and that unless and until the courts are more predisposed to enforce rights generally, and the right to equality more specifically, then the legal test itself is really not that significant.

While these other lines of inquiry into why the courts are so reluctant to enforce rights are obviously of great value, I would argue that focusing on the test itself is nonetheless important. As discussed earlier, the test leads to confused thinking about equality rights and

---

[95] In English, see for example, John O. Haley, "Judicial Independence in Japan Revisited" *Law in Japan: An Annual*, 1995, 1–18; John O. Haley, "The Japanese Judiciary: Maintaining Integrity, Autonomy and the Public Trust", (2003) *Lectures and Occasional Papers, Whitney R. Harris Institute for Legal Studies, No. 3, Washington University School of Law*; Malcolm M. Feeley, "The Bench, the Bar, and the State: Judicial Independence in Japan and the United States", in Malcolm M. Feeley and Setsuo Miyazawa eds. *The Japanese Adversary System in Context* (Hampshire: Palgrave MacMillan, 2002); Setsuo Miyazawa, "The Administrative Control of Japanese Judges" in Curtis J. Milhaupt, J. Mark Ramseyer, Michael K. Young eds. *Japanese Law in Context: Readings in Society, the Economy, and Politics*, (Cambridge: Harvard University Press, 2001); J. Mark Ramsayer, "Judicial (In)dependence in Japan" in *Japanese Law in Context*; J. Mark Ramsayer and Eric B. Rasmusen, *Measuring Judicial Independence: The Political Economy of Judging in Japan* (Chicago: University of Chicago Press, 2003); Frank K. Upham, "Polictical Lackey or Faithful Public Servents? Two Views of the Japanese Judiciary" (2005) 30 *Law & Social Inquiry: Journal of the American Bar Association* 421; Hidenori Tomatsu, "Judicial Review in Japan: An Overview of Efforts to Introduce U.S. Theories" in Yoichi Higuchi, ed. *Five Decades of Constitutionalism in Japanese Society* (Tokyo: University of Tokyo Press, 2001).

discrimination, and provides no assistance to judges grappling with the issue in concrete cases. To the extent that one accepts the basic premise that courts are constrained and guided by the analytical models and legal principles established in precedents, and that the conclusions that judges reach tend to be consistent with the application of such principles, then the inadequacy of the "reasonable discrimination" test can be argued to be one reason for the failure of the courts to enforce the right to equality under the law.[96]

More importantly, however, while the broader explanations are important in trying to understand why the courts are so conservative or timid when it comes to rights enforcement, as a basis for pragmatic normative arguments they become less attractive. They lead to arguments for solutions that are deeply structural and political, and beyond the ability of the judicial system itself to remedy. In contrast, the normative argument for the adoption of a legal test or analytical framework that is more consistent with the right to equality in the constitution, proposes a solution that is more modest and realistic, and yet potentially effective, even if one accepts all the arguments regarding the conservatism and lack of independence of the judiciary.

The argument for the development of a more rigorous legal test can appeal to and potentially persuade individual judges, and the development of the test itself can be advanced incrementally by courts developing analytical approaches to equality that more closely conform to equality rights theory and the values of the constitution, one judgement at a time. If more judgements, even if only those by more liberal-minded judges at the district and high court level, began to employ a more rigorous legal test, incorporating the elements that have been discussed here, then those judgements could develop an increasing influence on future decision making, leading finally to a paradigm shift in the judicial approach to the issue.

---

[96] This premise, of course, is the subject of great theoretical debate, which I do not intend to elaborate on here. As a purely factual matter, it should be noted that while *stare decisis* (the doctrine in common law according to which courts are bound by precedent) is not formally a feature of the Japanese legal system, it is well recognized that the courts do place a great deal of importance on precedent, and lower courts do feel constrained by higher court decisions. It is interesting to note that even Mark Ramsayer, *supra* note 95, while arguing that the judiciary lacks independence and does the bidding of the LDP in certain types of cases, argues that judges in Japan take doctrine and legal principles seriously. See Uhpham, *supra* note 95, at 435 and 449 for an interesting discussion of Ramsayer's and Haley's differing views on this issue.

Even at a less ambitious or optimistic level, it could be suggested that if a more rigorous and sophisticated analysis of equality rights issues works its way into the jurisprudence, then even those judges who are most predisposed to dismiss discrimination claims will arguably be forced to give reasons that to some extent address the rights-based analytical model, and it will become much harder to short-circuit questions regarding the unfairness of the distinction at issue and the harm it caused, or how it can be justified in accordance with the values of a democratic society. In short, the "reasonable discrimination" test may become increasingly inadequate, even for those judges predisposed to dismiss discrimination claims, as it is incapable of responding in a sophisticated and convincing manner to the approach of a rights-based model; and judges may become increasingly uncomfortable with the exposure created by employing what is a simplistic test by comparison.

There are other examples of legal doctrines and analytical models in Japan, such as that of the "abuse of right" doctrine as applied to termination in employment law, that have spread incrementally in lower court decisions until a critical mass was reached and they became the dominant doctrines and analytical approaches to the issue in question.[97] And there is some basis for very cautious optimism regarding a similar development of a more meaningful analysis and rigorous legal test for equality rights. In the *Tokyo Metropolitan Government* case, the Tokyo High Court found there to be discrimination, and in looking at the issue of justification it applied the principle of "less restrictive alternative" in inquiring into whether the objectives of the integrated personnel selection system could have been achieved through means that would have been less discriminatory. Those arguments were picked up by the dissenting judges in the Supreme Court decision.

The opinions of both Justice Takii and Justice Izumi, in contrast to the rest of the court in the *Tokyo Metropolitan Government* case, properly characterized the question before the court as being whether the unequal treatment of foreigners constituted discrimination, and if so, whether it could be justified. In the justification analysis, which they each purported to develop within the concept of the "reasonableness"

[97] See, for example, on the abuse of right doctrine, Foote, *supra* note 16, at 644 *et seq*; and also Michio Aoyama, "*Wagakuni ni okeru kenri ran'yo rinen no hatten*" [The Development of the Abuse of Right Doctrine in Our Country], in *Suekawa Sensei koki kinen—kenri no ran'yo* [In Honour of Professor Suekawa—Abuse of Rights] (1965), translation in John. O. Haley et al. (1994) II *Law and the Legal Process in Japan* 112.

test, they nonetheless looked to external and objective criteria as we have discussed here, so that, in addition to questioning whether there was simply a rational connection between the means chosen and the objectives identified, they went on to inquire into the actual importance of the purpose of excluding foreigners and the necessity of the integrated personnel system, and to examine whether there were less restrictive alternatives available to achieve the underlying objectives of the system.

Moreover, they both made clear that the onus of proving that the discrimination was justified rested with the government, and they each examined closely the evidence the government had advanced for that purpose. Finally, as a final stage of his analysis, Justice Izumi explicitly examined whether the benefit to the system of the government's policy outweighed the harm to foreign residents such as the applicant. Indeed, both justices considered the harm caused, particularly to special permanent residents such as the applicant, by the discrimination in question. In contrast, as we saw earlier, the majority of the Court had failed to examine in any way the nature of the discrimination in question. Both dissenting justices concluded that the blanket exclusion of foreigners from taking the exams for promotion constituted discrimination, and was not justifiable.[98]

There was a similarly strong dissent in an equality rights case before the Supreme Court ten years earlier, regarding the constitutionality of the *Civil Code* provision that limited the inheritance of illegitimate children to one half of that received by legitimate children, when the deceased died intestate.[99] The majority held that the discrimination against illegitimate children occasioned by the law was not "unreasonable", in light of the objective of fostering respect for the legitimate children of spouses married by law, and thus respect for the institution of marriage itself, while nonetheless affording illegitimate children with some level of protection.[100]

Six Justices joined in two very strong dissenting opinions. Again, elements of what we have discussed here as being essential to an equality rights analysis were reflected in the dissenting judges' reasons. The

98 *Tokyo Metropolitan Government* case, *supra*, note 68, dissenting opinions of Justices Takii and Izumi.

99 Supreme Court Judgement, Grand Bench, 5 July 1995 (*Illegitimate Child Inheritance* case). The provision of the *Civil Code* in question was article 900.

100 Ibid., reasons of majority, sections 2 and 3.

opinion of five of the dissenting judges inquired into the nature of the discrimination in relation to the dignity of the individual, emphasizing that the equal status of the child as an individual ought to be stressed over his or her status as an outsider to the marital family. Moreover, they pointed out that the status of the person as being illegitimate is an immutable characteristic, beyond the control of the person to change, but having been within the power of the deceased to have altered—in other words the law stigmatized persons who had no control over the issue for the alleged purpose of encouraging respect for the institution of marriage. In their view, there was thus not even a rational connection between the objective and the means of the provision.[101]

Moreover, in addition to focusing on the nature of the discrimination and the harm that it caused, particularly in terms of perpetuating the social stigma of illegitimacy and fostering further private discrimination against those born out of wedlock, both dissenting opinions attempted to establish a standard of "higher reasonableness". Justice Ozaki argued that such a test for "higher reasonableness" should require that "the level of reasonableness or necessity of the purpose of the legislation itself on the one hand, and the nature, content, and extent of the rights or legal value which is to be restrained by discrimination on the other hand should be fully considered, and whether there is a substantial link between them both should be determined."[102]

There are, therefore, attempts even at the level of the Supreme Court to develop the test for discrimination in a manner that better incorporates the fundamental elements of equality rights analysis, and to make it more consistent with the values of the Constitution. How are we to assess these developments? Is it a basis for the optimistic view that momentum is building towards a majority decision that will establish a new analytical approach to discrimination claims? I think that it is too difficult to say at this stage. After all, Justice Tanaka's dissent in the *Patricide* case was similarly strong and well reasoned, and yet it did not become the basis for any significant change. It is not yet possible to argue that there is a trend or an evolution in progress. But I would argue that there is reason to believe that, as the number of such judgements increase, and if they increasingly incorporate a

[101] Ibid., dissenting reasons of Justices Nakajima, Ono, Takahashi, Ozaki, and Endo, at section 2 and 3.

[102] Ibid., reasons of Justice Ozaki, section 1.

more sophisticated analytical framework that establishes a rigorous logic for the test to be applied to discrimination issues, the "reasonable discrimination" test has to come under pressure, and the influence of these judgements should increase. Moreover, that pressure and influence may not only operate at the level of individual judges, but may begin to have some traction with the Secretariat of the Supreme Court, which all agree is the single greatest influence over the thinking and conduct of the judiciary.[103] For the continued use of the "reasonable discrimination" test in the face of increased equality rights litigation may run counter to government policy for the ageing society, and will give rise to mounting social and institutional costs, issues to which the Secretariat may well be sensitive.

Indeed, in discussing why the legal test matters, the social cost of continuing to employ the test should not be underestimated. If, as has been argued in this article, there are indeed increased claims of discrimination as society ages in the coming decades, the issue of discrimination and how the courts deal with it will assume much higher visibility over time. If the courts continue to routinely dismiss the mounting claims of discrimination on the grounds that such treatment is reasonable, then it is likely that there will be increased resentment and bitterness among the vulnerable groups from which the claims arise. Such bitterness and sense of social injustice can lead to social conflict and anti-social behaviour. The riot in Los Angeles following the Rodney King trial is only an extreme example of how the sense of injustice and powerlessness in the face of perceived systemic failure by the justice system to recognize persecution can manifest itself in destructive ways. Finally, there are potential political costs to Japan as a state with growing leadership ambitions in the international arena, and particularly within the U.N., to having increasing complaints of fundamental human rights issues being apparently ignored by its judiciary.

In addition to the social and political costs that such tensions could have, there are possible economic costs to continued routine denial of the right to be treated equally. As discussed earlier, the government has identified increased employment of women, the elderly, and foreigners as being necessary for the continued economic growth of Japan. To

---

[103] Ramsayer and Haley, for example, while they disagree fundamentally on the political independence of the judiciary, agree that individual judges are heavily influenced by the administrative control of the Secretariat. See Ramsayer, Haley, and Upham, *supra* note 95.

the extent that members of those three groups are discouraged from participating in the labour market, because of the perception of systemic discrimination and the refusal of the courts to address the issue, there will be real costs to the economy.

Finally, there could very well be significant institutional costs to the courts caused by their continuing to employ the simplistic and arguably unfair "reasonable discrimination" test in denying increasing numbers of discrimination claims. Again, as the manner in which courts deal with such claims gain increased visibility as the number of claims grow, it is reasonable to expect that the reasoning of the courts will also come under increased scrutiny, even in the mainstream media.[104] While foreigners currently only comprise 2 per cent of the population, and so may not garner much sympathy from the rest of society, women and the elderly together constitute a large majority of the population. It is not unreasonable to speculate that the reasoning of the courts in denying the equality rights claims of women and the elderly may come under increasing criticism. The credibility and legitimacy of the courts could very well be eroded if they continue to dismiss in a cavalier fashion claims of discrimination on the simplistic grounds that the discrimination is reasonable in light of the reasons for it. Maintaining the public trust of the courts has been identified as a high priority for the Secretariat of the Supreme Court.[105]

If a more sophisticated and rigorous analytical model had been applied in the cases discussed in this article, the treatment would not necessarily have been found to be discriminatory or held to be unjustifiable in all of them. But the results would certainly have been different in some of them. Moreover, the judgements of the courts would have been more credible, more just, and more consistent with the values of the Constitution. How the judicial system responds to the tensions around equality rights in the ageing society will be important, not only in terms of how significant and disruptive those tensions may become, but also with respect to how Japan's legal system itself develops in the coming decades. The coming era may be seen as providing the courts with an opportunity to make a significant contribution to how Japan responds as a democratic society to the challenges of the ageing

---

[104] *Tokyo Metropolitan Government* case, for instance, received considerable press coverage, and a great deal of academic scrutiny.

[105] See Upham, *supra* note 95.

of society. If the courts can rise to the opportunity and develop a discrimination analysis that is more rigorous and just, then not only will the courts ease the tensions in an increasingly diverse society, but equality rights may finally come of age in Japan.

CHAPTER TWENTY-THREE

# COMING TO TERMS WITH AGE: SOME LINGUISTIC CONSEQUENCES OF POPULATION AGEING

Peter Backhaus

## 1. Introduction*

Chronological age is an important measurement in human development. Counting the years of life since birth is the commonest and apparently most objective way to determine an individual's age throughout the life span. Accordingly, people are teenagers or centenaries, 18 or 80, in their early thirties or well beyond 40. It is chronological age that legally determines when we reach school age, majority, and the age of retirement. This being said, however, it is also clear that age to an individual means more than just accumulating years of life like the annual rings in a tree trunk. Age is an important sociocultural variable as well. Who and what is considered to be old differs from individual to individual and from one society to the next.

What does it mean to be old, then? According to a German saying, old is what everybody wants to become but no one wants to be. In other words, while the dramatic rise in life expectancy in most modern societies is considered a great feat, the individuals of these societies share a general dislike of being old themselves. Japan, where the mean age rose from around 27 years in the 1920s to over 42 years in 2005, is one of the best examples for this development. While the average life expectancy back in the 1920s was around 45 years for both sexes, it today stands at 78 years for men and 85 years for women, respectively (IPSS 2005: 30, 80). This makes Japan the country with the oldest population worldwide, the so-called *chōju taikoku Nippon* ['long-life country Japan'].

As a society gets older and older, it is to be expected that its conceptions of what it means to be old get reconsidered. These conceptions are communicated through language. They are no fixed entities, but subject to negotiation and renegotiation by linguistic expression. As such they are subject to change. The basic question to be dealt with in this paper is in how far population ageing influences the linguistic encoding of age in Japan. To this end, three recent examples of change in the Japanese lexicon of age are discussed: (1) the reduced use of fictive kinship terms when talking to the elderly, (2) the emergence of some newly coined expressions to refer to the elderly, and (3) the official promotion of a new term for 'dementia'. The general relationship between population ageing and the linguistic encoding of age will be reflected on in the concluding section. We start with a brief general introduction to the Japanese lexicon of age.

## 2. Age in Japanese: Some General Observations

Japanese is known as a strongly socially encoded language that provides a rich formal repertoire for the expression of variables such as the interactants' relative status, sex, and age. Age relationships play an important part in everyday linguistic interaction in Japan and are assessed by both chronological and institutional age. The former refers to one's years of life, the latter is determined on the basis of the length of time one belongs to an institution. In most forms of social organization the seniority principle provides the basic frame of reference. It is usually taken for granted that one chooses a different vocabulary towards people of higher age than towards one's peers or people younger than oneself (Coulmas 2005: 59f).

One particularly age-indexical word field are kinship terms. Compared to most Western languages, the Japanese lexicon is rather fine-tuned when it comes to the expression of age differences within the family. For instance, apart from the non-age indexical terms *musume* [daughter] and *musuko* [son] there are special expressions to distinguish between first and second born children. The former are referred to as *chōjo* [firstborn daughter] and *chōnan* [firstborn son], while the latter are called *jijo* [second daughter] and *jinan* [second son], respectively. This distinction is not without relevance, since the firstborn son in Japan has traditionally inherited the family estate and therefore been expected to live with and take care of his parents in their later life.

Another lexical distinction within the Japanese family is between older sister (*ane*) and younger sister (*imōto*), and between older brother (*ani*) and younger brother (*otōto*). Noteworthy in the case of these two pairs is that a 'neutral', that is, non-age indexical term like the English *brother* or *sister* doesn't exist in Japanese. In other words, the age rela-

Table 1. Age-indexical kinship terms in Japanese.

| Japanese | Reading | English |
|---|---|---|
| 長女 | *chōjo* | first daughter |
| 長男 | *chōnan* | first son |
| 次女 | *jijo* | second daughter |
| 次男 | *jinan* | second son |
| 姉 | *ane* | older sister |
| 兄 | *ani* | older brother |
| 妹 | *imōto* | younger sister |
| 弟 | *otōto* | younger brother |

tionship is no supplementary information which may be omitted where considered unnecessary, but it is simply impossible to not make an age-based distinction when talking about brothers and sisters. The terms discussed are given in table 1.

One noteworthy aspect of Japanese kinship terms is their use in situations where they do not correctly reflect the relationship between two family members. The basic principle is that older family members adapt their use of kinship terms to the youngest member's perspective. Thus, husband and wife may refer to each other and themselves as *okāsan* [mother] and *otōsan* [father] and address their children as *onēsan* [older sister] and *onīsan* [older brother], respectively (see Carroll 2006: 114). This 'fictive' use of kinship terms can even be expanded to situations where no real kinship relationship applies at all. Consequently, it is common to address non-kin and even unknown children as *onēsan* and *onīsan*, and use terms like *okusan* [wife] and *goshujin* [husband], *okāsan* [mother] and *otōsan* [father], or *obasan* [aunt] and *ojisan* [uncle] towards non-relative adults up to a certain age. When addressing non-kin persons of higher age, *obāsan* [grandmother] and *ojīsan* [grandfather] serve as fictive kinship terms. This practice will be discussed in more detail below.

While language provides various ways of expressing the high prestige of age in a given society, it also has the potential to do just the opposite. It has frequently been observed that terms related to higher age show a tendency to be negative or even derogatory. This tendency, which is discernible in many languages, has been referred to as 'ageism' or 'ageist language' (Wilkinson and Ferraro 2002). As Nuessel (1982) has pointed out, 'the language used to depict the elderly is overwhelmingly negative in its scope.' Focusing on dictionary entries and the characterisation of elderly people in the mass media, Thimm (2000: 49–73) has examined this tendency with regard to German. Her analysis reveals that the term *alt* (old) in German dictionaries over the years has acquired increasingly negative connotations. Thimm also identifies various derogatory expressions about the elderly which of late have gained some currency in everyday language.

Similar tendencies have been identified in Japanese, too. Usami and Yoshioka (2004: 34–37) discuss various terms and expressions referring to elderly people with an unambiguously negative connotation. An example is the phrase *toshiyori kusai* [lit.: 'smelling of old age'] used to derogatively describe behaviour considered typical of older adults. Other stereotyping and role-enforcing expressions are *toshigai mo nai* [lit.: 'unworthy of one's age'], *toshiyori no kuse ni* [lit.: 'despite being old'] or *toshiyori no hiyamizu* [lit.: 'the elderly's cold water'], referring to behaviour considered unbecoming of old age. Particularly prominent are discriminatory terms towards elderly women such as *rōba* and *rōjo* ['old bag'], which, like in many other languages, have no direct male equivalents. Both terms contain the morpheme *rō* [old], to which we will come back in section 4.

In summary, it can be said that Japanese is a language with a particularly rich vocabulary to represent age-related characteristics. While seniority plays an important part in linguistically expressing social relationships, the Japanese lexicon also contains expressions conveying a negative, derogatory, and stereotypical image of people of higher age. As the examples below will show, this is of some relevance with regard to Japan's recent demographic developments.

## 3. 'I'm not your Grandma': Addressing the Elderly

As discussed in the previous section, it has been considered common practice to address unacquainted older adults as *obāsan* [grandmother] and *ojīsan* [grandfather] or even attach the diminutive ending *-chan*, which is normally used towards younger children and expresses a sense of intimacy. That this is not necessarily perceived of as an appropriate way of speaking is demonstrated by regular complaints in letters to the editor in which elderly people throughout Japan express their resentment at being called this way. Here are a few examples from the past two decades:

A 68 year old woman from Yamanashi Prefecture describes how she was so infuriated when being called *obāsan* by an unknown man asking her the way that she deliberately gave him wrong directions, in the pouring rain (*Asahi Shinbun* 22 September 1991: 17); a 73 year old woman from Kobe felt hurt by being addressed as *obāchan* in public by a woman of about the same age who wanted to compliment her on the dress she was wearing (*Yomiuri Shinbun* 25 September 1997: 14); a 77 year old man from Fukuoka Prefecture protests against him and his wife regularly being called *ojīchan* and *obāchan* at the medicine counter of their local hospital (*Yomiuri Shinbun* 11 August 1999: 18); a 38 year old woman from Hyogo Prefecture complains that her mother, who is just recovering from a stroke, now frequently is called *obāchan* by strangers in public (*Asahi Shinbun* 14 July 2002: 36); and a 71 year old woman from Okayama Prefecture describes her embarrassment when being offered a seat in the train by two middle-aged women calling her *obāchan* (*Asahi Shinbun* 4 October 2005: 34).

Another frequent target of criticism expressed in letters to the editor is the use of *obāchan* and *ojīchan* towards elderly people interviewed on TV (e.g., *Asahi Shinbun* 26 April 1988: 4; *Mainichi Shinbun* 28 April 1998: 4; *Yomiuri Shinbun* 2 July 1997: 20). Back in 1987, the national broadcasting corporation NHK in an issue of their monthly report on broadcast research had warned that *obāchan* and *ojīchan* in interviews with elderly people should be used with great care. It was held that though the terms might be intended to create a warm atmosphere, they were prone to be felt offensive by the persons spoken to (NHK 1987: 64). This stance has been repeated in various subsequent NHK publications (e.g., NHK 1990: 66f; NHK 2005: 216).

Another problem is the fictive use of kinship terms in institutional settings like hospitals and caring facilities. Drawing on personal experience, Ogasawara (1999) gives the following account of the situation:

> Until about ten years ago it was common practice both in nursing homes for the elderly and in ordinary hospitals to call elderly people *obāchan* and *ojīchan*. Thus, my late father when being called *ojīchan* by the nurses in hospital told me with a bitter smile: 'It seems I'm [their] granny'. It is said that in hospitals this way of address has finally been discontinued and people are now instructed to use the surname of their patients. In home care services for the elderly, however, *ojīchan* and *obāchan* are still very common.

The fictive use of kinship terms in the care sector has recently also attracted the attention of Japanese sociolinguists. Usami and Endō (1997: 66) criticize this way of address as an expression of unequal power relationships between older and younger adults. They hold that a phrase like *Ojīchan, onetsu hakarimashō* ['Now let's take gran's temperature'] is an unacceptable and yet widespread way of speaking to the elderly. Though there may be people who consider the fictive use of kinship terms an expression of intimacy, Usami (1997: 61) stresses that it is clearly a top-down type of intimacy rather than the articulation of closeness between equals.

A look at recent guidelines and manuals about communication with the elderly in the care sector suggests that there is a growing awareness that the fictive use of kinship terms is inappropriate. One of four basic principles given in *Kōreisha kea no manā to kotobazukai* [Manners and language usage in caring for the elderly] (Nishiguchi 2003: 3), for instance, stipulates that the relationship between caregiver and care recipient is of a professional nature and not one between family members. Therefore, it is emphasized, intimate or child language is inappropriate. A similar point is made in a care manual called *Kōreisha to no komyunikēshon sukiru* [Skills for communication with the elderly] (Tanaka 2001: 106):

> Addressing elderly people one meets for the first time as *ojīsan* or *obāsan*, one may be retorted: 'My name is So-and-so. I'm not your grandma (or grandpa)'... A term of address that carries an image of old age may be disgraceful to the elderly. It is not appropriate for use in the professional care sector.

Two things become obvious from the examples discussed. One is that the fictive use of kinship terms towards the elderly still seems to be a widespread phenomenon; otherwise there would be no need to criticize and regulate this practice in the first place. On the other hand, it can also be seen that explicit attempts are being made to eradicate these terms from the mass media, the care sector, and other arenas of public life.

## 4. From Seniority to Senility: Terms Referring to the Elderly

One of the Japanese key expressions with regard to ageing and age is the term *rōjin*. It refers to both female and male single persons of higher age, but also is a common expression to denote the elderly in general. Morphologically speaking, *rōjin* is a compound of the two morphemes *rō* [ageing, old age] and *jin* [man, human]. While the latter is a semantically neutral concept, *rō* has both positive and negative connotations. On one hand, it is associated with properties like wisdom, experience and maturity, as reflected in terms like *rōkai* [crafty, astute,

Table 2. Compounds containing the morpheme *rō* [old].

| Japanese | Reading | English | Connotation |
|---|---|---|---|
| 老獪 | *rōkai* | crafty, astute, wily | positive |
| 老巧 | *rōkō* | veteran, experienced | positive |
| 老成 | *rōsei* | mature, experienced | positive |
| 老練 | *rōren* | experienced, skilled | positive |
| 老眼 | *rōgan* | farsightedness | negative |
| 老弱 | *rōjaku* | infirmity with age | negative |
| 老朽 | *rōkyū* | decrepitude | negative |
| 老衰 | *rōsui* | senility | negative |

wily], *rōkō* [veteran, experienced], *rōsei* [mature, experienced], and *rōren* [experienced, skilled]. On the other hand, *rō* is also associated with the weaknesses and frailties of old age, such as in *rōgan* [farsightedness], *rōjaku* [infirmity with age], *rōkyū* [decrepitude], and *rōsui* [senility]. The two groups of expressions are juxtaposed in Table 2.

Given the above two connotations of the morpheme *rō*, the term *rōjin* in principle can be interpreted in both positive and negative ways. Recently, however, the negative associations seem to prevail. According to Usami (1999: 86), the term is now mostly used in contexts like *netakiri rōjin* [bedridden old person] or *hitorigurashi no sabishii rōjin* [old lonely person living on her/his own]. Another highly negatively connoted expression is the derogatory but commonly used term for senility, *rōjin boke*. As a result of the semantic shift from seniority to senility, *rōjin* came to be associated mainly with the burdens of ageing and age rather than with its positive facets.

With the use of *rōjin* getting increasingly problematic, various terminological alternatives have shown up to replace it. The most common option is *kōreisha*. It literally means 'person(s) of high age' but so far has retained a much more neutral image than *rōjin*. As will be seen below, it is now the default choice when talking about the elderly. Another frequent option is the term *toshiyori* [lit.: 'higher in age'], often used with the respectful prefix *o-* attached.

In addition, various neologisms have been created. Two such expressions are *jukunen* and *jitsunen*. The former literally means 'maturity years' and according to the widely used *Kōjien* Dictionary first gained currency in the second half of the 1970s (Shinmura 1998: 1229). Supposed to refer to the pre-*rōjin* years, it has much more positive connotations than *rōjin*. *Jitsunen* literally means 'true years' and is a more recent coinage. It was introduced by the Ministry of Health and Welfare in 1985 in order to refer to people between 50 and 70. Though *jitsunen* has been a *Kōjien* entry since the dictionary's fourth edition in 1991 (Shinmura 1991: 1153), it is commonly held that the term failed to take root in everyday language (e.g., *Asahi Shinbun* 14 September 2003: 33; *Yomiuri Shinbun* 22 June 1987: 2).

Another common strategy to refer to the elderly is relying on English loans. Two widely used expressions are *shirubā* [derived from English 'silver'] and *shinia* [English 'senior']. *Shirubā*, a metonymic euphemism based on what is supposed to be the colour of elderly people's hair, has become particularly common in welfare terminology. The *Shakai fukushi kihon yōgoshū* [Basic glossary of social welfare] (Kawamura 2004) contains the following entries: *shirubā sābisu* ['silver service'] and *shirubā sābisu shinkōkai* [association to promote 'silver services'], *shirubā jinzai sentā* [employment centre for retired persons], *shirubā haujingu* ['silver housing'], *shirubā bijinesu* ['silver business'], *shirubā hyakutōban* [support centre for the elderly], and *shirubā māku* [a 'silver mark' indicating cars driven by the elderly]. Another popular term is *shirubā shīto* ['silver seat'], a seat reserved for the elderly in buses and trains. It has been a *Kōjien* entry since the dictionary's third edition of 1983 (Shinmura 1983: 1227).

Due to its high prominence in welfare-related terminology, the term *shirubā* has experienced a semantic narrowing that makes its usage in other contexts problematic. Therefore, when referring to the elderly in more general terms, the loan *shinia* is usually preferred. Its morphological productivity allows for expressions like *shinia-tachi* ('seniors'), *shinia-sō* ('senior layers'), and *shinia-sedai* ('senior generation'). It is particularly popular in the commercial domain (see *Senden Kaigi* 1998). Table 3 provides a list of the terms discussed.

Another domain where the growing dislike of the term *rōjin* has become manifest is the print media. As Higuchi (1997) has remarked, *rōjin* in the newspapers in recent years has increasingly been replaced by *kōreisha* or (*o*)*toshiyori*. The quantitative validity of this assessment can be tested by taking a closer look at three major Japanese papers. An electronic full text survey of *Asahi*, *Mainichi*, and *Yomiuri Shinbun* shows that into the late 1990s, *rōjin* was used more frequently than *kōreisha*. It was not before 2000 that *kōreisha* surpassed *rōjin* in frequency to become the more common of the two terms ever since.

Table 4 gives the hits for the two terms in the three papers since 1990. It also includes the five other expressions discussed so far. The overall increase for virtually all terms throughout the 1990s reflects growing attention given to problems of ageing and age in general, which only

Table 3. Terms referring to the elderly.

| Japanese | Reading | English |
|---|---|---|
| 老人 | *rōjin* | elderly woman/man; the elderly |
| 高齢者 | *kōreisha* | lit.: person(s) of high age |
| (お)年寄り | *(o)toshiyori* | lit.: higher in age |
| 熟年 | *jukunen* | lit.: 'maturity years' |
| 実年 | *jitsunen* | lit.: 'real years' |
| シルバー | *shirubā* | 'silver' |
| シニア | *shinia* | 'senior' |

Table 4. Terms referring to the elderly: Hits in three major Japanese newspapers.

| Year | *rōjin* | *kōreisha* | *toshiyori* | *jukunen* | *jitsunen* | *shirubā* | *shinia* |
|---|---|---|---|---|---|---|---|
| 1990 | 5,262 | 3,017 | 3,664 | 152 | 106 | 1,733 | 369 |
| 1992 | 7,118 | 4,649 | 4,821 | 194 | 51 | 818 | 530 |
| 1994 | 7,175 | 5,961 | 6,246 | 267 | 74 | 906 | 799 |
| 1996 | 10,888 | 9,717 | 8,963 | 403 | 88 | 1,260 | 1,024 |
| 1998 | 11,944 | 10,403 | 9,800 | 519 | 76 | 1,290 | 1,153 |
| 2000 | 16,056 | 20,064 | 16,279 | 492 | 105 | 1,876 | 1,731 |
| 2002 | 13,441 | 15,940 | 12,058 | 444 | 134 | 1,879 | 2,397 |
| 2004 | 12,300 | 16,811 | 11,851 | 403 | 145 | 1,856 | 2,730 |

Source: *Asahi Shinbun, Mainichi Shinbun, Yomiuri Shinbun.*
Data base: Nikkei Telekom 21.

recently seems to have slightly weakened. The data also indicate that the two indigenous neologisms *jukunen* and especially *jitsunen* failed to become established terms, whereas the English-based *shirubā* and *shinia* have gained some currency in the print media. Use of the latter, in particular, shows a remarkable increase since the early 1990s.

The problem of how to properly refer to old age also becomes manifest with regard to recurring name changes of the national holiday dedicated to Japan's elderly. On 15 September 1947, a small town in Hyogo Prefecture first celebrated a day for the elderly, then called *otoshiyori no hi* [lit.: 'Day of those higher in age']. In the following years similar festivities were held in other communities throughout Japan until in 1963, September 15 was officially determined as *rōjin no hi* ['Day of the elderly']. However, when it became a national holiday in 1966, it was renamed into *keirō no hi* ['Day of respect for old age']. The expression *rōjin no hi* all but disappeared, and few people in Japan know that it has re-entered official terminology since 2001, when *keirō no hi* was moved from 15 September to the third Monday of September in order to create a long weekend. September 15 as the original date was re-designated as *rōjin no hi*, but ceased to be a national holiday unless coinciding with the new *keirō no hi* (*Asahi Shinbun* 15 June 2001: 2; *Asahi Shinbun* 14 September 2005: 37).

A Japanese institution particularly suffering from the negative image of *rōjin* are local clubs for the elderly, commonly known as *rōjin kurabu*. Between 1980 and 1996, their members dropped from 51% to 34% of the 60+ population nationwide. Conspicuous within this general trend is a high proportional decrease of members younger than 70. The main reason for this development is assumed to be that many people in their 60s do not want to see themselves as *rōjin* and either refrain from joining their local *rōjin* club or postpone entry to a later date. In order to counter this trend, various renaming initiatives have been going on. For instance, a *rōjin* club in Okayama Prefecture introduced a *toripuru hatachi kinen shikiten* ['triple-twenty ceremony']; a *Gold Egg Club* was founded in Osaka to attract younger members; and the *rōjin* club alliance of Kanagawa Prefecture reinvented itself as *Yume Kurabu Kanagawa* ['Dream Club Kanagawa'] (*Asahi Shinbun* 24 February 1997: 6; *Asahi Shinbun* 10 March 1997: 1; *Mainichi Shinbun* 30 October 1994: 19).

As the above initiatives suggest, the main problem with *rōjin* is not the term itself but the age of the reference group it denotes. In other words, what age is the beginning of *rōjin* age? The Hakuhodo Institute of Life and Living has asked 1,650 elderly people in the Tokyo metropolitan region about this (HILL 1996: 218). The two consecutive surveys of 1986 and 1996 clearly show that the beginning of the *rōjin* age is on the rise. As can be seen in Table 5, most of the subjects think that it is not before the early 70s that one starts to be *rōjin*. The period most frequently identified in both surveys is the 70 to 74 age bracket, with 49% in 1986 and 41% ten years later. A direct comparison of the two surveys reveals that the rate of people locating the coming of the *rōjin* age below 75 is dropping, while people who consider it to start later than that—particularly between 75 and 79, and even 80 and 85—are growing in number. Overall, the mean entrance age to the *rōjin* age rose by more than two years between the two surveys, from 71.5 years in 1986 to 73.6 years in 1996. It is not far-fetched to consider this development a by-product of Japan's recent demographic developments. With life expectancy on the rise, entry into old age is postponed.

Table 5. 'At what age starts the *rōjin* age?' 1986 vs. 1996.

| Age | 1986 | 1996 |
|---|---|---|
| 40–59 | 0.2% | 0.2% |
| 60–64 | 5.4% | 2.5% |
| 65–69 | 11.6% | 6.3% |
| 70–74 | 49.0% | 41.3% |
| 75–79 | 13.4% | 19.7% |
| 80–84 | 15.4% | 27.2% |
| 85–89 | 0.7% | 1.3% |
| 90+ | 1.1% | 1.5% |
| Mean/years | 71.46 | 73.64 |

Source: HILL 1996: 218.

## 5. *Chihō* vs. *Ninchishō*: In Search of Non-Discriminatory Language

A third noteworthy change in the Japanese lexicon of age concerns the word for dementia. The common expression in both everyday language and medical nomenclature used to be *chihō*. Like *dementia*, a Latin-derived term literally meaning 'out of one's mind', *chihō* has a rather unsavoury etymological origin. The word consists of the two morphemes *chi* and *hō*, each of which has highly negative connotations. The meaning of *chi* is 'stupid' or 'crazy', as in compounds like *chijin* [idiot, fool] or *hakuchi* [mentally retarded]. It is also contained in the frequently used *chikan*, a man groping women in crowded trains and other public places. The concept of *hō* is no better. Contained in compounds like *bōzen* [blank surprise, bewilderment] and *akke* [blankness, bafflement], it refers to a state of absent-mindedness or confusion. It is best-known as a component in the term *ahō*, which means 'idiot' or 'fool'. The terms discussed are enlisted in Table 6.

In April 2004, the directors of the three national research centres on dementia formally submitted a note to the Minister of Health, Labour and Welfare[1] which requested that use of the term *chihō* be reconsidered. Acknowledging that any other name for this disease would eventually acquire a negative connotation as well, it was emphasized that it would still be desirable to adopt a term with a less problematic etymology.

[1] The Ministry of Health, Labour and Welfare (*Kōsei Rōdōshō*) was created in 2001. It is a merger of the former Ministry of Health and Welfare (*Kōseishō*) and the former Ministry of Labour (*Rōdōshō*).

Table 6. Compounds containing *chi* and *hō*.

| Japanese | Reading | English |
|---|---|---|
| 痴人 | *chijin* | idiot, fool |
| 白痴 | *hakuchi* | mentally retarded person |
| 痴漢 | *chikan* | pervert, molester of women |
| 痴呆 | *chihō* | dementia |
| 呆然 | *bōzen* | blank surprise, bewilderment |
| 呆気 | *akke* | blankness, bafflement |
| 阿呆 | *ahō* | idiot, fool |

The Minister accepted the request and subsequently entrusted a commission with finding a new name. They took up work in June 2004 and by the end of the same year issued a summary report about the renaming of the disease (*Asahi Shinbun* 20 April 2004: 37; *Asahi Shinbun* 25 December 2004: 3; *Asahi Shinbun* 27 December 2004: 9).

The document, titled *'"Chihō" ni kawaru yōgo ni kansuru kentōkai' hōkokusho* [Report by the 'commission for renaming *chihō*'], was published on the ministry's homepage on 24 December 2004 (MHLW 2004, Internet). It outlines the three basic problems of the term *chihō* as follows: It is (1) discriminatory on account of its etymology; (2) conveys a misleading view of dementia and the rising number of dementia patients nationwide; and (3) evokes feelings of fear and shamefulness that are counter-productive to adequately dealing with the problem. The report stresses that many people today refuse to acknowledge suffering from senile dementia, thus delaying timely counter-measures that would abate or retard its progress. According to the commission report, this is largely due to the term's negative connotation.

The historical development of *chihō* as outlined in the report shows that the term was already sporadically in use in medical studies of the late Edo era (1603–1867). It remained one of various concurring expressions until the end of Meiji (1868–1912), when it had finally superseded all alternative expressions in medical nomenclature. Around the same time, *chihō* also entered everyday speech in the sense of 'idiot' or 'fool'. The first edition of the *Kōjien* Dictionary, published in 1955, gives both the popular and the technical meanings of *chihō* (Shinmura 1955). However, the former soon became obsolete and is no longer mentioned in the *Kōjien*'s second edition (Shinmura 1969). *Chihō* as a technical term gained wider currency in official language in the late 1970s. This is testified by the foundation of a *Chihōsei rōjin taisaku honbu* [*chihō* head office] within the Ministry of Health and Welfare in 1986 and the mentioning of *chihō* in various subsequent laws and ordinances (MHLW 2004, Internet).

As described in the report, the renaming commission drew up a list of six possible alternatives to replace *chihō*: (1) *ninchi shōgai* [lit.: 'recognition impediment'], (2) *ninchishō* ['recognition disease'], (3) *monowasure shō* ['forget-things disease'], (4) *kioku shō* ['memory disease'], (5) *kioku shōgai* ['memory impediment'], and (6) *arutsuhaimā* (*shō*) [Alzheimer('s disease)]. After the list had been widely publicized, a public opinion poll with over 6,000 votes cast showed that the most favoured term among the six suggestions was *ninchi shōgai*, with 22.6% of the votes. It was followed by *ninchishō* (18.4%), *kioku shōgai* (13.6%), *arutsuhaimā* (*shō*) (11.4%), *monowasure shō* (11.3%), and *kioku shō* (7.5%). The problem with the highest-ranked *ninchi shōgai* was that the term had already been in use in the field of psychiatry, albeit with a separate meaning. It was to be expected that this would create confusion and might eventually impede the new term's spread in medical nomenclature. It was therefore decided that the second-ranked *ninchishō* should become the new term for dementia (MHLW 2004, Internet).

The report emphasizes that the new term should be adopted in official terminology as soon as possible and be disseminated through large-scale PR campaigns throughout the following year. As another look at the three papers *Asahi*, *Mainichi* and *Yomiuri Shinbun* shows, these efforts have not been fruitless. Before 2005, *chihō* is the common term in the print media, with hits rising from 1,126 in 2000 to 1,730 in 2004. *Ninchishō* is only sporadically mentioned. Things change dramatically in the following year, when hits for *chihō* drop to little above 1,000, whereas the frequency of *ninchishō* explodes from former 494 hits in 2004 to 2,356 hits in 2005. The figures are given in Table 7.

In general, the efforts to remove the discriminatory term *chihō* from the lexicon of age suggests a rise in consciousness of problems related to ageing and age—at a time when these problems have started to concern an ever increasing part of the population.

## 6. Conclusions

The changes in the Japanese lexicon of age as discussed in this paper have been brought about by the general difficulties of how to properly refer to age and age-related concepts. Motivations underlying these

Table 7. Old and new term for dementia in three major Japanese newspapers.

| Year | *chihō* (痴呆) | *ninchishō* (認知症) |
|---|---|---|
| 2000 | 1,126 | 398 |
| 2001 | 1,238 | 505 |
| 2002 | 1,412 | 443 |
| 2003 | 1,699 | 536 |
| 2004 | 1,730 | 494 |
| 2005 | 1,027 | 2,356 |

Source: *Asahi Shinbun*, *Mainichi Shinbun*, *Yomiuri Shinbun*.
Data base: Nikkei Telekom 21.

changes can be summarized as (1) semiotic and (2) social in nature. The basic problem is that age and age-related concepts in many societies tend to have a negative, taboo-like image. Where that is the case, alternative terminology is introduced in order to express the same concept in a less straightforward manner. In the present context this is exemplified by the great variety of expressions used to avoid the term *rōjin* [old], which we have discussed in section 4.

The semiotic problem with all taboo-related terms is that whatever alternative expression one chooses, frequent use of the new term will result in a loss of euphemistic potential. Eventually, the new term will end up being as negatively connoted as the old one used to be. This development has been anticipated by the commission entrusted with the coinage of a new term for *chihō* [dementia] as discussed in section 5 above. As mentioned in the commission report, it would be naïve to believe that a new term would not eventually assume a negative connotation as well.

The social motivation for the recent changes in the Japanese lexicon of age is the country's demographic development. Particularly two trends seem to have an impact on how the meaning of age is communicated today. Firstly, as discussed in section 1, life expectancy has been constantly on the rise. At the beginning of the last century, most people in Japan did not live to see their 50th birthday. Being old under such circumstances necessarily meant something different than it does today, when people commonly turn 60, 70, 80, and older. People's aversion to being considered to belong to the *rōjin* population reflects this impact of the demographic development on the lexicon of age.

Secondly, Japan's demographic transition does not only involve a rise in life expectancy, but also a shift in proportions between the age groups. As a recent survey by the Ministry of Internal Affairs and Communications reveals, Japanese aged 65 or older topped 20% for the first time in fiscal 2005 (*Mainichi Shinbun* 5 August 2006: 2). With this part of the population increasingly gaining demographic weight, it is felt necessary to reconsider the way these people are being talked to and about. Both the official initiatives of discarding the derogatory term *chihō* [dementia] and an increased consciousness of the inappropriateness of the fictive use of kinship terms towards the elderly testify to this development.

The recent changes in the Japanese lexicon of age thus reflect a combination of universal tendencies of language change and specific socio-demographic circumstances. It is not entirely clear whether the instances discussed must be attributed to the greying of Japan or whether they would occur under different demographic circumstances as well. However, the developments we are presently observing, their overall scope, and the planned nature of certain changes suggest that the relationship between population ageing and the linguistic encoding of age is a field of growing interest both to sociolinguists and students of ageing societies.

* I would like to thank Takehiro Shioda (NHK Broadcasting Culture Research Institute) for his kind support with literature research for this project.

## References

*Asahi Shinbun* (26 April 1988): Obāchan to yobanaide [Don't call me *obāchan*], p. 4, morning edition.

—— (22 September 1991): 'Obāchan' to kiyasuku yobuna [Don't easily say *obāchan*], p. 17, morning edition.

—— (24 February 1997): Rōjin kurabu 'wakate' tsunoru [Elderly people's clubs recruiting the 'young'], p. 6, morning edition (Nagoya).

—— (10 March 1997): Rōjin kurabu [Elderly people's clubs], p. 1, evening edition.

—— (15 June 2001): Kaisei shukujitsuhō ga seiritsu [Revised public holiday law enacted], p. 2, evening edition.

—— (14 July 2002): Obāchan no yobikata kaete [Change the *obāchan* address], p. 36, morning edition (Osaka).

—— (14 September 2003): 'Otoshiyori' ni nayamu [In trouble with *otoshiyori*], p. 33, morning edition (Yamagata).

—— (20 April 2004): 'Chihō' to yobanaide [Don't call it *chihō*], p. 37, morning edition.

—— (25 December 2004): 'Chihō', 'ninchishō' ni kaishō [*Chihō* renamed into *ninchishō*], p. 3, morning edition.

—— (27 December 2004): 'Chihō' kara 'ninchishō' [*Chihō* becomes *ninchishō*], p. 9, morning edition.

—— (14 September 2005): Keirō no hi to rōjin no hi? ['Respect Day for the Aged' and 'Day of the Aged'?], p. 37, morning edition.

—— (4 October 2005): Yobikata: Okori shintō da ga gutto korae [Way of address: Infuriated but enduring it], p. 34, morning edition.

Carroll, Tessa (2006): Changing language, gender and family relations in Japan. In: Marcus Rebick and Ayumi Takenaka (eds.): *The Changing Japanese Family*. London and New York: Routledge, pp. 109–129.

Coulmas, Florian (2005): *Sociolinguistics: The Study of Speakers' Choices*. Cambridge: Cambridge University Press.

Higuchi, Keiko (1997): 'Obāchan' ni hisomu doku [The poison hidden in '*obāchan*']. In: *Yomiuri Shinbun*, 12 October, p. 12, morning edition.

HILL (Hakuhodo Institute of Life and Living) (1996): *Shirubā* 10 *nen henka: Seikatsu kizoku e mukau kōreishatachi—Shiryōhen* [Silver 10 years of change: Elderly people on their way to becoming life aristocracy—Data edition]. Tokyo: Hakuhodo Institute of Life and Living.

IPSS (National Institute of Population and Social Security Research) (2005): *Jinkō no dōkō: Nihon to sekai* [Population trends: Japan and the world]. Tokyo: Health and Welfare Statistics Association.

Kawamura, Masayoshi (ed.) (2004): *Shakai fukushi kihon yōgoshū (goteihan)* [Basic glossary of social welfare (Revised fifth edition)]. Kyoto: Minerva.

*Mainichi Shinbun* (30 October 1994): Rōjin wa nansai kara? [From what age on is one 'old'?], p. 19, morning edition.

—— (28 April 1998): Kōreisha e no yobikake ni kikubari o [Attention when addressing the elderly], p. 4, morning edition.

—— (5 August 2006): Jinkō, zennenhi 3505 nin genshō [Population shrinks 3505 people in comparison to previous year], p. 2, morning edition.

MHLW (Ministry of Health, Labour and Welfare) (2004): *'"Chihō" ni kawaru yōgo ni kansuru kentōkai' hōkokusho* [Report by the 'Commission for renaming *chihō*']. http://www.mhlw.go.jp/shingi/2004/12/s1224–17.html (found 8 August 2006).

NHK (Japan Broadcasting Corporation) (1987): *Hōsō kenkyū to chōsa* [The NHK monthly report on broadcast research] 1987, 4. Tokyo: NHK.

—— (1990): *Hōsō kenkyū to chōsa* [The NHK monthly report on broadcast research] 1990, 7. Tokyo: NHK.

—— (2005): NHK *kotoba no handobukku* [NHK Handbook on Language]. Tokyo: NHK Broadcasting Culture Research Institute.

Nishiguchi, Mamoru (ed.) (2003): *Kōreisha kea no manā to kotobazukai* [Manners and language usage in caring for the elderly]. Tokyo: Hitotsubashi Shuppan.

Nuessel, Frank H. (1982): The language of ageism. In: *The Gerontologist* 22, 2, pp. 273–276.

Ogasawara, Kyō (1999): Watashi no rōrō kaigo [My care for the very old]. In: *Mainichi Shinbun*, 13 June, p. 38, morning edition.

*Senden Kaigi* (1998): Gōruden eiji AD: Shinia jidai no kōkoku [Golden age AD: Advertising in the senior age]. In: *Senden Kaigi* 1998, 4, pp. 20–25.

Shinmura, Izuru (ed.) (1955): *Kōjien* (First edition). Tokyo: Iwanami.

—— (1969): *Kōjien* (Second edition). Tokyo: Iwanami.

—— (1983): *Kōjien* (Third edition). Tokyo: Iwanami.

—— (1991): *Kōjien* (Fourth edition). Tokyo: Iwanami.

—— (1998): *Kōjien* (Fifth edition). Tokyo: Iwanami.

Tanaka, Kimiko (2001): *Kōreisha to no komyunikēshon sukiru* [Skills for communication with the elderly]. Tokyo: Chuohoki Shuppan.

Thimm, Caja (2000): *Alter—Sprache—Geschlecht: Sprach- und kommunikationswissenschaftliche Perspektiven auf das höhere Lebensalter*. Frankfurt/Main: Campus.

Usami, Mayumi (1997): Kōreika shakai no komyunikēshon kankyō seibi no tame ni [Providing the communicative environment for the ageing society]. In *Gengo* 26, 13 (315), pp. 60–67.

—— (1999): Kōreisha to no komyunikēshon [Communication with the elderly]. In: Tokyo Metropolitan Institute of Gerontology (ed.): *Otoshiyori no komyunikēshon o kangaeru* [Thinking about communication with the elderly]. Tokyo: Tokyo Metropolitan Institute of Gerontology, pp. 58–91.

Usami, Mayumi and Orie Endō (1997): Kōreisha to gengo: (2) Kōreisha ni taisuru kotoba [Elderly people and language: (2) Language towards the elderly]. In: *Nihongo* 10 (October), pp. 66–71.

Usami, Mayumi and Yasuo Yoshioka (2004): *Kōreisha komyunikētā kōza: Tekisuto* [Lessons for communicators with the elderly: Text]. Tokyo: Nichii Gakkan.

Wilkinson, Jody A. and Kenneth F. Ferraro (2002): Thirty years of ageism research. In: Todd D. Nelson (ed.): *Ageism: Stereotyping and Prejudice against Older Persons*. Cambridge, Massachusetts: MIT Press, pp. 339–358.

*Yomiuri Shinbun* (22 June 1987): Jitsunen wa 'hatarakizakari' [*Jitsunen* in their prime], p. 2, morning edition.

—— (2 July 1997): Kōreisha no yobikata ni hairyo o [Consideration for the way older people are addressed], p. 20, morning edition.

—— (25 September 1997): Jibun ni iya na kotoba, tanin mo onaji [Language one dislikes equally disliked by others], p. 14, morning edition.

—— (11 August 1999): Kōreisha mo namae yonde [Also call elderly people by their name], p. 18, morning edition.

CHAPTER TWENTY-FOUR

# POPULATION AGEING AND LANGUAGE CHANGE

Fumio Inoue

## 1. Introduction

Several problems concerning language and ageing will be discussed in this paper. In Japan before and just after the Second World War, one could see many children and relatively few old people. Nowadays, however, only a few children and many old people (both healthy and infirm) can be seen. This kind of population change, owing to the decline in the number of children and population ageing, often has notable effects on the language. As language is a major means of transmission of culture, population ageing may eventually ensure transmission of culture between different generations, because periods of contact between young and old generations become longer.

However, population ageing in present-day Japan has already reached a sufficient level for this to happen, so the effect is limited. The "law of diminishing marginal utility" in economics is applicable. Furthermore, two social changes inhibit transmission of culture: first, discontinuation between generations because of the predominance of the nuclear family; and second, the increase of information from the mass-media.

The essence of this paper can be summarized as follows. Population ageing is a phenomenon owing to medical and hygienic improvements, but it is reflected as economic and cultural phenomena in contemporary society; its relation to language is a cultural phenomenon and higher social mechanisms are influential.

## 2. Language Tradition and Language Change

### 2.1. *Language acquisition throughout a whole lifetime*

Let us ascertain the process of language acquisition in order to observe the actual process and mechanism of language change. Language acquisition basically continues throughout one's whole lifetime, adjusting to the environment. The language acquisition of infants is said to be overwhelmingly influenced by the mother. There is a critical period for language acquisition and the basis of language, such as phonology, is stabilized by the teens. Later in life, there are influences from family members and peer groups, and at school, there are influences from classmates. As a young adult one adopts the language of the same generation, and also acquires the language of the workplace as a socialized person. Some areas of sociolinguistic competence, such as honorific language, manners and conventions (what to say on occasions such as births, marriages and deaths) are acquired still later in life. Not only knowledge of individual words, but sociolinguistic competence and communicative competence too are acquired outside school. When the mechanism of language acquisition does not work well, acquisition remains incomplete.

However, transmission from the generation above (parents, for example) is ordinarily sufficient, and transmission from two or three generations above (grandparents, for example) is not necessary. As for the transmission of culture among other primates, contact with one generation above is usual. Transmission of culture from two or three generations above while living together seems to be unique to the human species.

### 2.2. *When language changes occur*

Considering the processes discussed above, language changes typically appear as errors of acquisition. Discontinuation of transmission is realized as adoption of different word-forms and expressions. The following types, arranged according to life stage, have been actually observed (Inoue 2000).

1. Erroneous acquisition and simplification by analogy among infants.
2. Diffusion among groups of children and playmates (transmission from grandparents will be discussed later).
3. Acquisition of youth language among youth groups.
4. Acquisition as a socialized adult (honorific language and technical words).
5. Acquisition from younger people of youth language in later stages of life.

In conclusion, the basis of language is constituted by acquisition in infancy. Acquisition from older people is exceptional at this first stage, and it is observed only among children who have been brought up by older people and among those who have regular conversations with older people. Concrete examples will be given below.

### 2.3. *Possibility of age-linguistics*

There are various issues concerning the relationship between language change and age, and an independent field of study of age-linguistics can be established ("gerontolinguistics" is part of this research field, cf. Backhaus 2006). However, theoretical considerations will be omitted here (Inoue 2000).

Population ageing has a bearing on mutual influences between older people and children; however, it is difficult to establish the influence of recent population ageing on the language conclusively for lack of a control group. Experiments are impossible and observation is difficult. One of the rare cases where comparisons would seem to be possible are children brought up in an environment without intergenerational contact with old people, such as immigrant communities. How does their speech behaviour differ from that of children growing up with regular contact with speakers of two preceding generations? The northern pioneer land of Hokkaido is typical: new conventions and usages have been formed here. The koineization of language is conspicuous as several surveys carried out since the end of the Second World War have demonstrated (Sibata 1998). Language formation in new towns and housing developments in the late twentieth century can be another model of non-influence from older people. To add more cases, there are many Japanese immigrants and their descendants in Hawaii and Brazil, but here, the influence of local languages must also be taken into consideration.

As a contrast group, dialect surveys in agricultural and fishing villages, where there are many three-generation families, can be utilized. However, this kind of interest in the influence of older people living together has not been common, because language standardization has been ubiquitous nationwide. A new approach from a fresh point of view is needed to assess the impact of population ageing on language change.

## 3. Linguistic Surveys of Local Communities and Population Ageing

### 3.1. *Time span necessary for language change*

The progress of population ageing influences linguistic surveys. When glottogram surveys (age-area surveys) were first carried out in the past, the upper age limit of informants was thought to be the 70s, according to the usual convention of dialect geographical surveys. When the actual field research was carried out in rural areas, many healthy speakers in their 80s were found, so informants in their 80s were included in many communities. In one community it was possible to question a female informant over 100 years old. Using this kind of data, language change for time spans of 70 or 80 years can be inferred making use of the apparent time method. By making use of surveys carried out in the past, changes over more than 100 years can be ascertained. Some typical examples will be given here; more concrete data are found in Inoue (1997).

*Long-term language change in kusuguttai [ticklish]*

In one village on the Shimokita peninsula at the northern tip of Aomori prefecture, follow-up surveys were conducted 20 and 40 years after the original one carried out in 1964 (Inoue 2000). The data collection method changed, from individual interviews to distribution of questionnaires by hand. The return rate fell as a result. The first and third surveys, carried out in 1964 and 2005, are shown in figure 1. The informants are arranged according to year of birth. Informants of the middle generation are listed twice in order to show that the same informants (cohort) exhibit increased use of new dialect forms 40 years later. As is shown in the graph, replacement of four forms is clearly demonstrated.

In this settlement *mochokoe* has been in use since the nineteenth century to mean "ticklish". A new dialect form, *mochokari*, spread among people who were born after the Second World War. The morpheme *kari* is a dialectal expression for "itchy". A newer form partly influenced by the standard language, *mochokayui*, appeared in the later stages of the twentieth century. Young people nowadays use standard Japanese *kusuguttai*.

Population ageing is not so conspicuous in this village, as people seem to have a less than average life expectancy. According to an interview

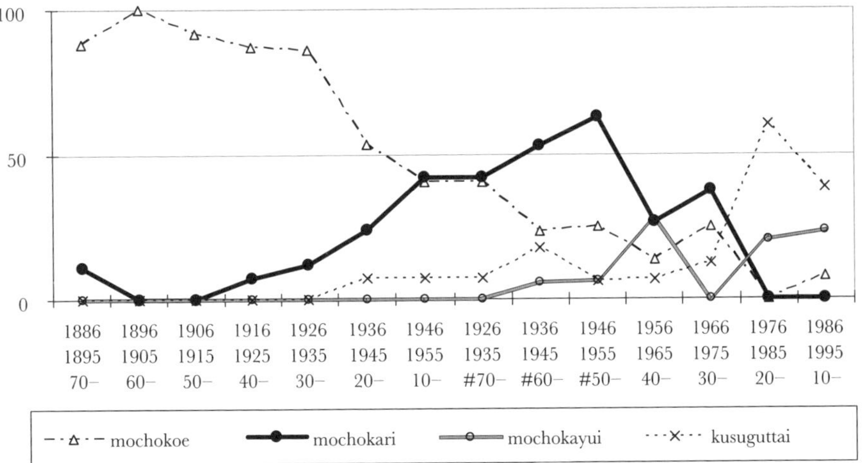


Figure 1. Replacement of new dialect form of *mochokoe* [ticklish] in Shimokita, 1964 and 2005.

with a community leader, the oldest informants of the survey carried out 40 years ago were about 70 years old. If life expectancy here were as high as for the Japanese population at large, old people in their 80s and 90s would be found and residents themselves might have the opportunity to notice language differences between generations, as in the case of *kusuguttai*. That is to say, they might have the opportunity to witness the birth and death of certain new word forms. However, language change generally needs more time than a regular human lifespan.

*Language change in the Tsuruoka survey*

The actual state of language change can be studied by making use of cohort analysis of the same age groups on the basis of repeated surveys. Since three large-scale surveys have been conducted so far at intervals of about 20 years in Tsuruoka city, Yamagata prefecture, language changes in real time and apparent time can be observed there (Inoue 1997, 2000; Yoneda 1997).

Given that the generation curve for accent in the 1991 survey is similar to that for phonology in the 1950 survey, it is possible to hypothesize that the accent shows the first half of the S-shaped diffusion curve of language change, and that the phonology shows the second half of the S-shaped curve (Aitchison 1981; Inoue 1997). When the curves for phonology and accent are combined, language changes can be interpreted as being completed in about 130 years. As for the time span of language change, more than 100 years are generally necessary in the case of phonology and accent (Inoue 1997, 2000).

### 3.2. *Social change, the mass media and language*

The examples above (of replacement of new dialect forms and language standardization) were collected in the 1970s and 1980s, and they may have become rather old-fashioned. Glottogram surveys widely used in Japan today, and some examples of language use by old people of young people's expressions have been observed. This shows that grandparents nowadays adapt their language use to that of their grandchildren. The influence seems to be working in the opposite direction, and language seems to have lost its function for the transmission of culture.

For language transmission from more than one preceding generation, further population ageing is not necessary. Cohabitation of three generations is effective, but that of four generations is not necessary. Grandparents 60 or 70 years old can take care of grandchildren, but great-grandparents of 80 and 90 years old are not expected to influence them linguistically, because they are not expected to participate in child-rearing.

#### *Data showing discontinuation between parents and children*

The mechanism of discontinuation of linguistic tradition from grandparents can be conjectured from data about linguistic behaviour. Interlocutors in daily conversation have been investigated in several dialect surveys to date, in order to understand the linguistic networks of a community. One of the results obtained in the Yamazoe area of Tsuruoka city, Yamagata prefecture will be presented here. This is an area of typical rural suburbs, and there are few young residents because they move to urban areas after graduation from junior and senior high schools. If there are children, they form three-generation families because they live together with grandparents.

Two dialect surveys were carried out at an interval of 15 years (Inoue 2000). The results are shown by dividing the respondents into 15-year age cohorts. The two surveys are shown side by side putting the same cohort on the same line as in Figure 2. The results of grandchildren and grandparents are shown here among many interlocutors in daily conversations. Age differences are conspicuous both in 1976 and 1991. Younger people talk with grandparents and older people talk with grandchildren. In 1991 younger people seem to speak more with grandparents than in 1976.

However, when the most frequent interlocutor is asked about in a later question, the proportions of both grandchildren and grandparents are small or near zero. The proportion of grandparents featuring as the most frequent interlocutor is very small, especially for children. Conversations across two generations are important for older people who have fewer interlocutors to talk to, but less important for young people who have many people to talk to. This means that the linguistic influence of two preceding generations is not so significant.

*Data showing effect of the media*

In investigating factors which hamper conversations across two generations, the length of time spent watching television is conspicuous. According to a nationwide NHK survey (cf. chapter 26), the average time spent watching television is about two hours a day, but in the rural Yamazoe area informants of all generations answered that on average they spent three to four hours daily watching television. In the second survey, 15 years later, the time had decreased to two to three hours among the socially active generations, but this is still a long time. Although much time is spent watching television, the language with which one is thereby in contact is linguistically only receptive, and so is not considered influential enough to have an effect on usage, at least for adults. (An exceptional phenomenon is accent change in the repeated surveys in Tsuruoka city; see Yoneda 1997.) The influence of television is most conspicuous in the diffusion of neologisms, loanwords and youth language. Language in television is, however, basically language in a theatre in a box, and residents in rural areas do not have direct contact with the users of new expressions.

*Language discontinuation in "long life" Okinawa*

There is also some counter-evidence to the conjecture that population ageing impedes or decelerates language change. The Okinawa Islanders are known for their longevity. Here, however, old people speak Okinawan dialects which the younger generations have abandoned. Young people with little or no contact with elderly Okinawans have difficulty even understanding the dialects. This is a typical case of language discontinuation.

In the areas where population ageing has become conspicuous recently, there is little evidence of slowed-down language change (other than the intrusive power of the standard language). The influence of population ageing upon language change thus appears to be limited.

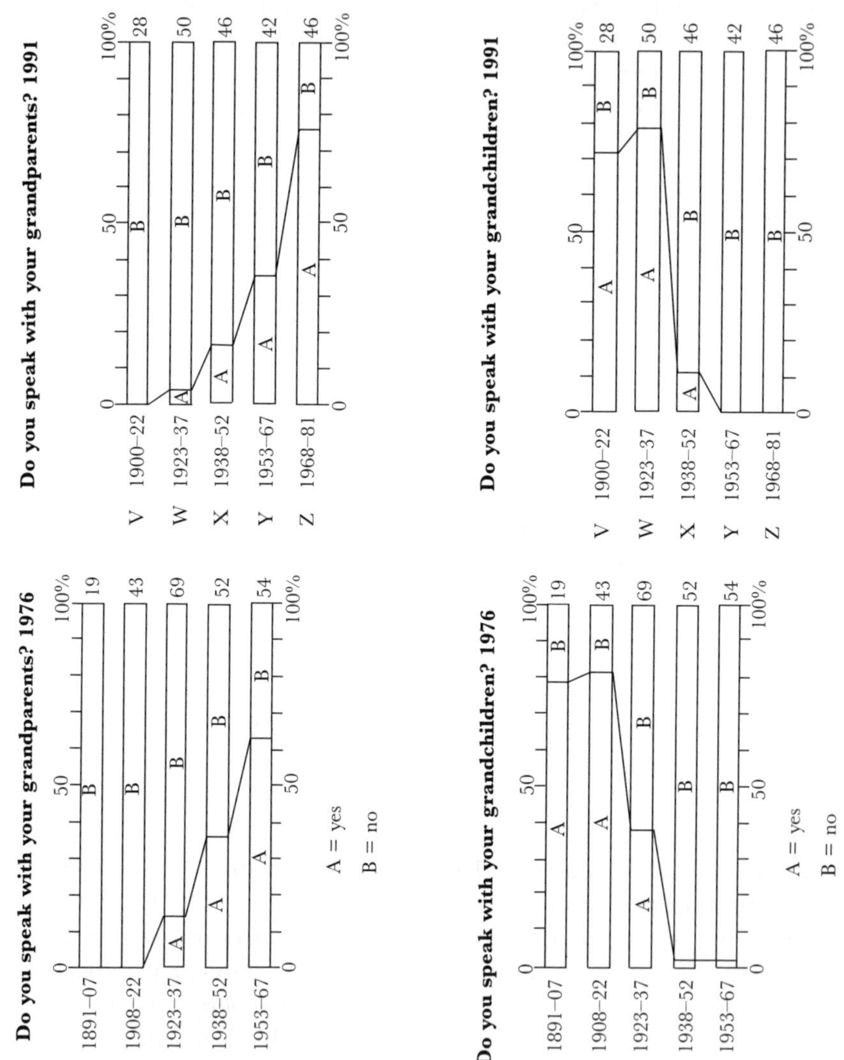


Figure 2. Communication across generations, grandchildren and grandparents.

*Maintenance of endangered languages*

However, population ageing seems to work favourably for languages in danger of disappearing. At least the time of death of the last speakers will be delayed. There will be more opportunities and time to record language and traditions, but in the end traditions will die out. The same is true for local dialects.

In the meantime, some languages and dialects are becoming the object of deliberate instruction and other revival measures. Elderly people are active in these movements which benefit from population ageing. Examples in Japan are education and broadcasting in the Ainu language of Hokkaido on the basis of the so-called "new Ainu law", speech contests by children in Okinawan dialects, and dialect training for employees in the Okinawa Islands. In the case of radio news in Okinawan dialects, for example, elderly people who otherwise might have already retired in former times are working actively on the programmes.

These are, however, cases of continuation of language use, which should be distinguished from language change within linguistic systems as discussed above.

*Law of diminishing marginal utility of population ageing*

A theoretical paradox is realized in relation to population ageing. Generation differences of more than 70 years can be observed in the same family because of recent population ageing, but the social structure of the family has also changed. Nuclear families have increased, and the numbers of elderly people living alone have increased. Grandchildren meet grandparents less often, and there are fewer chances of meeting elderly people in newly developed housing areas in the suburbs. Although living with great-grandparents has theoretically become more possible because of population ageing, in fact it is not likely, because the average age at first marriage has also increased. Moreover, older people are not expected to live with young infants and children. Increases in the numbers of solitary elderly people, single-person households and nuclear families all contribute to a lack of contact between young people and the elderly.

The law of diminishing marginal utility of economics is applicable to the influence of population ageing. Giving a person who has just one slice of bread an extra slice has an effect; but providing a person who has difficulty in consuming ten slices with an additional one makes little difference. In the same way, the extension of life expectancy in a society with a low median age has a great impact, while its effect is limited in a society where population ageing has already progressed to a certain extent. Although language acquisition continues throughout the speakers' lifetime, most language is acquired in the first stages of an individual's life during the "language formation period" (Sibata 1998). Population ageing, therefore, does not contribute much to the formation of individual speakers' language. Inhibition of language change among children may be an effect of communicating with grandparents, but population ageing does not necessarily increase the incidence of contact with grandparents.

In societies with a low life expectancy, such as Japan in the early twentieth century, the average age at first marriage is generally low, and grandparents are younger on average than in "old" societies, such as present-day Japan. This means that the effect of grandparents (and older people in one's environment) on slowing down language change is relatively strong, even though there is no population ageing.

## 4. Knowledge and Awareness in Opinion Polls

### 4.1. *Acceptance of new linguistic phenomena and population ageing*

In this section, the relation between acceptance of new linguistic phenomena and population ageing will be analyzed, focusing on neologisms, fashionable expressions and honorific language. It is conjectured that differences between the youngest and the oldest generations become greater because of population ageing, all other conditions being equal.

*Generation differences in aged people*

If we take into consideration the general tendency that a period of more than 100 years is needed for language change to arise and be completed, older people can experience part of the process, even though it may be difficult to ascertain the whole process. Expressions used by people when they are young often become obsolete, sometimes even incomprehensible. At the same time, new words appear that the elderly do not understand. Public opinion polls sometimes pick up language problems. In particular, in nationwide opinion polls carried out by the Agency for Cultural Affairs, various words are surveyed every year, and reports are published regularly.

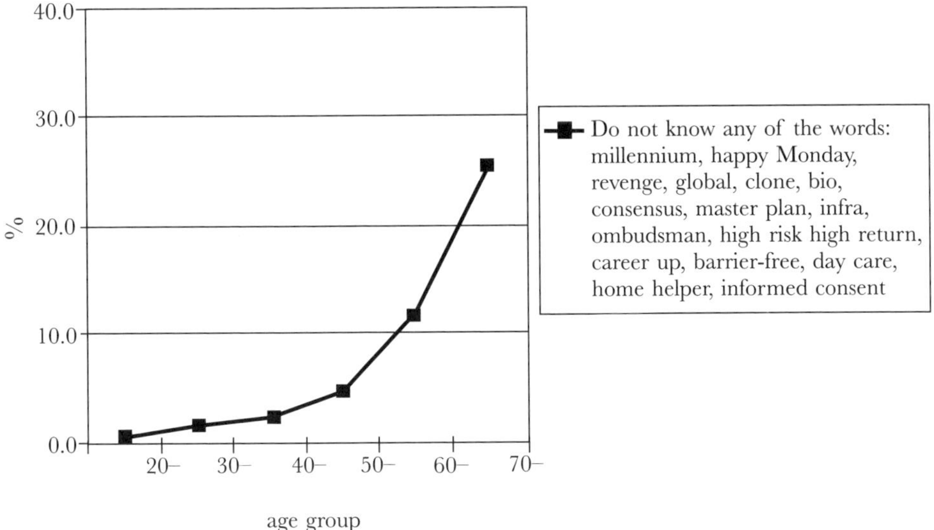


Figure 3. Age differences in knowledge of loanwords, 1999.

*Comprehensibility of loanwords among the ederly*

Generational analysis of increasing usage of loanwords shows a similar trend of generational differences. There are many surveys and tabulations relating to loanwords. The results of a nationwide survey by the Yomiuri newspaper (1999, 12) are examined here from a different point of view. In this survey respondents were asked to tick words whose meaning they knew. Figure 3 shows the proportion of people who knew none of the 16 words listed, exhibiting significant age differences. More than a quarter of the elderly answered that they knew none of the words, even though terms relating to welfare, which are important for the elderly, were included. Similar tendencies can be observed in a survey by the Agency for Cultural Affairs. Although the generation gap for individual loanwords is widely acknowledged, it is noteworthy that there are conspicuous differences among the generations in the proportions answering that they "knew none of the words".

To better understand the background of the incomprehensibility of loanwords to the speakers of a certain age cohort, it is necessary to note that the Japanese language has been taking in foreign words for more than five centuries (for more than a millennium, if we include Chinese) (Inoue 2005).

Lack of comprehension of the meaning of loanwords is widespread, and there are also great differences in knowledge of neologisms, fashionable words and youth language. The perception that the Japanese language is deteriorating arises from this phenomenon.

### 4.2. *Perception of language deterioration*

*Perception of language deterioration in opinion polls*
In this section, the perception that the Japanese language is deteriorating will be analyzed, and its relation to elderly people will be studied. It is expected that the perception that the language is deteriorating will increase with population ageing.

Population ageing has a bearing on the popular notion that the Japanese language is deteriorating in yet another way. When people live longer, old people notice more differences in the language of young people than before. This will lead to the perception that the language is becoming different, standards are undermined and Japanese is degenerating. The consistent trend in public opinion polls after the Second World War for language to be seen as deteriorating can be explained by this logic. The increase in opinion polls of the view that the Japanese language is deteriorating is caused by the swelling numbers of old people who become increasingly aware of differences between their language and the language of young people.

The perception that language is deteriorating has been established several times in opinion polls by the government and the mass media. The data presented here is an aggregate of repeated surveys by the Agency for Cultural Affairs, NHK (Japan Broadcasting Corporation) and other organizations. Different wordings and different choices were used in each survey, but contradictory tendencies do not appear. As shown in figure 4, the opinion that the Japanese language is deteriorating has increased steadily over the last 25 years, which is shown in concrete numerical values. It was below 80% in the past, but it is over 80% at present. (The proportion of people holding this opinion is low in the 2002 survey because the question was asked at the beginning of the questionnaire.)

*Age differences in the perception of language deterioration, 1977 and 2002*
Let us further analyze age differences within individual surveys. The opinion that Japanese is deteriorating is prevalent among older generations in many surveys. For example, in the left part of figure 5 (opinion

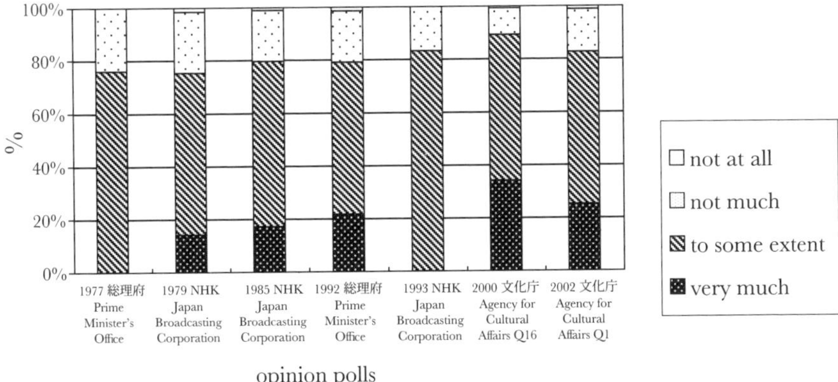


Figure 4. Is Japanese deteriorating?

polls carried out in 2002 by the Agency for Cultural Affairs) the peak appears in the socially active middle-aged generation. This must be because middle-aged people have contact with the speech of young employees in their workplaces. In surveys by NHK in which answers are divided into four choices, the proportion of those who thought that Japanese was deteriorating increased, and the peak is again in middle age.

The two surveys in figure 5 (opinion polls carried out in 1977 by the Prime Minister's Office and in 2002 by the Agency for Cultural Affairs) cannot be compared, as the survey methods are different, strictly speaking. However, when the same cohorts are compared by plotting the results from both surveys on the same graph, a significant trend appears. In the latter survey, the same cohort shows an increased proportion of people who think the language is deteriorating. The age group in their 20s in 1977 corresponds to the middle-aged in their 40s and 50s in the 2002 survey. The view that the language is deteriorating increased further. Meanwhile, the age group in their 40s in 1977 corresponds to the age group over 65 in 2002, and shows the same proportion in both surveys. This can be interpreted as meaning that people do not change their opinions after a certain age. It is thus shown that the same cohorts tend to strengthen their opinion that there is "deterioration" of the language over time.

The lower dark part of figure 5 shows the percentage who thought there was "strong deterioration" in the language, a view that is prominent among older people, in the 2002 Agency for Cultural Affairs survey. Large differences are found between the generations: 4% among males

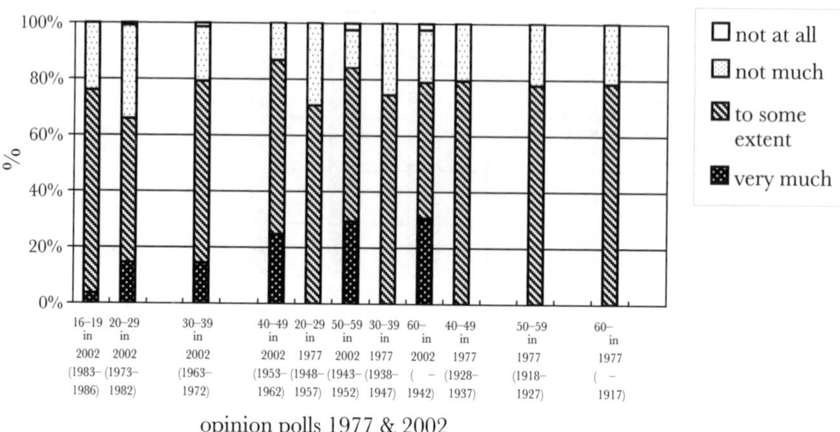


Figure 5. Age differences in the perception of deterioration.

in their teens (18% among females in their teens) and 30% among males over 60 (29% among females over 60). One might expect the opinion of "strong deterioration" to decrease in subsequent surveys, because of the increasing mortality of older respondents. But repeated surveys do not show the expected tendency.

The proportion of those who think the language is deteriorating also increased in all age groups in NHK surveys carried out from 1979 to 1986. This can be interpreted not as cohort change, but rather as life-stage change of the same groups of respondents because of ageing. That is to say, the same individuals get older and notice differences between their speech and that of younger people more keenly, and acquire the opinion that the language is deteriorating. At the same time, the mass media also spread the view that the language is deteriorating. Such opinions frequently appear in letters to the editor, and concrete examples are sometimes provided. This contributes concrete evidence to the process of raising the awareness of perceived deterioration.

### 4.3. *Dissatisfaction with usage of honorifics among the elderly*

Thus far, the extent of age differences of language use and perceptions of language between young and old generations have been discussed. Another important factor will be discussed here, that is, honorific language used to elderly people.

*Changes in honorific usage*

Another language problem connected to ageing is changes in Japanese honorific expressions. Changes in usage of honorifics in Japanese upset older people, because they are addressed with honorific expressions less frequently. The choice of use or non-use of honorific expressions is compulsory in normal conversation between adults. Non-use and use of sentence-final auxiliary verbs *desu* and *masu* correspond to usage of pronouns T/V (tu/vous in French and du/Sie in German). However, Japanese honorific usage is now experiencing a long-term historical change in the same direction as honorifics in western languages. In the past, Japanese honorifics were related to age, and honorifics were used to elderly people. Nowadays a different principle based on solidarity rather than age is becoming prominent. This is a change from power to solidarity (Brown & Gilman 1960), and it also corresponds to a social change from ascribed status to acquired status. It can be also interpreted as a shift from vertical (superior—inferior) relations to horizontal (right—left) relations and in the direction of democratization and equalization. This produces a tendency of "non-necessity of usage of honorifics to elderly people", and respectful expressions once prevalent are no longer used to the elderly.

Many elderly people find this trend hard to bear because they are not as clearly treated with verbal respect as they were in the past.

*Changes in honorific principles: belittling of age*

Young people no longer feel obliged to use honorifics just because an interlocutor is senior. Consider some actual survey data. Figure 6 shows the results of a nationwide survey by the Agency for Cultural Affairs. Age differences show that older generations admit the necessity of honorific usage to seniors, while the younger generation tends to use honorifics to senior people depending on the occasion. That is to say, in present-day Japan, honorific usage to older people is declining. In the world of work nowadays, promotion is based not on seniority, age or academic background, but on merit. The principle of seniority or age to determine honorific usage is difficult to apply to this fluid modern society, and is becoming old-fashioned. Language used to address one's seniors does not seem as important to young people these days. This trend is a reflection of long-term (and universal) historical change in honorifics.

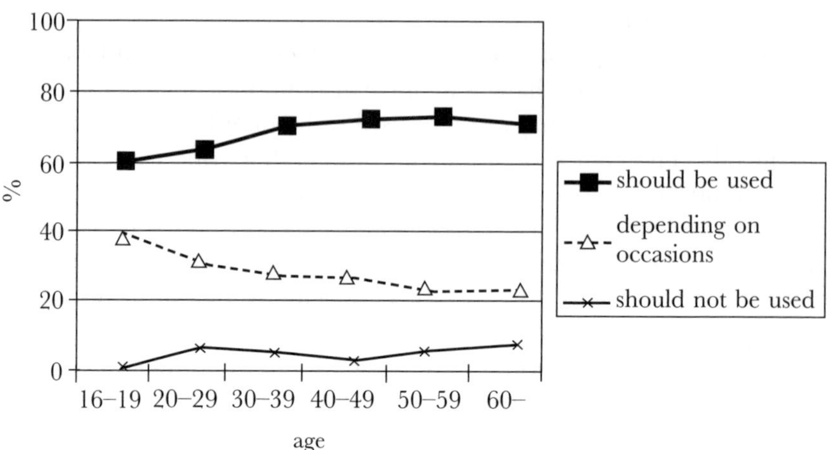


Figure 6. Should honorifics be used from juniors to seniors?

*Language used to the disadvantaged*

Another problem of language used to the elderly is also related to honorifics. There is no definite appropriate style to be used to elderly people. Current language usage in nursing of elderly people needs to be reconsidered, because old people are often talked to—and treated—like young children or babies. Appropriate usage for the elderly needs to be developed (Backhaus 2006).

There is incremental change of honorific usage in the direction of democratization and greater equality. Sometimes letters to the editor appear in which a young salesperson complains about older customers who do not use honorifics. The beneficial principle has been introduced for usage of honorifics. For instance, the notion that an elderly man with a physical handicap should use honorifics addressing a young carer is unfamiliar if not outright uncomfortable for the elderly speaker. The language used by nurses to the elderly is often similar to that used to children. It may be because expressions of empathy with the infirm or disadvantaged are not sufficiently differentiated. Language use of nursing for the elderly people at present should be reconsidered and appropriate usage for the elderly should be developed.

This use (or non-use) of honorifics is connected to the emotional function of language, while incomprehension of loanwords, neologisms and new dialect forms as discussed above is connected to the intellectual function of language. That is to say, the use or non-use of honorifics is related to emotion and sometimes brings displeasure to the interlocutor. As it is strongly influential in human relations, this problem should be reconsidered in society as a whole. The principle of maintaing the dignity of the elderly will naturally lead to an appropriate choice of expressions.

## 5. Conclusions: Language Change and Population Ageing

### *Social factors*

To conclude, at present population ageing does not have the effect of impeding or slowing down language change. Language changes generally proceed over a time span of more than 100 years. That is to say, more than three generations are necessary from the beginning to the completion of a particular language change in a community. As for language shift, 90 years at least are necessary, because three generations (one generation = 30 years) are necessary. An extreme example of language shift is exemplified by Japanese immigrants in Hawaii where the first generation spoke only Japanese, the second generation was bilingual speaking both Japanese and English, and the third generation is again monolingual, but in English.

When various language changes are taken into consideration, most changes need more than 100 years to complete, longer than a normal human lifespan. The effect of population ageing, in which life expectancy increases from 50 to 80 years, is not enough for influences to be measured. The law of diminishing marginal utility of economics is applicable to population ageing, and increases in the numbers of nuclear families and the preponderance of information from the media are also crucial.

Although language shift on the basis of economic principles is rare, most languages and dialects are likely to become obsolete in the future. According to the consideration described above, co-residence with the elderly is the most effective means for retaining a linguistic tradition. Without intergenerational co-residence, population ageing does not significantly affect the transmission of language.

In summary, social factors like urbanization, the spread of the nuclear family and discontinuation between generations have more impact on present states of language change than demographic factors such as population ageing. Population ageing is proceeding at great speed in present-day Japan, but on the other hand, there are great linguistic differences between generations, because many language changes are progressing simultaneously, and various new expressions are being adopted by younger people. Language differences between the young and the elderly seem to be great. However, it is difficult to estimate the extent or scale of language changes in progress at present because we observe them as they are happening. It is also difficult to assess the strength of the effect of population ageing on language change.

However, if the social conditions of the elderly are taken into consideration, voices of complaint from the elderly will clearly be heard. They tend to lag behind changes in the language, feel opposed and lament the deterioration of Japanese. The dissatisfaction of elderly people revealed in opinion polls should be included in the study of linguistics and language change, in particular.

## References

Aitchison, Jean (1981): *Language Change: Progress or Decay?* London: Fontana.

Backhaus, Peter (2006): *Care, Control, and Communication: Linguistic interaction between staff and residents in a Japanese nursing home for the elderly, Working Paper* 06/6. Tokyo: Deutsches Institut für Japanstudien.

Brown, R. and A. Gilman (1960): The pronouns of power and solidarity. In T. A. Sebeok (ed.) *Style in Language*. Cambridge, MA: The MIT Press, pp. 253–267.

Inoue, Fumio (1997): S-shaped curves of language standardization. In Alan R. Thomas (ed.) *Issues and Methods in Dialectology*. Bangalore: University of Wales, pp. 79–93.

—— (2000): *Tohoku-hogen no Hensen* [Transitions of the Tohoku Dialect]. Tokyo: Akiyama Shoten.

—— (2005): Econolinguistic Aspects of Multilingual Signs in Japan. In *Changing Language Regimes in Globalizing Environments: Japan and Europe, IJSL* 175/176 pp. 157–177.

Sibata, Takesi (1998): *Sociolinguistics in Japanese Contexts* (T. Kunihiro, F. Inoue, D. Long eds.) Berlin, New York: Mouton de Gruyter.

Yomiuri Zenkoku Yoronchōsa (1999, 12) [Yomiuri Nationwide Opinion Survey December 1999].

Yoneda, Masato (1997): Survey of standardization in Tsuruoka, Japan. In *Nihongo Kagaku* 2. http://www.dijtokyo.org/doc/NL28_english.pdf

CHAPTER TWENTY-FIVE

# AGE AND AGEING IN CONTEMPORARY JAPANESE LITERATURE

Lisette Gebhardt

This article examines representative texts of Japanese literature regarding age and ageing in terms of certain central features. Here the question will be explored according to relevant contexts, terminology, and concepts concerning age, for example, *pokkuri*, *keirō*, *yamauba*, *ubasute*, *inkyō*, *kanreki*, *rōgo*, *boke*, as well as decade-specific interpretations of age, life-stages, and death. The eight sections, including the introduction, are structured according to the following aspects:

1. The topic of age in contemporary Japanese literature
2. "Rice-devouring ghosts": Age and care as a crisis experience
3. The folklore of age or Japanese psycho-archeology
4. Obsessive old-age eroticism
5. Generational transition, ageing, and questions of meaning
6. Death scenarios, death initiations, and posthumous options
7. Advice literature and old-age philosophical discourse
8. The "nice old lady"? Old-age wisdom, emancipation, and a liberated life-sense

## 1. The Theme of Old Age in Contemporary Japanese Literature

The years between 1947 and 1960 saw a significant ageing of Japanese society. In the perceptions of the twenty-first century the so-called ageing boom is proving to be a weighty demographic development. During this period the birth rate declined, and life expectancy rose considerably, from 50.1 to 65.3 for men, and from 54. to 70.2 for women. As Imhof argued with his sociohistorical findings, Japan experienced an "ageing shock" from 1950 to 1960 (Imhof 1986: 368).

Ariyoshi Sawako's *Kōkotsu no hito* (lit. The Ecstatic; tr. 1984 *The Twilight Years*) is probably the best-known literary work concerning ageing in Japanese society. Published in 1972, it sold over two million copies. The story, to which Imhof's work also refers, treats the theme of senility and the question of how care-dependent elderly people are to be looked after. It is regarded as pivotal for Japan's "literature of ageing", although the subject was, to be sure, already being discussed before the novel became a bestseller.

There are inventories and extensive studies related to the representation of age and ageing for the pre-modern era. For example, Formanek (1994, 2005) provides a critical revision of the stereotype of Japanese respect for the aged, and a historical study of "the wicked old woman" (see also Scheidt 1996). However, similar studies are lacking for modern and contemporary times in both Occidental and Japanese research. Articles by Tsukimura (1978), Skord (1989), Loughman (1991), and Yoshitake (2003) contain individual analyses. Books written or edited by Higuchi (1979), Satō (1991), Mizuno (1991), and, more recently, Nagai (2004), Umetani (2003), and Suzuki (2005) likewise present collections of individual depictions.

This article examines texts from the decades after 1945, focusing on the literary treatment of the topic for that phase in which the old-age boom falls. The aforementioned crisis in care for the aged is only one aspect of how the issue is presented in contemporary literature. The following themes are introduced:

– ageing and care of the aged as a crisis experience;
– generational transition;
– concepts of age and awareness of stages in ageing;
– sex and the aged;
– death scenarios;
– advisory literature and philosophical discourse on ageing;
– emancipation of the elderly and aged.

Among the standard texts of Japanese literature related to age and ageing are, in addition to Ariyoshi's classic novel of 1972, Niwa Fumio's (1904–2005) *Iyagarase no nenrei* (1947, tr. 1956 *The Hateful Age*), Fukazawa Shichirō's (1914–1987) *Narayama bushi-kō* (1956, tr. 1966 *The Song of Oak Mountain*), Inoue Yasushi's (1907–1991) *Waga haha no ki* (1964–1975, tr. 1982 *Chronicle of My Mother*), and Irokawa Takehiro's (1929–1989) *Hyaku* [One Hundred] (1981). The theme also turns up, however, in such works as Tanizaki Jun'ichirō's (1886–1965) *Kagi* (1956, tr. 1971 *The Key*), *Fūten rōjin nikki* (1962, tr. 1991 *The Diary of a Mad Old Man*) and Kawabata Yasunari's (1899–1972) well-known *Nemureru bijo* (1961, tr.

1969 *House of the Sleeping Beauties*). More recent texts are, for example, Murata Kiyoko's (1945–) *Warabinokō* [To the Bracken Fields] (1994), Sae Shūichi's (1934–) *Kōraku* (1995, Yellow Leaves Fall), as well as Mobu Norio's (1970–) *Kaigo nyūmon* [Introduction to Care] (2004) und Kirino Natsuo's (1951–) *Tamamoe!* [Soulfire] (2005), both close to twenty-first century realities.

Variations in the thematization of age and ageing in contemporary Japanese literature over the decades, as well as in the cultural discourse being conducted by literary figures and critics, can be classified as follows:

A *social-critical-documentary/gerontological-philosophical* approach that seeks to offer enlightenment concerning the conditions of age and death in Japanese society and to stimulate contemplation about the issue of age and the human condition (for example, Niwa, Inoue, Ariyoshi, Mobu).

A *folkloristic, atavistic* approach that juxtaposes ageing as a rite of passage with the paradigms of today's achievement/consumption-oriented society (Fukazawa, Murata).

A *psycho-pathological/aestheticizing* approach (Tanizaki, Kawabata), spotlighting age and ageing within an obsessive battleground of eros-thanatos, typically in deliberate dialectal opposition to the vapid, convention-bound, utilitarian-capitalist society of the post-war era.

A *traditionalistic* approach, interpreting age according to Sino-Japanese worldviews and concepts relevant to the history of ideas and relating itself to Buddhist, Confucian, and Taoistic ways of thinking (cultivation of longevity = *rōjū; okina* = venerable old man). Also relevant here may be the concepts of the different stages of age (*sōnen* 'prime of life', *chūnen* 'middle age', *rōnen* 'old age'); of respect for the elderly (*keirō*), *keirō-no hi* (Respect-for-the Aged Day) having been declared an official holiday in 1966; of old-age wisdom, as reflected in the concept of *bannen no bungaku* [literature of the later years]; as well as of the tradition of retiring to one's hermitage (*inkyō*), as can be seen, for example, in the later work of Uchida Hyakken; and of the modern documentation of death [*tōbyōki*, "chronicle of doing battle with illness"], which is closely related to the tradition of the classical death poem *jisei*.

A *cultural-critical-journalistic* or *documentary-philosophizing* approach, which may be included in currently popular advice literature ([*ikikata no hon*] and which, beyond the realm of literary fiction, offers informative discussions for a broad readership. Among the popular contributors are Itsuki Hiroyuki (1932–), Setouchi Jakuchō (1922–), Sono Ayako

(1931–), Yanagida Kunio (1936–), Yōrō Takeshi (1937–), Hinohara Shigeaki (1911–), and Yanagisawa Keiko (1938–). Since the 1980s and 1990s this setting has produced ongoing cultural discussions on the topics of quality of life in old age, authentic life/authentic death, and thantatology [*shiseigaku*].

*Emancipatory texts* that enhance the role of older women (Enchi, Ōba) or that attribute positive aspects to age, as well as the importance of senior citizens as a psycho-hygienic element in families (for example, Yumoto Kazumi) and advocate a liberation of the elderly in keeping with the times.

## 2. "Rice-devouring Ghosts": Age and Care as a Crisis Experience

In her overview "Withered Blossoms: Aging in Japanese Literature," referring to the short story *Iyagarase no nenrei* by Niwa Fumio, Virginia Skord comments: "Turning to modern literature, we find a generally pessimistic view of aging." Skord hints at the "brutal and physical depiction of a senile grandmother, no more than a wasted bag of flesh greedily demanding to be fed, who destroys the lives of her resentful family members with her insatiable wants and compulsive habits." (Skord 1989: 136). Whether *Iyagarase no nenrei* echoes the post-war ageing-boom or reflects Niwa's personal experiences, he seems to have set the tone for contemporary Japanese literature of ageing and old age.

The elderly are not represented as beings worthy of veneration in the sense of Confucian conventions, but rather are exposed as burdensome old folk. The care of senior citizens appears as such a disruptive experience that it threatens to destroy the family. Centre-stage is the lament of family members who, because of social constraints, economic exigencies, and inadequate geriatric facilities, are obliged to take on the care of the very old themselves. It is above all female next-of-kin and relatives who have been—and right up to the present day continue to be—confronted with the physical and mental manifestations of the declining years and the different stages of senility (Alzheimer's, forgetfulness [*boke*], confusion, change of personality, incontinence).

In Niwa Fumio's *Iyagarase no nenrei*, the 86-year-old Ume is passed from one member of the extended family to another, as though in an involuntary game of musical chairs [*taraimawashi*]; looking after her wears to a frazzle her granddaughter Senko, her husband Itami, and other relatives. Even before Ariyoshi, Niwa discusses the issue: "People had been complaining for years, but the familial system still lingered on, with all its inefficiency, hypocrisy, sentimentality, and injustice. It was high time for something to be done—not by sociologists, but by people all over Japan who were themselves suffering from these anachronistic traditions" (Niwa 1962: 340).

He depicts impressively the mental decline of the old Ume, who has lost all human emotions, so that those around her let off steam by describing the forever hungry, troublesome old woman with the hostile expression "rice-devouring ghosts." When Ume is sent to her granddaughter Sachiko, her husband Minobe, a sensitive painter, observes the old woman. He imagines that he sees a last remnant of her humanity, but then she again reacts with disturbing signs of dementia. Niwa's story is characterized by a humanistic-enlightened attitude, as represented by Minobe. The author calls for a rethinking of mandatory care within the family, but also for thoughtfulness and consideration towards the elderly, whose fate one will share oneself some day. The story is nonetheless conditioned by its time, with a somewhat negative view of elderly women.

Inoue Yasushi, who had already taken up the theme of *ubasute* (granny abandonment) in the 1950s, describes in his autobiographical narrative series *Hana no shita* [Beneath the Blossoms] (1964), *Tsuki no hikari* [Moonlight] (1969), and *Yuki no omote* [Snow Cover] (1974), later compiled as *Waga haha no ki*, the observations and reflections of the son, as he sees his mother age, enter second childhood, and, as a result, retreat into her own isolated world.

In *The Twilight Years*, Ariyoshi Sawako describes from the point of view of the protagonist, Tachibana Akiko, the problems that result from the worsening senility of Shigezō, the 84-year-old father of her husband, Nobutoshi. Her father-in-law's wife, though ten years younger, dies unexpectedly of a stroke. When Akiko looks into the possibility of old people's homes or care facilities that might accept the disoriented and often wandering old man, she learns to her dismay that there are virtually none available. At first she is indignant at how both the state and her own husband simply take it for granted that the burden will fall to her. Nevertheless, drawing strength in part from a female social worker, she takes up the task and does her duty in accordance with the Confucian value of care for the elderly as mandated by traditional filial piety. She informs herself about the medical aspects of advancing senility and reduces her professional workload as a secretary in an attorney's office in order to give the evening of Shigezō's life a measure of dignity. Moving impressions of the old man are recounted: he is capable, for example, of finding joy in nature. Akiko reinforces this in her selfless activities. The family recognizes that old age is not merely a curse. While Akiko's son is still suggesting at the beginning of the story, "Dad, Mum, please don't live this long," he wishes at the end that his grandfather had lived longer.

In Irokawa Takehiro's *Hyaku* [One Hundred], the protagonist speaks without hedging about his wish for a quick end for his father and earlier patricidal visions entertained in puberty. He offers moral justification for his fantasies of liberation by pointing to the militaristic past of his domineering 95-year-old father, a former professional soldier, who tyrannizes his nearly 80-year-old mother and even threatens her with physical violence. The father and mother live with the younger son. The protagonist, a lone-wolf writer, who suffers from a nervous illness that is clearly related to his traumatic childhood, often comes to visit. He observes the behaviour of his father, even as he seeks finally to emancipate himself from his filial role and, at the same time, feels sympathy for the old man, as he steadily advances into senility. Having begun to suffer incontinence a year earlier, he appears likely to live to see his 99th birthday, an event known as *hakuju* (lit. "white life", a play on Chinese characters, the character for "white" being the same as the one for "100" but without a crowning "one"—a single horizontal stroke)—though such can hardly be seen as a cause for celebration, either by his family or even himself.

A military past also plays a key role in a father-son relationship in Abe Akira's (1934–1989) *Shirei no kyūka* [Commander on Leave] (1992). The father, a former low-ranking naval officer, is suffering from terminal cancer. The third and youngest son Teisuke at first leaves the care of his parents in the hands of his wife Tamako. He hesitates to come to grips with the fact of his father Teisaburō's imminent death and initially avoids contact, though in the end he is at his side. As is usual in Japan, the patient is not informed of his grave condition. As he quickly loses his strength, he is certainly aware that he has no hope of a cure. Teisuke ponders his difficult relationship with his father, that of his parents with each other, and the tragedy of his handicapped elder brother, who was subjected to castration in puberty and who subsequently died while still in his thirties.

As in Irokawa Takehiro's *Hyaku*, the wife languishes under the egotism and gross insensitivity of her husband, a representative par excellence of old-school Japanese maleness. Through alcohol abuse in his youth, he had his hopes for fame and prosperity dashed. Teisuke also notes the character weaknesses of his once vain and ambitious mother. She demonstrates a passive aggression that manifests itself as growing indifference in the face of her husband's sufferings. As his death approaches, she appears to enjoy a sense of power and to triumph to some degree. She speaks to all and sundry about the upcoming funeral and of how it should best be carried out. If the revenge of the oppressed is witnessed here, its consequences are also the expression of a difficult relationship, disappointed expectations, and ultimately of a failed domestic life and of the inability of the marriage partners, with their assigned gender roles, to communicate with each other, to share feelings that do, in fact, exist.

In *Kōraku* [Yellow Leaves Fall] (1995), a novel classified as *chūkan shōsetsu*, that is, literature falling between the genres of *belles lettres* and entertainment, Sae Shūichi again takes up the theme of parents being taken care of by married couples. The relationship between husband and wife, whose task it is to take care of the former's father and mother, is strained by the degenerating health of the hard-of-hearing 87-year-old mother. She develops signs of dementia and is soon behaving violently towards the father. She finally refuses all food and dies. The son and daughter-in-law, who had been contemplating separation, need now only care for the 92-year-old father.

In Japan, suicide among the elderly includes culture-specific aspects, in that family-provided care is justified in terms of the Confucian ethic of filial piety, leading old people to feel that, with no alternative, they are a burden on their children. Relying on relevant reports, Ariyoshi Sawako's novel appeals to readers not to provoke the deaths of the old, whatever the burden of their care may be. The well-known avant-garde magazine *Shūmatsu kara* (From the Last Days), which in the 1970s had as its theme various social and political scandals of a self-destructive capitalistic Japan, has in its edition of June 1973, a polemical article, illustrated by Akasegawa Genpei, concerning the tragic suicide of an old woman who, at 102, was bedridden and wished to burden her family no longer. In this context, the concepts of the *ubasute* and the *pokkuri* come to the fore. *Pokkuri* refers to a quick and gentle old-age death, one that many elderly people prefer to lengthy infirmity. To that end, as portrayed in an essay called, "Escape into Death, Old People, and their Wish to Die" by Fleur Wöss (1984), *ubasute* refers to a legendary practice in Old Japan, as a reflection of grim socio-economic realities. Driving the old into a limited number of overcrowded nursing homes, in which many lie on their beds in nappies, is seen as a modern variant of the same.

The point of view of the aged themselves is largely missing in the texts mentioned over the period from 1947 to 1997. Central to their depiction is how their relatives interact and cope with them and the changes brought on by the ageing process. Such family members look on those in their care as strange, dehumanized beings and are endeavouring to preserve their *own* humanity in the stressful situation in which they find themselves. In *Shinigami* [God of Death] (1996), Shinoda Setsuko (1955–) points once again to the inadequacies in Japanese welfare policies as well as to the lack of social and medical facilities.

Before representing the perspective of the elderly in *Tamamoe!*, Kirino Natsuo, who is increasingly proving herself to be a taboo-breaker on the contemporary Japanese literary scene, sounds a defiant call for desperate measures on the part of their beleaguered attendants in her highly successful crime fiction novel *OUT* (1997). A story about four homicidal housewives, it includes the widow Yoshie, who breaks out of care hell by setting fire to the old house of her bedridden, malevolent mother-in-law.

In *Kaigo-nyūmon*, Mobu Norio makes an interesting, autobiographical attempt to sketch a model of a new conviviality on the part of young and old. The young protagonist, a musician without any set routine or work habits, patiently and sympathetically dedicates himself—when not spending time with hiphop and marijuana—to the care of his demented grandmother, who, born in the fifth year of the Taishō Era (1916), was Miss Nara in her youth. He shows great indignation when he sees a "robot for taking care of the elderly" (*kaigoyō robotto*) and declares himself as favouring instead a "natural Japanese way of life." The novel suggests that for old people, like youthful dropouts, there is no place in a meritocracy that has already driven many to suicide.

## 3. The Folklore of Age or Japanese Psychoarcheology

In his oft-filmed *Narayama bushi-kō* (1956), Fukazawa Shichirō testifies to an historical form of treating old people. The well-known short story takes up the theme of *ubasute*; it depicts life in a poor mountain village, which is marked by labour, hunger, and precious few moments of happiness. Its tradition decrees that on reaching the age of 70, old people, now regarded as superfluous food consumers, must be taken by their children to the top of a mountain, where they can expect a swift demise. The old Orin adapts herself bravely to her fate and on the mountain is blessed with the coming of winter, which hastens her death. Matayan, a selfish old man, comes to an inglorious end when, on resisting the inevitable, he is thrown into a ravine by his own son. The atavistic text, which subordinates human beings to the cycle of nature and advocates a vitalistic model (celebrating human energy and youth), is an impressive example of the Japanese folklore renaissance in the post-war decades and represents a search for national identity through a collective recollection of rural roots.

*Warabinokō* (1994), a novel in lyrical-historicizing style by Murata Kiyoko, is regarded as *ubasute* updated to the Heisei Era. Whoever lives to complete the sexagenary cycle (*kanreki*), that is, reaches the age of 60, is abandoned at a specified place. There immediate death does not necessarily lurk; instead, the autumn of one's years is spent in a kind of old people's commune. The inhabitants nonetheless manage to gain something good from their burdensome situation. To the extent possible, they support themselves, or, as with Umakichi and Ren, find their way back to youthful loves. The novel, which has been filmed, draws on stories from old "abandonment legends" (*kirō-densetsu*) passed on to the compilers of the classical collection *Konjaku Monogatari* [Tales of a Time that is now Past], and foregrounds not only the tragic sides of *ubasute* but also the possibility of an alternative way of life for the elderly.

Furui Yoshikichi's (1937–) psycho-archeologically structured texts from the 1970s and 1980s likewise lead to a folkloric-religious level by treating in *Sansōfu* [Mountains Disturbed] (1987) and in *Hijiri* [The Sage] (1987) a constellation of disease, age, sexuality, and death. In *Sennen no yuraku* [The Joy of a Thousand Years] (1982) as well, Nakagami Kenji (1946–1992) creates in Oryū the figure of an archaic powerful grandmother, who represents, as midwife and occasionally still sexually active woman, the collective memory of the community.

Issuing a femininist-emancipatory challenge, the well-known writer Ōba Minako (1930–) gives shape to the classic *yamauba* motif in *Yamauba no bishō* [The Smile of a Mountain Witch] (1976), emphasizing that age is a sign of the maturity a woman has gained and the basis of her self-assertion. Enchi Fumiko in *Onnamen* (1958, tr. *Masks* 1983) and Mori Makiko (1934–) in *Toraware* [Obsessed] (1989) leave the purely folkloric level in favour of the classical court tradition of the Noh Theatre, in order to demonstrate via the masks (*ryō no onna* [ghost woman], *masugami* [young madwoman], *fukai* [deep]) the existence already in the pre-modern period of a sublime psychology of the ageing stages of women.

## 4. Obsessive Old-Age Eroticism

It is a world of ageing determined by aestheticism and the theme of sexuality that we encounter in the works of Tanizaki Jun'ichirō und Kawabata Yasunari, whose texts present an old-age eroticism that is oriented toward the paradigms of *fin de siècle* European thought. Kawabata creates in *The House of Sleeping Beauties* a gothic romance focusing on the 67-year-old Eguchi and an enigmatic realm of eros-thanatos and virgin worship. A small, left-handed woman in her mid-forties rules over a secret house that is a realm of the senses for rich senior citizens. Eguchi utilizes a service of the house that offers the opportunity for them to sleep side-by-side with young girls rendered senseless by sleeping medicine. The situation makes it possible for Eguchi to feast his eyes on the girls and to be delighted at their youthful beauty and life energy; an artificial Buddhist-esoteric quality rubs up against *fin-de-siècle* necrophilic impulses, creating an atmosphere of morbid sensuality. Eguchi, who unlike other clients, does not yet suffer from senile impotence, experiences in the sublime erotic play of restraint and depersonalisation an initiation into the realm of the dead.

The image of the protagonist's erotic-spiritual symbiosis with a *femme fragile* or *femme fatale* also manifests itself in Tanizaki Jun'ichirō's *The Diary of a Mad Old Man*. Tanizaki's last important work once again subsumes one of the dominant themes of his work: sexuality and sexual obsession in old age. Tanizaki initially writes in *The Key* of uncommunicativeness between husband and wife, of dwindling potency, and of the erotic *mises-en-scènes* of a professor—and self-confessed foot fetishist—in his fifties. Now in *The Diary of a Mad Old Man*, Utsugi Tokusuke cultivates an intense passion for his beautiful daughter-in-law. This obsession of a dying man, who suffers from neural impairment and cardiac defects, breaks through his isolation within the empty formalisms of family etiquette. His euphoria-inducing erotic fantasies and his anarchic momentum forward lead him, even as he is aware of the tragicomedy of his venture, back to the source of his vitality.

Mishima Yukio (1924–1970) continues the tradition of aestheticism in his portrayal of old-age eroticism. *Kinjiki* (1950–53, tr. 1968 *Forbidden Colors*) is about the latently homosexual relationship between the young

Minami Yūichi and the writer Hinoki Shunsuke, who, at the end of the novel, commits suicide. No less versed in the canon of aestheticism, though from a woman's perspective, is the writer Enchi Fumiko (1905–1986), who, in her novel *Onnamen*, interprets a mature intellectual's erotic-pedagogical game of manipulation with younger men as her prey. Her heroine, Toganō Mieko, an older, attractive, educated, and cruel woman, has two university males, Ibuki Tsuneo and Mikame Toyoki, on her string. With a talent for psychological games, Toganō induces the younger Mikame to be an involuntary sperm donor, the resulting impregnation being the fulfillment of her plans. The erotic is transported through allusion to the Japanese classics, as manifested in the guise of the battle of the sexes in the academic and educated upper-middle classes of the 1950s.

Since the 1990s, Ogawa Yōko (1962–) has been cultivating old-age eroticism in the style of the Japanese aesthetic school. In her work, there is a change of perspective in that her protagonists are young girls who discover older men as lords and masters of their desires. In *Hoteru Airisu* [Hotel Iris] (1996), 17-year old Mari makes the acquaintance of an older man. A translator of Russian literature, he is in himself quite unremarkable, but he nonetheless fascinates her. She follows him to his island and plays the role of his maid in sadomasochistic games. The scenario created by Ogawa in accordance with certain mannerisms characterized by retroaestheticism plays with incestuous desires; it constitutes a regressive, nostalgically encoded, ghostly-playful world of the father complex. Here a gothic Lolita and her older lover find themselves in a comfortable arrangement, while the perennial girl escapes the mother as her nemesis and avoides reality of life, with its demands for achieving mature adulthood.

The obsessive relationship between younger women and older men is also described in Mori Makiko's *Toraware* and in Kawakami Hiromi's (1958–) *Sensei no kaban* [Teacher's Bag] (2001), while Yamamoto Michiko's (1936–) short story *Onoroi* [Curse] (1978) tells of a strange love affair between an old man and a old woman.

## 5. Generational Transition, Ageing, and Questions About Meaning

Issues regarding life stages frequently involve the theme of sexuality. Through encounters with a woman, men in their fifties have a renewed experience of sex and love, something that their life up until now has made them overlook. These are the representatives of those generations that took part in the war and Japan's reconstruction and who now look back on their lives and what they have achieved in their professions and families and ask themselves: How should I regard my deployment in the war? Did my lifelong work have any meaning? What is my relationship to my family like? What can I now still expect from the future? Am I already too old, or may I yet hope for something from life? What will my declining years be like? How should I come to grips with those last years and my death?

In *Fukai kawa* [Deep River] (1993) Endō Shusaku succeeds in categorizing those related considerations as they might have engaged the Japanese during the prosperous days of the bubble economy in the 1980s. The *point de départ* in his portrayal of a journey to India taken by six Japanese is that, despite material wealth, a feeling of meaninglessness and a paralyzing void in values has spread across the entire consumption- and achievement-oriented society. He seeks a spiritual-religious dimension. Informative here are three central figures: the former soldier Kiguchi, aged about 65, fought in Burma and is seeking to process the terrible war experiences that still burden him: he had, for example, eaten the corpse of a dead comrade. Isobe, in his mid-fifties, mourns his recently deceased wife and hopes to meet her reincarnated in India. He bears a sense of guilt, as he paid little attention to her in the course of their long marriage. Communication difficulties are also a problem for Numata, who cannot open up to his wife. Though Endō as a so-called Christian writer hints at concern for one's fellow man and urges concern and charitable involvement in the name of Christ, he makes it clear that it is vital for the older generations to ask themselves urgent questions about the meaning of life, ultimately also in order to be able to die a good death.

In many texts by the scriptwriter Yamada Taichi (1934–), the issue is a man's self-awareness. His protagonists end up in crisis situations, separate themselves from their families, and meet a woman who accompanies them into an enigmatic world between reality, dream-world, and death. In *Tobu yume o shibaraku minai* [I Haven't Dreamt of Flying in a While] (1985), a man named Taura is obliged to spend some time in hospital, where he makes the acquaintance of what turns out to be a 67-year-old woman, Mutsuko. When he later encounters her, she is an attractive, middle-aged woman. A passionate love relationship ensues. Curiously enough, however, Mutsuko's rejuvenation continues. Even though their love grows all the more intense, she is finally transformed into a young girl, who, at the end of the story, disappears amidst a burgeoning crowd of suits and ties in Shinjuku. In *Ijintachi to no natsu* (1987, tr. 2003 *Strangers*) as well, the protagonist, who fears he has cancer, meets a woman who lures him off into another world. He knows, however, that he must leave and eventually finds the way back to his old life. Yamada's visions of longing bespeak the wounded souls of elderly Japanese men, who in the nostalgic realm of the other world rediscover their own vulnerability in the form of *shōjo* (nymphette) fantasies.

There is something similar in Hino Keizō's (1929–2002) *Yume no Shima* [Isle of Dreams] (1985), in which the widower Sakai Shōzō, a construction engineer, reflects on what he has done over many years of vocational endeavour. He has believed that he has contributed to the reconstruction of Tokyo after the war and thereby to a positive future for Japan. Now in the face of the city's development into a cold, gloomy, life-hating metropolis of "concrete and iron", he feels enormous regret. The engineer meets two strange young women. With a female motorcyclist he goes to an artificial island in an inlet of Tokyo Bay, though it is off-limits, and there spends the night with her, rediscovering his sexuality. In the morning he sees herons that have been caught in nylon lines discarded by anglers and have suffered painful deaths. He later attempts to bury them but in the process becomes caught in the fork of a tree and dies of shock-induced heart failure. Hino offers an interpretation of the text, thereby questioning the endeavours of the construction generation: the blood sacrifice of the construction engineer has brought reconciliation with the powers of nature, which now deign to accept an alliance for a new and better Neo-Tokyo.

Ōe Kenzaburō (1935–) also offers a critical reflection on Japan and its generational transition in a novel entitled *Torikaeko: Chenjiringu* [Changeling] (2000), arriving just in time for the new millennium. This is the first part of a trilogy, with the first-person narrator, Cogito Chōkō, writer and intellectual, as well as the *alter ego* of the author, presenting, as it were, an auditor's report. Prompted by the suicide of his brother-in-law Gorō, he undergoes, in his mid-sixties, a life-goal evaluation.

In the novel, Ōe succeeds in producing an interesting composition, containing reflections on age, sexuality, and death, as well as the history of modern Japan, the trauma of the American occupation, and the major change in Japan's educational culture during the 1990s. The author, who celebrated his 70th birthday in 2005, has clearly reacted with painful sensitivity to the change of the times. His *alter ego* Cogito, whose friends have for the most part already died, feels strange in today's Japan. In the 1950s Cogito graduated in philological studies, with renowned tutors, from the University of Tokyo. In the eyes of the Japanese media public in the year 2000, such a scholarly horizon appears to have receded into the distance, a circumstance that causes the writer to have doubts about his own existence, and he momentarily even contemplates suicide. The central theme of the novel is the dangers of old-age depression and the crisis that Cogito overcomes during a stay in Berlin. The author Ōe, who had already in 1963 published *Keirō shūkan* [Respect for Old People's Week], in which he enlists a sly old man as a social critic, continues to deal in his current novel, *Sayōnara, watashi no hon yo!* [Farewell, My Books!] (2005), with the theme of senectitude and the meaning of an artist's later work.

Finally, the old men that Furui Yoshikichi puts on stage in his play *Funnō* [Angry Old Men] (2002) make a most disgruntled appearance.

## 6. Death Scenes, Death Initiation, and Posthumous Options

If in *Torikaeko* Ōe stages a hereafter dialogue between the protagonist and his dead brother-in-law, which may be interpreted more as a psychologically explainable obsession than as anything related to the occult, Endō Shūsaku's *Fukai kawa* hints at the actual existence of dimensions beyond this world. The aforementioned meaning vacuum, frequently affirmed in Japanese literary and intellectual circles, has brought with it since the 1980s the phenomenon of a spiritual and religious search that publishing houses and the media have eagerly served. In the framework of the age theme discussed here, the models of the hereafter, that is, the conceptions of life's end and posthumous existence that the ageing person invokes, are of special interest.

A masterful parody of a virtual journey into the underworld is Abe Kōbō's (1924–1993) *Kangarū nōtō* (1991, tr. 1996 *Kangaroo Notebook*). If it reads as on the one hand a report on popular near-death experiences (*rinshi taiken*), it is on the other a satire on the Japanese longing for a traditional hereafter and the healing effect of such. After an odyssey on his sickbed, the protagonist finds himself in Chapter 6 in an underworld hospital. The exclusively male patients are served by female nurses. Even as thought is being given to how the death of a moribund old man might be eased, including contemplation of euthanasia [*anrakushi*], not because he is loved as a fellow human being but rather because he is an annoyance, the patients are concerned with food and their sexual fantasies. Although Abe takes up the theme of spirituality, he puts forward no claim to the promise of salvation in the Japanese hereafter. Quite the contrary. When a man runs across his old shrew of a mother in the land of the dead, he wants to drive her away. Here for the reader there turns out to be no post-mortem option (Gebhardt 2001).

Murakami Masahiko's (1958–) novel *Maō* [Demon King] (1994) and Date Ikkō's (1950–) *Babironki 1980* [Chronicles of Babylon 1980] (1988) lead straight into the realm of new religions, both taking a critical stance. Murakami describes a euthasizing rest home for old people from rich families. There the date of death is set on the very day that the resident arrives. Date Ikkō depicts the initiation into ageing in which a girl takes part; for this, she is supposed to offer an old man sexual services, so that she can gain an intimately skin-to-skin sense of what it is like to be old. In the process, the old man enjoys a lustful death (Kamata 1990: 20).

With compendia such as Yamada Taichi's *Kore kara no ikikata, shinikata* [Up-and-Coming Ways of Living, Ways of Dying] (1994), one must take into account the growing need to come to grips with the theme of ageing and death. These writings are still the subject of discussion in connection with advice literature [*ikikata no hon*]. There are also anthologies with essays by literary figures and culture critics: *Shi* [Death] (1983), *Shinu tame no ikikata* [A Way of Life in Preparation for Death] (1980), and the current volume, *Shinu made shitai 10 no koto* [Ten Things I Want to Do Before I Die] (2003), which contains contributions by Kakuta Mitsuyo (1967–) and Yokomori Rika (1963–) among others.

Of interest are the popular *tōbyōki*, the chronicles of illness battled, that is, documentations of sickness and death that were initially composed by literary figures and critics as they pertain to their own fates or those of others within the literary scene. Thus, for example, Honda Keiko, the daughter of Niwa Fumio, the author of *The Hateful Age*, writes about his struggle with Alzheimer's. Today many Japanese outside the literary world also write such accounts.

Under the mottos *jibun no shi o tsukuru jidai* [the era when one creates one's own personal death] and *shi no shakaika* [the socialization of death], the genre has broad appeal (Wöhr 1997: 389–391). An impressive example is the photo-documentation of the death of the writer Nakai Hideo (1922–1993), which Honda Shōichi compiled under the title *Suisei to no hibi* [Days With the Comet]. When the literary critic Etō Jun (1933–1999) published *Tsuma to watashi* [My Wife and I] (1999), depicting his wife in the last stages of cancer, the book received considerable attention. Etō shows himself to be a caring husband, at first reacting with horror to the news he receives from the physician and then movingly seeing to her needs. Again, as is the custom in Japan, he does not inform her of her condition. Shortly after her death, Etō committed suicide. Tanabe Seiko (1928–) has written *Naniwa no yūnagi* [Evening Calm in Naniwa] (2003), a story of how she nursed her dying husband.

Books such as *Konna fū ni shinitai* [This is the Way I Want to Die] (1987) by Satō Aiko (1923–) lead the way into occult visions of posthumous existence. Satō (1923–) is a well-known woman writer with a pronounced propensity for the occult. In the above-mentioned work, she delves into the death of her 76-year-old father, while also opining about the *shigo no sekai*, the afterworld, and reports from the realm beyond. In a contemporary Japan where many Japanese define themselves as non-religious [*mushūkyō*] and no longer find any orientation, council, or solace in institutionalized faiths (cf. chapter 21), the occult twist on the afterworld offers a model that may ease the fear of death. Also to be mentioned here is the cheerful compendium on death by the *manga*-artist Mizuki Shigeru (1924–) *Sanzu no kawa no watarikata. 'Ano yo' to 'reikai' ga miete kuru* [How to Cross the River Sanzu: Glimpsing "The Next World" and "The Spirit Realm"] (2000).

## 7. Advice Literature and Old-Age Philosophical Discourse

Riding the boom of advice literature in the last two decades, those who offer information regarding an improved quality of life in old age, ways to fulfilled twilight years, and *ars moriendi* have been churning out published material in large quantities. The 1990s were the decade of the great commentators on culture; first and foremost among those relevant to our theme are Yanagida Kunio and Hinohara Hideo. To the literary figures who have already published several volumes of advice literature relevant to age, we can add Itsuki Hiroyuki, Setouchi Jakuchō, Uno Chiyo (1897–1996), Sono Ayako, and Genyū Sōkyū (1956–).

Itsuki Hiroyuki, a writer of entertainment fiction, has been primarily known since the 1990s as a provider of advice. In 2000, he published *Urayamashii shinikata* [Enviable Ways to Die], in which he collects commentaries of various elderly people. In the epilogue, Itsuki speaks about the Japanese view of life and death [*shiseikan*]. In a volume entitled *Watashi nan daka shinanai yō na ki ga suru n desu yo* [Somehow I *do* Have the Feeling That I Won't Die], Uno Chiyo discusses the motto *ikijōzu, yamijōzu, oijōzu, shinijōzu* [Life, Illness, Ageing, Dying: Doing it All With

Panache]. The Christian writer Sono Ayako develops an aesthetics of old age: *Bannen no bigaku o motomete* [Towards an Aesthetics of the Later Years] (2006], while Setouchi and Genyū, both Buddhist clerics and writers, exchange opinions in the monograph *Ano yo, kono yo* [This World, The Next World] (2003).

Genyū carries on with the topic in *Shindara dō naru* [What Happens when we Die?] (2005). Ishihara Shintarō (1932–), formerly a writer, now a conservative politician and the governor of Tokyo, contributes to the discourse by authoring *Oite koso jinsei* [Getting Old Means True Human Life] (2002). Yanagida Kunio is a popular representative of "the critics' era": he writes, for example, in a volume entitled *Shi no henyō* [Changing Patterns of Death] (1997) about self-determined death, about death with dignity [*songenshi*], and about euthanasia [*anrakushi*]. The physicians Hinohara Shigeaki (1911–) and Yōrō Takeshi (1937–) have compiled numerous works of advice, for example, Hinohara's *Oi to shi no juyō* [Receptivity to Old Age and Death] (1998), *Jinsei hyakunen* [Centenarian] (2004), and *65. 27sai no ketsui • 92 no jōnetsu* [65: The Determination of 27; The Passion of 92] (2003), together with Ototake Hirotada; Yōrō's *Rinshō tetsugaku* [Deathbed Philosophy] (1997) und *Shi no kabe* [The Wall of Death] (2004). Hinohara represents himself as an active elderly citizen. He advocates the movement of the new elderly and supports the New Elderly Society [*Shin Rōjin no Kai*]. Like her two colleagues, Yanagisawa Keiko, a scientist, discusses aspects of life processes, ageing and death, thereby also seeking to explore spiritual dimensions and the momentum of healing [*iyashi*]. Solace and healing for each life situation and also for old age have been a publicized megatrend since the end of the 1990s (Gebhardt 2004).

Further texts in the popular age debate are: *Oikata no jōzu na hito, heta na hito* [People Who Age Well, People Who Don't] (1986) by Higuchi Keiko (1932–); *Dai ōjō* [The Great Crossing] (1994) by Rokusuke Ei (1933–), a million-seller in the year it appeared; Shikita Kazuko's (1925–) numerous writings, for example, *Toshi o kasaneru no mo waruku nai* [Piling Up The Years Isn't So Bad (1997), as well as Akasegawa Genpei's (1937–) *Rōjinryoku* [Old People's Power] (1999).

## 8. The "Nice Old Lady"? Old-age Wisdom, Emancipation, and a Liberated Life-sense

Newer publications, those of Uno, Itsuki and Sono, for example, emphasize a positive, active side of old age. They demonstrate how one can live as an elderly person, integrated and content. Then too there are Yumoto Kazumi (1959–), in whose work a "good granny" appears, and Kirino Natsuo, with her current contribution to senior citizen emancipation. (Note: The "good granny" stands in contrast to the "mean granny" [*ijiwaru-bāsan*], a famous cartoon character created by Hasegawa Machiko, 1920–1992.)

In Yumoto Kazumi's *Popula no aki* [Poplar Autumn] (1997), Chiaki, a young woman in crisis, contemplates the most important episode in her life: her encounter with Mrs. Yanagi. A telephone call informs her that the woman is still alive at nearly 100. As a young child Chiaki lived with her mother after the death of her father in the house of the old lady. In the small, quiet residence with its poplar tree, they feel as though they have been rescued. The mother finds employment, while the daughter gradually becomes accustomed to her new environment. The landlady is an eccentric old woman, whom Chiaki at first takes to have an antipathy towards children; we learn that she is the widow of a professor of Chinese literature. She succeeds in releasing Chiaki from her paralyzed mental state, brought about by the tragic loss (suicide) of her father, which has deprived her of all self-confidence. When Chiaki falls ill, the landlady declares that she is willing to take the place of the working mother to assume the care of the sick girl. As the six-year-old and the old woman come to know each other better, Mrs. Yanagi confides in her a secret that becomes the key to Chiaki's recovery. She tells her of letters that she collects to take with her and forward to those in the hereafter. Chiaki finds in this an opportunity to write letters to her father care of Mrs. Yanagi. The activity helps her over her problems. Now as she travels to the funeral of the old woman, dead at 100, the reader can well expect that she will meet the new challenge she faces, as she recalls the kindness and wisdom of the old woman.

In the world experienced by the children whom Yumoto creates, eccentric old folk play a central role. They tend to see things in a much more relaxed fashion than do the parents, driven as they are by longings and desires, and help the children to find themselves and to gain self-confidence. Their very pecularities, which they fearlessly live out, underline their balanced, positive outlook.

Kirino Natsuo likewise deals with the emancipated elderly. Three decades after Ariyoshi's *Kōkotsu no hito*, Kirino gives the themes of old age an up-to-date flavour in her novel *Tamamoe!* From the perspective of the old and mature, Kirino takes on the question of how one can make something pleasant of the last decades of life. Her old people's novel about the self-assertion of the elderly and (what in Anglo-Japanese is called) *romance grey* sets out a beacon of hope for the literary "silver market". The publication, placed with extreme adroitness, follows the current trend of advice literature and offers instructions for ageing, commenting on the various stages of the process, from 59 to the mid-70s.

Her husband's sudden death from a heart attack sends 59-year-old Sekiguchi Toshiko plunging from the sheltered existence of a housewife into raw reality. Several unpleasant facts are waiting for her: first the knowledge that her husband Takayuki has for many years had a lover; then she is confronted with the selfish desires of her son Akiyuki, who wants to terminate his unsuccessful stay in America and move into his mother's small house, together with his wife and children; and her daughter Miho is thinking about claiming a share of the inheritance. Toshiko takes time off from all of this and leaves her home for a few days. She finds refuge in a capsule hotel, where she has some decisive experiences, which demonstrate to her just how "out of it" she has been and how many other lifestyles and ways of survival there are. Her meeting with a "professional granny" is most instructive: this is an old woman who has taken up residence in the hotel and pockets money for the advice she forces on the guests.

The protagonist, who begins to reflect intensely on her environment and her own concepts and goals, comes to see her family from a markedly more distant perspective. Emotionally still unstable, she seeks contact with the outside world in order to reorient herself. Finally she dares to confront Itō Akiko, her dead husband's lover. Amazingly enough, Akiko is not a younger woman; at 63, she is, in fact, older than Toshiko. She owns a restaurant into which the greater part of Takayuki's money has gone. Toshiko, who had associated mostly only with three female friends from her school days, becomes acquainted with her husband's male friends, among them Tsukamoto, an older but very attractive married man. This leads to a night of love in a luxurious hotel in Shinjuku. In the course of weeks and months after the death of her husband, Toshiko succeeds in conquering her feelings of loneliness, disappointment, and rage towards Takayuki and her family. During the involuntary maturation process, she learns to assert herself, to live with self-doubts, and to gain a new attitude towards life. Toshiko makes it clear to her children that she will not sell the house to provide them with their share of the inheritance, demands of Itō that she return the money she owes the Sekiguchi family, and daringly embarks—as the last passage of the novel suggests—on a relationship with the married man Tsukamoto (Gebhardt 2006).

Kirino pleads the case of sexual freedom for both men and women and sees it as a matter of course to make these needs known. With her 2005 novel, the treatment of the topic of old age in contemporary Japanese literature has finally and decisively shifted: the rice-devouring ghosts have become self-aware senior citizens.

## Conclusion

Over the period from 1945 into the first decade of the twenty-first century, Japanese literature has been treating the theme of age and ageing, mirroring current reflections on the part of Japanese society and providing for its part much thoughtful insight. This literature ranges from commentary about senility and the care crisis to the depiction of lengthy farewells for the fathers who went off to war and finally to folkloristic endeavours and the invocation of power on the part of demonic women. Contemporary texts question conventional ideas about old age and demand new life models for older people, together with a pleasant life for them in retirement (*rōgo*).

It is worth noting that it is above all female authors who are presently revising the previously negative picture of ageing in Japan. They depict courageous older women who want to actively shape and enjoy their lives. Their works are directed to the literary "silver market" but also to readers who, on the verge of *kanreki*, wish to inform themselves about the various phases of ageing.

## References

Formanek, Susanne (1994): *Denn dem Alter kann keiner entfliehen. Altern und Alter im Japan der Nara- und Heian Zeit* [For no one can escape ageing: Ageing and age in Japan in the Nara and Heian Periods]. Vienna: Verlag der österreichischen Akademie der Wissenschaften.

—— (2005): *Die „böse Alte" in der japanischen Populärkultur der Edo-Zeit* [The "wicked old woman" in Japanese popular culture of the Edo period]. Vienna: Verlag der österreichischen Akademie der Wissenschaften.

Gebhardt, Lisette (2001): *Japans Neue Spiritualität* [Japan's New Spirituality]. Wiesbaden: Harrassowitz.

—— (2004): Der Konsum von Heilung (*iyashi*) in der japanischen Gegenwartskultur und die Religio-Reise nach Asien [Healing (*iyashi*) as a commodity in contemporary

Japanese culture and the religious journey to Asia]. In: Piegeler, Hildegard *et al.* (eds.): *Gelebte Religionen: Untersuchungen zur sozialen Gestaltungskraft religiöser Vorstellungen und Praktiken in Geschichte und Gegenwart.* Würzburg: Königshausen & Neumann, pp. 325–338.

—— (2006): *Im Alter frei, selbstbewußt und nicht ganz ohne Sex: Kirino Natsuos Wegweiser für ein erfülltes Seniorendasein* [Age-free, self-aware, and not entirely without sex: Natsuo Kirinos guide to successful ageing (March 2006). Japanologie Frankfurt am Main, Johann Wolfgang Goethe University, Germany. http://www.japanologie.uni-frankfurt.de/links.php?topic=53 (found 11 December 2006).

Higuchi, Keiko (1979): *Itoshiki wa oi: Bungaku no naka no rōjintachi* [Sweet old age: The elderly within literature]. Tokyo: PHP Kenkyūjo.

Imhof, Arthur E. (1986): Individualismus und Lebenserwartungen im Alter. Japans Interesse an uns [Individualism and life expectations in old-age: Japan's interest in us]. In: *Leviathan* 14, pp. 361–391.

Kamata, Tōji (1990): *Oi to shi no fuōkuroa* [The folklore of old age and death] Tokyo: Shinyōsha.

Loughman, Celeste (1991): The Twilight Years: A Japanese View of Aging, Time, and Identity. In: *World Literature Today* 65, 1, pp. 49–53.

Mizuno, Yumiko (1991): *Nihonbungaku to oi* [Japanese literature and old age]. Tokyo: Shintensha.

Nagai, Sonoko (2004): *Ikitsuzukeru to iu koto. Bungaku ni miru yamai to oi* [What it means to go on living. Illness and old age within literature]. Tokyo: Medical Review sha.

Niwa, Fumio (1962): The Hateful Age. In: Morris, Ivan (ed.): *Modern Japanese Stories.* Tokyo: Tuttle, pp. 320–348.

Satō, Yasumasa (1991): *Bungaku ni okeru oi* [Ageing in literature]. Tokyo: Kasama Shoin.

Scheidt, Bernhard (1996): *Im Innersten meines Herzens empfinde ich tiefe Scham. Das Alter im Schrifttum des japanischen Mittelalters* [In my innermost heart I feel shame: Age in the writings of medieval Japan]. Vienna: Verlag der österreichischen Akademie der Wissenschaften.

Skord, Virginia (1989): Withered Blossoms. Aging in Japanese Literature. In: Bagnell, Prisca von Dorotka und Patricia Spencer Soper (eds.): *Perceptions of Aging in Literature.* New York: Greenwood Press, pp. 131–143.

Suzuki, Akira (2005): *Ikiru chikara o ataeru bungaku—Fukai kandō, shisaku no chūshin o yomu* [Literature that gives the power to live: Reading deep affection and thought]. Tokyo: Toshishobō.

Tsukimura, Reiko (ed.) (1978): *Life, Death, and Age in Modern Japanese Fiction.* Toronto: University of Toronto, York University.

Umetani, Kaoru (2003): *Shōsetsu de yomu shōrōbyōshi* [Reading illness, old age and death within novels]. Tokyo: Igaku Shoin.

Wöhr, Ulrike (1997): Death in Present Day Japan: Changing the Image of an Immutable Fact of Life. In: *AS* 51, pp. 387–419.

Wöss, Fleur (1984): Escape into Death. Old People and Their Wish to Die. In: Daniels, Gordon (ed.): *Europe Interprets Japan.* Tenterden, Kent: Norbury Publication, pp. 222–229.

Yoshitake, Teruko (2003): Writing on Aging: Changes over Two Decades. In: *Japanese Book News* 41, pp. 1–3.

CHAPTER TWENTY-SIX

# MEDIA USE IN THE AGEING SOCIETY

Nobuko Shiraishi

## Introduction

Using various public opinion surveys, mainly the results of the "TV and the Japanese" surveys that NHK has been conducting every five years since 1985, this article analyses contemporary media use, focusing primarily on television viewership. In addition, we will examine media use by the age group 60 years and older, and how the special characteristics of this increasing proportion of the national population may affect media use more generally in the future.

## 1. Television Viewership

### 1.1. *TV viewing time continues to rise*

NHK is often asked whether on account of the proliferation of cell phones and increasing Internet use people are spending less time watching TV. However, a look at the statistics on viewing time reveals no such trend. According to the National Survey of Individual Viewing Rates (see Figure 1), which NHK has been conducting regularly since 1971, people have been watching plenty of TV in recent years. The latest data from 2005 show 3 hours and 43 minutes of TV a day for the average person during an average week.

Figures 2 and 3 give viewing times broken down for sex and occupation. The unemployed and the elderly 60 years and over spend upwards of 5 hours a day watching TV, much longer than those in other categories. After the elderly, those who spend the longest time watching TV (more than four hours per day) are women in their 40s and 50s, as well as homemakers and the self-employed. People under the age of 20 spend the least amount of time watching TV.

Since the elderly, who also watch the most TV, continue to become an ever larger percentage of the national population, they are driving up the national viewing time average. Therefore it is reasonable

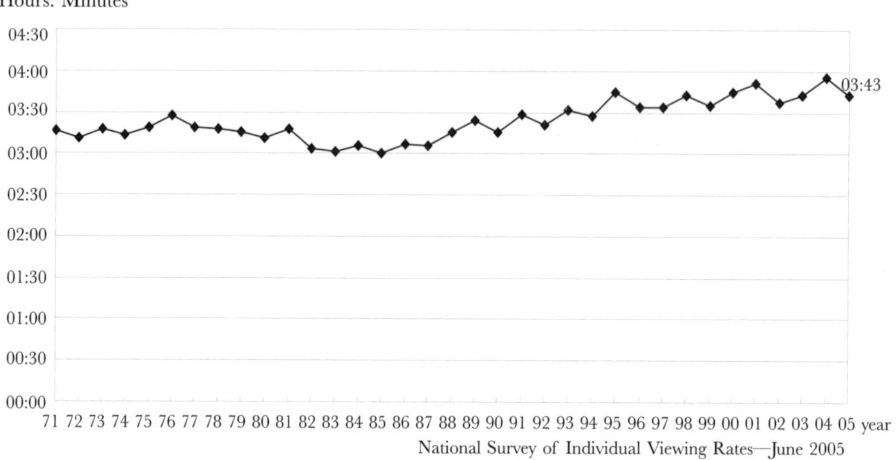


Figure 1. Changes in TV viewing duration, 1971–2005 (daily average per week).

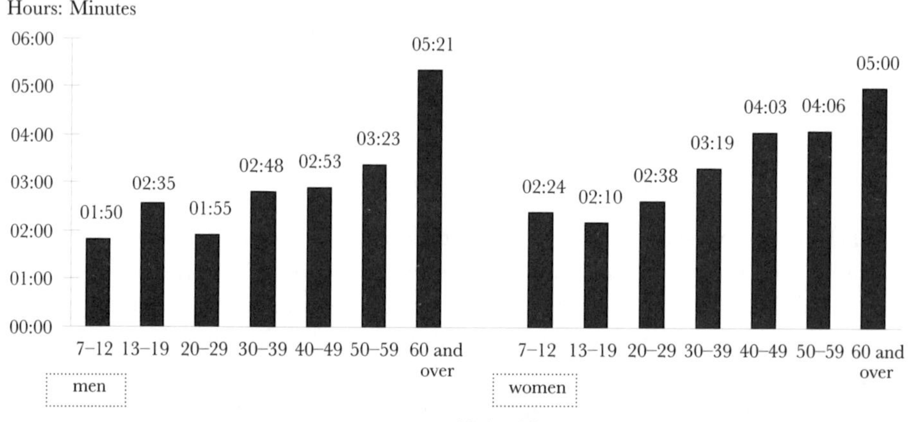


Figure 2. Viewing duration by sex (daily average per week).

to predict that viewing time will continue to rise as a function of our ageing society.

The rise in TV viewing time may also be due to changing viewing habits. In 2005, 39 per cent of respondents said "I prefer watching TV alone" while 30 per cent said "I prefer watching TV together with others." If we look at the change in responses over 20 years (Figure 4), we see that "I prefer watching alone" has increased slightly with every survey, which in the event focuses on women over 50 years and older. On the other hand, "I prefer watching with others" has declined

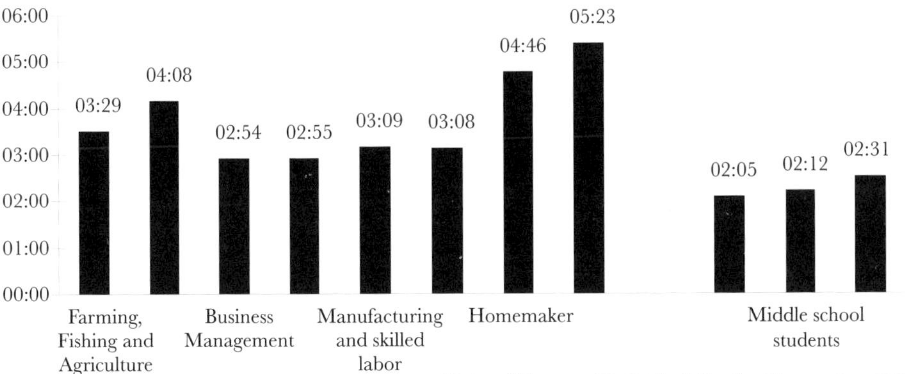


Figure 3. Viewing duration by profession (daily average per week).

little by little; in fact, between 1985 and 2005, the two categories have inverted their relationship. Since many of those who responded with "I prefer watching alone" were also those who said they watched "four hours or more" a day (46 per cent), we can probably assume that this attitude has some effect on the rise of viewing time.

The recent and striking trend towards leaving the TV on continuously ("I leave the TV on but watch only when I'm interested" ["Often" + "Sometimes" = 65 per cent], "When I come home, I turn the TV on right away" [62 per cent cumulatively]), as seen in Figure 5, is also related to the increase in viewing time. The group of those who responded with "Often" to these two queries overlapped with that of the respondents who watch TV "four or more hours" per day.

Even if we limit the set to those who use the Internet on a daily basis, a good number of respondents said that they "leave the TV on" either "often" or "sometimes" (61 per cent). In other words, the spread of Internet use in and of itself cannot be correlated with decreased TV viewing time.[1]

### 1.2. *The importance of TV has reached its limit*

As we can see, TV is an integral part of contemporary everyday life. People are watching TV while they do other things, whether shaving, ironing, or talking with family. One could even say that "watching TV"

[1] Compare NHK BCRI (NHK Broadcasting Culture Research Institute) (ed.) (2006): Growing Internet Use and TV Viewing Patterns (Japanese only). In: *The NHK Monthly Report on Broadcast Research* (March).

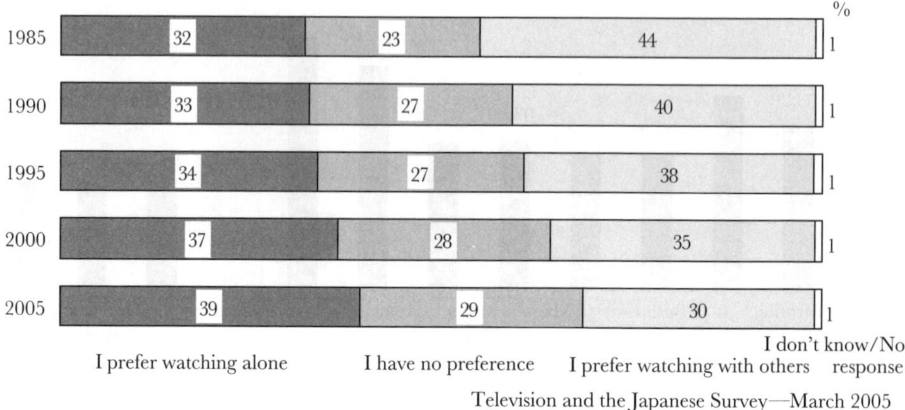


Figure 4. Watching alone *vs*. watching with others.

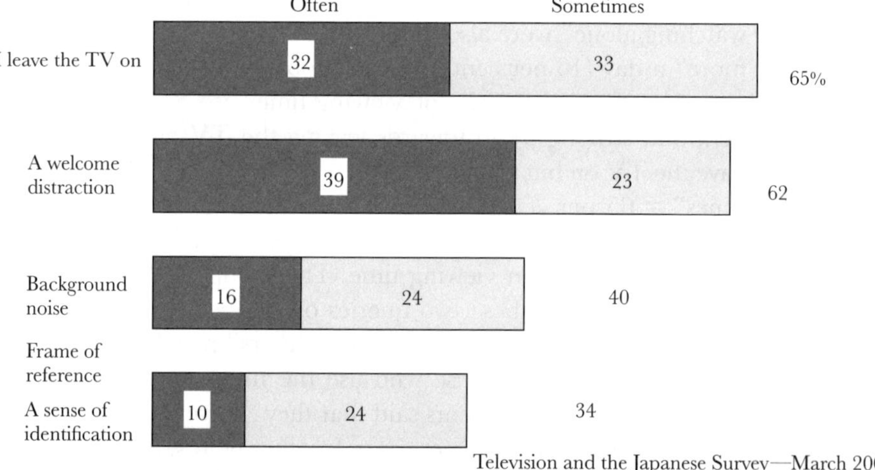


Figure 5. Modern TV viewing habits.

has become such an inseparable part of daily life that it has in fact has changed the way we look at the course of time.[2]

According to the National Time Use Survey (October 2005), the average person (aged 10 years and over) spends an average of 1 hour and 18 minutes a day watching TV while doing something else. This

[2] Compare NHK BCRI (ed.) (2006): Closeup of TV Viewing (Japanese only). In: *NHK Monthly Report* (May).

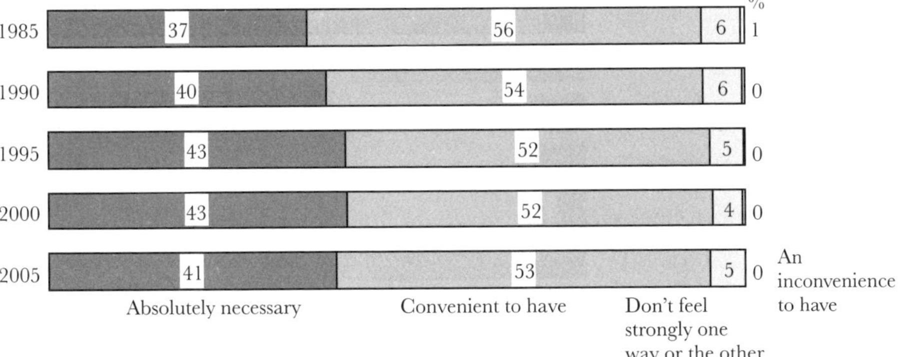


Figure 6. "How important is TV to you?"

is a little over a third of total viewing time (3 hours and 39 minutes).[3] However, we have not collected data that shows whether the importance of TV in everyday life as a whole has expanded along with increased viewing time.

Showing changes over the past twenty years, Figure 6 tracks responses to the question, "how important is TV to you?" In spite of the increase in viewing time between 1985 and 1995, we can see that the percentage of those who responded that TV was "Indispensable" to them has hardly changed at all over the last three surveys. It also seems that over the past twenty years, the estimation of TV's function has also decreased. Between 1985 and 2005, responses to "Source of dialogue with family members" decreased from 70 per cent to 63 per cent; "TV allows me to experience what I cannot do in real life" went down from 61 per cent to 52 per cent; and "I think of TV as a conversation partner" fell from 27 per cent to 19 per cent.

In other words, though viewing time continues to increase, this does not mean that the function and importance of TV in people's lives is increasing as well.

[3] Compare NHK BCRI (ed.) (2006): National Time Use Survey—2005 (Japanese only). In: *NHK Monthly Report* (April).

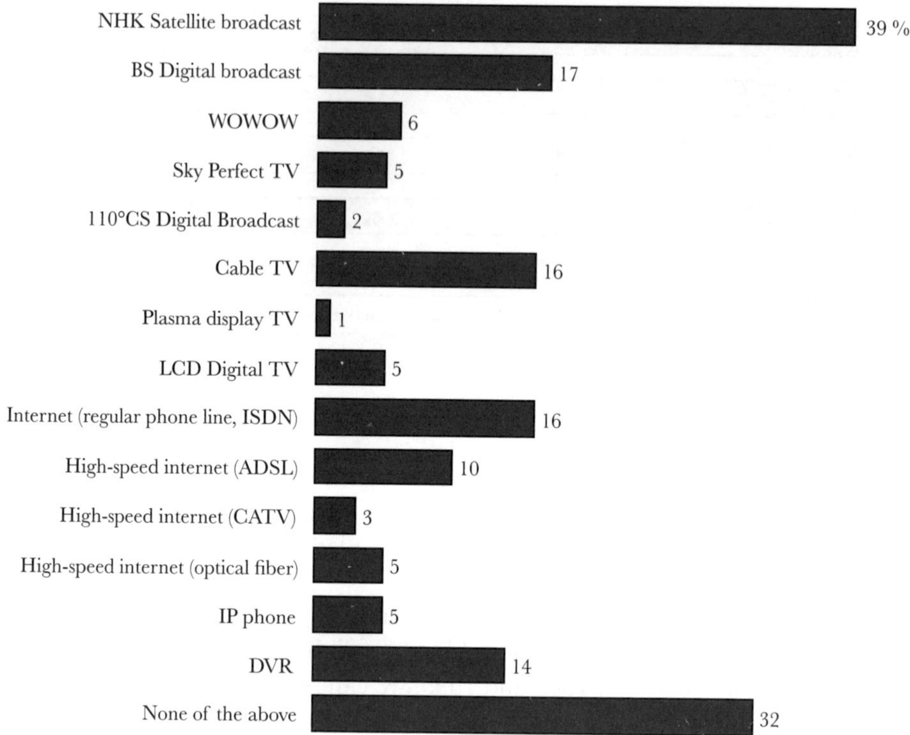


Figure 7. Equipment owned; services in use.

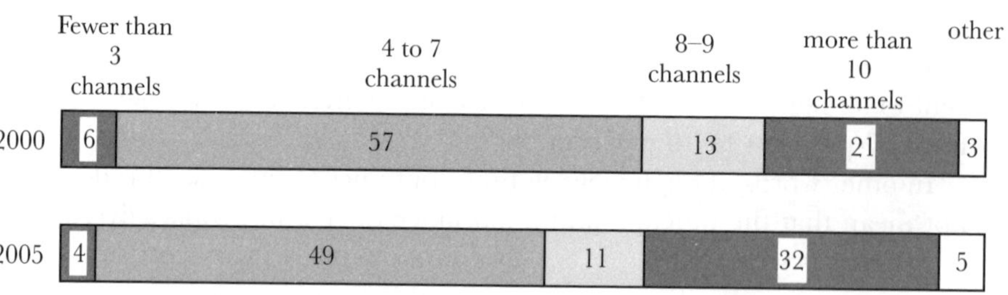


Figure 8. Channels available through commercial broadcast.

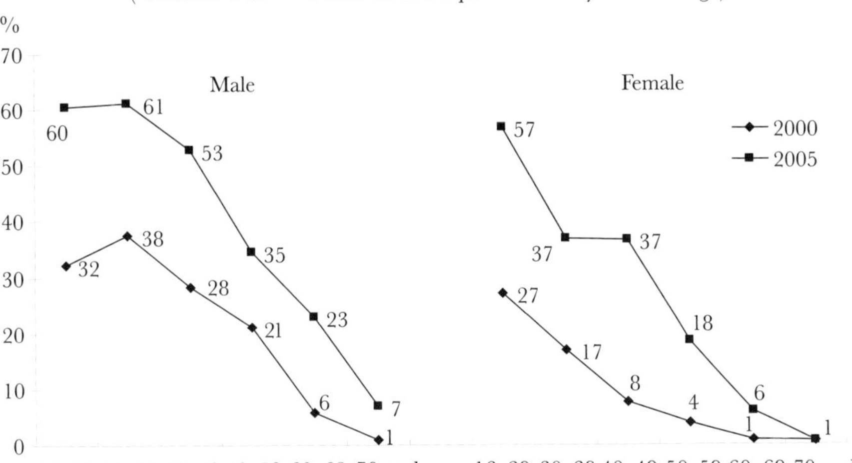


Figure 9. Frequency of Internet use (more than once a week).

## 2. Media Use

### 2.1. *A rich media environment*

In January 2006, media use in the home makes for a wide variety of channels available to viewers. As Figure 7 shows, 39 per cent of respondents receive NHK satellite broadcast, 17 per cent get BS digital cable, and 16 per cent make use of cable TV.[4] What is more, this availability has increased greatly over the past five years. In 2000, the percentage of households with access to 10 channels or more was 21 per cent. This number rose to 32 per cent by 2005 (see Figure 8).

As far as domestic use of digital media equipment is concerned, 5 per cent responded they had a LCD digital TV, and 14 per cent responded that they used a DVD, hard disk or some other digital recording device. The diffusion of DVR is still in an early phase.

In contrast, the Internet environment is expanding rapidly for home use. 16 per cent of households use regular or ISDN phone lines to access

[4] Compare NHK BCRI (ed.) (2006): Digital Media: How Far will the Number of Users Expand?" In: *NHK Monthly Report* (June).

the Internet; 10 per cent use ADSL high-speed service, 3 per cent use CATV, while another 5 per cent use fibre optic cable access (2006).

Actual use of the Internet has also increased since 2000, with 17 per cent responding that they "use the Internet every day"; another 30 per cent (twice the amount of 2000) report that they "use the Internet more than once a week."

Use is expanding among both men and women over a wide range of ages. According to Figure 9, the most active users are those under 40, a fact that has not changed much in the past five years, but there have been significant increases in Internet use among other age groups: 23 per cent of men in their 60s (compared with 6 per cent five years ago), and 18 per cent of women in their 50s (as opposed to 4 per cent five years ago). Looking by occupation, it is evident that Internet use has extended beyond the business sphere: 16 per cent of homemakers (as opposed to 5 per cent five years ago), and 16 per cent of the unemployed (as compared to 2 per cent five years ago).

### 2.2. *TV and the Internet: complementary media*

The "Television and the Japanese" survey asked respondents to choose their single most preferred medium (among a total of eleven which included TV, newspaper, radio, Internet, movies/video, books, CD/MD/cassette tape, etc., eleven media) for each of a variety of seven different functions, such as: "News"—world events and trends; "Commentary"—discussion of political and social issues; "Entertainment"—excitement and enjoyment; "Information"—information on hobbies and lifestyle issues; and so on. Table 1 displays the relative ratios for respondents who chose TV, newspapers, radio, or the Internet for the four functions "News," "Entertainment," "Commentary," and "Information."

TV rated the highest for all four of the functions. Other media cannot compare, particularly in the categories for "News" (66 per cent) and "Entertainment" (51 per cent).

TV led in the category of "Commentary" (51 per cent), followed by newspapers (35 per cent). In the category of "Information," TV fell below the 50 per cent mark (to 35 per cent), and lined up more closely with newspapers (12 per cent) and the Internet (11 per cent).

Table 2 narrows down the respondent pool to Internet users, particularly those who use it every day. As it shows, for these respondents, the Internet made the top three in the categories of "News," "Information," "Commentary," and "Socializing." 39 per cent of these respondents

Table 1. Useful Media.

(%)

| | TV | | Newspaper | | Radio | | Internet | |
|---|---|---|---|---|---|---|---|---|
| | 2000 | 2005 | 2000 | 2005 | 2000 | 2005 | 2000 | 2005 |
| News | 65 | 66 | 24 | 18 | 7 | 8 | 1 | 4 |
| Entertainment | 58 | 57 | 2 | 2 | 2 | 2 | 0 | 0 |
| Explanation Commentary | 48 | 51 | 41 | 35 | 3 | 2 | 0 | 2 |
| Information | 38 | 35 | 11 | 12 | 3 | 2 | 4 | 11 |

"News" World Events & Trends
"Entertainment" Excitement & Enjoyment
"Commentary" Discussion of political and social issues
"Information" Information on hobbies & lifestyle issues

Television and the Japanese Survey—March 2005

Table 2. Comparison of Media Use (Useful Media—"Routine Users").

(%)

| | Users—"Every Day" | | Users—"1–4 times a week" | |
|---|---|---|---|---|
| News | TV | 56 | TV | 68 |
| | Internet | 20 | Newspaper | 21 |
| | Newspaper | 18 | Radio | 7 |
| Entertainment | TV | 47 | TV | 44 |
| | Movies/Video | 26 | Movies/Video | 25 |
| | Books | 13 | Books | 13 |
| Education | Books | 42 | Books | 39 |
| | TV | 20 | TV | 23 |
| | Newspaper | 17 | Newspaper | 19 |
| Information | Internet | 39 | TV | 24 |
| | TV | 23 | Internet | 21 |
| | Local Information/Newsletters | 10 | Local Informations/Newsletters | 17 |
| Commentary | Newspaper | 42 | TV | 47 |
| | TV | 42 | Newspaper | 44 |
| | Internet | 9 | Talking with Family | 2 |
| Relaxation | TV | 28 | TV | 30 |
| | CDs, etc. | 23 | CDs, etc. | 21 |
| | Talking with Family | 21 | Talking with Family | 18 |
| Socializing | Talking with Friends | 41 | Talking with Friends | 49 |
| | TV | 17 | TV | 20 |
| | Internet | 11 | Talking with Family | 8 |
| | | (317人) | | (268人) |

"Education" Learning new things
"Relaxation" Taking a break, resting
"Socializing" Deepening and expanding relationship with other people

Television and the Japanese Survey—March 2005

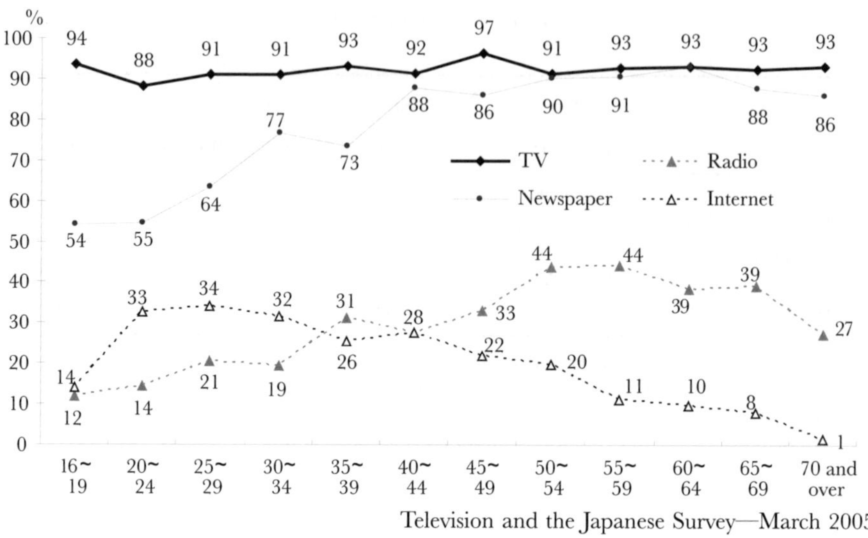


Figure 10. Frequency of media use ('daily' users by age).

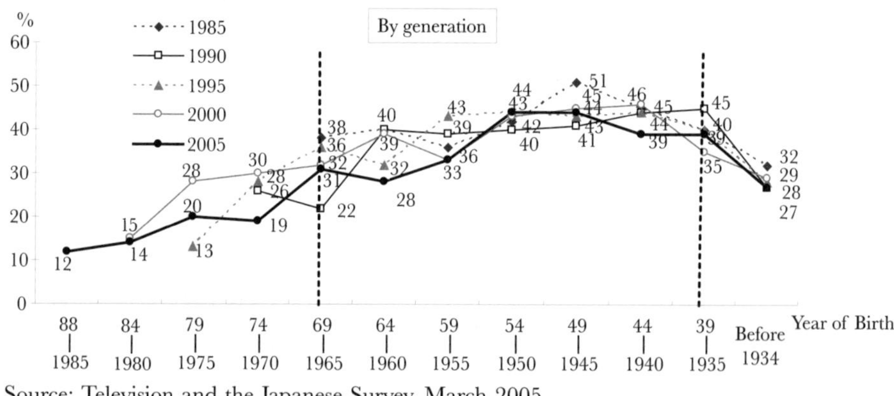


Source: Television and the Japanese Survey, March 2005.

Figure 11. Frequency of radio use ('daily' users).

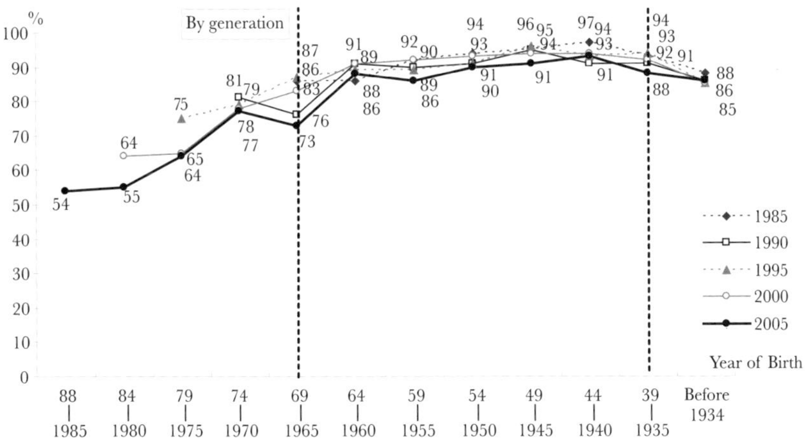


Source: Television and the Japanese Survey, March 2005.

Figure 12. Frequency of newspaper use ('daily' users).

preferred the Internet for "Information," which far exceeds TV (23 per cent).

However, for functions besides pure information transmission, such as "Entertainment," "Education" and "Relaxation," it seems that even daily Internet users do not necessarily prefer the Internet. In this sense, the power of the medium is still restricted, and as yet is no match for TV.

Table 3 tabulates the nationwide response to the question "What is the best medium for obtaining news and information, TV, newspapers, radio or Internet?" TV captured the overwhelming majority in terms of "speed" and "ease." Newspapers won out in the "quality" category. For "selectivity", TV was still ahead (35 per cent), but closer to newspapers (24 per cent) and the Internet (22 per cent).

TV is perceived to be extremely effective as a form of mass communication, in terms of both currency and ease of comprehension. On the other hand, the Internet seems to rate highly in terms of users being able to choose individually the information most suitable for their purposes.

Given the results of this survey, it seems that at the present stage, TV and the Internet are not in a conflicting, competitive relationship with one another. In other words, they are not interchangeable in terms of their function to users. We might say that the Internet is making a niche for itself by fulfilling functions that TV cannot perform as well.

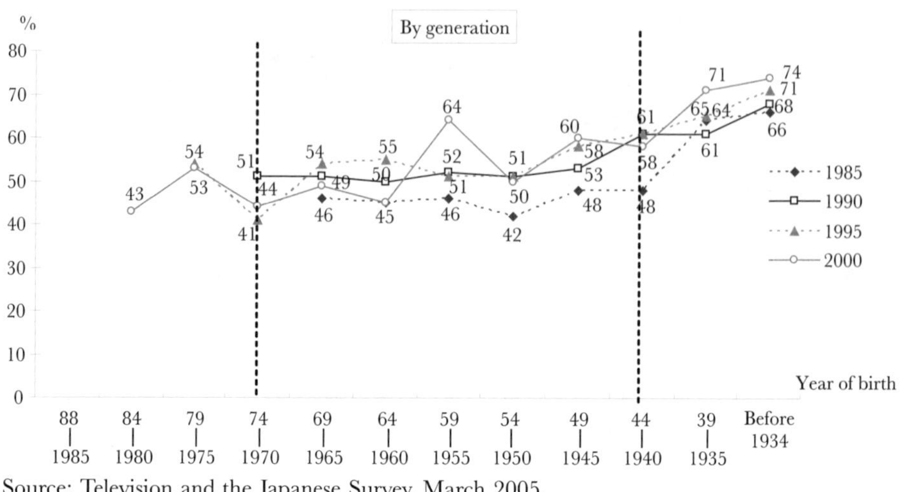


Source: Television and the Japanese Survey, March 2005.

Figure 13. 'An indispensable medium: TV' (1985–2000).

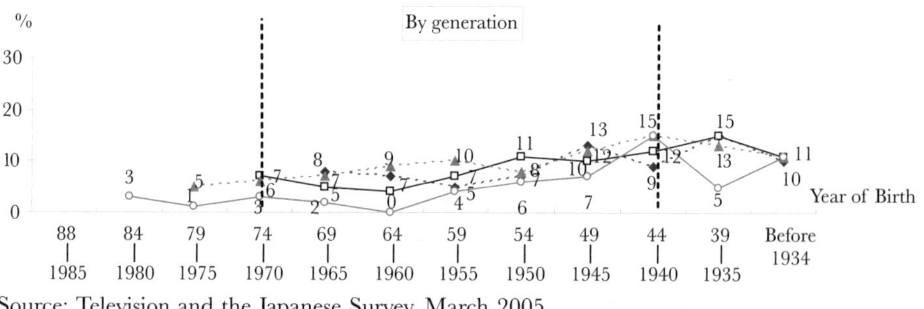


Source: Television and the Japanese Survey, March 2005.

Figure 14. An indispensable medium: Radio' (1985–2000).

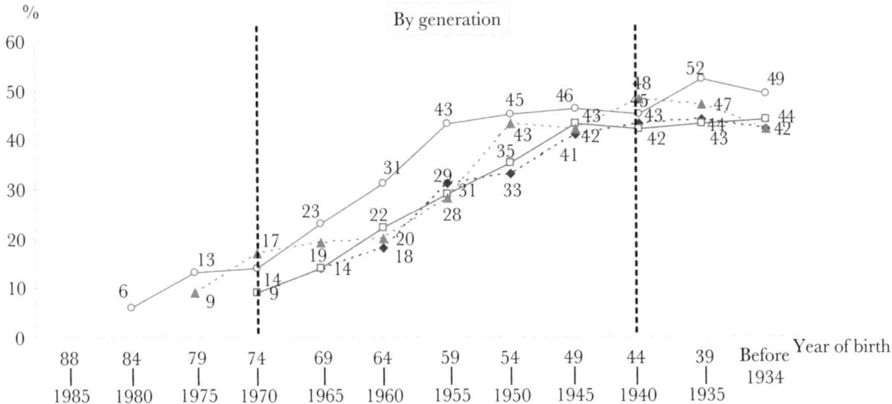


Source: Television and the Japanese Survey, March 2005.

Figure 15. 'An indispensable medium: Newspaper' (1985–2000).

Table 3. The Best Media for Obtaining News and Information.

(%)

| | TV | | Newspaper | | Radio | | Internet | |
|---|---|---|---|---|---|---|---|---|
| | 2000 | 2005 | 2000 | 2005 | 2000 | 2005 | 2000 | 2005 |
| Speed | 82 | 78 | 2 | 1 | 12 | 12 | 3 | 6 |
| Ease | 69 | 67 | 23 | 21 | 2 | 3 | 0 | 2 |
| Quality | 37 | 37 | 51 | 46 | 1 | 2 | 3 | 8 |
| Choice | 38 | 35 | 33 | 25 | 2 | 3 | 13 | 22 |

Speed — Has the most current information
Ease — The easiest to understand
Quality — The most accurate
Choice — Easiest to choose only what one needs

Television and the Japanese Survey—March 2005

### 2.3. *Media use and the generation gap*

Figure 10 reports the daily use of TV, radio, newspaper and the Internet by age group. Every age group, without exception, has daily contact with TV. Daily radio and newspaper use is concentrated among those in their 50s and 60s. Most everyday Internet users, by contrast, are between 20 and 34. In other words, there is no other medium quite as consistently pervasive as TV across generations.

As seen in Figure 11, any survey of radio use based on year of birth will show a peak between 1935 and 1954, demonstrating that radio is oft-used by this generation.

If we do the same with newspapers, as in Figure 12, we can see similarly high results from the same generation, years of birth 1935–1964. Thus we can see a connection between radio/newspaper use and year of birth.

So, what do these respondents view as "indispensable media"? Figures 13 through 15 show the preferences, by birth year, for TV, radio or newspapers. We can see that, with the exception of the newspaper results of 2000, there is great uniformity of results within each of the seven age cohorts.

Given these generational differences in media use, we can see that today's elderly (60 years and over) are highly partial to TV and newspapers. However, when those in their 50s now enter their 60s, we may imagine that the percentage of the population who use the radio and the Internet will increase proportionately.

## 3. Media and the Ageing Society

### 3.1. *Changing perceptions of old age*

Next, we will examine the changing perceptions of lifestyle during old age, using data from the Japanese Public Opinion Survey, which NHK has conducted once every five years since 1973.

Figure 16 and Table 4 record responses to questions about how one would like to spend one's old age. The majority of those who responded with "Live companionably with my children and grandchildren" in 2003 were age 60 and over. Nevertheless, this was much lower than the 1973 results, since affirmative responses in this category fell to between 30 per cent and 40 per cent in all three age groups over 60.

In these three age groups, there was an increase instead in positive responses to "live harmoniously with my spouse" and "enjoy my old age by pursuing my hobbies." Compared with the past, we can see an increasing desire to live independently of one's children and grandchildren.

Today's people in their 60s want to "retire" from the responsibilities of parenthood earlier, and embark on a "second life" in which they can enjoy themselves through actively engaging in hobbies and continuing education. This strong desire is markedly different from the elderly of previous generations.

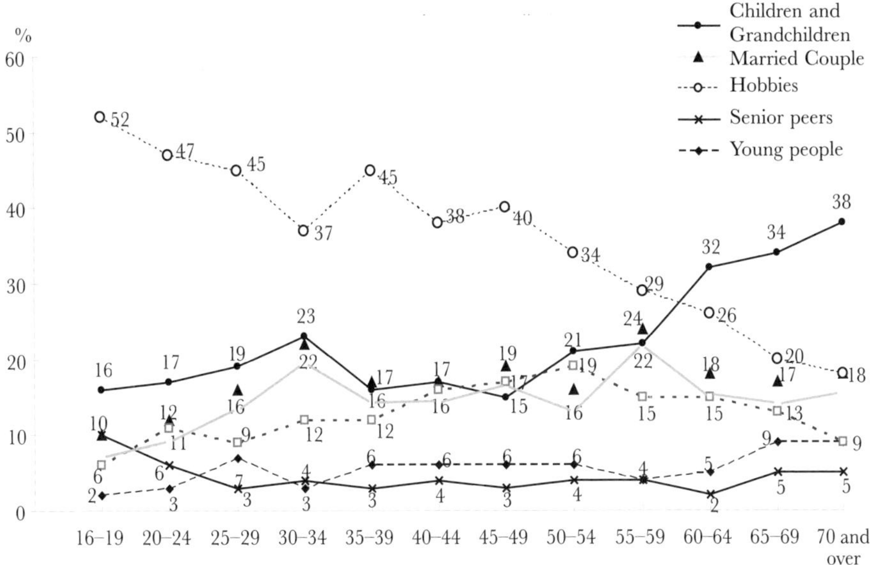


Figure 16. Lifestyle in old age (2003).

Table 4. Lifestyle in Old Age.

(By Age group) (%)

| | | total | 60–64 | 65–69 | 70 and over |
|---|---|---|---|---|---|
| To live companionably with my children & grandchildren | 1973 | 38 | 54 | 52 | 62 |
| | | ∨ | ∨ | ∨ | ∨ |
| | 2003 | 24 | 32 | 34 | 38 |
| To live harmoniously with my spouse | 1973 | 10 | 9 | 10 | 7 |
| | | ∧ | ∧ | ∧ | ∧ |
| | 2003 | 18 | 18 | 17 | 18 |
| Enjoy my old age by pursuing my hobbies | 1973 | 20 | 9 | 9 | 11 |
| | | ∧ | ∧ | ∧ | |
| | 2003 | 33 | 26 | 20 | 18 |
| Have fun with lots of friends who are my age | 1973 | 2 | 1 | 7 | 6 |
| | 2003 | 4 | 2 | 5 | 5 |
| Stay young at heart by associating with young people | 1973 | 8 | 10 | 6 | 3 |
| | | | ∨ | | ∧ |
| | 2003 | 6 | 5 | 9 | 9 |
| To work the job I have for as long as possible | 1973 | 20 | 15 | 16 | 7 |
| | | ∨ | | | |
| | 2003 | 13 | 15 | 13 | 9 |

Source: Japanese Public Opinion Survey, October 2003.

### 3.2. *The importance of TV to the elderly*

As mentioned at the beginning, the elderly aged 60 and over watch more TV than anyone else in the population generally. The elderly watch more TV than the national average during at virtually any time.

Figure 17 maps those who responded "can't do without TV" by age group. As of the age of 50, the numbers of those who responded in the affirmative grows exceeding 50 per cent by age 65. Again, the number of people who agree that they "think of TV as a conversation partner" increases dramatically after 65. It is clear that in the life of the elderly, TV occupies an important position both in terms of time as well as in terms of perception.

If we revisit Figure 10, Frequency of Media Use, we see that those 60 and over have a very high rate of contact with TV and newspapers. Radio use among this group is also on the high side at 39 per cent, while Internet use is not even at 10 per cent.

Table 5, which tabulates the daily time the elderly spend using various media, shows a clear dominance of TV. Newspapers and radio are also worth noting, but other media are barely represented.

Thus, TV and newspapers constitute the major proportion of media use by the elderly.

### 3.3. *The baby boomer generation: "the new elderly"*

However, the baby boomer generation (born 1947–1949) will soon be entering their 60s. When this group, now in their late 50s, enter their sixth decade, will their use of media differ much from that of the current elderly?

Given what has been discussed above, it is not difficult to predict that once the baby boomers turn 60, retire from their jobs, and find themselves with more free time, that they will make more use of various media. Certainly, TV will secure a definite position within that context. However, what other media might come into play? As mentioned above, this generation has active contact with radio. Why is that so?

TV broadcasting began in 1953; over 20 million households had subscriptions to the service by 1967 when the baby boomers were just entering their 20s. Thus TV was something they came into contact with largely as adults. Radio, on the other hand, was already quite widespread in their childhood. They remember the popular radio shows that broadcast at the height of radio, around 1955: *What is your name?*, *20 Doors*, and *The Piper*.

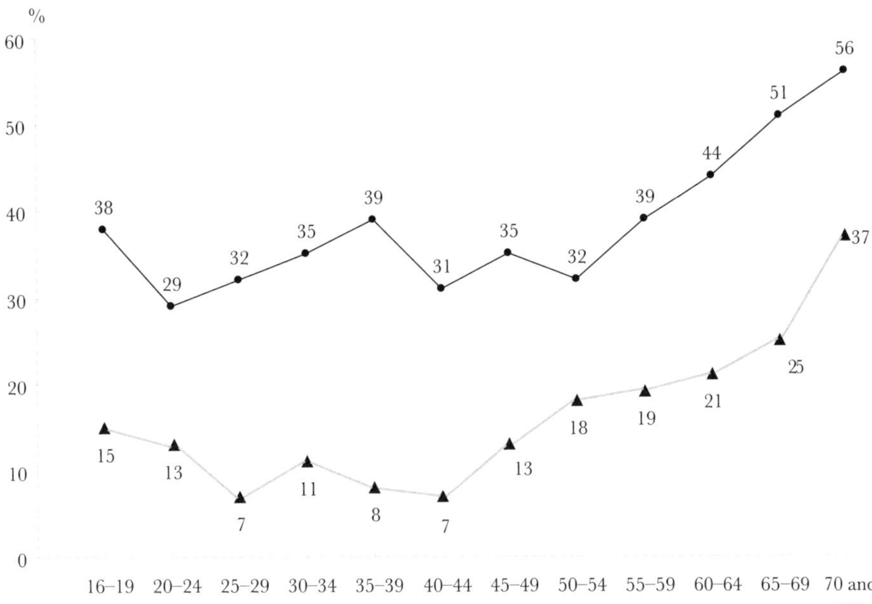


Source: Television and the Japanese Survey, March 2005.

Figure 17. Attitudes to TV.

Table 5. Media exposure.

Hours:Minutes

| | TV | Newspaper | Radio | Magazines, Comics, Books | Video | CDs•MDs Cassette tapes |
|---|---|---|---|---|---|---|
| Males 60–69 | 04:18 (96%) | 00:44 (73%) | 00:40 (24%) | 00:14 (17%) | 00:04 (5%) | 00:03 (4%) |
| Males 70 and over | 05:22 (96%) | 00:51 (71%) | 00:29 (21%) | 00:17 (18%) | 00:05 (6%) | 00:03 (2%) |
| Females 60–69 | 04:37 (94%) | 00:29 (62%) | 00:41 (25%) | 00:09 (14%) | 00:04 (5%) | 00:06 (6%) |
| Females 70 and over | 05:29 (95%) | 00:32 (51%) | 00:30 (18%) | 00:08 (10%) | 00:03 (3%) | 00:03 (3%) |

National Lifestyle Time Distribution Survey—October 2005

The tendency of adults to maintain a favourable attitude towards a mature medium first encountered in their teens has been demonstrated elsewhere.[5] Though it is somewhat dependent on programming, of course, it stands to reason that this generation, once liberated from their jobs and with some free time available, will naturally gravitate towards the radio.

The proportion of the baby boomer generation who have used the Internet is greater than that of the current generation of elderly (see Figure 9). Many have used the Internet during the course of their work. One can say that they have to a degree understood the advantages and disadvantages of the medium, and that many of them are quite comfortable using it selectively, more so than the current generation of elderly.

Moreover, it is said that the baby boomers are a particularly "outgoing" group. It seems certain that once they have more free time, they will pursue their "second life" with gusto. It is possible that, as a result, they will spend less time cooped up at home watching TV.

It is clear that, compared with the current generation of elderly, baby boomers use a wider range of media. Beyond this narrow realm, they also have a positive attitude toward enjoying their old age, which may result in lifestyles quite different from their immediate predecessors.

Even so, TV, esteemed for being "easy" and "convenient," is the medium most closely intertwined with everyday life. This perception of TV will probably remain firmly anchored in the minds of people, regardless of age, for years to come.

---

[5] See The Japan Society of Information and Communication Research (JSICR) (ed.) (2006): Difference in Media Use by Generation. In: *Journal of The Japan Society of Information and Communication Research* (June).

CHAPTER TWENTY-SEVEN

# GENDERED AGE

Sumiko Iwao

## 1. The Importance that Gender has According to Generation

When one walks around town in Japan, one sees many elderly women, and one experiences the reality of how the ageing of Japanese society is progressing: the average life expectancy has risen to the highest in the world, and, furthermore, women live longer than men. In 2004, the average Japanese lifespan was 78.64 years for men and 85.59 for women, and it is predicted to go on rising. In comparison, the average lifespan in Germany in 2002–03 was 75.59 for men and 81.34 for women.

The gap of approximately seven years between Japanese male and female life spans has consistently been seen in the past too. As a result, a situation has arisen where almost 60 per cent of the population over 65 years old and more than 70 per cent of those over 75 are women. Half of elderly people would like to live with their married children, but in reality, the number of households consisting of one person or a couple continues to rise steadily. In particular, 50.6 per cent of elderly women are living alone, compared to 14.1 per cent of men (*Danjo kyōsankaku hakusho* 2005) and this is one factor in gender-related problems in old age. The proportion of elderly people in Japan has risen to 21 per cent of the population today, and is estimated to increase to 35.7 per cent by 2050 (KSJK 2003). In other words, Japanese society will be full of more and more single-person elderly female households.

One characteristic of Japanese society is the fact that the changes in population structure brought about by falling birth rates and rising average life expectancy are progressing at a speed unprecedented anywhere else in the world; what other countries have experienced over a long time is happening many times faster in Japan. This means that the situation has progressed/developed without appropriate policies being established and concrete measures being taken to deal with the changes and without people having enough time and psychological space to adjust to the new circumstances. It seems that each generation is living using the generation before it as an example of how not to behave. Consequently, because the social conditions differ greatly for each generation, the details of their experiences also differ greatly. The awareness of gender, role expectations and patterns of behaviour also differ according to generation, so it is necessary to discuss gender with regard to each generation.

## 2. The Elderly

This generation experienced defeat in World War II when they were between the upper years of elementary school and early adulthood. The vestiges of the paternalistic family system were still strong in both the families in which they grew up and those they established themselves. The tendency to respect one's elders still held when they were young. However, as many people who left the provinces to work in the cities had arranged marriages, and formed nuclear families of just couples and children, contact with elderly people decreased, and elderly people began to carry less weight in society. They themselves grew up in households with an average of five children plus grandparents living together, and it was certainly not unusual to have six or seven siblings. They also grew up seeing plenty of the hardships of their mothers waiting upon their parents-in-law. This meant that, for women, the presence of elderly people was accompanied by a sense of burden. It is therefore understandable that this generation, particularly the women, yearned to establish salaryman households consisting just of couples and their children in the cities.

The men worked hard from morning until night to rebuild Japan, while the women stayed at home and devoted themselves to bringing up the children. Gratefully accepting the salaries brought home in cash by her husband, eking out the housekeeping until the next payday, and saving little by little to buy their own dream home was the lot of a typical salaryman's wife. Even though the constitution declared that men and women were equal, male and female roles gradually became established according to which it was the men who worked and earned the salaries and the women who stayed at home and devoted themselves to the housework and childrearing.

In these circumstances, work became a man's main purpose in life, while a woman's identity was invested in her husband's success at work and in childrearing. In other words, a man was valued for his own work in the seniority promotion system where experience carried weight, but a woman was valued in terms of other people, so there was nothing by which to assess her value as an individual human being. What is more, women accepted this as natural. So if a child got into a good university, that was an achievement for the mother, and there were women who worked really hard as cheerleaders in the intensifying examination competition. Women's purpose in life was to do their best for their families. In short, what was expected of women was to support others.

In cases where families struggled financially, women who contributed to the family budget by doing a side-job were not unusual, but the main earner in the household was the man. Daily budgeting was the responsibility of the women, but important decisions in the household were made by men, and men who did not do this were ridiculed as being "under the thumb".

This generation of women did not have the luxury of questioning the meaning of their lives, nor did they have that kind of consciousness. The groups that represented women at that time were called housewives' unions, and the sight of them participating in demonstrations in their aprons, with their wooden rice paddles, symbolised the role of women at that time perfectly.

However, as ordinary homes became equipped with washing machines, vacuum cleaners, refrigerators and other electrical goods, women were freed from the toil of housework. As their children graduated from high school and became university students and began to find the overprotectiveness and heavy interference of their mothers oppressive, they detached themselves from their mothers. On the other hand, their husbands in the prime of life became more and more like worker ants, responsible for the Japanese economy that continued to grow, and just left their families for their wives to deal with. It was rare for couples to have a real conversation. People joked that, when the tired husbands came home, all they said was the three words, "Food! Bath! Bed!". Nevertheless, the existence of couples at that time was like air: obvious and ignored. In other words, the presence of each half of the couple was something so important that the other could not live without it, but usually each lived without noticing the other; if anything, noticing it was a sign of crisis in the couple.

For women at home, television had an important influence as a window onto society. They learnt about the workings of society through the television screen, and gained information about how women lived. As Satō Tadao states, "whereas films were made on the premise that women were only valued until they got married, television dramas showed women even in their forties and fifties getting all dressed up and chattering away, greatly prolonging the years of their prime of womanhood. Housewives started to see in these images idealised self-portraits of how they themselves ought to be" (Satō 1995: 18).

In the world of home dramas in which women were absorbed, at first the family was depicted above all as a place of calm, where all the family members helped each other. However, changes anticipating reality gradually began to take place in the world of home dramas. As Japan shifted from rapid economic growth to a slowdown after the 1973 oil shock, the distortions brought about by rapid growth became evident throughout the whole of society. What the family ought to be also came into question.

The watershed in home dramas was *Sorezore no Aki* [Pieces of Autumn] (1973, TBS), broadcast in the year of the oil shock. This was a production that showed in detail the situation of a middle-class family breaking up and going their separate ways: a middle-aged couple who had finally built the home that they had long dreamed of, thanks to a long-term loan, and their three children growing up and leaving home one after another (Iwao 2000). Gradually, as the strains in society, such as environmental problems and domestic violence, became evident, home dramas depicted the reality of families with various problems, and provided the material for the women watching them to think about their own lives.

In addition, news about the effects of International Women's Decade started in 1975, and about the activities of women's movements in other countries, particularly America, that were demanding independence and liberation, began to reach Japanese women. As a result, the number of women having vague doubts about their own lives and traditional gender roles slowly began to grow. They also began to question the fact that there was limited freedom of choice and behaviour in the clothes they wore, since certain colours and shades were considered showy or subdued, appropriate or inappropriate according to one's age. Inspired by such developments, and responding to women's interest, many lecture courses furthering the cause of women's independence were started and were greeted with great enthusiasm by women. However, men either did not notice such changes in women, or, if they did notice, thought they were of little consequence.

From existing as "Mr X's wife" or "Y's mother", women began to seek to be valued in their own right as individual women. However, since they had no economic power, they were unable to put this into practice. As the 1980s began, the word "mother" appeared less frequently in television drama titles, and instead the word "woman" turned up more and more in titles such as *Tonari no Onna* [The Woman Next Door], *Yama o Hashiru Onna* [Woman Running in the Mountains] and *Watashi wa Tafu-na Onna* [I am a Tough Woman]. Women who had until then stayed at home taking on the role solely of housewife gradually started to appear as individual women.

Almost a decade after the awakening of women, signs of changes in men began to be seen too. In films in America, where family breakdown and changes in gender roles were ahead of Japan, there are indications of the influence of the big hit *Kramer versus Kramer*, which depicted a divorced family, but in Japan too, dramas taking the theme of the role of fathers began to come to the fore, such as *Papa, Sukāto Haite yo* [Dad, Put on a Skirt] (1983, NHK) and *Shufū Monogatari* [The Tale of a Househusband] (1986, NHK). One can also say that these dramas reflect the reality of men who, while swamped with work, completely lost the support of their families and their place in the family, and whose presence became relatively weak, as well as the men's frustration about this situation.

In contrast, women who needed to spend less time looking after their children began to find meaning in their lives in places that were close by but had nothing to do with their husbands: spending time on cultural activities and classes typified by those on offer at culture centres, and increasing the number of their female friends. Having husbands who were busy socializing with work colleagues and often tended to be away was convenient for such women. The saying, "It's good to have a husband who is healthy and away from home," expresses very well the feelings and pragmatism of this generation of women.

Until the 1970s, men were content to be the economic support of the family, but that alone gave their lives no more than the value of self-satisfaction. However, compared to women, men were bad at considering the feelings of their spouses, and had to wait until they retired to become aware of the gulf between them and their wives.

This generation of men depended totally on their wives for housework and personal care. When their wives went out without their husbands, they would prepare meals for them in advance. Nevertheless, if the man was working, this was an exceptional situation, so it was not unusual that it would cause trouble between husband and wife. But when the husbands retired and were at home all day, the circumstances changed completely. Their wives had not forgotten that they had not been treated with kindness and consideration by their husbands when they were working.

Because these men had had the workplace as the focus of their lives, including their leisure activities, and had had no connection at all with their local neighbourhood, they had no friends there at all. Their wives, on the other hand, had participated in various local activities, and had made many friends. A husband who could not live without depending on his wife in all aspects of daily life, including his three daily meals, became a nuisance to her. Far from speaking to her with affectionate words, he would boss her around and shout if he did not get his own way. Tenderness towards their wives was not in the nature of what the awkward men of this generation thought indicates "manliness". On the contrary, they were inhibited by the misapprehension that affectionate expressions and tender words were a sign of weakness. Men also thought wrongly that standing on their dignity was a symbol of manliness.

On the other hand, a husband had worked as hard as he could for the sake of the family for many years, including the weekend golf, so he expected that he would be taken good care of by his wife and family. So it must have been an enormous shock when he was called "large rubbish",[1] meaning he was useless, or one of the "Terrifying 'Me Too' Tribe" for wanting to go with his wife when she went out. This generation of Japanese men and women had lived in completely separate worlds over many years, without showing their real feelings to each other. The women had built up close relationships with their children and female friends, and one can even say that sometimes the children took on the role of the absent father. The wider the gulf between husband and wife became, the closer she grew to the children.

Among these wives there were some—not many—who took the opportunity to petition for divorce when their husbands retired. This was the beginning of middle-aged divorce in Japan. There were women who demanded half of their husbands' retirement lump-sums, and others who had managed to put by savings in their own name little by little from the housekeeping money over many years, planning to use them to start a new life after divorce. For the men who had never

[1] Household rubbish in Japan is sorted and put out for collection on different days; "large rubbish" [*sodai gomi*] are large items, such as televisions, furniture and refrigerators.

anticipated such a situation, the shock was immense. If their wives left them, they had to do the housework, which was quite unfamiliar to them, and cope with being alone. In contrast, for their wives, it was not simply that they could not stand living under the same roof as someone with whom they had nothing in common and no interests they could enjoy together, but that the freedom they had had until now had been extremely restricted, and they could no longer put up with someone bossing them around. Moreover, it was not even just that, but they refused to be made to take care, as a result of greatly increased average life expectancy, of someone for whom they could not feel any affection. Nevertheless, there were not that many among this generation of men and women who in the end went as far as getting divorced. The difficulty of being economically independent was probably also a factor. The phrase "divorce within the household" arose to refer to couples who were psychologically strangers to each other but who continued to live together under the same roof. According to the 2000 national census, the number of divorced people over 65 is increasing: 2.2 per cent of men and 3.5 per cent of women.

## 3. Impoverished Elderly Women

How their lives will come to an end is a matter of great concern for the elderly, but this is not something of their own choosing. A long life, which ought to be something to be happy about, is not necessarily only a pleasant thing.

It is only natural that, as age rises, the number of people who need nursing and care increases. Over 70 per cent of these elderly people are women; moreover, over 76 per cent of the people being looked after are taken care of by women. In other words, women are the core both of those being taken care of and of those providing the care.

In the past, it was the eldest son's wife who would look after her parents-in-law. This tendency is still evident in areas where three-generation families are relatively common, but in the cities, nuclear families are the norm, so elderly people living in the cities rely on public nursing care or on being looked after by their own daughters who have their own families. Apart from the men who can depend on their spouses, the feelings of those being cared for are complex: while they find it hard to turn to their daughters, who are busy with their own lives, when they look back over their own lives, which they have devoted to their families, they cannot abandon the feeling that they should be able to look to their daughters for help. Elderly people, particularly women, who are still in good health, are terrified of becoming bedridden and needing nursing care; they visit so-called *pokkuri* temples to pray for a quick and easy death while they are still well, but it is by no means necessarily the case that things will go as they wish.

The problem is that, because many elderly people thought they would only live until around 50, they do not have sufficient financial reserves to spend comfortably the lengthy old age that is the result of their unforeseen life expectancy. In the poverty that followed defeat in World War II, it was as much as they could do to bring up and educate their children. Many people vaguely thought that they would spend their old age living with their children and would end their lives there. There are many people who need public welfare assistance because they have lived to a far greater age than they expected: 46.7 per cent of the 1,420,000 people receiving welfare are elderly. Naturally, elderly people also need to consult doctors frequently, and the burden imposed by medical care for the elderly is a great strain on the national budget.

For their children, elderly impoverished parents in need of care are a burden. Looking at their aged parents, the children's generation resolve to work hard at part-time jobs to save for their own old age, if they do not want to follow the same path. This in turn means that they have less and less time available to look after their parents. In such situations, the elderly parents realise that, if it is the case that even their own daughters place great value on their own lives, they cannot place their hopes in their daughters-in-law either. The generation of women who have seen the current circumstances of their elderly parents, came to prefer to have daughters rather than sons. With a daughter, even if it was impossible to be looked after by her, at least they could expect to have someone to talk to.

## 4. The Baby Boomers

Within this generation are the so-called baby boomers born 1946 to 1949. Because they account for a large proportion of the whole population, they are thought to exert a great influence on society. This is the generation that received all its public education in co-educational schools, and so, compared to the generation above, they have quite a strong awareness that men and women are equal. In particular, the women were burdened with the fervent hopes of their mothers, who wanted their daughters to follow the paths that they themselves had not been able to take, bound by traditional gender role expectations and marrying whom their parents told them to, and regretting that they had not been given enough opportunity to choose how they wanted to live.

Nevertheless, the proportion of this generation of women who went on to higher education, combining the figures for junior colleges and four-year universities, added up to no more than 30 per cent, 10 percentage points less than men. Moreover, most of the women went to junior college, because people thought that women were not going to work throughout their lives so junior college was enough. Opinion surveys showed that many parents would give a son preference over a daughter if it was a case of sending only one child on to higher education.

It was considered normal that women too would work after finishing their education, but they were considered as staff to do the support work that carried no responsibility in the workplace, and called "office flowers" or "serving-tea-girls". Rather than seeking equal promotion with men, they wished to be treated protectively at work simply because they were women.

The concept of marriageable age still existed for these women, and most of them married by 25 and took this opportunity to stop working and become full-time housewives, devoting themselves to full-time child care as long as the children needed it, and then taking on part-time jobs when the children grew older and needed less looking after. This was the general pattern. This generation of women, who have used the generation above as an example of how not to behave, have asserted their independence regarding marriage by finding their own husbands, and the trend grew for them to strive for a way of life that they themselves could accept. They were not content simply to be cheerleaders for their husbands and children: they began to join in the race themselves.

In contrast to the generation above, who had filled their spare time with hobby activities, a trend amongst this generation towards activities in a broader social context is seen. They were able to use their own abilities to obtain an income, and moved enthusiastically into local activities such as cooperatives and neighbourhood children's associations. Sometimes they involved men in these activities, and one started to see cases where several couples acted together as a group.

The relationship between husband and wife also changed from being something taken for granted like air to being something to share, and the relationship became more equal. At the same time, changes in the parent-child relationship can also be seen, and the attitude that children's lives were their own grew stronger. Even so, for this generation, getting married was natural, and it was also considered natural to have children once one had got married. Accordingly, the proportion of unmarried people in this generation is less than 5 per cent.

This generation, in particular the baby-boomers, will start to reach retirement age in 2007, and there is concern about the impact of the arrival of a period of mass-retirement. Most men work as regular employees in management and administrative roles, or in industries such as transport and communications. The majority of working women, on the other hand, are employed as manufacturing and production workers, office workers, or in the service industry, in that order. In this generation of women, the proportion of those working part-time is greater than those working as regular employees. Women's income was strongly tinged with being subsidiary, set aside for children's education fees and leisure activities, and for their own activities and enjoyment, while the main breadwinners were strictly the men. However, after the bubble burst, as families suffered the repercussions of Japan's economic slump, these women's incomes became more important and they worked even harder at their part-time jobs.

In particular, most of the home helpers who are the backbone of personal care and nursing services are women of this generation, and when one considers that demand for these services is going to grow and grow in the future, it becomes clear that it is necessary to make even better use of the drive of these women. However, there are many women who have no choice but to give up work to look after their own parents, even if they want to continue working. The difference between them and the previous generation is that they feel little hesitation about entrusting the care of their parents to others, and, unlike the generation above, who tended to carry on out of a feeling of duty until they too collapsed, find a solution by making use of public support as much as possible to look after their own parents, while they themselves work looking after other people.

One sees signs that the men who are coming up to retirement now have learnt from seeing the example of the pitiful state of those of the generation above, who are lost and can do nothing for themselves if their wives are not there. In preparation for retirement, they are making efforts to secure a place for themselves—going to cookery classes, finding interests that they can enjoy together with their wives, and taking part in local community activities. The lifetime employment system that they thought would last semi-permanently has begun to collapse, and they have come to realise that, even if they sacrifice their personal lives, prioritise their jobs and devote themselves to their work, their workplace may in its turn be subject to restructuring. This has made them realise that they need to become independent of the workplace, and they have recognised the importance of making friends and a place for themselves outside work. They understand afresh the importance of the bonds with their families and their wives, and have come to be interested in their wives' lives and activities. One might also say that they are making efforts to bridge the gender gap between themselves and their wives.

In the 2000 national census, the largest number of divorced people were men in their late fifties (4.9 per cent) and early sixties (4.7 per cent), and women in their early fifties (7.3 per cent) and late forties (7 per cent). This generation of women are very dynamic; they tend to think that, if they are going to live until they are 80, it would be better to dissolve their marriages and start again, and moreover, as long as they can somehow get by on their own incomes, to take the step of getting divorced. Amongst women in their forties, 70 per cent are in paid work, the second highest proportion after women in their late twenties. This probably indicates that they have been freed from child care at this time in their lives. Nevertheless, it is clear that this figure is still low compared to men in the same generation, of whom 97 per cent are working.

In relation to this generation, it seems that there are couples who are waiting to get divorced until the system whereby the state pension is split on divorce comes into force in April 2007. Under the new system, it will be possible to divide the pension between the couple, up to a maximum of half of their combined average income, based on their mutual agreement or on a court settlement. Since the age for receiving the state pension is generally 65, if we assume that these couples are waiting until the husband is 65 to get divorced, it will be five or six years until this is reflected in the actual divorce rate.

For this generation, rather than additional years indicating greater maturity as a human being, their needs focus on preserving their youth as long as possible, and anti-ageing products are a huge market. Their clothes and activities are not restricted by age, and they tend to make decisions on the basis of their own likes and dislikes. One sees an enthusiasm and independence in study and cultural activities that did not exist in the generation above. Moreover, the women try to include men in the changes they themselves are undergoing. In contrast to the generation above, where men and women made their own separate worlds, in this generation the trend can be seen for men and women to strive to extend the parts of their worlds that overlap.

## 5. The Young

The Equal Employment Opportunity Law came into force in 1986, and people younger than those who began work in 1986 are sometimes called the "equal law generation". Here, there has been a shift away from the attitude that had prevailed until then, that women being the object of protection was for their own benefit, towards the attitude that women being given equal opportunities with men is desirable for them. As well as the rise in women's academic achievements and the upsurge in demands for equality between men and women, part of the background to this shift are the great improvements in the workplace environment and the fact that the tertiary sector has become the main employer for the majority of women.

Looking at the percentage of the population going on to higher education, there is a trend for the gap between men and women to shrink: in 2004, 49.3 per cent of men went to four-year universities, and 35.2 per cent of women. If we add to this the 14.4 per cent of women going to junior colleges, the gap between men and women disappears. Nevertheless, the imbalance remains that those specializing in science and technology are overwhelmingly men, and the government is placing great emphasis on improvements here.

## 6. Diversification of Life Choices

Rather than differences according to gender, women's diversification means that it has become difficult to discuss women of this generation as a single group. On the other hand, in comparison, men have diversified to a lesser extent.

There is a variety of lifestyles amongst women in this younger age-group: if there are those who choose to remain single, focus on their careers and work wherever in the world they can make the most of their abilities, there are also those who marry but do not have children and continue working, others who marry and have children but continue to work, and still others who accept the myth that they should look after their children themselves until they are three years old and take the opportunity of giving birth to stop working. The proportion of women in their late twenties who work is 74 per cent, the highest of all the age-groups; this falls to just over 60 per cent for women in their thirties, at which point a 30 per cent gap opens up compared to men in the same age-group, indicating that women stop working at this point to bring up children.

There are many different options regarding work patterns too. While there are professional women working on equal terms with men and seeking promotion, there are also those who want work patterns that prioritise compatibility of work with family life over promotion prospects and choose workplaces that do not require long commutes and where they have some freedom; then again, there are others who set up their own businesses so they can be flexible; and still others who are content to be part-timers rather regular employees. The range of workplaces where women are employed has also expanded, and it is now not unusual for women to be working in areas that in the past were practically all-male and where very few women were successful, such as building sites and taxi-driving. Increasing numbers of women are also making inroads into places where, at least superficially, they can work on equal terms with men, if they are qualified as lawyers, architects, teachers or in other professions.

Young people's attitudes towards marriage and having children have also diversified. One can say that the idea of marriageable age is completely obsolete for this generation. Marriage has changed from being a matter of course to just one option in life. They think there is no need to rush into marriage until they meet someone suitable. The average age at first marriage in 2000 was 29.4 for men and 27.6 for women; the proportions of those who were single in their late twenties are 54.0 per cent of women and 69.3 per cent of men, while 13.8 per cent of women and 25.7 per cent of men in their early thirties were unmarried.

To put it another way, for this generation, marriage has lost the attraction and advantages it had for the generation above. Permissiveness in sexual relations between men and women before marriage is relatively high. If you go to a convenience store, you can select foodstuffs and delicious-looking ready meals for one. It is not necessarily the case that women are competent at housework simply because they are women, since they have grown up without the experience of being made to help with housework because they were girls. Their mothers *were* made to help with housework when they were young because they were girls, and feel strongly that they were not given enough freedom and opportunity to make the most of their abilities. Now, the most popular requirement that women look for in a potential husband after personality is competence in housework and childrearing (KSJK 2003).

Having had the value of freedom instilled in them by their parents, and not having been taught to put up with things, this generation feel strongly that they want to avoid having their freedom restricted, psychologically, economically and in terms of time. For them, marriage has the aspect of entailing the drawback of losing one's precious freedom. Not many people actively decide to choose to stay single their whole lives, but the tendency to put off marriage is striking, and this links to the falling birth rate. Many women cannot feel positively about marriage and having children because of the difficulty of combining work and family. In fact, 70 per cent of women stop working after the birth of their first child, showing the reality of the difficulty of combining work and family, and the rate of women who take child-care leave is 70.6 per cent. In contrast, the rate of men who take child-care leave is only 0.56 per cent (2004 figures). For this generation, who are looking for a partnership in their marriages across the board, including child care, the situation where the burden of childrearing falls solely on women is quite likely to be connected to their hesitation about getting married and about having children, and even to their breaking off engagements. Amongst people in their thirties, the proportion of divorced people is not high, at 4–5 per cent for women and 2–3 per cent for men, but as long as there is no adjustment of the minimal time that men spend on housework and childrearing, women's hesitation about marriage and childbirth are likely to increase even more, as is the divorce rate.

Compared to the generation above, it is clear that the gender gap in this generation has shrunk in terms of their actions and attitudes. In the past many men were resistant to having a woman as a boss, but of late there are more men who think that gender is irrelevant as long as someone is competent, and who want women with ability to participate more actively. There is a clear trend for them to value honestly suggestions about plans and product development from a new perspective from their female colleagues.

In the midst of expected labour shortages, some big companies are making the retention of superior female employees one of their business strategies. The issue is probably that, rather than thinking that equal opportunities are natural and becoming positive about remedying the inequalities and disparities between men and women, one wonders how much can be expected from this generation, who have a marked tendency to pursue their own individual gratification. The government has stated its aim to have women filling 30 per cent of managerial positions in all areas of society by 2020, but this requires this generation to take the long view and strive for the creation of a gender-equal society as something of their own. There is still some anxiety about the extent to which this generation has such insight. It is desirable that the concept of fixed gender roles is swept away and a gender-sensitive viewpoint is adopted; that men and women work together and make the most of their abilities and that relations between them are such that each can take pleasure in the presence of the other.

## References


*Danjo kyōsankaku hakusho* [White Paper on Gender Equality] (2005): http://www.gender.go.jp/whitepaper/h17/danjyo_hp/danjyo/html/honpen/index.html.

Iwao, Sumiko (2000): *Terebi dorama no mesēji: Shakaishinrigakuteki bunseki* [The messages in television drama: A social-psychological analysis]. Tokyo: Keisō Shobō.

KSJK (Kokuritsu Shakai Hoshō Jinkō Mondai Kenkyūjo) [National Institute of Population and Social Security Research] (2003): *Dai 12 kai shussan dōkō kihon chōsa*

Satō, Tadao (1995): *Nihon Eiga Shi Dai 3 kan* [History of Japanese Cinema Vol. 3]. Tokyo: Iwanami Shoten.

Case in point: A pet culture in the making

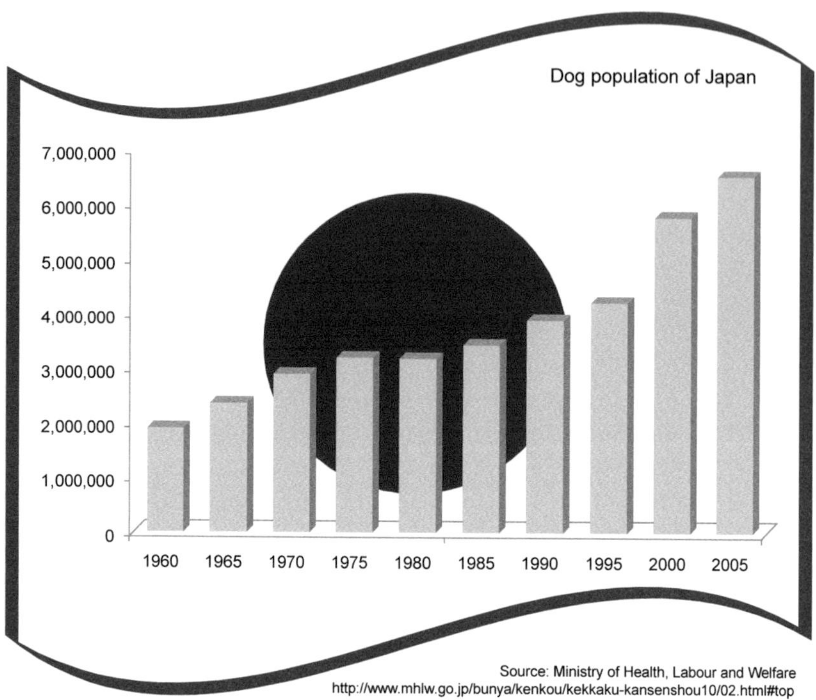


Source: Ministry of Health, Labour and Welfare
http://www.mhlw.go.jp/bunya/kenkou/kekkaku-kansenshou10/02.html#top

"So while the number of children in Japan is declining, the number of animal companions is on the rise. [...] Development of robotic pets is booming in Japan too." (Hidehiko Sekizawa, p. 999 of this volume).

CHAPTER TWENTY-EIGHT

# EDUCATION IN THE AGED SOCIETY: THE DEMOGRAPHIC CHALLENGE TO JAPANESE EDUCATION

Roger Goodman

## 1. Introduction

The story of how Japan's third post-war baby boom never materialised is well known and is told elsewhere in this volume. The effect on the Japanese education system of the shrinking of the number, both in absolute and in relative terms, of children in the Japanese population is much less well-known and forms the subject of this chapter.

The number of children attending the compulsory six-year elementary (*shōgakkō*) school system peaked first in 1958 at around 13.5 million, then declined again by over 3 million over the next decade, before peaking a second time at 11.9 million in 1981, since when the number of children in the sector has continuously declined to around 7.2 million in 2004 and will continue to decline in future years as its mirrors the declining national birth-rate. As one would expect, the same story can be seen as the cohort of children moved through the compulsory three-year junior high school (*chūgakkō*) sector which peaked first in 1962 at around 7.3 million, then declined by over 1.2 million over the next decade before peaking a second time at 6.1 million in 1986 since when the number of children in the sector has continuously declined to around 3.66 million in 2004, a drop in eighteen years of over 40 per cent.

This demographic shift has had a number of major effects on the compulsory school system. Interestingly, for example, while the number of schools has reduced over the past four decades, this has not been by the same proportion as the number of pupils taught in them. The number of elementary schools, for example, peaked in 1957 at 26,988 and fell back to 23,420 in 2004, a decline of only 13.2 per cent. The main reason for this was that class sizes have become much smaller although they remain some way above the OECD average: average sizes in elementary schools were 45 in 1952, 34 in 1986 and 26 in 2004; in junior high schools, they were 46 in 1955, 38 in 1987 and 31 in 2004. Almost all of the education in the compulsory sector of the education system up to the age of fifteen is delivered through the public system—only around 1 per cent of pupils in elementary school and 6.5 per cent of pupils in junior high schools receive private education—and the government kept rigidly to its commitment to principles of equality and meritocracy which sometimes meant that schools were kept open in outlying rural areas which had only two or three children in them. In Suginami Ward in Tokyo, the local government did experiment in the 1990s with a British system which allowed parents to determine which elementary school their children attended and for the local authority to close down unpopular schools on the basis that it was the parents and not the local government which had implicitly made this decision, but in most areas the policy was to reduce the number of children in schools rather than to merge or rationalise the local system as a whole. The contraction in both the number of schools and pupils also meant that fewer new appointments were needed and that—combined with the fact that the teaching profession offered a relatively high status and good salary compared to graduates of a similar background—has led to the average age of teachers increasing: for elementary school teachers in 2004, it was almost 44, while the figure for those in junior schools it was around 42. Older teachers and smaller classes have meant that spending per student has risen by around 25 per cent over the past decade (OECD 2005: 4–5).

The effect of the declining number of children in the education system on senior high schools has been slightly more complicated than on the lower levels of the system. There are two reasons for this. The first is that this system is not compulsory and many of the first baby boom generation were leaving the education system at the age of fifteen at the first opportunity which was available at that period. The number of those attending senior high school did not peak, therefore, until 1989 when around 94 per cent of those leaving middle schools continued into senior high school and the second baby boom generation passed through the system with 5.64 million children attending senior high schools across Japan. Since 1989, the number of those in senior high school has dropped rapidly to around 3.72 million in 2004 (a drop of 34 per cent over 15 years). The other complicating factor is the role of private education. At senior high school level in Japan around 30 per cent of schools are private. Many of these schools were established in the 1950s and 1960s to meet the expanding demand for education beyond the compulsory system which the Japanese state either could not or decided that it would not meet out of its own resources. According to James and Benjamin (1988: 56), "[t]he private sector...serves as a shock absorber, responding rapidly to ups and downs in the relevant population, while the public sector gradually adjusts." We can see this effect much more clearly when we turn our attention to the higher education sector in Japan.

## 2. The Demographic Shift and the Challenge for Japanese Higher Education

The Japanese higher education system is facing a contraction, possibly better described as an implosion, of a type not ever seen before. The bursting of the Japanese economic bubble at the start of the 1990s coincided almost exactly with the peak of the number of eighteen-year-olds (the group who have provided well over 90 per cent of all university entrants) in the Japanese population. This generation, the second post-war baby boom, peaked at 2.05 million in 1992 and then began a steady decline (31.2 per cent) in numbers to around 1.41 million in 2004. As we have seen, there has been no third baby boom nor is there any serious immigration on the horizon and so we can confidently predict that the number of eighteen-year-olds will continue to decline to under 1.2 million by 2012 (an overall decrease of 42.8 per cent over twenty years).

The widely-held view, therefore, that higher education is 'difficult to get into and easy to graduate from' (*hairinikui, deyasui*) has begun to be turned on its head. Far from being difficult to get in to, universities increasingly face great problems filling their government-authorised number of places. In 2004, just under 30 per cent of all four year private universities and over 40 per cent of all two-year colleges were already failing to fill their quotas and, as many commentators pointed out, the demographic shrinking of the typical university cohort still had several years to go. This did not mean, of course, as some have intimated (Obara 1998), that competition to get into university would disappear; rather it would be replaced by conspicuous polarisation of higher education institutions which had previously been part of a rather smooth hierarchy.

According to a detailed study carried out by the huge Mainichi newspaper group (and published in the weekly magazine *Sunday Mainichi* over a number of weeks at the end of 2003), one can already begin to see a clear bifurcation in the situation of Japanese universities based around the *hensachi* mark (the average score of their entrants) in 1992. Those which at that time had an average *hensachi* of fifty-five or over have maintained, and in many cases increased, their competition-for-places rate and the average score of their entrants; those which had an average *hensachi* under fifty-five in 1992 have seen both plummet. It should be no surprise therefore that a spate of popular books have appeared in recent years which reflect this situation such as Furusawa's *Daigaku sabaibaru* [University survival] (2001), Satō's *Daigaku no ikinokori senryaku* [Universities' strategies for survival] (2001), and the Yomiuri Shinbun Osaka Honsha's *Tsubureru daigaku; tsuburenai daigaku* [Universities which will collapse; Universities which will not collapse] (2002).

While Japan's leading national universities will continue to be protected by state support (despite technically in 2004 being turned into so-called Independent Administrative Institutions) and the leading private universities by their reputation and alumni networks, rural public and local universities and lower-level private universities face a bleak future, if indeed they have a future at all. Private universities rely, for example, on student fees for over 80 per cent of their annual income on average and 95 per cent of their students have been drawn from the school-leaving population.

In order to meet the challenge of the demographic time-bomb, some universities have worked hard to diversify their entrants. In this context, it is important to point out that other countries have faced similar challenges due to demographic shifts in the number of traditional-aged entrants. A forty per cent drop in enrolments was predicted in the US in the 1970s (see Kelly 1999: 41) and a very similar situation was predicted in the UK in the 1980s (Saul 1988). Both the UK and US were able to meet these demographic threats, however, by increasing very substantially the proportion of the traditional age group who went to university. In the US and UK in the 1970s and 1980s, higher education systems were still in the 'elite' phase, to use Martin Trow's categorisation (Trow 1973): in the UK, for example, the proportion of the school leaving age group continuing in to higher education was still only around 16 per cent in 1988. This meant that the decline in the absolute number in the age group could large be compensated for by an increase in the proportion going on to higher education; indeed in 2004, the UK government announced a target for 50 per cent of school leavers to go on to higher education by the time they reach the age of 30 by 2010. The difference in Japan has been that its demographic shift has arrived at a time when it already operated a 'universal' rather than an 'elite' or even a 'mass' higher education system.

As one might expect, in Japan also, in the past decade, there has been a very rapid increase in the proportion of eighteen-year-olds going to four-year universities. Between 1992 to 2002—despite the 31 per cent drop in the number of those leaving senior high outlined above—the proportion going to university actually increased by 31 per cent as the rate of advancement to universities of this group went up from around 37 per cent in 1992 to just under 49 per cent in 2002. This increase, of course, was explained in large part by the fact that it became increasingly easy during the 1990s to find a university place: in 1992 only 55 per cent of those who applied for higher education in Japan were successful; by 1995 this figure has risen to 65 per cent and by 2000 to just over 80 per cent (Ishikida 2005: 151). Sometime around 2009 according to Doyon (2001: 445), the places available in higher education institutions will be the same as the number of applicants, an era which is already dubbed in Japanese as '*zennyū jidai*' ('The Era of Open Entry').

The main way in which UK and US universities met the challenge of the demographic shift however was by expanding into new markets such as graduate students, mature students, part-time students, and overseas students. This has proven much more difficult in Japan, for a number of reasons which we need to examine.

In 1999, the ratio of graduate students to the overall population was 1.4 per 1000 in Japan, less than a fifth of the ratio in the US (Ishikida 2005: 158). This was still despite the fact that Japan during the 1990s substantially expanded its graduate population following a report at the beginning of the decade which placed it second among industrialised nations in the percentage of its college-age youth going to university and last in the proportion going on to graduate school. The low proportion of undergraduate proceeding to graduate work (in 2002, this was 8.9 per cent compared to 21 per cent in the UK and 22 per cent in France) has, in part, been put down to the reluctance of Japanese employers to hire those they feel already so qualified that they will be difficult to train in their own company way of doing things (Urata 1996: 189–90). Ogawa (1999) explains that graduate education in Japan has generally been seen only as a training ground for those who want to go on to be academics and that there has been little use of it for gaining professional and other non-academic skills. Teichler (1997: 286–287, 293) has pointed out that major Japanese manufacturing companies changed their policies in the early 1990s in favour of recruiting science and engineering graduates from Master's programmes—which largely explains the doubling in the number of graduate students from the mid-1980s to the mid-1990s—but while the number of undergraduate students in engineering and the natural sciences going on to graduate courses rose during the 1990s, it remained stuck around 3 per cent in the social sciences where graduate study was still not seen as having employment value other than for those who wanted to be academics.[1]

The current decade has seen a substantial growth in professional schools, which can be described as a form of specialist graduate education and for which universities can charge high fees. Almost 70 universities opened Law Schools on 1 April 2004, as part of the process of reforming radically the training—and increasing the number—of lawyers in Japan.[2] At the same time, there has been the development of MBA (Master of Business Administration) and MOT (Management of Technology) courses (see Yamada 2002).

The new professional schools and graduate programmes are having the effect of bringing *shakaijin gakusei* (mature students) into universities; the number of adult students in graduate university programmes increased by 65 per cent to 41,000 between 2000 and 2004 and the proportion rose to 15 per cent. Most of these students, however, are

---

[1] The graduation rate from advanced research programmes, such as PhDs, remains comparatively very low in Japan despite the increase in Master's courses. Among 27 OECD countries with available data, Japan in 2005 came 22nd on this measure. Furthermore, because of the emphasis on scientific higher degrees, there is a big gender gap in such programmes: only 27 per cent of the Japanese second-degree graduates and only 25 per cent of Japanese advanced research graduates are women while the corresponding OECD averages are 52 per cent and 41 per cent (OECD 2005: 2–3).

[2] The future of these Law Schools, however, does not lie in their own hands, but will rely heavily on how many graduates go on to pass the notoriously difficult bar examinations to become fully-fledged lawyers. Many fear that with the Japanese Bar Association (Nichibenren) currently setting the figure at around 34 per cent of graduates (as opposed to the 75 per cent originally proposed by the Ministry of Education) many of these new Schools will founder and, indeed, applications for entry in 2005 were around 30 per cent lower than those of the year below. Others, however, predict that the Bar Association will be forced to increase its quota as demand for lawyers in Japan increases and point out that before the establishment of the Law Schools the success rate in the bar examinations was less than 3 per cent. See Arakaki (2004) for an overview of these arguments.

taking courses in the evening and at weekends so that they can combine them with their jobs; there is not much practice of students taking career development breaks and there is even less of housewives coming back to university once their children are old enough to go to school (which were a huge new market for universities and community colleges in the US in the 1970s when they were facing the same drop in eighteen-year-olds as currently faced in Japan, see Kelly 1999). Of the roughly 76,000 students who entered master's programmes in 2003 in Japan, almost 80 per cent were in their twenties with the rest being equally divided between overseas and 'adult working' entrants (Ishikida 2005: 158). Given the economic recession and employment retrenchment since the early 1990s in Japan, it has become increasingly difficult for those in work to voluntarily resign and enrol on graduate programmes.

While some private universities have been aggressively pursuing the graduate market as a means of developing new income streams, most of them have discovered that establishing such courses involves considerable investment; there are strict minimum requirements for staff: student ratios which are much tougher than for undergraduate courses and often 'big name' professors have to be hired on high salaries in order to 'head up' the programmes. The number of graduates and mature students will need to increase much more, therefore, before they become a significant means for struggling higher education institutions to increase their income.

The biggest difference from the UK and US in the area of recruiting mature students, however, has been the inability of universities to persuade individuals, particularly women, who missed out on higher education when they left school to enrol later in life. In the UK, for example, almost 55 per cent of all those enrolled in first-year undergraduate programmes in 2005 were officially classified as 'mature entrants', meaning aged over 21 on the day of entry (THES 9 June 2006). There are a number of possible explanations for the lack of similar groups of mature students in Japan: unlike in the UK and US, returning to higher education, especially for women, is not seen as a good career investment, in part because the skills learned at university are not sufficiently vocational to be sold on the labour market and partly because the labour market still prefers to employ at the bottom of the age range in order to train people as early as possible in their own company practices and to keep down costs. The other reason is the availability of very high quality, subsidized education programmes for adult students, either through the public Bunka Kaikan or the private Asahi Cultural Centres that exists throughout Japan.[3]

It is perhaps indicative of the lack of development of this market, therefore, that there does not seem to be in Japan an official definition of who constitutes a mature student (*shakaijin gakusei*). Universities which operate special entrance categories for '*shakaijin gakusei*' seem to have developed their own definitions—most of which include the idea that the candidate either currently is, or in the past has been, in full-time paid employment while not receiving full-time education—but these definitions are not consistently applied across the sector as a whole.

It is also indicative of the lack of development of recruitment that there is no official definition of—or indeed national figures on—part-time students in Japan. The development of the market in part-time students was one of the biggest growth areas in the UK and the US when faced with a dramatic drop in the number of traditional university entrants; it has remained almost untapped in Japan despite Monbushō guidelines in 1991 that allowed universities to accept such students. In the UK, for example, about 25 per cent of all students on course in 2005 were officially registered as part-time, generally taking roughly double the length of time over their degree courses of full-time students (THES 9 June 2006).[4] Some argue, semi-jokingly, that because Japanese students already do so many hours of part-time paid work (*arbeit*) while on course—the average in 2005 was around 15 hours a week, which meant that many students were working far more hours than this—they are already *de facto* part-time students. The reason why universities have not become more flexible in the way they treat the idea of part-time students, however, is not widely discussed or understood in the literature on university reform.

Another source of possible students has been those from overseas (known as *ryūgakusei* in Japanese). As Walker (2005) points out, this is another category which has constituted a major source of university income in Anglophone countries such as the UK, US and Australia over the past decade. In 2003, Japan did finally achieve the target of enrolling 100,000 overseas students (26 per cent at graduate schools; 53 per cent on undergraduate programmes; 19 per cent at vocational schools) that had been set by then-Prime Minister Nakasone in 1984.

---

[3] Ishikida (2005: 168) quotes a 1995 survey which suggests that over 1.5 million students participated in courses at 723 Cultural Centres in 1995.

[4] From 1989–1999, full-time students have been defined in the UK as those studying for at least 24 weeks a year (THES 9 June 2006).

Much of this rise came about in the previous five years when the numbers doubled from 51,000 to almost 110,000 and it was largely the result of the easing of immigration requirements for overseas students in 1997 and the rapidly growing demand for higher education in China and South Korea. Nearly 65 per cent of all *ryūgakusei* come from China and a further 15 per cent from South Korea reflecting the fact that almost all university teaching in Japan is provided through a Chinese character-based Japanese language medium and very little through English.

One of the reasons for introducing *ryūgakusei* into the Japanese higher education system was as part of former prime minister Nakasone's drive to internationalise Japanese society—up to the year 2000, about 15 per cent of all *ryūgakusei* were on Japanese government scholarships and government funding for overseas students in Japan is still categorised as part of its overseas development aid (Tsuruta 2003).[5] A more recent driver has been to keep lower-level universities solvent and hence the increase in foreign students in Japan can be directly linked to the demographic shift which has left these institutions in such a vulnerable position. *Ryūgakusei* are highly concentrated, however, in the metropolises, with more than 30 per cent in Tokyo, which means that rural universities, which are most under financial threat, have found it difficult to recruit them as a mean of easing their financial situation.[6] Even in urban areas, though, it is generally agreed that *ryūgakusei* programmes are more closely related to the image and public relations of universities than their finances; many such programmes indeed are run at a loss.[7] Perhaps more significantly, the number of Japanese students studying overseas is still larger than the number of foreign students who come

[5] While Japan with a market share of 4 per cent of all overseas students now stands fifth in the world rankings—and has seen its share grow faster over the past five years than that of any other country—this still means that less than 2 per cent of higher education students enrolled in Japan are not citizens of the country, which is far below the OECD country mean of 5.9 per cent.

[6] One university in Tohoku set up classrooms in Tokyo and taught some of its *ryūgakusei* via video-links so that they could combine their studies with doing part-time jobs in the capital where such jobs are much easier to come by than in the countryside.

[7] The vulnerability of this market, and in particular its over-reliance on students from China, was clearly demonstrated in March 2004 when the Japanese immigration authorities refused to give student visas to a substantial proportion of students from China who had been offered places for the academic year that was about to begin. This was in the wake of a series of highly publicised crimes committed by Chinese *ryūgakusei* during the previous year.

to study in Japan, resulting in a net outflow of just under 1 per cent of total tertiary enrolment.

The higher education institutions which have suffered the most in the past decade from the demographic squeeze have been the two-year junior colleges (*tanki daigaku*). In 1992, with 541 institutions (88 per cent of them private) *tanki daigaku* constituted over 44 per cent of all of Japan's higher education institutions and catered for nearly 23 per cent of all higher education students (around 92 per cent of their in-take being female); by 2004 they catered for only 9.6 per cent of all higher education students, as more and more women chose to enter higher status four-year institutions. In order to survive financially, close to fifty junior colleges converted to four-year universities (and many others were absorbed into their attached four-year institutions) during the decade after 1992.[8]

By far the major beneficiaries of the current uncertainty in the higher education sector have been the vocationally-oriented higher education institutions known in Japanese as *senmongakkō*. The proportion of higher education students going to vocational schools has doubled over the past twenty years from 10 per cent to 20 per cent of all school leavers. Courses in these institutions involve much more focused teaching and learning and employers have a much clearer sense of the value-added of the tertiary educational experience for individual students.

It is important to point out that some junior colleges and lower level institutions have carved out a niche for themselves through offering more vocationally-oriented courses or accepting part-time students or recognizing credits from other institutions, but partly due to economic conditions, partly due to linguistic conditions and partly due to internal organizational structures which have made it very difficult for institutions to institute reforms (see Goodman, 2008), there is little evidence that the vast majority of the lower-level colleges and universities will

[8] It is interesting to note, in this context, that junior colleges (*tanki daigaku*) were initially established only on a provisional basis in 1950—because not all institutions which wanted to upgrade to universities in the post-war system were considered to be of a high enough standard—and they were only accepted as a permanent feature of the education system in 1965 (Teichler 1997: 278). Not long after, in 1969, as Cummings (1976: 69) recounts, several junior colleges went bankrupt as the level of debt in all private institutions increased severely, precipitating the student revolts which marked universities in Japan during the early 1970s. There is no doubt, therefore, that the junior college sector in Japan, which caters almost exclusively to female students, provided a useful 'buffer zone' during the development of higher education in the post-war period, but that role is fast disappearing as the supply of places across the sector as a whole begins to equal demand.

be able to rise to meet the demographic challenges that currently face them. The government has made it clear that, as with the banks in the 1990s, it has no intention of bailing them out. The result is that many institutions—high estimates suggest as many as 40 per cent, low around 15 per cent—will go bankrupt, or will merge or be taken over within the next decade.

## 3. The Demographic Shift and the Development of a New Idea of Higher Education

If, as suggested above, a very large proportion of Japanese higher education institutions are unable to meet the challenges of the demographic shift—and it is important to stress that there are options which would allow them to meet such challenges, not only through diversifying their students whose fees currently constitute 80 per cent of the income of private universities but actually diversifying their income streams and earning money through undertaking contract research or raising endowments—then what will be the effect on the higher education system as a whole?

There are those, such as the sociologist Takehiko Kariya (in English, see Kariya and Rosenbaum 2003; in Japanese, see Kariya and Shimizu 2004), who point towards the increasing educational differentiation of outcomes by class that is taking place directly as a result of the polarization in the higher education system. Put simply, as entry to lower-level (mainly private) universities becomes essentially a 'free pass' (up to 50 per cent of applicants to such universities already are exempt from taking any exam at all), students who decide to go to such universities will not need to do any work while at school, and the higher education institutions themselves will end up admitting lower and lower level students with little or no motivation to study, simply because they need their fees. It has of course always been the case that there is a very significant element of class reproduction in the Japanese education system (see Ishida 1993), but there is little doubt that the polarization that is taking place in the higher education system will greatly exacerbate this trend and educational and life chances will increasingly become more visibly related to family income. The long-term effect of this trend will be that life-time and secure full-time jobs will become increasingly limited to graduates of top institutions where entry continues to be via a competitive examination system. The consequent undermining of the 'myth of meritocracy' which has sustained, to a large degree, the emphasis on effort that has characterized practice in both the educational and work environments will have major knock-on effects throughout the society as a whole, as is already beginning to be documented by social scientists such as Genda (2005), Miura (2005) and Tachibanaki (1998).

There is also, however, a more optimistic view of the current demographic pressure which is that it will force private universities, particularly the lower-level ones, to become more aware of their social role, leading to a shift from them playing, as during most of the post-war period (see, for example, McVeigh 2002), a mainly screening and private money-making function to adding practical and academic value to the skills set and experience of their student entrants and thereby contributing to the public good. In order to support this cultural shift in the higher education institutions, we are likely to see a dramatically changing structure in their teaching staff, in particular the employment of more women (currently 14 per cent of total staff against an OECD country mean of 36 per cent), more foreign staff (currently less than 5 per cent of total staff, very few of whom are on anything more than one year contracts); and more foreign PhDs. We are likely to see many more classes taught in English as part of the internationalization of higher education in general in Japan and the search for overseas markets in particular. We are likely to see increased competition for funding leading to higher quality teaching and research. We are also likely to see a vigorous and open discussion about what is the role of higher education in Japan, and a serious challenge to the notion that it is primarily a site for social rather than intellectual or vocational development.

It is unlikely of course that the outcome of the current pressures on, and reforms of, Japanese universities will be clear-cut or homogenous across the sector. There will be unpredictable outcomes and changes that will be both positive and negative for the society as a whole. What is clear, however, is that the demographic shift in Japan will continue to play a major role in the reorganization of the education system in general and the higher education system in particular.

## References

Arakaki, Daryl Masao (2004): "Please Teach the 3 H's", a Personal Request to Japan's New American-Style Law Schools. In: *Osaka Gakuin Daigaku Hōgaku Kenkyū* (Osaka Gakuin law review) 30, 1–2, pp. 107–46.

Cummings, William K. (1976): The Problems and Prospects for Japanese Higher Education. In: Austin, Lewis (ed.): *Japan: The Paradox of Progress*. New Haven and London: Yale University Press.
Doyon, Paul (2001): A Review of Higher Education Reform in Modern Japan. In: *Higher Education* 41, pp. 443–70.
Furusawa, Yukiko (2001): *Daigaku sabaibaru* [University survival]. Tokyo: Shūeisha.
Genda, Yuji (2005): *A Nagging Sense of Job Insecurity: The New Reality Facing Japanese Youth* (Japanese title: *Shigoto no naka no aimai na fuan*). Translated by Jen Connell Hoff. Tokyo: LTCB International Library Trust / International House of Japan.
Goodman, Roger (forthcoming): Understanding University Reform in Japan through the Social Science Prism. In: *Learning and Teaching in the Social Sciences*. Special issue edited by David Mills on University Reform.
Ishida, Hiroshi (1993): *Social Mobility in Contemporary Japan*. Stanford: Stanford University Press.
Ishikida, Miki Y. (2005): *Japanese Education in the 21st Century*. New York, Lincoln, Shanghai: iUniverse Inc.
James, Estelle and Gail Benjamin (1988): *Public Policy and Private Education in Japan*. Basingstoke: Macmillan.
Kariya, Takehiko and James E. Rosenbaum (2003): Stratified Incentives and Life Course Behaviors. In: Mortimor, Jeylan T. and Michael J. Shanahan (eds.): *Handbook of the Life Course*. New York: Kluwer Academic / Plenum Publishers, pp. 51–78.
Kariya, Takehiko and Kokichi Shimizu (2004): *Gakuryoku no shakaigaku* [The sociology of scholastic ability]. Tokyo: Iwanami Shoten.
Kelly, Curtis (1999): The Coming Educational Boom in Japan: Demographic and Other Indicators that Suggest an Increase in the Number of Adults Seeking Education. In: *Japanese Society* 3, pp. 38–57.
McVeigh, Brian J. (2002): *Japanese Higher Education as Myth*. Armonk, New York and London, England: M. E. Sharp.
Miura, Atsushi (2005): *Karyū shakai* [Downstream society]. Tokyo: Kobundo.
Obara, Yoshiaki (1998): 'A Presidential Perspective from Japan', in *International Higher Education*, 10: 11–12.
OECD (2005): *Education at a Glance 2005: OECD Briefing Note for Japan*. Paris: OECD Directorate.
Ogawa, Yoshikazu (1999): Japanese Higher Education Reform: The University Council Report. In: *International Higher Education* 18, pp. 22–23.
Satō, Susumu (2001): *Daigaku no ikinokori senryaku* [Universities' strategies for survival). Tokyo: Shakai Hyōronsha.
Saul, Berrick (1988): Education Agenda: Struck by Market Forces. In: *The Guardian* (4 October 1988).
Tachibanaki, Toshiaki (1998): *Nihon no keizai kakusa* [Japan's economic disparities]. Tokyo: Iwanami Shoten.
Teichler, Ulrich (1997): Higher Education in Japan: A View from Outside. In: *Higher Education* 34, pp. 275–298.
THES (Times Higher Education Supplement) (2006): 9 June, 20–1.
Trow, Martin (1973): *Problems in the Transition from Elite to Mass Higher Education*. New York: Carnegie Commission on Higher Education.
Tsuruta, Yoko (2003): Globalisation and the Recent Reforms in Japanese Higher Education. In: Goodman, Roger and David Phillips (eds.): *Can the Japanese Change their Education System?* Oxford: Symposium Books, pp. 119–150.
Urata, Nobuchika (1996): Evaluation Issues in Contemporary Japanese Universities. In: Hayhoe, Ruth and Julia Pan (eds.): *East-West Dialogue in Knowledge and Higher Education*. New York and London: M. E. Sharpe, pp. 177–191.
Walker, Patricia (2005): Internationalising Japanese higher education: Reforming the system or re-positioning the product? In: Eades Jerry, Roger Goodman and Yumiko

Hada (eds.): *The 'Big Bang' in Japanese Universities: The 2004 Reforms and the Dynamics of Change*. Melbourne: TransPacific Press, pp. 170–188.
Yamada, Reiko (2002): *Shakaijin daigakuin de nani o manabu ka?* [What does one learn at professional schools?]. Tokyo: Iwanami Shoten.
Yomiuri Shinbun Osaka Honsha (ed.) (2002): *Tsubureru daigaku, tsuburenai daigaku* [Universities which will collapse; universities which will not collapse]. Tokyo: Chūō Shinsho.

CHAPTER TWENTY-NINE

# AGEING JAPAN AND THE TRANSMISSION OF TRADITIONAL SKILLS AND KNOW-HOW

Takanori Shintani

## Three Waves of Folkloric Transmission

Various facets of Japanese society are grappling with the question of how skills and know-how, as inherited from early modern times and as newly developed in the post-war high economic growth period, are now to be passed on to the next generations.

I have argued elsewhere that the transmission of customs and etiquette in modern and contemporary Japanese society consists of three waves (Shintani 2006). Moreover, the hypothesis sees these as generally applicable to the transmission of folk culture itself in the modern and contemporary periods. The first (Alpha Wave) refers to the folkways passed on from long before the eve of the Meiji Era (1868–1912) through the Taishō (1912–1926) Era, when Japan was undergoing modernization and many folklorists, notably Yanagita, initially set about conducting surveys and collecting data in farming, mountain, and fishing villages throughout Japan and in urban areas as well. The second (Beta Wave) runs from the Meiji Era of "civilization and enlightenment" through the Taishō and prewar Shōwa eras, when in the modernization of Japanese society, a new urban, upper-class culture was established, led and dominated by the aristocratic and bourgeois classes as part of the introduction and imitation of Occidental culture that characterized that modernization.

The lifestyle culture of this Beta Wave, including housing, food, and clothing, ceremonial occasions, the arts and the performing arts, differed greatly from that of the preceding Alpha Wave. Even as it took root within the urban upper classes as the way of life to be passed on, emblemizing modern Japanese society for the Meiji and Taishō eras, the general populace, i.e. of farming, mountain, and fishing villages as well as of the cities' commercial districts, strongly clung to the older ways. The decisive contrast lay on the one hand between commercial manufacture relying on the mechanical power born of the epoch-changing industrial revolution, along with a lifestyle based on a capitalist manufacturing economy that made possible mass distribution, and, on the other, a lifestyle based on a self-reliant production economy, using such traditional and natural resources as human and domestic animal power, wind and water power. Japan between the Meiji and the pre-war Shōwa eras was characterized by the existence of these two parallel cultures, these overlapping waves of folkway transmission, the one innovative, the other traditional, separated by differences of class and region.

In the post-war era period of high economic growth, 1960–1970, the Gamma Wave swept in a new and unprecedented mass culture, based on and drawing from the Beta Wave of modern urban bourgeois society. An entire way of life, including its economic and social transmission, was affected. Here is but one concrete example: the unravelling of the web of societal customs and taboos surrounding the realities of birth and death.

First, child delivery came to be included in the health-care system and, in a sense, "commercialized," as modern hygienic considerations led to the abandonment of do-it-yourself births, with expectant mothers' relying on the local, unlicensed midwife. The latter was replaced by licensed midwives as a transition toward full obstetric and nursing staffs.

Similarly, death had traditionally been a family matter, with the remains of the deceased treated at home and burial or cremation procedures carried out as part of neighbourhood mutual aid. Now the hospital came to be the place where one died, and professional undertakers assumed responsibility for funeral rites, with the body being cremated not in open fields but rather in publicly administered heavy-oil furnaces. The shift again pointed to a form of commercialization.

The Gamma Wave also brought with it such changes as the mechanization of agriculture and fishing and, with the massive shift of the work force to the urban centres, family nuclearization. The coexistence of the Alpha and Beta waves came to an end, the latter having been absorbed by the Gamma Wave, the former now having been rendered nearly extinct.

## The Advent of the Grey Society

On September 17, 2006, the Prime Minister's Office released statistics estimating Japan's senior-citizen population as of September 15, the announcement being timed to coincide with the observation of Respect for the Aged Day, falling that year on September 18. According to the report, the figure of those 65 and older had increased by 830,000 from 2005, for a total of 26.4 million, 11.2 million men and 15.2 million women. The population stood at 127.72 million, a decrease of 20,000 from the previous year; of this total, the Japan's senior citizens now reportedly accounted for an all-time high of 20.7%, an increase of 0.7%.

The first White Paper on the Greying of Society (*Kōreishakai-hakusho*) was published in 1996. The previous year life expectancy for men stood at 76.36, for women at 82.84; senior citizens then accounted for 14.6% of the population, at 18.28 million. They were divided into two groups, those between 65 and 74 and those 75 and older, the former amounting to 11.1 million, the latter to 7.18 million.

The 1996 white paper reported that senior citizens now constituted 15.1% of the population of 125.86 million, their total number standing at 19.02 million. Three categories were given: (1) an ageing society, defined as having 7–14% of the population 65 or older; (2) an aged society, with the figure of 14–21%; (3) a hyperaged society, with a figure of 21% and above. Japan had entered the first category in 1970, the second in 1995. The latter estimate had already come the year before. The government had thereafter resolved to publish a white paper annually as a means of coping with the problem.

The greying of Japanese society steadily continued, so that by the time the 2006 white paper was published (on the basis of statistics available as of October 1, 2005), senior citizens constituted 20.04% of the total population (127.76 million); for 2005, the figure had been 19.5% of 127.78 million. For the first time since the end of the war, Japan had undergone a population decrease; it was clear that the country was about to fall into the hyperaged category. There were now, by way of contrast to the statistics for a decade before, since 1995, 14.03 million Japanese aged 65–74, 11.57 million aged 75 and above, indicating not only an overall increase but also a relative rise in the latter group. With most of the members of the baby-boom generation having passed their *kanreki* (60th birthday) and now on the verge of passing the 65-mark, we can clearly foresee a society heavily tipped into Category #3.

## The Sites for the Transmission of the Traditional Arts

Japan's traditional technology falls into two broad divisions. One consists of skills and know-how—principally related to handmade artefacts—passed down and constantly improved upon from pre-modern times, the other of those that date from the era of mechanization. In terms of the three-way dichotomy discussed above, the first corresponds to the Alpha Wave, created and preserved in folk traditions, the second to the Beta-Gamma-Wave technology, born of the merger of modern elite culture and contemporary mass culture.

The transmission of traditional Alpha-Wave know-how through training and practice was principally concentrated (1) in the home, (2) in the village and hamlet, and (3) by merchants and artisans. In agriculture, forestry, and fishing, one acquired the necessary knowledge and skills by assisting in the family enterprise; in village and hamlet, technical guidance and exchange of information were carried out in various cooperative and mutual-benefit endeavours. To receive needed instruction, merchant-class youths were sent to mercantile houses, their artisan-class counterparts to independent masters as indentured labourers and apprentices. In modern times, teaching and training for the young has shifted to (4) schools, where both normal and practical education has been provided, including, by extension, such skills and know-how as Japanese dressmaking and Western-style couture.

As government and corporation assumed responsibility and leadership for modern society, various forms of practical and effective skills training became indispensable, resulting in the creation of (5) study programs for civil servants and corporate staff, including the sending of some to sites both within Japan and abroad for training and research. With constant improvements being introduced to this approach, such contributed to the development of human resources possessed of expert knowledge. This kind of training falls into the category of the Beta-Gamma Wave.

In Japan's ageing society, the decade between 1955 and 1965 has become quite the fashion rage. One reason that we can offer is the simple fact that as members of the baby-boom generation reach the age of sixty and mandatory retirement, they look back with the zeal of nostalgia to the years when they were growing up, thus creating quite a profitable media market for cinema, television, and publishing. That alone makes the era a valuable commodity. Yet there is also surprising interest on the part of the younger generations. One reason for this may be a yearning for the traditional handicraft skills and know-how whose loss is a mark of the period, when, it is thought, there was still a warm, human touch in dealings between people, when, in terms of transmitting the knowledge of those endeavours, the Alpha Wave lingered.

Nevertheless, if we consider the matter calmly and objectively, we may well wonder whether such a view is historically realistic. Is it appropriate for us, under the influence of today's secondary and tertiary mass media, to wax one-sidedly enthusiastic about how the pre-modern technical arts and their perpetuation were characterized by overflowing compassion and the eccentric old virtuoso's obstinate commitment to excellence? If we listen to experienced observers regarding the relationship between Alpha Wave and the Beta-Gamma Wave, we can recognize that the former had, in reality, its serious limitations.

## Artisan Skills and Modern Technology

Though journalists are inclined to romanticize the transmission of skills and know-how cultivated by handicraft makers and artisans, we must not forget that amidst the extraordinarily rapid advance of technological innovation, modernization, and rationalization, traditional artisanship was not without negative aspects.

Early on in Japan's post-war recovery during the first half of the 1950s, Hisashi Shintō, who was first president of Ishikawajima-Harima Heavy Industries Co, Ltd (IHI), and then of National Bulk Carriers Kure Shipbuilding, when it split off from the parent company, pointed the way toward constructing ships through full-welding as opposed to riveting. In 1951, the American naval corporation NBC leased the former Kure Naval Shipyard for nine years.

Block construction under Shintō's direction, with its emphasis on full-welding, made NBC famous as a cost-cutting, highly productive, pioneering maker of supertankers. In 1952, the company manufactured the first ship, the 38,000 DWT tanker Petrokure; in 1956 came the 85,515 DWT Universe Leader and in 1959 the 104,520 DWT Universe Apollo, thereby continuing in the tradition of building the world's largest ships.

Shintō saw that the bending of steel had hitherto depended on highly skilled workers, rendering operations management quite difficult. The entire process was entrusted to an experienced staff, whose authority in the workplace was considerable. Nevertheless, the excellence of the work was contingent on capabilities gained from learning handed down within specific facilities, involving specific materials; from the standpoint of overall construction operations, such was extremely limited. Crucial design, facilities, along with reform and rationalization of, for example, the construction process lay outside the competence of skilled workers, as were issues related to the vital management steps required for hull production. Here Shintō succeeded in carrying out ongoing reforms in design, facilities, the construction process, and operations management, enhancing the capabilities of young technicians, boosting efficiency, reducing dependence on the expertise of older workers, and introducing labour-saving plans. Thus were cultivated on-the-jobsite engineers, possessed of new knowledge and not dependent on the experience and skill of their predecessors, whose range of capabilities was highly limited. Shintō reformed the work place, clearly restricting the role of traditional skilled workers in the production process, providing concise job descriptions for the new breed of technicians, and turning actual operations over to them (Shintō and Yuri 1958).

Kō Tani, who graduated from the University of Tokyo in 1944 and joined Aioi Dockyard, explains how at the time Japan possessed superb shipbuilding technology, as exemplified in the construction of the Battleship Yamato. It progressed from simple riveting to full-production welding, the latter achieved in 1960–61. Yet even after the full-welding stage was achieved, there were two places where reinforcement through riveting was still the only method: the one, in the curve of the ship, the other in the upper deck, with the top corner of the outer plate being joined to the bottom of the outer plate. When Tani was first employed, traditional fitters controlled the work division, leaving him, a university graduate, with nothing to do. Yet as the welding stage was reached, those men were unable to judge for which parts such would be appropriate. Now at last the time of university-trained technicians had arrived. They reversed roles with the skilled workers, becoming their instructors. This new level of industrialization, brought about by the transition from traditional artisanship to modern engineering teams, began in the latter half of the 1950s (Sekizawa 2006).

## The Transmission of Traditional Culture

The generation that propelled technological innovation and industrialization over the 1955–65 era is entering the twilight years. In Japan's current ageing society, we are seeing in various fields a growing movement to encourage and enable senior citizens to pass on the precious skills and know-how they have preserved to the next generations. The experience of active technicians who have been at the corporate cutting edge would naturally be thought valuable. In fact, however, with the arrival and extremely rapid development of information technology (IT), high-tech, and super-information, that judgment will vary from field to field. If this is true for the Beta-Gamma-Wave skills that were a mainstay of post-war economic development, it is only to be expected that all the more doubt will be cast on the economic value of Alpha-Wave skills, as exemplified by farmers reliant on beasts of burden, as well as their own strength, and fishermen using manually operated boats.

Thus, attempts to do something to pass on antiquated skills and know-how are a cultural concern; that is, they are seen as other than economic resources. For human beings surrounded by nature, the knowledge and practices of farmers, fishermen, and artisans in times past, when work was largely carried out by hand, are meaningful, whether for children engaged in education and training or for senior citizens with the leisure to seek culturally enhancing hobbies and pastimes.

With such a perspective in mind, I should like to introduce as one example a foundation that has been established with the aim of activating and passing on the traditional culture that we are in the process of losing. It is called the *Dentō-bunka-kasseika-kokumin-kyōkai* [Citizens' Cooperative Association for the Activation of Traditional Culture].

It was established in 2001, centred on the *Nihon-dentō-bunka-kasseika-giin-renmei* [Parliamentarian league for the Japanese traditional culture activation], which itself was formed in 2000 by volunteers among Liberal Democratic Party Diet members. Its senior advisor was Diet member Tamisuke Watanuki; the chair and managing director was Ikuo Hirayama, former president of Tokyo Gakugei University. After all, political processes necessarily have their role to play in influencing culture, and now as a sign of the times at the dawn of the 21st century, there was the intense and urgent realization that "Japan" and "traditional culture" were being forfeited.

Then in 2003, the *Dentō-bunka kodomo-kyōshitsu* [the children's classroom for traditional culture] was launched, having been commissioned by the Agency for Cultural Affairs. The aims are: (1) to enable children, the torch-bearers of the next generation, to experience and learn about traditional culture; (2) to ensure that the precious treasure that is traditional culture—created, preserved, and perpetuated throughout Japan's long history—is passed on and further developed; (3) to deepen children's interest in and understanding of history, tradition, and culture, nurture an attitude of respect, and cultivate a rich and abundant sense of humanity. The project focuses on such endeavours as providing financial support to leaders of the children's classroom, as attended by primary- and middle-school pupils throughout Japan, sponsoring symposia at which reports concerning the results are presented (Dentō-bunka-kasseika-kokuminkai 2004a, 2005a, 2006a), collected samples are published (Dentō-bunka-kasseika-kokuminkai 2004b, 2005b, 2006b), and the exchange of views and information among leaders is encouraged. The most important subjects, covering a broad range, include: folk entertainment, craftsmanship, traditional Japanese music, traditional Japanese dance, the martial arts (kendō, jūdō etc.), tea ceremony, flower arrangement, the game of go, shōgi (Japanese chess), traditional children's games, nursery songs, folktales, regional events, traditional handicrafts, local cuisine, history and visits to historical sites. The following are the numbers of applying organizations and applications accepted from fiscal 2003 through fiscal 2006: 2003: 1,866/1550; 2004: 2634/2023; 2005: 2726/2595; 2006: 3449/3365. Both the total number of applications and the number accepted have obviously risen. The upper limit on monetary amounts for which applications are submitted is 900,000 yen, but, in fact, most receive between 500,000–600,000 yen.

Most of the money goes for tool repair, renovation, and teaching materials. Funds are going to support local activities whose leaders have already been zealously engaged in the same. One can also sense their enthusiasm when they attend symposia reporting on the results of the nationwide programmes.

One entirely legitimate concern is the question of political interference in cultural matters. In my own involvement in the endeavour as an advisor, I intend to give full and careful consideration to issues regarding the relationship between the two realms. The sound operation of these projects is vital. As we see the family, regional societies, and schools losing their capacity to educate children in the above-mentioned manual skills of Alpha Wave, we recognize all the more clearly the importance of the assistance being provided by such foundations.

Particular attention is being given to the fact that those able to pass on the knowledge and know-how of the Alpha Wave are in late old age (75 and above). At present, the leaders of the children's classrooms are either baby boomers or those in early old age (65–74), which is to say those that benefited from post-war mechanization. According to the half-joking comment of those who genuinely personify the Alpha Wave, the younger generations are still wet behind the ears. I should like to see those still healthy members of the older generation find satisfaction in their remaining years by passing on their knowledge and skills to today's children. Mindful that without such, this heritage will vanish forever, I continue to contribute to the cause.

## References


Dentō-bunka- kasseika-kokuminkai, ed. (2004a, 2005a, 2006a): *Dentō-bunka—(Dentō-bunka kodomo-kyōshitsu-tokushū-gō)* [Traditional culture—special edition of the children's traditional culture classroom]. Tokyo: Dentō-bunka- kasseika-kokuminkai.

—— (2004b, 2005b, 2006b): *Dentō-bunka wo kodomo ni* [Providing children with traditional culture]. Tokyo: Dentō-bunka- kasseika-kokuminkai.

Sekizawa Mayumi (2006): *Kōreika-shakai ni okeru inkyo to teinen wo meguru minzokugaku-teki kenkyū* [A Folkloric Approach to the Study of Retirement in an Ageing Society], Grants-in-Aid for Scientific Research Bulletin, 2006, Ministry of Education, Culture, Sports, Science and Technology.

Shintani Takanori (2006): Girei no Kindai [Custom and Etiquette in Modern Times]. In: *Toshi no Kurashi no Minzokugaku 3*, [Folklore Studies of Urban Life, Vol. 3], Yoshikawa Kōbunkan, pp. 1–34.

Shintō Hisashi and Yuri Kenichi (1958): *Tōtetsu-kōji no shinpo-katei no ichirei* [An example of progress in the bending steel process], in *Seibu-zōsenkai-kaihō* (*Transactions of the West-Japan Society of Naval Architects Bulletin*) 16: pp. 51–67.

CHAPTER THIRTY

# AGE-SPECIFIC TECHNOLOGY: A DEMOGRAPHIC CHALLENGE FOR DESIGN

Fumihiko Satofuka

## 1. Introduction

Changes in demography have recently generated considerable interest in designing products for the over-60s, by implication, 'the older generation'. However, the ageing process is insidious, with different rates for different individuals. The onset and speed of the ageing process are also fairly individual, depending upon the decade of birth, and on health, nutrition, exercise, work and social activities throughout life. It is therefore more useful to think in terms of functional ability, particularly at the extremes of the population, and design accordingly. As a result, all those who are younger and stronger, with better eyesight, hearing or manipulative skill should also be able to use the product.

Designing or marketing products purely for the population aged 60 years and older does not necessarily make economic sense, since this group currently accounts for less than 50 per cent of the adult population. A 'design for all' philosophy could make a product attractive to and usable by perhaps 80 per cent of the adult population, thus achieving a greater return for research and development.

To follow this principle and achieve functional, efficient, safe and attractive design which enhances our abilities or compensates for our limitations, it is necessary to consider what is known about how our senses and physical capabilities change with age, and to revise the guidance available to designers. The user of a product needs to be able to see it, understand it, possibly hear it and probably manipulate it in some way consequently the most relevant physical capabilities to consider are eyesight, hearing and hand function. Mental abilities are related to the information obtained from the interaction of senses and feedback, and a discussion of the mental changes associated with ageing is included.

## 2. Physical Aspects of Ageing

### 2.1. *Vision*

There is a deterioration of vision due to changes in the normal ageing eye which may be exacerbated if the individual has a degenerative eye disease, the likelihood of which increases with age. The vision of older product users may not be an insurmountable problem, however, given the correct provision and use of vision aids and access to corrective surgery, such as cataract removal.

Visual capabilities can be assessed in terms of: acuity, accommodation, contrast sensitivity, glare sensitivity, dark adaptation, colour vision and stereopsis.

#### 2.1.1. *Visual acuity*

Acuity refers to the ability of the eye to see the shapes of objects, that is, the ability to see fine detail sharply. The ability of the pupil to change size in response to ambient light reaches its maximum in the early teens and progressively diminishes thereafter, with the effect of reducing the amount of light transmitted to the retina, particularly after the age of 60. The lens also tends to discolour with age: less light enters the eye and an increase in illumination is necessary for older people to overcome these effects. It has been estimated that the average 60-year-old eye requires three times as much light as a 20-year-old eye to see the same object (Weale 1963).

#### 2.1.2. *Accommodation*

Accommodation is the ability of the eye to focus on near and far objects. The near point of accommodation recedes from approximately age 8 to age 50, when it begins to level off after a 55 per cent decrease. (Pitts 1982) The loss of elasticity with age also causes a reduction in the speed of accommodation. As a consequence, older people have difficulty reading without glasses. This loss of ability to focus the eyes on near objects, which occurs with age, is called presbyopia.

#### 2.1.3. *Contrast sensitivity*

Contrast sensitivity is the ability to distinguish between light and dark; this affects the ability to see the outline of an object clearly. An increase in illumination can improve performance until a point is reached at which glare begins to decrease performance. Between ages 20 and 80 there is a progressive decrease in contrast sensitivity. The main decline begins at around 40 or 50 years of age, and is due to less light being transmitted via the lens to the retina (Pitts 1982).

2.1.4. *Glare*
The discomfort, even disability, which arises from harsh excess light in the form of glare is more troublesome to those over 40 than to the young. Glare is associated with the scattering of light within the eye; the increased opacity of the lens of the older eye enhances this effect, contributing to the glare.

2.1.5. *Dark adaptation*
The human eye is capable of adjusting to extremely wide limits of light intensity by a process known as adaptation, whereby the pupil size increases and decreases to admit more or less light on to the retina. Light adaptation occurs when moving from a dark to a light environment. Dark adaptation occurs when eyes are exposed to a dark environment after previous exposure to light. Light adaptation is rapid; dark adaptation is a slower process.

2.1.6. *Colour vision and colour discrimination*
There is a gradual development of normal colour perception from birth to age 30, and a gradual decline after the age range 30–40. Generally a marked loss in blue-green discrimination is believed to begin around 30 and a red-green deterioration is believed to begin around 55–60. (Voke 1981)

2.1.7. *Stereopsis*
The fact that we use both eyes to judge not only distance but also depth is known as binocular depth perception or stereopsis. There is a loss of stereopsis with increasing age. There is an improvement in the ability to judge distance up to age 7–8 years followed by a small decline to the age of 12 and a further improvement to adulthood (Pitts 1982).

2.1.8. *Summary*
The lens of the eye becomes more opaque and less elastic in adult life, and less able to focus. Changes in the muscle controlling the shape of the lens also reduce accommodation, and convergence of the lines of sight from both eyes becomes less efficient in later life because the muscles become weaker. After the age of about 10 the best viewing distance

lengthens gradually until around 50, by which point many people need to wear glasses to correct this long-sightedness (presbyopia).

Recession of the near point means that retinal images are smaller, so greater acuity is required, which in turn requires an increase in illumination. Twice as much light is required at age 40 as at 20, and three times as much is needed at 60. From the 20s there is a decrease in contrast sensitivity, but the main decline begins at around 40 to 50 years of age. The discomfort, even disability, which arises from harsh excess illumination in the form of glare is more troublesome to those over 40 than to the young.

## 3. Hearing

There are changes in the ear due to normal ageing which may be exacerbated by illness, disease and/or cumulative workplace effects.

Hearing begins to decline in the age group 10 to 19 years and becomes more pronounced as age advances (Beales 1965). It is difficult to determine when normal ageing deterioration begins, since the process is affected by many factors, such as exposure to noise throughout life, genetic influences and diet. However, by about age 50, there is sufficient hearing loss on average to bring about impairment in some demanding listening situations, such as faint sounds, background noise, and multiple sources. Such listening requires more effort and so becomes tiring and subject to error. Ageing also affects the ability to interpret and respond to complex auditory information.

Hearing impairment can be ameliorated by amplification but is sometimes characterized by an inability to discriminate or understand speech sounds even with amplification. The appreciation of higher tones is affected first and the lower tones are the last to be affected.

## 4. Hand Function

Consideration of hand function and how this may change with age is important, because it affects people's ability to hold and use tools, and to manipulate controls and products. With age there is a decrease in hand strength, dexterity, precision, coordination, joint mobility and sensitivity. Older people may also suffer from diseases such as arthritis, which can result in swollen and painful hands. Unfortunately there are very few data based on research into the changes in the ageing hand.

### 4.1. *Size*

One study noted that there is no change in hand seize with age. (Molenbroek 1987) Static measurements are of little help to designers of products where dynamic, object/task-specific measurements are required.

### 4.2. *Grip*

There is a decrease in grip strength and grip endurance with age, that is, in the amount of force that can be exerted when clamping something in the hand and the length of time this concentrated pressure can be maintained.

### 4.3. *Turning, twisting and similar actions*

Other studies of the hand have concentrated on older people's wrist-twisting strength in opening jars and bottles, and on their grip strength (Holland and Rabbit 1981).

However, none of these studies has presented the data in a form which could be used by designers of products and equipment.

## 5. Mental Aspects of Ageing

As well as being able to see, hear and manipulate a product, the older user also needs to be able to understand it.

Studies have detected age-related changes in mental ability, starting early in adult life. Screenings of large populations have shown the beginnings of declines in performance on timed pencil-and-paper tests of intelligence and creativity as early as the late 30s and early 40s. Studies have found deterioration in the ability to master a fast, complex interactive video game toward the higher end of the 18 to 36 age range. In spite of these findings, those aged 35 to 50 have seldom been included in laboratory studies. As a result, there is little precise information about age-related changes. Most information is based on analysis of the most demanding lifetime achievements of scientists, men of letters, and other professionals. Studies have suggested that in all professions in which notable achievements can be precisely documented a plateau of maximum productivity and originality in the late 20s and 30s is followed by a marked decline in quantity and quality of output (Holland and Rabbit 1981).

### 5.1. *Mental abilities and experience*

Experience reduces age differences in mental abilities, allowing overall effectiveness to be maintained either by preserving the original levels of basic abilities or through the development of compensatory skills: in other words, tasks one has knowledge of are less likely to cause mental difficulties than something completely new encountered at the age of 60.

### 5.2. *Ageing and divided attention*

A great deal of research has shown that older people have more difficulty in doing two things at once than younger people: for example, driving and making a telephone call, reading a document and typing it; reading and listening to the radio (Salthouse 1990).

### 5.3. *Ageing and problem solving*

There is an increase in the ability to solve problems up to the age of 40 or 50 and a decline thereafter; the rate of decline is thought to be related to the experiences of the individual (Denny and Palmer 1981).

### 5.4. *Summary*

Age-related changes in mental ability appear early in adult life and there is increasing evidence that individuals age at markedly different rates, especially beyond the age of 50. Mental abilities appear to deteriorate at different rates, depending on whether they are based on bodies of information acquired over long periods of time or whether they require the rapid assimilation and analysis of new information. An implication of this view is that, while age differences might not be evident in typical activities, they may become apparent if some type of unusual stress or complication is present, as is often the case when learning new skills or the use of new equipment. Since a large percentage of a product-user group could comprise individuals over the age of 60, it is necessary, if not essential, that human—machine control systems (such as the design and layout of control buttons and dials) fit the capabilities of the older user. The mental capacities and limitations of ageing individuals can be compensated for by the ergonomic design of the system.

## 6. Conclusions

Ageing is not a single process and some ageing processes begin early in life. By taking the design-for-all approach, a wider range of user needs can be accommodated, which also makes good economic sense. To use the motto of the Centre for Applied Gerontology at the University of Birmingham: 'Design for the young and you exclude the old; design for the old and you include the young.'

There is some specific design guidance as follows:

> Avoid the possibility of confusion, for example by not placing 'stop' buttons next to 'start' buttons

Remove choices in tracking tasks, as in steering a car or operating a robot. As complexity is increased, choice reaction time is degraded more for older than for younger people.

Avoid irrelevant information: if older people have to deal with a lot of information they are likely to take longer to perform the task.

Much else is of a very general nature, although ergonomic principles will always help in determining the details. However, there are gaps in age-specific knowledge that could be given to the designer and that need to be addressed.

## References

Birren, James E. and K. Warner Schaie (2001): *Handbook of the Psychology of Aging.* 5th edition. New York: Academic Press.

British Standards Institution (1991): *Guide to Dimensions in Designing for Elderly People. BSI. Standard BS4467.* London: British Standards Institution.

Coleman, R. (1988): *The Art of Work: An Epitaph to Skill.* London: Pluto Press.

Denny, N. W. and Palmer, A. M. (1981): 'Adult age differences on traditional and practical problem-solving measures'. In: *Journal of Gerontology*, 36/3, pp. 323–328.

Holland, C. A. and Rabbitt, P. (1991): 'The course and courses of cognitive change with advancing age', *Review of Clinical Gerontology*, 1, pp. 81–96.

Konz, S. (1990): *Work Design: Industrial Ergonomics.* 3rd edition, Worthington: Publishing Horizons.

Molenbroek, J. F. M. (1987): Anthrometry of elderly people in the Netherlands;research and applications. *Applied Ergononomics*, 18 (3), pp. 187–199.

Noro, K. and Andrew S. Imada (eds.) (1991): *Participatory Ergonomics.* London: Taylor & Francis.

Office of Technology Assessment (2005): *Technology and Aging in America.* Washington DC, US Congress, Office of Technology Assessment, Congressional Board of the 119th Congress.

Pitts, D. G. (1982): The effects of aging upon selected visual functions; colour vision, glare sensitivity, field of vision and accommodation in aging and human visual function,' in: R. Sekuler, D. W. Kline and K. Dismukes (eds.) *Aging and Human Visual Function*, New York: Alan R. Liss, pp. 131–160.

Salthouse, T. A. (1990): Influence of experience on age differences in cognitive functioning. In: *Human Factors* 32 (5), pp. 551–569.

Voke, J. (1963): Eyes at work: another look. In: *Occupational Safety and Health* (11) 12, pp. 36–39.

Weale, R. A. (1963): *The Aging Eye.* London: H. K. Lewis.

CHAPTER THIRTY-ONE

# AGEING TOURISTS, AGEING DESTINATIONS: TOURISM AND DEMOGRAPHIC CHANGE IN JAPAN

Carolin Funck

Changing demographics in the developed world as well as in economies such as China are considered one of the major shifts in the world tourism industry (Tretheway and Mak 2006: 21). However, the fact that demographic changes will affect not only the demand side of tourism, but also the supply side, is often neglected. This paper examines the influence of demographic changes on tourism in Japan from these two aspects. On the demand side, demographic changes offer new possibilities for the tourism market, but also new challenges, as destinations and tourism industries have to adapt to the increasingly varied and sophisticated demands of senior travellers as well as to new types of group tours such as special interest trips.

On the supply side, many established tourist destinations go through a stage of decline that is connected not only to ageing facilities, but also to the ageing of the population that provides services for tourists. In this part of the paper, factors of decline but also trends towards rejuvenation and changes in the structure of ownership and services are examined with regard to different destinations.

## 1. Ageing Tourists

In Japan, the percentage of senior citizens has increased at an extremely fast rate. The country also consistently ranks among the top ten countries regarding tourism spending and number of trips abroad, and possesses a highly developed domestic tourist market. It can be expected to act as a predictor for the dramatic changes in worldwide tourism that will be caused by ageing populations.

### 1.1. *Senior travellers as an attractive target market*

The "mature", "older" or "senior" market (Shoemaker 2000: 11) is of growing interest for service providers as well as scholars. Escalating numbers of ageing consumers with growing incomes, time flexibility, more independence and better overall health are known to travel more frequently, for longer distances and to stay longer at destinations. Increasing levels of educational attainment will also positively impact on seniors' quality of life and their travel behaviour (Faranda and Schmidt 1999). Furthermore, a tendency to favour packaged travel has been observed in older tourists, which makes this market segment even more attractive to the tourism industry (Tretheway and Mak 2006: 23).

However, it has been repeatedly pointed out that this large emerging market is not yet well understood.

The first problem is defining age ranges. When considering age structures, the percentage of population over the age of 65 is generally used for international comparisons. However, at the age of 55, major changes like early retirement may have already occurred. On the other hand, those over 75 are normally less mobile and require higher levels of medical treatment. This paper will use retirement as a major indicator for the senior market segment. As this may occur at different ages and as many major Japanese companies have a retirement age of 55, data on those aged 50 and over will be included as far as possible. However, some statistics use the age of 65 as a borderline to separate demographic bands.

Research has shown that the senior market is highly diverse with respect not only to socio-economic characteristics, but also to health, lifestyles, attitudes and other factors (Hornemann *et al.* 2002: 23). Faranda and Schmidt (1999) offer an overview of studies on the segmentation of the senior market. Most of the major markets have been examined: Germany (Romsa and Blenman 1989), the USA (Anderson and Langmeyer 1982, Shoemaker 1989, Shoemaker 2000), Canada (Zimmer, Brayley and Searle 1995), Australia (Hornemann *et al.* 2002), Japan (You and O'Leary 2000, Cha, McCleary and Uysal 1995) and, most recently, Taiwan (Jang and Wu 2006). However, one basic question that cannot be answered by these studies is the problem of continuity. As Zimmer, Brayley and Searle point out (1995: 9), the continuity theory suggests that, as individuals age, they tend to sustain consistent patterns of behaviour rather than undergo major shifts in activities and tastes according to their age. Faranda and Schmidt (1999: 16) also emphasize the importance of generation cohort typical behaviour. Replications of previous studies like those by Shoemaker (1989, 2000), which might show differences between generation cohorts, are rare; data on tourist behaviour by age groups taken with a consistent method over a longer period are also few. In this paper, a survey on travel conducted regularly in Japan is used to address the question of age or cohort typical behaviour.

Finally, an important problem for the tourism industry is the difference between biophysical versus psychosocial age (Faranda and Schmidt 1999: 6). This basically connects to the question of how to sell "senior" tourism, as the target group will not readily define itself by this attribute.

Generally, a variety of variables are seen to influence seniors' travel behaviour. The basic factors most commonly agreed on are income, health, family life cycle or family situation and education. Psychological factors such as life satisfaction and affects (Jang and Wu 2006) or willingness to participate (Faranda and Schmidt 1999) also play an important role. In the following section, the living conditions of seniors in Japan will be examined to see how these basic factors influence the senior travel market.

### 1.2. *Seniors' living conditions in Japan*

Comparing the percentage of the population over the age of 65 in developed countries, Japan was in the lower rankings until the 1980s, and has since reached the highest in the world in the twenty-first century (Cabinet Office 2005, Internet). The country experienced its first post-war baby boom from 1947 to 1949. This generation, called *dankai no sedai*, will soon boost the ranks of senior citizens when it starts to retire en masse in 2007. To examine the socio-economic background for travel participation among Japanese seniors, we will consider types of households, income, work situation, health and overall life satisfaction and then take a closer look at the baby boom generation.

The types of households with seniors have changed considerably over the last 20 years. As opposed to 1980, when half of all households with seniors were composed of three generations, couples-only households have become the most prevalent type (28.1 per cent). This is followed by three-generation households (24.1 per cent) and singles (19.7 per cent) (Japanese Cabinet Office 2005, Internet). In three-generation households, seniors often take responsibility for certain household tasks or participate in child rearing. For example, 41.9 per cent of seniors over 60 living in three-generation households do the washing, 35.4 per cent cook and 15.3 per cent look after their grandchildren (Cabinet Office 2004, Internet). These household chores might inhibit free travel. On the other hand, households consisting only of elderly couples have a lot of disposable time and income. Single households, especially older females, are often restricted by a lack of financial resources and travel partners. Changing family life cycles also affect travel behaviour. For example, a tendency for first births at later ages will lead to a later empty-nest stage. As the average age at first marriage is increasing, single children stay with their parents longer to avoid high living costs, a phenomenon known as "parasite singles".

Concerning income, senior households where all family members are either above 65 or under 18 years old do not differ much from the average income when calculated on a per household member basis. In 2003, the annual average for all households stood at 2,047,000 yen, compared to 1,961,000 yen for senior households. The percentage of senior households that described their financial situation as tight or very tight was 47.6 per cent, which is 6 per cent lower than the rate for households overall. However, single female senior households have to deal with a much tighter situation, with an average personal income of 1,124,000 yen (Cabinet Office 2002, Internet).

One demographic characteristic of Japan is the high percentage of the senior population in the labour force, which also explains the relatively stable economic situation of senior households. In 2000, over 50 per cent of men were working up to the age of 69. Only 30 per cent of men and 55 per cent of women aged 65–69 have no desire to work (Cabinet Office 2005, Internet). The main reasons for the wish to work are to stay healthy (29 per cent) and to gain necessary income (20 per cent) (Data from 2003, Sōgō Yunicomu 2005: 514).

Another major factor influencing travel behaviour is health. Japan is famous for its high average life expectancy, 85 years for women and 78 for men. However, 13.8 per cent of men and 16.1 per cent of women between 65 and 74 years have an illness that affects their daily life. This percentage increases to 27.3 per cent of men and 31.6 per cent of women for those over 75 (Cabinet Office 2002, Internet).

As for life satisfaction, in a recent survey of 3,000 senior citizens carried out by the Cabinet Office, 82.5 per cent felt satisfied with life. However, this very high percentage was down 7.3 per cent from the same survey in 1994 (Cabinet Office 2004, Internet).

To summarize the situation of seniors, the generation now in or approaching retirement enjoys a relatively stable economic footing. However, full or part-time work after retirement and family responsibilities tend to restrict travel behaviour. The connection between work situation and travel participation will be further examined below.

It is widely accepted that a person's life history influences their travel behaviour (Faranda and Schmidt 1999: 10). It is therefore useful to consider some major collective events in the biography of the first baby-boomers, who started retiring in 2007. They were born 1947–49 and as teenagers experienced fast economic growth, and, in 1964, the Tokyo Olympics, the construction of the Shinkansen and the end of restrictions on foreign travel. In their prime of life around 40, when they were busy raising families and working, the yen started to rise after the 1985 Plaza Agreement, making foreign travel widely affordable. They enjoyed another several years of boom during the bubble economy from 1987 until 1992, when the economy started a major downturn leading to large-scale restructuring in companies. This meant the end of professional careers for some of them. In spite of the prolonged downturn, a large percentage of this generation will have had an economically stable life and will be able to enjoy its benefits upon retirement. Questions like how they will travel, whether they will create a new cohort trend, whether they will prefer international or domestic destinations, whether they will travel in groups or as individuals, and whether they will enjoy active or passive forms of recreation will affect the Japanese travel market, and possibly the world's, in the upcoming years.

### 1.3. *How do Japanese seniors travel?*

Until the 1980s the Japanese domestic tourism market was not affected very much by international tourism. Thus it has long enjoyed a rather uncompetitive, predictable and stable situation. This has started to change with the steep increase in outbound travel since the late 1980s, the economic downturn of the 1990s, a lesser but visible increase in the number of inbound tourists and the restructuring of the travel industry in response to globalization and information technology in the twenty-first century.

Due to the long phase of stability and the maturity of the market, some basic aspects of Japanese tourism have almost acquired the quality of myths; two of these will be examined below.

The most common image of Japanese tourists is their tendency to travel in groups. "Japan is a group-oriented society in which travel traditionally has been undertaken in groups" (March 2000: 188). Or, in an earlier study by Graburn (1995: 48), "compared to most Europeans and North Americans, the Japanese have a low sense of cultural self-confidence and they usually only travel in groups". This tendency was certainly true until the 1980s and has influenced the structure of domestic tourist destinations and services. However, the percentage of group travel for domestic trips declined from 32 per cent in 1987 to 24 per cent in 2002, due to a decreasing number of trips organized through companies or schools. The number of trips with over 10 persons has declined and trips with 2–3 persons now have the highest share (34 per cent), compared to 21 per cent in 1984. However, seniors over 60 show a higher tendency to travel in groups with over 15 persons. The percentage travelling with local or religious groups is also significantly higher than the average (NKK 2004: 55, 112). Among farmers over 50, regular group tours with organizations are the most important reason (~60 per cent) to travel (Zenkoku Nōgyō Kankō Kyōkai 1997: 55). As for outbound travel, 48 per cent of tourists who booked through a travel agency used package tours and 6 per cent group travel (2003), while the rest made individual travel arrangements. Among the elderly, both percentages are higher: 50.3 per cent of men over 60 use package tours and 10.1 per cent group travel, compared to 57.7 per cent and 6.8 per cent of women over 60 (JTB 2003: 46). Generally, the emphasis has shifted from large groups to small groups or families.

The second aspect concerns the market structure. "The Japanese travel market is very much controlled by a small number of large wholesalers.... As a result, trade- not consumer marketing is the critical factor for marketing." (March 2000: 189). This observation is supported by the fact that the top five companies have a market share of around 50 per cent among the top 50 agencies (JATA 2006, Internet). This may lead to a restricted choice for senior consumers.

In the following section, we will consider whether and how these patterns of uniformity in behaviour and market structure have changed pertaining to the senior market segment. Unfortunately, data on travel behaviour by age are somewhat limited. The "Survey on Time Use and Leisure Activities" conducted every five years by the government analyzes travel participation in overnight trips inside and outside Japan for sightseeing, VFR (Visit Friends and Relatives) and business purposes according to age, gender, work situation and other variables (Ministry of Internal Affairs and Communication Statistics Bureau 2001, Internet). A yearly survey by the Japan Tourism Association (*Nihon Kankō Kyōkai*) gives detailed account of travel behaviour by age groups; however, with fewer than 3,000 respondents, the survey is not representative (NKK,

Table 1. Travel Intensity and percentage of business trips.

| Work situation | Age | Domestic | | International | |
|---|---|---|---|---|---|
| | | Travel intensity % | % of trips for business | Travel intensity % | % of trips for business |
| Working | All ages | 71.2% | 32.9% | 14.0% | 25.1% |
| | >60 years old | 64.3% | 21.6% | 11.6% | 20.2% |
| Not working | All ages | 58.7% | 7.9% | 8.6% | 9.5% |
| | >60 years old | 57.6% | 5.8% | 9.3% | 4.3% |

Source: Ministry of Internal Affairs and Communication Statistics Bureau 2001.

yearly). This is especially so for the section on international travel. For travel abroad, the Japan National Tourist Organization publishes data on the number of trips made by different age groups compiled from immigration data (JNTO yearly, Internet), and the Japan Tourism Bureau, the largest travel agency, analyzes bookings through travel agencies (JTB, yearly).

Generally, travel intensity is higher among the working population than among the non-working population (Table 1). Among those working, business trips account for one-third of domestic trips and one-quarter of trips abroad. The same tendency is true for seniors, as those working travel more than their non-working counterparts, with the exception of 50–54 year olds travelling abroad. Business trips form an important segment of travel, because they make up one-fifth of all trips by working seniors over 60.

Except for men aged 55–59, men above 50 show a 1–3 per cent higher travel intensity than women. However, for those over 70 years old, the total number of women travellers is higher than men, mirroring the population structure.

Total numbers by gender and age for international trips show that travel patterns have not changed much over the last 13 years. According to immigration statistics from 1991 and 2004, as shown in Figure 1, women aged 10–29 travel more than men. The situation is reversed for groups aged 30–59, and among seniors, the disparity becomes smaller. These figures imply that family life restricts women's travel, while work creates chances for international trips for men.

With regard to travel companions, travel with work colleagues declines to below average after the age of 55. Instead, friends and, for trips abroad, family and neighbours become ever more frequent travel partners. Neighbours play an increasing role for those over 65.

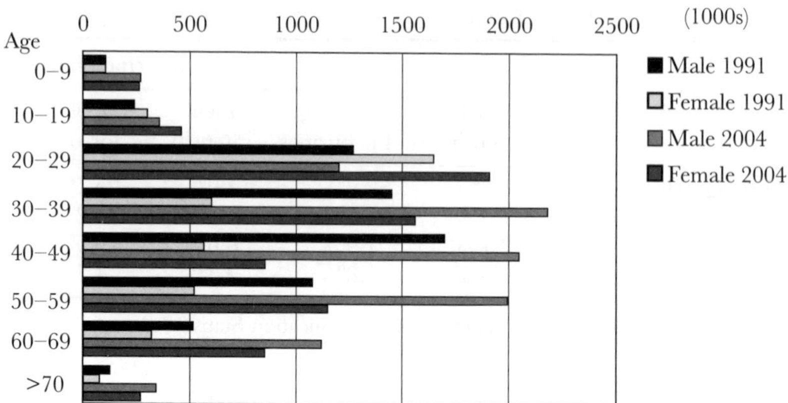


Source: Ministry of Land Infrastructure and Transport 2005, Internet.

Figure 1. International trips by gender and age (1991 and 2004).

According to the yearly survey by the Japan Tourism Association (NKK, yearly), seniors' travel behaviour on domestic trips differs from the general average on a number of points. Seniors between 60 and 69 spend more money on group travel or accommodation. They are more likely to use a tour bus, stay in a *ryokan*, (traditional Japanese style accommodation), and travel in October. The main purpose of trip shifts according to age: the percentage of those citing hot springs rises from 18 per cent (40–49) to 29 per cent (over 70); those citing sports correspondingly decrease from 21 per cent to 4 per cent.

Comparing activities at destinations recorded in the surveys of 1992, 1998 and 2003, respondents over 50 show clear preferences compared with other age groups, but follow the general trends with only a few exceptions (NKK, 1993, 1999, 2004). Activities which seniors are involved in more significantly than average include visits to hot springs, natural and cultural sightseeing and visits to shrines and temples. Elderly women also show more than an average interest in seasonal flower viewing and shopping for souvenirs. At the other end of the spectrum, participation is low for visits to theme parks, swimming in the sea, going for drives, skiing or camping. Among outdoor activities, men over 50 increasingly show a higher interest in golf and fishing and women in hiking.

Some changes over the period between 1992 and 2003 can be observed. Due to the increasing popularity of hot springs, the difference between senior and general respondents participating in this activity has shrunk. It has also decreased for shrine and temple visits. These two activities are now less age-specific. On the other hand, between 1998 and 2003, differences in participation percentages have increased for cultural sightseeing for men in their 60s, natural sightseeing for men and women in their 60s, and shopping for souvenirs for women in their 50s. Disparities have become wider for visits to theme parks. Therefore, the preference among seniors for cultural and natural attractions has apparently been consolidated.

To further examine activities and behaviour of senior tourists inside Japan, it is important to look at surveys conducted at destinations or places of residence. Few such surveys have been published, but from the examples given below, it is possible to identify some trends.

The author has conducted tourist surveys at several destinations in the Seto Inland Sea Area in Western Japan. In 2004, a questionnaire administered in Onomichi City (Hiroshima Prefecture) was taken by 431 tourists at different spots throughout the city (Funck 2005). Among the respondents, 17 per cent were in their 50s and 15 per cent over 60 years old. Onomichi City is famous for its picturesque location on a hillside overlooking the Onomichi Channel. It is also known for its many temples, a rich heritage of art and literature and as a location for movies. Asked about their general travel preferences, those over 50 put a higher emphasis on food quality and less on relaxation. In contrast to the younger age group below 30 years old, who had a strong image of Onomichi as a place where it is possible to relax, respondents over 50 saw the city mainly as a place with history and tradition. In the evaluation of their experience, they gave high marks for temples and shrines. These results confirm high cultural and historical interests among senior tourists, but also an emphasis on the quality of experiences expressed in the preference for food. Relaxation, on the other hand, is less important.

Surveys conducted at places of residence give a more localized pattern of tourism and leisure behaviour. A survey among residents over 50 years old in Gifu City (Gifu Prefecture) and Nagoya City (Aichi Prefecture) showed a high interest in travel as a leisure activity (Gifuken Sangyō Keizai Shinkō Sentā 2004). The main purpose of travel was to relax in hot springs, to enjoy nature and scenery, to visit historic or cultural sights and to enjoy regional food, customs and history.

A recent questionnaire in a smaller regional city, Higashihiroshima City (Hiroshima Prefecture) with about 160,000 inhabitants, gives some clues about general leisure behaviour (Asano *et al.* 2006). Here, a high percentage of those in their 50s spend their leisure time with people from the local area or with neighbours. Among seniors in their 60s, many want to spend their leisure time in natural surroundings, engage in local activities or experience a sense of fulfilment.

It can be concluded that in domestic tourism, natural, cultural and historical tourism resources play an important role for senior tourists, as do local or regional attractions like food specialities. While the tendency to travel in groups is higher than in other age groups, independent travel is also common.

### 1.4. *The tourism industry adjusts*

In the tourism industry, expectations for the burgeoning new silver market are high. At the same time, the industry has to adjust its services to ageing clientele. In 2006, a business hotel chain caused a major scandal as they removed extra parking lots and rooms for handicapped visitors after the initial construction inspection and replaced them with other facilities and normal rooms. The company argued that the special facilities for handicapped people were seldom used and therefore inhibited their business. The hotel chain was ordered by the city of Yokohama to restore the parking lots for the handicapped; this was the first such case under the Heart Building Law (Asahi Shinbun Chōkan 25.02.2006, Yokohama: 31).

Services and facilities have gradually been adjusted to the needs of aged and handicapped customers under the keywords of "barrier-free" and "universal design". The Heart Building Law, designed to make large buildings more accessible, was introduced in 1994 and expanded in 2003. The Law for Barrier-free Transport was implemented in 2000 to establish escalators, elevators and ramps in transport facilities. From 2001 onwards, a project to create barrier-free tourism spaces aims specifically at tourism facilities like information centres, public bathrooms etc.

For travel agents, senior outbound tourism is the more attractive market segment. Although many seniors have some travel experience abroad and should have no problems visiting Paris or London on their own, they will still require some kind of advice or guide for longer, more intensive experiences that allow for some immersion in regional culture or visits to more peripheral tourism locations. To answer this demand, Japans' biggest travel agent JTB created a new division for travel abroad, called JTB Grand Tour, in 2006 (JTB Grandtours 2006,

Internet). It offers individual package tours for "new seniors". Of the 50 tours introduced, 34 have European destinations. The company promises authentic travel, accompanied by competent guides, and integrates customers' individual wishes into the programme. A 10-day tour "Holidays in German Forests", for example, includes sightseeing and walks in smaller towns along the Mosel and Rhine rivers. Specialised agents like this cater to the diversifying needs of the senior market, which range from luxurious cruise trips to long-stay programs organized by grass-root groups or NPOs (Murata 2002).

Although government plans in the 1980s to relocate Japan's retired population in specially developed resort areas around the world never materialized, an increasing interest in long-stay tours seems to point to more flexible ways of enjoying life on an international basis. Buying second homes abroad and multinational living might never become as popular in Japan as it is in Europe. However, the concept of *kōryū jinkō*, a kind of temporary re-population scheme that was originally developed by the government to revive depopulated rural areas of Japan, might well be applied internationally by Japan's new generation of seniors.

## 2. Ageing Destinations

The second part of this paper will turn its attention to destination areas and examine how ageing affects tourist destinations. To this purpose, some terminology needs to be defined. Ageing processes affect tourism resources as well as the tourism industry. Tourism resources are defined as existing natural and cultural resources that were not originally created for the purpose of tourism, but attract visitors from outside the area. They are normally divided into three categories: natural resources like mountains, rivers, coasts or temporary phenomena like blooming flowers; cultural resources like castles, temples, pictures, but also customs or festivals; and integrated resources like cultural landscapes or towns and villages. The latter category is most closely interwoven with social and economic life and therefore most prone to be influenced by changes in population structure.

Tourism industry is comprised of tourism resources such as travel or communication infrastructure, receptive facilities like restaurants and accommodation, entertainment and sports facilities and tourism reception facilities like guides, tourist information offices etc. (Shaw and Williams 1994, 98).

These two sectors are affected by an ageing population structure in the following ways. Tourism resources, especially integrated resources like cultural landscapes or townscapes, have been created through certain forms of interaction between humans and their surroundings. Typical examples in Japan would include port towns, terraced rice fields or farmhouses adapted for silk cultivation. Production processes and means of transport change over time, resulting in buildings or townscapes losing or changing their former functions. Ageing processes further affect the material and cultural heritage of an area negatively as buildings fall empty, traditional methods of maintenance are forgotten and inhabitants lack the strength and energy to keep up cultural activities. Ageing of whole communities, for example, in remote areas or in designated protected historic districts, also inhibits the introduction of modern resource management due to lack of interest and human resources.

In the tourism industry, small-scale family-run businesses, which offer a large proportion of the services available, face difficulties in securing business successors or service personnel. In comparison to other service industries, accommodation facilities in Japan rely heavily on personnel over 55 years old, often female part-time workers (Funck 1999: 169). Many tourism facilities that were constructed during the economic boom of the 1960s are in need of reconstruction, but planning and investment require a smooth generational transition. Ageing demographics at tourist destinations also affect the ability of destinations to adjust to new, more diverse patterns of demand, to offer new or trendy forms of recreational activities and to cope with the increasing influx of foreign tourists.

### 2.1. *Regional structures of ageing*

Due to imbalances in population distribution, strong regional differences in ageing can be observed among the 47 prefectures of Japan. Basically, all prefectures belonging to the Kantō, Nagoya and Kansai conurbation areas and those with a capital city of over one million inhabitants have a lower percentage of senior citizens than the national average, which stood at 20.3 per cent in 2000. Figure 2 relates these data to the number of rooms in accommodation facilities per 1,000 inhabitants.

While the strength of the tourism industry in any given area is normally measured by the number of overnight stays per 1,000 inhabitants (Flohr 2000: 98), in countries lacking statistics on overnight stays,

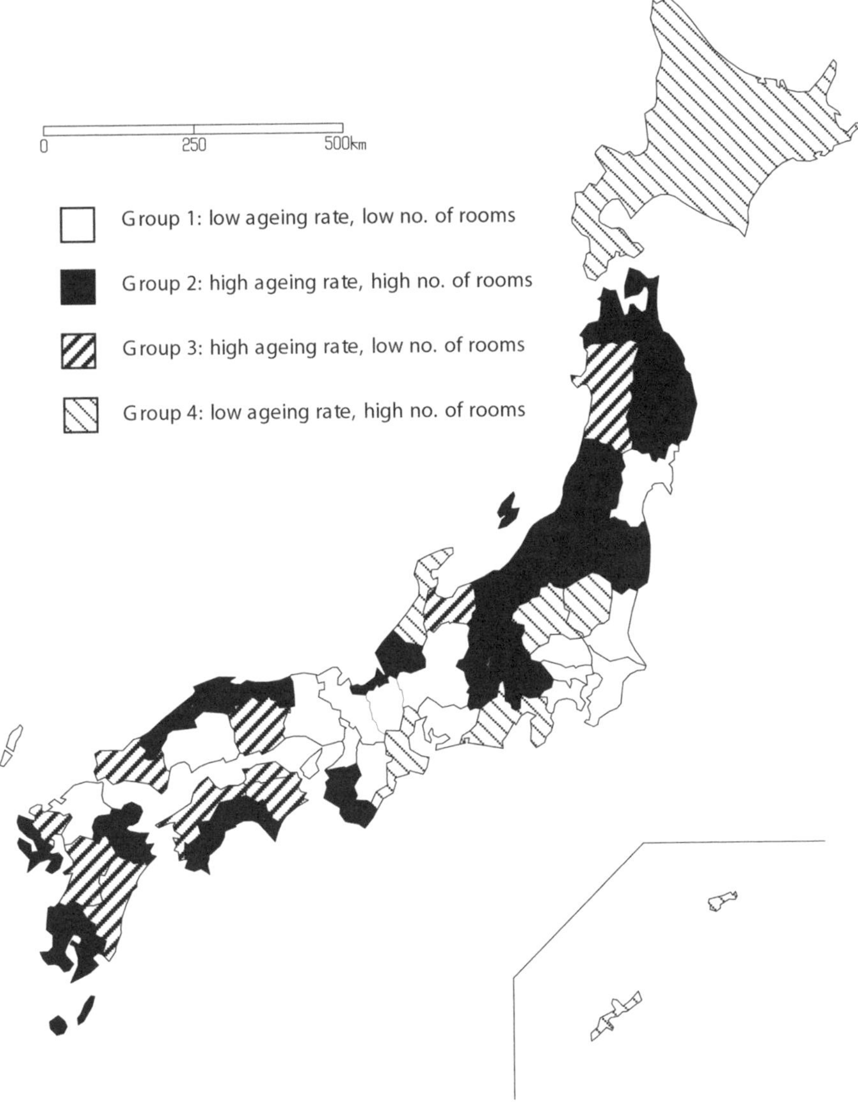


Source: author's own draft; data: Population Census of Japan 2000; Ministry of Health, Labour and Welfare 2004, Internet.

Figure 2. Regional differences in percentage of population older than 65 and number of rooms in accommodation facilities.

like Japan, rooms per inhabitants can be used as an indicator. Of the 47 prefectures, 15 fall in the category of low ageing rate and low number of rooms relative to population size, indicating an urbanized structure with high population density (Group 1). On the other hand, 15 prefectures with a high percentage of senior citizens feature many rooms per inhabitants, the most extreme examples being Nagano and Yamanashi (Group 2). Both prefectures have long-established tourism industries based on the attractions of the Japanese Alps and Mount Fuji and the closeness to the capital metropolitan area. Ten prefectures with an older population but lower than average number of rooms have poorly developed tourism structures (Group 3). Finally, seven prefectures with a young population and many accommodation facilities include well-known tourist destinations like Hokkaido and Okinawa, but also the inner areas of the pleasure periphery of the capital metropolitan area, where urbanization processes and attractive tourism resources overlap (Group 4). It can be concluded that prefectures in group 2, peripheral areas with sufficient natural and cultural tourism resources to have experienced tourism development, are most likely to face problems in keeping up tourism as a viable industry because of their age structure.

### 2.2. *Preserving historic townscapes*

One important tourism resource mainly found in peripheral areas are historic townscapes that have thus far escaped the pressures of urbanization. Since 1975, 66 districts (Dec. 2004, Agency of Cultural Affairs 2006, Internet) have been designated as "Important Preservation Districts for Groups of Historic Buildings" (*Jūyō dentōteki kenzōbutsugun hozon chiku*). Many are located in remote areas with bad transportation access; depopulation and ageing have led to an increasing number of empty houses.

For example, in the Preservation District of Takehara City (Hiroshima Prefecture), it was estimated that 30 houses were uninhabited in 2005. Based on this situation, the city applied for and received recognition as a "special area for structural reform" (*Kōzōkaikaku tokubetsuku*) to improve the management of uninhabited housing stock. A NPO now handles the intermediation procedures, which is normally not possible without an official certification as a real estate agent (*Asahi Shinbun* 2.05.2005, Hiroshima Edition: 19). While Takehara pioneered the use of structural reform areas, the problem of uninhabited buildings is common in most preservation districts. The problem appears in two variations. In peripheral areas without sufficient access to major tourism markets, buildings fall empty and municipalities try to attract new users, tenants or owners. In established tourist destinations, on the other hand, a policy of "don't sell, don't let, don't tear down" tries to prevent the influx of souvenir shop chains and other capital investment from outside the area that would destroy their local character (Tsumago Kankō Kyōkai, Internet). Such replacement processes are common in destinations where senior shop or land owners give up their property due to a lack of successors. Both policies stem from the same roots. A shrinking and ageing population in peripheral areas leaves a vacuum that becomes visible in empty buildings. And while renovated *machiya* (townhouses) have become fashionable in Kyoto and other urban areas, this process does not translate easily to more remote areas and spurs further debates about authentic use of historic townscapes.

### 2.3. *Shrinking communities and tourism development*

Some other examples will illustrate the consequences of the ageing process on tourism resources and industry. In the town of Yutakamachi (Hiroshima Prefecture) on Osakishimojima Island, the small port town of Mitarai was designated as a Preservation District in 1994. It was a thriving port not only in the Edo Period, when ships had to wait here for tides and winds to change, but until the 1950s as an entertainment quarter for sailors (Funck, 2006). Nowadays, the percentage of senior citizens in Yutakamachi Town is about 50 per cent, and even higher in the historic port town area. Although the place has become popular with tourists due to the efforts of a local volunteer guide group, there are very few accommodation and restaurant facilities available. The existing few mainly cater to temporary construction workers or other work-related travellers; on Sundays, no restaurant is open inside the old port town. The number of tourists, estimated at about 30,000 per year, is not sufficient to attract new inhabitants who would engage in the tourism industry, therefore the existing tourism resources have not yet been commercialized. In and of itself, this could be considered a positive aspect, except for the threat of a hollowed-out town that would leave well-preserved houses without inhabitants.

Tourism is part of most regional and local development strategies in Japan. However, ageing in remote peripheral areas also negatively impacts on the development of new tourism industries promoted by prefectures and municipalities. In the case of Yamanomura (Hida City), a village situated high up in the mountains of Gifu prefecture, the population shrank from around 1,000 in the 1960s to about 200 in 2004 after mining was abandoned (Funck 2004). As a result, the local community is struggling to keep up local festivals and other basic community functions. The municipality has recently engaged in green tourism, developing a horse-riding facility and a farm park where visitors can experience dairy and sausage production and buy or eat the products. However, instructors for the horse-riding club commute more than an hour from a neighbouring city, as nobody inside the village has sufficient expertise with horses. The farm park also relies on outside resources for know-how and investment. A local group has started to develop its own ideas for green tourism, such as renovating an empty house for visiting student seminars or offering farming experiences for visitors. Although tourism development started by the local administration has successfully created some private initiatives, both the public and private sector face a serious lack of manpower due to ageing.

Smaller regional cities are shrinking too. The city of Onomichi (Hiroshima Prefecture), introduced above in connection with a questionnaire on travel behaviour, has experienced changes in population structure due to changes in industry and transport. The central part of the city, where tourists concentrate, is characterized by a maze of temples and houses situated on a hillside parallel to the coast and a commercial district centring on a long shopping arcade that runs between the coast and the hill (Funck 2005). Houses along the hillside have deteriorated, but are difficult to renovate or rebuild, as they are mainly connected by small lanes and stairways (Figure 3). No sewage system is available in this district; decaying houses and empty lots are a common sight.

This is true also for the shopping arcade, which, as in many other cities, has lost customers to suburban shopping facilities. In 2001, 23 per cent of the 368 shops stood empty. In 1999, 88 per cent of the shop owners were over 50 years old and 29 per cent expected to close their shops in the future as they had no successor (Onomichi Shōkōkaigisho 2001). Recently, this decline has shown signs of reversal. Some young artists have moved into the houses along the hillside, students from the local university have started to plan events and the number of shops catering for tourists is increasing. At the same time, plans to construct a high-rise apartment building have led to a discussion on whether and how to preserve the townscape along the hillside. It remains to be seen

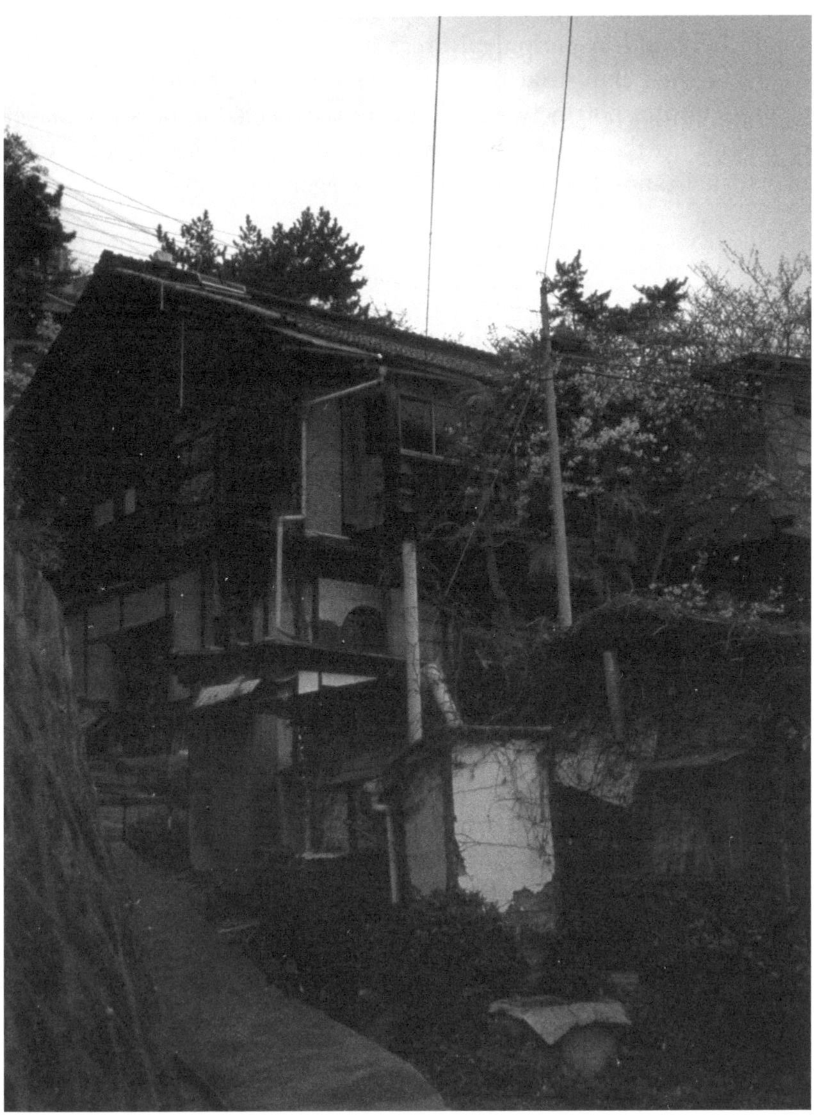

Figure 3. Decaying houses are a common sight in many districts with traditional houses (Onomichi City).

whether the equation of old houses = ageing = decline can be replaced without destroying the townscape.

The examples given above are not exceptions. Shrinking communities, a phenomenon which includes a high percentage of senior citizens, are to be found in peripheral areas as well as in regional cities that have lost their industrial base or their economic hinterlands due to changes in transport networks. Tourism is expected to be a key player in revitalizing these areas, but the resources and services necessary for that revitalization are threatened by the ageing process.

## 3. Conclusions

In the Japanese tourism industry as well as in destinations around the country, expectations are high for a larger, diversified target group as the first baby-boomers start to retire in 2007. Statistical evidence points to a strong tendency among senior tourists to enjoy natural and cultural tourism resources and attractions. However, the data basis is not sufficient enough to judge whether age or cohort effects will show up. For example, while group travel has been declining generally, baby-boomers might still feel more comfortable with this style of travel, as many of them had their first travel experiences in a group. Although the tourist industry is eager to develop new products for senior travellers, the infrastructure and services at destinations are not yet modified for their needs.

Ageing processes also affect tourist destinations. Peripheral areas and smaller regional cities struggle to preserve their cultural heritage as populations decline and/or age. While integrated tourism resources like townscapes and agricultural landscapes increasingly attract visitors, they lack owners, users, inhabitants or managers. Services and recreation activities, even if there is a demand for them cannot be provided. On the other hand, successful tourism development might in time attract investment and a working population to eventually reverse the effects of ageing. However, solutions will probably change the character of destinations no less dramatically than could be expected with a continuously shrinking and ageing population.

## References

Agency for Cultural Affairs (2006): *Jūyō dentōteki kenzōbutsugun hozon chiku* (Important Preservation Districts for Groups of Historic Buildings) http://www.bunka.go.jp/ (found 8.6.2006).

Anderson, Beverlee B. and Langmeyer, Lynn (1982): The Under-50 and Over-50 Travelers: A Profile of Similarities and Differences. In: *Journal of Travel Research* 20–4, pp. 4–10.

Japanese Cabinet Office (2002): *Heisei 14 nendō kōreisha no kenkō ni kansuru ishiki chōsa* [Comprehensive Survey of Living Conditions of People on Health and Welfare] http://www8.cao.go.jp/kourei/ishiki/h14_sougou/h14_gaiyou.html (found 15.5. 2006).

—— (2004): *Kōreisha no nichijō seikatsu ni kansuru ishiki chōsa* [Attitude Survey on the Daily Life of the Elderly] http://www8.cao.go.jp/kourei/ishiki/h16_nitizyou/index.html (found 15.5.2006).

—— (2005): *Report on the Aging Society 2005*. http://www8.cao.go.jp/kourei/english/annualreport/2005/05wp-e.html (found 19.3.2006).

Cha, Sukbin, McCleary, Ken W. and Uysal, Muzaffer (1995) Travel Motivations of Japanese Overseas Travellers: A Factor-Cluster Segmentation Approach. In: *Journal of Travel Research* 34–1, pp. 33–39.

Faranda, William T., Schmidt, Sandra L. (1999): Segmentation and the Senior Traveler: Implications for Today's and Tomorrow's aging Consumer. In: *Journal of Travel & Tourism Marketing* 8–2, pp. 3–27.

Flohr, Susanne (2000): Inländische Reiseziele. In: Institut für Länderkunde, Leipzig (Hg) (2000): *Freizeit und Tourismus* (= Nationalatlas Bundesrepublik Deutschland, Bd. 10). Heidelberg/ Berlin, Spektrum Akademischer Verlag, pp. 98–99.

Funck, Carolin (2006): Von der Mülldeponie zum Tourismusparadies? Strukturveränderungen in der Seto-Inlandsee-Region. In: Vollmer, Klaus (Hg): *Ökologie und Umweltpolitik in Japan und Ostasien. Transnationale Perspektiven* München: Iudicium Verlag, pp. 123–144.

—— (2005): Machinami, tenbō to engankankō—kankō shigen toshite no shamen chiku [Townscape, views and coastal tourism—hillsides as tourism resource]. In: *Nihon Kenkyū Tokushū* 3, 2005–10, pp. 49–62.

—— (2004): Diversifizierung im innerjapanischen Tourismus. In: *Petermanns Geographische Mitteilungen* 2004/5, pp. 36–43.

—— (1999): *Tourismus und Peripherie in Japan*. Bonn: Dieter Born Verlag.

Gifuken Sangyō Keizai Shinkō Sentā (2004): Kōreisha shijō no kasseika ni kansuru chōsa kenkyū hōkokusho kara [From the research report on activation of the senior market]. *Gekkan Rejā Sangyō Shiryō* 2004–8, pp. 125–128.

Graburn, Nelson (1995): The past in the present in Japan: nostalgia and neo-traditionalism in contemporary Japanese domestic tourism. In: Butler, Richard and Pearce, Douglas: *Change in Tourism*. London and New York: Routledge, pp. 47–70.

Hornemann, Louise, Carter, R. W., Wei, Sherrie and Ruys, Hein (2002): Profiling the Senior Traveler: an Australian Perspective. In: *Journal of Travel Research* 41–1, pp. 23–37.

Jang, SooCehong and Wu, Chi-Mei Emily (2006): Seniors' Travel Motivation and the Influential factors: An Examination of Taiwanese Seniors. *Tourism Management* 27, pp. 306–312.

JATA (Japan Association of Travel Agents) (2006): *Jūyō ryokō gyōsha 50sha no ryokō toriazukai jōkyō sokuhō*. [Announcement on the situation of 50 important travel agencies] http://www.jata-net.or.jp/tokei/001/1.htm (found 10.5.2006).

JNTO (Japan National Tourist Organization) (2006): *Visitor Arrivals and Japanese Overseas Travelers*. http://www.jnto.gp.jp (found 20.4.2006).

JTB (Japan Travel Bureau) (2003): *JTB Report 2003: All about Japanese overseas travelers.* Tokyo: JTB.

JTB Grandtours: http://www.jtb-grandtours.jp/ (found 27.2.2006).

March, Roger (2000): The Japanese Travel Life Cycle. In: Chon, K. S./Inagaki, Tsutomu/ Ohashi, Taiji (eds.): *Japanese Tourists. Socio-Economic, Marketing and Psychological Analysis.* New York/ London/Oxford: Haworth Hospitality Press, pp. 185–200.

Ministry of Health, Labor and Welfare (2004): *Eisei gyōsei hōkokurei heisei 16nendo* (Report on sanitation administration) http://wwwdbtk.mhlw.go.jp/IPPAN/ippan/scm_k_Ichiran (found 25.5.2006).

Ministry of Internal Affairs and Communication Statistics Bureau (2001): *2001 Survey on Time Use and Leisure Activities.* http://www.stat.go.jp/english/data/shakai/2001/kodo/zenkoku/travel.htm (found 25.5.2006).

Ministry of Land Infrastructure and Transport (2005): *Heisei 17nendo kankō hakusho* (White Book on tourism 2005). http://www.mlit.go.jp/hakusyo/kankou-hakusyo/kankou-hakusyo_.html (found 25.5.2006).

Murata, Hiro (2002): Kusanone sākuru gata ni mukau shinia no kaigairyokō [International trips by seniors tending to grass-root style]. *Rejā Sangyō* 2002–11, pp. 118–122.

NKK (Nihon Kankō Kyōkai) (1993, 1999, 2004): *Kankō no jittai to shikō* [State of and Trends in Tourism]. Tokyo: Nihon Kankō Kyōkai.

Onomichi Shōkōkaigisho (2001): *Onomichishi chûsho kouri shōgyō kōdōka kōsō "Onomichi TMO kōsō"* [The concept for the improvement of small- and medium-size retail trade in Onomichi City: "Onomichi TMO Concept"]. Onomichi: Onomichi Shōkōkaigisho.

Romsa, Gerald and Blenman, Morris (1989): Vacation patterns of the elderly German. In: *Annals of Tourism Research* 16, pp. 178–188.

Shaw, Gareth and Williams, Allan M. (1994): *Critical Issues in Tourism: A Geographical Perspective.* Oxford UK & Cambridge USA: Blackwell.

Shoemaker, Stowe (1989): Segmentation of the Senior Pleasure Travel Market. In: *Journal of Travel Research* 27–3, pp. 14–21.

—— (2000): Segmenting the Market: 10 Years Later. In: *Journal of Travel Research* 39–1, pp. 11–26.

Sōgō Yunicomu (2005): *Rejā sābisu sangyō tōkei chōsa fairu 2005* [Statistical Survey File of Service and Leisure Industries 2005]. Tokyo: Sōgō Yunicomu.

Tretheway, Michael and Mak, Doris (2006): Emerging Tourism Markets: Ageing and Developing Economies. *Journal of Air Transport Management* 12, pp. 21–27.

Tsumago Kankō Kyōkai (n.y.): *Hozon no aramashi* [An outline of conservation] http://www.dia.janis.or.jp/%7Etumago/hozon.html (found 15.5.2006).

You, Xinran and O'Leary. Joseph T. (2000): Age and Cohort Effects: An Examination of Older Japanese Travellers. In: Chon, K.S., Inagaki, Tsutomu, Ohashi, Taiji (eds.) *Japanese Tourists. Socio-Economic, Marketing and Psychological Analysis.* New York/ London/Oxford: Haworth Hospitality Press, pp. 21–42.

Zenkoku Nōgyō Kankō Kyōkai (1997): *Nōka no yoka/ryokō hakusho* [White Book on Leisure and Travel of Farm Households]. Tōkyō: Zenkoku Nōgyō Kankō Kyōkai.

Zimmer, Zachary, Brayley, Russell E. and Searle, Mark S. (1995): Whether to Go and Where to Go: Identification of Important Influences on Seniors' Decisions to Travel. In: *Journal of Travel Research* 33–1, 3–10.

CHAPTER THIRTY-TWO

# PASTIMES

John Clammer

The demographic changes in Japan described and analyzed in this book have profound implications for the whole range of social and institutional structures of the country, including not only such areas as the economy, politics, family, health, and rural depopulation, but also cultural dimensions such as leisure, entertainment and pastimes. This essay will examine the implications, both immediate and long term, of demographic change, and specifically ageing, on leisure and pastime activities in Japanese society.

With the expected decline in the Japanese population from its current 127 million to by some estimates approximately 70 million by 2050, and with the age structure of the population changing so that already the percentage of the population aged 80 or over is 5 per cent and the number of those aged 65 and above is 20 per cent—figures that will rise still further in the near future—Japan can expect to have a social composition tilted decisively towards the elderly, many of whom will be female, and who will for the most part enjoy reasonably good health (approximately three quarters of over 65 year olds report that they do not have serious physical ailments that effect their everyday lives) and be moderately affluent. Over fifty per cent of those aged over 60 report that they go out almost daily and many still drive cars.

While earlier studies of Japanese society tended to concentrate on work as the paradigmatic feature of modern Japanese life, both the slow shift to a much more consumption-based society concerned with lifestyle choices in the last two decades on the one hand, and the ageing of Japanese society on the other, have drawn more attention to the subject of leisure, especially amongst the rapidly expanding population of the retired. Age, which is a social and cultural category as much as a biological one, is as a result constantly reinterpreted, by many actors in society. These include gerontologists, medical specialists, marketeers and advertising copywriters, sociologists, life course planners (a slowly emerging group in Japan where few men in particular seem to make any systematic plans for post-retirement life) and psychiatrists concerned with post-work adjustment disorders, and leisure providers, both local government officials and commercial interests. The professional interests of all or many of these groups coalesce around the demography-driven issue of leisure, care and well-being of the aged. While some of these issues are seen as problems—rising health-care costs and the question of funding pensions in a rapidly ageing society for example—others, such as the provision of leisure activities, fashions, reading material, tourist facilities and fitness facilities—are seen as new and potentially enormous possibilities, especially for businesses willing or able to respond creatively to the emerging demographic reality. We will now turn to a review of these major shifts in pastime activities for the elderly, while noting that there are class and income differentials amongst them. While many enjoy substantial post-retirement incomes in the form of pensions, savings, stocks and income from property and can afford to lead an affluent lifestyle without the constraints of the necessity to work, the problem of poverty amongst the aged is a growing one, and with rising medical costs and recent cuts in special allowances to the elderly, the incidence of deprivation amongst the aged is likely to increase. Similarly there are urban/rural differences, with formerly salaried company workers and their spouses often having access to urban leisure and entertainment facilities, but without facilities for any income generation, while rural elderly, while cut off by distance and expense from urban entertainment, are more likely to have facilities for income and/or food generation from farming and gardening or handicrafts even after formal retirement age.

## 1. Patterns of Leisure

In the context of a long post-retirement life with an income that sustains a reasonable level of leisure activities, interest in pastimes expands and individual life-plans have begun to incorporate education and planning for activities well beyond the traditional roles of grandparenting. In fact my own data suggests both of a convergence of elderly/youth leisure activities, and a gender convergence with post-working age men and their spouses beginning to adopt the same pastimes together, something rare during their working lives and child-rearing periods.

Here in fact we see an interesting interweaving of individual and commercial interests centred on the consumption of things, services and images. It has not surprising occurred to many businesses that there are a large number of affluent aged in Japan, and responses to this fact have included the publication of magazines specifically aimed at the over 60s (for example *NK* and *Rakura*), featuring consumer goods, vacations, lifestyle options, fashion advice, health tips and cultural resources such as concerts, art shows, new books and music. A natural result of this kind of publicity is the popularity of consumption of fashions, foods, coffee, tea and cakes as pastimes in themselves, often in a combination and quite probably also including an art gallery visit or some other form of cultural consumption. Many cinemas have begun to respond to this trend by extending discounts to seniors or by encouraging the retired to attend the morning shows which are usually poorly attended on weekdays for a fixed ticket price of 1000 Yen, down from the 1800 Yen normally charged for an adult. Most art galleries similarly offer discounts to over 60s or certainly to over 65s and a recent survey by my own students revealed that the weekday attendance at galleries in Tokyo comprised mostly late middle-aged and retired people of both genders, mainly of quite affluent appearance. At weekends younger people made up a much higher proportion of art gallery attenders, but the middle aged and elderly were still abundantly present (the ratio to a great extent depending on the nature of the show, old master, classical Asian or European art and modern painting attracting a proportionately older audience, while not unexpectedly contemporary art drew a younger crowd).

While attendance at art galleries is a favourite activity amongst active, affluent and educated elderly, creating art is also highly popular across all class groups (painting and pottery especially, but also photography) as a visit to any scenic park on a sunny day will attest. Less immediately visible, but all the more interesting for that reason, has been the rapid expansion of music and dance facilities for the retired or late middle-aged. These include live music houses where both the performers and clientele are older and dance studios or clubs where the students or participants are likewise in the retired category. The music in these live houses is likely to be folk or the pop music familiar to the older generation rather than contemporary music or "J Pop" and so significant is this phenomenon that NHK, the national TV broadcasting channel, has devoted a whole programme to the subject (*Close-Up Gendai*, 19 April, 2006).

Technological change has also certainly not left the elderly behind. Television has long been a major form of entertainment for the aged, especially for the home-bound, and it continues to be and with the advent of cable television actually attracts an even larger elderly audience, especially in the countryside (although an emerging problem of technological inequality is that many areas of the countryside with low populations are not served by cable or even by broadband internet access). This latter fact is important, as in urban areas in particular, internet use amongst the elderly is increasing and has already achieved a high level of access, both email for constant contact with children and other family members and friends, as a way of shopping and utilizing the internet as a source of information and entertainment that is virtually unlimited and effectively free. The *ketai denwa*—the ubiquitous mobile phone, of which Japan has one of the highest usage/ownership rates in the world, has likewise spread to the elderly and it is now a common sight, again especially in urban areas, to see elderly people quite expertly using their mobiles and utilizing the many functions that they can perform in addition to talking—including texting, checking train routes and schedules, delivering music, weather forecasts and a host of other uses.

Tourism, both domestic and international (discussed in detail in chapter 31) also provides a major source of leisure activity. International travel by the retired is a major factor in the travel market already, especially in the low seasons when fares are reduced and hotel and tour prices to many destinations are discounted and substantially cheaper than during Golden Week, and the New Year and August holiday seasons when most salaried workers are required to take their vacations. Trips within the country are highly popular and are marketed through the airlines, the railway companies which offer weekend and weekday package deals, and bus companies which offer even cheaper tours. In Japan where bus and rail companies are often integrated, such tours are often quite affordable and transport the elderly comfortably to places of scenic beauty or historical interest. The *Bikkuri Bas* tours for example, visiting places where local specialities can be sampled and bought and in which the entertainment in the bus is the singing of *enka* (the traditional and indigenous form of popular vocal music technically known as *ryūkōka* distinguished by the slow vibrato or *kobushi* in which the melodies are sung), are specifically marketed to the retired, many of them widows, of modest means.

Convergence of leisure activities across age groups can be seen in another range of activities—notably sport, education, and food. While the playing of low intensity sports, such as the very popular game of gate ball (a form of croquet) or of more "mental" games such as *shōgi* (Chinese chess) or *go* and of course golf, have long been common amongst the older generation, other trends are also apparent. One is the expansion of playing active sports—tennis being a good example—amongst the retired. Other examples of this trend include swimming and some municipal and private pools now have special mornings or days for the elderly where they can swim or at least play in the water in the company of their peers and where physical presentation of the ageing body is in no way stigmatized. Attendance at fitness clubs is also popular for the "silver generation", especially those in suburban areas where again either special times or special sessions of lower intensity aerobics or exercise regimes and/or access to the exercise machines, massage, sauna and so forth are available, under the eye of trained instructors and usually at times of day when the clubs are relatively quiet, such as weekday mornings (Spielvogel 2003: 14–15, 129), and indeed in suburban fitness clubs clients in their late fifties and above can constitute 70% or more of the total membership and in the daytime hours virtually monopolize club facilities (along with younger housewives who are free after their children have left for kindergarten or school).

Japan has traditionally been a society in which if you miss your chance for an education at the "appropriate" time (for example entering university or college at around the age of eighteen), it is difficult if not impossible to get back into the system at a later date—unlike in north America and some European countries where it is quite common to meet mature students on a university campus and in the classrooms. While various forms of vocational education are essentially available to anyone who can pay (*semmon gakkō*), tertiary education largely excludes the aged. This however is beginning to change and will almost certainly greatly accelerate. Many of the universities in Japan are private institutions, reliant on fees for their survival at a moment when the birth rate is dropping and the number of eighteen year olds is declining rapidly, a fact that is already having a major impact on enrolments and applications to in particular the less prestigious universities. Many retired people in Japan however desire further education, whether to actually acquire an undergraduate or graduate degree, or simply for self-cultivation and pleasure. Some universities are now beginning to respond to this need and this huge untapped market, by opening regular classes to auditors or part-time students, by opening evening classes or by creating or expanding "community colleges"—essentially adult education institutes that provide a wide range of vocational or simply educational courses—in more technical subjects such as management, through languages, to agreeable subjects like poetry or art appreciation, creative writing and topical subjects such as current world affairs. It turns out that despite the theory that language learning gets harder with age, language study is a major activity amongst the retired, whether in a formal school setting or at home or with friends, Chinese being a very popular option, and currently Korean to some extent, although the elderly except those with memories of colonial life in Korea, are less effected by the "Korean boom" currently sweeping Japan and visible in popular culture, movies, music and foods in particular. There is also a relationship between previous occupation and leisure activities, not only in terms of class-based cultural consumption and preferred sports or reading material, but also in the probability of maintaining ties with the work or profession. Retired academics for example are very much in evidence at conferences and workshops and frequently maintain membership in *kenkyūkai* or study circles devoted to their speciality or to an interest and Japan has very many such circles, the number devoted to some aspect of English studies alone (literature, history, culture or language), being sufficient to warrant a substantial British Council sponsored directory the size of a small book. Another form of gender convergence occurs in the context of food, not simply eating out, but learning how to prepare and cook it. Cooking schools, which were until quite recently considered the preserve of young women, newly married or preparing for marriage, are now attracting both young men who are concerned to be more democratic in their marital relationships at least by helping with the cooking, and retired men who have no idea of how to cook and are interested in learning, wish to help around the house now that they are retired and have surplus time or wish to take the burden of housework off the shoulders of their also not so young spouses who have been preparing food for them for years as part of their role expectations. A major shift in post-retirement activities is indeed this tendency to do things together and share interests, rather than to have very separate interests and pursue them apart.

## 2. Ageing and Leisure in the Japanese Context

The sociology of ageing is necessarily contextualized in terms of the wider culture in which it is embedded, or globalizing forces that bring new possibilities and alternatives, and social change within the broader society, including gender convergence in terms of dress, language and pastimes. This is of course equally true of Japan and whereas a number of "modern" innovations have significantly effected the structuring of time and activity by the elderly (televison (see chapter 26) and the Internet for example), "traditional" activities still play a major and perhaps the central role in the organization of leisure amongst Japan's post-retirement generation. These activities include the much enjoyed visits to *onsen* or hot springs, where interestingly it is young people, exposed to more modernist concepts of modesty, that feel less comfortable with the shared nakedness (or in the countryside even mixed sex bathing) than older people for whom this is quite natural and unexceptional and indeed enjoyable. Similarly attending traditional spectator sporting events and in particular *sumo* is an activity concentrated amongst the older generation and is far less popular with younger people and attendance at the major *basho* (the public *sumō* contests held in Tokyo, Osaka, Nagoya and Fukuoka on an annual cycle) with their convivial and casual atmosphere enlivened by the consumption of beer, snacks and *obentō* or lunch-boxes, is for many retired people a event to be looked forward to with pleasure and anticipation.

Likewise participation in many other forms of cultural event is age structured, including attending *kabuki* or Noh dramas, concerts in which *enka*, the popular songs of loss, yearning and regret are the main entertainment, enjoying *bunraku* or traditional puppet plays or *rakugo* (comic story-telling), or participation in *hyakunin isshu*, a game requiring extensive knowledge of traditional poetry, which are clearly biased towards the late middle aged and elderly. Other events are mixed-age, for example participation in the *bon* dances that accompany the many festivals that punctuate the summer in particular in Japan and are usually organized on a community basis, especially in the older and more traditional districts of cities (Bestor 1989). In these cases some of the dance troupes that perform during the festivals, either in the shrines or in the streets, are composed of the elderly, usually women, but other troupes are of mixed age groups from the very young to the very old. Other traditional activities, especially amongst elderly women include flower-arranging (*ikebana*) and the tea ceremony, and in both cases the elderly appear not only as participants, but also often as teachers, as custodians and transmitters of the cultural heritage, although interestingly, even when the majority of students of these practices are female, the senior teachers, as is so often the case in Japan, are male.

Often overlooked too are quite everyday activities. Amongst the rural elderly these include gardening, television watching in quite substantial amounts and, especially amongst men, drinking. Maintaining, sweeping and serving the local shrine or Buddhist temple, upkeeping small neighbourhood parks even to the extent of posting seasonal information on the local flowers, plants and insect life, filling the food and water containers in bird-houses or small mammal refuges and keeping the immediate area of the residential house swept and tidy and possibly decorated with pot plants are important activities that maintain in the elderly a sense of social usefulness, provide contact with neighbours, and keep up a sense of liveliness through chance encounters with passers by, opportunities to chat or gossip and to play with passing children, cats and dogs, and to interact with postmen and delivery people. Much of the street life of suburban and older inner-city residential neighbourhoods in Japan is created not by the young who use the streets merely as thoroughfares, but by the elderly who use them as social spaces and as extensions of their own domestic environments. Another neglected subject is collecting. Many Japanese elderly, particularly men, are engaged in collecting something, whether objects of quite high value and cultural significance such as tea ceremony utensils (Guichard-Anguis 2000) or of quite everyday objects—stamps, baseball cards, dolls. As Ashkenazi (2000) points out, collections have an economic value too and may be a store-house of value and also provide a social function as collectors meet to compare, buy, exchange and chat about the objects that are their speciality. Collecting represents an interesting intersection of leisure, economic investment and in some cases what Olmstead calls "obsession"—a pastime that can now after retirement be indulged to its full without constraints of time (Olmstead 1991). The daily "management" of collections takes up a substantial part of the collector's time—dusting, polishing, rearranging, showing, just looking and as the time available to many retired people is overlong in relation to the amount of activity that they have to fill it, such preoccupations play an important part in the structuring of everyday life. So too do newspaper reading, pet care and exercise and in some cases visits to the hospital, which as in other countries also provide a legitimate excuse for an outing, a chance to meet people and a reassuring context in which medical advice and care are available. With the rising costs of medical care for the elderly, whose contribution for each visit or treatment for the over 70s has recently been raised by the government at the same time as special allowances for the elderly are being cut, it remains to be seen whether attendance at medical institutions will continue to have this role or will become too expensive for the non-affluent (see chapter 60).

A similar role is played by day care centres for the elderly in which two or three days a week can be spent in the company of peers, with lunch and tea provided and in which gossip, games, sexual banter (very much in evidence), talks, concerts, visits by elementary school children and simple nursing care are available. While residential homes are increasingly becoming a private sector initiative and indeed a substantial business, day centres tend to be run by local governments to ensure access to some leisure and social activities for the non-bedridden elderly citizens of specific wards or towns. Other city organized activities include talks and outings. Shibuya ward in central Tokyo for example arranges free series of lectures held in conjunction with the local campus of the United Nations University on topical and global themes and these are well attended by retired people from within the ward. Another example from the greater Tokyo area is that of the Ikiiki Plaza, opened in Chiba in 1998 and which is a centre for the elderly of the area and contains meeting rooms, holds seminars and classes in such subjects as calligraphy, folk songs and literature, promotes visits from and to local kindergartens, elementary and junior high schools, contains *karaoke* facilities and hobby rooms and an exercise and recuperation room with equipment for fitness training and recovery from minor injuries, and provides counsellors and nurses to deal with minor health problems and help with daily living. Available free to citizens of Chiba City, non-residents from the surrounding area are also welcome to attend at the very modest rate of 100 yen a day.

Also of note is the rise in volunteering in which the active elderly participate in the care of house-bound peers, help in park cleaning or street rubbish collection, and visits to kindergartens and elementary schools where they can play with the children and possibly help in simple maintenance tasks. At an elementary school in Ichikawa City in Chiba Prefecture for example the retired provide voluntary services that include a magic club where the elderly visit the school and demonstrate and teach magic tricks. Again these activities are often arranged through the local ward offices, or other organizations including trades unions, religious organizations, especially the *shin-shūkyō* or "new religions", and other organizations that help to provide sports and leisure activities as well as mutual help to the elderly. Ben-Ari in his study of a commuter village and a new suburban housing estate in the city of Otsu, Shiga

Prefecture, devotes an entire chapter to the subject of the "Old-Folks' Clubs". This study, which could be replicated for most neighbourhoods of Japan, demonstrates the rich network of such provision of activities for the elderly which include gateball games, parties and feasts, participation in the *bon* dances, singing of Noh, recitation of Chinese poetry, *bonsai* or minature tree cultivation, walking and hiking, the occasional *sake* drinking party, calligraphy, cultivation of a vegetable garden, visits by local kindergarten children, shrine cleaning and participation in the annual *undōkai* or sports day and at the party given for the elderly on *keirō no hi*—Respect for the Aged Day (Ben-Ari 1991: 161–179).

Other activities not mentioned by Ben-Ari in other localities include clubs for the writing and recitation of *haiku* poetry, regimes of physical fitness, including exercises based on the Chinese *tai chi*, newer exercise regimes such as the Pilates exercises, painting classes and excursions and pottery. One that he does mention is passing is quite widespread—notably mountain walking clubs for the fit elderly who will travel by van or minibus to various mountains in their general area and undertake quite lengthy and strenuous walks along the mountain trails (often well marked and laid out in Japan) on a regular basis. All this activity and the significance of sports of various kinds fits well with the assertion that sport in Japan is considered socially beneficial if it is properly organized: even play must be structured to a considerable degree to ensure that it is "useful" and can be visibly seen to promote the well-being of the target group (Edwards 2005) as well as having an aesthetic role in the promotion of both national and appropriate age-grade identity (Inoue 1998).

## 3. Leisure and the Sociology of Ageing in Japan

The increasing cohort of the elderly in Japan find themselves at an interesting historical juncture. They are becoming, if not a majority, certainly no longer a marginalized minority statistically, commercially and subjectively. They find themselves at a moment when globalization of cultural products and practices—food, musics, fashions, sports, film amongst other elements, have reached a fairly advanced level, despite Japan's actually undeserved reputation for being a "closed" country. The *reja bumu* or 'leisure boom" of the 1960s, then just overcoming its status as *rejā mondai*—as a problem—has long since turned into the vast leisure, sports and entertainment industry of today, and is indulged in without any of the feelings of time-wasting or frivolousness still common in the middle of the last century. The range of choices is now enormous—an aspect of the hyper-consumption oriented society that is now Japan for many of its denizens (Clammer 1997). The status of gateball as the game of choice amongst the elderly in the early 1980s (Iwamoto 1984) is no longer true, popular as it remains, and when one traces the changes in the range of pastime activities for the elderly from the 1980s when scholarly interest in leisure was high as Japan was entering a new phase of economic and cultural development (e.g. Koseki 1989), to the present, a large range of changes and expanding opportunities are discernible, together with the perception by both the elderly and the wider society of the appropriateness of the aged engaging in such a range of activities. The range of leisure activities in Japan as a whole has expanded of course across all age groups (Linhart and Frühstück 1998), but what is significant in this context is not only the maintenance of traditional games, sports and arts by the elderly, but their colonization of leisure spaces formerly assumed to be reserved for the young or younger. The status of *asobi* (play), *goraku* (amusement) and *rekuriēshon* (recreation) have not only become central to Japanese society as a whole, but are now the spaces where the time-rich elderly can sport, and indeed for many after a long life of company work and long hours, retirement is in many ways quite literally a second childhood.

The positive aspects of age have indeed been finally recognized even by the Ministry of Health, Labour and Welfare, which formerly tended to see ageing as a looming problem, but have shifted their official position to noting that the elderly have active "second lives" and that a fulfilled and active existence both in terms of leisure and of contribution to local communities and voluntary activities can be enormous (Kōseisho 1997). While retirement may be a period of financial and health anxiety, the research carried out by the Hakuhodo Institute of Life and Living has shown that for many elderly it is a time of optimism, hobbies and the self-cultivation that time-starved company workers simply do not have (McCreery 2000: 187–205).

Two additional and usually neglected factors should also be mentioned. The first is the role of religion. Not only do the elderly involve themselves in cleaning of shrine compounds and the material aspects of religious existence—many are active as lay members of temples—and a large number are to be found in the plethora of "new religions" that are such a prominent aspect of the Japanese religious and social landscape. These religions themselves (as do the more traditional schools of Buddhism) have substantial numbers of elderly members and many, such as the internationally well known *Sōka Gakkai* actively promote the welfare of their aged members and have activities both spiritual and social to meet the needs of their older members. The second is sexuality. In discussions of ageing this is a frequently ignored dimension, but there is no evidence to suggest that interest in sex and actual sexual activity necessarily declines with age. On the contrary the retired in Japan are sexually active and whereas sex is normally seen as a pastime for the young, it is rarely recognized as such amongst the elderly. Yet in Japan it continues to play an important role, and sex manuals for the elderly are readily available with advice on non-strenuous sex and techniques based usually on Chinese Taoist notions of longevity practice, continuing a tradition that anthropologists have long noted to be an important if rarely discussed aspect of Japanese folk culture (Campbell and Noble 1993: 1354). The aged in Japan are as much concerned with the presentation of the self, problems of identity and self-creation and finding meaning in their activities as anyone else. Ageing does not mean dehumanization and the concern with empowerment and self realization that Chizuko Ueno discerns amongst the ageing (Ueno 2005) signals the recognition of this in Japanese society. There is an aesthetics of ageing and it is through pastimes that many Japanese in or approaching more advanced years find a relationship to the world that not only fills their hours, but creates an active and agent driven identity.

## References


Ashkenazi, Michael (2000): Swords, Collections and *Kula* Exchanges. In: Ashkenazi, Michael and John Clammer (eds.): *Consumption and Material Culture in Contemporary Japan*. London and New York: Kegan Paul International, pp. 121–142.

Ben-Ari, Eyal (1991): *Changing Japanese Suburbia: A Study of Two Present-Day Localities*. London and New York: Kegan Paul International.

Bestor, Theodore, C. (1989): *Neighborhood Tokyo*. Tokyo and New York: Kodansha International.

Campbell, Alan and David. S. Noble (Executive Editors) (1993): *Japan: An Illustrated Encyclopedia*. Tokyo: Kodansha.

Clammer, John (1997): *Contemporary Urban Japan: A Sociology of Consumption*. Oxford and Malden MA: Blackwell.

Edwards, Elise (2005): Theorizing the Cultural Importance of Play: Anthropological Approaches to Sports and Recreation in Japan. In: Robertson, Jennifer (ed.): *A Companion to the Anthropology of Japan*. Oxford and Malden MA: Blackwell, pp. 278–296.

Guichard-Anguis, Sylvie (2000): Cultural Heritage and Consumption. In: Ashkenazi, Michael and John Clammer (eds.), *Consumption and Material Culture in Contemporary Japan*. London and New York: Kegan Paul International, pp. 97–120.

Inoue Shun (1998): Kindai nihon ni okeru supōtsu to bushidō [Sports and the Martial Arts in Modern Japan]. In: Henyō suru gendai shakai to supōtsu. Nihon Supōtsu Shakkaigakkai, pp. 225–235. Kyoto: Sekai Ahisōsha.

Iwamoto Masayo (1984): Gētobōru kyōgi no hassei to sono fukyū katei [Gate ball competitions and the process of their diffusion]. In: *Minzokugaku kenkyu*, 49, 2. pp. 174–82.

Kōseisho (1997): *Kōsei hakusho* [Health and Welfare White Paper]. Tokyo: Gyōsei.

Koseki, Sampei (1989): Japan: Homo Ludens Japonicus. In: Olszewski, Anna and Kenneth Roberts (eds.): *Leisure and Lifestyle: A Comparative Analysis of Free Time*. London: Sage Publications, pp. 115–42.

Linhart, Sepp and Sabine Früstück (eds.) (1998): *The Culture of Japan as Seen Through its Leisure*. Albany: State University of New York Press.

McCreery, John (2000): *Japanese Consumer Behavior: From Worker Bees to Wary Shoppers*. Honolulu: University of Hawai'i Press.

Olmstead, A. D. (1991): Collecting: Leisure, Investment or Obsession? In Rudmin, Floyd (ed.), *To Have Possessions: A Handbook on Ownership and Property*. Special number of *The Journal of Social Behavior and Personality*, 6, 6, pp. 287–306.

Spielvogel, Laura (2003): *Working Out in Japan: Shaping the Female Body in Tokyo Fitness Clubs*. Durham and London: Duke University Press.

Ueno Chizuko (2005): *Oiru Junbi* [Preparation for Ageing]. Tokyo: Gakuyo Shobō.

CHAPTER THIRTY-THREE

# SPORTS AND DEMOGRAPHIC CHANGE IN JAPAN

Wolfram Manzenreiter

## 1. Introduction

Japanese society has developed its own agenda and set of images associated with the body, sport,[1] fitness, health and beauty. Ideas of what sport is, and what it is good for, are to the same extent socially constructed as the social institutions in which practice and consumption of sports are embedded. These constructs are related to conventions, roles, behaviour and values associated with mainstream society and the capability of dominant ideologies to bear up against contending claims. The notion of sport, based on the outcome of social interaction between various groups of society and their underlying power relations, therefore is fluid, unstable and open to transformation, triggered by shifting constellations of the broader environment. Japan's enforced integration into the world economy in the later 19th century, the defeat in World War II, the rise of the consumption-led economy and recent globalisation processes influenced the role of sport in society. At the outset of the 21st century, it is the greying of society which most conspicuously causes changes in Japan's sport system.

Changes in the demographic stratification of society affect sport basically at both ends of the age strata. First, the declining birth rate is curtailing the population share of the young generation. Since sport in Japan has been largely promoted as an educational device and firmly established within the school curriculum, pupils and university students have traditionally accounted for the largest segment of the active sport

[1] In the context of this chapter, I refer to sport in the broadest sense of meaning, following the definition of the Council of Europe stating that "sport means all forms of physical activity which, through casual or organised participation, aims at improving physical fitness and mental well-being, forming social relationships, or obtaining results in competition at all levels". From a sociological perspective, sport cannot be reduced to its essentialist dimension since its discursive formation must be equally taken into consideration.

population. But the proportion of Japanese youths up to high school (6 to 18 years of age) decreased from roughly 20 per cent in 1970 to 14 per cent in 2000 and will continue to fall to a level of about 10 per cent by 2030. Second, the prolongation of the average life span is fuelling into the growth of old age groups that so far have largely been neglected by public and private sport suppliers. Japanese aged 60 and older, standing in the shadow of school sport, corporate welfare (company sport) or commercial sport programmes, contributed with 11 per cent to the entire population in 1970, 24 per cent in 2000, and they are forecasted to reach 37 per cent in 2030 (IPSS 2006).

Sport thus has become very important as a means to counter some of the problems associated with the ageing society. This chapter will identify the way sport in Japan is affected by demographic change directly and indirectly. My analysis focuses on the elderly and their sport experience, although outcomes of this ongoing process of change are of concern for the entire population. First I will sketch out the discussion on the widely claimed benefits of rising sport participation rates. Then I will demonstrate how government agencies use sports to address the challenges of ageing and old age. The next parts will identify some outstanding aspects of the demographics of sport and the way sport is accommodated by the consumer industry. In a concluding section, I will discuss the most urgent problems associated with Japan's sports policy, and finally, how the notions of sport and age themselves are affected by the changes within the broader social environment.

## 2. The Benefits of Sport Participation in the Ageing Society

The close association of sport with physical health, mental sanity and social skills has been at the core of the modern sport ideology ever since it started to spread from English boarding schools throughout the Victorian Empire and the rest of the world. Since its early years, the Olympic Movement has been a powerful agent behind the international dissemination of a sport ideology that too often is taken at face value and regards doping, cheating and hazing as aberrations deviating from the idealised norm of healthy sport. Since Jerry Morris' landmark study on the importance of physical activity as a cardio-protective factor in 1953, medical research into the health benefits of sport has provided solid evidence that regular physical exercise reduces the risk of developing diabetes, high blood pressure and colon cancer, and of dying prematurely. Singular voices in Japan occasionally echo concern about the lack of well-designed and large-scaled research in this country because of "obvious differences in the disease patterns of Japanese and Europeans", as well as in their genetic background and lifestyle routines (Miyachi 2005: 3). However, a cross-sectional study to determine the physical-fitness levels of more than one thousand older Japanese confirmed that declines in physical fitness, especially those that are related to mobility and risk for falls, occur with rising age, yet not at a uniform rate (Demura *et al.* 2003). A *Nikkei Science* report on the findings of the Ageing Bio Marker Research Team at the Tokyo Metropolitan Institute of Gerontology hinted at the surprising variations in the pace at which the ageing process takes place over the body, its parts and functions, indicating that many physiological aspects of ageing are still wanting explanation, notwithstanding any differences in genetic or cultural background (Shimizu and Shirasawa 2006: 16). Hence the general consent among Japan's gerontologists, physicians and health professionals is echoing the Western view, as represented by Amaha (2003: 20–35), a specialist in critical care medicine, who quotes the positive impact of physical leisure time activity on the most widespread age-related symptoms of physical decay, including ischemic heart disease, hyperlipidemia, hypertension, diabetes, obesity, osteoporosis, and postmenopausal syndrome.

By comparison, a substantial body of Japanese research into the psychological effects of sport participation supports the assumption that sports and physical activities lead to a higher level of daily life activities and thus enhance both self-rated health, quality of life and communal networking (e.g., Yasunaga, Yaguchi and Tokunaga 2002; Yoshiuchi *et al.* 2006). The close link between physical fitness, life satisfaction and social integration has been hinted at as early as the 1980s (Sugiyama *et al.* 1986). A recent survey among 1,500 physically active and non-active elderly confirmed the assumption since active elderly gave higher ratings to health, physical fitness and their capabilities of coping with everyday activities (KTJZ 2004). The relationship between physical mobility and life satisfaction may appear self-evident in such societies that highly esteem autonomy and independence of the individual. Thinking about the preference of living in multi-generational households after old age and the well known essay in psychology on *amae* ("anticipating indulgence", or "indulgent dependence") as a structuring principle of social relations in Japan (Doi 1973), the Japanese elderly may have quite different ideas of the self in communal life or family relations. Certainly there is a need to differentiate between physical, mental and emotional kinds of independence. Opinion surveys on life after retirement age by the Japanese government do not feature questions on independence, which ranks very high on the agenda of health programmes related to senior citizens in the Western world (Cameron 2004). But if independence means the physical capacity to get up from bed and walk freely outside the house, then Japanese elderly do not differ much. According to the governmental opinion survey among the elderly in 1998, about two third of the sample felt worried or at least uncertain about life in old age, with most quoting some kind of severe health condition that may request long-term care or medical treatment. When asked during a follow-up survey in 2005 what they would want society to pay attention to, more than five out of 10 respondents said health management (*kenkō kanri*), including physical activity (*shintai undō*), while only one out of 10 wished recreational activities, including sport, to be on the political agenda (SCK 1999, 2005). The data indicate a strong correlation between social and physical characteristics. People who felt healthy and participated regularly in social affairs gave higher ratings to their capabilities of coping with everyday activities, health and physical fitness (self-assessment) and had a more positive image of physical exercise (KTJZ 2004). In the Japanese Government's survey on people's lifestyle (NDK 2005), nearly every second adult (47.6 per cent) called the future state of health a troubling point of concern in old age, topped only by financial worries; and the older respondents were, the more attention shifted from money to the body.

The connection between physical health, fitness and finances is another argument featuring predominantly in debates on the benefits of sports. If sport participation contributes to health promotion, it also helps both the individual and the state reducing medical expenses. A survey in Miyagi prefecture among the local members of the National Health Insurance System aged 40 and older found out that those living a healthy life (no smoking, holding adequate weight and taking regular physical exercise) spent 35 per cent less on medical expenses (SSF 2001: 21). Health related expenses in Japan amounted to 30 trillion yen per year at the beginning of this decade and were projected to reach as much as 81 trillion in 2015 (Iwamoto 2004: 225). The average Japanese (without elderly aged 65 and above) generates medical expenses of about 150,000 Yen per year, while four times more (645,000) is spent on the average elderly, and a quarter of all medical expenses (26.3 per cent) on the high age group of 75 years and older; both total volume and the distributional imbalance have shown a sharp increase over the past 15 years (KRDK 2003). Other countries facing a rapidly ageing population and a similarly fast increase in lifestyle-related diseases,[2] have commissioned research on the economic impact of mass sport participation. According to the findings from Australia, the outcome can be as much as a quarter of GDP if the rate of people participating regularly in sports is raised by 40 per cent (Okada 1999: 112). The Canada Fitness Lifestyle Research Institute asserted in 1997 that a reduction of the inactive population share by one per cent translates into 10 Million Canadian Dollar less on expenses for coronary diseases (SSF 2001: 21). The UNESO Declaration of Punta del Este also proclaimed in 1998 that "one dollar invested into physical activity means 3.2 dollars saved on medical cost" (SSF 2001: 18).

## 3. Sport Policy for the Ageing Society

The Japanese government recognised the instrumental potentials of sport for public health and community building quite early. Under the influence of European national fitness programmes, such as Germany's 'Golden Plan' from the 1960s, guidelines for the regional bureaucracy were issued in order to guarantee sport opportunities for all. Sport participation rates beyond the primary target group of youth and young adults started to rise modestly when community sport appeared on the agenda of regional politics in the wake of the welfare state in the 1970s and lifestyle changes established new business opportunities for private sport suppliers in the following decade. Concerning health promotional activities directing toward enhancement of better nutrition and physical fitness of the elderly, the Ministry of Health and Welfare launched the National Movement for Health Promotion in 1978 and the second instalment dubbed Active 80 Health Plan in 1988. A certification system of health trainers was initiated, and fitness clubs having a certain number of qualified health trainers were granted preferential tax treatment and special designation by the government (JPHA 2006: 16). Coevally, the Ministry of Education acted on

[2] The term "lifestyle-related disease" was introduced in 1996, replacing the former name of "adult disease". This new term represents a concept of "a group of diseases whose symptomatic appearance and progress are affected by living practices including eating, exercising, rest, smoking, and drinking" (Kōseishō 1999: 269).

suggestions from the November 1989 report of the Health and Physical Education Council entitled "Strategies for the Promotion of Sports towards the 21st Century" and issued new guidelines to improve the supply of public sport in 1991. However, the shift in emphasis from 'social education' (*shakai kyōiku*) toward lifelong sport (*shōgai supōtsu*) was largely confined to rhetoric without bringing about true changes in the supply and demand of sports (Kiku 1998: 18).

Due to the heavy emphasis on infrastructure building, the number of public sports facilities[3] increased six-fold from the 1970s to the late 1990s; in addition, 90 per cent of elementary and middle schools and 50 per cent of high schools opened their sport facilities to the public (Manzenreiter 2004). However, the eventually achieved ratio of roughly one facility per 2,000 people, or of 0.9 to 1.3 sq m per capita was much lower than for instance Germany's 3 to 4.5 sq m per capita (Takahashi 2003: 14). Government sport funding (0.08 per cent of BIP in 2000) also had never come close to the spending ratio of Germany (0.35 per cent), Japan's paragon in terms of public sport administration. Under the double pressure of shrinking public funds and increasing medical costs, the Ministry of Education set out to revise its politics in the mid-1990s. The Council on Sport Issues (Hoken Taiiku Shingikai) filed a new mandatory programme for all communal authorities which was enacted in 2000 by what later became the Ministry of Education, Culture, Sports, Science, and Technology (MEXT). The 'Basic Plan for the Promotion of Sports' (*Supōtsu shinkō kihon keikaku*; MEXT 2000) was designed to refashion the domestic sport landscape according to the German role model of civil association sport (*Vereinssport*). Instead of facility supply, social and organisational conditions of sport participation advanced into the focus of the new sport policy. In many regards, the Ministry's policy shift acknowledged the limited efficiency of former programmes and conceded as legitimate the critical stance of prominent sports sociologists such as Nakamura (1995), Uchiumi (2005) and Seki (1997).

[3] The Ministry of Education, which is formally in charge of public sport facilities (*shakai taiiku shisetsu*), operates a very broad definition of sport facilities and these include anything from swimming pools, sports arenas and multiplex stadia, to gateball pitches (gateball is a variant of croquet particularly popular amongst Japanese senior citizens), sport parks (*undō kōen*), martial arts *dōjō* and mountain paths.

The preamble of the Basic Plan refers to the various changes in the social environment which have had a lasting impact on lifestyles of the young and the old, including urbanisation, erosion of social bonds, increases in convenience of life, leisure time and esteem for leisure activities, and demographic change. Facing the rapidly ageing society and decreasing birth rates, but also the decline in fitness and strength among the younger population, the Ministry acknowledges its responsibility to promote sports by establishing "sports as a form of culture essential to the Japanese lifestyle", and by encouraging the individual to independently address sports in order to maintain happiness of the individual as well as strength and vigour for the nation as a whole. For the sake of the Japanese nation, the Ministry aspires to achieve "a society that is active in sports throughout life by giving everybody the opportunity to engage in sport anywhere, anytime and forever, regardless of physical strength, age, capability, interest and purpose."

In marked difference to former programmes, the Basic Sport Promotion Plan specifies some concrete target numbers to evaluate policy outcome. First, as soon as possible a level of engagement in sport should be achieved whereby one out of every two adults engages in sport activities at least once a week. Second, regional authorities throughout the nation were requested to create at least one comprehensive community sports club on the local level (city, town, village), and to create at least one advisory sports centre covering a wide area in each prefecture until 2010. 'Comprehensive community sports clubs' (*sōgō-gata chiiki supōtsu kurabu*), the new key concept for the promotion of lifelong sport,[4] were designed to provide a rich diversity of sport available to people of all ages from children to senior citizens and of all levels of skill from beginners to top-level athletes in competitive sport.[5] Run independently by the local communities, the clubs should comprise facilities, a club house and highly qualified instructors in order to provide an opportunity for

[4] A further change in terminology concerns the widely used term 'Sports-for-All' which had also been borrowed from Europe. The new term 'Sports-for-Everyone' indicated the diversity of motives, capabilities and objectives of an active sport life.

[5] Attempts to establish the community as the social centre of sports clubs go back to the 1970s and the regional restructuring policy administered by the Economic Planning Agency. This strategy showed modest results yet the scope of the former community clubs was strongly limited in terms of sex, age and type of sport. 90 per cent of all sports clubs centred exclusively on a single sport and listed an average of less than 30 members. Next to shortage of facilities, funds and instructors (see Manzenreiter 2004) provided the ageing of club members a common threat to the continuity of the clubs (Kado *et al.* 1998: 98).

regular and constant participation in sport and social exchange activities. A national football lottery was started in 2001 to generate funding for the promotion of community sport.

Concise target numbers also appeared within the third instalment of the national health programme in 1998. Covering the period between 2000 and 2010, 'Healthy Japan 21' (Kenkō Nihon 21) identified 70 numerical targets in nine areas, including physical activities and exercise to promote people's health comprehensively through the extension of the healthy life span, i.e., the period during which people can live without suffering dementia or being bed-ridden (SSF 2001: 25). Training physical strength is at the core of all efforts to counter the "deflationary spiral of health" (Shirai 2000: 126), which is propelled as the fragile and unfit are more susceptible to injury and immobility. The new emphasis on "primary prevention" replaced traditional efforts having prioritised "secondary prevention", which aimed at early detection and early treatment. Actions related to physical activity intended to increase the number of persons who intentionally exercise from a base value of 50 per cent to 63 per cent; to increase the number of people who exercise regularly from a base value of 24.6 per cent (women) and 28.6 per cent (men) to a minimum of 35 per cent and 39 per cent respectively. In addition, the number of walking steps of men and women per day should be raised by roughly 15 per cent (WHO 2005: 15). As in the case of the Basic Plan, Healthy Japan 21 takes an all-encompassing look at public health in Japanese society, identifying points of concern for all age groups. With regard to pre-school and school-age children, the programme noted the negative impact of reduced playtime in the school yard, the vanishing of open space and an increase in sedentary activities such as watching TV and playing video games which all have contributed to the decrease in daily physical activity. With regard to the elderly, Healthy Japan 21 notes with concern their propensity to stay at home instead of adopting a more physically active lifestyle. Four target values of the national health programme aiming particularly at the elderly thus explicitly refer to regular exercise, extensive walking, and participation in social activities out of the home (WHO 2005: 24).

Maintaining physical mobility as long as possible is an essential prerequisite for the government-sponsored ideal of an "ageless life". Since 1998, the Cabinet Office solicits nominations for show case practices of an ageless life (*eijiresu raifu jissensha*) every year. Appropriate candidates are defined as persons aged 65 years and above who regardless of their age, in self-responsibility and according to their capabilities live their life in an unconstrained and spirited way (Naikakufu 2004a). Many seniors have been nominated as role models for achievements in sport. For example, 72 years-old Shichirō Midorikawa from Iwaki in Fukushima Prefecture has been nominated for holding six records in track and fields. He first got into track and fields as a youth but stopped after graduating from high school until the age of 43. Today he continues his daily training aiming at a future world championship title. Marathon runner Arata Momoda from Shimonoseki in Yamaguchi Prefecture is ninety years old. He took up long distance running at the age of sixty and has participated since then in numerous road races in Japan and abroad. Thanks to his physical fitness, the senior runner is proud of never having been hospitalized. Another nominee from 2004 is Shōgorō Azuma, aged 92, from Yokohama, who got into competitive swimming at the age of 69. Since then, he has won 22 world championship titles and 32 Japanese records (Naikakufu 2004). While these senior athletes are far from being representative for their age cohort, their public appraisal serves the objective of any role model: to inspire successors and to invite emulation.

## 4. Patterns of Sport Participation in Ageing Japan

While there are notable differences to participation rates of advanced sport nations such as Canada, Australia, or the UK, statistical data on the Japanese' sport participation undeniably reflect favourable changes in lifestyle behaviour. According to the Sasakawa Sports Foundation (SSF) biannual surveys on sport life of the Japanese adult population, the totally inactive sport population shrank over the past years from one out of two Japanese (49.3 per cent) in 1992 to one out of four adults (26.6 per cent) in 2004. By contrast, the active sport population, that is, according to the SSF definition, those who exercise at least twice a week for a minimum of 30 minutes to maintain and improve health and physical fitness, has shown a similarly remarkable progress from 6.5 per cent (1992) to 16.1 per cent (2004). The share of Japanese that take it more easily but nonetheless exercise at least twice a week nearly tripled over the period from 16.2 per cent to 45.3 per cent.

As tables 1 and 2 show, rising participation rates are evident in all age groups. Generally sports participation declines with advancing age. This tendency clearly reflects both physical and social processes related to the lifecourse. According to the 2001 Sasakawa Sports Foundation

Table 1. Share of inactive sport population in age groups.

| | 20–29 | 30–39 | 40–49 | 50–59 | 60–69 | 70+ |
|---|---|---|---|---|---|---|
| 1992 | 31.5 | 39.9 | 46.3 | 57.7 | 66.1 | 73.1 |
| 1994 | 40.3 | 38.5 | 44.0 | 57.8 | 63.5 | 71.8 |
| 1996 | 24.2 | 24.9 | 29.1 | 40.5 | 51.0 | 60.4 |
| 1998 | 22.4 | 26.6 | 26.2 | 38.1 | 47.1 | 61.7 |
| 2000 | 19.3 | 20.8 | 26.6 | 28.0 | 41.0 | 48.4 |
| 2002 | 19.8 | 22.9 | 30.7 | 30.8 | 39.5 | 51.1 |
| 2004 | 17.2 | 20.2 | 20.5 | 26.2 | 32.5 | 44.8 |

Source: Sasakawa Sports Foundation, *Sport Life Japan*, various years.

Table 2. Share of active sport population in age groups.

| | 20–29 | 30–39 | 40–49 | 50–59 | 60–69 | 70+ |
|---|---|---|---|---|---|---|
| 1992 | 9.1 | 7.4 | 5.6 | 5.8 | 5.8 | 5.8 |
| 1994 | 9.2 | 9.5 | 7.8 | 3.9 | 9.4 | 4.3 |
| 1996 | 15.0 | 9.3 | 10.3 | 8.2 | 8.2 | 1.8 |
| 1998 | 15.2 | 11.9 | 12.7 | 16.0 | 11.2 | 9.0 |
| 2000 | 18.4 | 14.8 | 21.4 | 20.2 | 14.4 | 13.7 |
| 2002 | 17.4 | 14.3 | 11.1 | 12.3 | 13.8 | 11.1 |
| 2004 | 15.7 | 14.8 | 16.4 | 16.4 | 18.9 | 13.5 |

Source: Sasakawa Sports Foundation, *Sport Life Japan*, various years.

survey (SSF 2001), less than a fifth of young adults in their twenties were completely inactive, compared to 20.5 per cent in their forties, 32.5 per cent in their sixties and 44.8 per cent of the elderly aged seventy and older. But in 1992, the respective shares of non-participants among the age groups were at much higher levels, comprising of about one third of young adults, roughly half of the middle aged and two thirds of the aged Japanese. This shift indicates a tremendous change having taken place in terms of physical awareness, health consciousness and lifestyle choices over the 1990s. Sport has become a viable and respectable option for everyday life activities among senior citizens. At the level of regular exercising, the formerly distinctive gap between active young and inactive old has almost disappeared. The share among younger adults has shown only moderate increase, while the shares of middle aged and older Japanese exhibits not only the highest growth rates, they have also replaced the young in relative terms as the age groups with the largest share of active sport participants. These data imply that demographic change in combination with lifestyle changes lead to a bifurcation in the population: both the numbers of exercising elderly, who regard sport as an essential part of their daily life routines, as well as of non-participants, are growing.

According to the SSF surveys, sport participation of the elderly is no longer restricted to light gymnastics or gateball, a Japanese variant of croquet that gained nationwide popularity in the 1980s. Initially, this game was applauded for its easy accessibility; offering sport novices and physically impaired the opportunity to meet with like-minded people for the enriching purposes of meaningful leisure, light physical exercise and social contacts (Kalab 1992). Gateball clubs, tournaments and local leagues were established all over Japan, while municipalities built gateball grounds. About two decades later, gateball is still played by many, but younger seniors seem to shun the game because of its reputation as a silver sport. Instead, they prefer to play golf, both on the green or at the driving range, or the simplified version of ground golf, another Japanese invention and contribution to the category of play-like, low-competitive "new sports". Strolls, walking and light calisthenics, including the early morning radio or television gymnastics, exhibit participation rates of more than 10 per cent and take the lead among the 15 most often practised sport activities by seniors. Still among the top 15, yet with notably lower participation rates, are hiking, golf, swimming, cycling and work outs in the gym (SSF 2004: 25).

Various tournaments and sport festivals are opened every year for those who continue competitive or social sport throughout their life. Sports Masters Japan is an annual all-Japan tournament for high-aspiring athletes aged 35 and older. Competitions are organised according to age groups of the participants, numbering about 6,000 a year. Age-specific competitions have also been added to the programme of the annual National Sports Festival (Kokumin Taiiku Taikai). On a more playful level, the broader public in general and the elderly more specifically are encouraged to participate at sport events such as the Nenlympics (Nenrinpikku, literally Tree-ring Olympics), the All Japan Sports and Recreation Festival (Zennihon Supo Reku Matsuri), or the Challenge Day (Ikeda, Yamaguchi and Chogahara 2001: 32). Some of these annual events containing a number of non- or low-competitive "new sports" attract some hundred thousands participants. These and other mass sport events put more emphasis on the social merits than on the competitive aspect of sport involvement. Such a reengineering of the notion of sport makes perfect sense since senior citizens typically are less inclined to get into serious sport training than into some kind of light physical exercise, social integration or entertainment. And it seems they are willing to spend on it.

## 5. The Silver Business of Sport in the Greying Consumer Industry

Amidst the current upswing of Japan's economy, the consumer industry is facing the first wave of the *dantai sedai*, Japan's baby boomers of the immediate post-war years, hitting retirement age in 2007. Since the average retiree will receive 20.5 million Yen in severance pay upon retirement, consumer industries eagerly await the unprecedented total spending power of 75 trillion yen over the second half of the decade (METI 2006). According to a government report, the entire silver market has a huge growth potential. Care and welfare related expenses were expected to compose about one tenth of the entire silver market and medical expenses between two and three tenth, with the overwhelming rest flowing into final consumption (SKS 2000: 60). Marketers of leisure and sport-related goods and services have begun designing their products for the ageing population and particularly those 70 to 80 per cent that report no health problems. Outdoor recreational activities, particularly hiking and mountaineering, were among the pioneering sectors of the leisure industry foreshadowing the demographic change. Major apparel producers such as Asics and Mizuno established R&D departments on senior sport and contributed actively to the promotion of new sport programmes for health conscious middle aged and older customers. When the walking boom hit Japan in the late 1990s, Mizuno utilised its own dense net of local retailers to offer encompassing packages of goods and services related to the new fashion. Special corners geared at the middle-aged were opened in more than hundred Mizuno shops. Shifting the sales concept from the traditional sport shop that sells goods for competitive sport to health shops offering diverse goods and services to the middle-aged is a long-term strategy of small-sized retailers to survive under the pressure of large retailers and sport shop chains (Matsunaka 2001: 338).

Since the most often practiced sport activities hardly require access to facilities and regular training partners, most of the elderly exercise either at home or somewhere in the public, in the streets, parks, or along the riverside (SSF 2004: 35). Only 17 per cent have enrolled in sport clubs, usually a community sports club. Occasionally the elderly, especially women, join a commercial sports club (SSF 2004: 156–157). But the fitness industry is setting high expectations in the silver sport market. When rising medical costs generated a national concern with health, memberships of fitness clubs began to rise, particularly among the middle-aged and postretirement population that emerged as the fastest growing group of new members at health clubs (Spielvogel 2003: 3; SCSK 2002: 11).[6] Renaissance, the third largest fitness club chain in Japan, operates about 80 stores throughout the country with a membership of 260,000. In-house data show that the proportional share of senior members nearly doubled over the years from 1998 to 2006 to reach nearly 20 per cent. The share of the middle-aged also increased, while younger age groups declined.

The senior generation is not a homogeneous group of hard-to-please consumers but is differentiated into lifestyle groups as any other segment of society (Carrigan 1998). Product development for life-stage segments targeting chronological age groups, commonly fail since disposable income, health perception and social independence are more important variables than age. Marketing specialists point out the necessity of understanding the psychosocial needs of the fifty-plus members. While larger fitness clubs can afford to rely on the mass market approach, including the expansion of age-adequate sport programmes such as yoga or *t'ai chi*, and fee reductions for off-peak visits, smaller clubs have to be more aware of local needs. One sport club in the rural part of Chiba Prefecture sent its staff around to visit every household within a radius of three kilometres, asking the residents for their needs and wishes. Another company operating six clubs in the suburbs of Tokyo realised the importance its senior members attach to social life. Holding culture classes, cooking courses and lectures on dietary and health issues, the chain tried to establish the gym as a kind of local meeting place. Providing sport medical advice and health checks have been identified as another best practice of Japanese fitness club operators targeting the elderly (CKSJ 2001).

It is easier to keep people involved than to introduce them to new activities (see Long 2004: 34). Thus, "catching them young" is the key solution to enhance participation rates among the society of lifelong sport. A large panel survey among Japanese aged 65 and older shows that socially active seniors differ from less active seniors in as far as they

[6] Japan's fitness market has an annual turnover of 323 billion Yen; about 3.4 million members are affiliated with more than 2,000 private fitness clubs. While Japan is leading the Asia Pacific in terms of turnover, total number of clubs and memberships, its penetration rate (share of entire population) of 2.7 per cent is lagging far behind New Zealand (10.4), Australia (9.0), Singapore (7.1), Hong Kong (4.7) and Korea (3.0); by comparison, the US penetration rate is 15.7 per cent, Canada's 14.6 per cent, and the average of the EU 25 nations is 8.1per cent (IHRSA 2006).

had participated in more hobbies during middle age, had higher levels of education, and had had a more varied diet between the ages of 30 and 50. In other words, maintaining general health habits and lifestyles from middle age on are the foundations for successful ageing and high social activity in old age (Ohno *et al.* 2000). But the process of successful sport socialisation starts at a much younger age. Looking at sport participation patterns of the middle aged, Kiku (1996) found out that the experiences of sport during school age was a major determinant of the level and the kind of sport activities of adult athletes. Therefore he suggests that sport and health politics in the ageing society should adopt an all-encompassing approach stretching over the entire lifecourse.

## 6. Concluding Observations

In this chapter I have shown how public and private actors in contemporary Japan have impacted upon the position of sport in the ageing society. Sport certainly has been adopted as a valuable resource to navigate through the three successive phases of the "ageing shock" at age 50, 60 and 70 because of its supportive qualities for the "eventide dowry" of the three K: *kenkō* (health), *keizai* (economics), and *kokoro no hari* (determination, or spirit).[7] However, the link between age and sport activities still is very weak since the share of non-active adults shows a disproportionate increase among the old, and within the older age groups, there is a preponderance of non-active women, who are consistently in all age groups less likely to fall short to the appeal of sport. While Japanese elderly are healthy by international comparison, this seems to be a cohort effect and should not be the cause for overt optimism. Observations on the present elderly hardly allow reliable predictions about the future shape of eventide lifestyles. Rather it is likely that a future breed of older people will not evidence the same robust health conditions. Particularly the prolongation of old-old age is likely to aggravate the "double dichotomy of ageing": we may expect a growing number of physically active and health conscious seniors in correspondence to what Höpflinger (2005) called the "socio-cultural

---

[7] See Emi's booklet (2005) on the three phases of ageing, beginning with presbyopia and wrinkling at age 50, the rising probability of cancer or hypertrophy at the second stage about a decade later, and the increasing dependency on artificial devices such as dentures or hearing aids at the third stage.

juvenescence of age", but the group of non-active seniors will concurrently increase at a much faster pace. No "ageless living" campaign is ultimately able to annihilate the risks of age-related disease and disability in the later stage of old age.

I have also argued that the discussion of sport and demographic change cannot be reduced to the role of sport for the aged. The current rhetoric of sport and health politics clearly shows that the government has acknowledged the significance of sport for all age groups. Over the past years, remarkable changes in lifestyle behaviour have equally contributed to rising sport participation rates among all age cohorts. In terms of growth rates, the gap to the more advanced sport nations is decreasing. But Japan started from a very low level, and all post-industrial societies are facing similar problems of obesity and lifestyle related atrophy among the young generations. Since the late 1980s, the level of physical fitness and athletic ability in Japanese children has dramatically decreased. The Ministry of Education attributes this to the common neglect of the importance of sports, a lack of factors needed to be involved in sports (time, space and friends) and a disorderly lifestyle. The ideological link between healthy body and sound mind triggered a moral panic echoing through the media. A commentary by the *Yomiuri Shinbun* (9 August 2002), for example, portrayed the decline of children's physical strength as a "reflection of the decline of Japanese society". It seemed that during the so-called lost decade the nation also lost its children's physical strength.

There is one more reason to be concerned. In its midterm revision of the Basic Plan,[8] the Ministry of Education conceded that the current sport participation rate of 38.5 per cent (based on the governmental opinion survey on physical strength from 2004; Naikakufu 2004b), was way below the targeted 50 per cent. Progress is also wanting in the case of the establishment of comprehensive community sport clubs. According to the midterm revision, the goal of opening at least one such sport club in all municipalities until 2010 was realized only in 33 per cent of all designated districts: at halftime, a total of 2,155 clubs were registered in 783 municipalities (Naikakufu 2006: 79). The

[8] Revisions have been added to the Basic Plan for the Promotion of Sports following a public hearing on July 29, 2006. The updated version, including some reference material on the current progress, was at the time of writing only available from the e-government online database (http://search.e-gov.go.jp/servlet/Public?ANKEN_TYPE=2; refer to project no. 185000217).

majority of local communities still lack a single club, and progress in establishing new clubs has slowed down. Particularly smaller and rural municipalities are struggling to fulfil their task. Research on the implementation of central government health politics at local level indicates that the progress in rural and small communities is lagging far behind the results metropolitan and large municipalities have achieved so far (Katanoda, Hirota and Matsumura 2005).

Poor public funding and lack of other resources are very likely to be a major cause for the slow progress. Public expenditure in general has been drastically curtailed over the past years. In the case of sports, despite all promotional programmes sport-related spending by the central government shrank from 453 billion Yen in the peak year of 1996 to 269 billion Yen in 2005 (Shibuya 2005).[9] Funding dedicated explicitly to mass sport promotion, has fallen from 3.3 billion in 2002 to 166 million in 2005. To a large extent the decrease results from a dramatic loss of income from public gambling. Transfer of revenues from *keirin* (cycling races) and horse races to the Japan Amateur Athletic Association went down from 760 million Yen in 1998 to 315 million Yen in 2004. A severe shock for the Basic Plan has been the lukewarm reception of the new football lottery toto, which the Ministry of Education had created for the purpose of financing public sport. Despite numerous attempts to facilitate lottery sales and to increase betting games, toto turnover has fallen from 64.2 billion Yen in fiscal 2001 to 5.7 billion in 2006. Toto sport subsidies accordingly decreased from 5.9 billion to 118 million Yen in fiscal 2006, when 108 community sport clubs received an average of 800,000 Yen each.[10]

The decrease in revenues for the promotion of public sport is a potential threat to the prospects of the lifelong sport society. Data from the national household survey (*Kakei chōsa*; see STK 2000, 2005) clearly indicate that the willingness—or capability—to spend on sport has decreased in general during the long recession and particularly

[9] In the past, local government expenditure hardly exceeded the national budget. In 2000, when the national budget was already down at 380 billion, local governments still spent 480 billion Yen on sports. Facility maintenance and public building projects consume the largest proportions (see Manzenreiter 2004).

[10] The remaining 30 per cent were spent on the promotion of top sport. All data according to the annual reports by the National Agency for the Advancement of Sport and Health, published on the agency's website http://www.naash.go.jp/sinko/happyou.html.

among lower income groups. Their sport budget comprises an increasingly smaller share of total household spending than the sport budget of higher income groups, and the gap has been widening. Disposable income also correlates strongly with active sport involvement. The 2001 Survey on Time Use and Leisure Activities (*Shakai seikatsu kihon chōsa*; STK 2001) reveals that higher income groups have higher participation rates and spend in average more time on sport per day than lower income groups. Hence public sport supply fulfils the important task of securing the less wealthy equal health chances.

But the central government seems to be torn apart between contemporary financial constraints and intervention for the sake of future benefits. Shifting the responsibility for health and physical fitness to local communities and ultimately to the individual is a notable concession to the lurking spirit of neo-liberalism which has left its impact on Japan's sport politics since the late 1980s (Uchiumi 2005: 220). Sport and health promotion politics nowadays are characterised by a previously unknown style of accountability and controllability expressed by the numerical targets for action by public bodies as well as physical bodies. The meaning of sport, in the context of public management, has expanded; it still is a disciplinary tool, a business and a source of individual pleasure, and now also an instrument of social engineering. In the culture of accountability, ageing is not a natural process but something that can and should be managed. The biological component certainly is still of importance for determining who are the old. But social components, crafted by the individual in its interactions with the social world, mediated through the body and linked to sociability, autonomy and self-perception, are increasingly gaining in significance for the new old.

## Acknowledgements

I want to thank Prof. Kōichi Kiku (Tsukuba University) for the concise research reports on sport participation of the middle-aged. I am also deeply indebted to Ryō Katō and Yasuko Kudō (Sasakawa Sports Foundation) for generously providing me with raw data and printed material of the SSF National Sport Life Surveys. Last, but not least, I express my gratitude to Dr. John Horne (Edinburgh University) for valuable comments on earlier versions of this chapter.

## References

Amaha, Keisuke (2003): Supōtsu de rōka o fusegō [Fending off ageing by sport]. In: *Supōtsu Shisutemu Kōza* 4, pp. 15–40.

Cameron, Heather (ed.) (2004): *Strategies for seniors and sport.* Conference report. Berlin: Anglo-German Foundation.

Carrigan, Marylin (1998): Segmenting the grey market. The case for fifty-plus 'lifegroups'. In: *Journal of Marketing Practice* 4, 2, pp. 43–56.

CKSJ (Chūshō Kigyō Sōgō Jigyōdan) (2001): *Juyō dōkō chōsa. Kōrei shakai sangyō yoka amenity bunya* [Demand trend survey. Field of leisure amenities among industries of the aged society]. Tokyo: Chūshō Kigyō Sōgō Jigyōdan.

Demura, Shinichi *et al.* (2005): Physical-fitness declines in older Japanese adults. In: *Journal of Aging and Physical Activity* 11, 1, pp. 112–121.

Doi, Takeo (1973): *The Anatomy of Dependence.* New York: Kodansha International.

Emi, Kōichi (2005): *'Oiru shokku' wa sando kuru!* [The ageing shock comes thrice!]. Tokyo: Kanki Shuppan.

Höpflinger, François (2005): Alternde Gesellschaft—verjüngte Senioren. Über die doppelte Dynamik des Alterns [Ageing society—rejuvenated seniors. On the double dynamics of ageing]. In: *Neue Zürcher Zeitung* (27 September 2005), pp. 00–00.

IHRSA (International Health, Rackets and Sportsclub Association) (2006): *The 2006 IHRSA Global Report on the State of the Health Club Industry.* Excerpts available at http://cms.ihrsa.org/IHRSA/ (found 31 July 2006).

Ikeda, Masaru, Yasuo Yamaguchi and Makoto Chogahara (2001): *Sport for All in Japan.* Tokyo: Sasakawa Sports Foundation.

IPSS (National Institute of Population and Social Security Research) (2006): *Population Statistics of Japan 2006.* Tokyo: IPSS.

Iwamoto, Yasushi (2004): Issues in Japanese health policy and medical expenditure. In: Tachibanaki, Toshiaki (ed.): *The Economics of Social Security in Japan.* Cheltenham: Edward Elger, pp. 219–232.

JPHA (Japan Public Health Association) (2006): *Public Health of Japan 2005.* Tokyo: Japan Public Health Association.

Kado, Osamu (1998): Chūkōnen no supōtsu sanka o meguru tayōka to soshikika ni kansuru kenkyū no matome to teigen [Summary of research on organisation and diversification of sport participation by the middle aged and final declaration]. In: Kado, Osamu *et al.* (eds.): *Chūkōnen no supōtsu sanka o meguru tayōka to soshikika ni kansuru shakaigaku kenkyū—dai 3 hō* [A sociological study on organisation and diversification concerning sport participation of the middle-aged]. Tokyo: Nihon Taiiku Kyōkai, Supōtsu I + Kagaku Senmon Iinkai, pp. 96–100.

Kalab, Kathleen A. (1992): Playing gateball: A game of the Japanese elderly. In: *Journal of Aging Studies* 6, 1, pp. 23–40.

Katanoda, Kōta, Kōichi Hirota and Yasuhiro Matsumura (2005): Jichitai kubun-betsu ni mita Kenkō Nihon 21 chihō keikaku ni okeru sūji mokuhyō sakutei jōkyō [State of the establishment of numerical targets in regional plans of Healthy Japan 21, according to local community type]. In: *Nihon Kōshū Eisei Zasshi* 52, 9, pp. 817–823.

Kiku, Kōichi (1996): Kako no supōtsu katsudō no jōkyō [Situation of former sport involvement]. In: Kado, Osamu *et al.* (eds.): *Chūkōnen no supōtsu sanka o meguru tayōka to soshikika ni kansuru shakaigaku kenkyū—dai 1 hō* [A sociological study on organisation and diversification concerning sport participation of the middle-aged]. Tokyo: Nihon Taiiku Kyōkai, Supōtsu Kagaku Senmon Iinkai, pp. 31–41.

—— (1998): *Shōgai supōtsu taikei no kōzō to undō ni kansuru Nichiei hikaku kenkyū* [A comparative study on structure and movement of lifelong sport systems in Japan and England]. Research report to a grant-in-aid for scientific research in fiscal 1997.

Kōseishō (ed.) (1999): *Heisei 11-nendo kōsei hakusho. Shakai hoshō to kokumin seikatsu* [White Book on Welfare 1999. Social security and the life of the people]. Tokyo: Gyōsei.

KRDK (Kōsei Rōdōshō Daijin Kanbō Tōkei Jōhō Bu) (2003): *Heisei 14-nendo kokumin iryōhi no gaikyō* [General conditions of national medical expenses in fiscal 2002]. Tokyo: Kōsei Rōdōshō Daijin Kanbō Tōkei Jōhō Shitsu.
KTJZ (Kenkō Tairyoku-zukuri Jigyō Zaidan) (2004): *Kōreisha no undō jissensha to hijissensha ni okeru seikatsu ishiki to seikatsu no sōi ni kan suru kenkyū* [Research on life perceptions and differences of lifestyle among aged participants and non-participants in sport activities]. Tokyo: Kenkō Tairyoku-zukuri Jigyō Zaidan.
Long, Jonathan (2004): Sport and the ageing population: Do older people have a place in driving up participation in sport? In: Sport England (ed.): *Driving up participation: The challenge for sport*. London: Sport England, pp. 28–38.
Manzenreiter, Wolfram (2004): Sport zwischen Markt und öffentlicher Dienstleistung. Zur Zukunft des Breitensports in Japan [Sports between market and public service. On the future of mass sports in Japan]. In: *SWS-Rundschau* (Journal für Sozialforschung) 44, 2, pp. 227–251.
Matsunaka, Keiko (2001): Shirubā bijinesu to supōtsu [The silver business and sport]. In: Harada, Munehiko (ed.): *Supōtsu sangyō nyūmon* [An introduction to the sport industry]. Tokyo: Kyorin Shoin, pp. 332–347.
METI (Ministry of Economy, Trade and Industry) (2006): *This new generation of Japanese seniors is a consumer powerhouse.* Press release delivered by PR Newswire, March 22, 2006. http://sev.prnewswire.com/household-consumer-cosmetics/20060322/NYW07322032006–1.html (found 23 March 2006).
MEXT (Ministry of Education, Culture, Sports, Science and Technology) (2000): *Supōtsu shinkō kihon keikaku* [Basic plan for the promotion of sports]. http://www.mext.go.jp/b_menu/houdou/12/09/000905.htm (found 18 February 2002).
Miyachi, Motohiko (2005): Laboratory of physical activity and health evaluation. In: *Health and Nutrition News* 11, p. 3.
Naikakufu (2004a): *Heisei 16-nendo 'ejiresu raifu jissensha' oyobi 'shakai sanka katsudō jirei' senkō kekka* [Results from the selection of 'ageless life practicioners' and examples of 'participation in social activities']. http://www8.cao.go.jp/kourei/kou-kei/h16ageless/h16agefront.html (found 15 August 2006).
—— (2004b): *Heisei 16-nen tairyoku supōtsu ni kan suru yoron chōsa* [Opinion survey on sport and physical fitness 2004]. Tokyo: Naikakufu.
—— (2006): *Heisei 18-nenban seishōnen hakusho* [White Book on Youth 2006]. Tokyo: Kokuritsu Insatsukyoku.
Nakamura, Toshio (1995): *Nihonteki supōtsu kankyō hihan* [Critique of the Japanese sport environment]. Tokyo: Taishūkan Shoten.
NDK (Naikakufu Daijin Kanbō Seifu Kōkoku Shitsu) (2005): *Heisei 17-nendo kokumin seikatsu ni kan suru yoron chōsa.* Tokyo: Naikakufu Daijin Kanbō Seifu Kōkoku Shitsu.
Ohno, Yoshiyuki *et al.* (2000): Successful aging and social activity in older Japanese adults. In: *Journal of Aging and Physical Activity* 8, 2, pp. 129–139.
Okada, Kei (1999): Nihon ni okeru supōtsu seisaku no genjō to kadai—ASC (Australia Sports Commission) to no hikakuteki kenchi kara [Current state and task of Japan's sport politics in comparison with Australia]. In: *Dōshisa Seisaku Kagaku Kenkyū* 1, pp. 111–128.
SCK (Sōmuchō Chōkan Kanbō Kōrei Shakai Taisaku Shitsu) (1999): *Heisei 10-nendo koreisha no nichijō seikatsu ni kan suru ishiki chōsa* [Survey on attitudes of the elderly towards everyday life in 1998]. Tokyo: Sōmuchō Chōkan Kanbō Kōrei Shakai Taisaku Shitsu.
—— (2005): *Heisei 16-nendo koreisha no nichijō seikatsu ni kan suru ishiki chōsa* [Survey on attitudes of the elderly towards everyday life in 2004]. Tokyo: Sōmuchō Chōkan Kanbō Kōrei Shakai Taisaku Shitsu.
SCSK (Shinkin Chūō Sangyō Kenkyūjo) (2002): *Kitai sareru shirubā bijinesu* [The expected silver business]. *Sangyō Chōsa Jōhō* 66.

Seki, Harunami (1997): *Sengo Nihon no supōtsu seisaku. Sono kōzō to tenkai* [Sport policy in post-war Japan]. Tokyo: Taishūkan Shoten.
Shibuya, Shigeki (2005): Opinion: *Nihon wa supōtsu senshinkoku?* [Is Japan an advanced sport nation?]. *Sports for Everyone Network*, Online Magazine, September 2005. http://www.sfen.jp/opinion/shibuya/shibuya1_3.html (found 1 August 2006).
Shimizu, Takahiko and Takuji Shirasawa (2006): How to stay young while getting old. In: *Japan Close-Up* (July 2006), pp. 12–18.
Shirai, Shōzō (2000): Fittonesu sangyō to wa nani ka [What is the fitness industry?]. In: Uenishi, Yasufumi (ed.): *Supōtsu bijinesu senryaku* [Strategies in sport business]. Toyko: Taishūkan, pp. 113–139.
SKS (Sangyō Kōzō Shingikai) (2000): 21-seiki keizai sangyō seisaku no kadai to tenbō. Kyōsōryoku tasanka shakai no keisei o megutte [Prospects and tasks of industrial politics for the 21st century. On the formation of a society enhancing its competitive power]. Tokyo: Ministry of Economy, Trade and Industry.
SKSH (Shakai Keizai Seisansei Honbu) (2003): *Rejā hakusho 2003. Arata-na yoka shijō no kanōsei* [Leisure White Book 2003. Potentials of new leisure markets]. Tokyo: Shakai Keizai Seisansei Honbu.
Spielvogel, Laura (2003): *Working Out in Japan: Shaping the Female Body in Tokyo Fitness Clubs*. Durham: Duke University Press.
SSF (Sasakawa Sports Foundation) (ed.) (2001): *Supōtsu hakusho 2010. Supōtsu foa ōru kara supōtsu fō eburiwan e* [White Book on sport 2010. From 'sport for all' to 'sport for everyone'). Tokyo: Sasakawa Sports Foundation.
—— (2004): *Supōtsu raifu dēta 2004* [Data on sports life 2004). Tokyo: Sasakawa Sports Foundation.
STK (Sōmushō Tōkei Kyoku) (2000): *Kakei chōsa nenpō: Heisei 12-nen* [Annual report on household income and expenditure survey 2000]. Tokyo: Sōmushō Tōkei Kyoku.
—— (2001): *Heisei 13-nen shakai seikatsu kihon chōsa* [Basic survey on time use and leisure 2001]. Tokyo: Sōmushō Tōkei Kyoku.
—— (2005): *Kakei chōsa nenpō: Heisei 17-nen* [Annual report on household income and expenditure survey 2005]. Tokyo: Sōmushō Tōkei Kyoku.
Sugiyama, Yoshio *et al.* (1986): Kōreisha no supōtsu katsudō to 'ikigai' ishiki no kanren [The relationship between sport activities of elderly and their sense of 'purpose in life']. In: *Rōnen Shakaikagaku* 8, pp. 161–176.
Takahashi, Hirokazu (2003): *Taiiku supōtsu shisetsu no seibi unei hōhō ga toshi no jizokusei ni ataeru eikyō ni kansuru kenkyū* [Influences of provision and management of PE and sport facilities on urban sustainability]. M.A. thesis approved by the Division of Environmental Engineering and Architecture, Nagoya University.
Uchiumi, Kazuo (2005): *Nihon no supōtsu fō ōru—mijun-na fukushi kokka no supōtsu seisaku* [Japan's 'sport for all'. The sport politics of an immature welfare state]. Tokyo: Fumaidō Shuppan.
WHO Centre for Health Development (2005): *Public Health Policy and Approaches for Noncommunicable Disease Prevention and Control in Japan: A Case Study* (Ageing and Health Technical Report, 6). Kobe: WHO Centre for Health Development.
Yasunaga, Akitomo, Kōichi Yaguchi and Mikio Tokunaga (2002): Kōreisha no shukanteki kōfukukan ni oyobosu undō kanshū no eikyō [Effects of exercise habits on subjective well-being among the elderly]. In: *Taiikugaku Kenkyū* 47, 2, pp. 173–183.
Yoshiuchi, Kazuhiro *et al.* (2006): Yearlong physical activity and depressive symptoms in older Japanese adults: cross-sectional data from the Nakanojo study. In: *American Journal of Geriatric Psychiatry* 14, pp. 621–624.

PART FOUR

# POLITICAL ASPECTS OF DEMOGRAPHIC CHANGE

# INTRODUCTION

Many states have tried to manage their people's fertility behaviour both to curb and to promote population growth. China's one-child-policy comes to mind or Russia's recent bids to boost birth rates. Japan, too, has a history of population policies. However, the real success of state intervention into population behaviour is a matter about which scholars are divided. Although it is a central issue, it is not exclusively fertility behaviour that is the interest of politics when dealing with a nation's demographic development. Questions that arise in this field of research are numerous; they include, for example, policy making for specific groups, such as the elderly or students, people living in rural, gradually depopulating areas, labour migrants crossing borders to compensate for shrinking national workforces, and many others. Questions that need to be addressed in a political science setting concern not only the contents of these policies, but also the underlying process of political agenda setting and decision making, which may provide general insights into how policy making works.

This part of the *Handbook* focuses on political aspects of Japan's demographic change. It takes a two-sided approach of studying, on the one hand, the multiple policy making actors and the interdependence between them, and, on the other hand, the contents of actual policy outcomes. In detail, the chapters of this part fall into three groups. First, the three chapters by Schoppa, Campbell, and Talcott discuss issues of demographics and state institutions, in other words, so-called traditional political actors. The second group, Potter, Pekkanen and Tsujinaka, as well as Ogawa focus on how Japan's civil society, a relatively new political actor in Japan, is reacting to the nation's demographic development. The third group, Kreitz-Sandberg, Coleman, Roberts, Feldhoff, and Maclachlan highlight frameworks and challenges within specific policy fields. The following paragraphs offer brief introductions to each of these chapters.

Schoppa acquaints the reader with the Japanese state's attempts to manage its people's fertility behaviour. Attempts to reverse the current trend of population decline through political interference in people's fertility behaviour so far have failed, because of a taboo on pro-natalism which has its roots in the *umeyo fuyaseyo* [give birth and multiply] policy of the period during World War II. Campbell addresses the other end of the population pyramid, introducing three areas of policy making for the increasing number of senior citizens: public pensions, medical care, and long-term care. At the core of this chapter are numerous close-up studies of how bureaucrats and leading politicians within the Liberal Democratic Party have influenced and bargained with each other over specific policy guidelines. Talcott takes a deeper look at the role of political parties in the policy-formation process. He argues that policy making in Japan is shaped by coalition party officials, ministry officials, academic experts, business representatives, and, on a case by case basis non-governmental organizations. It is a top-down process initiated to some degree by party elites which Talcott analyses step-by-step.

Since state actors are reaching their limitations in coping with the challenges of ageing and depopulation, civil society actors are more often called upon to step in. Potter's chapter provides a bird's-eye view of Japan's non-profit organization (NPO) sector and its role for elderly care. NPOs indeed answer a need not fulfilled by public welfare. However, the small size of NPOs in Japan, their limited resources and their reliance on volunteer staff are challenges to their becoming influential political actors. Pekkanen and Tsujinaka focus on another form of civil society organization, neighbourhood associations (NHA). On the one hand, the local and non-professional nature of NHAs prevents them from being effective avenues for setting new political agendas or proposing new policy visions. On the other hand, it is this very character of NHAs that makes them a central part of local life for citizens all over Japan: NHAs are essential for community building. Ogawa sheds light on the changing role of schools in Japan's ageing society. He argues that schools aim at creating what he calls "volunteer subjectivity" internalized in human nature. Ogawa illustrates this argument by discussing the *hōshi* [service] programme, introduced into the curriculum of public high schools in Tokyo in 2004.

Kreitz-Sandberg shows that the declining birth rate has manifold impacts on the education system. Classes will have fewer pupils and, in the short run, the student-teacher ratio falls. A second change ahead is the closing down of schools due to falling student numbers. Thirdly, she argues, entrance exams are becoming less competitive as the number of applicants declines. Admission rate is approaching one hundred per cent. Coleman draws a close-up picture of Japan's family policy, known as *shōshika taisaku* [measures to counter the declining birth rate]. She argues that, particularly since the "1.57 shock" of 1990, when the total fertility rate for the previous year fell to a post-war low, family policies have increasingly taken issue with the declining fertility rate. In particular, these policies were developed through three successive five-year plans: the Angel Plan, the New Angel Plan, and the Children and Childrearing Support Plan. Roberts discusses the question of how immigration policy could be reformed so as to counteract the demographically induced labour shortage without leading to wage dumping and cultural clashes. She introduces the latest policy outline by the Ministry of Justice, which advocates the acceptance of foreign workers in restricted numbers, and only if integration efforts, such as their willingness to acquire Japanese language proficiency, can be proved. Feldhoff's chapter on infrastructural policy deals with population and urban decline, that is the spatial implications of demographic change. Demographic ageing and shrinking is not only related to depopulation, but also to a loss of functions, de-economization and de-socialization. He discusses current concepts of infrastructural policy, such as "Urban Renaissance" and "Universal Design", questioning their effectiveness in bringing about economic and social revitalization of shrinking cities and regions. The final chapter of this part is a case study. Machlachlan analyzes the privatization of the postal system and its implications for the nation's local—and mostly aged—society.

To sum up, this part of the *Handbook* provides insights into how state institutions and civil society organizations address the multifaceted challenges current population development pose to Japan's political system in general and exemplified policy areas in particular.

G.V.

CHAPTER THIRTY-FOUR

# DEMOGRAPHICS AND THE STATE

Leonard Schoppa

## 1. Introduction

States have concerned themselves with the size of their populations since soon after they developed their modern form (Gauthier 1996). In the first half of the 20th Century, their concerns grew out of worries that states with slow-growing populations risked falling behind those with higher fertility rates. Viewing today's babies as tomorrow's soldiers and factory workers, many states adopted policies and organized propaganda campaigns aimed at encouraging higher rates of fertility. After World War II, many of these same states came to look at population numbers in exactly the opposite way. Today's babies were now seen as tomorrow's poor and needy welfare cases. Smaller families were seen as being able to invest more in the education of their children. Many states therefore began encouraging families to limit themselves to two or three children (in the case of China, just one) through usually subtle but sometimes brutal means. Today, however, demographic trends have shifted to a point where many states once again see danger in *low* fertility rates. Today's babies are now seen as tomorrow's taxpayers, and there aren't enough of them to pay for the health and pension benefits retiring baby boomers are counting on.

Japan has experienced each of these twists in a particularly pronounced way, pushing aggressively to boost its population size in the period before World War II with its *umeyo fuyaseyo* [give birth and multiply] policies and then reversing course sharply in the aftermath of its defeat when the state embraced modern methods of family planning, including access to abortion on demand. Recently, it is again in the front ranks of states struggling to respond to rapidly falling fertility rates that threaten the fiscal sustainability of social insurance programs. Since 1994, starting with its Angel Plans, and more recently with the provocatively-named Plus One Plan, it has been implicitly or explicitly committed to reversing the fall in fertility rates through a wide range of policies.

Although this chapter focuses in greatest detail on Japan's most recent "twist" in this saga, it begins by examining the earlier two periods of active state efforts to shape demographic trends. Ironically, I argue, past experience attempting to influence fertility rates has not given the Japanese state much of an advantage in its latest campaign to increase the number of babies being born. On the contrary, memories of aggressive pro-natal policies during the war have made it difficult for the government to adopt (or even *discuss*) policies aimed at boosting fertility rates while post-war policies encouraging small families with mothers devoted to raising and educating their children have made the task of reversing fertility trends in the most recent period all the more difficult. Meanwhile, the fiscal challenge facing the Japanese state has been made urgent by the rapid pace of Japan's demographic transition. Japan faces particular difficulty financing its social insurance obligations because it is ageing more rapidly than any nation in the world, a "problem" that is in part the product of past efforts to boost and then suppress fertility rates.

## 2. Demography and the State during Wartime

The last time the Japanese worried about a population deficit was during wartime, when the architects of Japan's planned Greater East Asia Co-prosperity Sphere dreamed of populating much of East Asia, including Australia and New Zealand, with transplanted members of the Yamato race (Dower 1986: 275). Japan at this time was already a crowded country. Mortality rates were falling much more rapidly than birth rates as the nation industrialized, helping to make it one of the most densely-populated nations in the world. Yet as leaders of the Japanese state looked at neighbours with larger populations, they calculated that they needed the nation's population to grow from 70 million to at least 100 million if they expected to compete militarily with their rivals. Japan was growing, they knew, but its birth rate was falling rapidly, from 36.2 births per 1,000 members of the population in 1920 to 26.6 in 1939 (see Figure 1). If this rate continued to fall, the Japanese population was destined to remain much smaller than neighbouring China and Russia, which had birth rates of 45 and 43.3 respectively.

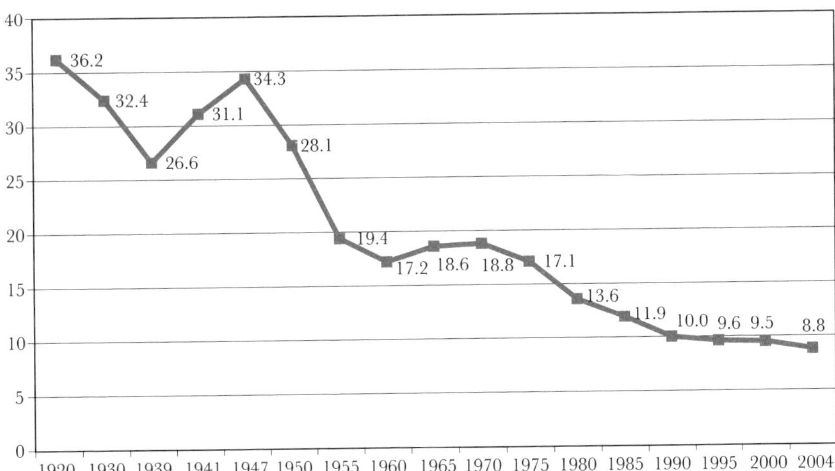


Note: births per 1,000 population
Source: NIPSSR 2006, p. 17.

Figure 1. Japan's Crude Birthrate, 1920–2004.

Government propaganda made it clear to Japanese women that it was their responsibility as citizens to "give birth and multiply." Fertility choices were not private matters. Women were obligated to take on *kokkateki bosei* [motherhood-in-the-interest-of-the-state] (Norgren 2001: 33–34).

Meanwhile, it was the responsibility of the Japanese state to take on the powerful social and economic forces that were driving birthrates down. Everywhere, as nations industrialize, fertility rates fall, and Japan was industrializing very quickly in the 1920s and '30s. When nations were predominantly agricultural, there was some symbiosis between the interests of states (which needed larger populations to staff growing armies) and the interests of families (who counted on children to help out on the farm). By the time the Japanese state took up its campaign to boost birth rates in the late 1930s and early 1940s, however, it found itself asking the growing number of urban families to *sacrifice* by feeding and educating larger families that were not contributing to the family income, merely to serve the interests of the state.

Urbanization and Japan's interactions with the world also brought to Japanese society new ideas and new movements interested in improving the quality of children by reducing their number. Although abortion was illegal, couples in this era used a variety of contraceptive techniques, most frequently the condom, but also contraceptive pins, rings, and intrauterine devices. Contraceptive supplies were "displayed prominently in drug stores during the 1920s and early 1930s" (Whelpton 1950: 35), and many urban areas had local birth control clinics to offer advice on how to use them correctly. There were 60–70 in the Tokyo metropolitan area alone (Norgren 2001: 26). There are no reliable statistics on birth control use in pre-war Japan, but post-war demographers looking back at birthrates in the era argue that "the practice of contraception became well established among certain groups" by the 1920s, and "an increase in use of preventive methods played an important role in causing the decrease in the birth rate that occurred from 1920 to 1938" (Whelpton 1950: 35).

With the nation at war with China in the mid-1930s, the government decided to begin restricting access to birth control. An ordinance passed in 1930 banned the sale and display of "harmful" birth control devices (but not the condom), and in 1937 the government extended the ban to written publications on birth control. The police monitored and harassed birth control activists, and they also stepped up prosecution of doctors and others performing illegal abortions. While these actions did not close off all access to birth control (the condom was kept freely available because the army valued its utility in preventing the spread of venereal disease), post-war demographers attribute the rise in birthrates from 26.6 in 1939 to 31.1 in 1941 in part to the way these prohibitions restricted the use of certain birth control techniques "by making it more difficult for people to learn of their contraceptive qualities" (Whelpton 1950: 38).

The Tōjō Cabinet in 1941 adopted an explicitly pro-natal policy aimed at using all of the persuasive powers of the state to encourage marriage and childbearing. The Population Problems Institute of the newly-formed Ministry of Health and Welfare (MHW) declared that year that in order to reach the state's target of five babies per woman, it would adopt policies aimed at lowering the marriage age for women from 24.4 to 21. With government support, patriotic young women's groups set up marriage counselling centres designed "to cause women to move from an individualistic view of marriage to a national one."[1] The state also established matchmaking centres, asked employers to offer special bonuses to workers who had babies, and promised free

[1] Nihon Seinenkan, *Dai Nihon Seishonendanshi* [History of the Greater Japan youth and child group], quoted in Havens (1975: 927).

higher education to families who had more than ten children (Havens 1975: 928). Finally, to encourage soldiers to marry and start families, the government offered special furloughs to single soldiers before deploying them for duty overseas. It also gave inductees advance warning so that they could get married before joining the military (Whelpton 1950: 35).

These extra efforts in the early 1940s helped keep birth rates above the lows of the late 1930s in 1940–42, and probably kept birth rates higher than they would have been during the years when World War II imposed the greatest deprivations on the Japanese home islands, but they ultimately could not prevent a steep fall in births as families faced growing difficulty obtaining food and other necessities of life (Whelpton 1950: 34–35). By the final year of the war, the birth rate had fallen to a record low of 23.2.

## 3. Demography and the State in the Early Post-war Years

When the MHW's Population Problems Institute was founded in 1939, it had conceived of the "population problem" referred to in its name as involving a birth *dearth*. Almost overnight with the conclusion of the war, this institute, the bureaucracy as a whole, and Occupation authorities all came to regard the "population problem" as one of *over*-population. Defeat had led to the repatriation of eight million Japanese who had been living or fighting battles overseas. As these citizens (most of them male) returned to the home islands, many married or rejoined spouses and immediately began adding to their families, causing the birth rate to peak in 1947 at 34.3 births per 1,000 residents. Between repatriation and the baby boom, Japan's population grew by 11 million in the first five years after the war, leaving Japan with a 1950 population of 83 million that was far larger than could be sustained by its post-war economic base.

This time the state apparatus found itself pushing in the same direction as economic and social forces. Mothers struggling to find enough food to feed their families were eager to gain control their fertility, and the prewar pro-family-planning group, the Japan Birth Control League, began actively pushing for the liberalization of birth control and abortion rules as early as 1947 (Norgren 2001: 88). Furthermore, the effort to rebuild the Japanese economy after the war led to the resumption of urbanization and industrialization trends that encouraged families to limit the number of their offspring.

In 1948, the new Pharmaceutical Affairs Law repealed restrictions on sales and marketing of contraceptive drugs and compounds. Many such pharmaceuticals were approved in the year after it went into effect and were widely advertised (Whelpton 1950, 39). Reported rates of contraceptive use rose from just 19.5 per cent of women under 50 in 1950 to 40 per cent in 1957.[2]

Also in 1948 the legislature passed the Eugenic Protection Law, authorizing abortion when the health of the mother was in jeopardy or when the child was likely to be born "eugenically inferior." Just one year later, the law was revised to allow for abortion when an additional child would threaten the economic welfare of the family. While the Eugenic Protection Law initially set up special medical committees to evaluate cases before authorizing abortions, after another set of revisions in 1952 abortions were allowed at the discretion of the physician. The number of abortions performed increased quickly after the passage of these laws, rising from 320,000 in 1950 to over a million in 1953.[3]

Together, these measures helped Japan record a sharp decline in the birth rate, from 34.3 in 1947 to 19.4 in 1955—a pace of decline that was "unprecedented in recorded world history" (Oakley 1978: 620). By 1954, when the government's Council on Population Problems came out with a report stating explicitly that "it is necessary for the Government to adopt a policy designed to check the growth of population," it was in fact ratifying what had already been done (Taeuber 1956: 32–33).

## 4. Demography and the State Since 1990

According to the fertility surveys the Populations Problems Institute conducted every five years, Japanese couples had their fertility firmly under control at a level that was projected to take Japan to zero population growth by early in the 21st century. Cohorts of women born between 1932 and 1952, the first generation to come of age in post-war Japan, had children at a remarkably stable rate. The cohorts had on average 2.01 children, with no pronounced trend upward or downward. The

[2] Figures are for the percentage of women under 50 who are currently practicing contraception, reported in NIPSSR (n.d., Internet), Table 11.

[3] Norgren (2001: 36–52) offers an extended discussion of the Eugenic Protection Law and its revisions, emphasizing the role of the ob-gyn doctors' lobby in pushing for liberalization. Data on abortions performed are from NIPSSR (n.d., Internet), Table 10.

1932 cohort had 2.03 children, and the 1952 cohort had 2.01—numbers that were very close to the population replacement rate of 2.07 (NIPSSR 2003: 31–33).

Yet by the time the organization got around to removing the "problem" from the English version of its name in 1996, when it became part of the National Institute of Population and Social Security Research (NIPSSR), the institute's demographic data and fertility surveys were already signalling the emergence of a new population problem.

The latest problem had its roots, as noted at the start of this essay, in the demographic after-effects of the state's first attempt to boost Japan's fertility rates in wartime Japan. Combined with the post-war baby boom, this effort to urge Japanese to "give birth and multiply" had created an extra large cohort of individuals born between 1941 and 1950 that was roughly 20 million strong. Japan's demographers had known since that time that this generation, when it retired, would give Japan a much older population profile than it had had up to that point, but the gravity of the challenge the state faced did not start to sink in until after the 1973 oil crisis. As early as 1975, the MHW and the associated policy community began talking about the looming "ageing society problem" Japan faced as this large cohort (then aged 25–34) approached retirement age (Campbell 1992: 210). What made their retirement years a concern was the fact that Japan had in the interim begun promising this generation of workers that they would be well-taken-care-of in their golden years. Pension programs had been established and expanded. The government had even established a program of free health care for those over 70. While these programs cost little in the 1970s, when retirees made up just eight per cent of the population (NIPSSR 2003: 14), it didn't take much mathematical skill to calculate that the cost was going to soar when the 1941–50 generation retired.

Compounding this concern about the retirement of this large cohort was evidence that this generation was going to *live longer* than expected (NIPSSR 2003: 52). Between 1997 and 2002, projected life expectancies for 2050 went up from 80 to 81 for men and from 86 to 89 for women. In the process, Japan added over three million very-old citizens to the number of elderly it expects to have to support in that year.[4]

Japan's most recent "population problem" started with this concern about a surplus of old people, but there was little the state could do to

[4] Data for the 1997 projections are from Takahashi *et al.* (1999: 108, 113); Data for the 2002 projections are from NIPSSR (2002: 12, 17).

alter this demographic projection. Instead, the Japanese state's efforts to deal with its new population problem have again focused on *fertility*. Here again, its latest efforts are being shaped in various ways by its previous attempts to influence fertility trends. The problem is that the Japanese government's attempts to use "birth control as a fundamental solution" to its population problems, as Prime Minister Yoshida put it in 1949, proved too successful too quickly. Each 10–year cohort born since 1941–50 has been smaller than that one, and recent ones have been much smaller. Between 1991 and 2000, just 12 million babies were born, making this cohort just 62 per cent the size of the one born between 1941 and 50. Japan's birth rate, which stood at 34.3 in 1947, was down to 8.8 in 2004 (see Figure 1 above). Cohorts of women *completing* their periods of fertility recently continue to have about two children on average, but the "total fertility rate"—which captures the fertility behaviour of women aged 15 to 40—has fallen to one of the lowest levels in the world. It stood at 1.29 in 2003 and 2004.[5]

The demographers working at the Populations Problems Institute saw this trend emerging and began to fret about it as early as the 1980s, but most of Japan did not wake up to Japan's "declining fertility problem" (*shōshika mondai*) until 1990 when the institute reported that the total fertility rate (TFR) for the previous year had fallen to 1.57. This report came to be known as the "1.57 shock," not because the rate was that much lower than rates up to that point (it had been 1.66 the year before), but because the TFR had fallen below the previous record low recorded in 1966 when it fell abruptly for one calendar year as couples adjusted family planning to avoid giving birth to a daughter during the Chinese zodiac year of the fire-horse (*hinoeuma*). According to superstition, women born in one of these years are likely to gnaw their husbands to death, a prospect that makes them unattractive candidates for marriage.[6] That the fertility rate had fallen below the 1966 level even though 1989 was *not* an unlucky year signalled to many that the falling fertility rate was a real problem. As one government commission noted in 1990, "Just

[5] NIPSSR (2006: 18). The total fertility rate is a demographic statistic that is calculated by taking the actual number of children born to all women between 15 and 40 and then adding to this an extrapolated number of children younger women between these ages can be expect to have if they give birth at the rates of those above them in age. Thus, for example, if women aged 27 give birth to an average of 0.12 children in a given year, the TFR is calculated by assuming all women between 15 and 26 will go on and have 0.12 children during the year when they are 27.

[6] The year of the fire horse arrives once every 60 years. See Ueno (1998: 103).

as in the last days of the Roman empire, the decrease in the number of children is a sign of the decline of civilization."[7]

What worried government demographers more than a "fall of civilization," in fact, was the implications of the declining fertility rate for the fiscal sustainability of state social insurance programs for the elderly. It was bad enough that the retirement of the 1941–50 generation was going to cause the costs of these programs to soar in the 2010s and beyond. Now the state was faced with the prospect of having to finance these costs on the backs of cohorts even smaller than the 12 million born in 1991–2000. How much smaller were these cohorts going to be? Was there anything the government could do to reverse recent trends and encourage Japanese couples to have more babies—more future *taxpayers*? The goal was no longer an increase in the number of soldiers and colonists to carry the Japanese flag across Asia, but government demographers in the 1990s began to study and brood about fertility trends in much the same way their predecessors had in wartime.

For many reasons, however, the state could not return to the policies that had boosted Japanese birth rates in the early 1940s. A constitution guaranteeing freedom of the press made it impossible to ban advertising for contraceptives. The fact that women now had a vote, and after fifty years of access to abortion were not about to let the state take this option away, ruled out any effort to restrict the availability of abortion services. Even less threatening policy proposals, like the suggestion that the government promote marriage or expand the size of the child allowance, caused women's groups to raise objections on the grounds that decisions about whether to marry or have children were *private* matters and should not be subject to influence by the state. As Yuriko Ashino, the deputy director of the Family Planning Federation of Japan put it, "Population control deserves praise rather than criticism. You won't find today's women having babies for the sake of their country or because someone told them to."[8]

As Ashino's reference to "*today's* women" suggests, much of the resistance to the government's new pro-natalism was a direct reaction to the way *yesterday's* women had been pushed into having babies on behalf of the state under wartime *umeyo fuyaseyo* policies. Not only professional feminists like Ashino but rank and file members of the

[7] Quoted by Suzuki (1995: 14).
[8] Quoted in Suzuki (1995: 16).

government bureaucracy working on the government's policy response were constrained by this historical memory. When I asked MHLW officials whether they considered raising fertility rates a goal, they uniformly brought up this historical legacy to explain why the government could not make this an explicit goal.[9] One official who had worked for many years with like-minded officials to advance women's issues within the ministry recalled the "repulsion" (*hanpatsu*) expressed by members of her group when it was proposed that they seek to use the decline in fertility as a reason for advancing policies promoting gender equality. "Many didn't want to say anything that suggested women needed to have more children," she recalled. Over time, they have become more comfortable with using the declining fertility trend as a reason to "create an environment in which women who want to have children can do so," but the goal is always expressed in this way in order to avoid arousing memories of the *umeyo fuyaseyo* period.[10] The government's challenge in the latest period of concern about demography has therefore been to find ways of reversing the downward trend in fertility rates without using any of the aggressive tactics that worked (to some degree) in the 1940s and *without even openly discussing* the goal of influencing fertility rates.

As a result of this constrained deliberative process, the steps the government took in the period immediately after the "1.57 shock" were tentative and ultimately ineffectual. The first policy package, the Angel Plan of 1994, focused narrowly on the goal of expanding child-care services. Replicating the model of the Gold Plans for the elder care services, it set specific targets for expanding child-care services: an increase in the number of spaces in child-care centres (especially for children aged 1–2); longer hours of service (so that parents would have an extra hour in the evening before they needed to pick up their children); and specialty services (sick child-care centres; weekend coverage). That there was pent up demand for child-care spots was clear, since many centres, especially in growing suburban areas of Tokyo and Kansai, had long

[9] Interviews with MHLW officials, April and May 2001. It seems that attitudes have changed (or have been over-ruled) since these interviews were conducted. In November 2006, the MHLW announced that it was going to set a fertility target of 1.4 and attempt to boost fertility to this level through a variety of policies (*Daily Yomiuri* 11 November 2006: 3).

[10] Interview with Chihoko Asada, May 9, 2001.

waiting lists. It was also clear that these expanded services would make life easier for working parents, and especially working mothers.[11]

What was not clear was whether these expanded services would have any impact on fertility rates. There was little deliberation about the relationship between this policy initiative and fertility behaviour, and fertility rates kept falling after 1994. By the time NIPSSR announced its new population projections in 1997, the total fertility rate had fallen to 1.39.

MHW officials gradually came to the realization that their efforts to address child-care service needs, by themselves, were not going to address the deeper causes of the declining fertility problem. Through discussions of the Council on Population Problems (*Jinkō Mondai Shingikai*), culminating in the publication of its analysis of the causes of declining fertility in 1997, policymakers came to realize that the roots of the problem lay in the structure of Japan's employment system, which imposed steep opportunity costs on working mothers (JMS 1997, Internet). Even with expanded child-care services and a program of child-care leave introduced in 1992, mothers of young children were finding it difficult to meet the expectations of their employers, but the system provided little room for such mothers to slow down or take a break while their children were young. If they quit or went part-time, they were likely to find it difficult ever to move back onto the career track since Japan's "lifetime employment system" continued to reserve the best jobs for young people hired right out of college or in their first years out of school. Neither did this system give these women's husbands much opportunity to help out at home. This basic incompatibility between the Japanese employment system and childrearing, the advisory council argued, was causing couples to have fewer children and turning off young women to the idea of marriage.

Michiko Mukuno, the MHW official who took the lead in overseeing the work of the *Jinkō Mondai Shingikai*, admits that government officials failed to grasp the extent of social change that would be needed to tackle the declining fertility problem when they began addressing the issue with the first Angel Plan.[12] Only after the publication of this commission's report, and the adoption of a more comprehensive approach to the declining fertility problem with the New Angel plan in 1999 and

[11] For details on the Angel Plans, see Schoppa 2006: 170–174.
[12] Mukuno is quoted in Kabashima (2000: 99).

the Plus One Plan in 2003, did the government begin putting in policies based on a clear *logic* linking them to increased fertility rates. The approach was also based on social scientific evidence which showed that fertility rates were higher in nations such as Sweden that imposed lower opportunity costs on working mothers. In the Swedish case, fertility rates went up after the state made child-care leave more generous.

The problem Japanese officials have confronted, in the years since they began putting in place policies based on this design, is that they are once again confronting powerful social and economic forces that lie behind the opportunity cost structure they blame for the steep fall in fertility rates. The government has attempted to make the Japanese employment system more accommodating for working parents by introducing a year of paid child-care leave (now compensated at a rate of 40 per cent of income), requiring firms to offer shorter hours and flex time to working parents of children under three, and further expanding child-care services, but it has been unwilling to challenge the broader structure of the lifetime employment system that makes moving in and out of careers so costly for Japanese women. The government's leave and flex-time programmes, moreover, have failed to challenge entrenched gender-role norms that cause *mothers* to claim most of the new benefits for working *parents*. The only attempt to push fathers to do more to help out at home was legislation passed in 2003 obliging employers to fashion "specific plans" for helping employees balance work and family lives. The Ministry of Health, Labour, and Welfare announced at the time this legislation passed that it hoped many firms would adopt plans encouraging fathers to take time off from work to spend time helping with newborns, but it betrayed its limited expectations by suggesting that it hoped *ten per cent* of fathers would take advantage of plans allowing fathers *five days* of leave after the child was first born (Schoppa 2006: 167). Even this degree of intrusion in employment practices was strongly criticized by employers' organizations.

Ten years after the *Jinkō Mondai Shingikai* revealed its strategy for boosting fertility rates by reducing the opportunity costs of motherhood, the state has so far had little impact on either opportunity costs or fertility rates. The proportion of mothers working full-time with young children is actually *down* since 1992. The proportion working part-time with young children has barely changed.[13] The number of

[13] See data cited in Schoppa (2006: 179).

fathers taking child-care leave is miniscule. In 2005, the total fertility rate fell to a new record low of 1.25.[14]

## 5. Conclusion

The history of the Japanese state's attempts to shape demographic trends makes it clear that Japanese officials care deeply about the size and structure of their population. They need people to man the Japanese military and the nation's industrial base and to pay the taxes needed to cover the government's fiscal commitments, but they also worry when the population has *too many* poor or old people that require large transfer payments and social services. The state has attempted to steer population trends between the shoals of too few and too many, making extraordinary efforts to influence demographics in wartime, after the nations' defeat, and since 1990. What we also see in this history, however, is the way social and economic forces and prior policies condition the degree to which the state is able to achieve its demographic objectives.

When it attempted to boost fertility rates through aggressive interference in birth control efforts of private citizens during the war, the Japanese state was able to temporarily increase birth rates, but only at the cost of burdening future efforts with memories of these very controversial interventions. After the war, in contrast, the state was able to accelerate the sharp reduction in fertility rates with very little backlash since it was working with social and economic forces that were compelling couples to control family size for their own reasons. In the most recent period, the state has had virtually no success in influencing fertility rates because it is working against powerful social and economic forces and a historical legacy that made explicit pro-natalism a taboo. Though the government eventually identified a relatively uncontroversial logic designed to boost fertility rates by reducing opportunity costs, it has been unable to shift policies that define the opportunity cost structure sufficiently to reverse the decline in birth rates.

[14] See data in *Daily Yomiuri* (11 November 2006: 3).

## References

Campbell, John C. (1992): *How Policies Change: The Japanese Government and the Aging Society*. Princeton: Princeton University Press.

*Daily Yomiuri* (11 November 2006): Government eyes fertility rate of 1.4 kids by 2050, p. 3.

Dower, John (1986): *War without Mercy: Race and Power in the Pacific War*. New York: Pantheon Books.

Gauthier, Anne Hélène (1996): *The State and the Family: A Comparative Analysis of Family Policies in Industrialized Countries*. Oxford: Clarendon Press.

Havens, Thomas (1975): Women and War in Japan, 1937–1945. In: *The American Historical Review* 80, 4 (October), pp. 913–934.

JMS (Jinkō Mondai Shingikai) (1997): *Shōshika ni kansuru kihonteki kangaekata ni tsuite* [Fundamental thinking on the low birth rate]. http://www1.mhlw.go.jp/shingi/s1027–1.html (found 17 November 2006).

Kabashima, Hideyoshi (2000): *Seifu wa musaku dattanoka* [Was the government without a policy?]. In: *Chūō kōron* 115, 13 (December), pp. 96–103.

NIPSSR (National Institute of Population and Social Security Research) (n.d.): *Selected Demographic Indicators for Japan*. http://www.ipss.go.jp/index-e.html (found 15 May 2006).

—— (2002): *Population Projections for Japan: 2001–2050*. http://www.ipss.go.jp/pp-newest/e/ppfj02/ppfj02.pdf (found 17 May 2006).

—— (2003): *Population Statistics of Japan, 2003*. http://www.ipss.go.jp/p-info/e/psj2003/PSJ2003.pdf (found 17 May 2006).

—— (2006): *Population Statistics of Japan, 2006*. http://www.ipss.go.jp/p-info/e/PSJ2006.pdf (found 17 May 2006).

Norgren, Tiana (2001): *Abortion Before Birth Control: The Politics of Reproduction in Postwar Japan*. Princeton: Princeton University Press.

Oakley, Deborah (1978): American-Japanese Interaction in the Development of Population Policy in Japan, 1945–52. In: *Population and Development Review* 4, 4 (December), pp. 617–643.

Schoppa, Leonard J. (2006): *Race for the Exits: The Unraveling of Japan's System of Social Protection*. Ithaca: Cornell University Press.

Suzuki, Kazue (1995): Women Rebuff the Call for More Babies. *Japan Quarterly* 42, 1 (January–March), pp. 14–20.

Taeuber, Irene B. (1956): Recent Population Developments in Japan: Some Facts and Reflections. In: *Pacific Affairs* 29, 1 (March), pp. 21–36.

Takahashi, Shigesato, Ryuichi Kaneko, Akira Ishikawa, Masako Ikenoue and Fusami Mita (1999): Population Projections for Japan: Methods, Assumptions and Results. In: *Review of Population and Social Policy* 8, pp. 75–115.

Ueno, Chizuko (1998): The Declining Birthrate: Whose Problem? In: *Review of Population and Social Policy* 7, pp. 103–128.

Whelpton, P. K. (1950): The Outlook for the Control of Human Fertility in Japan. In: *American Sociological Review* 15, 1 (February), pp. 34–42.

CHAPTER THIRTY-FIVE

# POLITICS OF OLD-AGE POLICY-MAKING

John Creighton Campbell

## 1. Introduction

This chapter will concentrate on three important areas: public pensions, medical care, and long-term care. By the turn of the millennium Japan's pension and health-care programs for older people had reached the standard of the rich nations.[1] In the field of long-term care it had become a world leader. Since the substance of ageing-society problems and Japan's policies are treated elsewhere in this volume, this chapter will concentrate on the policy-making process—in particular, the most important policy-change events over a fifty-year span. This process cannot be described either as a smooth and rational policy development or as a series of political clashes—in fact, it cannot be described in general at all. Periods of expansion alternated with periods of reform, and some policy changes were dominated by bureaucrats largely working behind the scenes, while others were much more open and political. Such differences in process inevitably had effects on the resulting policies.[2]

## 2. Building the Pension System: The 1950s

In the early 1950s, as Japan was emerging from the immediate post-war recovery and from being ruled by foreigners, problems of the elderly were hardly at the top of the policy agenda. Economic rebuilding and the political controversies about occupation reforms and the "reverse

[1] Under OECD definitions, in 2002 Japan spent 9.7% of GDP on old age and survivor pensions, long-term care insurance, and other direct services for the elderly other than medical care. In 2001, France and Germany spent 12.1%, Sweden 9.8%, the UK 9.2%, and the US 6.1% (IPPS 2006: 52). In medical care service levels are high and outcomes are excellent though spending is moderate. For more detail see chapters 58 and 60 in this volume.

[2] The approach to policy change, and most of the description and analysis up to 1990, is drawn from Campbell (1992).

course" were the main concerns. Even within the social policy domain, taking care of all the people left bereft or impoverished by the war was a persistent worry, while the toughest problem for the immediate future was what to do with the children of the post-defeat baby boom. Beyond immediate problems, public and officials shared the goal of building a Japanese "welfare state"—one component of the ubiquitous desire to catch up with the West.

The most important old-age policy developments of the decade were the reconstitution of the Employees' Pension System (EPS) in 1954, to cover workers in all but the smallest companies, and the creation of the National Pension System (NPS) in 1959, to cover everyone not covered by an employment-related pension. The processes of designing the EPS and the NPS were quite different. The two-year negotiations over EPS included powerful interests—notably big business, big labour, and the Ministry of Finance (MOF). The MOF's influence is seen in an unusual feature of the EPS, that it was supposed to be "funded"—twenty years of contributions were required before benefits would be paid, reflecting a concern for capital accumulation to finance economic growth. Despite the importance of the decisions reached there was not much public attention and the Ministry of Health and Welfare (MHW) was able to preside; political parties were not much involved.

Creation of the NPS, in contrast, was political from beginning to end. It was proposed as election slogan, "pensions for all" (*kainenkin*), by the conservative Liberal Democratic Party (LDP) to co-opt a perceived threat from the Japan Socialist Party (JSP) particularly in rural areas since most of the enrolees would be farmers. A leading role was played by Kishi Nobusuke, Prime Minister 1957–60, a conservative who believed in an activist state including social policy (Ōtake 1983). Important and difficult issues (who to cover, contributory or not, fixed benefits or not, how to cover women, etc.) had to be settled under a tight political deadline, with participation by politicians and pressure groups as well as MHW bureaucrats. Most of the latter were opposed to many aspects of the new plan but they were ineffectual amidst so much political pressure.

## 3. The High Growth Era

It is generally true that as countries get richer they spend a higher percentage of their income on social policy (Wilensky 1975). The level of expectation about what is needed for a decent life goes up, and so do the resources to finance higher benefits. In the 1960s GDP grew over 10 per cent a year, and social security spending grew even a little faster (IPSS 2006, Internet). However, policy change was more incremental than dramatic until the early 1970s. Spending increases mainly came from periodic improvements in pension and health-care benefits.

### 3.1. *Welfare services*

Yet a quiet development within the MHW portended major policy change in the future. Officials in the Social Affairs Bureau proposed a new "Welfare Law for the Aged" (*Rōjin Fukushi-hō*). The law was passed in 1963 and in the following year the Welfare of the Aged Division (Rōjin Fukushika) was established—it would gradually be expanded and elevated over the years to become the Health and Welfare Bureau for the Elderly.

Social welfare specialists in and around the MHW hoped to expand this narrow policy niche into a comprehensive and rational set of programs to provide both welfare and health-care services to the elderly. The official in the forefront of this effort was Ibe Hideo. Ibe had been in charge of the 1962 edition of the annual MHW White Paper (*Kōsei hakusho*), which featured the government's first extensive treatment of the "old-people problem" (*rōjin mondai*). He headed the Pensions Bureau for four years, where he brought about several incremental but substantial benefit increases, and in 1969 became head of the Social Affairs Bureau. Ibe's perception was that the Social Affairs Bureau should take responsibility for the elderly as a whole and their role in society, rather than just providing services to poor or sick old people as under the Welfare Law for the Aged.

To provide some solutions, in 1969 Ibe established a new high-powered advisory body on old age welfare. The final report, "Concerning Comprehensive Measures to Meet the Old People Problem," was approved and published by the group's parent body, the permanent Central Social Welfare Council, in November, 1970.

The report begins with a two-page preamble which discusses demographic trends, how far ahead foreign countries are, how economic growth has left serious "gaps" (*hizumi*) that the nation must think about, and the sad plight of Japanese old people—high suicide and accidental death rates, many on public assistance, many bedridden and people living alone. It points out that national policies so far have been inadequate.

This preamble is followed by 16 pages of detailed recommendations: five major headings (income, health, housing and institutions, in-home services, and research and training) with a total of 21 subheads and 75 new program ideas or specific reforms or expansions of existing programs. An appendix presented 76 statistical tables (CSFS 1970).

This report was soon overwhelmed by a political surge that took policy in quite a different direction.

### 3.2. *Free medical care*

Although everyone in Japan was covered by one or another health insurance system, good and readily available evidence demonstrated that older people were not getting the medical care they needed. For example, the MHW's annual surveys of patients were showing that people over 65 were three times more likely than younger people to get sick, but used medical facilities at only a slightly higher rate (YRKKI 1971: 225). Moreover, only 20 to 30 per cent of the elderly were taking advantage of the free medical examination program—asked why, many responded that if the doctor found something wrong, they couldn't afford the 30 to 50 per cent of medical bills they would have to pay (MacDougall 1975: 367).

While experts in and around the MHW were formulating their comprehensive services approach to older people's health-care needs, a more grass-roots movement was pushing a simpler and more radical solution. Sōhyō, the largest union federation, convened its first Central Conference of the Elderly in September, 1967, and one of its four top demands was that older people should get free medical care. In 1968, union-connected opposition Dietmen picked up on this idea and raised the issue of free medical care in the national Diet.

Health and Welfare Minister Sonoda Sunao replied quite positively and then at an old-age welfare convention in Tokyo, he declared

> I will risk my political fate to bring about medical care for the aged (rōjin iryō). Probably I will soon be leaving the Cabinet, but I know I can count on the cooperation of my colleagues from the Diet here today, so you all should rest assured [...] (KSRF 1974: 35).

Objections from both his bureaucratic subordinates and senior LDP politicians meant the idea did not go any further at the national level, but Tokyo Governor Minobe Ryōkichi said "If the national government won't do it, Tokyo will do it on its own" (*Asahi Shinbun* 27 August 1969: 1). Minobe, in his first term as the first progressive governor of

Japan's leading metropolis, was alert to popular issues which would sharply contrast his people-oriented administration with the conservative national government. He submitted a bill to the Metropolitan Assembly, which passed easily, and in December 1969, Tokyo began to cover all medical costs—that is, cover the 30–50% co-pay—for all its residents over 70 who could pass a rather lenient income test.

By spring of 1972 all but three of Japan's 47 prefectures (and quite a few cities besides) had passed some kind of measure to alleviate older people's medical bills. However, few localities had Tokyo's resources to support such a generous program; even though most of the new initiatives were more limited in coverage or benefits, the new costs soon led to pressure on the national government to take over.

It is safe to say that virtually no MHW official, and hardly any Dietmen in the LDP, really wanted to approve the extremely generous Tokyo-model program. However, pressure from public opinion and opposition parties meant that something would have to be done. In the end, the full Tokyo version of *rōjin iryōhi muryōka* [lit. no-fee-ization of medical charges for old people] was approved by the party, passed by the Diet in June 1972, and implemented at the start of 1973.

In one sense the free medical care initiative was anomalous in that is was considerably more generous than nearly any of the decision makers preferred. In another sense it was part and parcel of the explosion in overall government spending in the early 1970s. This was the climax of the super high growth period under Prime Minister Tanaka Kakuei. Along with his famous slogan of "reconstructing the Japanese archipelago," Tanaka dubbed 1973 as *fukushi gannen*, the "first year of the welfare era," which along with free medical care included the *goman'en nenkin*, meaning a hike in the "model" monthly benefit for the Employee Pension from ¥20,000 to ¥50,000 (note that not many were yet eligible for this benefit, but the small "welfare pension" that was still the most common was also raised, from ¥2300 to ¥5000).

## 4. Consolidation

The 1973 oil shock threw the Japanese economy into short-run turmoil, and cut the long-term growth rate in half. Tax revenues plummeted. Despite attempts to retrench in the 1974 budget, spending levels remained high and the budget went into the red. Although in fact social spending had not been a disproportionate share of the problem, the ambitious projects of the early 1970s, particularly the free medical care program that nearly all officials and politicians had disliked from the start, were an obvious target for blame.

However, no important change in policy toward older people occurred from the mid-1970s until 1982. It was not for lack of trying: the MOF and the MHW, backed by the political leadership, proposed cutbacks in free medical care on several occasions, and in 1979 a plan to reduce pension spending by raising the pensionable age from 60 to 65 got as far as cabinet approval but then was withdrawn from consideration in the Diet. The proximate cause of these failures was the unwillingness of the ruling LDP to support proposals to cut social spending coming from the bureaucracy or even their own leaders.

Why were LDP politicians unwilling? It was not that they had become enthusiasts for the welfare state, nor that they were getting pressured by powerful interest groups. They were simply afraid of voters. One point is that the late 1970s was the era of *hakuchū* or conservative-opposition near-parity in the Diet, meaning that the LDP's majority was precarious. Another is that the media attacks on the welfare state had not gotten much response from the general public, where the general sentiment was that social policy was still inadequate and should be strengthened.

What was wrong with the proponents? One key was indecision and confusion within the leadership of the MHW. Different bureaus disagreed too much to formulate a ministry-wide position, or no one paid enough attention to political strategies to get a proposal enacted. Another possibility never to be ignored was that no leader with sufficient talent and energy happened to be present.

There is a clear contrast with two successful reform proposals shortly thereafter. First was the Health Care for the Aged Law in 1982, which made "free medical care" not quite free by introducing small co-pay, and more importantly fixed the problems with financing. Second was a major pension reform in 1985 that trimmed future benefits and raised contributions a bit, fixed some (not all) of the problems created by the National Pension's bad design, and put the system on a more secure financial basis than earlier.

Changes in the political context held account for this change. The era of parity had ended with a big election victory for the LDP in 1980 (though it was partially reversed in 1983). Bureaucratic leadership is another important explanation. In fact, both successes were directly managed by individual bureau chiefs: Yoshimura Hitoshi for health-care reform and Yamaguchi Shin'ichirō for pension reform. These two men had been recognized as standouts in their fields within the ministry for at least twenty years, and they were masters of policy substance, political strategy, and perhaps most importantly the ways to generate consensus and enthusiasm within the ministry.

## 5. Back to Expansion: Caring for Frail Older People

The reforms of the 1980s, while substantial, were hardly a permanent solution to the "ageing society problem." Officials, conservative politicians, and experts of all stripes continued to worry and write about burdens on the economy in general and government spending in particular. But the broader political context had shifted. The sense of crisis generated by the administrative reform campaign had dissipated in the economic "bubble" of the late 1980s and the LDP was under attack—partly about scandals but mainly about taxes. A window of opportunity for expanding old-age policy opened.

One of the most influential actors here was MOF, which got three prime ministers to propose a new indirect tax. Ōhira and Nakasone tried in 1979 and 1987 but failed due to intense public reaction; Takeshita succeeded in late 1988. The MOF had several reasons for wanting a new consumption tax but it thought the most attractive argument for the general public was that the ageing society required more public revenue. In response, during the campaign for the summer 1989 Upper House election, the Socialists pointedly asked how the government planned to spend this new money on old people. In fact the LDP had increased spending on a few programs, but it really had no convincing response, which was one reason it lost the election and the JSP won.

Hashimoto Ryūtarō had resigned his post of LDP Secretary General to take responsibility for the election loss, but he was appointed Finance Minister in the next government. With his encouragement in fall, 1989, MHW officials started working overtime on a new set of proposals that were passed by the Cabinet in December as the "Gold Plan" or the "Ten-Year Strategy on Health and Welfare for the Aged" (*Kōreisha Hoken Fukushi Suishin Jūkanen Senryaku*). In televised debates during the election campaign, when opposition party members criticized the consumption tax, the LDP spokesman would bring up the Ten-Year Strategy to show how new revenues would be used to help the elderly.

The Gold Plan set concrete targets for expansions over ten years: for example, 30,000 to 100,000 home helpers, 200,000 to 500,000 nursing home beds, 1,000 to 10,000 adult day-care centres. Actually, the services were pretty much the same ones that old-age welfare officials and experts had been calling for since the 1970 "Comprehensive Measures" report—but now, instead of lower-level specialists trying (and failing) to get the attention of higher-ups, a top-level politician was reaching down for ideas he could use in an election campaign.

Some thought that Japanese preferred family care and would not welcome this intrusion of government into care giving, but the opposite was the case—people responded to the availability of services by demanding more, and the Gold Plan targets had to be revised upward in 1994. The problem was that rapidly increasing spending brought a threat of future tax hikes, and management was faltering as local governments tried to administer a broad program through structures designed to serve a small number of poor people. Standards for eligibility, oversight, and accountability were vague at best.

The MHW's answer was to create a new social insurance system, called *Kaigo Hoken* [lit. care insurance], so that much of the revenue could come from contributions rather than taxes, eligibility could be determined by objective test, and consumers could choose and evaluate the services they wanted.[3] Most of the key details were worked out behind the scenes, between July 1989 when the first MHW advisory committee on care giving was appointed, and March 1994 when its plans were first made public as the "welfare vision" report (Nichisōken 1997). From then to when Kaigo Hoken passed the Diet in 1997 the process was more open and indeed more political.

Political but fuzzy. Partisan politics were confused in this period—three different coalitions came into power and parties themselves changed their names and shapes. No political party opposed Kaigo Hoken though there were some different views. As to other groups, while social and fiscal conservatives carped about this welfare state expansion as a blow to traditional family values or as too expensive, they did not mount an effective attack.

Quite a few mayors were worried about the point that municipalities would become the insurers, a heavy new responsibility, and they raised

---

[3] See chapter 58 in this volume for information on how the program works. Eto (2000, 2001) and Talcott (2002) have the best accounts in English of the politics of establishing the system; Campbell (2002) contrasts it with German politics. A report from Nichisōken (1997) includes a detailed account of the early process by Masuyama.

many problems. The most publicized debate was whether to pay cash benefit for family caregivers (the pillar of the German system) or offer only formal services. The latter prevailed, partly because of an effective argument by feminists who defined the real care giving problem as oppression of women, particularly daughters-in-law. In fact, Keiko Higuchi and other leaders had started a lively association to agitate for better long-term care back in the 1980s, but the fact that—unusually for Japan—these feminist voices were well represented on official advisory committees hints that MHW officials favored this approach as well.

These conflicts along with political complications slowed the process of making the proposal into a bill to be submitted for over a year. Three factors finally led to success. One was that other politicians then allied with the LDP (particularly Socialists) were considerably more enthusiastic, and the issue became a factor in interparty horse-trading (Eto 2000). Another was effective organizational mobilization, by a cleverly named "Committee of ten thousand citizens to advance the socialization of care" (*Kaigo no shakaika o susumeru ichimannin shimin iinkai*) as well as women and mayors (Eto 2001). Most important was probably poll results that showed 70–80 per cent of the Japanese public in favour of the idea.

The scope and generosity of Kaigo Hoken gives Japan one of the most highly developed long-term care systems in the world—for example, more than double the size of the German program, the other major example of the social insurance approach. This is the first time that any aspect of the Japanese welfare state has been out in front of the world. Here it was politicians who brought about the expansion by sponsoring the Gold Plan, and bureaucrats who took the lead in making it work through long-term care insurance.

## 6. Reform Again After the Bubble

After the bursting of the economic bubble in 1990 tax revenues and social insurance contributions fell; even when the government wanted to spend more for economic stimulation it concentrated on public works. Fiscal conservatives saw social spending as out of control while free-market neoliberals thought government should back out anyway. Social policy retrenchment became a normal component of the verbal campaign for "reform" of practically everything (companies, labour markets, bureaucracies, political relationships, etc.) that became the hegemonic discourse of the political world in the 1990s and into the new millennium.

The impact on actual policy was more modest though not insignificant. In the health-care system, where spending on the elderly was a major concern, leaders talked of radical reform (*bappon kaikaku*) but actually settled for a series of restraints on public health insurance deficits such as higher co-pays and contributions. The MHW also chipped away at pension finance—for example, finally getting the future pensionable age hiked in steps to 65 (in 1994 for the National Pension and 2000 for the Employees Pension), raising contribution rates, adjusting pension formulas to restrain future benefits, and trying to get people who were not part of an employment-related pension plan to pay their premiums.

Another incremental reform was in Kaigo Hoken, stemming from its scheduled fifth-year review. The program had started smoothly and was quite popular with older people and their families, to the extent that spending was outrunning forecasts. Officials in the Ministry of Health, Labour, and Welfare (MHLW—it was amalgamated in 2001) identified the problem as big increases of eligible people in the lightest categories. Their solution was to create a new system called "preventive care" (*kaigo yobō*) with a lower level of services, which would save money and perhaps make the program less attractive to those without much need. It was also designed to reduce dependency and, at least as a *pro forma* goal, to lower frailty in the future.

Some of these incremental reforms in social policy engendered controversy, particularly battles over medical spending between the MHW and the Japan Medical Association (and its supporters in the LDP), but they mainly took place within accustomed channels without engaging heavyweight political forces. The Kaigo Hoken reform is a case in point: it represented a real reduction in available benefits, and so also of revenues for providers, but the opposition amounted to little more than a few rallies late in the process when the reform was already settled.

The exception to this pattern, and indeed an exception to the entire political history of Japanese policy toward the elderly, was the issue of pension reform in the early 2000s.[4] Pension policy became a bone of contention between political parties in the election campaign of 2003.

[4] The substance of the pension debate is covered in chapters 61 and 62; this brief account is mainly based on Yoshida, Guo and Cheng 2006.

A major plank in the pre-election platform or "manifesto" published by the opposition Democratic Party of Japan (DPJ) before the election campaign called for a radical restructuring of pensions, including unification of the system and covering the National (or "Basic") Pension benefits completely from tax revenues. In its own answering manifesto, the LDP argued that restructuring should be more moderate and the National Pension should continue as a social insurance system, in effect echoing the view of MHLW officials.

The clashes during the election campaign aroused interest still further, to the point that the 2003 campaign came to be called the "pensions election." Actually, it would be hard even for a pension expert to choose between the stated positions of the parties, and the concerns voiced by voters were mostly about their lack of trust in the system and their future benefits rather than any policy preference.

The DPJ did well in the election, but the LDP kept its majority and proceeded to introduce another rather incremental pension reform drafted by the MHLW in 2004. At this juncture the political system was further inflamed by a colourful if essentially irrelevant scandal about many prominent politicians who somehow had not paid their own National Pension premiums. The DPJ decided pensions were a good issue for a dramatic protest and walked out of Diet proceedings, so the government's bill had to be passed by forceful tactics.

The National Pension mess aside, Japan is basically in the same boat as all rich nations in trying to decide on the right balance between benefits for an expanding old-age population and premiums (or taxes) paid by the hard-pressed working population. The magnitude of the problem and the strong concern of the Japanese public mean that pensions will be high on the policy agenda for some time.

## 7. Conclusion

This account has traced the decision-making process for each of the major policy changes in pensions, health care, and long-term care, the three most important areas of public policy that explicitly target older people.[5] A few generalizations emerge. First, to refer to the main

[5] The elderly are of course much affected by policies that are not so specific, such as tax policy. There are also many specific programs that are not so important, such as for old-age employment (particularly interesting in Japan), education, recreation, and so forth. Many policy changes regarding the latter are described in Campbell (1992).

academic controversy about policy making in Japan, both bureaucrats and politicians have participated heavily. Second, the Ministry of Health and Welfare (MHW) and the majority opinion in the Liberal Democratic Party (LDP) have generally been in broad agreement (albeit often with different emphases), that Japan should have a welfare state up to Western standards, and that social programs must be sustainable in the sense of effective and not too expensive.

Third, their roles have been different: the major expansions of the welfare state have come at the initiative of politicians; bureaucrats have initiated smaller expansions, but often as not have been engaged in repairing or consolidating programs that had been pushed through by the LDP—"free medical care," the Gold Plan, and particularly the National Pension.[6]

Fourth, individuals have been more important than one might expect. Individual political entrepreneurs like Kishi, Sonoda (though he failed), Minobe, Tanaka, and Hashimoto were willing to make a bet that expanding old-people policies would give an advantage to their parties or themselves. And individual bureaucrats have played crucial roles too: Ibe as an entrepreneur promoting a new direction for the MHW, Yoshimura and Yamaguchi by taking charge of a difficult situation with energy and skill. Moreover, the lack of such leadership helps account for the ministries lacklustre performance in the late 50s and late 70s.

Fifth, actual conflicts between political parties have been rare. Politicians' motives generally have to do with securing an electoral advantage, typically by coopting an issue that opposition parties were even more enthusiastic about, but the only major partisan disagreement in this set of policy change processes was over pension policy in the 2000s—and even in the 2003 "pensions election" that was not really about clear-cut and fundamental issues.

This pattern may well not continue. All rich countries have been more in a retrenchment, reform or consolidation mode than an expansion mode for some time, and there have sharp clashes between political parties or even in the streets in Europe and the United States between

[6] One might argue that the failure to fix the National (or Basic) Pension over fifty years is partly due to the MHLW's commitment to the social insurance principle when covering it through taxes would seem to make much more sense. That could be due to the bureaucrats' attachment to the cushy postretirement jobs for managing the money, as suggested by Estevez-Abe (2006), or to ideology or sentiment.

those who want to dismantle various elements of the welfare state and those who want to preserve them. Whether and how that happens in Japan is the key question for future old-age policy making.

## References

*Asahi Shinbun* (27 August 1969): Kōseishō tsurenai shiuchi: To no rōjin iryō muryō keikaku [Action disdained by the Ministry of Health and Welfare: Tokyo's plan for free medical care for old people], p. 1, morning edition.

Campbell, John Creighton (1992): *How Policies Change: The Japanese Government and the Aging Society*. Princeton, N.J.: Princeton University Press.

—— (2002): How Policies Differ: Long-Term-Care Insurance in Japan and Germany. In: Conrad, Harald and Ralph Lützeler (eds.): *Aging and Social Policy—A German-Japanese Comparison*. Munich: Iudicium, pp. 157–187.

CSFS (Chūō Shakai Fukushi Shingikai) [Central Social Welfare Council] (25 November 1970): *Rōjin mondai ni kansuru sōgōtekina shisaku ni tsuite* [Concerning comprehensive policies for the old people problem]. Tokyo: CSFS.

Estavez-Abe, Margarita (2006): *Welfare and Capitalism in Postwar Japan*. New York: Cambridge University Press.

Eto, Mikiko Murase (2000): The Establishment of Long-term Care Insurance. In: Ōtake, Hideo (ed.): *Power Shuffles and Policy Processes: Coalition Government in Japan in the 1990s*. Tokyo: Japan Centre for International Exchange, pp. 21–50.

Eto, Mikiko (2001): Public Involvement in Social Policy Reform: Seen from the Perspective of Japan's Elderly-Care Insurance Scheme. In: *Journal of Social Policy* 30, 1 (January), pp. 17–36.

IPPS (2006): *The Cost of Social Security in Japan: Fiscal Year 2003*. http://www.ipss.go.jp/ss-cost/e/cost03/data/cost2003.pdf (found 6 January 2006).

KSRF (Kōseishō Shakaikyoku Rōjin Fukushika) (1974) (ed.): *Rōjin Fukushi no Jūnen no Ayumi* [The ten-year advance of old-age welfare] Tokyo: Rōjin Fukushi Kenkyūkai.

MacDougall, Terry (1975): *Political Organization and Local Government in Japan* (unpublished Ph.D. dissertation, Yale University)

Nichisōken (1997): *Kaigo hoken dōnyū no seisaku kettei katei* [Decision-making process for the introduction of Kaigo Hoken]. Tokyo: Nihon Ishikai Sōgō Seisaku Kenkyūjo.

Ōtake, Hideo (1983): Sengo hoshu taisei no tairitsu jiku [The axis of confrontation in the post-war conservative structure]. In: *Chūō Kōron* (April), pp. 137–51.

Talcott, Paul (2002): The Politics of Japan's Long-Term Care Insurance System. In: Conrad, Harald and Ralph Lützeler (eds.), *Aging and Social Policy—A German-Japanese Comparison*. Munich: Iudicium, pp. 89–138.

Wilensky, Harold (1975): *The Welfare State and Equality*. Berkeley: University of California Press.

Yoshida, Kenzo, Yung-Hsing Guo and Li-Hsuan Cheng (2006): The Japanese Pension Reform of 2004: A New Mode of Legislative Process. In: *Asian Survey* 46, 3 (May/June), pp. 381–400.

YRKKI (Yutaka na Rōgō no tame no Kokumin Kaigi Linkai) (1971): *Yutaka na Rōgō no tame ni* [For a rich old age] Tokyo: YRKKI.

CHAPTER THIRTY-SIX

# POLITICAL PARTIES IN AN AGEING SOCIETY

Paul Talcott

## 1. Introduction

The ageing society in Japan presents formidable policy challenges for the political system and the political parties in Japan. Coalition government (since 1994) makes the triangulation between party policies, voters, and policy problems even more complex. Political institutions and the policy process in Japan, however, have reduced the impact of broader internal party debates or policy discussions, particularly in recent years. The arena of policy has shifted strongly to the Office of the Prime Minister due to administrative reforms strengthening the cabinet structure of government and increasing emphasis on fiscal restraint. Moreover, the long-governing and increasingly successful Liberal Democratic Party (LDP) has only recently begun to make detailed campaign promises. As a result, policy emerges during the legislative process, not before, and is coordinated by the Office of the Prime Minister.

This chapter therefore explains the basic outlines of institutions and parties in Japanese politics (Section 1), how the electoral process works (Section 2), how the governing coalition and opposition parties develop policy (Section 3), the relative success of the LDP in recent elections (Section 4), the origin and development of the LDP and major opposition parties in the House of Representatives (Section 5), and their recent policy positions regarding policy in the ageing society (Section 6).

### 1.1. *Structure*

The 1947 Constitution establishes the Japanese Diet (House of Representatives and House of Councillors) as the highest political power. Within the Diet, the House of Representatives has power to enact legislation even over the objection of the House of Councillors.

### 1.2. *Governing coalition*

The LDP governed alone from 1955 until 1989, and in coalition with one or more smaller parties since then except for one ten-month period between 1993 and 1994. Since the landslide election of September 2005 the LDP controls nearly two-thirds of the seats in the House of Representatives, a feat unprecedented since 1986. This chapter focuses more on LDP party politics, but also features the coalition partner since 1999, the New Kōmei Party, which is vital for the governing coalition majority in the House of Councillors.

### 1.3. *Key opposition parties*

Two opposition parties also matter for current and future policy regarding demographic change: the Democratic Party of Japan (DPJ) and the Japan Communist Party (JCP). In the past, particularly in social policy, the LDP has picked up popular local initiatives from opposition parties in order to appeal in national elections to those who do not vote for them at the local level. Below the national level, JCP and DPJ have a large number of mayors, governors, and representatives on local councils and prefectural legislatures. The DPJ also has the most number of seats in the Diet after the LDP, and in future elections has the best chance of any opposition party to replace the LDP. Or, in keeping with recent reshuffling of political parties including the LDP, parts of the DPJ may rejoin the LDP. Therefore, the structure and policies of the JCP and the DPJ are also critical for the next directions of policy dealing with the ageing society.

### 1.4. *Japan as a dominant party democracy*

Japan has long been characterized as a dominant party democracy (Pempel 1989). Opposition party strategy failed spectacularly to capture the majority in the House of Representatives (HR) (Kohno 1997). Since 1989, the LDP has not had a majority in the House of Councillors (HC), and it has only occasionally had a majority in the HR. Only once has a coalition government formed without the LDP, from 1993–1994. Since 1994, all governments have been coalition governments led by the LDP. Other than the LDP and New Kōmei Party, the identity and composition of all other parties has changed dramatically due to splits, mergers, and failure to attract enough votes (Johnson 2000; Scheiner 2005). Other than the DPJ, no party or coalition comes close to rivalling the LDP since 1994. The election of August 2006 cemented the LDP with nearly 2/3 of the seats in the HR. The election of July 2007 for the HC will determine whether the LDP can regain a majority alone. Despite the loss of majority in the HC in July 2007, the LDP continues to set the agenda. The DPJ must, however, be consulted more closely than before. Part of the reason for the long stability of LDP power is its flexibility in policy that makes sudden and permanent reversals in direction quite common (Pempel 1998).

### 1.5. *Role of parties & politicians with respect to other sectors*

Although scholars of Japanese politics have debated vigorously about whether politicians or bureaucrats affect policy more, the change to coalition governments and the re-emergence of the dominant LDP have made the role of political parties more relevant than ever. While there is a considerable disagreement about who has the most influence over and/or the final say about the content of government policy, almost all research point to the same central arenas. Policy is made within and among political parties in party policy committees, coalition policy coordination committees, advisory councils within ministries (often more than one for the same policy), and advisory councils convened by the Prime Minister. In all of these venues, meetings among politicians, bureaucrats, lobbyists from the private sector, academic experts (some of which are independent) and occasionally nongovernmental organizations discuss major problems and a few alternative proposals to address them. The centre of gravity has shifted from the LDP and its internal policy process of the Policy Affairs Research Council (PARC) and its subcommittees to the Office of the Prime Minister.

### 1.6. *Party membership and composition*

Questions of policy concerning demographic change concern party elites, rather than the broader party membership. None of the major parties in Japan are mass-membership parties. Data on the composition of membership is available only at aggregate levels. In all major parties, leadership selection and policy positions almost always favour the preferences of Diet members or an executive committee, not the membership as a whole. Even the party trying to be a catch-all party, the LDP, has recently emphasized top-down reform from the Office of the Prime Minister. The consequence is that Diet members representing groups affected by demographic change, such as retirees, or women in the workforce, have fewer avenues to participate in the policy process through the LDP, or through the Diet at all.

1.6.1. *LDP*
The LDP has fewer than two million members in a population of nearly 130 million. There is no fixed rule about how party members count in party leadership selection or other decisions. For each election the party president (and the executive committee he appoints) sets the rules, which currently favour the votes of the Diet members (although somewhat less than before). As the leading member of the governing coalition, LDP party policy deliberation is closely linked with the cabinet policy process, described in section 3.3 below.

1.6.2. *New Kōmei Party*
The LDP's coalition partner since 1999, the New Kōmei Party, has 400,000 members. It has over 3,200 local, municipal and prefectural assembly representatives, and the third-largest Diet delegation (New Kōmei Party 2006). Party leadership is selected by an executive committee which also coordinates policy decisions directly.

1.6.3. *DPJ*
In September 2006, the DPJ had 239,238 individual members. At the local and prefectural levels, 1,915 elected officials belong to the DPJ (DPJ 2006, Internet). In leadership elections, Diet members get two votes, while the entire membership in each election district gets only one vote (a majority of the votes in the election district). Party policy is coordinated by the leadership in wide consultation with an array of civil society groups in addition to Diet members.

1.6.4. *JCP*
The long-time opposition Japan Communist Party has 400,000 members. It has over 3,800 local elected officials, but only 9 members in the HC and HR, all from proportional representation. Policy and party leadership are proposed by an executive committee and ratified by an annual Party Congress (JCP 2006).

## 2. How Do Parties Get Elected?

Demographic change affects the composition of the overall electorate. But election systems and election district rules determine a critical ratio for politics: the relationship between the number of votes a party receives and the number of seats it gets in the legislature. The multi-member district system in Japan in the HR until 1994 froze the demographic profile from the 1950s and made change difficult. In the ageing society, the current Japanese single-member district electoral system may directly benefit districts with relatively larger numbers of elderly people. These districts are typically rural. While the end of multi-member districts for HR elections in 1994 shifted the balance away from the overrepresentation of rural areas, and younger, urban areas received more seats, the House of Councillors and the proportional representation districts in HR still guarantee a large number of seats that do not reflect national changes. The 11 HR districts preserve some influence for the older, rural areas.

### 2.1. *House of Representatives*

In Japan until 1994, voters in 151 multi-member districts voted for one candidate by name. Up to six seats were elected for each district, based in part on population. Since gaining a majority of the seats in the Diet required winning more than one seat per district, members of the same party had to run against each other. LDP voters chose candidates based on highly personal connections in the community rather than on programmatic differences (Curtis 1983). The long-dominant Liberal Democratic Party was the first party to capture a majority without a coalition, since business leaders forced the outright merger of the Liberal and Democratic Parties in 1955. Election reform in 1994 replaced the multi-member district system with a two-part system of 300 single-member districts and 11 regional proportional vote districts with between 6 and 30 members. Initially there were 200 seats allocated by a second ballot from party lists for the proportional vote. In 1999, the number of proportional seats was lowered to 180. The transformation to single-member districts was expected to create a system in which two major parties competed on policy, rather than on personal characteristics such as the ability to bring home favours for constituents. Recent elections for the House of Representatives in September 2005 and September 2004 have featured new policy platforms, known as "*manifestos*" in Japanese, promising an overview of what parties will do if elected to office. Their existence is partly due to the proportional representation component in which 180 seats are allocated in 11 regions according to the share of the vote for a party. To get voters to write the party name on the party ballot, parties issue much clearer and more detailed outlines than ever before. The content of these manifestos regarding the ageing society is presented in Section 6. Complicating the picture of parties and policy is the longstanding and growing disaffection between voters and even the ruling party. Unaffiliated voters have long decided elections in Japan (Flanagan 1991) and since the 1990s have been a majority of all voters (Kabashima and Sugawara 2004).

### 2.2. *House of Councillors*

One-half of the members of the House of Councillors are elected every three years in a system that has changed much more than the system for the HR. The current system establishes prefectural election districts for each of the 47 prefectures with between 2 and 8 members depending on population. 149 of the members are elected through prefectural districts. A national list of 98 members is elected by proportional vote. There are two ways to cast a proportional ballot: by party name or by candidate name. The list allows opposition parties to win representation without winning in a single election district. In practice since 1989 the LDP has had to depend on a coalition to pass legislation in the HC. This allows non-LDP parties in coalition the ability to greatly affect the content of all policies, even though they have far fewer seats in the HR.

## 3. How Do Parties Develop Policy?

### 3.1. *Election of PM*

The first task of parties after an election in any parliamentary democracy is the selection of the prime minister. In Japan this must be done by a majority vote in both the House of Representatives and House of Councillors. If one party does not have a majority of seats, it may elect to form a coalition. This has been the case since 1993. Prime Ministers in Japan must be Diet members. They have come from three different backgrounds: senior civil servants who resign to run for office, party politicians from a provincial political background, and the sons and grandsons of former prime ministers or cabinet officials. Since 1947, all but three PMs (from August 1993 to January 1996) have been LDP Diet Members. Candidates for prime minister from the LDP must usually be the party president as well. Therefore an understanding of internal party politics is essential to understand how and why prime ministers are selected. Factional politics formed the basis for electing party presidents (and thus prime ministers) in the LDP from its formation in 1955 until at least the 2001 party president election (Iyasu 1996). Until campaign finance reform shifted donations from individuals to parties, and added a strong measure of public funding, individual politicians could gain support for their own election and power within the party policy organizations through factions which collected political contributions and then distributed them to other party members, individually or in groups. This competition escalated into routinized corruption by the late 1970s (Blechinger 1998; Schlesinger 1999). If the party president wins decisively, he can name all the top posts in the party after winning an election. If he has more mixed support, he must balance party leadership appointments across different groups which supported different candidates for party president. Party President and Prime Minister Shinzō Abe won with over two-thirds of the votes in the party, the same margin as his predecessor Junichirō Koizumi (April 2001–September 2006). Both used their advantage to not balance their appointments in party leadership among factions and instead focused on appointing only members of their own faction or outsiders.

### 3.2. *Cabinet ministers*

In addition to critical party leadership posts, the prime minister names ministers to head the ten Cabinet ministries. Depending on his internal strength within the party, he can appoint members of his own or allied factions, or must appoint members of rival factions to positions of leadership. Cabinet meetings approve all legislation for submission to the Diet. On all but rare occasions, the Diet then approves the legislation with only minor modifications. Cabinet ministers need not be elected members of the Diet (PM Koizumi made the first extensive use of non-legislators). Although previously they were informally expected to represent the views of the ministry to the cabinet, some ministers such as Naoto Kan in the Ministry of Health and Welfare in 1996–7 took a much more confrontational role, with dramatic consequences in the case of the HIV-tainted blood products scandal (Kan 1996). Currently ministers are expected to advocate the reform initiatives led by the PM in the ministries rather than represent the views of the ministries to the PM.

### 3.3. *Cabinet Office*

The Cabinet Office itself also expanded dramatically under reforms led by PM Hashimoto Ryūtarō and implemented in January 2001 (Connors 2000). A new range of appointments within this office are also available to the PM to carry out his preferred policies by loyal legislators. The question of the effectiveness of PM appointments within the Cabinet Office—which is staffed largely by bureaucrats on secondment from other agencies—reopens the old debates about the role of politicians and bureaucrats in general. Nevertheless, the new power of the PM to appoint directly mid-level officials, and assistant cabinet ministers, is more than before. Some of the new initiatives concerning demographic change originated with the Cabinet Office. For example, the new Council for Measures for Society with Decreasing Birthrate established in 2003 is chaired by the PM, and its members are the ministers of almost all the other ministries. These new offices and councils add to the complexity of coordination and development of policies to address demographic change. The official inter-ministerial coordination takes place through the Cabinet Office Vice Secretary (*Kambō Fukuchō-kan*). The tension between reform goals of the prime minister and the capacity to carry them out in the new institutional arrangements and even within his own party attract much criticism (Mulgan [2002] represents the most sceptical approach).

### 3.4. *Dissolving the Diet*

If the Prime Minister fails a vote of no confidence in the HR, he and the Cabinet must resign and a new election is then called. The PM may also dissolve the HR whenever he deems it necessary. This gives the PM power to discipline critics within his party or take advantage of high popularity. PM Koizumi used this power in August 2005 to thwart members of his party opposed to the partial privatization of the Japan Post Office and Postal Savings Bank that had been central to the support base of LDP Diet members in rural areas in the HR, and in the proportional list part of the HC (on postal privatization see chapter 44). Although it was argued that older voters would be negatively affected by postal reform, the LDP won in all demographic groups and in all kinds of districts, and also won the proportional vote.

### 3.5. *Parliamentary Committees*

The ruling coalition or party must appoint the leadership and membership of committees in the Diet. These committees must approve or modify Cabinet legislation before submitting it to the general body for approval. With a certain number of co-sponsors, Diet members can initiate their own legislation without going through the Cabinet. The main sponsors will usually bring the bill through the committee on which they serve. Ideally, the relevant ministry is agreeable to the legislation in question. The brain-death law to allow and regulate organ transplants in 1997 was one example of Diet-sponsored legislation relevant for the ageing society. The opposition coalition members have few tools in committee other than delay, but a few technicalities make it possible to stop votes by grabbing the microphone, rushing the podium to prevent the chair from taking a vote, or barricading the doors to prevent a quorum from taking a vote. These delay tactics have developed a counter-tactic by the ruling coalition: cash contributions to opposition party organizations (Krauss 1984). The role for these committees is usually limited to minor modifications. Real power over the content of policy lies in the party review committees and the governing coalition councils.

### 3.6. *LDP Policy Affairs Review Council*

Under LDP dominant rule until 2001, the party review took place first, in the Policy Affairs Review Council (PARC), so the role of legislative committees was limited to raising issues pressed by the relevant interests dissatisfied by the results of party review. Policy experts (*zoku giin*) shepherded through key legislation affecting their long-time donors, and could expect to be committee chairs both in PARC and in the legislature after enough years of service (Inoguchi and Iwai 1987). PM Hashimoto Ryūtarō developed this system all the way to the party presidency and the prime ministership. Under the new PM-centred policy system, set up under PM Koizumi in 2001, party experts, political appointees, and committee chairs are supposed to carry out Cabinet Office-set policy, not the other way around. The new system is argued by proponents such as Eisuke Sakakibara (2003) to be more transparent and efficient. Critics maintain that it is less democratic by removing lower-level input.

### 3.7. *Policy deliberation in other parties*

New Kōmei Party develops policy through an executive committee which develops recommendations in consultation with elected representatives at the national, prefectural, municipal, and town/village levels. New Kōmei Party is concentrated in urban areas. The DPJ develops policy in a "shadow cabinet." Each "shadow minister" develops policy proposals in reaction to existing policies and proposals from the governing coalition. A wide variety of non-profit organizations participate in formal and informal DPJ policy development. The DPJ has party organizations in some but not all election districts in both urban and rural areas. The JCP develops policy in accordance with the Leninist principle of democratic centralism through the Executive Council of the Central Committee, the twice-yearly Central Committee meeting and the bi- or tri-annual Party Congresses. The JCP has the most party-centred organization at all levels including many directly-affiliated unions and health-care providers in the public health and welfare sector.

## 4. Major Governing and Opposition Political Parties Overview

The LDP governed alone until 1989 and in coalition since 1989 with the exception of a ten-month period from July 1993 to May 1994. The share of seats in the HR since 1994 for parties have fallen dramatically for parties other than the LDP and the various combinations of catch-all opposition parties formed from former opposition parties and pieces of the LDP. Non-LDP losses in the HR are greater than those in the HC and in the single-member districts. Complicating the picture from 1994–1999 were the four times that the prime minister changed without an election due to additions, subtractions, and replacements in the coalition. The ruling coalition has been stable since the LDP, the New Kōmei Party and the Conservative Party formed a new governing coalition in 1999. The Conservative Party dissolved in 2004 and its four members joined the LDP. Tables 1 and 2 below show the share of seats in the HR and HC in the past three elections for the parties currently in existence.

Table 1. Seats in House of Representatives after elections (2000–2005).

| Seats in HR after elections (480 total) | LDP | New Kōmei Party | DPJ | Other (includes independents) |
|---|---|---|---|---|
| 2005 | 296 | 31 | 113 | 40 |
| 2003 | 237 | 34 | 177 | 32 |
| 2000 | 233 | 31 | 127 | 89 |

Source: Nikkei Net 2003; Nikkei Net 2005.

Table 2. Seats in House of Councillors after elections (1998–2004).

| Seats in HC after elections (total) | LDP (includes New Conservative Party) | New Kōmei Party | DPJ (includes New Green Breeze Party) | Other (includes independents) |
|---|---|---|---|---|
| 2004 (247) | 113 | 24 | 82 | 24 |
| 2001 (247) | 116 | 24 | 61 | 46 |
| 1998 (252) | 105 | 24 | 56 | 67 |

Source: Asahi Shinbunsha 1999; House of Councillors 2006.

## 5. Origin and Constituency of Major Political Parties

The political positions of parties in Japan have developed interdependently between the dominant LDP and the many opposition parties. Coalitions and rivalries among parties (and factions within parties) have shifted much more than any change in the basic constituencies, policy positions, and party leadership. The basic dynamic in governing coalitions since 1993 has been splits within the LDP and subsequent recruitment back into the party. The flexible strategy of the LDP in reaching out to former Diet members has thus proved catalytic in changing the governing coalition frequently without a general election (Curtis 2000). Since 1999 the coalition between New Kōmei Party and the LDP has remained unchanged. Unless the LDP wins a majority in the Upper House in 2007, or can persuade former members now belonging to the DPJ to return, a coalition with New Kōmei Party will continue, even as the LDP maintains a nearly two-thirds seat majority in the Lower House after the stunning Koizumi victory in September 2005.

The implications for the ageing society of the nature of party politics in Japan are complex. On the one hand, elderly voters have a far greater role, and have traditionally voted overwhelming for the LDP.

Moreover, the elderly are far more likely to turn out than voters of other age cohorts. At the same time, political scientists disagree about whether the elderly have fundamentally different preferences about policy than do younger people (Binstock 2000). Nevertheless, the New Kōmei Party has gone further than other parties in promoting the protection of low-income elderly, particularly on the issue of financing of long-term care insurance and exceptions for new health-care surcharges (Talcott 2002). As long as the LDP does not succeed in a simple majority (plus the extra seats needed to conduct smooth parliamentary business) in the Upper House, the strong policy preferences and fixed constituency of New Kōmei Party will continue to dominate policy towards the elderly. Critical issues approaching in 2007 include reform of the long-term care insurance system, implementation of the new health-care insurance system for the elderly over 75, and details of the privatization of the postal life insurance and savings system.

The complication for political parties in Japan, including the LDP, is that an ever-rising number of voters support no particular political party (Kabashima and Sugawara 2004). Furthermore, none of the major parties (other than Japan Communist Party) are mass membership parties. The opposition party with the best chance to take over if the LDP loses, the DPJ, has a combination of very different kinds of constituencies due to its origin combining social democratic and neo-liberal reformist politicians. The next section presents a snapshot of the origins and politics within each major party, focusing primarily on the LDP.

### 5.1. *LDP*

The Liberal Democratic Party formed when business donors forced a merger of the Liberal Party and the Democratic Party in 1955 to fend off the rising threat of a Japan Socialist Party victory. Since 1955 the LDP has attracted a decreasing share of the vote but a constant majority of seats in both houses of the Diet until 1989. After September 2005 it has nearly a two-thirds majority in the House of Representatives but needs a coalition partner to assure a majority in the House of Councillors. The Upper House election in July 2007 will test whether the LDP regains its role as the dominant party in both houses. The primary commitments in the LDP are to economic growth, anti-communism, and social order. In foreign policy the Japan-U.S. alliance takes centre stage, along with assurance of the supply natural resources of which

Japan has very few, particularly oil. As a political party, its domestic interests focus on staying elected, in part to assure the stability of the Japan-U.S. security treaty. Until 1994, the major opposition parties based their programmes on removal of Japan's Self Defence Forces and ending security cooperation with the United States. Domestic policy, including policies affecting demographic change, turned 180 degrees on several occasions, in an effort to stay elected. Opposition from business interests to public pensions gave way to an expanding effort to woo elderly voters, beginning with programmes for war veterans and their families, whose association is still central to becoming elected as LDP party president. Initial objections to pilot projects in communist-governed cities to provide free care for the elderly in the 1960s, and very young children in the 1990s, were later taken up enthusiastically in an effort to reach new voter groups (and reduce the appeal of non-LDP parties in local as well as national elections). Employer-based health insurance was expanded dramatically to cover all citizens. Long-term care insurance programs were designed to socialize care and change the role of women in the family from the default caregiver (Eto 2001), a shift which many LDP members opposed directly due to its conflict with what they considered to be core elements of Japanese tradition.

Prior to campaign finance reform in 1994, and party voting reforms in 2001, factional (*habatsu*) politics mattered greatly for distribution of party and cabinet positions. Within the LDP, the basic dynamic pitted a mainstream faction against an anti-mainstream faction (Muramatsu and Krauss 1987). The Tanaka/Takeshista/Hashimoto faction competed against a changing constellation of several anti-mainstream factions to attract members by providing campaign finance and other electoral assistance in return for voting for faction leaders as party president (who would then become Prime Minister). Certain factional bosses were also policy bosses (*zoku giin*) who served as brokers or gatekeepers for new policies or reforms in certain areas, including pensions, labour, health care, and care for the elderly. Many observers predict a demise of factions once their main functions of spreading money and offices have ended. Moreover, as policy shifts away from party members to the party leadership, the role for factional bosses as gatekeepers of policy areas has diminished. But recent events in the choice of party leadership and cabinet officials, and the continuing affiliation of old and new Diet members with factions (always identified in newspaper coverage), suggest that the role of factions may be changing rather than ending altogether. After 2001, the Mori faction, the leading anti-mainstream faction, dominated the assignment of party and cabinet positions, even naming non-politician experts instead of mainstream faction members to key cabinet positions. Prime Minister Abe has continued the direction of non-accommodation, shutting out the former mainstream faction entirely from senior party positions as well as most cabinet roles.

Conflict and reversal of direction for electoral expedience illustrates both the real tensions of different visions of the role of the party within the LDP but also the long tradition of a palliative effect of reversals that bring new voters to the party. Such conflict within a catch-all party is not unusual, but it means that the groups within the party have the potential to coalesce into institutional structures that reinforce conflict across a broad range of issues. Since the first schism within the LDP in 1976, and more damaging in 1993 which led to the loss of the majority in the HR, these disagreements also have the potential to threaten the primary goal of the LDP which is to remain the majority party. At the same time, the ideological flexibility and vagueness of the party program allows it to attract a wide range of voters. Some analysts attribute the vagueness to old features of the electoral system (discussed above) that pitted candidates of would-be majority parties against each other in the same multi-member electoral district. Since 1994 the introduction of single-member districts was supposed to have ended this policy vagueness and produced sharper policy contrasts. But the main focus on winning election in an environment where the number of non-aligned voters keeps rising provides another incentive to maintain vagueness and flexibility rather than sharp policy distinctions: maximizing the potential vote on election day by deciding policies at the last minute rather than far in advance.

### 5.2. *New Kōmei Party*

The New Kōmei Party (formerly Kōmeitō Clean Government Party) started in 1964 as an offshoot of a lay Buddhist movement, the Sōka Gakkai. Almost all of the voters and most of the party leaders are members of the Sōka Gakkai, but some prominent celebrities and academics have been invited to run under the party ticket for the House of Councillors, such as former Minister of the Environment Hiroko Wakamatsu, and Akira Matsu (the stage name of Reiko Nishikawa from the all-female Takarazuka Revue). The Sōka Gakkai is based in urban areas among workers and salaried employees in small and medium-sized firms, particularly in Tokyo, Kanagawa Prefecture, and

Aichi Prefecture. Its votes are reliable and vote totals for New Kōmei Party candidates track closely the number of Sōka Gakkai members (and their relatives) in a district (Hori 1999: 195). Since New Kōmei Party joined the coalition with the LDP in 1999, in several HR districts the LDP has agreed not to run a candidate against a New Kōmei Party incumbent, instead encouraging its voters to vote for the New Kōmei Party candidate (and the LDP for the party ballot). In the area of policy affecting demographic change, New Kōmei Party policies focus on protecting the weak and vulnerable: the elderly, children, women, and particularly low-income groups within these categories.

### 5.3. *DPJ and its predecessors*

The DPJ is an amalgam of several former parties and newly elected representatives (Köllner 2004). The main groups consist of former Social Democratic Party of Japan (SDPJ) members and Liberal Party members many of whom split from the LDP in 1993. Other conservative lawmakers who left the LDP in 1993 moved through several smaller parties before joining the DPJ in 1998. Within the DPJ, which formed as a fusion of several smaller and diametrically opposed parties, factional politics pits conservative reformers such as Ichirō Ozawa and Yukio Hatoyama against progressive (left-wing) NGO leaders Naoto Kan and former SDPJ members. Rapid success in recent elections has led to the election of a new generation of Diet members without direct affiliations, but the leadership remains in the hands of the veterans of other parties. The DPJ runs candidates in almost every electoral district. The DPJ has an ambitious program of policy reforms at every level of Japanese government, and has attracted much of the energy of the previous opposition parties along with new efforts at reform at the grass-roots level networking with civil society organizations.

### 5.4. *JCP*

The Japan Communist Party was long supported as part of the international communist movement by the Soviet Union. In recent years the party has made efforts to distance itself from calling for nationalization of industries and a dictatorship of the proletariat in its official party constitution. In local politics it campaigns on an image of clean politics and policies supporting families with generous tax-financed benefits. The JCP has a policy of running candidates in every district regardless of the likelihood of success. Since almost none of these candidates win, some efforts have been made to develop Italian-style cooperation between the JCP and other opposition parties. So far the practice of excluding the JCP from any cooperation or coalitions, even among the opposition, has persisted.

## 6. Party Platforms Regarding Demographic Change

Since the policy process winds through several stages before a final decision, political platforms are only one part of the analysis of the origins of policy for demographic change. Coalition government makes party platforms of smaller parties more important than in single-party governments, not because they are a roadmap to a complete policy, but because they indicate some of the limits that will be more difficult to push if policy is to change directions radically. In this case, the power of the small coalition partners is enormous, not to design entire policies, but to stop even strongly-held platform positions of the dominant LDP. The most concrete example of New Kōmei Party success as a small coalition partner is the insertion of provisions protecting low-income elderly in health insurance reforms since they joined the coalition in 1999.

Opposition party platforms matter, even in a parliamentary democracy. The opposition DPJ is in a position to make compromises and appear pro-reform by making agreements to cooperate even while in opposition. This lends legitimacy to the credibility of DPJ as a potential governing party, and even opens the opportunity to take credit for popular policies enacted while they are in opposition. In 1997 the DPJ signed an agreement over the course of health insurance policy that smoothed the way to reforms in the late 1990s. The negative example is the pension reform of 1999, which the DPJ boycotted throughout the policy process, refusing to attend Diet committee hearings, physically obstructing the chair when he declared committee approval by a majority vote, and storming the podium during the plenary session that ended up passing the legislation only after a major police presence restored just enough order to read the decision aloud.

The coalition agreement itself commits the LDP and New Kōmei Party to address the challenged of demographic change and names a wide range of policies but does not address specific targets or goals or plans. Given that the entire original document is a four-page outline, this lack of detail is not surprising. The key coordinating body, the

Coalition Policy Coordination Council, meets at the very late stages of the legislative process. The individual party platforms are somewhat more inclusive of targets, goals, and specific proposals, and are presented below.

### 6.1. *LDP*

As the governing party, the LDP strives to develop policy that meets a wide range of needs, including solving the problems raised by demographic change. The budget drives some of the policy process (Campbell 1977), particularly when shortfalls in pensions, health care, and long-term care insurance programs require new measures for funding in the short or long term. The search for sustainable financing drove most of policy change since the LDP returned to the governing coalition in 1994. Major reforms of the pension system such as in 1999 have increased contribution rates and reduced pension benefits for the future. Major health-care insurance reforms raised the out-of-pocket costs to be equal across programs that formerly were cheaper for large company employees and their families. Long-term care insurance was created in 1997 in part to remove certain costs from the health-care system and create open-ended cost-sharing instead of closed-ended cost sharing in the health insurance system. All of these major policies went through a series of iterations as they moved their way through the policy process before arriving at these final positions. Since the LDP is the governing party, it is difficult to identify simple policy preferences for the LDP. Adding to the difficulty in identifying a single party position is the increasing role of expert committees convened by the Prime Minister, displacing the input from party policy committees. The job of Diet members is now to ratify decisions of the Prime Minister rather than to provide input at each stage.

Strong parts of the party remain committed to traditional views of the family and the role of women as caregivers rather than full participants in the workforce. Major efforts to socialize the burden care such as long-term care insurance are possible only insofar as they meet other goals such as cost-saving. The primary LDP policy priority affecting all decisions about policy addressing demographic change is to limit the costs to citizens (and businesses) of social security contributions and taxes. The principle of minimizing the "social burden" (*kokumin futan*) of all government programs overrides other goals such as providing a set of specific services to individuals with greater needs. This priority fits with the longstanding interest of the LDP in promoting economic growth first, then distributing the benefits of growth later. A major effort in 2006 in the Council on Fiscal and Economic Reform is underway to revisit all social security systems with this goal in mind.

### 6.2. *New Kōmei Party*

The New Kōmei Party models itself as the party for people other than big business and union members. As such it has a broad range of proposals for improving conditions for those left out, such as the elderly, children, and women. Gender equality is another strong commitment of the party, and proposals to improve it include human rights education in schools, greater attention to employment of more women in the judicial system, and to increase the number of women in politics. In its election manifesto for 2006, New Kōmei Party proposes a range of policies to achieve a "children first" society to address the causes of demographic change that have led to the first-ever absolute reduction in the Japanese population in 2005. Its policy proposal focus on improving labour force participation, promoting investment in research, better urban development, and mitigating growing social inequality. New Kōmei Party is committed to improving the workforce participation rate of women through policies to help balance child-raising and work. In addition, they urge increasing workforce productivity by creating expert innovator groups of older workers to advise younger workers, to transfer the skills and optimism from the "*monozukuri*" generation that built Japan's post-war success. The election manifesto also identifies the growing imbalances between different social groups (*kakusa shakai*) and urges the investment of sufficient resources in urban areas to make up for years of neglect in the post-war system of subsidies that benefited primarily rural areas. Moreover, growing concentrations of the elderly in urban areas need to have more facilities and programs available to ease their transition out of the workforce and into the community. For health-care insurance and long-term care insurance, New Kōmei Party focuses on the need to balance the growing costs fairly across generations, but acknowledges that individual contributions will need to be raised, and the age of contribution for long-term care insurance will have to be lowered. A new programmatic emphasis on prevention and lifestyle adjustment should help to reduce the growth of the demand for health care. Pension policy analysis focuses exclusively on the ability to sustain the current system by maintaining an average rate of economic growth above 1.39 per cent per year until 2050, rather than on the details of particular pension programs. The focus on sustainable financing of social policy, overall economic growth, and productivity increases fits well with most of the LDP policy directions. The tone about addressing imbalances between rural and urban areas, and mitigating social inequality, goes beyond the LDP commitment to minimizing permanent social inequality.

### 6.3. *DPJ*

The major initiatives with the DPJ focus on streamlining central government and increasing direct cash benefits for families with children. The DPJ favours merging all public pension plans, ending the divided system that benefits civil servants and company employees more than any other citizens. The DPJ proposed in 2005 a child benefit system of 16,000 yen per month payments per child. Other DPJ initiatives that have not been taken up in the legislature include a draft law for prevention of violence against the elderly in nursing homes. On almost every policy proposal from the government, the DPJ has a counter-proposal that seldom is reflected into the final policy. Despite serious attempts, such as the Cancer Basic Law proposal in spring 2006, without a legislative majority there are few possibilities for the DPJ to propose policies. Otherwise it is possible to stall legislative business completely through obstructing normal procedures necessary to pass legislation, which raises the costs in terms of time to consider other important legislation. This option was tried in 1999 to block pension legislation but failed. In 2006 DPJ Diet members did not attend the session that approved health-care reform legislation. If the DPJ can win enough seats in the HC election, it can affect the content of policy more strongly. Conversely, if the LDP wins the next HC election and gets a simple majority, the relative influence of the opposition parties and even coalition partners will be much smaller.

### 6.4. *Japan Communist Party (JCP)*

The other parties currently in the Diet are not in a position to affect policy directly, and have too few members to block legislative action indirectly. Although the JCP has only 9 seats currently in the HC and HR respectively, at the local level, however, there are thousands of municipal assembly representatives and some mayors. If decentralization takes place as scheduled in the next five years in Japan, the JCP stands to gain much more influence over local policy. Moreover, several closely affiliated unions of civil servants are active in all ministries, but also in service provision in the health and welfare sector. The JCP positions itself as an advocate for citizens in expanding the role of social policies funded through taxation, particularly corporate taxes and income taxes. In the 2005 election they called for a basic minimum pension of 50,000 yen monthly financed entirely through taxes. They opposed major revisions to the health-care system that would raise costs to patients and their families, including the reclassification of hospital wards with primarily long-term care patients (who paid a maximum monthly amount set by the medical care insurance system) into long-term care system nursing homes with unlimited cost-sharing. Without a legislative majority and with no party willing to add the JCP to its coalition, the only effect that the JCP at the national level can have is to ask provocative questions during Diet sessions based on embarrassing internal information passed on from its affiliated public sector unions in the ministries and public organizations such as the hospitals.

## 7. Conclusion

Demographic change in Japan has affected political parties tremendously. Party platforms and policies have changed to deal with problems raised by the ageing society. The process of change has not taken place through the rise of new parties or new policies from opposition parties. Changes in society and policy challenges are not easily converted into changes in the direction of policy, or of the parties elected to government, due to the nature of parties, electoral rules, and the top-down policy process. Furthermore, given the very low membership in parties and the limited input for non-Diet members in policy, changes take place at the elite level not at the level of the membership. Party policy platforms in recent elections address some of the components of demographic change, but people vote on very general understandings of reform rather than on single issues or policy areas. As a result, pensions, family policy, health insurance, long-term care insurance, and workforce policies have changed but not due to the replacement of one party with another. The policy processes have shifted, with more weight placed on decisions of committees convened by the Prime Minister directly, and a somewhat diminished role for LDP party committee chairs, but the general policy-making system remains detached from legislative politics, taking place in a zone where coalition party officials, ministry officials, academic experts, business representatives, and some non-governmental organizations contend and compete for reforms that benefit their own organizations, their members, and/or some vision of the common good. Therefore any changes in policy to address demographic change will result from only changes in the policies preferred by the elites within the governing coalition. At the same time, it is important to remember that the political structure and nature of political parties in Japan does not rule out the opportunistic adoption of policies from the opposition. The key actor, however, is the governing coalition, and increasingly the Prime Minister and his advisors, rather than the broader party or its membership.

## References


Asahi Shinbunsha (1999): *Japan Almanac 2000*. Tokyo: Asahi Shinbunsha.

Binstock, Robert (2000): Older People and Voting Participation: Past and Future. In: *Gerontologist* 40, 1, pp. 18–31.

Blechinger, Verena (1998): *Politische Korruption in Japan: Ursachen, Hintergründe und Reformversuche*. Hamburg: Institut für Asienkunde.

Campbell, John (1977): *Contemporary Japanese Budget Politics*. Berkeley: University of California Press.

Connors, Lesley (2000): Next Steps for Japan: Administrative Reform and the Changing Polity. In: *Asia Pacific Review* 7, 1 (May), pp. 107–130.

Curtis, Gerald (1983): *Election Campaigning Japanese Style*. Tokyo: Kodansha International.

—— (2000): *The Logic of Japanese Politics*. New York: Columbia University Press.

DPJ (Democratic Party of Japan) (2006): *2006-nen 9-gatsu daihyō senkyō no yūkenjasū ni kan suru kōkoku* [Press release about the number of voters in the September 2006 election of representatives], September 5, 2006. http://www.dpj.or.jp/news/dpjnews.cgi?indication=dp&num=8982 (found 17 January 2007).

Eto, Mikiko (2001): Women's Leverage on Social Policymaking in Japan. In: *PS: Political Science and Politics* 34, 2 (June), pp. 241–246.

Flanagan, Scott (1991): *The Japanese Voter*. New Haven, Conn.: Yale University Press.

Hori, Yukio (1999): *Kōmeitō ron: sono kōdō to taishitsu* [The study of the Kōmei Party: its activities and nature]. Tokyo: Nansōsha.

House of Councillors (2006): *Kaiha-betsu shozoku giin sū* [Number of councillors listed by Faction]. http://www.sangiin.go.jp/japanese/joho1/kousei/kaiha/giinsu.htm (found 23 November 2006).

Inoguchi, Takashi and Tomoaki Iwai (1987): *Zoku giin no kenkyū: jimintō seiken wo gyūjiru shuyaku tachii* [Research on "Policy Tribes": The Dominant Players in the LDP Government]. Tokyo: Nihon Keizai Shinbunsha.

Iyasu Tadashi (1996): Jimintō no habatsu [LDP Factions]. In: Nishikawa, Tomokazu and Junichi Kawada (eds.): *Seitō habatsu: hikaku seijigaku kenkyū* [Party Factions: Comparative Politics Research]. Tokyo: Minerva Shobō, pp. 133–218.

Japan Communist Party (2006): *What Is the JCP? A Profile of the Japan Communist Party*. http://www.jcp.or.jp/english/2006what_jcp.html (found 23 November 2006).

Johnson, Stephen (2000): *Opposition Politics in Japan: Strategies Under a One-party Dominant Regime*. London, U.K.: Routledge.
Kabashima, Ikuo and Taku Sugawara (2004): Prospects of a Two-Party System in Japan. In: *Japan Echo* 31, 1 (February), pp. 33–38.
Kan, Naoto (1996): *Nippon daitenkan* [Japan's great transformation]. Tokyo: Kobunsha.
Kohno, Masaru (1997): *Japan's Postwar Party Politics: A Microanalytic Reassessment*. Princeton, N.J.: Princeton University Press.
Köllner, Patrick (2004): Factionalism in Japanese political parties revisited or How do factions in the LDP and the DPJ differ? In: *Japan Forum* 16, 1 (March), pp. 87–109.
Krauss, Ellis (1984): Conflict in the Diet: Toward Conflict Management in Parliamentary Politics. In Krauss, Ellis, Thomas P. Rohlen and Patricia Steinhoff (eds.): *Conflict in Japan*. Honolulu: University of Hawaii Press.
Mulgan, Aurelia George (2002): *Japan's Failed Revolution: Koizumi and the Politics of Economic Reform*. Canberra: Asia Pacific Press.
Muramatsu, Michio, and Ellis Krauss (1987): The Conservative Policy Line and the Development of Patterned Pluralism Model. In: Yamamura Kōzō and Yasukichi Yasuba (eds.): *The Political Economy of Japan, Vol. 1*. Stanford, Calif.: Stanford University Press, pp. 516–54.
New Kōmei Party (2006): *Basic Information*. http://www.komei.or.jp/en/about/index.html (found 22 November 2006).
Nikkei Net (2003): *2003-nen shūgiin senkyo tokushū* [Special Report on 2003 House of Representatives Election]. http://www.nikkei.co.jp/flash3/election-after/ (found 17 November 2006).
—— (2005): *Shūgiin senkyo supesharu 2005* [Special Report on 2005 House of Representatives Election]. http://www.nikkei.co.jp/senkyo/200509 (found 17 November 2006).
Pempel, T. J. (1989): *Uncommon Democracies: The One-Party Dominant Regimes*. Ithaca, N.Y.: Cornell University Press.
—— (1998): *Regime Shift: Comparative Dynamics of the Japanese Political Economy*. Ithaca, N.Y.: Cornell University Press.
Sakakibara, Eisuke (2003): *Structural Reform in Japan: Breaking the Iron Triangle*. Washington, D.C.: Brooking Institution Press.
Scheiner, Ethan (2005): *Democracy without Competition: Opposition Failure in a One-Party Dominant State*. Cambridge, U.K.: Cambridge University Press.
Schlesinger, Jacob (1999): *Shadow Shoguns: The Rise and Fall of Japan's Postwar Political Machine*. Stanford, Calif.: Stanford University Press.
Talcott, Paul (2002): Renritsu seiken no iryō seisaku e no eikyō [The impact of coalition politics on Japanese health-care policy]. In: *Shakai kagaku kenkyū* [Annals of the University of Tokyo, Institute of Social Science] 53, 2/3 (March), pp. 243–268.

CHAPTER THIRTY-SEVEN

# CIVIL SOCIETY ROLES IN ELDERLY CARE: A NON-PROFIT ORGANIZATION CENSUS

David M. Potter

## 1. Introduction

A rapidly ageing society and the rise of an invigorated non-profit sector have been parallel trends in Japan in the last two decades. As the central and prefectural governments have begun to realize their economic and administrative limitations in coping with demographic change, localities and non-profits are called upon to fill in policy gaps. At the same time, the non-profit sector itself has grown in size and capability, and its visibility has prompted the public administration to take it more seriously as a potential policy actor.

This chapter surveys NPOs engaged in service provision for the elderly in Japan's 47 prefectures. This chapter examines opinion polls and government policy pronouncements to identify public expectations about NPO roles in coping with ageing population. It then surveys NPOs engaged in service provision for the elderly nationwide. The chapter attempts to measure the degree of NPO involvement in elderly care provision and examines the kinds of activities that NPOs themselves define as elderly care. The chapter concludes by assessing to what degree NPO activities reflect public expectations about their roles.

## 2. NPOs and the Need for Elderly Care

Is there a need for non-profit action in the provision of social services for the elderly? Recent public debate suggests that there is. Interest in a healthy non-profit sector that can contribute to the vitality of local communities can be found in both official circles and among non-profit organizations themselves. Citizens' affairs offices in prefectural governments keep data on NPOs, if only because prefectures are now partially charged with approving and regulating the activities of locally registered NPOs. In addition, citizen-organized NPO support centres have also cropped up.

Official attitudes toward NPOs, however, display a certain amount of ambivalence. Since the late 1990s, national government documents on ageing routinely mention the role of NPOs and the voluntary sector. The interest in relation to services for the elderly is frequently expressed in the press and other fora. While the official interest in non-profits may be increasing overall, it is not certain how this impacts elderly care. Recent sociological and anthropological research finds that care of older family members still falls heavily on the shoulders of younger women, especially daughters-in-law (Jenike 1998; see chapter 11 in this volume), rather than on institutions organized by public, non-profit or for-profit corporations. Hospice care is rare, and in principle most citizens still wish to avoid relying on public health facilities for the care of elderly relatives if possible. A 2003 poll conducted by the Cabinet Agency found that just under 45 per cent of respondents (and a slight majority of men) would prefer to receive care at home if possible (NDKSH 2004: 25), suggesting that institutional care, non-profit or otherwise, is still not a popular option.

Perhaps the best evidence of official ambivalence is in the structure of laws that govern the non-profit sector. This chapter follows Salamon and Anheier's (1998) definition of non-profit organization. The structural-operational definition they formulate highlights the bifurcated nature of Japan's non-profit sector (Yamauchi *et al.* 1999; Pekkanen 2002), a structure that has its basis in the law. Today, we may say that legally speaking there are two non-profit sectors in Japan. One is that organized and regulated by Article 34 of the 1877 civil code and subsequent statutes, which provides the legal foundation for public interest corporations (*kōeki hōjin*). These include the trusts (*zaidan hōjin*), foundations (*shadan hōjin*), social welfare institutions (*shakai fukushi hōjin*), and medical institutions (*iryō hōjin*) that make up the "established" non-profit sector closely regulated by the bureaucracy. Care for the elderly has been a long-standing concern of these organizations, of course.

The second is the much larger galaxy of heretofore mostly unincorporated citizens' voluntary organizations. Until the creation of the so-called NPO Law passed by the Diet in 1998, these organizations had no legal status. They were, and still are, mostly small, weakly institutionalized, and minimally capitalized. The 1998 NPO Law intended to provide them with a legal identity that would encourage organizational and financial stability. This second group of NPOs is also concerned with issues of the elderly but little is known about what exactly they do.

The 1998 NPO Law helps to clarify the situation, but the majority of voluntary organizations that make up the "non-profit sector" in Japan today are not registered with a relevant government agency and therefore do not have official non-profit status. Many of the smaller voluntary organizations are reluctant to register because of official interference in their activities or do not possess the financial and personnel resources to comply with the requirements of official status.

This chapter concerns itself with organizations registered as NPOs under the 1998 law. The older *hōjin* [legal persons] that have made up the mainstream NPO sector tends to be well-established, close to officialdom, and professionalized. The relationship between the social welfare corporations and the government tends to be so close and official supervision so strict, as to call into question whether they are really part of independent civil society (Amenomori and Yamamoto 1998: 5–6). The new NPOs, on the other hand, combine a degree of institutionalization with the spontaneity and voluntarism that has characterized the unincorporated non-profit sector. Because they are institutionalized and have legal status, however, they are systematically observable in ways the unincorporated voluntary sector is not.

Table 1 presents a summary of the Cabinet Agency's 2006 survey of these new registered NPOs arranged by category. The data make it clear that social services and health retain a dominant share among NPO activities, as they have in the past among the established NPOs (Yamamoto 1998; Yamauchi *et al.* 1999). Much of the activity associated with services for the elderly fall into this category of activities, suggesting the possibility that both the established *kōeki hōjin* NPOs and the newer NPO Law NPOs are active in providing services for the elderly.

An important feature of the registered non-profit sector has to do with these organizations' understandings of activity categories. Most prefectures and the Cabinet Agency allow volunteer organizations applying for NPO status to specify any sectors that they consider their activities to fall under. Activities that involve multiple sectors are common. In fact, the 2006 data finds that two-thirds of all registered NPOs engage in activities in between two and four categories. Some list all seventeen possible sectors. As a result, NPOs working with the elderly are likely to view "social welfare," a discrete category as used by officialdom, more broadly than do government agencies.

Table 1. Non-profit organizations' activities nationwide in per cent, 2006.

| | |
|---|---|
| Health, medicine, welfare | 57.2 |
| Social education | 46.8 |
| *Machizukuri* (community building) | 40.3 |
| Culture and arts | 32.2 |
| Environmental protection | 28.6 |
| International cooperation | 20.8 |
| Child development | 39.8 |
| Human rights protection | 15.3 |
| Gender equality | 8.9 |
| Disaster assistance | 6.6 |
| Local safety | 9.4 |
| Other | 34.4 |
| Networking support | 44.9 |

Source: Naikakufu (2006b).

## 3. NPOs and Elderly Care

To better understand how the "new" NPOs contribute to solution of problems related to an ageing society, the following section surveys organizations across the 47 prefectures. The analysis focuses on NPOs registered with the prefecture governments for two reasons. First, most are registered in a single prefecture (25,853 out of 28,240 organizations) rather than with national government agencies. Second, dividing the data thus allows analysis of potential differences among regions and prefectures.

Table 2 presents data on the number of NPOs that work with the elderly nationwide. The table includes total numbers of registered NPOs per prefecture, total NPOs claiming social welfare as an area of activity, and total NPOs claiming to work with the elderly. Figures for relevant social welfare corporations, part of the traditional non-profit sector, are also included. To ensure uniformity across prefectures, the table presents data collected from prefectural sites linked to the Cabinet Agency's homepage for registered non-profit organizations by prefecture and nationally. Prefectures do not use standard reporting procedures, so there are gaps in the data. Specific data on relevant NPOs from Akita, Iwate, Kyoto, and Tokushima were unavailable, and those prefectures are excluded from the following discussion.

NPOs are counted in the health and social welfare column even if that category of activity is not their main one. Prefecture data vary

Table 2. Overview of non-profit organizations related to elderly care.

| Prefecture | Total NPOs | Social welfare NPOs | Elder care NPOs | Other care facilities |
|---|---|---|---|---|
| Hokkaido | 1011 | 548 | 141 | 985 |
| Aomori | 203 | na | 80 | 395 |
| Akita | 130 | na | na | 374 |
| Iwate | 249 | 154 | na | 353 |
| Yamagata | 197 | 121 | 36 | 249 |
| Miyagi | 412 | 166 | 50 | 534 |
| Fukushima | 328 | na | 48 | 380 |
| Tochigi | 271 | 161 | 72 | 294 |
| Ibaraki | 337 | 204 | 83 | 425 |
| Gunma | 442 | 287 | 90 | 381 |
| Saitama | 882 | 556 | 179 | 799 |
| Chiba | 1690 | na | 231 | 685 |
| Tokyo | 4880 | 2541 | 654 | 1592 |
| Kanagawa | 1491 | 817 | 155 | 866 |
| Niigata | 357 | 187 | 45 | 565 |
| Toyama | 155 | 83 | 7 | 265 |
| Ishikawa | 194 | na | 54 | 228 |
| Fukui | 167 | 81 | 32 | 163 |
| Yamanashi | 108 | 46 | 17 | 158 |
| Nagano | 530 | 334 | 152 | 545 |
| Gifu | 345 | 104 | 50 | 379 |
| Shizuoka | 546 | 322 | 79 | 464 |
| Aichi | 890 | 340 | 136 | 952 |
| Mie | 201 | 116 | 44 | 379 |
| Shiga | 295 | 192 | 70 | 535 |
| Kyoto | 709 | 360 | na | 438 |
| Osaka | 1967 | 1153 | 447 | 1216 |
| Hyogo | 953 | 576 | 225 | 910 |
| Nara | 187 | 113 | 29 | 391 |
| Wakayama | 210 | 141 | 26 | 298 |
| Tottori | 77 | na | 7 | 205 |
| Shimane | 134 | 86 | 30 | 241 |
| Okayama | 303 | 216 | 65 | 454 |
| Hiroshima | 388 | 222 | 62 | 478 |
| Yamaguchi | 249 | na | 35 | 303 |
| Tokushima | 146 | na | na | 361 |
| Kagawa | 145 | 87 | 24 | 361 |
| Ehime | 218 | na | 43 | 341 |
| Kochi | 174 | na | 41 | 291 |
| Fukuoka | 865 | 516 | 185 | 509 |
| Saga | 179 | 104 | 34 | 213 |
| Nagasaki | 223 | 148 | 57 | 391 |
| Kumamoto | 333 | na | 60 | 547 |
| Oita | 280 | 146 | 63 | 384 |
| Miyazaki | 157 | na | 38 | 240 |
| Kagoshima | 294 | 180 | 55 | 500 |
| Okinawa | 225 | 111 | 36 | 163 |

Source: Naikakufu (2006b).

widely, from asking prospective NPOs to list only their main activity to not asking for this data at all. Therefore, no finer coding is possible. NPOs were counted as active in providing services to the elderly only if they specifically mentioned the elderly in their statements of objectives that accompany application for corporate status. Some NPOs that use wording such as "for all ages, from children to the elderly," sometimes found with sports NPOs, were also excluded.

The average of elderly care NPOs as a proportion of total NPOs identified is 18.6 per cent, just over one in five organizations. There is a wide range across prefectures, however; 39.4 per cent of all NPOs in Aomori, for example, claim to engage in activities for the elderly. Only nine per cent of those in Tottori and 4.5 per cent of those in Toyama do so. As the table shows, both of these prefectures have very small numbers of registered NPOs to begin with.

The author devised two simple measures to test the incidence of these NPOs relative to population and the existence of other social welfare foundations in each prefecture. The first compares elderly care NPOs as a percentage of total NPOs in each prefecture with the proportion of elderly citizens in that prefecture. It was hypothesized that the proportion of NPOs working with the elderly will be higher in prefectures with relatively high elderly populations. Operationally, therefore, prefectures with percentages of elderly residents above the national average (19.5 per cent) should have NPOs that target elderly citizens above the national average for total NPOs (18.6 per cent).

There does not seem to be a strong correlation between potential needs of older citizens and the existence of NPOs organized to serve them. 13 prefectures show both above-average elderly populations and relevant NPOs. Another eight show the opposite tendency, with both elderly populations and relevant NPOs below their respective national averages. The remaining 22 show mixed results. As noted above, sufficient data on NPOs for Akita, Iwate, and Tokushima are not available. This is unfortunate because these three have unusually high proportions of elderly populations.

The author then compared the ratio of social welfare foundations (*shakai fukushi hōjin*) dedicated to elderly care to their counterpart NPOs across the country. Population estimates of residents over 65 years of age in each prefecture were divided by the number of elderly care NPOs and *shakai fukushi hōjin* respectively to create values that measures the density of each type of organization by its target population.[1] This does not assume, of course, that senior citizens necessarily require the services of either. Rather, it is simply a measure of the relative density of these organizations in each prefecture. An average for each set of values was calculated; then raw values were compared to that average to determine each prefecture in relation to the average. Prefectures with raw scores above the average have relatively fewer organizations per target population, and those with scores below the average have relatively more organizations per target population. Therefore, an above-average score is an indication that, for whatever reasons, institutionalized civil society organizations are not responding sufficiently to potential need.

Scores for each prefecture were compared to determine whether the position of one value in relation to its average was congruent with the position of the other value in relation to its average. Congruence was determined to exist simply when both scores were either above or below their respective averages. Dissonance was determined to exist simply when each value was opposite its counterpart (i.e., above average relative to below average, and vice versa). Dissonance suggests that one kind of organization crowds out the other in that field of activity.

The results of this exercise are equivocal. In nineteen cases, values were congruent. Of those, 11 prefectures have above-average scores, meaning that both NPOs and *shakai fukushi hōjin* responding to needs of the elderly are less prevalent there than their respective national averages. Another eight have NPO and *shakai fukushi hōjin* densities below the national average. Four out of the eight are clustered in Kyushu (Saga, Nagasaki, Oita, and Kumamoto). In nineteen other prefectures the values were dissonant. In only 11 cases, however, were above-average *shakai fukushi hōjin* densities associated with below-average NPO densities, a situation that could be interpreted as one in which NPOs compensate for below average *shakai fukushi hōjin* presence. In the remaining eight, the opposite may be occurring: NPOs are in fact being crowded out by their better-established counterparts.

---

[1] Population estimates are taken from *Nihon tōkei nenkan heisei 18-nen-han* (STK 2006: 49). *Shakai fukushi hōjin* numbers are calculated from *Shakai fukushi shisetsu-to meibō* (KTK 2004: *passim*).

Table 3. NPO activities.

| |
|---|
| Home care/home support |
| Home helper dispatch, day service |
| Transportation services |
| Promotion of senior citizen revitalization and social participation |
| Group home operation |
| Health maintenance |
| Social and cultural activities |
| Network development among the elderly |
| Research and needs assessment |

Source: Naikakufu (2006b).

## 4. NPO Activities

What do these NPOs actually do? The range of activities and purposes provided in the organizations' self-descriptions is quite broad. As suggested above, NPOs' understanding of social welfare is much more inclusive than is found in the activities of the traditional *shakai fukushi hōjin*. Nevertheless, there appears to be a repertoire of collective action that is relatively uniform across the country. Table 3 presents a list of the most common activities mentioned by NPOs that target the elderly.

There is an overwhelming emphasis on social welfare activities. Indeed, NPOs that specifically identify the elderly as objects of their activities are a nearly perfect subset of the health/medicine/social services category presented in Table 2. Popular activities include "at-home living support", "rest home/day service support", and "cultural and social activities" aimed at shut-ins or those in institutional care. Another widely occurring subset consists of organizations that attempt to provide counselling and home visit support for the elderly and their families. Given the fact that primary responsibility for care of older citizens falls disproportionately on younger female family members, this focus of activity appears to try to alleviate the stresses on those women.

Aside from home helper provision, day service, meal delivery or other social welfare services, much of the support provided by NPOs is in the nature of cultural and social activities. A few organizations provide counselling services but it is unclear whether this is professional service. A few provide employment support and retraining for older workers, and others provide personal computer training. A very few see older citizens as bearers of specialized cultural and technical knowledge and have organized to provide them the opportunity to pass that knowledge on to younger generations.

One result of this emphasis on social welfare provision appears to be that NPO organizers have absorbed, and now reproduce, a perspective that sees the elderly as passive recipients of needed care and social services. Nakano noted this perspective in her study of Yokohama volunteer organizations that provide meal service and social and cultural activities for senior citizens living by themselves at home (Nakano 2005).

There appears to be a division of labour between the established *shakai fukushi hōjin* and the new NPOs in the field of elderly care. The former operate care facilities used by the elderly; the latter provide a variety of auxiliary services to those facilities or provide services they do not cover. Group homes are an exception (see below). To put it simply, the established non-profits provide the hardware of social services for the elderly while the new NPOs provide the software of social and community contact.

An important factor in NPO choice of activity, then, may be the density of broad non-profit sector (all types of non-profits regardless of type of legal incorporation) activity related to care of the elderly. It was noted above that several types of mainstream non-profit sector organizations already provide social services, and elderly care is no different. Registered NPOs have emerged in what is already a crowded field. Partial insights into this point can be gleaned from examining sector-specific data. For example, according to a 2006 directory of elder care facilities and group homes NPOs are active across the country in operating group homes for the elderly, one of the few areas in which they operate facilities *per se*. Although the data is not as complete as one would hope, a survey of sixteen group home associations from across the country shows that 227 of 1264 total members are registered NPOs, just under one in six organizations (CLSC 2006). The average masks the fact, however, that NPO membership in specific associations ranges widely. The numbers here are too small to provide anything more than an impression, but the density of NPO involvement in a prefecture-wide association appears to be inversely related to the density of participation by other non-profit organizations. In other words, the more social welfare or medical corporations there are, the less room there is for NPO participation.

Table 4. Sectoral distribution of NPO activities in Aichi.

| Activity | Number (%) |
|---|---|
| At-home living support | 31 (30) |
| Rest home/day service support | 20 (19.6) |
| Cultural and social activities | 37 (36) |
| Provision of goods tailored to elderly | 3 (3) |
| Other/undefined | 14 (13.7) |

Source: ASS, 2004.

## 5. Aichi Prefecture: A Comparison

Unfortunately, the quality and coverage of nationwide data is inconsistent. One would like to know, for example, about participation rates by senior citizens in NPOs, those organizations' resources, or about the distribution of those NPOs within prefectures. To get a sense of these dimensions this chapter turns to survey data published by Aichi Prefecture. The data used come from a 2003 survey conducted by the Aichi prefectural governments' citizens' affairs office.[2] The survey provides some level of information on over 1,400 organizations, so it is possible to measure the level of NPO activity in any particular field in proportion to all NPO activity, and to consider the resources that those organizations bring to bear on the problem.

Table 4 presents a breakdown of NPO activities in Aichi. The Aichi data aggregate both recognized non-profits registered with an appropriate government agency under the 1998 NPO Law and so-called voluntary organizations that define themselves as NPOs. This makes it possible to compare registered NPO characteristics with those of their informal counterparts.

Two main conclusions can be drawn from the survey data. First, welfare, health, and health NPOs are among the numerically dominant organizations (along with children's services and culture and recreation), just as they are nationally and among the established *kōeki hōjin*. 471 out 1,447 organizations included in the Aichi survey are in this category. Second, further investigation reveals that 100 of them are active in providing social services of one kind or another to the elderly. In other

[2] Unless otherwise specified, data discussed in the following sections come from the prefectural survey.

words, 21 per cent of all health and welfare NPOs, and almost seven per cent of all organizations in the survey, are active in this area.

The nationwide division of labour between the new NPOs and the established *kōeki hōjin* in the field of elderly care is present in Aichi. The latter operate care facilities used by the elderly; the former provide a variety of auxiliary services to those facilities. In fact, there is considerable overlap between the table categories of "at-home living support," "rest home/day service support", and "cultural and social activities." Except in cases such a meal delivery or other social welfare services, much of the support provided by NPOs is in the nature of cultural and social activities. A few organizations listed under "other/undefined" appear to provide counselling services but it is unclear whether this is professional service. As seen in the national data, the established non-profits provide the hardware of social services for the elderly while the new NPOs provide the software of social support. Their activities also favour those senior citizens living at home, either alone or with relatives, although they also provide services for citizens receiving institutional care, too.

This is consistent with the organizational character of the new NPOs. Many simply do not possess the finances, personnel, or organizational capacity to manage highly regulated social service facilities (CKS 2004).[3] Nor does it appear that they want to. Nor is the kind of specialized care associated with the old-line *kōeki hōjin* a part of the new NPO toolkit. Second, note that in-home support service outnumbers rest home and day service support. Again, this suggests that volunteer organizations composed mostly of women charged with care of elderly family members are pooling their efforts. In-depth research on this point needs to be conducted.

## 6. Geographic Distribution of Elderly Care NPOs in Aichi

Is the number of NPOs providing services to the elderly related to the proportion of elderly in an urban area or to its overall population? In other words, do NPOs form in response to need or do they organize

---

[3] A survey of 238 elderly care facilities listed in the 2004 Aichi edition of the *Kōreika shisetsu dētabukku* (CKS 2004) turned up only one facility incorporated as a NPO according to the 1998 law. The rest were incorporated as various entities under the *kōeki hōjin* classification or as for-profit businesses.

when an area has a critical mass of people capable of sustaining the organization? The national data analyzed above suggest that this is not necessarily so across prefectures. This section considers the geographic distribution of relevant NPOs within one prefecture, Aichi.

The population of Aichi was 7,205, 625 in 2004, with 16.5 per cent of the population was over the age of 65 (ATK 2004: 34). Incidentally, this was the third-lowest figure among the 47 prefectures (Naikakufu 2005: 5). A rough breakdown of the three major areas of the prefecture—Owari (including Nagoya City), Western Mikawa, and Eastern Mikawa (both southeast of Nagoya)—shows that they have 16.9 per cent, 14.3 per cent, and 18.6 per cent, respectively, of their populations aged 65 or older.

Assuming that the survey reflects the relative density of NPOs in any given area, population seems to be a significant factor in explaining the presence of NPOs providing services to the elderly. The Owari area, which includes Nagoya, has 68.5 per cent of the prefecture's total population, and is home to just over half (54) of the NPOs investigated here. The rest of the NPOs are spread rather thinly across the prefecture. Eastern Mikawa has a relatively older population, suggesting need for services, but has a lower population than Western Mikawa and fewer NPOs. Some cities report no NPOs at all active in this field even though they have relatively high elderly populations. If NPOs are supposed to be supplementing services provided by the public administration, then serious issues of equity are raised by this finding.

## 7. NPO Organizational Structure

Three features of Aichi NPO organization stand out. First, as far as the directory data reveal, they are in fact new. Second, they are composed largely of volunteers. Third, they are highly local. These conclusions are substantiated by available data on date of establishment, employment structure, and finance.

Survey responses to queries about staffing and finances are too inadequate to allow rigorous analysis, but NPOs that provide support for the elderly tend to look like the *machizukuri* [community building] organizations surveyed elsewhere (Potter 2004). Most organizations rely heavily on volunteers, do not maintain paid staff, and have small budgets (typically the equivalent of a few thousand dollars). This has consequences for the kinds of activities that these organizations conduct

Table 5. Main ages of ageing care NPO members in Aichi.

| Age group | Organizations | Women predominate |
|---|---|---|
| Students | 3 | 2 |
| 20s–30s | 1 | 1 |
| 40s–50s | 51 | 35 |
| 60s and above | 34 | 11 |

Source: ASS, 2004.

because most do not have the capitalization or expertise to carry out professionalized social services.

The 2003 survey asked for information about the main age of members in each group, and also for gender ratio. Respondents were much more forthcoming with this data, which is summarized in Table 5. Clearly middle-aged volunteers form the core of NPOs working with the elderly. More significantly, these organizations tend to have more women than men in them.[4] Absent interviews with volunteers it is possible only to speculate, but the impression one takes away from this data is that the people most likely to be assigned care of elderly family members—middle-aged women—are using the opportunities for NPO establishment to build social organizations with which they can assist each other. This is a hypothesis that awaits confirmation.

## 8. NPOs as Centres of Senior Activity

In addition to caring for the elderly, one public expectation about NPOs seems to be that they will provide suitable outlets for senior citizens' energies. Indeed, the 1995 Basic Law on Measures for the Ageing Society (*Kōreishakai Taisaku Kihon-hō*) and the 2001 Charter on the Ageing Society (*Kōreisha Taisaku no Taiko*) commit the government to promoting volunteer activities among seniors after retirement age (Naikakufu 2006a: 188–204). Voluntary activity in NPOs and other civil society organizations is seen as an appropriate transition to retirement (Naikakufu 2006a: 166). It is widely taken for granted that older citizens will form the core of *chōnai-kai* [neighbourhood association]

[4] "Women predominate" in the table means simply that the NPO reported a higher proportion of women than men.

administration, the criminal justice parole system, and traffic and neighbourhood safety activities.

How well NPOs contribute to senior involvement in civil society, however, is problematic. Three issues in particular stand out. The first has to do with data. This author knows of no nationwide survey of NPO participation by age group. The prefecture data used in the previous sections vary greatly in depth of information made public, and in any case do not poll NPOs about age-based participation rates as a precondition for obtaining non-profit status.

A second problem has to do with attitudes about NPOs and volunteering in general. For one thing, it is not clear that old stereotypes about volunteering, as egoistic or associated with the political and religious fringe (Stevens 1997: 145–165, 230), have been dispelled. It is likely that prejudices against volunteering, which may be on the wane among younger generations, will still be held by older citizens. In 2000 Yokkaichi City, Mie Prefecture, polled 119 workers in their fifties about their post-retirement plans (all but fifteen were men). Only eight responded that they saw themselves doing any kind volunteer or NPO activity. Only one envisioned doing volunteer work directly with the elderly, box lunch delivery in this case (Yokkaichi-shi Shiminbu 2000b: 1–9).[5] In a broader survey of 1439 Yokkaichi workers (86 per cent of whom were men) in their fifties concerning their post-retirement plans, few reported that either they or their spouses were currently engaged in volunteer activity outside of *chōnai-kai* activities (about 7 per cent and 17 per cent, respectively, with a full 10 per cent of the latter being taken up by volunteering at consumer cooperatives) (Yokkaichi-shi Shiminbu 2000a: 9).

This is consistent with national data. A 2005 poll conducted by the Cabinet Agency found that 91.8 per cent of 1,863 citizens queried had not participated in NPO activities in the last five years, and 48.9 per cent indicated no interest in doing so henceforward. The national poll data also reveal that, even when citizens are inclined to contribute in one way or another to voluntary organizations, they do not necessarily favour NPOs (NDKSH 2006: 9, 11). Similarly, a 2004 national poll of senior citizens' involvement in community activities revealed that 68 per cent of them have no particular affinity with NPOs, by far the largest response (Naikakufu 2005: 46).

[5] It is not clear whether these options were from open-ended questions or from prompts.

There are, of course, alternative outlets for social participation. Today, there are about 130,000 old people's clubs in Japan with approximately 8.4 million members (Naikakufu 2005: 117). Kaplan *et al.* (1998: 105–106) point out that these clubs typically start focused on providing activities for members but over time often add a community service component. A few appear to have become NPOs and therefore show up in the prefecture lists analyzed above. The *chōnai-kai* and traffic safety drives organized by local authorities are stereotypical locations for social participation by retired citizens (see also chapter 38 in this volume).

This does not mean necessarily that the elderly do not participate in NPO activities. Surveying all of the registered NPOs currently active reveals an extraordinary variety of purposes and activities that cross the range of civil society. National poll data cited above shows that middle-aged respondents are interested in volunteering in park cleaning and other local *machizukuri* activities after retirement even if they do not envision participating in a NGO. A 2002 national poll of citizens over age 50 found that nearly one-third of respondents in their sixties and seventies report participating in *machizukuri* activities, an extraordinarily broad field of activity. As might be expected, participation rates decline as citizens enter their late seventies and eighties (Naikakufu 2005: 44).

To be sure, there are some NPOs that seek to organize the talents and energy of older citizens. For example, the NPO "Umibudō" in Kitakyushu City has as its purpose *senior-centred* social contribution through participation in *machizukuri* and promotion of science and technology. Others see the elderly as a valuable repository of cultural and artistic knowledge and thus formed to provide a place for these people to pass on that knowledge to younger generations. The survey conducted above, however, identified only a handful across the country, with no more than one or two per prefecture. It is not at all clear that NPOs themselves see fostering senior participation as their role. The modal NPO concerned with elderly issues, however, focuses on elderly assistance; few deliberately have organized to promote the participation of older people in society.

Table 6 provides information on volunteer organization participation by age group in Aichi. Please note that respondents were asked to specify a main age group of their members rather than a complete distribution of membership by age. It is therefore possible that a group composed mainly of students might have some members in their forties, and so on. The table makes clear that senior citizen participation drops

Table 6. Main ages of NPO membership in Aichi.

| Age group | Organizations |
|---|---|
| Students | 70 |
| 20s–30s | 201 |
| 40s–50s | 703 |
| 60s and above | 277 |

Source: ASS, 2004.

off compared to peak participation by people in middle age, but note that reported participation by older citizens is still higher than that of younger adults and much higher than that of students. The numbers are too small for nuanced statistical analysis, but it appears that the incidence of organizations with participants predominantly over sixty years of age increases outside of metropolitan areas. In other words, in smaller communities with fewer NPOs to begin with those groups with membership cores of older citizens are especially prominent. Without more detailed data, however, it is impossible to determine the incidence of senior citizen participation in NPOs nationwide or potentially interesting variations in that participation.

## 9. Conclusion

NPOs see social welfare in broad terms, which means they are in a position to provide the kinds of services that fill in social gaps in the hardware of public welfare services for the elderly. This is especially visible in the widespread repertoire of home care and home service provision. In this sense, it can be said that NPOs are answering a public need not fulfilled by public social welfare policies. They also function as outlets for social participation for the elderly. At the same time, however, they face competition from other civil society and quasi-public entities that have established histories and reputations. This competition is evident both in service provision for the elderly and in outlets for social participation for the same. Senior citizens are active in a wide array of volunteer and quasi-volunteer activities, but they do not necessarily equate those with participation in NPOs.

Finally, while NPOs are increasing in numbers they are not necessarily evenly distributed. In particular, rural areas with high proportions of older residents tend to have low incidences of NPO formation. This is seen not only in nationwide comparisons of prefectures but among communities within prefectures as well. Practically all analyses of NPOs in Japan note their small size, limited resources, and overwhelming reliance on volunteer staff. Whether they are equipped to stem the crises of depopulation and ageing in rural areas is open to question.

## References


Amenomori, Takayoshi and Tadashi Yamamoto (1998): Introduction. In: Yamamoto, Tadashi (ed.): *The Nonprofit Sector in Japan*. Manchester: Manchester University Press, pp. 1–18.

ASS (Aichi-ken Shimin Seikatsubu) (2004): *Aichi NPO jiko shōkai gaidobukku* [Aichi NPO self-introduction guidebook]. Nagoya: Aichi-ken Shimin Seikatsubu.

ATK (Aichi-ken Tōkei Kyōkai) (2004): *Aichi no jinko (nenkan)* [Population of Aichi (annual)]. Nagoya: Aichi-ken Kikaku Shinkūbu Tōkeika.

CKS (Chubu Keizai Shinbunsha) (2004): *2004-nen-han kōreisha shisetsu dētabukku* [2004 data book on senior homes]. Nagoya: Chubu Keizai Shinbunsha.

CLSC (Community Life Support Center) (2006): *Takurōsho/gurūpu hōmu hakusho* [White paper on assisted living and group homes]. Tokyo: Community Life Support Center.

Jenike, Brenda Robb (1998): Parent Care and Shifting Family Obligations in Urban Japan. In: Trapaghan, John W. and John Knight (eds.): *Demographic Change and the Family in Japan's Aging Society*. Albany, New York: State University of New York Press, pp. 177–202.

Kaplan, Matthew, Nancy Henkin and Atsuko Kusano (1998): *Intergenerational Programs: Support for Children, Youth, and Elders in Japan*. Albany, New York: State University of New York Press.

KTK (Kōsei Tōkei Kyōkai) (2004): *Shakai fukushi shisetsu-to meibō* [Directory of social services facilities], Vol. 1. Tokyo: Kōsei Rōdōsho Daijin Kanbō Tōkei Jōhōbu.

Naikakufu (2005): *Kōrei shakai hakusho, heisei 17-nen-han* [White paper on ageing society, 2005]. Tokyo: Gyōsei.

—— (2006a): *Kōrei shakai hakusho, heisei 18-nen-han* [White paper on ageing society, 2006]. Tokyo: Gyōsei.

—— (2006b): *Tokute hieri katsudō hōjin no katsudō bunya ni tsuite (2006/03/31 genzai)* [On types of activities among no-profit organizations (as of 2006/3/31)]. http://www.npo-homepage.go.jp/data/bunnya.html (found 1 May 2006).

Nakano, Lynne (2005): *Community Volunteers in Japan: Everyday Stories of Social Change*. London and New York: Routledge Curzon.

NDKSH (Naikakufu Daijin Kanbō Seifu Hōkokushitsu) (2004): *Gekkan yoron chōsa, ichi-gatsu* [Opinion poll monthly, January]. Tokyo: Dokuritsu Gyōsei Hōjin Kokuritsu Insatsu-kyoku.

—— (2006): *Gekkan yoron chōsa, san-gatsu* [Opinion poll monthly, March]. Tokyo: Dokuritsu Gyōsei Hōjin Kokuritsu Insatsu-kyoku.

Pekkanen, Robert (2002): *Japan's Dual Civil Society*. Ph.D. diss., Harvard University.

Potter, David (2004): Machizukuri and the Nonprofit Sector in Central Japan. In: *Academia* 79, 1, pp. 405–416.

Salamon, Lester and Helmut Anheier (eds.) (1998): *Defining the Nonprofit Sector*. Manchester: Manchester University Press.

Stevens, Carolyn (1997): *On the Margins of Society: Volunteers and the Welfare of the Urban Underclass*. London and New York: Routledge.

STK (Sōmusho Tōkei Kenshūsho) (2006): *Nihon tōkei nenkan heisei 18-nen-han* [Annual statistics on Japan, 2006] Tokyo: Sōmusho Tōkeikyoku.

Yamamoto, Tadashi (ed.) (1998): *Japan's Nonprofit Sector*. Manchester, UK: Manchester University Press.

Yamauchi, Naoto, Hiroko Shimizu, S. Wojciech Sokolowski and Lester Salamon (1999) Japan. In: Salamon, Lester, Helmut K. Anheier, Regina List, Stephan Toepler, S. Wojciech Sokolowski, and Associates (eds.): *Global Civil Society*. Manchester, UK: Manchester University Press, pp. 243–260.

Yokkaichi-shi Shiminbu (2000a): *Chi'iki shakai ni okeru shimin katsudō no sanka ni kansuru iyoku chōsa* [Survey of attitudes concerning participation in civic activities in regional society]. Yokkaichi, Mie Prefecture: Yokkaichi-shi Chi'iki Seisaku Kenkyūjo.

—— (2000b): *NPO katsudō e no sanka iyoku ni kansuru rōdōsha mensetsu chōsa: Shimin katsudō to no shien hōshin ni tsuite no teigen*. [Interview survey of interest in participation in NPO activities among working people: suggestions for policies in support of civic activities]. Yokkaichi, Mie Prefecture: Yokkaichi-shi Chi'iki Seisaku Kenkyūjo.

CHAPTER THIRTY-EIGHT

# NEIGHBOURHOOD ASSOCIATIONS AND THE DEMOGRAPHIC CHALLENGE

Robert Pekkanen and Yutaka Tsujinaka[1]

## 1. Introduction

This chapter focuses on how neighbourhood associations respond to the demographic challenge. Neighbourhood associations are an appropriate locus to examine for such a response, because, with nearly 300,000 groups[2] across the archipelago, they are Japan's most numerous form of civil society organization,[3] and because, in formal membership, they encompass a large majority of Japanese. Moreover, there are subgroups attached to most neighbourhood associations (NHAs) that seem perhaps particularly well-suited to respond to either the ageing society or declining fertility aspects of the demographic challenge: elderly people's clubs (*rōjin-kai/rōjin kurabu*) for the former problem, and children's associations (*kodomo-kai*) and women's associations (*fujin-kai*) for the latter.

Civil society organizations could, broadly speaking, address large-scale societal problems such as the demographic challenge in two ways. The first is to tackle the problem. This comes about largely through the provision of social capital (Putnam *et al.* 1993; Putnam 2000; Pekkanen 2006) and the effective implementation of specific policies. We argue below that neighbourhood associations are effective in mitigating some of the problems facing the aged, but not as effective in mitigating the

---

[1] Authorship is equal.

[2] According to *The Survey on Neighborhood Associations with Legal Status 2003 (LS-NHA Survey)*, there were 296,770 NHAs in Japan as of 1 November 2002, out of which 22,050 NHAs had acquired a legal corporation status from municipalities (Ministry of General Affairs 2003).

[3] See Tsujinaka 2002, 2003; Pekkanen 2006 on Japanese civil society organizations in general. In addition to the NHAs, there are more than 100,000 social associations (according to the telephone directory), 30,000 registered non-profit organizations (NPOs), or NGOs, 230,000 religious corporations, 15,000 social welfare corporations, 16,000 private school corporations, etc.

problems faced by potential parents. The second way civil society organizations can help to address large-scale problems is by improving the solution. Civil society groups can monitor the state's solutions, as well as themselves formulate and propose new policy ideas. We argue below that, in contrast to, say, US advocacy groups such as AARP (American Association for Retired Persons) and NOW (National Organization for Women), Japan's NHAs are by their nature unsuited to this type of contribution: they are congenitally unable to formulate or articulate alternative policy visions.

## 2. Neighbourhood Associations

Neighbourhood associations[4] are an important aspect of civil society in Japan. Their names have some variations in different areas, such as *jichi-kai* [self-government association], *chōnai-kai* or *chō-kai* [town block association], *buraku-kai* [village district association], *ku* or *ku-kai* [district association], etc.[5] All these are groups based on residential proximity, most often comprising from one hundred to one thousand households. Most Japanese are members in one or another NHA.

We adopt here Pekkanen's definition of neighbourhood associations:

**Neighborhood associations** are voluntary groups whose membership is drawn from a small, geographically delimited, and exclusive residential area (a neighbourhood) and whose activities are multiple and are centered on that same area (Pekkanen 2006: 87, bold in the original).[6]

---

[4] See Read and Pekkanen 2005; Nakata 2000; and Nakamura and Kojima 2007 regarding the NHAs in an international comparative perspective. The description here is mainly based on the surveys of Yokohama, Mie, and Tsukuba in addition to Pekkanen's data (2006). See the Table 1 notes for the source.

[5] According to the LS-NHA survey of 2003, out of a total 296,770, there were 114,222 *jichi-kai* (38.5%), 83,498 *chōnai-kai* or *chō-kai* (28.1%), 15,851 *buraku-kai* (5.3%), 48,653 *ku* or *ku-kai* (16.4%), and 34,546 NHAs with other names (11.6%).

[6] See also Pekkanen (2003, 2004a, 2004b, 2006) and the Ministry of General Affairs in the Local Autonomy Law: Article 260–2, which formally defines NHAs as "an association based on a district of municipalities, with the conditions of 1) having a purpose and actual functions to conduct collective activities such as maintaining mutual communication, keeping good surroundings, and maintaining their community assembly hall, etc.; 2) having a specific objective area; and 3) open to all residents in the area, of whom most have in fact become members."

The members pay dues, choose leaders, and participate in a variety of activities together. Their activities are centred on the local community, ranging from cleaning up a local park to neighbourhood watch type programmes to organizing local athletic meets or children's outings, to running the local festival (see Table 1).

Table 1. Activities of NHAs in several cities and prefectures (by % of NHAs which engage in the activity).

| Type of Activity | Activity | LS-NHA 2003 (1) | Yokohama 2003 (2) | Mie prefecture 2005 (3) | Tsukuba 2005 (4) | Ueda NHAs 1985 (5) |
|---|---|---|---|---|---|---|
| Welfare | Supporting affiliated children and/or their groups | | 71.9% | | Child care 3% Day care 27% | 89.50% |
| | Supporting affiliated elderly people and/or their groups | Welfare visit 15.5% | Aged Day Party 75.2% Delivery 18.9% | Aged Day Party 72% | 27% | 83.10% |
| | Supporting affiliated women and/or their groups | | 51.5% | | | 51.60% |
| | Supporting affiliated youth and/or their groups | | 59.6% | | 38% | 24.20% |
| Commons | Building or maintaining a community centre | 81.5% | 67.7% | | 61% | 83.90% |
| | District Planning | | | 43% | 17% | |
| | Cleaning and repairing gutters, rivers and streams, street lamps and roads | 23.3% | 76.6% | Lamps 84% | Gutters 27% Roads 88% | 91.10% |
| | Cleaning and maintaining the environment | 85.8% | 81.7% | Cleaning 67% Greening 28% | 81% | |
| | Constructing or maintaining parks | | 35.4% | 77% | | 39.50% |
| | Recycling | | 70.4% | 47% | 17% | |
| Social | Organizing a local festival | 30.8% | 50.8% | 75% | 58% | 85.50% |
| | Organizing local sports events | 36.3% | 53.1% | 59% | 36% | 79.00% |
| | Running club activities | 35.4% | 20.3% | | | 75.80% |
| | Publishing newsletters | | 45% | 25% | | 26.60% |
| | Running study groups | | 36.4% | 17% | | 39.50% |
| | Gifts for congratulations or condolences | 12.7% | 74.2% | 59% | 52% | |
| Security | Crime prevention, road safety | 29.4% | Roads 54.7% | Crime 50% Road 53% | Crime 43% Road 29% | 84.70% |

Table 1 (*cont.*)

| Type of Activity | Activity | LS-NHA 2003 (1) | Yokohama 2003 (2) | Mie prefecture 2005 (3) | Tsukuba 2005 (4) | Ueda NHAs 1985 (5) |
|---|---|---|---|---|---|---|
| | Disaster and fire prevention | 31.9% | Crime/Fire 79% | 64% | Disaster 23% Fire 47% | |
| Government Relations | Distribution of government notices* | 88.3% | −100% | 90% | | 89.50% |
| | Cooperating with government collections* | | −100% | 75% | | 87.10% |
| | Presenting petitions from residents to local government* | 16.1% | | 69% | | 84.70% |
| | Support of politicians | | | | | 25.00% |
| | | N=22050 | N=2829 | n=420 | N=279 | n=408 |

Note: *= Activities directly related to interaction with local governments.
Source: (1) *LS-NHA Survey 2003* (Ministry of General Affairs 2003); (2) Yokohama City Government 2003, 2004a, 2004b. (3) Mie Prefecture 2005; (4) Tsukuba City Survey (unpublished);[7] (5) Ueda 1985; Yasui 1985.

Table 2. Frequency of participation in NHAs.

| more than 4 times a week | 2 to 3 times a week | Once a week | 2 to 3 times a month | Once a month | A few times a year | No answer |
|---|---|---|---|---|---|---|
| 0.8% | 2% | 3.9% | 14.1% | 30.6% | 45.3% | 3.3% |

Note: N=5,607.
Source: Nihon Sōgō Kenkyūjo 2003: 147.

Their activities also include cooperation with local government, primarily in disseminating information from government to local residents.[8] In addition, the chairs of NHA and quasi-governmental voluntary

[7] The Tsukuba City Survey 2006 was done as a preparatory survey for the comprehensive national survey in late 2006 by Tsujinaka Yutaka and his survey team, and it consisted of two slightly different surveys using slightly different survey questionnaires in order to test their answerability. One targets 142 cases and the other 137. The total is 249.

[8] Tsujinaka is currently leading the first ever nationwide survey of NHAs in Japan, as part of the Civil Society Organizations and Governance project based at University of Tsukuba. The survey, taking place mainly from August to December 2006, covers more than 18,000 NHAs out of 300,000 associations throughout Japan. It includes a variety of questions related to their activities, group networks and policy affairs, most of which have not been asked in the previous surveys.

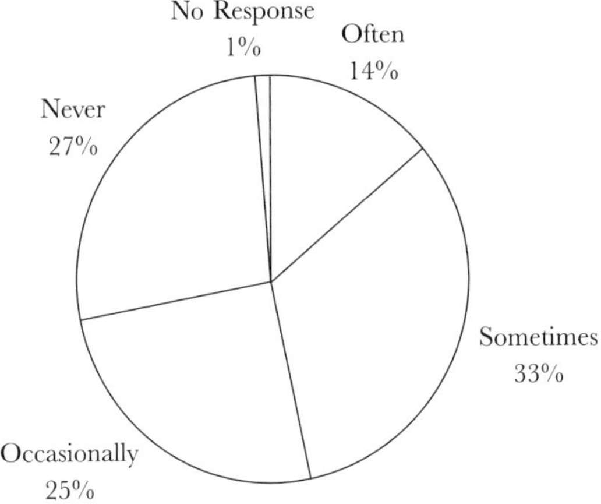


Note: N = 2947.
Source: Roper Center 1997.

Figure 1. NHA participation (National Survey 1997).

professionals,[9] such as welfare commissioners (*minsei i'in*), case workers (*hogoshi*), traffic councillors, and civil liberty commissioners, overlap in many cases. Even when the positions are not concurrently held by the same individual, many NHA chairs have prior experience as having been the head, or at least a member of, these organizations. This means that NHAs are the real nucleus of the respective district in municipalities for the local government.

As for the organizational structure, NHAs often have sub-district units called *han* or by some other names, consisting of ten to 30 households. They also often have some functional groups named *bu-kai* for various activities as shown in Table 1. The NHA's budget depends on the size of their membership. But because their membership fee is very small, roughly between 100 and 500 yen (less than 5 U.S. dollars) a month, their budget is also not large, on average between 500,000 and 6 million yen. They receive subsidies, commissions, and so on as fund transfers from local governments. In general, the proportion of these would be between 10 and 50 per cent of the total NHA budget.

[9] They are "quasi-governmental" professionals because they are formally appointed by ministries or municipalities, and also "voluntary" because they are paid very little or nothing considering the amount or quality of their work.

Neighbourhood associations typically contain several hundred households.[10] Although NHA membership levels hover around 80 to 90 per cent in general, and two-thirds of them have a membership rate higher than 90 per cent, participation is predictably lower, if still quite robust, showing about half of the adult population in Japan are active in NHAs (see Figure 1 and Table 2).

The above should make it apparent that NHAs are a nationwide form of civil society organization. Their ubiquity is what makes it relevant for us to consider how they relate to Japan's demographic challenge.

## 3. The Ageing Society

As mentioned in our introduction, we argue that NHAs can respond to the challenges of Japan's ageing society in two ways. NHAs effectively sustain social capital, and assist with the implementation of government policies towards the aged. However, they are congenitally ineffective in formulating or articulating alternative policy visions.

### 3.1. *NHAs and social capital*

NHAs are important to the generation of social capital in Japan. NHAs cooperate closely with local governments (Pekkanen 2004b, 2005, 2006). Through this cooperation, NHAs can improve government performance, while lowering costs. At the same time, participation in face-to-face group activities contributes directly to social capital stocks in the community. As nucleus organizations, NHAs also contribute indirectly to social capital by providing the base for clusters of related groups, including the seniors' clubs or elderly people's clubs (*rōjin-kai/rōjin kurabu*).

As Table 3 shows, in the Tsukuba city case, NHAs closely cooperate with seniors' clubs or elderly people's clubs (*rōjin-kai/rōjin kurabu*). More than half of the Tsukuba NHAs reported having cooperative linkages with those clubs. In addition, while having no strong ties with NPO-type care and welfare associations (6 per cent), NHAs have strong connections with Social Welfare Councils (54 per cent) and

[10] The range is very wide, from less than 50 households (6 per cent) to more than 1,000 households (11 per cent), depending on areas, according to the survey in 2003 (Ministry of General Affairs 2003).

Table 3. Cooperative networks between NHAs and other organizations.

| Name of organization having cooperative linkage | | % |
|---|---|---|
| Children's association | 96 | 67.6% |
| Women's association | 41 | 28.9% |
| Youth club | 14 | 9.9% |
| Aged people's club | 73 | 51.4% |
| Fire brigade, Crime prevention association, Vigilance group | 102 | 71.8% |
| Physical education promotion association etc. | 48 | 33.8% |
| PTA for primary and secondary school | 85 | 59.9% |
| Temples, Shrines, Churches | 37 | 26.1% |
| Religious related groups (parishioners) | 57 | 40.1% |
| Other NHAs | 44 | 31.0% |
| Federation of NHAs | 55 | 38.7% |
| Rotary and Lions clubs | 1 | 0.7% |
| Stores' association, Shopping arcade, Chamber of Commerce, Junior Chamber | 9 | 6.3% |
| Agricultural, Fishery, and Forest cooperatives | 44 | 31.0% |
| Consumer cooperatives | 4 | 2.8% |
| Social Welfare Council | 76 | 53.5% |
| Company, Factory | 4 | 2.8% |
| Labour union | 2 | 1.4% |
| Town Planning | 12 | 8.5% |
| Environmental, Ecological organization | 5 | 3.5% |
| Child-care circle | 4 | 2.8% |
| Children sports circle and sport corps | 10 | 7.0% |
| Hobby club | 12 | 8.5% |
| Handicapped organization | 4 | 2.8% |
| Care and welfare volunteer | 9 | 6.3% |
| Other citizen groups | 3 | 2.1% |
| Total | 142 | — |

Note: The Tsukuba City Survey consists of two similar but slightly different surveys of NHAs in Tsukuba. This survey includes 142 associations.
Source: Tsukuba City Survey (unpublished).

other religion-related groups (parishioners'), such as those belonging to Buddhist temples and Shinto shrines (40%) and with temples and shrines themselves (26%).[11]

[11] For example, the *Shakyō*, Social Welfare Council, with which 54 per cent of NHAs reported having close links. This organization also shows the unusual nature of the relationship or boundary between the state and society in Japan. Their office is always located within the municipality office (city, town or village hall), as if it were one of

Frequent interaction with others is not only enjoyable, but for many elderly people, it has important health benefits. The trips to local health facilities familiarize the elderly with the available health resources and how to access them. They also provide a chance for both health professionals and peers to observe the health of the group members, giving an opportunity for early detection of health concerns. Putnam argued that social connectedness correlates with better health for the elderly in the United States, and these arguments apply in full measure to the Japanese NHAs and seniors' clubs (Putnam 2000: 327–329).

It should not be forgotten that NHAs themselves provide a good opportunity for the elderly to enjoy social life: 90 per cent of NHA chairs recruited are men, one-third from the retired elderly, and two-thirds are older than 60. Thus, a typical chair of an NHA would be in his sixties, retired or self-employed (for example, farmers, shop owners) (Yokohama City Government 2003; Mie Prefecture 2005; Tsukuba City Survey, unpublished).

Looking again at Table 1 above creates the impression that no group contributes more directly to Japan's social capital. The informational role they play is certainly crucial, with high levels of communication flowing through embedded networks that provide multiple opportunities for sanctioning of defectors. A recent survey presented interesting findings about NHA participation and levels of generalized trust at the individual level. It is not surprising that NHA participants are more than twice as likely as non-participants to say that they can rely on their neighbours (Nihon Sōgō Kenkyūjyo 2003: 171). More importantly, the survey reveals that individuals who participate in NHAs have higher levels of trust in *anyone*. They are more likely than non-participants to agree with the statement that most people can be trusted. This suggests that NHA participation could directly increase levels of generalized trust and thus contribute to the building of social capital, although irrefutable evidence on causal direction is needed to be conclusive.

Based on high quality social capital created by NHAs, some of the more advanced and active NHAs have started to take measures to deal by themselves with the problems of the ageing society. Besides ordinary activities like Respect for the Elderly Day[12] parties, some NHAs,

---

the divisions of the administration. Since this is one of the social welfare and security organizations based on the Social Welfare Service Law of 1951, we will not elaborate on it in this chapter. See Tsujinaka (1988).

[12] Respect for the Elderly Day (*keirō no hi*) is a public holiday in Japan. It is celebrated on the third Monday in September.

in cooperation with Social Welfare Councils, municipalities and other organizations, deliver meals to the lonely elderly, have regular lunch parties, make regular care visits, and so on. (*Ashita no Nihon wo Tsukuru Kyōkai* 2000).

In short, we contend that NHAs and their associated seniors' clubs are well suited to mitigating some of the challenges of the ageing society. They create social capital, integrate elders into community networks, and are likely to be associated with superior individual and community health outcomes and integration.

### 3.2. *NHAs and policy on the ageing society*

On the other hand, NHAs are not capable of formulating or articulating policy proposals. There is no comprehensive central national organization of NHAs in Japan. Although there is a National Federation of Neighbourhood Associations (*Zenkoku Jichikai Rengo-kai*), which has existed since the 1990s, it covers only one-third of the total number of NHAs in 31 prefectures out of 47, and it has no independent office.[13] Its function is mainly holding an annual convention and recommending individuals to be decorated by the government.[14]

This presents a vivid contrast with the organizational form that represents elderly Americans. The American Association of Retired Persons or AARP is a classic interest group and a quintessential advocacy group. The AARP claims over 35 million members (AARP 2005). It also boasts 160,000 volunteers, 1,837 employees, and, through its dozens of registered lobbyists and more than 150 policy and legislative staffers, an important influence on policymaking (Pekkanen 2006: 9). The AARP budget in 2003 was $689 million, with $58 million of that going to lobbying activities (legislation and research) and a further $146 million to disseminating AARP publications (AARP 2003).

Although they have a comparable membership base, the seniors' clubs in Japan are outclassed by the AARP in terms of professional staff, lobbying ability, and policy expertise. The Japan Federation of Senior Citizens' Clubs, Inc. (JFSCC) started its activity in 1962, and

---

[13] Their office is within the municipality office (city hall) of the presiding community. Presently it is located in the Okayama city hall, Citizen Planning and General Affairs Division (Zenji-ren 2007).

[14] There is another national federation in Japan acting more like an "interest group", the National Council of Residents of the Japan Housing Corporation, covering 250 NHAs. Its scope is mainly the interests of members as residents, such as rent and the living environment.

covers 128,897 clubs with 8,277,911 members as of March 2005 (its peak was 1998, when there were 134,285 clubs with 8,869,086 members). Its budget in 2005 was 199 million yen (less than 2 million U.S. dollars) (JFSCC various years). Its scope is limited mainly to senior life and health on the one hand and volunteer activities and social advocacy to the local government on the other. There seems very little ambition to lobby the national government concerning policy involving the elderly.

In fact, although they have modest budgets, NHAs and seniors' clubs as a rule have no professional staff, being community affairs. This means that NHAs and seniors' clubs are incapable of devising policy solutions to address the challenges posed by the ageing society. The flip side to being poor vehicles for interest articulation is they are also ill-positioned to block legislation, unlike the AARP's powerful ability to block social security reform.

## 4. Declining Fertility

Neighbourhood associations are not as well-suited to facing the second aspect of Japan's demographic challenge: declining fertility rates.

As Table 3 shows in the Tsukuba city case, quite a few NHAs cooperate closely with the children's associations (*kodomo-kai*, whose nature is not that of children's groups but more like parents' clubs) and women's associations (*fujin-kai*, whose nature is more like housewives' clubs, formed by relatively older women): 68 per cent of all NHAs reported having a cooperative linkage with the *kodomo-kai* and 29 per cent with the *fujin-kai*.

In addition, while there are no strong ties to NPO-type care and welfare associations (6 per cent), NHAs have strong connections with Social Welfare Councils (54 per cent), and other religion-related groups (parishioners'), such as those belonging to Buddhist temples and Shinto shrines (40 per cent), and with temples and shrines themselves (26 per cent).

Although there are subgroups dedicated to children (*kodomo-kai*) and women (*fujin-kai*), these are hardly sufficient to make parenthood more tempting. For one thing, these groups are only effective outlets for members (families with children), not inducements for potential members. More importantly, even the most active *kodomo-kai* falls far short of offering full-time child care or similar benefits that could make the difference to a person or family contemplating parenthood. Nor does the womens' association necessarily do anything to make motherhood more attractive.

### 4.1. *NHAs and policies to address declining birth rates*

Neither are NHAs or their associated subgroups effective vehicles to change government policies, for the reasons discussed above.[15] The problem is perhaps more acute in this arena, too, as policy measures have been successfully adopted in other nations. However, compared to, say US women's groups such as NOW, Japanese groups remain small and relatively weak.

The largest women's association in Japan is the National Federation of Regional Women's Organizations (NFRWO, or *Zenchifu-ren*). This organization is the national centre of *fujin-kai* associated with NHAs, but it is not very centralized. It covers roughly 5 million members under the umbrella of 47 prefectural organizations and three metropolitan federations. Its total membership has been declining gradually since the mid-1960s, when it recorded its peak with around 7 million members.[16] *Zenchifu-ren* has been active as a policy advocacy organization in many fields such as gender-equal society programmes, consumer issues, environmental problems, welfare and health, the peace movement and even Japan's Northern Territories issue.

While *Zenchifu-ren*, unlike NHAs or JFSCC, is oriented more to policy advocacy, its budget is limited, with less than 77 million yen (around 700,000 US dollars), and it employs only three professional staff (Ichikawa Fusae Kinenkai 2002; Park 2006; Zenchifu-ren 2007).[17]

---

[15] For an intriguing discussion on the sources of change (and non-change) in Japan's fertility policies, see the thought-provoking book, *Race for the Exits*, by Leonard Schoppa (2006).

[16] Data are drawn from the annual reports (1958 to 2004) by the Ichikawa Fusae Kinenkai.

[17] *Zenchifu-ren* is not necessarily a small resource in the world of Japanese women's organizations. Its membership is the largest except for the Federation of Consumer Cooperatives in Japan (FCCJ), which has 22 million members, but is not a genuine women's organization. Its budget size and staff are close to those of the FCCJ and the New Japan Women's Association, which is closely related to the Japan Communist Party. Other feminist-oriented organizations are very small in terms of their memberships (less than 3,000) and budgets (less than 20 million yen). See the annual reports (1958 to 2004) by the Ichikawa Fusae Kinenkai and Park (2006: 47–52).

In addition, *Zenchifu-ren*'s policy focus seems so comprehensive that it is not very effective in influencing the constant declining fertility rate.

The national centre of *kodomo-kai*, children's (parents) associations, is the National Federation of Children's Associations (*Zenko-ren*). *Zenko-ren*'s policy also puts emphasis on training, educating, and communicating with children, their parents and leaders of both children and parents. It has a relatively weak desire to lobby and influence national policy, especially countermeasure policies against declining fertility (Zenko-ren 2007).

## 5. Conclusion

Our review of the contributions of NHAs to facing the demographic challenge leaves us with a mixed conclusion.

Japanese neighbourhood associations are effective in the provision of social capital. Their organizational infrastructure and networks provide a bulwark that mitigates enfeeblement and loneliness. Together, these factors ameliorate the effects of the ageing society. In this context at least, NHAs are effective "problem-solves" for the state.

However, NHAs and their women's and children's subgroups are not as effective in mitigating declining fertility, because social capital is not as relevant for reproductive decisions as it is for health.

Finally, NHAs are not good solution-providers for the state or society as it seeks to create new solutions to meet the demographic challenge. Because of their intrinsically local and non-professionalized nature, NHAs are not effective avenues for formulating or articulating new policy visions.

## References

AARP (American Association for Retired Persons) (Various years): *Annual Report*. http://www.aarp.org (found 26 February 2007).

Ashita no Nihon wo Tsukuru Kyōkai (2000): *Jichi-kai, chōnai-kai no kōreisha ni kansuru hōkokusho* [Report on the NHAs' support to aged people]. Tokyo: Ashita no Nihon wo Tsukuru Kyōkai.

Ichikawa Fusae Kinenkai [The Fusae Ichikawa Memorial Association] (2002): *Zenkoku Soshiki Josei Dantai Meibo 2002 nen-ban* [Directory of National Women's Organizations in Japan, 2002]. Tokyo: Ichikawa Fusae Kinenkai.

JFSCC (Japan Federation of Senior Citizens' Clubs, Inc.) (Zenkoku Rōjin Kurabu Rengo-kai, Zenrō-ren) (Various years): *Annual Report*. http://www4.ocn.ne.jp/~zenrou/ (found 25 February 2007).

Mie Prefecture (2005): *Jichi-kai nado no jūmin iichi soshiki ni kansuru ankēto chōsa kekka hōkokusho* [The result of the NHA survey in Mie]. Mie: Prefecturural Government, Machizukuri Support Congress.

Ministry of General Affairs (2003): *Chien ni yoru dantai no jyōkyō nado ni kansuru chōsa kekka* [Results of a survey on neighbourhood associations with legal status]. Tokyo: Ministry of General Affairs, Bureau of Self-autonomous Administration, Administration Division.

Nakamura, Itsuro and Katsuko Kojima (eds.) (2007): *Sekai no jūmin soshiki to funsō* [Neighbourhood associations and conflict in the world]. Tsukuba: University of Tsukuba Press.

Nakata, Minoru (2000): Kenkyū no mokuteki, hōhō, kadai [Themes, methods, and aims of the research]. In: Nakata, Minoru (ed.): *Sekai no jūmin soshiki* [Residents' associations around the world]. Tokyo: Jichitai Kenkyūsha, pp. 1–21.

Nihon Sōgō Kenkyūjo (2003): *Sōsharu kyapitaru: yutaka na ningenkankei to shiminkatsudō no kōjunkan o motomete* [Social capital: for a virtuous circle of rich human relationships and citizen activities]. Tokyo: Nihon Sōgō Kenkyūjo.

Park, In Kyoun (2006): *Nihon no josei seisaku katei ni okeru josei-dantai, sono eikyōryoku to genkai* [Women's associations in the women's policy process in Japan: their influence and limitation]. Ph.D. Dissertation, University of Tsukuba.

Pekkanen, Robert (2003): Molding Japanese Civil Society. In: Schwartz, Frank J. and Susan J. Pharr (eds.): *The State of Civil Society in Japan*. Cambridge and New York: Cambridge University Press, pp. 116–134.

—— (2004a): After the Developmental State in Japan. In: *Journal of East Asian Studies* 4, 3, pp. 363–388.

—— (2004b): Japan: Social Capital without Advocacy. In: Alagappa, Mutiah (ed.): *Civil Society and Political Change in Asia: Expanding and Contracting Democratic Space*. Stanford, CA: Stanford University Press, pp. 223–255.

—— (2005): Neighbourhood Associations and Public Policy in Japan. In: *Journal of Public Policy Studies* 5, pp. 27–52.

—— (2006): *Japan's Dual Civil Society: Members without Advocates*. Stanford, CA: Stanford University Press.

Putnam, Robert D. (2000): *Bowling Alone: The Collapse and Revival of American Community*. New York: Simon & Schuster.

Putnam, Robert D., Robert Leonardi and Raffaella Nanetti (1993): *Making Democracy Work: Civic Traditions in Modern Italy*. Princeton, NJ: Princeton University Press.

Read, Benjamin L. and Robert Pekkanen (2005): Straddling State and Society: Challenges and Insights from Ambiguous Associations. Conference paper read at Shambaugh Conference held on Nov. 10–12, 2005, at the University of Iowa.

Roper Center (University of Connecticut) (1997): *Japan Broadcasting Survey*. http://www.ropercenter.uconn.edu/jpoll/JPOLL.html (found 9 November 2003).

Schoppa, Leonard (2006): *Race for the Exits: The Unraveling of Japan's System of Social Protection*. Ithaca, NY: Cornell University Press.

Tsujinaka, Yutaka (1988): Fukushi shakai no mosaku to Nihon no fukushi shakai no genzai [Japanese welfare interest groups in a transition period]. In: *The Welfare State in Transition and Political Science, The Annuals of Japanese Political Science Association*. Tokyo: Iwanami Shoten, pp. 163–178.

—— (ed.) (2002): *Gendai Nihon no shimin shakai, rieki dantai* [Civil society organizations and interest groups in contemporary Japan]. Tokyo: Bokutakusha.

—— (2003): From Developmentalism to Maturity: Japan's Civil Society Organizations in Comparative Perspective. In: Schwartz, Frank J. and Susan J. Pharr (eds.): *The State of Civil Society in Japan*. Cambridge, UK; New York: Cambridge University Press, pp. 83–116.

Tsukuba City Survey (unpublished): *Tsukuba-shi jichikai-tō chōsa* [Neighbourhood associations survey in Tsukuba City], a survey conducted in 2006 by Tsujinaka Yutaka and his team (University of Tsukuba).

Ueda, Korekazu (1985): Gyōsei, seiji, shūkyō to chōnai-kai' [Local government, politics, religion and neighbourhood associations]. In: Iwasaki, Nobuhiko, *et al.* (eds.): *Chōnai-kai no kenkyū* [Research on neighbourhood associations]. Tokyo: Ochanomizu Shōbō, pp. 439–468.

Yasui, Kouji (1985): Seibi sareta zenchiteki chōnai-kai taisei [Citywide neighbourhood association system]. In: Iwasaki, Nobuhiko, *et al.* (eds.): *Chōnai-kai no kenkyū* [Research on neighbourhood associations]. Tokyo: Ochanomizu Shōbō, pp. 195–214.

Yokohama City Government (2003): *Jumin soshiki no genjō to katsudo* [The situation and activities of NHAs in Yokohama]. Yokohama: City Government.

—— (2004a): *Yokohama-shi jichi-kai chōnai-kai ankēto chōsa kekka* [The result of the NHA survey in Yokohama]. Yokohama: City Government.

—— (2004b): *Yokohama-shi jichi-kai chōnai-kai no genkyō to yosan kessan jokyō shirabe hōkokusho* [Report of NHAs' budgets and settlements in Yokohama]. Yokohama: City Government.

Zenchifu-ren (2007): *Zenkoku Chiiki Fujin Dantai Renraku Kyōgikai* [National Federation of Regional Women's Organizations]. http://www.chifuren.gr.jp/ (found 25 February 2007).

Zenji-ren (2007): *Zenkoku Jichikai Rengo-kai* [National Federation of NHAs]. http://www.city.okayama.okayama.jp/shimin/zenjiren/ (found 25 February 2007).

Zenko-ren (2007): *Zenkoku Kodomo-kai Rengo-kai* [National Federation of Children's Associations]. http://www.kodomo-kai.or.jp/ (found 25 February 2007).

CHAPTER THIRTY-NINE

# "INDUCED" VOLUNTARISM: A NEW ROLE FOR SCHOOLS?

Akihiro Ogawa

## 1. Hōshi [service] in the School Curriculum

In November 2004, the Japanese media reported that the Tokyo Metropolitan Government had decided to introduce a new course from the 2007–08 academic year as part of the core curriculum at all public high schools supervised by the government (see, for example, *Asahi Shinbun* 11 November 2004). The course is titled *hōshi*, which literally translates as "service" in English. It targets some 45,000 students in 207 high schools in the Tokyo metropolitan area. According to the interim report produced in March 2006 by the curriculum development committee of the Tokyo Metropolitan Government Board of Education (TMG 2006a), the course is to be taught over at least 35 hours (1 credit unit) as a graduation requirement. During the course, it is expected that students will spend ten hours hearing from their teachers what *hōshi* is, and then, for the remaining 25 hours, they will "experience" (*taiken suru*) various kinds of volunteering opportunities beyond the conventional classroom, arranged by their schools in the area of social welfare, environmental protection, and so on. In the last phase of the course, the students are expected to have some reflective sessions on their *hōshi* activities. Furthermore, this policy implementation addresses a key problem faced by contemporary Japanese society: the increase of young people known as "NEET" (Not in Education, Employment or Training) and "Freeters" (temporary or part-time workers) (Honda 2004; Genda 2005; Kosugi 2006). By giving wider opportunities to know and experience the real world, policy makers and educators expect that students will think realistically about their job possibilities after graduating from school. This is the first kind of policy attempt in the country to introduce such a course requirement at school.

The interim report construes the purpose of this policy development as outlined below:

> In life, it is extremely important to do something for others, not for oneself, and to feel happiness through those experiences. "Thank you." This single phrase means we are acknowledged by other people and makes us feel we have been useful to them; this contributes greatly to developing mature adults. Through *hōshi* activities, we can nurture a sense of independence and spontaneity among students [...]. We believe that it is particularly important to use this opportunity for students to start participating in these activities, so that through these activities they can realize the significance of doing something for others and continue them. Above all, we believe that it is important for schools to provide students with various kinds of opportunities and settings for the *hōshi* activities, and then, as a result of this education, we hope that students will display this voluntarism fully in the future (TMG 2006a: 1).

The interim report goes on to say why they call the course *hōshi*, instead of *borantia*, which can be roughly translated as "volunteering" in English—a more popular word among Japanese people.

*Hōshi* is an activity responding to the actual needs of society. We believe that it goes beyond conventional *borantia* activities generated through individual spontaneous will. We locate such *hōshi* activities in the regular school curriculum, and then expect that, through the activities, students will come to feel that they are members of society. The new course aims for students to feel happiness through the actual activities and being useful to society (TMG 2006a: 3–4).

This curriculum is based on a pilot programme that the Tokyo Metropolitan Government had previously implemented. Since the 2004–05 school year, all Tokyo public high schools set one day in November as Volunteering Day (*borantia no hi*), and since 2005, the Tokyo government tentatively introduced a course titled *borantia* in 21 high schools (TMG 2006a: 36). However, this one-day activity was not successful, because most of the schools just spent the day on cleaning activities around the schools, according to a newspaper report (*Yomiuri Shinbun* 11 November 2004).

In this policy implementation—introducing *hōshi* as a core requirement—however, the Tokyo government seems to have become more strategic. First, by changing the course name from *borantia* to *hōshi*, they bestow the nuance that the activities are more or less to be forced on students, and are made to sound mandatory. Furthermore, they prepared a pamphlet for local people and communities in order to ask for their cooperation (TMG 2006b). In the strong linkage of schools and communities, students are placed to work as interns with local social welfare facilities and non-profit social service providers. The pamphlet prepared by the Tokyo government's board of education introduces the kind of activities expected with real pictures taken in the pilot programme. The activities include gardening with kindergarten students; listening to stories from senior citizens; campaigning to decrease the number of abandoned bicycles; and cleaning and repairing wheelchairs. The pamphlet is distributed by the metropolitan government when it asks local communities to accept students. In a Q & A format, the government tells the local people and communities that they will not need to pay the students any transportation expenses or rewards (both commonly paid in Japan); and students would be provided with casualty and damage insurance under the programme.

In this paper, I discuss an implication of the ongoing government-sponsored "induced" volunteerism in Japan society. In particular, I focus on the role of the school in developing a coercive sense of volunteerism. I see state-supervised education today as an agency in generating a particular form of human nature that becomes internalized in what I call "volunteer subjectivity"—Foucauldian, normative self-disciplined subjectivity—as an ideal social identity. In fact, the policy process has been strategically implemented with a series of revisions to education-related laws in order to support such subjectification, in other words, subjugation of the individual to a norm by means of internalisation. Concerning demographic changes—ageing, in particular—my argument further focuses on the fact that this education policy plays a significant role in generating a convenient subject, from a policy maker's perspective, to support the social welfare system originally operated by the government. The newly generated individuals who experience the current coercive volunteer mobilization, or *hōshi* programme, are strongly expected to work to take care of the expanding number of ageing people as non-paid workers organized under the voluntary non-profit-based social service providers like the Non-Profit Organizations (NPO), a new third sector incorporated under the 1998 NPO Law (formally Law to Promote Specified Non-profit Activities).[1]

[1] I use the term "third sector," which usually implies "citizens' sector" and is associated neither with government nor business. The third sector stands beside the first sector (the government) and the second sector (for-profit businesses). In Japanese, there is a direct translation for "third sector": *daisan sekutā*. However, this term refers to corporations established through joint investments of the government and for-profit businesses. In the present context, I am referring to the common usage (Van 1995), not to the Japanese term.

I explore the following key questions: What are the ways in which states seek to shape their relations with their populations, and how effective are those policies likely to be? What are students experiencing and how do they feel about what they are doing or are forced to do? For data collection, I employ the methodology of qualitative ethnography. The data this paper cites were collected during 22 months of fieldwork in downtown Tokyo from September 2001 through 2003, followed by additional research in summer 2004. In addition, I conducted some document research in order to update my knowledge of policy developments at the national, prefectural and municipal levels. Ultimately, this paper calls into question the relationship between the state and civil society in contemporary Japanese social and political life. Furthermore, the paper has some policy implications for any state seeking to mould its society in specific ways.

## 2. Volunteer Mobilization Programme

The Tokyo case I introduced at the beginning is not an exception. Nowadays the government-sponsored volunteer mobilization programme is a solid trend in Japanese society. The Ministry of Education, Science, Sports, Culture, and Technology (MEXT) funded more than 120 billion yen (approximately USD 1.1 billion) for implementing policies in volunteer mobilization or "promotion" (*suishin*, as it is called in the official policy report's language) in fiscal 2006 starting April of that year (MEXT 2006b). The policies include research funds in the area; training instructors; networking for generating internship opportunities among schools and local communities; curriculum development; and so on. The policies broadly cover formal education, including elementary and secondary schools, colleges, and lifelong learning. One of the key policies of the ministry is the introduction of a nationwide programme for experiencing volunteering within the regular school curriculum, as in the Tokyo case. The formal state programme title in Japanese is *yutakana taiken katsudō suishin jigyō* [programme for promoting rich experience activities], and it intends to give students some real experiences beyond the classroom and to make them realize the significance of volunteerism. Emphasizing *taiken*, or experiencing activities, is located as one of the key agenda items in the programme. The ministry has currently appointed 893 pilot schools at all levels in every region of Japan (MEXT 2006a) and asked for programme development of activities of "social service" (*shakai hōshi*) in the policy report. The programme further aims to generate a nationwide structure to promote *shakai hōshi* activities for students at elementary, secondary, and college levels through actual volunteer experiences. Meanwhile, the programme has established support centres (*shien sentā*) at both national and prefectural levels for promoting such activities and maintaining information on the issue. Across the country, there are 1,194 support centres (MEXT 2004).

This kind of education policy might remind some readers of service learning programmes developed in the United States, for example, a teaching and learning strategy broadly used in K-12 institutions (from kindergarten through the last year of high school), colleges and universities. The National Service-Learning Clearinghouse of the United States defines service-learning as follows (NSLC 2006): "Service-learning combines service objectives with learning objectives with the intent that the activity changes both the recipient and the provider of the service. This is accomplished by combining service tasks with structured opportunities that link to self-reflection, self-discovery, and the acquisition and comprehension of values, skills, and knowledge content." Further, "Service-learning links to academic content and standards; involves young people in helping to determine and meet real, defined community needs; is reciprocal in nature, benefiting both the community and the service providers by combining a service experience with a learning experience; can be used in any subject area so long as it appropriates to learning goals; and works at all ages, even among young children" (NSLC 2006). In a Japanese context, however, the term service learning is not (yet) used in the official policy documents I examined in analysing the ongoing volunteer mobilization policies, nor was the term itself well-known among ordinary people. But I believe the concept itself has permeated the Education Ministry's thoughts, and that service learning is in fact just being introduced to Japanese society. A couple of universities have introduced service-learning as credit courses. For example, the International Christian University in Tokyo set up a Service Learning Center and offered service learning courses in 2006, actually using the term "service learning" (ICU 2006). The MEXT has funded programme development in the area of international service learning and is building information networks with foreign universities over four years from 2005 (MEXT 2005a). It also funded a programme development initiative on community-based service learning at Showa Women's University in Tokyo in 2005 (MEXT 2005b).

The implementation of volunteer mobilization programmes was originally supported by the revision of the School Education Law in 2001 mentioning the introduction of social service experiences in school education. Further, it was supported by a report released in 2002 by the Central Council for Education, an advisory body to the education minister, recommending *hōshi* activities in regular school curricula as part of their core courses, such as in moral education and social studies classes at elementary, secondary and college levels (CCE 2002). In the report, *hōshi* is located as "a key for solving problems we are facing" and it "provides an opportunity for the social participation of independent, autonomous individuals." Further, a new term, New Public (*atarashii kōkyō*), was introduced in the same report. This is a sphere in which people in general or people who are interested in a particular cause can voluntarily participate, and the report sets this sphere as a foundation of solidarity for good citizens to promote a better society. In the following year's report by the Central Council for Education, the concept of the New Public was actively discussed with a view to supporting the sphere (CCE 2003). The report explicitly stated, "To support the *New Public*, what one needs is self-awareness as an active participant in the making of state and society, courage in order to practise social justice, and an attitude of respect for Japanese traditional norms." Trained under this educational philosophy, students are expected to realize what civic engagement is. These conceptualizations have been embodied in the new guidelines for school education (*gakushū shidō yōryō*) in 2002 for elementary and junior high schools and in 2003 for senior high schools. The current introduction of *hōshi* courses in Tokyo metropolitan high schools and the nationwide MEXT-sponsored *taiken* programme can be located as parts of this series of the revision of education-related laws in Japan. In tandem with this policy development, the Japanese government was trying to revise the Fundamental Law of Education, a basic charter defining the direction of state-supervised education, in order to situate *borantia*, volunteering, as one of the core courses in the Japanese school system. The revision was approved by the National Diet in December 2006—the first change since its enactment during the US-led post-war occupation in 1947. It aimed to generate a subjectivity focused on civic engagement called *hōshi*, in which people can spontaneously participate in problem-solving processes in public affairs.

## 3. Cultural Production of Volunteer Subjectivity

During the course of my ethnographic fieldwork from September 2001 through April 2003, I was based at a third-sector NPO organization incorporated under the 1998 NPO Law in Japan. My field site, SLG (pseudonym), was an NPO promoting lifelong learning in a local community in downtown Tokyo. What I primarily observed and experienced there was the mobilization of a type of subjectivity supporting the new social institution, the NPO. As I have already argued elsewhere (Ogawa 2004, 2005a, 2005b, 2005c, 2005d), this subjectivity is a Foucauldian coercive subjectivity—what I call "volunteer subjectivity." I have identified the phenomenon from a viewpoint heavily influenced by Michel Foucault's notion of governmentality, which refers not only to political processes or state agencies, but also, in a more general sense, to the art of guiding people (Foucault 1977, 1991). This theoretical perspective highlights the interplay among forms of knowledge, power strategies, and modes of subjectivation. It concentrates on those rationalities and technologies that aim to systematically direct and control individuals and collectives containing forms of self-government as well as forms of governing others. At the micro-political level, this normative, self-disciplined subjectivity is recognized as important and ideal for society, and it is reproduced as a desirable social identity through education as a national project and a nationwide campaign promoting volunteerism.

At my field site, the local government invites—or, more accurately, *mobilizes*—its residents to become volunteers and organizes them under NPOs to provide basic social services originally furnished by the government (Ogawa 2004). The Japanese Law for the Promotion of Lifelong Learning, enacted in 1990, states that both national and municipal governments must support the promotion of lifelong learning. In 1994, the municipal government in downtown Tokyo opened a public facility for promoting lifelong learning in the ward where SLG is currently located. In order to operate the centre, the fiscally constrained government, which did not want to spend more money on social services, decided to ask that course-content creation be carried out by local residents as volunteers. The government initially organized the local volunteers as a citizens' group, which functioned as part of the government. Following the enactment of the 1998 NPO Law, the government decided that this citizens' group, SLG, should apply for NPO status. Taking on the government's role, SLG offered a variety of lifelong learning courses to the local residents—a total of 190 individual courses over the two years from 2001 to 2003. The courses included not only cultural activities and hobbies, but also career development, languages, and sports, and local residents could take these courses on their own initiative to enrich and improve their lives. This local action was primarily established and copied by municipal governments as part of the devolution of social services or the withdrawal of the state from social services—a key feature of neoliberal governmentality—primarily aimed at cost-cutting in public administration (Dean 1999). Such policy collaboration between the state and third sector is known as *kyōdō* in Japanese, and has become a fashionable administrative technique in Japanese local politics. In fact, providing this social service was something inevitable in the downtown Tokyo community where more than one-fifth of the total population was elderly, aged 65 years or older, more than the Japanese national average.[2] SLG played a significant role in providing learning opportunities to this expanding, aged population, giving their lives meaning through learning.

One of the major differences I noticed between the initial and final stages of my fieldwork from 2001 through 2003 and follow-up research in summer 2004 at my field site was that the number of students participating in the NPO's activities as volunteers gradually increased. SLG regularly accepted students from local junior high schools and colleges as interns. SLG has accepted two or three students from local junior high schools each month during semesters and college students in summer. The students were invited to the work experience (*shokuba taiken*) programme, developed jointly by local schools and SLG. They worked with paid staff at the organization for a week or so, and they earned credits needed for graduation. Through this programme, students were expected to learn how volunteer activities actually worked in real settings, and, furthermore, how third-sector organizations like NPOs work with the other existing sectors, the government and for-profit businesses, as well as other third-sector organizations. SLG assigned some projects to the students. The projects include data entry using computers with secretariat staff members, helping instructors and resident volunteers in course administration, and delivering newsletters on

[2] According to the 2005 White Paper on the Ageing Society, among the total population of 127.69 million people, the number of elderly people aged 65 or over reached a new high of 24.88 million people in 2004. The percentage of elderly people in the total population also increased to 19.5% (Cabinet Office 2005).

lifelong learning to such local facilities as the city hall, public libraries, senior citizens' centre, banks, metro stations, and neighbourhood associations. One local junior high school student who had an internship at SLG commented that he was impressed with SLG activities primarily organized by volunteers. He said, "I helped with administrative work at the secretariat. Before doing this internship, I thought that this kind of experience would not mean so much to me. But, having actually done it, my impression has totally changed. I learned a lot from this experience." Another intern, a college student majoring in business administration, said, "By experiencing a job in a real setting, I myself became aware of many things. It was important to process what I was assigned quickly and correctly, and what is more, I also learned that taking care of others is important too." By actually experiencing these activities, those students were expected to realize the meaning of what they were doing, and to internalize "volunteer subjectivity." (Cf. Coleman in this volume, 749–763).

Nowadays the Japanese state at many different levels—national, prefectural, and municipal—is trying to systematically produce this particular type of individual, who has internalized volunteer subjectivity through education. This could be a prototype for so-called *shimin* [citizens], and I would argue that *shimin* are cultural products of discursive norms—"a category of individuals to be governed" (Wedel *et al.* 2005: 30)—in contemporary Japan. The standardized volunteer subjectivity embodied in *shimin* is expected to produce docile subjects in the current neoliberal system. They are merely expected to be collaborative partners participating in public affairs for the betterment of society by being organized under NPOs. The Japanese NPOs were originally believed to provide greater accommodation and space for diversity in contemporary Japan, while breaking the rigid bureaucratic rationality. Japanese people were expected to play a significant role in the newly created social space. However, the NPOs were strategically co-opted into the social and political system under neoliberal governmentality, and *shimin* as a key actor in politics. The process of dispersal from the state to the third sector or the NPOs even strengthened government control through performance targets, or cost cutting in public administration, and the growth of managerialism by the government as a mode of collaboration with the NPO.

## 4. Policy Implications in an Ageing Society

The current policy developments relating to *hōshi* [volunteer mobilization] programmes have significant meaning in contemporary Japanese society, which is facing a huge demographic change: ageing. In December 2005, the Japanese government announced that the national population started shrinking in 2005 for the first time on record. The Ministry of Health, Labour and Welfare's annual survey (MHLW 2005) shows that the balance of domestic births of Japanese minus deaths in the year is estimated to be minus 10,000 people, marking the first "natural decline" since the data were first compiled in 1899. This figure represents pressing social and economic challenges for the Japanese state, such as how to sustain its social security system and secure the labour force. With society ageing and women having fewer children, social security costs are likely to increase for future generations. This will increase the pressure on the government to secure a budget by raising social security contributions.

Under the circumstances, the ongoing volunteer mobilization programme is a political technique. It has been generated by a particular type of population who can or will support the social welfare system originally operated by the government. The individuals are expected to work to take care of the expanding ageing population as volunteers under social-service NPOs. What they are expected to do is to work to maintain and even strengthen the existing social and political system of the Japanese state. Underlying this is the "induced" volunteerism I have discussed in this paper, and such volunteerism is eagerly promoted by conservative politicians, such as Tokyo Governor Shintarō Ishihara. They have long been dissatisfied with the post-war US-drafted laws, which they say eroded the pride of Japanese in their culture and history, and negated legitimate patriotic sentiment. In fact, current policy development in the series of education laws, primarily including the revision of the Fundamental Law of Education, makes it a goal to cultivate an attitude that respects tradition and culture, and love of the nation and the homeland that has fostered them. Within this particular political philosophy, participating in *hōshi* activities equates to contributing to the nation and the homeland or the state. This again creates a synergy effect to enhance a sense of patriotism—*hōshi* activities stimulate a sense of patriotism, and a sense of patriotism encourages participating in *hōshi* activities. The ongoing "induced" volunteerism is expected and intended to generate such Japanese young people who will work for the state.

## References

*Asahi Shinbun* (11 November 2004): Toritsu kōkō 'hōshi' hisshū e, Tōkyō-to Kyōi ga 07 nendo ni [Tokyo Metropolitan Government Board of Education to introduce *hōshi* as a core requirement in 2007], p. 1, evening edition.

Cabinet Office (2005): *Kōreikashakai hakusho* [White Paper on the ageing society]. Tokyo: National Printing Bureau.

CCE (Central Council for Education) (2002): *Seishōnen no hōshi katsudō—taiken katsudō no suishin hōsaku nado ni tsuite* [On promoting youth volunteerism]. Tokyo: Central Council for Education.

—— (2003): *Atarashii jidai ni fusawashii Kyōiku Kihon-hō to kyōiku shinkō kihon keikaku no arikata ni tsuite* [On the Fundamental Law of Education and basic plan for education promotion for the new era]. Tokyo: Central Council for Education.

Dean, Mitchell (1999): *Governmentality: Power and Rule in Modern Society*. London: Sage Publications.

Foucault, Michel (1977): *Discipline and Punish: The Birth of the Prison*. New York: Vintage Books.

—— (1991): Governmentality. In: Burchell, Graham, Colin Gordon and Peter Miller (eds.): *The Foucault Effect: Studies in Governmentality*. Chicago: University of Chicago Press, pp. 87–104.

Genda, Yuji (2005): *A Nagging Sense of Job Insecurity: The New Reality Facing Japanese Youth*. Tokyo: International House of Japan.

Honda, Yuki (2004): The Formation and Transformation of the Japanese System of Transition from School to Work. In: *Social Science Japan Journal* 7, 1 (April), pp. 103–115.

ICU (International Christian University) (2006): *Service Learning Center, ICU Service Learning Program*. http://subsite.icu.ac.jp/slc/e/about.html#a (found 17 May 2006).

Kosugi, Rieko (2006): *Youth Employment in Japan's Economic Recovery: 'Freeters' and 'NEETs'*. http://www.japanfocus.org/products/details/2022 (found 10 February 2007).

MEXT (Ministry of Education, Science, Sports, Culture, and Technology) (2004): *Heisei 16-nendo Monbukagaku hakusho* [English title: White Papers on education, culture, sports, science and technology 2004]. Tokyo: National Printing Bureau.

—— (2005a): *Heisei 17-nendo daigaku kyōiku no kokusaika suishin puroguramu* [Programme for internationalization of university education in 2005]. http://www.mext.go.jp/a_menu/koutou/kaikaku/kekka/05080201/003.htm (found 17 May 2006).

—— (2005b): *Heisei 17-nendo 'gendaiteki kyōiku nīzu torikumi shien puroguramu'* [Support for programmes addressing contemporary education needs in 2005]. http://www.mext.go.jp/b_menu/houdou/17/08/05080601/005.htm (found 17 May 2006).

—— (2006a): *Mitemiyō, furetemiyō, yattemiyō, taikenkatsudō no susume* [Recommendations on seeing, feeling and experiencing activities]. http://www.mext.go.jp/a_menu/shougai/houshi/pdf/06030109.pdf (found 4 May 2006).

—— (2006b): *Monbukagakushō ni okeru hōshi katsudō, taiken katsudō no suishin ni kansuru seisaku* [MEXT Policies on promoting social service activities and experience activism]. http://www.mext.go.jp/a_menu/shougai/houshi/05112201.htm (found 4 May 2006).

MHLW (Ministry of Health, Labour and Welfare) (2005): *Heisei 17-nendo jinkō dōtai tōkei* [Population vital statistics for 2005]. Tokyo: Ministry of Health, Labour, and Welfare.

NSLC (National Service-Learning Clearinghouse) (2006): *Service Learning Is*... http://www.servicelearning.org/welcome_to_service-learning/service-learning_is/index.php (found 4 May 2006).

Ogawa, Akihiro (2004): Invited by the State: Institutionalizing Volunteer Subjectivity in Contemporary Japan. In: *Asian Anthropology* 3, pp. 71–96.

—— (2005a): *Mobilizing Volunteer Subjectivity: Japanese "Civil Society" and Volunteerism.* Paper presented at the annual meeting of American Anthropological Association, Washington, DC. November 30, 2005.

—— (2005b): *Power and Contested Rationalities: Policy Collaboration in Continuing Education between an NPO and the State.* Paper presented at the annual meeting of Association for Asian Studies, Chicago. April 1, 2005.

—— (2005c): Shimin shakai ron e no atarashii apurōchi [New approach to civil society studies]. In: National Museum of Ethnology, Osaka, Japan (ed.): *Gekkan Minpaku* 29, 4. (April 2005), p. 6. Available at http://www.minpaku.ac.jp/publication/gekkan/200504txt.html (found 17 May 2006).

—— (2005d): *When the NPO Law Sinks: Japanese Civil Society, Shimin, and Neoliberalism.* Program on US-Japan Relations Occasional Paper Series. Harvard University.

TMG (Tokyo Metropolitan Government) (2006a): *Chūkan hōkokusho: hōshi no hisshūka ni mukete* [Interim report: towards making social service activities required]. Tokyo: Tokyo Metropolitan Government Board of Education.

—— (2006b): *Heisei 19-nendo kara subete no toritsu kōkō de hōshi taiken katsudō ga hajimarimasu* [Service activities to be introduced to all Tokyo public high schools in the 2007–08 academic year]. Tokyo: Tokyo Metropolitan Government Board of Education.

Van, Jon (1995): Theory of the Third Sector. In: *Nonprofit and Voluntary Sector Quarterly* 24, 1, pp. 3–4.

Wedel, Janine R., Cris Shore, Gregory Feldman and Stacy Lathrop (2005): Toward an Anthropology of Public Policy. In: *The Annals of the American Academy* 600, pp. 30–51.

*Yomiuri Shinbun* (11 November 2004): Toritsu kōkō katsudō" hisshū kamoku ni, 2007–nendo zen-200–kō de [Social Service Activities to be required in all 200 Tokyo public high schools from 2007], p. 1, evening edition.

Case in point: Age structure of volunteers

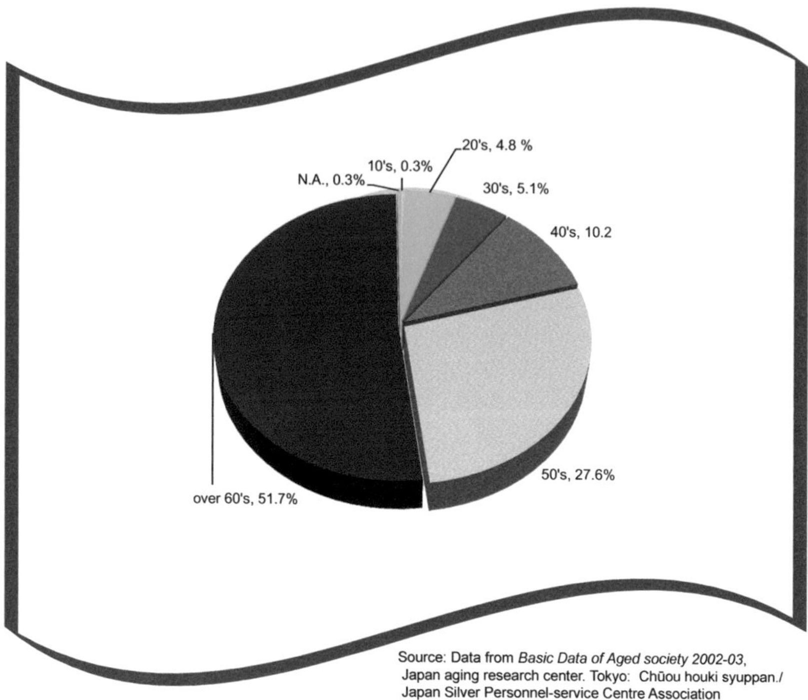


Source: Data from *Basic Data of Aged society 2002-03*, Japan aging research center. Tokyo: Chūou houki syuppan./ Japan Silver Personnel-service Centre Association

CHAPTER FORTY

# EDUCATIONAL POLICY: FRAMEWORK AND CHALLENGES

Susanne Kreitz-Sandberg

## 1. Introduction

Changes in the birth rate influence the situation in schools and other educational institutions. With a decline in the birth rate, school class sizes are falling, universities are entering into new competition for students, and generational relations within educational institutions are changing. Obviously, demographic change is one, but not the only, factor triggering change. It co-exists and interacts with other factors, such as value change, internationalization and specific youth problems. In this chapter the following questions will be addressed: Is demographic change an obvious factor influencing educational policy? How is the situation in educational institutions affected by demographic change? How are demographic developments and their consequences discussed in Japanese educational policies, and how do educational policies respond to questions of demographic change?

Each of these questions will be analysed in separate sections with the aim of investigating the challenges and opportunities of demographic change for schooling and educational policies in Japan. A brief literature review will deal with the question of whether demographic change is perceived to be an obvious factor affecting Japanese educational policy (section 2). In section 3, the actual influence of the declining birth rate on the reality in schools is investigated. I will focus my analysis on the developments in the school population in public schools, and on the consequences of the changing student-teacher ratio, including its influence on classroom interactions and on central measures in educational reform, for example, high school admission reform. In section 4, I will analyse policies of the Ministry of Education addressing the challenges of a declining birth rate for society in general and for education and education policies in particular. Finally, I will summarize the overall effects of demographics on education and discussions evolving around educational policy.

## 2. Literature Review on Educational Policy

Educational crisis and reform have been popular topics in Japan for decades (e.g. Cummings *et al.* 1984). While some educational researchers point out the need for liberalization and individualization in the school system (Amano 1998), others remind us of the need to build a social system that builds on cooperation (Fujita 1997) and are keenly aware of increasing social inequality within the school system (Kariya 2001). Some of the most recent problems faced by the educational system are related to demographic change. For example, the so-called "2009 crisis" is predicted to bring serious consequences for the study habits of school students, as all students will easily be able to enter higher education because they belong to such small age cohorts graduating from high school. Goodman's introductory chapter to the edited volume *Can the Japanese Change Their Education System* (Goodman and Phillips 2003) already hint that education and education reform are obviously linked to demographic change.

Back in the early 1990s, Leonard Schoppa (1991) described Japanese immobilist politics concerning education. Various actors involved in the design of educational policies discuss the reasons and need for change in different ways. The Ministry of Education, Science, Sport and Culture had to reach a compromise on many of its ideas with other influential actors such as teachers' unions and employers' organisations. This led, according to Schoppa's analysis, to an almost complete inability to change educational policies. Further studies on educational reforms during the 1980s came to slightly different conclusions. Both Marie Roesgaard (1998) and Christopher Hood (2001) described how educational policy is in fact changing. Did something relevant change during the 1990s which helped them develop this argument? The hypothesis to be investigated in the following discussion is that attention to demographic developments gave new impetus to the need for and perspectives on reform of educational policy.

Demographic change is more obvious in discussions on higher education than in those on school reform. Higher education reforms build on the prediction that Japan will be challenged in many respects, and the first factor mentioned in the most comprehensive report issued by the University Council[1] in 1998 under the title "A Vision for Japanese Universities in the 21st Century and Reform Measures" is in fact the rapidly ageing population (Tsuruta 2003: 127). In connection with the fast decline in the number of 18 year-olds it "was proposed that more global cooperation, and co-existence in higher education is necessary, as well as interdisciplinary research and lifelong learning" (Tsuruta 2003: 128). Reforms aim at more flexibility and more variation in entrance procedures. Graduate schools are opening up to adult learners with a new focus on lifelong learning, recurrent education and collaboration with the community and industry.

Lifelong learning is gradually becoming more favoured in an aged society with fewer children. However, even if adult education has gained importance, Japan is still a highly school-centred society where much of further learning is left to training within companies (Fuwa 2001: 132). Nevertheless, issues arising from the ageing society have also fuelled discussions on lifelong education through the 1990s and on the influence of demographics, specifically "how the social issue of the birth of fewer children impacts on lifelong learning in Japan" (Ogawa 2005: 352). Obviously demographic processes are favouring institutions other than the conventional school system (see also chapter 28 in this volume).

## 3. Changing Schools In or For a Society with Fewer Children

The intention in this section is to demonstrate how a declining birth rate influences the schooling situation and education policy decisions. The term demography will be used as a synonym of social ageing, characterising the decline of population which follows low numbers of births combined with a stagnating high life expectancy.

[1] The so-called University Council Report was published by the Planning Division of Higher Education Bureau in the Ministry of Education, Science, Sport and Culture in 1998.

### 3.1. *Development of school population in the compulsory school system*[2]

The first baby boomers (born 1948–51) entered primary school in 1954, junior high school six years later, and senior high school in 1963. Within one year, primary school teachers had to take care of 2.5 million new pupils instead of fewer than two million per year. The number declined to 1.5 million children within a decade, only to rise again to two million with the so-called second baby boomers, the children of this big post-war cohort, who entered primary school 1978–1980. After this, the number of children and therefore of pupils entering school declined steadily to less than 1.2 million in 2004 (MEXT 2005: 22).[3] The consequence of this process is that Japanese primary schools experienced a decade of comparatively low student numbers after a period of frequent change.

For junior high schools a similar process can be described. For the years between 1955 and 1965, there were almost six million junior high school students in grades 7 to 9. The same was true for 1985, when the second baby boom generation had reached secondary school age (MEXT 2005: 43). In between and after that the numbers were substantially lower, with around 4.7 million through the 1970s and then again below 4.5 million from 1995 onwards. In 2004 the lowest number was reached, with 3,663,513 pupils in junior high school.

Concerning the relation of demographics and educational policies, these numbers can teach us the following points. First of all, it is interesting to observe that, in the mid-1980s, that is, the years when Prime Minister Nakasone Yasuhiro (1982–1987) was determined to realize school reforms, student numbers in junior high schools were peaking. It is not surprising that youth problems were the most prominent topic of debate during this wave of education reform. At the same time, the decline in the birth rate and its consequences was already becoming obvious.

---

[2] "The post-war Japanese education system is patterned on the American model. At the age of six, children enter primary school, which has six grades. They then proceed to middle school, which comprises three years; completing is mandatory. Some 97 per cent of those who complete compulsory education then progress to three-year high school [data from 2000]. Thus more than nine out of ten students complete twelve years of schooling, making high school education virtually semi-mandatory. All governmental schools are co-educational, but some private schools are single-sex." (Sugimoto 2003: 115).

[3] The number of students in the first grade rose slightly in 2005, but is still under 1.2 million (MEXT 2006).

### 3.2. *Student-teacher ratio*

The average class size in a primary school was 26 pupils in 2004 (MEXT 2005: 40). It has steadily declined over recent decades. Class size varies greatly between different residential areas. The smallest classes resulting from the decline in the birth rate are found in many schools in the countryside and in some inner city areas where families have been moving away because of high apartment prices. In these areas, some of the schools have even had to close. In other areas we can still find class sizes of 36 to 40 pupils. This was the case in about 20 per cent of the primary schools in 1995. Such big classes are also common in the popular state schools and some of the private schools (MEXT 2005: 40). In junior high schools, the same pattern becomes obvious, with big classes continuing in the elite schools and a steady decline in class sizes in average state schools. The size in the local junior high schools reached an average of 31 students per class in 2004 (MEXT 2005: 43).

What are the consequences of this process? In comparison to European standards, over 30 pupils per class does not seem very small. And American commentators also criticize class size in Japanese schools (Nemoto 1999). However, smaller classes do not necessarily carry a positive connotation:

> In Japan, where the students' passivity and obedience to school rules allow the teacher to concentrate on instruction according to the Education Ministry's standardized national curriculum, children learn very effectively in large classes. [...] Even so, class sizes have been reduced considerably since World War II, when classes of 60 children were normal. By 1958 the average was 50. The maximum was set at 45 in 1963 before being lowered to the current figure of 40, which was introduced for elementary and middle schools in 1980 and extended to high schools in 1993. Some local school officials have requested further reductions but the Education Ministry is content with the current number (Nemoto 1999: 50).

The upper limit of 40 pupils per class was set during the years when the large cohort of the second baby boom just had entered school age. As a result, a considerable number of additional teachers were employed during the 1980s. This group is still active in the teaching profession, as becomes obvious looking at the percentages of full-time teachers by age group: in 2001, 57.7 per cent of the teachers belonged to the 39 to 53 age group, forming the largest age group of all teachers. Only 13 per cent of primary school teachers were aged 32 years and under. The same trend becomes obvious for junior high school teachers, with the only difference being that the teaching cohorts are a few years younger, as the baby boomers entered their schools a few years later. Here two-thirds of the teachers were 33 to 50 years old in 2001. Only 17 per cent of junior high school teachers were aged 32 years or under (MEXT 2005: 41–45).

As a result, we have an aged teacher population, and young teachers have almost no chance of entering employment in the state school system. The absolute number of teachers has been declining since 1985 for primary schools and since 1990 for junior high schools. The fact that fewer teachers have been employed affected female university graduates especially, as 63 per cent of the full-time teaching staff in junior high schools and 75 per cent in primary schools are women (MEXT 2005: 41, 45). This proportion has been stable for over three decades.

Fewer newly trained teachers, threatened survival for some schools in the countryside and inner cities, and smaller classes for a majority of children are the consequences of the declining birth rate.

### 3.3. *Senior high school and university admission*

The number of senior high school students (grade 10 to 12) peaked for the first time in 1965. The advancement rate, which describes the percentage of pupils going on from junior high school to senior high school, was around 70 per cent at that time and rose rapidly over the following years, reaching 82 per cent in 1970 and 92 per cent in 1975. However, even with these rising percentages, the absolute number of senior high school students was not only stable but even declined from over 5 million in 1965 to around 4.3 million through the 1970s. With an advancement rate of around 94 per cent, the absolute number of senior high school students rose to 4.6 and then 5.1 million between 1980 and 1985, reaching the high numbers of the mid-1960s once again. In 1990, competition was at its peak, with 5.6 million teenagers attending senior high school, and from that time the number declined steadily.

In these years of large age cohorts, competition for university places was extreme, and the key phrase "examination hell" (*juken jikoku*) was heard everywhere (Frost 1991). Japanese education became known for its strongly standardized entrance system. Entrance to senior high schools used to be regulated through entrance examinations developed by local education boards (*kyōiku iinkai*). The content of these examinations is almost exclusively retrospective, testing knowledge studied during junior high school years—either in the respective school or in one of the private study academies often called cram schools (*juku*). The examination combines standardized tests in multiple-choice form and questions to be completed in the following subjects: Japanese (language and literature), mathematics, natural science, history, geography and English (von Kopp 1997: 42). The prestige of a school is connected to the points needed to enter it, as well as to the number of its pupils who manage to enter prestigious national universities, such as the University of Tokyo, or the well-known private ones, for example, Waseda or Keio University. Competing for the rare places in the Japanese equivalent of Ivy League Universities in the United States became the tip of the iceberg, with entrance examinations even for the institutions paving the way to these universities. The system established applies these meritocratic standards more or less to all high schools. Even entrance to the less prestigious schools and professional high schools used to be determined by entrance examinations, sometimes combined with grades and recommendation letters from the junior high school. The number of points needed according to a so-called *hensachi* [deviation index][4] were recorded and, in combination with mock examinations, provided pupils with quite a clear picture of which school they might be able to enter.

A diversification of high school admission procedures can already be observed in the early 1980s. A "Committee to Improve Systems of Selecting Entrants to Senior High Schools" was formed in 1983, and published a report "On Systems of Selecting Entrants to Senior High Schools" the following year. This advised local boards of education to diversify selection methods and to employ various selection criteria. The awareness of the negative impact of examination competition on the healthy development of students was a central reason for this process (Nemoto 1999: 105). A closer analysis of demographic development and the number of entrants to senior high school also makes it obvious that the most competitive years for entrance to senior high schools, especially to those with the best reputations, were expected.

From the beginning of the 1990s, the Education Ministry advocated further diversification of selection methods. Nemoto (1999: 106) cites the Ministry's Central Council for Education expressing the view that

---

[4] This index provides information on the average number of points needed in order to enter a school; through mock tests, students have some knowledge of how many points they are likely to get in an average entrance exam.

these changes were vital "in order to create an education system that respects individuality and emphasizes humanity". However, demographic processes influenced these reforms. As the numbers of children and adolescents in inner city areas had declined rapidly, senior high schools started competing for students. In Tokyo the number of primary school pupils had declined from around 930,000 in 1985 to 700,000 in 1990. Von Kopp (1997: 44) presents and interprets these data from the annual statistics on education (*Monbu tokei*). Some primary schools had already closed, and keeping strongly regulated school districts would limit the opportunities of some senior high schools so much that they might also suffer severely.

In connection with liberalization (*jiyūka*), the question of which high schools are forced to close depends on the choice of the students, and perhaps even more on that of the parents (Goodman 2003: 19). And in connection with the school reforms of 2002, schools are allowed and, moreover, required to build up their individual profiles. Therefore, one might argue, it was their own fault if they fail to attract a sufficient number of students. Through this choice, schools are becoming part of a market: which schools are able to survive is no longer a political decision made by the local or national government, but a market-based effect.

Demographic change has severe consequences for university entrance. With fewer children and fewer students graduating from senior high schools, competition for university places, which is also regulated through entrance examinations, is becoming less intense.[5] On one hand, this endangers less prestigious institutions, which are no longer able to attract a sufficient number of students. This is the case especially for junior colleges and for many of the private universities, which depend directly on their income from tuition fees. However, even the leading institutions and well-established universities feel the effects. Even if they have no problems filling their places, they are not always able to attract only the most brilliant students, since this group is much smaller. And, last but not least, a decline in competition is being felt. While the "examination hell" gave cause for concern for many years,

[5] There are also other ways in which the decline of the birth rate affects higher education: since the demand for primary and secondary teachers is declining the universities were confronted with the need to reorganize the relevant faculties. This led to the creation of new departments and academic subjects, often with an international or interdisciplinary focus (Tsuruta 2003: 127).

now there is concern that an insufficient sense of competition hinders young people from aiming to do their best and engaging wholeheartedly in their studies. Today there is concern about students lacking the competence to lead Japan into the next decade of successful international competition, because, since 2002, fewer hours are being taught in the main subjects along with a radical reduction in the core subjects (Kreitz-Sandberg 2001). Why did the reform councils take these radical steps? This question underlies the following analysis of reform papers, focusing on questions of demographic change and its influence on education policy discussions.

## 4. Measures for a Society with Fewer Children within Education Policies

How is Japan's demographic change being addressed by the Ministry of Education? What is the character of the discussion and who took the initiative in this matter? Are the policies just coping with the change inflicted or do they take the initiative in influencing demographic processes?

The national curriculum standards reform of 1998 is the basis for the educational reforms that were carried out in the compulsory school system. The Curriculum Council developed basic principles for this reform, which, besides moral education, were also supposed to respond to social changes such as internationalization, the information-oriented society, environmental issues and an ageing society with a declining birth rate (Curriculum Council, Monbushō 1998).[6] In 2000, the Central Council for Education (Chūō Kyōiku Iinkai) published a report on "Education and the birth of fewer children" (*Shōshika to kyōiku ni tsuite*). The key phrase for demographic change in this report is the term *shōshika*, describing the process or state of a society with few children. The declining birth rate is linked to an increasing number of unmar-

[6] "Children need to deepen their understanding of the ageing society with declining birth rate and the significance of childrearing by the united efforts of both sexes. They also need to develop practical minds to voluntarily take actions for the elderly. For these purposes, related classes and the 'Period for Integrated Study' will provide children with opportunities to have basic idea of the ageing society with declining birth rate, to learn the meaning of family and child-rearing and to deepen their understanding of such related issues as nursing and welfare. Specifically, great emphasis will be placed on actual interaction with infants and elderly people and volunteer activities related to nursing and welfare" (Curriculum Council, Monbushō 1998).

ried women and men and an increased average age at first marriage. Reasons for this are seen in the difficulty of bringing up children (or, more precisely, in the difficulty for parents of combining a profession and bringing up children); individual views on marriage and value change; and finally in the extended phase of dependency of children on their parents. This process has resulted in fewer children per family and in a decline of children in the local community. By analysing the ratio of adults and pupils in individual school districts we see that, if there were 55 children for 100 adults in Japanese society in 1955, there are only 17 children for the same number of adults today (Chūkyōshin 2000a; 2000b). The specific consequences for education are seen in the fact that opportunities for children to interact with each other are decreasing and wisdom about child education is lacking. Overprotection of children by their parents can be observed; the organization of informal teaching environments in the neighbourhood or clubs, and even in school, is getting more difficult; and finally the report even mentions that competition in a positive sense is weakening. These characteristics are seen as consequences of the trend to nuclear families living in bigger cities, where their whole life takes place in the house or apartment and where outdoor activities have low priority. However, even if the whole process is described very critically there are positive elements to be mentioned. With the decline of student numbers and accordingly fewer pupils per teacher, schools become quieter[7] and conditions for education which can respond to the needs of individual students can be realized. The report mentions the examples of foreign language teaching, literacy and gaining skills in computer competence or debating. Last but not least, the situation in universities is relaxing and opportunities for choice can be introduced (Chūkyōshin 2000a).

Different perspectives on educational policies that are adequate to respond to this process are being discussed. This includes the question of how to cope with the situation, but also how the trend might be countered by means of education. Generally the policies aim at providing a social climate where children are welcome and which is supportive in the child-rearing process. These policies address the need to let children find

[7] This observation is not in accordance with recent descriptions of collapsing discipline in the classroom (*gakkyū hōkai*). Smaller classes do not automatically lead to a "quiet" learning environment. Teaching styles have a much stronger influence on the climate in schools.

their place in society, appeal to all institutions in society to contribute to bringing up children, and express the wish that adults taking care of children should be supported in this process. In combination with these common views the report also takes a variety of positions. These include questions around individual rights to decide on marriage and childbirth, concentrating on forming a supportive environment for child education, and the importance of children being taken care of by the whole society, as well as questions of equal rights in a society where men and women cooperate (*danjo kyōdō sankaku shakai*).

The committee also describes specific measures for how education should respond to the change in the demographic situation. The following five areas form the core of the report:

1. Concrete measures concerning the role of family education;
2. Concrete measures concerning the role of school education;
3. Concrete measures concerning the role of education in the local community;
4. Connections with education reform as a whole;
5. Reduction of financial burden of education fees.

The second, fourth and fifth areas focus on immediate school policies, which deserve some further attention in this article. From primary school onwards children should receive opportunities to experience themselves as human beings, as members of a family, and as members of the society and the nation. An appropriate understanding of "family" should be approached partly through the strengthening of the subjects of technical and home economics (*gijutsu kateika*). Home economics (*kateika*) became obligatory for both boys and girls in senior high schools from 1994 (Tanaka and Hong 2007), and the committee sees room to integrate areas such as educational practice in kindergartens and similar activities, which should give adolescents opportunities for practical experience in interaction with and education of young children (Chūkyōshin 2000b).

Interdisciplinary studies and project learning gained with the so-called "Period for Integrated Study" (*sōgōtekina gakushū*) new attention in the context of remedies for the rapid ageing of Japanese society. This was an area that had long been favoured by progressive teachers (Motani 2005). When the new reforms were carried out, one of the most surprising areas was the radical reduction of core subjects like mathematics, science and Japanese lessons from an average four lessons per week to three and the introduction of this new subject. This included the need for completely new teaching materials for many classes. In most subjects there were detailed teaching manuals on what and even how students could absorb the learning content. Both, the detailed regulation in connection with the course of study and the development of model lessons in the context of lesson studies have contributed to detail compiled lessons in core subjects. In the context of integrated studies, teachers needed to develop new plans. A reason that this teaching approach, which had already been practised by some progressive teachers, for example, in environmental subjects or gender studies, found the acceptance of other members in the reform council is that this pattern of teaching became even attractive for conservative members; they saw it as an additional way of strengthening moral education, something they wanted to revive. In the above quoted report, this trend becomes very obvious. *Sōgōtekina gakushū* is a core area where social problems of present and future can be addressed, including the challenges of an aged society.

There are many areas in this report which are interesting to discuss in the context of a changing stance towards educational reform. As a general impression, we might summarize that consensus building among the various actors seems to be facilitated by the new pressure resting on the shoulders of the educational system, which includes coping with demographic change, but also other areas, such as the need to adapt the education system to an economic system in crisis, and the needs of internationalization and globalization. This might be one of the reasons why the "immobile pattern in educational policies" observed until the early 1990s has changed over the last decade.

Key phrases in this report are individuality (*kosei*), ability (*nōryoku*), fitness (*tekisei*), interest (*kyōmi*) and concern (*kanshin*). They play a central role in a system where standardized entrance examinations are presently losing some of their influence and a new integration of knowledge, values and social participation is aimed for.

The report concluded with remarks concerning policies which extend over the range of educational institutions. A certain distance towards the belief in the role of schools in relation to countering the effects of ageing is becoming obvious, as well as an awareness of the limits of educational policies in the process of changing population developments. This impression is strengthened by the constitution of this subcommittee. Obviously, for a long time, school education reform committees paid less explicit attention to questions of demographic change than other ministries. The idea or initiative for this report, or, more concretely, the foundation of this subcommittee, has its origin in 1998. The topic came up during the 223rd meeting of the Central Council of Education in November 1998, which initiated the formation of a subcommittee on the topic "Education in a society with fewer children" (*Shōshika to kyōiku ni kansuru shōiinkai*). The committee met 12 times between December 1998 and February 2000, and its report on the decline of children and education was published in April of the same year (Chūkyōshin 2000b). Interestingly enough, an official of the Ministry for Home Affairs, who also coordinated a Committee concerning demographic change there, was appointed as chairperson of this subcommittee. According to the report of the first meeting the initiative takes up discussions which were conducted in the Ministry for Home Affairs in order to discuss the consequences of the declining number of children for education (Chūkyōshin 1998).

The report discussed here should be interpreted as an attempt to interpret and form an overall social approach towards education as a context to the present educational policy changes within the school system (Curriculum Council, Monbushō 1998). Demographics must be seen as a piece of a much more complex puzzle of the changing social reality in a quite traumatized Japanese society during the 1990s,[8] which made educational reform necessary. Demographic change supports the process of consensus building between actors which had previously strongly opposed each other, but it was not the most important factor for change itself.

## 5. Conclusion

In summary we can state that demographic change is still not very obvious in the international debate on education and educational policy. This debate has long been caught up in questions of whether or not the Japanese can change their educational system. The stagnation which Schoppa (1991) described, and which became obvious with individual policies taking almost 30 years to be put into practice, has changed into vital discussions. When Nakasone called for reforms, it

[8] Japan's crisis in the 1990s is extensively dealt with in Foljanty-Jost (2004).

was not yet the time for real change, but from the 1990s on, the reform process was speeding up. The background to this acceleration is the economic crises and the general political climate calling for reforms. In this climate, even the analysis of reform was changing, as evidenced in Hood's and Roesgaard's works on education reform. Then, in the late 1990s, discussions on demographic change and falling birth rates received the explicit attention of reform councils.

Educational policies respond to questions of demographic change in as far as the falling birth rate had a very strong effect on the reality in schools. This has been shown through various examples:

1. The decline in the population after the second baby boom entering primary, junior and senior high schools led among other things to smaller classes and fewer pupils per teacher. This could facilitate a certain change in teaching methods. At the same time, however, the low numbers of young teachers employed, together with the decline in the number of students does not necessarily facilitate change concerning the introduction of new teaching methods.
2. Schools are actually in danger of being closed and need to attract pupils with specific school profiles. This goes hand in hand with the diversification of entrance examinations: *Hensachi* is no longer the only parameter, and, for example, interviews or compositions gain importance. There are also factors other than demographic change, for example, issues of integrating children returning from abroad.
3. Competition is declining with rising numbers of students: almost everybody who wants to do so can enter university.

As overall effects of demographic change on educational policies we can consider that these challenges have some positive effects, because they lead to a situation where the need for reform can no longer be ignored. Whether and how the policies can really respond to the change must be observed in the future. However, it will also be interesting to observe how the policies are realized in the future. This might also be of interest for policy makers in other nations under the impact of demographic change, where similar challenges will have to be faced.

## References


Amano, Ikuo (1998): *Kyōiku kaikaku no yukue. Jiyūka to koseika o motomeru* [In search of educational reform: calling for liberalisation and individualisation) Tokyo: Tōkyō Daigaku Shuppankai.

Chūkyōshin (Chūō Kyōiku Iinkai) [Central Council for Education] (1998): *Shōshika to kyōiku ni kan suru shō-iinkai (Dai ikkai) 1998/12/11 gijiroku* [Report of the first meeting of the subcommittee on education in a society with fewer children, 1998/12/11]. www.mext.go.jp/b_menu/shingi/12/chuuou/gijiroku/001/981201.htm (found 12 February 2007).

—— (2000a): *Shōshika to kyōiku ni tsuite (hōkoku) no yōshi* [Central points of the report on education in a society with fewer children]. http://www.mext.go.jp/b_menu/shingi/12/chuuou/toushin/000402.htm (found 12 December 2005).

—— (2000b): *Shōshika to kyōiku ni tsuite hōkoku* [Report on education in a society with fewer children]. http://www.mext.go.jp/b_menu/shingi/12/chuuou/toushin/000401.htm (found 12 December 2005).

Cummings, William K.; Beauchamp, Edward R.; Ichikawa, Shogo; Kobayashi, Victor N.; Ushiogi, Morikazu, eds. (1984): *Educational Policies in Crisis*. New York, Westport, London: Praeger.

Curriculum Council, Monbushō (1998): *National Curriculum Standards Reform for Kindergarten, Elementary School, Lower and Upper Secondary School and Schools for the Visually Disabled, the Hearing Impaired and the Otherwise Disabled* (Synopsis of the Report). July 29, 1998. http://www.monbu.go.jp/series-en/00000016/ (found 1999; now available via the homepage of MEXT) http://www.mext.go.jp/english/news/1998/07/980712.htm (found 1 March 2007).

Foljanty-Jost, Gesine (2004) (ed.): *Japan in the 1990s. Crisis as an Impetus for Change*. Münster: Lit.

Frost, Peter (1991): Examination Hell. In: Edward R. Beauchamp (ed.): *Windows on Japanese Education*. Westport: Greenwood Publishing Group, pp. 291–305.

Fujita, Hidenori (1997): *Kyōiku kaikaku—kyōsei jidai no gakkō zukuri* [Educational reform—building schools for times of symbiotic living]. Tokyo: Iwanami Shoten.

Fuwa, Kazuhiko (2001): Lifelong education in Japan, a highly school-centred society: educational opportunities and practical educational activities for adults. In: *International Journal of Lifelong Education* 20, 1–2 (January–April), pp. 127–136.

Goodman, Roger (2003): The Why, What and How of Educational Reform in Japan. In: Goodman, Roger and David Phillips (eds.): *Can the Japanese Change Their Education System?* Oxford: Symposium Books, pp. 7–30.

Goodman, Roger and David Phillips (eds.) (2003): *Can the Japanese Change Their Education System?* Oxford: Symposium Books.

Hood, Christopher (2001): *Japanese Education Reform: Nakasone's Legacy*. London and New York: Routledge.

Kariya, Takehiko (2001): *Kaisoka nippon to kyōiku kiki* [Social stratification in Japan and education crises] Tokyo: Yushindo Kobunsha.

Kreitz-Sandberg, Susanne (2001): Reformen im japanischen Schulwesen [Reforms in the Japanese School System]. In: Bosse, Friederike and Patrick Köllner (eds.) *Reformen in Japan [Reforms in Japan]*. Hamburg: Institut für Asienkunde, pp. 265–284.

MEXT (Ministry of Education, Culture, Sports, Science and Technology) (2005): *Statistical Abstract (Education, Culture, Sports, Science and Technology) 2005 edition*. Tokyo: National Printing Bureau.

—— (2006): *Statistics. Elementary Schools*. http://www.mext.go.jp/english/statist/index03.htm (found 12 December 2006).

Motani, Yoko (2005): Hopes and challenges for progressive educators in Japan: assessment of the "progressive turn" in the 2002 educational reform. In: *Comparative Education* 41, 3 (August), pp. 309–327.

Nemoto, Yasuhiro (1999): *The Japanese Education System*. Parkland, Florida: Universal Publisher.

Ogawa, Seiko (2005): Lifelong learning and demographics: a Japanese perspective. In: *International Journal of Lifelong Education* 24, 4 (July–August), pp. 351–368.

Planning Division of Higher Education Bureau, Monbushō (1998): *University Council Report. "A Vision for Universities in the 21st Century and Reform Measures" To Be Distinctive Universities in a Competitive Environment.* http://www.mext.go.jp/english/news/1998/10/981010.htm (found 12 December 2006).

Roesgaard, Marie H. (1998): *Moving Mountains. Japanese Educational Reform*. Aarhus: Aarhus University Press.

Schoppa, Leonard J. (1991): *Education Reform in Japan: A Case of Immobilist Politics*. London and New York: Routledge.

Sugimoto, Yoshio (2003): *An Introduction to Japanese Society*. Cambridge, New York, Melbourne, Madrid and Cape Town: Cambridge University Press.

Tanaka, Hiromi and Hong, Mihee (2007): Dynamics of Global Gender Politics: A Comparative Analysis of the Implementation of the *Convention on the Elimination of All Forms of Discrimination Against Women* (CEDAW) in Japan and South Korea. In: Claudia Derichs and Susanne Kreitz-Sandberg (eds.): *Gender Dynamics and Globlisation. Perspectives on Japan within Asia*. Münster: Lit, pp. 49–76.

Tsuruta, Yoko (2003): Globalization and the Recent Reforms in Japanese Higher Education. In: Roger Goodman and David Phillips (eds.): *Can the Japanese Change Their Education System?* Oxford: Symposium Books, pp. 119–150.

von Kopp, Botho (1997): Stuktur und Funktion des Prüfungssystems in Japan [Structure and Function of the Education System in Japan]. Frankfurt am Main: Deutsches Institut für Internationale Pädagogische Forschung.

CHAPTER FORTY-ONE

# FAMILY POLICY: FRAMEWORK AND CHALLENGES[1]

Liv Coleman

## 1. Introduction

Family support policies are typically categorized according to the nature and level of social rights and services available, such as paid child-care leave, child-care services, family and child allowances, tax policies, and early-childhood education (e.g., Gauthier 1996; O'Connor, Orloff and Shaver 1999; Schoppa 2006; Ueno 1998; Boling 1998; Peng 2002). In Japan, these policies are not "family policies" (*kazoku seisaku*) per se, but rather "measures to counter the declining birth rate" (*shōshika taisaku*). Accordingly, Japanese family policies have developed closely with concerns about declining fertility rates, particularly since the "1.57 shock" of 1990, when the total fertility rate for the previous year fell to a post-war low. The family policy framework has broadened significantly over time, as the government has attempted to counteract more causes of the declining birth rate, and existing educational and social welfare policies have been adapted to reflect concerns about the low birth society. Even so, government expenditures for children and families account for about 3.8 per cent of the social security budget, compared to 70 per cent for the elderly. About three-quarters of Japanese family policies fall under the jurisdiction of the Ministry of Health, Labour, and Welfare (MHLW). This chapter examines the development of Japanese family policies and considers various challenges to program success and further development of family policies.

[1] Research for this chapter could not have been accomplished without generous support from the KCC Japan Education Exchange.

## 2. Development of Japanese Family Policies

Japanese family policies have developed through three successive five-year plans: the Angel Plan, New Angel Plan, and the Children and Childrearing Support Plan. The Japanese government initially hesitated to tackle family policies openly and assertively due to its history of aggressively pro-natalist wartime policies exhorting women to "give birth and multiply" (*umeyo fuyaseyo*) for the sake of the nation (Miyake 1991), though the government has played a crucial role in regulating reproduction even in the post-war era (Norgren 2001; Takeda 2005; chapter 34). After the 1.57 shock, some women's groups and feminists invoked the wartime mantra to ward off government intervention in women's private reproductive choices, while suggesting that the declining birth rate represented a "birth strike" by women against male-dominated society (Ogino 1993). Over time, however, voices opposing policy intervention waned and government policymakers turned their attention to explicit analysis of the causes of the declining birth rate and policy remedies (Schoppa 2006). As MHLW policymakers have begun to realize that the declining birth rate is a much bigger issue than a working women's problem, they have also targeted support for stay-at-home mothers and encouraged fathers to take on greater domestic responsibilities. Moreover, social problems ostensibly unrelated to the declining birth rate such as child abuse have been incorporated into the policy framework. The declining birth rate has spurred interest in a wide variety of issues related to the healthy upbringing of children, especially given concern about the faltering ability of families to bring children in the world and help them grow into self-sufficient adults.

### 2.1. *Angel Plans*

The Japanese government was slow to develop its first programmatic response to the declining birth rate, the Angel Plan, although it organized a meeting of twelve relevant ministries and agencies to study the childrearing environment in August 1990 immediately after the 1.57 shock. Following these meetings, the Ministry of Health and Welfare (MHW)[2] took the lead in sponsoring a two-year "Welcome Baby" campaign to raise awareness about childrearing. The campaign featured a

[2] In 2001 the Ministry of Health and Welfare (MHW) and the Ministry of Labour (MOL) merged to become the so-called Ministry of Health, Labour and Welfare (MHLW).

song composition contest and surveys of young men and women about the childrearing environment. The Angel Plan Prelude, a one year plan, was launched in December 1993 to fill the childrearing assistance gap before the Angel Plan itself would begin. At the same time, the MHW and Nikkeiren [Japan Federation of Employers' Associations] planned the establishment of the Children's Future Foundation (*Kodomo Mirai Zaidan*), largely staffed by retired MHW bureaucrats to assist childrearing support efforts such as company on-site child care, child-care centres located near train stations, babysitters for employees working overtime, and nursing corners at department stores and supermarkets.

The Angel Plan (1995–1999) came together with the joint efforts of the Ministry of Health and Welfare, Ministry of Labour, Ministry of Education, and Ministry of Construction. From the beginning, the Angel Plan was narrowly designed to provide child-care support for working mothers, despite its ostensibly wide-ranging inclusion of education, welfare, housing, and employment policy objectives. The main reason for the primary focus on support for working mothers was that the *21-seiki fukushi bijon* [21st century welfare vision], the overarching framework for the Angel Plan, sought to rectify future labour shortages by increasing the number of women in the workforce. The Welfare Vision aimed that by 2025 child-care services would be easily accessible to all, allowing up to 70 per cent of women to work outside the home, in line with other advanced industrial countries such as the United States (*Asahi Shinbun* 4 October 1994). Accordingly, the Angel Plan's centrepiece, the Basic Proposal for Urgent Child-care Measures, set numerical targets to increase the number of young children under three years old in child care from 450,000 to 600,000, more than double the number of child-care centres with extended hours from 2,230 to 7,000, increase the number of drop-in or emergency child-care facilities from 450 to 3,000, and nearly double the number of after-school clubs for kids from 4,520 to 9,000. Although demographers believed that the primary cause of the declining birth rate was delayed marriage, some analysts thought the Angel Plan would boost birth rates because many young couples reported they would like to have three children, but most were having only one or two.

Although the Angel Plan primarily targeted working mothers, it also provided some early support for beleaguered stay-at-home mothers and attempted to prod working fathers to participate more in childrearing (Roberts 2002). The burden on isolated, urban homemakers first attracted public concern beginning in the 1970s, after sensational cases of child abuse and neglect. The Angel Plan's two primary initiatives for stay-at-home mothers were drop-in child-care services and community childrearing support centres. Drop-in child care provides parents of children below elementary school age with child care while parents run errands, recuperate from illness, or refresh themselves. Community childrearing support centres offer free counselling and advice for parents, places for young children to play, and meeting space for childrearing circles and parents' groups. The Ministry of Education also sponsored seminars encouraging fathers to participate in childrearing.

The subsequent family policy trajectory was also significantly shaped by the 1997 Population Problems Advisory Council's (*Jinkō Mondai Shingikai*) research report, which was largely responsible for the sea change toward greater support for gender equality as remedy for the declining birth rate, while also providing the government's first basic stance toward policies for the declining birth rate. The report analyzed the causes of the declining birth rate, pointing to delayed marriage and the increasing unmarried rate. The report identified the major obstacles to recovering fertility rates as the traditional sexual division of labour hindering women's social advancement and rigid employment practices, especially a corporate culture prioritizing work over family life. To address the causes of the birth rate, the report suggested revising employment practices, tackling the gendered division of labour, and facilitating balance between work and home life. Public debate about the declining birth rate regularly featured calls for gender equality, promotion of women's participation in the workplace, and encouragement of men's childrearing beginning with the 1.57 shock. But this report marked the first official indication of a shift in family policy from a traditional family model to a gender equality model (Atoh 2000). The findings of the advisory council were incorporated into the White Paper for Health and Welfare for 1998 and its analysis grounded the development of the New Angel Plan.

The New Angel Plan (2000–2004), produced by six ministries, still centred on child care for working mothers, but strengthened support for children of stay-at-home mothers and newly emphasized family-friendly workplace changes to revise corporate culture and the gendered division of labour. The child-care targets were to increase once again the number of children under three in child care, child-care centres with extended hours, after-school clubs for kids, child-care centres open on holidays, and family support centres providing services such as picking children up after day care when their parents unexpectedly work overtime. Labour objectives included strengthening existing initiatives to reduce working hours, encourage employees to take allotted vacation days, promote women's employment and men's childrearing, and provide subsidies for companies that facilitate child-care leave and establish on-site child-care centres. Finally, the New Angel Plan set new targets for expansion of maternal-child health facilities and infertility consultation centres, and included educational objectives such as lightening the burden on students through a lighter curriculum and a five-day school week, thereby also reducing pressure on families.

In addition to the Angel Plans, the Zero Waiting for Day Care Program (*taiki jidō zero sakusen*) provided child-care support for working parents frustrated by long waiting lists to enrol their children in child care, particularly in urban areas. To address these concerns, Prime Minister Jun'ichirō Koizumi announced in May 2001 his intentions to eliminate waiting lists for child care, primarily by relaxing regulations. The Japanese government has long played a major role in regulating and administering child-care centres by licensing centres that meet personnel and facility standards, providing subsidies, and, in earlier years, providing guidance to low-income parents (Uno 1999; Wada 2002; Oishi 2002). The Zero Waiting for Day Care Program relaxed facility regulations, loosened the child-staff ratio requirements, and allowed entities other than municipalities and social welfare corporations to provide child-care services for the first time. Through these measures, the government sought to create spaces for another 50,000 children in day care between fiscal 2002 and 2004. In 2004 the strategy was extended to create an additional 50,000 spaces in urban areas of particular need, though funding was cut over the previous year (*Asahi Shinbun* 19 June 2004). Koizumi claims credit for creating a total of 150,000 additional child-care spaces from the time he became prime minister until the end of fiscal 2005 (Koizumi 2006).[3] Long waiting lists remain in urban areas, however, while rural areas have empty spaces. The longest lists are for children under three years old because these services are costly and child-care providers must meet additional requirements, such as keeping a nutritionist on staff (Nakamura and Wada 2001: 14). Additionally, in areas with the longest waiting lists, licensed child-care facilities are sometimes only available to mothers

[3] The Japan Federation of Bar Associations reports that waiting list numbers went down for Koizumi in part because the government changed the definition of children on the waiting list to exclude children in unlicensed child-care facilities (JFBA 2003: 142).

with a fixed workplace, so it can be difficult for stay-at-home mothers to find licensed child care while seeking reemployment (JFBA 2003: 141; *AERA* 3 October 2005).

### 2.2. *Next generation childrearing support*

As the birth rate continued to fall, including reduced marital fertility, and demographic projections were revised to indicate hastened societal ageing, the MHLW embarked on next generation childrearing support measures, approaching the problem of the declining birth rate comprehensively for the first time, rather than focusing almost exclusively on day care, especially as far as budgeting was concerned. Next generation childrearing support measures significantly expanded the scope of Japanese family policies by attempting to include all childrearing households, all working parents including fathers, and young people who would be parents of the next generation. To suggest that they were adding another layer of policies to earlier Angel Plans, the MHLW called the new initiative Measures to Cope with a Fewer Number of Children Plus One (*shōshika taisaku purasu wan*), known hereafter as the Plus One Plan. This plan formed the foundation for all subsequent family policy-related legislation and the newest iteration of the Angel Plan, the Children and Childrearing Support Plan.

The Plus One Plan featured wide-ranging labour, health, residential, welfare, and educational objectives. The Plan's four major planks were 1) revising work styles, including those of men; 2) community childrearing support; 3) next generation childrearing support in social security; and 4) improving children's sociality and promoting self-sufficiency. Each of the four areas contained specific policy objectives and sometimes numerical targets, such as encouraging 10 per cent of fathers and 80 per cent of mothers to take child-care leave. The Plan's premiere objective, to reconcile work and family life, was to be achieved by changing the corporate work environment by promoting child-care leave, reduced overtime, flextime systems, work sharing, telecommuting, and shorter hours for parents of young children. The MHLW hoped that they could lead companies to adopt family friendly policies and publicized companies meeting ministry standards. In addition to workplace-changing initiatives, the Plan expressed support for expanding the number of after-school clubs, home education, child-care support for part-time and temporary workers, community childrearing lectures to prevent and reduce child abuse, student scholarships to reduce the educational cost burden on families, and "barrier-free" public facilities to make it easier to bring children on personal outings. The Plus One Plan has been bolstered by two significant pieces of legislation, both passed in 2003: the Next Generation Childrearing Support Measures Law (*Jisedai Ikusei Shien Taisaku Suishin-hō*) and the Basic Law for a Low Birth Society (*Shōshika Shakai Taisaku Kihon-hō*).

The Next Generation Law, drafted by MHLW bureaucrats, spans ten years (2005–2015) and requires local governments and companies with over three hundred employees to create action plans to implement next generation childrearing support objectives. The MHLW's guidance for company action plans includes suggestions based on the Plus One Plan to promote work-family balance, family-friendly corporate work styles, and measures for the community such as barrier-free facilities and internships for young people to foster their steady employment and self-sufficiency. A MHLW official explains, however, that the aim of the law is not to force companies to implement action plans but to get them to start thinking about childrearing support (*Chūnichi Nyūsu* 5 May 2005); accordingly, the ministry assesses no penalties for non-compliance. Action plans were to be submitted by March 2005 and to last from two to five years. Local governments also play a significant role under the Next Generation Law. Local plans were not required under the Angel Plan, so only about half of municipalities and prefectures participated (Asai 2004: 28); now all local governments must draft action plans reflecting citizen input. The MHLW provides local government guidelines for seven action areas including community childrearing support, maternal and child health, housing, and safety.

The Next Generation Law has a number of limitations, mostly stemming from tepid corporate support for the action plans. Mandatory action plans for large companies were enacted in spite of early opposition from Nippon Keidanren [Japan Business Federation]. Large companies have been slow to respond to the law but have gradually fallen into line. Only 36.2 per cent of companies submitted their action plans by the April 2005 deadline, but compliance rates soared to 97 per cent by the end of year (MHLW 2006b). Small and medium-sized companies with 300 or fewer employees are only required to make an effort to create action plans. In a survey of action plans of fifty companies popular with recent college graduates, most companies reported that they want at least one working father to take child-care leave during the course of their 2–5 year action plans (*Sankei Shinbun* 12 April 2005). If the primary challenge for companies is to muster the will to change corporate culture, the main challenge for local governments is to secure adequate funding sources. Some local governments have had to opt for low-cost plans or cut other programs (such as ageing society programs), issuing complaints that the central government failed to budget for the action plans properly (Sakakibara 2006). As a result, local action plans vary considerably.

Additional legislation has also been required to work to achieve the centrepiece of the Next Generation Law, improving child-care leave taking rates. Child-care leave has been expanded several times since the 1.57 shock through revisions of the Child Care and Long-term Care Leave Law. Child-care leave for fathers came to be an important policy topic beginning with the next generation childrearing support measures out of concern about falling marital fertility rates, suggesting a need to revise work styles even for men. The law currently guarantees 40 per cent of wages (from the employment insurance system) over a 12-month leave; leave takers are also exempt from social insurance payments during leave. Ten years after the law was first implemented in 1992, however, 38.5 per cent of companies still did not have explicit child-care leave systems (Satō and Takeishi 2004: 35). Moreover, the MHLW does not sanction employers who fire or mistreat employees who take leave. In 2002, 0.33 per cent of men took child-care leave, compared to 64 per cent of women (Satō and Takeishi 2004: 15). Men's low child-care leave rates are partially attributable to the fact that they cannot take leave if they have wives engaged primarily in childrearing. Men also report that they are reluctant to take leave because it would cause trouble for their workplace or be hard on family finances (Satō and Takeishi 2004: 27). The situation for women is not necessarily much better. Many women are employed as part-time or temporary workers and thus find it practically impossible to take child-care leave. Some companies have reportedly responded to the law by hiring fewer full-time women out of fear they will inconvenience the firm by taking child-care leave (*AERA* 3 October 2005).

Complementing the Next Generation Law, the Basic Law for a Low Birth Society provides a basic political framework for subsequent policies to boost the declining birth rate. The Basic Law was sponsored by a cross-party coalition of Diet members, led by a group centred on the LDP's Tarō Nakayama, a paediatrician best known for his lifelong efforts to revise the constitution. The Basic Law dramatically states that the declining birth rate is a problem "unprecedented since the dawn of history" (*yūshi irai no mizō no jitai*). To meet this formidable challenge, the Basic Law imposes obligations on the national government, regional public bodies, corporations, and individual citizens. The duties are, respectively, to formulate and implement policy, craft policy in response to community needs in cooperation with the national government, support a family-friendly work environment, and create a society where people dream of family life and can bear and raise children with peace of mind. The law asserts priorities such as changing workplaces, strengthening child-care support, lessening the economic burden on families, and improving the maternal and child health-care system. The law also mandates an annual white paper on the low birth society and establishes an administrative framework to create and implement family policy. The law does not offer policy specifics, however: a MHLW official describes the Next Generation Law as the "engine" of the Basic Law (*Mainichi Shinbun* 6 June 2003).

The Basic Law also touched off a debate about whether the current trajectory of Japanese family policy was sufficiently mindful of reproductive rights for two primary reasons. First, specific language about reproductive rights did not appear in the original draft bill and was only added to the preamble following opposition protests about the lack of safeguards for freedom of individual choice regarding marriage and childbirth.[4] This stance represents a notable reversal from the early years of family policy debate following the 1.57 shock, when officials assiduously declared the importance of reproductive rights at the beginning of all policy documents (Ōhinata 2005: 20–22). The Japan Federation of Bar Associations issued an opinion paper arguing that the original draft of the bill violated the spirit of the constitution because it lacked a reproductive rights position; they found the notion of obligating citizens to "dream of having children" particularly incongruent with respect for individual choices about marriage and childbirth (JFBA 2001). Female politicians of the Democratic Party of Japan (DPJ) and the Social Democratic Party of Japan (SDPJ) made the same type of argument, successfully arguing in Diet debates for inclusion of language explicitly protecting reproductive rights. Second, the law controversially identifies a need to support fertility treatment, which critics saw as adding social pressure to have children. In response to these types of concerns, Tarō Nakayama replied, "Marrying or not is up to the free choice of

[4] Basic Law sponsors argued that reproductive rights were so obvious that they did not merit mention in the bill (*Asahi Shinbun* 12 June 2003).

the person involved [...]. No matter how many laws we make, people who won't have children won't have children" (*Asahi Shinbun* 12 June 2003). Turning the critics' reproductive rights argument on its head, a co-sponsor of the basic law argued that social support for fertility treatment is the very essence of reproductive rights because it allows people to make reproductive choices free of economic necessity.

The Children and Childrearing Support Plan (2005–2009), also known as the New New Angel Plan, represents the first programmatic response by the government since the passage of the Basic Law and Next Generation Law (MHLW 2005). A Cabinet-level group headed by Prime Minister Koizumi drafted a low birth society policy framework (*shōshika taisaku taikō*), largely resembling the Plus One Plan; ministry bureaucrats based the Children and Childrearing Support Plan on this framework. The plan's standout objectives are to increase the number of men and women taking child-care leave, bring the amount of time men spend on childrearing and housework in line with men in other advanced industrial countries (from 48 minutes per day to two hours), shorten overtime hours at work, increase child-care support, strengthen the child abuse prevention network, teach young people the significance of children and families, and boost young people's self-sufficiency. The plan's aims are mostly achieved through the Next Generation Childrearing Support action plans administered by the national government, local governments, and companies.

The Children and Childrearing Support Plan significantly features more explicitly pro-natalist measures to build "parents of the next generation" (*jisedai no oya*). Most scholars of comparative family policy overlook these types of family formation policies, focusing instead on the more prominent policies to provide child-care support, reduce the economic burden on families, and to promote work-life balance. Yet the expansion of Japanese family policy to include targeted support of youth themselves arguably represents the most distinctive feature of next generation childrearing support policies. Policies to build parents of the next generation reflect two major strains of argument: the inability of "parasite singles" to marry and children lacking traditional values failing to grasp the importance of societal and family duties. First, the parasite singles thesis posits that young people enjoy high living standards by continuing to live with their parents who provide them with housing, meals, and, frequently, housekeeping services in a carefree "moratorium" from adulthood (Miyamoto, Iwakami and Yamada 1997; Yamada

1999). In recent years, the parasite singles thesis has shifted somewhat in recognition of structural changes in the economy and young people's lack of stable employment as an obstacle to family formation (Yajima and Mimizuka 2001; Miyamoto 2002). Sociologist Masahiro Yamada (2005) provocatively points out that women aren't going to marry freeters no matter how charming their personalities might be. The second significant discourse discusses family formation in the context of the bitter fruits of modernization: urbanization, industrialization, loss of extended families, breakdown of traditional community support networks, and profound alienation and social isolation—particularly concerning children themselves (e.g., Kadowaki 1999; Sagaza 2001; Hayashi 2002). According to this line of argument, children have been crowded out of public spaces and rarely interact with adults or other children outside their parents, teachers, and immediate siblings—if they have any. As a result, children lack sociality and are out of touch with traditional values that prize families and life.

Programs to build parents of the next generation respond to these concerns with educational, economic, and health objectives.[5] Educational programs include career education, mandatory voluntary service (chapter 39), excursions to the countryside, and interaction between students and babies.[6] The latter activity (*fureai*), having young people interact with babies, is one type of program designed to inculcate a healthy respect for family and life. Activities vary considerably by location, but junior and senior high school students receive brief training lessons, spend time holding babies, and try on pregnancy simulation jackets. The hope is that adolescents will naturally incorporate childrearing into their life plan through activities giving them some basic childrearing experience in school and will learn how to become good parents. Both boys and girls are encouraged to participate. Economic programs are designed to foster young people's self-sufficiency and career consciousness. These programs include promotion of trial employment programs, job cafes, college scholarships, and internships. Health programs include adolescent health-care programs to reduce infertility by promoting healthy eating and reducing teenage abortions and sexually transmitted

[5] For an overview of the full list of activities, see the 2004 White Paper on the Low Birth Society (Naikakufu 2004: 143–154).

[6] Many of these programs are part of ongoing efforts by the Ministry of Education to instill a "zest for living" (*ikiru chikara*) in schoolchildren (Motani 2005).

diseases; subsidies for fertility treatment; and efforts to improve obstetric services and enhance the image of childbirth to make it appear less painful and scary. Many of the programs to build parents of the next generation are administered through the Ministry of Education and the MHLW's *Sukoyaka Oyako 21* [Healthy families 21] framework.

The other type of policy support aimed at children, albeit indirectly, are child allowances. These allowances have expanded over time, but still remain far below levels of Western European countries (Fukuda 1999); this might be surprising given that the top reason for having fewer children usually cited in public opinion polls is the financial burden associated with childrearing, especially educational expenses. Established in 1971, Japan's child allowance system from its inception partially grew out of concerns about changes in population structure and the declining birth rate, which was creeping toward population replacement level (Kojima 1994). Payment levels have risen modestly over time, while income limits have dropped. The current child allowance system provides monthly payments of 5,000 yen for the first and second children and 10,000 yen for the third child and beyond, for all children who have not yet finished elementary school. Effective April 2006, the annual income limits for receiving allowances are 8.6 million yen for salaried workers and 7.8 million yen for self-employed workers (MHLW 2006a). As Schoppa notes, however, child allowances are so modest that it appears that the Japanese government "has not even made a pretense of activism in the area of child allowances" (Schoppa 2006: 179). Financial support for lone parents has also dropped in recent years. To qualify for child allowances, residents must submit an application to local authorities, so some qualified residents do not receive allowances. Some municipalities offer additional child allowances.

## 3. Looking Back, Looking Forward

As seen in programs from the Angel Plan to the Next Generation Childrearing Support Measures, Japanese family policy has been driven by concerns about declining fertility rates and remains an eclectic combination of family-oriented social welfare and education programs adapted to concerns about the low birth society. Some government programs are designed to spur a gender-role revolution; some are designed to reinforce traditional values and life courses. In this way, as analysts have noted before, Japanese family policy does not present a coherent, unified image of the "ideal family" (Shimoebisu 2000).

The daunting challenges of implementing largely voluntary Japanese family policy action plans through intermediaries such as companies and local governments suggest the difficulty of raising fertility rates through existing government policies. Moreover, given the already broadly encompassing nature of childrearing support policies and the contested nature of debate, it seems unlikely that family policy goalposts will move anytime soon. Analysts say, though, that the next five years will be critical for Japan to avert demographic disaster. MHLW bureaucrats are increasingly looking abroad to foreign models, particularly French and Northern European models. Masahiro Yamada calls for Japan to approach the low birth society as if it were the next "Guadalcanal," requiring a clear strategy and massive infusion of resources (ESRI 2004). But even some government demographers are growing gloomy about prospects for the efficacy of family policy as pro-natalist stimulant. Toru Suzuki of the National Institute for Population and Social Security Research claims that "[i]t is just a fantasy that the [Total Fertility Rate] would return to a moderately low level if Japan adopted policy interventions used in Western and Northern Europe" (Suzuki 2006: 16). Given debates about the breakdown of the family, however, Japanese analysts increasingly argue that family policy may be necessary or desirable, regardless of its effectiveness as fertility policy.

## References

*AERA* (3 October 2005): Ikuji kore dake no kibishī genjitsu [The harsh reality of child-care leave], pp. 20–21.

*Asahi Shinbun* (4 October 1994): Shōshika taisaku, ikuji sasaeru hiyō wa zōdai [Policy measures to counteract the declining birth rate: Expansion of Expenditures to Support Childrearing], p. 11, morning edition.

—— (12 June 2003): Shōshika taisaku 2 hōan, nerai to mondaiten, Nakayama Tarō-shi to Iwao Sumiko-shi ni kiku [2 Bills to counter the declining birth rate, aims and problem points: asking Nakayama Tarō and Iwao Sumiko], p. 15, morning edition.

—— (19 June 2004): Shusshōritsu 1.29 shokku, niwaka ni sōten [Total fertility rate 1.29 shock, suddenly a point of debate], p. 3, morning edition.

Asai, Haruo (2004): "Jisedai ikusei shien" de kawaru, kaeru kodomo no mirai, kosodate o ōen suru kōdō keikaku zukuri [Changing children's future through "next generation childrearing support"—Making childrearing support action plans]. Tokyo: Yamabuki Shoten.

Atoh, Makoto (2000): *Gendai jinkōgaku, shōshikōreika no kiso chishiki* [Contemporary demography: Basic knowledge of ageing and declining fertility]. Tokyo: Nihon Hyōronsha.

Boling, Patricia A. (1998): Family Policy in Japan. In: *Journal of Social Policy* 27, 2 (April), pp. 173–190.

*Chūnichi Nyūsu* (5 May 2005): Omoikitta shisaku de jinzai kakuho, Jisedai-hō shikō kara ikkagetsu [Securing talent with decisive policy—One month since the Next Generation Law went into effect], p. 26.

ESRI (Economic and Social Research Institute) (2004): *Minutes of Forum "In Search of Effective Measures to Slow Japan's Declining Birthrate."* ESRI Economic Policy Forum: Vision of Japan in the 21st Century Series (December 14). http://www.esri.go.jp/en/forum1/minute/minute21st_2-e.html (found 5 June 2006).

Fukuda, Motō (1999): *Shakai hoshō no kōzō kaikaku, kosodate shien jūshi gata shisutemu e no tenkan* [Structural reform of social security: Shift to a system emphasizing childrearing support]. Tokyo: Chūō Hōki.

Gauthier, Anne Hélène (1996): *The State and the Family: A Comparative Analysis of Family Policies in Industrialized Countries*. New York: Oxford University Press.

Hayashi, Michiyoshi (2002): *Kazoku no fukken* [Restoring the Family]. Tokyo: Chūō Kōron Shinsha.

JFBA (Japan Federation of Bar Associations [Nihon Bengoshi Rengō Kai]) (2001): *'Shōshika Shakai Taisaku Kihon-hō' ni tai suru ikensho* [Opinion paper concerning the 'Low Birth Society Law']. http://www.nichibenren.or.jp/ja/opinion/report/2001_33.html (found 05 June 2006).

—— (2003): *Alternative Report to the Second Report of the Japanese Government on the Convention on the Rights of the Child (May).* http://www.nichibenren.or.jp/en/activities/statements/data/INT03_09_PS.pdf (found 5 June 2006).

Kadowaki, Atsushi (1999): *Kodomo no shakairyoku* [Children's social power]. Tokyo: Iwanami Shinsho.

Koizumi, Junichiro (2006): *Dai 164-kaikokukai ni okeru Koizumi naikaku sōridaijin shisei hōshin ensetsu* [General policy speech by Junichiro Koizumi to the 164th session of the diet] (January 20). http://www.kantei.go.jp/jp/koizumispeech/2006/01/20sisei.html (found 5 June 06).

Kojima, Seiyō (1994): Seitō no kazokukan to jidō teate seidō [Parties' view of families and the child allowance system]. In: Shakai Hoshō Kenkyūjo (ed.): *Gendai kazoku to shakai hoshō* [Contemporary families and social security]. Tokyo: Tokyo University Press, pp. 273–291.

*Mainichi Shinbun* (6 June 2003): Kuni no kanyo de ronsō, shōshika taisaku [Debate about National Intervention: Measures to Counteract the Declining Birth rate], p. 2.

MHLW (Ministry of Health, Labour and Welfare) (2005): *Kodomo kosodate ōen puran, kodomo no sodachi ya kosodate o shakai zentai de shikkari to ōen suru kankyō zukuri o mezashite* [Children and childrearing support plan: Toward creating an environment where all of society firmly supports children's upbringing and childrearing]. Tokyo: Ministry of Health, Labour and Welfare.

—— (2006a): *Child Support Allowance System is Expanded.* http://www.mhlw.go.jp/english/topics/child-support/index.html (found 5 June 2006).

—— (2006b): *Ippan jigyōnushi keikaku sakutei todoke no todokede jōkyō (12-getsumatsu genzai) ni tsuite* [On the state of general entrepreneurs' action plan submissions (as of the end of December)] http://www.mhlw.go.jp/houdou/2006/01/h0116-1.html (found 5 June 2006).

Miyake, Yoshiko (1991): Doubling Expectations: Motherhood and Women's Factory Work under State Management in Japan in the 1930s and 1940s. In: Bernstein, Gail Lee (ed.): *Recreating Japanese Women, 1600–1945*. Berkeley: University of California Press, pp. 267–295.

Miyamoto, Michiko (2002): *Wakamono ga shakaiteki jakusha ni tenraku suru* [Young people have fallen to a socially weak position]. Tokyo: Yōsensha.

Miyamoto, Michiko, Mami Iwakami and Masahiro Yamada (1997): *Mikonka shakai no oyako kankei* [Parent-child relations in unmarried society]. Tokyo: Yūhikaku.

Motani, Yoko (2005): Hopes and Challenges for Progressive Educators in Japan: Assessment of the 'Progressive Turn' in the 2002 Educational Reform. In: *Comparative Education* 41, 3 (August), pp. 309–327.

Naikakufu [Cabinet Office] (2004): *Shōshika shakai hakusho* [White paper on the low birth society]. Tokyo: Gyōsei.

Nakamura, Minoru and Ritsuko Wada (2001): *Setting Social Policies for Japan's Declining Birthrate and Growing Elderly Population.* NRI Papers 32 (1 September). http://www.nri.co.jp/english/opinion/papers/2001/pdf/np200132.pdf (found 5 June 2006).
Norgren, Tiana (2001): *Abortion before Birth Control: The Politics of Reproduction in Postwar Japan.* Princeton: Princeton University Press.
O'Connor, Julia S., Ann Shola Orloff and Sheila Shaver (1999): *States, Markets, Families: Gender, Liberalism and Social Policy in Australia, Canada, Great Britain and the United States.* New York: Cambridge University Press.
Ogino, Miho (1993): Japanese Women and the Decline of the Birthrate. In: *Reproductive Health Matters* 1 (May), pp. 78–84.
Oishi, Akiko S. (2002): The Effect of Childcare Costs on Mothers' Labor Force Participation. In: *Journal of Population and Social Security Research* 1, 1 (August), pp. 50–65.
Ōhinata, Masami (2005): *"Kosodate shien ga oya o dame ni suru" nante iwasenai* [Don't say: "Childrearing support spoils parents"]. Tokyo: Iwanami Shoten.
Peng, Ito (2002): Gender and Generation: Japanese Child Care and the Demographic Crisis. In: Michel, Sonya and Rianne Mahon (eds.): *Childcare Policy at the Crossroads: Gender and Welfare State Restructuring.* New York: Routledge, pp. 31–56.
Roberts, Glenda S. (2002): Pinning Hopes on Angels: Reflections from an Aging Japan's Changing Landscape. In: Goodman, Roger (ed.): *Family and Social Policy in Japan: Anthropological Perspectives.* New York: Cambridge University Press, pp. 54–91.
Sagaza, Haruo (ed.) (2001): *Shōshikōrei shakai to kodomotachi* [The ageing society with declining fertility and children]. Tokyo: Chūō Hōki.
Sakakibara, Noriko (2006): Local govts more child friendly. *Daily Yomiuri* (9 May), p. 4.
*Sankei Shinbun* (12 April 2005): Dansei no ikukyū, michi nakaba [Men's Child-care Leave, Half Way down the Road], p. 1, morning edition.
Satō, Hiroki and Emiko Takeishi (2004): Dansei no ikuji kyūgyō, shakai no nīzu, kaisha no meritto [Men's Child-care Leave: Societal Needs, Company Advantages]. Tokyo: Chūkō Shinsho.
Schoppa, Leonard (2006): *Race for the Exits: The Unraveling of Japan's System of Social Protection.* Ithaca: Cornell University Press.
Shimoebisu, Miyuki (2000): 'Kosodate no shien' no genjō to ronri [The state and logic of childrearing support]. In: Fujisaki, Hiroko (ed.): *Oya to ko: kōsaku suru raifu kōsu* [Parents and children: Entwined life courses]. Tokyo: Minerva, pp. 271–295.
Suzuki, Toru (2006): Fertility Decline and Policy Development in Japan. In: *The Japanese Journal of Population* 4, 1 (March), pp. 1–32. http://www.ipss.go.jp/webj-ad/WebJournal.files/population/2006_3/suzuki.pdf (found 5 June 2006).
Takeda, Hiroko (2005): *The Political Economy of Reproduction in Japan: Between Nation-State and Everyday Life.* New York: Routledge.
Ueno, Chizuko (1998): The Declining Birthrate: Whose Problem? In: *Review of Population and Social Policy* 7, pp. 103–128.
Uno, Kathleen S. (1999): *Passages to Modernity: Motherhood, Childhood, and Social Reform in Twentieth Century Japan.* Honolulu: University of Hawaii Press.
Wada, Junichiro (2002): Political Economy of Nurseries in Japan. Unpublished paper prepared for the Childcare Workshop at Yale University (18 January).
Yajima, Masami and Hiroaki Mimizuka (2001): *Kawaru wakamono to shokugyō kankyō* [Changing young people and the work environment]. Tokyo: Gakubunsha.
Yamada, Masahiro (1999): *Parasaito shinguru no jidai* [The age of the parasite singles]. Tokyo: Chikuma Shobō.
—— (2005): Shōshika no genjō to seisaku kadai [The state of the declining birth rate and policy topics]. In: *Jurist* (1–15 January), pp. 126–131.

CHAPTER FORTY-TWO

# IMMIGRATION POLICY: FRAMEWORK AND CHALLENGES[1]

Glenda S. Roberts

## 1. Introduction

Changes in Japan's migration policy are occurring, both in response to Japan's recent economic restructuring, and in response to a more heightened sense of urgency for national security after the 9/11 attacks. Perceived increases in crimes by migrants in Japan, abetted by disproportionate focus in the media in recent years, also affect the policy framework. Furthermore, the spectre of the impending population decline also influences migration policy discourse. Governmental agencies as well as economic organizations realize that migration policy must react to these trends, but there is as yet little consensus around what exactly a new vision should be. That the old framework is flawed and inadequate to meet current concerns is obvious. The Ministry of Justice (MOJ) has stated as much in the 9/26/2006 report of a project team related to the reception of foreigners in the future, later analyzed in this chapter. The Ministry has also recently published a 3rd edition of the Basic Plan for Immigration Control, in which they state, "The time has come to decide what the role of Japanese administration of immigration control should be in this age of population decline" (MOJ 2005: 216).

In this chapter, I will first acquaint the reader with the general trends in migration to Japan from the late 1980s onward, and then turn to the question of how Japanese intellectuals and others have responded to the suggestion that low birth rate projections should be compensated for by increased migration. In the final section, I will discuss the latest government responses toward changing the migration policy framework. Due to spatial limitations, it is impossible to cover the migration policy framework in all its intricacy, but I would urge the interested reader to

[1] The author extends warm thanks to James E. Nickum for his editorial assistance on this paper.

refer to Tsuda (2006), Douglass and Roberts (2003), Sellek (2001) and Iyotani (2001) for more comprehensive treatment.

## 2. Current Migration Trends and Policy

Before the 1980s, the majority of "foreign workers" in Japan were South Korea and North Korea-affiliated Koreans, as well as some Taiwanese, who, as a legacy of Japan's imperialist past, had remained in Japan after WWII and whose relationship to the Japanese state as citizens of the Empire had been nullified. They were given the status of "special permanent resident" (*tokubetsu eijūsha*). In 2005, 451,909 special permanent residents remained in Japan (MOJ 2006a). These peoples are often referred to as "old-comer" residents. The number of people in this category is shrinking steadily in recent years as those who seek to become naturalized citizens increases.

The status of "permanent resident" (*eijūsha*), is granted only after the person has lived for a period of time in Japan, generally at least ten years, although this is now being revised. Granting of the status is at the discretion of the MOJ. This group of people has been increasing as "long-term residents" (*teijūsha*) seek a status that will allow them to remain and work in any occupation permanently in Japan, without rescinding their citizenship in their homelands. There were 349,804 permanent residents in 2005 (MOJ 2006a).

Legal benchmarks leading to new immigration were made when MOJ revised the Immigration Control and Refugee Recognition Law (*Shutsunyūkoku Kanri Oyobi Nanmin Nintei-hō*) in 1989, allowing peoples of ethnic Japanese descent, mainly from Brazil and Peru, to come to Japan with their families to work in any category (including unskilled work) for periods of up to three years. This coincided with extremely high inflation in Brazil, so there were many Brazilians desirous of seeking out job opportunities in Japan, where the yen was very strong, and it seemed possible to accumulate funds even given Japan's much higher cost of living. Many of these people became employed in the auto parts and automobile industry, as well as in welfare care-giving work. This group of people comes into Japan under the status of "long-term resident" (*teijūsha*), numbering 265,639 registrants in 2005 (MOJ 2006a). Japanese nationals who had been stranded in China at the end of WWII (*zanryū koji* and *zanryū fujin*) who repatriated to Japan, and persons granted asylum as refugees, also are included in the long-term resident category.

The category "spouses of Japanese nationals" (*Nihonjin no haigūsha*) has been growing steadily. According to Yamawaki (2006: 11), one out of eighteen matches in Japan involves a foreign spouse, and almost 80 per cent of these marriages consist of a foreign woman and a Japanese man. In 2005, there were 259,656 people with the status of spouse of a Japanese national.

In 1990, pre-college students of Japanese language (*shūgaku*), as well as college students (*ryūgaku*), were also encouraged to come to Japan. These students are legally allowed to work for up to twenty hours per week at any job. In 2005, there were 129,568 college students, and 28,147 pre-college students, registered in Japan. This immigration status, and in particular the pre-college student status, has come under increasing scrutiny as students have often been found to use the status as a means to enter Japan to work.

The category of "trainee" (*kenshū*) and "technical intern" (*ginōjisshū*) has also allowed foreigners, especially from developing countries, to enter Japan with the ostensible purpose of technology transfer. The current system allows people to be trained and later take up technical internships at firms for up to three years. The trainee program began in 1981 and grew throughout the recession to the present, with modifications through the years. Kawakami notes that despite the recession, small to medium-sized firms brought in trainees and technical interns under the lowest possible allowances and wages as they still had a demand for labour (Kawakami 2005). This trainee and internship system has been heavily criticized by academics and NGOs as a loophole for bringing in manual workers under the guise of technical transfer, for extremely low wages and poor conditions (Sellek 2001; Kawakami 2005; Torii 2006; GKMN 2006). The majority of trainees come from China, followed by Indonesia and the Philippines. In 2005, the total number of registered trainees stood at 54,107 (MOJ 2006a).

Another significant group of foreign workers until 2005 were those in the 'entertainment' (*kōgyō*) category. Oishi notes: "The immigration category of 'entertainment' was introduced in 1981 in response to the strong demand for overseas entertainment workers. From the beginning, this category was seen as breaching the state policy of not accepting unskilled foreign labour. Work visas in Japan were supposed to be for 'skilled workers'" (Oishi 2005: 35). Although bona fide entertainers also enter Japan in this category, the majority of women on this visa are channelled to work as bar hostesses, where sex work may also come with the job (Douglass 2003). The Ministry of Justice in 2005 remarked that the number of foreigners newly entering Japan in this category had been steadily on the rise since 2000, reaching 134,879 in 2004. In 2005, Japan imposed severe restrictions on the qualifications for those granted this status, responding to Japan's being listed as a "Tier 2—Watch List" country on the 2004 U.S. State Department watch list for international trafficking in women and children, together with countries such as the Philippines, Thailand and Zimbabwe (Oishi 2005; see also USDS 2004). As a result, the numbers of people submitting alien registrations as entertainers has fallen sharply, from 64,742 in 2004 to 36,376 in 2005 (MOJ 2006a).

Furthermore, during the 1980s especially, many people from the region and beyond, who learned of the high demand for unskilled labour in Japan's construction and small-to-medium size manufacturing industries, as well as service industries such as restaurants and bars, came to Japan as tourists or in other statuses such as pre-college student or technical intern or trainee, found jobs, and overstayed. Their estimated number peaked at 298,646 in 1993, but diminished over the economic recession period and particularly under a stringent MOJ campaign instituted in December 2003 that aims to cut in half the number of undocumented foreign residents by 2008. The three pillars of this policy are "Forbid them to come," "Forbid them to enter," and "Forbid them to stay" (MOJ 2006b: 2). Their estimated number stood at 193,745 in January 2006, down 6.5 per cent from 2005. There has been no general amnesty for overstayers, and those discovered to be overstaying are summarily deported. In a few cases, however, the MOJ has granted permission for overstayers to remain in Japan. Typically in such cases, the parents have stable jobs, and the children have done well in the Japanese school system and cannot speak their native languages (Yoshinari 2005).

Finally, political asylum seekers are also found among Japan's migrant population. Aside from Indochinese refugees, of whom Japan accepted as residents 10,941 persons from 1978–2002, Japan approved 313 applications out of 3,544 for asylum seekers through 2004 (*Asahi Shinbunsha* 2006: 90; MOFA 2006: 3).

The year 2005 saw the largest number of foreigners ever register as residents in Japan, the first year to top the two million mark, at 2,011,555 people. They made up 1.57 per cent of Japan's total population, which was 127,756,815 in 2005 (MOJ 2006a). The nationality of the majority of foreign residents is South or North Korea (29.8% of all foreign registrants), followed by China (25.85%), Brazil (15%), the Philippines (9.3%), and Peru (2.5%). Although foreign residents can be found all over the country, in both rural and urban areas, their

Table 1. Shifts in numbers of foreign registrants by status, 2001–2005

| RESIDENCY STATUS | 2001 | 2002 | 2003 | 2004 | 2005 | Total% |
|---|---|---|---|---|---|---|
| **TOTAL** | **1.778.462** | **1.851.758** | **1.915.030** | **1.973.747** | **2.011.555** | **100,00%** |
| **PERMANENT RESIDENT** | **684.853** | **713.775** | **742.963** | **778.583** | **801.713** | **39,90%** |
| General resident | 184.071 | 223.875 | 267.011 | 312.964 | 349.804 | 17,40% |
| Special permanent resident | 500.782 | 489.900 | 475.952 | 465.619 | 451.909 | 22,50% |
| **NON-PERMANENT RESIDENT** | **1.093.609** | **1.137.983** | **1.172.067** | **1.195.164** | **1.209.842** | **60,10%** |
| Long-term resident | 244.460 | 243.451 | 245.147 | 250.734 | 265.639 | 13,20% |
| Spouse of Japanese | 280.436 | 271.719 | 262.778 | 257.292 | 259.656 | 12,90% |
| College student | 93.614 | 110.415 | 125.597 | 129.873 | 129.568 | 6,40% |
| Accompanying family | 78.847 | 83.075 | 81.535 | 81.919 | 86.055 | 4,30% |
| Spec. in humanities/ international services | 40.861 | 44.496 | 44.943 | 47.682 | 55.276 | 2,70% |
| Trainee | 38.169 | 39.067 | 44.464 | 54.317 | 54.107 | 2,70% |
| Entertainer | 55.461 | 58.359 | 64.642 | 64.742 | 36.376 | 1,80% |
| Engineer | 19.439 | 20.717 | 20.807 | 23.210 | 29.044 | 1,40% |
| skilled labour | 11.927 | 12.522 | 12.583 | 13.373 | 15.112 | 0,80% |
| Intra-company transferee | 9.913 | 10.923 | 10.605 | 10.993 | 11.977 | 0,60% |
| Spouse of permanent resident, etc. | 7.047 | 7.576 | 8.519 | 9.417 | 11.066 | 0,60% |
| Education | 9.068 | 9.715 | 9.390 | 9.393 | 9.449 | 0,50% |
| Professor | 7.196 | 7.751 | 8.037 | 8.153 | 8.406 | 0,40% |
| Other | 155.405 | 170.999 | 182.547 | 190.858 | 209.964 | 10,40% |

Note: Figures are from year-end of each year. Total per cents are rounded.
Source: Adapted from MOJ 2006a.

heaviest concentration is in Tokyo, followed by Osaka, Aichi, Kanagawa, Saitama, Hyogo, Chiba, and Shizuoka prefectures (MOJ 2006a). While 1.57 per cent may seem inconsequential compared to the proportions of foreign residents in the rest of the developed world,[2] to the Japanese, it is apparent and a cause for comment. It should be noted, however, that many of the people included as "foreign residents" in the statistics are Japan-born, but Japan's citizenship principle is based on *jus sanguinis* rather than *jus soli* (Kashiwazaki 1998).

[2] According to the OECD, in 2002, the foreign population made up 8.9% of the population in Germany, 5.6% in France, 4.9% in Denmark, 4.5% in the UK, 4.3% in the Netherlands, 3.1% in Spain, 2.6% in Italy, and 0.5% in Korea (OECD 2003).

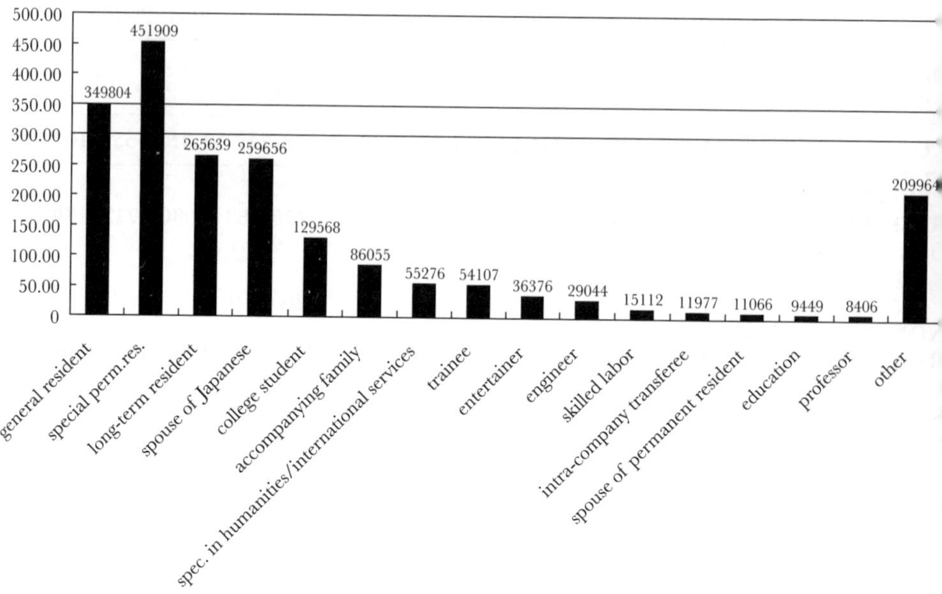


Source: Adapted from MOJ 2006a.

Figure 1. Residency status in 2005.

## 3. Population Decline and Response

In 2000, a United Nations report suggested that in order for Japan to maintain its population in the face of the coming population decline, it would need to accept about 381,000 foreign migrants annually, and if Japan desired to keep the size of the working-age population constant at the 1995 level (87.2 million), Japan would need to allow 609,000 migrants to enter per year to 2050. In this latter scenario, the report notes, "The number of post-1995 immigrants and their descendants would be 46 million, accounting for 30 per cent of the total population in 2050." (UNPD 2000: 49–51). At the time, this declaration made big headlines, and indeed, it has reverberated in academic writings as well as policy documents. While the projection by the United Nations report may have been a kind of unwelcome wake-up call, it certainly was not taken as a serious policy direction. There is a range of opinion among academics, as well as amongst economic federations, NGOs, and government ministries, as to how the immigration framework should be changed. None of the above parties look to immigration as the main solution to the problem of the low birth rate. On the other hand, no one is calling for a cessation to migration. Parties differ as to what sort of migrant workers should be encouraged to come to Japan, in what sort of occupations, and under what kind of conditions.

In his book *Amerikagata fuan shakai de ii no ka* [Do we want an anxiety society like that of the US?] (2006), Toshiaki Tachibanaki, Professor of Economics at Doshisha University, brings to his discussion of the low birth rate society the question of whether Japan must open to foreign migrants. Tachibanaki's opinion on opening the country to foreign labour is that it is effective as a means of economic invigoration. He cites the USA, Canada and Australia as cases in point. Furthermore, in post-war Europe, the economic recovery was successful due to the importation of migrant workers. Such workers, he notes, tend to be 'low-wage' workers, hence cost-saving to firms. This would be especially attractive to firms in Japan, where wages are on the comparatively high side (Tachibanaki 2006: 149). Yet Tachibanaki is aware of the costs of labour migration as well. He notes that in economic downturns, migrants become the first to be unemployed and form an economic underclass. Second, he mentions that migrants' families also come to stay, so social diversity (*ishitsusei*) as seen in religion, language, culture, and race, increases. Third, social unease arises due to the above mentioned increased diversity. As examples, he gives Germany's unease with the Turks, France's unease with Arab population, and England's unease with Indians, Pakistanis and Caribbean peoples in their midst. His solution to minimize such costs is to introduce migrants not as permanent labour, but as fixed-term labour, and not at low wages, but at the same or slightly higher wages as their Japanese counterparts. As to the question of what type of worker should be received, he notes: "The proposal to accept only skilled workers is a selfish argument on the part of the receiving country, and I am of the opinion that unskilled workers should also be accepted in the same way." (Tachibanaki 2006: 150).

Selfish argument notwithstanding, the Japan Business Federation (Nippon Keidanren) in May 2006 issued a set of resolutions for FY 2006, *Tapping Human Potential: Creative Solutions for a New Era*, in which the acceptance of foreign labour is only mentioned once, under "Rapid responses to the decline in Japan's population." The policy recommended is "Controlled admission of more highly qualified foreigners in greater numbers; development of new mechanisms to ensure this goal" (Nippon Keidanren 2006a). Another response to the threat of economic decline is the argument that Japan will make up in high technological prowess what it lacks in bodies. That is, it does not matter if low-value-added industries decline and die, because hi-tech industries requiring fewer but better educated workers will make up the difference in productivity (Usui 2006).

This line of reasoning is also taken up by Prime Minister Shinzō Abe in his book, *Utsukushii kuni he* [Toward a Beautiful Country]. In his chapter "Japan and Asia, and then, China", he notes, "If there are people who are appreciative of the Japanese national essence (*kunigara*) and ideals, and wish to educate their children in Japan, or if there are people who wish to become Japanese, we must open the doors wide for them. Needless to say, this is for the dynamism of Japan" (Abe 2006: 158). In his chapter on the low birth rate, however, Abe does not mention migration at all. He believes that the shrinking labour force will be compensated for by productivity gains and changing the pension system, as well as by progress in preventive medicine for the elderly.

Governmental officials disagree over the question of whether and to what extent migration should be encouraged in the future. According to the *Yomiuri Shinbun* (3 August 2006), the Ministry of Health, Labour and Welfare (MHLW) crossed swords with the Council on Regulatory Reform and Promotion of the Liberalization of the Private Sector (*Gyōsei kaikaku minkan kaihō suishin kaigi*) over a midterm report the latter had issued, in which they encouraged the acceptance of foreign social welfare workers and welfare caregivers. While the MHLW argued that supply of labour in the care fields exceeds demand, and that importation of foreign labour would lead to job losses for women and Japanese youth as well as worsened conditions, the Council rejected this view, stating "This will not lead to an oversupply of labour or a worsening of labour conditions." The major private-sector economic organization, Nippon Keidanren, was positive about the so-called Economic Partnership Agreement (EPA): "Nippon Keidanren has been calling to date for the acceptance of foreign human resources in the fields of nursing and care-giving, where a labour shortage is expected. For this reason, it warmly welcomes the creation within the Japan-Philippine EPA of a basic framework for the acceptance of nurses and careworkers (Nippon Keidanren 2006b: 11).

According to the EPA agreement which was supported by both the Ministry of Foreign Affairs (MOFA) and the Ministry of Economy, Trade and Industry (METI), Japan was to accept up to 1,000 nurses and welfare caretakers from the spring of 2007, who would be given six months' training in Japanese language before being sent to facilities where they would assist in nursing and care-giving tasks respectively. The nurses would be required to have a nursing degree and three years of experience; the caregivers, a four year college degree and care experience or a degree from a Philippine nursing school. Both would be required to pass the Japanese national exams for nurses or welfare caretakers, respectively, by the end of a three or four year term, respectively. If they fail the exam, they would not be allowed to remain in Japan. If they pass, they could remain and work as regular workers on three year renewable visas (*Chunichi Shinbun* 12 September 2006). Apparently it took two years to negotiate this agreement because of the strong stance of labour against it (*Shizuoka Shinbun* 25 September 2006). The Japan Nurses Association issued a public statement on 12 September 2006, in which, after noting that while there are some 550,000 qualified Japanese who are currently not working in medical fields, "We should not simply bring in foreign nurses with the notion of solving Japan's nurse shortage" (*Tōkyo Shinbun* 12 September 2006).

There are also many citizen groups in Japan working toward improving living and working conditions for foreign residents and lobbying the government actively to create what is called a "Multicultural Coexistence Society" (*tabunka kyōsei shakai*). Beginning with groups that supported the *Zainichi* [residing in Japan] Korean "oldcomer" population and expanding to numerous support organizations for "newcomer" foreigners living in Japan, they have proved essential in upholding the rights of the foreign population and contributing in crucial ways where government assistance was totally lacking (see Roberts 2003; Shipper 2005; Milly 2005; Yamanaka 2005). Many of these groups challenge the current immigration policy framework, by, for instance, advocating that overstayers who have lived peaceful and productive lives in Japan for many years now, should be granted amnesty, or by insisting that the current technical trainee system is a sham and should be replaced by a system allowing migrant workers to perform blue-collar work as regular workers under the Labour Standards Law (Torii 2006; GKMN 2006; Miyajima 2006; Nakajima 2006). Some write books to expose the scapegoating by politicians and media of foreign migrants as criminals (GSUN 2004). Some oppose the new move toward heightened surveillance and control through ID cards (Nichibenren 2006). The citizens groups' voices may lack the strength of the economic organizations, but they do maintain international networks and are savvy about using external pressure and human rights arguments to bolster their concerns. Of course these groups have differences among themselves, and one cannot claim they pose a united front on all issues.

## 4. A New Basic Stance on Immigration?

In September 2006, the Ministry of Justice's 'project team on the future admittance of foreigners' (Kongo no Gaikokujin no Ukeire ni kansuru Purojekuto Chīmu) issued a report entitled "Basic stance on admittance of foreigners in the future" (*Kongo no gaikokujin no ukeire ni kansuru kihontekina kangaekata*). The principal investigator on this team was the Vice Minister of Justice, Tarō Kōno. In general, this document seems to lean toward rationalizing the current system of migration, and points toward the creation of a 'more finely-tuned residence management system' for foreigners (MOJ 2006c: 1), wherein foreigners must be given wages equal to those of the Japanese, and will be obliged to enrol in pension and social insurance systems. The new policy document definitely does not lean in the direction of welcoming foreign permanent residents in large numbers. In the following I will highlight two sets of policy proposals to be found in this document, which have a direct impact on the legal status of migrant workers.

The project team recommends changing the systems and policies regarding people who are being used for the securing of cheap labour, (they mention the intern and technical trainee program as well as the entry system for people of Japanese descent).Concretely, they suggest thoroughly overhauling the intern/trainee system to one where such workers are accepted under employment contracts with firms, as "special skills workers" (*tokutei ginō rōdōsha*) whose fields of work are not recognized as skilled under the current framework. They note, "The industries to be allowed to hire such foreign labour are those for which it is deemed necessary for the development of the industry, only after they have carried out policies to hire domestic workers" (MOJ 2006c: 3). Furthermore, they suggest that such workers attain a certain level of proficiency in Japanese, and that their children must obtain compulsory education (in Japanese schools). Family reunification is also being considered: "Those on this system may, after a certain period has passed, and after having attained a certain level of skill and Japanese ability, bring over their family members. In that case, the spouses and so on must also have a certain level of Japanese proficiency" (MOJ 2006c: 3).

Another notable feature is that they plan to restructure the current acceptance scheme for *Nikkeijin* [of Japanese descent] migrants such that they must fulfil the same requirements as those mentioned above in the new 'special skills workers' category, once it is implemented, rather than giving them special admittance privileges "just because of shared blood." (MOJ 2006c: 3). This appears to be an attempt to ensure that Japanese Brazilian workers, as well as their accompanying family members, learn Japanese and are covered by health and social insurance programs.[3] They also mention that one of their basic stances in future policy will be to contribute to the diversification of Japanese society by way of refraining from favouring particular nationalities in their admittance policies (MOJ 2006c: 2, item #7). Furthermore, those *Nikkeijin* already in Japan for the purpose of working will have to have acquired a certain level of proficiency in Japanese (after the Japanese language support policies are actualized), and will have to demonstrate their ability to support a household stably (through stable employment) if they wish to continue their residency. Admittance for co-residing direct relatives and dependents would also depend on these conditions (MOJ 2006c: 4). Taken together with the comments on rehauling the admittance policies for *Nikkeijin*, one might conclude that the Ministry of Justice project team is rethinking its descent-based policies, probably due to problems with the education of *Nikkeijin* children,[4] and related juvenile crimes.

Although the Basic Stance lays out a general scheme for immigration policy and control in the future, it is currently only a set of recommendations, subject to negotiation and amendment. Shortly after the Stance document was published, the *Asahi Shinbun* (23–24 September 2006: 25) noted that although the MOJ project team announced plans to abolish the current trainee-internship program, this is being contested

[3] Failure of many employers to enter *Nikkeijin* workers into the social and health insurance schemes has been a major problem in past years (see Roth 2002).

[4] While young children of *Nikkeijin* families are more easily able to adjust to the local Japanese school curriculums, older children have more difficulties with learning to read and write as well as to keep up with the level of their studies in their home countries. The number of unschooled immigrant children has been increasing since the mid-90s. Furthermore, often both parents work, so unschooled children must fend for themselves during the day. Sometimes these children end up in the juvenile justice system (interview, Kurihama Juvenile Justice Home for Youths, 26 July 2005). See also Yamanaka (2005). Problems of this sort might be mitigated by fashioning school systems with far greater support for bilingual students than is now provided.

by the business community, who "has asked for an extension of the current trainee-technical internship program." Furthermore, they note the MHLW wants to keep the current system but hold businesses strictly to the rules, while METI wants to consider extending the length of time foreigners may stay under the current system.[5] There is a new Minister of Justice since the project team issued the Basic Stance, and how it fares will also be influenced by his opinion. One wonders how many of the Stance's plans will be eventually put in place, but one can look at it as a text illustrating the policy directions advocated by one group at the MOJ.

## 5. Conclusion

The economic malaise of the post-Bubble period, accompanied by various social ills that garnered much news coverage, contributed to Japan's caution toward increasing foreign migration. If 9/11 had not occurred, if Germany and France had not had so much unrest with their migrant populations, and if England had not experienced terrorist bombings in 2005, the tone regarding immigration might be more positive. A heightened sense of awareness of security issues is brought up regularly in policy documents related to migration.[6] Clearly, the Japanese government will not be moving forward swiftly to increase the numbers of migrants allowed into Japan, despite the accelerating population decline. Indeed, as the Basic Stance document illustrates, there is a strong current toward revising the existing framework, and toward more strict control of immigration. Perhaps they are waiting for the labour market to tighten. One reason it has not done so, as Torii (2006) observes, is that migrant workers, including the undocumented and trainees, are already making substantial contributions. The details of who will be encouraged to come to Japan, under what conditions, are the subject of considerable debate among ministries, economic federations, and local officials. The main challenge to Japan in the years ahead, as with all rich, ageing countries of migration, lies in recognizing the necessity of migration at some level, and in setting out a framework to deal justly with the peoples in its midst.

---

[5] See also Miyajima (2006). Takashi Miyajima is a professor in the graduate Sociology program at Hosei University and the head administrator for the NPO, RINK.

[6] See, for instance, MOJ (2005: 216–228).

## References

Abe, Shinzō (2006): *Utsukushī kune e* [Toward a beautiful country]. Tokyo: Bungeishinju.

*Asahi Shinbun* (23–24 September 2006): Foreign trainees may get boot: A Justice Ministry team says the current program allows too many abuses, p. 25.

*Asahi Shinbunsha* (2006): *Japan Almanac 2007*. Tokyo: Asahi Shinbunsha.

*Chunichi Shinbun* (12 September 2006): *Hi kara ukeire: Kangoshira 1000-nin 07-nendo hajime ni mo* [Bringing them in from the Philippines: 1,000 people from as early as the beginning of the fiscal year 2007]. Factiva Press Release Service: http://global.factiva.com/ha/default.aspx (found 15 October 2006).

Douglass, Mike and Glenda S. Roberts (eds.) (2003): *Japan and Global Migration: Foreign Workers and the Advent of a Multicultural Society*. Honolulu: University of Hawaii Press.

Douglass, Mike (2003): The singularities of international migration of women to Japan: past, present and future. In: Douglass, Mike and Glenda S. Roberts (eds.): *Japan and Global Migration: Foreign Workers and the Advent of a Multicultural Society*. Honolulu: University of Hawaii Press.

GKMN (Gaikokujin Kenkyūsei Mondai Nettowāku) (2006): *Gaikokujin kenshūsei: jikyū 300-en no rōdōsha, yabureru jinken to rōdō kijun* [Foreign trainees: workers at 300 yen per hour, shattered human rights and labour standards]. Tokyo: Akashi Shoten.

GSUN (Gaikokujin Sabetsu Uotchi Nettowāku) (2004): *Gaikokujin hōimō, 'chian akka' no sukēpu gōto* [Foreigners' alliance: scapegoats of the "worsening law and order"]. Tokyo: Gendai Jinbunsha.

Iyotani, Toshio (2001): *Gurōbarizēshon to imin* [Migration in an age of globalization]. Tokyo: Yūshindō Kōbunsha.

Kashiwazaki, Chikako (1998): Jus sanguinis in Japan: the origin of citizenship in a comparative perspective. In: *International Journal of Comparative Sociology* 39, 3 (August 1998), pp. 278–301.

Kawakami, Sonoko (2005): Gaikokujin kenshūsei: rōdō jittai to sono kadai [Foreign trainees: labour reality and issues]. In: Nishikawa, Jun (ed.): *Gurōbaru-ka jidai no gaikokujin shōsūsha no jinken: Nihon o dō hiraku ka* [The human rights of the minority foreign population in an age of globalization: how shall we open Japan?]. Tokyo: Akashi Shoten.

Milly, Deborah (2006): Policy Advocacy for Foreign Residents in Japan. In: Tsuda, Takeyuki (ed.): *Local Citizenship in Recent Countries of Immigration: Japan in Comparative Perspective*. Lanham, Maryland: Lexington Books, pp. 123–151.

Miyajima, Takashi (2006): Gaikokujin ukeirekoku Nihon no kadai [Issues for Japan as a receiving country for foreigners]. In: *Gekkan Oruta* 11, pp. 6–8.

MOFA (Ministry of Foreign Affairs) (2006): *Refugees*. http://www.mofa.go.jp/policy/refugee/japan.html (found 1 November 2006).

MOJ (Ministry of Justice) (2005): *Basic Plan for Immigration Control, 3rd Edition*. http://www.moj.go.jp/ENGLISH/information/bpic3rd.html (found 1 October 2006).

MOJ (2006a): *Heisei 17-nenmatsu genzai ni okeru gaikokujin tōrokusha tōkei ni tsuite* [Current statistics on foreign residents, year end 2005]. http://www.moj.go.jp/PRESS/060530–1/060530–1.html (found 10 February 2006).

—— (2006b): *Heisei 18-nenkan 'shutsunyūkoku kanri' no pointo* [Points on immigration control for 2006]. http://www.moj.go.jp/PRESS/060911–1/060911–1.pdf (found 1 October 2006).

—— (2006c): *Kongo no gaikokujin no ukeire ni kansuru kihontekina kangaekata* [Basic stance on the admittance of foreigners in the future], written by Kongo no Gaikokujin no Ukeire ni kansuru Purojekuto Chīmu [Project team for the future admittance of foreigners]. Report from 26 September 2006. http://www.moj.go.jp/NYUKAN/nyukan51–3.pdf (found 1 November 2006).

Nakajima, Hiroshi (2006): *Gaikokujin kenshū/ginojisshū wa na bakari machiukeru kakokuna rōdō* [Foreign trainees and technical interns in name only: harsh labour lying in wait]. In: *Shūkan Economisuto* (7 November), pp. 206–107.

Nichibenren (Japan Federation of Bar Associations) (2006): *Hōmufukudaijin 'kongo no gaikokujin no ukeire to ni kansuru purojekuto' 'Kongo no gaikokujin no ukeire ni tsuite' (chūkanmatome) ni taisuru ikensho' 2006.7.20* [Opinion report (20 July 2006) on the Vice-Minister of Justice's project team for the future admittance of foreigners' mid-term report, 'Basic Stance on the Admittance of Foreigners in the Future']. http://www.nichibenren.or.jp/ja/opinion/report/data/060720_000.pdf (found 1 December 2006).

Nippon Keidanren (2006a): *Tapping Human Potential: Creative Solutions for a New Era: FY 2006 General Assembly Resolutions, May 24, 2006*. http://www.keidanren.or.jp/english/policy/2006/031.html (found 1 December 2006).

—— (2006b): *Towards Broader and Deeper Economic Partnership Agreements, 17 October 2006*. http://www.keidanren.or.jp/english/policy/2006/072/proposal.html#part3 (found 1 December 2006).

OECD (2003): *Stocks of foreign and foreign-born populations in selected OECD countries, 1995 and 2002*. http://www.oecd.org/dataoecd/7/49/24994376.pdf (found 1 December 2006).

Oishi, Nana (2005): *Women in Motion*. Stanford: Stanford University Press.

Roberts, Glenda S. (2003): NGO Support for Migrant Labor in Japan. In: Douglass, Mike and Glenda S. Roberts (eds.): *Japan and Global Migration: Foreign Workers and the Advent of a Multicultural Society*. Honolulu: University of Hawaii Press, pp. 275–300.

Roth, Joshua (2002): *Brokered Homeland: Japanese Brazilian Migrants in Japan*. Ithaca, N.Y.: Cornell University Press.

Sellek, Yoko (2001): *Migrant Labor in Japan*. Houndmills, Basingstoke, Hampshire: Palgrave.

Shipper, Appichai (2005): Criminals or Victims? The Politics of Illegal Foreigners in Japan. In: *Journal of Japanese Studies* 31, 2, pp. 299–327.

*Shizuoka Shinbun* (25 September 2006): *Rōdōkaikoku: kyōsei e no kankyō seibi o* [Opening the country to labour: preparing the way for an environment of co-existence]. Factiva Press Release Service: http://global.factiva.com/ha/default.aspx (found 1 October 2006).

Tachibanaki, Toshiaki (2006): *Amerika gata fuan shakai de ii no ka. Kakusa, nenkin, shitsugyō, shōshikamondai e no shohōsen* [Do we want an anxiety society like that of the US? Recipes for questions on difference, pension, unemployment, and declining birth rate]. Tokyo: Asahi Shinbunsha.

*Tokyo Shinbun* (12 September 2006): *Hi kara ukeire, kangoshira 1000 nin 07 nendo hajimenimo* [1000 nurses to be admitted from the Philippines as early as the beginning of the 2007 fiscal year]. Factiva Press Release Service: http://global.factiva.com/ha/default.aspx (found 1 October 2006).

Torii, Ippei (2006): 'Gaikokujin kenshū' ga utsushidasu gendai Nihon: jikai suru kōkyōsei [Contemporary Japan as imaged in 'foreign trainees': the disintegration of commonality]. In: *Gekkan Oruta* (November), pp. 12–15.

Tsuda, Takeyuki (ed.) (2006): *Local Citizenship in Recent Countries of Immigration: Japan in Comparative Perspective*. Lanham, Maryland: Lexington Books.

UNPD (United Nations Population Division) (2000): *Replacement Migration: Is it a Solution to Declining and Ageing Populations?* Report for Japan. http://www.un.org/esa/population/publications/migration/japan.pdf (found 4 December 2006).

USDS (U.S. Department of State) (2004): *Trafficking in Persons Report*. Released by the Office to Monitor and Combat Trafficking in Persons, June 14, 2004. http://www.state.gov/g/tip/rls/tiprpt/2004/33191.htm (found 18 December 2006).

Usui, Chikako (2006): Japan's Demographic Future and the Challenge of Foreign Workers. In: Tsuda, Takeyuki (ed.): *Local Citizenship in Recent Countries of Immigration: Japan in Comparative Perspective*. Lanham, Maryland: Lexington Books.

Yamanaka, Keiko (2006): Immigrant Incorporation and Women's Community Activities in Japan: Local NGOs and Public Education. In: Tsuda, Takeyuki (ed.): *Local Citizenship in Recent Countries of Immigration.* Lanham, MD: Lexington Books, pp. 97–119.

Yamawaki, Keizo (2006): Tabunkakyōsei shakai ni mukete [Towards a multicultural, co-existent society]. In: *Meiji Foramu* 6, pp. 10–15.

*Yomiuri Shinbun* (3 August 2006): *Gaikokujin rōdōsha ukeire kakudairon gikushaku 'ginōjisshū' kakujū de dakyō?* [The debate over expanding the number of foreign workers admitted gets rough: Will a compromise be reached to expand the number of 'technical trainees'?]. Factiva Press Release Service: http://global.factiva.com/ha/default.aspx (found 15 October 2006).

Yoshinari, Katsuo (2005): Zairyūtokubetsu kyoka o motomeru hiseiki taizai gaikokujin [Undocumented foreigners who apply for special permission for residency]. In: Yorimitsu, Masatoshi (ed.): *Nihon no imin seisaku o kangaeru: jinkō gensho shakai no kadai* [Considerations to immigration policy in Japan: measures against decreasing population]. Tokyo: Akashi Shoten.

CHAPTER FORTY-THREE

# INFRASTRUCTURAL POLICY: FRAMEWORK AND CHALLENGES

Thomas Feldhoff

## 1. Introduction

In the post-war period, national and local governments in Japan made their spatial planning policies assuming ever-growing socio-economic conditions. Today's reality, however, looks quite different: demographic change is leading to population and urban decline. Issues of communities losing vitality are becoming more and more evident (Flüchter 2005; Fujii 2005). Shrinking regions and cities are a phenomenon that will provide considerable challenges to infrastructural planning.

Policy makers need to create strategies to deal with the spatial implications of demographic change. However, the already high public debt combined with rising financial obligations resulting from the changing social and economic environment will increasingly restrict the government's ability to act. Innovative ways of building, managing and using infrastructural facilities as well as integrated planning and development approaches are under consideration even though they run contrary to the vested interests of powerful lobbying groups.

In this chapter, the challenges and prospects resulting from the demographic ageing and shrinking processes will be analysed, based on a description and evaluation of the traditional framework of Japan's infrastructural policy related to the "construction state" issue. With regard to the spatial dimension of these processes, regional population projection results have to be taken into account. To exemplify the ongoing challenges in spatial development processes and planning policies, selected governmental strategies for policy reorientation will be discussed. Finally, from the standpoint of institutional stability and change, some evaluative remarks on Japan's reform approaches that focus on sustainable regional development are offered for further discussion.

## 2. Traditional Framework of Infrastructural Planning Policies

Since the 1950s, Comprehensive Plans for the Development of the Country (*zenkoku sōgō kaihatsu keikaku*) and strategic infrastructure investment plans characterized by very high levels of central government control have been implemented. Based on these plans, infrastructure development made a major contribution to economic growth, social welfare improvement, and regional development through the decades of Japan's post-war high growth. As a result, the construction and public works sector became Japan's largest industry. Throughout the 1990s in particular, the government spent vast sums of public money on economic stimulus packages. In fact, much of this money was devoted to public works in Japan's low-income and depopulating peripheral areas. From the standpoint of social and regional policies, the government justified the public investment as a contribution to a more equitable distribution of wealth among people and regions. In consequence, the level of public investment per capita in remote rural areas exceeded by far that for metropolitan areas (Kajita 2001).

Since 1998, due to greater economic and fiscal restraints, public construction investment has continued to decline. By international comparison, however, in relation to GDP, the level of investment is still far higher than in any other OECD country (see Figure 1). Correspondingly, the Japanese construction business constitutes a vast public employment system, composed of nearly 559,000 companies that directly employ about 5.84 million people or 9.2 per cent of the total working population in fiscal year 2004 (JFCC 2005: 11, 16). It is especially in remote rural areas in Hokkaido, Northeastern and Southwestern Japan that construction employment ratios of more than 20 per cent of the total employment are the norm (Feldhoff 2005: 102–104).

Since the early post-war years, the government has adopted the concept of balanced regional development, aiming to supply hard infrastructure in the form of highways, railways, airports and large dams in the structurally weak regions. However, the intended economic growth failed to occur and public works have not scored any real success in lessening the regional disparities. On the contrary, the most obvious outcomes of regional planning were the unprecedented concentration of wealth and power in the metropolitan areas in the Pacific Coast Industrial Belt and the "Unipolar Concentration" in Tokyo (*Tōkyō ikkyoku shūchū*). Furthermore, public works have aggravated the regional

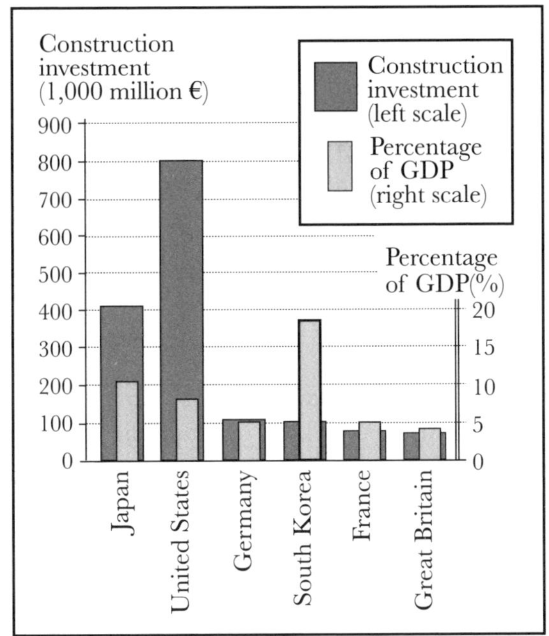


Note: Author's calculations of JFCC data.
Source: JFCC 2005: 37.

Figure 1. Japan's construction investment by international comparison 2003.

economies' dependence on construction to an irrationally high level. Therefore, a large number of government-financed projects, some of them absurdly expensive and paying no regard to environmental concerns or future costs, are still under construction or under planning in the remote regional areas.

Over the past decade, these so-called "wasteful public works" (*muda na kōkyō jigyō*), compensating declining rural areas through fiscal redistribution, have become subject to mounting public criticism to the effect that public works appear to be little more than a costly large-scale advancement and employment programme for the construction industry (Bowen 2003; Feldhoff 2002a; Feldhoff 2002b; Er 2005). From the standpoint of sustainability—managing the interplay of nature, society, and the economy—there are three main problems with Japan's traditional infrastructure planning policies (McCormack 2001, 2002; Feldhoff 2002a, 2005). Firstly, the fiscal crisis of local and national governments in Japan is a major issue of concern. The debt-financed allocation of public funds for public works projects to stimulate the economic cycle has incurred massive public debts, inviting an enormous misallocation of resources. Japan's fiscal condition is among the worst of all major industrialized nations, with an estimated year 2006 national debt of 160.5 per cent of nominal GDP (OECD 2005, Internet).

Environmental devastation is a second negative outcome of the "construction state" (Guo and McCormack 2001). It is the result of intense industrialization and urbanization processes induced by strong agglomeration economies, especially during the rapid growth period, and "wasteful public works" that contributed to the construction boom of the post-bubble era.

Thirdly, it is worth noting that in recent years, local protest movements and referendums against large-scale public works projects have become a new trend on the landscape of local politics in Japan (Jain 2000; Er 2005). These movements and referendums symbolize the growing opposition of potentially affected local residents to Japan's public works policy. Moreover, they also reflect a growing indignation among urban citizens at the waste of taxpayers' money on projects in rural areas with only little benefit to the people and to future infrastructure needs in socially essential sectors such as health and welfare, elderly care, education or housing (Kabashima 2000; McCormack 2002: 20).

One main reason for these negative outcomes of modern Japanese infrastructural planning is the institutional arrangements of the so-called "construction state" (*doken kokka*) (McCormack 2001, 2002). According to regional development theory, infrastructure was seen as having a positive effect on the regional economy by producing accessibility. On the surface, therefore, its significance for regional development served as grounds for investing billions of yen. In reality, this was but a disguise for robust power politics. According to Broadbent (2002: 43), a "construction state" can be defined as a government which puts much more public investment into the construction of public works than can be realistically justified by public need. At its heart, a system of collusion between politicians, ministerial bureaucrats, especially from the Ministry of Land, Infrastructure and Transport (MLIT), which is in charge of infrastructural and regional planning, and construction-related businessmen can be identified. Under Liberal Democratic Party (LDP) long-term one-party rule in post-war Japan, these actors became linked by an extensive network of formal and informal ties and bound in a so-called "iron triangle" of benefit and influence (Woodall 1996; Feldhoff 2002a; McCormack 2002).

For many decades, this "iron triangle" of major actors was considered the symbol of the country's economic prosperity. However, with the revelations of illegal practices and abuse, the system of mutual give-and-take connections threw Japan's democracy into crisis. As Bowen (2003: 3) points out, "Japan's democracy [...] suffers from personalism, graft, cronyism, favoritism, bribery, money politics, factionalism and collusion [...]." The resulting severe public criticism gave support to those wishing to initiate a structural reformation of Japan's political system. The advent of non-governmental organizations, local referendums and governors who rely on grassroots, non-partisan support is challenging the traditional top-down approach of Japanese planning practices (Er 2005; Feldhoff 2005). With the unprecedented demographic changes, the bottom-up pressure to overcome traditional framework-based development will become even more severe.

## 3. The Demographic Challenge: Regional Population Projection Results

Population projections are a key instrument for appraising future development processes. At the regional and local level, they can help to increase the awareness of decision-makers of certain problems by indicating a need for action. There are, indeed, a number of research institutions that have constructed various national population projections for Japan. While the predictions of each body are somewhat different, the general pattern of all the projections is basically the same.

- The Ministry of Health, Labour and Welfare (MHLW), for example, estimates that there will be just 500 Japanese left by the year 3000, if the demographic situation remained unchanged (cited after Hewitt 2003: 4).
- According to a 2004 United Nations projection, Japan's population is poised to peak at about 128 million people in 2005. From that point on, it will begin a reverse track, contracting to an estimated 112 million people by 2050 according to the medium variant (UNPD 2005).
- The Japanese National Institute of Population and Social Security Research (IPSS 2002, Internet) forecasts that the population will fall to somewhere between 92 and 108 million by mid-century, with a medium-case prediction of about 100.6 million people in 2050.

Concerning the spatial impacts of the ageing process, a brief look at regional population projection results is illuminating. In 1997, the National Institute of Population and Social Security Research projected the total population by prefecture from 1995 to 2025 (IPSS 1997, Internet). The major findings of this projection, which is based on regionally differentiated assumptions regarding factors such as fertility, survivorship, and net migration rates, will be summarized below. In this context, it is important to note that, according to the results of population censuses, the population had already decreased in 13 prefectures between 1990 and 1995, in 23 prefectures between 1995 and 2000, and in 32 prefectures between 2000 and 2005 (STK 2000, 2005, Internet).

Without going into too much detail, we come to realize that by 2025, the total population will decline in most prefectures (see Figure 2). When we examine the population in 2025 using an index in which the population in 1995 is set as 100, the indices of 17 prefectures, including Akita, Shimane, and Yamaguchi, are below 90. That indicates a high population decline of more than 10 per cent. Until recently, the problem of ageing primarily belonged to the countryside. The percentage of the aged population to the total population was markedly high in those prefectures on the periphery, such as Akita, Yamagata, Shimane, Kochi and Kumamoto. This percentage will consistently increase nationwide, and thus ageing is becoming a concern in all prefectures (see Figure 3). According to the projection, the number of prefectures where the percentage of those aged 65 and above exceeds 30 will be just four in 2015 and eight in 2020, but already fourteen in 2025. Thus, "rural Japan will experience an increasing number of communities in which there are virtually no children" (Traphagan 2005: 103).

The process of spatial differentiation becomes even more pronounced at the sub-regional or local level. In the coming era, depopulation and ageing are most severe in towns or villages in rural and remote areas as well as in small cities with fewer than 50,000 inhabitants. Moreover, many cities with around 50,000 to 100,000 people will lose much of their population and become very aged local societies. It should also not be forgotten that remote port cities and old industrial cities will continue to lose population together with their economic bases (Fujii 2005: 96–97). At the same time, the percentage of people living in large cities of more than 200,000 inhabitants will increase further. As a consequence, the population in the highly urbanized prefectures surrounding Tokyo in particular will increase their share of the overall

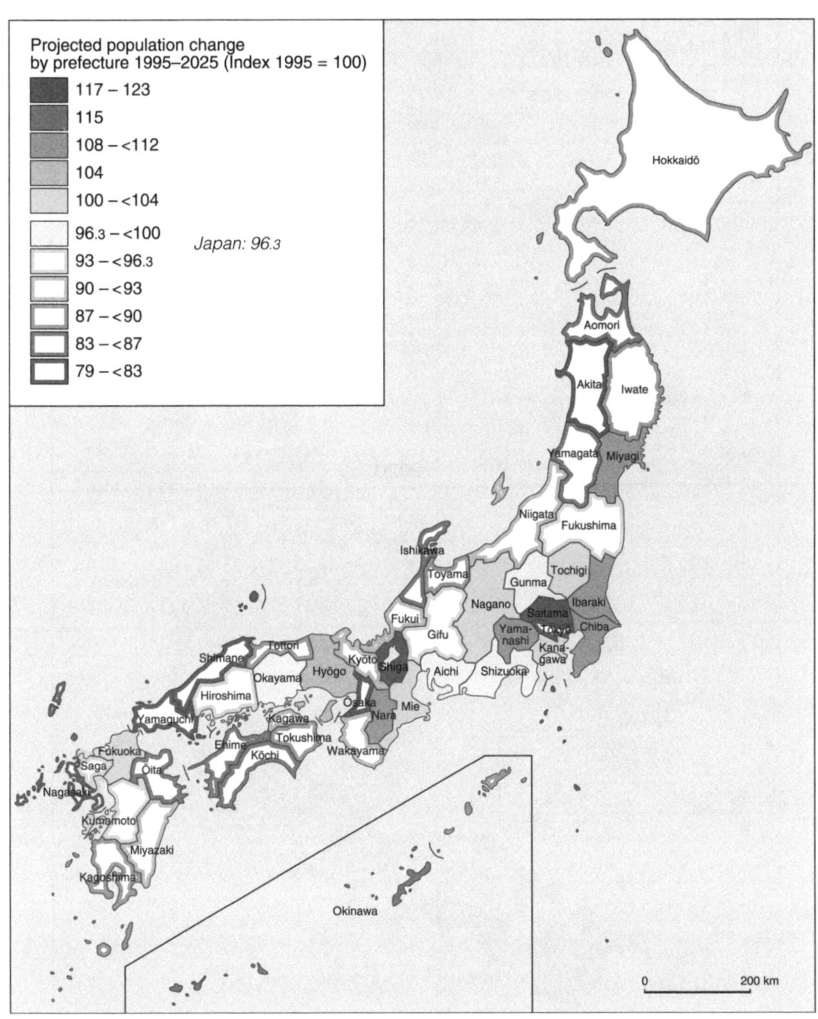


Source: Author's own calculations of IPSS (1997) data.

Figure 2. Per cent change in population by prefecture 1995–2025.

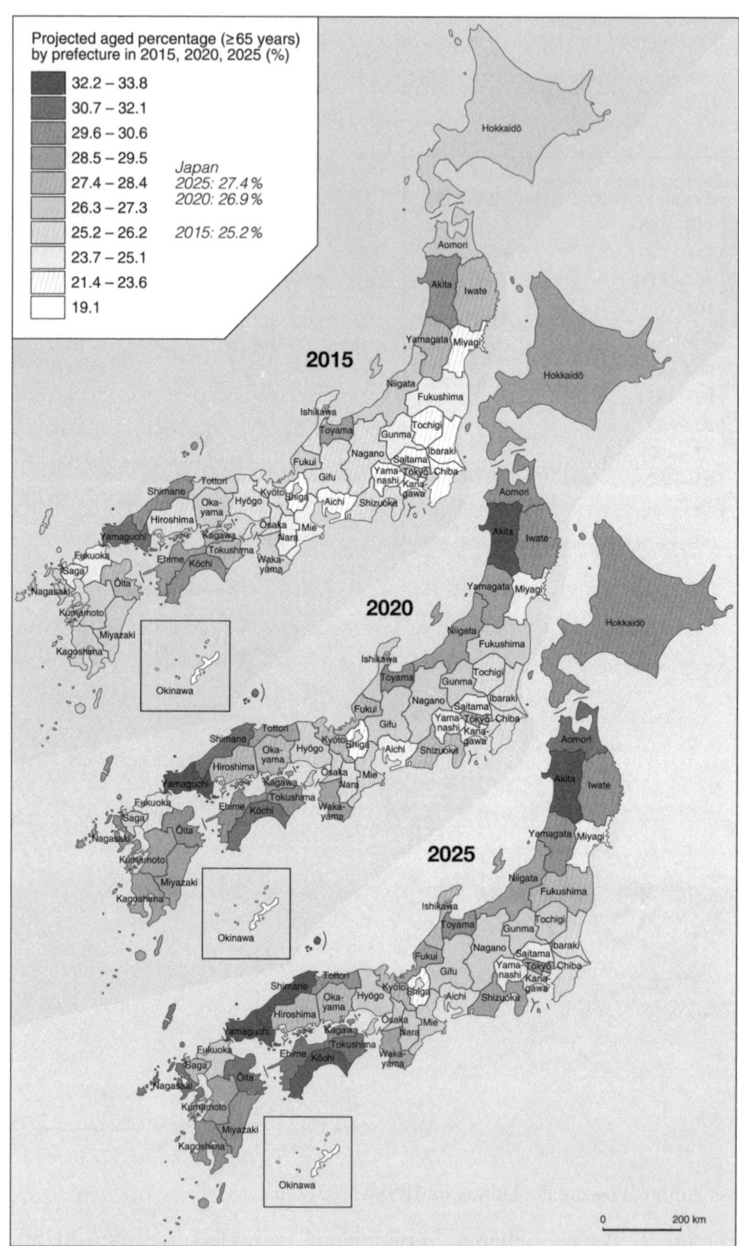


Source: Author's own calculations of IPSS (1997) data.

Figure 3. Projected percentage of aged population (65 years and older) by prefecture 2015, 2020 and 2025.

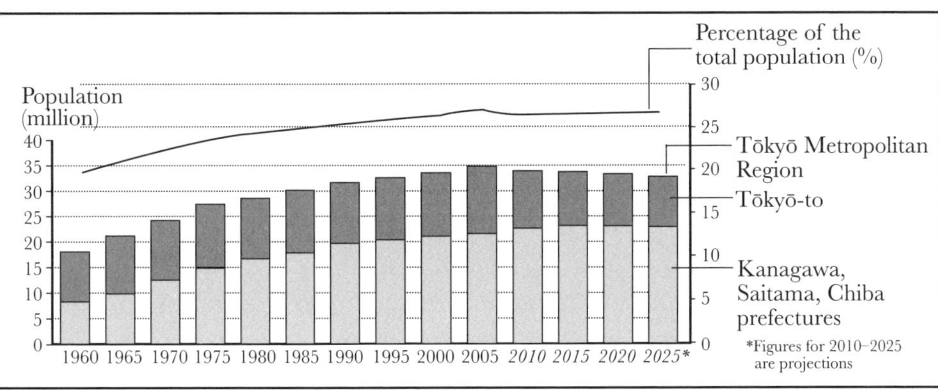


Source: Author's own calculation of STK (2000, 2025) and IPSS (1997) data.

Figure 4: Tokyo Metropolitan Region: Absolute population and percentage of the national total population 1960–2025.

population in the future, and the imbalance in regional population distribution will grow (see Figure 4).

To sum up the regional population projection results, firstly, we can observe divergent processes of urban growth and shrinkage, with urban growth being centred on large cities. Secondly, demographic ageing and the issue of shrinking relating not only to depopulation, but also to the loss of functions, de-economization, and de-socialization, describe closely intertwined processes. According to Flüchter (2005: 91), "shrinking" is almost always associated with deindustrialization and the ageing of society, particularly in monostructured areas based on so-called "sunset industries", such as mining, that can no longer compete in the global economy. Thanks to substantial governmental subsidies, the quantity and quality of public infrastructure services in such cities is still much better than one would expect. However, the situation will change dramatically when subsidy programmes are reduced or terminated and urban and regional restructuring policies fail.

## 4. Challenges and Prospects for Japan's Infrastructural Policy

In an era of ageing and shrinking, it is a major duty of policy makers to ensure that residents in shrinking, thinning regions are provided with an appropriate range of infrastructural facilities in a coordinated,

Table 1. The contraction of urban spaces in Japan: Total area of Densely Inhabited Districts (DID) by type of city region 2000–2030.

| | Actual | | | Projected | | |
|---|---|---|---|---|---|---|
| | 1980 | 1990 | 2000 | 2010 | 2020 | 2030 |
| Tokyo, Osaka, and Nagoya Metropolitan regions (1980: 5,261 km$^2$) | 100 | 118 | 123 | 124 | 124 | 121 |
| Cabinet order designated city regions (1980: 972 km$^2$) | 100 | 121 | 130 | 132 | 131 | 129 |
| City regions with at least 300,000 inhabitants (1980: 1,956 km$^2$) | 100 | 123 | 133 | 133 | 131 | 127 |
| City regions with at least 100,000 inhabitants (1980: 1,277 km$^2$) | 100 | 117 | 125 | 124 | 121 | 116 |

Note: Densely Inhabited District (DID, *jinkō shūchū chiku*): Statistical area with a population density over 4,000 persons per km$^2$ and a resident population of over 5,000 people.
Source: MLIT 2003a.

accountable, and affordable manner. With special reference to demographic changes, the following kinds of infrastructure are of particular importance:

- educational and social facilities, including kindergartens and schools as well as medical services and health-care systems;
- public transport, including measures to promote social inclusion for those living in rural areas and to design a barrier-free travel environment for the elderly;
- the supply of commerce and other services including recreational facilities and specialized social services for the elderly;
- urban landscape design, including the planning of housing and public spaces, the contraction of urban spaces (see Table 1), and the revitalization of urban centres.

Facing these challenges, the MLIT decided to revise its planning policies and instruments. In 2003, the Priority Plan for Social Infrastructure Development (*shakai shihon seibi jūten keikaku*) replaced the nine special infrastructure development plans for roads improvement and management, airports, ports, traffic safety facilities, city parks, sewerage, flood control, collapse of steep slopes, and seacoast. These plans were traditional framework-based and orientated towards quantitative development, aiming to implement monolithic standards nationwide.

In contrast, the new integrated Priority Plan is intended to shift infrastructural planning policies from the emphasis on quantitative to qualitative, sustainable development. In order to improve the transparency of decision-making processes, the ministry introduced a new evaluation system. "Plan-Do-See" is a method of infrastructure lifecycle management intended to achieve cost reductions by optimizing all project phases, including public involvement (PI). With regard to efficiency, equity, and accountability, the shortening of project periods, clearer objectives for procurement, tendering and contracting procedures as well as private finance initiatives (PFI) are required (MLIT 2003a: 33–34).

To facilitate the process of policy reorientation, in 2005, the government abolished the "old" Comprehensive National Land Development Act and enacted the "new" National Land Sustainability Plan Act (*Kokudo Keisei Keikaku-hō*) (MLIT 2006, Internet). Based on the new law, so-called "National Land Sustainability Plans", consisting of a national plan and wide-area regional plans, will be drafted. They should be different from the past plans in terms of both planning processes and contents, as they intend to do the following:

- create a national and regional planning vision in cooperation between the national and local governments;
- foster participation of a variety of bodies in planning processes;
- establish an integrated national and regional planning system (MLIT 2006, Internet).

By introducing this act, the government was reacting to long-standing criticism of the traditional planning policies, which were too state-centralized, too uniform countrywide, and led by vested interests (Feldhoff 2005: 205). Whereas the new "sustainability plans" are still under discussion and a subject for future research, two concrete outcomes of the changing planning paradigm have already been translated into action: the "Urban Renaissance" and "Universal Design" policies.

As the contraction of urban space on the edge of metropolitan regions is a future trend, one major concept of city planners is "Urban

Renaissance" to encourage compactness in urban development in favour of the central areas (MLIT 2003b, Internet). With regard to the everyday needs of an aged (and possibly more disabled) population, the MLIT launched the "General Principles of Universal Design Policy" in 2005 (MLIT 2005a, Internet). According to the Center for Universal Design (CUD 1997, Internet), universal design is "the design of products and environments to be usable by all people, to the greatest extent possible, without the need for adaptation or specialized design". It developed from past efforts to remove barriers to the use of public infrastructural facilities by elderly and handicapped people and intends to simplify life for everyone at little or no extra cost. Currently, the Japanese government's aims for concrete action in this field are as follows (MLIT 2005a, Internet):

1. Constructing a participation society from the perspective of users;
2. Integrating barrier-free policies;
3. Public transportation that all people can use safely and smoothly;
4. Creating communities where everyone can live safely and comfortably;
5. Providing for diverse activities based on technology, methods, etc.

To put Universal Design into practice, various efforts are being made, such as remodelling existing buildings and infrastructural facilities (see Figure 5), introducing new standards for transit vehicles and other transport services, public-private partnerships in product development, and educating entrepreneurs, public administration staff and residents. One important element in all the activities is public involvement, and, indirectly at least, the evolution of new forms of governance. Instead of the traditional top-down approaches in Japan's infrastructural policy domain, it seems necessary to promote bottom-up involvement and citizen participation in policy shaping and implementation. This process should be carried out in a community-based way, which means providing opportunities for citizens, community reference groups, non-profit organizations (NPO), relevant funding agencies, specialized consultants, and local authorities to be heard.

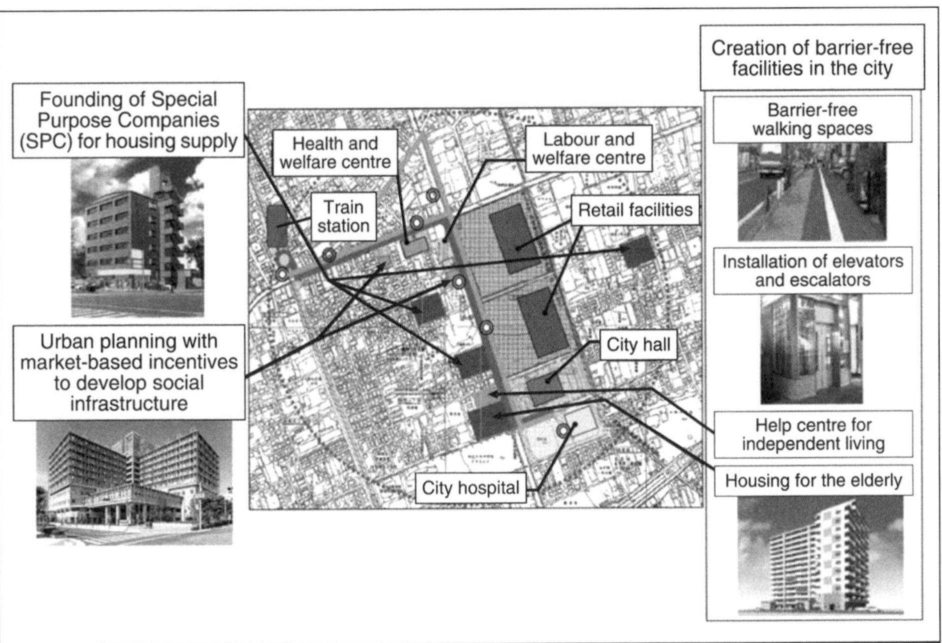


Source: Based on MLIT 2005b: 12.

Figure 5. Consideration of Universal Design aspects in urban planning.

## 5. Evaluation and Conclusion

Facing diminishing legitimacy, severe budgetary pressures, and the nation's demographic transition, the actors of the "construction state" have been forced to react. Many of their "new" concepts are, however, old empty phrases well-known from earlier documents, routinely appealing to emotions, but more or less meaningless in terms of altering the current consciousness of the main actors. The main problems associated with the "new" policies will be briefly discussed below.

Infrastructural policy adjustments are intended to reduce the capital and running costs of infrastructural facilities while increasing the accessibility and levels of their utilization. Meanwhile, within the government's extensive programme of capital investment, private finance initiatives that could be an adequate instrument make up only a few per cent, whilst the vast majority remains conventionally procured. Moreover, the official promotion of private finance initiatives conceals the fact that private investors are only interested in lucrative investments that are most unlikely to be made in rural peripheral areas.

As a consequence, urban renaissance projects are almost exclusively a phenomenon of the metropolitan regions. Urban renaissance is thus a concept for the consolidation of the metropolises, further accelerating the decline of peripheral cities and regions. More compact settlement structures, including services for the elderly, may also be interpreted as a response to sustainability challenges (Fujii 2005). Additionally, the Universal Design policy is important in adjusting public spaces to the everyday needs of an ageing society. At the same time, it creates new business opportunities for the construction business. However, this policy is more or less meaningless with regard to the economic and social revitalization of shrinking cities and regions.

The same holds true for many public works projects that still seem to be based on predictions of growth, ignoring the problem of "shrinking cities". Though criticism of public works funding has increased sharply and all political parties have called for reduced public investment, money is, even today, often spent to the benefit of the construction lobby, due to regional lobbying and a lack of political imagination. Since 1999, the LDP-led coalition government has pursued an official policy of reviewing public works, but this has mainly been a face-saving exercise. The necessity of public works projects is in many cases not critically evaluated; rather, the time of realization is merely prolonged due to fiscal restraints (McCormack 2002: 17).

Officially, the involvement of local stakeholders and citizens in public affairs is a major tool in dealing with regional and urban development processes since the enactment of the Law to Promote Specified Non-profit Activities in 1998. Nevertheless, public involvement is still more of an alibi strategy to dampen citizens' resistance to public works and to incorporate divergent interests into governmental planning structures to legitimize state authority, rather than substantive bottom-up policy-making or local self-governance. A true consultation mechanism empowering citizens to influence substantively all the processes, from proposal formulation and planning to the implementation of public works projects, is still lacking (Bothwell 2003: 147).

This is particularly due to the fact that administrative reforms have failed to weaken the power of the ministerial bureaucracy in policy-making and the centralism of the state administration. The bureaucrats successfully obstructed any radical change of their exclusive dominance in public works matters intended by the reorganization of central government in 2001, which involved the reform of public corporations and administrative deliberation councils as well as plans for decentralization and deregulation. In particular, the highly centralized nature of the public finance system, including investment programmes, specific tax revenues and special accounts earmarked for construction purposes, has remained virtually unchallenged (Feldhoff 2005: 376–384). In fact, the new Priority Plan for Social Infrastructure Development is very much left to bureaucratic discretion, as it contains neither project details (*kashozuke*) nor concrete investment expenditures, but only broad, long-term objectives.

At the same time that administrative reforms failed, political reforms in the fields of the electoral system and the regulation of political donations were unsuccessful in weakening systemic corruption and the strong regionalism built into Japan's political system. The LDP, although facing a steady decline in voter support, still controls the government, as the parties in opposition to the LDP ruling coalition are programmatically weak parties with more or less weak leadership (Stockwin 2005: 68). Although the two major opposition parties (Democratic Party of Japan and Liberal Party) combined into one shortly before the general election of November 2003, the scandal-ridden LDP still retained power, and in the autumn of 2005 won an even larger majority (McCormack 2005, Internet).

Finally, several informal institutions of Japan's political economy that circumvent the constraints of formal ones still persist. That holds especially true for "old boys" networks based on study or university cliques (*gakubatsu*), informal pre-negotiations among decision makers (*nemawashi*), family ties based on traditional marriage and adoption policies, the high proportion of hereditary politicians (*seshū giin*) in national, prefectural and municipal assemblies, and the unwritten rules of political payback (Feldhoff 2005; McCormack 2005). That makes us realize that changes in the formal institutions will remain more or less toothless as long as the informal institutions are left untackled.

From a structural point of view, the importance of new forms of governance becomes obvious when we stress the importance of institutional innovation and legitimacy in overcoming the lock-in of regional development processes. The dynamic nature of institutional innovation poses a challenge, not only to the traditional institutional arrangements of Japan's powerful construction lobby, but also to the social stability these arrangements had guaranteed until the present. In light of our reform evaluation, indicating a relative stability of the "construction state" mechanism, it seems fair to conclude that sustainability still remains an unattainable ideal in Japanese infrastructural policy (Flüchter 2005). The new governmental strategies are a step in the right direction to addressing key issues of Japan's ageing society, but need to be enforced by breaking up vested interest coalitions and traditional, growth-orientated development patterns.

For the very densely settled Japanese society, however, does shrinkage necessarily need to be regarded as a disadvantage? Could it not rather be seen simply as a great opportunity to improve the quality of life, including affordable housing, relief of traffic congestion, and improved environmental conditions? Much more political and public discussion about the positive aspects of shrinkage seems to be inevitable. Whether new forms of bottom-up urban and regional governance instead of top-down urban and regional planning will be born out of the ongoing changes in society is thus a question that has yet to be answered.

## References


Bothwell, Robert O. (2003): The challenges of growing the NPO and voluntary sector in Japan. In: Osborne, Stephen P. (ed.): *The Voluntary and Non-Profit Sector in Japan. The Challenge of Change*. London, New York: RoutledgeCurzon, pp. 121–149.

Bowen, Roger W. (2003): *Japan's Dysfunctional Democracy. The Liberal Democratic Party and Structural Corruption*. Armonk, New York, London: M.E. Sharpe.

Broadbent, Jeffrey (2002): Comment on: The Institutional Roots of the Japanese Construction State. In: *Asien* 84, pp. 43–46.

CUD (The Center for Universal Design) (1997): *About Universal Design*. http://www.design.ncsu.edu/cud/about_ud/about_ud.htm (found 20 May 2006).

Er, Lam Peng (2005): Local Governance. The Role of Referenda and the Rise of Independent Governors. In: Hook, Glenn D. (ed.): *Contested Governance in Japan. Sites and Issues*. London, New York: RoutledgeCurzon, pp. 71–89.

Feldhoff, Thomas (2002a): Japan's Construction Lobby Activities—Systemic Stability and Sustainable Regional Development. In: *Asien* 84, pp. 34–42.

—— (2002b): Japan's Regional Airports: Conflicting National, Regional and Local Interests. In: *Journal of Transport Geography* 10, 3, pp. 165–175.

—— (2005): *Bau-Lobbyismus in Japan. Institutionelle Grundlagen—Akteursnetzwerke—Raumwirksamkeit*. Dortmund: Dortmunder Vertrieb für Bau- und Planungsliteratur.

Flüchter, Winfried (2005): Megalopolises and Rural Peripheries. Shrinking Cities in Japan. In: Oswalt, Philipp (ed.): *Shrinking Cities. Vol. 1: International Research*. Ostfildern-Ruit: Hatje Cantz, pp. 83–92.

Fujii, Yasuyuki (2005): Shrinkage in Japan. In: Oswalt, Philipp (ed.): *Shrinking Cities. Vol. 1: International Research*. Ostfildern-Ruit: Hatje Cantz, pp. 96–100.

Guo, Nanyan and Gavan McCormack (2001): Coming to Terms with Nature: Development Dilemmas on the Ogasawara Islands. In: *Japan Forum* 13, 2, pp. 177–193.

Hewitt, Paul S. (2003): The Grey Roots of Japan's Crisis. In: *Asia Program Special Report* 107, pp. 4–9.

IPSS (Institute of Population and Social Security Research) (1997): *Population Projection by Prefecture.* http://www.ipss.go.jp/pp-fuken/e/ppp_h9/gaiyo.html (found 15 August 2005).

—— (2002): *Population Projections for Japan: 2001–2050.* With Long-range Population Projections: 2051–2100. http://www.ipss.go.jp/pp-newest/e/ppfj02/ppfj02.pdf (found 30 July 2005).

Jain, Purnendra (2000): Jumin Tohyo and the Tokushima Anti-Dam Movement in Japan—The People Have Spoken. In: *Asian Survey* 40, 4, pp. 551–570.

JFCC (Japan Federation of Construction Contractors) (2005): *Kensetsugyō handobukku* [Construction handbook]. Tokyo: Tanaka Insatsu.

Kabashima, Ikuo (2000): The LDP's 'Kingdom of the Regions' and the Revolt of the Cities. In: *Japan Echo* 27, 5, pp. 22–28.

Kajita, Shin (2001): Public Investment as a Social Policy in Remote Rural Areas in Japan. In: *Geographical Review of Japan* 74 (Ser. B), 2, pp. 147–158.

McCormack, Gavan (2001): *The Emptiness of Japanese Affluence.* Rev. edn. Armonk, London: M. E. Sharpe.

—— (2002): Breaking the Iron Triangle. In: *New Left Review* 13, pp. 5–23.

—— (2005): *Koizumi's Kingdom of Illusion.* http://japanfocus.org/products/details/1924 (found 23 May 2006).

MLIT (Ministry of Land, Infrastructure and Transport) (2003a): *Heisei 15-nendo kokudo kōtsū hakusho* [White Paper on Land, Infrastructure and Transport in Japan 2003]. Tokyo: Gyōsei.

—— (2003b): *Toshi saisei bijon* [A vision of urban renaissance]. https://www.mlit.go.jp/kisha/kisha03/04/041224/01.pdf (found 30 May 2006).

—— (2005a): *General Principles of Universal Design Policy.* http://www.mlit.go.jp/kisha/kisha05/01/010711/04.pdf (found 30 May 2006).

—— (2005b): *Yunibāsaru dezain seisaku taikō. Sankō shiryō* [General principles of Universal Design Policy. Illustrative materials]. http://www.mlit.go.jp/kisha/kisha05/01/010711/02.pdf (found 30 May 2006).

—— (2006): *The New National Land Sustainability Plan.* http://www.mlit.go.jp/english/2006/b_n_and_r_planning_bureau/01_duties/New_NLSP_060515.pdf (found 13 June 2006).

OECD (2005): *OECD Economic Outlook December No. 78—Statistical Annex.* http://miranda.sourceoecd.org/upload/annextable78.zip (found 10 June 2006).

STK (Sōmushō Tōkeikyoku) (2000, 2005): *Kokusei chōsa* [Population census]. http://www.stat.go.jp/data/kokusei/index.htm (found 30 May 2006).

Stockwin, J. A. A. (2005): Governance, Democracy and the Political Economy of the Japanese State. In: Hook, Glenn D. (ed.): *Contested Governance in Japan. Sites and Issues.* London, New York: RoutledgeCurzon, pp. 54–70.

Traphagan, John W. (2005): Aging Cities. In: Oswalt, Philipp (ed.): *Shrinking Cities. Vol. 1: International Research.* Ostfildern-Ruit: Hatje Cantz, pp. 101–104.

UNPD (United Nations Population Division) (2005): *World Population Prospects. The 2004 Revision. Highlights.* New York: United Nations.

Woodall, Brian (1996): *Japan Under Construction—Corruption, Politics and Public Works.* Berkeley, Los Angeles: University of California Press.

CHAPTER FORTY-FOUR

# POSTAL PRIVATIZATION AND ITS IMPLICATIONS FOR THE AGEING SOCIETY

Patricia L. Maclachlan

## 1. Introduction

From the early days of his political career, Prime Minister Junichirō Koizumi (2001–2006) has upheld privatization of the postal system as the ultimate prerequisite for the reform of the Japanese political economy. Koizumi firmly believes that subjecting the mail collection and delivery services to market competition will provide new opportunities for entrepreneurship while lowering communication costs for both individual and corporate consumers. By sounding a death knell for public corporations that receive funds from the postal system, moreover, privatizing the postal savings and insurance systems should help rid the country of both wasteful public works programs and patronage appointments for retired bureaucrats, while injecting much-needed funds into the country's beleaguered private financial sector. These changes should in turn loosen the ties that bind Liberal Democratic Party (LDP) politicians, bureaucrats, and private businessmen into sector-specific iron triangles, thereby paving the way for reform in other political-economic areas. All told, Koizumi views postal reform as a long overdue step toward enhancing the flexibility of the political system to respond to new challenges and improving the health of the public and private financial system—all at a time when Japan's rapidly ageing society is putting increased pressures on the government for bigger and better social welfare programs.

Postal privatization has been an issue for Japanese governments since the late 1960s, when it became increasingly clear that the booming economy no longer required injections of funds amassed from the state-run postal savings and insurance systems. Koizumi, however, is the first prime minister to succeed in subjecting the postal services to the principles of private competition, a feat made possible by his landslide electoral victory in September 2005. To Koizumi's supporters, postal privatization marks a major victory for free-market principles and a wholesale attack on financial mismanagement by the state. His critics, however, fear the decline of one of Japan's most socially and culturally significant government institutions and the potential impact on local society—particularly as communities grapple with a rapidly ageing society and increasing fiscal constraints at the local governmental level (*The Japan Times* 24 July 2006).

The purpose of this chapter is three-fold. I explore the history of the Japanese postal services from the early Meiji period, paying close attention to the services' political, economic, social, and cultural functions at the local level. I then present the arguments for and against privatization, focusing on the implications of both for the future of local communities. The chapter concludes with a brief overview of Koizumi's postal reform agenda and its impact on the future of local Japan, especially small, rural communities that are disproportionately occupied by the nation's elderly (also see chapter 47 in this volume).

## 2. The History of the Japanese Postal System[1]

The modern Japanese postal system was introduced in 1871 as an essential component of the Meiji state's long-term plans for state-building and rapid industrialization. Led by Maejima Hisoka, a mid-level bureaucrat and devoted Anglophile, the architects of the new system looked to the post-1840 British Post Office for guidance. Accordingly, a two-tiered system was introduced that by the early 1940s consisted of large post offices headed by civil servants (*futsū yūbinkyoku* [general or ordinary post offices]), and a vast network of tiny post offices administered by private citizens working under contract with the state (*tokutei yūbinkyoku* [commissioned post offices]). In 2003, there were 24,778 post offices in Japan, 18,916 of which were commissioned (Sōrifu 2003).[2]

The hiring and duties of the commissioned postmasters are key to understanding the social and political nature of the modern Japanese postal system. Unlike the postmasters of the general post offices, who were (and continue to be) chosen on the basis of seniority in the postal

[1] For more on the history of the Japanese postal system, see Westney (1987), Calder (1990) and Maclachlan (2004).

[2] Of that total, 1,312 are general post offices, and 4,550 "simple post offices" (*kan'i yūbinkyoku*) located in small retail shops that deal mostly in mail collection and stamp sales.

bureaucracy and their performance on competitive examinations, the commissioned postmasters were hand-picked by bureaucrats in regional bureaus of what is now the Ministry of Internal Affairs and Communications (MIC). During the Meiji period, most commissioned postmasters were "men of distinction" (*meibōka*), former landlords or village headman of financial means and good education who worked without salary from their own homes; in return, they reaped the social benefits of serving the state at a time when the feudal social-class system had all but disappeared.[3]

The Meiji state benefited immensely from the commissioned postal system. Spared the prohibitive expense of establishing postal facilities throughout the country and providing their contracted servants with salaries, the state was able to extend its reach to all corners of the country through the post offices while channelling its scarce resources into industrial and military pursuits. The commissioned postmasters also facilitated the expansion of the postal savings system by using their vaunted social status to teach ordinary Japanese the advantages of saving and to gain the trust of potential depositors.[4] The postal savings system soon provided the state with a vast reservoir of funds that could be used at its discretion for investment in state projects. Even today, the commissioned postmasters collect the vast majority—roughly 75 per cent—of deposits into the system.

As a result of their local roots,[5] social status, and the fact that they provided the facilities with which to administer postal services in their communities, the commissioned postmasters quickly evolved into local authority figures that passed their positions on to their sons. Although the exact rate of inheritance is unknown,[6] the postmasters themselves estimate that by 1945, roughly half of these positions were inherited. Today, on the eve of privatization, the total stands at approximately

---

[3] Since the early Occupation period, the commissioned postmasters have received salaries and benefits like other public servants, but they continue to be selected from among local candidates instead of on the basis of their performance on competitive exams.

[4] The postal savings system was introduced in 1875 and was modelled on the British system.

[5] Unlike the postmasters of the general post offices, who are transferred to new post offices every few years, the commissioned postmasters spend their entire careers with one facility.

[6] The MIC does not keep statistics on inheritance rates because they do not recognize the existence of such practices. (Interviews with two MIC officials, 3 March 2003).

25 per cent.[7] These inheritance practices reinforced the commissioned postmasters' position as local personages comparable to temple priests, school principals, police chiefs, and other local leaders who were noteworthy for their contributions to local cultural life and infrastructural development.

Of particular note were the postmasters' political functions—functions that firmly entrenched them by the end of the 20th century as defenders of the state-run postal system. Before World War II, individual postmasters often served as local assemblymen and contributed to the election campaigns of conservative politicians at both the national and local levels. During the early post-war period, they quickly evolved into active and influential allies of conservative politicians, replacing the now displaced landlord class as local opinion leaders and mobilisers of the vote. During the occupation (1945–52), the newly established national commissioned postmasters association (now known as *Zentoku*) appealed regularly to the conservative parties to assist them in their fight against *Zentei*, the highly militant postal workers union that opposed the commissioned postal system as a semi-feudal and economically incompetent institution.[8] The conservative parties, recognizing in the postmasters a potential source of long-term political support, backed the postmasters by pressuring the then-Ministry of Communications not to cave in to union demands and by supporting petitions submitted to the Diet that called for the protection of the commissioned postal system.

This informal marriage of convenience between the conservative parties and the commissioned postmasters was consummated following the LDP's establishment in 1955. Led by Tanaka Kakuei, who served as minister of posts and telecommunications for a brief period toward the end of the decade, the party embarked on a long-term plan to weaken the political influence of *Zentei* and to increase the number of commissioned post offices throughout the country, particularly in rural areas where the LDP was struggling to expand its base of support (*jiban*). After leaving his position, Tanaka and his supporters, including Takeshita Noboru and Kanemaru Shin, went on to control most

---

[7] Interviews with commissioned postmasters, Kamakura and Kitakyūshū City, summer 2002.

[8] *Zentei*'s criticisms were not unfounded. Many commissioned postmasters neglected their duties and contributed to poor working conditions for postal employees, while their nepotistic inheritance practices prevented talented employees from assuming postmasterships.

of the top appointments to the ministry until well into the post-war period (Calder 1990: 47).

The commissioned postmasters repaid Tanaka's benevolence with votes. Taking advantage of their social status and extensive personal ties, the postmasters persuaded local residents to vote for LDP candidates—particularly in Upper House elections[9]—or to join the party or the support organizations (*kōenkai*) of individual politicians. The postmasters circumvented legal bans on electoral activities by public servants by performing these tasks after hours or by mobilizing their wives and retired colleagues as proxies. Bureaucrats in the former Ministry of Posts and Telecommunications, meanwhile, did little to correct these legal infractions; in fact, some observers have argued that the bureaucrats themselves were actively involved in these electoral campaigns.[10] Japanese conventional wisdom has it that this virtual "vote gathering machine"—known to many insiders as the postal system's "fourth service"—mobilized roughly one million votes behind LDP politicians at election time.

In sum, the commissioned postmasters comprised an essential cog in one of post-war Japan's most influential iron triangles—an iron triangle that made immeasurable contributions to post-war LDP dominance. From the mid-1980s, however, the alliance was transformed as *Zentei* gradually dropped its longstanding demand for the abolition of the commissioned postal system, the postmasters experienced a gradual erosion in their sense of occupational unity, and more and more LDP politicians began calling for market-oriented changes within the postal system. Nevertheless, the postmasters and their political and bureaucratic allies remained an important political force by functioning as a brake on demands for postal reform; their ranks, meanwhile, continued to swell with the addition of the postal workers, their political allies in the Democratic Party, and other anti-reformers. It was the postal lobby that unleashed a public-relations offensive against Koizumi's privatization crusade following his ascension to the prime ministership in spring 2001—an offensive that highlighted the positive contributions of the state-run postal services for ordinary Japanese and, consequently, that

---

[9] Since their numbers are geographically dispersed, the postmasters have been most effective in gathering the vote in the large constituencies of Upper House elections.

[10] Interview with *Mainichi Shinbun* reporter, Tokyo, 23 January 2003.

underscored the conflicting values of Japanese society in an era of globalization and rapid social change.

## 3. Koizumi's Reform Philosophy

As noted earlier, Prime Minister Koizumi has focused much of his political career on the comprehensive reform of the postal system and the various institutions it supports, including the Fiscal Investment and Loan Program (FILP) and the special corporations (*tokushū hōjin*) that are lent FILP funds. At the root of his reform campaign is a deep-seated belief that postal privatization is a necessary prerequisite for political and economic reform more generally. As he wrote in 1999, "Administrative and financial reform without postal privatization" was like "trying to swim with one's hands and feet tied" (Koizumi 1999: 1–4).

Postal privatization accomplishes several inter-related objectives that are symbolized by Koizumi's favourite political slogans. One of those slogans is "Rely on the private sector to do what the private sector does best." Koizumi is certainly not the first politician to extol the virtues of minimal government and a vigorous private sector; the slogan actually has precedents in Meiji history and was routinely evoked during the administrative reform campaigns of the 1980s. For the postal system, relying on the private sector means subjecting the various services to free market mechanisms, including private-sector competition, in the interests of reviving the commercial banks and other private sector financial institutions; reinvigorating the financial sector should in turn help meet the growing financial needs of a rapidly ageing society and shrinking labour force by stimulating economic growth. In Koizumi's view, postal privatization will do more for the country's fiscal health than any other policy instrument at the state's disposal, including tax rate increases (Koizumi 1999: 2).

Koizumi also called for "Structural reform with no sacred cows," a slogan that symbolized his determination to reform even the most vaunted of Japanese institutions, particularly when they were the locus of economic inefficiency and political corruption. In so doing, finally, Koizumi strived to "Reform Japan by reforming the LDP." By loosening the hold of vested interests like the postal lobby over the ruling party, Koizumi hoped to pave the way for quicker and more comprehensive reform of other dimensions of the political economy.

In the wake of Prime Minister Hashimoto Ryūtarō's (1996–1998) disappointing stab at postal reform during the late 1990s, Koizumi helped launch the Postal Privatization Study Group (*Yūsei min'eika kenkyūkai*) that eventually produced a broad template for postal privatization. Of primary concern during the group's deliberations was the Hashimoto government's decision to turn the government-run postal services into a public corporation, effective in 2003. Arguing that corporatization was a poor solution to the fiscal problems confronting the postal services—since it would not solve such problems as high, fixed labour costs in the postal system and the economic inefficiencies of the commissioned post offices—the study group called for a complete abolition of the state's monopoly over the system and the break up and privatization of all three services. In the interests of creating a level playing field between the postal services and the private banking and insurance sectors, moreover, the group proposed breaking up the savings and insurance services into regional entities along the lines of Nippon Telegraph and Telephone (NTT) after 1999. Koizumi later explained that the proposal was designed to illustrate that postal privatization could be carried out in ways that were both economically efficient and attentive to the needs of ordinary consumers (Mizuno *et al.* 2001: 19–25).

Koizumi's thinking about postal reform is rooted in a distrust of public enterprise's ability to guarantee the "public interest" as the state grapples with increasing demographic pressure for enhanced social programs. He therefore advocates a more market-oriented approach to meeting the economic needs of ordinary citizens—an approach that is informed by liberal economic principles and a willingness to conform to the forces of globalization. As such, his postal privatization proposals received strong support from the big business community (as represented by Nippon Keidanren [Japan Business Federation]), the commercial banking and insurance sectors, parcel delivery firms, and many economists and social critics. Members of the postal lobby and concerned citizens, however, lambasted his plans as a repudiation of Japanese culture and a sell-out to free-market economists.

## 4. The Case Against Reform[11]

The postal lobby opposed postal privatization for a number of reasons, not least of which were the potential long-term repercussions for the postmasters and the 280,000 or so full-time employees of Japan Post, the public corporation in charge of postal services since 2003. Whether postal services were ultimately subjected to organizational streamlining or wholesale privatization, the lobby feared the closure of unprofitable post offices, most of which were concentrated in small rural or semi-rural areas. The reduction in the number of post offices could in turn put many postmasters and their employees out of work, a development that was anathema to the long-standing Japanese values of full employment and social stability.

Publicly, the postal lobby cast its opposition to postal privatization largely in terms of its possible effects on "universal service." As in most other advanced industrialized economies since the mid- to late-19th century, the Japanese state's administration of mail collection and delivery services is based on the principle of uniform postage rates for mail, regardless of their destination within predefined geographic areas. Thus, a letter mailed from Tokyo to Yokohama will cost the same for consumers as one mailed from Naha to the tip of Hokkaido; the state, meanwhile, covers the losses resulting from long-distance mailings with the profits accrued from letters sent short distances. Thus universal service also entails a commitment to service all communities, no matter how small or geographically isolated. The postal lobby contended that liberalization would lead to the neglect of small, rural postal districts that had trouble turning a profit and contribute to the closure of unprofitable post offices. This would be especially troublesome for small communities that depended heavily on the post office for financial services.[12]

Another widely trumpeted reason for opposing comprehensive reform was that it might bring about the demise of the highly distinctive social services provided by the post offices. Not surprisingly, the commissioned postmasters have been quick to extol their own selfless contributions to their communities and the broader public interest since the introduction of the modern postal system during the early Meiji period. They refer,

---

[11] For more on the arguments against privatization, see Maclachlan (2006).

[12] According to one estimate, as many as 540 towns and villages in 2001 relied almost exclusively on post offices for their financial needs, since they were not served by banks, credit unions or credit associations. (*Asahi Shinbun* 27–28 April 2002).

for instance, to their willingness to perform their duties without salary before the mid-1940s, to help cultivate a penchant for savings among the population, and, in some cases, to fund the expansion of postal, telephone, and telegraph services with their personal savings—sacrifices that saved the cash-strapped state significant resources while contributing to the expansion of commerce, national communications, and hence the integration of local communities.[13]

Since World War II, as their identities as "men of distinction" steadily weakened, many postmasters have worked hard to maintain their positions as community leaders by participating in local organizations and performing volunteer services. They serve, for instance, as leaders or members of neighbourhood associations (*chōnai-kai*) (also see chapter 38 in this volume) and parent-teacher associations, contribute to the planning and implementation of seasonal festivals, and coach children's sports teams. Even more significant is their work as informal social workers (*minseiin*) for the elderly in their communities. Many postmasters will routinely call on the homes of their elderly customers to check on their safety and offer at-home banking, insurance, and mail delivery services. Some post offices take these services a step further by assisting the infirm with their essential shopping needs, including the purchase of medicines. Postal workers are also doing their bit to enhance the well being of their communities. After shedding their opposition to the commissioned postal system, they have promoted *fureai yūbin* [lit.: contact mail], the practice of making direct contact with elderly residents during normal mail rounds to ensure their safety. Mail carriers have also taken it upon themselves to report potholes, automobile accidents, and illegal dumping to local authorities, help children walking to and from school who run into trouble, and the like. Like the postmasters, mail carriers take great pride in these informal welfare services, referring to local post offices as the "legs of the region" (*chiiki zentai no ashi*) (Kano 2001: 42). Taken together, these volunteer activities are known as *himawari* [lit.: sunflower] services, and they have become increasingly important in small communities that are suffering from the ill effects of depopulation or areas where local governments

[13] The historical accomplishments of the commissioned postmasters are chronicled in the many publications produced by *Zentoku* and its regional chapters. See, for example, Kyūshū chihō tokutei yūbinkyokuchōkai (2000).

have cut back on services due to fiscal constraints or administrative amalgamation.

When all is said and done, these volunteer services should not be viewed as simple acts of altruism on the part of the postmasters; to the contrary, they are closely entwined with the economic and political requirements of their positions. As residents of the communities they serve, postmasters who do not gain the trust of their neighbours will have trouble meeting their quotas (*noruma*) for the sale of stamps, postal savings accounts, and insurance policies. They will also have difficulties mobilizing the electorate behind conservative politicians, a task that is governed by an elaborate set of directives and quotas emanating from *Zentoku*. Moreover, it is no accident that the primary focus of the postmasters' volunteer services is the elderly—those who are most likely to make use of their local post office for their financial needs and, in some communities, who comprise the bulk of the local electorate. In short, strong ties to the locals are the currency of the political and economic success of the commissioned postal system. That said, the economic and political imperatives of the commissioned postal system have resulted in certain practices that meet some very real social needs; these benefits, the postmasters are quick to remind us, could very well decline should local post offices disappear as a result of privatization.

In addition to the informal social welfare functions performed by the postmasters and their employees for their communities, the postal system as a national institution has provided an array of important economic and social services of its own. The state, for example, long provided guarantees of postal savings accounts, a benefit not offered to the commercial banks. The postal savings system, which advantages small-scale deposits typical of lower-income groups, has also offered tax-exempt status to elderly depositors and single mothers, and the postal insurance system, introduced in 1916, issues low-cost life insurance policies without requiring comprehensive medical examinations. The mail collection and delivery service provides discounted rates for the handicapped, offers many services in Braille, and encourages the dissemination of information in society by lowering postage rates for newspapers and magazines. The postal savings system encourages charitable contributions by charging reduced fees for the transfer of funds from postal savings accounts to domestic NGOs and by establishing special accounts that channel donations to international NGOs. Until 2001, postal savings deposits and life insurance premiums were channelled into the massive Fiscal Investment and Loan Program

(FILP) administered by the Ministry of Finance (MOF); government institutions then used these funds to issue low-interest loans to local governments for the purpose of local infrastructural and community development (Kobayashi 2001: 130). Community development is also served by the *furusato kotsuzumi* [lit.: hometown packages] program, in which the postal system advertises and distributes products specific to local communities; the program is widely praised for promoting small businesses and boosting local employment. Finally, Japan has scores of postal savings halls and welfare centres around the country that cater to citizens with postal savings accounts and postal insurance policies, respectively. The postal savings halls provide hotel and banquet services, and the welfare centres recreational and medical services; both are popular gathering places for the elderly and other local residents and, as such, social hubs at the local level.[14]

Those connected to the postal system argue that these informal social welfare services have transformed the postal system into an institution that is at the very heart of local society and culture; remove these services, or so the argument goes, and local communities that are already suffering from depopulation, unemployment, and a decline in local government services will deteriorate even further. Of particular concern is the fate of *himawari* services in areas where the post office is the only contact local residents have with the state, and where alternative methods for caring for the elderly are poorly developed. Proponents of the status quo conclude that the needs of society will receive short shrift under a more competitive postal system driven by the profit motive (see Arai 2003). Many critics, on the other hand, brand the postal system and the FILP as examples of "financial socialism," a disparaging shorthand term for the inefficient financial practices of state-run or public institutions that promote social objectives while nurturing vested interests, promoting governmental mismanagement, and discouraging market competition (Matsubara 1996: 221). At the same time, critics are quick to argue that even private enterprise can tend to the social needs of local populations, if given the right incentives (see Matsubara 2001).

Permeating these arguments against postal privatization is a belief that the postal system is the embodiment of Japanese culture. In the

---

[14] Interviews with commissioned postmasters, Kamakura and Kitakyūshū City, summer 2002.

words of Hiroyuki Arai, a Diet member and former LDP politician who built much of his career on opposing Koizumi's reform movement, the modern mail carrier trudging through the snow to deliver letters and postcards symbolizes such quintessentially Japanese virtues as honesty, diligence, and concern for the welfare of others; the Japanese citizen who does not recognize this is not a true Japanese. (Never mind that the modern mail carrier was invented in Britain!) In the spirit of economic nationalism, individuals like Arai also tend to brand Koizumi and his allies as thoughtless mouthpieces of "made-in-America" globalization who are all too willing to sacrifice the distinctive welfare functions of the postal system on the altar of profit. Privatize the postal system, Arai goes on to warn, and Japan opens up new opportunities for American corporations to enter and even control the Japanese economy (Arai 2003: 44).

## 5. Koizumi's Privatization Package

Since 2001, the postal lobby, with the postmasters at its core, lobbied long and hard to bring a decisive end to Koizumi's privatization plans. And they almost succeeded. Koizumi's efforts in 2002 to introduce competition into the mail delivery services ended in a legislative reform package that was so riddled with loopholes that to date, not one private company has applied to the MIC for entry into the national mail sector. More recently, in the summer of 2005, Koizumi's comprehensive privatization package was defeated by the Upper House by a fairly comfortable margin. In both instances, Koizumi's defeats were mainly attributable to pressures from the postmasters, postal workers, and sympathetic LDP politicians.

Following the Upper House vote in August 2005, however, Koizumi did the unthinkable by dissolving the Lower House and calling a general election, which was to be fought on a platform of postal privatization. He then withheld the LDP's support from all party candidates who had voted against the privatization bills over the summer, and unleashed a slew of young, attractive LDP "assassins" to run in their stead. The results on 11 September caught everyone by surprise: the now pro-privatization LDP won 296 of 480 seats in the Lower House, its biggest win ever. A month later, Koizumi's privatization bills sailed through the Diet.

What does all this mean for the postal system and the communities it serves? It does *not* mean that the Japanese people have experienced a sea change in their thinking about the economy. Although Koizumi clinched the September 2005 election by a landslide, the LDP's share of the popular vote did not significantly increase over the previous election. Furthermore, while many former LDP "rebels" who opposed postal reform were defeated in the cities, several did quite well in non-urban areas where the postmasters and other LDP clients are most entrenched. Since Koizumi's pro-reform allies did far better among the urban floating vote (*Yomiuri Shinbun* 9 December 2005), it appears that there is a significant urban-rural divide in terms of Japanese views of the political economy; while the cities may be leaning toward Koizumi's more liberal economic thinking, the countryside still tends to favour the values of state-led capitalism and the institutions—like the postal system—that embody those values.

Reflecting the inherently conservative values of much of the Japanese population is a postal privatization package that will subject the services to private sector competition while preserving many of the essential values of the old system. Beginning in October 2007, the services will be divided into four corporations, one each for the postal savings, postal insurance, and mail delivery services, and one for the facilities that will provide those services. All four corporations will fall under the control of a government holding company that will gradually sell its shares in the postal savings and insurance corporations by 2017. In the meantime, all three services will be subjected to private competition.

The 2005 privatization legislation and supporting resolutions include several provisions that will soften the effects of privatization on the economy and society. First, contrary to the wishes of the private banking sector and many economists, the postal savings system will remain a national entity. Critics oppose this provision on the grounds that it will give the postal savings system a size advantage over the private banks, which are organized at the regional and city levels (*The Japan Times* 13 September 2005). Others view this as a measure to guarantee uniform financial service to all parts of Japan, regardless of geographic location and the profitability of local post offices. Second, during the final phases of the deliberative process surrounding privatization, provisions were introduced that allow the government to buy back shares in the postal savings and insurance companies, thereby blunting the effects of future private-sector competition within the services. Third, although the commissioned postmasters will lose their status as public servants and will have to function in a more competitive economic environment, the government has not taken steps to abolish the commissioned postal system as an institution. This increases the likelihood that the postmasters will continue to bequeath their postal businesses to their offspring—in fact, it will be easier for them to do so now that their appointments will not be controlled by the state—and function as key members of local economic and social life.

Fourth, and perhaps most importantly, the privatization package contains several provisions for guaranteeing the longevity of the "postal network." One of the most contentious issues over the past several decades of Japanese postal politics has been the impact of reform on the survival of small post offices, particularly in under-populated areas. To counter resistance to postal privatization, Heizō Takenaka, Koizumi's key policy-maker on postal reform, publicly committed the government to maintain at least one post office in each and every village of Japan.[15] In addition, Koizumi's team agreed to establish a massive (two trillion yen or more) government fund to supplement struggling post offices and guarantee postal services to all communities. This measure was clearly an act of political compromise on Koizumi's part[16]—the price paid for building support for privatization among conservative LDP politicians that depended heavily on the postal network for electoral support.

These and related measures can be interpreted in part as economically rational steps to guarantee employment stability within the postal services; after all, if the postmasters and their employees are not given incentives to stick with the postal services during and after the privatization process, the privatization experiment may very well fail. But the measures also represent a willingness on the part of Koizumi and other proponents of freer markets to preserve some of the essential values of Japanese society and culture that have been defining features of the old state-run postal services. These values, moreover, are precisely those that stand to protect local communities in changing times. In the words of Naoyuki Yoshino, an economist who served on several of Koizumi's postal-privatization advisory councils, competition may be necessary to make the postal services more efficient, but the new system must also

[15] Interview with Naoyuki Yoshino, Department of Economics, Keio University, Tokyo, 15 July 2006.

[16] Interview with Yuri Okina, Japan Research Institute, Tokyo, 13 July 2006.

respect Japan's penchant for equality (a value protected by universal service), its preference for financial security and risk avoidance, and its valorisation of community. "This is why postal privatization is not only an economic issue, but also an issue that is deeply indebted to the culture."[17]

The question we must then ask ourselves is, will the postal network continue to protect local communities from the ill effects of depopulation, unemployment, and social instability after 2007? There is certainly good reason to conclude that it will. In anticipation of reform, Japan Post, which will be dissolved in October 2007, has been taking numerous steps to transform local post offices into multi-faceted service centres. Even now, on the eve of privatization, the postal system offers an expanding variety of financial services, including investment trusts (mutual funds), and many local post offices provide local government services, such as issuing alien registrations and copies of family registers, services that will be particularly useful in communities that are not well serviced by local government offices (*Asahi Shinbun* 3 April 2003). With privatization, moreover, the post offices will be encouraged to transform themselves into convenience stores that offer all manner of products in addition to postal services, and some are likely to venture into travel-related services as well. If all goes according to plan, in short, the postal network should be even *more* attuned to the needs of their ever-changing communities.

Not surprisingly, the postmasters themselves remain sceptical about the market's promises and are regrouping in the wake of the 2005 election to lobby government to soften the effects of change as it hammers out the details of privatization. Meanwhile, many postmasters lament the loss of a spirit of community service that permeated the postal system since its inception during the early 1870s. With privatization, they argue, the post offices will become just another business governed by the profit motive; as a result, individual post offices will lose their distinctive personalities as they are subjected to the homogenizing influences of the market.[18] This, they believe, will be of enormous consequence to the cultural heart of local Japan.

[17] Interview with Naoyuki Yoshino, Department of Economics, Keio University, Tokyo, 15 July 2006.

[18] Interviews with four commissioned postmasters, Kitakyūshū City, 10 July 2006.

As of this writing, it is too soon to tell how the local post office—that quintessential symbol of paternalistic values in a rapidly ageing society—will adapt to the requirements of privatization, particularly since the details of privatization have yet to be finalized. We do know, however, that the privatization process will continue to be an emotional issue for many Japanese, particularly the elderly residents of rural Japan who stand to lose the most as the post office's myriad social functions are subjected to the vicissitudes of market competition.

## References


Arai, Hiroyuki (2003): *Yūbinkyoku o amerika ni uriwatasuna* [Don't sell out the post office to America]. Tokyo: Asuka Shinsha.

*Asahi Shinbun* (27–28 April 2002): Privatize postal savings, insurance for reform, p. 27.

—— (3 April 2003): Japan Post starts life a step ahead of rivals, p. 23.

Calder, Kent E. (1990): Linking Welfare and the Developmental State: Postal Savings in Japan. In: *The Journal of Japanese Studies* 16, 1 (Winter), pp. 31–59.

Kano, Kazuhiko (2001): *Chiiki to kurashi o posuto ga tsunagu* [The postal system is tied to our communities and lives]. Tokyo: Nihon Nōritsu Kyōkai Management Center.

Kobayashi, Masayoshi (2001): *Minna no yūbin bunkashi: kindai nihon o sodateta jōhō dentatsu shisutemu* [A history of mail for everyone: A system for disseminating information that raised contemporary Japan]. Tokyo: Nijūni.

Koizumi, Jun'ichirō (1999): Foreward. In: Koizumi, Jun'ichirō and Matsuzawa Shigefumi (eds.): *Yūsei min'eikaron: Nihon saisei no daikaikaku* [The postal privatization debate: A big reform for regenerating Japan]. Tokyo: PHP Kenkyūjo, pp. 1–13.

Kyūshū Chihō Tokutei Yūbinkyokuchōkai (2000): *Kyūshū tokutei yūbinkyokuchōkai-shi* [A history of the Kyūshū commissioned postmasters association]. Kyūshū: Kyūshū Chihō Tokutei Yūbinkyokuchōkai.

Maclachlan, Patricia L. (2004): Post Office Politics in Modern Japan: The Postmasters, Iron Triangles, and the Limits of Reform. In: *The Journal of Japanese Studies* 30, 2 (Summer), pp. 281–313.

—— (2006): Storming the Castle: The Battle for Postal Reform in Japan. In: *Social Science Japan Journal* 9, 1 (April), pp. 1–18.

Matsubara, Satoru (1996): *Gendai no yūsei jigyō* [The contemporary postal business]. Tokyo: Nihon Hyōronsha.

—— (2001): *Yūseimineika de kō kawaru: Kokuei shinwa ni wa, mō damasarenai* [Things will change this way with postal privatization: We can no longer stay silent on the myth of government enterprise]. Tokyo: Kadokawa.

Mizuno, Kiyoshi, Satoru Matsubara, Ushio Chūjō and Makoto Matsuda (2001): *Yūsei min'eika: Koizumi gen'an* [Postal privatization: Koizumi's plan]. Tokyo: Shogakukan Bunko.

Sōrifu Tōkeikyoku (Statistics Bureau, Prime Minister's Office) (ed.) (2003). *Nihon tōkei nenkan* [Japan statistical yearbook]. Tokyo: Nihon Tōkei Kyōkai.

*The Japan Times* (13 September 2005): Koizumi's act to be his toughest yet, p. 10.

—— (24 July 2006): 91 per cent of local leaders fear their cities won't survive, p. 1.

Westney, D. Eleanor (1987): *Imitation and Innovation: The Transfer of Western Organizational Patterns to Meiji Japan*. Cambridge, Mass.: Harvard University Press.

*Yomiuri Shinbun* (9 December 2005): Jimintō ha beddo taun de gisekizō [The LDP increases its seats in bed towns], p. 23.

# PART FIVE

# ECONOMIC AND SOCIAL SECURITY ASPECTS OF DEMOGRAPHIC CHANGE

# INTRODUCTION

In recent years the economic implications of population ageing have received increasing attention among researchers, policy makers and the general public. Most of this attention has focused on the increasing burden on the active members of the labour force who will have to meet the income-maintenance, health and long-term care needs of the nonworking members of the ageing society. Although these aspects are unquestionably very important and make up a large proportion of this part of the *Handbook*, we have also tried to cover a variety of other economic issues, such as business and management aspects, which are not directly related to the social security debate but which are nevertheless extremely important.

The chapters in this part of the *Handbook* address both the economics of the aged, in other words, the present economic status of the elderly, and the economics of ageing—the economic changes that result from population ageing. These issues are naturally interrelated and some aspects of both are discussed in a number of chapters. For example, the economic wellbeing of today's elderly people is the obvious starting point for the discussion of how population ageing will affect the economic wellbeing of future generations.

Although the following chapters deal with a variety of subjects, sometimes with overlapping topics, we have arranged them loosely into four groups. Beginning in the first few chapters with a macroeconomic perspective, we then move on to some that are more microeconomic in nature. These are followed by a few chapters dealing with business and management issues and finally a larger number analysing various social security aspects of demographic change in Japan.

In the first chapter, Ogawa discusses the impact of falling fertility, rapid shifts in the age composition of the population, and unprecedented population ageing upon the Japanese economic system over the period 1950–2025. He highlights the important linkages between demographic transformations and economic growth and examines two economic policy options for coping with Japan's population ageing. Kawase and Ogura's joint chapter takes an even more forward-looking macroeconomic perspective by assessing the public finance perspectives of Japan's ageing society up to the year 2100. This chapter presents an overall picture of social insurance costs and the portion of the tax revenue already earmarked for maintaining the most important social security systems through the twenty-first century. How the ageing society will influence the regional economies is discussed by Elis, who highlights the complexity and interrelatedness of the various factors affecting the metropolitan and non-metropolitan areas. He concludes that, as labour supply becomes scarcer and the purchasing power of both the younger population and the affluent elderly is needed to fuel the regional economies, domestic migrants will become the focus of regional development policies in the future. Household saving behaviour is one of the important factors that will determine how the Japanese economy will be able to deal with the impact of the ageing society. Horioka argues that, despite the fact that Japan's household saving rate has been falling substantially since the mid-1970s and is projected to fall in future, this will not pose a major problem for the economy. The chapters by Ohtake and Fukawa both deal with issues of economic inequality. Ohtake analyses the various factors behind Japan's rising economic inequality and concludes that, since income inequality is usually greater among the elderly and the elderly now make up a higher proportion of society, the overall level of economic inequality has risen quite naturally as a result of the ageing factor. Taking these findings as the starting point of his discussion, Fukawa deals with the rather limited public policy response to growing economic inequality and discusses the issue of rising poverty and increasing numbers of welfare recipients among the elderly. Yashiro's chapter focuses on the economic factors explaining the declining birth rate, highlighting the comparatively high opportunity costs of childrearing and structural problems in both labour markets and child-care services. According to his analysis, more flexible labour markets, as well as a market-based supply of nursery services, are needed to reverse the declining fertility trend. The labour market and labour-market policies for the elderly are the topic of Meyer-Ohle's chapter, which analyses the factors underlying the comparatively high labour force participation of the elderly and recent policy developments to support such employment. Labour market issues are also the focal point of Shire's chapter, which considers the gender dimensions of the ageing workforce and discusses the economic risks of ageing posed by the ways in which men and women are currently employed in Japan. Following on from these discussions of labour market issues, Conrad discusses from a management perspective how the ageing workforce reshapes typical human resource management practices such as lifetime employment and seniority-based pay in Japanese companies. The impact on private businesses is the topic of the chapters by Sekizawa and Moerke. Sekizawa discusses how consumer behaviour and consumer markets are affected by the ageing society and what roles cultural ageing, social ageing and physiological ageing play in this respect. Related to this, Moerke's case study analyses in detail how the automobile industry has adapted its technologies and marketing activities to the growing numbers of elderly people.

The chapters on social security aspects begin with Peng's overview of social security and the social welfare implications of population ageing and fertility decline. This chapter highlights three major concerns that Japan's policy makers have to confront: the increasing dependency ratio, elderly care, and work-life balance. The first two of these concerns are the topics of the following chapters, while the latter is touched upon in the preceding chapters by Yashiro and Shire. Elderly and health-care issues are taken up in the chapters by Ikegami, Arai and Fukawa, and the issue of an increasing dependency ratio is at the heart of those by Oshio, Takayama, and Kubo on public and corporate pensions. Ikegami presents an historical overview of the developments which led to the present delivery system of health and long-term care and focuses on how the introduction of public long-term care insurance in 2000 has changed payment mechanisms and affected the delivery of care. Arai's chapter deals with an important legal aspect related to the introduction of long-term care insurance, namely the system of legal support in the form of guardianships for the growing number of people suffering from mental disorders. The public health-care system is the topic of Fukawa's chapter, which provides a detailed overview of health-care provision and financing mechanisms and discusses current and future reforms from a financial perspective. The sustainability of public pension finances and the impact of current and future demographic developments are the focus of Oshio's chapter. He argues that, although the latest pension reforms have greatly improved pension finances, there are still huge net pension liabilities which later generations will have to pay if no further adjustments are made. These intergenerational equity issues are also the topic dealt with by Takayama, who suggests that future pension policy should seek to separate the legacy pension problem stemming from benefit promises in the past from the problem of rebuilding a sustainable and intergenerationally equitable pension system. To this end, he suggests that future contributions and future promised pension benefits should be handled within a new, yet-to-be-established notional defined-contribution system, as can be found, for example, in Sweden. Finally, Kubo's chapter presents the situation of corporate pensions in Japan, highlighting current problems and possible future developments as well as the potential of these types of pensions for old-age income security in the future.

With the 19 chapters of Part V of this *Handbook*, we have aimed to cover the most important economic and social security related issues of demographic change. Nevertheless, we are the first to acknowledge that the informed reader will probably find other issues that should also have been covered here. In such cases, we hope that you will find the list of references helpful to direct you to papers which deal with such issues in more detail.

H.C.

Case in point: "Silver" customers: Japan's centenarians 1963-2005

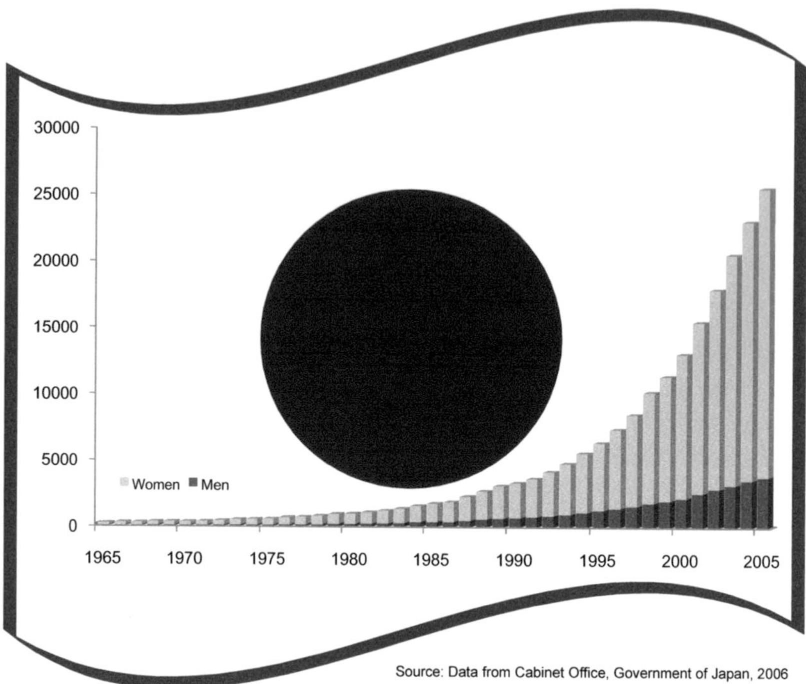


Source: Data from Cabinet Office, Government of Japan, 2006

CHAPTER FORTY-FIVE

# POPULATION AGEING AND ECONOMIC GROWTH: THE ROLE OF TWO DEMOGRAPHIC DIVIDENDS IN JAPAN

Naohiro Ogawa

This chapter discusses the impact of falling fertility, rapid shifts in the age composition of the population, and unprecedented population ageing upon the Japanese economic system over the period 1950–2025. In addition, this chapter examines two economic policy options available to twenty-first century Japan in coping with the formidable problems likely to be caused by these demographic developments.

## 1. Falling Fertility and Declining Population in Japan

After World War II, Japan's fertility decline was both the earliest to occur and the greatest in magnitude among all the industrialized nations. Subsequent to its short-lived baby boom period (1947–1949), Japan's fertility plummeted dramatically, as shown in Figure 1 (Hodge and Ogawa 1991; Ogawa and Retherford 1993; Ogawa 2003; Retherford and Ogawa 2006). Between 1947 and 1957, the total fertility rate (TFR) dropped by more than 50 per cent, from 4.54 to 2.04 children per woman. This 50-per cent reduction in fertility over a ten-year period was the first such experience in the history of mankind. After this dramatic fall in the 1950s, there were only minor fluctuations around the replacement level until the first oil crisis occurred in 1973. Thereafter, TFR started to fall again, and the post-1973 fertility decline is often referred to by some demographers as Japan's "second demographic transition" (Ogawa and Retherford 1993; Retherford and Ogawa 2006). In 2005, TFR reached 1.25 children per woman, an all-time low in post-war Japan. If fertility were to remain constant at this level, each successive generation would decline at a rate of approximately 35 per cent per generation.

In recent years, Japan's very low fertility has attracted a great deal of attention both inside and outside the country (Retherford and Ogawa 2006). In contrast to such increased attention to falling fertility trends,

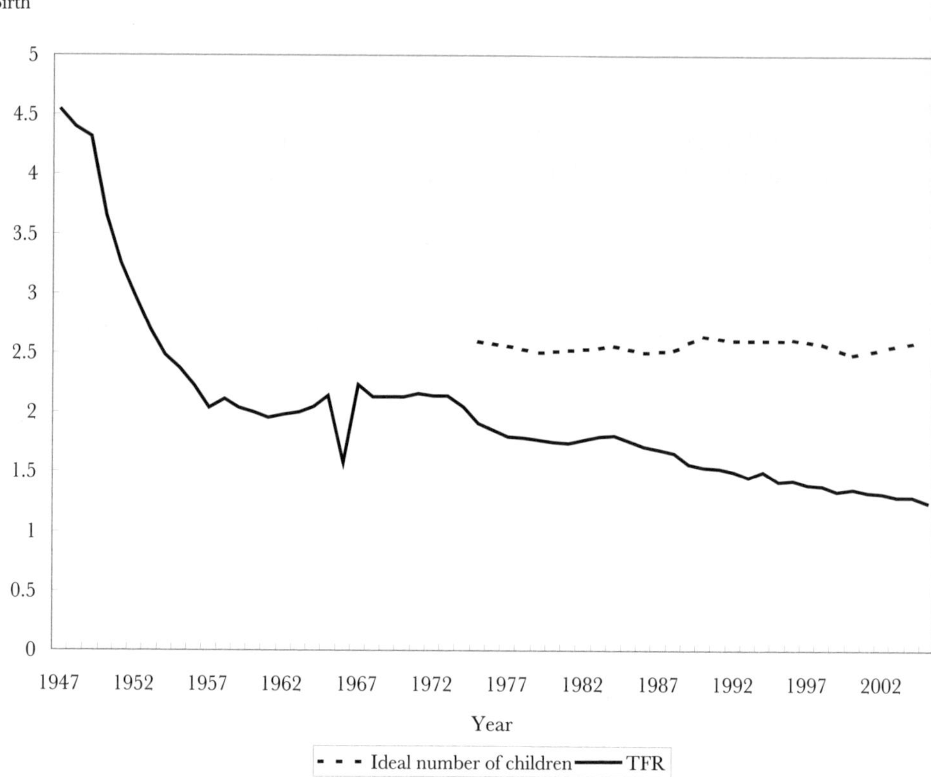


Source: TFRs up to 2005 are from Ministry of Health and Welfare, *Vital Statistics*, various years. Values of ideal family size are from various rounds of the National Survey on Family Planning, and the 2004 round of the National Survey on Population, Families and Generations, conducted by the Mainichi Newspapers of Japan.

Figure 1. Total fertility rate (TFR) and ideal family size, Japan, 1947–2005.

only a limited amount of attention has been paid to the unprecedented rapidity with which Japan's mortality transition has been under way. Age-specific mortality rates have declined remarkably over the past several decades. From 1947 to 1965, Japan's life expectancy at birth rose from 50.1 to 67.7 years for men and from 54.0 to 72.9 years for women. When Japan joined the OECD at the end of 1964, the country's life expectancies for both men and women were the lowest among all the OECD member countries at that time (Mason and Ogawa 2001). By the early 1980s, however, Japanese life expectancy had become one of the highest among all the OECD members. In 2004, male life expectancy at birth reached 78.6 years, becoming the second highest in the world after Iceland, and female life expectancy reached 85.6 years, the highest in the world. Moreover, between 1964 and 2004, life expectancy at age 65 grew substantially, from 12.2 to 18.2 years for men and from 14.8 to 23.3 years for women, thus implying a marked increase in the retirement period and in the joint survival to older ages of both husbands and wives. Primarily because of such long-term improvements in mortality, the number of centenarians has been increasing at an annual rate of 13 per cent over the past four decades.

These rapid improvements in mortality in post-war Japan are shown in Figure 2. In this graphical exposition, the data on the average age of the 50 oldest deaths in each year over the period 1950–2003 are plotted separately for men and women. As can be clearly seen, the average age of the 50 oldest deaths increased substantially over the second half of the twentieth century for both sexes. In the case of women, the average age of the 50 oldest deaths rose from 101 years old in 1950 to 108 years old in 2003. Similarly, it increased from 99 to 106 years old during the same period for men.

As a consequence of these rapid demographic transformations, the age distribution of the Japanese population has been changing to a marked extent over the past several decades, and such trends are predicted to persist over the next few decades. In Japan and other countries, both developed and developing, population age distributions are changing markedly, with a relative increase in the number of the elderly and a relative decrease in the number of the young. Thus, the twenty-first century is likely to become the century of population ageing (Lutz, Sanderson and Scherbov 2004). In addition, with no end in sight to the falling fertility trends, the twenty-first century may turn out to be an era of population decline for many of these countries.

There seems to be little new to be said about the demographic mechanism of population ageing. A greater interest lies in the policy responses to these demographic trends (McNicoll 2002). Undoubtedly, the policy responses to these population changes will influence economic growth and poverty, intergenerational equity, and social welfare for decades ahead. For instance, how do we sustain economic productivity with an ageing labour force, and maintain economic growth with a declining population? How do we manage transfers between age groups under the new age structures that are emerging? What are the roles of the public sector, the market, the family, and individual life-cycle saving strategies? Are there acceptable means to raising low fertility nearer to a replacement level? What are the prospects for accepting immigration?

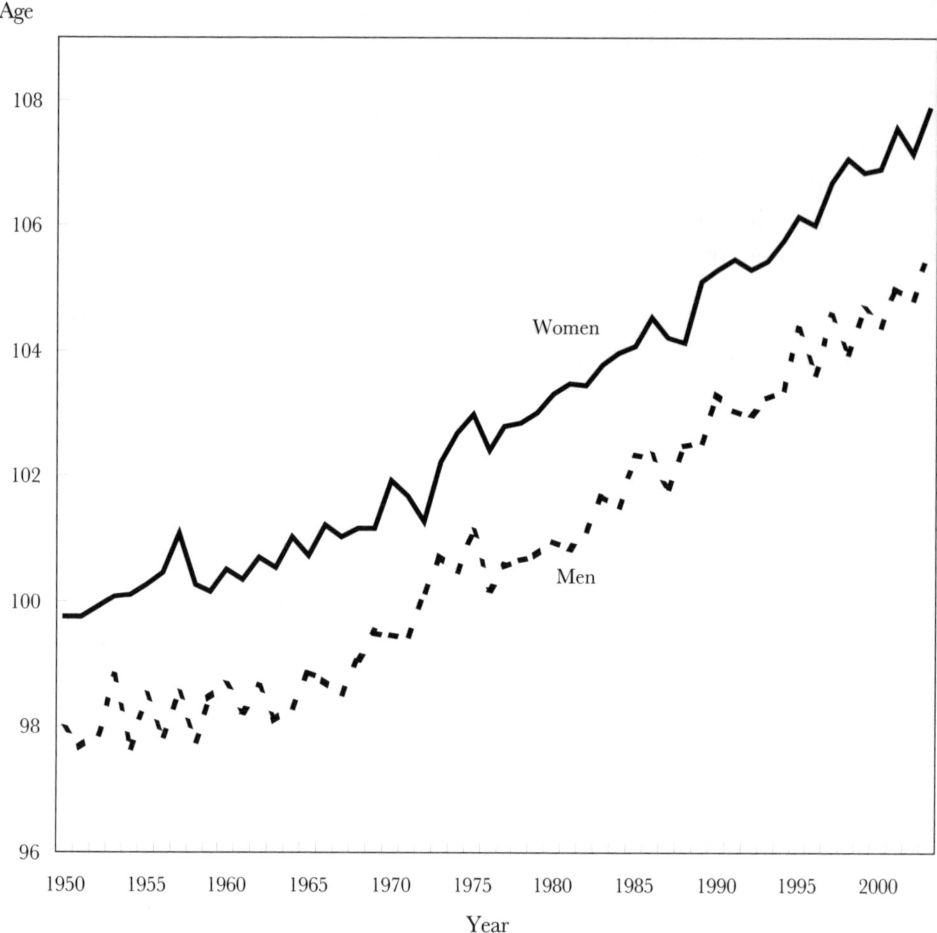


Source: Ministry of Health and Welfare, *Vital Statistics*, various years.

Figure 2. Change in average age of death among 100 oldest persons by sex, Japan, 1950–2003.

These policy-oriented issues are particularly important in a number of countries in East Asia. At present, fertility in East Asia is the lowest in the entire world (McDonald 2005), and Japan is the most aged society in the region. In fact, Japan is considered to have become the most aged society in the entire world in 2005, overtaking Italy. The total population of Japan peaked in the same year only to start declining thereafter (Ogawa 2005; Ogawa and Takayama 2006). More importantly, as shown in Table 1, these demographic trends of very

Table 1. Population change in Japan, 1950–2025.

| Year | Total population (1000 persons) | 0–14(%) | 15–64(%) | 65+(%) | Total Dependancy Ratio | 75+/65+(%) | Women 40–59/ 65–84 |
|---|---|---|---|---|---|---|---|
| 1950 | 83200 | 35.4 | 59.7 | 4.9 | 67.5 | 25.7 | 1.8 |
| 1955 | 89276 | 33.4 | 61.3 | 5.3 | 63.1 | 29.2 | 1.8 |
| 1960 | 93419 | 33.0 | 64.2 | 5.7 | 60.4 | 30.4 | 1.8 |
| 1965 | 98275 | 25.6 | 68.1 | 6.3 | 46.8 | 30.3 | 1.8 |
| 1970 | 103720 | 23.9 | 69.0 | 7.1 | 44.9 | 30.2 | 1.7 |
| 1975 | 111940 | 24.3 | 67.8 | 7.9 | 47.6 | 32.0 | 1.6 |
| 1980 | 117060 | 23.5 | 67.4 | 9.1 | 48.4 | 34.4 | 1.5 |
| 1985 | 121049 | 21.5 | 68.2 | 10.3 | 46.7 | 37.8 | 1.4 |
| 1990 | 123611 | 18.2 | 69.7 | 12.1 | 43.5 | 40.1 | 1.3 |
| 1995 | 125570 | 16.0 | 60.5 | 14.6 | 50.4 | 39.3 | 1.1 |
| 2000 | 126926 | 14.6 | 68.1 | 17.4 | 46.9 | 40.9 | 0.9 |
| 2005 | 127449 | 13.8 | 66.2 | 20.0 | 50.6 | 45.1 | 0.8 |
| 2010 | 127013 | 13.0 | 64.0 | 23.0 | 55.6 | 48.0 | 0.7 |
| 2015 | 125603 | 12.1 | 61.0 | 26.9 | 63.2 | 48.4 | 0.6 |
| 2020 | 123235 | 11.0 | 59.5 | 29.5 | 67.6 | 52.1 | 0.6 |
| 2025 | 120094 | 10.2 | 58.8 | 31.0 | 70.0 | 60.0 | 0.6 |

Source: Statistics Bureau, *Population Census*, various years.
Nihon University Population Research Institute Population Projection, 2003.

low fertility and population decline are expected to persist over the period 2005–2025.

## 2. Age Structural Transformations and Two Demographic Dividends

These demographic trends, particularly in the change of age composition, have been closely intertwined with changes in economic growth performance in post-war Japan (Ogawa, Kondo and Matsukura 2005; Ogawa 2005; Ogawa and Matsukura 2005). As has been extensively discussed elsewhere (Mason 2001; Mason 2005; Mason and Lee 2006), one of the important linkages between demographic transformations and economic growth is the role of demographic dividends in the process of economic development. As a country advances through the stages of demographic transition, it undergoes considerable age structural shifts. When the country's fertility begins to fall, the first demographic dividend arises because changes in population age structure

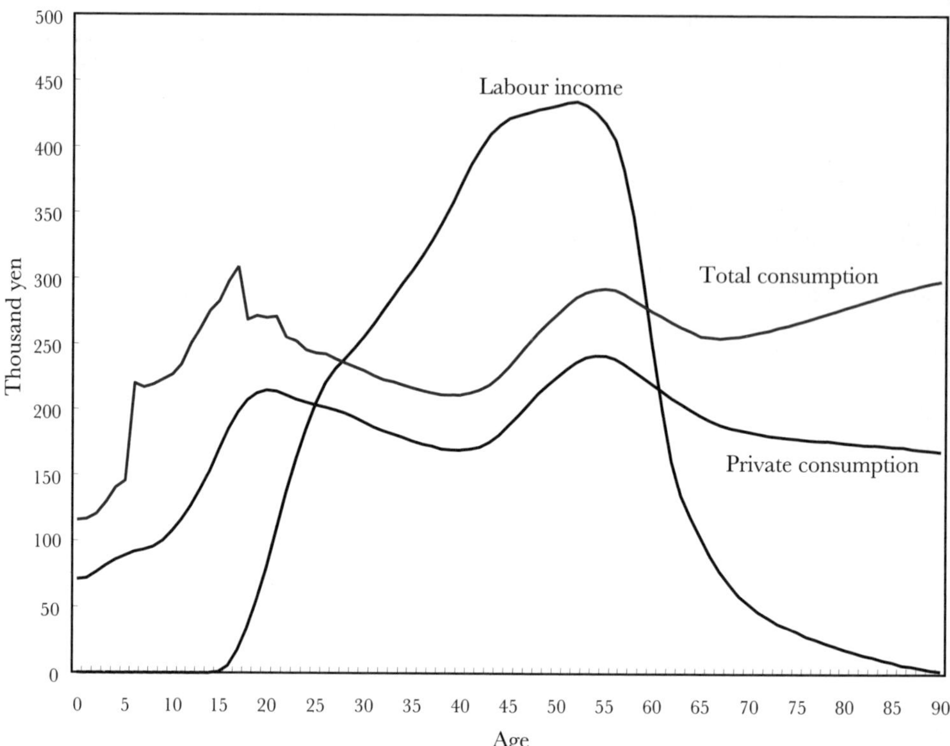


Source: Nihon University Population Research Institute Projection based on *Family Income and Expenditure Survey* (1999), Statistics Bureau, Ministry of Internal Affairs and Communications, Japan.

Figure 3. Age profiles for labour income and consumption, 1999.

have led to an increase in population of working age relative to those of non-working ages. In other words, the first demographic dividend arises because of an increase in the proportion of the population in age brackets during which production exceeds consumption. That is, the first demographic dividend is positive when the rate of growth in output per effective consumer exceeds the rate of growth in output per effective producer (Mason 2005).

In order to calculate the first demographic dividend, we have estimated the age-specific profiles of consumption with both private and public sectors combined and the age-specific profiles of production in contemporary Japan. The estimated results are presented in Figure 3. These profiles have been produced by drawing upon private-sector infor-

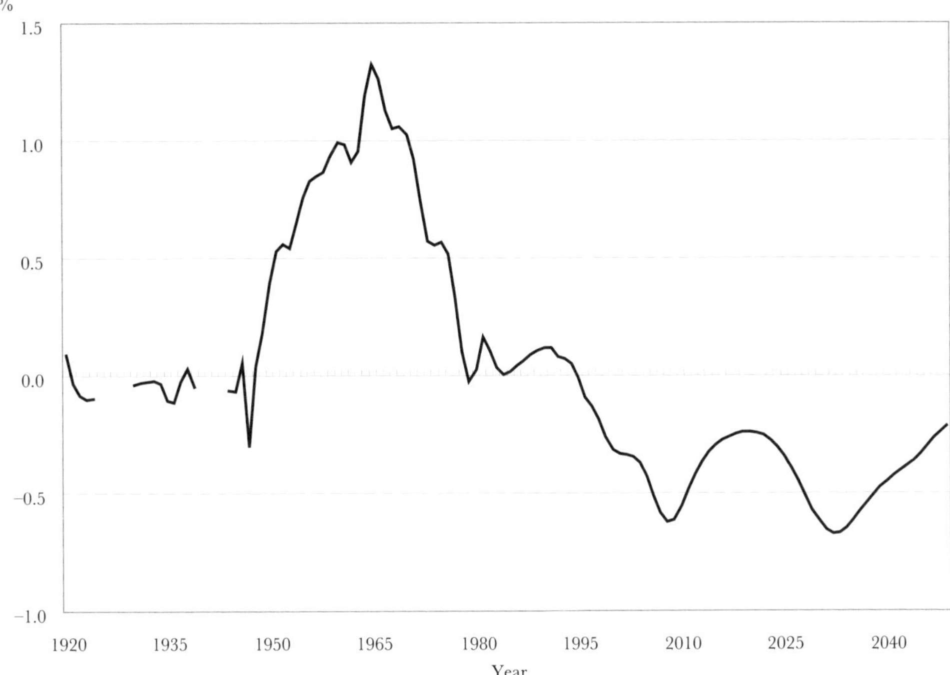


Source: Nihon University Population Research Institute Projection based on *Family Income and Expenditure Survey* (1999), Statistics Bureau, Ministry of Internal Affairs and Communications, Japan.

Figure 4. Trend in first dividend in Japan, 1920–2025.

mation derived from the *National Survey of Family Income and Expenditure* (NSFIE) for 1999, carried out by the Statistics Bureau of Japan, and public-sector information for 1999 gleaned from various government publications. By applying the computed age-specific results displayed in this graphical exposition as statistical weights to adjust for the entire population over the period 1920–2025, we have calculated the annual growth rate of output per effective consumer and the annual growth rate of output per effective producer over this period. As regards the population for the period 2000–2025, we have used the population projection prepared by the Nihon University Population Research Institute (hereafter NUPRI population projection). Because a detailed description of the NUPRI population projection has been provided elsewhere (Ogawa *et al.* 2003), no further discussion relating to it is given here. The computed results are shown in Figure 4.

Caution should be exercised with regard to interpreting the computed results. We have applied the same age-specific profiles of consumption and production calculated from the data for 1999, on the assumption that these profiles remain unchanged throughout the entire period under review. It should be noted, however, that both age-specific profiles of consumption and production have been adjusted on the basis of the observed growth rates of consumption and production for each decade over the period 1920–2000 and that the average growth rates observed between 2001 and 2004 have been applied throughout the period 2000–2025. It should also be added that, although we have attempted to apply the different age-specific profiles estimated from the 1989 and 1994 rounds of NSFIE, essentially the same results have been obtained.

A brief glance at the computed results illustrated in Figure 4 reveals that Japan's first demographic dividend, which corresponds to the difference between the annual growth rate of output per effective consumer and the annual growth rate of output per effective producer, was positive for 46 years from 1949 to 1995, except for 1980. But the magnitude of the positive first demographic dividend was extremely large during the rapid economic growth of the 1960s and the early 1970s, as presented in Figure 5.

As has been the case with post-war Japan, the first demographic dividend typically lasts for decades, but it is inherently transitory in nature. The same demographic forces that bring an end to the first dividend lead to a second demographic dividend. That is, in the process of age structural transformations, the second dividend arises in response to the prospect of population ageing. For instance, in countries that rely on capital accumulation to meet the retirement needs of the elderly, population ageing provides a powerful incentive to accumulate wealth. It is important to note, however, that in countries that rely on transfers, both public and familial, in meeting the retirement needs of the elderly, the second demographic dividend may not emerge. While the first dividend is purely accounting-oriented, the second dividend consists of both compositional and behavioural effects (Mason 2005; Ogawa and Matsukura 2005). The second dividend is affected not only by the numbers of elderly people relative to younger people, but also by the extent to which consumers and policy makers are forward-looking and respond effectively to the demographic changes that are anticipated in the years ahead. When life expectancy is increasing, for example, the impetus for accumulating wealth is stimulated, which, in turn, leads to

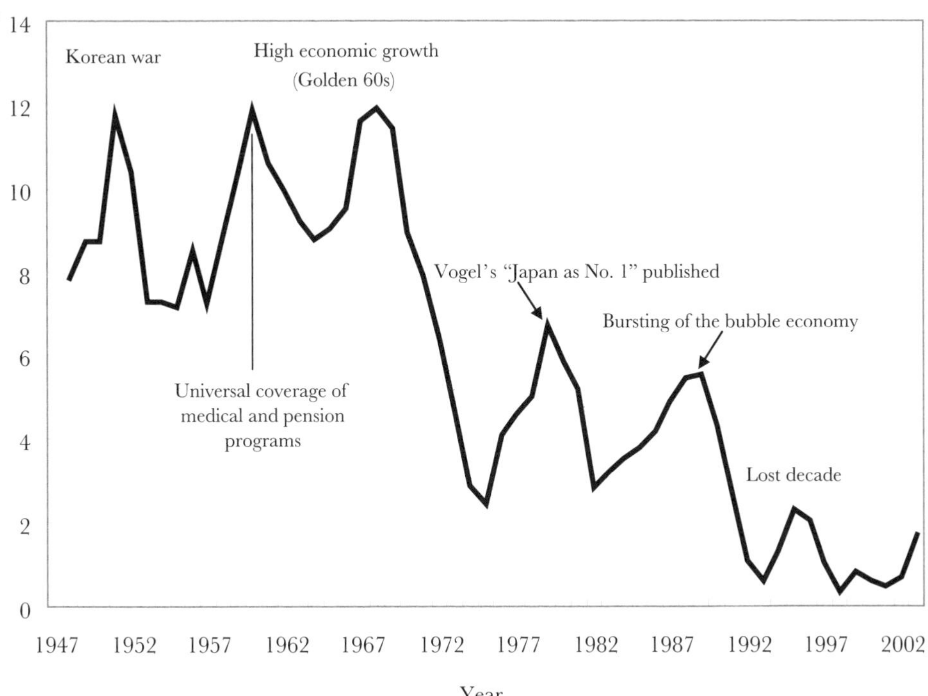


Source: Economic and Social Research Institute, Cabinet Office, Government of Japan, *Annual Report on National Accounts*, various years.

Figure 5. Trend in real GDP growth rate: Japan, 1948–2003.

a permanent increase in income. This implies that, if capital accumulation rather than familial or public transfer programmes dominate the age reallocation systems for supporting the elderly, population ageing may yield a second demographic dividend in the form of higher rates of saving and capital intensification of the economy (Mason 2005).

Compared with the first dividend, measuring the amount of the second dividend is considerably more difficult, in part because the accumulation of wealth is intrinsically forward-looking. In the present study, as in previous studies (Mason 2005), we have simplified the computational procedure by making the following two major assumptions. First, we have assumed that the growth rates of the capital and lifecycle wealth are equal, and the elasticity of labour income with respect to capital is set equal to 0.5. Second, we have assumed that the wealth held by those aged 50 and older is closely connected with the effect of demography on life cycle wealth and the second demographic dividend. It should

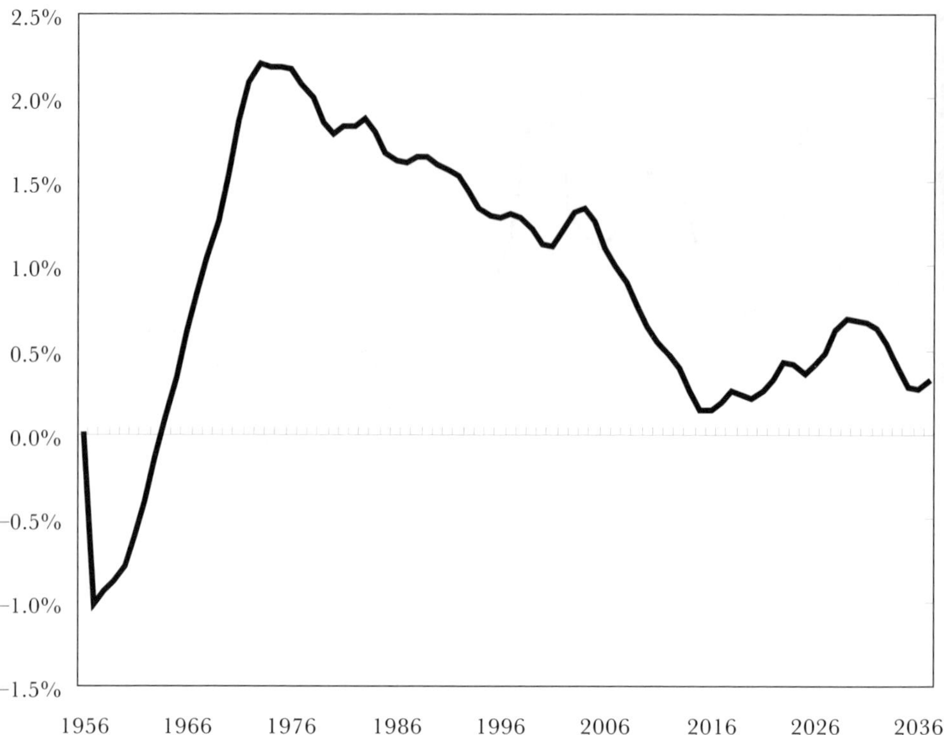


Sources: Nihon University Population Research Institute Projection (2003).
*Family Income and Expenditure Survey* (1999), Statistics Bureau, Ministry of Internal Affairs and Communications, Japan.

Figure 6. Trend in second dividend in Japan, 1950–2030.

also be noted that the population for the period 2000–2050 has been projected by extending NUPRI's population projection beyond 2025.

As discussed elsewhere (Mason 2005), the second demographic dividend is calculated as the growth rate of the wealth-income ratio, which corresponds to 0.5 times the difference between (i) the present value of future lifetime consumption of all persons at a certain cut-off age (50 years old in this exercise) or earlier per effective consumer in year t, and (ii) the present value of future production of all persons at the cut-off age earlier per effective producer in year t.

The estimates of the second demographic dividend over the period 1950–2050 are shown in Figure 6. A few points of interest emerge from Figure 6. First, Japan's second demographic dividend was negative up to 1958. Apparently, this result reflects the fact that the Japanese

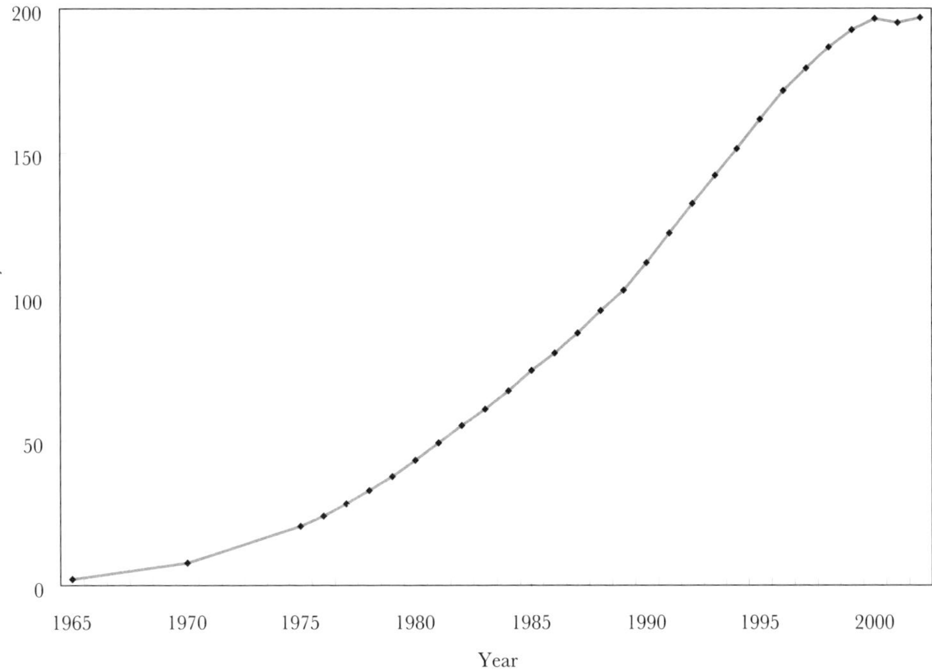


Source: Ministry of Health, Labour and Welfare, *Financial Report on the Public Pension System: Fiscal Year 2003*, 2004.

Figure 7. Growth of reserved funds for all public pension schemes combined, 1965–2002.

economy was destroyed during World War II and was still in shambles for most of the 1950s. Second, Japan's second demographic dividend increased remarkably in the 1960s and 1970s, and remained at a considerably high level for the latter half of the twentieth century. One salient example of the rapid increase in wealth in the early 1960s was the establishment of universal pension plans. Their reserved funds have accumulated at a phenomenal rate, as shown in Figure 7. Third, from the 1990s onwards, the amount of the second demographic dividend fluctuates to a considerable extent, with a pronounced trough in the 2010s, followed by a substantial upsurge in the 2020s and 2030s. These oscillations are substantially attributable to the rapid age compositional shifts in the early part of the twenty-first century.

These computational results relating to both first and second demographic dividends provide an additional piece of empirical evidence pointing to the high likelihood that the unprecedented fertility reduc-

Table 2. Estimates of the first and second dividends, actual growth in GDP per effective consumer, 1950–1995, Japan.

| Time period | Demographic dividends | | | Actual growth in GDP per effective consumer | Actual dividend |
|---|---|---|---|---|---|
| | First | Second | Total | | |
| 1950–1960 | 0.61 | –0.49 | 0.13 | 7.00 | 6.87 |
| 1960–1970 | 1.07 | 1.67 | 2.74 | 10.55 | 7.81 |
| 1970–1980 | 0.64 | 1.89 | 2.53 | 12.67 | 10.14 |
| 1980–1990 | 0.05 | 0.02 | 0.07 | 6.22 | 6.15 |
| 1990–1995 | 0.09 | 1.24 | 1.33 | 2.50 | 1.17 |

Source: Nihon University Population Research Institute Projection based on *Family Income and Expenditure Survey* (1999), Statistics Bureau of Internal Affairs and Communications, Japan.

tion subsequent to the baby boom (1947–1949) played an important role in boosting the phenomenal growth of per capita income during this high economic growth period. As presented in Table 2, among the five time periods in question, the sum of the first and second demographic dividends was the largest during the period of rapid economic growth. In contrast, it was miniscule in both the 1950s and 1980s. It is also interesting to note that, in the first half of the 1990s, the second demographic dividend was quite large as a result of increased wealth during the bubble period.

The age compositional transformations, induced by declining fertility and improved longevity, produce the positive forces for boosting economic growth, but with a lag of a couple of decades, they also cause formidable population ageing problems.

## 3. Utilization of Resources Owned by the Elderly in the Twenty-First Century

What should the Japanese people do in order to cope with the numerous difficulties arising in the process of rapid population ageing? In recent years, not only demographers but also scholars in other disciplines have discussed a variety of population ageing scenarios and policy options (MacKellar 2003; Onofri 2004). For instance, Sinding (2002) listed the following four broad alternative scenarios: (i) the slow fadeout (in this scenario, population ages without any policy responses), (ii) healthy ageing (in this scenario, public policy recognizes the necessity of increasing the longevity and effectiveness of the labour force), (iii) replacement migration, and (iv) successful pronatalism. Bongaarts (2004) recently analysed the impact of population ageing on public pension plans. He discusses some policy options from the following four angles: (i) counteracting population ageing (encouraging higher fertility and permitting more immigration), (ii) increasing labour force participation, (iii) raising the retirement age, and (iv) reducing public pension benefits.

Because various policy options available to twenty-first century Japan in coping with population decline and ageing have already been discussed in detail elsewhere (Ogawa 2005), here only two ways to utilize the resources owned by the elderly in Japan to cope with its unprecedented population ageing will be examined: (i) more effective utilization of the wealth of the elderly, and (ii) better utilization of healthy elderly workers and extension of the retirement age.

### 3.1. *More effective utilization of wealth owned by the elderly*

As has been examined in the previous section, both first and second demographic dividends have been generated over the course of Japan's demographic transition after World War II. Figure 8 plots the age profile of asset holdings in Japan in 1999. Using the 1999 round of NSFIE, we have estimated the age-specific pattern of holding real and financial assets. In addition, we have calculated the present value of the expected future stream of public pension benefits. To be consistent with the data on real and financial assets, we have calculated the present value of public pension wealth, evaluated in 1999. In this computation, we have incorporated the structural change in the contributions and benefits amended by the 1999 and 2004 pension reforms. The discount rate used for calculation was 1.25 per cent, which corresponds to the average interest rate for the long-term government bonds over the period 1999–2004.

A quick glance at this graph reveals that Japanese elderly people are wealthy. At age 60, the total amount of assets an average person owns is more than 50 million yen, or US$0.5 million. In fact, they are wealthier than this graph shows, because private pensions are not included in the calculation. Moreover, various types of familial transfers have not been included.

It is interesting to observe that the amount of public pension wealth is greater than that of real assets at a relatively early stage of retirement life, but the latter exceeds the former by a great margin at a later

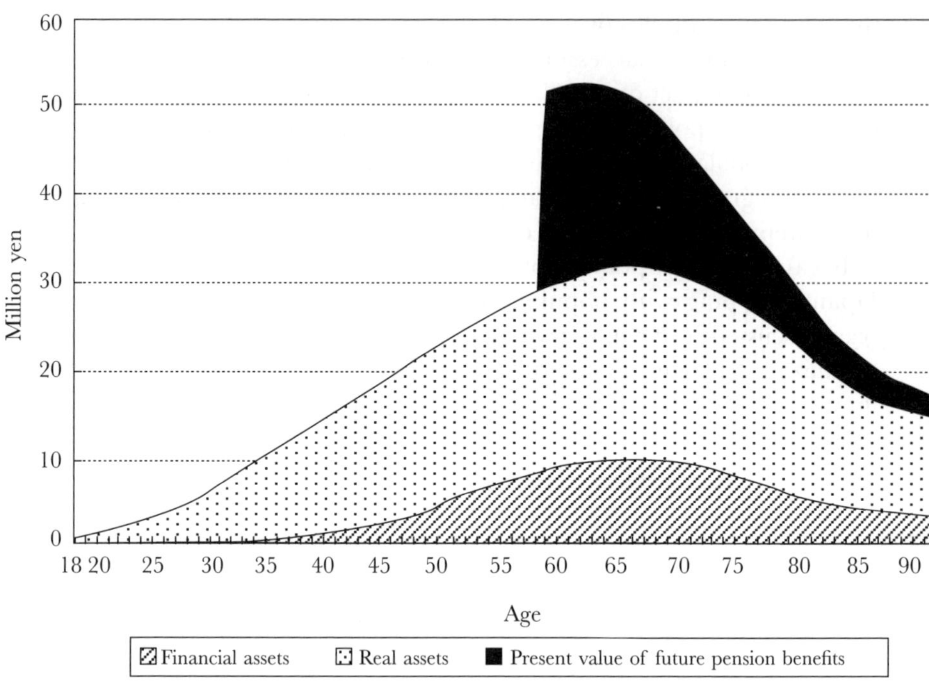


Sources: Nihon University Population Research Institute Projection (2003). *Family Income and Expenditure Survey* (1999), Statistics Bureau, Ministry of Internal Affairs and Communications, Japan.

Figure 8. Age profile of assets and pension wealth in Japan, 1999.

stage of retirement life. This seems to suggest that the liquidation of real assets such as land and housing is crucial for very old persons, particularly those who are living alone. There seems to be substantial potential for developing various financial schemes, such as the reverse mortgage plan.

Attention should also be drawn to the fact that the Japanese people's preference for land has been changing to a considerable degree over the last decade or so, during Japan's "lost decade", the period of low economic growth after the burst of the bubble-economy at the beginning of the 1990s. According to the National Opinion Survey on Land Issues conducted by the Ministry of Land, Infrastructure and Transport in 2004, the proportion of those aged 20 and over who think that land is a better asset than financial assets such as savings and securities declined from 62 per cent in 1993 to 33 per cent in 2004.

This result may suggest that an increasing proportion of the Japanese elderly need more information regarding investment opportunities. Caution should be exercised, however, with regard to the lack of knowledge about financial markets. According to a recent report released by the OECD (2005), 71 per cent of the population aged 20 and over have no knowledge about investment in equities and bonds, 57 per cent have no knowledge of financial products in general, and 29 per cent have no knowledge about insurance, pensions, and tax.

However, if Japanese elderly persons are provided with sufficient knowledge about the dynamics of the financial market, there may be good opportunities for them to invest their accumulated assets, possibly outside Japan. Moreover, as analysed by Cheung *et al.* (2004), the timing of the "first demographic dividend" for selected Asian countries varies considerably. As examined earlier, Japan's first dividend ended in 1994. In contrast, in the case of China, for instance, its first dividend will last for 40 years, from 1990 to 2030, as shown in Figure 9. In an era of globalisation, the wealthier Japanese elderly will be able to invest their assets in a dynamically growing Chinese economy, and bring financial gains back to Japan. Obviously, to facilitate such international transactions, proper institutional and legal arrangements need to be developed to protect elderly investors.

### 3.2. *Better utilization of aged workers and extension of the retirement age*

A variety of quantitative research studies have recently shown that supply factors, particularly labour supply, constitute a major bottleneck in sustaining Japan's economic growth after 2010 (Ogawa *et al.* 2003). One of the ways to overcome this supply-constrained growth scenario is to facilitate a better utilization of human resources among the elderly.

In order to assess such potential, we have run the following two simulation exercises. In Simulation 1, we assume that all healthy elderly persons (no matter how old they are) participate in the labour force over the period 2005–2025. As a detailed description of these estimation methods has already been provided elsewhere (Ogawa and Matsukura 2005), no further discussion relating to the estimation of the number of elderly persons by health status will be given here.

In Simulation 2, we assume that the labour force participation rates for both men and women aged 60–64 have risen to the level equal to that of their counterparts aged 55–59. In other words, in Simulation 2, the legal age of mandatory retirement is raised from 60 to 65 and

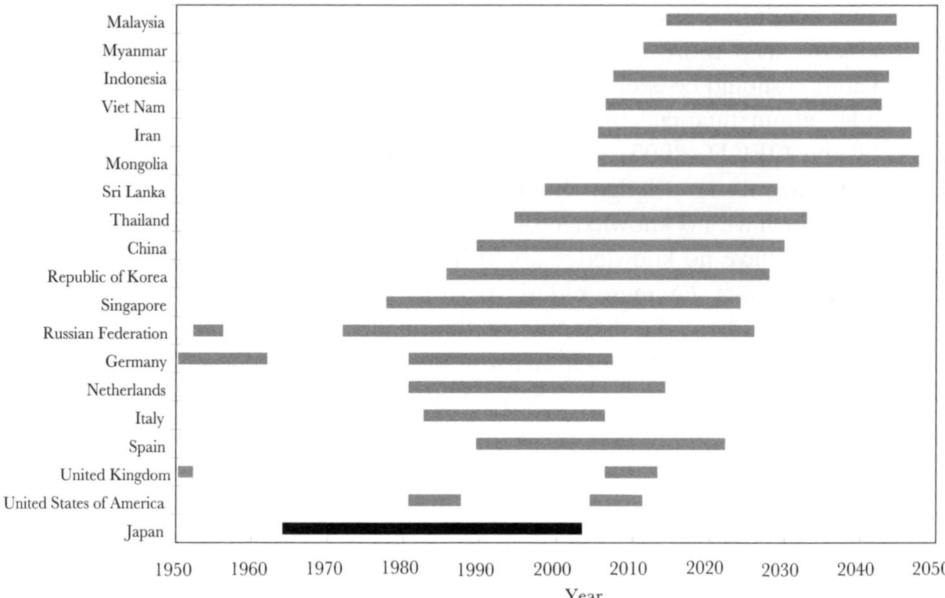


Sources: United Nations, *World Population Prospects: The 2004 Revision*, 2005. United Nations, New York. Nihon University Population Research Institute Population Projection, 2003.

Figure 9. Timing of first demographic dividend (Dependency ratio <0.5).

companies are assumed to comply with this change. Furthermore, Simulation 2 assumes that the labour force participation rates for both men and women aged 65 and over are higher by 10 percentage points than those currently observed.

These two simulation exercises have been undertaken, by utilizing the newest version of the long-term simulation model constructed by the Nihon University Population Research Institute (NUPRI) in 2002. The simulated results for these two exercises are presented in Table 3. In the first simulation exercise, the difference between the base run result derived from the NUPRI model and the counterfactual case is 27.8 per cent in terms of real GDP (in 1990 constant prices) and 26.7 per cent in terms of GDP per capita. In the second simulation exercise, the change in the employment rates of older persons would produce in 2025 approximately 12 per cent higher real GDP and real GDP per capita than those implied by the base run, yielded from the NUPRI model.

Table 3. Simulation exercises for alternative labour force participation among the elderly in Japan, 2005–2025.

| NUPRI Model projection (Base run) | | Simulation 1 | Simulation 2 |
|---|---|---|---|
| Potential GDP (Trillion yen) | | | |
| 2005 | 561.2 | 653.8 (16.5%) | 576.4 (2.7%) |
| 2015 | 600.6 | 747.2 (24.4%) | 661.8 (10.2%) |
| 2025 | 619.1 | 791.3 (27.8%) | 692.3 (11.8%) |
| Potential GDP per capita (Million yen) | | | |
| 2005 | 4.4 | 5.1 (16.5%) | 4.5 (2.9%) |
| 2015 | 4.8 | 5.9 (23.9%) | 5.3 (10.8%) |
| 2025 | 5.1 | 6.5 (26.7%) | 5.7 (12.3%) |
| Labor force (1000 persons) | | | |
| 2005 | 66958 | 86803 (29.6%) | 70386 (5.1%) |
| 2015 | 62827 | 89107 (41.8%) | 73938 (17.7%) |
| 2025 | 59172 | 87880 (48.5%) | 70921 (19.9%) |

Simulation 1: We assume that all the healthy persons aged 65 and over will participate in the labour force throughout the projection.
Simulation 2: We assume (1) that the labour force participation rates of those aged 60–64 are raised to those of people aged 55–59 and (2) that the participation rates of those aged 65 and over are raised by 10 percentage points above the current rates.

If the health status of Japanese older people continues to improve and life expectancy at age 60 continues to increase, it is highly conceivable that more Japanese over the age 60 will wish to remain in the labour force. These two simulation exercises suggest that, if appropriate changes in industrial relations policies are made to accommodate this desire, the contribution to be made to the labour force by Japanese older persons could be quite substantial. It may be worth remarking that a larger workforce to be generated by higher labour force participation among older but healthy people may lead to a considerable increase in the first dividend, although it may reduce the amount of the second dividend as a result of the shorter period of retirement life.

## 4. Concluding Remarks

This chapter has reviewed the evidence supporting the impact of fertility decline and age compositional shifts of the Japanese population upon the Japanese economy. It has also highlighted the important roles played by both first and second dividends induced by rapid fertility decline and massive age structural transformations in the past several decades. The accumulated resources yielded by these two demographic dividends are expected to alleviate the numerous difficulties likely to arise in the years to come in the Japanese economy in the future. For instance, through these demographic dividends, the Japanese elderly have been and will be healthier and wealthier in many more years to come. Because many of them will be healthier, they appear to have great potential for saving Japan from its financial crisis to a considerable extent, by working beyond the age of mandatory retirement. Furthermore, because many of them will be wealthier, they will be able to earn substantial financial resources from abroad, by taking advantage of the differential timing of the first demographic dividend among different countries. Through these two policy options available to Japan, the elderly will contribute to achieving healthy ageing and retaining the dynamism of the country's economic growth. However, depending upon government policies adopted, the effectiveness of these two policy options may vary considerably.

This chapter has shown that Japanese elderly people will generally be very healthy and wealthy. It is important to note, however, that income disparities have been expanding at an alarming rate in Japan, not only among the population in general but also among the elderly (Time Asia 2005). Thus, more research on demographic changes and the deterioration of income distribution needs to be conducted urgently in order to improve the quality of life for the Japanese population, both young and old.

## References

Bongaarts, John (2004): Population Aging and the Rising Cost of Public Pensions. In: *Population and Development Review* 30, 1(March), pp. 1–23.

Cheung, Siu Lan K., Paul Yip, Iris Chi, Antonio Golini and Jean-Marie Robine (2004): Change in Demographic Window in Low Fertility Countries. A paper presented at the International Seminar on the Demographic Window and Healthy Aging: Socioeconomic Challenges and Opportunities, Beijing, May 10–11, 2004.

Hodge, Robert W. and Naohiro Ogawa (1991): *Fertility Change in Contemporary Japan*. Chicago: University of Chicago Press.

Lutz, Wolfgang, Warren C. Sanderson and Sergei Scherbov (eds.) (2004): *The End of World Population Growth in the 21st Century: New Challenges for Human Capital Formation and Sustainable Development*. London and Sterling, VA: Earthscan/James & James.

Mason, Andrew (ed.) (2001): *Population Change and Economic Development in East Asia: Challenges Met, and Opportunities Seized*. Stanford: Stanford University Press.

—— (2005): Demographic Transition and Demographic Dividends in Developed and Developing Countries. A paper presented at the United Nations Expert Group Meeting on Social and Economic Implications of Changing Population Age Structure, Mexico City, August 31–September 2, 2005.

Mason, Andrew and Naohiro Ogawa (2001): Population, Labor Force, Saving and Japan's Future. In: Bloomström, Magnus, Byron Gangnes and Sumner La Croix (eds.): *Japan's New Economy: Continuity and Change in the Twenty First Century*. Oxford: Oxford University Press, pp. 48–74.

Mason, Andrew and Ronald Lee (2006): Reform and Support Systems for the Elderly in Developing Countries: Capturing the Second Demographic Dividend. In: *Genus* 62, pp. 11–35.

McDonald, Peter (2005): Low Fertility in Singapore: Causes, Consequences and Policies. A paper presented at the Forum on Population and Development in East Asia, Beijing, May 16–17, 2005.

McNicoll, Geoffrey (2002): The World after Demographic Transition. In: *East Asian Perspectives* 13, Special Issue 2 (March), pp. 98–104.

MacKellar, F. Landis (2003): The Predicament of Population Aging: A Review Essay. In: Lutz, Wolfgang, Selgei Scherbov and Alexander Hanika (eds.): *Vienna Yearbook of Population Research*. Vienna: Verlag der Österreichischen Akademie der Wissenschaften, pp. 73–99.

OECD (2005): *Recommendation on Principles and Good Practices for Financial Education and Awareness*. Paris: OECD.

Ogawa, Naohiro (2003): Japan's Changing Fertility Mechanisms and its Policy Responses. In: *Journal of Population Research* 20, 1 (May), pp. 89–106.

—— (2005): Population Aging and Policy Options for a Sustainable Future: The Case of Japan. In: *Genus* LXI, 3–4 (July–December), pp. 369–410.

Ogawa, Naohiro and Robert D. Retherford (1993): The Resumption of Fertility Decline in Japan: 1973–92. In: *Population and Development Review* 19, 4 (December), pp. 703–741.

Ogawa, Naohiro, Makoto Kondo, Masao Tamura, Rikiya Matsukura, Tomoko Saito, Andrew Mason, Shripad Tuljapurkar and Nan Li (2003): *Long-term Perspectives for Japan: An Analysis Based on a Macroeconomic-Demographic-Social Security Model with Emphasis on Human Capital*. Tokyo: Nihon University Population Research Institute.

Ogawa, Naohiro, Makoto Kondo and Rikiya Matsukura (2005): Japan's Transition from the Demographic Bonus to the Demographic Onus. In: *Asian Population Studies* 1, 2 (July), pp. 207–226.

Ogawa, Naohiro and Rikiya Matsukura (2005): The Role of Older Persons' Changing Health and Wealth in an Aging Society: The Case of Japan. A paper presented at the United Nations Expert Group Meeting on Social and Economic Implications of Changing Population Age Structure, Mexico City, August 31–September 2, 2005.

Ogawa, Naohiro and Noriyuki Takayama (2006): Demography and Aging. In: Clark, Gordon L., Alicia H. Munnell and J. Michael Orszag (eds.): *The Oxford Handbook of Pensions and Retirement Income*. Oxford: Oxford University Press, pp. 163–182.

Onofri, Paolo (ed.) (2004): *The Economics of an Ageing Population: Macroeconomic Issues*. Cheltenham: Edward Elgar.

Retherford, Robert. D. and Naohiro Ogawa (2006): Japan's Baby Bust: Causes, Implications, and Policy Responses. In: Harris, Fred (ed.): *The Baby Bust*. Boulder: Rowman and Littlefield, pp. 5–47.

Sinding, Steven W. (2002): Policies at the End of the Demographic Transition: A Speculation. In: *East Asian Perspectives* 13, pp. 85–97.

Time Asia (2005): *A Deepening Divide*. http://www.time.com/time/asia/magazine/article/0,13673,501050718-1081429,00.html (found 7 April 2006).

CHAPTER FORTY-SIX

# MACROECONOMIC IMPACT AND PUBLIC FINANCE PERSPECTIVES OF THE AGEING SOCIETY[1]

Akihiro Kawase and Seiritsu Ogura

## 1. Introduction

During the next fifty years, the population of Japan is expected to age at an unprecedented speed rate. The proportion of those aged 65 years or over is about 20 per cent of the population now, and the government expects it to exceed 40 per cent in fifty years' time. Since most of these people will be retired, their living expenditures will have to be financed either by liquidating their private wealth, or by private or public transfers from the working generation. During the last few decades, the increase in life expectancy, the increase in the incidence of so-called "life-style diseases" and long-term care needs have greatly added to financial uncertainty in old age.

In response to these increased risks, universal coverage in the public pension plan and the health insurance system was established in the early 1960s, and finally in 2000, long-term care insurance was introduced. These social security programmes are operated, by and large, as pay-as-you-go systems. This is clear for health-care and long-term care insurance programmes that hold only minimal financial reserves. While some of our pension programmes still have substantial reserve funds, these are small relative to their liability, and, in the long run, they have to be operated under a modified pay-as-you-go principle.

Under a pay-as-you-go system, as the population ages, social insurance contributions from the younger generations inevitably increase in order to maintain constant benefits. If the population ages rapidly, the

[1] This research is supported by a Grant-in-Aid for Scientific Research from the Ministry of Education, Culture, Sports, Science and Technology to Hitotsubashi University on the Economic Analysis of Intergenerational Issues. This research is also a part of the International Research Project on Aging (Japan, China and Korea) at Hosei Institute on Aging, Hosei University, supported by the Special Assistance of the Ministry of Education, Culture, Sports, Science and Technology.

insurance cost must increase sharply. Japan is having misgivings about the consequences of such a steep increase for the coming generations (see, for example, Ogura 1994). The motive may be very selfish. The government has now learned that a social insurance programme can lose its credibility very quickly once the public realizes that its cost is rising too fast to be honoured by future generations.

The problem is further complicated in Japan, where, so far, only estimates of the costs of benefits have been published by the government. In these estimates, the insurance contribution costs are usually calculated according to the current financing framework, leaving substantial portions to general tax revenue, and thus effectively hiding them from the public eye. Looking at the government's future projection of individual programmes, it is easy to overlook the overall implication of the hidden costs, particularly when close to a third of public expenditure is financed by public debt. This is precisely what we want to accomplish in this paper: namely, to present an overall picture of social insurance costs and the size of the general tax revenue already earmarked to maintain them through this century.

This chapter is organized as follows. In section 2, the relationship between social security and demographic change in the future is described. In section 3, we outline the model used in our paper. In section 4, the simulation result is described. Section 5 concludes the paper.

## 2. Demographic Change and Social Security

It is useful to review the basic relationship between the tax rate of the pay-as-you-go social security system and the dependency ratio (see, for example, Rosen 2002).

If $b$ is the benefit per retiree and $N_b$ is the number of retirees, then total benefits are $b \times N_b$. The taxes paid by current workers are the products of tax rate $t$, the average covered wage per worker $w$, and the number of workers $N_w$. Hence, equality between benefits received and taxes paid requires that

$$b \times N_b = t \times w \times N_w \qquad (1)$$

Rearranging this equation gives us

$$t = \frac{N_b}{N_w} \times \frac{b}{w} \qquad (2)$$

The first term on the right-hand side of equation (2) is the *dependency ratio*, the ratio of the number of retirees to the number of workers. The second term is the *replacement ratio*, the ratio of average benefits to average wages. The long-term problems with the social security system arise from the fact that Japan has an ageing population, which implies that the dependency ratio is increasing over time.

In Figure 1 we have shown how the elderly dependency ratio for Japan has changed since 1960, and how it is expected to change during this century. The data for the period from 1960 to 2000 are taken either from the *Population Census* or from the *Annual Report on Current Population Estimate* published by the Ministry of Public Management. The data for years 2001 to year 2100 are taken from the *Population Projections for Japan* (January 2002) published by the National Institute of Population and Social Security Research (NIPSSR), and three different paths are shown for the three fertility scenarios, low, medium and high.

In 1961, when the universal coverage was achieved for both public pensions and public health insurance, the elderly dependency ratio was only 0.11, and, in 1973, which used to be referred to as "the first year of the welfare era", (*fukushi gannen*), it was still only 0.12. In other words, in 1973, there were 8.1 workers to support one retiree. Population ageing accelerated in the 1970s and 1980s, however, and the elderly dependency ratio reached 0.17 in 1985, when the basic pension was introduced for all adults, and was 0.28 in 2000. We had only 3.6 workers to support one retiree in 2000. Further ageing will raise the elderly dependency ratio to 0.5 in 2020, when two workers will be expected to support one retiree. The timing of the peak year is different in different fertility scenarios: in the high fertility scenario, the peak is in 2051, at a dependency ratio of 0.67; in the medium fertility scenario, it is in 2054, at 0.73; but in the low fertility scenario, it is in 2072, at 0.89. In all three scenarios, however, the dependency ratios are expected to decline after these peak values.

In a pay-as-you-go social security system, an increase in the dependency ratio implies that, for each contributing worker, more elderly people are receiving the benefits. Given fixed retirement benefits, in

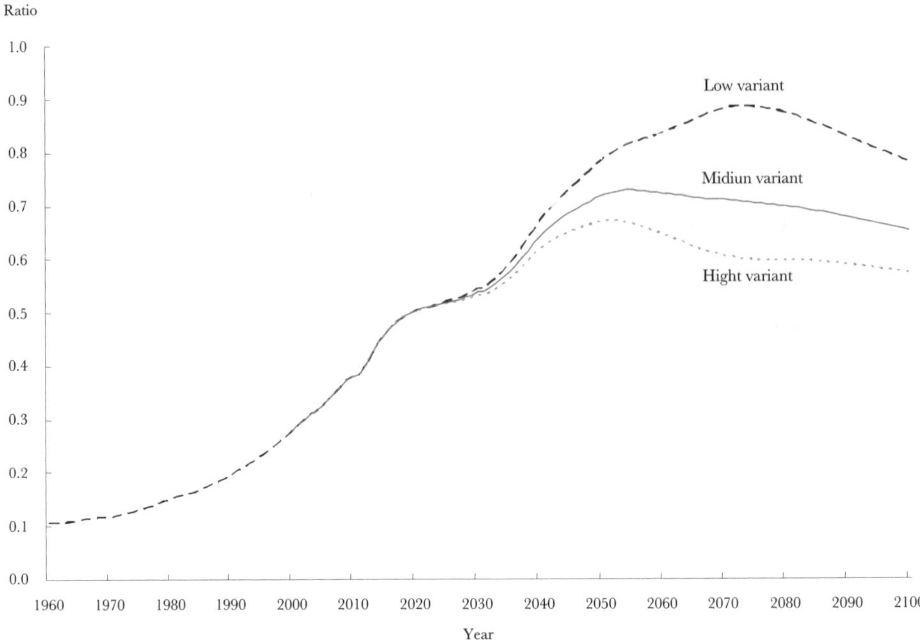


Sources: Statistics Bureau, *the Population Census* and *the Annual Report on Current Population Estimates*, and National Institute of Population and Social Security Research, *Population Projections for Japan* (January 2002).
Note: Elderly dependency ratio is the population aged 65 and over divided by the population aged 20–64.

Figure 1. Actual and Projected Elderly Dependency Ratio in Japan.

particular, rapid ageing of society will require a rapid increase in the contributions made by current workers, which may create serious intergenerational conflicts and destabilize the social security system. As the society ages, the aggregate risks of long life, chronic diseases and long-term care increase, and structural adjustments are needed to stabilize the system once more.

Perhaps, in the long-run, it may be still possible for Japan to push the elderly dependency ratio downwards by effective pro-fertility policies and thus remove substantial pressure on its social security. It will take, however, at least 20 years before such policies start making a difference in the ratio, and another 40 years to realize their full effects. Moreover, the causes of low fertility seem to be rooted deep in the structures of our market economy and our society. It may not be easy, and it may very well be extremely costly, to put effective pro-fertility policies into place. In any case, for the first half of this century, we can ignore the effects of pro-fertility policies as they will make little difference in our analysis during this period.

Given the official population projection, and given the present benefit policies of our social insurance programmes, therefore, we will first calculate the overall burden of these programmes. We will then examine whether the current fiscal system provides sufficient funds to pay for these benefits.

## 3. The Model

In what follows, we first outline the framework of our simulation model, developed by Kawase *et al.* (2007). The entire model consists of three sectors: the macroeconomic sector, the social insurance sector, and the general government sector. For each year, first, the basic economic environments are derived from the macroeconomic sector of the model, and second, the expenditures and the revenues of the three social insurance programmes (public pension, public health insurance and long-term care insurance) are calculated. Thirdly, the expenditures and revenues of the public sector are calculated. Finally, the capital stock and the public debt are recalculated, and new population structure data are given.

### 3.1. *Economic assumptions*

For our macroeconomic sector, we adopt a simple growth model that was used in the last official pension projection of public pensions by the Ministry of Health, Labour and Welfare (MHLW). The official 2004 pension projection, however, focuses exclusively on the cost of public pensions in the context of a growing economy. In order to grasp fully the burden of the ageing population on the public sector, however, it is clear that we have to extend the analysis to include all three major social insurance programmes, namely, public pension, health insurance and long-term care insurance. In addition, we have to take into account the general tax burden as well as the public debt. It is also necessary for us to adopt identical assumptions to those used by the government on such important macroeconomic indicators as the economic growth rate, the interest rate, and the inflation rate, as well as on the population structure.

Following the set of assumptions employed for the public pension projection of 2004, we have set the rate of growth in the real wage rate at 1.1 per cent, the rate of inflation at 1.0 per cent, and the real rate of return on pension funds at 2.2 per cent. The economic growth rates and the long-term interest rates during the period from 2000 to 2008 are identical to those used for the Cabinet Office's middle-term economic and fiscal projection of 2003.

The economic growth rates and the long-term interest rates beyond year 2009, on the other hand, are generated by the macroeconomic model presented at the Pension Subcommittee of Social Security Council on 27 August 2003.

We can write the Cobb-Douglas production function as

$$Y = AK^{\alpha}L^{1-\alpha} \qquad (3)$$

where $Y$ is GDP, $A$ is total factor productivity (TFP), $K$ is capital, $L$ is labour, and $\alpha$ is the capital share of income. The growth rate of this economy can be expressed as

$$\frac{\dot{Y}}{Y} = \frac{\dot{A}}{A} + \alpha\frac{\dot{K}}{K} + (1-\alpha)\frac{\dot{L}}{L} \qquad (4)$$

where $\dot{Y}$, $\dot{A}$, $\dot{K}$, $\dot{L}$ represents the time derivatives of these variables respectively.

If we define per capita GDP as $y = Y/L$, the growth rate of per capita income can be expressed as

$$\frac{\dot{y}}{y} = \frac{\dot{A}}{A} + \alpha\left(\frac{\dot{K}}{L} - \frac{\dot{L}}{L}\right) \qquad (5)$$

Denoting the rate of depreciation by $\delta$, the rate of growth in capital stock is expressed as

$$\frac{\dot{K}}{K} = \frac{I}{K} - \delta \qquad (6)$$

where $I$ is the gross investment of the economy, a policy variable in this simulation. The rate of growth in labour, $\dot{L}/L$, on the other hand, is an exogenous variable in our model. We define the net profit rate $r$ as the marginal product of capital net of depreciation, or

$$r = \alpha \frac{Y}{K} - \delta \qquad (7)$$

Our long-term interest rate is derived from this profit rate, as the real long-term interest rate is, by and large, proportional to the net profit rate. More specifically, the real long-term interest rate will be produced by multiplying the average real long-term interest rate of the last 15 years (2.8 per cent) and the ratio of the net profit rate to the average net profit rate of the last 15 years (9.9 per cent).

The constant parameters of this model are the capital income share $\alpha$, the rate of depreciation $\delta$, and the rate of technological change. The growth rate of labour is not necessarily constant over time, but will be given from outside of the system. Under normal circumstances, the policy variable of the model is the gross investment: given the path for $I$, the model will determine the complete paths for the wage rate, the net profit rate, the growth rate of the economy, and the growth rates of per capita income.

Specifically, in this model, the capital share $\alpha$ is set at 37.3 per cent, the rate of depreciation $\delta$ is set at 8.2 per cent per year, and the rate of technological progress is set at 0.7 per cent per year. The labour supply data are taken from the labour force projection of the MHLW until 2025, and they were calculated by the authors from the population projection of the NIPSSR for the years beyond 2025. For the gross investment, we have used the figures used by the MHLW for their official pension projection: they have assumed that the gross investment ratio will slowly decline from 24.7 per cent in 2001 to 21.4 per cent in 2032. Furthermore, for the years beyond 2032, it is held constant at 21.4 per cent.

Using this model, we has obtained 1.1 per cent as the average growth rate of per capita GDP. This is exactly the figure obtained for the average real wage growth rate by the MHLW, which they decided to use in their pension simulation as far as 2100. This completes our attempt to reproduce the MHLW economic growth model.

The MHLW has added a 0.5 percentage point to the estimated real long-term interest rate (1.8 per cent–2.1 per cent) as the additional return from the diversification of portfolios on public pension funds. Rather than using a variable rate, they have used the mid-range value of the sum (2.2) as the real rate of return in their official pension projection. We have followed their assumption to reproduce their results faithfully.

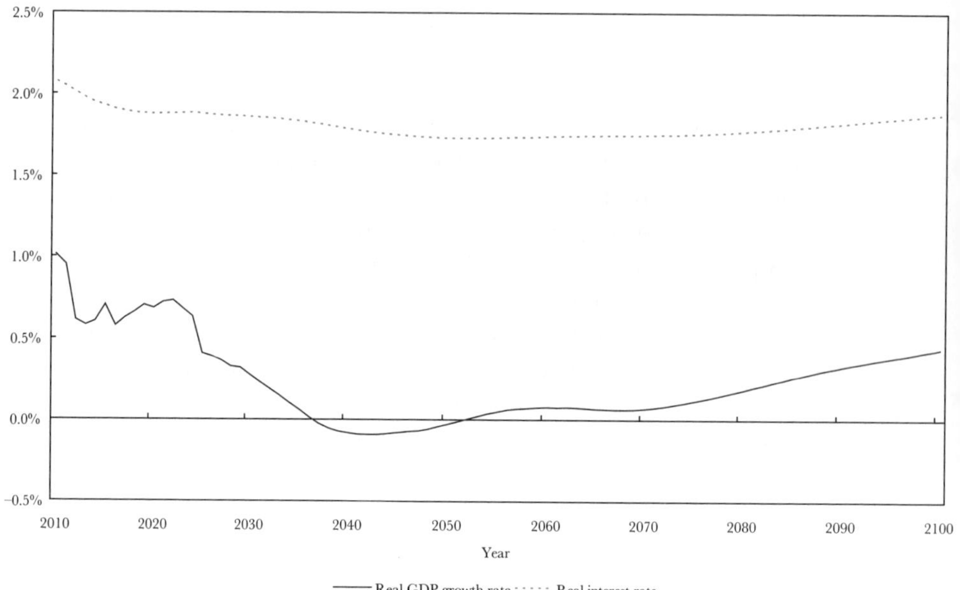


Source: Simulation by the authors.

Figure 2. Economic growth rate and interest rate.

In Figure 2, we have shown the results of our simulated growth rates of real GDP and the real long-term rate of interest. Throughout this 90-year period, the real long-term rate of interest remains fairly stable around its mean of 1.8 per cent. The growth rate of real GDP for this period is far from stable: first it falls for the next 30 years, then stays around zero for another 30 years, and gradually recovers up to 0.5 per cent. The average growth rate of real GDP (not per capita) during this period is only 0.2 per cent.

### 3.2. *Public pension programmes*

(1) *Revenue from contributions*

Revenue from contributions in each programme is obtained as the product of the numbers of insured workers and their average contribution.

In Japan, the population is classified into three major groups according to their basic pension status: Category 1 for self-employed, Category 2 for employees, and Category 3 for dependent spouses of Category 2 individuals. First, the number of insured workers (Category 2) for each year is obtained from the population projection and the labour force participation rate projection, and then the number of dependent spouses (Category 3) is obtained by multiplying the dependency ratio. The number of Category 1 individuals is obtained as a fixed proportion of the difference between the population and the sum of Category 2 and Category 3. This process is repeated for each age and for both sexes.

For the average contribution values, for Category 1 insured, we have used the projected contribution values in the MHLW projection, and, for Category 2 insured, we have used the product of the projected payroll tax rates in the MHLW projection and their estimated average payroll.

(2) *Cost of benefits*

The cost of benefits for each kind of pension is calculated by multiplying the per capita benefit and the number of beneficiaries. The number of beneficiaries is estimated from the population projection.

To obtain the cost of the basic pension benefits, first, we add the number of those aged 65 or over and the number of those who opt for early retirement benefits to obtain the number of basic pension beneficiaries, which we multiply by the estimated per capita benefit. Incidentally, the subsidy of the national government is calculated as a fixed proportion of the cost of the basic pension benefit.

As for the cost of public pensions for employees, we have generated the total number of entitled retirees by taking into account their mortality and the inflow of new retirees, from which the numbers of those receiving full benefits and partial benefits are calculated. The latter are those individuals who continue to work after they become eligible for a pension. For each benefit, the average cost is calculated as a weighted average of the existing claims and the average new claims. The scheduled changes in benefit parameters are duly taken into account to calculate the value of the average new claims, including the increasing pensionable age. This process is repeated for each age and both sexes.

(3) *Simulation of revenue and payment balances*

Given these estimates of revenues, benefit payments, and national government subsidies, the only missing link for the financial projections of the basic pension programme and employees' pension programmes are the returns on their accumulated funds. These are obtained simply by multiplying the end of year figures of the funds by the assumed rate of return. In the simulation, we have used all the basic system parameters published by the MHLW. In order to reproduce the official financial balance projection faithfully, we have further adjusted the estimated data to the official figure when necessary.

### 3.3. *Health insurance*

We have first estimated future national health-care expenditure using the population projection and our per capita health-care projection. The latter has been obtained by simply assuming that the per capita health-care costs will grow at 2.1 per cent per year for individuals below age 70, and at 3.2 per cent per year for individuals aged 70 or over, which is exactly the same assumption as that used in the *Projections of the Cost and Benefits of Social Security* (*Shakai hoshō no kyūfu to futan no mitōshi*) produced by the MHLW. Using the latest data, we distributed a fixed proportion of the national health-care expenditure thus obtained as the cost of public health insurance benefits. The health insurance charges and government subsidies of each year have been obtained based on the cost of the public health insurance benefits of the year.

### 3.4. *Long-term care insurance programme*

The cost of the benefits of Long-term Care Insurance has been obtained by totalling the costs of benefits of each care level. For each care level, we have calculated its cost as the product of the number of beneficiaries and the average cost of benefits in that level.[2] The number of beneficiaries is obtained by applying the present long-term care incidence rate of the elderly to the projected elderly population. The average cost of benefits is assumed to grow at 2 per cent per year until 2025, and at 1 per cent per year thereafter, which is the assumption employed in the *Projection of the Cost and Benefits of Social Security* by the MHLW. After the cost of benefits is calculated, it is distributed to insurance charges and government subsidies, following the present legal framework.

[2] Care levels in Japan's long-term care insurance are classified into six levels as follows: support level, and care levels 1 to 5. Authorization boards composed of public health, medical treatment and welfare specialists determine the level of need for long-term care.

### 3.5. *General government sector*

The general government sector consists of the combined national and local government financial transactions. The expenditure items consist of the cost of subsidies to social insurance programmes, interest payments for public debts, and other government expenditures. The revenue items consist of the total tax revenue, the (non-insurance) charges, and the net deficit.

The cost of the subsidies to social insurance programmes is the sum of the government subsidies calculated in the social insurance sector. The interest payment for public debt is calculated by multiplying the long-term interest rate generated by the macroeconomic sector by the stock of last year's public debt. The cost of other government expenditures is assumed to grow at the same rate as GDP. The total tax revenues and the revenue from charges are assumed to grow 1.1 times faster than the GDP growth rate. The net deficit is the difference between the sum of government expenditures and the sum of the total tax revenue and revenue from charges.

## 4. Simulation Results

### 4.1. *Cost of social insurance programmes*

In Figure 3, we have shown the burdens of pension, health insurance and long-term care insurance contributions as percentages of GDP.

The size of the combined contributions increases rapidly for the first 20 years, but grows more slowly until it exceeds 14 per cent of GDP in 2050. After reaching its peak at 14.54 per cent in 2060, it remains around 14 per cent. The most important component is the public pension contribution, whose level has been fixed by the pension reform of 2004 for the years beyond 2018. The contribution of health-care insurance increases more steadily, and approaches public pensions in importance. The contribution of long-term care insurance grows gradually until it reaches 1.6 per cent.

In Figure 4, we have shown the burdens of public pensions, health insurance, and long-term care insurance, including government subsidies, as ratios to GDP. The government subsidies have to be financed either by tax revenues or by public debt, but the choice does not concern us here. Incidentally, the jump in 2009 reflects the scheduled increase (from one-third to one-half) in the government subsidy to the basic

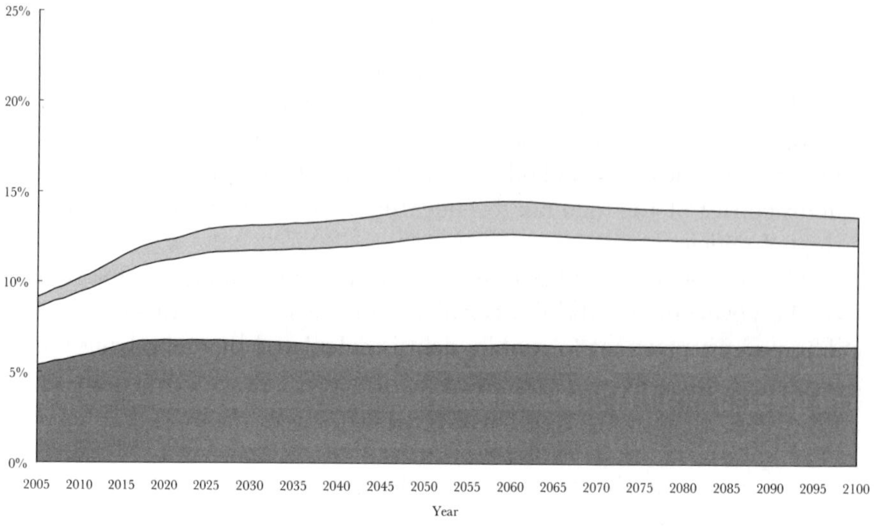


Source: Simulation by the authors.

Figure 3. Social security contributions as a percentage of GDP.

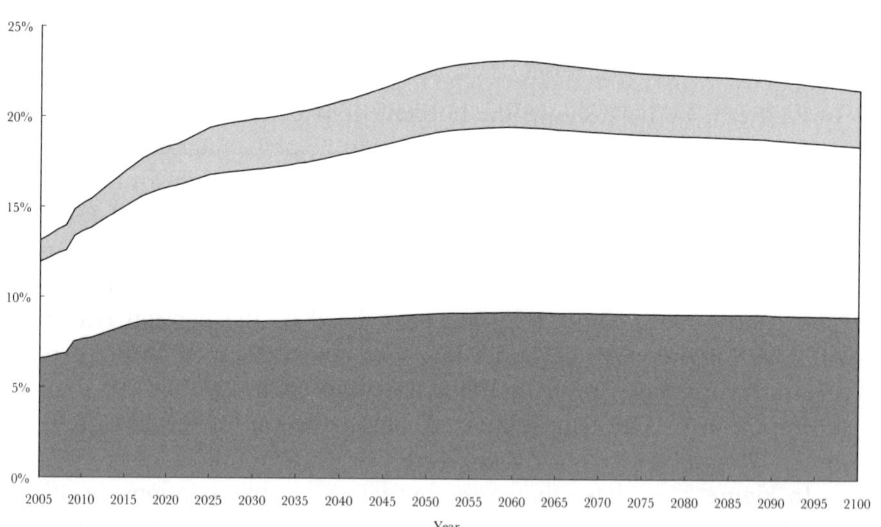


Source: Simulation by the authors.

Figure 4. Social security contributions including government subsidies as a percentage of GDP.

pension introduced in the 2004 pension reform legislation. The overall burden of social security programmes relative to GDP will exceed 20 per cent in 2033, and, in 2060, it will reach almost 23 per cent. It will remain around 22 per cent thereafter.

As we can see from Figure 4, the introduction of a mechanism for automatic adjustment of benefit level, called "macroeconomic slide", and a fixed contribution programme will start to stabilize the public pension cost relative to GDP around 2015, which is a substantial accomplishment. For health insurance and long-term care insurance, on the other hand, we still have a progressive cost structure with respect to ageing. The costs of these programmes still seem to be too large to be sustainable, particularly in the second half of this century, when more than 20 per cent of GDP will be used to finance the programmes.

### 4.2. *Potential national burden and financing methods*

We have seen how the cost of social security programmes changes as our population ages, particularly relative to the size of our future GDP. So far, we have not addressed the question of financing methods. When we allow the possibility of financing part of these costs through public debt, or deficit financing, we need a new comprehensive index, called the potential national burden, to capture the burdens under different financing policies. The potential national burden ratio is the ratio of the sum of the tax revenue, social security contribution and fiscal deficit to the GDP, or

Potential National Burden Ratio
= Total taxes as a percentage of GDP
+ Social security contribution as a percentage of GDP (8)
+ Fiscal deficit as a percentage of GDP

In Figure 5, we have shown how the overall national burden changes over time. From Figure 5, we can see that the general tax burden is stable at around 17 per cent, and the social security burden is also stable at around 14 per cent, but the fiscal deficit as a proportion of GDP keeps on growing throughout this period. Not only does our present fiscal structure place an enormous burden on future generations, but it is also not sustainable under the expected population ageing. As the public debt to GDP ratio keeps on growing without limit, sooner or later, the capital market will refuse to finance any more deficits. For

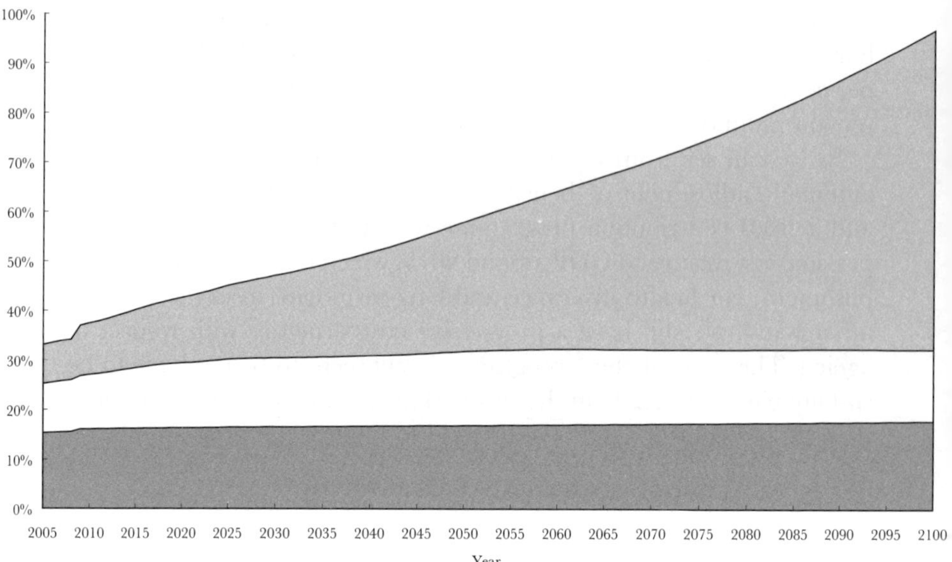


Source: Simulation by the authors.

Figure 5. Potential National Burden Ratio.

sustainability, the primary fiscal balance has to be restored at some point. To put it differently, all other things being equal, the current system of taxes and contributions is not sufficient to finance the costs of Japan's ageing society as projected by the government.

One way for the government to reduce the fiscal deficit is through a reduction in public expenditures by "cutting the fat". Given the size of the current fiscal deficit or the implied future fiscal deficits, however, it is not realistic to restore the primary balance by cutting expenditures alone. At some point, the government will have to resort to increases in taxes or contributions at the same time as cutting benefits. Practically speaking, striking a proper balance between the two will be very important, but for the rest of this section, as a first approximation, we will ignore the latter and concentrate on the former.

For Japan, the obvious candidate for such an increase is consumption tax. The rate of consumption tax in Japan is only 5 per cent, and it yielded revenue of 12.5 trillion yen in FY 2004. Thus an additional 1 per cent of consumption tax would add 2.5 trillion yen. Compared with such European nations as Sweden (25 per cent), Italy (20 per cent),

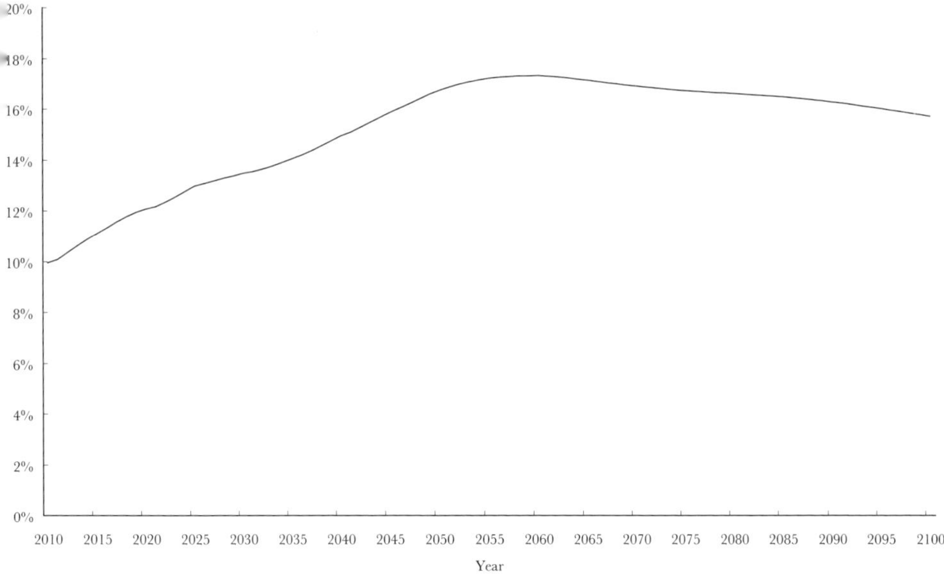


Source: Simulation by the authors.

Figure 6. The required rate of an earmarked consumption tax.

France (19.6 per cent), United Kingdom (17.5 per cent) or Germany (19 per cent), Japan has a very low rate. An important aspect of a fundamental reform in a social security programme is whether or not we should maintain the framework of social insurance. For public pensions or public health insurance, for instance, some argue very strongly that we should abandon the social insurance principle and adopt a complete tax financing scheme. It may be difficult to do away completely with the social insurance framework that has almost one hundred years of history. For this reason, we will adopt the middle ground for our financing reform: we maintain the basic social insurance framework but finance the required increase in government funding through an earmarked consumption tax.

Let us consider introducing the new earmarked consumption tax to finance the public subsidy to the social security programmes in 2010. The required rate of such an earmarked consumption tax is given in Figure 6.

It is, however, difficult to adjust the consumption tax rate every year, and for this reason, we considered an alternative scenario in which the consumption tax rate is raised by a further 15 percentage points in

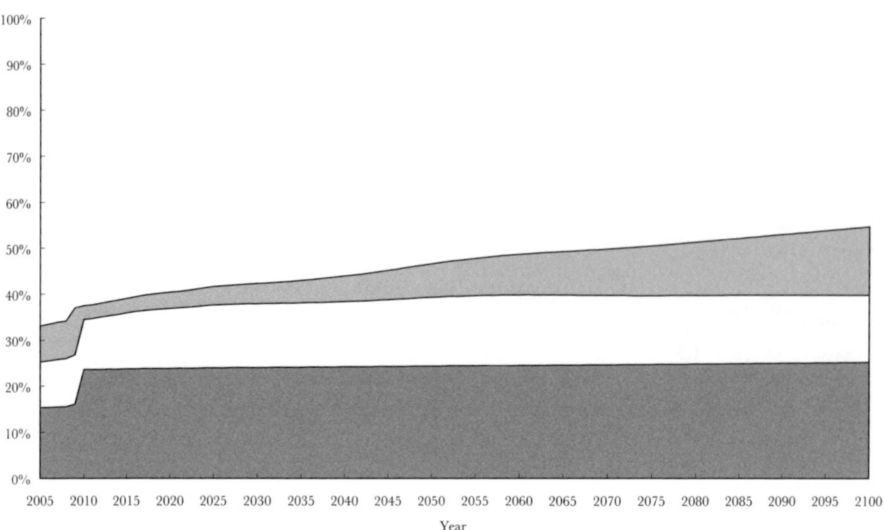


Source: Simulation by the authors.

Figure 7. Potential National Burden Ratio (the consumption tax rate is raised by 15 percentage points in 2010).

(percentage points in 2030)

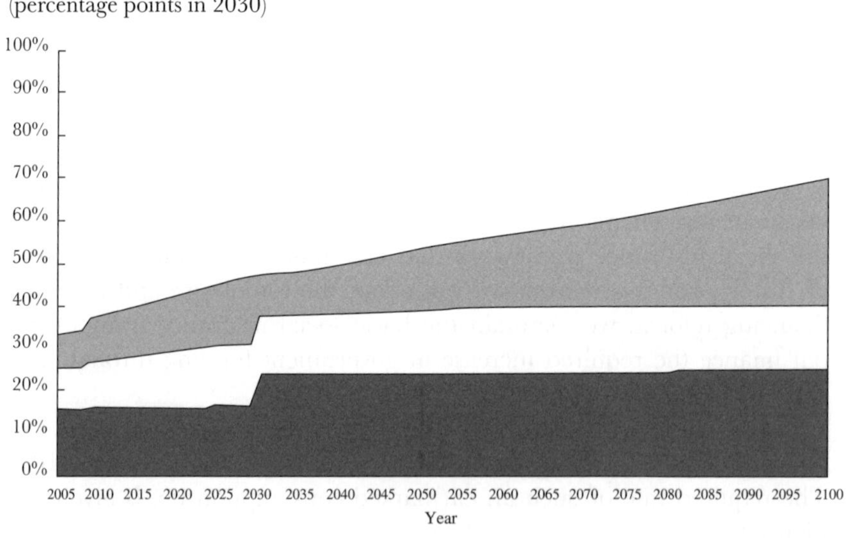


Source: Simulation by the authors.

Figure 8. Potential National Burden Ratio (the consumption tax rate is raised by 15 percentage points in 2030).

2010 once and for all, that is, to 20 per cent. Needless to say, we may need to increase the consumption tax rate by less than 15 per cent, if the primary fiscal balance is improved sufficiently through cuts in government expenditures. We have shown the changes in the potential national burden under this scenario in Figure 7.

By increasing the consumption tax rate in 2010, the potential national burden jumps to 23.6 per cent that year, but, under this policy, the potential national burden is reduced almost by half of Figure 5 in subsequent years. Clearly a bold and early increase in consumption tax will improve the primary fiscal balance and reduce the public debt to GDP ratio, and it could effectively halve the future national burden.

What if the tax increase is delayed due to political procrastination? What if politicians procrastinate for 20 years, and they finally decide on the 15 per cent increase in consumption tax rate in 2030? This scenario is shown in Figure 8.

The potential national burden is reduced to about 70 per cent of the no-tax-increase case of Figure 5, but it is substantially higher than the case in Figure 7. As the consumption tax increase is delayed, not only does the public debt keep on growing, but the reduction of the public debt to GDP ratio becomes much harder and a larger increase is required to achieve the same goal.

Recently, many have argued that fiscal balance can be restored through economic growth and the resulting increase in tax revenues. Such a policy, called a "Deficit Gamble", could leave an enormous burden for future generations if the policy fails (Ball *et al.* 1998). The current Japanese policy of postponing the tax increase necessary to restore the primary fiscal balance is a good example of a gamble. If we consider the increasing future burden of social security programmes, however, the probability of winning such a gamble is extremely small, which makes it a very irresponsible policy.

## 5. Concluding Remarks

According to our analysis, if we are to maintain the current social security benefit levels, the public sector will be certain to consume a proportion of GDP that most regard as excessive and unsustainable. Substantial reductions in these benefits will be necessary. However, at the same time, fiscal reconstruction is difficult to achieve by cuts in expenditures alone, and tax increases are clearly needed. What taxes can we rely on? In the face of a declining labour force and a declining share of labour income, there will be a natural limit on the increase in the income tax burden, and most of the burden will have to be borne by the consumption tax.

The timing of the tax increase may be very important, too. In an economy with a declining population, as we have shown in our simulation, postponing the necessary tax increase will greatly add to the burden of future generations. It is therefore essential for us to form a consensus as quickly as possible on how to finance the inevitable increase in the cost of social security programmes. Earmarking part or all of the consumption tax revenue for these programmes will help this process a great deal.

Since the 1970s, Japan's social security system of has allocated huge resources to unconditional benefits to the elderly. However, continuing such an intergenerational transfer system has become impossible because of a rapidly falling birth rate and the ageing of society. The purpose of social security is to provide a scheme in which all generations can live without anxiety. The success or failure of social security reform in the future depends on whether we will be able to design a system in which fairness among the generations is considered.

What about economic growth? Can't we hope for economic growth to restore fiscal balance and put off painful tax increases for some time? Economic growth is known to be an indispensable part of fiscal reconstruction, but putting off necessary tax increases on the basis of very optimistic economic growth expectations is an extremely risky policy. It can be compared to borrowing money in one's child's name, hoping to repay the debt by the child winning in a lottery. The child will be left with a large burden if he or she fails to get a winning lottery ticket.

Uncertainty is inherent in the prospects of the economic growth rate, the interest rate, population dynamics, and other factors. The amount by which it will be necessary to raise the rate of consumption tax increases by putting off the decision. It is necessary to accomplish a bold and accountable reform.

## References

Ball, Laurence, Douglas W. Elmendorf and N. Gregory Mankiw (1998): The Deficit Gamble. In: *Journal of Money, Credit, and Banking* 30, 4, pp. 699–720.

Kawase, Akihiro, Yoshiaki Kitaura, Shin Kimura and Satoko Maekawa (2007): 2004-nen nenkin kaikaku no shimyureshon bunseki [The 2004 public pension reform in Japan: A simulation analysis]. In: *JCER Economic Journal*, No. 56.

Ogura, Seiritsu (1994): The Cost of Aging: Public Finance Perspectives for Japan. In: Yukio Noguchi and David Wise (eds.): *Aging in the United States and Japan*. Chicago: The University of Chicago Press, pp. 139–173.

Rosen, Harvey S. (2002): *Public Finance* (6th edition). New York: McGraw-Hill.

CHAPTER FORTY-SEVEN

# THE IMPACT OF THE AGEING SOCIETY ON REGIONAL ECONOMIES

Volker Elis

## 1. Introduction

The aim of this chapter is to examine the way demographic change will influence the economic wellbeing of different regions in Japan. Decision makers and actors in various fields of Japanese society are in need of rules of thumb concerning the question of which regions will prosper and which will suffer, in order to adjust their reactions, measures, and policies to the upcoming developments. A failure to choose the right path now could obviously result in serious difficulties in the future. It is important to know beforehand what is going to happen and why. This chapter is an attempt to clarify what kind of demographic and economic mechanisms will be at work during the adjustment process. The task is to shed light on the effects those mechanisms are likely to bring about and to examine how they are interrelated. As a first step, we will look at the population projections available.

## 2. Regional Population Change and Economic Development

Although this chapter is a treatise on the *economic* effects of demographic change, the whole argumentation must be based on forecasts about population development. Firstly, one has to consider the estimates of both natural population movement and domestic migration broken down into regions or municipalities.

### 2.1. *Regional population projections*

The most obvious and clear-cut way to produce forecasts about population movement is simply to extrapolate into the future developments that have taken place in a given time span in the past. If this method is chosen, the outcome is something that is completely in line with the expectations that the man on the street in Japan has about the coming developments: The metropolises will be less affected, as young people continue to flock to the metropolitan regions as before, while the situation will worsen in the peripheral regions, which will be hit hard both by a population exodus and by the ageing of its resident population. This is, in simplified form, the outcome that has been suggested by a population projection published by the National Institute of Population and Social Security Research, which covers population development in the period from 2000 to 2030 on a municipal scale (IPSS 2004). On the basis of these data, the Ministry for Land, Infrastructure and Transport (MLIT) has compiled a report on future population development in Japan's urban areas (MLITCRDB 2005a), which comes to the conclusion that population decline will occur in 87 per cent of all areas surveyed. The remaining 13 per cent of urban areas, which can expect their population to stay constant or rise marginally, generally have in common that they are either located in or near the three large conurbations centring on the cities of Tokyo, Osaka and Nagoya, or near the so-called regional capital cities (*chihō chūsū toshi*) of Sapporo, Sendai and Fukuoka, which are at the core of the larger regional units of Hokkaido, Tohoku and northern Kyushu respectively. Booming manufacturing regions, which have experienced large scale immigration in the 1990s, are also on the list, such as the urban area including Toyota city in Aichi prefecture and the urban area located on the shores of Lake Biwa in Shiga prefecture. A special case is the city of Naha, the capital of Okinawa prefecture, which shows a comparatively advantageous population development mainly due to its above-average birth rate.

On the other hand, population losses will be a distinctive feature of urban areas formed by cities which are not prefectural capitals (*kenchō shozai toshi*). Urban areas endangered by especially pronounced population losses exceeding 20 per cent in 30 years' time can be found scattered on Hokkaido, in the Tohoku and Inland Sea regions, and on the island of Kyushu. It is possible to summarize the trend forecast by the projection as follows: the smaller the urban area's core city is, the higher the actual danger of population decline (MLITCRDB 2005b).

This is what comes out of a simple examination of long-term population development in Japan on a regional scale. However, what happens if we add a simulation which takes into account the economic effects of population movement as well? The Ministry for Economy, Trade and Industry (METI) has created a comprehensive simulation model, which forms the basis for forecasts about both population movement and economic development in urban Japan for the period from 2000 to 2030. The simulation is based on a detailed input-output model in five-year steps, which takes into account the direct and indirect effects that demographic change has on labour supply and demand, labour productivity, local production capacity, and the gross regional product in 269 urban employment areas (KSCKK 2006a: 1–3; 7–9). A central assumption of the simulation model is that regions which are experiencing a positive economic development will in turn become target regions for immigration again (KSCKK 2006b: 10).

The simulation provides results which point in a similar direction to the population forecast mentioned above: the Tokyo metropolitan region will be the only sample unit in which population will rise. In the urban areas belonging to special status cities[1] (*seirei shitei toshi*), the population will decline by 6.6 per cent, a figure which compares favourably with the national average of 10.7 per cent. In comparison to this, the population is estimated to shrink by 14.3 per cent in those prefectural capitals that are not designated as special status cities, while other cities which do not belong to this group are even worse off and have to reckon with a population decrease of 16.2 or 24.6 per cent respectively, depending on their population size. The worst prospects are calculated for the rural areas, whose population will shrink by 29.7 per cent (see table 1).

The main result that can be extracted from the population projection by the MLIT is that the higher the urban area is ranked in the Japanese city hierarchy, the smaller the estimated loss of population expressed as a percentage.

The METI projection also includes forecasts about growth rates of gross regional product in Japan's urban employment areas (see table 2). It is apparent that the urban zones higher up the urban hierarchy fare better. While the gross regional product is predicted to shrink in 87 per cent of the areas covered, it will rise in, for instance, the agglomerations of the Tokyo metropolitan area, Sendai, Nagoya, Osaka, Okayama, Hiroshima, Fukuoka and Naha. With regard to regional economic growth too, this supports the general picture that the regions with bigger

[1] Special status cities have administrative powers and rights nearly comparable to a prefecture. Cities aspiring to become special status cities must have at least 700,000 inhabitants to be eligible for designation. Many special status cities double as prefectural capitals, but some do not (Kawasaki, Hamamatsu, Sakai, Kitakyushu).

Table 1. Population development according to the METI simulation.

| Type of urban area | population (2000) (million) | population (2030) (million) | rate of increase |
|---|---|---|---|
| Tokyo metropolitan area | 31.8 | 32.0 | +0.8 |
| Special status cities | 31.5 | 29.5 | –6.6 |
| Prefectural capitals | 20.2 | 17.3 | –14.3 |
| Urban zones > 100,000 | 26.8 | 22.4 | –16.2 |
| Urban zones < 100,000 | 7.0 | 5.2 | –24.6 |
| Rural areas | 9.7 | 6.8 | –29.7 |
| Total | 126.9 | 113.3 | –10.7 |

Note: Special status cities which double as prefectural capitals are included in the category "special status cities" (see also footnote 1).
Source: Based on KSCKK 2006b.

Table 2. Development of Gross Regional Product according to the METI simulation.

| Type of urban area | GRP (2000) (trillion ¥) | GRP (2030) (trillion ¥) | rate of increase |
|---|---|---|---|
| Tokyo metropolitan area | 159.6 | 176.8 | +10.7 |
| Special status cities | 132.8 | 141.9 | +6.9 |
| Prefectural capitals | 78.8 | 76.3 | –3.2 |
| Urban zones > 100,000 | 106.1 | 99.3 | –6.4 |
| Urban zones < 100,000 | 24.4 | 20.7 | –15.1 |
| Total for urban areas | 501.7 | 514.9 | +2.6 |

Source: Based on KSCKK 2006b.

core cities and larger commuting zones will show better performances in the face of demographic change.

Both the projection of the MLIT and that of the METI convey the impression that bigger cities will experience less serious population losses than smaller cities. Even if the natural decrease in population is on a comparable scale, the metropolitan areas should profit from net migration gains.

On the basis of this perception, the METI has developed a scenario which in turn forms the starting point for various recommendations concerning regional policy. It proceeds on the assumption that regional economies will be increasingly affected by sluggish intraregional demand, insufficient utilization of public infrastructure and a deterioration of regional finances (KSCKK 2006b: 14–15).

Newspaper articles commenting on the findings of the two government-financed projections have tended to emphasize the point that demographic change will lead to a widening of interregional disparities in Japan between metropolitan and non-metropolitan areas (*Asahi Shinbun* 7 May 2006: 9; *Nihon Keizai Shinbun* 22 May 2006: 1).

### 2.2. *The population structure approach*

In marked contrast to the government forecasts explained above, the Japanese economist Matsutani Akihiko (2004a: 5–6) holds the view that it will be the big agglomerations that have to worry most about the economic effects of demographic change, not the peripheral regions. He supports his claim by an argument which emphasizes the importance of regional differences in population structure. His approach is to project changes in the percentages of the younger population cohorts of the workforce on a prefectural scale and to calculate prefectural income on the basis of these data (Matsutani 2004b: 102–116).

According to his analysis, Japan's non-metropolitan regions are facing greater population decline, while the speed of the ageing process will be higher in the metropolitan regions, so that the decline in the working-age population will be above the national average. As important variables like economic growth and the per capita growth of the gross regional product are largely determined by the speed of ageing and not by the absolute decline in total population, the metropolitan regions are in trouble. According to his analysis, the special characteristics of the ageing process in Japan's metropolitan regions will lead to a gradual convergence of age structures in metropolitan and peripheral regions, leading in the long run to a leverage of regional disparities (Matsutani 2004b: 85–94).

Contrary to public opinion, it is less important to look at the absolute decrease in overall population than at the ratio of the working-age population to the total population, in order to make statements about the future economic wellbeing of given regions. The reason for this is that the economic capacity of firms will be determined by the amount of available labour in the future. With regard to this hypothesis, Matsutani (2004b: 123–126) even goes so far as to state that, with the labour market becoming a seller's market, firms will have to move to regions where sufficient labour is still available. The economic impact of this new trend will lead to income increases in the non-metropolitan prefectures of Japan, so that regional disparities will shrink. According to this argument, decentralization of industrial locations in Japan due to changes in regional labour demand will thus offer new opportunities for peripheral regions to improve their economic base and to raise living standards, so that it will no longer be necessary to move to Tokyo or Osaka to enjoy a good life.

Matsutani's argumentation stands or falls by the notion that it is crucial to look at the decline in the proportion of the population that is of working age in order to make statements about the development of particular regions. He stresses the fact that the upper limit of the economic capacity of firms is determined by the labour supply, which is likely to become a crucial factor in future. The next section will elaborate on the question of whether this argument holds or not.

## 3. Does Demographic Change Lead to a Demand-led Labour Market?

There can be no doubt that macroeconomic factors like economic growth and the future development of the labour market will have repercussions on regional economic development. If reliable estimates for these factors were available, it would make it much easier to draw conclusions about the impact of demographic change. The problem is that these two factors cannot be easily forecasted, because the mechanisms at work are fraught with many uncertainties. It is therefore still a controversial issue what will happen in a—probably shrinking—economy with a rapidly declining working population. However, to shed some light on the relationship between demographic change and labour market effects it is useful to refer to some German research on this point.

German researchers in particular have dealt in detail with such issues, because Germany, together with Japan, belongs to the group of countries in which the ageing process is most advanced. Although these studies focus on different aspects of the economic impact of demographic change, the bottom line of all the studies is that labour issues play a central role.

In the case of Germany, it will not be possible to prevent a decrease in working population, even if measures to raise the labour participation rate bear fruit. This will effectively put a brake on economic growth, since economic capacity depends on the development of labour input (Grömling 2005: 79). Although this seems inconceivable from a current point of view, it can even be assumed that population ageing in Germany will lead to a veritable labour shortage in the higher qualified sectors of the labour market, mitigating the unemployment problem. As labour scarcity leads to a higher price of labour, labour has to be substituted by capital (Börsch-Supan 2004: 3–5). However, it is questionable whether the current level of prosperity can be raised or maintained by this, because human capital cannot be substituted by capital in all cases. Kaufmann (2005: 66–67) even argues that overconfidence in the neoclassical assumption that the market mechanism will be sufficient to balance any changes in factor combinations constitutes the core of the common trend to play down the consequences of demographic change in Germany.

It has also been argued in the German case that many urban agglomerations and especially the suburban belts at their fringes might be seriously affected by demographic change, as above-average increases in the proportion of elderly people lead to an especially marked decrease in the working-age population. Without a considerable population inflow from other regions to compensate for this, the effects of demographic change will make themselves felt in the majority of urban agglomerations in Germany (Röhl 2005: 329–331).

The findings presented above show that there is a tendency to emphasize the importance of a declining labour supply when dealing with the effects of demographic change in Germany on both a macro- and a regional scale. This shows that the population structure approach with its labour market focus championed by Matsutani for the Japanese case should not be seen as an isolated opinion, but has counterparts in German research as well.

## 4. Regional Effects of a Labour Shortage

Will a labour shortage in the metropolitan areas really induce corporations to relocate facilities in search of suitable employees? Matsutani (2004b: 119–124) thinks that this new situation could be a big opportunity in the efforts to decentralize, which have never borne fruit, despite great efforts in the past. He forecasts a decentralization of Japanese industry and income increases in the non-metropolitan regions. According to his analysis, it is highly unlikely that a lack of employment opportunities will become a problem in the areas outside the metropolises.

However, there are several arguments which imply that the Japanese economist might be going too far with his conclusion. Firstly, the scenario he is drawing upon tends to overemphasize the importance of manufacturing while neglecting the implications of a growing tertiary sector. Secondly, a labour shortage due to the ageing society in Japan will lead to a situation in which companies will shift their production facilities to other countries (Matsubara 2006: 3), rather than seeking new locations in Japan's non-metropolitan regions. Thirdly, Matsutani fails to take into account the fact that the current income disparities among Japanese regions are not a result of the different population structure in metropolitan and non-metropolitan areas, but of differences in labour productivity (Suzuki and Harada 2006: 6).

While Matsutani's conclusion overshoots the mark to some degree, the core of his deduction is still plausible. Even if the inflow of younger population to the three big metropolitan regions continues, it can be forecast that this will not suffice to make up for the loss of younger population due to the ageing process. It is therefore plausible that the metropolitan regions will also be substantially affected by the lack of population of working age, which could lead to a contraction of their regional economies.

## 5. Regional Policy Implications

What can be done to react to the new challenges arising from a shrinking population? Are there measures which should be taken to prepare for those challenges? The problem in answering these questions is that there are not only demographic factors that need to be taken into account, but also political and economic processes. Moreover, in the case of Japan's regional economies, the answer will be different depending on the particular situation of the prefecture or municipality involved.

Actors on the political stage tend to hang on to their preoccupation with growth targets for fear of losing support and popularity, while an active management of the inevitable shrinking process might be the right reaction. However, it is necessary to keep in mind that a failure to convey a positive regional image could also prove counter-productive.

### 5.1. *Cumulative downward spirals looming*

An important factor not to be neglected is the danger of downward spirals of demographic and economic development triggered by downsizing of public infrastructure. I will elucidate this point using the example of a closing school.

In a society with fewer children, deciding whether or not an elementary school in a particular municipality should be closed will be a common problem. A decision to close a school could lead to a situation in which it is possible that young families with younger children or intending to have children will consider moving to another town, because there is no longer an elementary school within reach. Population exodus has different negative effects, such as a reduction of local tax income and a decline in demand for goods and services produced inside the region. As demand falls, retail shops and shops offering personal services might have to close, which in turn has a negative effect on the municipality's tax income. While tax income dwindles away, the pressure to get rid of infrastructure which cannot be used to capacity grows, so that the vicious circle is set into motion again.

The example given is only one of the vicious circles which can occur because of the effects of the ageing society on regional economies. Figure 1 shows how the processes involved are interrelated. If mechanisms like the vicious circle described above are at work across the whole country, some municipalities will become problem areas, while others could even profit economically from population gains. In a zero-sum game scenario in which one side wins what the other side loses, it becomes important to determine whether the losers should be compensated through state intervention.

### 5.2. *No help when most needed?*

Just when a considerable number of Japanese municipalities are threatened by the prospect of population exodus and ensuing economic decline, Japan's central government is taking steps to withdraw some of the support which has been guaranteed to weaker administrative units since the period of rapid growth (1955–1973). Those steps were taken by the Koizumi government (2001–2006) under the name of *sanmi ittai kaikaku* [trinity reforms].[2] The aim was to replace a system characterized by redistributive centralism by a new system in which

[2] The trinity reforms were a central part of Koizumi's reform agenda and were intended to bring about a reorganization of local government finance by three means: a cut in the amount of local allocation tax grants (*chihō kōfuzei*); the reduction of central government disimbursements (*kokko shishutsukin*); and a transfer of additional tax income resources to local governments.

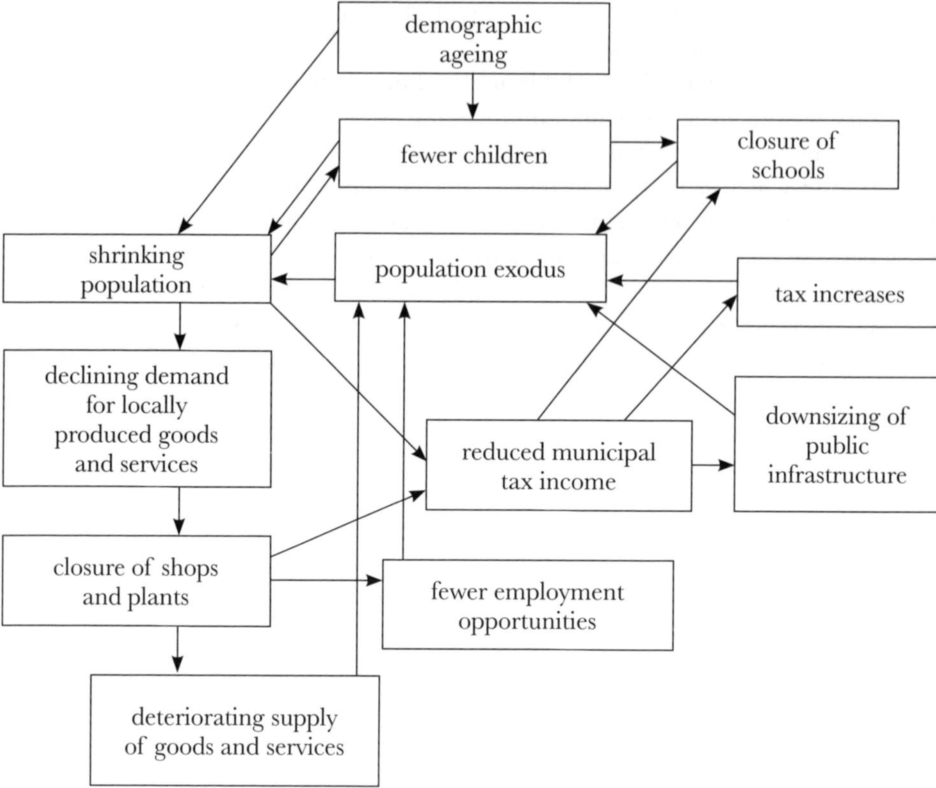


Source: Figure based on concept by the author.

Figure 1. Interrelations between different vicious circles in a municipality affected by demographic ageing.

federal elements and incentives for independent policy-making play a bigger role. This policy shift was foreshadowed by a paradigm change from Keynesian regional policy to a market-oriented neoliberal approach that took place in the 1990s.

Koizumi's policy stance to "enhance the autonomy of localities and expand their discretionary capabilities" and "leave to the localities what they can do" (OCPRCS 2004) has its supporters and its critics both inside Japan and abroad. While a detailed discussion of those reforms is beyond the scope of this chapter, it is possible to say that they were a political reaction to budget constraints stemming in part from the higher costs caused by an ageing society (De Wit and Yamazaki 2004: 3) and will definitely have repercussions on the financial leeway that Japanese self-governing bodies have in view of the challenges of demographic change.

While the course suggested by the trinity reforms is well-defined, it is not clear whether they will be wholeheartedly implemented under the agenda of the Abe government, which came into power in September 2006. Be that as it may, in terms of the scope of political action, three alternatives seem possible. The first is to offer even stronger support to the affected municipalities by means of intra-regional transfers to enable them to manage the new challenges. The second stance would be to postpone the problem by pushing on the process of municipal amalgamation, so that the weaker villages and towns are added to stronger neighbouring municipalities. The third alternative, which is not the least likely to be favoured in the end, is to leave some of the problem-ridden municipalities to their fate and accept a shrinking process in which a gradual downsizing of public infrastructure will finally lead to the depopulation of some areas and the abandonment of some settlements to become ghost towns.

### 5.3. *What will happen in the countryside?*

While it has been indicated by some academic authors (Yoshida 2005: 145; Harada and Suzuki 2006: 6) that the negative effects of the ageing society will mainly affect the rural periphery of Japan, this picture could be misleading. As has already been mentioned, the consequences of the ageing society will hit the metropolitan regions as well, especially through a reduced labour supply. Moreover, it is important not to lump all rural areas together. As Motani (2006: 79–80) indicated, there are very pronounced differences even among those areas already designated as underpopulated areas[3] (*kaso chiiki*). Some of those areas can recently boast of considerable population inflow and a positive development of employment.

Nevertheless, rural areas are certainly especially vulnerable to downward spirals of regional development, as the ageing process of the population has begun earlier there and is already in full swing in some of the regions. A deterioration of the regional economic situation will

[3] Designated municipalities which are eligible for special grants and subsidies from the central government. *Kaso chiiki* are determined by fiscal capacity, age structure and population decrease in the last 25 years. In fiscal year 2004, 38 per cent of all Japanese municipalities were considered *kaso chiiki*; 7 per cent of Japan's population lives in those predominantly rural areas (KTKK 2006: 4).

be difficult to stop, if the vicious circles leading to repeated contraction processes are once set in motion. The delicacy of regional policy measures in Japan's rural areas in the future is determined by the need to avoid repeated shrinking processes with regard to the regional economy and infrastructure until the municipality can benefit from an advantageous population structure after the adjustment process has been accomplished. If downward spirals are triggered, the ensuing outflow of population can have a devastating effect on the regional economy, so that population falls short of the critical mass necessary for upward economic development in the future. The opportunity for the rural areas lies in the fact that they have already lost a large part of their baby-boomer generation to the metropolitan areas, so that there will be fewer problems with replacement by younger workers when this generation retires. The metropolitan areas, on the other hand, have to cope with an age structure that will be much more unbalanced. The ageing process of the younger generation, which is also overrepresented there because of the impact of the descendants of the baby-boomers, will cause major problems.

Since not all of the municipalities in the rural periphery will be able to maintain regional vitality, it is conceivable that a concentration process will ensue in the non-metropolitan areas, in which municipalities successfully adjusting to the new requirements will gradually gain new economic functions and administrative power.

### 5.4. *The situation in the conurbations*

Demographic ageing in Japan's large cities will be characterized by the following characteristics: a rapid ageing process, which will occur later here than elsewhere; a slow population decrease mitigated by the convergence of younger people; a shrinking workforce with the consequence of a sharp decline in value added; and a concentration of elderly people (Matsutani 2006: 177–178). Even in the metropolitan area of Tokyo, the workforce will steadily decline, unless there is a large increase in economically active women and senior citizens. The gap opened by the retirement of employees will not be fully compensated for by younger ranks (Motani 2006: 78–79). As the natural shrinking process of the younger population in metropolitan and non-metropolitan areas is going on at the same time, the number of people migrating to the Tokyo metropolitan area is almost sure to decline, if no dramatic change in migration behaviour occurs (Esaki 2006: 67).

The impact of demographic change on the metropolitan areas will be ambiguous. While there will also be negative effects that have to be dealt with, it is conceivable that negative agglomeration effects could be mitigated. Land prices could drop or stagnate, the lack of housing space could be alleviated and traffic congestion reduced. This could again enhance the attractiveness of the urban agglomerations, especially for younger people (Yoshida 2005: 138).

On the other hand, it has to be emphasized that the financial burden resulting from the need to offer adequate infrastructure for the growing number of elderly people in metropolitan areas should not be underestimated.

### 5.5. *Measures to attract the affluent elderly*

Japan differs from other developed countries with regard to the fact that there is still no marked migration of the elderly, and retirees' cities have not appeared so far (Lützeler 2004: 43–44). However, there has been much media attention lately on the topic of municipalities trying to attract senior citizens. There are frequent offers for members of the baby-boomer generation to move to the countryside. Hoping to profit from their economic affluence, cities and towns offer a wide range of incentives to attract people willing to move to the countryside after retirement: sheltered housing and collective taxis for senior citizens; professional help to find a job and a place to live; subsidies for renovation, house-building and house purchases; reimbursement of real-estate costs; refunding of commuter tickets; and taster weeks for those interested. All of these incentives aim at the demand-boosting effect expected from investments like housing, real estate and automobile purchases, if silver agers from the metropolitan regions decide to spend their old age in the countryside. Although at first sight these measures to attract the baby-boomer generation seem to be a practicable way to give a new stimulus to regional economies, it also has to be taken into consideration that when the affluent senior citizens' savings are used up, the rising costs of social welfare could place a heavy burden on municipal finances (*Asahi Shinbun* 26 November 2006: 9).

## 6. Prospects for Different Sectors and Industries

The aim of this section is to give a short overview of the issue of which branches of the economy will benefit from demographic ageing.

The Japanese Ministry of Economy, Trade and Industry asserts that it is crucial for sustainable development of regional economies and societies to generate income from industries which have their sales market outside the region, such as the manufacturing sector, agriculture and tourism. It propagates a regional policy concept in which the income generated by those industries is multiplied by the branches of the regional economy which have their sales market inside the region, such as services and trade (KSCKK 2006b: 1). Retailing and personal services are considered most vulnerable to ageing and population decline (KSCKK 2006b: 14).

This argument is largely supported by Grömling (2005: 84–86), who stresses that branches of industries producing place-bound goods and services are likely to be more affected by a shrinking population than those producing goods and services that are tradable on international markets. The latter could possibly even benefit from a still-rising world population. While this means good prospects for the capital goods industry, consumer goods industries have to be concerned about diminished domestic demand, as spending on consumer goods declines as individuals grow older (Grömling 2005: 88–90).

Diametrically opposed to this forecast is the argument of Matsutani (2006: 65–67), whose focus lies on macroeconomic changes. As consumption will replace investment as the driving dynamic of the Japanese economy, he predicts that consumer goods industries and service industries will rise, while the capital goods industries will decline. Particularly affected will be those industries which rely heavily on public sector demand, like the construction and basic materials industry, because of the decline in spending on public works (Matsutani 2006: 116–117).

While the conclusion that consumer industries are going to surge is a minority opinion, the notion that the construction industry will be a possible loser in demographic change is generally accepted in Germany as well as in Japan (Kaufmann 2005: 89; Grömling 2005: 86–87). The construction industry might come under pressure, because the main consumers of new housing are younger people and families (Grömling 2005: 86).

On the other hand, there could be growth opportunities for industries which produce goods that will be increasingly consumed by the growing cohorts of the elderly. These include the pharmaceutical industry, biotechnology, medical technology and medical equipment (Grömling 2005: 86).

Because assessments of the impact of demographic ageing on the development of particular branches of industry are not yet comprehensive and reliable, it is still too early to derive regional policy recommendations from them. Future forecasts about sectoral economic development in particular regions of Japan need to be based on detailed case studies considering regional conditions and requirements.

## 7. Conclusion

The attraction of domestic migrants will become the focus of regional development policy, as labour supply becomes scarcer and the buying power of both the younger population cohorts and of the affluent elderly is needed to fuel the regional economy. As labour cannot simply be substituted by capital in all cases, labour supply will set the upper limit of regional output. To prevent cut-throat competition among Japan's municipalities, the central government has to moderate the adaptation process and put forward a conclusive concept which determines what should be done about the losers in the race. The most important choice will be between continued support and tacit abandonment of problem-ridden municipalities by the central government.

Recent research indicates that there will be challenges both for metropolitan and non-metropolitan areas in the wake of demographic ageing. The metropolitan areas have to cope with the ageing process of their large younger population cohorts, which cannot be replaced by a matching number of young people in the future. On the other hand, they might benefit from mitigated negative agglomeration effects and a continuing influx of young people from non-metropolitan areas. The rural areas face the task of avoiding cumulative shrinking processes resulting from population exodus, before positive effects generated by an adjustment process accomplished faster than in the metropolitan areas may gain a foothold.

A crucial issue that will determine which options municipalities have at their disposal in the future is whether the market-oriented Koizumi reforms concerning regional policy will also be on the agenda of the present and future governments of Japan, or if the new policy stance will soon be replaced by the customary patronage of the countryside, including pork-barrel spending, which prevailed up to the late 1990s. However, the future of the reforms is still a matter of political arbitration and it is still too early to make a final judgement.

If possible negative effects stemming from prolonged adherence to the growth paradigm are to be avoided, it will be paramount to convey to the public that an adjustment process is inevitable. If it were commonly accepted that responsible management of the shrinking process on municipal and regional scales could be the best option, this would lead to an enhanced likelihood of appropriate policy responses.

## References


*Asahi Shinbun* (7 May 2006): Hirogaru "toshi to chihō" no kakusa. Anata no sumu machi wa? [Widening disparities between metropolitan and non-metropolitan areas. What about the town where you live?], p. 9, morning edition.

—— (26 November 2006): Kore kara doko ni sumimasu ka. Jichitai o erabu jidai desu [Where are you going to live from now on? The age has come in which you can choose your place of residence], p. 9, morning edition.

Börsch-Supan, Axel (2004): Was bedeutet der demographische Wandel für die Wirtschaft Baden-Württembergs? In: *Mannheimer Forschungsinstitut Ökonomie und Demographischer Wandel* [Mannheim Research Institute for the Economics of Ageing], Discussion Paper 56–2004. http://www.mea.uni-mannheim.de/mea_neu/pages/files/nopage_pubs/t7yoakcvicon8w7_dp56–2004.pdf (found 18 December 2006).

DeWit, Andrew and Yukiko Yamazaki (2004): Flawed Political Economy of Decentralization. In: *Japan Focus*. http://japanfocus.org/article.asp?id=166 (found 22 June 2006).

Esaki, Yūji (2006): *Shutoken jinkō no shōraizō. Toshin to kōgai no jinkō chirigaku* [A vision of the future for the population of the national capital region. Population geography of the inner city area and the suburbs of Tokyo]. Tokyo: Senshū Daigaku Shuppan-kyoku.

Grömling, Michael (2005): Wirtschaftswachstum. In: Institut der deutschen Wirtschaft Köln [Cologne Institute for Economic Research] (ed.): *Perspektive 2050. Ökonomik des demographischen Wandels.* Cologne: Deutscher Instituts-Verlag (2nd revised edition), pp. 67–96.

IPSS (National Institute of Population and Social Security Research) (ed.) (2004): *Nihon no shikuchōson-betsu shōrai suikei jinkō. Heisei 12 (2000) ~ 42 (2030) nen* [Population projections for Japan by municipality. 2000–2030]. (= Jinkō mondai kenkyū shiryō [Research materials on population issues] 310). Tokyo: National Institute of Population and Social Security Research.

KTKK (Kaso Taisaku Kenkyū-kai) (ed.) (2006): *Kaso taisaku dētabukku. Heisei 16 nendo kaso taisaku no genkyō* [Statistical compendium on measures for underpopulated areas. Present situation of measures for underpopulated areas 2004]. Tokyo: Marui Kōbunsha.

Kaufmann, Franz-Xaver (2005): *Schrumpfende Gesellschaft. Vom Bevölkerungsrückgang und seinen Folgen.* Frankfurt/Main: Suhrkamp.

KSCKK (Keizai Sangyō-shō, Chiiki Keizai Kenkyū-kai) (2006a): *Chiiki keizai no shōrai suikei ni tsuite* [On estimation methods for regional economies]. www.meti.go.jp/press/20051202004/4-sannkou2-set.pdf (found 8 May 2006).

—— (2006b): *Jinkō genshō ka ni okeru chiiki keiei ni tsuite—2030 nen no chiiki keizai no shimyurēshon* [On the management of regions with regard to population decline]. www.meti.go.jp/press/20051202004/2-honnbunn-set.pdf (found 8 May 2006).

Lützeler, Ralph (2004): Demography. In: Kreiner, Josef, Ulrich Möhwald und Hans Dieter Ölschleger (Hg.): *Modern Japanese Society* (= Handbook of Oriental Studies/

Handbuch der Orientalistik; Section 5, Japan, Vol. 9). Leiden and Boston: Brill, pp. 15–61.
Matsubara, Hiroshi (2006): Shōshi kōrei-ka jidai no chiiki saihen [Regional reorganization in the age of population ageing]. In: *Keizai Chirigaku Nenpō* 52, 4, pp. 1–17.
Matsutani, Akihiko (2004a): Jinkō genshō ka no Nihon keizai, chiiki keizai [Japan's national and regional economy with regard to population decline]. In: *Chiginkyō Geppō* 10, pp. 2–15.
—— (2004b): *"Jinkō genshō keizai" no atarashii kōshiki* [The new formula for an economy with a shrinking population]. Tokyo: Nihon Keizai Shinbunsha.
—— (2006): *Shrinking-Population Economics. Lessons from Japan* (Japanese title: *"Jinkō genshō keizai" no atarashii kōshiki*). Tokyo: International House of Japan.
MLITCRDB (Ministry of Land, Infrastructure and Transport, City and Regional Development Bureau) (2005a): *Toshi/chiiki repōto 2005* [Report on Cities and Regions 2005]. Tokyo: Ministry of Land, Infrastructure and Transport.
—— (2005b): *Toshi/chiiki repōto 2005 (gaiyō)* [Report on Cities and Regions 2005 (overview)]. http://www.mlit.go.jp/kisha/kisha05/04/040726/01.pdf (found 10 October 2006).
Motani, Kōsuke (2006): Ikinokoru machi, kieru machi [Surviving towns, dying towns]. In: *Chūō Kōron* 6, pp. 72–83.
*Nihon Keizai Shinbun* (22 May 2006): Toshi-ken no 9-wari jinkō-gen [Population losses in 90 per cent of urban areas], p. 1, morning edition.
OCPRCS (Office of the Cabinet Public Relations, Cabinet Secretariat) (2004): *General Policy Speech by Prime Minister Jun'ichiro Koizumi to the 159th Session of the Diet* (Provisional Translation). www.kantei.go.jp/foreign/koizumispeech/2004/01/19sisei_e.html (found 23 June 2006).
Röhl, Klaus-Heiner (2005): Räumliche Entwicklung. In: Institut der deutschen Wirtschaft Köln [Cologne Institute for Economic Research] (ed.): *Perspektive 2050. Ökonomik des demographischen Wandels*. Cologne: Deutscher Instituts-Verlag (2nd revised edition), pp. 321–344.
Suzuki, Hitoshi and Yutaka Harada (2006): *Jinkō genshō to chiiki keizai* [Population decline and regional economy]. Daiwa Institute of Research. http://www.dir.co.jp/research/report/capital-mkt/capmkt/06051002capmkt.pdf (found 12 January 2007).
Yoshida, Yoshio (2005): Shōshi-ka ni tomonau chiiki shakai no shomondai [The problems fertility decline brings for regional communities]. In: Ōbuchi, Hiroshi and Hiroyuki Kanekiyo (eds.): *Shōshi-ka no shakai keizaigaku* [Socioeconomics of fertility decline] (= Jinkōgaku Raiburarī 2). Tokyo: Hara Shobō, pp. 133–151.

CHAPTER FORTY-EIGHT

# A SURVEY OF HOUSEHOLD SAVING BEHAVIOUR[1]

Charles Yuji Horioka

## 1. Introduction

It is often claimed that the Japanese are big savers and that they save a lot because it is part of their national character to do so and/or because of the influence of Confucian teachings, which regard frugality as a virtue. In this paper, I examine (1) whether or not the Japanese really do save a lot and whether or not they have always saved a lot, (2) why the Japanese save a lot (if indeed they do), and (3) whether or not we can expect the Japanese to continue saving a lot in the future as well.

The organization of the paper is as follows: In section 2, I present data on trends over time in Japan's household saving rate and on household saving rates in international perspective; in section 3, I consider the reasons for Japan's high household saving rate; in section 4, I consider the reasons for the recent decline in Japan's high household saving rate; in section 5, I project future trends in Japan's household saving rate; in section 6, I consider the implications of my findings; and section 7 is a brief concluding section.

To preview my main findings, I find, first, that Japan's high household saving rate was a temporary phenomenon and that it was high in both absolute and relative terms during the 1955–95 period (especially during the 1960s and 1970s) but that it was not unusually high during the pre-war and early post-war periods or after 1995; second, that Japan's temporarily high household saving rate was due not to culture but to temporary economic, demographic, and institutional factors such as the high growth rate of income, the low level of household wealth holdings, the unavailability of consumer credit, the young age structure

[1] I am grateful to Harald Conrad, Fumio Ohtake, Masaru Sasaki, and Midori Wakabayashi for their valuable comments and assistance.

of the population, the bonus system of compensation, tax breaks for saving, the low level of public pension benefits, and saving promotion activities; third, that the decline in Japan's household saving rate since the mid-1970s is due to the weakening of these factors and that Japan's household saving rate can be expected to decline even further as these factors become even less applicable and that the rapid ageing of Japan's population has played the most important role; and fourth, that there is nothing to worry about even if Japan's household saving rate falls to zero or even negative levels because the other sectors of the economy will at least partly take up the slack, because investment can also be expected to decline, and because Japan always has the option of borrowing from abroad.

## 2. Do (Did) the Japanese Really Save a Lot?

In this section, I present data on trends over time in Japan's household saving rates and on household saving rates in international perspective in order to shed light on whether Japan's household saving rate is high in absolute and/or relative terms. I present data on net saving (saving net of depreciation on fixed capital) because it is net saving that leads to an increase in wealth or assets and is thus the more meaningful concept.

### 2.1. *Trends over time in Japan's household saving rate*

I look first at trends over the past century in Japan's household saving rate. As I have shown in Horioka (1993a), Japan's household saving rate was volatile during the pre-war, wartime, and early post-war periods. It was low, sometimes even negative, during about half of the years in this period (1907–15, 1921–30, and 1946–49) but was high and generally in the double digits during the other years (1906, 1916–20, 1931–44, and 1950–54). In fact, it exceeded 30 or even 40 per cent at the height of World War II (1941–44), but during the war years, goods were scarce or rationed and the state encouraged and often forced people to save. If we exclude the war years (1937–45), Japan's household saving rate was low, on average, during both the pre-war and early post-war periods, averaging only 4.3 per cent during the pre-war period (1906–1936) according to the Long-Term Economic Statistics and only 5.6 per cent during the early post-war period (1945–54) according to the former System of National Accounts (hereafter SNA).[2]

Turning to the post-1955 period, a continuous time series is unfortunately not available for the entire post-1955 period. The Japanese government switched from the 1968 United Nations SNA to the 1993 United Nations SNA in 2000, and thus data based on the 1968 SNA are available only for the 1955–1998 period whereas data based on the 1993 SNA are available only since 1980.[3] Two further complications are that the 1995 benchmark revision was implemented at the same time as the conversion to the 1993 SNA and that the 2000 benchmark revision was implemented in 2005. As a result, there are three different data series for the 1955–2004 period, with data based on the 1968 SNA (1990 benchmark revision) being available only for the 1955–1998 period, data based on the 1993 SNA (1995 benchmark revision) being available only for the 1980–2003 period, and data based on the 1993 SNA (2000 benchmark revision) being available only for the 1996–2004 period.

In the case of the 1993 SNA, I present data on the adjusted household saving rate because it includes social transfers in kind (i.e., social benefits in kind and transfers of individual non-market goods and services from the government and from private non-profit institutions serving households) in both the numerator and the denominator and hence is the correct theoretical concept and because it is consistent with the household saving rate based on the 1968 SNA.

Figure 1 and Table 1 show data on all three series for the 1955–2004 period, and as can be seen from this figure and table, Japan's household saving rate showed a steady upward trend from the mid-1950s until the mid-1970s, increasing from 11.9 per cent in 1955 to a phenomenal level

---

[2] However, Japan's household saving rate was high (in excess of 15 per cent) during the 1935–37 period according to the former System of National Accounts.

[3] A detailed discussion of the conceptual differences between the 1968 SNA and the 1993 SNA is beyond the scope of this paper, but the main difference between the two lies in their treatment of bad loans. Under the 1968 SNA, write-offs of bad loans to households and unincorporated businesses are treated as a current transfer from financial institutions to households. Thus, bad loan write-offs increase the incomes of households, and because their consumption does not change, their measured saving increases. By contrast, the 1993 SNA treats write-offs of bad loans to households and unincorporated businesses as a decline in the asset holdings of financial institutions, and thus they do not affect the saving rate of households.

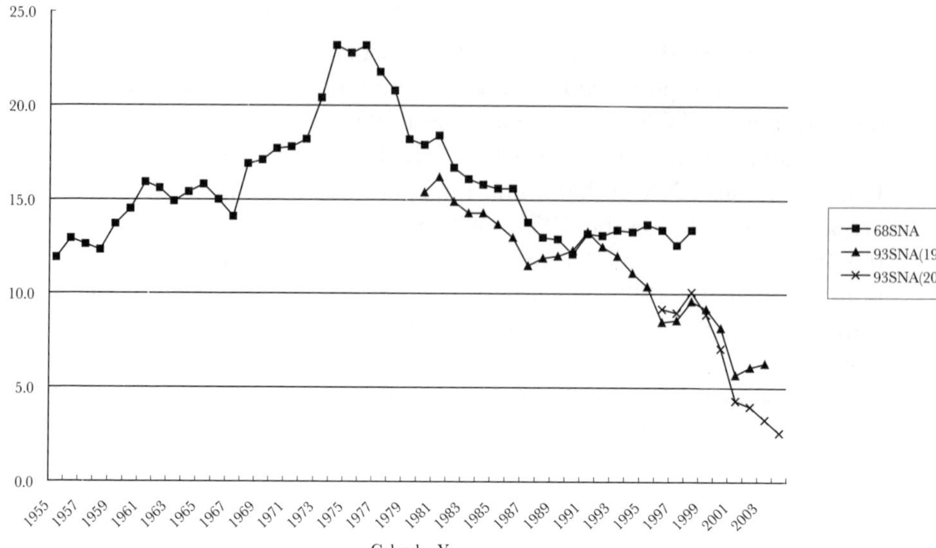


Notes: The line marked "68SNA" shows data based on the 1968 United Nations System of National Accounts, whereas the line marked "93SNA" shows data based on the 1993 United Nations System of National Accounts. The 68SNA figures show the net household saving rate, while the 93SNA figures show the adjusted net household saving rate.
Source: Department of National Accounts, Economic and Social Research Institute, Cabinet Office, Government of Japan, ed., *Annual Report on National Accounts*, 2006 edition (Tokyo: Mediarando Kabushiki Kaisha, 2006), and the 2004 and 2005 editions of the same.

Figure 1. Trends in Japan's net household saving rate (1955–2004).

Table 1. Trend in Japan's net household saving rate (1955–2004).

| | SNA68 | SNA93 | |
|---|---|---|---|
| Calendar Year | 1990 Benchmark Revision | 1995 Benchmark Revision | 2000 Benchmark Revision |
| 1955 | 11.9 | | |
| 1956 | 12.9 | | |
| 1957 | 12.6 | | |
| 1958 | 12.3 | | |
| 1959 | 13.7 | | |
| 1960 | 14.5 | | |
| 1961 | 15.9 | | |
| 1962 | 15.6 | | |
| 1963 | 14.9 | | |
| 1964 | 15.4 | | |
| 1965 | 15.8 | | |
| 1966 | 15.0 | | |

Table 1 (*cont.*)

| Calendar Year | 1990 Benchmark Revision | 1995 Benchmark Revision | 2000 Benchmark Revision |
|---|---|---|---|
| 1967 | 14.1 | | |
| 1968 | 16.9 | | |
| 1969 | 17.1 | | |
| 1970 | 17.7 | | |
| 1971 | 17.8 | | |
| 1972 | 18.2 | | |
| 1973 | 20.4 | | |
| 1974 | 23.2 | | |
| 1975 | 22.8 | | |
| 1976 | 23.2 | | |
| 1977 | 21.8 | | |
| 1978 | 20.8 | | |
| 1979 | 18.2 | | |
| 1980 | 17.9 | 15.4 | |
| 1981 | 18.4 | 16.2 | |
| 1982 | 16.7 | 14.9 | |
| 1983 | 16.1 | 14.3 | |
| 1984 | 15.8 | 14.3 | |
| 1985 | 15.6 | 13.7 | |
| 1986 | 15.6 | 13.0 | |
| 1987 | 13.8 | 11.5 | |
| 1988 | 13.0 | 11.9 | |
| 1989 | 12.9 | 12.0 | |
| 1990 | 12.1 | 12.3 | |
| 1991 | 13.2 | 13.3 | |
| 1992 | 13.1 | 12.5 | |
| 1993 | 13.4 | 12.0 | |
| 1994 | 13.3 | 11.1 | |
| 1995 | 13.7 | 10.4 | |
| 1996 | 13.4 | 8.5 | 9.2 |
| 1997 | 12.6 | 8.6 | 9.0 |
| 1998 | 13.4 | 9.6 | 10.1 |
| 1999 | | 9.2 | 8.9 |
| 2000 | | 8.2 | 7.1 |
| 2001 | | 5.7 | 4.3 |
| 2002 | | 6.1 | 4.0 |
| 2003 | | 6.3 | 3.3 |
| 2004 | | | 2.6 |

Notes: SNA68 denotes the 1968 United Nations System of National Accounts, while SNA93 denotes the 1993 United Nations System of National Accounts. The SNA68 figures show the net household saving rate, while the SNA93 figures show the adjusted net household saving rate.
Source: Department of National Accounts, Economic and Social Research Institute, Cabinet Office, Government of Japan, ed., *Annual Report on National Accounts*, 2006 edition (Tokyo: Mediarando Kabushiki Kaisha, 2006), and the 2004 and 2005 editions of the same.

of 23.2 per cent in 1974 and 1976, but has shown a downward trend since then, falling to the 2 to 3 per cent level in recent years.

If we give precedence to data based on the 1993 SNA whenever possible, Japan's household saving rate exceeded 20 per cent only during the six-year period from 1973 until 1978, exceeded 15 per cent only during the 21-year period from 1961 until 1981, and exceeded 10 per cent only during the 41-year period from 1955 until 1995.

To sum up, Japan's household saving rate was not always high. It was high during much of the post-war period (especially during the 1960s and 1970s), but it was not necessarily high during the pre-war and early post-war periods and has by no means been high in recent years.

### 2.2. *International comparison of household saving rates*

I turn now to an international comparison of household saving rates. Horioka (1989: Table 1) shows data on household saving rates for the 1975–84 period for the sixteen Organization for Economic Cooperation and Development (OECD) member countries for which data are available, while Table 2 shows data on household saving rates for the 1985–2005 period for the 23 OECD member countries for which data are available. Data are available only on gross household saving rates for five of these countries, but since net household saving rates are, on average, about 70 per cent of gross household saving rates, the figures on the gross household saving rate were converted to a net basis using this conversion factor in the case of the five countries for which only gross data are available.

As can be seen from Horioka (1989: Table 1) and Table 2, Japan's household saving rate was one of the highest among the OECD member countries during the 1975–85 period. It ranked first in 1975, was second only to Italy in 1980 and 1985, and was 1.79, 1.61, and 1.81 times the OECD average in 1975, 1980, and 1985, respectively. However, Japan's rank among the OECD member countries as well as the ratio of her household saving rate to the OECD average both fell steadily during the subsequent twenty years. For example, by 1990, Japan had fallen to fourth place (tie) and her household saving rate had fallen to 1.43 times the OECD average. By 1995, Japan had fallen further to seventh place, and her household saving rate had fallen further to 1.25 times the OECD average. By 2000, Japan had fallen further to tenth place although her household saving rate rose slightly to 1.32 times the OECD average. Finally, by 2005, Japan had fallen further to 17th

Table 2. Net household saving rate of selected OECD countries (1985–2005).

| | 1985 | | 1990 | | 1995 | | 2000 | | 2005 | |
|---|---|---|---|---|---|---|---|---|---|---|
| Australia | 10.8 | 7 | 8.5 | 12 | 6.7 | 18 | 2.8 | 19 | −2.6 | 22 |
| Austria | 10.5 | 8 | 13.3 | 6 | 10.9 | 11 | 8.4 | 8T | 9.5 | 6T |
| *Belgium | 11.1 | 6 | 9.2 | 11 | 13.2 | 5 | 9.8 | 5 | 7.8 | 10 |
| Canada | 15.8 | 3 | 13.0 | 7 | 9.2 | 13 | 4.7 | 15 | −0.2 | 18 |
| Czech Rep. | na | | na | | 9.0 | 14 | 3.6 | 16 | 3.3 | 16 |
| *Denmark | na | | 1.3 | 19 | 0.9 | 22 | −1.3 | 21T | −0.6 | 21 |
| Finland | 3.4 | 14 | 3.6 | 16 | 4.7 | 19 | −1.3 | 21T | −0.5 | 20 |
| France | 8.9 | 10 | 9.3 | 10 | 12.7 | 6 | 11.4 | 3 | 11.6 | 3 |
| Germany | 12.1 | 5 | 13.9 | 4T | 11.0 | 10 | 9.2 | 7 | 10.7 | 4 |
| Hungary | na | | na | | 15.6 | 3 | 16.0 | 1 | 17.7 | 1 |
| Ireland | na | | 6.1 | 13 | 8.5 | 16 | 9.6 | 6 | 10.9 | 5 |
| Italy | 21.5 | 1 | 23.8 | 1 | 17.7 | 1 | 8.4 | 8T | 9.5 | 6T |
| Japan | 16.5 | 2 | 13.9 | 4T | 11.9 | 7 | 8.3 | 10 | 2.4 | 17 |
| South Korea | 14.8 | 4 | 22.5 | 2 | 17.5 | 2 | 10.7 | 4 | 4.3 | 14 |
| Netherlands | 5.6 | 13 | 17.7 | 3 | 14.6 | 4 | 7.0 | 12T | 5.7 | 13 |
| New Zealand | 1.3 | 16 | 0.7 | 20 | −3.8 | 23 | −4.1 | 23 | −7.1 | 23 |
| Norway | −3.3 | 17 | 2.2 | 18 | 4.6 | 20T | 5.2 | 14 | 11.8 | 2 |
| *Portugal | na | | na | | 10.1 | 12 | 7.0 | 12T | 6.9 | 12 |
| * Spain | 7.8 | 11 | 9.8 | 8 | 11.5 | 9 | 7.8 | 11 | 7.3 | 11 |
| Sweden | 2.2 | 15 | 3.2 | 17 | 9.1 | 15 | 3.2 | 18 | 7.9 | 9 |
| Switzerland | na | | 9.6 | 9 | 11.6 | 8 | 11.8 | 2 | 8.8 | 8 |
| *United Kingdom | 6.9 | 12 | 5.6 | 15 | 7.0 | 17 | 3.5 | 17 | 3.5 | 15 |
| United States | 9.2 | 9 | 7.0 | 14 | 4.6 | 20T | 2.3 | 20 | −0.4 | 19 |
| OECD Mean | 9.1 | | 9.7 | | 9.5 | | 6.3 | | 5.6 | |

Notes: The left-hand figures denote the household saving rate, defined as household saving as a ratio of disposable household income, while the right-hand figures denote the rank of each country. "na" denotes "not available," while "T" denotes "tie." The first figure for New Zealand is the figure for 1986 because the figure for 1985 was not available. The figures include the saving of households as well as that of non-profit institutions except in the case of the Czech Republic, Finland, France, Japan, and New Zealand. For countries marked by an asterisk, only figures on gross household saving rates were available, and the gross figures were converted to a net basis by using a conversion factor of 0.7 (which is the approximate ratio of the average net household saving rate to the average gross household saving rate for the countries and years used in the present analysis). In the case of Italy and Sweden, the figures for 1985 were computed from figures on the gross household saving rate.
Source: For 1985 data, *OECD Economic Outlook*, vol. 2003/1, no. 73 (June 2003), Annex Table 24; for 1990, 1995, 2000, and 2005 data, the same source, vol. 2006/1, no. 79 (June 2006), Annex Table 23 (in the case of Hungary and New Zealand, the same source, vol. 2004/2, no. 76 (Dec. 2004), and in the case of Ireland, the same source, vol. 2005/2, no. 78 (Dec. 2005), Annex Table 23).

place and her household saving rate had fallen to only 43 per cent of the OECD average.

Thus, Japan's household saving rate was formerly high not only in absolute terms but also relative to the other developed countries and was at one point the highest in the developed world, but it has since fallen not only in absolute terms but also relative to the other developed countries and is no longer high by any standard.

What is especially striking is that Japan's relative ranking fell sharply during the 1985–2005 period even though 17 of the 23 OECD member countries for which data are available as well as the OECD average showed downward trends during the same period (with the OECD average falling to only 62 per cent of its 1985 level by 2005). This is because Japan's household saving rate declined even more sharply than that of the other OECD member countries.

Incidentally, what OECD member countries have shown the highest household saving rates? Japan occupied the number one position in 1975; Italy occupied the number one position in 1980, 1985, 1990, and 1995; and Hungary occupied the number one position in 2000 and 2005. Moreover, these countries have ranked relatively high in other years as well (except for Japan in 2005). France, Germany, South Korea, and Switzerland have also shown relatively high household saving rates (except for South Korea in 2005). By contrast, the Scandinavian countries (Denmark, Finland, Norway, and Sweden), the Czech Republic, New Zealand, the United Kingdom, and the United States have shown relatively low household saving rates (except for Norway in 2005). Thus, the rank ordering of the OECD member countries has been relatively stable over time.

An exploration of the reasons for these inter-country differences in household saving rates is beyond the scope of this paper, but many of the countries with low household saving rates have generous social insurance systems, and thus households in these countries may not feel the need to save for retirement and/or for precautionary purposes.

Note, however, that these inter-country differences in household saving rates have not necessarily been stable over time. For example, the relative positions of Australia and Canada fell as much as that of Japan during the 1985–2005 period (from seventh place to 22nd place and from third place to 18th place, respectively), and Finland, South Korea, New Zealand, and the United States also showed sharp declines in their relative positions. By contrast, Norway showed a sharp increase in its relative position (from 17th place in 1985 to second place in 2005), and France, Ireland, and Sweden also showed substantial increases. An interesting case is that of the Netherlands, whose rank increased sharply from 13th place in 1985 to third place in 1990 before falling back down to 13th place in 2005.

The fact that inter-country differences in household saving rates are relatively stable but sometimes show sharp variations over time suggests that these differences are due partly to long-term factors and partly to short-term factors.

To sum up, Japan's household saving rate was high in both absolute and relative terms during the 1955–95 period (especially during the 1960s and the 1970s) but has declined in both absolute and relative terms since the mid-1970s and is no longer high by any standard.

## 3. Why Did the Japanese Save So Much?

In the previous section, we found that the Japanese saved a lot during the 1955–95 period (especially during the 1960s and 1970s) but not before or after. In this section, we consider the reasons why the Japanese saved so much during this period.

### 3.1. *The impact of culture*

One oft-heard hypothesis is that Japan's household saving rate has been high for cultural and/or religious reasons. One variant of this hypothesis is that it is part of the national character of the Japanese to save a lot, and another variant is that the Japanese save a lot because of the influence of Confucian teachings, which regard frugality as a virtue. In this subsection, I consider how much explanatory power this hypothesis has.

First, if Japan's household saving rate was high for cultural reasons, it should always have been high because culture is presumably relatively invariant over time. As we saw in section 2, however, Japan's household saving rate was high primarily during the 1955–95 period (especially during the 1960s and 1970s) and was not unusually high during the pre-war and early post-war periods or after 1995.

Second, since culture presumably weakens over time as better transportation and communication systems facilitate the influx of foreign influences, we would expect Japan's household saving rate to show a downward trend over time if culture is an important determinant thereof. However, as we saw in section 2, Japan's household saving rate did not show any clear trend during the pre-war period and showed a clear *upward* trend during the early post-war period (until the mid-1970s) although it has shown a downward trend since the mid-1970s.

These two pieces of evidence strongly suggest that culture is not an important explanation of why Japan's household saving rate was high during much of the post-war period.

### 3.2. *The impact of economic, demographic, and institutional factors*

What then can explain why Japan's household saving rate has been high during much of the post-war period? My hypothesis is that Japan's household saving rate was high during the 1955–95 period (especially during the 1960s and 1970s) because of various temporary economic, demographic, and institutional factors that were applicable during this period. Horioka (1990) lists more than thirty such factors, and Hayashi (1986, 1997) and Horioka (1993b, 2006a) are also useful summaries of the literature on household saving behaviour in Japan. Here, I examine what I consider to be the eight most important explanations of why Japan's high household saving rate was high during the 1955–95 period (especially during the 1960s and 1970s).

(1) The High Growth Rate of Income: The high growth rate of income during the high-growth era from the 1950s to the early 1970s undoubtedly helped raise Japan's household saving rate. When income grows rapidly and/or unexpectedly, households often cannot adjust their living standards and consumption patterns at the same pace, and as a result, saving (the difference between income and consumption) tends to increase, at least temporarily.

(2) The Low Level of Household Wealth Holdings: Household wealth holdings were very low in Japan just after the Second World War because the war destroyed much of Japan's housing stock and the post-war hyperinflation reduced the real value of financial assets. Japanese households presumably saved as much as they did in part to restore their wealth holdings to desired levels.

(3) The Unavailability of Consumer Credit: Consumer credit was not readily available in Japan until recently, and thus Japanese households found it necessary to save in advance of purchases of such big-ticket items as housing, automobiles, furniture, and electrical appliances. Moreover, the paucity of credit also increased the need for precautionary saving because Japanese households knew that they would not be able to borrow in times of emergency.

Table 3. Share of the aged population in selected OECD countries (1975–2025).

| Country | 1975 | | 2000 | | 2025 | |
|---|---|---|---|---|---|---|
| Australia | 8.7 | 19T | 12.3 | 19T | 18.6 | 19 |
| Austria | 14.9 | 2 | 15.6 | 10T | 24.3 | 7 |
| Belgium | 13.9 | 5 | 17.0 | 4T | 23.7 | 8 |
| Canada | 8.5 | 21 | 12.6 | 18 | 20.7 | 17T |
| Czech Rep. | 12.9 | 9 | 13.8 | 16 | 23.1 | 10 |
| Denmark | 13.4 | 8 | 15.0 | 13 | 22.5 | 11 |
| Finland | 10.6 | 15 | 14.9 | 14 | 25.2 | 5 |
| France | 13.5 | 7 | 16.0 | 7T | 22.2 | 12 |
| Germany | 14.8 | 3 | 16.4 | 6 | 24.6 | 6 |
| Hungary | 12.6 | 10T | 14.6 | 15 | 21.2 | 16 |
| Ireland | 11.0 | 13 | 11.3 | 22 | 16.3 | 23 |
| Italy | 12.0 | 12 | 18.1 | 1 | 25.7 | 3 |
| Japan | 7.9 | 22 | 17.2 | 3 | 28.9 | 1 |
| South Korea | 3.6 | 23 | 7.1 | 23 | 16.9 | 22 |
| Netherlands | 10.8 | 14 | 13.6 | 17 | 21.9 | 13T |
| New Zealand | 8.7 | 19T | 11.7 | 21 | 18.5 | 20T |
| Norway | 13.7 | 6 | 15.4 | 12 | 21.8 | 15 |
| Portugal | 9.9 | 18 | 15.6 | 10T | 20.7 | 17T |
| Spain | 10.0 | 17 | 17.0 | 4T | 23.6 | 9 |
| Sweden | 15.1 | 1 | 17.4 | 2 | 25.4 | 4 |
| Switzerland | 12.6 | 10T | 16.0 | 7T | 27.1 | 2 |
| United Kingdom | 14.0 | 4 | 15.8 | 9 | 21.9 | 13T |
| United States | 10.5 | 16 | 12.3 | 19T | 18.5 | 20T |
| OECD Mean | 12.6 | | 16.0 | | 24.4 | |

Notes: The left-hand figures denote the share of the population aged 65 or older to the total population, while the right-hand figures denote the rank of each country. "na" denotes "not available," while "T" denotes "tie."
Source: United Nations, *World Population Ageing, 1950–2050* (New York: United Nations, 2002).

(4) The Young Age Structure of the Population: The age structure of Japan's population was one of the youngest among the industrialized countries until recently. As Table 3 shows, in 1975, the share of the elderly (those aged 65 or older) in Japan's total population was only 7.9 per cent, which was the lowest among the OECD member countries at the time (this ratio was 3.6 per cent in South Korea in 1975, but South Korea was not yet an OECD member country at the time). According to the life cycle hypothesis, the aggregate household saving rate will be higher in a country with a young population because the young typically work and save, whereas the elderly typically retire from work and dissave, and thus the young age structure of Japan's population

can help explain her high household saving rate in the past (see, for example, Modigliani and Brumberg 1955). Indeed, Horioka (1989) finds that the low ratio of the aged population to the working-age population was by far the most important cause of Japan's high private saving rate during the 1975–84 period, and the same undoubtedly holds for her household saving rate.

(5) The Bonus System of Compensation: Japan's bonus system of compensation, whereby a large chunk of employee compensation is paid in the form of semi-annual lump-sum bonuses, is often said to have encouraged, or at least facilitated, saving (see, for example, Ishikawa and Ueda 1984).

(6) Tax Breaks for Saving: The Japanese government introduced many tax breaks for saving such as the *maruyū* system (tax-exempt system for small savings) whereby the interest income on bank and postal deposits and on government bonds was tax-exempt, up to a limit), and these tax breaks for saving may have induced Japanese households to save more than they would have otherwise.

(7) The Low Level of Public Pension Benefits: Public old-age pension benefits were relatively low in Japan until 1973. This made it necessary for Japanese households to save on their own to prepare for their life after retirement.

(8) Saving Promotion Activities: The Japanese government and the quasi-governmental Central Council for Savings Promotion engaged in a variety of saving promotion activities such as the preparation and distribution of magazines, statistical handbooks, booklets, leaflets, posters, films, household financial ledgers, and money boxes, the appointment of private citizens as saving promotion leaders, etc., during much of the post-war period, and Garon (1997: Chapter 5) has argued that these saving promotion activities helped to raise Japan's household saving rate.

## 4. Why Don't the Japanese Save As Much Now?

In the previous section, I discussed why Japan's household saving rate was so high in the past, but in this section, I discuss why Japan's household saving rate has shown a downward trend since the mid-1970s. My thesis is that Japan's household saving rate has declined since the mid-1970s because the factors that caused Japan's household saving rate to be high until the mid-1970s gradually became less applicable after the mid-1970s.

(1) Double-digit rates of economic growth ended in the early 1970s, and income growth rates have been low in recent years, especially in the 1990s.

(2) The wealth holdings of Japanese households increased rapidly as a result of their high saving rates, and by 1990, the ratio of household wealth holdings to household disposable income in Japan was by far the highest among the Group of 7 (G7) countries (Canada, France, Germany, Italy, Japan, the United States, and the United Kingdom) (see Horioka 2006a: Table 5.3).[4]

(3) Consumer credit has become more and more available over time, and by 1990, the ratio of household liabilities outstanding to household disposable income in Japan was by far the highest among the G7 countries (see Horioka 2006a: Table 5.3).

(4) Japan's population is ageing at an unprecedented rate, with the share of the population aged 65 or older to the total population rising from 7.9 per cent (lowest among the OECD member countries at the time) in 1975 to 17.2 per cent (third place among the OECD member countries) in 2000 (see Table 3).

(5) According to the Basic Survey on Wage Structure (*Chingin Kōzō Kihon Tōkei Chōsa*), conducted annually by the Ministry of Health, Labour and Welfare, there has been a long-term decline in the ratio of bonus income to regular employee compensation since 1975: the ratio of "average annual special cash earnings" to "average monthly scheduled cash earnings" showed an upward trend until 1975, peaking at 3.92, but has shown a downward trend since then (except for a temporary increase during the 1979–92 period when economic conditions were favourable), falling to 3.00 by 2005.

(6) Most tax breaks for saving including the aforementioned *maruyū* system were abolished (except for the elderly) in 1988.

(7) Public old-age pension benefits were dramatically improved in 1973, and a public long-term care insurance program was introduced in 2000.

(8) Government saving promotion activities have been scaled back, and the Central Council for Savings Promotion was renamed the Central Council for Savings Information in 1987 (and renamed the Central Council for Financial Services Information in 2001), gradually shifting

[4] The sharp decline in land and equity prices during the 1990s led to a temporary reversal in the increase in the level of household wealth holdings, but both land and equity prices seem to have bottomed out.

from the active encouragement of saving to providing consumers with information on the array of financial services available and helping them with life planning.

Moreover, I concluded earlier that culture was not an important determinant of Japan's high household saving rate, but to the extent that it is important, it can help explain the decline in Japan's household saving rate since culture presumably weakens over time due to the increasing influx of foreign influences.

Thus, virtually all of the factors that caused Japan's household saving rate to be high have weakened over time, and this can explain why Japan's household saving rate has declined so sharply since the mid-1970s.

## 5. How Much Will the Japanese Save in the Future?

In this section, I speculate about future trends in Japan's household saving rate. In my opinion, the most important factor determining future trends in Japan's household saving rate will be the rapid ageing of her population. Japan's population is ageing at the fastest rate in human history and has already become the most aged in the world. As Table 3 shows, the share of the population aged 65 or older to the total population in Japan is projected to increase from 17.2 per cent in 2000 to 28.9 per cent in 2025, rising from third to first place among the OECD member countries. This will cause her household saving rate to continue its rapid decline if the life-cycle hypothesis, which assumes that the elderly finance their living expenses during retirement by drawing down their previously accumulated savings, is valid, and Horioka (1993b, 2002, and 2006b) argues that it is. Indeed, a number of authors, myself included, have projected that the rapid ageing of Japan's population will cause Japan's household saving rate to decline to zero or even negative levels by around 2010 (see Horioka 1989; Horioka 1991; and for a useful survey Horioka 1992).

I should note, however, that the discussion thus far has focused exclusively on the impact of the ageing of the population on the household saving rate. The other factors that caused Japan's household saving rate to be high during most of the post-war period will continue weakening, and this will cause Japan's household saving rate to decline even more sharply.

For example, the growth rate of income can be expected to recover somewhat as the economy recovers but is very unlikely to return to the levels of the high-growth period; the level of household wealth holdings can be expected to resume its increase as land and equity prices stabilize and/or recover; the ratio of bonus income to regular employee compensation shows no signs of recovering; the special tax breaks on capital gains on stock sales and dividend income, which were introduced in 2003, are scheduled to be abolished shortly; saving promotion activities have already been discontinued; and the impact of culture can be expected to continue weakening due to the continued influx of foreign influences.

The primary exceptions are uncertainty about the future of the public pension system and changes in the lending law. The rapid ageing of the population, combined with the pay-as-you-go nature of the public pension system, is causing the finances of the system to deteriorate, which in turn is necessitating cuts in benefits, increases in contribution rates, and considerable uncertainty about the future of the system. This is likely to cause Japanese households to save more for life during retirement, thereby putting upward pressure on Japan's household saving rate.

In addition, the lending law was revised in December 2006, and as part of this revision, the ceiling on the lending rate for unsecured consumer loans was reduced and a limit was imposed on loan amounts. It has been projected that this will cause the outstanding loans of consumer finance companies to be halved, and the reduced availability of consumer loans may cause households to spend less and save more.

In my opinion, however, the factors putting downward pressure on Japan's household saving rate far exceed the factors putting upward pressure thereon, and thus there is no doubt that Japan's household saving rate will continue to decline sharply in the coming years.

## 6. Policy Implications

In this section, I present the policy implications of my finding that Japan's household saving rate was high during much of the post-war period but that it has been falling since the mid-1970s and is projected to continue declining in the future as well.

First, however, I would like to step back and consider the role that saving plays in the economy as a whole. Saving is indispensable in any economy because it provides the funds for financing investment in plant and equipment, housing, social infrastructure, etc. Investment cannot be done without a corresponding amount of saving from somewhere—either from the same sector, from another sector of the same economy, or from abroad.

In the case of Japan, the household sector saved at high levels throughout most of the post-war period, and this abundant saving of the household sector was used in a variety of different ways. For example, during the high-growth period of the 1950s, 1960s, and early 1970s, household saving was used primarily to finance corporate investment in plant and equipment, and hence was instrumental in increasing the productive capacity of the economy and in achieving rapid economic growth. Since the 1970s, however, a considerable share of household saving has been used to finance investment in housing and social infrastructure, thereby contributing toward improving the quality of life of the Japanese people and toward facilitating economic growth. And since the 1980s, a considerable share of household saving has been lent abroad (either directly or indirectly via financial intermediaries), thereby helping to alleviate saving shortages in the United States and other countries but at the same time leading to enormous capital account deficits that had to be offset by correspondingly large trade and current account surpluses. Thus, Japan's abundant supply of household saving has played an important role throughout the post-war period, but the nature of its role has shifted over time.

Since the abundant supply of household saving in Japan has played such an important role in the past, one might be tempted to conclude that the sharp decline in Japan's household saving rate that began in the mid-1970s and that is projected to continue in the future as well will lead to a severe saving shortage, spelling disaster for the Japanese economy, if not the world economy. However, I do not share this view for the following reasons.

First, even if the household saving rate declines, the overall level of national saving in Japan will not decline if there is a corresponding increase in the saving of the other sectors of the economy such as the government and corporate sectors. The Japanese government is currently giving top priority to reconstructing its finances (reducing its fiscal deficits) by cutting expenditures and raising taxes, and assuming it succeeds, government saving will increase. Moreover, as the economy recovers, the profits of corporations will presumably increase, enabling them to retain more earnings, which count as corporate saving. Thus, it is likely that the saving of both the government and corporate sectors will increase in the coming years, thereby at least partially offsetting the decline in household saving.

Moreover, even if the overall level of national saving declines because the decline in household saving is not fully offset by increases in the saving of other sectors of the economy, a saving shortage will not necessarily emerge because investment may also decline. Japan's population has been declining since 2005, and a declining population means that there is less need to increase the productive capacity of the economy and hence less need for investment. And if the decline in investment demand is comparable to the decline in saving, no saving shortage will emerge.

Moreover, even if a saving shortage emerges because the decline in investment demand falls short of the decline in saving, this does not necessarily spell disaster either because Japan always has the option of borrowing from abroad. There are currently many countries with very high saving rates such as China, Hong Kong, Taiwan, and Singapore, and Japan should be able to borrow from these countries.

Thus, I conclude that the prolonged decline in Japan's household saving rate does not necessarily spell disaster for the Japanese economy.

## 7. Conclusions

This paper presented a variety of data on Japan's household saving rate and found that Japan's high household saving rate was a temporary phenomenon: Japan's household saving rate was high in both absolute and relative terms during the 1955–95 period (especially during the 1960s and 1970s) but it was not unusually high during the pre-war and early post-war periods or after 1995.

Moreover, this paper found that Japan's temporarily high household saving rate was due not to culture but to temporary economic, demographic, and institutional factors such as the high growth rate of income, the low level of household wealth holdings, the unavailability of consumer credit, the young age structure of the population, the bonus system of compensation, tax breaks for saving, the low level of public pension benefits, and saving promotion activities.

This paper then argued that the decline in Japan's household saving rate since the mid-1970s is due to the weakening of these factors and that Japan's household saving rate can be expected to decline even further as these factors become even less applicable and that the rapid ageing of Japan's population has played the most important role.

Finally, this paper considered the policy implications of my findings and concluded that there is nothing to worry about even if Japan's household saving rate falls to zero or even negative levels because the other sectors of the economy will at least partly take up the slack, because investment can also be expected to decline, and because Japan always has the option of borrowing from abroad.

## References

Garon, Sheldon (1997): *Molding Japanese Minds: The State in Everyday Life*. Princeton, N.J.: Princeton University Press.

Hayashi, Fumio (1986): Why Is Japan's Saving Rate So Apparently High? In: Fischer, Stanley (ed.): *NBER Macroeconomics Annual*. Cambridge, Massachusetts: MIT Press, vol. 1, pp. 147–210.

—— (1997): A Review of Recent Literature on Japanese Saving. In: Hayashi, Fumio: *Understanding Saving: Evidence from the United States and Japan*. Cambridge, Massachusetts: MIT Press, pp. 289–330.

Horioka, Charles Yuji (1989): Why Is Japan's Private Saving Rate So High? In: Sato, Ryuzo and Takashi Negishi (eds.): *Developments in Japanese Economics*. Tokyo: Academic Press/Harcourt Brace Jovanovich, Publishers, pp. 145–178.

—— (1990): Why Is Japan's Household Saving Rate So High? A Literature Survey. In: *Journal of the Japanese and International Economies* 4, 1 (March), pp. 49–92.

—— (1991): The Determinants of Japan's Saving Rate: The Impact of the Age Structure of the Population and Other Factors. In: *Economic Studies Quarterly* 42, 3 (September) [now called *Japanese Economic Review*], pp. 237–253.

—— (1992): Future Trends in Japan's Saving Rate and the Implications thereof for Japan's External Imbalance. In: *Japan and the World Economy* 3, 4 (April), pp. 307–330.

—— (1993a): Consuming and Saving. In: Gordon, Andrew (ed.): *Postwar Japan as History*. Berkeley, California: University of California Press, pp. 259–292.

—— (1993b): Saving in Japan. In: Heertje, Arnold (ed.): *World Savings: An International Survey*. Oxford, UK, and Cambridge, USA: Blackwell Publishers, pp. 238–278.

—— (1994): Japan's Consumption and Saving in International Perspective. In: *Economic Development and Cultural Change* 42, 2 (January), pp. 293–316.

—— (1995): Is Japan's Household Saving Rate Really High? In: *Review of Income and Wealth* 41, 4 (December), pp. 373–397.

—— (2002): Are the Japanese Selfish, Altruistic, or Dynastic? In: *Japanese Economic Review* 53, 1 (March), pp. 26–54 (the 2001 JEA-Nakahara Prize Lecture).

—— (2006a): Are the Japanese Unique? An Analysis of Consumption and Saving Behavior in Japan. In: Garon, Sheldon and Patricia Maclachlan (eds.): *The Ambivalent Consumer: Questioning Consumption in East Asia and the West*. Ithaca, New York: Cornell University Press, pp. 113–136.

—— (2006b): Do the Elderly Dissave in Japan? In: Klein, Lawrence R. (ed.): *Long-Run Growth and Short-Run Stabilization: Essays in Memory of Albert Ando.* Cheltenham, UK, and Northampton, MA, USA: Edward Elgar, pp. 129–136.

Horioka, Charles Yuji; Hideki Fujisaki, Wako Watanabe and Takatsugu Kōno (2000): Are Americans More Altruistic than the Japanese? A U.S.-Japan Comparison of Saving and Bequest Motives. In: *International Economic Journal* 14, 1 (Spring), pp. 1–31.

Ishikawa, Tsuneo and Kazuo Ueda (1984): The Bonus Payment System and Japanese Personal Saving. In: Aoki, Masahiko (ed.): *The Economic Analysis of the Japanese Firm.* Amsterdam: North-Holland, pp. 133–192.

Modigliani, Franco and Richard Brumberg (1955): Utility Analysis and the Consumption Function: An Interpretation of Cross-Section Data. In: Kurihara, Kenneth K. (ed.): *Post-Keynesian Economics*. New Brunswick, N.J.: Rutgers University Press, pp. 388–436.

CHAPTER FORTY-NINE

# THE AGEING SOCIETY AND ECONOMIC INEQUALITY

Fumio Ohtake

## 1. Introduction

For many years, opinion surveys among the Japanese population have shown that most Japanese consider themselves to belong to a middle-class society with a comparatively equal income distribution. However, Tachibanaki (1998) claims that the degree of inequality in Japan has recently become greater than in the United States. For example, there is a tendency for many Japanese enterprises to shift the basis of their wage systems from seniority to achievement. Although it would seem that Japan is becoming a society with greater economic inequality, it is in fact difficult to prove that this is actually happening, because reliable income data are scarce, and the suitability of annual income as a criterion for measuring living standards is debatable. Despite these statistical and definition problems, we can, however, trace time-series changes in the degree of inequality within a particular country according to one particular kind of survey, in order to shed some light on the inequality issue.

In the following sections, this chapter discusses some general data on inequality (section 2) and the various causes of a growing disparity in personal incomes (section 3). Sections 4 to 5 consider the impact of changes in the wage system and the issue of consumption inequality. Finally, the paper finishes with a short conclusion.

## 2. Degree of Income Inequality in Japan

Let us first examine the question of how the degree of inequality in Japanese incomes has been changing. Figure 1 shows the trend in the Gini coefficient of annual pre-tax household incomes, calculated from quintile ranking data in the Family Income and Expenditure Survey of the Management and Coordination Agency. Table 1 shows the Gini coefficient calculated from several income surveys.

Roughly speaking, the distribution of Japan's household incomes grew more equal during the period of high growth, and has been dispersing since the mid-1980s. The widening inequality since the mid-1980s is observable in every kind of relevant data. Is it safe to say, then, that Japanese society, which achieved relative equality while the economy was expanding, is now moving towards inequality?

It is well known that, during the last 20 years, the degree of income inequality has substantially increased in the U.S. and the U.K. On the other hand, many of the countries of continental Europe, which have preserved equality of incomes by maintaining all kinds of restrictions on the labour market (such as high minimum wages, wages set by centralized labour unions, and strict restrictions against dismissals) are suffering high rates of unemployment.

Japan's unemployment rate, though relatively high in a historical perspective, maintains a low level by global standards. On the surface, the combination of a relatively low unemployment rate and an increasing degree of inequality resembles the patterns in the U.S. and the U.K.

Inequality in Japan is in fact increasing, but around half of the increase can be explained by the ageing factor. In this respect, it differs from the U.S. and U.K., where inequality increase is independent of changes in their population structure. In Japan, the degree of inequality within particular age groups has not increased so greatly, but the degree tends to be greater in the higher age groups. This is attributable to an accumulation of chance factors affecting the individual and to the fact that returns from investment in human capital, such as education and development of skills, tend to become more apparent in the later stages of life.

In Japan, this tendency for inequality to increase with age is particularly marked on account of the narrow range of income inequality among the young. It was in the context of this relationship between income inequality and the age distribution of the population that the rapid increase in the older generation seen in the 1980s brought about a widening of overall economic inequality in Japan. The policy implications of this will be discussed in the concluding section.

## 3. Causes of Income Inequality in Japan

When looking at the growing disparity in personal incomes in Japan since the mid-1980s it is easy to imagine that the bubble boom in the late 1980s widened income inequality. One reason is that an increase in asset income created a large difference in incomes between stock and land holders and non-holders. Another reason is that wages in industries such as finance, real estate, and construction increased more than those in other sectors, which created dispersion among industries.

Even though soaring asset prices widen differentials, asset income does not contribute very much to overall income inequality, because only a small proportion of all holders realize their capital gains. Furthermore, if fluctuations in asset prices were indeed a major cause of widening income inequality, it would not be possible to explain why this has continued despite the end of the bubble.

It is possible that wage gaps between industries, in particular the high salaries in the financial sector, were the cause of income differentials in the late 1980s. However, this cannot explain the long-term trend, since it is not clear that this is applicable after the collapse of the bubble economy. In fact, wage gaps between industries narrowed in the 1990s.

Have wage gaps among different educational levels, then, become wider in Japan, as in the U.S.? Taken as a whole, wage differentials among male workers with different educational levels have stayed more or less flat over the years. However, the trend for the middle-aged or older age groups differs from that for the young. Among the former group, the wage gap between university graduates and high-school graduates has progressively narrowed since the mid-1980s. On the other hand, it is becoming wider among the latter group.

The contraction of wage differentials among middle-aged and older workers in terms of educational levels reflects the fact that the proportion of people with higher education has risen sharply as better-educated cohorts have moved into this age group. The greater wage differentials among the younger age group are caused by the concentration of labour demand in new technology on young people who have received higher education. Does this mean, then, that wage gaps in relation to age differences have widened? It is often asserted that the seniority wage system has begun to collapse, and wage differentials among highly educated persons in relation to age have indeed been narrowing. This implies that wage dispersion in relation to age is not a cause of the present widening inequality.

One wonders then what the actual explanation of the trend towards inequality is. A feature of income and wage dispersions in Japan is that the dispersions within age groups widen in the higher age groups.

Moreover, there are remarkably stable trends in income and wage dispersions within the same age group (Figure 3). The correct understanding of the cause of widening inequality in Japan is that, because of the ageing labour force, the proportion of the age group with potentially wide income and wage dispersions has increased, so that inequality in the economy as a whole has been widening since the mid-1980s.

Using the *Income Redistribution Survey*, Ohtake and Saito (1998) showed that about 30 per cent of the increase in income inequality during the 1980s is explained by the ageing of the population. Iwamoto (2000) finds that about 10 per cent of the increase in inequality can be explained by the ageing factor in the 1990s.

The following are possible explanations for the source of the difference between Ohtake and Saito (1998, 1999) and Iwamoto (2000).

(1) The differences of data source: Ohtake and Saito (1998) used data for households of two or more persons from the *National Survey on Family Income and Expenditure*. Ohtake and Saito (1999) used the data for all types of households from the *Income Redistribution Survey (IRS)*. Iwamoto (2000) used the data for all types of households from the *Basic Survey of People's Life (BSPL)*. The IRS and BSPL are sampled from the same population because the samples of the IRS are sub-samples of the BSPL. The percentage of single-person households in Japan increased during the 1980s and 1990s. Because the average income of single-person households is lower than that of households with two or more members, the increase in the ratio of single households has a positive effect on income inequality.

(2) The differences of time period: Ohtake and Saito (1998) used data from 1979 to 1989. Ohtake and Saito (1999) used data from 1986 to 1992. Iwamoto (2000) used data from 1989 to 1995.

In this section, I quantify how much population ageing and the increase in single-person households contributed to the increase in income inequality during the 1980s and the 1990s. To this purpose, I decompose the change in income inequality into three factors: demographic effects (the effects of population ageing and those of the increase in single-person households); within-age-households effects; and between-age-households effects.

To carry out this decomposition, we collect the following data from the *Income Redistribution Survey*:

(a) the population proportion by age and household type:
$s_t = \{s_{tjh}\}, {}^{75}_{j\,25\,=,\; h\,=\,single\ or\ not},$
(b) the within-age-household log income variance:
$\sigma_t = \{\sigma_{tjh}\}^{75}_{j\,=\,25,\; h\,=\,single\ or\ not},$
(c) the average of log income within the same age and household group:
$Y_t = \{Y_{tjh}\}^{75}_{j\,=\,25,\; h\,=\,single\ or\ not}$

where $t$ denotes a point of time, $j$ the age group and $h$ the household type (single-person households or households with two or more members).

As shown by Ohtake and Saito (1998, 1999), the log-income variance (Var ln $y_{it}$) can be decomposed as follows:

$$\text{Var In Var In } y_{it} = V(s_t, \sigma_t, Y_t) = \sum_{j=25}^{75} s_{tjh}\sigma^2_{tjh} + \sigma^2_{bt}, \qquad (1)$$

Where $\sigma^2_{bt} = \sum_{j=25}^{75} s_{tjh} Y^2_{tjh} - \left( \sum_{j=25}^{75} s_{tjh} Y_{tjh} \right)^2$. Equation (1) shows that the log-income variance can be decomposed into two terms. The first term in equation (1) is the effect of the increase in the inequality within an age group and within the same household type (single-person household or household with two or more members). The second term is the effect of the increase in the inequality between age group and household type.

Using the log variance decomposition in equation (1), I define demographic effects, within-age-households effects, and between-age-households effects as follows between year T1 and year T0.

$$\text{Demographic Effects} = V(s_{T1}, \sigma_{T0}, Y_{T0}) - V(s_{T0}, \sigma_{T0}, Y_{T0}) \qquad (2)$$

$$\text{Within-Age-Household Effects} = V(s_{T0}, \sigma_{T1}, Y_{T0}) - V(s_{T0}, \sigma_{T0}, Y_{T0}) \qquad (3)$$

$$\text{Between-Age-Household Effects} = V(s_{T0}, \sigma_{T0}, Y_{T1}) - V(s_{T0}, \sigma_{T0}, Y_{T0}) \qquad (4)$$

I decompose income inequality using data from the *Income Redistribution Survey* (IRS) of the Ministry of Health and Welfare. The notion of "initial [*tōsho*] income" in this survey is, however, substantially different from the definition of income used in the *Family Income and Expenditure*

*Survey* (FIES) of the Management and Coordination Agency. One primary difference is that "initial income" includes a lump-sum retirement allowance and insurance benefits, but not public pension payments, which tends to exaggerate the degree of inequality.[1] Thus, I use the adjusted initial income, which is a similar definition of income to that used in FIES, for the decomposition. Figure 4 shows the Gini coefficient for various definitions of income. As Ohtake and Saito (1999) showed, income inequality for "adjusted initial income" is much lower than that for "initial income." Surprisingly, income inequality defined by adjusted initial income decreased after 1989.

Table 2 summarizes the results of the above decomposition. Concerning the increase in income inequality by 0.076 from 1983 to 1995, about 80 per cent was caused by demographic change, while 16 per cent was due to the increase in within age and household group effects. Figure 5 shows the change in inequality and its decomposition. From 1986 to 1992, however, within age and household effects make the largest contribution to the increase in income inequality. This period coincided with the "bubble period" in Japan. As Figure 5 shows, the long-term trend of income inequality can be explained by demographic change. However, short-term change in income inequality is affected by the business cycle.

Figure 6 shows the result of the decomposition of income inequality when we only take into account the ageing effects and we ignore the change in the proportion of single households as a factor in demographic change, as in Ohtake and Saito (1998, 1999) and Iwamoto (2000). In this case, the contribution of demographic change to the increase in inequality from 1983 to 1995 is much smaller than that shown in Figure 5, in which demographic change includes the change in the proportion of single-person households as well as change in the age distribution of household heads.

Background data for the inequality decomposition are shown in Figures 7, 8, and 9. Figure 7 shows the change in proportions of households by age of household head and type of household (single-person households or other households) between 1983 and 1995. This change affects the demographic effects in the inequality decomposition in Table 2. First, the proportion of households with two or more members shifted to the aged group in 1995. Second, the proportion of single households

[1] For further details, see Ohtake and Saito (1999).

increased in most age groups. Both of these changes raise economy-wide inequality, because within-age income variance increases as age of household increases, as shown in Figure 8, and because the average income of single-person households is lower than other households, as shown in Figure 9.

## 4. A Pyramiding Wage System?

It has been argued that the seniority wage system cannot be maintained as the population ages: in short, the seniority wage system is destined to collapse. On the surface, the argument sounds plausible, in that managers of individual firms might hope to hire young workers at the expense of currently employed older ones in order to save labour costs.

Given that middle-aged and older workers undertake different work from younger workers, it is natural that an increase in the number of workers in higher age groups should reduce their wages and diminish the role of seniority in the system. This is the situation in Japan. However, a flattening of the age-wage profile caused by the ageing society is not the same as the collapse of the seniority wage system (see chapter 54).

In fact, no drastic change has occurred in the seniority system, although it has become somewhat weaker. Although the wage gap among highly educated workers employed in large companies is widening, this is mainly confined to the group around 30 years old and does not affect other age groups.

Economics frequently explains the seniority wage system in terms of the human capital theory and the incentive theory. The human capital theory asserts that education and training improve labour productivity. It explains that the accumulation of occupational experience increases skills, which in turn brings about higher wages, so that the seniority wage system is justified by increasing productivity. On the other hand, the incentive hypothesis perceives the seniority wage system as an encouragement to employees to work hard over a long period of time. In other words, employees receive wages that are low in relation to their productivity while they are young, and high when they have become senior. Since wages exceeding productivity are withheld until employees have acquired long-term tenure, if they are found not to be diligent and are dismissed midway through their career, their opportunity cost incurred by the loss of the job will be much higher. Thus, the system provides an incentive to all employees to work hard.

Neither hypothesis, however, demonstrates that ageing of the labour force causes the collapse of the seniority wage system. The human resource hypothesis sees the high productivity of older workers as justification for the seniority system; the incentive hypothesis says that the rise in expenditure on wages caused by an increased number of ageing workers is a delayed payment to cover earlier inadequate wages.

The argument that the seniority wage system cannot be retained in an ageing society resembles the argument that a public pension system cannot be retained under the same demographic pressure, in that the seniority wage system is likened to a kind of a pay-as-you-go pension system that transfers income from the younger to the older generation. While public pensions are compulsory, workers can choose the company where they work. Is it likely that young employees will join a firm—which by its nature will have its ups and downs—that employs a wage system predicated on constant growth? It is unreasonable to believe that many workers would be deceived by a wage system resembling a pyramiding system.

Admittedly, as explained in the following section, both theories allow for the possibility that the seniority wage system could temporarily break down. It should be realized, however, that this is different from the "pyramiding" hypothesis.

## 5. The Baby-Boom Generation and Wages

The baby-boom generation (those born immediately after the end of World War II) is typically affected by the collapse of the seniority wage system and company restructuring. How does it differ from other generations?

Assuming that the work done by experienced employees is different from that performed by newly employed persons, then the initial salary should be considered as the wage rate for unskilled workers. When the baby-boom generation entered the labour market after school or university, the wage rate for unskilled workers should have dropped, because the supply of unskilled labour was greater than in previous years.

Suppose, on the contrary, that both experienced and recently hired employees performed the same work; then the downward wage pressure should have affected all the employees in question. In short, workers of all ages should have faced a fall in their wages. However, if the work they do is different, then the effect of the mass entry of the baby-boom generation into the labour force should simply have resulted in a fall in that generation's initial salaries.

This argument can be applied not only to the issue of initial salaries but also to managers' salaries. Suppose that the proportion of managers to all employees is fixed and that managerial posts are assigned to workers with longer tenure. Then, when the baby-boom generation reaches the age level for managerial posts, the supply of appropriate workers outnumbers the demand, leading to a drop in the salaries paid for the posts. Consequently, salaries for managerial posts should, when occupied by baby-boomers, be lower than when other generations occupy the posts.

Therefore, in a society where the jobs people do are determined to a certain extent by age, a change in demographic structures, such as the emergence of baby-boomers, should tend to cause wage decreases limited to the particular generation with a high population.

One of the causes of growing inequality in relation to educational levels in the U.S. is a rapid increase in the demand for educated workers. In Japan, too, it is true that the wages of well-educated young workers have for the same reason increased relatively more than those of other types of workers. However, among middle-aged and older workers, whose proportion to the entire population is relatively large, and whose proportion of educated workers is rapidly increasing, the effect of the rise in the supply of highly educated workers is greater than that of the increase in demand.

Of course, there are other possible explanations, apart from an oversupply of labour in that generation, for the brake on wage increases and employment insecurity among middle-aged and older people at the moment. First, a sharp growth in technological innovation may have made previously acquired skills and experience out-dated. Second, assuming that the level of education and training in workplaces is higher when the number of subordinates per superior is smaller, one might say that the human capital of the baby-boomers is lower than that of other generations. Furthermore, the rise in the proportion of university graduates among baby-boomers may simply mean that the quality of university graduates has declined. If so, then the increase in the number of workers with higher education could bring a drop in wage inequalities between workers of differing educational levels, a trend that might continue in the future.

## 6. Consumption Inequality

We have seen how the rise in income inequality in Japan has its roots in the ageing of the population. Now let us consider whether income and wages are appropriate means of gauging inequality. Let us take the following example: A and B earn the same wages, but A is from a poor family, whereas the parents of B own a large area of land. Since B can certainly rely on inheritance from his parents in the future, he travels abroad every year. On the other hand, A cuts down on his expenditure so that he can buy a home in the future.

Although the two seem to be equal in terms of present income, B is obviously richer when future bequests are taken into account. The implications of this comparison are important when one considers inequality between generations in a society with intergenerational income transfers through pension systems. That is to say, in considering inequality it is not enough to use current income differentials to gauge actual dispersions. To measure inequality accurately, it is necessary to measure life-time income dispersions.

In practice, it is difficult to estimate future incomes of individuals. Nevertheless, consumption expenditure, it is safe to say, closely approximates lifetime income: individuals make decisions about their current level of consumption on the basis of their expected future incomes. Of course, individuals are restrained by their current income levels in that they cannot borrow money on their future income even if they are sure that they will receive a certain amount of income in future. Nonetheless, in a society such as Japan, in recent years, where stock accumulation is substantial, it is more likely that consumption levels rather than income levels reflect more accurately the degree of inequality.

Ohtake and Saito (1998) have analysed the characteristics of inequality of consumption expenditure and how it changed during the 1980s. The study revealed that consumption inequality increases according to age. In particular, inequality rises sharply among people aged 40 or older, a rise that is brought about by sudden, unpredictable threats to future income. The differences in consumption levels cited above, which depend on future inheritances, can be foreseen; this is precisely why they appear in the form of such consumption differentials. On the other hand, sudden dismissals, accidents, illnesses, and the like are unforeseeable, and in such cases people adjust their consumption levels once what has happened is apparent. In Japan, people aged 40 or older face various unexpected threats to their income. In the 1980s, when the baby-boomers passed the 40 years' mark, consumption inequality in the economy as a whole rose sharply. Thus, in the case of consumption as elsewhere, the greying of the population is the major cause of increases in inequality in Japan.

## 7. Conclusion

The rise in income and consumption inequality seen in Japan since the mid-1980s can be explained to a large extent by the greying population. This is a major difference from the situations in the U.S. and the U.K., where the rise in income inequality was induced by rises in inequality between various groups and within those groups, not by the ageing of the population as a whole.

What policy measures are desirable where, as in Japan, economic inequality is caused by demographic pressure? One important aspect is to treat the two factors involved—prolonged longevity and the declining birth rate—separately. With prolonged longevity, the accumulation of unexpected threats to income over the years means a rise in uncertainty concerning lifelong income. If people are unwilling to accept uncertainty in their living standards when they get old, then an ageing society needs to establish security systems that will allay their fears. In this sense, the improvement and expansion of public pension systems and of services for caring for the aged is crucial. What should be taken into account here, however, is that the need for such security systems should be satisfied by pooling risks within each generation—that there should be a redistribution among those who are fortunate enough to live comfortable lives in their old age and those who are unfortunately unable to do so. Of course, it is also true that some generations are more fortunate than others, but the issue of intergenerational redistribution is beyond the scope of public security systems or public schemes of caring for the aged, and should be left to a system of progressive taxation.

On the other hand, what happens in a society whose ageing is caused by a declining birth rate? In such a case, the uncertainty concerning the individual's lifelong income remains unchanged regardless of the number of children. In this sense, a reinforcing of existing security systems is hardly necessary. Yet one should remember that the family incorporates a complementary security system in areas that private and public security systems cannot cover. A large family functions as a security system in itself. However, as family units shrink due to the declining birth rate, diminishing the family's value as a security unit, public or private income security systems will become more necessary.

In a demographically young society, many of the population have not yet drawn their "lots" in life, whereas in an ageing society many already know the outcomes of the lots they drew. The important thing is that a preponderance of people who are already aware of these outcomes should not hinder appraisal of the element of chance in the "lottery." To treat those who were unlucky in the lottery as "losers" will have a demoralizing effect on people. The distinction here is significant in fashioning economic policies. There must be income redistribution policies to take care of what happens after the unexpected.

## References

Deaton, Angus S. and Christina H. Paxson (1998a): Measuring Poverty among the Elderly. In: Wise, David A. (ed.): *Inquiries in the Economics of Aging*. Chicago: University of Chicago Press, pp. 169–204.

—— (1998b): Economies of Scale, Household Size, and the Demand for Food. In: *Journal of Political Economy* 106, pp. 897–930.

Iwamoto, Yasushi (2000): Ruifusaikuru kara mita fubyōdōdo [Inequality from the viewpoint of lifecycle]. In: Kokuritsu Shakai Hoshō · Jinkō Mondai Kenkyūjo (ed.): *Kazoku · setai no henyō to seikatsu hoshō kinō*. Tokyo: Tōkyō Daigaku Shuppankai, pp. 75–94.

Ohtake, Fumio (1994): 1980-nendai no shotoku shisan bunpai [Income and wealth distribution in the 1980s in Japan]. In: *Economic Studies Quarterly* 45, 5, pp. 385–402.

Ohtake, Fumio and Makoto Saito (1998): Population Aging and Consumption Inequality in Japan. In: *Review of Income and Wealth* 44, 3, pp. 361–381.

—— (1999): Shotoku fubyōdōka no haikei to sono seisakuteki gan'i—nenrei kaisō nai kōka, nenrei kaisō kan kōka, jinkō kōreika kōka [On income inequality during the 1980s: causes and implications]. In: *Kikan Shakai Hoshō Kenkyū* [Quarterly of Social Security Research] 35, 1, pp. 65–76.

Tachibanaki, Toshiaki (1998): *Nihon no keizai kakusa* [Economic Inequality in Japan]. Tokyo: Iwanami Shoten.

Table 1. Gini Coefficients According to Various Income Surveys.

| | The Family Income and Expenditure Survey (FIES) (Calculated from the Yearly Income Quintile Group data) Household with two or more members | Basic Survey on People's Life (Yoshida (1993) docile Group Data) All households | Basic Survey on People's Life (quartile Group Data) All Households | Income Redistribution Survey ("initial income" micro data) All households | Income Redistribution Survey ("adjusted initial income, micro" data) All Households | National Survey of Family Income and Expenditure (Docile data) Households with two or more members |
|---|---|---|---|---|---|---|
| 1962 | | 0.376 | | | | |
| 1963 | 0.310 | 0.361 | | | | |
| 1964 | 0.299 | 0.353 | | | | |
| 1965 | 0.282 | 0.344 | | | | |
| 1966 | 0.284 | — | | | | |
| 1967 | 0.280 | 0.352 | | | | |
| 1968 | 0.267 | 0.349 | | | | |
| 1969 | 0.257 | 0.354 | | | | |
| 1970 | 0.253 | 0.355 | | | | |
| 1971 | 0.259 | 0.352 | | | | |
| 1972 | 0.256 | 0.357 | | | | |
| 1973 | 0.260 | 0.350 | | | | |
| 1974 | 0.269 | 0.344 | | | | |
| 1975 | 0.276 | 0.353 | | | | |
| 1976 | 0.267 | 0.360 | 0.333 | | | |
| 1977 | 0.258 | 0.342 | 0.331 | | | |
| 1978 | 0.264 | 0.354 | 0.323 | | | |
| 1979 | 0.260 | 0.336 | 0.312 | | | 0.271 |
| 1980 | 0.260 | 0.337 | 0.315 | 0.349 | | |
| 1981 | 0.258 | 0.352 | 0.325 | | | |
| 1982 | 0.263 | 0.351 | 0.324 | | | |
| 1983 | 0.261 | 0.351 | 0.325 | 0.398 | 0.349 | |
| 1984 | 0.260 | 0.350 | 0.322 | | | 0.280 |
| 1985 | 0.272 | 0.359 | 0.333 | | | |
| 1986 | 0.278 | 0.356 | 0.328 | 0.405 | 0.364 | |
| 1987 | 0.273 | 0.359 | 0.334 | | | |
| 1988 | 0.268 | 0.375 | 0.345 | | | |
| 1989 | 0.273 | | 0.346 | 0.433 | 0.391 | 0.293 |
| 1990 | 0.276 | | 0.342 | | | |
| 1991 | 0.282 | | 0.353 | | | |
| 1992 | 0.278 | | 0.353 | 0.439 | 0.389 | |
| 1993 | 0.278 | | 0.348 | | | |
| 1994 | 0.278 | | 0.341 | | | 0.297 |

Table 1 (*cont.*)

| | The Family Income and Expenditure Survey (FIES) (Calculated from the Yearly Income Quintile Group data) Household with two or more members | Basic Survey on People's Life (Yoshida (1993) docile Group Data) All households | Basic Survey on People's Life (quartile Group Data) All Households | Income Redistribution Survey ("initial income" micro data) All households | Income Redistribution Survey ("adjusted initial income, micro" data) All Households | National Survey of Family Income and Expenditure (Docile data) Households with two or more members |
|---|---|---|---|---|---|---|
| 1995 | 0.281 | | 0.360 | 0.441 | 0.353 | |
| 1996 | 0.283 | | 0.346 | | | |
| 1997 | 0.284 | | 0.362 | | | |
| 1998 | 0.278 | | 0.364 | 0.472 | | |
| 1999 | 0.286 | | 0.354 | | | 0.301 |
| 2000 | 0.284 | | 0.366 | | | |
| 2001 | 0.280 | | 0.368 | 0.498 | | |
| 2002 | 0.284 | | 0.366 | | | |
| 2003 | 0.272 | | 0.369 | | | |

Table 2. Sources of Increase in Economy-wide Income Inequality in Japan: 1983–1995.

| | Actual Change in Income Inequality | Demographic Effects | Between-Age-Household Effects | Within-Age-Household Effects |
|---|---|---|---|---|
| 1983 | | 0 | 0 | 0 |
| 1986 | 0.243 | 0.011 (4.47%) | 0.075 (31.03) | 0.155 (63.83) |
| 1989 | 0.389 | 0.040 (10.17) | 0.083 (21.35) | 0.226 (58.12) |
| 1992 | 0.387 | 0.056 (14.58) | 0.093 (24.00) | 0.182 (47.09) |
| 1995 | 0.076 | 0.061 (80.13) | 0.009 (11.51) | 0.013 (16.63) |

Note: The number in parentheses denotes the contribution of each effect to the increase in economy-wide inequality.
Source: Own calculation.

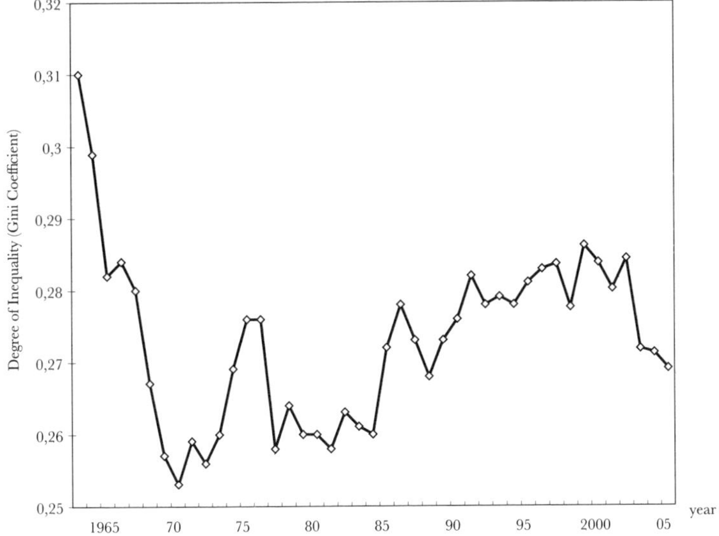


Source: Author's calculation from the Family Income and Expenditure Survey of the Management and Coordination Agency.

Figure 1. Trends in Income Inequality in Japan.

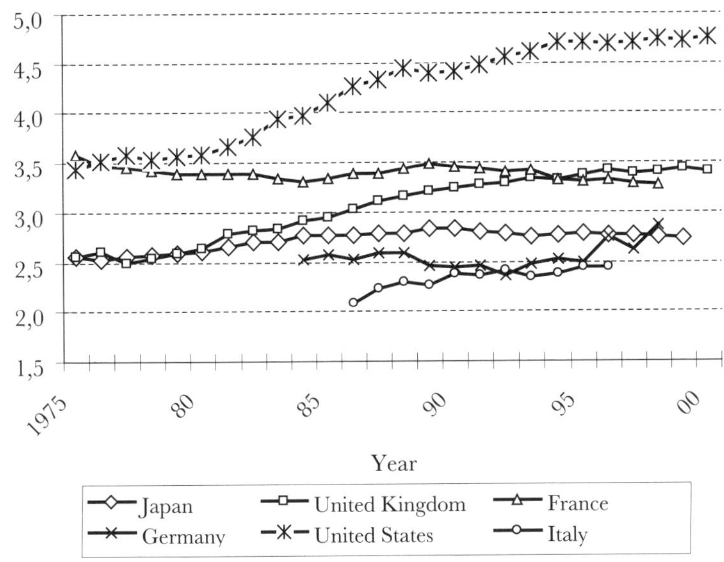


Source: OECD.

Figure 2. Trends in Wage Differentials (Males).

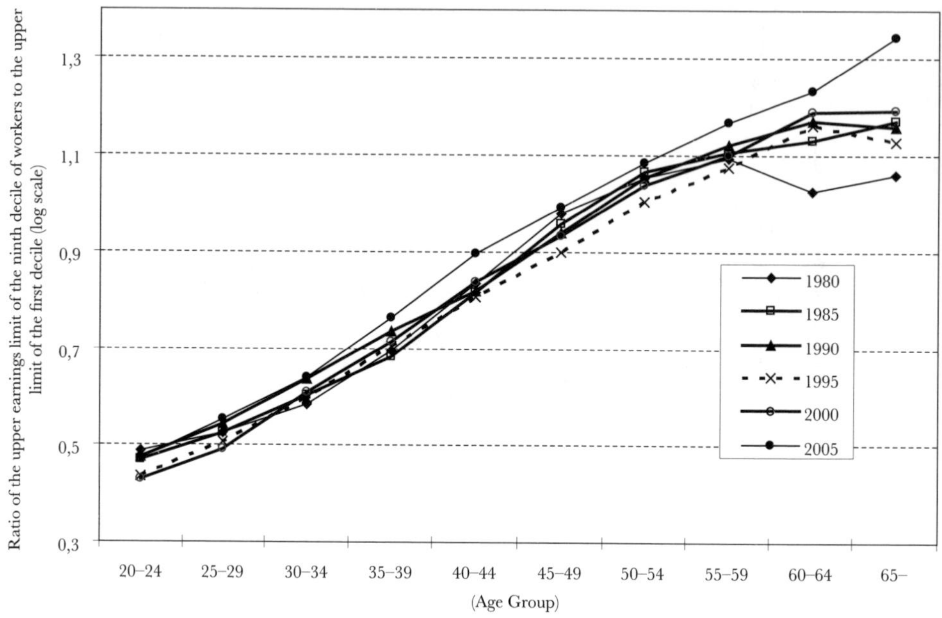


Source: Basic Surveys on Wage Structure, Ministry of Labour.

Figure 3. Stability of Wage Differentials within Each Age Group (Males).

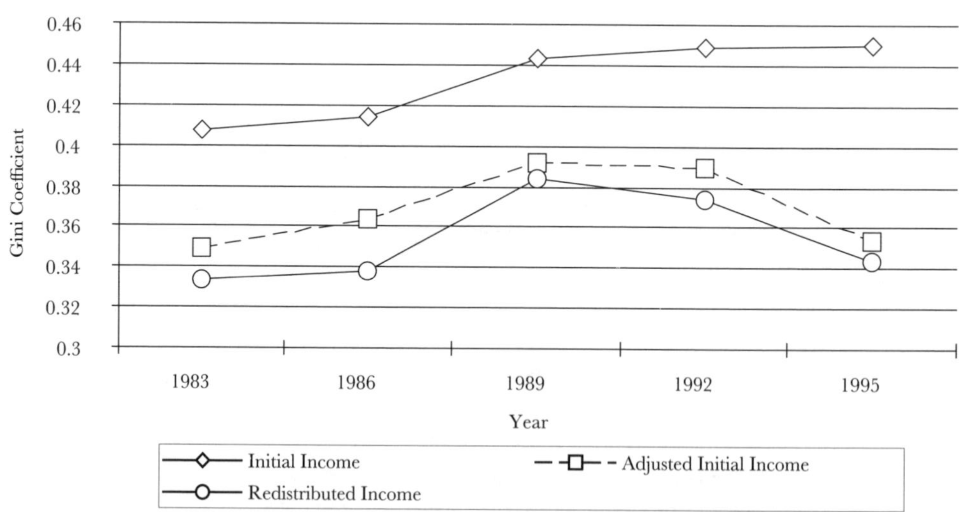


Source: Own calculation.

Figure 4. Gini Coefficients by Income Definition from Income Redistribution Survey.

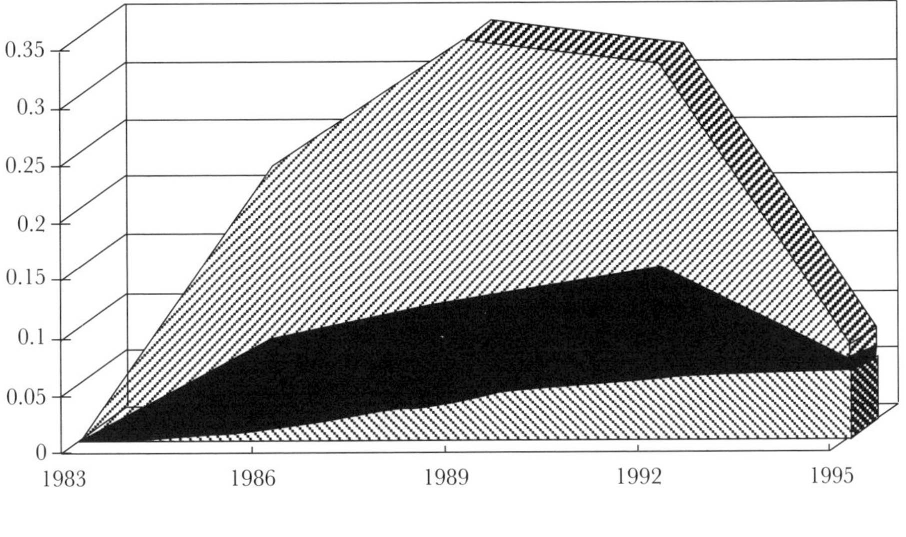


Source: Own calculation.

Figure 5. Decomposition of Log Variance of Income.

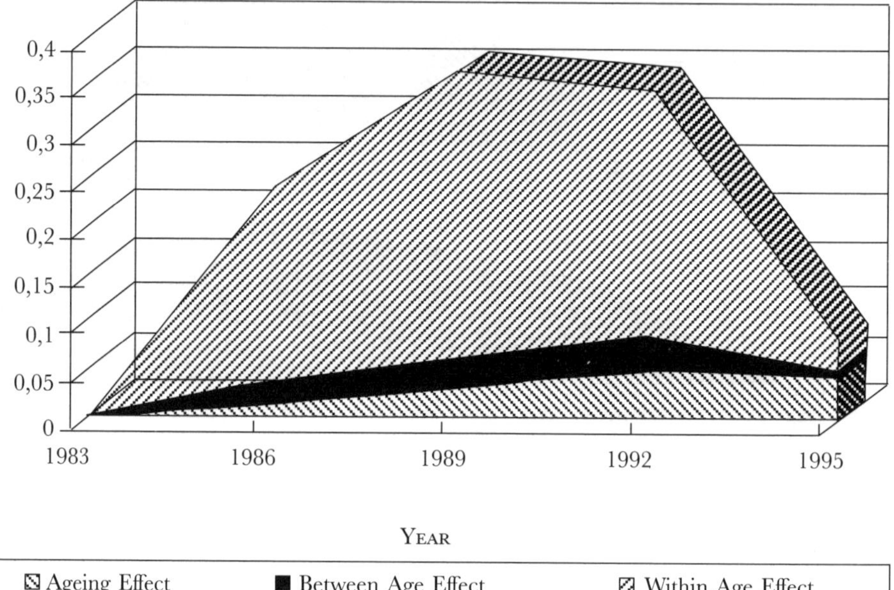


Source: Own calculations.

Figure 6. Decomposition of Log Variance of Income—Ageing Effects.

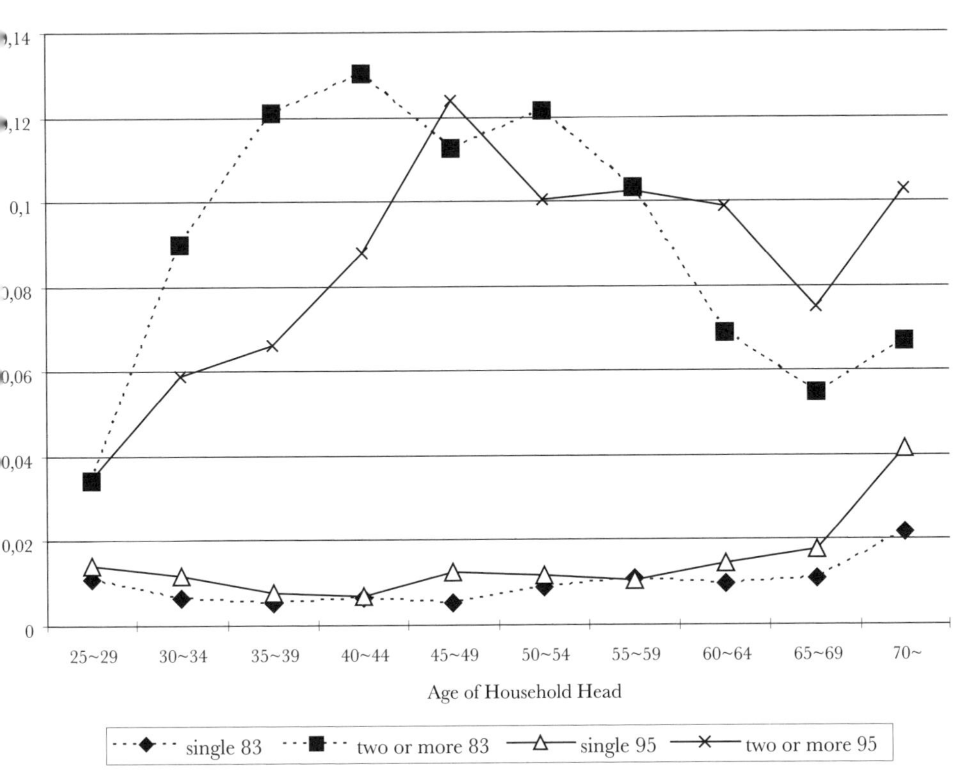


Source: Own calculation.

Figure 7. Changes in the Proportions of Households by Age of Household Head and Type of Household (1983–1995).

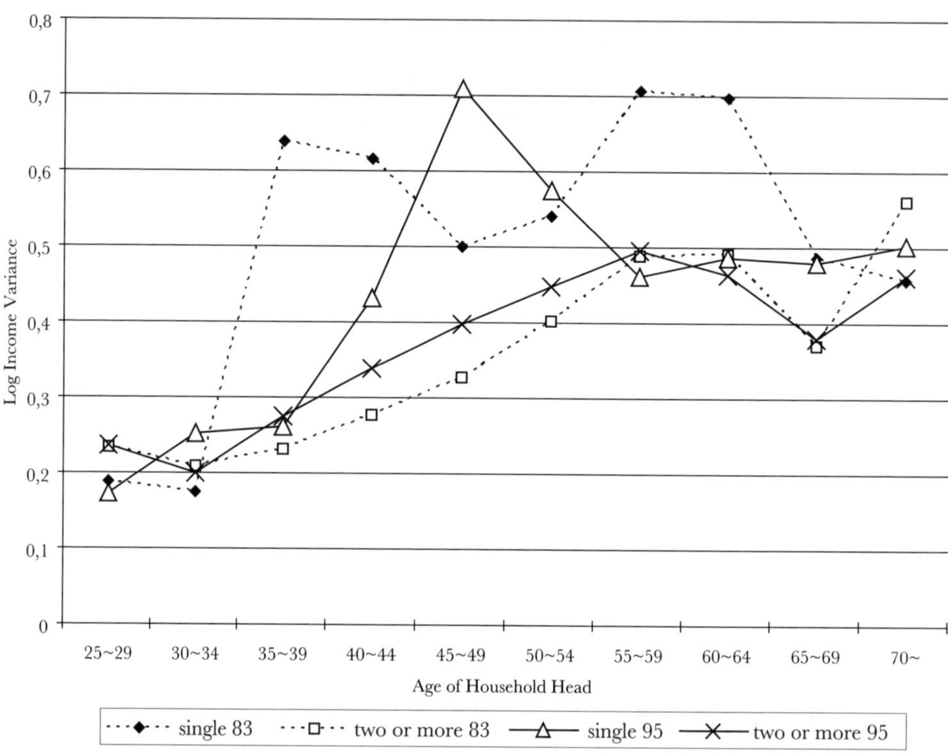


Source: Own calculation.

Figure 8. Log Income Variance Within Age Group and Household Type.

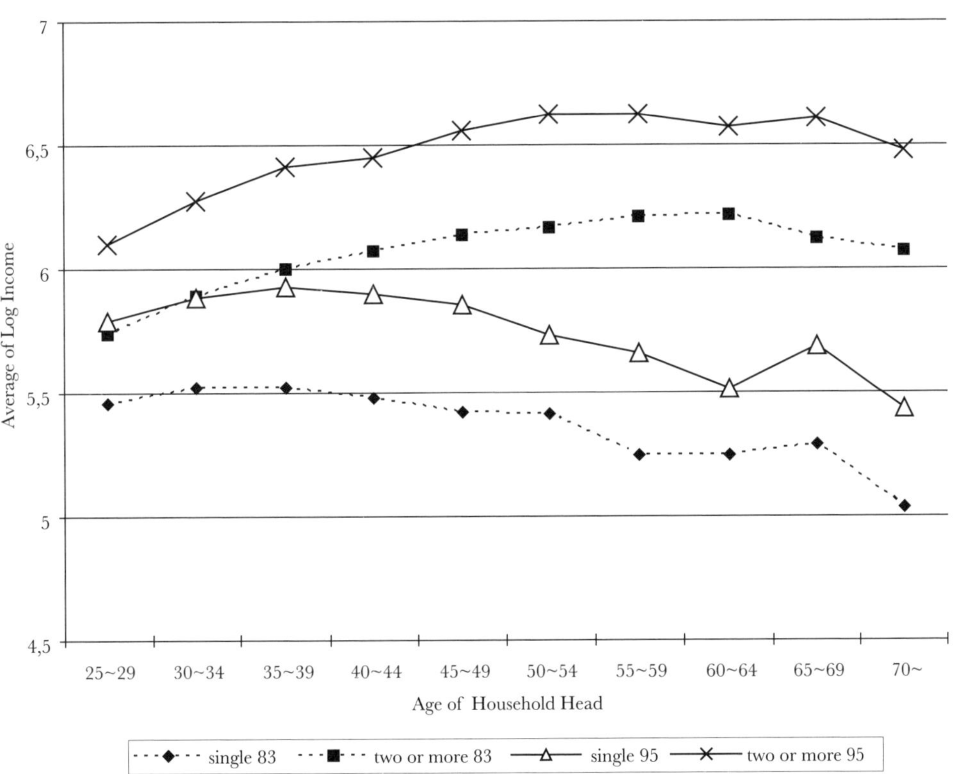


Source: Own calculation.

Figure 9. Average Log income by Age of Household Head and Household Type (1983–1995).

CHAPTER FIFTY

# POVERTY AMONG THE ELDERLY

Hisashi Fukawa

## 1. Introduction

Increasing inequality and rising poverty in Japan are the subject of debate. Points of contention cover many areas, but most authors agree that, with regard to both these issues, the main factors are the size of disparities in wealth and the high rate of poverty among the elderly.

Given that this is the case, one might think that Japan is progressing in a direction that will alleviate the growing inequality and poverty among the elderly, but this is not the case. Rather, the view that rising inequality and poverty are inevitable phenomena accompanying the ageing of society is mainstream thinking. In the ultimate safety net that is public assistance, there have been cuts in the minimum levels of social security benefits for the elderly. Moves to make the threshold for public assistance even stricter, and to make further cuts in the basic amounts of the minimum levels of social security, are gaining strength. However, in the midst of such trends developments aiming at social inclusion of the elderly must also not be overlooked.

## 2. Growing Inequality and Rising Poverty among the Elderly in Japan

### 2.1. *The inequality debate and ageing*

Debate among researchers about the causes of growing inequality and poverty began at the end of the 1990s (see, for example, Tachibanaki 1998; Ohtake and Saitō 1999), prompted by the fact that the Gini coefficient, which shows the level of inequality in income distribution, had been tending to rise. There was also a debate in the Diet on "An unequal society" at the beginning of 2006. That inequality is growing is not in dispute, but in the debate are the causes of growing income inequality, that is the increase in the rate of inequality. The argument that it is an effect of the ageing society has become mainstream. This analysis argues that since income inequality is usually greater among the elderly, if the elderly make up a higher proportion of society, the overall level of inequality will appear to rise (see chapter 49). Although data from the *National Expenditure Survey* [Zenkoku shōhi jittai chōsa] indicate that there is a trend for inequality among the elderly to shrink, the rate of inequality itself is still high (Naikakufu 2006c: 262). The Cabinet Office's *Materials from Cabinet Meetings on Monthly Economic Reports etc.* (Naikakufu 2006a) and the *2006 White Paper on Economic and Fiscal Policy* (Naikakufu 2006c) also cite ageing as the main cause of increasing inequality in Japan. Ageing has thus not lost its importance as a factor in widening income disparity in Japan.

The fact that there are large inequalities among the elderly has been made clear through this debate, but it is striking that the need to rectify these inequalities has not been recognized. According to those leading the debate, the elderly are people who have drawn that lot in life's lottery, and it is inevitable that income inequalities will rise (Ohtake 1999). The growth of inequality is treated as if it were a natural phenomenon. The debate has not led to a re-examination of how income redistribution ought to function in order to take the elderly, who are at the bottom of this wealth gap, out of poverty.

### 2.2. *From inequality to poverty*

In Japan today, where prosperity is said to have continued as never before, it is not just a matter of increasing inequality: rising poverty has also attracted attention. The trigger was a recent OECD Working Paper, which reported that relative poverty in Japan had risen from 13.7 per cent in 1994 to 15.3 per cent in 2000, reaching a higher level than in any of the other developed countries (Förster and Mira d'Ercole 2005). As is clear from Table 1, even though the poverty rate among the elderly has fallen somewhat, it is still overwhelmingly higher than the rate among young people. As the proportion of elderly people in the population increases, the effect of that alone means that the overall rate of poverty rises. The ageing of society is the main cause of the increase in the rate of poverty.

Table 1. Shifts in the Poverty Rate.

| Age (years) | 0–17 | 18–25 | 26–40 | 41–50 | 51–65 | 66–75 | over 76 | Total |
|---|---|---|---|---|---|---|---|---|
| Poverty rate | 14.3 | 16.6 | 12.4 | 11.7 | 14.4 | 19.5 | 23.8 | 15.3 |
| 1994–2000 | +2.3 | +2.5 | +2.0 | +1.5 | +1.0 | –1.7 | –2.3 | +1.6 |

Source: Förster and Mira d'Ercole 2005: 73.

However, this does not mean that the debate is moving in the direction of raising poverty among the elderly as an issue in itself and saying that its alleviation ought to be striven for. Rather, it is argued that the reason the number of poor households among the elderly is rising is that their absolute numbers are rising as a consequence of the ageing of the population (Ohtake 2006). Just as in the debate on inequality, the increase in poverty among the elderly is treated as a natural phenomenon accompanying the ageing of society. If this is the case, it is quite possible for the growth of poverty in Japan overall too to be seen as an inevitable natural phenomenon resulting from changes in the population structure.

Poverty among the elderly has also been raised as an issue in itself, along with the idea that the system of income redistribution must be improved (Abe 2006). According to this argument, the main cause of the increase in the rate of poverty among the elderly between 1993 and 2002 is the income factor that is the result of changes in market income and of the tax and social security system. Changes in household structure are only a small factor, and the influence of ageing is even smaller.

Attention is shifting to the rapid increase in non-regular employment among young people as a factor in the rise in the poverty rate, and this has become a new policy issue. It is certain that the shift to non-regular employment among young people is something that threatens to continue long-term and to destroy the basis of Japanese society. However, being poor is just as serious whether one is old or young, and poverty should not be accepted simply because it is the elderly who are poor. Policy measures ought to be seen as just as necessary.

## 3. Ageing and the Reality of Inequality and Poverty

### 3.1. *Living arrangements*[1]

On 1 October 2005, there were 25.6 million people in Japan aged 65 and over: 14.77 million women and 10.84 million men. This meant that elderly people accounted for 20.04 per cent of the total population.

At the same time as the numbers of elderly people are rising, the shift to single-person households is also advancing among the elderly.

[1] All data in this section are from Naikakufu 2006b.

In 2004, there were 17.86 million households with one or more elderly persons aged 65 and over, and of these, no more than 3.92 million households (21.9 per cent) were "three-generation households" where elderly people were living with their children and grandchildren. The majority, 5.25 million (29.4 per cent) were households consisting of just elderly couples, while 3.73 million households (20.9 per cent) were single-person households consisting of elderly people living alone. Because of the fall in the number of three-generation households and the rise in the number of single-person households, their respective numbers have ended up almost the same.

If we look at the increase in elderly single-person households, we see that, in 1980, there were 190,000 elderly men and 690,000 women living alone, but by 2000, these numbers had increased dramatically to 740,000 men and 2.29 million women. Currently, 13.8 per cent of the elderly are living alone—8.0 per cent of men and 17.9 per cent of women.

The increase in the numbers of elderly people living alone is predicted to continue, increasing by 6.35 million to reach 34.56 million by 2020, when 18.4 per cent of elderly people will be living alone. Until now, the number of women living alone has grown, but the proportion of elderly men living alone is expected to rise considerably in the future.

However, even though these elderly people are classified as living alone, this does not necessarily mean that that they are living on their own in real terms. There are cases where the households are separate according to the residents' register, but their children and their families are living under the same roof as the elderly people, and there are also cases where siblings are living nearby. There are no national statistics on how many elderly people are living alone in real terms. However, according to a survey on independence carried out by Minato Ward in Tokyo (MSFK 2006), 45 per cent of elderly people classified as living alone were doing so in real terms, in other words, without any family in the neighbourhood. The number of elderly people living alone in real terms was 1,889 out of 16,660 elderly households (11 per cent) in 1985, and had increased to 3,665 out of 21,420 households (17 per cent) in 2000.

### 3.2. *Poverty among the elderly*

Regarding the average annual income of the elderly, 60 per cent of elderly households have an annual income of less than 3 million yen (see Figure 1). Overall, no more than 30 per cent of households fall into this category, so it is clear that elderly households are clustered together at the bottom of the income classes. It is difficult for elderly households to pull themselves out of income equality by themselves. In cases where they do not have enough money to live on, they are no longer able to rely on their children either. If we compare surveys from 2001 and 1995, the largest category in 1995, "living with and/or being helped by one's children", had fallen to third place by 2001, and instead, "saving for living expenses and making do" and "meeting costs by using up savings" had risen to first and second places. The number of elderly people who try to get by through their own efforts without relying on their children has increased (Naikakufu 2006b).

Elderly people whose own incomes are low and who cannot expect support from their children cannot help but fall into poverty. Poverty is growing above all among those living alone. Looking at the results of the estimates of the poverty rate of the elderly using 50 per cent of the equivalent disposable income level as a base, we see that in 2002, 20.05 per cent of those aged 60 and over were categorized as poor. The poverty rate rises with age and with the shift to living alone: 44.44 per cent of households of people in their 70s, and 55.90 per cent of households of people in their 80s are categorized as poor by the above standard (Abe 2006).

The level of pension benefits is hitting its peak because of pension reforms, so improvements in the income of the elderly cannot be expected. Poverty among the elderly, particularly those living alone, is certain to become a great problem in Japan in the future.

### 3.3. *Rapid increase in people receiving elderly public assistance*

Public assistance is the public support system targeting poor relief in Japan. Public assistance is the last safety net, but the fourth article of the Public Assistance Law states the "principle of want" as a condition of receipt of assistance.[2] It is well-known that this principle has

---

[2] (1) Public assistance comes into effect on the condition that the impoverished person uses any possible assets and uses all his or her powers in order to maintain a minimum standard of living for him or herself. (2) Support for people whom it is an obligation to assist as determined in the Civil Code and aid as determined in other laws all come into effect taking precedence over the aid provided by this law. (3) The two aforementioned provisions are not intended to prevent providing necessary aid in urgent cases.

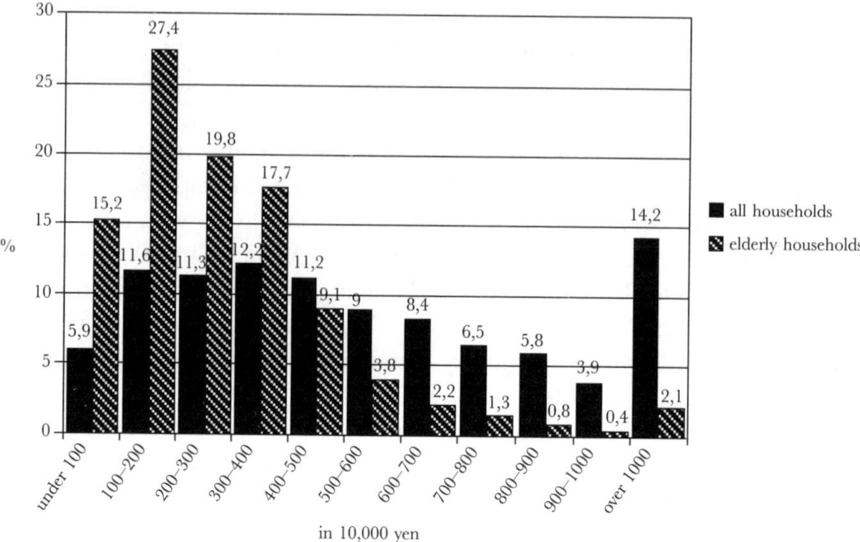


Note: Elderly households are those consisting only of people aged 65 and over, including those with unmarried persons aged under 18. Average for all households: 57,970,000 yen; average for elderly households: 29,090,000 yen; median for elderly households: 2,340,000 yen.
Source: Naikakufu 2006b.

Figure 1. Distribution of Household Income.

been excessively emphasized and has resulted in a situation where even people who really ought to receive support are not deemed eligible. Public assistance tells us the proportion of poor households receiving this support, and, according to the research cited above, it is no more than 20 per cent (Komamura 2002).

Even though the public assistance system is one in which it is difficult to qualify for support, poverty among the elderly was already becoming apparent at the beginning of the 1990s, and the numbers of people aged 65 and over receiving public assistance have increased rapidly (see Figure 2).

In 2004, 525,131 people aged 65 and over were receiving public assistance (see Table 2), and 40 per cent of those receiving public assistance are elderly. Of the 25.6 million elderly people in the population, the proportion receiving public assistance is 2.00 per cent, twice the proportion of the 1.11 per cent in the overall population. Poverty is undergoing an ageing process.

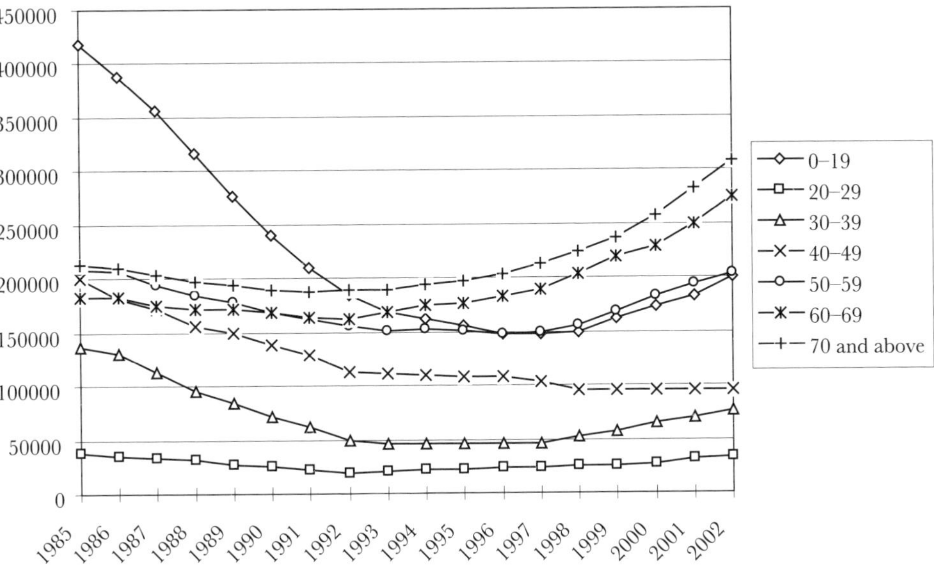


Source: Ministry of Health, Labour and Welfare *"National Mass Survey on People Receiving Public Social Assistance (basic survey)."*

Figure 2. Shifts in people receiving public assistance by age group.

Table 2. People Receiving Public Assistance by Age and Sex.

| | | 2004 | | | 2003 | | |
|---|---|---|---|---|---|---|---|
| | | Total | Aged 65 and over | | Total | Aged 65 and over | |
| | | | | Single-person households | | | Single-person households |
| Number of people | Total | 1,375,926 | 525,131 | 371,763 | 1,291,212 | 489,843 | 347,353 |
| | Men | 636,946 | 216,319 | 147,972 | 594,618 | 199,861 | 136,354 |
| | Women | 738,980 | 308,812 | 223,791 | 696,594 | 289,982 | 210,999 |
| Proportion (%) | Total | 100.0 | 38.2 | 27.0 | 100.0 | 37.9 | 26.9 |
| | Men | 46.3 | 15.7 | 10.8 | 46.1 | 15.5 | 10.6 |
| | Women | 53.7 | 22.4 | 16.3 | 53.9 | 22.5 | 16.3 |

Source: Ministry of Health, Labour and Welfare *"National Mass Survey on People Receiving Assistance (basic survey)".*

### 3.4. *Poverty among elderly people living alone*

Special mention should be made of the fact that the majority of elderly people receiving public assistance are living alone: 371,763 people, or 70.8 per cent of the elderly receiving public assistance.

There are 3.73 million households consisting of elderly people living alone, so this means that 10 per cent of them are receiving public assistance. The proportion of people receiving public assistance overall in Japan is no more than 1 per cent, so it is clear that poverty among the elderly living alone is becoming apparent.

However, if we take the statistic that over 40 per cent of the elderly living alone are in poverty, as mentioned above, it becomes clear that there are still many elderly people living in poverty who are nevertheless not receiving public assistance. The public assistance system needs to be made more user-friendly.

### 3.5. *Living circumstances of elderly people receiving public assistance*

Although elderly people receiving public assistance are supposed to be guaranteed a basic standard of living, if we look at their actual living circumstances, the reality is that they have lost touch with people and are living in isolation (see Figure 3). The reason is that they are forced to restrict their outgoings related to having a social life, because the level of public assistance is low. To encourage participation in society among those receiving public assistance, it is necessary to improve the level of public assistance. Moreover, it is also necessary to provide places for elderly people to get together and more opportunities to encourage them out of their homes.

## 4. Policies to Combat Poverty among the Elderly

Against a background of increasing poverty among the elderly, it is striking that recently in Japan policy measures have been taken that will increase poverty even more. Pension reforms and medical treatment system reforms have made the burden on the elderly on low incomes even heavier. In public assistance too, reductions in the levels of payments have been made.

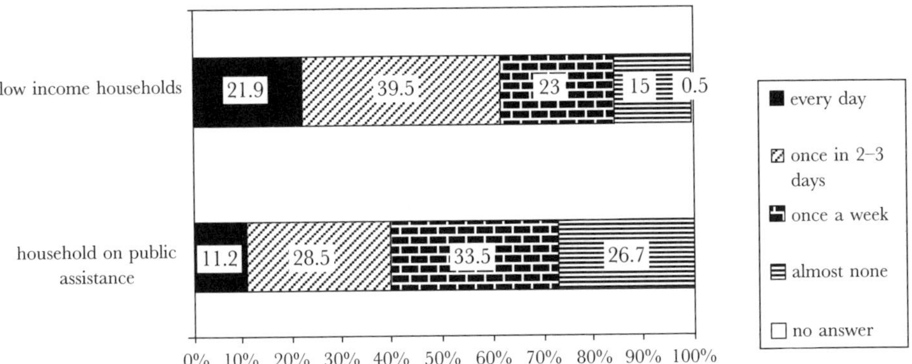


Source: SSKCK 2003: 10.

Figure 3. Social Life of the Elderly—Number of Telephone Calls Made.

### 4.1. *Abolition of public assistance age additional allowances*

As elderly people get older, they start to need easily digestible food, and their heating, clothing, hygiene, social and other costs rise. Additional age allowances for those aged 70 and over (or the infirm aged 68 and over) are what meet these special needs that accompany ageing. The amount varied between the big cities and the provinces, but if we take the big cities as an example, 17,930 yen was paid monthly as an additional age allowance to people aged 70 and over receiving public assistance.

This additional age allowance has undergone phased reductions since April 2004 and was abolished in April 2006. The reason for abolishing it is that, if we look at the spending patterns of elderly people overall, it is not the case that expenditure particularly increases with age after 70, so there are no special needs corresponding to the age additional allowance (SHSFB 2004).

As of July 2006, 64 people receiving elderly public assistance have taken out lawsuits opposing this move in five areas—Tokyo, Akita, Hiroshima, Niigata, and Fukuoka—on the grounds that they can no longer afford even a minimum standard of living because of the abolition of the additional age allowance. What happens in the hearings will be watched carefully as an indication of whether minimum living expenses for elderly people are still sufficient after the loss of the additional age allowance, or are now inadequate.

### 4.2. *Beginnings of support for independence in everyday life and social life*

In accordance with the 2004 Special Committee Report on the Desirable Form of the Public Assistance System, a programme of support for independence has been implemented in public assistance since 2005. In these cases, the important thing is that independence does not only mean independence in terms of work and economic independence. Combining what public assistance calls independence and the social welfare law, independence has been redefined as going about everyday life, living socially and being integrated into the local area, while continuing to take advantage of public assistance. This marks a watershed in terms of the direction of development of the public assistance system: it is not just a matter of financial benefits, but rather the aim is to create a system of phased-in support, with welfare offices providing a choice of personal service benefits at different levels and of various kinds for people in need of assistance.

The choice of kinds of support for independence covers a wide range, and new programmes have begun for elderly people receiving public assistance, such as support in daily life in their own homes, and "making meeting places" as support for participation in society. There is a danger that elderly people receiving public assistance have been forced to economise on social spending because of the abolition of the additional age allowance and that social isolation has deepened; but on the other hand, services supporting elderly people's lives have begun to be provided. For example, Shinjuku Ward in Tokyo, which is running advanced programmes, has drawn up the "Shinjuku Support Plan", raising the "capacity to live" of elderly people who have a tendency to shut themselves away at home, by setting up karaoke classes and handicraft workshops for single elderly people receiving public assistance (Fukawa 2006).

## 5. Conclusion

To prevent poverty among the elderly, it is absolutely essential to increase the basic pension and guarantee to all elderly people an income above the level of public assistance benefits. However, in reality, the pension level is not being raised, and there are even moves to cut the benefit levels of public assistance. Together with the age additional allowance lawsuits, how this situation will develop is something that will be keenly watched.

Moreover, the newly started independence support programmes are positive programmes aiming at social inclusion, and their expansion must be closely watched.

## References


Abe, Aya (2006): *1980–2000-nendai no nihon no bōkon ritsu no idō to yōin bunseki (Shakai seisaku gakkai dai-112 kai taikai jiyū rondai hōkoku)* [Analysis of changes and factors in the poverty rate in Japan in the 1980s to 2000s. (Report on open theme section at 112th Social policy conference). Unpublished.

Förster, Michael and Mira d'Ercole, Marco (2005): *Income Distribution and Poverty in OECD Countries in the Second Half of the 1990s. OECD Working Paper 22.*

Fukawa, Hisashi (ed.) (2006): *Seikatsu hogo jiritsu shien puroguramu no katsuyō* [Application of programmes supporting independence in public assistance]. Tōkyō: Sekibundō.

Komamura, Kōhei (2002): Sēfutinetto no saikōchiku—tei shotoku setai no jōkyō [Reconstructing the safety net—circumstances of low-income households]. In: *Shūkan Shakai Hoshô [Social Security Weekly]*, 228, November: pp. 24–27.

MSFK (Minato-ku Shakai Fukushi Kyōgikai) (2006): *Minato-ku ni okeru hitori kurashi kōreisha no seikatsu jittai to shakaiteki koritsu ni kansuru chōsa hōkokusho* [Report on survey on living conditions and social isolation in elderly people living alone in Minato ward]. August.

Naikakufu [Cabinet Office] (2006a): *Getsurei keizai hōkoku nado ni kansuru kankei kakuryō kaigi shiryō* [Materials from cabinet meetings on monthly economic reports etc.]. January.

—— (2006b): *Heisei 18-nenpan kōrei shakai hakusho* [2006 White Paper on the aged Society]. http://www8.cao.go.jp/kourei/whitepaper/w-2006/zenbun/18index.html (found 12 April 2007).

—— (2006c): *Heisei 18-nenpan keizai zaisei hakusho* [2006 White Paper on Economic and Fiscal Policy]. http://www5.cao.go.jp/j-j/wp/wp-je06/06–00000.html (found 12 April 2007).

Ohtake, Fumio (1999): Kōreika to shotoku bunpai no fubyōdō—fubyōdō no honshitsu o mikiwame seisakuteki taiō o [Ageing and inequality in income distribution—ascertaining the real nature of inequality and making policy responses to it]. In: *Nihon Keizai Kenkyū Sentā Kaihō [Japan Economic Research Centre Bulletin]*, 825, June, pp. 17–20.

—— (2006): "Kakusa wa ikenai" no fumō—seisaku toshite tou beki shiten wa doko ni aru no ka [The sterility of "inequality is wrong"—where are the viewpoints that ought to be sought in terms of policy?]. In: *Kōza [Lectures]*, 131, April, pp. 104–109.

Ohtake, Fumio and Saitō, Makoto (1999): Shotoku fubyōdōka no haikei to sono seisakuteki gan'i—nenrei kaisō nai kōka, nenrei kaisō kan kōka, jinkō kōreika kōka [The background and policy implications of the trend towards income inequality—effects within and among age groups and effects of population ageing]. In: *Kikan Shakai Hoshō Kenkyū* 35, 1, pp. 65–76.

SHSFB (Shakai Hoshō Shingikai Fukushi Bukai—Seikatsu Hogo Seido no Arikata ni Kansuru Senmon Iinkai) (2004): *Seikatsu hogo seido no arikata ni kansuru senmon iinkai hôkokusho* [Report of Special Committee on the Desirable Form of the Public assistance System].

SSKCK (Shakai Seikatsu ni Kansuru Chōsa Kentōkai) (2003): *Shakai hoshō seikei chōsa kekka* [Survey results on social security livelihood]. Tokyo: Kōseirōdōshō.

Tachibanaki, Toshiaki (1998): *Nihon no keizai kakusa* [Economic inequality in Japan]. Tokyo: Iwanami Shinsho.

CHAPTER FIFTY-ONE

# ECONOMIC FACTORS IN THE DECLINING BIRTH RATE

Naohiro Yashiro

## 1. Introduction

Japan's total fertility rate has continued to decline since the mid-1970s, from an annual average of 2.1 during the 1960–74 period to 1.26 in 2005. Despite a series of policy measures aimed at countering the trend, such as increases in nursery schools or in maternity-leave benefit, there are no signs of the declining trend stopping. As a result of low fertility rates in the past, which have been well below the population reproduction level of 2.1 for many years, the Japanese population reached a peak in 2005 and has started to decline steadily; it is predicted to fall from 127.7 million in 2005 to about 100 million in 2050, approximately the same level as in 1967. The declining and ageing population is now one of the most important policy issues in Japan. Nevertheless, there are no consensus views on what the major factors in the persistent decline in fertility are, and thus, there are no concrete ideas for strong policy measures to reverse the trend. In fact, current policies to counter the decline in the population are simply incremental measures based on existing schemes and institutions.

In this chapter, we try to explain the fertility decline mainly in terms of economic factors, for example, the increasing costs of childrearing. The costs for child care include not only pecuniary expenses for childrearing, but also the opportunity costs of women who have to leave full-time work to take care of their children and have to sacrifice substantial lifetime earnings which they would otherwise receive. This trade-off between continuing in full-time work and full-time child care at home is particularly important in Japan, because it is quite difficult to return to full-time jobs after childrearing. Common work practices for core workers have been modelled on an "ideal" type of household where the husband is supposed to be supported by a full-time housewife. In contrast, traditional work practices do not assume households where both husband and wife work full-time.

Another factor that makes the cost of childrearing expensive is insufficient and poor nursery services. This problem arises from various regulations and institutions which fail to support the growing numbers of families in which both husband and wife work full-time. Nursery schools are mainly provided by the public sector as part of welfare programmes for those poor families that cannot afford to take care of their children at home, although those who are in this traditional category have recently been in the minority.

Although the government has tried to expand the pubic supply of nursery schools, there is still not enough supply to meet the increasing demand from working women in the urban areas. The main reason for the lack of public child-care services is high costs due to public employees' seniority-based wages, which are subject to public budget constraints.

Removing the obstacles for working women to reconcile gainful employment and childrearing is a top priority on the policy agenda, but it is politically difficult, because labour unions and traditional child-care providers object to necessary structural changes. Nevertheless, such structural problems in both labour markets and child-care services will have to be overcome in order to cope with the rapidly ageing Japanese society.

## 2. Labour Market Reforms

The trend of Japan's total fertility rates in the post-war period can be divided into three periods according to various factors affecting the trend (Figure 1).

The first period is reflected in the rapid fall in the fertility rate, from 4.5 to 2.1 in the 1947–1959 period, which was mainly due to a declining proportion of self-employed families, chiefly in the agricultural and retail sectors: self-employed families need many children as a labour force and to inherit the family business, while having children is optional for an employee family.[1] In other words, whereas children can be regarded as a "capital good" for the self-employed, they constitute "consumption goods" for employees. Thus, an increasing proportion of

[1] The total fertility rates of agricultural self-employed, other self-employed and employees were 2.39, 2.06, and 1.79 respectively in 1997 (Basic Survey on Marriage and Childbirth, National Institute of Population and Social Security Research).

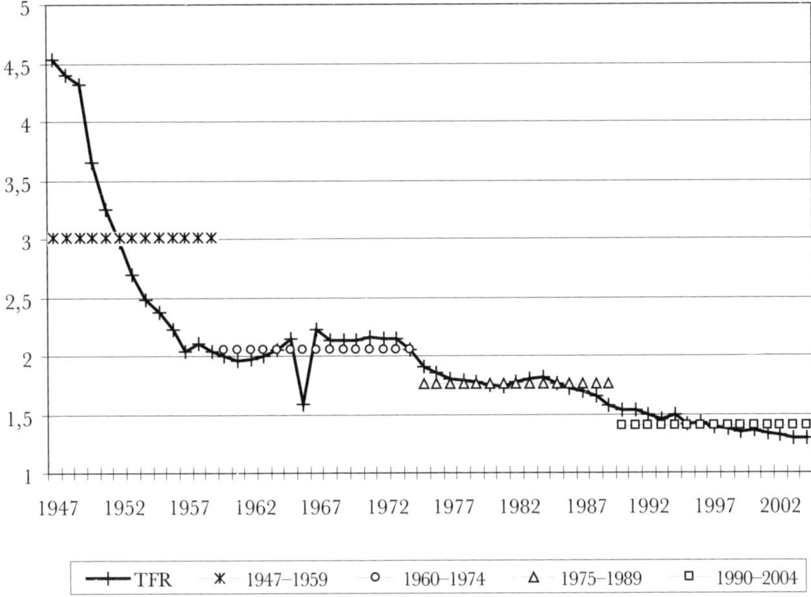


Note: The numbers refer to the medium official fertility projections.
Source: National Institute of Population and Social Security Research, IPSS.

Figure 1. Trend of the total fertility rate in Japan.

employees in the population lead to a decrease in the average number of children per family.

The second period is 1960–1974, when fertility rates were virtually constant at 2.1, with the downward pressure on fertility due to the fall in self-employed people and the increase in employed people fading away. The third is the period of continuous decline from 1975 to the present, which is the focus of this paper.

Since 1975, Japan has been experiencing a continuous decline in the total fertility rate. This decline was not entirely expected by demographers, and official projections have frequently been too optimistic in assuming an automatic recovery of fertility, which, however, has never materialized[2] (see Figure 2).

[2] There are three kinds of fertility projections: high, low and middle, of which the middle projection is used for the official social security estimates and other policy planning.

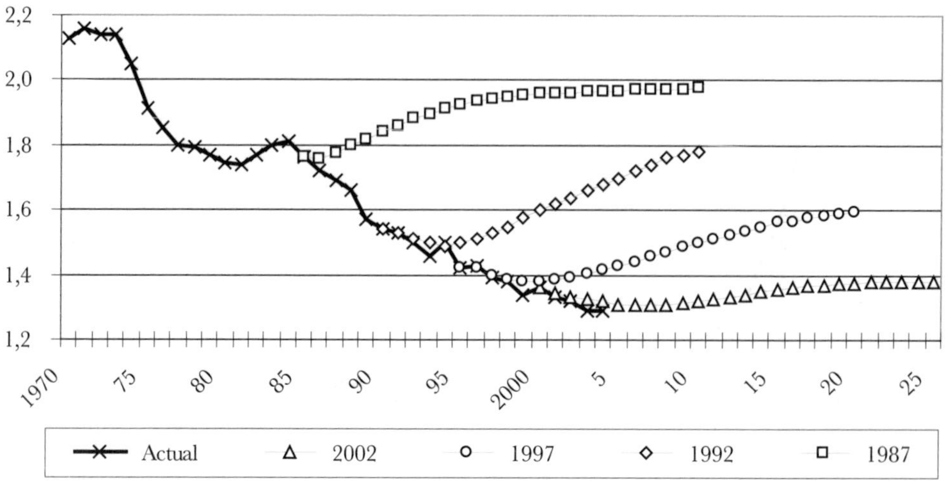


Note: The numbers refer to the middle official fertility projections.
Source: National Institute of Population and Social Security Research, IPSS.

Figure 2. Projections of the fertility rate in Japan.

Even in the most recent official projection, the actual fertility rate has already dipped below the predicted one.

This persistent prediction error in only one direction (upside risk) indicates the presence of an underlying force lowering the fertility rates that is not being accounted for in the traditional demographic projections. The single most important missing factor is the increasing labour force participation of women in more qualified jobs. This reflects an expansion of service industries providing better job opportunities for women (demand side factor), and women's higher enrolment in college education, thus improving the quality of labour (supply side factor).

With the ratio of female to male university enrolment rising to over 70 per cent, the gap in male and female higher education has been diminishing rapidly. This is reflected in an increase in the ratio of employed women to men from 40 per cent in 1960 to 70 per cent in 2005 (Figure 3).

Higher labour force participation of women alone does not necessarily lower fertility rates, as shown by the experience of some Scandinavian countries like Sweden or Norway, where fertility rates are higher than Japan's, despite equally high labour force participation of women. However, under Japan's traditional employment practices, the opportunity costs of marriage and childrearing are especially high, so

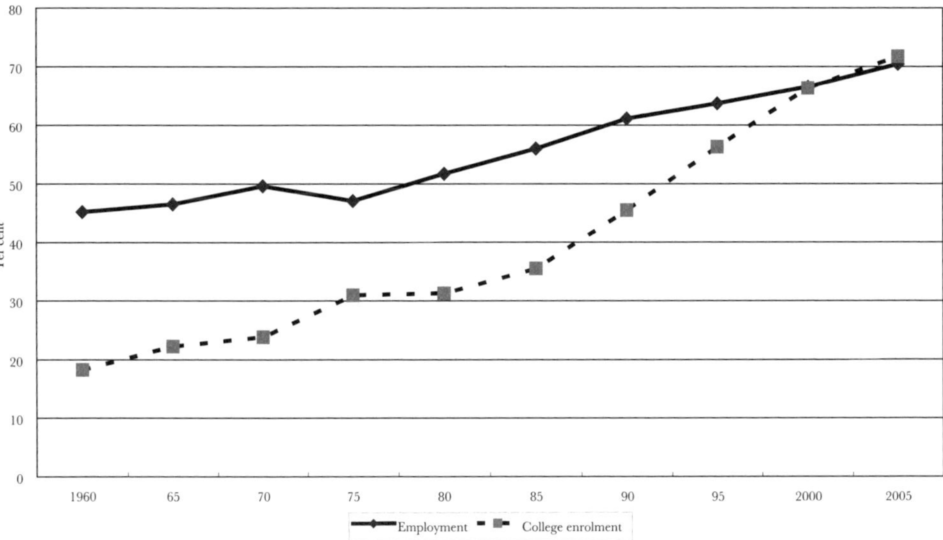


Source: Ministry of Education and Ministry of Health, Labour and Welfare.

Figure 3. Increasing ratio of women to men in both employment and university enrolment.

that the desire for children is likely to fall, with more women coming into the labour market on a full-time basis. The high opportunity costs for women of bringing up children are closely related to the long-term job security and seniority-based wage structures found in many Japanese companies.

Traditional employment practices, which guarantee long-term employment and seniority-based wages, are not attributable to paternalistic behaviour on the part of employers, but are economically rational practices which help companies to retain workers in whose human resource development they have invested through long-term on-the job training. Because such employment guarantees are costly for companies, particularly in recessionary periods, workers are supposed to show high flexibility in terms of overtime work and frequent job rotations. The long working hours by international standards in Japanese companies function as a sort of employment protection, because companies can reduce labour costs during recessions by merely cutting overtime hours.

The long-term employment commitment between companies and workers, and the resulting burden on workers is implicitly based on a vertical division of labour between a husband concentrating on work and his wife being responsible for child care and other home activities. The husband's sustained long hours of work, which are necessary for preventing lay-offs, make it difficult to share the burden of child care at home. Frequent job shifting in the company or across company groups, which is another means of providing job security, require the spouse not to commit herself to permanent jobs. Such a traditional workstyle is, however, quite costly for couples where both partners work full-time, as one of them has to give up his/her current job or has to live separately when required to move to other areas by the company.

As a result, if Japanese women follow a similar workstyle to Japanese men, no one can afford to take care of the children at home. Thus, Japanese women usually face a trade-off between continuing to work without having children or leaving the company to concentrate on bringing up children at home. However, once women leave the company to bring up children, it is hard to return to their previous full-time jobs, because entry into large companies is usually restricted to new graduates, under long-term employment protection.

This trade-off was not significant when most women's jobs were unattractive, with low wages and less possibility for promotion; in that case, marriage might well be a better long-term commitment than job security. With the improvement of women's status in the labour market, however, the trade-off becomes a more important factor in discouraging the demand for children. The opportunity costs (foregone earnings) of an average woman incurred by leaving a company to bring up children can be approximated by comparing the following two standard cases: one is the lifetime earnings of a full-time worker starting at age 20 (junior college graduate) who stays with a company until the normal retirement age of 60; another is the case of a woman starting work at age 20, leaving a company at age 25 and rejoining the labour market as a part-time worker at age 40 (when the youngest children have reached school age). Comparing the life-cycle patterns of the two women, the difference in lifetime earnings amounts to 220 million yen (White Paper on Peoples' Life 2005). With average wages increasing, more and more women are becoming conscious of these "opportunity costs of marriage". This is why there exists a strong potential demand for marriage, but the actual marriage rates have continued to decline.[3]

[3] According to surveys on unmarried women, close to 90 per cent of them wish to marry sometime.

To sum up, the direct cause of the fertility decline is the increasing labour force participation of women, reflecting good job opportunities for them. But what is more important as an underlying factor is the inflexibility of labour markets based on a traditional division of labour between men and women. As it is unrealistic to encourage women to stay at home, and since Japan's economy is not sustainable without an increasing supply of qualified women workers, a possible policy option has to be the reform of labour markets so that households with two earners can manage to bring up children without incurring a heavy economic burden. Alternatively, a more flexible labour market, where second chances for full-time jobs are abundant, is needed.

The lack of flexible labour markets is a reflection of rigid employment protection. Although employment contracts are based on agreements between companies and labour unions, there are various laws protecting firm-specific internal labour markets by excluding flexible labour markets. For example, the labour law prohibits certain occupations (for example, the medical service or legal service sectors) for temporary workers, and sets the limit for contract work at 3 years in most occupations. These prohibitions are based on the idea that regular workers should be protected from being replaced by temporary workers with fixed-term contracts. Such policies regulating the various employment contracts limit the choices of married women who would like to pursue jobs and have children. Once they have left work, such rigid employment protection reduces opportunities to return to full-time jobs, including for those who leave the labour market to bring up children. In Japan, dismissal of workers due to lack of competence is usually not admitted in court. Although employment protection is a safety-net for the benefit of the workers who are already employed, it is unfair to workers of higher quality outside the company, including women after the childrearing period.

The government is basically negative towards more flexible labour market policies where both men and women can move from one company to another at lower opportunity costs. Instead, the government has encouraged women to stay in companies by extending their maternity leave.[4] However, this implies only a minor change to traditional

[4] Maternity leave is legally assured for six weeks before and eight weeks after birth.

employment practices, which are implicitly based on the assumption that men work outside the home and that women stay at home.

## 3. Efficient Supply of Child-Care Services

In Japan, nursery schools are mainly provided by the public sector as part of welfare programmes. This is because child care is generally considered to be a responsibility of the family, and public nursery[5] schools are provided only for those families that cannot afford to take care of their children at home because both parents have to earn money. Also, public nursery schools are established based on the law for the protection of children, that is, as a welfare policy, not as a labour policy to support the work of parents with small children. This has led to the basic concept of public nursery policies according to which the government should be responsible for allocating nursery services for the benefits of the children rather than for their parents. The law implicitly assumes that there is a possibility of a conflict of interests between parents and their children, that is, the parents may act for their own convenience rather than that of their children. This view that the consumers' sovereignty should not be allowed is marked in the nursery services, but is contrary to the case for other services in the market.

The basic characteristics of the current nursery administration are the following. First, nursery services are allocated by the municipal administration based on the "need" of the children. The first priorities in the allocation of the public nursery school quotas are single-parent families, followed by those with both parents working full-time, although they do not necessarily belong to the low income classes. However, public nursery schools have limited opening hours and are thus difficult for women in full-time jobs to utilize. This reflects the principle that public nursery schools are for the benefits of children, not for providing services for the parents.

Second, the costs of nursery services, particularly of those schools managed by the municipality with public employees, are quite high, as their salaries are linked to seniority just like those of other public employees.

---

[5] Public nursery schools are either managed by municipalities using government employees, or by social welfare corporations, which are private non-profit organizations but strictly regulated by the government, just like those in the public sector.

Third, the user charges for the nursery services are generally low, and they do not cover the total costs of the services. Also, the user charges are proportional to the *incomes* of the family (based on the principle of welfare) and the lowest income classes are free from charges.[6] This is contrary to the cases of health or elderly care services, where the user charges are basically proportional to the *costs of services* (just like normal services in the market), except for low income classes.

The combination of low prices and high costs of nursery services naturally stimulates a large demand for nursery services in the middle-class, but the supply is limited due to public budget constraints. This results in excess demand for public nursery services, reflected by long waiting lists, particularly in urban areas where young families with two earners are prevalent. Although the government has tried to increase nursery services simply by expanding the current capacities of nursery schools, there is obviously a limit to supplying services within the existing institutions. Furthermore, the target of the government policy to increase supply is only based on the "revealed demand" for such services from people already registered with the municipal authorities. However, the potential demand is even higher and will reveal itself only after more opportunities for using such services are provided.

Thus, with an increasing number of working women who are not necessarily poor, this traditional scheme of nursery services within the framework of welfare has become inefficient. A more efficient provision of nursery services in terms of both quantity and quality would be to provide them as market services, so that the mechanism that the demand creates the supply is incorporated just as with any other normal services in the market.

### 3.1. *Major reform issues*

A major factor in why there is not a sufficient supply of child-care services lies in the "dual structure" in the nursery school market. On the one hand are nursery schools officially approved by the government, which are financed by public subsidies covering most of the costs. In these cases, three-quarters of the capital costs (excluding the land) are financed by the government. On the other hand, there are private

[6] User charges based on a household's income are not necessarily fair, as the self-employed can manage their incomes by controlling their expenses, unlike employees whose salaries are captured by the tax authorities through company reports.

nursery services that are not financially supported by the government which are financed mainly by user fees and receive few public subsidies. The dividing line between the two categories of nursery schools in terms of spaces and allocation of staff per children is uniform nationwide, and is too rigid in urban areas with high land prices, resulting in an insufficient supply of such services. The administration's view is that the current dividing line is based on a minimum standard for the certified nursery schools, but actually there are many nursery schools of various qualities based on the various demands of the consumers.

In this sense, the way that public support is provided to nurseries should be incremental according to the quality of the services, rather than all or nothing between certified and non-certified, in order to give incentives to non-certified nursery schools to improve their quality. Also, support should not be provided to the nursery schools but to the users, so that the more children the nursery schools attract, the more subsidies they receive, which would stimulate mergers and acquisitions by excellent nursery schools over less popular ones. The basic framework for reform should be the following:

First, nursery services should be supplied based on a "contract", rather than allocation by the administration. It is important for the users to choose freely nursery schools with adequate services, so that those nursery schools which are chosen by the consumers can expand their supply. This is closely related to the way prices of services are set; the user charges should be set in proportion to the costs, not by the income of the households, so that the quality of the services is balanced with the price.

Second, it is important to induce competition among nursery schools to stimulate the supply of various types of services in the market. Removing the entry barriers to the nursery service market for firms is necessary to stimulate such competition. Although for-profit firms are already allowed to enter the market, they have to follow the general practices of the social welfare corporations, and implicit penalties are charged for dividends.

Third, public subsidies to nursery services should be directed to the consumers, rather than to the existing nursery schools,[7] so that com-

[7] Subsidies to public nursery schools are not directly related to the numbers of children, so those with low quality services can survive.

petition between service providers is stimulated on a level playing field to improve quality with a variety of services.

### 3.2. *Budgetary policy for financing child-care services*

A major characteristic of Japan's social security expenditure is a heavy emphasis on the elderly. The share of the public social security expenditure for the elderly was over 70 per cent in 2003, while that for children and the family was less than 4 per cent. The expansion of social security expenditure for the elderly has been mainly due to increases in pensions and, to a lesser extent, health expenditure (see Figure 4). The current expenditure distribution has developed mainly because child care is thought to be a responsibility of the family, and working-age families were usually better-off than the retired during the period of high economic growth. However, with slowing economic growth and the deterioration of the function of the family during the 1990s, more public support for children and the family is needed. Such support for the family also helps to restore a fair distribution of budget resources across generations.

Another factor explaining the disparity in expenditure between the elderly and children lies in the different ways of financing their support. Most social expenditure for the elderly is in the form of social insurance, collected mainly through social insurance premiums, while social expenditure for children is mainly financed by the general tax revenue. Raising social insurance premiums meets less resistance politically than raising tax rates for expenditure that is not necessarily specified.

However, there are various reasons that financing child-care services in the form of social insurance is desirable. Although "social insurance" for child-care services seems odd at first sight, as having a child cannot be considered to be an insurable "risk" in the strict sense, it is to a certain extent the same as insurance for the frail elderly.

Social insurance is simply a mechanism to share the burden of taking care of the elderly and children in society. What is more important is that there is no "moral hazard" problem with social insurance for child care. In fact, a "moral hazard", in the sense that people are induced to have children because of this insurance, would actually be the aim of such a policy countering the declining fertility trend.

The major aims of social insurance for child care would be the following. First, to secure the social security budget financing for child-care services in the form of social insurance premiums. Second, to

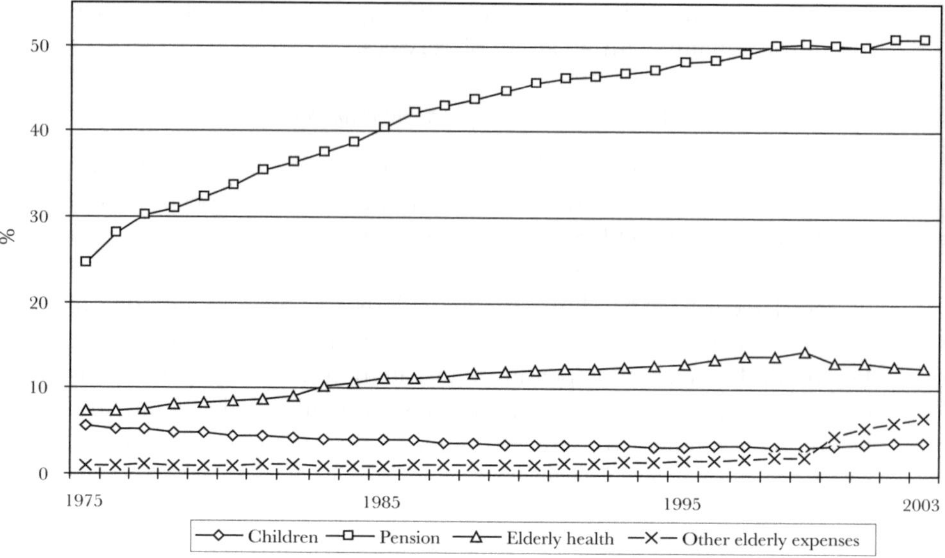


Source: National Institute for Population and Social Security Research, IPSS.

Figure 4. Comparison of social expenditure for children and the elderly in per cent of total social expenditure.

concentrate the existing subsidies on the users in the form of vouchers for such services. Third, to allow users to choose child-care services freely in the market, so that the growth of the child care industry would be stimulated, just as was the case with the industry for care services for the frail elderly after the introduction of public long-term care insurance. Public insurance for the frail elderly was established in 2000 and has completely changed the traditional framework of care services, as access to such services is based on a contract between users and providers. Users are basically those aged 65 and above who, based on an assessment of the need for such services, can receive care service benefits (in kind) to a certain amount. The contributors to the insurance are those aged 40 and above, and the scheme is managed by the municipalities. The same basic framework could be applied to child-care services.

## 4. Conclusion

A major economic factor in the declining birth rate is the increasing opportunity costs for women of childrearing. Thus, policy to reverse the declining birth rate has to aim to reduce the opportunity costs of bringing up children. This means that more flexible labour markets, as well as a market-based supply of nursery services, are needed. Nursery schools, which are currently based on a welfare approach, should be reformed to become market-based services for ordinary families, who share the costs related to the quality of the services. A similar kind of reform has already been undertaken in care services for the frail elderly and has created a growing variety of services and employment. What is important now is to offer care services for the frail elderly and children under a social insurance scheme for the family. In this respect, it will become necessary to revise the composition of social security expenditure, which is heavily biased toward the elderly.

Such regulatory and institutional reform is, however, difficult, as it conflicts with the vested interests of specific groups such as labour unions and providers of current child-care services, which tend to favour the status quo. In this sense, countering declining fertility is at the core of the structural reform of Japan's economy and society, where many people are still dreaming of the recovery of the high rate of economic growth and the resulting abundant tax revenues of the past. In this sense, the continuously declining fertility rates are a symbol of insufficient efforts towards the necessary structural reform.

## References

Hurd, Michael D. and Naohiro Yashiro (eds.) (1997): *The Economic Effects of Aging in the United States and Japan*. Chicago: The University of Chicago Press.

Yashiro, Naohiro (1999): *Shōshi · kōreika no keizaigaku* [Economics of a Declining Population and Ageing]. Tokyo: Toyokeizai Shuppansha.

—— (2001): Social Implications of Demographic Change in Japan. In: Little, Jane Sneddon and Robert K. Triest (eds.): *Seismic Shifts: The Economic Impact of Demographic Change*. Federal Reserve Bank of Boston, Conference Series No. 46, June.

—— (2003): Demographic Changes and their Implications for Japanese Household Savings. In: Robert M. Stern (ed.): *Japan's Economic Recovery*. Northampton, MA: Edward Elgar Publishing, pp. 375–395.

Yashiro, Naohiro, Wataru Suzuki and Sayuri Shiraishi (2006): Hoikusho no kisei kaikaku to ikuji hoken [Regulatory reform in nursery schools and social insurance for child care]. In: *Nihon Keizai Kenkyū* [Japan Economic Journal] 53, pp. 194–220.

CHAPTER FIFTY-TWO

# LABOUR MARKET AND LABOUR MARKET POLICIES FOR THE AGEING SOCIETY

Hendrik Meyer-Ohle

## 1. Introduction

Compared to other advanced economies, Japan ranks very highly in terms of the economic activity of older people. This not only points to a high degree of willingness on the part of older people to work, or to the necessity for them to do so, but also indicates the existence of employment opportunities for older people. Therefore, the issue of labour market participation of older people seems to be less pressing for Japan than for most other comparable countries. Indeed, policy makers from other countries have been studying Japan's labour market situation and labour market policies for older people. However, with the number of older people increasing, as well as changes in the factors that have so far supported the high labour market participation rate among older people in Japan, concerns have increasingly been raised as to whether this favourable situation will continue. Others have pointed to shortcomings in regard to the quality of work offered to older people in Japan. Faced with an increasing number of older people, Japanese policy makers have come up with a number of initiatives to sustain this high participation rate and to improve the employment situation of older people.

## 2. Japan's High Labour Force Participation Rate among Older People

Any discussion of the labour market for older people in Japan needs to start from the comparatively high rate of older people who are still economically active. With 71.2 per cent of all men aged between 60 and 64 years still working, Japan stands out among countries of comparable economic development, such as the US, Germany, France, Sweden and Korea (see Table 1). Even after age 65, 31.1 per cent of Japanese men

Table 1. Working population among older people (in per cent).

| Age/gender | Japan | US | Germany | France | Sweden | Korea |
|---|---|---|---|---|---|---|
| Men | | | | | | |
| 60–64 years | 71.2 | 57.6 | 34.0 | 17.3 | 60.1 | 66.5 |
| 65 years and above | 31.1 | 17.9 | 4.4 | 3.3 | — | 42.7 |
| Women | | | | | | |
| 60–64 years | 39.2 | 44.1 | 16.4 | 15.1 | 53.4 | 46.4 |
| 65 years and above | 13.2 | 9.8 | 1.8 | 2.5 | — | 23.0 |

Source: ILO LABORSTA, France and Korea OECD LABOUR STATISTICS PORTAL, compiled in: Kōsei Rōdōshō 2005a: 163.

continue to be economically active, a figure only exceeded by Korea. For older Japanese women, the situation is, however, less unusual, with women in the US, Sweden and Korea all showing higher participation rates.

A large scale survey conducted by the Japanese Ministry of Health, Labour and Welfare in 2004 shows that, in addition to elderly people already working, there is a significant number of people who are not working but who want to work (Kōsei Rōdōshō 2005b).

The high Japanese participation rate seems to run counter to developments in western countries, especially those in Europe. Here, older employees have increasingly been encouraged or given the opportunity to retire before reaching the official retirement age. The situation in Japan has therefore received some attention. For example, Japan is one of three countries looked at by the United States General Accounting Office in a comparative report on policies to increase labour force participation (GAO 2003). In November 2005, Singapore sent a delegation to Japan to study the country's employment policies for older workers (*The Business Times*, Singapore 9 November 2005).

## 3. Factors Underlying Japan's High Participation Rate

A person's decision to retire or to continue working depends on a number of factors: the availability and appropriateness of employment opportunities; the desire to work; the ability to work; and finally the necessity to work, based on current and previous income as well as future needs.

Table 2. Distribution of employees by age group and size of establishment (in per cent).

| | 25–29 | 30–34 | 35–39 | 40–44 | 45–49 | 50–54 | 55–59 | 60–64 | 65–69 | 70 and above |
|---|---|---|---|---|---|---|---|---|---|---|
| 1 to 4 | 4.9 | 6.6 | 7.2 | 7.9 | 8.1 | 9.8 | 9.9 | 14.6 | 19.0 | 26.2 |
| 5 to 29 | 23.7 | 23.5 | 23.4 | 23.5 | 24.2 | 23.9 | 27.3 | 32.7 | 38.7 | 41.6 |
| 20 to 99 | 17.7 | 17.2 | 17.1 | 16.5 | 19.2 | 19.4 | 18.8 | 19.7 | 17.5 | 15.5 |
| 100 to 499 | 22.5 | 22.7 | 20.8 | 20.7 | 20.0 | 20.0 | 20.1 | 17.4 | 14.6 | 11.9 |
| 500 to 999 | 7.7 | 7.6 | 6.6 | 7.2 | 6.5 | 6.4 | 6.4 | 5.8 | 3.6 | 2.4 |
| 1000 and above | 23.5 | 22.3 | 24.9 | 24.2 | 22.1 | 20.5 | 17.5 | 9.9 | 6.6 | 2.4 |

Note: Labour Force Survey November 2005, excluding public employees and employees of associations and foundations.
Source: Somushō Tōkeikyoku 2005.

Looking at factors underlying the employment situation of older people in Japan, the first noticeable point is the importance of jobs in smaller establishments. Table 2 shows the distribution of employees by age group across establishments of different sizes. Although the importance of small businesses and establishments firms for employment overall is high, this is even more pronounced with regard to the employment of older people. From age 45 upwards the proportion of employees working in smaller establishments increases, with the most significant increase occurring among people over 60 years of age.

The above data are a reflection of the retirement policies of Japanese corporations, with many companies asking their employees to retire around the age of 60. The 2004 Survey Concerning the Working Situation of Older People (Kōsei Rōdōshō 2005b) found that, overall, 74.4 per cent of establishments firms asked employees to retire at a fixed age. Out of these, 98 per cent applied the same age to all employees regardless of occupation. Practically all establishments with more than 100 employees enforced retirement at a fixed age, with the figure dropping to 95.1 per cent for establishments with more than 30 and fewer than 100 employees and further to 70.6 per cent for establishments with fewer than 30 employees. Among those establishments that had a fixed retirement age, the most common age was 60 (88 per cent) (Kōsei Rōdōshō 2005b).

The existence of a fixed retirement age does not, however, necessarily mean that all employees who have reached that age have to leave the company either to retire or to find a new job elsewhere. Many companies operate schemes that enable employees to continue

Table 3. Jobs held by older people by industry (in per cent).

| Age Groups | Agriculture, Fishing, Forestry | Construction | Manufacturing | Transport | Retail, Wholesale | Other Services |
|---|---|---|---|---|---|---|
| Total | 4.1 | 8.8 | 18.1 | 5.1 | 17.7 | 14.6 |
| 35–39 | 1.3 | 8.6 | 21.5 | 5.2 | 16.6 | 13.3 |
| 55–59 | 3.7 | 10.4 | 20.1 | 6.5 | 17.9 | 14.0 |
| 60–64 | 7.1 | 10.8 | 17.7 | 6.2 | 16.8 | 18.7 |
| ≥ 65 | 23.1 | 7.2 | 13.1 | 2.8 | 18.5 | 16.7 |
| Men | | | | | | |
| Total | 4.1 | 12.9 | 20.8 | 7.2 | 14.9 | 14.1 |
| 35–39 | 1.2 | 11.9 | 25.1 | 6.8 | 14.6 | 12.2 |
| 55–59 | 3.3 | 15.1 | 21.5 | 9.0 | 14.3 | 14.3 |
| 60–64 | 6.0 | 15.5 | 18.1 | 9.4 | 13.6 | 18.1 |
| ≥ 65 | 22.9 | 10.1 | 13.4 | 4.2 | 16.3 | 17.3 |

Note: Labour Force Survey November 2005, excluding public employees and employees of associations and foundations.
Source: Somushō Tōkeikyoku 2005.

working, albeit usually with a change in contractual conditions. The 2004 Survey on the Situation of Older Employees showed that 67.5 per cent of establishments had introduced such schemes. Such schemes are, however, normally not made available to all employees. Only 23.3 per cent of establishments offer this opportunity to every employee approaching retirement age, while the majority (61.9 per cent) only offer it to employees deemed worthy by management (Kōsei Rōdōshō 2005b). In addition to in-house schemes, companies often also help older employees to transfer to other companies. This can be to subsidiaries or affiliates, but can also be to business partners, such as suppliers or distributors. Often employees are first loaned out on a temporary basis [*shukkō*] with their original contract staying intact. Later this transfer then might become permanent with a new employment contract being concluded [*tenseki*] (Dirks 1999).

Looking at the distribution of employees across industries, older employees play a larger role in agriculture and the service sector, as well as in construction (see Table 3).

Another factor contributing to high rates of economically active older people is self-employment. While in the 45 to 49 age bracket only around 10 per cent of all working men are self-employed, this figure increases to 24 per cent for men between 60 and 64 and finally to 55 per cent for working men aged 70 and above (Somushō Tōkeikyoku

Table 4. Reasons for older Japanese people to continue working.

| Age<br>Reasons | 55–59 | | 60–64 | | 65–69 | |
|---|---|---|---|---|---|---|
| | Men | women | men | women | men | women |
| To support myself and my family | 88.7 | 62.7 | 67.4 | 56.9 | 53.9 | 46.6 |
| To raise my standard of living | 2.1 | 7.9 | 3.6 | 7.6 | 4.9 | 6.0 |
| Health reasons | 0.6 | 5.1 | 6.3 | 5.6 | 9.6 | 9.3 |
| To provide purpose, to participate in society | 2.4 | 9.4 | 9.3 | 11.3 | 11.8 | 12.5 |
| Asked to do, spare time available | 1.1 | 8.1 | 6.1 | 9.1 | 12.1 | 10.8 |
| Other | 4.4 | 7.6 | 5.5 | 5.8 | 5.3 | 10.8 |

Note: Survey of 25224 people, response 17853, conducted November 2004.
Source: Kōsei Rōdōshō 2005b.

2005). With many sectors like agriculture, retailing and wholesaling, as well as parts of manufacturing, still being largely composed of smaller companies, entry barriers are relatively low, and people can often use the substantial lump sum payments that are paid by employers upon resignation or retirement to set up a new business. In addition, in manufacturing, employers often engage former employees as subcontractors, or in retailing, new entrants into the sector can make use of the support of powerful wholesalers. In the service and retail sector, franchise schemes that reduce the risk of setting up new businesses have become increasingly popular.

The next point that needs to be discussed is the motivation of older Japanese people to continue working. While some authors see a generally higher willingness to work among Japan's elderly population (Iwata 2003), results from the 2004 Survey on the Situation of Older Employees show that economic necessity should not be underestimated (see Table 4).

Finally, Japan's policy makers support older people who want to continue working by having put in place schemes that allow people to work while already receiving pensions (Iwata 2003; Casey 2004). Indeed, a survey by the OECD (2000) showed that, in international comparison, Japan had the highest number of working pensioners.

Thus, a number of factors contribute to the high rate of economic activity among Japan's elderly, and at the same time another feature becomes apparent: the possibility for people to retire gradually. Casey (2004) argues that it is the abrupt fashion in which people change from work to retirement that causes a number of problems: on an individual level, with people having to cope with sudden changes in lifestyle, but also on the macro level, with people becoming dependent on income transfers, an economic loss of productivity, and finally, companies losing experience and knowledge. For Japan, Casey points to the above mentioned mechanisms, such as the flexibility of Japan's pension system; the possibility of inter- and intra-company job transfers as well as re-employment on temporary and part-time contracts; opportunities to set up one's own business; and the possibility of returning to family agricultural or retail businesses. He therefore sees Japan as one of the very few countries that have found ways to ease people into retirement gradually.

While Japan therefore seems to have come up with ways to keep its older people employed and to offer them a gradual path into retirement, the situation still has its question marks. A major problem here is the remuneration of older employees. The contractual situation of most employees changes at the age of 60, or even before that, and this frequently leads to a quite drastic drop in remuneration (Kōsei Rōdōshō 2004).

A major concern among Japanese policy makers is that Japan's first post-war baby boom generation, born between 1947 and 1949, is in the process of reaching retirement age. This is the group that has grown up in economic stability and affluence, and many in this group could therefore be expected to have accumulated enough resources to simply retire upon reaching 60. A survey carried out by the Nomura Research Institute among 500 privately and publicly employed people shows, however, that members of this generation plan largely to follow the established pattern and continue working (NRI 2005). However, while policy makers are concerned about the economic and social effects of a large number of employees suddenly retiring and should therefore welcome the continuing willingness of people to continue working, they at the same time face significant problems in providing adequate work opportunities.

Such concerns are further aggravated by changes in the industrial structure of Japan, as well as in the management practices of corporations. As outlined earlier, companies have often assisted employees in finding re-employment in other companies. However, the internal organization of companies and corporate relationships in Japan are changing. Many corporations have reorganized their corporate affiliates and have also loosened relationships with suppliers and distributors. At the same time, companies themselves are in the process of introducing new evaluation and remuneration systems that take individual achievements more into account and make it more difficult for companies to reserve positions for non-productive employees (see chapter 54). Companies therefore have more and more difficulty catering for their older employees, who are increasingly forced to find new employment in the open labour market. Another problem is the higher numbers of white-collar employees who will retire from their long-term employers but who might not be content to be offered employment that is of lower pay and status than their previous position.

## 4. Policy Development

Japan's policy makers have come up with a number of policies to support the employment of older people. These can be categorized into five areas (Iwata 2002).

- Creating employment security until age 65
- Supporting and promoting re-employment of the elderly
- Providing employment opportunities according to the desire to work and physical fitness
- Eliminating mismatches in job skills
- Promoting an environment where elderly people can continue working regardless of age

### 4.1. *Creating employment security until age 65*

To counter changes in pension eligibility (a raise in the age from which pensions can be drawn), Japanese lawmakers have instituted measures to lengthen the period that employees can work before they have to retire.

The "Law Concerning the Stabilization of Employment of Older Persons" [*Kōnenreisha nado koyō antei nado ni kansuru hōritsu*] lays down stipulations in regard to the employment of older people. This law was originally passed in 1971 but has since gone through several rounds of revisions. The latest major revision was passed in June 2004, with the changes having come into effect in April 2006. While the general provisions still state rather broadly that "Employers shall endeavour to secure employment opportunities for their older employees in accordance with their desires and abilities by taking measures for the development and improvement of occupational ability, improvement of working facilities and other conditions and assistance in re-employment for their older employees, etc. and the like" (*Kōnenreisha*, Article 4), other provisions specify employer's responsibilities more concretely.

Article 8 states that, if employers specify a retirement age, this shall not be below 60 years of age. Having gradually raised the eligibility for pension payments to 65 years, it could have been expected that lawmakers would change this provision accordingly, but this did not happen. Article 9 does, however, ask employers to provide for employees between age 60 and 65 via several alternative routes: "In cases where the employer fixes the retirement age (limited to under 65 years old: hereinafter the same shall apply) he or she shall conduct any of the measures listed in the items below in order to secure stable employment for older workers until the age of 65" (*Kōnenreisha*, Article 9).

1) Raising the retirement age;
2) Introduction of a continuous employment system;
3) Abolition of retirement age.

In deciding on continuous employment systems companies have to reach an agreement with their union or labour representatives in regard to the standards that will be employed to decide which workers are eligible for the system (Article 10).

Employers were given some time to comply with these provisions. Not until 2013 are companies required to cater for all employees up to age 65.[1] Several surveys were conducted in anticipation of April 2006, the date when companies had to come up with provisions for employees up to 62 years of age. Here the most comprehensive data come from surveying the 11,169 medium-sized and larger companies with more than 300 employees that were visited by employees of Japan's Ministry of Health, Labour and Welfare or participated in instructional meetings to prepare for the new regulations (Kōsei Rōdōshō 2005c). As of the second half of 2005, only 23.6 per cent of companies had already adopted measures, while 63.1 per cent were preparing for their introduction. Thus the large majority of companies were prepared to offer their employees more employment opportunities. Many of these

[1] From April 2006 up to age 62, from April 2007 up to age 63, from April 2010 until age 64, from April 2013 until age 65.

companies (39.4 per cent) even went beyond the stipulations of the law by deciding to immediately offer employment opportunities until 65 years of age.

However, most companies did not raise the mandatory retirement age, but limited their actions to introducing continuous employment systems. Only 7.5 per cent of companies decided to raise their mandatory retirement age beyond 60 or even to totally do away with a mandatory retirement age. The remaining 92.5 per cent decided to introduce continuous retirement systems, under which employees are employed under revised employment conditions once they have reached 60.

### 4.2. *Supporting and promoting re-employment of older employees*

To increase the chances of older people finding new employment, the Law concerning the Stabilization of Employment of Older Persons stipulates that, when middle aged and older workers (between 45 and 65) leave their jobs due to mandatory retirement, redundancy or some other reason at the convenience of the employer, employers must come up with employment support plans. Employers that demonstrate action taken in this regard are eligible for grants from the Public Employment Security Offices.

Policy makers have also realized the willingness of people in Japan to set up their own businesses. To promote such activities, in 2001 the Ministry of Health, Labour and Welfare introduced a scheme that subsidizes businesses set up by three or more people over the age of 60.

To help older employees find re-employment, Japan's Public Security offices have also set up so-called Human Resource Banks in larger Japanese cities. They try particularly to match the skills of older workers with the needs of smaller companies that are looking for employees with engineering and administrative experience. Another initiative is the creation of so-called Career Exchange Plazas at local employment office branches. These focus on the needs of middle-aged and older white-collar employees, by holding seminars and also giving job seekers the opportunity to exchange experiences (Naganawa 2002).

To provide some institutional framework, the various schemes to promote older employees in terms of the provision of subsidies as well as information and consultation were brought together under the Japan Organization for Employment of the Elderly and Persons with Disabilities in October 2003.

### 4.3. *Providing employment opportunities according to the desire to work and physical fitness*

While many employees would prefer to stay with the company and in the occupation where they have spent most of their career, there are also those who prefer less demanding employment with advancing age. In this regard, another building block in Japan's system providing employment opportunities for older people is the Silver Human Resource Centre [*shirubā jinzai sentā*] scheme, which is regarded as largely unique to Japan.

Silver Human Resource Centres operate locally and arrange for short-term employment opportunities for older people with either public or private employers. Employers pay employees through the centres, and the running of the centres is financed partly through employers' contributions and partly through government funding. The centres are prohibited from putting their workers in competition with younger workers and therefore provide jobs that are only temporary and outside the normal labour market (Weiss *et al.* 2005). People work in a variety of jobs, such as in the running of community centres, as parking lot attendants, distributors of leaflets, instructors, clerical workers, public park maintenance personnel, or home helps. Some centres run their own businesses, such as bicycle rental stations. The first such centre was set up in Tokyo in 1975. Later the status of this initiative was gradually upgraded and it became part of Japan's legislation in 1986. Elderly people interested in working become members of their local centres. As of 2004, there were 1,820 local centres with a total of 772,197 members, 513,763 male and 258,434 female. The total value of contractual services provided stood at 306.7 billion yen, roughly 400,000 yen per member. Private companies or individuals provided 69 per cent of work opportunities, while the rest were provided by public bodies (Shirubā Jinzai Sentā Jigyō Kyōkai 2004).

While the Human Silver Resource Centres are largely seen as a success story, some problems still need to be mentioned. Statistics show that the jobs offered to members are largely low-skilled and undemanding in nature and therefore might not cater for the wishes of people who have previously worked in white-collar occupations. As of 2004, only 2 per cent of jobs were administrative. Therefore demands have been made for the provision of a wider variety of jobs, for jobs that might lead to continuous employment, for the enlargement of the scope of work, and, finally, for the enrichment of programmes to develop job skills (Naganawa 1997).

### 4.4. *Eliminating mismatches in job skills*

Under a system where long-term employment was the norm, employees in the past largely relied on their employers to provide them with the necessary skills and guide them in their career development. Companies trained employees as generalists, and with employees staying in one company throughout their careers, employees often developed company-specific skills.

Since the 1990s, the number of companies that have gone bankrupt, undergone restructuring, or instituted large-scale early retirement exercises has increased significantly. Therefore, it has increasingly become the responsibility of the individual employee to take care of his or her own skills and career development. The Japanese government has implemented several measures to support employees in developing skills that are recognized in the open labour market. These include the training of a large number of career counsellors to support middle-aged employees and older white-collar job leavers, as well as placing older employees with the various private and public institutions that offer training and education programs (Iwata 2002).

### 4.5. *Creating an environment where the elderly can work regardless of age*

The policies outlined above largely focus on providing remedies for current pressing problems. Nevertheless, Japan's policy makers have formulated a long-term vision that sees the creation of an environment in which people have opportunities to work regardless of age.

Guidelines for the future direction of labour policies for older people are regularly drafted by the Labour Policy Advisory Council (Rōdō Seisaku Shingikai), an advisory council to the Ministry of Health, Labour and Welfare that is composed of representatives from academia, corporations and the media. The latest guidelines in regard to the employment of older persons were finalized in 2005, building heavily on earlier guidelines from 2000 (Rōdō Seisaku Shingikai 2005).

The guidelines show that Japanese policy makers realize that they are largely dependent on the collaboration of employers. To really achieve the goal of an employment system where people can work regardless of age, companies would have to make substantial changes to the way they manage their human resources. For example, while many companies prefer to hire fresh graduates or younger employees, the advisory council requires that employers do not discriminate against older workers in the hiring process; if they do so they must give their reasons in detail. Another area of change is skills development and recognition. Instead of regarding employees as generalists, the guidelines require companies to come up with systems that properly assess and recognize necessary job skills, specialist knowledge and qualifications. Another requirement is more flexible handling of working hours. Finally, the guidelines call for changes in remuneration systems, namely a shift from age-based systems of remuneration and treatment to systems that build on skills and occupational principles.

Following the demands outlined above would lead to fundamental changes in the way Japanese corporations manage their employees, basically removing many of the elements that were regarded as characteristic of Japanese management. Nevertheless, administrators have made some efforts to promote change. A first step in this direction was a change in the Employment Measures Law [*Koyō Taisaku-hō*]. The law formulates guidelines for employment based on two principles. First, employers should make efforts not to exclude employees based on grounds of age; and second, employers should clearly outline job content and the abilities needed when recruiting employees.

However, the law still leaves a lot of room for employers to apply age restrictions. For example, companies are allowed to make exceptions when they want to hire fresh graduates for the purpose of long-term career development, or when they want to restore the age balance between employees of different age groups. Exceptions are also allowed when the hiring of employees of a certain age would lead to distortions in existing pay systems that are based on seniority. The law has therefore been criticised for its exceptions as well as for the fact that it does not include penal provisions for employers who do not comply with its stipulations (Iwata 2002).

## 5. Discussion and Conclusions

Iwata (2002) states that, in 1997, a study group of the Japanese Ministry of Labour presented a report that suggested three different approaches to ageing and employment, under the keywords of a) age 60-plus, b) age 65 minus beta, and finally c) age-free. So far Japan largely maintains an age 60-plus approach, with age 60 being seen as the legitimate retirement age and the government and companies making efforts to keep people somehow employed until age 65. While guidelines have clearly pointed out what companies would have to do to really remove age restrictions, this general orientation allows companies to leave their employment and remuneration systems largely intact.

Consequently, Taylor (2002) argues that Japan's policy for the employment of elderly people is somewhat ineffective and might sometimes even result in the opposite of what was originally intended. He points to the above-mentioned exceptions in the Employment Measures Law, which, since October 2001, has stipulated that companies need to carry out hiring and recruitment activities regardless of age. More importantly, he draws attention to the point that the implementation of schemes that provide financial support to employers for the hiring and employment of older people might lead to the stigmatization of older employees, or, even worse, might encourage employers to move workers out of normal employment into types of employment that are financially supported, thereby institutionalizing age barriers instead of doing away with them.

Overall, this situation somehow mars Japan's positive record as one of the few countries to have achieved gradual retirement opportunities for its people. It has been demonstrated that Japan is a forerunner in terms of labour force participation and employment rates of older people; however this picture changes somewhat when we look at wages, types of work and modes of working.

This does not, however, mean that Japan will not change further in this regard. So far the country has largely pursued a soft approach that builds on the cooperation of employers and strives to overcome non-compliance by providing counselling and financial assistance. This soft approach may be related to the fact that new regulations were formulated in a period when Japanese corporations were in the process of restructuring their operations and also introducing new policies in regard to employment and remuneration generally. Policy makers might therefore not have wanted to stand in the way of Japanese companies regaining competitiveness.

Indeed, Japanese corporations have reduced the weight placed on seniority elements and introduced more individual assessment of skills and achievement, both factors that were seen as necessary towards the removal of age barriers. However, it remains to be seen whether they have done so to an extent that will lead to offering quality employment to their older employees.

Another development that is difficult to forecast is labour supply and demand. On the supply side, the number of people aged between 15 and 64 years of age is expected to shrink from about 85 million people in the year 2003 to only 70 million people by the year 2030. Based on current labour force participation this means a drop from 66 million employees to just 56 million employees over the same period (Koyō Seisaku Kenkyūkai 2005). Forecasting labour demand is more difficult; however, most studies that attempt to do so predict a shortage of labour. For example, a very detailed study by the Mizuho Research Institute predicts a shortage of 2.3 million employees by the year 2015, albeit with significant sector-specific differences (Mizuho Sōgō Kenkyūjo 2006). This explains the interest of policy makers in increasing the labour force participation not only of older people, but also of women and among younger people.

With a record number of employees approaching retirement age and a lower number of younger people available, corporations might therefore well discover the value of their older employees by themselves. However, should this not happen, Japanese policy makers might well introduce stricter measures, as has often happened in the past when relatively soft initial policy measures based on voluntary cooperation by the corporate sector have failed to show the hoped for results.

## References


Casey, Bernard H. (2004): *Why are Older People not More "Active"?* Discussion Paper PI-0408, Pensions Institute, May 2004. London: Pensions Institute City University.

Dirks, Daniel (1999): Limits and latitudes of labour adjustment strategies in Japanese companies. In: Daniel Dirks, Jean-Francois Huchet and Thierry Ribault (eds.): *Japanese Management in the Low Growth Era.* Berlin: Springer, pp. 267–294.

GAO (United States General Accounting Office) (2003): *Older Workers—Policies of Other Nations to Increase Labor Force Participation.* Report to the Ranking Minority Member (February 2003), Special Committee on Aging, U.S. Senate, GAO-03-307. http://www.gao.gov/cgi-bin/getrpt?GAO-03-307 (found 30 January 2001).

Iwata, Katsuhiko (2002): *Employment and Policy Development relating to Older People in Japan.* The Japan-side Background Document of 9th Japan-EU Labour Symposium, March 2002. http://europa.eu.int/comm/employment_social/international_cooperation/docs/eu_japan_symposium9/doc_iwata_en.pdf (found 13 December 2006).

—— (2003): *Labor Market Policies in the Era of Population Aging: Japan's Case. International Seminar on Labor Market Policies in an Aging Era* (22 October 2003), organised by the

Korean Labour Institute, Seoul. http://www.jil.go.jp/english/documents/aging_policy-e.pdf (found 12 January 2006).

*Kōnenreisha nado koyō antei nado ni kansuru hōritsu* (Law Concerning the Stabilization of Employment of Older Persons), (Law No. 68 of May 25, 1971). English translation available from Japan Institute of Labour Policy and Training. http://www.jil.go.jp/english/laborinfo/library/documents/llj_law16.pdf (found 15 January 2006).

Kōsei Rōdōshō (2004): *Heisei 15 nen koyō dōkō chōsa* [Survey on Employment Trends 2003]. http://www.mhlw.go.jp/toukei/itiran/roudou/koyou/doukou/03–2/index.html (found 15 January 2006).

—— (2005a): *Rōdō keizei hakusho, heisei 17-nenban, jinkō genshō shakai ni okeru rōdō seisaku no kadai* [White Paper on the labour economy 2005: Labour policy issues in a society with a declining population]. Tokyo: Kokuritsu Insatsukyoku.

—— (2005b): *Heisei 16-nen kōnenreisha shūgyō jittai chōsa kekka no gaikyō* [Outline of survey concerning the working situation of older people 2004]. http://www.mhlw.go.jp/toukei/itiran/roudou/koyou/keitai/04 (found 30 January 2001).

—— (2005c): *Keisei Kōrei-hō no jikkō ni muketa kigyō no torikomu jōkyō ni tsuite* [Survey on the preparation of companies in regard to the enforcement of the revised older persons law]. www.mhlw.go.jp/houdou/2005/12/h1216–1.html (found 17 January 2006).

Koyō Seisaku Kenkyūkai (2005): *Jinkō genshō shita ni okeru koyō—rōdō seisaku no kadai* [Issues in regard to labour and employment policies under a shrinking population]. http://www.mhlw.go.jp/houdou/2005/07/h0727–2.html (found 5 July 2006).

Mizuho Sōgō Kenkyūjo (2006): *Rōdō fusoku wa dō sureba kaishō suru ka* [How can the shortage of labour be reduced?]. Mizuho Ripōto (13 March 2006). http://www.mizuho-ri.co.jp/research/economics/pdf/report/report06–0313.pdf (found 5 July 2006).

Naganawa, Hisao (1997): The Work of the Elderly and the Silver Human Resources Centers. In: *Japan Labor Bulletin* 36, 6, pp. 5–7. Also available online at: http://www.jil.go.jp/bulletin/year/1997/vol36–06/05.htm (found 12 December 2006).

—— (2002): Re-employment of Older White-collar Workers. In: *Japan Labor Bulletin* 41, 2. http://www.jil.go.jp/bulletin/year/2002/vol41–02/05.htm (found 30 March 2006).

NRI (Nomura Research Institute) (2005): *Dankai sedai no sekando raifu ni kan suru chōsa* [Survey concerning the second life of the baby boom generation]. http://www.nri.co.jp/news/2005/051118_1.html (found 15 February 2006).

OECD (2000) *Ageing and Income. Financial Resources and Retirement in 9 OECD countries*. Paris, OECD Publishing.

Rōdō Seisaku Shingikai (2005): *Kōreisha nado shokugyō antei taisaku kihon hōshin an* [Proposal for guidelines concerning policies for securing employment for older people and others] (March 28, 2005). http://www.mhlw.go.jp/shingi/rousei.html (found 20 February 2006).

*Rōdo Taisaku-hō* (Employment Measures Law (Law No. 132 of July 21, 1966)). English translation available from Japan Institute of Labor Policy and Training. http://www.jil.go.jp/english/laborinfo/library/documents/llj_law13.pdf (found 12 December 2006).

Shirubā Jinzai Sentā Jigyō Kyōkai (2004): *Keiyaku kingaku, kanyū kaiinsū, dantai sū no suii* [Development of contract price, number of members, number of groups], http://www.zsjc.or.jp/rhx/upload/Statistics/2.pdf (found 17 March 2006).

Somushō Tōkeikyoku (2005): *Rōdōryoku chōsa: Heisei 17-nen 11-gatsu* [Labour force survey, November 2005). http://www.stat.go.jp/data/roudou/200511/index.htm (found 15 January 2006).

Taylor, Philip (2002): Working at the Margins: Public Policy, Age and Firms in Japan. In: *Japan Labor Bulletin* 41, 8, pp. 13–16. Also available online at: http://www.jil.go.jp/bulletin/year/2002/vol41–08.pdf (found 12 December 2006).

*The Business Times, Singapore* (9 November 2005): Singapore to get Japanese tips on hiring older workers; Team to study employment strategies for ageing workforce. (found via LexisNexis 25 April 2005).

Weiss, Robert S., Scott A. Bass, Harley K. Heimovitz and Masato Oka (2005): Japan's Silver Human Resource Centers and Participant Well-being. In: *Journal of Cross-Cultural Gerontology* 20, 1, pp. 47–66.

CHAPTER FIFTY-THREE

# GENDER DIMENSIONS OF THE AGEING WORKFORCE

Karen A. Shire

## 1. Introduction

This chapter discusses the economic risks of ageing posed by the ways in which men and women are employed in Japan.[1] The focus is on the extent to which forms of employment make it possible for employees to achieve economic security during and after active employment. The concept of security, and its antonym, risk, are not new ways of framing the question of the social and economic consequences of ageing, but the concepts of employment performance and security have gained importance recently for analyzing new dimensions of social inequality emerging in relation to the liberalization of employment institutions in the context of economic globalization. In particular, paying attention to the "unequal distribution of insecurities" between social groups in the workforce (ILO 2004: 3) and viewing forms of employment contracts in relation to the types of security they offer (Kim and Kurz 2003) contribute to identifying new dimensions of social exclusion in the labour market. This is particularly important in Japan, where the crisis of employment performance is not rooted in long-term unemployment as in Germany, but rather in the expansion of non-regular employment forms (Osawa 2006).

The gender dimension of the ageing workforce is approached from a relational and institutional perspective, highlighting how employment contracts and social policy shape opportunities for securing a livelihood, for men and women as individuals, but also as partners in households and families. The concept of the "male breadwinner" (Ostner and Lewis 1995) refers to a particular model of gendered employment and

[1] The author wishes to thank Jun Imai for data and research assistance, Mari Osawa, Margarita Estevez-Abe and Karin Gottschall for comments and help in improving the data and argument.

social policy, considered dominant in Japan and Germany (Gottfried and O'Reilly 2002). As a model of livelihood security (Osawa 2007), the "male breadwinner model" points to how social policies intersect with gender relations, to define men as workers and women as wives and/or mothers. In the Japanese case, the model of the male breadwinner is rooted in particularly strong employment protections for male regular workers, who receive a family wage. The dominance of this model is evident in the comparatively high contribution of male wages to total household income, and pension policies delivering the highest rate of benefits to full-time employees with dependent spouses (Osawa 2006). Pension reforms in the 1980s actually strengthened the male breadwinner model in Japan, in part by adding a third class of insured to National Pension Insurance (NPI) for dependent spouses and improving survivor benefits. The intersection of employment practices and social policies in Japan had, by the end of the 1980s, established regular employment for men, and marriage to a regular employee for women, as the best security against the risks of ageing. In practice however, the dual structure of the Japanese labour market and high levels of non-agricultural self-employment well into the 1980s have meant that the "model male breadwinner" really only existed for male employees of large companies. So despite the policy dominance of the male breadwinner model, the majority of women were also regularly employed (see below), and dual earning couples outnumbered households with the "model" male breadwinner/full-time housewife throughout the 1980s (Osawa 2007).

In the 1990s, corporate restructuring in response to the long recession brought declines in regular employment and lower rates of wage growth over the life course for younger cohorts of Japanese men, including those regularly employed in large companies (Osawa 2006). At the same time, the strengthening of the Equal Employment Opportunity Law enacted in 1999, and the passing of the gender equality act in the same year, which launched a discussion of social policy reform in the direction of supporting an alternative "dual-earner/dual-care-giver" livelihood security system in place of the male breadwinner model, seemed to create an improved context for qualitative improvements in women's employment in Japan. These hopes have been dashed however, in the wake of a fundamental deregulation of employment, and a consequent expansion of non-regular employment (Imai 2004), both of which changed the structure of women's employment more fundamentally than men's employment. In contrast to employment policy in the European Union, there is no tendency to treat non-regular employees in Japan equally to regular workers. As a result, the expansion of female employment through non-regular employment has deepened gender inequalities within the Japanese workforce.

Employment changes and the social risk of ageing are analyzed in this chapter in relation to three main sources of employment insecurity: temporal, material and social (Kim and Kurz 2003). The three sources of insecurity refer respectively to the length and protection of the employment relation, the possibilities for earning a living wage, and access to social insurance and benefits. Attention is paid throughout, to rising insecurities overall, and specifically to the unequal distribution of insecurities between men and women in the Japanese workforce.

## 2. The Gender Divide in Economic Security

In Japan, a basic distinction is made between *regular* (*sei-sha'in*) and non-regular (*hi-sei-sha'in*) employees, a contractual distinction not unlike that between 'unlimited' and 'limited-term' employment in Germany. Regular employment is typically a full-time, unlimited employment relation, with strong protections against unfair dismissals. Japan is considered to have one of the strongest systems of employment protection in international comparisons (OECD 1999: 47–132). About 63 per cent of all Japanese employees were in regular employment in 2002, down from 75 per cent in 1987. (Fig. 1) Firm size has historically made a difference in the extent of employment security, wages and corporate welfare in Japan, with large firms guaranteeing the most security. In 1987, when 75 per cent of all workers were regularly employed, only 16.4 per cent of all workers were in the most protected sector of large firm (> 1000) employment. By 2002, this proportion had dropped to 12 per cent of all regular employment in the most secure sector of large firm employment (Sōmushō Tōkeikyoku 1988, 2004).

The overall decline in regular employment has hit regular female workers harder than men. (Table 1) Depending on the survey used, 84 to 85 per cent of men remain regularly employed, while the proportion of women's regular employment has, in some estimates, dropped by 20 per cent since 1985 to 49 per cent of all female employees in 2002 (Osawa 2006; Sōmushō Tōkeikyoku 1998, 2004). Overall part-time employment has expanded from 14 to 22 per cent of all employment between 1987 and 2002, and non-regular work altogether rose to nearly

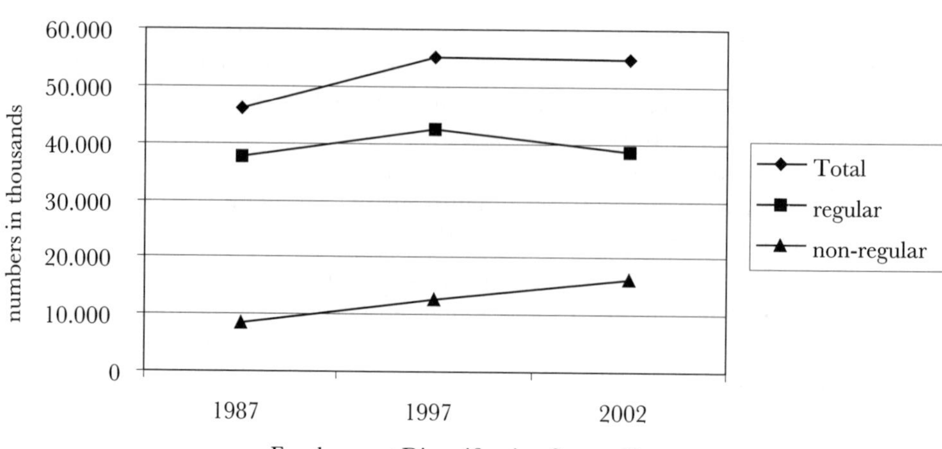


Source: Sōmushō Tōkeikyoku 1988, 1998, 2004.

Figure 1. Change in employment contracts: Total employment, and divided into regular and non-regular employment, 1987–2002.

30 per cent of all employment. The rise of non-regular employment overall, and especially for women, is primarily due to this expansion of part-time employment.[2]

Employment deregulation by the Japanese government in the late 1990s also led to an exponential expansion of temporary employment, especially limited-term contract work. Still almost 75 per cent of all non-regular workers (over 12 million employees) are in one of two forms of part-time work (employment contracts of less than 35 hours, *pāto*, and casual work, *arubaito*), in contrast to 2.5 million in various forms of fixed-contract work and 700,000 in temporary agency (*haken*, literally dispatched) work. The largest single category of non-regular work (*pāto*) is over 90 per cent female. Temporary agency work is also dominated by women. Within the general category of agency work,

[2] Part-time work contracts are often limited term, but even when they are unlimited, they are subject to greater fluctuations as part of corporate employment adjustments. In the late 1990s, lay-offs of temporary and part-time workers were one of several measures used by large companies to reduce their workforces (Hiwatari and Miura 2001: 24).

Table 1. Employment contracts and employment forms by gender, 1987–2002.

| | 1987 | | | 1997 | | | 2002 | | |
|---|---|---|---|---|---|---|---|---|---|
| | total | male | female | total | male | female | total | male | female |
| Total employee | 46,153 | 29,154 | 16,998 | 54,997 | 33,130 | 21,867 | 54,733 | 32,201 | 22,531 |
| Regular employee | 37,653 | 24,256 | 10,309 | 42,392 | 29,760 | 12,632 | 38,452 | 27,369 | 11,083 |
| Non-regular employee | 8,500 | 2,427 | 6,071 | 12,590 | 3,358 | 9,231 | 16,206 | 4,781 | 11,425 |
| Part-time (*pāto)* | 4,677 | 215 | 4,462 | 6,998 | 436 | 6,562 | 7,824 | 628 | 7,196 |
| Casual (*arubaito*) | 1,886 | 953 | 932 | 3,344 | 1,652 | 1,692 | 4,237 | 2,096 | 2,141 |
| Temporary agency (*haken*) | 87 | 38 | 49 | 257 | 53 | 204 | 721 | 204 | 517 |
| Limited-term (*keiyaku, shokutaku*) | 1,848 | 1,221 | 628 | 966 | 605 | 361 | 2,477 | 1,309 | 1,169 |
| Others | | | | 1,025 | 612 | 412 | 946 | 544 | 402 |

Note: The category "executives" in the Japanese survey has been added to "regular workers". This category is not broken down by gender in 1987, thus the total employment includes this category, but not the gender breakdowns.
Source: Sōmushō Tōkeikyoku 1988, 1998, 2004, presentation by author.

Japanese women also dominate the most precarious forms of *tōroku-gata* or *registered* temporary employment (Shire and Imai 2000).[3]

These developments show that in the span of the 1990s, increasing female employment in sectors of the labour market with little employment protection created a gender divide in the temporal security of work. The temporal insecurities of non-regular employment were coupled with material and social insecurities, in terms of pay gaps and inclusion in employee pension insurance. In international comparisons, Japan has one of the highest rates of part-time work among advanced economies (behind Australia and the Netherlands), but unlike these and other European countries, Japan has a very wide gap in pay between full- and part-time workers, with part-timers earning just 66.4 per cent of full-time hourly pay (compared to 87.5 per cent in the Netherlands and 74.5 per cent in Australia) (OECD 1999, cited in Osawa 2006: 23).

[3] There are two types of temporary agency work in Japan: registered type (*tōroku-gata*) temps, dispatched by agencies on an on-call basis and employed type (*kōyō-gata*), whereby temporary workers are employees of the agencies dispatching them. Registered temporary work is more precarious, since workers are not paid between dispatch assignments.

Even wages for so-called "full-time part-timers"[4] in Japan, who work more than 35 hours per week, are well below those of regular full-time workers (Nagase 1995, cited in Osawa 2001: 185). The gap between part-time and full-time wages also holds between women, with female part-timers earning 65.7 per cent of female full-time wages. This rate has in fact worsened since 1990, when female part-timers could earn 75 per cent of female full-time wages (Osawa 2006: 23). While wages of temporary workers are generally higher than for other forms of non-regular work, female temps earn just 78 per cent of male temp wages (based on hourly wage averages, as reported in *Rōdōsha haken jigyō jittai chōsa*, cited in Imai 2004: 50).

Part-time (and other non-regular) workers are covered under employee pension insurance schemes if they work at least 30 hours or more per week (i.e., 75 per cent of the regular hours). Employees who work fewer hours are able to register in the National Pension Insurance (NPI) as Class 1 insured, along with non-employees (e.g., self-employed and unemployed). As Class 1 insured however, they are responsible for paying their own contributions. In contrast, employers bear 50 per cent of contributions for class 2 insured, and individual contributions are not paid for Class 3 insured. For spouses earning less than 1.3 million yen a year, and whose marriage partners are employees registered as Class 2 insured under the NPI, pension coverage is extended as a dependent spouse (Class 3), a coverage first enabled by pension reform in the 1980s. Thus part-time workers, depending on their inclusion in employee pension schemes, their hours, earning and marital status, may be classified as either Class 1, Class 2 or Class 3 insured in national schemes.

Since employers are not required to register part-time workers with less than 30 hours as pensionable employees, interpretations about the actual hours part-timers perform opens up a route for Japanese employers to escape pension contributions. With the rise of part-time work in Japan, and pressures on corporations to reduce their labour costs, there are reports recently of increasing non-registration and thus, no

[4] There are two definitions of part-time (*pāto*) work in Japan. In the part-time law (*pāto hō*) part-time work is defined as scheduled working hours less than those of regular workers. Statistics gathered for most official surveys use this definition, and depend on employer self-reports of who is part-time. This relative definition is the source of 'full-time' part-time work in Japan (see Osawa 2001). The Japanese labor force survey defines part-time workers as those working less than 35 hours.

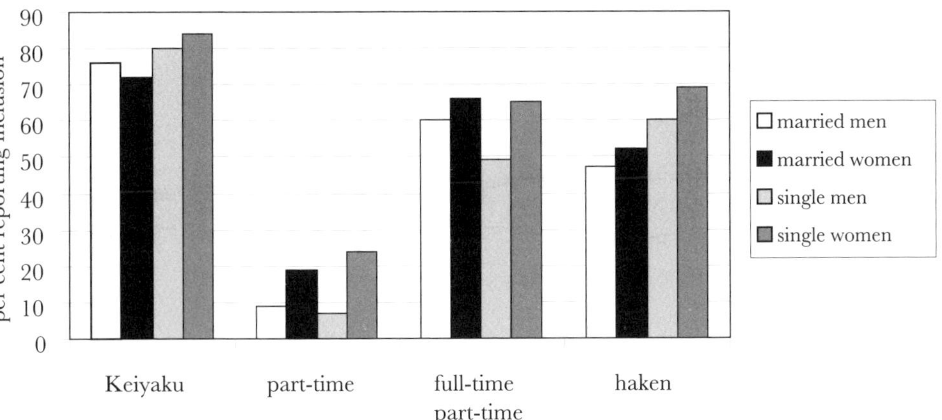


Source: Nagase 2003, Table 15, figure by author.

Figure 2. Inclusion of non-regular employees in employee pension insurance.

coverage of employees normally eligible for Class 2 status, for whom employers share 50 per cent of the social insurance burden. Case studies of part-time workers suggest that hours under 30 are not so common (Broadbent 2003). Recently, increases in the numbers of employed workers joining the class 1 insured category of the NPI system has spurred speculation, that employers may be escaping their contributions by refusing to enrol otherwise eligible non-regular workers into their social insurance schemes. Osawa (2006) views the non-inclusion of part-timers in employees' social insurance as evidence of the casualization and extra-legality of part-time employment, not unlike the increasing informalization of women's work in developing countries.

One study of a sample of employees from firms included in the 1997 Employment Status Survey examined the extent to which men and women in various forms of employment reported inclusion in employee pension insurance schemes. (Fig. 2) Coverage of part-time workers is the lowest of all categories, though this is the largest category of non-regular work in Japan. Certainly part of the exclusion from employee pension plans has to do with the fact that this category subsumes those who work less than 75 per cent of regular hours. Full-time part timers in Figure 2 account for less than 17 per cent of all non-regular workers, meaning they, like *keiyaku* and *haken* workers, are a small proportion of

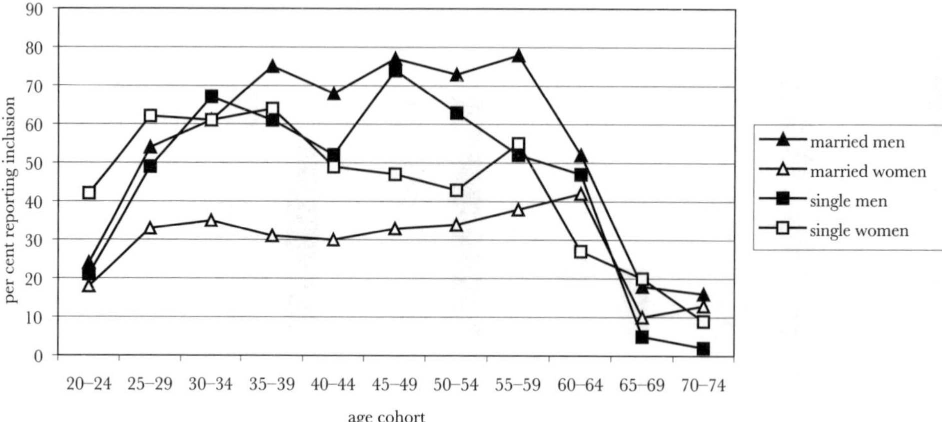


Source: Nagase 2003: table 15, figure by author.

Figure 3. Per cent of men and women in non-regular employment reporting inclusion in employee pension insurance schemes by marital status and age cohort.

the non-regular workforce. Actual inclusion of employees in pension insurance may be even lower than the results for non-regular workers in Figure 2 suggest. Referring to recent media reports, Osawa cites estimates that some 9.26 million individuals who should be eligible for supplementary (class 2 NPI) coverage are not enrolled (a rate of 10 to 20 per cent failure to enrol). She also cites a survey, which estimates the failure to enrol part-time and temporary workers in employee pension insurance schemes at 68 per cent (Osawa 2006: 26).

In terms of age cohorts of workers covered, the relatively low overall pension inclusion of married women in all age cohorts of non-regular employment, compared to the relative high inclusion of married men, especially from middle-age through to retirement, points to much better social protection of men, essentially casting even men in non-regular employment as 'breadwinners'. (Fig. 3) In most age cohorts, including mid-life through retirement age employees, even single men are better included than women. These results show that the gender divide in temporal insecurity extends far deeper into other dimensions of material and social insecurity, positioning women in the most precarious domains of relatively low wage and low insurance employment.

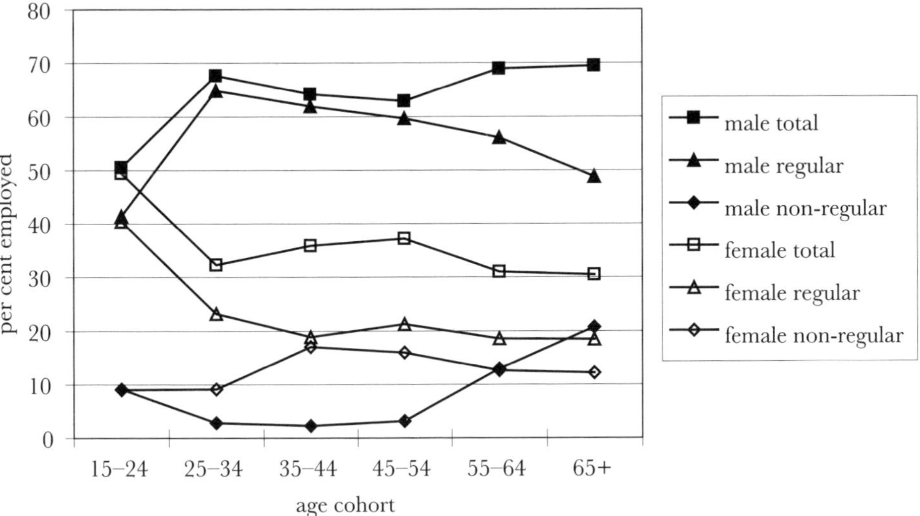


Note: In the 1987 survey reported in 1988, executive employees were not reported by age cohort, so that the total employment levels are higher than the sum of regular and non-regular employment in this year only.
Source: Sōmushō Tōkeikyoku 1988, figure by author.

Figure 4. Regular and non-regular employment by gender and age cohort 1987.

## 3. Cohort Dimensions of the Gender Divide in Economic Security

Insecure employment, if it is confined to certain stages of the life course, for example, entry into the labour market, as a transition to more secure forms of employment, or at the exit stage, when pension contributions have already accumulated to secure retirement, may not be so meaningful for raising the risks of ageing. Figures 4, 5 and 6 document how employment is shifting over the life course in Japan, comparing men and women in regular and non-regular employment from 1987 to 2002. The pattern of male employment in 1987 follows a standard male biography of entry into the workforce in the early 20s, with employment levels peaking between the ages of 25 and 44, there after declining as men reach pre-retirement age. Almost all male employees are regular employees, with relatively low levels of non-

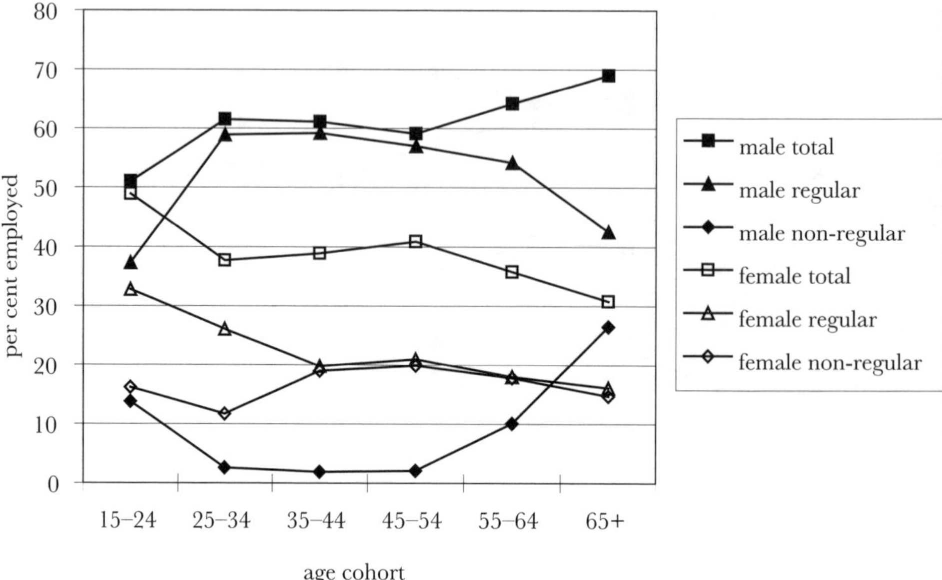


Source: Sōmushō Tōkeikyoku 1998, figure by author.

Figure 5. Regular and non-regular employment by gender and age cohort 1997.

regular employment clustered at the points of labour market entry and exit (15–24 and 55–64 age cohorts). The pattern for women follows the dominant female biography of entry into regular employment in the early 20s, a decline overall and for regular employees in the typical (for the 1980s) marriage and childbirth age cohort of 25–34 and re-entry during the late 30s/early 40s as a non-regular worker. Throughout however, regular employment levels for women were higher than non-regular levels throughout the life course.

While men's work biographies experienced a degree of volatility at mid-life, overall the pattern of continuous and high regular employment at mid-life holds, without any change in the clustering of relatively small levels of non-regular employment at the point of labour market entry and exit. In fact, for the age cohort 45–54 employment in 1997 was even higher and more stable than in 1987. This is consistent with other findings on the strong employment performance for baby boomer men in Japan, despite the deep and prolonged recession of the 1990s (Osawa 2007). For women, the well-known shift of marriage

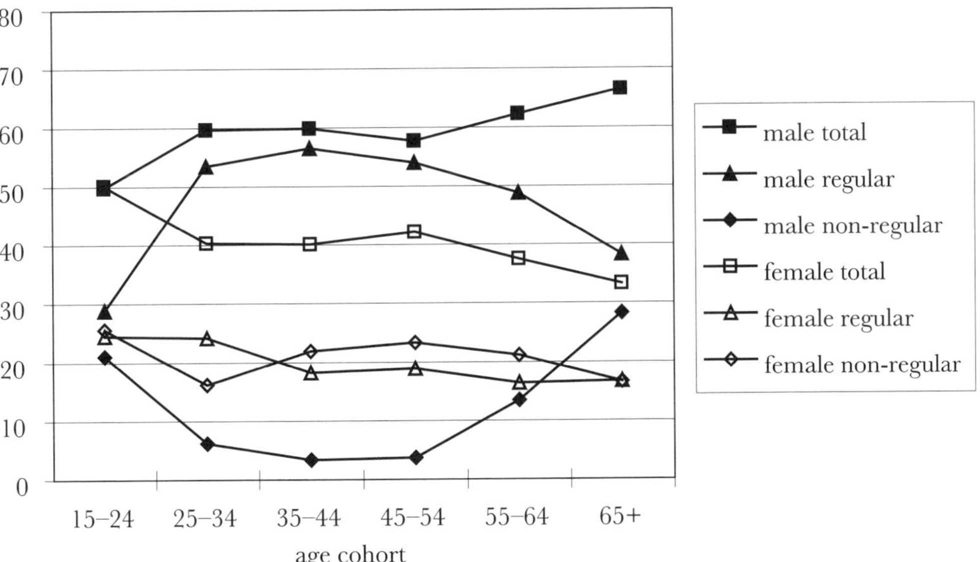


Source: Sōmushō Tōkeikyoku 2004, figure by author.

Figure 6. Regular and non-regular employment by gender and age cohorts 2002.

and childbirth from the mid- to late 20s and early 30s is evident in a later dip in overall employment levels. As in 1987, women's regular employment remained slightly higher than non-regular employment, except for women over the age of 65.

Non-regular employment for men in 2002 remains the same, with men in regular employment throughout mid-life, and in non-regular employment at the point of labour market entry and exit. The pattern of employment for women however, changes dramatically, with non-regular employees outnumbering regular employees for all age cohorts except one: the cohort of women aged 25 to 34. For the first time since 1987, the levels of non-regular employment for women age 35 and older are higher than for regular employment.

Non-regular work in general, but especially part-time work is much less secure, in material and social dimensions, than regular work. At the same time however, regular employment, including at large firms, and especially for younger cohorts of regular workers, is undergoing change as part of corporate restructuring and changes in personnel management practices, making even regular work less secure than in

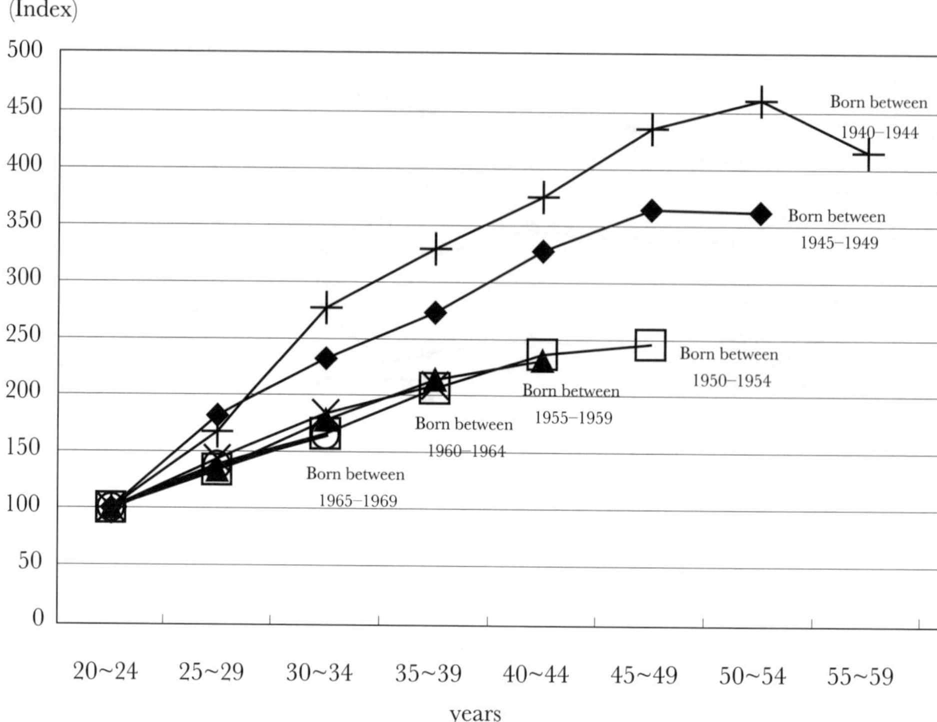


Note: Real wages are calculated by age bracket with those regularly paid to 20 to 24 year olds and their annual bonuses as 100.
Source: Reprinted from Osawa 2007, Figure 4.1, original source cited is Basic Statistical Survey on Wage Structure (annual edition), Ministry of Health, Labour and Welfare; Consumer Price Index, Ministry of Public Management, Home Affairs, Posts and Telecommunications.

Figure 7. Real wage growth of male employees by birth and age cohorts.

the past. While temporal dimensions of security have changed little for middle-aged and older workers, reductions in wage growth and cut-backs in non-wage benefits are beginning to call the provision of a "family wage" through regular long-term employment into question. Figure 7 presents average wage growth for both age and birth cohorts, and illustrates how wage conditions are deteriorating for younger generations of workers affected most by the introduction of performance-based wages and other cost reduction measures.

Declining material security is also evident in recent analyses of household income, especially among younger cohorts of household heads.

Comparing the GINI coefficient, across age cohorts and by household types, Shirahase finds a steady rise in income inequality between 1986 and 2001, especially among younger cohorts in comparison to retirement age households (Shirahase 2006: 59). Further, she finds that the incidence of low income households rose considerably between 1986 and 2001 for the age cohorts 30–39, but only slightly for the 40–65 cohorts, and an actual decline of the frequency of low income for household cohorts between the ages of 65–75 and older (Shirahase 2006: 61). The social divide in *insecurity* between age cohorts in Japan is thus also a social divide in *inequality*, with middle-aged and elderly cohorts faring better overall than younger cohorts of Japanese. Thus generational dimensions are interacting with gender dimensions in changing the distribution of economic insecurities, with young women seemingly in the worse possible positions in terms of securing a livelihood during and after active employment.

## 4. The Impasse in the Japanese Male Breadwinner Model

Growing inequalities and insecurities in the Japanese labour market, especially for younger cohorts of workers, can be seen as a consequence of the weakening of the male breadwinner, and at the same time, the failure to strengthen the female wage earner. While men continue to enjoy high levels of temporal security through high levels of full-time employment over their life courses, overall shifts out of regular work and changes in personnel management practices are affecting the degree of economic and social security even for highly protected male regular employees, and by association, for their families, dependent on a family wage. Younger cohorts of men cannot necessarily expect to earn a family wage, or at least they can expect to face more uncertainty over the life course in their capacity to do so. This situation is best described as an impasse in the transition from a male-breadwinner to a dual earner model of employment/welfare mix (Osawa 2007). Yet in most advanced countries exactly such a transition toward a dual earner/dual career work/family balance is seen as important, not only for achieving ideals of better gender equality, but also to improve the use of a broader population of qualified workers in the knowledge-based economy and to improve the fiscal health of social insurance program in the context of ageing societies.

Just how poorly young female employees fare in the Japanese workforce is exemplified by the case of single working mothers, who can be viewed as a test case for the capacity of women to establish economic independence. While single mothers have a very high employment rate in Japan, only women in the high qualified and traditionally female occupations of the public sector (e.g., teachers) actually manage to earn enough income to place themselves above the threshold for receiving public transfers for dependent children (Ezawa 2007). Nearly 40 per cent of female heads of households work in non-regular forms of employment. Even single mothers in private sector full-time jobs are employed mainly by very small firms, where wages are low (JIL 2003).

## 5. Conclusion

In Japan, insecurities are rising for both men and women, regular and non-regular employees, in the Japanese workforce. These insecurities are however, unequally distributed for men and women. Insecurities are also unequally distributed across generations, with younger Japanese at higher risk of being unable to secure a livelihood during and after active employment, than those older cohorts of employees now nearing or in retirement. Regular employment has traditionally insured workers against the risk of ageing, because it secures material, temporal and social security. Non-regular employment, especially part-time employment, is materially and temporally insecure, and secures only a minimum of pension support in old age. The new segmentation of the Japanese workforce into regular and non-regular workers, together with the age and gender dimensions of this segmentation, will increase the risk of ageing for both men and women, because these developments mean that increasing female labour force participation cannot contribute to improving the economic independence of women or to establishing dual-earner type households.

## References

Broadbent, Kaye (2003): *Women's Employment in Japan: The Experience of Part-time Workers*. London: RoutledgeCurzon.

Ezawa, Aya (2007): How Japanese Single Mothers Work. In: *Japanstudien* 18, pp. 59–83.

Gottfried, Heidi and Jacqueline O'Reilly (2002): Re-regulating Breadwinner Models in Socially Conservative Welfare Regimes: Comparing Germany and Japan. In: *Social Politics* 9, 1, pp. 29–59.

Hiwatari, Nobuhiro and Mari Miura (2001): *Export Sector-led Adjustment in Trouble? Unemployment, Fiscal Reconstruction and Welfare Reform in Germany and Japan*. Paper prepared for the 2001 Annual Meeting of the American Political Science Association, 33 pages.

ILO (International Labor Office) (2004): *Economic Security for a Better World*. Geneva: ILO.

Imai, Jun (2004): The Rise of Temporary Employment in Japan: Legislation and Expansion of a Non-Regular Employment Form. In: *Duisburg Working Papers on East Asian Studies* 62, 64 pages.

JIL (Japan Institute of Labor) (2003): New Law to Support Employment of Single Mothers. In: *Japan Labour Bulletin* 42, 9, pp. 6–7.

Kim, Anna and Karin Kurz (2003): Prekäre Beschäftigung im Vereinigten Königreich und Deutschland. Welche Rolle spielen unterschiedliche institutionelle Kontexte? In: Müller, Walter and Stefani Scherer (eds.): Mehr Risiken—Mehr Ungleichheit? Abbau von Wohlfahrtsstaat, Flexibilisierung von Arbeit und die Folgen. Frankfurt/New York: Campus Verlag, pp. 167–197.

Nagase, Nobuko (1995): "Pāto sentaku" no jihatsusei to chingin kansū [The voluntariness of the 'choice to work part-time' and the wage function]. In: *Nihon Keizai Kenkyū* 28, pp. 162–184.

—— (2003): Hi-seiki koyō to shakai hoken [Non-regular employment and social insurance]. In: Sato, Hiroki (ed.) *Hi-seiki koyō rōdōsha no tayō na shūgyō jittai: 'shūgyō keitai no tayō-ka ni kansuru sōgō jittai chōsa' tō ni yoru jisshō bunseki* [Diversified employment among non-regular workers: empirical analysis of the employment diversification survey]. Japan Institute of Labour Research Report No. 158. Tokyo: Japan Institute of Labour, pp. 142–168.

OECD (1999): *OECD Employment Outlook*. Paris: OECD.

Osawa, Mari (2001): People in Irregular Modes of Employment: Are They Really Not Subject to Discrimination? In: *Social Science Journal Japan*, 4, 2, pp. 183–199.

—— (2006): *The Livelihood Security System Works as a Mechanism for Social Exclusion: The Reverse Function of Japan's Male Breadwinner Model*. Unpublished paper, 36 pages.

—— (2007): Comparative Livelihood Security from a Gender Perspective, with a Focus on Japan. In: Walby, Sylvia, Heidi Gottfried, Karin Gottschall and Mari Osawa (eds.): *Gendering the Knowledge Economy: Comparative Perspectives*. London: Palgrave, pp. 201–259.

Ostner, Ilona and Jane Lewis (1995): Gender and the Evolution of European Social Policies. In: Leibfried, Stephan and Paul Pierson (eds.): *European Social Policy Between Fragmentation and Integration*. Washington: Washington Brookings Institution, pp. 159–194.

Shirahase, Sawako (2006): Fubyōdo-ka nihon nakami—setai to gendā [The nature of growing inequalities in Japan—A household and gender analysis] In: Shirahase, Sawako (ed.): *Henka suru shakai no fubyōdō: shōshi kōreika ni hisomu kakusa* [Inequality in a changing society: hidden disparities behind the demographic shift in Japan]. Tokyo: University of Tokyo Press, pp. 47–78.

Shire, Karen and Jun Imai (2000): Gender and the Diversification of Employment in Japan. In: Brose, Hanns-Georg (ed.): *Reorganisation der Arbeit.* Frankfurt: Campus Verlag, pp. 117–136.

Sōmushō Tōkeikyoku (1988): *Showa 62-nen shūgyō-kōzō kihon chōsa hōkoku* (English title: 1987 Employment Status Survey), Tokyo: Nihon Tōkei Kyōkai.

—— (1998): *Heisei 9-nen shūgyō-kōzō kihon chōsa hōkoku* (English title: 1997 Employment Status Survey). Tokyo: Nihon Tōkei Kyōkai.

—— (2004): *Heisei 14-nen shūgyō-kōzō kihon chōsa hōkoku* (English title: 2002 Employment Status Survey]. Tokyo: Nihon Tōkei Kyōkai.

CHAPTER FIFTY-FOUR

# HUMAN RESOURCE MANAGEMENT PRACTICES AND THE AGEING WORKFORCE

Harald Conrad

## 1. Introduction

Demographic developments, especially the ageing of the Japanese labour force, pose challenges for all major human resource management (HRM) functions, namely recruitment and placement, training and development, and appraisal and compensation. The purpose of this paper is to discuss and analyze the nature of these challenges and the strategies adopted to cope with them. The underlying assumption of the analysis is that the different HRM functions are interrelated and that the HRM system—as a nexus of HRM functions—is itself interdependent with other domains such as the social policy framework. This interdependence should therefore be considered when assessing changes.

The next section will discuss the internal logic of the "traditional" HRM functions in Japanese companies, how they are affected by ageing workforces, what kind of strategies are adopted to cope with change, and what kind of adjustment problems remain. The third section will assess these strategies briefly from a wider perspective, taking into account the design of and recent changes in the social policy framework. The fourth and final section will offer some concluding remarks.

## 2. HRM Functions and the Ageing Labour Force

If we consider the development of the composition of the Japanese labour force since the mid-1980s (see Figure 1), it is clear that the percentage of older age cohorts within the total labour force has been constantly increasing, with the ratio of employees who are 55 and older increasing from 18% in 1985 to 24.4% in 2003. This section will discuss how this ageing process is affecting "traditional" HRM practices in Japanese companies.

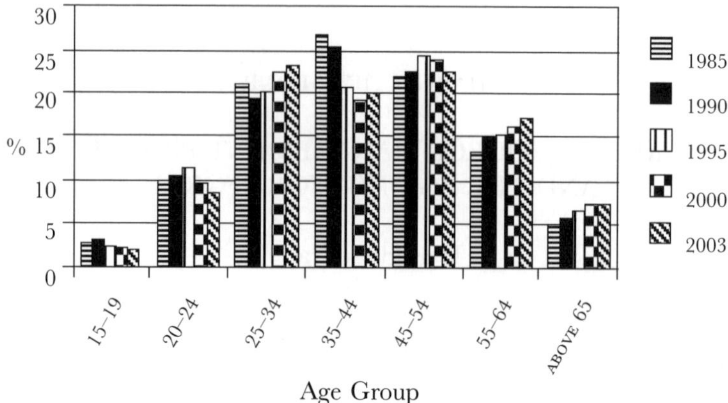


Source: Own calculations based on Sōmuchō Tōkeikyoku 2004: 492.

Figure 1. Japanese Labour Force by Age Group.

In the large body of literature on Japanese human resource practices, the main focus of attention is on discussions of the so-called "three pillars of the Japanese employment system," i.e. lifetime employment (*shūshin koyō*), seniority-based pay (*nenkō joretsu chingin*), and in-house company unions (*kigyōbetsu kumiai*). With regard to the impact of ageing on HRM practices, lifetime employment and seniority-based pay are the most affected.

Before we discuss these issues in more detail, we should, however, briefly consider the question of how universal these practices are. Within the dual structure (*nijū kōzō*) of the Japanese employment system, the 'traditional' or 'prototypical' employment practices pertain mainly to the core male labour force of large companies. These practices have never applied to the same extent for other employees, such as workers in small and medium-sized companies, and the increasing number of marginal workers in larger companies (consisting mainly of women, temporary and part-time workers). In fact, it can be argued that these practices could only be applied to the core male labour force in larger companies because the rest of the labour force was or had to be more flexible.

### 2.1. *Recruitment, placement and retirement*

The dual structure is especially pronounced when it comes to the lifetime employment system, which most authors still consider to be one of the core institutions of the Japanese management system in large corporations (Inohara 1990; Matanle 2003). Ono (2005), who elaborates various problems of definition and measurement, nevertheless estimates that roughly 20% of the Japanese labour force enjoy lifetime employment, pointing out that the participation rate varies considerably according to gender, firm size, and education level. Although there is no coherent definition in the literature, most authors (for example Cole (1979) and Koike (1980)) understand lifetime employment as a system in which school or university graduates join the core labour force of a large company and remain there for their entire working careers.

The system was established during the high economic growth period of the 1960s when many companies were not able to hire the necessary human resources from outside, and so started to invest in in-house training (JILPT 2004a). Since labour contracts rarely contain explicit clauses concerning lifetime employment, it should be understood as an implicit mutual commitment between employer and employee that significantly effects career development. Employees are expected to show a high degree of loyalty to the firm, and flexibility with regard to working hours and assignments to different jobs and locations. In return, the company avoids lay-offs during times of financial hardship and invests in in-house training and the development of multiple skills through job rotation. Younger entrants are usually not trained in just one specific type of job, but are trained to become multi-skilled generalists with a deep understanding of the workings of the company.

Given the fact that the average age of the labour force has constantly been increasing as shown in Figure 1, the lifetime employment system together with seniority-based pay structures causes a quasi-automatic increase in labour costs. Furthermore, the economic downturn of the post-bubble years has put additional pressure on companies to restructure and implement cost-saving measures. The issue to be discussed here is whether and how these pressures have affected the lifetime employment system. Effects on seniority-based compensation practices will be discussed in section 2.3.

Although the end of the lifetime employment system has been announced repeatedly in the popular media since the mid-1990s, the empirical evidence for such a change is rather mixed. Whereas various studies either indicate a decrease in the core labour force or point to an increase in separation rates, both of which support the notion of a decline in the lifetime employment system, other indicators, such as length of tenure, have either increased or not shown any significant change, as in the case of retention rates (Ono 2005). Offering a convincing interpretation for these mixed findings, Ono (2005: 35) states "...that although the population of workers who are ex-ante covered by lifetime employment may be shrinking, the likelihood of job separation has remained stable for those who are already in the system."

After the sharp rise in the unemployment rate since 1997, public awareness focused mainly on the rise in unemployment among middle-aged and older graduate workers. However, as Genda (2001) has pointed out, the overall position of these groups in the unemployment statistics has not really changed significantly since the early 1990s, and increasing unemployment has mainly affected young people and those over sixty. Ono (2005) notes a pattern of bifurcation between young people entering bad jobs and old people remaining in good jobs, which has resulted in the erosion of employment stability among young workers and continued stability among older workers.

Calculations by Genda (2001) clearly show a correlation between the greying of the workforce (measured as the ratio of employees over 45) and hiring trends in companies with more than 500 employees. For example, according to his calculations, when the ratio of workers over 45 increases by one percentage point, the hiring rate for full-time employees drops by 0.0510 per cent. In order to compensate for retaining middle-aged and older workers, employment opportunities for younger workers had to be reduced, a development which Genda describes as a 'displacement effect'.

What factors explain the displacement effect? Economically speaking, the lifetime employment system not only offers benefits to employees, but it also allows companies to make long-term investments in human capital development. Employees are intensively trained and rotated throughout the company. Reducing older workers thus generates high costs because companies are no longer able to recover these human resource investments. Dismissing older workers is also legally very problematic, because Japanese case law has established various requirements which companies have to meet. In fact, Japan has some of the strongest employment protection laws in the OECD (Waldenberger 2003).

Another reason why companies have tried hard to fulfil the implicit lifetime employment contract is to protect their reputation among employees and the public. They found it easier to reduce recruitment, which led to increasing unemployment, especially among younger age groups during the 1990s and the early 2000s, as can been seen in Figure 2.

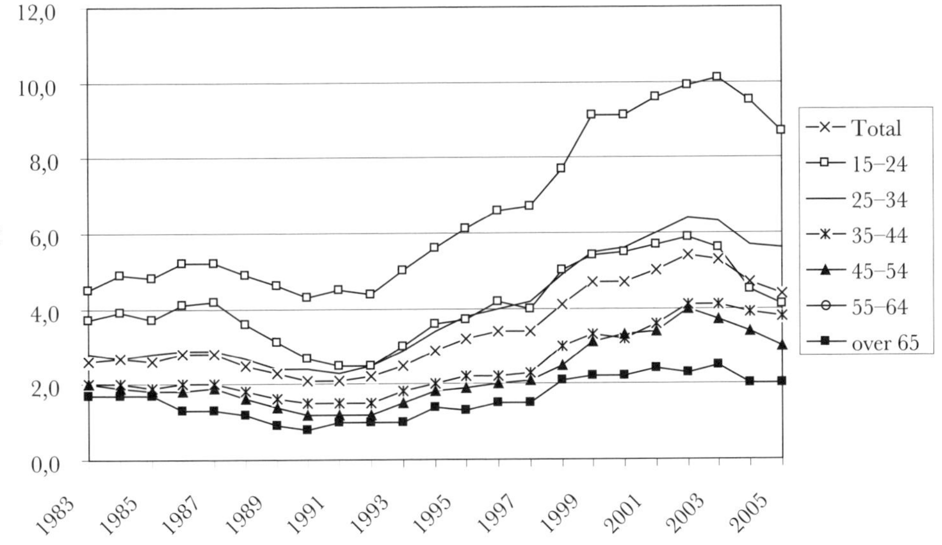


Source: Sōmuchō Tōkeikyoku 2006.

Figure 2. Unemployment rates of different age groups.

Whether and to what extent the lifetime employment system will be maintained in the forthcoming years remains unclear. Since around 2002, the improving economic climate has led to a recovery in the labour market. In December 2005, the ratio of overall job offers to seekers reached parity for the first time in about 13 years (*Nikkei Weekly* 6 February 2006: 1) and, after declining for seven years, the full-time workforce increased slightly for the first time again in 2005 (*Nihon Keizai Shinbun* 1 February 2006: 3). In March 2006, the number of regular employees grew by 0.6 per cent, twice the rate of recruitment for part-time work and temporary contracts.

Improvements in the labour market thus give companies some leverage in sticking to established HRM practices. What is more, the general attitude of companies towards lifetime employment is still very positive. In a 2003 survey, conducted by the Japanese Institute for Labour Policy and Training, 36.1% of companies answered that they would basically maintain the practice, and another 40% answered that partial adjustments were inevitable. On the other hand, only 15.3% answered that a fundamental review was necessary, and only 5.2% stated that they did not have a lifetime employment system (JILPT 2004a).

The positive attitude of companies is matched by a generally positive attitude among Japanese employees towards lifetime employment. Although younger employees have on average a less favourable view of the system, even among the 20–29 year-olds 21.8% strongly favour such a system, and 42.2% favour it somewhat (JILPT 2004a). The Japan Institute for Labour Policy and Training therefore concludes that only a few companies are implementing major reviews of their lifetime employment systems, most are instead resorting to a strategy of restricting the number of regular workers that are subject to the system, and of increasing the number of non-regular employees such as part-time workers. However, since part-time workers largely belong to younger age cohorts, maintaining lifetime employment in this fashion means reducing the chances of younger age cohorts receiving proper training, a point which will be discussed in more detail in section 2.2.

Apart from lifetime employment, another practice closely related to the ageing issue is mandatory retirement. Japan currently has no law which forbids age discrimination. According to a 2004 survey of the Ministry of Health, Labour and Welfare, 91.5% of companies with more than 30 employees have a mandatory retirement system (Kōseirōdōshō Daijin Kanbō Tōkei Jōhōbu 2004a). Article 8 of the Law Concerning the Stabilization of the Employment of Older Persons (*Kōnenreisha tō no kōyō no antei tō ni kan suru hōritsu*) stipulates that employers may not fix the mandatory retirement age under 60.

In April 2006, there was a revision of this law so that employers are now obligated to continue employing workers up to the age of 65. The employer must either raise the mandatory retirement age from the current age of 60, adopt a continued employment scheme while leaving the mandatory retirement age at 60, or abolish the mandatory retirement age as such. Although employers have opposed the latest revision of the law, 80.4% of firms in a Nippon Keidanren survey replied that they would adopt or expand continued employment, and another 11.9% said that they would not take any particular steps because they already satisfied the new requirements.

Continued employment will, in principle, be available for all workers who wish to continue working, but firms can use labour-management agreements to limit the range of eligible workers, for example to "those who have held posts in three or more branches across the country." Furthermore, until 2009, temporary measures make it possible for companies with more than 300 employees to limit the workers eligible for continued employment by stipulating conditions in working rules.

Companies with less than 300 workers have an even longer grace period until 2011 (JILPT 2006).

How these legal changes will impact employment and recruiting practices remains to be seen. Genda (2001) argues that the protection of employment opportunities for older workers might have a detrimental effect on the hiring of younger people. His calculations show that the percentage of companies which do not hire high school and college graduates annually is higher in companies with a mandatory retirement age of 61 and older than in companies with a mandatory retirement age of 60. If we apply this argument, which is based on 1998 data, to the situation created by the 2006 revisions of the Law Concerning the Stabilization of the Employment of Older Persons, we might conclude that the new legal requirements for the longer employment of older workers will counteract the general improvement in the labour market for younger employees mentioned above.

However, this forecast is called into question by the '2007 problem' (*2007-nen mondai*). This refers to the mass retirement between 2007 and 2009 of the first baby boomer generation (those born between 1947 and 1949), which is expected to have repercussions on human resource training and development.

### 2.2. *Training and development*

The hiring freezes since the early 1990s have aggravated the ageing of the Japanese labour force because they have negatively impacted the age structure of companies. In some sectors, especially manufacturing, companies like the JFE Steel Corporation and Mitsubishi Heavy Industries have workforces where more than 40% of workers are over 50 years old and very few employees are in the 35 to 45 age bracket. When the '2007 problem' starts, these companies will loose many experienced workers and so fear a decline of technical know-how and product quality.

The reason these fears are so pronounced is closely linked to the way training and development takes place in a typical Japanese company. Since Japanese schools provide a broad general education rather than specialized knowledge and skills, companies need to train and develop new recruits in in-house training programs. On-the-job experience and learning-by-doing as part of a team of experienced and less-experienced workers is the most common mode of training in Japanese companies. Through frequent job rotations employees are trained to become generalists, with a broad understanding of the workings of their companies, rather than specialists who are assigned a limited range of tasks. Through this kind of in-house training Japanese employees tend to amass company-specific knowledge which cannot easily be applied elsewhere. Therefore, there is only a limited chance of recruiting suitable workers from the external labour market to fill the gap which will result from the retirement of the baby-boom generation. Instead, companies will need to engage in the training of new personnel themselves.

According to a summer 2005 survey by Tohmatsu Consulting of 136 listed and 63 unlisted companies, 70% of corporations answered that they are already suffering or expect to suffer shortages of white-collar workers, and 65% stated that they had the same problem with blue-collar workers (*Nikkei Weekly* 23 January 2006: 21). In the electronics and car industries, the shrinkage of the older core labour force and the increased use of younger temporary and part-time labourers in the late 1990s have negatively affected product quality, job rotation practices, skills transfer, and quality improvement systems (Nakamura 2005). A government survey from 2004 shows that 63% of companies are in fact less concerned about the labour shortage problem as such, but more worried about maintaining and handing down workplace skills in the manufacturing sector (*Nikkei Weekly* 7 March 2005: 21).

To confront this situation, manufacturing companies have recently started to develop mechanisms for technical skills transfers to younger workers. Mitsubishi Heavy Industries has, for example, created special training schools for 'man-to-man' skills transfers, and Ishikawajima Harima Marine United Inc. has introduced a new system of using re-employed senior workers as full-time service instructors to train younger employees (*Nihon Keizai Shinbun* 19 April 2006: 1).

These kinds of developments are stimulating the labour market for younger workers, and the hiring of new college graduates by major corporations is expected to rise by more than 20% in the year 2007, a gain of 20% or more for the third consecutive year. Therefore, the increase in or abolition of the mandatory company retirement age may not necessarily have the kind of negative impact on the employment of younger age cohorts that Genda (2001) forecast.

In order to moderate the negative impact of the '2007 problem', companies will also use employment practices which have always provided flexibility once employees reach the mandatory retirement age, namely the extension of the employment contract (*kinmu enchō*) and the re-employment (*saikoyō*) of retired workers (Suzuki 2004). Among companies (with over 30 employees) with a uniform mandatory retirement age, 67.4% use these systems. More specifically, 14.3% have an employment extension option, 42.5% use the re-employment option, and 10.7% apply both practices (JILPT 2004a).

From the company perspective, the extension of the employment contract or the re-employment of retired workers is doubly advantageous. Firstly, companies can freely choose only workers they consider to be especially capable, possibly for the explicit purpose of training younger workers and facilitating skills and knowledge transfers. Secondly, wages are usually adjusted downwards, with re-employment and contract extension wages both being up to 30% lower (Rōdōshō 1997: 261, appendix 141). Re-employment and employment extension are thus also attractive in terms of cost saving, although Suzuki (2004) estimates that the structure of personnel expenses will not change considerably due to the massive retirement of the baby-boom generation.

For a long time, a relatively low mandatory retirement age, which was often below 60 before the lower limit of 60 became legally obligatory in April 1998, together with the described wage cuts for re-employment and employment extension, have enabled companies to keep their labour costs under control, even if wages were in principal seniority-oriented. However, the increase in the average age of employees in companies and the legal requirement to either abolish or raise the mandatory retirement age, while staying committed to lifetime employment, is now putting considerable cost pressure on companies to adjust their seniority-oriented wage systems, an issue that will be discussed next.

### 2.3. *Appraisal, promotion and compensation*

In the traditional HRM model, promotion and compensation are strongly influenced by the seniority principle. This does not, however, mean that employees rise in the company's hierarchy just by virtue of age; that no competition between employees takes place, or that appraisals are deemed unnecessary. In fact, appraisals are a very common feature in Japanese companies, and do not focus solely on performance but also take behavioural aspects and future potential into account. Since many work processes in a Japanese company are group processes, distinct incentives are necessary so that individual workers commit themselves to the team-based effort (Aoki 1988, 1990, 1994). Japanese companies have therefore designed incentives that are not tightly related to a specific job category but rather motivate employees to acquire wide-ranging job experiences.

At the centre of their incentive schemes are rank hierarchies for blue-collar workers, white-collar workers, and engineers as well as for the supervisory and managerial employees. Each rank is usually associated with a certain pay range, which consists of several pay elements. Employees of the same educational background commence their company careers with identical pay, and for approximately 15 years after entering the company are promoted at an equal rate. It is only after this period that they start to compete for promotion in rank. The central criteria for such promotions are the number of years of continuous employment and merit.

According to the underlying skill-grading system (*shokunō shikaku seido*), merit does not so much depend on a particular job or output, but is broadly defined by problem-solving and communication skills as well as other qualifications. Thus, employees are neither rewarded for achieving a well-defined objective nor due to some subjective evaluation of their performance. Frequent appraisals assess their potential ability based on adaptability to technical changes as well as soft skills such as loyalty and the ability to cooperate with other employees. It is also important to note that speed of promotion varies in later years—with some employees only reaching the higher ranks just before mandatory company retirement, whereas others proceed to supervisory ranks mid-career—and those who do not show continuous progress might be posted to minor subsidiaries or affiliated companies.

Although there is a strong relationship between the rank-hierarchy system and compensation practices, compensation in large Japanese companies is not merely a function of rank. In fact, pay systems are highly complex. Typical pay components in a Japanese company include base pay, family pay, overtime pay and various allowances. According to the Basic Survey on Wage Structure, which covers all major Japanese industries including the finance and service sector, base pay is the most important pay component and comprises 58.4% of total compensation in Japanese companies with more than five employees. Other important pay components are bonuses, 18%, retirement benefits, 5.4%, and statutory benefits, 9.6% (MHLW 2001). Base pay closely reflects the position of employees in the rank-hierarchy and is a function of ability/skills, age and performance. However, the latter has so far played only a marginal role, whereas ability/skills and age are the most important factors. Most companies have a pay component that is explicitly and directly linked to age, but ability/skills as evaluation criteria of the skill-grading system are generally the most important factor of base pay.

As the data from the Basic Survey on Wage Structure indicate, bonuses and retirement benefits are also important pay components. Bonuses are traditionally paid bi-annually. They are sometimes viewed as a kind of profit-sharing scheme, but there is little evidence to support such a view (Morishima 2002).

As a matter of fact, bonus payments are negotiated twice a year between employers and labour unions, and the latter have considered bonuses as part of the regular pay, which should not be linked to company profits. Accordingly, severe bonus cuts have only occurred in companies that encountered financial difficulties (Demes 1998).

During the 1990s and early 2000s, compensation practices met with increasing criticism. What are the most important factors that challenge the status quo? As pointed out above, the single most important challenge is the ageing of Japanese society and the resulting increase in the number of older employees.

Given the age-related compensation and promotion practices, seniority-oriented compensation leads to a quasi-automatic increase in labour costs and a need to create more managerial positions, although the worsening business climate in recent years and a general trend towards organizational structures with less managerial layers and flatter hierarchies would suggest steps in the opposite direction. Another important factor is the fast-changing business environment, which makes it harder to rely on continuous technological progress and generalist skills, which have so far been the comparative strengths of Japanese companies. Related to this point is the problem that the skill-grading system assumes a constant accumulation of skills and, in principle, does not take into account the fact that certain skills may have become obsolete due to technological changes. There is now a growing demand for more creative personnel with more specialised skills. The resulting requirement is to change compensation practices to pay the employees commensurate with their actual value to the firm, rather than equalizing pay over the long run.

In 2000, the Japan Productivity Center for Socio-Economic Development conducted a survey in which human resource managers were asked to indicate three major problems with the skill-grading system (Shakai Keizai Seisansei Honbu 2000). Most notably, 72.2% of the 317 responding companies stressed that skill-grading systems had in fact turned into seniority-based systems, 52.1% remarked that they do not allow demotion based on actual performance, and 39.7% pointed out that the concentration of workers in higher ranks causes increasing labour costs.

As a result of these pressures, a growing number of Japanese companies have acknowledged the need for new incentive tools and the term *seikashugi*, roughly translated as 'performance-ism', has became a frequent buzzword in the Japanese media. However, the performance-oriented restructuring of compensation and appraisal systems has not been easy.[1] Data from one of the most statistically representative surveys covering pay practices in Japan, the "General Survey on Working Conditions" conducted by the Ministry of Health, Labour and Welfare, which consists of a sample of about 5300 companies with 30 employees or more (Kōseirōdōshō Daijin Kanbō Tōkei Jōhōbu 2001), shows that many companies have implemented changes in their pay determination variables.

Whereas factors like age/length of continuous employment and schooling have decreased in importance, others such as performance, skills/qualifications and job content have gained in importance. Other data from the same survey indicate that employers are not simply shifting to new variables, but are making their wage determination systems more complex by considering a larger number of determinants. Although performance has gained in importance as a determination variable, skill-grading systems have not been abolished. This view is also confirmed by a smaller survey of the 199 largest employers on the Tokyo Stock Exchange, which found that only 23.9% of employers that use employee performance to determine employee wages plan to discontinue the skill-grading system (Morishima 2002).

Another interesting question is how performance-based pay elements have influenced actual wage setting. Data from the "General Survey on Working Conditions" show that actual wage increases and decreases for those performing better and worse than their peers are still rather small. Wage cuts in particular appear hard to implement, so that 50% of all companies surveyed have limited their wage cuts for the lowest performers among non-managerial staff to below 5%.

[1] For a more detailed discussion of recent changes in compensation practices see Conrad and Heindorf (2006).

Such data might suggest that compensation practices have not really changed much. However, if we take a closer look at individual companies such a conclusion is not tenable. Although wage disparity is still rather low, this does not mean that companies are not willing to establish stronger performance-related compensation. The ongoing changes are tentative and require fine-tuning to fit the changing demands of employees as well as changes in the business and legal environment. Generally, pay systems in Japan have become more diverse. Therefore, it has become much harder to pinpoint 'Japanese-style' reward practices. Nevertheless, we can identify some general trends. An increasing number of companies are testing pay practices that incorporate different appraisal and reward systems. In contrast to most other industrialized nations, reward systems for white-collar and blue-collar workers in Japan have so far been very similar in the sense that the same systems apply to all members of the core labour force up to a certain level in the hierarchy (Genda 2001).

Recently, companies have started to seek different kinds of reward systems for different groups of personnel. For example, they have largely maintained a seniority-oriented reward system for blue-collar workers, while introducing new wage systems for technical and white-collar personnel. In the latter, seniority might still play a key role in the early years of company employment, but performance factors increase in importance after several years of employment, while seniority factors are subsequently lowered or abolished. This diversification of pay practices can be understood as a strategy to maintain institutional complementarities between human resource management practices and the production system of companies. For the blue-collar workforce, job rotation, on-the-job training and teamwork are still regarded as essential for an effective production process. Human resource departments consider stronger performance-based pay for these groups unsuitable because it could have negative effects on knowledge-sharing and teamwork. At the same time, some companies still regard seniority-oriented rewards as a good measure of employees' productivity. Thus, a change to more performance-based pay is not believed to increase efficiency.

Overall, many companies have increased the weight of performance-based pay elements, especially for white-collar staff. However, as shown above, this has not yet translated into greater intra-firm wage disparities. The main reasons for this discrepancy are problems with the appraisal system and the performance evaluation criteria. Almost 30% of large companies are currently reporting difficulties with their appraisal systems after the introduction of new compensation practices (Kōseirōdōshō Daijin Kanbō Tōkei Jōhōbu 2004b). Consequently, they are in the process of reforming these appraisal systems and will in the future attach greater importance to the evaluation of processes and skills.

Most companies have decided to keep wage disparity narrow until these problems are solved. Although employee appraisals were frequently practiced in Japan, the results of such appraisals usually had little immediate influence on rewards, and the results were often not communicated to employees. Once performance-based pay started to increase in importance, workplace morale declined and employees complained about evaluations conducted by inexperienced managers. Companies had to realize that they had prematurely opted for an increase in performance-based pay without establishing clear criteria for evaluating performance, and without institutionalizing evaluation processes which allowed managers and subordinates to discuss evaluation results.

Companies are now fine-tuning their reward systems to meet these challenges. However, determining clear criteria for individual performance is not always easy, because job descriptions in operational types of work are not usually very clear, and the line between individual job and team activities is frequently blurred. For this reason, some companies focus more on team performance than individual performance.

While performance-oriented pay elements are increasing in importance, this does not mean that companies are giving up on long-term-oriented pay practices. On the contrary, as indicated above, skills and qualifications have actually gained as determinants for base pay. However, in contradiction to former practices where the skill-grading system was seniority-oriented due to a semi-automatic link between age and accumulated latent skills, the reformed skill-grading systems aim to reflect actual skills and qualifications rather than latent skills.

Job ranking and job-group ranking systems are growing in importance. The former are mainly adopted for specialists, where job content and career development can be clearly circumscribed. The latter have, for example, been adopted for clerical/professional and manufacturing staff at Mitsubishi Motors, and for non-managerial employees at Canon. Mitsubishi's 2003 system distinguishes four job categories of clerical/professional white-collar staff (*gyōmu shoku* [operational work], *tantō shoku* [managerial work], *shutantō shoku* [chief managerial work], *shidō senmon shoku* [leading expert work]) as well as four categories of manufacturing blue-collar staff (*ippan ginō shoku* [technical work], *jōkyū ginō shoku* [higher technical work], *kantoku kōginō shoku* [supervisory higher technical work] and *shidō senmonshoku* [leading expert work]).

Each category has a fixed sum job-rank related pay component and a flexible performance-related pay component. For flexible performance-related pay, the appraisal not only evaluates results but also work behaviour and competency. Thus, although there is a strong move to performance-related pay at Mitsubishi, performance is not simply measured in terms of output but also takes the work process and soft skills of employees into consideration (Mitsubishi Motors 2003).

Canon introduced a similar system in 2002. Each job-rank has a monthly wage band, so that wages cannot rise above a certain level without employees engaging in jobs associated with higher ranks. The flexible pay component at Canon aims to reflect not only performance but also ability improvement, another sign that long-term oriented practices continue to play an important role (Fujimura 2003).

Although many companies have introduced stronger performance-based wage factors, this reform process has not yet come to an end. In this respect, it is especially noteworthy that companies are struggling with the definition and assessment of performance. A first wave of companies opting for stronger performance-based pay had to realize that neither their performance criteria nor their evaluation processes were sufficiently clear. Many of them are now redefining their understanding and evaluation of 'performance'. The result might well be a definition of performance that remains distinctly different from western concepts.

## 3. Related Changes in the Social Policy Framework for Older Workers

This section examines how the social policy framework of public pension arrangements interacts with HRM practices. In international comparison, Japan has one of the highest labour force participation rates among the major OECD countries. For example, in 2000 the labour force participation rate of men aged 60–64 was still 71.2% (ILO 2003). Despite this generally positive state of affairs, the efficient use of older employees will become an even more important task in future, when the size of younger age cohorts will shrink due to demographic developments. In this regard, public pension arrangements are important because they have an impact on incentives to work. Seike and Yamada

(2004) demonstrate that Japan's pension schemes currently lead to a reduction in labour supply because of the effect of the earnings test of public pensions. In order not to exceed the earnings test ceiling and to remain eligible to receive at least 80% of their pension benefits, many workers reduce their labor supply. Seike (2003) argues that the earnings test should eventually be abolished, in order to encourage older workers' participation in the labour market.

Another interesting aspect is how public pensions might influence the utilization of skills and abilities of older workers. According to Seike and Yamada (2004) workers aged 60 to 69 who receive public pension benefits and/or have a mandatory retirement experience are statistically less likely to be in the same occupation that they were in at age 55 than workers who do not receive pensions and/or are without mandatory retirement experience. They interpret this correlation as a sign that pension and mandatory retirement schemes obstruct the full utilization of the skills of older workers.

However, it can be expected that the scheduled increase in the normal retirement age to 65 by 2013 and 2025, for the basic pension and for the remuneration-proportional pension respectively (Conrad 2001), will naturally moderate such problems in the future. The same is probably true for the effects of the mandatory retirement system, because of the changes in the Law Concerning the Stabilization of the Employment of Older Persons, as mentioned above.

In this sense, it can be said that the social policy framework has at least in part been adjusted so that public rules and incentives will have a less negative impact on the efficient employment of older workers.

## 4. Conclusions and Outlook

This article has sought to shed light on the impact of the ageing workforce on Japanese human resource management practices. Since the different HRM functions of recruitment and placement, training and development and appraisal and compensation are interrelated, it is not surprising that changes in one domain depend very much on changes in other domains. In this respect, one interesting finding is that the lifetime employment system has largely been upheld at the expense of younger workers who had to face much higher unemployment due to hiring freezes in the 1990s.

The main reason for sticking to lifetime employment is that training and development still takes place within companies, and a way to secure investment in human resources is to bind employees to the company by this implicit employment guarantee. During the post-bubble period of the 1990s and early 2000s, maintaining lifetime employment for the ageing core labour force meant fewer opportunities for younger graduates, who filled the fast growing ranks of temporary and part-time workers. Now, with the retirement of the baby-boom generation between 2007 and 2009, the fallacy of the hiring policies of the recession period is becoming apparent. More and more companies are already facing a shortage of qualified labour and are struggling to maintain and transfer skills to their younger workers.

However, companies are likely to overcome these problems because older Japanese still show a great willingness to work, and companies can use traditional measures, such as the extension of employment contracts and the re-employment of retired workers, to make use of the skills of older workers even after they have reached the mandatory retirement age.

Therefore, the most pressing age-related problem for human resource management is the restructuring of seniority-based pay practices. Many companies are currently experimenting with new remuneration systems, and performance-related pay components are becoming increasingly important. Despite current problems in this area, it can be expected that Japanese HRM practices will be fit to face the ageing labour force once appraisal systems and pay systems have been sufficiently fine-tuned. Although the "age factor" will continue to play a role in remuneration systems, performance measures in the broadest sense will gain in importance so that the cost automatism of seniority pay can be overcome.

## References

Aoki, Masahiko (1988): *Information, Incentives and Bargaining in the Japanese Economy*. Cambridge: Cambridge University Press.

—— (1990): Toward an Economic Model of the Japanese Firm. In: *Journal of Economic Literature* 28, 1, pp. 1–27.

—— (1994): The Japanese Firm as a System of Attributes: A Survey and Research Agenda. In: Aoki, Masahiko and Ronald Dore (eds.): *The Japanese Firm: The Sources of Competitive Strength*. Oxford, pp. 11–40.

Cole, Robert E. (1979): *Work, Mobility and Participation: A Comparative Study of American and Japanese Industry*. Berkeley: University of California Press.

Conrad, Harald (2001): *The Japanese Social Security System in Transition—An Evaluation of the Current Pension Reforms.* Munich: Iudicium Verlag.

Conrad, Harald and Viktoria Heindorf (2006): Recent changes in compensation practices of large Japanese companies: wages, bonuses and corporate pensions. In: Matanle, Peter and Wim Lunsing (eds.): *Perspectives on Work, Employment, and Society in Contemporary Japan.* Houndmills and New York: Palgrave Macmillan, pp. 79–97.

Demes, Helmut (1998): Arbeitsmarkt und Beschäftigung. In: Deutsches Institut für Japanstudien (ed.): *Die Wirtschaft Japans—Strukturen zwischen Kontinuität und Wandel,* Berlin: Springer, pp. 135–164.

Fujimura, Hiroyuki (2003): Changes in the Spring Wage Offensive and the Future of the Wage Determination System in Japanese Firms. In: *Japan Labour Bulletin* (May 1), pp. 6–12.

Genda, Yūji (2001): *Shigoto no naka no aimai na fuan* [A vague sense of job insecurity]. Tokyo: Chuokoran Shinsha.

Inohara, Hideo (1990): *Human Resource Development in Japanese Companies.* Tokyo: Asian Productivity Organization.

ILO (International Labour Organization) (2003): *Yearbook of Labour Statistics.* Geneva: International Labour Organization.

JILPT (Japan Institute for Labour Policy and Training) (2004a): *Labour Situation in Japan and Analysis 2004/2005.* Tokyo: The Japan Institute for Labour Policy and Training.

—— (2004b): *The Japan Labour Flash No.7,* Email Journal (January 15).

—— (2006): *The Japan Labour Flash No.60,* Email Journal (May 1).

Koike, Kazuo (1980): Nihonteki kanko [Japanese employment practices]. In: *Keizaigaku Daijiten II,* Tokyo: Tōkyō Keizai Shinposha, pp. 100–108.

Kōseirōdōshō Daijin Kanbō Tōkei Jōhōbu (2001): *Heisei 13-nen shūrō jōken sōgō chōsa* [General survey on working conditions]. Tokyo: Rōdō Kosei Kenkyūjo.

—— (2004a): *Koyō kanri chōsa* [Survey on employment management]. http://www.mhlw.go.jp/toukei/itiran/roudou/koyou/kanri/kanri04/07.html (found 19 June 2006).

—— (2004b): *Heisei 15-nen shūrō jōken sōgō chōsa* [General survey on working conditions]. Tokyo: Rōmu Kosei.

Matanle, Peter (2003): *Japanese Capitalism and Modernity in a Global Era. Re-fabricating Lifetime Employment Relations.* London and New York: Routledge Curzon.

MHLW (Ministry of Health, Labour, and Welfare) (2001): *Basic Survey on Wage Structure,* Tokyo: Ministry of Health, Labour, and Welfare.

Mitsubishi Motors (2003): *Kumiaiin shain no jinji seido kaisei keikaku ni tsuite* [Reform of the new human resource management system for union members]. Tokyo: Mitsubishi Motors.

Morishima, Motohiro (2002): Pay Practices in Japanese Organizations: Changes and Non-changes. In: *Japan Labour Bulletin* (April 1), pp. 8–13.

Nakamura, Keisuke (2005): Koyō shisutemu no keizoku to henka—chiteki jukuren to seika shugi [Continuity and change of the employment system—skill formation and performance principle]. In: Tōkyō Daigaku Shakaikagaku Kenkyūjo (ed.): *Ushinawareta 10-nen wo koete 1: Keizai kiki no kyōkun.* Tokyo: Tōkyō Daigaku Shuppankai, pp. 145–173.

*Nihon Keizai Shinbun* (1 February 2006): Rōdōryoku jinkō sakunen 7-nen buri ni zōka [Work force increased last year for first time in 7 years], p. 3, morning edition.

—— (19 April 2006): Seizōgyō, ginō denshō wo kasoku [Manufacturing industry, accelerating skill transfer], p. 1, morning edition.

*Nikkei Weekly* (7 March 2005): Continuity major issue as boomers retire, p. 21.

—— (23 January 2006): Problem of finding, keeping core staff already begun, p. 21.

—— (6 February 2006): Shortage of skilled workers looms, p. 1.

Ono, Hiroshi (2005): *Lifetime Employment in Japan: Concepts and Measurements.* http://swopec.hhs.se/hastef/papers/hastef0624.pdf (found 10 May 2006).

Rōdōshō (1997): *Rōdōhakusho Heisei 9-nenban* [Labour white book 1997]. Tokyo: Nihon Rōdō Kenkyū Kikō.

Seike, Atsushi (2003): Pension Reforms toward an Aging Society. In: *The Japanese Journal of Social Security Policy* 12, 1 (June 2003), pp. 1–5.

Seike, Atsushi and Atsuhiro Yamada (2004): *Kōreisha shūgyō no keizaigaku* [Economics of employment of the elderly]. Tokyo: Nihon Keizai Shinbunsha.

Shakai Keizai Seisansei Honbu (2000): *Nihonteki jinji seido no genjō to kadai* [Current situation and issues of Japanese-style human resource management]. Tokyo: Shakai Keizai Seisansei Honbu.

Sōmuchō Tōkeikyoku (2004): *Nihon tōkei nenkan—Heisei 17-nen* [Japan statistical yearbook 2005]. Tokyo: Nihon Tōkei Kyōkai.

—— (2006): *Rōdōryoku chōsa* [Labour force survey]. http://www.stat.go.jp/data/roudou/longtime/03roudou.htm (found 10 May 2006).

Suzuki, Hitoshi (2004): Dankai sedai to kigyō no jinkenhi futan [The baby-boom generation and companies' personnel expenses]. In: Higuchi, Yoshio et al. (eds.): *Dankai seidai no teinen to nihon keizai*. Tokyo: Nihon Hyōronsha, pp. 149–166.

Waldenberger, Franz (2003): Japans Arbeitsmarktlage und Arbeitsmarktpolitik aus deutscher Sicht, In: Conrad, Harald and Rolf Kroker (eds.): *Deutschland und Japan—Mit Reformen zu neuer Dynamik*, Cologne: Deutscher Instituts-Verlag, pp. 103–127.

CHAPTER FIFTY-FIVE

# THE IMPACT OF THE AGEING OF SOCIETY ON CONSUMER BEHAVIOUR AND CONSUMER MARKETS

Hidehiko Sekizawa

## 1. The Three Impacts of Ageing on Consumer Behaviour

There are three types of ageing (HILL 2003). *Cultural ageing* refers to the changes that occur in one's values and tastes with advancing years, and alters one's lifestyle as a consumer. *Social ageing* is the phenomenon whereby one is deemed elderly in accordance with social conventions; specifically, it refers to the transition in life stages from a work-centred to a leisure-centred existence that occurs upon retirement. *Physiological ageing* is the deterioration of one's physical and mental abilities, in other words, the process of senile decay; in the end, it reduces the individual to a state where he or she finds it difficult to lead an independent existence.

Cultural ageing alters consumer behaviour: for example, people's tastes in food and clothing change. Among the Japanese, preferences in food, for example, change noticeably with the advance of years. While 74.3 per cent of men in their twenties enjoy steak, only 38.0 per cent of those in their sixties do (HILL 2004). When today's sexagenarians were still in their twenties, steak was already a highly popular item on restaurant menus in Japan. They ate plenty of steak back then, but in growing older they have developed a preference for plainer-tasting traditional foods. Only 30.9 per cent of men in their twenties enjoy the unobtrusive flavour of vegetables stewed in traditional Japanese style (*nimono*), but that figure rises to 58.0 per cent among those in their sixties (HILL 2004).

Regular employees of large Japanese firms typically retire at 60; they may then either be rehired on contract or find a new position at a small or medium-sized company. Many individuals thus continue working until their mid-sixties, although they have plenty of leisure time, since they are not as busy as they were in their old jobs. The age of retirement is determined by explicit social rules or conventions, as indicated by the fact that it varies from country to country. When people reach a certain age, they are expected to retire, regardless of how physically aged they actually are as individuals. Retirement may therefore be defined as social ageing par excellence.

Social ageing leads to consumption of services that require time on the part of the consumer. It is predicted that in the Japan of tomorrow, an increasing number of people will take trips, attend concerts, visit art galleries, and go to watch sports. In particular, the number of retirees who travel abroad, an activity that requires plenty of leisure time, is likely to increase. When travelling, Japanese retirees prefer to visit cities with long histories or archaeological sites redolent of ancient cultures, rather than stay at a resort; thus the intersection of cultural and social ageing has in effect created a new market.

Finally, there are changes in consumer behaviour attendant on physiological ageing, which manifests itself in the final stage of life. As people grow older and find it increasingly difficult to lead an independent existence, they start to purchase various nursing care goods and services. Even people in the early stage of old age, who are still independent, are frequent buyers of dentures, reading glasses, wigs, and other such aids.

With the increase in the number of senior citizens who are to all appearances healthy, there has been a growing tendency to become complacent about the ravages of physiological ageing. But according to a large-scale survey of individuals aged between 70 and 100, it is more and more often the case that senior citizens who could stem the decline in their physical powers if they took steps soon enough are, in an excess of optimism, letting the best time to do so slip by (Baltes and Mayer 1999). While becoming psychologically depressed because of excessive pessimism about the prospect of physiological ageing is something to be avoided, nor is it wise to be overly optimistic and just let things take their course.

These three forms of ageing—cultural ageing, social ageing, and physiological ageing—each lead to differences in consumer behaviour from those seen in the regular market; and the magnitude of those differences increases in that order. Individuals at the later stages of old age, being ill yet able to act on their own, must even depend on others to engage in consumer behaviour on their behalf, which is in sharp contrast to the normal pattern of consumer behaviour. In the following sections of this chapter, the impacts on consumer behaviour of each of these three forms of ageing are examined in more detail.

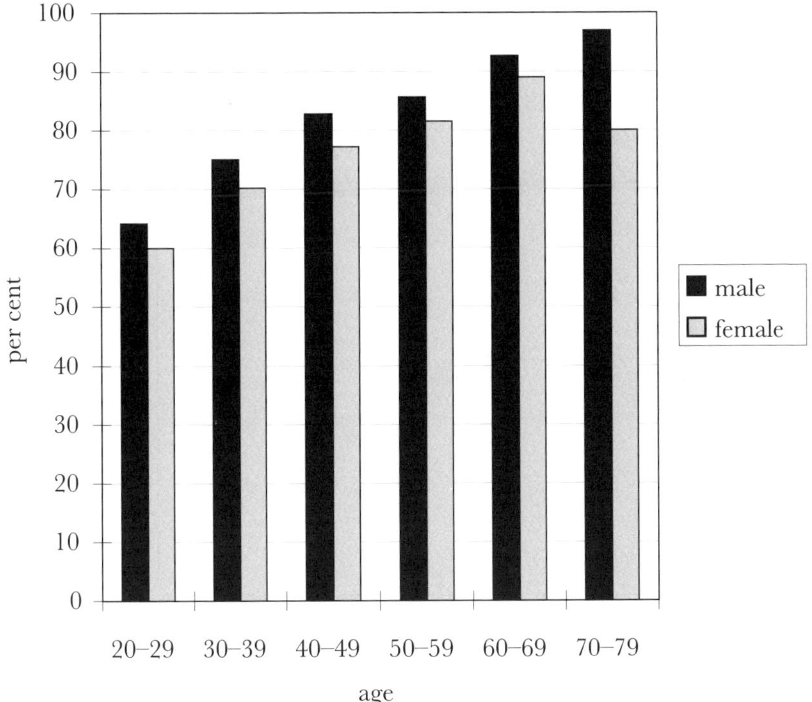


Source: Hill 2004.

Figure 1. "When buying something, I place a higher importance on the features and functions than on the design."

## 2. Cultural Ageing: Getting Older Alters Values and Tastes

As consumers age, they come to favour practical convenience over outward show. Figure 1 illustrates how, when selecting a product, older people place greater importance on features and functions than on design (HILL 2004). As the figure shows, considerable differences are to be observed by sex as well as by age: a greater percentage of men than women place higher importance on features and functions. Nonetheless, women too place steadily greater importance on features and functions as they grow older, at least until their sixties.

Figure 2 shows how attitudes to price change with age. Note how men and women differ in their pattern of change. Until their fifties, men display an increasing reluctance to buy expensive items even if they like them. Women in their thirties and beyond, by contrast, display an

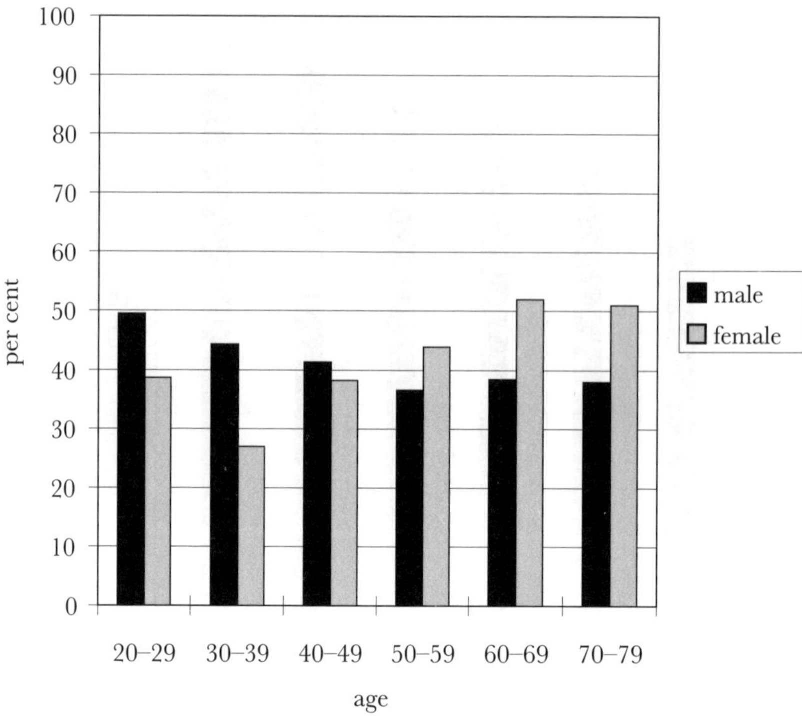


Source: HILL 2004.

Figure 2. "I buy items I like even when they are expensive."

increasing tendency to buy items they like even when they are expensive. It will also be observed that in the fifties and older age brackets, women exhibit a higher propensity to consume than do men.

Young people tend to act in accordance with their desires, a tendency that, in terms of consumer behaviour, manifests itself in the form of impulse buying. Figure 3 illustrates how impulse buying decreases with age. By sex, women are the more impulsive consumers. The percentage of women who buy on impulse declines with age between the twenties and the fifties, but then it jumps again in the sixties. A conspicuous phenomenon in today's Japan is women in their sixties descending on redeveloped commercial centres in the company of friends the same age. Females in their twenties and those in their sixties thus constitute two primary targets for businesses these days.

The longer you live the more knowns there are, and the fewer unknowns to surprise you. Figure 4 shows how the propensity to

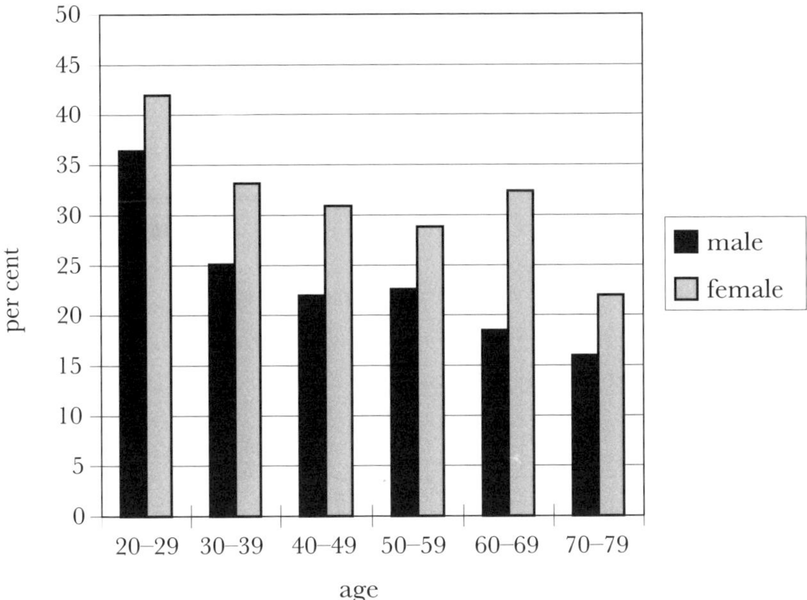


Source: HILL 2004.

Figure 3. "I often buy on impulse."

consume declines overall with age. Among women in particular, the percentage of individuals who do not have anything in particular that they want rises sharply in the seventies age bracket. Impulse buying also declines among women in their seventies, as Figure 3 reveals. Women are more avid consumers than men, but once they reach their seventies their energy flags. Among Japanese couples it is very common for the husband to be around three years older than the wife. Many women in their seventies thus are widows or have an older spouse who is in need of care, which appears to be a reason that they channel less energy into consumption.

Figure 5 reveals a peculiarly Japanese form of cultural ageing: how, as they grow older, people develop a craving for rice, the traditional staple of the Japanese diet. The percentage of individuals who feel that something is missing from their diet if they do not eat rice at least once a day rises gradually until the fifties age bracket, then shoots up from the sixties age bracket. Diet is thus the area where the traditional Japanese lifestyle persists most strongly.

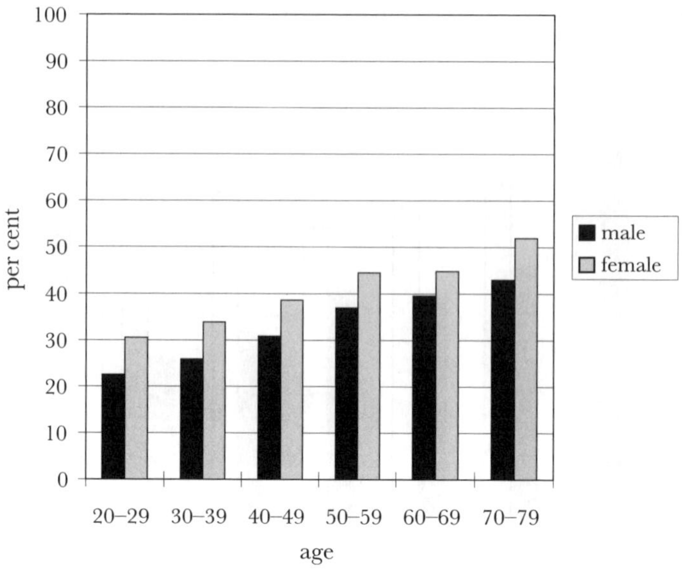


Source: HILL 2004.

Figure 4. "I don't have anything in particular that I want very badly."

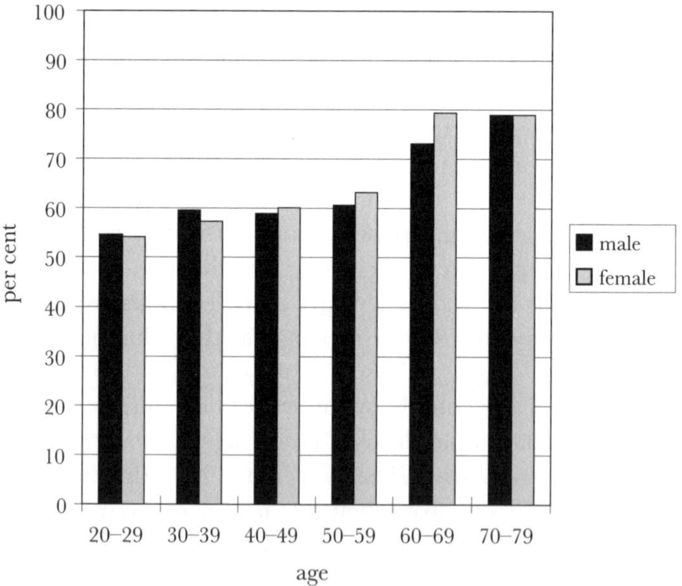


Source: HILL 2004.

Figure 5. "Something is missing in my diet if I don't eat rice at least once a day."

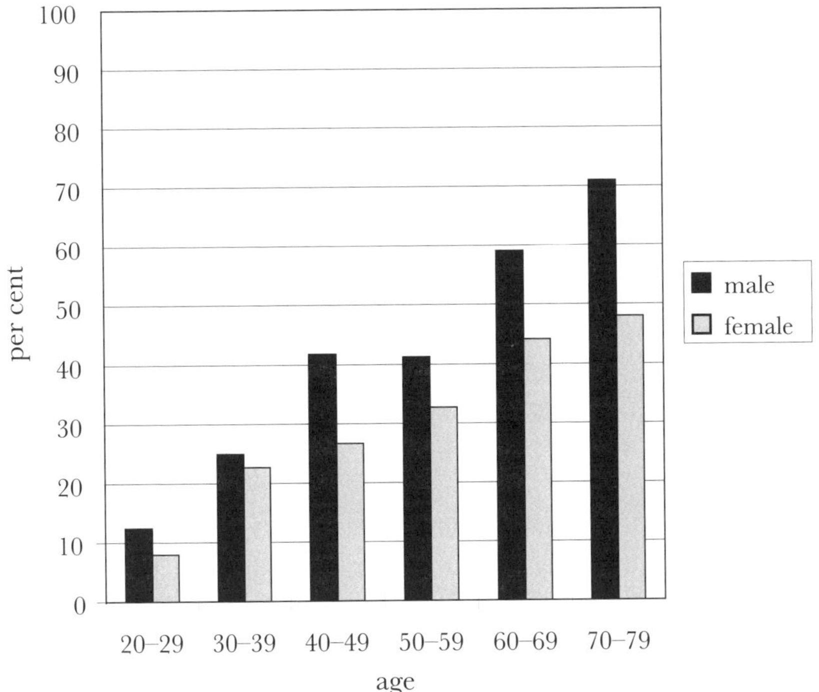


Source: HILL 2004.

Figure 6. "I feel I'm missing out on something whenever I don't read the morning newspaper."

Figure 6 shows a similar pattern to Figure 5. The percentage of people who make it a habit to read the newspaper rises with age. But eating rice and reading the paper differ in one regard: while older people's predilection for rice can be expected to remain fairly strong, older people in the future may not necessarily stick to the habit of reading the paper every morning as they do today.

Another form of cultural ageing is to be seen in the tendency of older people to take an interest in high culture. In Japan, fans of classical music are commonly in their fifties or older. Similarly, the most frequent visitors to museums are men in their sixties and women in their fifties and above. This tendency is also related to the fact that older people have more time to observe paintings at leisure, thanks to the phenomenon of social ageing (or retirement), to which we turn next.

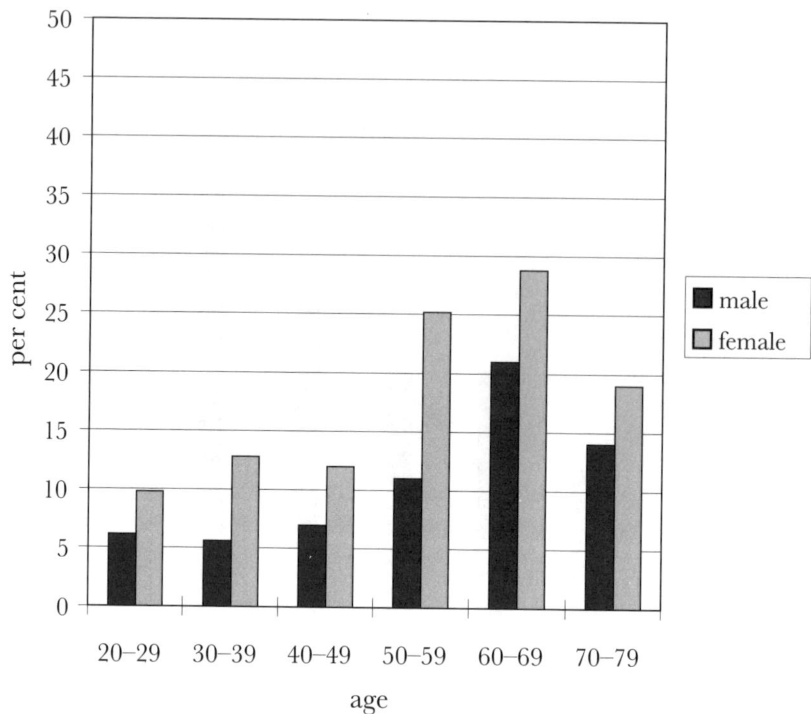


Source: HILL 2004.

Figure 7. "I frequently go to museums."

## 3. Social Ageing: Retirement Leaves More Time for Consumption

In 2007 began the retirement of Japan's baby boomers—the generation born between 1947 and 1949—who, at some seven million people, constitute a massive segment of the population. Although many of them will go on to do light jobs, their having more leisure time than before will affect patterns of consumption considerably.

Table 1 compares availability of spare time among individuals in their fifties, when retirement rates are low, with that among individuals in their sixties, when retirement rates are higher (HILL 2004). According to the HILL survey, 3.4 per cent of men in their fifties and 33.0 per cent of those in their sixties were without work; 21.8 per cent of women in their fifties and 58.4 per cent of those in their sixties were without work. "Without work" means having no employment whatso-

Table 1. Availability of spare time compared between individuals in their fifties and sixties.

| | Men in their 50s | Men in their 60s | Women in their 50s | Women in their 60s |
|---|---|---|---|---|
| Have plenty of spare time | 55.8% | 72.8% | 69.1% | 77.9% |

Source: HILL 2004.

Table 2. Classification according to availability of spare time and economic leeway.

| | Men in their 50s | Men in their 60s | Women in their 50s | Women in their 60s |
|---|---|---|---|---|
| A. Considerable economic leeway, plenty of spare time | 24.7% | 34.1% | 32.4% | 43.4% |
| B. Considerable economic leeway, little spare time | 11.0% | 8.7% | 9.7% | 7.5% |
| C. Little economic leeway, plenty of spare time | 31.1% | 38.8% | 36.7% | 34.5% |
| D. Little economic leeway, little spare time | 33.2% | 18.5% | 21.2% | 14.6% |

Source: HILL 2004.

ever, including a part-time job. While among women the difference in availability of spare time between the fifties and sixties age bracket is insignificant, among men it is considerable.

Availability of spare time is significant as a determinant of one's level of consumer behaviour; economic leeway is even more so. Table 2 presents a classification into four categories defined by a combination of the two factors (HILL 2004).

Of the four groups, Group A probably has the most active consumers. In percentage terms it is dominated by women in their sixties, followed by men in their sixties. Group B has low percentages in all four brackets; in relative terms, it accounts for a higher percentage of individuals in their fifties than of those in their sixties. People in this group have the money to spend, but not the time to shop. In Group C, the largest segment constitutes men in their sixties; having little economic leeway

Table 3. Areas of consumption on which people plan to spend money (multiple answers; top five responses).

| Baby boomers, male | | | Baby boomers, female | | |
|---|---|---|---|---|---|
| 1 | Domestic travel | 54.4% | 1 | Domestic travel | 53.7% |
| 2 | Cars | 31.6% | 2 | Remodelling the home | 33.1% |
| 3 | Overseas travel | 29.8% | 3 | Mastering a new skill | 30.0% |
| 4 | Remodelling the home | 26.8% | 4 | Overseas travel | 29.6% |
| 5 | Mastering a new skill | 16.7% | 5 | Cars | 13.6% |

Source: NRIIM 2003.

but plenty of time on their hands, individuals in this group frequently go away on low-cost tours. Group D, consisting of inactive consumers, accounts for a higher percentage of individuals in their fifties than of those in their sixties.

Table 3 summarizes how baby boomers replied to the question, "When you or your spouse retire, what consumer goods and services do you plan to spend money on?"

As can be seen, both men and women are eager to travel, whether at home or abroad. On the domestic travel front, hot springs are a highly popular destination. The traditional Japanese-style inn-cum-spa facilities to be found throughout the country were once geared primarily to tour groups, but of late they have switched to a strategy of providing extended accommodation to retired couples. These inns have been successful by overhauling themselves to look like Asian resort hotels or equipping individual rooms with outdoor baths in place of the communal bathing facilities that were once the norm. People can take frequent domestic trips even before they retire, but overseas travel is a major focus of consumer spending for retirees in particular. As Figure 8 shows, Japan's most frequent overseas travellers are women in their twenties, followed by women in their fifties, women in their sixties, men in their sixties, and women in their seventies. With the exception of women in their twenties then, retirees thus account for the highest percentage of overseas trips.

Besides travel, other areas where baby boomers intend to spend money after retirement are cars, remodelling the home, and mastering a new skill. Young men exhibit less interest in cars than they used to in the old days; as long as a vehicle offers a certain level of performance, this is enough to keep them happy. Baby boomers, on the other hand, have a genuine enthusiasm for cars, since it was in their younger days

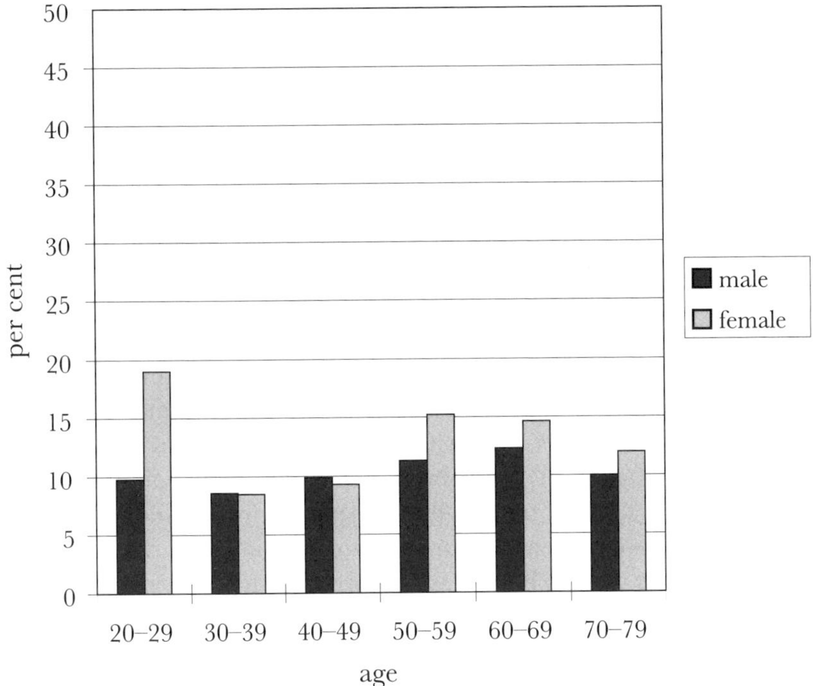


Source: HILL 2004.

Figure 8. "I have travelled overseas in the past year."

that the wave of motorization first swept over Japan, and they are looking for the sheer joy of being behind the wheel. Baby boomers account for the lion's share of sales of two-seater sports cars in Japan; they are also the primary purchasers of heavyweight motorcycles.

When it comes to remodelling the home, a favourite renovation is installing larger windows in the room with the bath (traditionally separate from the toilet in Japan) so as to offer a view of the trees in the garden, the idea being to create the effect of bathing at a hot spring. Many people also want a sunroom or a terrace. Other projects that baby boomers are eager to undertake upon retirement include installing a home theatre for watching movies on a big screen, and building a well-appointed study.

In the area of mastering new skills, many people take classes in things like pottery, yoga, dance, or playing a musical instrument. More and more individuals are also taking advantage of the availability of places for mature students at university to start specialized studies in subjects such as foreign languages and literature, whether at undergraduate or graduate level.

Buying a car, remodelling the home, and mastering a new skill are forms of consumption that may be said to improve the quality of time spent on the road, in the home, and on leisure activities respectively.

## 4. Physiological Ageing: The Effects of Physical and Mental Decline on Consumption

In April 2000 Japan launched a public nursing care insurance system. All Japanese aged 40 and over must obtain cover by enrolling in the programme. Municipalities actually run the programme, collecting premiums from insurees and paying out benefits when an insuree who requires care makes use of nursing services. With the establishment of a well-funded system of nursing care in Japan, advances have also been made in the development of nursing care equipment and supplies.

A wide range of such items has appeared: foods for people who have trouble swallowing; eating utensils designed not to spill their contents; aids to help one in getting dressed; special writing utensils designed for individuals with disabled hands; sensors that let caregivers know when the person in their charge has wet his or her incontinence pants; walking aids; apparatus that makes it easier to take a bath; products for wiping the bodies of bedridden patients; tooth-brushing devices for elderly people with disabled hands; portable toilets; homecare beds that sit one up mechanically; products designed to prevent bedsores; and so forth. More and more models of wheelchairs that are outstanding in terms of design as well as function have also come onto the market. A host of new products that tap into information technology have also been developed, such as a device with a Global Positioning System (GPS) function designed to keep track of Alzheimer's patients when they stray from home.

Work is even under way on the development of nursing care robots, which may in the near future be able to take over the job of getting elderly people in nursing homes out of bed and into a wheelchair, or cheering them up with a bit of friendly conversation. As of fiscal year 2004, the Japanese market for incontinence pants, wheelchairs, and other nursing care supplies totalled 1.1821 billion yen, and the market for home nursing care services totalled 2.67 billion yen.

## 5. Ageing and the Consumer Market

Consumer demand manifests itself on the market in basically one of two forms: either as a desire for ways to reduce the negatives in daily life by supplementing what is lacking or lost, or as a desire for ways to increase the positives by enhancing the joy of being alive.

Although it may assume different aspects—cultural, social, and physiological—the ageing process is inevitably accompanied by some form of loss. But precisely because they stand on the threshold of physical and mental decline, the elderly have that much stronger an urge to enjoy the present moment. Focusing on these conflicting demands for ways to allay fears and ways to enhance pleasure, it is possible to forecast future directions in the senior citizens' consumer market.

Next, therefore, we turn to the question of what opportunities will arise in individual markets as the number of senior citizens rises.

### 5.1. *The clothing market*

Clothes are designed to regulate temperature, correct the bodyline, and serve as articles of fashion. Functional clothing shows particular promise for the future. Garments that warm or cool the body in response to changes in temperature will be useful for those of such an age that their body's own temperature adjustment mechanism no longer works as well as it used to. In the case of individuals with a dysfunctional body part—say a bad knee—it will be possible to warm just that area. One department store has been highly successful in selling the idea of clothes designed to be worn in several layers to older women who have lost their body shape. Conversely, there are those senior citizens, albeit few, who are eager to try showy fashions precisely because they are old. Such individuals often take advantage of mail order sales and the like to buy flashy clothes that they would be embarrassed to buy in a shop. Ordering from the television or radio, a catalogue, or the Internet is more than just a matter of convenience; it also caters to this facet of the female psyche.

### 5.2. *The food market*

For seniors, diet is the most important aspect of life. In a survey conducted by the Japanese government (Naikaku Sōri Daijin Kanbō Kōhōshitsu 2004), the top response to the question "What will be the most important area of your life from now on?" was, as averaged out for the overall survey sample, leisure time. However, among women in their sixties (41.2%), women in their seventies (35.3%), and men in their seventies (28.3%), it was diet. In Japan, foods designed to maintain and enhance health, or "functional foods" as they are called, have witnessed phenomenal growth. Products already on the market include foods that help blood pressure, regulate the gastrointestinal system, assist in keeping the teeth healthy, regulate blood sugar, lower cholesterol, supplement minerals, and reduce triglyceride levels. In today's Japan with its growing number of old people, the market for such items promises to grow even further.

As already noted, the percentage of people eating traditional Japanese cuisine rises with age. But quite a few individuals find such a diet monotonous on its own. Hence there is a growing appetite for Western-style dishes made with Japanese-style ingredients, and things like hamburger steaks made with sardines and Western-style cakes made with soybeans have appeared on the scene. Retro-style restaurants where people can dine in the ambience of yesteryear are on the increase. Especially popular among the middle-aged and elderly are restaurants that look like theme parks recreating the mood of the 1960s. But for a store or restaurant, dedicating yourself exclusively to the senior citizens' market entails considerable risk. In that regard an effective strategy is to focus on different target markets depending on the time of day (Wilson 2000).

### 5.3. *The housing market*

A massive market is beginning to emerge for home remodelling services as people seek to make their homes barrier-free by, for example, installing stair rails and eliminating steps from hallways. A growing number of older couples are also eager to renovate their homes so that they can better enjoy their life together now that the children have moved out. Today's Japan with its dwindling population offers little prospect of growth in the market for new homes, but demand for home renovation services is considerable.

The garden is an important part of the home, and the gardening market is growing. Many people attend culture classes to study English gardening, French gardening, Japanese gardening, and various other styles of horticulture, and to learn how to take care of trees and plants.

More and more people can be expected to install home theatres with large screens. Some will presumably invite friends of the same age over for house parties complete with screenings of videos from the good old days. Remodelling the bathroom is another popular project among older Japanese. These investments are designed to enhance people's enjoyment of the time they spend at home.

### 5.4. *The recreation and travel market*

Markets that cater primarily to retirees need to create ways for them to enjoy the abundant time they have on their hands. As we have already observed, the travel market shows great potential. Growing numbers of Japanese are interested in spending extended periods abroad, and more and more of them can be expected to stay for long periods at, say, European-style spa resorts, which are quite different from their Japanese counterparts.

Japan's retirees are youthful enough in spirit that they are willing to throw themselves into new adventures. They display a growing fondness for physically challenging activities such as climbing, diving, hiking, and rowing. But they also have a strong predilection for visiting historical sites of cultural interest. Many of them want to re-experience the long and glorious history of other lands. Because Japan's elderly consumers are remarkably keen to learn, tours that cater to them should preferably come complete with lectures.

Japan's baby boomers are part of the Beatles generation. Some of them actually attended the Fab Four's concerts in Japan, and many more played an instrument in their younger days. One instrument manufacturer has launched a program to help people "relearn" how to play using the piano that is collecting dust in their home. Digital instruments have been developed that can be muted at the flip of a switch, and growing numbers of older music lovers practise late into the night on them. We can also expect a proliferation of services that put individuals who want to organize a band, as in the old days, in touch with other musicians of the same generation.

### 5.5. *The IT equipment market*

Widescreen flat-panel televisions are selling briskly, and members of the baby boom and older generations are among their most avid buyers. They tend to purchase them in conjunction with an HDD recorder. These devices are especially attractive to people of such an age as to have the time to watch movies. Digital cameras too have become all the rage among older Japanese.

It was once thought that elderly consumers would be uninterested in mobile phones that provide Internet access or come with a built-in camera, but nowadays they take such technology for granted. It is not at all rare for Japanese women in their seventies to send friends digital photos of grandchildren taken and stored on a mobile phone.

As of 2004 there were eighty million people in Japan with Internet access, whether via computer, cell phone, game console, or other means, and 60 per cent of these were broadband users. By age group, Internet use stood at 66 per cent in the fifties age bracket, 49 per cent in the 60 to 64 age bracket, and 18 per cent among those over 65. In the past there were concerns that the elderly would end up on the wrong side of the digital divide, but in fact they have rapidly taken to the Internet. As of 2004 there were 3.35 million blog users throughout the country, among them many retirees who post diaries or personal histories on the Web.

### 5.6. *The therapeutic market*

The pet market is expected to grow as the population ages. There are currently some twenty million dogs and cats kept as pets in Japan, which is more than the number of children aged fourteen and under. So while the number of children in Japan is declining, the number of animal companions is on the rise. There is thus a considerable market for such emotional companionship, which caters to the need for a source of relaxation and a way to relieve stress among couples living by themselves now that the children have left home, as well as among old people living alone.

Development of robotic pets is booming in Japan too. Also available are crime-fighting robots that automatically keep an audiovisual record if anything moves or makes a sound in the house when the owner is out. Another type of robot has been developed that, with a vocabulary of 1,000 to 2,000 words, is capable of holding a conversation and can thus cheer up lonely elderly people.

The reception area of the international Expo held in Aichi Prefecture in 2005 featured a humanoid robot able to understand Japanese, English, Chinese, and Korean. In the near future, according to predictions, we will see the advent of robots capable of performing household chores for elderly people.

Table 4. The three stages in the 30,000 days of life.

| Stage One | Stage Two | Stage Three |
|---|---|---|
| 7,500 days | 15,000 days | 7,500 days |
| Age 0–20.5 | Age 20.5–61.5 | Age 61.5 and over |

Source: HILL 2003.

## 6. Life: The 30,000-Day Adventure

As of 2004, the life expectancy of the average Japanese was 79 years for men and 86 years for women, which works out to roughly 30,000 days. Those 30,000 days can be divided into three life stages (HILL 2003). Stage One, 7,500 days in length (about 20.5 years), is spent on the process of socialization through upbringing and education. Stage Two, 15,000 days in length (about 41 years), comprises the period when people are busy performing their social roles, either by participating in the labour market or by having a family and bringing up the next generation. Stage Three, 7,500-odd days in length, comprises the period after retirement when people are liberated from their social responsibilities.

Note here the similarity between Stage One and Stage Three. Stage One tends to be regarded as a period of education in preparation for Stage Two. But it also has value in its own right, for it generates youth culture and thereby invigorates society as a whole. Stage Three, on the other hand, is the period when individuals can take back their private lives, having been freed from the constant pressures imposed by their social roles. People at this stage of life are poised to create a new subculture that might be termed "old folks' culture" (Sekizawa 1997).

If Stage One can be defined as a moratorium period in preparation for one's entrance into the present world, then Stage Three may be considered a moratorium period in which awareness of the limited time left looms large as one faces the prospect of the next world. At both stages it is important to ask oneself where, personally, the true value of life lies.

Consumption expands as the number of people with plenty of time on their hands increases. Consumers at Stages One and Three of life have an abundance of such spare time. On the stage of Japan's consumer society, youth culture and old folks' culture can be expected to evolve in new directions, sometimes in competition, sometimes in concord.

## References

Baltes, Paul B. and Karl Ulrich Mayer (1999): *The Berlin Ageing Study*. Cambridge/New York: Cambridge University Press.

HILL (Hakuhodo Institute of Life and Living) (2003): *Kyōdai shijō erudâ no tanjō* [The birth of the massive "elders" market). Tokyo: Purejidentosha.

—— (2004): *The Biannual Data Book on the Japanese People*. Tokyo: Hakuhodo Institute of Life and Living.

Naikaku Sōri Daijin Kanbō Kōhōshitsu (2004): *Kokumin seikatsu ni kan suru yoron chōsa* [Opinion survey on national living standards]. Tokyo: Naikaku Sōri Daijin Kanbō Kōhōshitsu.

NRIIM (Nikkei Research Institute of Industry and Markets) (2003): *Dankai-sedai no shōhi to kōdō* [Consumption and behaviour among the baby boom generation]. Tokyo: Nikkei Research Institute of Industry and Markets.

Sekizawa, Hidehiko (1997): Shin-rōnen bunkaron [A new theory of old folks' culture]. In: Inoue, Shun and Kazuo Aoi (eds.): *Seijuku to oi no shakaigaku* [The sociology of maturity and ageing]. Tokyo: Iwanami Shoten.

Wilson, Gail (2000): *Understanding Old Age*. London: SAGE.

Case in point: A ward that takes pride in being traffic safe for the elderly

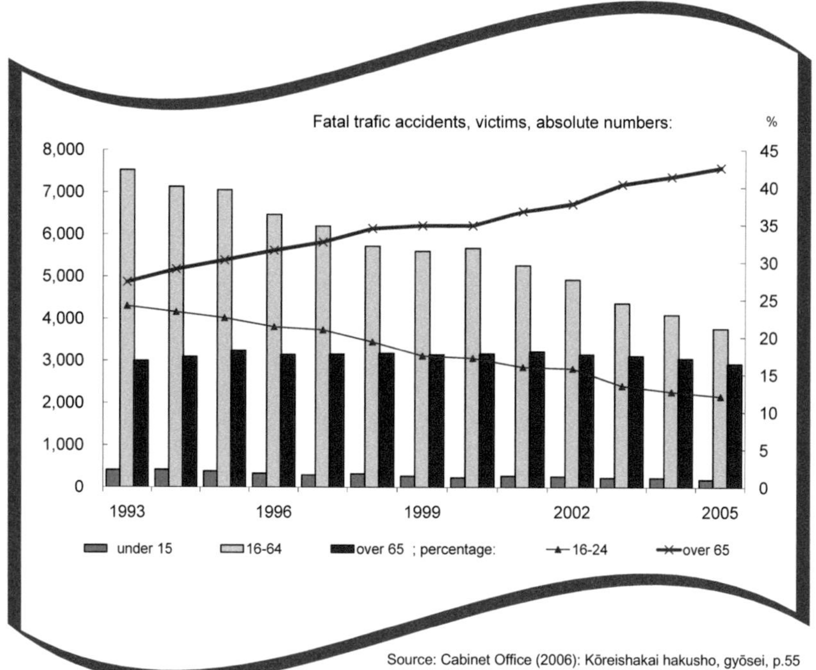


Source: Cabinet Office (2006): Kōreishakai hakusho, gyōsei, p.55

CHAPTER FIFTY-SIX

# THE AGEING SOCIETY AND REACTIONS OF THE AUTOMOBILE INDUSTRY—A CASE STUDY

Andreas Moerke

## 1. Introduction

The automobile industry in Japan is among the most important industries and has been making a decisive contribution to the gross domestic product for a number of years now. In 2004, the total value of automotive shipments in Japan was about 45.4 trillion yen, which equals 16.1% per cent of the entire manufacturing industry (JAMA 2006: 4). With its production of more than 11.48 million vehicles (including about 9.76 million passenger cars), Japan is the second largest producer in the world, right after the United States of America (JAMA 2007). Despite slightly decreasing domestic sales numbers, it there is still a large and attractive market for the industry, with about 5.74 million new-registration sales (JAMA 2007).

However, questions, remain: How does the industry deal with the fact that Japan's population structure is changing so fast, and how does it react to the ever increasing number of elderly drivers who demand vehicles appropriate to their needs? While in 2005, about 20% per cent of Japan's population were aged 65 years and older, their share proportion is expected to increase and reach around 39% per cent by 2050 (IPSS 2000). It is therefore only natural that keywords like Barrier-free Mobility (Kamata 2006) or Universal Design (Iwakata and Atsumi 2006; Yogo 2006) shape a good part of the discussion on Japan's automobile future.

This chapter presents results from a research project concerning the adjustments of Japan's automobile industry to the ageing society.[1]

[1] In preparation for this article we communicated with all Japanese car makers, conducted personal interviews with Honda, Nissan and Toyota, and paid company visits to the following plants: MFBTC, Kawasaki Plant, 29 January 2007; Nissan Motor Co., Ltd., Oppama Plant: Aug. 2, 2005; Toyota Motor Corporation, Motomachi Plant

All OEMs (original equipment manufacturers) and the major first-tier suppliers in Japan were contacted, asked for interviews, and asked to fill-in a questionnaire covering the following areas: products and technologies to be implemented in cars for elderly[2] drivers; questions about the marketing of these products to potential customers; the integration of experienced employees' know-how in the factories; and the adjustments on the part of the companies to the ageing of their employees (cf. Moerke and Kamann 2005). For reasons of clarity and consistency, this chapter will concentrate on parts one and two, that is, on products and technologies as well as on marketing questions.

## 2. Ageing Drivers as a Challenge for the Automobile Technology

Although it is known that elderly people are, in absolute terms, less involved in accidents, the situation changes once we relate those numbers to the miles (or kilometres) driven. Elderly people cause more accidents on the few kilometres they drive, and both injury and fatality rates increase dramatically with advanced age.

With these statistics in mind, it is imperative that car makers and suppliers, as well as researchers from universities and research institutions, investigate how ageing affects driving, and what solutions (technical or other) can be found to make help elderly people drive safely.

As a matter of course, the process of ageing is an individual one, but there are parallels between this process and elderly drivers' needs. Generally speaking, driving fitness deteriorates, and reduced physical resilience has to be taken into account. In the following discussion, we will refer to a selection of the most obvious occurrences of these phenomena.

The Fitness to drive is understood as the ability to drive a vehicle safely. In this regard, the process of ageing has three implications: Ageing affects apperception as well as the motoric skills and cognitive abilities (Koppa 2004: 228). Increasing age severely affects visual apperception (in other words, deteriorating eyesight) (cf. Atsumi & Kanamori

8 August 2005; Toyota Motor Corporation, Sapporo Plant, 5 August 2005; Toyota Motor Corporation, Tsutsumi Plant, 17 November 2006.

[2] In this article, we use the terms silver generation and others as synonyms, and do not intend to discriminate against one group or single persons.

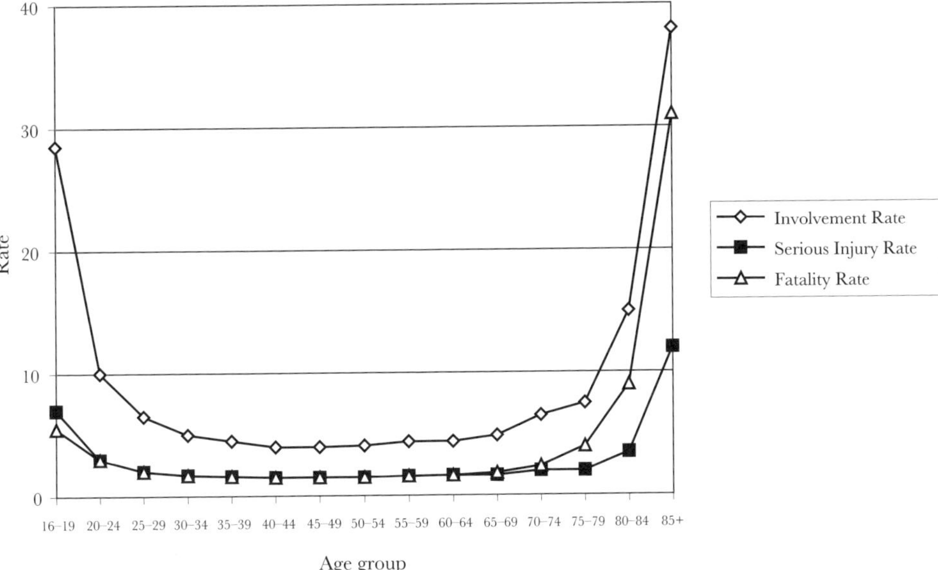


Source: UMich 2001: 14.

Figure 1. Involvement, Injury and Fatality Rates.

2006), especially visual acuity, the responsiveness to contrasts, and stereopsis. The following illustration gives an example of two possible derogations of eyesight.

With respect to the musculoskeletal system, ageing results in reduced physical strength, reduced flexibility, a diminished ability to coordinate one's movements, and a decreasing sense of balance. It also affects people's cognitive abilities: reaction time slows down, and other mental changes become evident, especially selective perception and divided attentiveness (Glenstrup and Engell-Nielsen 1995).

In addition, one should keep in mind that the intake of medicine, sometimes necessary due to a driver's age, can lead to a decreased fitness to drive.

With increasing age, the ratio of fatal accidents increases as well. The body shows less tolerance to external impact, and is therefore more vulnerable. Bone density, decreasing muscle mass, and a less efficient cardiovascular and respiratory systems are all factors (Alicandri *et al.* 1999). The following figure shows the relationship between age and fragility and makes it clear that people get injured more often and more severely with increasing age.

Source: ACT n.y.

Illustration 1. Examples for Long-sightedness, Nearsightedness and a Diminished Field of Vision.

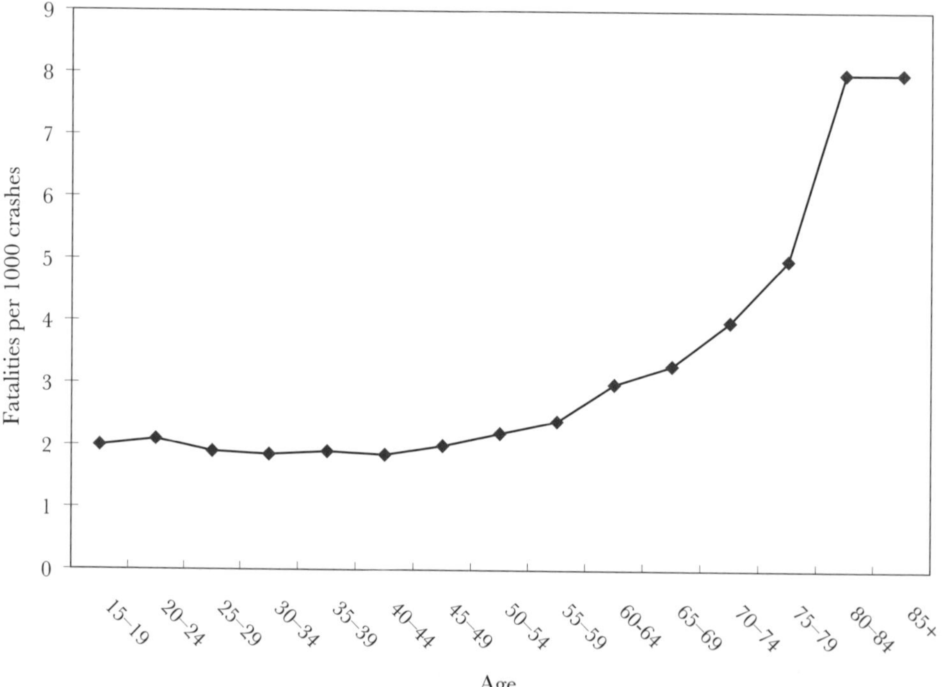


Source: UMich 2001: 16.

Figure 2. Age Fragility Relationship.

It turns out that elderly people are especially vulnerable in the neck and ribcage. A person aged 65 and over, for instance, can cope with only one quarter of the force younger people can handle when the seat belt is activated in case of sudden stops. In case of an accident, elderly people are therefore more likely to suffer from rib fractures which can also harm their lungs and inner organs (Fildes 2002: 89, cited in RSC 2003: 206).

The above is only a small selection of examples, but it should make sufficiently clear what kind of problems need to be dealt with. The following section will introduce some technical solutions to these challenges.

## 3. Technical Solutions for Elderly Drivers

Even though restricted eyesight is one of the major constrictions, the solution is not necessarily to enlarge the instruments on the dashboard, but rather to create instruments providing clear contrast, easily readable numbers, and a clear-cut structure (cf. Atsumi and Kanamori 2006; Konishi and Kodera 2006). Contrast turns out to be more important than lighting: according to a one study it has to be three times stronger for elderly people than for younger ones (Schieber 1999: 21).

There is also new technology in use, for instance, driver-assistance systems such as blind-spot detection (covering the "full blind spot" in mirrors), head-up displays (to project information on the windshield and thus allow the driver to look ahead), night-vision devices, as well as adaptive (front) lighting, (that allows the driver to see ahead in the dark by lighting up corners,) and optical parking assistance with cameras.

To tackle the issue of cognitive abilities, it is important to minimize physical and psychological stress, for example, by arranging improved and easier apperception through the assistance systems mentioned above. However, there are also warnings claiming that such systems could distract drivers more than actually be useful (TRB 2004: 233).

With respect to motor skills, carmakers are taking measures such as providing their vehicles with additional grips, relocated pedals, or with turnable, lowering seats to ease ingress and egress.[3]

[3] For a quantitative analysis of muscular stress during vehicle ingress and egress, see Nakamoto et al. 2006.

In order to enable safe driving and minimize injuries despite decreased physical resilience, car makers and suppliers have also created passive safety systems, such as seatbelt airbags (dual airbags, side-airbags, etc.), seatbelt strength restrictors / seat belt load limiters, and active head protection. One concrete example for of this technology is the "smartbelt" system by Autoliv (http://www.autoliv.com).[4] In case of an accident, the seatbelt is tightened, which keeps the passenger in a less dangerous position. The accident is then analyzed with the help of sensors that take into account factors such as severity, the weight of the driver's and other passengers' weight, etc. According to the situation, the seatbelt is loosened or tightened, which regulates (and reduces) the exposure of the ribcage. The airbag absorbs the energy released through this process.

Apart from improved technology, though, a convincing marketing strategy is crucial when it comes to actually selling the vehicles. The major concern here must be to make them appear attractive and not appear to be adapted for "old" people. Carmakers, (regardless of the country,)[5] are trying very hard to not let the technical solutions indicate a (physical or other) handicap, but to have them appear as "smart support".

One way to achieve this is Universal Design, which means products that can be easily used by everyone, regardless of his or her age. Universal Design is being discussed intensively in Japan, and perhaps applied more often there then anywhere else. The "International Association for Universal Design" (AUD) is an example of how efforts are being made to deal with the challenges of demographic change without discriminating against people because of their age. It comes as no surprise that all Japanese carmakers are directly (or indirectly, through subsidiaries,) represented in the association. Universal Design is defined as follows:

Universal Design is about creating things that are easier to use by a greater number of people, whether or not they are elderly or not. Some of its features, as applied to automobiles, are more obvious than others (large assist grips for getting in and out of vehicles), some are more subtle (slightly oval steering wheels that make it easier to enter and exit the driver's seat). To the greatest extent possible, these features

[4] Autoliv Corp. supplies Toyota Motor, among others, but of course there are also other makers of such systems, for instance, BF Goodrich Aerospace (http://www.theautochannel.com/news/press/date/20000429/press014250.html).

[5] The actual comment was given by a representative from a German car company, but it holds for other OEMs as well.

are designed to fit into the overall styling of a vehicle in a natural (and sometimes sublime) way that presents neither a sense of intrusion nor awkwardness. They are also designed to be as intuitive as possible, requiring little or no additional thought on the part of the user.

It is obvious that all Japanese carmakers apply the ideas of Universal Design to their products. Some vehicles offer a higher seating position for drivers and co-drivers, as well as easy ingress and egress and good circumferential all-round visibility (for example: Daihatsu's *Move* and *Boon*; Honda's *Step Wagon* and *That's*; Mazda's *AZ Wagon* and *Verisa*; Mitsubishi's *Dion* and *eK Classy*; Nissan's *Cubic* and *Otti*; Subaru's *Pleo* and *R2*"; Suzuki's *Wagon R*, and, finally, Toyota's *Isis*, *Porte*, and *Raum)*. Technical solutions such as seatbelt-load limiters and belt pre-tension systems are already being applied in small and subcompact cars like Toyota's *Yaris C*, Nissan's *Micra* or Mitsubishi's *Colt*. Xenon headlights seem to be reserved for rather sporty vehicles such as Toyota's *Celica*, not designed exclusively for elderly drivers. According to our interview partners and to our own investigations at international exhibitions (Tokyo Motor Show, ITS Nagoya, and others), there is a clear tendency towards equipping vehicles with easily visible instruments and warning signals. To sum up: all Japanese carmakers are developing and bringing to market cars that are suitable for elderly drivers, without necessarily marketing them as vehicles for the "silver generation". In this respect, the development is very much like it in other countries, such as Germany. There is one area, however, in which the difference between Japan and other markets is quite obvious, namely when it comes to vehicles for welfare purposes, that shall support users whose ability to drive and ride is limited. The following section will deal with those "welfare vehicles" [*fukushi sharyō*] in more detail.

## 4. "Fukushi Sharyō"—Welfare on Wheels

The market for "welfare vehicles" in Japan seems to be larger than anywhere else. Yet, relating the number of about 42,000 vehicles sold in 2005 to the 5.85 million vehicles of new-registration sales, it is plain to see that the market is just starting to develop. Taking into account how quickly the Japanese society is ageing, it becomes clear that vehicles for drivers (and co-drivers) in need of assistance will become a major need. Japanese makers have recognized this need: while, at the Tokyo Motor Show back in 2004, only one-fourth of the exhibits were so-called "barrier-free" vehicles; by now every manufacturer is producing them. Basically, they all use the following techniques: sliding or wide opening doors, turnable and lowering seats, and facilities such as ramps or pulling tools to allow the ingress and egress of wheelchairs.

Although all manufacturers produce such "barrier-free" vehicles, the marketing of these products differs in various aspects and will be highlighted below.

Besides its Universal Design approach, Toyota is following another concept to integrate elderly and handicapped people and to give them the opportunity to be mobile. This concept is called "Welcab", which is a combination of "Welfare/ Well (being)/ Welcome" and "Cabin" (http://toyota.jp/welcab/index.html). The idea dates back to the 1960s, when Toyota attempted to secure mobility for everybody. Nowadays, a variety of technical features such as turnable and height-adjustable seats, the integration of wheelchairs (for drivers and co-drivers), or sliding doors are to be found. As of February 2007, a total of 21 different types of cars in categories as different as Sedan, Wagon, Minivan, and Box, as well as three different types of small trucks, could be ordered equipped as "Welcab" vehicles. In addition to the existing Universal Design showrooms, Toyota established "Toyota Heartful Plaza" showrooms, which focus on "Welcabs", in Sapporo, Sendai, Chiba, Chiba Chuo, Tokyo, Yokohama, Nagoya, Kobe, Hiroshima, and Fukuoka. Each site has 10 to 20 vehicles on permanent display, and employees are there to advise the customers. In other showrooms, "Welcabs" are often on display together with other vehicles.[6] In addition, Toyota also conducts marketing activities, such as the newsletter *Welcab Magazine*, distributed to interested readers, and the "Heartful Homepage".[7] The design is characterized by pastel colours and by a composition that is best described by the concept of *kawaii* (meaning *pretty, cute, sweet*). The slogan "motto yasashiku, anato no soba e" [Much easier, by your side] presents Toyota as a helper for the elderly, and—in a free interpretation of the iconography of the website and newsletter—as contributing to solidarity between the generations.

Nissan's concept to provide mobility for elderly people and for those affected by restricted driving ability is called the "Life Care Vehicle" (LV). Devices to support ingress and egress, the usage of wheelchairs,

---

[6] Personally checked in a showroom in Tokyo, Shirokanedai, January 2007.
[7] http://toyota.jp/heartful/index.html, last accessed 1 March 2007.

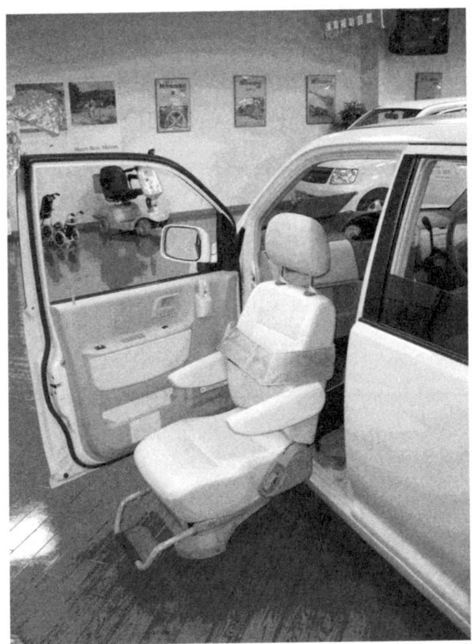

Source: Photograph by the author taken in a Mitsubishi "Hearty Run" Showroom.

Illustration 2. Vehicle with turnable, height-adjustable seat.

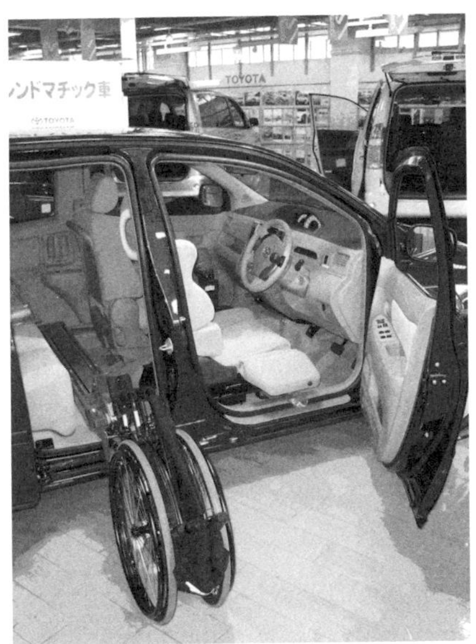


Source: Photograph taken by the author in a Toyota Showroom.

Illustration 3. Vehicle to be driven by wheelchair drivers.

Table 1. Life Care Vehicles—applicable vehicle categories and car types.

| Category | Sedan | Compact | SUV / Sportstype | Minivan/ Onebox | Station Wagon |
|---|---|---|---|---|---|
| Car Type | Cima<br>Teana<br>Latio | Tiida<br>Note<br>Cubecubic<br>Cube<br>March<br>Otti<br>Clipper | Fairlady Z<br>Skyline | Elgrand<br>Presage<br>Serena<br>Lafesta<br>Caravan<br>Civilian | Stageo |

Source: http://lv.nissan.co.jp/LINEUP/index.html.

and so on can already be applied to a total of 19 car types in five vehicle categories, listed in detail in the following table. LVs are produced by Nissan's subsidiary, Autech, Inc.

According to Nissan, much attention is paid to making "Life Care Vehicles" indistinguishable from other cars of the same type. The aim is to lower the psychological barrier that may prevent people from buying these vehicles, because elderly people—despite decreased driving ability—often do not want to be thought of as old. This point matches the viewpoint of customers in Germany: according to a study presented at the International Car Symposium in Essen in 2005, German customers do not identify themselves with a "senior car" (Hamburger Abendblatt 2004).

To market the LVs, Nissan has developed the "Life Care Vehicle Qualified Shop System", characterized by a complete barrier-free layout and by the display of LVs among ordinary vehicles. By displaying them together, Nissan wants to demonstrate the high degree of performance of the LVs. The sales personnel in these shops undergo special training courses where they experience movement and driving in a "third age suit"[8] for a better understanding of the older generation's needs, as well as special sales training to learn which vehicles of Nissan's portfolio fulfil these needs.

---

[8] The Third Age Suit was first developed by Ford Motor Corporation. It is a jumpsuit that integrates Velcro and other pieces of clothing to decrease mobility and give engineers and developers an idea of how elderly people s movements are constricted. Usually, goggles to cloud vision are worn in addition to the suit (Coughlin 2004: 40).

Nissan also uses marketing measures such as newsletters, a magazine, a designated homepage, and special events to promote the LVs. The magazine, named after the French greeting phrase "enchanté", is published on a quarterly basis. It uses cartoon elements, pastel colours, and a lot of photos showing members of several generations using the LV's jointly. The same holds true for the LV homepage. All in all, it seems fair to say that the "cuteness" (*kawaïirashisa*) characterizing Toyota's marketing approach can also be found at Nissan, at least on those sites that potential customers are expected to access on the internet. The homepage of Autech, the company that actually produces the LVs, is much less like a marketing device and rather neutral. The websites of Nissan and Autech (http://lv.nissan.co.jp/ and http://www.autech.co.jp/JP/ENTERPRISE/LV/index.html) both allow for a detailed comparison of their products.

Although Mitsubishi Motor Corporation (MMC) was not as cooperative as we had hoped, it was still possible to derive some basic points of MMC's approach to mobility for elderly drivers.

In order to open up the market, MMC also applies features of Universal Design. With respect to welfare cars, the company has followed the example of Toyota and established dedicated showrooms for welfare vehicles. In the case of Mitsubishi, the concept was named "Hearty Run", with reference to Mitsubishi's marketing slogan "Heartbeat Motors", as well as to the meaning of "hearty" as "affectionate", "integrated into something" and, in this case, intergenerational bonding (http://www.mitsubishi-motors.co.jp/japan/heartyrun/).

In comparison with other makers, especially Toyota and Nissan, the number of welfare vehicles is still very limited. The Full Line-up Catalogue of 2007 displays no more than eight models and has hardly changed since 2005, when nine models were shown.[9] "Hearty Run" models can be purchased in every ordinary showroom, but MMC has also established two designated "Hearty Run" showrooms, one in the suburbs of Tokyo, one in Osaka. Our trip to the Tokyo Showroom clearly showed a problem in terms of location: since it is situated in the suburbs, far away from public transport, visitors either have to drive or go by taxi or face a long walk. The showroom itself is completely

[9] Among the nine models, one minibus from the commercial vehicle division was shown. But since the division was a spin-off and acts as Mitsubishi Motors Truck & Bus Corporation (MTFBC) with DaimlerChrysler as the major shareholder, these products are no longer covered by MMC.

barrier-free, thus allowing a person in a wheelchair to move freely to the second floor, where the real exhibition takes place.

The quarterly magazine "Hearty Run Press" describes the concept as "cars that are easy and people-friendly" [hito ni yasashii jidōsha]. Topics often include stories of barrier-free driving with photographs and families, but seem to focus on physically handicapped people rather than on the elderly. The design is quite similar to that of the catalogues and clearly less *kawaii* than the material provided by Toyota, Nissan, or Honda. This holds true for the homepage as well, but we should add that the latter was designed also for elderly people, and therefore has to be easy to navigate and to understand. All in all, the segment of "welfare vehicles" does not seem to have the importance for MMC that it has for other makers.

Just like the other carmakers, Honda also produces welfare vehicles, nine types with different specifications, such as turnable and liftable seats and devices for wheelchairs. According to Honda's definition, welfare cars are vehicles everybody can ride in easily, feeling good (http://www.honda.co.jp/welfare). This includes physically handicapped people as well as elderly people who may not be able to drive on their own any more and who therefore need support (Honda 2007).

Although Honda has no designated sales outlets, as is the case with Toyota and Mitsubishi Motors, some qualified dealers called "orange dealers" do exist across Japan. They provide barrier-free layouts at the outlets, including all the facilities necessary for wheelchair users (such as sanitary facilities), offer test drives of welfare vehicles, and have sound knowledge about the products.

In 2005, our interview partners told us that Honda did not undertake any designated marketing activities to promote welfare vehicles. However, at the headquarters and showrooms relevant catalogues could already be found at that time. Both the catalogues and the homepage have the motto "Fun for everyone", and aim to include people with decreased driving abilities in society.

In terms of design, the homepage as well as the catalogues (see Illustration 4) allude to the image of a multi-generation family. showing comic-like elements and pastel colours. In comparison, the homepage is more functionally designed and gives a lot of information about the whole line-up of products and features. As an innovation in the field of marketing, Honda issues an e-mail magazine for those interested in welfare vehicles.

Source: Honda Headquarter 2005.

Illustration 4. Honda's Welfare Vehicle Catalogue of 2005.

Since other makers did not cooperate with our study, the following paragraphs present only a short summary of the information that can be derived from the internet.

Fuji Heavy Industries, Ltd.: The maker of Subaru cars call the welfare vehicles "Transcare Vehicles", but clearly positions them as insurance and care-related. Features include turnable and liftable seats, supporting steps for easy ingress and egress, devices to put a patient trolley into the car easily, and wheelchairs that also function as car seats (http://www.subaru.co.jp/transcare/). It seems that no specific marketing is done to promote the sales of "Transcare Vehicles"; at least, we were unable to obtain any information on e-mail magazines, publications, marketing events etc.

Mazda Motor Corporation: It is not surprising that Mazda also has welfare vehicles among its products. The homepage lists seven types of vehicles, from Sedan to Minivan, equipped with turnable or liftable co-driver seats, a ramp for wheelchair access, and additional steps for easier ingress and egress (http://www.welfare.mazda.co.jp/). Outlet stores also offer test drives. With respect to marketing, there is a section on the homepage introducing the vehicles, but it seems that there is no e-mail magazine or other regular publication.

Suzuki Motor Corporation: The market leader in the segment of small cars is also a major producer of motorcycles, sports utilities, trikes, and so on, and welfare vehicles are to be found in these categories too. The largest number consists of so-called "senior cars", a mixture of a chair and a four-wheeled electric bike. They are often equipped with shopping baskets, and of course they do not go at any great speed, but run rather slowly in order to avoid accidents. In addition, Suzuki offers electric scooters and motorized wheelchairs (http://www.suzuki.co.jp/welfare/main.html).

As far as marketing is concerned, information on the safety of senior cars, opportunities for rentals and so on are available on the homepage. Suzuki is also attempting to create an internet community of senior car users. Again, the design is comparable with that of Toyota, Honda, and Nissan: pastel colours, comic elements—in short, the application of "cuteness". The homepage, however, is a serious attempt to create a community, with explanations about seats, information on events, and even games.

## 5. Summary

The automobile industry in Japan is experiencing enormous changes due to the demographic change the whole society is being confronted with. An increasingly ageing population demands that cars be more comfortable, safer and easier to use without looking "old".

Universal Design, understood as user-friendly design for everybody (but, clearly, with the older generation as a target group), is one way. It includes not only the design itself (for instance, contrast or brightness), but also technical features, such as event-prevention systems and warning systems, and even the design of advertising material. It seems that, in contrast to countries like Germany, Universal Design is a suitable way of advertising.

The segment of "welfare vehicles", also aiming at elderly people, is especially strong, this time focusing on restricted driving abilities. While the number of vehicles sold is limited at present, the overall market will definitely grow, which is why all Japanese makers are already active in the field, albeit to varying degrees. It seems that Toyota is still ahead of the game, but considering the recent developments at Nissan and Honda, it is not certain that this will not change in the future.

Since other countries are experiencing similar ageing trends, the way Japanese automobile companies are reacting to the demographic challenge is surely worth a closer look.

## References

ACT (Australian Capital Territory) (n.y.): *Information for Older Road Users.* http://www.cota-act.org.au/Livedrive/ageing_ impact.html. (found 7 June 2005).

Alicandri, Elizabeth, Mark Robinson and Tim Penney (1999): *Designing Highways with Older Drivers in Mind.* http://www.tfhrc.gov/pubrds/mayjun99/Alicandri et al.htm (found 7 June 2005).

Atsumi, Bunji and Hitoshi Kanamori (2006): Sharyō untenji no shikaku jōhō shori no moderuka—nenreigoto no kanjiyomitori no suitei [Visual Cognitive Performance of Drivers—Age-Based Estimation of Reading Time of *Kanji* Characters]. In: *Toyota Technical Review* 54, 2, pp. 34–39.

BF Goodrich Aerospace. http://www.theautochannel.com/news/press/date/20000429/press014250.html (found 14 March 2007).

Coughlin, Joseph F. (2004): Not Your Father's Auto Industry? Aging, the Automobile, and the Drive for Product Innovation. In: *Generations* 28, 4, pp. 38–47.

Fildes, Brian (2002): *Vehicle Safety, Transcript of Proceedings, Mobility & Safety of Older People Conference.* Melbourne, 26–27 August 2002 (cited in RSC 2003, p. 206).

Glenstrup, Arne John and Theo Engell-Nielsen (1995): *Eye Controlled Media: Present and Future State.* Thesis, Institute of Computer Science, University of Copenhagen. http://www.diku.dk/~panic/eyegaze/article.html (found 30 August 2005).

Hamburger Abendblatt (24 February 2004): *Senioren wollen kein ‚Rentner-Auto'* [Older people don't want 'pensioners' cars]. http://www.abendblatt.de/daten/2004/02/14/262275.html?prx=1 (found 6 June 2005).

Honda (2007): *Honda welfare no rinen* [Honda's idea of welfare]. http://www.honda.co.jp/welfare/idea/index.html (found 1 March 2007).

IPSS (National Institute of Population and Social Security Research) (2002): *Population projections for Japan 2001–2050.* http://www.ipss.go.jp/ppnewest/e/ppfj02/top.html (found 12 February 2005).

Iwakata, Koji and Bunji Atsumi (2006): Sharyō no kaihatsu ni okeru yunibāsaru dezain [Universal Design in Car Development]. In: *Toyota Technical Review.* 54, 2, pp. 10–13.

JAMA (Japan Automobile Manufacturers' Association, Inc.) (2006): *The Motor Industry of Japan.* Tokyo: JAMA.

—— (2007): Active Matrix Database System. http://jamaserv.jama.or.jp/newdb/eng/print_stat.cgi (found 24 February 2007).

Kamata, Minoru (2006): Baria furī mobiritī no genjō to tenbō [Accessible Transport and Vehicles for Barrier-free Mobility]. In: *Jidōsha gijutsu* 60, 3, pp. 2–7.

Konishi, Makoto and Haruyuki Kodera (2006): Kānabigēshon shisutemu no ishō kaihatsu [Development of Screen Design for Car Navigation Systems]. In: *Toyota Technical Review* 54, 2, pp. 26–33.

Koppa, Rodger (2004): Automotive Adaptive Equipment and Vehicle Modifications. In: TRB (Transportation Research Board) (ed.): *Transportation in an Aging Society: A Decade of Experience*. Washington D.C.: TRB, pp. 227–235.

Moerke, Andreas and Simon Kamann (2005): *Herausforderungen des demographischen Wandels: Fallbeispiel Automobilindustrie* [Challenges of Demographic Change: A Case Study of the Automobile Industry]. Tokyo: DIJ Working Paper 05/04.

Nakamoto, Kazuhiko, Bunji Atsumi, Haruyuki Kodera and Hitoshi Kanamori (2006): Jōkōji no suji futan teiryōka kenkyū [Quantitative Analysis of Muscular Stress During Vehicle Ingress/Egress]. In: *Toyota Technical Review* 54, 2, pp. 20–25.

RSC (Road Safety Committee) (2003): *Inquiry into Road Safety for Older Road Users*. Victoria: Parliament.

Schieber, Frank (1999): Beyond TRB218. *A Select Summary of Developments in the Field of Transportation and Aging since 1988.* http://www.usd.edu/~schieber/pdf/Beyond218.pdf (found 7 June 2005).

TRB (Transportation Research Board) (2004): *Transportation in an Aging Society: A Decade of Experience.* http://gulliver.trb.org/publications/conf/reports/cp_27.pdf (found 7 June 2005).

UMich (University of Michigan) (2001): *Program for Injury Research and Education.* http://www-nrd.nhtsa.dot.gov/pdf/nrd-50/ciren/2001/1201UMich.pdf (found 28 February 2007).

Yogo, Takamori (2006): Raumu, porute, aishisu no yunibāsaru dezain [Universal Design in Vehicle Development of the Raum, Porte and Isis]. In: *Toyota Technical Review* 54, 2, pp. 14–19.

CHAPTER FIFTY-SEVEN

# AGEING AND THE SOCIAL SECURITY SYSTEM

Ito Peng

## 1. Introduction

Demographic ageing has been one of the main driving forces behind social security and social welfare reforms in Japan since the 1990s. Notwithstanding its impacts on programmes such as old age security and health care, the combination of rapid ageing and low fertility in Japan has also opened up intense public and policy debates on issues like tensions between family and work, changes in ideas and norms regarding family and gender relations, and the state's role in providing social care. These debates have led to significant reforms in the areas of family policy and social care. This chapter will examine how demographic changes in the 1990s have helped shape social policy reforms. In the following sections, I will first discuss demographic ageing and low fertility in Japan in the 1990s, and their implications for social security. I will then illustrate some of the key social policy reforms that were introduced. In the last section, I will conclude by reflecting on the Japanese experience in a global context.

## 2. Demographic Changes in Japan

The issue of population ageing in Japan has been around for several decades. In 1970, when the proportion of people over the age of 65 reached 7.1 per cent of the total population, it prompted the government to issue a number of social policy reviews. Claiming that Japan had become an "ageing society" (*kōreika shakai*), the government then introduced a number of health care and pension reforms (Campbell 1992). These included a five-year plan to develop social welfare institutions, particularly those related to care of the elderly (1970), the development of employment promotion centres for older workers (*shirubā jinzai sentā*) (1971), free medical care for people over the age of 70 (1973), and the rises in and the indexation of the national pension benefits (1973). The issue of population ageing *per se*, though, did not cause widespread alarm. The total fertility rate in 1970 was 2.13, and the economy had been growing at a rate of approximately 9 per cent per annum throughout the previous decade. Public support for welfare expansion was high, and the economic climate was also positive. There was no particular reason at that time to believe that demographic ageing would cause immediate or mid-term social or economic concern.

However, this situation changed markedly in 1989, when the total fertility rate dropped to 1.57, causing what came to be known as the "1.57 shock". By 1990, socio-economic conditions in Japan had changed quite substantially from those of 1970: it was clear that Japan's rapid economic development phase had come and gone, and the bubble economy, which had helped sustain economic growth for most of the preceding decade, was also beginning to show signs of strain. Family structures and gender relations had also changed over this period. For example, the proportion of three- or more generation households had declined from 19.2 per cent in 1970 to 12.7 per cent in 1994, while at the same time that of single-person households, which included a growing number of single-person elderly households, had grown from 18.5 per cent to 21.9 per cent (Kōseishō 1995). The proportion of elderly citizens living with their children also fell from 83.2 per cent in 1970 to 58.5 per cent in 1990 (Kōseishō 2000). During this time, the employment rate of married women rose. By 1990, the proportion of dual earning couples had exceeded that of salaryman and full-time housewife couples (Naikakufu 2001). In short, within two decades since 1970 Japanese families had become smaller in size, more nuclear, and less "traditional". These structural changes were reflected in a shift in public opinion as well. For example, whereas 60.1 per cent of people surveyed in the 1992 Cabinet Office's public opinion survey had agreed that "men should work and women should stay at home", by 2002 this figure had declined to 46.9 per cent (Naikakufu 2002). Public opinion surveys throughout the 1990s also show a steady increase in the proportion of people who believe that women should continue to work after marriage and childbirth. This was particularly evident amongst people under the age of 60 (Naikakufu 2006). Government white papers show a steady shift in public attitudes toward family and gender relations, with both women and men under 60 holding more liberal ideas about marriage, divorce and women's roles compared to people over 60.

Against this social and economic backdrop, the issue of demographic ageing and fertility decline had a very different resonance in Japan in 1990 as compared to 1970. First, by 1990 the proportion of the elderly population had reached 12 per cent, and the Japanese people had become much more aware of the country's new demographic reality. With a total fertility rate of 1.57 and a trajectory of steady fertility decline, the issue was no longer simply that of population ageing, but, more importantly, that of the *speed* of population ageing. Every demographic projection indicated that Japan was ageing faster than any other country in the world, and that, at this rate, it would become the demographically oldest nation by 2010 (Maruo 1992; Hori 1992; Takegawa 1992). This sense of urgency set in motion a wide range of policy debates and policy rethinks both within and outside the government. Second, the reality of rapid population ageing had also highlighted a number of impending social and economic issues, such as the increasing dependency ratio, the need for elderly care, labour shortages, economic slowdown, and eventual population decline. Finally, changes in social norms and expectations further underscored the complexity of social and demographic changes. For example, more liberal views on marriage and on women's work, combined with the decline in co-residency between elderly parents and their adult children, were rendering traditional family-based elderly and child care less tenable and more precarious. In short, the 1990s was a critical decade for Japan as rapid demographic ageing threatened to disrupt the country socially and economically.

## 3. Social Security and Social Welfare Implications of Population Ageing and Fertility Decline

The three main social security and social welfare concerns related to population ageing and fertility decline in Japan are: a) the increasing dependency ratio; b) elderly care; and c) family-work harmonization.

### 3.1. *Increasing dependency ratio*

The increase in the dependency ratio[1] between people over the age of 65 and those between 15 and 64 means that there will be more retired

[1] Dependency ratio is normally the ratio of economically inactive population over economically active population. Normally, this is calculated in terms of number of people aged 0–14 + 65 and over divided by the number of people aged 15–64. In

people relative to the working age population over time. According to the government projection, the old-age dependency ratio will increase from the current level of 25.5 per cent (approximately 3.9 people in the working age population to 1 senior citizen) to around 50 per cent in 2030 (approximately 2 working age people to 1 senior citizen). By 2050 the figure will reach 67 per cent (NIPSSR 2002). Since social security programmes are largely funded by general and payroll taxes, an increase in the old-age dependency ratio means that the employed population will have to pay out more in taxes in order to maintain the current level of provision for the senior citizens. This has led to calls for a reform of social security programmes, particularly public pensions. Since Japan's national pension scheme is based on a Pay-As-You-Go (PAYG) system, in which pension benefits provided to pensioners come directly from pension contributions paid by current workers, an increase in the old-age dependency ratio means that the current generation of workers will have to pay more into the pension fund in order to maintain the current level of benefits to the growing number of pensioners. Throughout the 1990s, policymakers and experts have called for reforms to balance the intergenerational burden of the public pension system. Experts have argued that the PAYG system would have to be replaced by a mix of defined contributions and private savings. Policymakers have also emphasized the need to raise the contribution rate while at the same time to reduce the level of benefits. Compounding the problem of the increasing dependency ratio since the mid-1980s is the rising divorce rate amongst couples who have been married for 20 years or more—what is commonly referred to as the *jukunen rikon* (mature-years divorce). Since Japan's national and occupational pension schemes are very much tied to men or husbands, women often risk not receiving any pension in their old age if they get divorced. Pension reforms have thus attempted to broaden the population coverage while at the same time balancing out the financial burden of pensions between older and younger generations.

In 1985, the government implemented a radical reform of the public pension system. Up until then, the pension system in Japan had followed a typical Bismarckian model of occupationally based pensions. The 1985 reform led to a two-tier system in which the first tier consists

---

Japan, dependency ratio is often calculated in terms of the number of people aged 65 and over divided by those aged 15–64.

of a basic universal pension (*kiso nenkin*) provided to all citizens; and the second tier composed of different occupational pension schemes. This reform was important for two reasons. First, it universalized the national pension through the basic pension scheme. It established an equal baseline for minimum old age security for all citizens. Second, it made the enrolment into the basic pension scheme compulsory for housewives who had been left out until this point. In other words, it legislated on married women's pension rights. The 1989 reform extended population coverage even further. This time enrolment was made compulsory for all citizens over the age of 20, including full-time students, who up until this point had been exempted from paying into the national pension plan. Thus, by 1990, all citizens over the age of 20 were obliged to enrol in the national pension plan regardless of their labour market attachment.

With the extension of compulsory pension enrolment to all adult citizens, the pension reforms of the 1990s began to pay more attention to the intergenerational burden. The 1994 reform set the process of gradually raising the pension age from 60 to 65 while increasing the individual pension contribution rate over time. In 1994, as part of the national plan to help families harmonize work and family responsibilities (the Angel Plan, discussed later), a special pension contribution exemption was introduced for workers on parental leave. The 2000 revision led to reduced employee pension benefits, an increased employee pension contribution rate, a further rise in pension age, and to the extension of the pension contribution exemption to low income students as well. In summary, the rising dependency ratio in Japan has resulted in a series of pension reforms since the mid-1980s. The reforms have resulted in the integration of previously occupationally separated pension schemes and the universalization of pension coverage. The reform also attempted to balance the intergenerational financial burden by raising the contribution rate and reducing the benefit level.

### 3.2. *Elderly care*

Population ageing also has had significant impacts on the elderly health and social care. The combination of rapid population ageing and the rise in married women's employment outside the home has resulted in an increasing mismatch between the need for elderly care on the one hand, and the decline in the availability of unpaid care provided by housewives on the other. Throughout the 1980s, women's groups have mobilized women, elderly people, and students to lobby the Japanese government and politicians to provide more social support for the elderly and for families taking care of their elderly relatives. Research studies and the media also highlighted women's care burden in Japan. In response to public pressure, the government introduced the Gold Plan (otherwise known as the Ten-Year Strategy to Promote Elderly Health and Welfare [*Kōreisha Hoken Fukukshi Suishin Jū-kanen Senryaku*]) in 1989 to develop and expand social services for the elderly. The Gold Plan resulted in an expansion of public services such as home help, day services, short stay services and elderly care institutions. As well, a significant amount of money has been transferred from the national to local governments to build the infrastructure for community-based elderly care. The demand for care, however, proved much greater than expected. In 1994, the Gold Plan was revised with new and more ambitious ten-year targets. As shown in Table 1, most of the targets set in 1989 were met or were close to being met by 1994, compelling the government to set new.

In the meantime, the pace of demographic ageing in Japan quickened as the total fertility rate continued to fall. Despite the expansion of public elderly care services, it was also found that the incidence of social hospitalization amongst the elderly in Japan was comparatively high. Studies show that many elderly people and their families who were not able to get adequate care services often turned to hospitals in order to receive care. Between 1989 and 1997, the total national annual health expenditure rose by 37.5 per cent (Kōseishō 1998).[2] During this time, the increase in elderly health care expenditure was particularly evident. The proportion of health expenditure for the elderly increased from 28.8 per cent to 33.1 per cent of total national health insurance expenditure within the five years between 1990 and 1995 (Kōseishō 2000). By the mid-1990s the cost of social hospitalization for national health insurance had become a serious policy concern. After several years of task force studies, research, and consultations the government introduced the Long-term Care Insurance Law in 1997 (Masuda 2003; Campbell and Ikegami 1999; see also chapter 58).

[2] It should be pointed out here that total national expenditure on pensions in 1997 was 48.5 per cent higher than 1989. In Japan, pension and health care made up 89 per cent of all social security expenditure in 1997 (Ministry of Health and Welfare, 1998).

Table 1. Gold and New Gold Plan Targets and Achievements.

| | Actual figure in 1989 | Initial Gold Plan targets for 1999 | Actual figure in 1994 | New Gold Plan targets for 1999 |
|---|---|---|---|---|
| Home helps | 31,405 | 100,000 | 79,689 | 170,000 |
| Short stay institutions | 4,274 | 50,000 | 27,127 | 60,000 |
| Day service centre | 1,080 | 10,000 | 3,993 | 17,000 |
| In-home care support centres | 0 | 10,000 | 1,777 | 10,000 |
| Special nursing homes for the aged | 162,019 | 240,000 | 217,417 | 290,000 |
| Health service facilities for the aged | 27,811 | 280,000 | 93,994 | 280,000 |
| Care home (spaces) | 200 | 10,000 | 9,889 | 100,000 |
| Living welfare centres for the aged | 0 | 400 | 158 | 400 |

Sources: Foundation for Social Development for Senior Citizens 1992; Kōseishō 1998: 243.

Long-term Care Insurance replaced the Gold Plan with a new compulsory social insurance insuring domiciliary and institutional care for people over the age of 65. Social policy experts in Japan attribute the speedy introduction of Long-term Care Insurance to four factors. The first is the sense of urgency felt by policy makers and the public, along with the realization that something had to be done about rapid population ageing. While both the Japanese government and the public had been aware of the country's demographic ageing, the issue became much more critical in the 1990s. Indeed, much was done in the media and in public debates in 1993, when it was revealed that a total of 2 million elderly people had some form of disability (Hiroi and Yamazaki 2001). Public opinion polls also showed strong support for the Long-term Care Insurance scheme throughout 1996 and 1997. A nationwide opinion poll in December 1997, shortly after the government had passed the Long-term Care Insurance legislation, also found 80 per cent of respondents in support of the new legislation (Mainichi Shinbun 1997).

Second, changes in the family structure, particularly the decline in the proportion of the three- or more generation households and the increase in the number of elderly people living on their own, had also helped raise policy attention for social care. The National Basic Household Survey in 1994 found that, amongst the households with at least one elderly member, 16.4 per cent were single-person households, 24.0 per cent were couple-only households, and 34.9 per cent were three-generation households (Kōseishō 1998). Similarly, the National Institute for Population and Social Security Research projected that the number of households with elderly heads would increase to 14.79 million by 2010 (NIPSSR 1993). Third, there was also strong social and political mobilization by civil society groups pushing for Long-term Care Insurance. Women's groups in Japan have been highlighting the family's (that is, women's) care burden since the 1980s. The call for more public support for elderly care grew after 1990, when women's groups were joined by community groups, social welfare organizations, and retired people's groups. When the government began to consider the issue of Long-term Care Insurance in 1994, these groups emerged as important actors in promoting and campaigning for the "socialization of care" [*kaigo no shakaika*] (Eto 2001; Peng 2002).

Finally, concerns over rising health care costs and the problem of social hospitalization were also important factors facilitating the passage of the Long-term Care Insurance Law. Within the Ministry of Health and Welfare, policy makers had become increasingly concerned about soaring elderly health care costs. To address the issue of social hospitalization, policy makers saw it necessary to create a separate programme able to provide long-term care for the elderly and thereby move those in need of care out of the hospital/medical stream. This coincided with the civil society groups' interest in social care and with the demand for more public care services for the elderly. Ministry of Health and Welfare bureaucrats were able to use this opportunity to forge consensus amongst various stakeholders, including academics, medical associations, business groups, women's groups and local governments, to pass the bill (Eto 2001; Masuda 2003; Peng 2002).

### 3.3. *Family-work harmonization*

Finally, in addition to the issues of dependency ratio and elderly care, demographic ageing in Japan has also focused people's attention on the issue of family-work tensions. In Japan, the steady fertility decline not only underscored the country's long-term ageing problem, but also cast a long shadow over the issue of long-term social and economic sustainability. By the mid-1990s, academics, demographers, and government policy makers came to agree that family-work tensions were the main cause of the fertility decline. As pointed out in the 1997 White Paper for Health and Welfare (Kōseishō 1998: 42), there is a growing consensus that the decline of the fertility rate can be traced to Japan's rigid social structure, which puts an undue burden on the family to raise children without any public support and thus "denies young people the dream of marriage and family" (see also chapter 51). In 1994, the government introduced a ten-year strategy called the Angel Plan to address the declining fertility problem. The Angel Plan tries to lessen family-work tensions and to encourage childbirth, by providing more public child care, after-school programmes, community-based support centres for families with children, a parental leave system, and a more generous child allowance system, and by reforming the child welfare system. As shown in Table 2, the number of child-care spaces, extended-hour child-care centres, temporary child-care centres, after-school programmes and other support programmes to help families with small and school-age children has increased since 1994. Like the Gold Plan, the Angel Plan was also revised in 1999 with more ambitious targets for the next ten years.

In addition to the expansion of child care and after-school programmes, a number of employment reforms were introduced, including one year of parental leave with 40 per cent income replacement, flexible hours, and the expansion of temporary and part-time work. The child allowance programme, which had been cut in the 1982 welfare reform, was reintroduced in 1996. To promote greater gender equality, the Council of Gender Equality was established within the Cabinet Office in 1996, and the Basic Law for a Gender-equal Society [*Danjo Kyōdōsankaku Kihon-hō*] was introduced in 1999 to institutionalize gender equality principles by setting up a monitoring system to measure the level of change. Finally, the Low Fertility Measures Plus One Programme [*Shōshika Taisaku Purasu Wan*] was put into place in 2001 as an extension of the Angel Plans. The programme includes targets of zero waiting lists for public day care, a parental leave take-up rate of 10 per cent for fathers and 80 per cent for mothers, a minimum of five days' paternity leave, and shorter work hours for workers with small children.

Table 2. The Angel Plan's Targets and Actual Figures.

| Target Activities/Services | Actual figures in 1994 | Angel Plan's target figures for 1999 | New Angel Plan's target figures for 2004 | Actual figures for 1999 |
|---|---|---|---|---|
| No. of child-care spaces for 0–2 year olds | 470,000 | 580,000 | 680,000 | 584,000 |
| No. of extended hours child-care centres | 2,530 | 7,000 | 10,000 | 7,000 |
| No. of child-care centres operating during weekends and holidays | N/A | 100 | 300 | No data available |
| No. of temporary child-care centres | N/A | In 450 local communities | In 500 local communities | 1,500 |
| Multifunctional child-care centres | 200 | 1,600 | 2,000 | 365 |
| Child-care support centres for stay-at-home mothers | 354 | 1,500 | 3,000 | 1,500 |
| Temporary child-care support for stay-at-home mothers | 600 | 1,500 | 3,000 | No data available |
| After-school programmes for elementary school age children | 5,220 | 9,000 | 11,500 | 9,000 |
| Treatment and counselling centres for infertile couples | N/A | 24 | 47 | No data available |

Source: Kōseishō (1999) and Kōseirōdōshō (2001).

## 4. Conclusion: Demographic Ageing in Japan within the Global Context

In the 1990s, Japan introduced a number of social policy reforms in an effort to avert and manage the impending demographic crisis. Pension and health care reforms were not unexpected, given the pace of demographic ageing. Since they constituted a significant portion of social security expenditure, pension and health care reforms were considered important for the purpose of fiscal control. The expansions of social care, particularly public child care, and firming up gender equality policies, however, came somewhat unexpectedly, because these were policy sectors that had received very little attention from the Japanese government up until then. To be sure, throughout most of the 1980s, the government was openly dismissive of these issues as a public responsibility, insisting that care of children and the elderly should be the family's responsibility (for example, debates on the Japanese-style welfare society). The fact that the government's attitude toward the elderly, children, and women changed during the 1990s shows the impacts of structural changes on social policy reforms. Demographic ageing and low fertility have underscored the issues of an increasing dependency ratio, increasing elderly care needs, labour shortages, and eventual population decline. Combined with this, the 1990s also witnessed significant changes in family structure and in ideas on marriage and gender relations in Japan. Moreover, there is increasing global economic pressure pushing for labour market restructuring, including increased deregulation and labour market flexibility. These factors have contributed to changes in the attitudes of government, business and the public towards family, women's roles as workers and mothers, and the state's role in social welfare provision. In summary, changes in demographic and socio-economic contexts in Japan over the last couple of decades have had a significant role in reshaping the social policy logic and strategies in the country.

From a global perspective, the phenomenon of demographic ageing and low fertility is no longer unique to Japan today. In fact, a similar pattern can also be observed amongst the other OECD countries. The Japanese case, however, still stands as a useful example because of the extent and the speed of ageing. By 2005, the proportion of people over the age of 65 in Japan had reached 20% of the total population—highest in the OECD countries. Whereas it took Germany 42 years, the UK 46, the US 69, and France 114 to double the proportion of people aged 65 and over from 7 per cent to 14 per cent, Japan accomplished this in a mere 24 years between 1970 and 1994. It is not surprising then that major reforms of social security and social welfare systems took place in the country in the 1990s. The Japanese case thus helps us understand the impact of rapid population ageing, and the extent to which social-demographic factors can influence social policy changes.

Like Japan, other OECD countries, such as Spain, Italy, South Korea and Taiwan, have also been experiencing fertility decline throughout the 1990s, and thus rapid demographic ageing. The total fertility rates in Spain and Italy in 2000 were both 1.24, while the proportions of people aged 65 and over in these countries were 18.27 per cent and 16.85 per cent respectively (OECD 2006). Although the total fertility rates in South Korea and Taiwan were relatively low in 2000, 1.4 for South Korea and 1.6 for Taiwan, they have been falling further since 2000. In 2005, the fertility rates in these countries were 1.0 and 1.1, respectively (KNSO 2006; CEPD 2006). Given its very low fertility rate, the proportion of people aged 65 and over in South Korea is projected to increase from 7.2 per cent in 2000 to 20.8 per cent by 2026. Similarly, Taiwan also predicts its ageing population will increase from 8.62 per cent in 2000 to 20.62 per cent by 2026 (KNSO 2006). These figures make Korea and Taiwan two of the fastest ageing countries in the world, along with Japan.

In response to the EU and OECD recommendations, efforts have been made to develop and expand social care in these countries as well (Sleebos, 2003; Mahon, forthcoming). In Italy and Spain, pension and health care reforms were introduced in the 1990s to offset the pressures of the ageing population. These countries have also introduced some expansion of elderly care services and public child-care programmes. The South Korean and the Taiwanese governments are also responding to the projected demographic crises by introducing family and gender policy reforms. In South Korea, Infant-Child Care Programmes expanded tenfold between 1991 and 2002, and the total number of children enrolled in public child care increased nearly threefold between 1995 and 2001 (Lee and Park 2003). The 2005 child-care reform also extended to governmental financial support for child care to middle-income families, and increased employers' obligations to provide workplace child-care facilities. A new universal Elderly Care Insurance (ECI) scheme has been legislated to commence in 2008. Like Japan's Long-term Care Insurance, the Korean ECI will cover home and institutional care for elderly people. In addition to child and elderly care, a number of gender equality measures have also been introduced in Korea, including gender mainstreaming in the public sphere, provisions for single mothers, extended maternity and parental leave laws, and workplace support for women (Sung 2003).

Similarly, the Taiwanese government introduced the Gender Equality Labour Law in 2001, which includes equal pay for equal work, a two-year maternity leave provision, monthly leave for women, and the formal codification of non-discriminatory hiring practices for married or pregnant women. Further reforms have been made since then to strengthen women's rights and protections in the workplace. In addition, the government has also proposed providing more support for parental leave allowances, child-rearing subsidies and affordable day care (Tsai 2006; Fang 2006; Taiwan Journal 2006; Hsiao 2006). Rapid population ageing in Taiwan has also led to the proposal to introduce a public pension scheme (Chen 2006) and to greater efforts to train and increase the number of licensed health care workers to work in the area of elderly care (Huang 2006). These policies to avert fertility decline and encourage childbirth by extending social care suggest the extent to which demographic changes can affect social policy reforms in many countries.

In summary, Japan stands out as an early example of a social security/social welfare restructuring case. Its social policy reforms in the 1990s serve as an important case of social and demographically driven policy reforms. However, a global demographic trend suggests that Japan is no longer unique. As other industrialized nations and Japan's East Asian neighbours are experiencing demographic shifts, the Japanese case will serve as a useful model for some, and as an important lesson for all.

## References


Campbell, John. C. (1992): *How Policies Changes: the Japanese Government and the Aging Society.* Princeton: Princeton University Press.

Campbell, John C. and Naoki Ikegami (eds.) (1999): *Long-term Care for Frail Older People: Reaching for the Ideal System.* New York: Springer.

CEPD (Council of Economic Planning and Development, Executive Yuan, Republic of China) (2006): *Population Projections for the Taiwan Area 2006–2051.* http://www.cepd.gov.tw/encontent/en_data/en_content.jsp?linkID=239&parentLinkID=112&businessID=3290&gosec2=y (found 7 March 2007).

Chen, Shui-bian (2006): *Chen Shui-bian's New Year's Address, 2006.* In: *Taiwan Journal,* January 6, 2006. http://www.theworldpress.com/press/worldpress/taiwanpress/taiwanjournal.htm (found 1 March 2007).

Eto, Murase Mikio (2001): Public Involvement in Social Policy Reform: Seen from the Perspective of Japan's Elderly-Care Insurance Scheme. In: *Journal of Social Policy* 30, 1, pp. 17–36.

Fang, Rita (2006): Taiwan Needs Solutions for Birthrate Headache. In: Taiwan Journal, July 7, 2006. http://www.theworldpress.com/press/worldpress/taiwanpress/taiwanjournal.htm (found 1 March 2007).

Foundation for Social Development for Senior Citizens (1992): *Health and Welfare for the Elderly: An outline of systems and trends,* Tokyo: FSDSC.

Hiroi, Yoshinori and Yasuhiko Yamazaki (2001): *Shakai hoshōron* [Social security theory]. Tokyo: Minerva.

Hori, Katsuhiro (1992): Public Pension System for the 21st Century, In: *Review of Population and Social Policy* 1, pp. 55–70.

Hsiao, Edwin (2006): Cabinet Agrees on US$5b Plan as Part of Big Warmth Objective. In: *Taiwan Journal,* September 29, 2006. http://taiwanjournal.nat.gov.tw/ct.asp?xItem=23318&CtNode=122 (found 1 March 2007).

Huang, Annie (2006): Taiwan Heading for Aging Milestone, Must Face Challenges "Beginning Now", In: *Taiwan Journal*, November 24, 2006. http://www.theworldpress.com/press/worldpress/taiwanpress/taiwanjournal.htm (found 1 March 2007).

KNSO (Korea National Statistics Office) (2006): *Highlights of Population Projections*. Seoul: KNSO. http://www.nso.go.kr/eng2006/emain/index.html (found 7 March 2007).

Kōseirōdōshō (Ministry of Health, Labour and Welfare) (2001): *Heisei 13-nen kōseirōdō hakuhso* [White paper on labour and social welfare 2001]. Tokyo: Gyōsei.

Kōseishō (Ministry of Health and Welfare) (1995): *Kokumin seikatsu kiso chōsa*. [Survey of national life]. Tokyo: Kōsei Tōkei Kyōkai.

—— (1998): *Heisei 10-nen kōsei hakusho* [White paper on social welfare 1998]. Tokyo: Gyōsei.

—— (1999): *Heisei 11-nen kōsei hakusho* [White paper on social welfare 1999]. Tokyo: Gyōsei.

—— (2000): *Heisei 12-nen kōsei hakusho* [White paper on social welfare 2000]. Tokyo: Gyōsei.

Lee, Hey-Kyung and Yeong-Ran Park (2003): *Families in Transition and the Family Welfare Policies in Korea*. The Canada-Korea Social Policy Research Symposium, Seoul, November 22–23. http://www.kihasa.re.kr/board/seminar/file/HyeKyung_lee-Yeong_Ran_Park.pdf (found 7 March 2007).

Mahon, Rianne (forthcoming): *Babies and Bosses: Gendering the OECD's Social Policy Discourse*. Draft chapter for the OECD and Global Governance.

*Mainichi Shinbun* (27 December 1997): Kaigo hoken seido ni tsuite 47-todofuken no kachokyu tantōsha ni taisuru ankēto chōsa [Public opinion survey among director level people across the 47 prefectures regarding long-term care insurance].

Maruo, Naomi (1992): The Impact of the Aging Population on the Social Security and the Allied Services of Japan. In: *Review of Population and Social Policy* 1, March, pp. 1–54.

Masuda, Masanobu (2003): *Kaigo hoken minaoshi no sōten: seisaku katei kara mieru kongo no kadai* [Long-term care insurance reform debate: emergent issues from the perspective of policy process]. Tokyo: Hoken Bunkasha.

Naikakufu [Cabinet Office] (2001): *Heisei 13-nen danjo kyōdō shakai sankaku hakusho* [White paper on gender equal society 2001]. http://www.gender.go.jp/whitepaper/h13/zentai/2001-index.html (found 13 March 2007).

—— (2002): *Danjo kyōdō sankaku shakai ni kan suru seron chōsa* [Public opinion survey concerning a gender equal society]. Tokyo: Naikakufu daijin kanbō seifu kōhō.

—— (2006): *Heisei 18-nen danjo kyōdō shakai sankaku hakusho* [White paper on gender equal society 2006]. http://www.gender.go.jp/whitepaper/h18/web/danjyo/pdf/DKH18H01.pdf (found 13 March 2007).

NIPSSR (National Institute for Population and Social Security Research) (1993): *Nihon no setaisū no shōrai shinkei* [Projections for Japan's household numbers]. Tokyo: NIPSSR.

—— (2002): *Population Projections for Japan: 2001–2050*. http://www.ipss.go.jp/index-e.html (found 8 March 2007).

OECD (2006): *OECD Country Statistical Profiles 2006—Population and Migration Data*. http://stats.oecd.org/WBOS/Default.aspx?QueryName=245&QueryType=View (found 2 January 2007).

Peng, Ito (2002): Social Care in Crisis: Gender, Demography and Welfare State Restructuring in Japan. In: *Social Politics* 9, 3, pp. 411–443.

Sleebos, Joelle E. (2003): *Low Fertility Rates in OECD Countries: Facts and Policy Responses*, OECD, DELSA, Social, Economic and Migration Working Papers No. 15. http://www.inomics.com/cgi/repec?handle=RePEc:oec:elsaaa:15-EN (found 1 March 2007).

Sung, Sirin (2003): Women Reconciling Paid and Unpaid Work in a Confucian Welfare State: the case of South Korea. In: *Social Policy and Administration*, 37, 4, pp. 342–60.

Taiwan Journal (3 November 2006): Premier outlines vision of affluent, caring society, editorial section. http://www.theworldpress.com/press/worldpress/taiwanpress/taiwanjournal.htm (found 2 March 2007).

Takegawa, Shogo (1992): The Need for Social Services for the Elderly. In: *Review of Population and Social Policy*, 1, March, pp. 117–139.

Tsai, June (2006): CLA proposal tackles gender inequality. In: *Taiwan Journal*, November 3, 2006 http://www.theworldpress.com/press/worldpress/taiwanpress/taiwanjournal.htm (found 2 March 2007).

CHAPTER FIFTY-EIGHT

# PROVIDING CARE FOR THE AGEING SOCIETY

Naoki Ikegami

## 1. Introduction

Health-care systems are primarily determined by how doctors and hospitals are organized, and these, in turn, reflect their social function and historical legacy. Although providers have become increasingly influenced by government policy and, in particular, by how they are paid, the rules and regulations on payment must be set after negotiations with provider organisations. This is especially true in Japan, where policy making has been made through an incremental approach and in collaboration with the Japan Medical Association (Campbell and Ikegami 1998). The first half of this chapter will be an overview of the historical developments that have led to the present delivery system. The second half will focus on the elderly and how payment mechanisms have affected the delivery of care.

## 2. Historical Background

### 2.1. *The indigenous system*

Japan already had a well established network of practitioners in Chinese medicine by the middle of the eighteenth century. Chinese medicine took a holistic approach, focusing on the need to restore the balance between the two opposing forces of yin and yang within the body. Medication was the main treatment, to the extent that these practitioners were often known as apothecaries. Payment was theoretically made only for the cost of the drugs, since it was regarded as morally unacceptable to accept fees for performing a humane service. However, the unstated quid pro quo was that patients were expected to pay according to their ability, and therefore to pay munificently if they had the means. This norm served a useful purpose for the government: it was absolved of the responsibility of providing public assistance for medical care because the practitioner's duty to provide services and the patient's obligation to pay were not directly connected.

Medical practice was an exception to the rigidly divided society of that time, because it was open to all classes and there was competition based on skill. Practitioners recognised a hierarchy among themselves, with those appointed as personal physicians to the feudal lords being ranked the highest. Despite the austere rule of not demanding payment from the patients, many practitioners were able to become quite wealthy. Indeed, it could be said that de-emphasizing money was part of their strategy to advance their position in society, because if it became explicit that they depended on the practice of medicine for their livelihood, they would be seen as having the same low rank as an artisan. It was as scholars possessing knowledge of medicine that they would rank highly, because such skills were esteemed in Confucian teaching, as they fulfilled the sacrosanct filial duty of maintaining the health of one's parents.

Compared with Western nations, there was little development of guilds and professional identity among medical practitioners in Japan, and there was also very little provision of institutional care for the sick and indigent, either by religious organisations or by government. The selfless practice of philanthropy was not a religious duty for the popular Buddhist and Shinto sects, which promised the granting of secular wishes, nor was it a secular duty under the Confucian ideology favoured by the rulers, which emphasized practical ethics. Care of the ill, the disabled and the elderly was regarded as the responsibility of the family (Ikegami 1995a).

### 2.2. *From the Meiji era to the end of World War II*

With the inauguration of the Emperor Meiji in 1868, the government embarked on a policy of rapid Westernization throughout society. The early years in particular were characterized by wholesale and enthusiastic adoption of Western ideas and institutions. In health care, the first edicts issued in 1875 proclaimed that in future only Western medicine would be given official recognition, and eventually all practitioners would have to sit for a national licensing examination. The first step was to invite German physicians to come and teach at the new government medical school in Tokyo in 1871. In retrospect, these edicts were very radical compared with the development of medical care in other non-Western countries. The Meiji leaders soon realized that they had to be more realistic, however. For one thing, little public money could be allocated to health care, because the country was facing foreign aggression and internal discord: available resources had to be invested in defence and building the industrial infrastructure. Moreover, to grant licences only to physicians trained in Western medicine would mean that most of the population would be denied access, and, equally importantly, existing practitioners would be deprived of their livelihood.

Compromises were therefore inevitable. First, most of the available resources were put into one medical school, that of the University of Tokyo. The students would be taught by German professors to the same high level as in Germany. After completing their training, they would be appointed as faculty at other schools. Later in the century, some of these schools were raised to university level, but others (including most of the private ones) remained at the vocational-school level. This pattern led to a difference in status among the physicians that in some ways reconstituted the hierarchical structure of the previous period. Indeed, many thought that university hospital professors behaved exactly like retainers of feudal lords, if not like the lords themselves. The second compromise occurred in 1882, the year before medical licences were to be granted only to those who had studied Western medicine. The government "grandfathered-in" the existing practitioners of Chinese medicine—and even their sons—so they could continue to practice indefinitely.

Thus, the pattern of medical practice was accordingly eventually transformed into the Western model, but the basic structure of the indigenous system was left intact. However, in one area, hospitals, it was necessary to adopt a completely new method of delivering care. As noted earlier, before the Meiji era there had been virtually no public or religious institutions that could serve as nuclei for hospitals. This institution therefore developed quite differently from in the West. For one thing, hospitals had no associations with care for the indigent (in fact, hospitals were the first to introduce regular fees because they were not constrained by the old rule of not demanding payment from patients). Another major difference was that, since Japan had no tradition of community-based philanthropic activities, the task of establishing hospitals was taken on by the government on the one hand or by individual physicians on the other.

Hospitals in Japan were therefore built for the following specific purposes. The first was for teaching and research. Since Western medicine could not be taught without studying patients, hospitals had to be built along with medical schools. The second was for the army and navy. The several rebellions and wars of the Meiji era created a pressing need for hospitals to treat combat-related diseases and injuries. The third type was established by local governments for quarantine of communicable and venereal diseases. The fourth type, which was to become the most numerous, was built by private practitioners as extensions to their offices. In all four cases, the hospital was regarded as very much the doctor's workplace, and, as the director, a medical doctor carried both clinical and administrative responsibilities. Hospitals therefore failed to develop an identity independent from physicians.

The independence of hospitals was further weakened by the control over their medical staff by the professors of prestigious medical schools. Physicians were rotated at the whim of the professor within the closed network of the university clinical department and its affiliated hospitals. Although this arrangement developed partly as a result of the acute shortage of physicians—hospital founders had to beg the professors to send physicians—it fitted very well with the vertical structure of Japanese society. Hierarchical relations were formed among physicians within the close-knit, family-like network in each clinical department, presided over by the patriarchal figure of the professor. The strength of these vertical relationships made the development of professional organisations difficult. As a result, practice patterns tended to differ even within the same university, if the physicians did not belong to the same clinical department. Another problem was that hospital doctors tended to be more concerned with research than with clinical medicine, because their career advancement depended on the approval of the professor. Young doctors concentrated on obtaining the research degree of Doctor of Medical Science, which came to be regarded as a mark of professional competence by the public because there was no formal system of accreditation for specialists.

Despite the tensions inherent in this hierarchical system, most physicians were relatively satisfied with their positions. Attaining a senior position in a prestigious hospital was denied to anyone not a graduate of the elite medical schools, but for the vast majority of physicians, hospital appointments were only a temporary stage in their careers. Even the most elite graduates expected eventually to go into private practice, where a high income was almost guaranteed because of the continued shortage of trained physicians. Doctors no longer had access to hospital facilities once they became private practitioners, but those who wanted to continue to perform surgical operations or provide inpatient care could do so by building small hospitals next to their offices. The most successful of these continued to expand until they rivalled the large hospitals in the public sector. Thus, there was a continuum from physicians' offices through small hospitals to large hospitals. There was also not much distinction between specialists and general practitioners. Those who went into open practice continued to regard themselves as specialists, but in fact they mostly provided primary care.

The general public did not see much change in medical care. Most went on seeing private practitioners and were treated mainly with medication obtained directly from the physician. People seldom visited hospitals. Even when they were hospitalized, apart from in military hospitals, nursing care continued to be provided primarily by family members, who would bring in bedding and prepare meals. Nurses were trained almost solely for the purpose of assisting physicians. However, despite all this continuity, it is important to observe that the government did eventually succeed in changing the basis of medical practice from Chinese to Western medicine. Unlike other Asian countries, independent schools or formal qualifications in Chinese medicine were not allowed to co-exist with Western medicine. Moreover, this transition was achieved with minimal cost and social disruption.

### 2.3. *Postwar development to the present*

After Japan's defeat in World War II, the occupying forces tried to restructure the health-care system as part of their goal of "democratizing" the entire fabric of society. However, their endeavours had only limited success. In medical education, the two-tiered system of university and vocational schools was abolished, but the hierarchical structure with the University of Tokyo at the top remained intact. The professors of clinical departments maintained their control within the encompassing networks of affiliated hospitals. The planned closure of small, sub-standard hospitals was forestalled when a time limit of 48 hours on stays in the "clinics-with-beds" [*yushō shinryojo*] was rendered meaningless by adding the clause, "unless unavoidable for medical reasons". At present, about a sixth of the clinics still have such beds, although they continue to be virtually solo-practices (MHLW 2006a). A move to prohibit doctors from dispensing was also thwarted.

Thus, the structure of the delivery system remained essentially unchanged. Despite the huge expansion of hospitals in the postwar period, their role as actors in the health policy arena has continued to be marginal because their interests have been divided between the private and the public sectors. The private hospitals owned and operated by physicians constitute 80 per cent of the total, but the public sector, which receives subsidies from the government, provides most of the high-tech care. Both sectors maintain large outpatient departments, so most of their patients come without referrals. This unrestricted access to tertiary hospitals means that there are no waiting lists for outpatient consultations. Although there are complaints about the long waiting time in hospitals, patients are seen on the same day. The delivery system is still weighted toward outpatient care, so that Japan has one of the highest rates of physician visits and the lowest rate of hospital admissions among advanced industrialized countries (OECD 2005). Waiting lists for inpatient care are limited to a few prestigious hospitals, and those patients who are not able or willing to wait are referred to their affiliated hospitals (Ikegami and Ikeda 1996).

### 2.4. *Containing costs through the payment mechanism*

Payment to physicians and hospitals is made on a fee-for-service basis, but strictly regulated by the government's fee schedule [*shinryo hōshu*]. Providers are prohibited from billing patients for services not listed, with the exception of private room charges and new technology still under development (Ikegami 2006).[1] Costs have been contained by the following mechanism. First, the global revision rate for fees and prices of drugs is politically determined in a process in which the government has generally been able to play a strong hand. Recently, the rate was decreased by 2.7 percent in 2002 and 3.16 per cent in 2006. Second, the fees for most surgical operations and high-tech new procedures have historically been set at a low level, so that providing these services tends to result in a net loss. These services are nevertheless provided because physicians find these services professionally rewarding and because their salary is not linked to the profits they may bring to the

[1] There is very little private medicine outside public insurance. Economists and business leaders who sit on the Economic and Fiscal Committee within the Cabinet Office have called for allowing balance billing but their views have had very limited impact (Ikegami 2006).

hospital. Moreover, three-quarters of the surgical operations requiring general anesthaesia are provided in public-sector hospitals and university hospitals (Ikegami 1995b), which can afford to do so because they receive additional subsidies from the government.

Third, when the fee schedule is revised, rather than adjusting by an across-the-board conversion factor, items are individually altered. In particular, fees for procedures that show inappropriately large increases in volume will be reduced. For example, the fees for laboratory tests and diagnostic imaging have been continuously lowered, either directly, or through "bundling" (per unit fees are lowered as the number of tests increases), or through restrictions on the number of times a particular test can billed within a calendar month. As a result, despite major advances in technology for diagnostic tests between 1979 and 1993, their average unit costs have remained the same (Ikegami and Campbell 1999). Another example is the MRI scan. In the 2002 fee schedule revision, the fee for a MRI head scan was further reduced from 16,600 yen to 11,400 yen, to offset their volume increase (Ikegami and Campbell 2004). However, Japan has the highest per capita number of MRI scans in the world (OECD 2005), because these fee cuts have spurred the development of low-priced types of MRI scan that have, in turn, led to increases in volume.

Despite the cost containment policy, doctors in clinics have managed to earn a relatively high income compared to those employed in hospitals because of their political power within the Japan Medical Association, and because of the incremental approach taken in the fee schedule revision that tends to favour providers originally having large shares in primary care.

## 3. Providing Care to the Elderly

### 3.1. *Before the expansion of health care*

Although universal coverage was achieved in 1961, the co-payment rate was at 50 per cent with the exception of those who were employees. As a consequence, access to medical care remained limited for the elderly. Care was provided by the family, in particular by the daughter-in-law of the eldest son. This was encoded in the old Civil Code, together with the right of primogeniture. This legal obligation is no longer in the new Civil Code which was promulgated after World War II, but has continued to be practised as a social norm.

Public welfare services were mainly limited to the indigent with no children. The first attempt to expand elderly people's access to services was the enactment of the Welfare Law for the Aged [*Rōjin Fukushi-hō*] in 1963. This led to the establishment of Special Homes for the Aged (SHA) [*Tokubetsu yōgo rōjin hōmu*] (sometimes translated as nursing homes) for those who had more serious physical and mental disabilities than the residents in the Homes for the Aged [*Yōgo rōjin hōmu*], which remained restricted to the indigent. The SHA's extent of medical care was limited, as licensed nurses were on duty only during regular work hours on weekdays. The Act also provided for home-help services but these were initially restricted to the indigent living alone. Access to welfare services was controlled by the local government's social welfare office and was means-tested. The services were provided directly by the local government, or by special welfare organisations closely supervised by the government. A stigma continued to be attached to their use and provision remained constrained by budgets which were financed entirely by taxes.

### 3.2. *Opening of the door to health care and past attempts at reform*

In 1973, health care became free (no co-payment) to all elderly people 70 and over, and to those with disabilities from 65 and over. This opened the door to health care for the elderly. The proportion of the general population aged 65 and over in hospitals doubled from 2 per cent in 1975 to 4 per cent in 1990, and constituted two-thirds of the institutionalized elderly (MHW 1975, 1992). A significant amount of this increase was due to admissions for "social reasons" arising from the following conditions. First, there was a lack of formal social services, both institutional and community-based. Second, small to medium-sized hospitals began to face difficulties in filling their beds, because patients began to turn to the large medical centres. Third, unlike social welfare, health-care costs were not capped by budget, but open-ended. Finally, the ageing of society led not only to increases in the number of elderly people, but also to decreases in the availability of informal care as the carers themselves aged.

Hospital admission for social reasons not only increased costs, but also led to inappropriate care, with the excessive use of laboratory tests, drip-infusions and medication under the fee-for-service method of payment. The government's first attempt to remedy this situation was to establish the Health Facilities for the Elderly (HFE) [*Rōjin hoken shisetsu*] in 1986. The HFE was intended to function as an intermediate care facility between the hospital and the community, and as such, the length of stay was officially limited to three months. However, instead of being a bridge between the hospital and home, most HFE patients are either admitted for extended respite care and are transferred back and forth between their homes and the HFE, or are transferred back and forth between the hospitals and the HFEs because their families are unwilling or unable to provide care (Ikezaki *et al.* 2005). It was also planned that some of the HFEs would be converted from hospitals but no hospitals actually did so, mainly because the physical facility requirement of 8 square metres per bed was too high a hurdle for hospitals (the minimum requirement for hospitals being 4.3 square metres).

Second, a new method of payment was devised in 1990: a relatively generous inclusive rate was offered to hospitals that could meet prescribed staffing levels and were willing to forgo itemized billing for medication and laboratory examinations. The problem with this solution was that the per diem payment was a flat rate (as for the HFE) and not adjusted for severity. Thus, those requiring heavy care, such as the use of respirators, faced difficulties in being admitted. This also meant that there was considerable overlap among the three types of facilities providing long term care (LTC): the social service SHAs, the intermediate care HFEs and the hospital LTC beds. As of 2006, the number of hospital LTC beds was still the greatest: 380,000 hospital beds (one quarter of all hospital beds excluding psychiatric and tuberculosis beds) (MHLW 2006a), compared with 364,000 for SHAs, and 283,000 for HFEs (MHLW 2006b).

### 3.3. *Development of social services with the Gold Plan*

In 1989, the government revealed the Gold Plan, a ten year plan to develop services for the elderly. It was part of the ruling Liberal Democratic Party's strategy to win back votes after nearly losing the election that followed the introduction of the sales tax. The Gold Plan proved popular, so it was subsequently revised with higher targets in the five year "New Gold Plan" in 1994. By the year of completion of both Plans in 1999, the number of full-time equivalent home-helps was planned to increase from the 1990 level of 38,945 to 100,000 in the Gold Plan, and to 170,000 in the New Gold Plan; and the number of adult day care centres to increase from 1,615 to 10,000 in the former and to 17,000 in the latter (Kōsei Tōkei Kyokai 1996, 2001).[2] These goals had generally been met when the plan ended in 1999 (MHLW 2001).

However, access to services continued to be controlled by the local government welfare departments and were means-tested, and the client had no choice of providers. Restrictions based on income and availability of family support were officially removed so that services became accessible to the middle-classes, but indigent elders living alone or with only a spouse continued to be preferentially provided with services, reflecting the institutional culture of the social welfare agencies and budget limitations. Moreover, although private enterprises were officially allowed to contract with the municipalities in 1989, few actually did so (Ogawa 1998). Another problem was the disparity across municipalities because the development of services was at the discretion of the mayors.

### 3.4. *Implementation of long-term care insurance*

The problems inherent in providing LTC within the health and welfare sectors were the key factors that led to the establishment of an independent LTC Insurance [*kaigo hoken*] (Campbell and Ikegami 2000). Home-helps for personal care (Activities of Daily Living support) and domestic tasks (Instrumental Activities of Daily Living support), bathing services, the loan of devices such as wheelchairs, home alterations (putting in ramps, hand-rails, and so on) and nursing homes were transferred from social services to LTCI. Two-fifths of the hospital LTC beds, all HFE beds, most visiting nurse and visiting rehabilitation services, and "medical management" (supervision of care by doctors) were transferred from health insurance to LTCI. Adult day care and temporary respite stays in institutional settings, which had been available from both sectors, were transferred to LTCI but were not unified and continued to maintain different staffing requirements. Doctors' services continued to be paid for in the same way as prior to the implementation of LTCI.[3]

[2] Some health-care services were also included in the Gold Plan, such as HFE and visiting nurse services, but, unlike social services, they were funded only for their capital costs, and their operating costs were paid by health insurance.

[3] On a fee-for-service basis in community care and in nursing homes by health insurance, and included in the per diem inclusive payment in hospital LTC beds and HFE by the LTCI.

There are no cash benefits for family carers, partly because these were opposed by feminist groups who claimed that their provision would further increase the social pressure to provide care for their in-laws.

Access to services became an entitlement, regardless of income or amount of family support available. After eligibility has been determined, the individual can go to any certified care management agency for community care and be covered for LTCI services up to the amount set for each level, which varies from 49,700 yen to 358,300 Yen per month. These amounts were derived from model care plans designed for each level by a government expert committee, and then multiplying the unit price of each service by the number of times it would be provided. The care manager agencies were newly created for the LTCI and virtually all were established by service providers. A licence for care managers was also newly created so that nurses and others working in the LTC field could easily become qualified.[4] The fact that provider agencies are dually registered as care planning agencies could lead to a conflict of interests, as they are able to draw plans that consist only of the services they could deliver themselves.[5] However, those who want visiting nurse service would be likely to go to a care manager agency that is dually certified as a visiting nurse station, while others who want IADL support service would go to one dually certified as a home-help agency. It should be noted that the client may ask for the care plan to be changed and, if dissatisfied, go to another agency.

After the care plan is drawn up based on the assessment of needs and client preferences, provider agencies are contracted and services delivered. In principle, anyone who prefers institutional care may go to any facility and will be admitted if a bed is available, with the exception of those requiring the lowest level of care, who are only eligible for community services. In place of means testing with a sliding scale of payment for social services and, at the time of LTCI implementation, a small flat payment for health care, a 10 per cent co-payment was introduced, which must be paid for all services except that of the

[4] Those who have had five or more years of experience are allowed to sit the examination; after passing, they are required to attend a 32-hour training course. As of 2005, 350,000 have received licences.

[5] Some of the agencies were also initially delegated the task of assessing eligibility using the 84 item form. However, this practice has been gradually phased out. From 2006, care planning agencies that contract most of the services to one provider agency have their fee reduced.

care manager.[6] After services have been provided, billing is made to the insurer and to the client on a calendar month basis, according to the prices and rules set by the government. For-profit and non-profit providers were allowed to contract with individual clients for home and community-based services (but not for institutional care settings), while local governments divested themselves of the responsibility of directly providing care.

In contrast to the expansion and improved access in community care, institutional care remained largely untouched by the implementation of the LTCI. They have maintained their different levels of staffing and reimbursement, and there was no system of triaging patients among the three types of LTCI facilities. Although the numbers of SHAs and HFEs increased, they could not match the growth in demand. In particular, the implementation of the LTCI led to the lengthening of waiting lists for the SHAs, because admissions were no longer triaged by the municipal social welfare offices. To meet this demand, the numbers of sheltered housing [*tokutei shisetsu*] and group homes (for those with mild to moderate dementia and officially categorized as "housing") increased tremendously.

### 3.5. *Government's efforts to contain costs*

LTCI expenditures were projected to increase, not only as a consequence of the ageing of society, but also because people would become more aware of their entitlement, and because supply would expand (unlike Germany, there are no cash benefits so that services had to be developed before those eligible could receive any benefits). Thus, the government stated that expenditures would increase from 4.3 trillion Yen in 2000 to 5.5 trillion Yen in 2005 (Ikeda 1997). However, actual expenditure turned out to be 6.8 trillion Yen (1.4 per cent of GDP) in 2005. The number of eligible care recipients has increased from 10 per cent of the elderly aged 65 and over to 16 per cent in these six years, with the greatest increase in the lowest care level (2.3 times), compared with 1.6 times for the highest care level (MHLW 2005).

The government has taken several measures to contain costs. First, the fee schedule for LTCI services was lowered by 2.3 per cent in 2003,

[6] In health insurance, a 10 per cent co-payment was introduced in October 2002, and from April 2003, elderly people with incomes higher than the average income of employees make a 30 per cent co-payment (with catastrophic ceilings).

and again by 2.4 per cent in 2006. Second, in community care, from April 2006, those in the two lowest eligibility levels are restricted to a new programme of "preventive services", consisting of muscle strength training, oral function improvement and dietary consultation provided in adult day centres.[7] Moreover, the drawing up of their care plans is now supervised by "Local Comprehensive Care Centres (LCCC)" [*chiiki hōkatsu shien sentā*], which are either established directly by the municipalities or contracted out to selected agencies. As a result, the provision of IADL support services (particularly house cleaning and so forth) is no longer available to those in the two lightest groups. The ostensible purpose is to prevent further physical decline, for which the provision of such services has been held responsible.

Third, in institutional care, whereas previously only the cost of food had been excluded from benefits, from October 2005, some, but not all, of the hotel costs must be paid. This would amount to an increase in out-of-pocket expenses for nursing home residents from about 56,000 yen per month to about 81,000 yen in a regular room with four beds, and 104,000 yen with the new surcharge for a single room. Those with low incomes are charged lower amounts, depending on their level of income, and those at the lowest level will not see any increase, the balance being paid by LTCI. This will have the effect of decreasing the disparity between "institutions" and the "housing" type of care.

Finally, the government announced that the number of hospital LTC beds will be decreased from the present 380,000 beds to 150,000 beds by the end of fiscal year 2011. All of the 130,000 beds covered by the LTCI (which are the most expensive type of institutional care within LTCI) will be abolished and encouraged to convert to HFEs or sheltered housing. In addition, the 100,000 beds covered by health insurance will be reduced by the introduction of a new payment mechanism in July 2006 (MHLW 2006b). Under this system, those grouped in the lowest of the three medical complexity groups will be paid only a third of the amount of the highest group, which will make their continued hospitalisation financially unviable to the hospitals. Thus, the door that had been opened to hospital admissions for social reasons in 1973 will finally be closed forty years later.

[7] The lightest level will only be eligible for preventive services. A secondary algorithm will separate out those in the second from lightest level into a preventive service group (about two thirds), and the rest (those with dementia and so forth) who will not be affected by this change.

### 3.6. *Future challenges for long-term care provision*

The government predicts that the number of elderly people certified to be eligible for LTCI benefits will increase from the 2004 level of 4.1 million to 6.4 million in 2014 as the population ages. However, with the implementation of the "preventive services", this number is expected to be reduced by 0.4 million to 6 million (MHLW 2004b). Whether these reductions can be realized remains to be seen. More radical efforts are likely be needed in order to contain LTCI expenditures within a fiscally sustainable level in the future. On the benefits side, the payment of accommodation costs should be made in full, with the balance paid by public assistance for those with low incomes, not financed by the LTCI. On the revenue side, premiums should be raised from those in the 20–39 age range. However, in order to do so, the eligibility algorithm must be revised and the benefit package redesigned in order to meet the needs of the non-elderly disabled population. Whether there is the political will to implement what is economically sustainable is the future challenge.

## 4. Closing Remarks

Policy cannot be written on a blank canvas, least of all the delivery of health services. In retrospect, it could be said that the following decisions played a crucial role in determining the system's present structure, although few immediate repercussions at the time that they were made. The first was the decision to initially concentrate available resources for medical education into one university. The second was the decision to formally recognize only Western medicine, which led to the closing of the door to the development of parallel schools of Chinese medicine. The third was the decision to open the door to the use of hospitals as de facto nursing homes by providing free medical care to elderly people. The fourth was the decision to legislate LTCI which established LTC as an entitlement and led to the development of home and community services. Whether the recent policy initiatives to contain costs in health insurance and LTCI will turn out to be successful or not remains to be seen. However, it is clear that providers will be increasingly caught between the rising demands of the ageing society and the fiscal limitations of, at best, a moderately growing economy. At the same time, given their past record, it is likely that most will manage to adapt successfully to changes in government policy.

## References


Campbell, John C. and Naoki Ikegami (1998): *The Art of Balance in Health Policy—Maintaining Japan's Low-cost, Egalitarian System*. Cambridge: Cambridge University Press.

—— (2000): Long-term care insurance comes to Japan. In: *Health Affairs*, 19 (1), pp. 26–39.

Ikeda, Shōzō (1997): Kaigo hoken no nokosareta mondai [Remaining problems in long-term care insurance]. In: Sato, Susumu and Masateru Kawano (eds.): *Kaigo hokenhō*. Tokyo: Hōritsu Bunkasha, pp. 225–250.

Ikegami, Naoki (1995a): Economic aspects of doctor-patient relationship in Japan. In: Kawakita, Yoshio, Shizu Sakai and Yasuo Otsuka (eds.): *History of the Doctor-Patient Relationship*. Tokyo: Ishiyaku EuroAmerica, Inc., pp. 131–140.

—— (1995b): Iryō kikan no kozoteki yōin to shinryo tokusei narabini sono hiyō kanren no nichibei hikaku [US and Japan comparison on structural factors, practice characteristics and related costs of medical facilities]. In: *Herusu risāchi wa iryō ni dō kōken suru ka*. Tokyo: Pfizer Health Research Foundation, pp. 24–27.

—— (2006): Should providers be allowed to extra-bill for uncovered services? Debate, resolution and sequel in Japan. In: *Journal of Health Politics, Policy and Law* 31(6), pp. 1129–1149.

Ikegami, Naoki and John C. Campbell (1999): Health care reform in Japan: The virtues of muddling through. In: *Health Affairs*, 18 (3), pp. 56–75.

—— (2004): Japan's health care system: Containing costs and attempting reform. In: *Health Affairs*, 23 (3), pp. 26–36.

Ikegami, Naoki and Shunya Ikeda (1996): Waiting lists in Japanese hospitals. In: Ikegami, Naoki and John C. Campbell (eds.): *Containing Health Care Costs in Japan*. Ann Arbor: Michigan University Press, pp. 176–183.

Ikezaki, Sumie, Yumiko Hoshishiba, Hiroshi Sakamaki and Naoki Ikegami (2005): Kaigo rōjin hoken shisetsu ni okeru zaitaku fukki ni kan suru shisetsu yōin to riyōsha yōin no bunseki (Analysis of facilities and user factors related to returning home in health service facilities for the elderly defined by long-term care insurance). In: *Byōin kanri* 43 (1), pp. 9–21.

Kōsei Tōkei Kyōkai (1996, 2001): *Kōsei no shihyō* [Health and welfare statistics], 43 (12), p. 199; 48 (12), p. 194.

MHW (Ministry of Health and Welfare (1975): *1973 Kanja chōsa* [Patient survey 1973]. Tokyo: Kōsei Tōkei Kyōkai.

—— (1992): *1990 Kanja chōsa* [Patient survey 1990]. Tokyo: Kōsei Tōkei Kyōkai.

MHLW (Ministry of Health, Labour and Welfare) (2001): *1999 Shakaifukushi shisetsuto chōsa* [Survey of social welfare facilities]. Tokyo: Kōsei Tōkei Kyōkai.

—— (2004a): *2004 Iryō shisetsu chōsa, byōin hōkoku* [Survey of medical institutions, report from hospitals]. Tokyo: Kōsei Tōkei Kyōkai, pp. 264, 288.

—— (2004b): *Kaigohoken seido ni okeru Dai-1 gō hokenryō oyobi kyūfu no mitoshi* [Health insurance premium levels of the first category and future benefit expenditures. MHLW Oct 21, 2004] http://www.mhlw.go.jp/houdou/2004/10/h1021-5.html (found 1 September 2006).

—— (2005): *Kaigo hoken seido kaikaku no saishin dōkō* [Most recent trends in LTCI]. Tokyo: MHLW.

—— (2006a): *2004 Kaigo service shisetsu, jigyo chōsa* [Survey of LTCI institutions and facilities]. Tokyo: Kōsei Tōkei Kyōkai, pp. 132, 208.

—— (2006b): *Ryoyō byōshō ni kan suru setsumeikai shiryō* [Debriefing meeting information for the LTC beds]. Tokyo: MHLW.

OECD (2005): *OECD Health Data 2005*. CD-ROM.

Ogawa, Eiji (1998): Homu herupu rōdō no arubeki sugata to kaikaku an [The preferred form of home help work and reform proposals]. In: Kawai, Katusyoshi (ed.): *Homu herupu no kōteki sekinin o kangaeru*. Tokyo: Akebi Shobō, pp. 80–116.

CHAPTER FIFTY-NINE

# GUARDIANSHIP FOR ADULTS

Makoto Arai

## 1. Introduction

At present, Japan is experiencing rapid ageing of its population and a steep decline in the number of children. In addition, the growing ranks of demented senior citizens and single-member or couple-only elderly families have become challenges urgently demanding effective countermeasures.

Against this background, a public long-term care insurance plan was launched in April 2000 which gives in principle all frail elderly citizens above 65 a legal right to receive long-term care benefits if their health deteriorates. If the need arises for services that are to be provided under this insurance, patients must first file an application for recognition of need and must then, once benefits have been granted, enter into a service contract. However, people suffering from senile dementia, impaired intelligence, or other mental disorders lack sufficient capacity of judgement and are therefore often unable to take such measures themselves. In these cases, a system of legal support must be in place to assist them to take the necessary steps to obtain long-term care insurance services. This chapter provides an overview of Japan's system of legal support before and after the introduction of a new guardianship system for adults in 1999 and discusses some of the remaining challenges.

## 2. Background

Until 1999, the Japanese Civil Code provided protection for people suffering from senile dementia, impaired intelligence or other mental disorders through guardianships or curatorships based on the concepts of incompetency and quasi-incompetency. It was pointed out long ago, however, that these protective arrangements were in many respects difficult to use (Arai 1990: 117–121). In addition, with the rapid greying of Japanese society and the heightening concern over the welfare of people with impaired intelligence or mental disorders, social needs gradually increased to the point that an overhaul of the traditional system into a more flexible and user-friendly system became necessary. In fact, the number of senile elderly people is estimated at 1.89 million today, but is expected to rise to about 3.37 million by 2035 (Kōreisha Kaigo Kenkyūkai 2003).

In reaction to these challenges Japan introduced a new system of voluntary guardianship in 1999.[1] The legislative reform to create a new system of guardianship for adults has been driven by both practical and ideological considerations. On the practical front, a more flexible system was needed that would make it easier for the elderly and mentally incapacitated to use. On the ideological front, there was a need to harmonize the traditional ideal of protection with new concepts such a respect for the autonomy of the principal, effective use of his or her mental capacity, and maximum normalization of their lives.

Before this reform, the Civil Code included a guardianship system based on incompetency and quasi-incompetency, corresponding to the statutory guardianship system discussed below. Under these protective arrangements, a guardianship commenced when a person in a persistent state of mental disorder was found to be incompetent by a family court and was placed under the care of a guardian. A guardian was authorized to revoke legal acts, such as contracts, made by the incompetent person (power of revocation), and to engage in legal acts on behalf of the principal (power of representation). The guardian thus undertook to supplement the principal's capacity of judgement and to protect his or her rights and interests by exercising those powers.

[1] The new system of guardianship for adults was introduced in Japan as a result of the following four laws, which were enacted on December 1, 1999, and officially published on the eighth day of that month: (1) The Law concerning Partial Amendment of the Civil Code (*Minpō no ichibu wo kaisei suru hōritsu*) (Law No. 149 of 1999); (2) The Law concerning Voluntary Guardianship Contracts (*Nini kōken keiyaku ni kan suru hōritsu*) (Law No. 150 of 1999); (3) The Law concerning Establishment of Legal Frameworks in Conjunction with the Enforcement of the Law concerning Partial Amendment of the Civil Code (*Minpō no ichibu wo kaisei suru hōritsu no shikō ni tomonau kankei hōritsu no seibito ni kan suru hōritsu*) (Law No. 151 of 1999); and (4) The Law concerning Registration of Guardianships, etc. (*Kōken tōkito ni kan suru hōritsu*) (Law No. 152 of 1999). These laws went into effect on April 1, 2000.

The arrangement based on quasi-incompetency operated similarly. A curatorship commenced when a family court found a person to be feeble-minded or a spendthrift and appointed a person to act as curator for him or her. Under this arrangement, the principal had to obtain the curator's consent before engaging in any important legal act designated in the Civil Code, and any such act made without such consent was revocable. With this power, a curator undertook to supplement the principal's decision-making capacity and to protect his or her rights and interests by deciding whether to consent to important legal acts intended by the principal that might prove adverse to his or her interests. Unlike a guardian, however, a curator has neither the power of revocation nor the power of representation.

It can hardly be said that the arrangements based on incompetency and quasi-incompetency were fully utilized. In 1998, for example, court proceedings that included rulings for incompetency and those for rescissions thereof totalled 1,709 across Japan. In that same year, rulings for quasi-incompetency and rescissions thereof totalled only 251.

Under these circumstances, there were many people who pointed out problems with the system based on competency and quasi-incompetency (Arai 1990: 117–121). Generally speaking, the system, introduced in 1898 and based on these two concepts, had undergone virtually no reform for almost 100 years. And from the perspective of a century later, that system put too much emphasis on the protection of principals, and the resultant lack of flexibility made it difficult to use on a practical level. In this sense, criticism that the system lacked modern ideals, such as respect for a principal's wishes, his or her autonomy, and maximum normalization of disabled principals' lives, appears to be accurate. Legislative reform was the answer to such criticism.

Discussions on the reform of the Guardianship Law in Japan were also strongly influenced by recent developments in European countries and the United States, where laws concerning guardianship for adults have been amended in quick succession.

In France, the 1968 amendment of the Civil Code abolished the system based on incompetency and quasi-incompetency and introduced a new system comprising three protective devices: guardianship (Tutelle), curatorship (Curatelle), and court protection (Sauvegarde de Justice). Likewise, in the Canadian province of Quebec, an amendment to the Civil Code replaced the traditional system based on incompetency and quasi-incompetency with three-stage protection through guardianship (*Tutelle*), curatorship (*Curatelle*), and Advisership (*Conseiller*). Similarly, Austria, through a 1983 amendment of the Civil Code based on the Custodian Law (*Sachwalterrecht*), abolished its system based on incompetency and quasi-incompetency and introduced a new system granting a court-appointed custodian (*Sachwalter*) three-stage authority to handle the principal's affairs: (a) in their entirety, (b) within certain limits, and (c) case by case. In Germany, too, an amendment to the Civil Code by the 1990 Caretaking Law (*Betreuungsrecht*) replaced the incompetency-based system with a new system in which a court appoints a caretaker (*Betreuer*) with authority granted case by case depending on the circumstances.

These developments in the continental-law countries invariably featured a review of the system based on incompetency and quasi-incompetency and focused on the creation of a flexible, user-friendly system of guardianship for adults. Moreover, all of these developments aimed to harmonize the traditional ideal of protection of the principal with such new concepts as respect for his or her autonomy and the aim that his or her life should be as normal as possible. The system reform carried out in Japan can be said to have followed these international trends (Arai 1990: 121–123).

Anglo-American law countries, for example, England and Wales, the United States, Canada, and Australia, have moved a step further in regard to such reforms. They have adopted special legislation to introduce an enduring power of attorney, which enables a principal to make a contract with a trusted guardian, providing for the handling of the principal's affairs before his or her mental capacity deteriorates. Such legislation includes the Enduring Powers of Attorney Act (1985) in England and Wales; the Uniform Durable Power of Attorney Act (1979) in the United States, and local versions of it in various states that have adopted its principles; the Uniform Powers of Attorney Act (1978) in Canada, and local versions in the provinces that have adopted its principles.

Among these jurisdictions, England and Wales, and the Canadian province of Alberta (Powers of Attorney Act, 1991) authorize the court to supervise a guardian-attorney's performance within certain limits after the principal has lost his or her competency. Also noteworthy in this respect is the 1997 amendment to the Uniform Guardianship and Protective Proceedings Act in the United States.

These laws invariably emphasize respect for the autonomy of the principal. Based on such a premise, the laws aim to establish a legal framework that empowers the principal to decide by a contract how his or her affairs should be handled by a guardian. The system of voluntary guardianship newly introduced in Japan follows in the footsteps of these laws.

Japan's legislative reform has been undertaken in light of developments at home and abroad as described above. The reform has focused on harmonizing the traditional ideal of protection of the weak with new concepts such as respect for a person's autonomy, effective use of one's remaining capacity, and enabling a person to live as normal a life as possible. Thus, the new guardianship-for-adult system constitutes a sweeping reform. It has replaced the traditional system based on incompetency and quasi-incompetency with a new system comprising adviserships, curatorships, and guardianships. At the same time, the new system introduces voluntary guardianships. It also establishes a guardianship registration procedure in place of entries in the family register, as was practised in the past.

## 3. The Legislative Reform Process

The reform process started in June 1995, when the Legislative Council, an advisory panel to the Minister of Justice, officially adopted a review of guardianship for adults for consideration by its Civil Code Committee. As a follow-up to this decision, a guardianship-for-adults study group was established within the Civil Affairs Bureau of the Ministry of Justice in preparation for the committee's deliberations. The study group worked on the subject until July 1997, and in September of that year it submitted its report, entitled *Study Group Report on Guardianship for Adults (Seinen kōken mondai kenkyūkai hōkokusho)*, to the Civil Code Committee.

Based on this report, the Civil Code Committee established the Subcommittee on Guardianship for Adults. This group energetically started its work in October of 1997 and compiled its results as a draft of reform recommendations. The Civil Code Committee approved the draft recommendations in April 1998 and invited comments from various concerned parties. The Subcommittee on Guardianship for Adults continued its study, taking into consideration many comments obtained through the consultation process, and then finalized its formal recommendations for reform. These recommendations were approved by the Civil Code Committee in January 1999. In February of that year, the recommendations were adopted as an official reform proposal of the Legislative Council and were immediately presented to the Minister of Justice.

Based on this reform proposal, the Civil Affairs Bureau of the Ministry of Justice prepared the four bills mentioned above, and on March 15, 1999, submitted them to the 145th Diet. These bills were unanimously approved by the House of Representatives on July 6, 1999, and were immediately forwarded to the House of Councillors, but the scheduled term of the 145th Diet expired without the House of Councillors completing its deliberations on the bills. However, in the 146th Diet, the bills were unanimously approved by the House of Councillors on November 24, 1999 and were then sent back to the House of Representatives, where they were once again approved unanimously on December 1.

## 4. The New System of Guardianship for Adults: An Overview

### 4.1. *Statutory guardianship and voluntary guardianship*

The new system of guardianship for adults broadly consists of statutory guardianship and voluntary guardianship. Of these, a statutory guardianship is imposed through legal action and takes the form of an advisership, curatorship, or guardianship. Of these arrangements, advisership is a new device, while guardianships and curatorships are the products of a major overhaul of the traditional system based on incompetency and quasi-incompetency. Under statutory guardianship, if the court deems that a principal has become insufficiently capable of making sound judgments, the court appoints an adviser, curator, or guardian (hereafter collectively referred to as "statutory guardian") based on the provisions of law, and grants powers as necessary to that protective agent. This reform of statutory guardianship has been based on the Law concerning the Partial Amendment of the Civil Code (listed as (1) in footnote 1). In addition, a network of relevant laws that have become necessary in conjunction with this reform has been established, based on the Law concerning the Establishment of Legal Frameworks in conjunction with enforcement of the Law concerning the Partial Amendment of the Civil Code (listed as (3) in footnote 1).

In contrast, voluntary guardianship is a contract-based protective arrangement introduced by this reform. As such, its use is optional. Any person with sufficient capacity to make judgements may appoint a voluntary guardian by contract in preparation for an eventual loss of full capacity and may give powers to the guardian as desired. This arrangement was created by the Law concerning Voluntary Guardianship (listed as (2) in footnote 1).

As mentioned above, voluntary guardianship respects as much as possible the autonomy of a principal and thus is compatible with the principle of private autonomy. Therefore, in principle, voluntary guardianship is applied in preference to statutory guardianship. The latter is reserved for situations where the principal does not opt for voluntary guardianship or where voluntary guardianship does not fully protect the principal's rights and interests.

### 4.2. *Registration*

The recent reform has created a new registration system for both statutory guardianship and voluntary guardianship. The traditional method of proclamation of guardianship, in which a guardian's name was entered in the family register pursuant to the provisions of the Family Registration Law, has been abolished. This change was based on the Law concerning the Registration of Guardianships (listed as (4) in footnote 1).

### 4.3. *Major changes*

The first of the five major changes surrounding the Adult Guardianship Law is the introduction of the voluntary guardianship system, a topic that is the subject of considerable attention.

The voluntary guardianship system is one that seeks to respect the right to self-determination. First of all, the principal and the voluntary guardian conclude a contract by signing the notarized documents. The principals choose their guardian whilst still competent, and determine the details of the guardianship of their own volition. In addition to the management of financial matters, livelihood care issues (such as securing medical treatment, housing, hospitalization, care, sustenance, education and rehabilitation) are decided upon, and subsequently registered. The creation of such a registration system means that courts of law will be able to verify the facts of a case if anybody petitions for statutory guardianship at a later stage.

A supervisor is also appointed in order to protect the principal. The supervisor is appointed by a family court, and the supervisor oversees the voluntary guardian at all times. The voluntary guardian is dismissed by a family court in the event that a problem arises. The protection of the principal is the purpose of the processes, from the family court to the voluntary guardian. The voluntary guardianship system is one that seeks to ensure not only self-determination but also the protection of the principal.

Under the contemporary legal code, it was difficult to assure the self-determination of principals who had lost their mental capacity, even with the application of the entire civil law system, including the will and testament system. The voluntary guardianship system involves a contract based on notarized documents, registration, and the surveillance of improprieties. It involves a great deal of work, but a system such as this is absolutely essential.

The voluntary guardianship system was introduced to Japan in a modified version of the Enduring Powers of Attorney Act of England and Wales.

The second major change brought about by the Adult Guardianship Law is that it reformed the two types of statutory guardianship that had hitherto existed, incompetence and semi-incompetence, turned these into guardianship and curatorship, and added the new form of advisership. The purpose of this is to make it a very user-friendly system by enabling people—even those whose mental capacity is relatively unimpaired—to freely, and with no reason for disqualification, choose the content and scope of the adviser's powers either through their own petitioning or after an agreement is reached between both parties. In addition to the reform of the previous system, the establishment of a new system capable of dealing with minor degrees of dementia, mental disabilities or psychiatric disorder is another major point.

The third major change concerns the enrichment of the guardianship system. Firstly, until now only individuals were allowed to become guardians or curators. Now it is possible for bodies such as social welfare services to assume these roles. Secondly, a provision that imposes the obligation to take the principal's livelihood into consideration during guardianship, curatorship, advisership and voluntary guardianship was added, in order to emphasize the protection of principals' livelihoods.

Thirdly, the posts of curatorship supervisor, advisership supervisor, and voluntary guardianship supervisor were created in addition to the solitary supervisor post that originally existed.

The fourth major change is the abolition of the practice of indicating in the family register that a person is incapacitated or semi-incapacitated, and the introduction of the registration of adult guardianship.

The fifth and final major change is that, in addition to the principal, the principal's spouse and people within the fourth degree of consanguinity, the right of petition was conferred upon the mayor of the village, town or city where the principal resides. It is hoped that this will assure the protection of people living on their own.

## 5. The System of Guardianship for Adults: An Assessment after Five Years

The new system of guardianship for adults has now been in operation for over five years. The development in the number of cases in the different legal categories can be seen in Table 1.

How can we interpret these numbers? I would first like to take a look at voluntary guardianship, because I believe that this area shows the most notable qualities of the Adult Guardianship Law. The number of voluntary guardianship supervisors actually appointed over the past five years was 467. Though this figure is small, the number of voluntary guardianship contracts concluded and registered reached 10,034. Since the purpose of the voluntary guardianship system is to prepare for the impairment or loss of the principal's mental capacities and thereby provide them with peace of mind, the conclusion of voluntary guardianship contracts is of greater importance than the appointment of supervisors. In this sense, the figure of 10,034 voluntary guardianship contracts concluded is a considerable number. When one considers that 42,405 registrations were made in the 11 or so years after the introduction of the Enduring Powers of Attorney Act in England and Wales in 1985, a law that can be regarded as having engendered Japan's voluntary guardianship legislation, there can be little doubt that the voluntary guardianship system needs to be more widely disseminated and more firmly established.

Despite advisership being another pillar of the new system for statutory guardianship, it has failed to catch on. Of the 50,058 cases requesting statutory guardianship that were judged, only 2,648 adviserships

Table 1. Number of Cases under the New System of Guardianship for Adults.

| | Statutory guardianship Number of cases accepted | Curatorship Number of cases accepted | Advisership Number of cases accepted | Voluntary guardianship contracts concluded and registered | Appointment of supervisors adjudicated |
|---|---|---|---|---|---|
| 2000 | 2,980 | 240 | 272 | 801 | 20 |
| 2001 | 6,630 | 713 | 472 | 1,106 | 67 |
| 2002 | 8,966 | 962 | 550 | 1,801 | 83 |
| 2003 | 12,023 | 1,316 | 670 | 2,521 | 147 |
| 2004 | 12,309 | 1,271 | 684 | 3,805 | 150 |
| Total | 42,908 | 4,502 | 2,648 | 10,034 | 467 |

Source: Saikō Saibansho Jimu Sōmukyoku Kateikyoku 2000–2004.

were approved. This is nothing less than a deviation from the basic philosophy of the Adult Guardianship Law.

Regarding petitions, the number filed by municipal mayors over the past five years was 1,342, just 1.9 per cent of the total figure. With a track record like this, one can hardly say that the aim of conferring the right of petition to mayors by law has been met. The purpose of the law was to secure appropriate protection for senile, mentally disabled and psychiatrically ill people without any relatives, by petitioning for judgement on the commencement of statutory guardianship swiftly, appropriately, and in line with information gained from social and welfare workers.

The prime motive for petitioning was to deal with the management of financial matters (an average of 61 per cent of the cases over the past five years), followed by livelihood protection (18 per cent over the same period). The Long-term Care Insurance System was introduced at the same time as the Adult Guardianship Law, in April 2000. Those wishing to enjoy the benefits of the long-term care insurance system have to conclude a contract. The number of demented elderly people whose main motive was concluding a long-term care insurance contract was extremely low, just 3 per cent annually on average over a five-year period.

The Adult Guardianship Law also seeks to provide improved support for legal actions concerning livelihood protection. The noticeable rise in the amount of petitions pertaining not only to the management of financial affairs, but also to livelihood protection, is gaining attention. However, I feel that the combined figure of 21 per cent for livelihood protection and long-term care insurance contracts is still extremely low. We clearly need to do more to spread knowledge about the importance of livelihood protection in the Adult Guardianship Law.

A look at the relationship between adult guardians and their principals suggests that, although an overwhelming percentage of those chosen as guardians are relatives of the principal, attention is being given to the fact that this percentage is gradually declining, falling from 90 per cent in 2000 to 86 per cent in 2001, 84 per cent in 2002, 83 per cent in 2003, and 80 per cent in 2004. Likewise, the number of third party guardianship chosen from outside the principal's family has grown steadily from 10 per cent in 2000 to 14 per cent in 2001, 16 per cent in 2002, 17 per cent in 2003, and 20 per cent in 2004. Considering that the Adult Guardianship Law actively encourages the use of third party guardians this upward trend is likely to accelerate.

## 6. Conclusion and Outlook

In summary, although the track record of the Adult Guardianship Law over its first five years shows that the concept of the new system is steadily taking root in Japanese society, it must be said that the number of people using the system is very small considering that there are thought to be 1.89 million senile elderly people in Japan. As mentioned already, the new Adult Guardianship Law came into force at the same time as the Long-term care insurance system in 2000. The intention was that the Adult Guardianship Law would offer care insurance services for use by elderly people with declining mental competence. But the reality is that the system is not being used in this way. Reasons for this low level of use include the public's lack of awareness of contracts, and the cumbersome red tape encountered when seeking to use the Adult Guardianship Law (Akanuma 2003: 71–72, 78–79). Moreover, the notion that adult guardianship is a "domestic" matter still lingers in the law itself; we need to foster the idea that adult guardianship is an issue for the whole of society.

Two fresh initiatives aiming to expand the use of the Adult Guardianship Law started in April 2006. Firstly, the Long-term care insurance law was amended, and the decision was taken to establish regional comprehensive support centres at 5,000 locations across the country. These centres will offer a comprehensive regional care system, a mechanism which provides a variety of continuous and comprehensive care service-oriented support, on an individual basis and according to the situation and changing needs of each elderly person. One of the tasks of these centres is spreading knowledge about the Adult Guardianship Law.

Secondly, the Law for the Prevention of Abuse of the Elderly (*Kōreisha Gyakutai bōshi-hō*) came into force in 2006. The law clearly defines abuse of the elderly, and stipulates that its prevention is the responsibility of both national and local government bodies, which should encourage utilization of the Adult Guardianship Law.

Thus, with the establishment of the regional comprehensive support centres and the arrival of the Law for the Prevention of Abuse of the Elderly, Japan's Adult Guardianship Law has entered a new phase. It remains to be seen whether these initiatives can have an impact on the utilization of the various forms of adult guardianship in Japan.

## References


Akanuma, Yasuhiro (2003): Seinen kōken seido kaisei e no teigen [Proposal for a reform of the legal guardianship system]. In: *Jiyū to seigi* 54, 11, pp. 71–72, 78–79.

Arai, Makoto (1990): *Zaisan kanri seido to minpō, shintaku-hō* [Asset administration system and the Civil Code and trust law]. Tokyo: Yūhikaku.

—— (2000): *Seinen kōken—hōritsu no kaisetsu to katsuyō no hōhō* [Adult guardianship—Explanation of the law and ways of utilization]. Tokyo: Yūhikaku.

Arai, Makoto, Yasuhiro Akanuma and Masao Ōnuki (eds.)(2006): *Seinen kōken seido—hō no riron to jimu* [Adult guardianship system—theory and practice of the law]. Tokyo: Yūhikaku.

Kobayashi, Akihiro and Tasuke Daimon (eds.) (2000): *Seinen kōken seido no kaisetsu* [An explanation of the adult guardianship system]. Tokyo: Monzai.

Kobayashi, Akihiro and Ichirō Ōtaka (eds.) (2006): *Wakariyasui seinen kōken seido* [An easy to understand adult guardianship system]. Tokyo: Yūhikaku.

Kōreisha Kaigo Kenkyūkai (2003): *2015-nen no kōreisha kaigo: kōreisha no songen wo sasaeru kea no kakuritsu ni mukete* [Elderly care in the year 2015: Towards a care system that respects the dignity of the elderly]. Tokyo: Hōken.

Saikō Saibansho Jimu Sōmukyoku Kateikyoku (2000–2004): *Seinen kōken kanren jiken no gaikyō* [General situation of cases concerning adult guardianship]. Tokyo: Saikō Saibansho Jimu Sōmukyoku Kateikyoku.

CHAPTER SIXTY

# THE PUBLIC HEALTH-CARE SYSTEM—A FINANCIAL PERSPECTIVE

Tetsuo Fukawa

Most health-care services in Japan are provided through the public health insurance system. The total population has been covered by public health insurance since 1961, but there are different schemes for employees and the self-employed in terms of contributions, national subsidy and benefit levels. There is also a special programme for the elderly which reduces patient cost sharing greatly. Although the private sector is important in delivering health-care services and maintaining public health, it only plays a minor role in terms of financing.

Japan enjoys the lowest infant mortality rate and the longest life expectancy in the world. Furthermore, the country's public health expenditure is only 6 or 7 per cent of GDP, and the health-care system appears to be functioning quite well. We should be careful, however, when drawing any conclusions from this, because infant mortality rate and life expectancy at birth are no longer proper indicators for an evaluation of a health-care system. Japan's health-care delivery system and patterns of patient flow indicate many problems, such as quality issues and the overuse of pharmaceuticals.

In this chapter,[1] we will describe the historical development of the public health-care system and evaluate problems up to the present day. We will then discuss current and future reforms from a financial perspective.

## 1. History of the Health Insurance System in Japan

### 1.1. *Until universal coverage*

Japan's public health insurance for private sector employees was introduced by the Health Insurance Law of 1922; implementation was

[1] This paper is based on Fukawa (2002).

delayed until 1927 because of the Great Kantō Earthquake of 1923. Prior to this, there were only a few private companies offering health insurance to their employees, and hardly any programmes had lived up to the Factory Law of 1911, according to which an employer had to provide assistance in case of a worker's injury or illness. The Health Insurance Law was enacted to protect workers, but its coverage was partial and its benefits were not comprehensive.

The health insurance system faced a financial crisis shortly after its establishment in 1929 resulting from the global Great Depression, but it gradually regained financial stability as the nation's economy started to grow again. The Ministry of Health and Welfare was established in 1938, and regional-based National Health Insurance was introduced in the same year.

After World War II, social security systems, including health insurance, were introduced and improved one after another. With the introduction of the Labour Standard Law and the Workers' Accident Compensation Law in 1947, health-care provision for work-related illnesses and injuries was excluded from the insurance coverage. In 1948, the National Public Service Mutual Aid Association Law was established, and various other insurance schemes for employed persons were institutionalized in the following years. In 1954, the central government set aside one billion yen to subsidize government-managed health insurance. The goal of universal public health insurance coverage was finally attained in 1961.

### 1.2. *Improvement of benefit levels in the 1960s and 1970s*

The public health insurance system took firm hold in the 1960s, and benefit levels were improved throughout the 1970s. When a health insurance system for the entire population was established in 1961, the benefits covered 100 per cent of the costs for insured persons and 50 per cent for their dependants through employer-based insurance schemes, while the National Health Insurance covered 50 per cent for both the head of a household and its members. Thereafter, these benefit levels were gradually improved and raised to 70 per cent for the subscribers of the National Health Insurance and the dependants of employer-based insurance in 1968 and 1973 respectively. Furthermore, the benefit level of inpatient care for dependants of those subscribing to employer-based health insurance was raised from 70 to 80 per cent in 1980.

A number of important measures were introduced in 1973. The 30 per cent patient cost sharing for the elderly aged 70 and over was paid out of public funds, with the implementation of a so-called Free Health Service System for the Elderly in this year. A ceiling on patient cost sharing was introduced for the first time in 1973, and whenever the monthly out-of-pocket amount exceeded the ceiling, the balance was paid back to the patient by the insurers. In addition, the public pension insurance was substantially improved by raising the benefit levels and by introducing a cost-of-living adjustment in line with the consumer price index increase. Therefore, the 1973 social security reform is remembered as an epoch-making move towards a welfare state (see Table 1).

As a result of the extended access to health services, health expenditures increased by double digit percentage points every year. After the first oil crisis of 1973–74, the Japanese economy changed from high to stable growth. Nevertheless, health expenditure kept on increasing in the latter half of the 1970s, owing to measures such as the Free Health Service System for the Elderly and an increased benefit level for younger people.

### 1.3. *Reforms in the 1980s and 1990s: cost-containment and pursuing quality*

In circumstances dominated by an ageing population and a mounting need to reduce the budget deficit, the containment of health expenditures was regarded as a matter of urgency, and the public health insurance system underwent several reforms in the 1980s. First, the Health Service Programme for the Elderly (HSE) was created in August 1982 and fully enforced on 1 February 1983. It was designed to spread the burden of health costs for this age group equally among various sickness funds and introduced cost sharing for elderly patients.

Government revised the health insurance system in 1984, which was the second important step in the reform process. The main point of the revision was the introduction of an excess, or 10 per cent cost-sharing to be paid by the insured person under an employer-based insurance. Before the revision, the insured person was granted full benefits for health-care expenses, except for the first visit consultation fee and hospitalization charge.[2] At the same time, a ceiling on total household out-of-pocket costs was introduced to relieve individuals and households affected by high expenditure (before the revision, cost sharing had been

[2] The first visit fee was 800 yen, and the hospitalization charge was 500 yen per day for the first month only.

considered on an individual basis). The 1984 reform also introduced another important measure: in the conventional system, the total costs had been treated as ineligible for insurance coverage whenever advanced technology not covered by health insurance was used. According to the new system, a patient receiving high-technology treatments in specially approved medical facilities is refunded the part corresponding to the conventional health service by the insurance and only pays the balance. This is called a high-cost relief scheme.

A separate programme for retired employees was also created in 1984 within the National Health Insurance System. This programme would transfer money from employer-based funds to the National Health Insurance Fund to help cover the costs of retired employees. The Health Service Programme for the Elderly was amended in 1987 to increase patient cost sharing and to change the method of calculating contributions from sickness funds.

The reformed Health Insurance for the Elderly is focused on the coordination between health-care and long-term care services and on the elimination of inappropriate long-term hospitalization. In December 1989, the Ten-Year Strategy for the Promotion of Health and Welfare for the Elderly, or the "Gold Plan", was formulated to improve underdeveloped long-term care and welfare services for the elderly, with substantial government commitment. It consisted of a large-scale budgetary allocation plan designed to increase both home- and community-based care, as well as facility-based care services, by March 2000. These target figures were revised upwards in December 1994.

The health insurance system was again revised in 1997—an important step toward the reforms of the 2000s. The most important points of the revision were (a) the increase in cost sharing to be paid by the insured person under employer-based insurance from 10 to 20 and eventually to 30 per cent; and (b) the introduction of the patient charge on pharmaceutical costs for outpatient care.[3]

In the mid-1990s, long-term care became one of the highest priority issues in Japan. The Long-term Care Insurance Act was finally passed by the Diet in November 1997 and was implemented in April 2000. The principles underlying this new programme are: universality of coverage (although benefits are available mainly for the elderly); financing

[3] This patient charge was introduced in 1997 for the first time, but terminated in 2000 for those who were eligible to HSE and in 2002 for the non-elderly.

Table 1. History of public health insurance in Japan.

| Year | Health | References |
|---|---|---|
| 1961 | Universal coverage | |
| 1972 | Revision of the Welfare Law for the Elderly (1973)<br>– Free medical care for the elderly | |
| 1973 | Revision of the Health Insurance Law<br>– Improvement of benefit level for families of the insured from 50 per cent to 70 per cent.<br>– Introduction of the upper ceiling for patients' cost-sharing.<br>– National subsidy of 10 per cent of health expenditure for government-managed Health Insurance. | First Year of Welfare State, First Oil Shock |
| 1982 | Law of Health Service Programme for the Elderly (HSE, 1983) | |
| 1983 | | "National burden < 50% of NI" |
| 1984 | Revision of the Health Insurance Law<br>– Ten per cent cost-sharing by the insured.<br>– Relaxation of regulations on high-technology health care.<br>– Introduction of the health care program for retired persons. | |
| 1985 | Revision of the Medical Service Law<br>– Medical plan by prefecture. | |
| 1988 | | Introduction of Consumption Tax (3%) |
| 1989 | Gold Plan | |
| 1990 | Welfare Reform (Wefare by municipalities) | 1.57 Shock (TFR=1.57 in 1989) |
| 1991 | Revision of the Law of HSE<br>– Visiting nurse care service for the elderly<br>– Increase in public funds for nursing care from 30 to 50% | |
| 1992 | Revision of the Medical Service Law.<br>– Classification of hospitals by function | |
| 1994 | Patient charge on inpatient meals<br>New Gold Plan, Angel Plan | Increase in Consumption Tax to 5% (April 1997) |
| 1995 | | The Hanshin Earthquake |
| 1997 | Revision of the Health Insurance Law.<br>– Twenty per cent cost-sharing by the insured.<br>– Introduction of the patient charge on pharmaceutical costs<br>Long-term Care Insurance Law (April 2000) | Administrative Reform Council |
| 1999 | | Economic Strategy Council |

Table 1 (*cont.*)

| Year | Health | References |
|---|---|---|
| 2000 | Healthcare reform<br>– Cost-sharing by elderly patients (70+) from fix amount to 10 %<br>– Increase in the upper ceiling of patient cost-sharing<br>Implimentation of the Long-term Care Insurance | |
| 2001 | | Koizumi Structural Reform |
| 2002 | Healthcare reform<br>– Unification of benefit level to 70 %<br>– Termination of the patient charge on pharmaceutical costs | |
| 2003 | DPC reimbursement system for inpatient care at 82 hospitals | |
| 2006 | Healthcare reform<br>– New Health Insurance for 75+ (April 2008)<br>– Payment of "hotel cost" by long-term inpatient elderly (70+)<br>– Prevention of life-style related diseases | |

through social insurance (although the public fund finances 45 per cent of the cost); freedom of choice for the service users; and reliance on the service market. The main purposes of the programme are to share the burden of caring for the frail elderly among all members of society (in order to lessen the burden upon family caregivers) and to standardize facility-based care services.

### 1.4. *Reforms in the 2000s: Sustainability and "patients first health care"*

The main tool of health-care reforms in the 2000s has been an increase in patient cost sharing, mainly to control health expenditure on the elderly. In 2000, cost sharing for elderly patients (70+) was increased from a fixed amount to 10 per cent of the total cost; the upper ceiling on patient cost sharing in general was also increased. The benefit level was finally unified to 70 per cent for non-elderly patients; eligibility to the Health Service Programme for the Elderly (HSE) was raised from 70 to 75 years in the 2002 reform. The 2006 reform included the decision to create a new health insurance for the elderly aged 75 or over by April 2008 and to target lifestyle-related diseases, especially those linked to obesity. Informed consent and patient choice have been considered important since the reform of the 1990s, and this approach is formulated as "patients first health-care" in the 2006 reform.

## 2. Outline of the Present Health Insurance System

Japan has three major categories of public health programmes: employer-based health insurance, National Health Insurance, and Health Service Programme for the Elderly (see Table 2). The former two categories cover the entire population and there are hundreds of separate sickness funds (or insurers) linked to a person's employer, occupation or geographic location. Each fund provides coverage for a person and his or her dependants. Insured individuals cannot choose a sickness fund. While they are all quite similar in terms of health services and reimbursement procedures, there are systematic differences in the benefits available and in the level of national subsidy. Health Service Programme for the Elderly provides additional benefits to those who qualify; however, this will change in 2008.

### 2.1. *Employer-based insurance*

This category includes Society-managed Health Insurance, Government-managed Health Insurance, and Mutual Aid Associations (see Table 2). Society-managed Health Insurance covered 23.8 per cent of the population in 2005. The average contribution rate accounted for 7.6 per cent of an employee's wage, evenly shared between employer and employee. However, some employers agree to pay more than half of the contributions. The funds receive a small subsidy from the central government for administrative expenses.

Government-managed Health Insurance covers private sector employees who are not covered by Society-managed Health Insurance. The plan is administered by the government agency and insured 28 per cent of the population in 2005. Its premium is fixed at 8.2 per cent of the payroll, divided between employer and employee. While society-based plans may offer extra benefits, the government-managed plan only offers one package. Because its members generally earn less than those in society-managed plans, the central government contributes 13 per cent of the benefit and all administrative costs. Mutual Aid Associations cover public sector employees and insured 7.7 per cent of the population in 2005.

## 2.2. *National Health Insurance*

The National Health Insurance is a community-based health insurance covering those not eligible for employer-based insurance, in particular agricultural workers, self-employed individuals, and retirees, as well as their dependants. In April 2005, there were 3,144 municipal plans, and 166 separate National Health Insurance Associations serving separate categories of craftspeople; 40.4 per cent of the population were enrolled in such schemes in 2005. The services provided are generally equal to those of employer-based insurance, but cash benefits tend to be somewhat more limited. Contributions vary from community to community, based on an individual's income and assets. In the absence of an employer, the central government pays for 43 per cent of the costs under the municipal plans and for 32 to 55 per cent for the craft-based plans.

## 2.3. *Health Service Programme for the Elderly*

The Health Service Programme for the Elderly was introduced in 1983 to spread the burden of providing health for the elderly equally among various sickness funds. Membership is available for those aged 75 and over, as well as for disabled persons aged 65–74. These individuals may be in any fund, although they are most likely to be in the National Health Insurance. In this programme, patient cost sharing is 10 per cent (20 per cent for high income elderly) of the expenditure, although an excessive amount[4] is covered by the insurance. This system creates a pooled fund to which each individual fund contributes as if it had the same proportion of elderly people as in the national population.

---

[4] Upper ceiling on patient cost sharing per month (in yen; from October 2006):

- below 70 years old
  - (a) High income (530,000 yen or more per month): 150,000 + 1% of Exp. above 500,000
  - (b) Middle income: 80,100 + 1% of Exp. above 267,000
  - (c) Low income: 35,400
- 70 years old or older
  - (a) Class 1: (annual taxable income > 1,450,000 yen):<br>44,400 for outpatient care; 80,100 + 1% of Exp. above 267,000 for inpatient care
  - (b) Class 2: 12,000 for outpatient care (From 2008: 24,600 for age 70–74)<br>44,400 for inpatient care (From 2008: 62,100 for age 70–74)
  - (c) Class 3: (exempted from local tax): 8,000 for outpatient care;<br>24,600 or 15,000 for inpatient care.

Table 2. Outline of the health insurance system in Japan.

(As of April 2006)

| | Employer-based health insurance | | | National Health Insurance | Health Service Programme for the Elderly (HSE) |
|---|---|---|---|---|---|
| | Health Insurance | | Mutual Aid Associations | | |
| | Govt. managed | Society managed | | | |
| Insured Persons | Mainly employees at small and medium-sized companies | Mainly employees at large companies | National and local public service employees, etc. | Farmers, Self-employed, etc. | Persons aged 75+ as well as disabled persons aged 65–74 |
| Insurer | National Government | Health Insurance Societies: 1,584 | Mutual Aid Associations: 76 | Municipalities: 2,531 Associations: 166 | Municipalities: 2,531 |
| Coverage as % of Total Population | 28.0 | 23.6 | 7.6 | 40.6 | 11.4 |
| Benefit Level | (Note 1) 70% | | | | (Note 2) 90% |
| Contribution Rate | 8.2% | 7.6% on average | | (Note 3) | – |
| National Subsidy as % of Health Expenditures | 13.0% | 6.7 billion yen | None | 50% | (Note 4) |
| Proportion of those who are eligible to HSE | 4.6 | 2.1 | 3.8 | 22.9 | – |

Note 1: Patient cost sharing in excess of X per month is covered by the insurance.
X=35,400 yen (for low-income)
=72,300 yen + 1 per cent of health expenditure over 241,000 yen (for middle income)
=139,800 yen + 1 per cent of health expenditure over 466,000 yen (for high income)

Note 2: Patient cost sharing in excess of 40,200 yen (24,600 yen for low-income persons) per month is covered by the insurance.

Note 3: The amount of contribution is related to the income and assets of each insured person. Average annual contribution was 158,600 yen per household.

Note 4: 20% by central government, 5% by prefecture and 5% by municipality.

Source: Kōsei Rōdōshō 2006.

Patient cost sharing aside, 70 per cent of the total cost is covered by all sickness funds, 20 per cent by the central government, and 10 per cent by the local governments. In consideration of the importance of long-term care for the elderly, the proportion borne through public funds was raised in 1992 from 30 to 50 per cent in the case of long-term care services.

### 2.4. *Benefit coverage*

All funds cover a broad range of health-care services, including hospital and physician care, dental care, pharmaceuticals, and even some transport. The sickness funds also pay some cash benefits, such as for maternity leave, but society-managed funds generally pay greater cash benefits than National Health Insurance. Large employers provide some preventive care, but health insurance covers little preventive care in general. Normal pregnancy is not covered by the benefit catalogue, although there is some cash payment for it (see Fig. 1).

Patient cost sharing used to differ according to various schemes, but it has been unified to 30 per cent for all patients, except the elderly, since 2003. Moreover, there is a universal upper limit on patient cost sharing, and all sickness funds pay 100 per cent of any additional expenses. This cap is lower for those on low incomes and for those who have already paid the maximum for three months within a year. Because of this universal cap, the proportion of patient cost sharing to the total health expenditure amounted to 15.7 per cent in 2003 (see Table 3).

### 2.5. *Health-care service providers*

The supply-side of health-care services is a mixed system of both public and private health-care institutions. In 2004, there was a total of 9,077 hospitals (1,681 or 18.5 per cent of which were public). Due to the larger size of public institutions, there are far more public than private hospital beds (30 per cent). Patients are free to opt for any health-care institution where the service prices are basically the same. Although equality in health-care delivery should be regarded as a priority, the classification of hospitals according to their functions and streamlining patient flow are insufficient. The so-called "gate keeping" function of primary care physicians is weak and the referral system does not work well.

The number of beds in a region has been controlled according to the regional health-care plans made by the respective governments

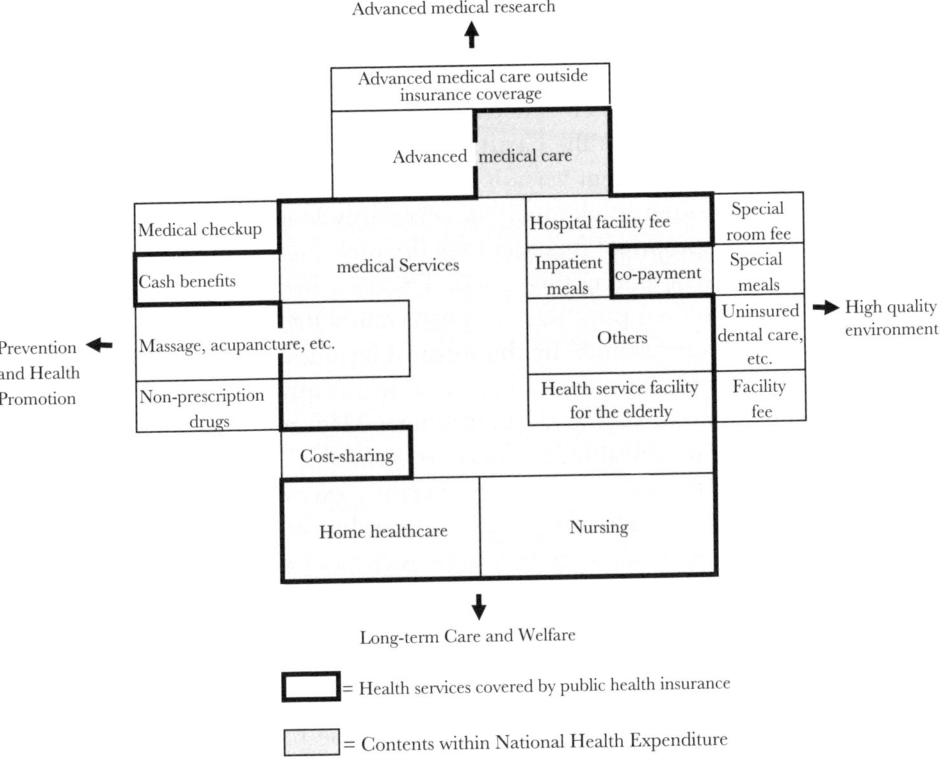


Source: Kōseishō 2000.

Figure 1. Health services covered by public health insurance.

(prefectures) since 1989. Among many health-care providers, the Japan Medical Association (JMA) is the most powerful one, representing mainly the interests of clinics and small and medium-sized private hospitals. The health-care-related industry includes various kinds of private enterprises, such as pharmaceutical companies, medical device manufacturers, and medical test companies. Many of these have their own interests in the health-care system, in particular, the reimbursement mechanisms.

### 2.6. *Reimbursement mechanisms*

The rules for paying doctors and hospitals are identical for all plans, and providers are paid in a centralized manner. Payment to the facility is basically on a fee-for-service basis, but package payment (bundling clinical tests, pharmaceuticals, injections and nursing charges) has been introduced to some extent in Health Service Programme for the Elderly. The price for each insurance-covered medical treatment is listed in the fee schedule, which is determined by the government based on recommendations from the Central Social Insurance Medical Council (see Figure 2). A different version of the fee schedule was prepared for the elderly in order to eliminate unnecessarily long hospital stays and to promote appropriate treatment for the physical and mental characteristics prevalent among this group. The fee schedule is revised every two years. The drug price standard determines the price of prescribed drugs that can be claimed by the medical facilities. Every month, bills are submitted to the regional offices of two central examination and payment organizations: the Social Insurance Medical Fee Payment Fund and the National Health Insurance Federation. These organizations examine the bills in order to detect errors, excessive utilization and fraud. Thus, a utilization review does exist, but its reviewing capacity is naturally limited and only very expensive cases or specified facilities are reviewed intensively. Once approved, the bills are forwarded to the individual funds. Payments to hospitals and physicians are again processed through these organizations.

Insurers and medical service providers are the principal actors at the Central Social Insurance Medical Council. The basic roles of central and local governments are twofold. One is the role of the insurer, the other of the general supervisor of the health-care system. The central government is responsible for health-care policy making in general and it is expected to coordinate the conflicting interests of the parties concerned at the national level.

### 2.7. *Financing*

Public health insurance in Japan is financed through contributions (from individuals as well as employers), government subsidies and out-of-pocket payments. Health services for needy persons, based on the Public Assistance Law of 1950, and public funding for specific diseases and disorders such as tuberculosis, nuclear irradiation and mental illness account for 5.8 per cent of all health expenditure. Direct patient payment for services not covered by insurance was 15.3 per cent in 2004. The proportion of patient cost sharing in national health expenditure decreased from 40 per cent in 1955 to 11 or 12 per cent in the 1980s and 1990s, but has started to increase again due to recent health-care reforms (see Table 3, Figure 3).

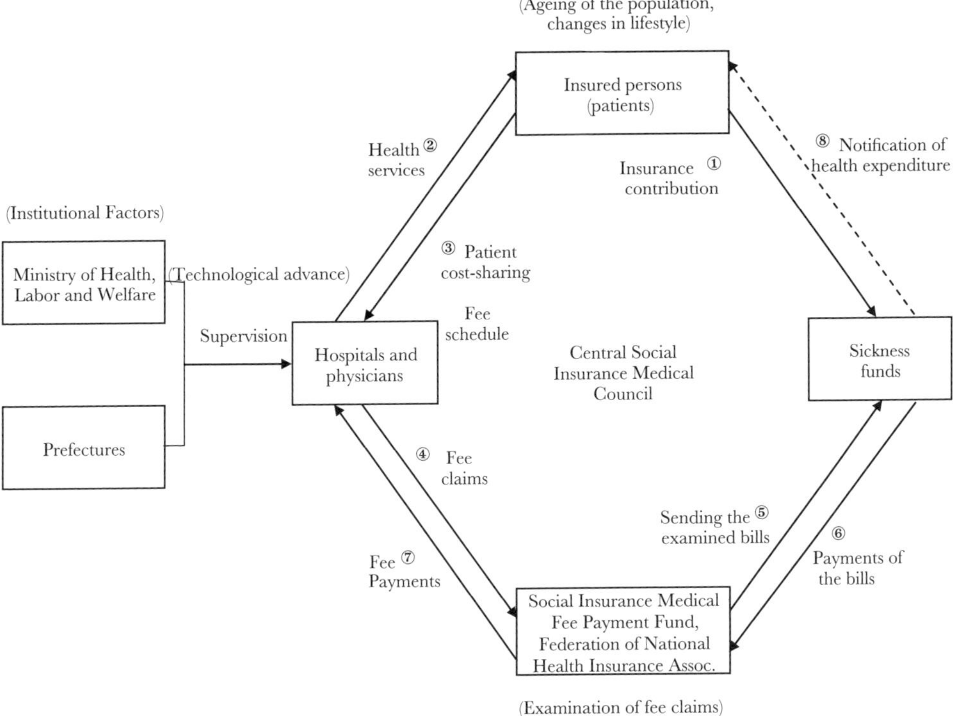


Source: Fukawa 2002: 17.

Figure 2. The public health insurance system in Japan.

The average per capita health expenditure for those aged 65 or over is four times as high as it is for the 0–64 age group (see Table 3). As a result, 20 per cent of the population is consuming 50 per cent of national health expenditure in Japan.

## 3. The Japanese Health-Care System from a Financial Perspective

Universal health care coverage through a public health insurance scheme with fee-for-service payment is the basic definition of the Japanese system, which has contributed to the equitable distribution of health services and relieved families from old-age support. Benefit levels were improved during high economic growth periods. Several mechanisms are necessary to make the fee-for-service system work, including

Table 3. Population and health expenditure in Japan.

| Year | Population | | Co-resident rate (%) | TFR | Life expectancy at birth (year) | | Health Expenditure | | | | | GDP |
|---|---|---|---|---|---|---|---|---|---|---|---|---|
| | | | | | | | National Source | | | | OECD | |
| | Total (million) | 65+ (%) | | | Male | Female | % of GDP | Share of 65+ (%) | 65+/ 0–64 | Out-of-pocket (%) | % of GDP | (trillion yen) |
| 1950 | 83.2 | 4.9 | | 3.65 | 59.6 | 63.0 | — | | | | — | |
| 1955 | 89.3 | 5.3 | | 2.37 | 63.6 | 67.8 | 2.8 | | | 38.7 | — | 8.60 |
| 1960 | 93.4 | 5.7 | 86.8 | 2.00 | 65.3 | 70.2 | 2.5 | | | 30.0 | 3.0 | 16.68 |
| 1965 | 98.3 | 6.3 | 83.8 | 2.14 | 67.7 | 72.9 | 3.3 | | | 20.6 | 4.4 | 33.77 |
| 1970 | 103.7 | 7.1 | 79.6 | 2.13 | 69.3 | 74.7 | 3.3 | | | 19.3 | 4.5 | 75.30 |
| 1975 | 111.9 | 7.9 | 74.4 | 1.91 | 71.7 | 76.9 | 4.3 | | | 12.9 | 5.6 | 152.4 |
| 1980 | 117.1 | 9.1 | 69.0 | 1.75 | 73.4 | 78.8 | 4.9 | 31.3 | | 11.0 | 6.5 | 246.3 |
| 1985 | 121.0 | 10.3 | 64.6 | 1.76 | 74.8 | 80.5 | 4.9 | 37.5 | | 12.0 | 6.7 | 327.4 |
| 1990 | 123.6 | 12.0 | 59.7 | 1.54 | 75.9 | 81.9 | 4.6 | 41.5 | | 12.1 | 5.9 | 450.0 |
| 1995 | 125.5 | 14.5 | 54.3 | 1.42 | 76.5 | 83.0 | 5.4 | 45.2 | | 11.8 | 6.8 | 495.7 |
| 2000 | 126.9 | 17.4 | 49.1 | 1.36 | 77.7 | 84.6 | 6.0 | 48.3 | 4.4 | 14.2 | 7.6 | 502.8 |
| 2005 | 127.8 | 21.0 | | 1.25 | 78.6a | 85.6a | 6.4a | 51.1a | 4.3a | 15.3a | 8.0b | 498.3a |
| 2025 | 121.1 | 28.7 | | 1.38 | 79.8 | 87.5 | | | | | | |
| 2050 | 100.6 | 35.7 | | 1.39 | 80.9 | 89.2 | | | | | | |

Note 1: a = 2004 b = 2003.
Note 2: Co-resident rate = co-resident rate of the elderly (65+).
65+/0-64 = Per capita (65+) / Per capita (0–64).
Source: Fukawa 2002: 11.

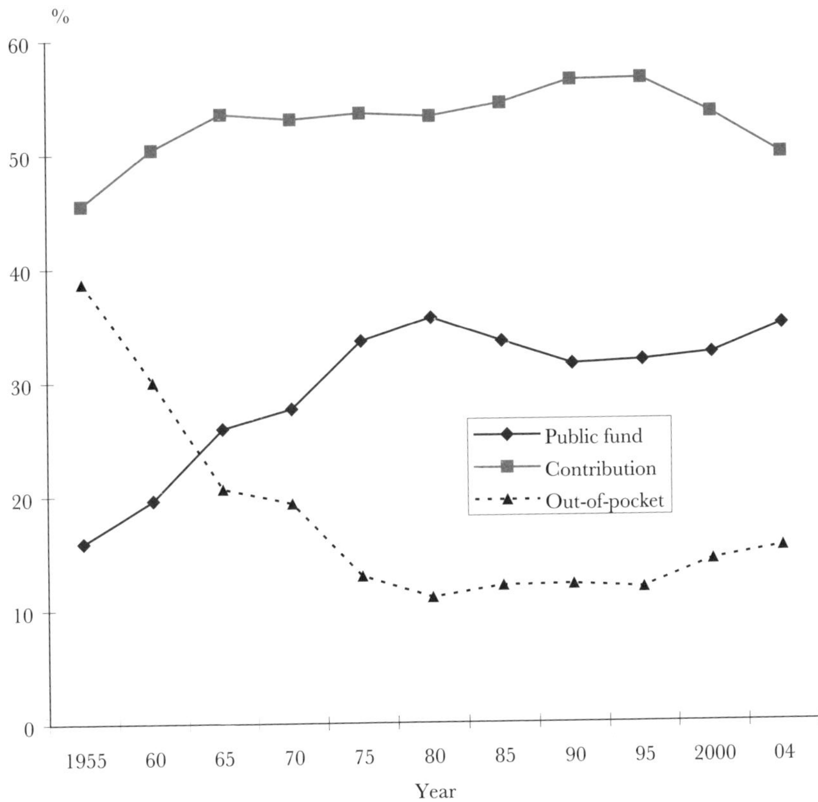


Source: Kōsei Rōdōshō 2006.

Figure 3. Sources of funds for health expenditure.

price-setting, utilization review (to control the volume of service), and regulations to minimize moral hazards tempting both physicians and patients. In Japan, the fee schedule is determined by the government, based on the recommendations of a powerful council which conducts intense negotiations between the parties concerned. Utilization reviews are carried out through the examinations of payment organizations on a rather limited scale. However, their mere existence has an important impact on the prevention of excessive utilization and fraud.

Life expectancy in Japan has been extended mainly because of improved living standards. The availability of health insurance has also helped to raise the quality of people's lives and to establish an equity-based society. Employer-based insurance eliminates the workers' fear of a possible financial burden imposed by illness. Community-based health insurance helps the individual not to become a recipient of public assistance too easily. Health Service Programme for the Elderly provides a remarkable example of nationwide solidarity.

Japan's health expenditure is low as a percentage of GDP compared to the other major developed countries, which might imply that the Japanese health-care system is efficient. Since the universal coverage of the nation through the National Health Insurance in 1961, the benefit level was improved considerably during the 1960s and 1970s. Cost containment and quality assurance have been major goals of health care reforms since the 1990s. The main reform issues in the Japanese health-care system identified since then are: (1) the reorganization of the health service delivery system; (2) reforms of the reimbursement system of medical fees and of the pharmaceutical pricing system; (3) the financing of health care for the elderly; and (4) quality assurance of health services and empowerment of patients. The health-care reform continues in the 2000s, and we will discuss several topics below.

*Health care for the elderly*

A special programme was introduced in 1983 to finance health care for the elderly (70 and over or 65–69 and disabled). Patient cost sharing aside, 70 per cent of this programme is covered by all health insurers and 30 per cent by the public fund. The eligible age of the programme was increased from 70 to 75 years. About half of national health expenditure in Japan is consumed by people older than 65 and about 40 per cent by those aged 70 and over. How to finance the health expenditure of the elderly has been a leading issue in recent years, as well as the reduction of so-called socially induced hospitalization, common among elderly patients. This is still the case to some extent, even after the implementation of the Long-term Care Insurance in April 2000. The per capita health expenditure for the elderly is much higher than that for younger people, and they usually stay in hospital much longer. Given the rapid ageing of the population, the question of how to finance the health expenditure of the elderly is certainly a serious issue, and a new health insurance for the elderly (75 and over) is supposed to be created by the year 2008, although the details of the new system are yet unclear.

*Patient cost sharing*

During the 1990s health-care reforms, special attention was drawn to the quality aspect. Because of the cap, patient cost sharing used to be low: about 15 per cent for the non-elderly and 5 per cent for the elderly. However, an increase in this cost sharing has been the main tool of recent health-care reforms, as well as the introduction of a patient charge on pharmaceutical cost for outpatient services (September 1997).[5] The latter in particular was reported to have a major impact on patients' behaviour. Although there is an upper ceiling, patient cost sharing amounts to 30 per cent of health-care costs for non-elderly and to 10 or 20 per cent for elderly patients.

*Right incentives in the reimbursement system*

If the person receiving fees (such as a physician) also controls the volume of services, he/she will respond to a fee reduction by raising the volume of services in order to restore his/her income. Japan is no exception. The fee schedule is the key factor in controlling the increase in health expenditure in Japan (Ikegami 1991). It clearly favours physicians in private practice over hospitals—fees are especially low for services such as surgery and intensive care (Hsiao 1996)—which is why hospitals compete with the clinic doctors by promoting their outpatient care. Clinic doctors and small hospitals counter by trying to buy prestige in form of high-tech equipment (White 1995). Japanese hospitals are generally not eager to perform services undervalued by the fee schedule. Experience has shown that fee regulation combined with utilization review can control costs without any supplementary measures to limit volume (White 1995). Despite the large number of hospital beds in Japan, the health-care system operates at a low cost when judged against international statistics, largely because of the relatively low prices of the resources used (Mooney 1996). However, this approach faced serious limitations in the 1990s, and the Japanese government is searching for new measures to control the volume increase of health services.

Most health-care services in Japan are reimbursed on a fee-for-service basis, and the price of each service is specified on the Medical Fee Schedule. The same nationwide fee schedule is applied to general practitioners and hospitals. The fee schedule and the drug standard

[5] The first visit fee was 800 yen, and the hospitalization charge was 500 yen per day for the first month only.

(pharmaceutical version of fee schedule) have been the primary tools to pursue health-care reforms in Japan. It has become clear, though, that these tools are limited, and other measures are being studied to improve both the quality and the efficiency of health services. In order to correct false incentives in the fee-for-service system, a partial price bundling, mainly for chronic diseases of the elderly, was introduced in the 1990s. A nationwide feasibility study of a prospective payment system for inpatient services has been conducted since 2003, which is now known as DPC (Diagnosis Procedure Combination) system.

*Regional differences*

Regional differences in health expenditure are a prominent issue in Japan. Health expenditure does not coincide with life expectancy, but there is a strong relationship between health expenditure and the capacity of health services. If there are differences, such as one region's figure being twice as much as another's within the same country, and if they cannot be explained reasonably, the country's overall health expenditure might be reduced by half without affecting the outcome in health-care services. There are many factors that may cause regional differences in health expenditure: the population's demographic and epidemiological profiles; patients' and physicians' behaviour; institutional settings; and people's socio-cultural attitudes toward health-care services. However, service providers and institutional settings are considered the main causes for regional differences in health expenditures (Gunji 2001).

*Prevention: averting cost-push pressure*

Japanese health insurance in general pays relatively little attention to preventive care. However, in view of the importance of lifestyle-related diseases, prevention has slowly become one of the main issues in the 2006 health-care reform. Prevention is important not only for averting cost-push pressure to health expenditure but also for people's quality of life.

*Health-care for patients*

Patients' empowerment is another area that needs to be improved. In fact, from the consumers' point of view it is quite natural to demand coordination between health and welfare services. Amenities in Japanese hospitals are far inferior to those of other developed countries. A significant number of services is not reimbursed by sickness funds and may not be included in the calculations of national health expenditure.

There are also under-the-table payments to physicians for favours such as special attention and treatment or quick admission. It is necessary to set priorities based on objective analysis in order to use limited resources more efficiently. Who will finance the costs of health is another important issue for the maintenance of a fair and stable system.

## References


Campbell, John C. (1996): The Egalitarian Health Insurance System. In: Ikegami, Naoki and John C. Campbell (eds.): *Containing Health Care Costs in Japan*. Michigan: University of Michigan Press.

Fukawa, Tetsuo (2001): Japanese Welfare State Reforms in the 1990s and Beyond: How Japan is Similar to and Different from Germany. In: *Vierteljahrshefte zur Wirtschaftsforschung/Quarterly Journal of Economic Research* 70, 4, pp. 571–585.

—— (2002): *Public Health Insurance in Japan*. Washington DC: World Bank Institute Working Paper/ http://www.worldbank.org/wbi/pubsbysubject_socialandculturalissues.html (found 20 February 2007).

Gunji, Asuaki (ed.) (2001): *Iryō no chiikisa* [Regional differences in health expenditure]. Tokyo: Tōyō Keizai Shinposha.

Hsiao, William (1996): Costs—The Macro Perspective. In: Ikegami, Naoki and John C. Campbell (eds.): *Containing Health Care Costs in Japan*. Michigan: University of Michigan Press, pp. 116–145.

Ikegami, Naoki (1991): Japanese Health Care: Low Cost through Regulated Fees. In: *Health Affairs* 10, pp. 87–109.

Kōseishō (1998): *Heisei 10-nen kōsei hakusho* (White Paper on Health and Welfare 1998). Tokyo: Gyōsei.

—— (2000): *Heisei 12-nen kōsei hakusho* (White Paper on Health and Welfare 2000). Tokyo: Gyōsei.

Kōsei Rōdōshō (2006): *Heisei 18-nen kōsei rōdō hakusho* (White Paper on Health, Labour and Welfare 2006). Tokyo: Gyōsei.

Mooney, Gavin (1996): An International Perspective on Health Services Reform. In: *Journal of the Japanese Society on Hospital Administration* 33, 2, pp. 81–107.

OECD (2006): *Health Data 2006*. Paris: OECD.

White, Joseph (1995): *Competing Solutions: American Health Care Proposals and International Experience*. Washington, D.C.: Brookings Institution.

WHO (World Health Organization) (1996): *World Health Statistics Annual, 1995*. Geneva: WHO Press.

CHAPTER SIXTY-ONE

# THE PUBLIC PENSION SYSTEM AND THE AGEING SOCIETY

Takashi Oshio

## 1. Introduction

Population ageing will increasingly put strong pressures on the public pension system. To confront this situation, the Japanese government launched the 2004 pension reform, which aimed to put an upper ceiling on the payroll contribution rate, and to hold down total pension benefits within total contributions and government subsidies. Unlike previous reforms, the latest reform introduced an adjustment indexation to adjust benefits automatically in response to demographic and macroeconomic changes.

However, there are still concerns about the sustainability of the public pension system. In fact, the most recent population projections released by the government assume that the total fertility rate will keep falling from 1.32 in 2006 and just recover to 1.26 by 2055, and predict that the ratio of people aged 65 and older will rise from 20 per cent in 2005 to about 36 per cent in 2025. Moreover, as will be discussed in this chapter, net pension liabilities are high, reflecting the generous policies in the past, meaning that a large burden has been postponed and passed on to future generations.

Many previous studies, such as Seike and Yamada (2004), have shown that public pension benefits have a significant impact on incentives to work among the elderly. Ageing and a shrinking population will raise the relative importance of the participation of the elderly in the labour force, an important issue that should be taken into account when discussing pension reform. Furthermore, the impact of public pensions on income distribution among the elderly will become an increasingly important issue, because the household income of the elderly depends greatly on public pension benefits.

This article provides an overview of current issues regarding public pension programmes and their reforms under population ageing in Japan. It summarises basic institutional backgrounds, presents policy projections under population ageing, and addresses issues that remain unresolved—all of which are expected to help understand how the Japanese pension system is responding to population ageing. For these purposes, the remaining part of this article is structured as follows. Section 2 presents a brief overview of the institutional features of Japan's public pension system and discusses the basic features of the 2004 pension reform. Section 3 assesses the post-reform pension system from a balance sheet viewpoint and discusses future reform options. Section 4 discusses related issues regarding the public pension system—that is, the impact of pension benefits on the incentives to work for the elderly and on intra-generational income distribution. The final section summarizes the paper.

## 2. Institutional Background and the 2004 Pension Reform

### 2.1. *Japan's public pension scheme*

Japan's public pension scheme consists of three major components. The first is the National Pension Insurance (NPI) [*Kokumin Nenkin*] for self-employed workers, farmers, and other non-employed workers. The second is the Employees' Pension Insurance (EPI) [*Kōsei Nenkin*], which covers employed workers in the private sector. The third component is the Mutual Aid Insurance (MAI) [*Kyōsai Nenkin*] for employed workers in the public sector. The NPI has only a flat-rate benefit, while the EPI and MAI have both flat-rate and earnings-related benefits. Since the 1986 pension reform, all beneficiaries in these three programmes have received a common, flat-rate benefit, which is called the basic pension benefit. Accordingly, the flat-rate components of EPI and MAI, as well as the NPI benefits, are all the same under the current scheme.

For the NPI, the eligibility age for the full benefits is 65. More than a quarter of the insured, however, start to receive actuarially reduced benefits between the ages of 60 and 64 years. This is because their self-earned income is so low that they choose to draw pension benefits as soon as possible, even if they are actuarially reduced. An actuarial addition to the benefits is also available for those who are aged between 65 and 70 years, but few apply for it. Under the current programme, eligibility to receive NPI benefits requires a minimum of 25 years of contributions, and eligibility to receive full benefits requires 40 years of contributions. The benefits are price-indexed to reflect changes in the consumer price index in the previous calendar year. NPI contributions are flat-rate, and government subsidies are utilized to finance its benefits.

The EPI is the main part of the Japanese public pension programme. The benefits consist of a flat-rate component (basic pension benefits) as the first tier and an earnings-related component as the second tier. In principle, the eligibility age for the flat component used to be 65, but there was a special legal provision allowing employees to receive full benefits from age 60. Since 2001, however, the eligibility age has been raised by one year every three years, and it will eventually be raised to 65 in 2013. EPI contributions are wage-proportional (with an upper ceiling), paid equally by employee and employer.

The structure of the MAI, which covers employed workers in the public sector, is almost the same as that of the EPI, and MAI reforms tend to follow EPI reforms. These two pension schemes for employed workers are likely to be unified in the near future. In addition to these key public pension schemes, some people are covered by corporate pension insurances. There are also disability pensions under the public pension scheme but they are not taken as a major route to retirement, unlike in European countries.

### 2.2. *The 2004 pension reform*

A well-established view is that population ageing will increasingly put strong pressure on pension finances, as long as the pension scheme is managed under a pay-as-you-go system. Figure 1 compares the estimated numbers of contributors and beneficiaries of the public pension programmes as a whole, based on NPI membership, to illustrate roughly the demographic pressures over the next decades. The number of beneficiaries will keep increasing and that of contributors will level off, so that the ratio of contributors to beneficiaries will decline substantially from 4.0 in 2020 to 1.3 in 2050. This clearly suggests that a reduction in benefits and/or an increase in contributions will be required in order to keep the system balanced.

Over the past two decades, the Japanese government has repeatedly conducted piecemeal pension reforms every four to five years. As a result, the pension system has become less generous since the early 1990s, with benefits steadily declining and the eligibility ages for benefits rising step by step. At the same time, the government has been lifting the contribution rates to sustain the still generous level of benefits. Despite these reforms, the strong pressures from population ageing have been

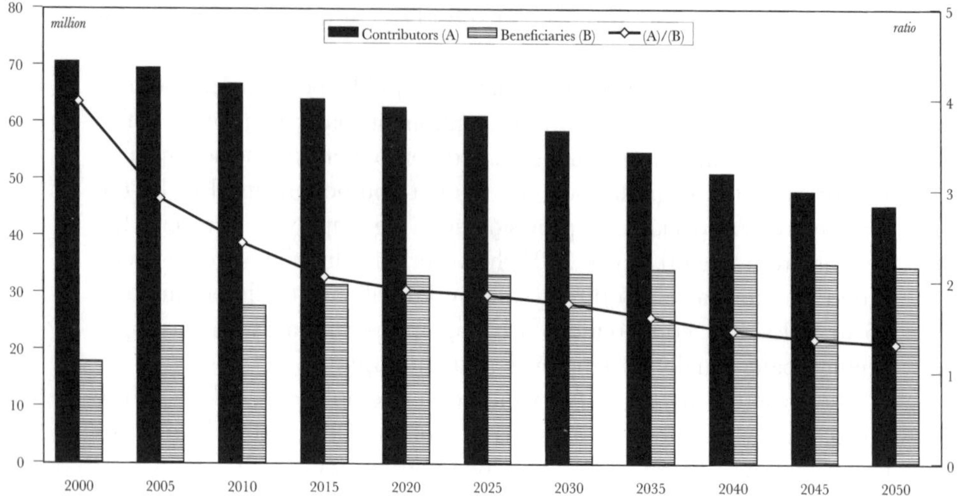


Note: The figures are the projected numbers of contributors and beneficiaries of the National Pension Insurance (NPI).
Source: Ministry of Health, Labour and Welfare (2004): Actuarial Valuation of Employees' Pension Insurance and National Pension in Japan.

Figure 1. Prospective public pension contributors and beneficiaries.

consistently underestimated. At the same time, these types of reforms have raised concerns among the young insured in particular as to how far burdens may keep increasing in future. This is often recognized as a key factor causing increasing drop-out from the public pension system among young and non-salaried workers.

The 2004 pension reform was quite different from previous reforms in several ways. First, it put an upper ceiling on the contribution rate: the EPI contribution rate is set to rise by 0.354 percentage points every year from October 2004, but it will be kept at 18.3 per cent after 2017. However, the revenue from contributions will not be enough to finance the pension system, so the government plans to gradually raise the government subsidy to the basic pension programme from one third to one half of its benefits during the period from 2004 to 2009. A rise in government transfers implies that the government will eventually have to increase tax revenues, most likely by an increase in the consumption tax rate, which is now at 5 per cent, exceptionally low among industrialized countries.

Second, the reform incorporated an *automatic adjustment* of benefit levels into the system, as already introduced in Sweden, Italy and some other countries. If the levels of contributions and the government subsidy are fixed, it becomes necessary to adjust pension benefits to keep pension finances balanced. The reform hence introduced the adjustment indexation to adjust benefits automatically in response to demographic and macroeconomic changes. In fact, the benchmark scenario adopted for the reform suggests that benefits will be reduced by 0.9 per cent in real terms every year for the next two decades, reflecting a shrinking labour force and lengthened life expectancy in future. The introduction of this adjustment indexation contrasts sharply with the previous reforms, which first determined the levels of benefits and then adjusted the contribution rates to balance pension finances.

Third, the reform changed the method of balancing revenues and expenditures from the *whole-future-balancing method*, which had been adopted in past actuarial valuations, to the *closed-period balancing method*. The whole-future-balancing method aims to balance finances into the indefinite future, requiring the public pension system to manage a huge fund in order to make use of the return on it in the future. The closed-period balancing method, by contrast, aims to balance finances over the predetermined finite period and to produce a large enough fund at the end of this financial period to meet a payment reserve. For the actuarial valuation in 2004, future projections were drafted based on a 95-year balancing period up to 2100. Subsequent actuarial valuations will be conducted at least every five years to balance finances over 95 years from the valuation year. Combined with an increase in the government subsidies to the basic pension, this was expected to help reduce an increase in the contribution rate.

Based on these changes, the net replacement rate—the average ratio of pension benefits to after-tax wage income obtained by the working generation—will decrease from the pre-Reform 59 per cent to 50 per cent by 2023. If the socio-economic situation deteriorates more than currently expected, then continued adjustment of benefit levels will lead the replacement ratio to fall below 50 per cent. And if the replacement ratio is projected to fall below 50 per cent before the next actuarial valuation, terminating benefit level adjustment will need to be examined.

How robust will the post-reform scheme be against demographic and macroeconomic shocks? The 2004 reform assumes that the total fertility rate will recover to 1.39 by 2050 from 1.29 in 2004. However, this projection is often criticized as too optimistic, given that there are no signs of near-term pickup in fertility. Indeed, according to the government, the replacement ratio will have to be reduced to 45.3 per cent if the total fertility rate falls to 1.10 and economic growth is correspondingly reduced. The 2004 Reform thus cannot make the pension system fully free from demographic risks, so another key reform in the future will presumably be required.

## 3. Balance-Sheet Assessment of the Public Pension System

### 3.1. *Assessing the 2004 pension reform*

This section assesses the 2004 Reform from a balance-sheet viewpoint, which highlights the key problem: how to finance net pension liabilities. Japan's public pension scheme has paid far more in benefits to early generations than their contributions could have financed. Consequently, later generations have to receive less in benefits than could otherwise be financed from their contributions, unless some additional sources of revenue are provided. As pointed out by Diamond and Orszag (2004), this is not a shortcoming in the design of the public pension scheme, but rather a legacy of the relative generosity of benefits provided to earlier generations. A crucial question is how to spread the cost arising from net pension liabilities—in other words, the legacy debt—fairly across different generations.

It is useful to examine the balance sheets of the pension programmes when we consider how to finance net pension liabilities. The Ministry of Health, Labour and Welfare has released the balance sheets of the EPI and NPI after the 2004 reform. Because the balance sheet structures of the EPI and NPI have many things in common, we can, in order to save space, focus on the balance sheet of the EPI (as of April 1, 2005), as illustrated in Figure 2.

The balance sheet of the public pension can be divided into two parts: the first (left) part shows the assets and liabilities accrued from past contributions, while the second (right) part shows those accrued from future contributions. To close the system as a whole, the total of assets in both parts must be equal to that of liabilities in both parts. It means that the net pension liabilities, which are defined as excess liabilities accrued in the past, must always be offset by the net pension *assets* in the future. This relationship—which is also satisfied in the post-Reform framework—roughly corresponds to the trade-off between elderly and young generations. As implied in this relationship, any pen-

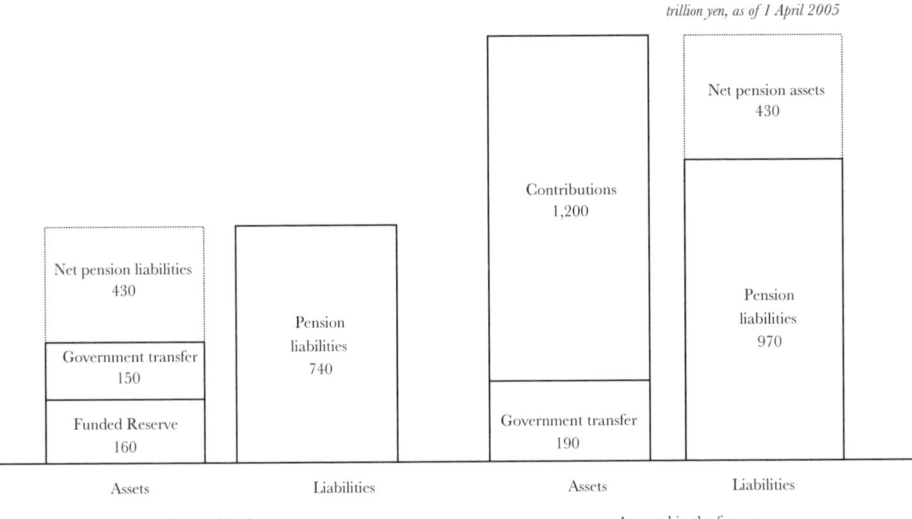


Note: The author's calculations based on the data published by the Ministry of Health, Labour and Welfare.

Figure 2. Balance sheet of the EPI after the 2004 pension reform.

sion reform will be a zero-sum game that cannot simultaneously make all generations better-off.

The left part of Figure 2 indicates that net pension liabilities amount to 430 trillion yen, which is equivalent to 86 per cent of nominal GDP. Pension liabilities accrued from past contributions are 740 trillion yen, which is 430 trillion more than the sum of the funded reserve (160 trillion yen) and expected government transfers (which are linked to past pension liabilities, 150 trillion yen). The accrued net pension liabilities must be financed in the future, especially by younger and future generations. Indeed, the right part of Figure 2 shows that pension liabilities accrued from future contributions (970 trillion yen) are 430 trillion yen less than the sum of future contributions and government transfers (which are linked to future pension liabilities).

This balance sheet structure means that future generations still have to finance a large part of the legacy costs, although the newly introduced automatic adjustment of benefits will help contain past pension liabilities. Therefore, the generational inequality regarding pension benefits and contributions remains almost intact after the Reform. In fact, Suzuki (2006) and others show that the reform failed to change significantly the gain and loss pattern among generations. In sum, the reform essentially repeated the previous reform pattern, in that it postponed most of the legacy costs, passing them on to current young and future generations.

### 3.2. *Future options*

It is sometimes argued that the government should shift from a pay-as-you go system to a funded system, which is neutral to demographics. The World Bank (1994) led this argument in the late 1990s, and Hatta and Oguchi (1999) explicitly proposed it in Japan. In fact, a shift to a funded system or downsizing a pay-as-you-go system into the basic benefit component with partial privatization was considered to be a reasonable reform option around the 2000 pension reform.

However, it is now widely accepted that a transition to a funded system cannot make anyone better off, so long as net pension liabilities are required to be financed. This has long been recognized as what is called a "double burden" problem, and stressed again by Geanakoplos, Mitchell and Zeldes (1998) and others. Feldstein and Samwick (1998) proposed a gradual transition to a funded system to make additional costs more equally spread and easily absorbed across generations in the transition period, and Oshio (1997) applied this idea to Japan. In principle, however, potential benefits from downsizing a pay-as-you-go system will be completely offset by additional costs to finance pension liabilities. In addition, experiences with the 401(k) plan in the United States and pension reforms in Chile and other countries suggest that privatizing the public pension programme may cause several problems such as risk management and administrative costs.

In recent years, around the time of the 2004 reform, there was no strong argument in favour of an explicit shift to a funded system or privatizing the public pension in Japan. Furthermore, the 2004 reform can be interpreted as *de facto* downsizing of a pay-as-you-go system, because it aims to contain the levels of benefits within contributions and tax revenues. There seems to be no substantial discrepancy as to the direction of pension reform in reform discussions, and current debates tend to concentrate on further reform options that can further solve the legacy debt problem or reduce intergenerational inequality, assuming the current scheme as the benchmark. Among others, Takayama (2004) proposes an interesting option (cf. chapter 62). He argues that net pension liabilities should be financed by introducing a new 3 per cent earmarked consumption tax and intensive injection of increased government transfers. Then, future contributions would correspond to pension benefits entitled by them, raising the incentive-compatibility of the pension system. He also insists that this strategy of separating the legacy debt problem from rebuilding a sustainable pension system for the future would make it possible to switch to a notional defined contribution (NDC) system, which has been introduced in Sweden and some other countries.

Takayama's proposal looks attractive and reasonable, but it should be noted that a substantial part of the newly introduced consumption tax will be paid by young and future generations. It is true that contributions and benefits will be linked more directly with each other under the new system, but most of the legacy costs will be financed by later generations. In other words, his proposal will be effective to the extent to which elderly generations will absorb additional costs to finance the legacy debt by paying additional consumption tax.

It is of interest to see what will happen if the government decides to keep the contribution and tax rates unchanged from the pre-reform levels and contain total benefits every year within contributions and government transfers (see Oshio 2006). In this case, the government will require elderly generations to forgo a part of their already-committed benefits—in other words, to pay more legacy costs than required by the 2004 reform. This option will make earlier generations worse off, but it will also reduce the burdens on future generations and improve intergenerational equity.

To assess this additional reform, let us consider three options. For option I, we will keep the EPI contribution rate unchanged at the pre-reform 13.58 per cent. For option II, we will keep the share of government transfer of the basic pension benefit unchanged at one third, which implies that the government will not raise the consumption tax rate to finance basic pension benefits. For option III, we will use a combination of options I and II. Option III is an extreme version of the 2004 reform-type automatic adjustment, which assumes no further rise in contributions and taxes from the current levels. For all these options, we will also front-load the pension fund utilization for the next forty years (instead of the officially scheduled ninety-five years) to mitigate a reduction in benefits in the interim.

The estimation results are summarized in Table 1, in comparison to what the 2004 reform implies.

Table 1. Results of future options for public pension reforms.

(trillion yen)

| | Pension liabilities | | | | Pension assets | | | | |
|---|---|---|---|---|---|---|---|---|---|
| | Total | Accrued in the past | [For retirees] | Accrued in the future (A) | Total | Contributions (B) | Government transfers (C) | Funded reserves | Net loss in the future (B)+(C)–(A) |
| 2004 Reform | 1,710 | 740 | [350] | 970 | 1,710 | 1,200 | 340 | 160 | 570 |
| Option I | 1,430 | 670 | [330] | 750 | 1,430 | 920 | 340 | 160 | 510 |
| Option II | 1,600 | 740 | [350] | 860 | 1,600 | 1,200 | 230 | 160 | 570 |
| Option III | 1,310 | 630 | [310] | 680 | 1,310 | 920 | 230 | 160 | 470 |
| Changes from 2004 Reform | | | | | | | | | |
| Option I | Δ 280 | Δ 70 | [Δ20] | Δ 220 | Δ 280 | Δ 280 | — | 0 | Δ 60 |
| Option II | Δ 110 | 0 | [0] | Δ 110 | Δ 110 | — | Δ 110 | 0 | 0 |
| Option III | Δ 400 | Δ 110 | [Δ40] | Δ 290 | Δ 400 | Δ 280 | Δ 110 | 0 | Δ 110 |
| % changes from 2004 Reform | | | | | | | | | |
| Option I | Δ16% | Δ9% | [Δ6%] | Δ23% | Δ16% | Δ23% | — | 0% | Δ11% |
| Option II | Δ6% | 0% | [0%] | Δ11% | Δ6% | — | Δ32% | 0% | 0% |
| Option III | Δ23% | Δ15% | [Δ11%] | Δ30% | Δ23% | Δ23% | Δ32% | 0% | Δ19% |

Note: Value figures are rounded at the second digit.
Source: Oshio 2006: 171.

We first find that option I will reduce total pension liabilities by 280 trillion yen (70 trillion for past liabilities and 220 trillion for future liabilities) from what the reform calls for. Second, option II will reduce total pension liabilities by 110 trillion yen, all of which is for future liabilities, suggesting that the front-loading of pension fund utilization will make it possible to pay benefits as initially scheduled in the 2004 reform. Option III, which is a combination of options I and II, will hold down total liabilities by 400 trillion yen (110 trillion for past liabilities and 290 trillion for future liabilities), equivalent to 23 per cent of what the reform implies.

These types of reform options will have a significant impact on intergenerational income distribution. In the case of option III, past liabilities will decline by 15 per cent as a whole and by 11 per cent for liabilities promised to those who have already started to receive pension benefits. It correspondingly implies a downward shift in the path of the replacement rate, which is projected to decline to 52 per cent (from the initially projected 59 per cent) in 2004 and to around 40 per cent (from 50 per cent) in 2023.

It is an open question whether such a reduction in already-committed benefits is politically acceptable, although there is no explicit legal restriction against it and previous pension reforms have repeated a gradual reduction in benefits. At the same time, however, option III will reduce a net loss in the future by 110 trillion yen, 19 per cent of what the reform implies. These options will make older generations worse off and young and future generations better off.

To some extent, it is a matter of value judgment how to spread the cost arising from the legacy debt across different generations. Option III, which calls for no further rise in contributions and taxes, is an extreme one that is not easy to implement. However, some business groups and labour unions actually argue that the contribution rate should be contained within 15 per cent or so, rather than 18.3 per cent as scheduled in the reform. On the other hand, it is sometimes politically necessary to sustain already-committed benefits, especially for current retirees and near-retirees. Indeed, the reform promises not to reduce benefits in nominal terms, although it incorporates their automatic adjustment to demographic and economic factors.

## 4. Related Issues

### 4.1. *Labour force participation of the elderly*

This section addresses two issues—labour force participation of the elderly and income redistribution among the elderly—both of which are closely related to the public pension and its reform. First, ageing and the shrinking population are likely to reduce labour force growth, which is one of the key determinants of long-term growth potential. Hence, policymakers are now considering policy measures to enhance labour participation to offset its reduction. In fact, the government is striving to raise the mandatory retirement age or to encourage firms to keep employing people after 60, which is currently the normal company retirement age (see chapter 52). A gradual increase in the entitlement age for public pension benefits, which has been incorporated in recent pension reforms, is also likely to raise incentives to work among the elderly, other things being equal.

The labour force participation rate in Japan is very high compared to other advanced countries, as shown in Figure 3. Along with increasing pension benefits, however, labour force participation has been declining over the past few decades, even allowing for cyclical swings. Also, a cross-country study by Gruber and Wise (1999) found that the existing pension schemes tend to reduce the incentive to work for the elderly to a greater or lesser extent in all industrialized nations. In Japan, the postwar baby-boomers, who were born in the late 1940s, are starting to leave their primary workplace in the early 2000s. Their response to pension benefits should be cautiously watched to assess the medium-term growth trend.

Many earlier studies indicated that pension benefits tend to reduce the incentive to work for the elderly. As one of the most recent examples, Seike and Yamada (2004) showed, the probability of retirement of people who are eligible to receive EPI benefits is about 15 per cent higher than that of those who are not. In addition, several empirical studies have confirmed that the means-tested [*zaishoku*] pension programme tends to reduce significantly incentives to work among the elderly, even after recent reforms. In this sense, pension benefits still operate as "penalties on employment" for the elderly. However, these studies were based on a static framework, where an old person compares pension benefits (which he/she will receive when retired) and wage income (which he/she will obtain when postponing retirement), without consideration of lifetime income and utility.

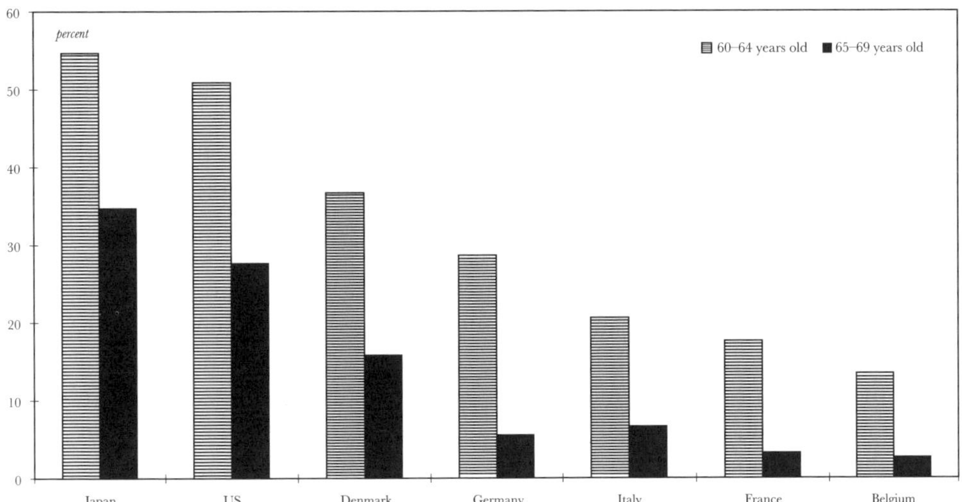


Note: Japan (2005), US, Denmark, Germany, and France (2004), and Italy and Belgium (2003).
Source: ILO, *Yearbook of Labour Statistics 2005*, Statistics Bureau: *Labour Force Survey* 2005.

Figure 3. Labour force participation rates among the elderly.

Most recently, the relationship between public pension benefits and retirement decisions is often analyzed in a dynamic framework. The discounted present value of net pension benefits obtained over a lifetime after retirement is defined as pension wealth (or social security wealth). If postponing retirement until the following year increases pension wealth, it is reasonable to stay in the labour force, other things being equal. Oishi and Oshio (2005) confirmed a negative correlation between accrued pension wealth and the probability of retirement. Moreover, because public pension benefits reduce the incentives to work, they are likely at least partly to crowd out the wage earnings of the elderly. In fact, Oshio and Shimizutani (2006) confirmed that 50–80 per cent of public pension benefits are translated into total household income on average (depending on estimation model specifications), by explicitly taking into account the endogenous feature of benefits.

The impact of pension benefits on the incentive to work for the elderly will be affected by two additional factors in the coming decades. First, the eligibility age for EPI benefits will be gradually raised: initially, the eligibility age for the flat-rate component is to be raised by one year every three years from 60 in 2001 to 65 in 2013; and subsequently the eligibility age for the earnings-related component is scheduled to be raised by one year every three years to 65 in 2025. Hence, it is natural to expect that the negative impact of pension benefits on labour force participation will gradually fade for those aged 60 to 64.

Second, the impact of pension benefits will be affected by the demand for elderly workers from firms. Currently, employed workers tend to retire from their primary workplace at the normal retirement age, 60 years old, and then enter the secondary labour market with lower wages as part-time workers if they want to stay in the labour force. If that is the case, the ratio of pension benefits to expected wage income tends to be so high that it often encourages people to retire. If firms flatten their wage profiles and make their employment and wage systems more "age-neutral," then elderly workers can be expected to stay longer in the labour force. Otherwise, those in their early sixties would face rising income uncertainty, without either stable wage income or sufficient pension benefits between retirement and eligibility ages.

### 4.2. *Income redistribution among the elderly*

The second related issue is income redistribution among the elderly. It is often discussed how unequal the current pension system is across different generations. Given net pension liabilities which reflect previous generous benefits, it is natural that net benefits in a lifetime are positive for early generations and negative for late ones. A pay-as-you-go system is in essence a mechanism of intergenerational income transfer, so population ageing is likely to make it work adversely on younger cohorts. It is equally important, however, to assess the public pension system in terms of intergenerational equity, although income redistribution itself is not a primary object of social security. For example, assume a pay-as-you-go system of flat-rate benefits which is financed by a wage-proportional premium. This system is equivalent to so-called "negative income tax" over a lifetime, and transfers income from higher income individuals to lower income ones within the same cohort, even if it subtracts from net lifetime income on average under population ageing.

Income inequality is now relatively high in Japan among industrialized countries and it continues to rise in terms of the Gini coefficient and other inequality measures, as stressed by Tachibakaki (2005). It is true, as pointed out by Ohtake (2005) and others that a substantial part of widening income inequality is due to population ageing as well as changes in household size. Income inequality tends to widen as people

Table 2. Income redistribution by age group.

(2001)

| Age group | Gini coefficient: Market income | Gini coefficient: Redistributed income | Reduction in Gini coefficient (%) | due to social security | due to taxation |
|---|---|---|---|---|---|
| 20~24 | 0.3397 | 0.3147 | 7.4 | 4.0 | 3.7 |
| 25~29 | 0.3243 | 0.2993 | 7.7 | 4.7 | 3.3 |
| 30~34 | 0.3327 | 0.2974 | 10.6 | 7.6 | 3.1 |
| 35~39 | 0.3548 | 0.3007 | 15.2 | 11.4 | 3.5 |
| 40~44 | 0.3251 | 0.2832 | 12.9 | 9.8 | 3.3 |
| 45~49 | 0.3265 | 0.2898 | 11.2 | 8.1 | 3.4 |
| 50~54 | 0.3350 | 0.3068 | 8.4 | 6.0 | 2.9 |
| 55~59 | 0.3837 | 0.3266 | 14.9 | 11.5 | 3.0 |
| 60~64 | 0.5020 | 0.3522 | 29.8 | 27.0 | 0.6 |
| 65~69 | 0.6073 | 0.3396 | 44.1 | 42.5 | −2.5 |
| 70~74 | 0.6566 | 0.3452 | 47.4 | 45.6 | −2.6 |
| 75 + | 0.6436 | 0.3751 | 41.7 | 40.3 | −1.8 |

Source: Ministry of Health, Labour and Wealth, *Survey on Income Redistribution* 2002.

age, and a rising proportion of the elderly in the total population naturally raises overall income inequality. However, the fact that the elderly face wide income inequality should not be ignored and it is important to address how the current redistribution policies respond to it.

To be sure, public pension benefits help to reduce income inequality among the elderly, because they raise their average income through income transfer from working generations. Indeed, as indicated by Table 2, the Gini coefficient drops sharply for those aged 60 and above, and social security explains almost all of the reduction in income inequality.

Excluding the effect of income transfer from younger generations via social security programmes, however, income redistribution within the elderly population is quite limited. In fact, Table 2 reveals that taxation *adds* to income inequality among the elderly. Moreover, Oshio (2005) confirmed the regressivity, albeit small, of redistribution policies for the elderly, based on the analysis of the micro-data of the official survey. As a result, the Gini coefficient for redistributed (post-tax and post-transfer) income is still significantly higher for the elderly than for the young. Limited income redistribution among the young probably reflects a series of tax reforms that have consistently flattened the tax curve and raised the minimum tax base.

Income inequality among the elderly will surely become more important as the population continues to age, and the risk is that income redistribution among them based on income transfer from the working population will become more difficult to sustain. The public pension is not expected to redistribute income among the elderly, however, EPI earnings-related benefits reflect wage income inequality when young, and the separated systems of EPI and NPI do not narrow the income gap between employed and self-employed workers. The income tax structure, which now has limited impact on income redistribution among the old, is likely to become a key focus in fiscal policy in Japan, especially if a hike in consumption tax, which is regressive in nature, is implemented to finance public pension and other social security expenditures.

## 5. Concluding Remarks

This chapter has focused on the sustainability of public pension finances in Japan and the impact of current and future demographic developments. The key points regarding the public pension programmes and their reforms can be summarized as follows. First, the 2004 Reform made remarkable progress in containing a future increase in pension benefits by introducing an automatic adjustment mechanism. Second, however, there are still concerns about the sustainability of the public pension system, because there are huge net pension liabilities which later generations are forced to pay. Third, as indicated by the balance-sheet analysis, any pension reform will be a zero-sum game which cannot make all generations better off. A crucial question is how to spread the cost arising from net pension liabilities fairly across different generations.

This chapter has also addressed two related issues, labour force participation of the elderly and income redistribution among them. An ageing and shrinking population will raise the relative importance of labour force participation of the elderly, and the impact of benefits on this participation should be more seriously addressed in future pension reform. Also, population ageing will increasingly highlight wide income inequality among the old and require further discussions about redistribution policies.

## References


Diamond, A. Diamond and Peter R. Orszag (2004): *Saving Social Security: A Balanced Approach*. Washington D.C., Brookings Institution Press.

Feldstein, Martin and Andrew Samwick (1998), The Transition Path in Privatizing Social Security. In: Feldstein, Martin (ed.): *Privatizing Social Security*. Chicago: The University of Chicago Press, pp. 215–260.

Geanakoplos, John, Olivia S. Mitchell, and Stephen. P. Zeldes (1998): Would a Privatized Social Security System Really Pay a Higher Rate of Return?. In: Arnold R., Douglas, Michael Graetz and Alicia H. Munnell (eds.): *Framing the Social Security Debate: Value, Politics, and Economics*. Washington D.C.: Brookings Institution Press, pp. 137–156.

Gruber, Jonathan and David A. Wise (eds.) (1999): *Social Security and Retirement around the World*. Chicago: The University of Chicago Press.

Hatta, Tatsuo and Noriyoshi Oguchi (1999): *Nenkin kaikakuron: Tsumitate hōshiki ni ikō seyo* [Pension reform: A shift to a funded system]. Tokyo: Nihon Keizai Shimbunsha.

Ohtake, Fumio (2005): *Nihon no fubyōdō* [Inequality in Japan]. Tokyo: Nihon Keizai Shinbunsha.

Oishi S., Akiko and Takashi Oshio (2004): Social security and retirement in Japan: an evaluation using micro-data. In: Gruber, Jonathan and David A. Wise (eds.): *Social Security and Programs and Retirement around the World*. Chicago: The University of Chicago Press, pp. 399–460.

Oshio, Takashi (1997): *Nenkin mineika eno kōsō* [Towards privatizing the public pension]. Tokyo: Nihon Keizai Shimbunsha.

—— (2005): *Jinkō genshō jidai no shakai hoshō kaikaku* [Social security reform under ageing population]. Tokyo: Nihon Keizai Shimbunsha.

—— (2006): *Baransu shīto kara mita nenkin kaikaku no kadai* [Pension reform issues from a balance sheet viewpoint]. In: Kaizuka, Keimei and Policy Research Institute, Ministry of Finance (eds.): *Nenkin o kangaeru* [Thinking of the public pension]. Tokyo: Chuō Keizaisha, pp. 147–176.

Oshio, Takashi and Satoshi Shimizutani (2006): The Impact of Public Pension Benefits on Income and Poverty of the Elderly in Japan. In: *The Japanese Journal of Social Security Policy* 2, 2, pp. 54–66.

Seike, Atsushi and Atsuhiro Yamada (2004): *Kōreisha shūgyō no keizaigaku* [Economics of employment of the elderly]. Tokyo: Nihon Keizai Shinbunsha.

Suzuki, Wataru (2006): *Genzai no shakai hoshō seido no moto ni okeru sedaikan jueki to futan no mitōshi* [Projected costs and benefits by generation under the current social security system]. In: Kaizuka, Keimei and Policy Research Institute, Ministry of Finance (eds.): *Nenkin o kangaeru* [Thinking of the public pension]. Tokyo: Chuō Keizaisha, pp. 7–33.

Tachibakaki, Toshiaki (2005): *Confronting Income Inequality in Japan: A Comparative Analysis of Causes, Consequences, and Reform*. Cambridge: MIT Press.

Takayama, Noriyuki (2004): *Anshin to shinrai no nenkin kaikaku* [Reliable and trustworthy pension reform]. Tokyo: Tōyō Keizai Shinpōsha.

World Bank (1994): *Averting the Old Age Crisis*. New York: Oxford University Press.

CHAPTER SIXTY-TWO

# THE SEARCH FOR MORE EQUITABLE PENSIONS BETWEEN GENERATIONS[1]

Noriyuki Takayama

## 1. Introduction

Today, Japan has the oldest population in the world. It has also built a generous social security pension programme, but since 2002, the income statement of the principal pension programme has shown a deficit. Consequently, public distrust in the government's commitment towards pensions has been growing steadily in recent years.

The current pay-as-you-go public pension system has been working, not as a pure insurance system, but rather as a tax-and-transfer system involving huge income transfers between generations. In such a pay-as-you-go (PAYG) system, pension benefits for the aged are financed mainly by contributions from the working generation.

However, the nature of such an intergenerational contract is difficult for many people to understand. Maintaining a fixed rate of replacement in gross income terms for the elderly is by no means a contract. In fact, increasing costs stemming from larger numbers of retirees can only to a limited degree be shouldered by the actively working generation or future generations, because an increasing contribution burden will ultimately inhibit their work incentives. Instead, benefits and contributions in PAYG defined-benefit plans should be changed flexibly to respond to changing circumstances. This is necessary also because planning for different possible outcomes in the future can never be complete. Consequently we have found that the replacement rate embedded in the law is not a promise in a strict sense, but is just the starting point for an ongoing process of adaptation to a changing and unpredictable world. Continual adjustments will be required to keep the system viable.

[1] This chapter is a revised version of Takayama (2007).

This chapter addresses pension issues in the context of intergenerational equity. Special attention is paid to the following two problems: first, how to find an intergenerationally equitable remedy for the mistakes made in the past; second, what pension schemes will be preferable for a nation to avoid any inequities between generations arising from uncertainties in the future.

The chapter is structured as follows. The next two sections will give a brief overview of the Japanese social security pension programme and its financing perspectives. This is followed by a discussion of the key problems of the public pension system in section 4 and an analysis of the most important reform measures of the last pension reform in section 5. Sections 6 and 7 deal with intergenerational equity issues in Japan's social security pensions and the future policy options to secure equity between generations. The chapter closes with some concluding remarks.

## 2. Pension Provisions Before the 2004 Reform

Since 1980, Japan has carried out piecemeal pension reforms every five years, mainly due to great stresses caused by anticipated demographic and economic factors. Since then, too generous pension benefits have been reduced step by step with an increase of the normal pensionable age from 60 to 65. The pension contribution rate has been lifted gradually as well. Yet, existing pension provisions still remain generous, and face serious financial difficulties in the future.

Japan currently has a two-tier benefit system, covering all sectors of the population in the first tier with a flat-rate basic benefit. The second tier, with earnings-related benefits, applies only to employees.[2] The system operates largely like a pay-as-you-go defined-benefit programme.

The flat-rate basic pension covers all residents aged 20 to 60. The full old-age pension is payable after 40 years of contributions, provided the contributions were made before 60 years of age. The maximum monthly pension of 66,000 yen at 2006 prices (with the maximum number of years of coverage) per person is payable from age 65. The benefit is indexed automatically each fiscal year (from 1 April) to reflect changes in the consumer price index (CPI) from the previous calendar

[2] A detailed explanation of the Japanese social security pension system is given by Takayama (1998, 2003).

year. The pension may be claimed at any age between 60 and 70 years. It is subject to actuarial reduction if claimed before age 65, or actuarial increase if claimed after 65.

Earnings-related benefits are given to all employees. The accrual rate for the earnings-related component of old-age benefits is 0.5481 per cent per year, and 40 years' contributions will thus earn 28.5 per cent of career average monthly real earnings.[3]

The career-average monthly earnings are calculated over the employee's entire period of coverage, adjusted by a net-wage index factor, and converted to the current earnings level. The full earnings-related pension is normally payable from age 65 to an employee who is fully retired.[4] An earnings test is applied to those who are not fully retired. The current replacement rate (including basic benefits) for take-home pay or net income is about 60 per cent for a model male retiree (with an average salary earned during 40 years of coverage) and his dependent wife. Its monthly benefit is about 233,000 yen in 2006.

Equal percentage contributions are required of employees and their employers. The contributions are based on the annual standard earnings including bonuses. The total percentage in effect before October 2004 was 13.58 per cent for the principal programme for private-sector employees, the Employees' Pension Insurance (*Kōsei Nenkin*), hereafter referred to as EPI. Non-employed persons between the 20 and 60 years pay flat-rate individual contributions. The 2004 rate was 13,300 yen per month. For those who cannot pay for financial reasons, exemptions are permitted. The flat-rate basic benefits for the period of exemption were one-third of the normal amount.

Under the current system, if the husband has the pension contribution for social security deducted from his salary, his dependent wife is automatically entitled to the flat-rate basic benefits, and she is not required to make any individual payments to the public pension system.

The government subsidizes one-third of the total cost of the flat-rate basic benefits. There is no subsidy for the earnings-related part. The government pays administrative expenses as well.

---

[3] A semi-annual bonus equivalent to 3.6 months' salary is typically assumed.

[4] The normal pensionable age of the Employees' Pension Insurance (EPI) is 65, although Japan has special arrangements for a transition period between 2000 and 2025. See Takayama (2003) for more details.

The aggregate amount of social security pension benefits was around 46 trillion yen in 2004, which is equivalent to about 9 per cent of Japan's GDP of the same year.

## 3. Demography and Its Impact on Financing Social Security

In January 2002, the Japanese National Institute of Population and Social Security Research (NIPSSR) released population projections according to which the total population would peak at 128 million around 2006 and then begin to fall steadily, decreasing to about 50 per cent of the current number by 2100.

The total fertility rate (TFR) was 1.26 in 2005. There is still little sign that the TFR will stabilize or return to a higher level. However, the 2002 *medium variant* projections assume that it will record a historical low of 1.31 in 2006 and will gradually rise to 1.39 around 2050, progressing slowly to 2.07 by 2150. The number of births, currently about 1.06 million in 2005, will continue to decrease to less than 1.0 million by 2014, falling further to 0.67 million in 2050.

Because it has the longest life expectancy in the world, Japan is now experiencing a very rapid ageing of its population. The number of elderly people (65 years and over) was 26.4 million in 2006. The number will increase sharply to reach 34 million by 2018, remaining around 34–36 million thereafter until around 2060. Consequently the proportion of the elderly will go up very rapidly, from 20.7 per cent in 2006 to 25.3 per cent by 2014, rising further to more than 30 per cent by 2033.

In Japan, nearly 70 per cent of social security benefits are currently distributed to the elderly. Along with the ailing domestic economy, rapid ageing will certainly put more and more stresses on financing social security.

In May 2006, the Japanese Ministry of Health, Labour and Welfare published the latest estimates of the cost of social security, using the 2002 population projections of the NIPSSR. According to these latest estimates, the aggregate cost of social security in terms of GDP was 17.5 per cent in 2006. It will increase steadily to 19.0 per cent by 2025.

Of the various costs, that of pensions is quite predominant, amounting to 9.2 per cent of GDP in 2006, with an expected slight decrease to 8.7 per cent by 2025. The cost for health care was 5.4 per cent in 2006, but will rise steadily to 6.4 per cent by 2025.

## 4. Current Problems of Japan's Public Pension System

The public pension system in Japan currently faces several difficulties. Among these, the following five problems are especially crucial.

1. Persistent deficit in the income statement: since 2002, the EPI has been facing an income statement deficit. It recorded a deficit of 1.3 trillion yen in 2002, and the deficit was expected to be 4.8 trillion yen in 2005. It is estimated that the deficit will persist for a long time, unless radical remedies are made in the EPI financing.

2. Huge excess liabilities in the balance sheet: the EPI balance sheet is shown in Figure 1. In calculating the balance sheet, we assumed that:

a) annual increases in wages and CPI are 2.1 per cent and 1.0 per cent respectively in nominal terms, while the discount rate is 3.2 per cent annually,
b) the current contribution rate of the EPI, 13.58 percentage points, will remain unchanged in the future, and
c) the period up to 2100 is taken into account.

Figure 1 indicates that, as of 31 March 2005, there were excess liabilities of 550 trillion yen, which is a quarter of the total liabilities.[5]

Part One of Figure 1 is assets and liabilities accrued from past contributions and Part Two is those accrued from future contributions. Figure 1 implies that, as far as Part Two is concerned, the balance sheet of the EPI has been almost cleaned up. The funding sources of the current provisions will be sufficient to finance future benefits, and the only task left is to slim down future benefits by 4.5 per cent.

But if we look at Part One of Figure 1, things look quite different. The remaining pension liabilities are estimated to be 800 trillion yen, while pension assets are only 300 trillion yen (a funded reserve of 170 trillion yen plus transfers from general revenue of 130 trillion yen). The difference is quite large—about 500 trillion yen[6]—which accounts for the major part of excess liabilities in the EPI.

---

[5] Excess liabilities of all social security pension programmes in Japan as of March 2005 amounted to around 650 trillion yen, which is equivalent to 1.3 times the fiscal year 2004 GDP of Japan.

[6] The amount of excess liabilities (EL) will vary depending on alternative discount rates. For example, a 2.1 per cent discount rate produces EL of 650 trillion yen, while

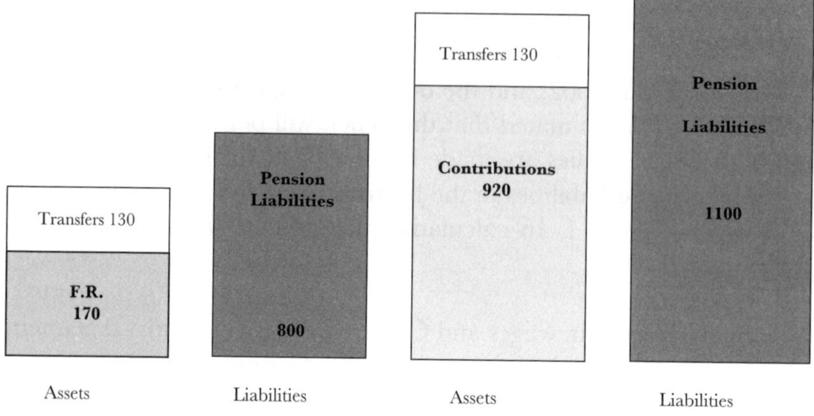


Source: Calculations by the author.

Figure 1. EPI Balance Sheet: Before Reform.

500 trillion yen is more than 60 per cent of Part One liabilities, equivalent to about 100 per cent of GDP of Japan in 2004. In the past, too many promises on pension benefits were made, while sufficient funding sources have not been arranged. The Japanese have enjoyed a long history of generous social security pensions. However, contributions made in the past were relatively small, resulting in a fairly small funded reserve. Consequently, the locus of the true crisis in Japanese social security pensions is how to handle the excess liabilities of 500 trillion yen to which people were entitled on the basis of their contributions made in the past.

3. Heavy burdens outstanding for pension contributions: in Japanese public debates, one of the principal issues has been how to cut down personal and corporate income tax. But recently the situation has changed drastically. Social security contributions (for pensions, health care, unemployment, work injury and long-term care) are 55.6 trillion yen (15.2 per cent of national income) for FY 2003. This is more

another 4.0 per cent discount rate produces EL of 420 trillion yen. Part One excess liabilities can be termed as "accrued-to-date net liabilities" or "net termination liabilities". See Franco (1995) and Holzmann *et al.* (2004).

than all tax revenues (43.9 trillion yen) of the central government for the same year. Since 1998, the central government has acquired more from social security contributions than from tax incomes. Looking in more detail, we can see that revenue from personal income tax is 13.8 trillion yen and corporate income tax is 9.1 trillion yen, while revenue from social security pension contributions stands out at 29.0 trillion yen. Needless to say, the last places a most heavy burden on the public. The Japanese now feel that social security pension contributions are too heavy; they operate as the most significant factor in determining the take-home pay from the gross salary. On the other hand, businesses have begun to show serious concerns about any further increases in social security contributions.

4. Overshooting in income transfer between generations: currently, in terms of per-capita income after redistribution, the elderly in Japan are better off than those aged 30 to 44 (see Figure 2). Undoubtedly, there must still be room for reductions in benefits provided to the current retired population.

5. Increasing drop-out: in the past 20 years, the Japanese government has made repeated changes to the pension programme, increasing social security pension contributions and reducing benefits by raising the normal pensionable age while reducing the accrual rate. Further such piecemeal reforms are very likely to follow in the future.

Many Japanese feel that the government is breaking its promise. As distrust against government commitment builds up, concern about such a 'problem of lack of trust' is also growing.

In 2005, nearly 33 per cent of non-salaried workers and people with no occupations dropped out from the basic level of old-age income protection, owing to exemption, delinquency in paying contributions or non-application (see Figure 3 for increasing delinquency).

Also, employers are discreetly trying to find ways to avoid paying social security pension contributions. The Ministry of Internal Affairs and Communications has estimated that nearly 30 per cent of the relevant business establishments did not participate in the EPI in 2004. Any further escalation in the social security contribution rate is likely to induce a higher drop-out rate.[7]

[7] Contributions to social security pensions operate as "penalties on employment." Further increases in the contribution rate will severely hit domestic companies, which have been facing mega-competition on a global scale, thereby exerting negative effects on the economy, leading to a higher unemployment rate, lower economic growth,

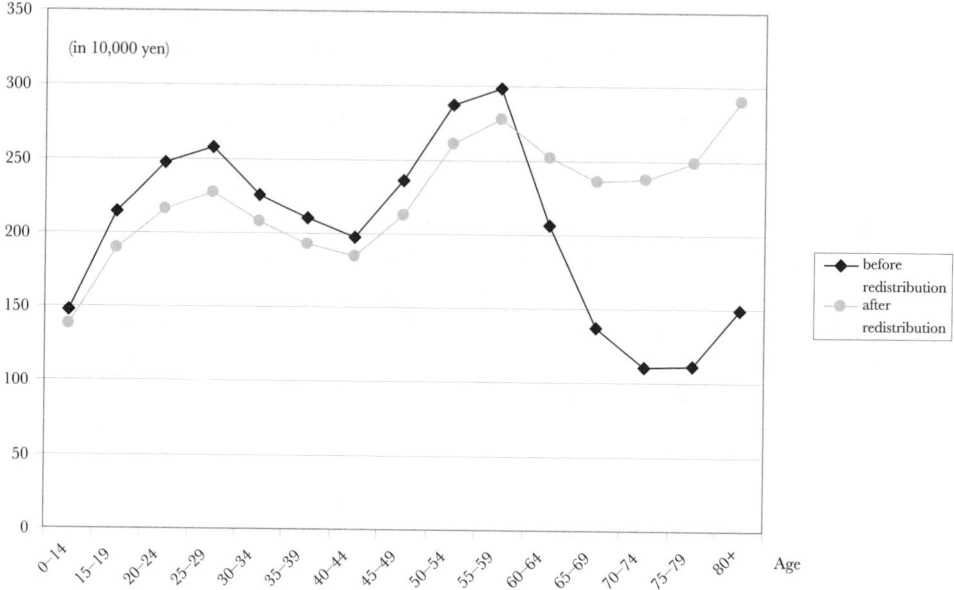


Source: Ministry of Health and Welfare, *The 1996 Income Redistribution Survey.*

Figure 2. Per capita income by age-group in Japan.

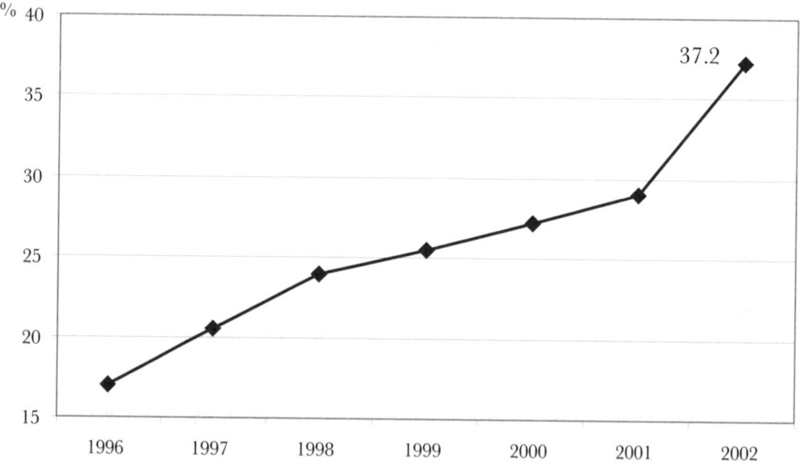


Source:

Figure 3. Drop-out rate in the National Pension Insurance (non-employees) (Percentage of those not paying pension contributions).

## 5. The 2004 Pension Reform: Main Reform Measures and Remaining Difficulties[8]

The administration of former Prime Minister Koizumi Jun'ichirō submitted a set of pension reform bills to the National Diet on 10 February 2004, and these were enacted on June 5. This section will describe the gist of the approved reforms and explore issues that remain to be addressed.

Salaried workers are, as a rule, enrolled in the EPI, which is part of the public pension system. Contributions under this plan had since October 1996 been set at 13.58 per cent of annual income, paid half by the worker and half by the employer, but the newly enacted reform has raised this rate by 0.354 percentage point per year starting in October 2004. The rate will rise every September thereafter until 2017, after which it will remain fixed at 18.30 per cent. The portion paid by workers will accordingly rise from 6.79 per cent of annual income in 2003 to 9.15 per cent in 2017.

For an average male company employee earning 360,000 yen a month plus annual bonuses equivalent to 3.6 months' pay, contributions will increase by nearly 20,000 yen a year starting in October 2004. By the time they stop rising in September 2017, they will have reached just under 1.03 million yen a year, and the share paid by the worker will be just over 514,000 yen. This amounts to a 35 per cent increase from current contribution levels.

Those who are not enrolled in the EPI or other public pension schemes for civil servants are required to participate in the National Pension Insurance (*Kokumin Nenkin*), which provides just the basic pension (the basic pension also forms the first tier of benefits under the EPI and other public pension systems for civil servants). Contributions under this plan will rise by 280 yen each April from the current 13,300 yen per month until they plateau at 16,900 yen (at 2004 prices) in April 2017. The actual rise in National Pension contributions will be adjusted according to increases in general wage levels.

In addition, the government will increase its subsidies for the basic pension. One-third of the cost of basic pension benefits is paid from

---

lower saving rates and so on. Further increases in the contribution rate will be sure to decrease the take-home pay of actively working people in real terms, producing lower consumption and lower effective demand.

[8] This section depends heavily on Takayama (2004).

the national treasury; this share is to be raised in stages until it reaches one-half in 2009.

Benefits under the EPI consist of two tiers: the flat-rate basic pension, which is paid to all public pension plan participants, and a separate earnings-related component. The latter is calculated on the basis of the worker's average pre-retirement income, converted to current values. Until now, the index used to convert past income to current values was the rate of increase in take-home pay. Under the 2004 reform, though, this index will be subject to a negative adjustment over the course of an "exceptional period" based on changes in two demographic factors, namely, the decline in the number of participants and the increase in life expectancy. This period of adjustment is expected to last through 2023.

The application of the first demographic factor will mean that benefit levels will be cut to reflect the fact that fewer people are supporting the pension system. The actual number of people enrolled in all public pension schemes will be ascertained each year, and the rate of decline will be calculated based on this figure. The average annual decline is projected to be around 0.6 point.

Introducing the second demographic factor, meanwhile, will adjust for the fact that people are living longer and thus collecting their pensions for more years; the aim is to slow the pace of increase in the total amount of benefits paid as a result of increased longevity. This factor will not be calculated by tracking future movements in life expectancy; instead, it has been set at an annual rate of about 0.3 percentage point on the basis of current demographic projections for the period through 2025. Together, the two demographic factors are thus expected to mean a negative adjustment of about 0.9 point a year during the period in question.

How will these changes affect people's benefits in concrete terms? Let us consider the case of a pair of model EPI beneficiaries as defined by the Ministry of Health, Labour, and Welfare: a 65-year-old man who earned the average wage throughout his 40-year career, and his 65-year-old wife, who was a full-time homemaker for 40 years from her twentieth birthday. In fiscal 2004 (April 2004 to March 2005), this model couple would receive 233,000 yen a month.

How does this amount compare to what employees are currently taking home? The average monthly income of a salaried worker in 2004 was around 360,000 yen, before taxes and social insurance deductions. Assuming that this is supplemented by bonuses totalling an equivalent of 3.6 months' pay, the average annual income is roughly 5.6 million yen. Deducting 16 per cent of this figure for taxes and social insurance payments leaves a figure for annual take-home pay of about 4.7 million yen, or 393,000 yen a month.

The 233,000 yen provided to the model pensioners is 59.3 per cent of 393,000 yen. But this percentage, which pension specialists call the "income replacement ratio," will gradually decline to an estimated figure of 50.2 per cent as of fiscal 2023 (assuming that consumer prices and nominal wages rise according to government projections by 1.0 per cent and 2.1 per cent a year respectively). Over the next two decades, then, benefit levels will decline by roughly 15 per cent by comparison with wage levels.

The revised pension legislation stipulates that the income replacement ratio is not to fall below 50 per cent for the model case described above, and so the exceptional period of negative adjustment will come to an end once the ratio declines to 50 per cent. This provision was included to alleviate fears that benefits would continue to shrink without limit.

How will the reforms affect those who are already receiving their pensions? Until now, benefits for those 65 years old and over have been adjusted for fluctuations in the consumer price index. This ensured that pensioners' real purchasing power remained unchanged and helped ease postretirement worries. But this cost-of-living link will effectively be severed during the exceptional period, since the application of the demographic factors will pull down real benefits by around 0.9 point a year. In principle, however, nominal benefits are not to be cut unless there has also been a drop in consumer prices. Once the exceptional period is over, the link to the consumer price index is to be restored.

Social insurance contributions in Japan already exceed the amount collected in national taxes, and contributions to the pension system are by far the biggest social insurance item. If this already huge sum is increased by more than 1 trillion yen a year, as the government plans, both individuals and companies are bound to change their behaviour. Government projections of revenues and expenditures, however, completely ignore the prospect of such changes. Companies are likely to revamp their hiring plans and wage scales to sidestep the higher social insurance burden. They will cut back on recruitment of new graduates and become more selective about mid-career hiring as well. Many young people will be stripped of employment opportunities and driven out of the labour market, instead of being enlisted to support the pension system with a percentage of their income. And most of the employment options for middle-aged women who wish to re-enter the work force will be low-paying ones. Only a few older workers will be able to continue to command high wages; there is likely to be a dramatic rise in the number of ageing workers who will be forced to choose between remaining on the payroll with a cut in pay or settling for retirement. Many more companies will either choose or be forced to leave the EPI, causing the number of subscribers to fall far below the government's projections and pushing the system closer to bankruptcy.

The jobless rate overall will rise. The Ministry of Economy, Trade, and Industry has estimated that higher pension contributions will lead to the loss of one million jobs and raise the unemployment rate by 1.3 points. The government plan to increase pension contributions annually for the next 13 years will exert ongoing deflationary pressure on the Japanese economy. For the worker, a rise in contribution levels means less take-home pay; as a result, consumer spending is likely to fall, and this will certainly hinder prospects for a self-sustaining recovery and return to steady growth.

Another problem with increasing pension contributions is that they are regressive, since there is a ceiling for the earnings on which payment calculations are based and unearned income is not included in the calculations at all.

One major objective of the reforms is to eventually eliminate the huge excess liabilities in the balance sheet of the EPI. The plan is to generate a surplus by (1) raising contributions, (2) increasing payments from the national treasury, and (3) reducing benefits. The policy measures adopted in the 2004 pension reform bill will induce huge excess assets of 420 trillion yen in Part Two of the balance sheet whereby offsetting excess liabilities of the same amount in Part One of the balance sheet, as shown in Figure 4. Huge excess assets of Part Two of the balance sheet imply that future generations will be forced to pay more than the anticipated benefits they will receive. Their benefits will be around 80 per cent of their contributions, on the whole.

It is like using a sledgehammer to crack a nut. Younger generations are most likely to intensify their distrust in the government. The incentive-compatibility problem or the drop-out problem will become graver. Business (represented by the Japan Business Federation, Nippon Keidanren) and trade unions (represented by the Japanese Trade Union Confederation *Rengo*) both oppose any further increases of more than 15 percentage points in the EPI contribution rate.

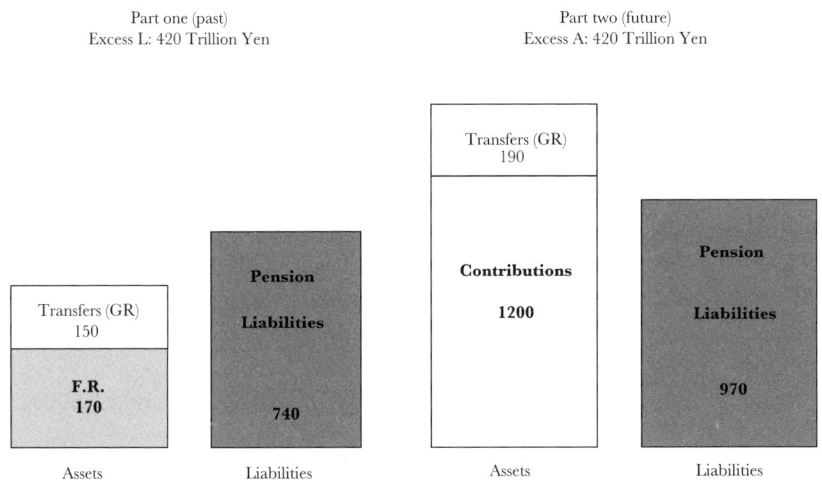


Source: Calculations by the author.

Figure 4. EPI Balance Sheet: After Reform.

As noted above, those who are already receiving their pensions will see their benefits decline in real terms by an average 0.9 per cent per year. The government scenario sees consumer prices eventually rising by 1.0 per cent a year and take-home pay by 2.1 per cent a year. This means that the model beneficiary who begins receiving 233,000 yen a month at age 65 in 2004 will get roughly 240,000 yen at age 84 in 2023; nominal benefits, in other words, will remain virtually unchanged for two decades, despite the fact that the average take-home pay of the working population will have risen by over 40 per cent. The income replacement rate, which stood at nearly 60 per cent at age 65, will dwindle to 43 per cent by the time the model recipient turns 84. The promise of benefits in excess of 50 per cent of take-home pay does not apply, therefore, to those who are already on old-age pensions.

The so-called demographic factors are likely to continue changing for the foreseeable future. The government itself foresees the number of participants in public pension plans declining over the coming century: the estimated figure of 69.4 million participants as of 2005 is expected to fall to 61.0 million in 2025, 45.3 million in 2050, and 29.2 million in 2100. This corresponds to an average annual decline of 0.6 per cent through 2025, 1.2 per cent of the quarter-century from 2025, and 0.9 per cent for the half-century from 2050. In other words, the decline in the number of workers who are financially supporting the public pension system is not likely to stop after just two decades.

However, the 2004 reform adjusts benefit levels in keeping with the decline in the contribution-paying population for the next 20 years only; the government's standard case does not foresee any further downward revisions, even if the number of participants continues to fall. If the government really anticipates an ongoing decline, there is no good reason to abruptly stop adjusting benefit levels after a certain period of time. Sweden and Germany, for instance, have adopted permanent mechanisms whereby benefit levels are automatically adjusted for fluctuations in demographic factors.

The decision to keep the model income replacement rate at 50 per cent at the point when pension payments commence represents, in effect, the adoption of a defined-benefit formula. Maintaining both fixed contributions on the one hand and defined benefit levels on the other is not an easy task, for there is no room to deal flexibly with unforeseen developments. The government will be confronted with a fiscal emergency should its projections for growth in contributions and a reversal in the falling birth rate be wide of the mark.

The government bases its population figures on the January 2002 projections of the National Institute of Population and Social Security Research. According to these projections, the medium variant for the total fertility rate (the average number of childbirths per woman) will fall to 1.31 in 2007, after which it will begin climbing, reaching 1.39 in 2050 and 1.73 in 2100. Actual figures since the projections were released have been slightly lower than this variant, and there are no signs whatsoever that the fertility rate will stop declining in 2007.

If the government is to keep its promise on an upper limit for contributions and a lower limit for benefits, the only policy option it will have in the event of a financial shortfall will be to raise the age at which people begin receiving benefits. The reform package makes no mention of such a possibility; the drafters of the bills no doubt chose simply to put this task off for a future date.[9]

By fiscal 2009, the share of the basic pension benefits funded by the national treasury will be raised from one-third to one-half. This means that more taxes will be used to cover the cost of benefits. Taxes are

---

[9] Later retirement would be preferable for the country to achieve active ageing, providing that this has little substitution effects on employment for young people.

by nature different from contributions paid by participants in specific pension plans, and there is a need to reconsider the benefits that are to be funded by tax revenues.

The leaders of Japanese industry tend to be quite advanced in years. For the most part, they are over the age of 65, which means that they are qualified to receive the flat-rate basic pension. Even though they are among the wealthiest people in the country, they are entitled to the same basic pension as other older people hovering around the poverty line. Using tax revenues to finance a bigger share of the basic pension essentially means asking taxpayers to foot a bigger bill for the benefits of wealthy households as well. For an elderly couple, the tax-financed portion of the basic pension will rise from 530,000 yen a year to 800,000 yen. If a need arises to raise taxes at a future date, who will then actually agree to pay more? Few people will be willing to tolerate such a wasteful use of tax money.

## 6. Intergenerational Equity Issues in Japan's Social Security Pensions

Huge excess liabilities of 500 trillion yen appearing in Part One of Figure 1 partly reflect mistakes made in the past.[10] It is true that any social security scheme for pensions faces great uncertainties for its future long-term scenarios: about the number of participants, the number of pensioners, the rate of increases in wages or the consumer price index, and the rate of return from investment. No one has precise information on these variables beforehand. Nevertheless, the system planners need some fixed figures on the system's future scenario when designing (or re-designing) the pension system. It is often the case, however, that the assumed figures differ to a greater or lesser extent from the actual ones. What really matters is whether or not the system planners adjust their system to correspond to the changing circumstances in a timely and proper way.

Japanese experience in the past 30 years shows that the adjustments were so slow and insufficient as to produce huge excess liabilities amounting to 500 trillion yen. It is evident that pension projections

[10] The excess liabilities arise partly from windfall gains given to the first generation in a pay-as-you-go pension system. This part should not simply be interpreted as "the mistakes made in the past."

always turned out to be too optimistic, and that politicians were always reluctant to introduce painful remedies for current pensioners and current contributors, leaving the pension system financially unsustainable and inequitable between generations.

The 2004 reform in Japan looks very drastic, since the introduction of the demographic factors will significantly reduce the level of pension benefits in real terms. These reductions are regarded as an inevitable reaction to make up for the mistakes or omissions made in the past, for which the current pensioners and the baby-boomers were responsible. Nevertheless, the 2004 reform still suffers from an incentive-compatibility problem, leaving the pension system inequitable from the younger generations' point of view.[11]

## 7. Future Policy Options for Securing Equity Between Generations

Are there any policy measures that could avoid the incentive-compatibility problem in Japan? This section tries to answer this question.

To begin with, how about separating the "legacy pension" problem from the problem of re-building a sustainable pension system for the future? The two problems are quite different in nature, and accordingly they require separate treatment.

The legacy pension problem of Japan looks like *sunk costs* from an economic perspective. It can be eased, not by increasing the EPI contribution rate, but by introducing a new 2.0 per cent earmarked consumption tax and intensive injection of the increased transfers from general revenue (see Figure 5). Needless to say, the current generous benefits have to be reduced more or less by the same percentage in the aggregate level as implemented in the 2004 pension reform.

All these measures are considered on the understanding that current pensioners and baby-boomers are mainly responsible for Part One excess liabilities, and that they are therefore first in line in diminishing

[11] Richard Musgrave once examined the credibility and long-run political viability of alternative contracts between generations, demonstrating that a "*Fixed Relative Position (FRP)*" approach is most preferable (Musgrave 1981). Following his suggestion, Germany and Japan had introduced a net indexation method in adjusting their social security pension benefits since the early 1990s. The FRP approach faces some difficulties, however. For example, this approach could be acceptable only if participation in the social security pension system pays for the younger generations.

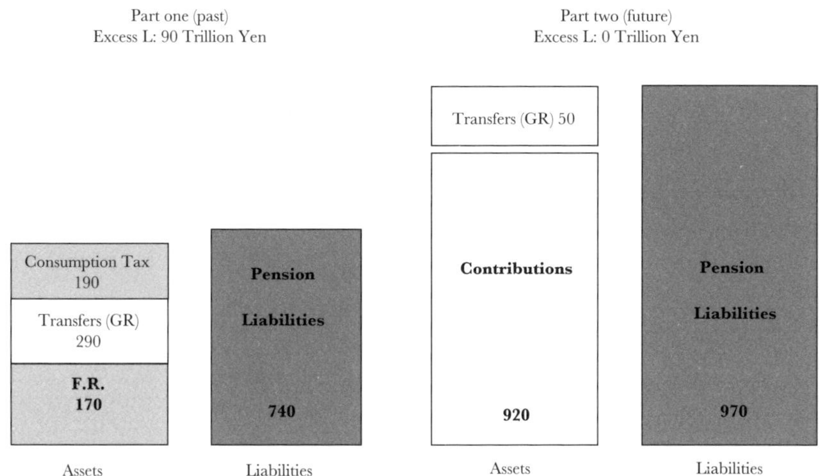


Source: Calculations by the author.

Figure 5. EPI Balance Sheet After Alternative Reform.

the existing excess liabilities. Note that any increases in the contribution rate for social security pensions will be paid by current younger and future generations. Current pensioners no longer pay them and baby boomers will pay them only to a small extent. They are not an appropriate measure for diminishing Part One excess liabilities. By contrast, an increase in the consumption-based tax will be shared by all the existing and future generations, including current pensioners and baby-boomers.[12] Increased transfers from general revenue can be financed by increases in inheritance tax and income tax on pension benefits as well.[13]

When it comes to Part Two of the balance sheet, which relates to future contributions and promised pension benefits to which people are entitled through future contributions, a switch to an NDC (notional

[12] The payroll tax and the consumption-based tax might be indifferent in a steady-state economy, although they will induce different economic impacts in a transition period.

[13] A 2 per cent earmarked consumption tax could be all right, since the remaining excess liabilities of 90 trillion yen might be acceptable as a "hidden" national debt. Even if all the alternative measures above stated are implemented, current young and future generations will still have to pay a substantial part of Part One excess liabilities. However, the current pensioners and baby boomers should still try to do as much as possible to diminish the excess liabilities before any further increases in the contribution rate are considered.

defined contribution) system is possible and preferable.[14] An NDC system follows the philosophy of a funded system of individual accounts, but with a pay-as-you-go financing structure. The main difference from a defined-benefit model is that NDC benefits are defined, not by a formula based on wages and years of service, but by a worker's accumulated account balance at retirement. Benefits are thus closely linked to contributions. With an NDC system in place, the EPI contribution rate can be kept unchanged at the current level, around 14 percentage points.

With an NDC plan, the incentive-compatibility problem can be avoided. Indeed, in an NDC system, every penny counts, and this would be the most important element, because it would demonstrate to the public that everybody gets a pension equivalent to his or her own contribution payments (see Könberg 2002; Palmer 2003).

In an NDC, the notional rate of return should be endogenous. It could be periodically adjusted by an automatic balance mechanism, such as was introduced in Sweden (see Settergren 2001). Alternatively, in 2004, Germany introduced a sustainability factor, whereas Japan implemented the demographic factors in the same year. Both factors operate more or less as an automatic balance mechanism. The automatic balance mechanism aims to avoid any political difficulties by flexibly adapting the pension system to a changing and unpredictable world.

We could also introduce a guaranteed pension (GP) to add to the NDC pensions. This would be to provide an adequate income in old age. However, this should be financed by sources other than contributions (payroll tax), since the policy objectives for a guaranteed pension and an NDC are quite different (see Figure 6).

## 8. Concluding Remarks

Regarding pensions, the Japanese are increasingly concerned with the "taste of the pie" rather than the "size of the pie" or the "distribution of the pie." When it comes to social security pensions, the most important question is whether or not they are worth buying. How big or how fair they are has become a secondary concern. The basic design of the pension programme should be incentive-compatible. Contributions

[14] A funded plan might be another alternative. However, it cannot escape the so-called "double burden" problem in the transition period, while the NDC is free from it.

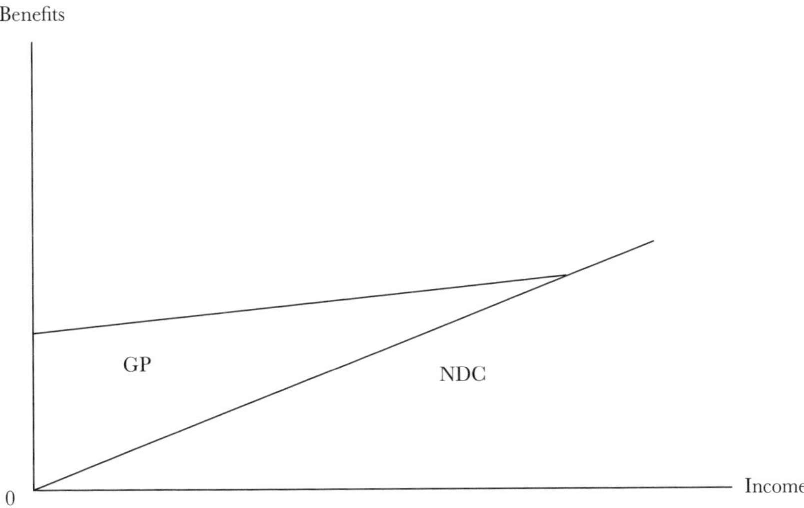


Source: By the author.

Figure 6. Notional Defined Contribution plus Guarantee Pension.

should be much more directly linked to old-age pension benefits, while an element of social adequacy should be incorporated in a separate tier of pension benefits financed by sources other than contributions.

Japan faces the problem of seeking to meet too many targets through the single policy instrument of pensions. This contradicts the standard theory of policy assignment, which suggests that each policy objective can be best attained only if it is matched with a different policy instrument of comparative advantage. A diversified multi-tier system is thus most preferable.

Also important is the separation of the legacy pension problem from the problem of rebuilding a sustainable and intergenerationally equitable pension system.

Social security pensions are consumption-allocation mechanisms, thereby transferring resources from workers to pensioners when pensions are paid. Under a pay-as-you-go system, the transfer is direct, through contributions or taxes paid by workers. Under a funded system, pensioners liquidate their accumulated assets by selling them to the current working generation. In both cases, workers' disposable income is reduced by the amount of resources transferred to retirees. Supporting an increasing number of retired people is possible if output grows. Economic output depends crucially on the supply of workers, and thus increasing labour force participation on the part of young retirees, women and young adults will be required.

No one can claim to see clearly all the changes that lie ahead in the decades to come. Nevertheless, the challenge is hard to ignore. What is missing is more explicit consideration of an automatic balancing mechanism for remedying possible mistakes in the projections towards the future.

## References

Franco, Daniele (1995): Pension Liabilities: Their Use and Misuse in the Assessment of Fiscal Policies. In: *Economic Papers* 110, Commission of the EC, Directorate-General for Economic and Financial Affairs (DG ECFIN).

Holzmann, Robert, Robert Palacios and Asta Zviniene (2004): Implicit Pension Debt: Issues, Measurement and Scope in International Perspective. In: *Social Protection Discussion Paper Series* No. 0403, Social Protection Unit, World Bank.

Könberg, Bo (2002): The Swedish Pension Reform: Some Lessons. In: *Discussion Paper* 46. Project on Intergenerational Equity, Institute of Economic Research, Hitotsubashi University.

Musgrave, Richard A. (1981): A Reappraisal of Financing Social Security. In: Skidmore, Felicity (ed.): *Social Security Financing*. Cambridge: MIT Press, pp. 89–125.

Palmer, Edward (2003): Pension Reform in Sweden. In: Takayama, Noriyuki (ed.): *Taste of Pie: Searching for Better Pension Provisions in Developed Countries*. Tokyo: Maruzen CO., Ltd., pp. 245–269.

Project on Intergenerational Equity, Hitotsubashi University (2005): *The Balance Sheet of Social Security Pensions*, Proceedings 6, PIE. Tokyo: Hitotsubashi University.

Settergren, Ole (2001): *The Automatic Balance Mechanism of the Swedish Pension System*. http://forsakringskassan.se/sprak/eng/publications/dokument/aut0107.pdf (found 29 November 2006).

Takayama, Noriyuki (1998): *The Morning After in Japan: Its Declining Population, Too Generous Pensions and a Weakened Economy*. Tokyo: Maruzen CO., Ltd.

—— (2003): Pension Arrangements in the Oldest Country: The Japanese Case. In: Takayama, Noriyuki (ed.): *Taste of Pie: Searching for Better Pension Provisions in Developed Countries*. Tokyo: Maruzen CO., Ltd., pp. 185–217.

—— (2004): Changes in the Pension System. In: *Japan Echo* 31, 5 (October), pp. 9–10.

—— (2007): Social Security Pensions and Intergenerational Equity: The Japanese Case. In: Roemer, John E. and Suzumura Kotaro (eds.): *Intergenerational Equity and Sustainability*. Houndmills and New York: Palgrave.

CHAPTER SIXTY-THREE

# THE RESTRUCTURING OF THE CORPORATE PENSION SYSTEM

Tomoyuki Kubo

## 1. Introduction

According to the 2004 Public Pension Reform Act, the replacement rate of public pensions in comparison to the net income of a typical employee household will be reduced to 50.2 per cent in 2050 from 59 per cent in 2004. With this substantial curtailment of public pension benefits, expectations that private pensions will close the emerging old-age security benefit gap have risen considerably. Private pensions have thus received more attention lately, and important corporate pension reforms were undertaken in the early 2000s.

This chapter presents some general information on the situation of corporate pensions[1] in Japan and discusses the potential of these types of pensions for old-age income security in the future. Section 2 gives a short overview of the history of corporate pensions in Japan; section 3 then discusses the contents and significance of the newly introduced corporate pension schemes in recent years. The fourth section highlights current problems and possible future developments of corporate pension insurance in this country.

---

[1] It is common to use the term "occupational pension" for pension plans financed by employers (or sometimes unions). However, there are few industry-wide pension plans in Japan. Usually, an employer or a group of employers with a special relationship, such as parent-subsidiary, establish a pension plan. Therefore, the terminology "corporate pension" is used in this article for plans financed by employers.

## 2. Historical Overview of the Corporate Pension System in Japan

### 2.1. *The retirement allowance system and the emergence of corporate pensions*

Since Japan's corporate pension system developed from a retirement allowance (lump sum) system, one must consider the retirement allowance first in order to understand the characteristics of today's corporate pension system. The start of the retirement allowance system is said to date back to *noren-wake* (shop-curtain division) in the Edo period. *Noren-wake* was a custom according to which employees who had been working at the same shop for years were finally permitted to open a shop themselves with the help of their former employer. The customer base was divided and sometimes money was also transferred to the former employees.

The retirement allowance system after World War II shows similar aspects of gratuity for employees. Because financial resources were scarce in the immediate postwar period, companies promised their employees future retirement benefits instead of paying them their whole salary. Since they were guaranteed long-term employment based on the so-called "lifetime employment system", employees were able to plan their lives on a long-term basis.

Although a company could not take back wages which had already been paid, it could give preferential treatment to those who had been working for a long period of time, by paying them progressively higher benefits. Of course this also worked the other way round: employees who left the company after only a few years were paid less. Thus, the retirement allowance also played a role in the personnel management of companies.

As the Japanese working population grew older and many employees retired at the same time, financing retirement allowances became hard to manage. Companies began to develop ways to spread these payments, such as by saving capital beforehand or by dividing the whole sum into a number of instalments. These attempts to level the burden of the funds were connected to the development of corporate pensions, which will be discussed next.

### 2.2. *The birth of Tax-qualified Pension Plans*

Tax-qualified Pension Plans (TQP) were created in 1962. After the Japan Federation of Employers' Associations had published a report

Table 1. Historical overview of the Japanese corporate pension system.

| Period | Event |
|---|---|
| Edo period | "Shop curtain division" started |
| Meiji period | Retirement allowance system developed |
| Taishō period | In-house pensions similar to civil servants' pensions appeared |
| Early postwar period | The retirement allowance system became popular against the background of the financial needs of companies |
| 1962 | Tax-Qualified Pension Plans (TQP) were introduced |
| 1965 | Employees' Pension Funds (EPF) were introduced |
| 2000 | Changes in the retirement benefit accounting |
| 2001 | New defined-contribution plans and defined-benefit plans were introduced |
| 2012 | Tax-Qualified Pension Plans (TQP) will be abolished |

Source: Kubo 2004: 23.

"Demand relating to the taxation policy of corporate pension plans" in 1957, parts of the Corporate Tax Law and the Income Tax Law were revised in order to allow companies tax preferences, so that they could establish corporate pension plans. A TQP is an agreement between a company and a financial institution which receives preferential tax treatment focusing on deductible contributions. It allows lump sum payments (see Fig. 1).

Because TQP were easy to establish and advantageous in the tax system, smaller companies in particular would use them for their retirement allowance payments. However, the TQP will be abolished at the end of March 2012 and be replaced by the new defined-benefit plans which will be discussed later.

### 2.3. *The introduction of Employees' Pension Funds*

The Employees' Pension Funds (EPF) were introduced in 1966. They provide a substitutional part to the public pension (*daikō*), as well as their own additional benefits. By assuming the responsibility for paying a substitutional part of the public pension, companies pay lower social security contributions, while the public pension insurance bears the cost for price- and wage-indexation (see Figure 2). The contributions to the substitutional component are equally divided between the worker and the firm, whereas additional benefits are paid mostly by the employer. Employer contributions are treated like business expenses and are therefore deductible from corporate income tax. The employees'

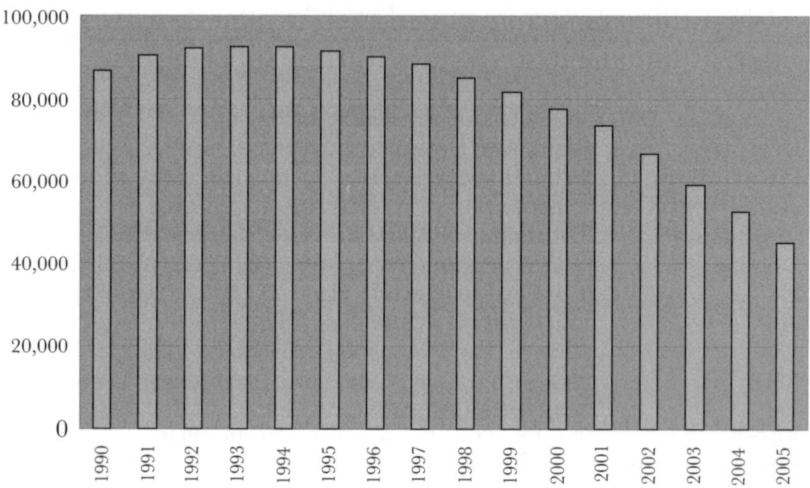


Source: Nikko Financial Intelligence 2006.

Figure 1. Development of the number of Tax-Qualified Pension Plans.

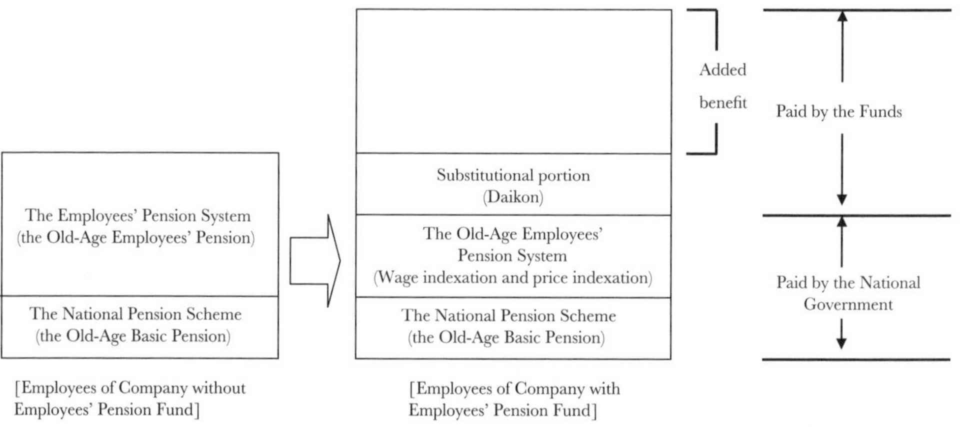


Source: MHLW 2005 (Chapter 9): 130.

Figure 2. The structure of Employees' Pension Funds.

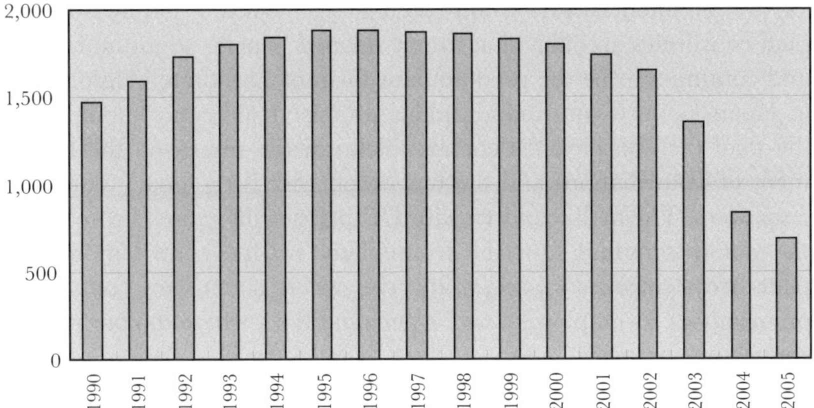


Source: Nikko Financial Intelligence 2006.

Figure 3. Development of the number of Employees' Pension Funds.

contributions to the EPF are exempt from income tax. EPF benefits are usually paid as annuities.

The EPF have played an important role in Japan, but have recently faced financial problems which have led to a dramatic reduction of these plans, from 1,883 in 1996 to 687 in 2005 (see Figure 3).

## 3. Recent Developments in the Corporate Pension System

In 2000, a new rule for the accounting of retirement benefits came into effect. It changed the pension accounting from a system that used to recognize only pension contributions as annual cost to one that acknowledged the full amount of the deferred payments on a market value basis. The pension liability should be recognized as a projected benefit obligation.

Owing to this change, future pension obligations and financing shortfalls became visible, and many companies had to start to review their management of corporate pensions. The ongoing restructuring process takes place against the background of new pension legislation, with the Defined Contribution Pension Law [*Kakutei Kyōshutsu Nenkin-hō*] and the Defined Benefit Corporate Pension Law [*Kakutei Kyūfu Kigyo nenkin-hō*], enacted in June 2001, as its heart. These new laws present companies with a number of new options to restructure their corporate pension plans, as shown in Figure 4.

New Defined Contribution (DC) Plans: While a defined-benefit plan constitutes an obligation to pay defined benefits to future retirees and continues to be the predominant form of corporate pension plan in Japan, defined-contribution plans promise fixed contributions, and the final pension payout depends solely on the return on the investment of contributions and the investment risk is essentially borne by employees. The main concern with DC plans is therefore how to invest the money stemming from the accumulated tax-free contributions. DC plans are divided into a corporate type, where a company contributes on behalf of its employees, and a personal type, where the participant contributes himself.

New Defined-Benefit (DB) Plans: The new defined-benefit plans are to ensure the continued protection of benefit rights in those plans where the sponsoring company terminates an EPF or a TQP plan. They guarantee fiduciary responsibility for the person in charge, and provide the disclosure of financial information to the participants and the beneficiaries. Although some companies might find these restrictions quite burdensome, corporate pensions are after all based on the trust between a company and its employees, and the responsibility of the company that promises benefits does not change in any way.

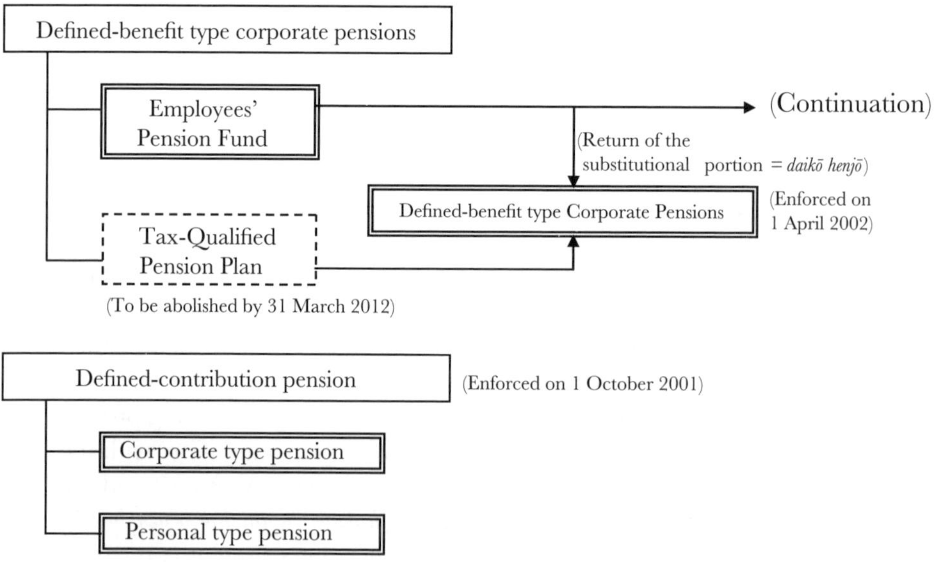


Source: MHLW 2005 (Chapter 9): 12.

Figure 4. Recent corporate pension restructuring.

Table 2. Historical data on Japanese corporate pension plans.

| Year (April–March) | Employees' Pension Funds | | Tax-qualified Pension Plans | | Defined-Benefit Plans | | Defined-Contribution Plans | |
|---|---|---|---|---|---|---|---|---|
| | Funds | Participants (in 1,000s) | Contracts | Participants (in 1,000s) | Plans | Participants (in 1,000s) | Plans | Participants (in 1,000s) |
| 1975 | 929 | 5,340 | ... | ... | - | - | - | - |
| 1980 | 991 | 5,964 | ... | ... | - | - | - | - |
| 1985 | 1,091 | 7,058 | 68,268 | 7,560 | - | - | - | - |
| 1990 | 1,474 | 9,845 | 86,648 | 9,370 | - | - | - | - |
| 1991 | 1,593 | 10,678 | 90,434 | 9,770 | - | - | - | - |
| 1992 | 1,735 | 11,571 | 92,082 | 10,400 | - | - | - | - |
| 1993 | 1,804 | 11,919 | 92,467 | 10,600 | - | - | - | - |
| 1994 | 1,842 | 12,051 | 92,355 | 10,751 | - | - | - | - |
| 1995 | 1,878 | 12,130 | 91,465 | 10,776 | - | - | - | - |
| 1996 | 1,883 | 12,096 | 90,239 | 10,626 | - | - | - | - |
| 1997 | 1,874 | 12,254 | 88,312 | 10,432 | - | - | - | - |
| 1998 | 1,858 | 12,002 | 85,047 | 10,297 | - | - | - | - |
| 1999 | 1,832 | 11,692 | 81,605 | 10,011 | - | - | - | - |
| 2000 | 1,801 | 11,396 | 77,555 | 9,656 | - | - | - | - |
| 2001 | 1,737 | 10,871 | 73,582 | 9,167 | - | - | 70 | 88 |
| 2002 | 1,656 | 10,386 | 66,741 | 8,586 | 43 | - | 361 | 325 |
| 2003 | 1,357 | 8,351 | 59,163 | 7,770 | 309 | - | 845 | 708 |
| 2004 | 838 | 6,152 | 52,761 | 6,545 | 1,103 | 3,140 | 1,402 | 1,255 |
| 2005 | 687 | 5,250 | 45,090 | 5,670 | 1,432 | 3,840 | 1,866 | *(Jan 31) 1,715 |

Source: Nikko Financial Intelligence (2006).

Cash-Balance (CB) Plans and Cash-Balance-like (CB-like) Plans: "Cash-Balance" is a form allowed in EPF and defined-benefit plans. Although it should rather be called "Cash-Balance Type" in defined-benefit plans, it is usually referred to as a "Cash-Balance Plan". A typical cash-balance plan credits the interest—(based on a given index) to the contribution—(calculated by a certain standard) via a virtual individual account balance, and provides the pension or the lump sum that corresponds to this balance. In terms of structure, CB and DC plans are quite similar. How DC, CB and DB plans differ in detail can be seen in Table 4.

Table 3. The current status of Japanese corporate pension plans (as of March 2006).

| | | Funds | Asset amounts (market value) | | | Participants (in 10,000) |
|---|---|---|---|---|---|---|
| | | | (100 million Yen) | Composition (%) | Compared to previous year (%) | |
| EPF | Trust banks | 512 | 346,309 | 92.30% | Δ0.3% | 435 |
| | Insurance companies | 175 | 29,073 | 7.70% | Δ21.7% | 89 |
| | sub total | 687 | 375,382 | 100.00% | Δ2.4% | 525 |
| TQP | Trust banks | 6,938 | 101,334 | 58.70% | 9.40% | 243 |
| | Insurance companies | 37,725 | 68,230 | 39.50% | Δ10.4% | 313 |
| | Others | 427 | 3,153 | 1.80% | 2.90% | 10 |
| | sub total | 45,090 | 172,718 | 100.00% | 0.50% | 567 |
| DB | Trust banks | 859 | 280,800 | 85.00% | 52.10% | 296 |
| | Insurance companies | 563 | 49,479 | 15.00% | 52.20% | 87 |
| | Others | 10 | 78 | 0.00% | 25.60% | 0 |
| | sub total | 1,432 | 330,358 | 100.00% | 52.10% | 384 |
| Total | | 47,209 | 878,458 | | 13.60% | 1,477 |

Source: Shintaku Kyōkai (2006).

A typical cash balance plan accumulates contribution credits with interest credits, but the concept can be extended. Essentially, the amount of the pension benefit is calculated from the account balance of the lump sum (cash balance).

A typical corporate pension in Europe or the US provides 3 per cent of the accumulated salaries after the age of 60. The amount of the pension benefit is based on the salary increase that would normally be expected in the future. An employee who leaves his company before retirement age will lose part of this benefit, even though it is possible to withdraw the pension as a lump sum and to transfer it to an individual saving plan at the time he leaves the company.

Japan's corporate pension system determines the retirement allowance through a labour agreement which has to be accumulated either through a traditional or a cash-balance method. However, once an employee leaves his company the employer needs a reasonable adjustment that must of course correspond to the economic conditions, but must also take into account the employee's need to protect his old-age

Table 4. Comparison of (corporate type) DC, CB and (traditional) DB plans.

| Category | DC | CB | DB |
|---|---|---|---|
| Benefit | – No guarantee<br>– Depends on investments<br>– No design flexibility<br>– Basically non-forfeitable<br>– Cannot be with-drawn before retirement | – Interest guaranteed<br>– Depends on interests<br>– No design flexibility<br>– Forfeitable in some cases<br>– Can be withdrawn before retirement | – Full guarantee<br>– Basically specified<br>– Flexible in design<br>– Forfeitable in some cases<br>– Can be withdrawn before retirement |
| Contributions | – Fixed amount<br>– With limit<br>– Only employer contributions<br>– Without actuarial calculations | – Variable amount<br>– Without limit<br>– Employee contribu-tions allowed<br>– With actuarial calculations | – Variable amount<br>– Without limit<br>– Employee contribu-tions allowed<br>– With actuarial calculations |
| Investments | – By participants<br>– Risk owed to participants<br>– Investment education required | – By the company<br>– Risk shared by participants and the company<br>– No need for education | – By the company<br>– Risk owed to the company<br>– No need for education |
| Accounting | – Contributions as cost | – Pension benefit obligations | – Pension benefit obligations |

Source: Yamaguchi and Kubo 2004: 54.

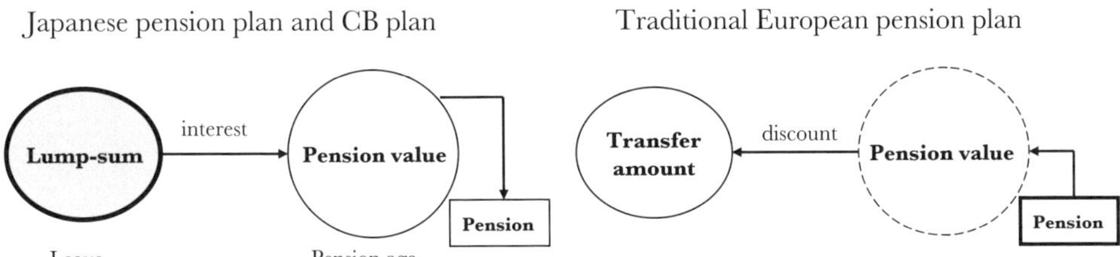


Source: Kubo (2004): 164.

Figure 5. The essential difference between Japanese and European corporate pensions.

Table 5. The difference between the CB plan and the CB-like plan.

| Category | While working | After leaving company |
|---|---|---|
| CB | Financial-policy oriented | Financial-policy oriented |
| CB-like | Personnel-policy oriented | Financial-policy oriented |

Source: Kubo 2004: 166.

income security. The linking of the pension benefit to a certain index was therefore allowed in 2002.

The term "Cash Balance-like Plan" is an alias of "Cash Balance Plan". It provides a traditional retirement allowance while the employee is working, but after he retires it converts the lump sum into a pension, referring to an index that reflects the economic conditions as well as a cash-balance plan. The comparison of a CB plan and a CB-like plan is shown in Table 5.

The reforms of the retirement allowance and the corporate pension system were accelerated by the introduction of retirement-benefit accounting. Under these circumstances, defined-contribution pension plans and the introduction of cash-balance plans became necessary. However, the core value of corporate pension plans must be based on human resource management and on a company's personnel strategy. A cash balance-like plan is suitable for the personnel strategy while the employee is still working. Financially speaking, it reduces cost volatility after he leaves the company.

## 4. Issues Concerning the Future of Corporate Pensions in Japan

### 4.1. *Adequate protection of beneficiaries*

In Japanese corporate pensions, the rights of beneficiaries are not necessarily protected very strongly. With some restrictions, employers can reduce the pension amount, something which is generally not allowed in European countries or the United States.

Some observers have therefore argued in favour of establishing a pension benefit guarantee system like the Pension Benefit Guarantee Corporation (PBGC) of the United States. However, it can be argued that such a system may actually prevent companies from undertaking the necessary funding efforts, because the more funding shortages occur, the higher will be the relief provided by the guarantee system, meaning that such a system faces a considerable moral hazard problem. And in fact, the American PBGC is now said to be at risk of bankruptcy.

Even so, if an individual company cannot take adequate action to protect beneficiaries, it is necessary to consider another protection mechanism. My idea would be to establish a "Pension Beneficiaries Pooling Fund". A company sponsoring a pension plan would still take the responsibility for active employees, but the PBPF would take on the responsibility for those who have left the company.

### 4.2. *The future significance of defined benefit plans*

The number of observers who think that DB plans will decrease or even disappear altogether in the not-too-distant future seems to be increasing, not only in Japan but also overseas. According to this view, DB plans will largely be replaced by DC plans. How should we evaluate such a trend?

A proper pension system should provide both a saving as well as an insurance function. However, a defined-contribution plan lacks the latter, and some people might therefore argue that it is no pension plan at all. It is certainly doubtful whether a defined-contribution plan can be classified as a pension scheme when we look only at its definition, but if we judge by its function, providing old-age income security, it might actually be called a pension plan.

However, if DC plans were really to remain the only sort of corporate pensions, the story would become quite different. In such a case, the favourable tax treatment of the pension system would become merely a privilege for a special type of saving. Although it is excellent that a lot of senior citizens have their own savings, favourable tax treatment for the pension system as a national policy can only be justified when it provides old-age income security beyond savings. From this point of view, favourable tax treatment should be directed first to public pensions, then to DB-type pensions with a mutual-help function, and only finally to an individual annuity. The DC plan without a mutual-help function should be treated the same way as an individual annuity.

On the other hand, let us consider this issue from the position of a company that offers such a pension plan. There are many who argue that prepayment as wages or contributions to a DC plan is better than providing DB plans, because such a system takes better care of ex-employees. To illustrate this point, let us draw an analogy with a basic business transaction. For example, an employee acquires the right to receive compensation as a reward for his or her labour. That is basically the same as when a merchant acquires the right to receive money when he or she sells goods. In the case of labour, an employee is a seller and his company is a buyer. For the seller, it is certainly safest to be paid the price at once. Therefore, the seller side will basically demand a lump-sum cash payment. If the buyer side responds with such a payment, the transaction is settled and another transaction will follow. Now let us assume that a company on the buyer side proposes to the seller side that the payment is deferred for some time. Behind such a request, there may be the financial need to retain money for the construction of a new factory, or various other reasons. How should the seller think about this offer? If the buyer worries, he should refuse the offer and demand instead a lump-sum payment. On the other hand, when he can trust the seller and the proposed bill payment is more advantageous or continuous dealings with the seller can be expected in future, he may choose to accept the proposal.

The same kind of situation applies to the corporate pension system. Although there might be a trend at the moment for companies to prefer prepayments because of changes in retirement benefit accounting and so on, there have also emerged some cases where employees demand prepayments instead of pensions because they are concerned about the future of their companies. In business, a company cannot expand simply by cash transactions. For a merchant, the most important thing is said to be trusted, and the ability to obtain deferred payments should be thought of as one sign of such trust. Of course, excessive deferred payments might cause problems, and the seller would not accept them. However, if all payments had to be in cash only, a company would face too many restrictions in its business activities. In short, it is desirable to have an adequate balance of prepayments and deferred payments.

Another important advantage of DB plans with deferred payments is that the level of payments and the manner of payment can be flexibly adjusted. Moreover, the benefits of these plans can be structured in such a way as to limit early employees' leaves and to make them stay longer with a company. That means that employees who leave a company after a relatively short period of time will not receive their full accrued benefits whereas benefits increase progressively for those who commit themselves longer to the company.

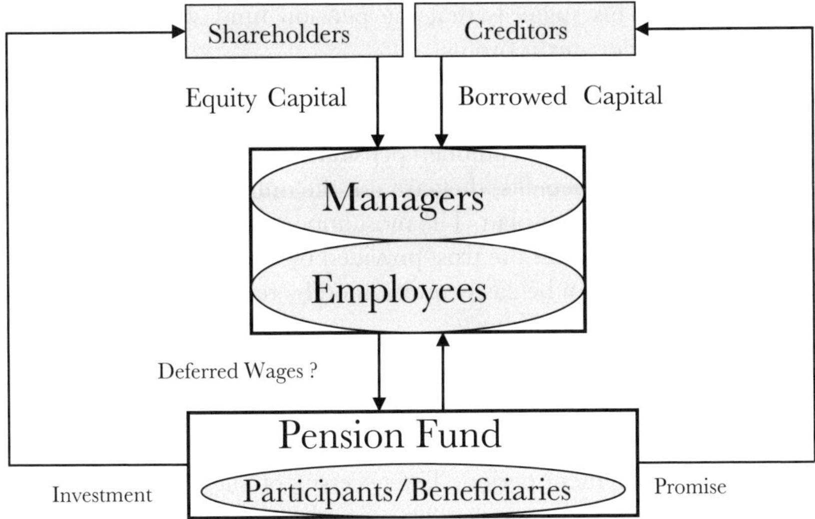


Source: Kubo (2003).

Figure 6. The relationship between pension fund, company and employees.

### 4.3. *The future role of corporate pensions*

If we think about the future of corporate pensions in Japan, it is necessary to think about the relationship between companies and their employees now and in the future. As for the companies, the power of shareholders represented by institutional investors has become much stronger in recent years, and voting rights are exercised more actively in order to influence management and corporate governance. Under such circumstances, some companies have started to focus too much on short-term profits, sometimes reducing wages and firing employees. Of course, a company that finds itself in financial trouble needs to reduce costs. However, this should not be carried out at employees' expense, for it is on them that the company's fate ultimately depends. Another important aspect is the relationship between employees and pension funds, as shown in figure 6.

Pension funds provide capital through stock investment and thus become shareholders of the company. However, the capital of pension funds stems ultimately from the deferred payments that employees have acquired by their labour. Consequently, pension capital will decrease if employees' pay is squeezed by wage reduction or restructuring. The entire mechanism may finally collapse if too much pressure is put on the company. This suggests that the pension fund should not focus excessively on short-term profits.

In a defined-benefit plan, the full amount of the benefit is not necessarily funded. It is quite common to observe funding deficiencies. How should we feel about this? Although pension assets are important for the security of pension benefits, they are not the only and most important part of a defined-benefit plan. The most important part is the company sponsoring the plan, and the trust provided by the participants and the beneficiaries. This can be easily understood by referring to the transaction example mentioned above.

### 4.4. *Post-employment benefit guarantee*

The most critical issue for private pensions is the guarantee of benefits in the post-employment period. The necessity of such a guarantee has increased and will increase even further with extended life expectancy. However, the institutions, which can provide this kind of guarantee—insurance companies, sponsoring companies and government—have in one way or another been weakened in recent years. Insurance companies have faced uncertain business circumstances; individual companies have abandoned their responsibilities to purchase annuities because of intense global competition and cost pressures; and even the government is reducing its role by cutting public pensions, so that the twenty-first century may be thought of as an era of "lost insurance".

To deal with this issue, it is necessary to clarify again the responsibilities of these three institutions. Employers can provide money for retirement to their employees, at least while they are still working. They have also been providing a post-employment guarantee of the conversion of such money into pensions. However, this kind of guarantee is now a heavy burden for them. Therefore, employers should focus on accumulating assets for retirement only for their active employees. The post-employment guarantee of annuities should be taken care of by insurance companies. If they cannot provide such protection, government should intervene to help and control them.

## 5. Conclusion

Corporate pension plans originally developed out of the employers' need to attract employees. As their use became more widespread, they took on the social purpose of protecting employees' old-age income security.

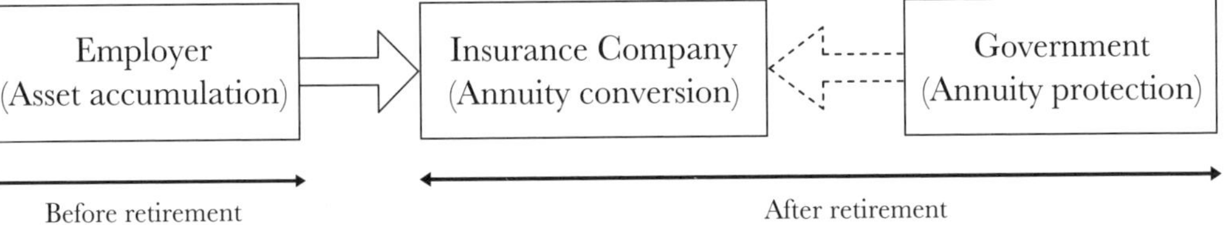


Source: Based on Kubo (2004): 215.

Figure 7. The three players in old-age income security.

Due to a long-lasting recessionary period over the 1990s and early 2000s and volatile investment performances, companies have started to shift from defined-benefit plans towards defined-contribution plans in order to limit their financial risks. Using the latter as a supplement of the former does make sense to a certain extent; however, defined-contribution plans alone seem to be too risky for employees, because the risk of market volatility is here essentially born by the employees only.

To the retirees, the security of their pension benefits is of course crucial. Such security includes non-volatile pension payments. Therefore, the significance of defined-benefit plans ought to be reviewed and an effective method of controlling their risk for companies needs to be created. One method of controlling such risks is through cash-balance type plans, which should be developed further. Finally, the roles of the "three players in old-age income security" (employers, insurance companies and government) ought to be reconsidered and clearly defined.

Japanese corporate pension plans are being restructured in order to strengthen and maintain their sustainability, which I find a well-considered approach. I am convinced that old-age security and happiness both depend on the collaboration of public and private pensions.

## References

Kigyō Nenkin Kenkyūjo (1998): *Heisei 10-nenban kigyō nenkin hakusho* [1998 White Paper on Occupational Pensions]. Tokyo: Life Design Kenkyūjo.

Kubo, Tomoyuki (1999): *Taishoku kyūfu-seido no kōzō kaikaku: jukyūken hogo wo chūkaku toshite* [Structural reform of Japan's retirement benefit system: focusing on the protection of benefit rights]. Tokyo: Tōyō Keizai Shinposha.

—— (2003): Kōporēto gabanansu to kigyō nenkin [Corporate governance and pension funds]. Tokyo: The Asia Foundation. http://tafjapan.org/english/forums/15–4–2003/material.html (found 16 February 2007).

—— (2004): *Wakariyasui kigyō nenkin* [Easy to understand corporate pensions]. Tokyo: Nikkei Shinbunsha.

McGill, Dan M., Brown, Kyle N., John J. Haley and Sylvester J. Schieber (1996): *Fundamentals of Private Pensions, Seventh Edition.* Philadelphia: Pension Research Council Publications.

MHLW (The Ministry of Health, Labour and Welfare) (2005): *Textbook for the Study Programme for the Senior Social Insurance Administrators: Chapter 3: Overview of the Pension System in Japan & Chapter 9: Overview of the Corporate Pension. Brief Overview of 2004 Pension Plan Revision* (2005.6). http://www.mhlw.go.jp/english/org/policy/p36–37a.html (found 16 February 2007).

Nikko Financial Intelligence (2006): *Pension Research.* http://www.nikko-fi.co.jp/modules/pension_e9/index.php?id=2&flow=0–2–15&tmid=15 (found 19 February 2007).

Shimada, Tomiko (1995): *Nenkin nyūmon* [An Introduction to Pensions]. Tokyo: Iwanami Shoten.

Shimazaki, Kenji and Miyazato Naomi (2005): *Kigyō nenkin wo meguru kokusaiteki chōryū to kigyō nenkin no yakuwari* [International Trends: Role of and Issues relating to Corporate Pensions]. In: *Kaigai Shakai Hoshō Kenkyū* [The Review of Comparative Social Security Research] 151 (Summer), pp. 4–20.

Shintaku Kyōkai [Trust Companies Association of Japan] (2006): *Kigyō nenkin ni jutaku gaikyō (Heisei 18-nen sangatsu matsu genzai).* [The current status of Japanese corporate pension plans (As of March 2006)]. News release of May 25, 2006. http://www.shintaku-kyokai.or.jp/ (found 19 February 2007).

Wooten, James A. (2005): *The Employee Retirement Income Security Act of 1974: A Political History.* Berkley: University of California Press.

Yamaguchi, Osamu and Kubo Tomoyuki (2004): *Kigyō nenkin no saisei senryaku* [Strategies for the revival of corporate pensions]. Tokyo: Kinyūzaisei Jijōkenkyūkai (Kinzai).

# LIST OF CONTRIBUTORS

Makoto Arai, University Tsukuba, Dean of Law School
Makoto Atoh, Waseda University, Graduate School of Human Sciences
John C. Campbell, Michigan University, Professor Emeritus
John Clammer, United Nations University, Advisor to the Rector and Director of International Courses
Harald Conrad, Ritsumeikan Asia Pacific University, Faculty of Asia Pacific Management
Liv Coleman, University of Wisconsin-Madison Department of Political Science
Florian Coulmas, German Institute for Japanese Studies Tokyo
David Blake Willis, Soai University, Faculty of Humanities
Peter Backhaus, German Institute for Japanese Studies Tokyo
Volker Elis, German Institute for Japanese Studies Tokyo
Thomas Feldhoff, University of Duisburg-Essen, East Asian Regional Geography
Susanne Formanek, Austrian Academy of Sciences, Institute for the Cultural and Intellectual History of Asia
Hisashi Fukawa, Shizuoka University, Faculty of Economics
Tetsuo Fukawa, National Institute of Population and Social Research, Social Security Research I
Carolin Funck, Hiroshima University, Faculty of Integrated Arts and Sciences
Lisette Gebhardt, Johann Wolfgang Goethe Universität Frankfurt, Japanese Studies
Roger Goodman, St Anthony's College, Oxford University, Faculty of Oriental Studies
Toshiko Himeoka, Tsukuba University, Institute of History and Anthropology
Charles Yuji Horioka, Osaka University, Institute of Social and Economic Research
Naoki Ikegami, Keio University, School of Medicine
Fumio Inoue, Meikai University, Faculty of Languages and Cultures
Kenji Ishii, Kokugakuin University, Faculty of Shinto Studies
Sumiko Iwao, Keio University, Professor Emeritus

Miho Iwasawa, National Institute of Population and Social Security Research, Department of Population Dynamics Research
Ryuichi Kaneko, National Institute of Population and Social Security Research, Director Department of Population Dynamics Research
Akihiro Kawase, Toyo University, Faculty of Economics
Matthias Koch, German Institute for Japanese Studies Tokyo
Shigemi Kono, Reitaku University, Economics & Business Administration
Susanne Kreitz-Sandberg, Linköping University, Department of Behavioural Sciences and Learning
Tomoyuki Kubo, Nissan Motor Co., Ltd., Global Pension Manager
Sepp Linhart, University of Vienna, Department of East Asian Studies
Susan Orpett Long, John Carroll University
Ralph Lützeler, German Institute for Japanese Studies Tokyo
Patricia Maclachlan, University of Texas at Austin, Department of Asian Studies
Wolfram Manzenreiter, University of Vienna, Department of East Asian Studies
Craig Martin University of Pennsylvania, Law School
Hendrik Meyer-Ohle, National University of Singapore, Department of Japanese Studies
Stephen Murphy-Shigematsu, Stanford University, Walter H. Shorenstein Asian Pacific Research Center
Andreas Moerke, Representative Director and President of Messe Düsseldorf Japan, Ltd., Tokyo.
Akihiro Ogawa, Ph.D., Stockholm University, Department of Japanese Studies
Naohiro Ogawa, Nihon University, Deputy Director, Population Research Institute
Takeo Ogawa, Yamaguchi Prefectural University, Graduate School of Health and Welfare
Seiritsu Ogura, Hosei University, Director General, Hosei Institute on Aging
Hans Dieter Ölschleger, University of Bonn, Japanese Studies
Fumio Ohtake, Osaka University, Institute of Social and Economic Research
Akiko Sato Oishi, Chiba University, Faculty of Law and Economics
Takashi Oshio, Kobe University, Graduate School of Economics
Robert Pekkanen, University of Washington, Japan Studies Program
Ito Peng, University of Toronto, Department of Sociology

David Potter, Nanzan University, Faculty of Policy Studies
James Raymo, University of Wisconsin-Madison, Center for Demography and Ecology
Glenda Roberts, Waseda University, Graduate School of Asia-Pacific Studies
Fumihiko Satofuka, Tokyo University of Agriculture and Technology, Institute of Symbiotic Science and Technology
Annette Schad-Seifert, Heinrich-Heine-University of Duesseldorf, Ostasien-Institut/Modernes Japan
Leonard Schoppa, University of Virginia, Department of Politics
Mayumi Sekizawa, National Museum of Japanese History
Hidehiko Sekizawa, Tokyo Keizai University, Faculty of Business Administration
Sawako Shirahase, University of Tokyo, Graduate School of Humanities and Sociology, Department of Sociology
Takanori Shintani, National Museum of Japanese History, The Graduate University for Advanced Studies
Nobuko Shiraishi, NHK Broadcasting Culture Research Institute
Karen A. Shire, University of Duisburg-Essen, Social Sciences
Noriyuki Takayama, Hitotsubashi University, The Institute of Economic Research
Paul Talcott, Health policy consultant, Berlin, Germany
Leng Leng Thang, National University of Singapore
Christopher S. Thompson, Ohio University, Department of Linguistics
John W. Traphagan, University of Taxes at Austin, Center for East Asian Studies
Yutaka Tsujinaka, Tsukuba University, Graduate School of Humanities and Social Sciences
Chikako Usui, University of Missouri-St. Louis, Department of Sociology
Gabriele Vogt, German Institute for Japanese Studies Tokyo
Naohiro Yashiro, International Christian University, Economics

# INDEX OF AUTHORS CITED


AARP (American Association for Retired Persons), 715
Abe, Aya, 291, 923, 925
Abe, Shinzō, 772
Acker, Joan, 218
*AERA*, 756
Agency for Cultural Affairs, 485, 592
Aikawa, Yoshihiko, 136
Aitchison, Jean, 477
Alicandri, Elizabeth, 1019
Amada, Josuke, 136
Amaha, Keisuke, 615
Amano, Ikuo, 734
Amenomori, Takayoshi, 691
Anbäcken, Els-Marie, 138, 206
Anderson, Beverlee B., 580
Anderson, Robert N., 269
Ando, Hidehiro, 222
Anheier, Helmut, 690
Anzo, Shinji, 259
Aoi, Kazuo, 135, 187
Aoki, Hisao, 10
Aoki, Masahiko, 987
Aoyama, Michio, 449
Aqua, Ronald, 364
Arai, Hiroyuki, 809, 810
Arai, Makoto, 1065, 1067, 1068
Arai, Yumiko, 206, 211
Arakaki, Daryl Masao, 552
Arakaki, Toyoko, 134
Araki, Takashi, 426
Arifin, Evi Nurvidya, 35
Arita, Eriko, 296
Ariyoshi, Sawako, 131, 331, 493
Arthur, W. B., 47
Arudou, Debito, 295, 428
*Asahi Shinbun*, 172, 173, 191, 398, 459, 462, 463, 464, 466, 468, 592, 656, 677, 721, 751, 753, 757, 758, 775, 806, 813, 865, 873
*Asahi Shinbun Chōkan*, 588
Asai, Haruo, 755
Asano, Hitoshi, 135, 136
*Ashita no Nihon wo Tsukuru Kyokai*, 715
Ashkenazi, Michael, 606
ASS (Aichi-ken Shimin Seikatsubu), 698
ATK (Aichi-ken Tōkei Kyōkai), 700
Atoh, Makoto, 8, 10, 11, 14, 15, 17, 18, 20, 35, 73, 75, 264, 266, 752
Atsumi, Bunji, 1017, 1019, 1021
Ault, Brian, 19
Averbuch, Irit, 369, 370
Axinn, William G., 267
Aymanns, Gerhard, 35
Ayumi, Takenaka, 297

Backhaus, Peter, 475, 488
Bähr, Jürgen, 26
Ball, Laurence, 857
Baltes, Paul B., 1000
Banks, James A., 297
Bass, Scott A., 956
Beauchamp, Edward R., 734
Becker, 267
Beer, Lawrence W., 426, 434, 435
Befu, Harumi, 296, 297, 298
Ben-Ari, Eyal, 608
Bestor, Theodore, C., 605
Binstock, Robert, 678
Blau, David M., 281
Blechinger, Verena, 673
Blenman, Morris, 580
Blossfeld, Hans-Peter, 256, 267
Boling, Patricia A., 749
Bongaarts, John, 7, 55, 833
Borowski, Alan, 166
Börsch-Supan, Axel, 867
Bothwell, Robert O., 794
Bourgeois-Pichat, Jean, 45
Bowen, Roger W., 783, 785
Bracher, Michael, 267
Brayley, Russell E., 580
Brinton, Mary, 176, 262
Brinton, Mary C., 262
Broadbent, Jeffrey, 784
Broadbent, Kaye, 969
Brooke, James, 308, 311
Brown, R., 487
Brumberg, Richard, 890
Bumpass, Larry, 260, 263
Bumpass, Larry L., 256, 260, 262, 263, 265, 266, 268

Calder, Kent E., 800, 803
Caldwell, John C., 31, 114
Campbell, Alan, 610
Campbell, John C., 137, 166, 207, 645, 653, 660, 663, 683, 1033, 1038, 1049, 1055, 1058
Carrigan, Marylin, 625
Carroll, Tessa, 457
Carruthers, Ashley, 311
Carter, R. W., 580
Casey, Bernard H., 951
Castells, Manuel, 167, 168
Caudill, William, 212
CCE (Central Council for Education), 725, 741
Cepaitis, Zygimantas, 33
CEPD (Council of Economic Planning and Development, Executive Yuan, Republic of China), 1044
Cha, Sukbin, 580
Chen, Shui-bian, 1045
Chesnais, Jean-Claude, 256
Cheung, Siu Lan K., 835
Chi, Iris, 835
Chimoto, Akiko, 241, 243
Choe, Minja Kim, 256, 262, 263, 265, 266, 268
Chogahara, Makoto, 623
Chūjō, Ushio, 805
Chūkyōshin (Chuo Kyoiku Iinkai) [Central Council for Education], 742, 743, 745
*Chūnichi Nyūsu* (5 May 2005), 755
*Chūnichi Shinbun* (12 September 2006), 773
CKS (Chubu Keizai Shinbunsha), 699
CKSJ (Chusho Kigyo Sogo Jigyodan), 625
Clammer, John, 298, 609
CLSC (Community Life Support Center), 697
Coale, Ansley, 11
Cohen, Joel. E., 43
Cole, Robert E., 221, 981
Connors, Lesley, 674
Conrad, Harald, 138, 990, 994
Cool, Linda, 324
Coughlin, Joseph F., 1026
Coulmas, Florian, 456
Council of Europe, 16
Crane, Gene A., 369
Crehan, Kate, 294
Crown, William H., 166
CSFS (Chuo Shakai Fukushi Shingikai) [Central Social Welfare Council], 656
CUD (The Center for Universal Design), 792
Cummings, William K., 556, 734
Curriculum Council, Monbusho, 741, 745
Curtis, Gerald, 671, 677

Daidō, Yasujirō, 130
De Rose, Alessandra, 267
Dean, Mitchell, 728
Demes, Helmut, 989
Demura, Shinichi, 615
Denny, N. W., 576
Dentō-bunka-kasseika-kokuminkai, 568
Detroit Eldernet, 125
DeWit, Andrew, 870
Diamond, A., 1102
Dickens, Bernard M., 445
Diène, Doudou, 309
Dirks, Daniel, 950
Doak, Kevin M., 298
Doi, Takeo, 615
Dore, Ronald, 221
Douglass, Mike, 766, 767
Dower, John, 639
Doyon, Paul, 551
DPJ (Democratic Party of Japan), 670
Dworkin, Ronald, 429, 431, 432

Earhart, H. Byron, 393
Edwards, Elise, 608
Eekelaar, John M., 423
Ehara, Yumiko, 246
Eldridge, H. T., 45
Elmendorf, Douglas W., 857
Emi, Koichi, 626
Emori, Itsuo, 353
Endō, Orie, 459
Engell-Nielsen, Theo, 1019
Er, Lam Peng, 783, 784, 785
Ermisch, John F., 262
Esaki, Yuji, 872
Esping-Andersen, Gøsta, 174
ESRI (Economic and Social Research Institute), 761
Estavez-Abe, Margarita, 664
Eto, Mikiko Murase, 660, 661, 679, 1040
Ezawa, Aya, 976

Fan, Jennifer S., 426
Fang, Rita, 1045
Faranda, William T., 580, 581, 583
Feeley, Malcolm M., 447
Feldhoff, Thomas, 782, 783, 784, 785, 791, 795
Feldman, Gregory, 729
Feldstein, Martin, 1104
Ferraro, Kenneth F., 457
Fildes, Brian, 1021
Flanagan, Scott, 672
Flohr, Susanne, 590
Flüchter, Winfried, 63, 67, 781, 789, 796
Foljanty-Jost, Gesine, 745
Foner, Nancy, 330
Foote, Daniel H., 422, 443, 449
Ford, Ramona L., 166
Formanek, Susanne, 126, 138, 325, 326, 327, 328, 329, 330, 331, 336, 337, 338, 339, 340, 492
Förster, Michael, 922
Foucault, Michel, 727
Franco, Daniele, 1120
Freeman, Michael D., 423
Frost, Peter, 738
Früstück, Sabine, 609
Fujii, Yasuyuki, 781, 786, 794
Fujimasa, Iwao, 19
Fujimura, Hiroyuki, 993
Fujisaki, Hiroko, 136
Fujita, Hidenori, 734
Fujita, Yoshihisa, 66
Fujitani, Masakazu, 105
Fujiwara, Kazuo, 370
Fukawa, Hisashi, 930
Fukawa, Tetsuo, 1077
Fukazawa, Shichirō, 129, 329
Fukuda, Moto, 285, 760
Funck, Carolin, 587, 590, 593, 594
Furusawa, Yukiko, 550
Fuwa, Kazuhiko, 735

GAO (United States General Accounting Office), 948
Garon, Sheldon, 890
Gauthier, Anne Hélène, 639, 749
Geanakoplos, John, 1104
Gebhardt, Lisette, 505, 507, 510
Genda, Yuji, 270, 558, 721, 982, 985, 986, 991
Getreuer-Kargl, Ingrid, 138
Gifuken Sangyō Keizai Shinkō Sentā, 587
Gilman, A., 487
GKMN (Gaikokujin Kenkyusei Mondai Nettowaku), 767, 773
Glenstrup, Arne John, 1019
Goldstein, Joshua A., 267
Goldthorpe, John H., 218
Golini, Antonio, 835
Goodman, Roger, 297, 556, 734, 735, 740
Gornick, Janet, 174
Gottfried, Heidi, 964
Goyette, Kimberly, 267
Graburn, Nelson, 583
Greenhalgh, Susan, 109, 114
Gribble, James N., 31
Grömling, Michael, 866, 874
Gross, Ames, 173
Gruber, Jonathan, 1108
GSUN (Gaikokujin Sabetsu Uotchi Nettowaku), 773
Guichard-Anguis, Sylvie, 296, 606
Gunji, Asuaki, 1094
Guo, Fang, 303
Guo, Nanyan, 784
Guthrie, Stewart, 393

Hakim, Catherine, 272
Haley, John O., 447, 449, 452
Hamaguchi, Haruhiko, 134, 135
*Hamburger Abendblatt*, 1026
Hamilton, Brady E., 34
Hanamaki City, 374
Hanashiro, Rieko, 134
Hani, Yoko, 190
Hannan, M. T., 45
Hara, Junsuke, 221, 222
Harada Toshiaki, 346
Harada, Akira, 133
Harada, Yutaka, 868, 871
Hasegawa, Kazuo, 131
Hashimoto, Akiko, 137, 207, 340, 341
Hashimoto, Juro, 13
Hashimoto, Kazuyuki, 136
Hashimoto, Masaaki, 133
Hauser, Jürg A., 27, 32
Havens, Thomas, 642, 643
Hayami, Akira, 25, 26, 73, 105, 113
Hayami, Toru, 7
Hayashi, Hiroko, 189
Hayashi, Michiyoshi, 759
Hayer, Hayes, 188
Hayward, Mark D., 269
Heimovitz, Harley K., 956
Heindorf, Viktoria, 990

Hewitt, Paul S., 785
Hideki, Shibutani, 425
Higashi Shakai Fukushi Kyōkai Hoikubu Tsūshin, 183
Higo, Kazuo, 346
Higuchi, Keiko, 462, 492
Higuchi, Yoichi, 447
Higuchi, Yoshio, 224
HILL (Hakuhodo Institute of Life and Living), 464, 999, 1001, 1006, 1007, 1015
Hinde, Andrew, 114
Hinohara, Shigeaki, 132
Hirao, Keiko, 256
Hiraoka, Kōichi, 132
Hirayama, Takeshi, 76
Hiroaki, Watanabe, 422
Hiroi, Yoshinori, 187, 197, 1039
Hirokado, Masako, 105
Hiroko, Miura, 206, 211
Hirota, Koichi, 628
Hirota, Masaki, 340
Hisamichi, Shigeru, 187, 703
Hisane, Masaki, 295
Hiwatari, Nobuhiro, 966
Hodge, Robert W., 821
Hodgson, Dennis, 114
Hoem, J., 45
Hogg, Peter H., 431
Hohn, Uta, 68
Holland, C. A., 575
Hollifield, James F., 296
Holzmann, Robert, 1120
Honda, 1028
Honda, Yasuji, 370
Honda, Yuki, 721
Hong, Mihee, 743
Honjō, Eijirō, 113
Honsha, Osaka, 550
Hood, Christopher, 734
Höpflinger, François, 626
Hori, Katsuhiro, 1035
Hori, Yukio, 681
Horioka, Charles Yuji, 880, 884, 888, 890, 891, 892
Horlacher, David E., 171
Hornemann, Louise, 580
Hoshishiba, Yumiko, 1057
House of Councillors, 677
Hsiao, Edwin, 1045
Hsiao, William, 1093
Huang, Annie, 1045
Huinink, Johannes, 267
Ichibangase, Yasuko, 136
Ichikawa Fusae Kinenkai [The Fusae Ichikawa Memorial Association], 717
Ichikawa, Shogo, 734
Ichinokura, Shunichi, 370
ICU (International Christian University), 725
IHRSA (International Health, Rackets and Sportsclub Association), 625
Iinuma Kenji, 334
Ikeda, Kazuo, 105
Ikeda, Masaru, 623
Ikeda, Shozo, 1060
Ikeda, Shunya, 1054
Ikegami, Hiromichi, 361, 367
Ikegami, Naoki, 1038, 1049, 1050, 1054, 1055, 1057, 1058, 1093
Ikenoue, Masako, 264, 645
Ikezaki, Sumie, 1057
ILO (International Labor Office), 172, 963, 993
Imada, Takatoshi, 221
Imai, Jun, 964, 967, 968
IMF, 19
Imhof, Arthur E., 491
Inada, Shunosuke, 106
Inoguchi, Takashi, 675
Inohara, Hideo, 981
Inoue Shun, 608
Inoue, Fumio, 474, 475, 476, 477, 478, 483, 493
Inoue, Teruko, 246
Institute of Statistical Mathematics National Survey Committee, 397
IPSS (Institute of Population and Social Security Research), 455, 614, 653, 655, 785, 786, 789, 862, 1017
Ishida, Hiroshi, 222, 557
Ishii, Kenji, 398
Ishikawa, Akira, 645
Ishikawa, Tsuneo, 222, 890
Ishikawa, Yoshitaka, 67
Ishikida, Miki Y., 551, 553
Itō, Mitsuharu, 132
Itoh, Hiroshi, 426
Itoh, Shigeru, 7
Iwai, Tomoaki, 675
Iwakami, Mami, 758, 759
Iwakata, Koji, 1017
Iwamoto, Masayo, 609
Iwamoto, Yasushi, 616, 902, 904
Iwao, Sumiko, 534

Iwasawa, Miho, 17, 256, 260, 264, 265, 266, 268, 269
Iwasawa, Yuji, 429
Iwata, Katsuhiko, 951, 953, 957, 958
Iwate Prefecture, 373
Iyasu, Tadashi, 673
Iyotani, Toshio, 310, 766

Jaffee, David, 165
Jain, Purnendra, 784
JAMA (Japan Automobile Manufacturers' Association, Inc.), 1017
James, Estelle and Gail Benjamin, 549
Jang, SooCehong, 580, 581
Japan Aging Research Center [JARC], 184, 185, 186
Japan Communist Party, 670
Japan Institute for Labour Policy and Training, 421
Japan Intergenerational Unity Association (JIUA), 187
Japan Society of Information and Communication Research (JSICR), 530
*Japan Times*, 422, 424, 800, 811
Japanese Federation of Bar Associations, 424, 446
JATA (Japan Association of Travel Agents), 584
Jenike, Brenda Robb, 204, 206, 690
JFBA (Japan Federation of Bar Associations [Nihon Bengoshi Rengo Kai]), 753, 754, 757
JFCC (Japan Federation of Construction Contractors), 782, 783
JGSS (Japanese General Social Surveys) Project, 404
JIL (Japan Institute of Labor), 976
JILPT (Japan Institute for Labour Policy and Training), 981, 983, 984, 985, 987
Jinkō Mondai Kenkyūjo, 100, 106, 107, 110, 129
JMS (Jinko Mondai Shingikai), 649
JNTO (Japan National Tourist Organization), 585
John, Daphne, 268
Johnson, Stephen, 668
Johnston, Eric, 307
JPHA (Japan Public Health Association), 617
JTB (Japan Travel Bureau), 584, 585
JTB Grandtours, 588
Jussaume, Raymond A., 387

Kabashima, Hideyoshi, 649
Kabashima, Ikuo, 672, 678, 784
Kado, Osamu, 619
Kadowaki, Atsushi, 759
Kagami, Masahiro, 76
Kajita, Shin, 295, 782
Kakumi, Kobayashi, 423
Kalab, Kathleen A., 623
Kamann, Simon, 1018
Kamano, Saori, 265, 272
Kamata, Minoru, 1017
Kamata, Toji, 505
Kameda, Toyojirō, 106
Kamiya, Nobuyuki, 105
Kamiyama, Takehito, 370
Kan, Naoto, 673
Kanamori, Hitoshi, 1019, 1021
Kaneko, Isamu, 135, 136
Kaneko, Ryūichi, 17, 260, 263, 645
Kang, Sang-jung, 310
Kano, Kazuhiko, 807
Kanomata, Nobuo, 222
Kaplan, Matthew, 180, 185, 187, 188, 189, 703
Kargl, Ingrid, 138
Kariya, Takehiko, 557, 734
Karsh, Bernard, 221
Kasahara, Masanari, 130
Kashiwazaki, Chikako, 769
Katano, Masayoshi, 136
Katanoda, Kota, 628
Katsutoshi, Kezuka, 422
Kaufmann, Franz-Xaver, 867, 874
Kawabata, Osamu, 136
Kawai, Hayao, 132
Kawakami, Sonoko, 767
Kawamura, Masayoshi, 462
Kawano, Satsuki, 389
Kawase, Akihiro, 845
Kazuka, Katsutoshi, 169
Kei, Kudo, 206, 211
Keigo, Kumamoto, 206, 211
Kelly, Curtis, 550, 553
Kenney, Catherine T., 267
Keyfitz, Nathan, 12
Kiefer, Christie W., 137
Kiku, Koichi, 618, 626
Kim, Anna, 963, 965
Kimura, Shin, 845
Kinoshita, Shone, 444

Kinoshita, Yasuhito, 133, 137
Kirisutokyō Shimbun, 401
Kishimoto, Shigenobu, 221
Kitamura, Akiko, 189
Kitaura, Yoshiaki, 845
Kitō, Hiroshi, 113
Knapp, Kiyoki Kamio, 426
Knight, John, 137, 387
KNSO (Korea National Statistics Office), 1044
Kobayashi, Kazumasa, 113
Kobayashi, Masayoshi, 809
Kobayashi, Victor N., 734
Kobayashi, Yotaro, 20
Kobe City Government, 306
Kodera, Haruyuki, 1021
Kögel, Tomas, 255
Kohler, Hans-Peter, 16, 256
Kohno, Masaru, 668
Koike, Kazuo, 981
Koizumi, Junichiro, 753, 804
Kojima, Katsuko, 708
Kojima, Seiyo, 760
Kojima, Setsuko, 369
Kokudochō, 67
Kokugakuin University Twenty-First Century Centre of Excellence Program, 402
Kokuritsu Shakaihoshō Jinkō Mondai Kenkyūjo (KSJK) (National Institute of Population and Social Security Research), 6, 7, 8, 9, 12, 13, 14, 15, 17, 19, 28, 29, 30, 35
Köllner, Patrick, 681
Komai, Hiroshi, 303
Komamura, Kohei, 926
Komine, Tatsuo, 20
Komiya, Emi, 136
Könberg, Bo, 1132
Kondo, Makoto, 825, 827, 835
Konishi, Makoto, 1021
Koppa, Rodger, 1018
Kōreisha Kaigo Kenkyūkai, 1066
Kōsei Rōdōshō, 948, 949, 950, 952, 954
Kōsei Tōkei Kyokai, 1058
Kosei-sho Jinkomondai Kenkyujo (KJK), 15, 17
Kōseirodōshō Daijin Kanbō Tōkai Jōhōbu (several years), 990, 992
Kōseirōdōshō Daijin Kanbō Tōkei Jōhōbu, 28, 32, 984
Kōseirōdōshō Tokeijyohobu (KRTJ) (Statistical and Information Division, Ministry of Health, Labour and Welfare), 16, 18
Kōseisho, 609, 617, 1034, 1038, 1040, 1041
Koseki, Sampei, 609
Kosugi, Reiko, 18, 270, 721
Koyama, Shizuko, 237, 242, 243
Koyano, Wataru, 136, 180, 340
Koyō Seisaku Kenkyūkai, 960
Krauss, Ellis, 675, 679
KRDK (Kosei Rodosho Daijin Kanbo Tokei Joho Bu), 617
KRDKTJ (Kōsei Rōdōshō Daijin Kanbō Tōkei Jōhōbu), 69, 74, 76
Kreitz-Sandberg, Susanne, 741
KSCKK (Keizai Sangyo-sho, Chiiki Keizai Kenkyu-kai), 863, 864, 874
KSJK/KSHJMK (Kokuritsu Shakai Hoshō Jinkō Mondai Kenkyūjo) [National Institute of Population and Social Security Research], 66, 69, 70, 71, 72, 76, 531, 544
KSRF (Koseisho Shakaikyoku Rojin Fukushika), 656
KTJZ (Kenko Tairyoku-zukuri Jigyo Zaidan), 615, 616
KTK (Kosei Tokei Kyokai), 695
KTKK (Kaso Taisaku Kenkyu-kai), 871
Kubo, Tomoyuki, 1137, 1143, 1147, 1149
Kumamoto, Keiko, 211
Kumamoto-Healey, Junko, 421, 444
Kurata, Washio, 135
Kuronuma, Yukio, 370
Kurosawa, Masako, 270
Kurosu, Satomi, 73, 105
Kurz, Karin, 963, 965
Kusano, Atusko, 187, 703
Kyōgoku, Takanobu, 136
*Kyūshu Chihō Tokutei Yūbinkyokuchōkai*, 807

Land, K. C., 45
Langmeyer, Lynn, 580
Larsen, Robert, 424, 426
Lathrop, Stacy, 729
Lee, Hey-Kyung and Park, Yeong-Ran, 1044
Lee, Ronald, 13, 825
Leonardi, Robert, 707
Leslie, P. H., 44
Lesthaeghe, Ron, 16, 255
Levine, Solomon B., 221
Lewis, Jane, 963

Lewis, Susan K., 269
Li, Nan, 827, 835
Lichter, Daniel T., 269
Lie, John, 302
Linck-Kesting, Gudula, 325
Linhart, Sepp, 132, 136, 138, 609
Lock, Margaret, 137
Long, Jonathan, 212, 625
Long, Susan Orpett, 137
Lopez, Alan D., 29
Lotka, A. J., 44
Loughman, Celeste, 492
Lutz, Wolfgang, 35, 823
Lützeler, Ralph, 27, 30, 31, 32, 36, 63, 68, 70, 73, 75, 76, 77, 138, 873

Mabuchi, Masaru, 365, 367
MacDougall, Terry, 656
MacKellar, F. Landis, 832
Maclachlan, Patricia L., 800, 806
Maderdonner, Megumi, 138
Maeda, Daisaku, 137
Maekawa, Satoko, 845
Mahon, Rianne, 1044
*Mainichi Shinbun*, 463, 464, 468, 757, 1039
Mainichi Shinbunsha Jinko Mondai Chosakai, 37
Mak, Doris, 579, 580
Maki, Masahide, 135
Makino, Noboru, 133
Mankiw, N. Gregory, 857
Manzenreiter, Wolfram, 618, 619, 628
March, Roger, 583, 584
Marschalck, Peter, 26
Martin, Joyce A., 34
Martin, Teresa Castro, 260
Maruo, Naomi, 1035
Masakazu, Washio, 206, 211
Mason, Andrew, 822, 825, 826, 827, 828, 829, 830, 835
Mason, Karen O., 256, 262, 263, 264, 265, 268, 272
Masuda, Kōkichi, 130
Masuda, Masanobu, 1038, 1040
Matanle, Peter, 981
Mathers, Colin D., 29
Matsubara, Hiroshi, 868
Matsubara, Satoru, 805, 809
Matsuda, Makoto, 805
Matsui, Shigenori, 425, 437
Matsukura, Rikiya, 75, 266, 825, 827, 828, 835
Matsumoto, Toshiaki, 135
Matsumura, Naomichi, 133, 136
Matsumura, Yasuhiro, 628
Matsunaka, Keiko, 624
Matsutani, Akihiko, 865, 867, 872, 874
Matsutani, Akihito, 19
Maxwell, Robert J., 323
Mayer, Karl Ulrich, 1000
McCleary, Ken W., 580
McCormack, Gavan, 783, 784, 794, 795
McCreery, John, 609
McDonald, Peter, 89, 256, 824
McGill, Dan M., 1150
McNicoll, Geoffrey, 823
McVeigh, Brian J., 558
Meadows, D. H., 45
Meguro, Yoriko, 251
Meishin Chōsa Kyōgikai, 403
Menacker, Fay, 34
METI (Ministry of Economy, Trade and Industry), 624
MEXT (Ministry of Education, Culture, Sports, Science and Technology), 618, 724, 725, 736, 737, 738
Meyers, Marcia, 174
MHLW (Ministry of Health, Labour and Welfare), 152, 155, 160, 169, 170, 218, 220, 223, 225, 227, 228, 229, 238, 277, 278, 279, 284, 288, 423, 465, 466, 467, 730, 755, 758, 760, 845, 988, 1038, 1042, 1053, 1057, 1058, 1061, 1062, 1138
MHW (Ministry of Health and Welfare), 642, 750, 1056
Mie Prefecture, 714
Mikami, Katsuya, 136
Milhaupt, Curtis J., 447
Miller, Robbi Louise, 421
Mimizuka, Hiroaki, 759
Minami, Ryōzaburō, 98, 111
Ministry of General Affairs, 707, 710, 712
Ministry of Land Infrastructure and Transport, 586
Minoguchi, Tokijirō, 106
Mira d'Ercole, Marco, 922
Mita, Fusami, 260, 264, 645
Mitchell, Olivia S., 1104
Mitsubishi Motors, 993
Mitsunari, Miho, 237
Miura, Atsushi, 558
Miura, Fumio, 133
Miura, Mari, 966

Miyachi, Motohiko, 615
Miyajima, Takashi, 773, 776
Miyake, Yoshiko, 750
Miyamoto, Michiko, 758, 759
Miyata, Noboru, 345
Miyazaki, Tetsuya, 361, 366
Miyazawa, Setsuo, 447
Miyazawa, Toshiyoshi, 432
Mizuho Sōgō Kenkyujo, 960
Mizuno, Kiyoshi, 805
Mizuno, Yumiko, 492
Mizushima, Haruo, 6
MLIT (Ministry of Land, Infrastructure and Transport), 790, 791, 792
MLITCRDB (Ministry of Land, Infrastructure and Transport, City and Regional Development Bureau), 862
Modigliani, Franco, 890
Moerke, Andreas, 1018
MOFA (Ministry of Foreign Affairs), 768
MOJ (Ministry of Justice), 299, 300, 302, 303, 420, 428, 765, 766, 768, 769, 774, 775, 776
Molenbroek, J. F. M., 575
Monbukagakusho [Ministry of Education, Culture, Sports, Science and Technology], 190
Montgomery, Keith, 26
Mooney, Gavin, 1093
Moreau, Sophia R., 429, 430, 431
Moriizumi, Rie, 262, 264
Morioka, Kiyomi, 135
Morishima, Motohiro, 989, 990
Morris-Suzuki, Tessa, 308, 312
Mosk, Carl, 28
Motani, Kosuke, 871, 872
Motani, Yoko, 743, 759
MSFK (Minato-ku Shakai Fukushi Kyogikai), 924
Mulgan, Aurelia George, 674
Munson, Martha L., 34
Murakami, Yasusuke, 221
Muramatsu, Michio, 679
Muramatsu, Minoru, 10
Murata, Hiro, 589
Murphy-Shigematsu, Stephen, 298, 309
Murray, Christopher J. L., 29
Musgrave, Richard A., 1130
Muta, Kazue, 237, 242
Myles, John, 165, 166

Nadaoka, Yoko, 105
Nagai, Sonoko, 492
Naganawa, Hisao, 955, 957
Nagaoka, Shinkichi, 238
Nagase, Nobuko, 20, 172, 968
Nagayama, Sadanori, 100
Naikaku Sōri Daijin Kanbō Kōhōshitsu, 1011
Naikakufu (Cabinet Office), 21, 179, 180, 182, 187, 202, 204, 205, 209, 210, 238, 244, 245, 248, 249, 399, 581, 582, 621, 627, 692, 693, 696, 700, 701, 702, 703, 728, 759, 922, 925, 1034
Nakabayashi, Itsuki, 135
Nakae, Katsumi, 337
Nakajima, Hiroshi, 374, 773
Nakajima, Michiko, 444
Nakakubo, Hiroya, 444
Nakamura, Itsuro, 708
Nakamura, Keisuke, 986
Nakamura, Minoru, 753
Nakamura, Toshio, 618
Nakamura, Yukihiko, 332
Nakanishi, Hiroyuki, 364
Nakano, Lynne, 697
Nakano, Mami, 444
Nakano, Mitsutoshi, 332
Nakata, Minoru, 708
Nambu Foreign Worker Caucus, 309
Namiki, Shokichi, 357
Nanetti, Raffaella, 707
Nanjo, Zenji, 9, 12
Naoi, Michiko, 133
Nasu, Sōichi, 130, 131
National Federation of Civic Halls, 185
National Institute of Population and Social Security Research, 50, 51, 53, 84, 217
NDK (Naikakufu Daijin Kanbo Seifu Kokoku Shitsu), 616
NDKSH (Naikakufu Daijin Kanbo Seifu Hokokushitsu), 690, 702
Nemoto, Yasuhiro, 737, 739
New Kōmei Party, 670
Newell, Colin, 114
Ngo, Hang-Yue, 262
NHK, 368, 459, 479, 484
NHK Broadcasting Culture Research Institute, 412, 515, 516, 517, 519
Nichibenren (Japan Federation of Bar Associations), 773
Nichisōken, 660
*Nihon Keizai Shinbun*, 865, 986
Nihon Kokugo Daijiten (NKD), 125
Nihon Sōgō Kenkyūjyo, 714

Nikkei Net, 677
*Nikkei Weekly* (7 March 2005), 983, 986
Nikko Financial Intelligence, 1141
Nippon Keidanren, 771, 772
NIPSSR (National Institute for Population and Social Security Research), 14, 257, 259, 260, 261, 262, 641, 644, 645, 646, 843, 1036, 1040, 1118
Nishiguchi, Mamoru, 460
Nishioka, Hachiro, 76
Nishishita, Akitoshi, 136
Nishizaki, Fumihira, 222
Niwa, Fumio, 129, 493, 495
NKBT (Nihon koten bungaku taikei), 326, 330, 331, 332, 333, 334, 335, 336
NKK (Nihon Kanko Kyokai), 584, 586
Noble, David. S., 610
Noguchi, Haruko, 288
Nomura, Kanetarō, 113
Norgren, Tiana, 37, 641, 642, 643, 644, 750
Notenstein, Frank W., 44
NRI (Nomura Research Institute), 952
NSLC (National Service-Learning Clearinghouse), 725
NST (Nihon shiso taikei), 327
Nuessel, Frank H., 457
Nyukan Kyokai, 71

O'Leary, Joseph T., 580
O'Reilly, Jacqueline, 964
O'Connor, Julia S., 749
Oakley, Deborah, 644
ōba, Saneharu, 106
Obara, Yoshiaki, 549
Oberländer, Christian, 138
Obuchi, Hiroshi, 111
Ōbuchi, Hiroshi, 19, 20
Ochiai, Emiko, 37, 236, 237, 244, 249
OCPRCS (Office of the Cabinet Public Relations, Cabinet Secretariat), 870
Ōe, Moriyuki, 67
OECD, 21, 45, 277, 548, 552, 769, 784, 835, 885, 951, 965, 967, 1043, 1054, 1055
Ogasawara, Kyo, 459
Ogasawara, Yuko, 256
Ogawa, Akihiro, 136, 727, 735, 759
Ogawa, Eiji, 1058
Ogawa, Makoto, 421
Ogawa, Naohiro, 14, 36, 75, 173, 262, 264, 266, 821, 822, 824, 825, 827, 828, 833, 835
Ogawa, Yoshikazu, 551
Ogino, Miho, 750
Oguma, Eiji, 302
Ogura, Chikako, 171
Ogura, Seiritsu, 842
Ohbuchi, Hiroshi, 28
Ōhinata, Masami, 278, 757
Ohno, Yoshiyuki, 626
Ohta, Kiyoshi, 224
Ohtake, Fumio, 218, 222, 902, 903, 904, 908, 921, 922, 923, 1110
Oishi F. (pseudonym), 381
Oishi S., 1109
Oishi, Akiko, 280, 282, 285, 289, 291, 753
Oishi, Nana, 767, 768
Oka, Masato, 956
Okada, Kei, 617
Okada, Minoru, 111
Okamoto, Hideaki, 206
Okazaki, Ayanori, 8
Okazaki, Yoichi, 6
Ōkouchi, Kazuo, 221
Olmstead, A. D., 606
Ölschleger, Hans Dieter, 36
Olshansky, Jay S., 19
Omran, Abdel R., 11, 30, 31
Ono, Hiromi, 256, 267, 268, 270, 271
Ono, Hiroshi, 981, 982
Onofri, Paolo, 832
Onomichi, Shōkōkaigisho, 594
Oppenheimer, Valerie K., 266, 268, 269
Orikuchi Shinobu, 345
Orloff, Ann Shola, 749
Orszag, Peter R., 1102
Osada, Hiroshi, 136
Osaka Prefectural Government, 305
Ōsawa, Mari, 218, 963, 964, 967, 968, 969, 973, 975
Oshio, Takashi, 1104, 1105, 1109, 1111
Oshiro, Noritake, 134
Ostner, Ilona, 963
Ōta Motoko, 335
Ōta, Hiroko, 133
Ōtake, Hideo, 338, 654
Otani, Kenji, 8

Palacios, Robert, 1120
Palmer, A. M., 576
Palmer, Edward, 1132
Palmore, Erdman, 137, 324, 326
Park, Kyoun, 717
Parsons, Talcott, 267
Peach, Ceri, 297

Pearl, David, 423
Pearl, R., 44
Peattie, Mark R., 298
Pekkanen, Robert, 690, 707, 708, 712, 715
Pempel, T. J., 668, 669
Peng, Ito, 749, 1040
Penney, Tim, 1019
Phillips, David, 734
Picheral, Henri, 31
Pieterse, Nederveen, 310
Pinelli, Antonella, 267
Pitts, D. G., 572, 573
Plath, David W., 137, 331, 390
Population reference Bureau, 34
Potter, David, 700
Potter, Robert C., 7
Prachuabmoh, Vipan, 35
Preston, Samuel H., 31
Putnam, Robert D., 707, 714

Rabbitt, P., 575
Ramsayer, J. Mark, 447, 452
Rasmussen, Eric B., 447
Rastenyte, Daiva, 33
Rausch, Anthony, 362, 364, 367, 368
Raymo, James M., 256, 260, 267, 268, 269, 270, 271
Read, Benjamin L., 708
Reed, L. J., 44
Reher, David, 255
Retherford, Robert D., 75, 264, 266, 821
Rindfuss, Ronald R., 256, 262, 263, 266, 268
Rinharuto, Zeppu (= Sepp, Linhart), 324
Ritsuko, Inokuma, 423
Roberts, Glenda S., 751, 766, 773
Robertson, Jennifer, 186
Robine, Jean-Marie, 835
Robinson, Mark, 1019
Rōdō Seisaku Shingikai, 957
Roesgaard, Marie H., 734
Rogers, A., 45
Röhl, Klaus-Heiner, 867
Rōjin Hoken Fukushi Jānaru [Journal of Elderly Healthcare and Welfare], 197
Romsa, Gerald, 580
Rosen, Harvey S., 842
Rosenbaum, James E., 557
Ross, Katherin, 174
Roth, Joshua, 775
Roth, Joshua Hotaka, 303
RSC (Road Safety Committee), 1021
Ruys, Hein, 580

Sadana, Ritu, 29
Sagaza, Haruo, 100, 134, 135, 136, 180, 184, 185, 187, 759
Saitō, Makoto, 222, 902, 903, 904, 908, 921
Saito, Sadao, 184
Saito, Tomoko, 827, 835
Sakai, Junko, 176
Sakaiya, Taichi, 12
Sakakibara, Eisuke, 675, 756
Sakamaki, Hiroshi, 1057
Sakamoto, Satomi, 264
Salamon, Lester, 690, 691
Salomon, Joshua A., 29
Salthouse, T. A., 576
Samwick, Andrew, 1104
Sanderson, Warren C., 823
*Sankei Shinbun* (12 April 2005), 755
Santow, Gigi, 267
Sarti, Cinzia, 33
Sasai, Tsukasa, 262, 265
Sasaki, A. (pseudonym), 381
Satō, Hiroki, 133, 756
Satō, Naoto, 133
Satō, Ryuzaburo, 266
Satō, Susumu, 550
Satō, Tadao, 534
Satō, Toshiki, 221, 222
Satō, Yasumasa, 492
Saul, Berrick, 550
Saunders, Peter, 230
Sauvy, A., 44
Sawano, Yukiko, 181, 186
Sawyer, Malcolm, 221
Scheidt, Bernhard, 328, 333, 334, 492
Scheiner, Ethan, 660
Scherbov,Sergei, 823
Schieber, Frank, 1021
Schlesinger, Jacob, 673
Schmidt, Sandra L., 580, 581, 583
Schoen, R., 45
Schoppa, Leonard, 650, 717, 734, 745, 749, 750, 760
Schulz, James H., 166
SCK (Somucho Chokan Kanbo Korei Shakai Taisaku Shitsu), 616
SCSK (Shinkin Chuo Sangyo Kenkyujo), 625
Searle, Mark S., 580
Sechiyama, Kaku, 171, 236, 243

Seikatsu Kagaku Chōsakai, 129
Seike, Atsushi, 159, 993, 994, 1097, 1108
Seiyama, Kazuo, 222
Seki, Harunami, 618
Sekiyama, Naotaro, 113
Sekizawa, Hidehiko, 1015
Sekizawa, Mayumi, 346, 565
Sellek, Yoko, 766, 767
*Senden Kaigi*, 462
Sepp, Linhart, 324
Settergren, Ole, 1132
Shakai Hosho Kenkyusho, 134
Shakai Keizai Seisansei Honbu, 989
Sharpe, F. R., 44
Shaver, Sheila, 749
Shaw, Gareth, 589
Shelton, Beth A., 268
Shibuya, Shigeki, 628
Shimamura, Toshihiko, 109
Shimizu, Hiroaki, 134
Shimizu, Hiroko, 690, 691
Shimizu, Kokichi, 557
Shimizu, Takahiko, 615
Shimizutani, Satoshi, 288, 1109
Shimoebisu, Miyuki, 760
Shin, Sumi, 420, 424
Shinmura Taku, 330, 333, 461, 462
Shinmura, Izuru, 466
Shintaku Kyōkai [Trust Companies Association of Japan], 1142
Shintani, Takanori, 358, 561
Shintani, Yuriko, 262
Shintō, Hisashi, 566
Shipper, Apichai W., 309, 773
Shirahase, Sawako, 228, 262, 975
Shirai, Shozo, 620
Shirasawa, Takuji, 615
Shire, Karen, 967
Shirubā Jinzai Sentā Jigyo Kyokai, 956
*Shizuoka Shinbun* (25 September 2006), 773
Shoemaker, Stowe, 579, 580
Shore, Cris, 729
Shorter, Edward, 15
SHSFB (Shakai Hosho Shingikai Fukushi Bukai—Seikatsu Hogo Seido no Arikata ni Kansuru Senmon Iinkai), 929
Sibata, Takesi, 475, 479
Siegel, Jacob S., 45, 114
Silverman, Philip, 323
Sinding, Steven W., 832
SJGKT (Sōmushō Jichi Gyōseikyoku Kaso Taisakushitsu), 63
Skord, Virginia, 331, 492, 494
SKS (Sangyo Kozo Shingikai), 624
Sleebos, Joelle, E., 1044
Smeeding, Timothy, 230
Smith, Robert J., 323, 389
Sodei, Takako, 133, 206
Soeda, Yoshiya, 130, 132
Sōgō, Yunicomu, 582
Sokolowski, S. Wojciech, 690, 691
Sōmuchō (Management and Coordination Agency), 204
Somūsho Tōkei Kyoku (STK) (Statistics Bureau, Ministry of General Affairs), 16, 61, 63, 66, 68, 69, 72, 103, 628, 629, 695, 786, 789, 950, 965
*Sōrifu Tokeikyoku* (Statistics Bureau), 800
Spielvogel, Laura, 603, 625
SSF (Sasakawa Sports Foundation), 616, 617, 620, 621, 622, 623, 624
Statistics Bureau, Ministry of Internal Affairs and Communication, 34, 155, 203, 219, 220, 277, 278, 584, 826, 827
Steffen, Christian, 174
Stevens, Carolyn, 702
Stockwin, J. A. A., 795
Suda, Keizō, 113
Sugano, Noriko, 326, 334, 338
Sugawara, Taku, 672, 678
Sugeno, Kazuo, 427
Sugimoto, Yoshio, 736
Sugiyama, Yoshio, 615
Sung, Sirin, 1044
Sutton, Paul D., 34
Suzuki, Akira, 492
Suzuki, Eriko, 21
Suzuki, Hitoshi, 868, 871, 987
Suzuki, Kazue, 647
Suzuki, Tohru, 269, 761
Suzuki, Wataru, 1103
Swanson, David A., 114
Sweeney, Megan M., 267, 268
Sweet, James A., 260

Tachibanaki, Toshiaki, 221, 222, 558, 771, 899, 921, 1110
Tadashi, Hanami, 421
Tadashi, Yamamoto, 691
Taeuber, Irene B., 37, 644
Tai, Eika, 308
Taiwan Journal, 1045
Takabayashi, Takashi, 354

Takahagi, Tateo, 136
Takahashi, Bonsen, 113
Takahashi, Hirokazu, 618
Takahashi, Shigesato, 645
Takahashi, Shinichi, 7
Takahashi, Yuetsu, 136
Takase, Masato, 6, 7
Takayama, Noriyuki, 824, 1104, 1115, 1116, 1117, 1123
Takeda, Hiroko, 750
Takeda, Kyoko, 135
Takegawa, Shōgo, 133, 136, 1035
Takeishi, Emiko, 756
Takeuchi, Kei, 98
Talcott, Paul, 660, 678
Tamada, Hirotake, 445
Tamaki, Takao, 134
Tamanoi, Mariko Asano, 298
Tamura, Masao, 827, 835
Tanaka Yoshiaki, 330
Tanaka, Hiromi, 743
Tanaka, Hiroshi, 298
Tanaka, Kimiko, 460
Tanimoto, Masayuki, 239, 240
Tarumoto, Hideki, 308
Tatsukawa, Shoji, 337, 338, 339
Taylor, Philip, 959
Teachman, Jay D., 267
Teichler, Ulrich, 551, 556
Teruko, Ueda, 206, 211
Tetsuya, Kazuaki, 446
Thang, Leng Leng, 181, 182, 187
*The Business Times*, 948
The Clearinghouse on International Developments in Child, Youth and Family Policies at Columbia University, 172
*The New York Times*, 294
THES (Times Higher Education Supplement), 553, 554
Thimm, Caja, 457
Thompson, Christopher, 362, 364, 365, 367, 373, 375, 379
Thompson, W. S., 44
Thompson, Warren S., 26
Thornbury, Barbara, 362, 370, 380, 383
Thornton, Arland, 267
Thornton, Arland D., 267
Time Asia, 838
TMG (Tokyo Metropolitan Government), 721, 722
Tobin, Joseph Jay, 137
Todd, Emmanuel, 87
Tokyo Metropolitan Government, 304
*Tokyo Shinbun* (12 September 2006), 773
Tokyo Volunteer Action Center, 190
Tomatsu, Hidenori, 436, 447
Tominaga, Kenichi, 221
Torii, Ippei, 767, 773, 776
Tōwa-chō Kikaku Zaiseika, 382
Tōwa-chō Kōhō, 375
*Tōwa-chō Shiryōhen*, 374
Tōwa-chō Sōgō Shisho, 381
Traphagan, John W., 137, 204, 355, 387, 388, 389, 390, 392, 393, 786
TRB (Transportation Research Board), 1021
Tretheway, Michael, 579, 580
Trow, Martin, 550
Tsai, June, 1045
Tsuboi, Hiroshi, 308
Tsuda, Takeyuki, 766
Tsuji, Ichiro, 187, 703
Tsuji, Shōji, 136
Tsuji, Yohko, 341
Tsujinaka, Yutaka, 707, 714
Tsukimura, Reiko, 492
Tsukuba City Survey (unpublished), 713, 714
Tsumago Kankō Kyōkai, 593
Tsurumi, Shunsuke, 132
Tsuruta, Yoko, 555, 735, 740
Tsuya, Noriko, 10, 256, 262, 263, 264, 265, 266, 268, 272
Tuljapurkar, Shripad, 827, 835
Tuma, N. B., 45
Tuomilehto, Jaakko, 33
Turner, Victor W., 345

Uchida, Kan'ichi, 113
Uchiumi, Kazuo, 618, 629
Ueda, Chiaki, 133
Ueda, Kazuo, 890
Ueda, Masao, 106
Ueda, Teijiro, 106
Ueno, Chizuko, 36, 237, 610, 646, 749
Ujiie, Mikito, 335
Umetani, Kaoru, 492
UNFPA, 13
United Nations, 82, 94, 156, 163, 421
United Nations, Department of Economic and Social Affairs, 35
United Nations, Department of Economic and Social Affairs, Population Division, 81, 85, 86, 90, 93

United Nations, Department of Economic and Social Affairs, Statistical Division, 34
Uno, Kathleen S., 753
UNPD (United Nations Population Division), 770, 785
Upham, Frank, 426, 427, 442, 447, 448, 452, 453
Urata, Nobuchika, 551
Usami, Mayumi, 458, 459, 460, 461
USDS (U.S. Department of State), 768
Ushiogi, Morikazu, 734
Usui, Chikako, 165, 166, 170, 772
Usui, Takashi, 136
Uysal, Muzaffer, 580

Van de Kaa, Dirk J., 36, 255
Van, Jon, 723
Vaupel, J. W., 47
Ventura, Stephanie J., 34
Vertovec, Stephen, 310
Vogel, Ezra, 221
Voke, J., 573
von Kopp, Botho, 739, 740

Wada, Junichiro, 753
Wada, Ritsuko, 753
Wagatsuma, Takashi, 17
Wahdan, M. H., 31
Waldenberger, Franz, 982
Walker, Patricia, 553
Wattelar, C., 44
Weale, R. A., 572
Webb, Philippa, 206
Wedel, Janine R., 729
Wei, Sherrie, 580
Weinstein, Helen, 212
Weintrub, Rachel, 173
Weiss, Robert S., 956
Westney, D. Eleanor, 800
Whelpton, P. K., 44, 45, 642, 643, 644
White, Joseph, 1093
White, Paul, 734
WHO (World Health Organization), 167, 620
WHOSIS (WHO Statistical Information System), 33
Wilensky, Harold, 654
Wilkinson, Jody A., 457
Williams, Allan M., 589
Willis, David B., 306, 307, 310
Wilson, Gail, 1012
Wiltshire, Richard, 67
Wise, David A., 1108
Wöhr, Ulrike, 505
Woodall, Brian, 784
World Bank, 45, 91, 1104
World Health Organization (WHO), 29
Wöss, Fleur, 136, 138, 497
Wu, Chi-Mei Emily, 580, 581
Wynder, Ernst L., 76

Xie, Yu, 267, 269

Yagi, Takumi, 222
Yaguchi, Koichi, 615
Yajima, Masami, 759
Yamada, Atsuhiro, 993, 994, 1097, 1108
Yamada, Masahiro, 17, 18, 248, 758, 759
Yamada, Reiko, 552
Yamada, Yasushi, 222
Yamaguchi, Osamu, 1143
Yamaguchi, Toru, 135
Yamaguchi, Yasuo, 623
Yamamoto Shigemi, 329
Yamamoto, Tadashi, 691
Yamamoto, Yoshihiro, 182
Yamanaka Akiko, 171, 773, 775
Yamaori Tetsuo, 327, 328, 340, 345
Yamashita, Kesao, 133, 136
Yamauchi, Naoto, 690, 691
Yamawaki, Keizo, 767
Yamazaki, Yasuhiko, 1039
Yanagawa, Yoshitoki, 105
Yanagita Kunio, 345, 350, 355
Yanaihara, Tadao, 106
Yano, Masahiro, 427, 445
Yasunaga, Akitomo, 615
Yasuo, Kuwahara, 421
Yazaki, Takeo, 64
Yeoh, Brenda S. A., 35
Yip, Paul, 835
Yogo, Takamori, 1017
Yokkaichi-shi, Shiminbu, 702
Yokohama City Government, 305, 714
Yokoyama, Gennosuke, 242
Yomiuri Shimbunsha Yoron Chosabu, 405, 406
*Yomiuri Shinbun*, 459, 462, 463, 468, 483, 627, 648, 651, 722, 772, 811
Yoneda, Masato, 477, 479
Yoshida, Yoshio, 20, 294, 871, 873
Yoshida, Yoshishige, 135

Yoshimi, Shunya, 310
Yoshinaga, Kazuhiko, 9, 12
Yoshinari, Katsuo, 768
Yoshioka, Yasuo, 458
Yoshitake, Teruko, 492
Yoshiuchi, Kazuhiro, 615
You, Xinran, 580
Young, Louise, 298
Young, Michael K., 447
YRKKI (Yutaka na Rogo no tame no Kokumin Kaigi Iinkai), 656
Yu, Wei-hsin, 256
Yukiko, Yamazaki, 870
Yumiko, Arai, 211
Yuri, Kenichi, 566
Yuzawa, Yasuhiko, 126, 130, 245, 246

Zarit, Steven H., 211
Zeldes, Stephen. P., 1104
Zenchifu-ren, 717
Zenji-ren, 715
Zenko-ren, 718
Zenkoku Nōgyō Kankō Kyōkai, 584
ZGHRK (Zenkoku Gakudo Hoiku Renraku Kyogikai), 290
Zhou, Yanfei, 285
Zimmer, Zachary, 580
Zviniene, Asta, 112

# INDEX OF SUBJECTS

Note: Page numbers in bold indicate illustrations.


1.57 shock, 35, 637, 646, 648, 749–50, 752, 756–7, 1034
"2007 problem", 985–6
21st Century Welfare Vision, 751

abortion, 37, 109, 639, 641–4, 647, 759; illegal, 11, 442; induced, 8, 10–11, 17
accessibility, 172, 623, 784, 793
accountability, 629, 660, 791
action plan, 755–6, 758, 761
active ageing, 155, 157, 159–60, 167, 1128n9
adolescent, 740, 743, 759
adulthood, 146–7, 171, 238, 501, 532, 573, 758
adults: young, 29, 63, 68, 387, 474, 617, 622, 1134; younger, 459, 622, 704
advisory council, 649, 669, 752, 812, 957–8
after-school: care, 196; centre, 182, 189n6; Children's Plan, 291; club, 751–2, 754; programmes, 1041–2
age: average, 8, 16, 36, 53–4, 171, 246, 257, **258**, 455, 481–2, 543, 548, 582, 742, 823, **824**, 981, 987; biophysical, 581; chronological, 125–6, 319, 455, 456; composition, 44, 46, **83**, 817, 821, 825, 831–2, 837; construction of, 319; discrimination (*see* ageism); distribution, 823, 900, 904; of fruition (*jitsunen*), 134, 153, 461–2, **463**; at giving birth, 53; grade, 319, 353, 608; of houseold head, **917–19**; lexicon of, 456, 465, 467–9; at marriage: 8, 15–16, 54, 73n4, 171, 246, 257, **258**–9, 481–2, 543, 582, 742; of maturity, 112, 134, 153, 461, **463**, 1036; mean, 8, 16, 36, 53, 257, **258**, 455; meaning of, 468; method of calculating, 346, 350n2; norm, **147**, 150; pensionable, 658, 662, 849, 968, 1116–17, 1121; prestige of, 457; psychosocial, 581; segregation, 122, 180–1, 188, 196; stratification, 319; very-old, 160
age cohort, 47, 71, 319, 325, **405**, 478, 483, 526, 621, 627, 678, 734, 738, 949, 969, **970–74**, 975, 979, 984, 986, 993
age group, 8, 27, 30, 41, 47, 49, 52, **53**, 130, 164, 170,181, 188n5, 192, 219, 226, **247**–8, 257, 259, 277, 353, 405, **406**, 408, 477, **483**, 485–6, 513, 520, 525, **526–7**, 528, 543, 550, 574, 580, 584–8, 602, 605, 609, 616, 620–1, **622**–3, 625–7, **701**–3, 704, 737, 823, 900–3, 905, **914**, **918**, **927**, **949–50**, 958, **980**, 982, **983**, 1014, **1019**, 1079, 1089, **1111**, **1122**
age structure, 27, 33n1, 46, 52, 73, 94, 319, 321, 580, 592, 599, 605, 823, 825, 828, 837, 865, 871n3, 872, 879, 889, 895, 985
age-integrated facility, 32, 191, 192n11, 196–7
age-linguistics, 475; encoding of linguistic age, 456, 469
aged society, 3, 132, 136, 154, 157, 547, 563, 637, 735, 744, 824
ageing: aesthetics of, 506–7, 610; body, representation of, 603; boom, 491; clientele, 588, 601; and cognitive abilities, 1018–9, 1021; economics of, 817; effects of: 321, 596, 744; index, 217; physiological, 615, 819, 999–1000, 1010–11; population, 133, 166, 175, 222, 294, 367, 579, 590, 593, 596, 689, 730, 735, 843, 845, 933, 1030, 1044, 1079 (*see also* population ageing); process, 332, 498, 571, 577, 593, 596, 786, 865–6, 868, 871–2, 875, 926, 979, 1011; regional differences in, 590; shock, 491; social, xiii, 121, 125, 127–8, 132, 133, 135, 137–8, 153, 397, 735, 819, 999–1000, 1005, **1006**; sociology of, 129–33, 136, 604; of whole communities, 59
ageing society, 121–2, 129–30, 132–6, 138, 145, 148, 150, 152–7, 163–4, 179–80, 186, 188, 190, 194, 197,

202, 217, 248, 319–22, 355, 367, 406, 419–20, 443, 452–3, 513–14, 526, 547, 563–4, 566, 600, 614, 617, 619, 626, 636, 645, 653, 659, 667–8, 671, 675, 677, 686, 689, 692, 701, 707, 712–18, 728n2, 735, 741, 744, 756, 794, 796, 799–800, 804, 814, 817–19, 824, 841, 854, 861, 868–71, 899, 905–6, 909–10, 921, 1017, 1033, 1049, 1062, 1097
ageism, 50, 125, 136, 150, 180, 321, 418, 423, 427, 445, 457, 984, 1022
Agency for Cultural Affairs, 400, 482–5, 487, 567
agriculture, 112, 239, 243, 296, **515**, 562, 564, 874, **950**–1
Aichi, 61n1, 64, **66**, **68–9**, 303, 587, 680, **693**, **698–701**, 703, **704**, 769, 862, 1014
AIDS, 31, **33**
Ainu, 294, 302, 311, 481
Akita, **66**, **69–70**, 383, 387, **388**–9, 391–2, 692, **693**–4, 786, 929
alien registration, 422n14, 768, 813
allocation, 320, 783–4, 829, 869, 940, 942, 1080, 1133
Alzheimer's disease, 205, 467, 494, 505, 1010
amalgamation, 123, 361–70, 373–4, 379–82, 808, 871
Amendment Act of Job Security for Older People, 159
ancestor, 146, 148, 239, 242, 246, 320, 326, 345, 355–6, 358, 387, 389–3, 396–7, 414
Angel Plan, 123, 286, 639, 648–55, 760, 1037, 1041, **1042**, **1081**; New Angel Plan, 172, 272, 637, 649, 750, 752–3, **1042**; New New Angel Plan, 758
Annales School, 237
apparent-time method, 476
assets, 9, 182, 833, **834**–5, 880, 881n3, 901, 925n2, 1084, **1085**, 1102, **1106**, 1119, **1120**, 1126, **1127**, **1131**, 1133, **1142**, 1148, **1149**; cultural, 376; financial, 833, **834**, 888; land, 834; real, 833, **834**
assimilation, 309, 383, 576
asylum political, 766, 768
attitudinal change, 265–6
Australia, 48, 81–2, **86**, 89–**90**, 93–4, 267, **304–6**, 413, 554, 580, 617, 621, 625n6, 640, 771, **885**–6, **889**, 967, 1068
automobile industry, 165, 766, 819, 986, 1017, 1030
average income, 173, 541, 582, 902, 905, 1060n6, 1111

baby, 10, 29, 108, 110, 123, 169, 488, 639, 640, 642, 646–7, 650, 759
baby boom, 10, 12, 34, 35n6, 37, 45, 110, 244, 259, 366, 547–9, 563–4, 581, 643, 645, 654, 736, 737, 746, 821, 832, 906–7, 952, 986–7, 995, 1013
baby boomers, 12n7, 149, 156–7, **158**–9, **408**, 528, 530, 538, 540, 568, 583, 596, 624, 639, 736, 738, 872–3, 907, 909, 985, 1006, **1008**–9, 1013, 1108, 1130, 1131; second, 736
babysitting, 193, 240, 751
bank, 42, 45, 158, 243, 557, 674, 729, 804–5, 807–8, 811, 890, 955, 957, 1104, **1142**
"barrier-free", 205, **483**, 588, 755, 790, 792, 1012, 1017, 1024, 1026, 1028
Basic Law for a Gender-equal Society, 250, 1041
Basic Law for a Low Birth Society, 755–6
Basic Law on Measures for the Ageing Society, 154, 420, 701
Basic Law on Measures for the Society with Declining Birth Rate, 21
Basic Plan for Immigration Control (3rd edition), 765
Basic Proposal for Urgent Child-Care Measures, 751
"Basic stance on admittance of foreigners in the future", 774
Basic Survey of People's Life, 902
Basic Survey on Wage Structure, 891, 988–9
bill: medical, 656–7, 1054–5, 1057, 1060, 1088, **1089**, 1123, 1129, 1146; political, 427, 657, 661, 663, 675, 757, 810, 1040, 1070, 1123, 1126, 1128
birth: age at giving, projected, 53; cohort, 8, 9n5, 10, 15, 17, 52, 974; control, 11, 36–37, 211, 642–3, 646, 651; dearth, 643; extra-marital, 15, 17n10; "strike", 750
birth rate, xiii, 6, 27, **28**, 34, 36–7, 160, 174, 291, 603, 643, 646, 733, 770; boost, 635, 641, 647; decline in,

10, 26, 45, 121, 123, 173, 201, 203, 383, 491, 531, 544, 547, 613, 618–9, 636, 640, 642, 644, 651, 733, 735–9, 740–1, 746, 749–52, 749–52, 754, 756, 760, 818, 858, 862, 909–10, 945, 1128; crude (CBR), 6, **28**, 34; high, 27, 69; increase, 651; low, xi, 81–2, 159, 248, 251, 765, 770–2; measures to counter the declining, 20, 291, 636, 749, 758, 1041; national, 367, 547; peak of, 643; projection of, 765, 1128
border: cultural and psychological, 293, 297, 310; migration across, 25, 310, 635
bottom-up activities, 785, 792, 794
Brazil, 21, **85**, **299–301**, **304–306**, 475, 766, 768
breadwinner-homemaker system, 15, 18
breadwinner, male, 540, 963–4, 969, 975
"bubble" *see* economy, "bubble"
Buddhism, 112, 138, 327–8, 331, 333–4, 339, 355, 369, 372, 389–90, 393, **400**, 401, **402–3**, 404–5, 407, 409, 410, 414, 493, 500, 507, 606, 610, 680, 713, 716, 1056
Burakumin, 76, 294, 302, 0309
bureaucracy, 25, 106–7, 191, 207–8, 363, 365–7, 375, 381, 427, 617, 636, 643, 648, 653–4, 656, 658, 661, 664, 669, 674, 690, 729, 751, 755, 758, 761, 784, 794–5, 799–801, 803, 1040

Cabinet (Office/Agency), 104–7, 109–10, 153, 157, 399, 420, 582, 620, 642, 656, 658–9, 667, 670, 672–6, 679–80, 690–2, 758, 790, 829, 846, 922, 1034, 1041, 1054n1
Canada, 82, **90**, 92, 94, **304–6**, **413**, 430–1, 431n52, 441n74, 580, 617, 621, 625n6, 771, **885**–6, **889**, 891, 1068
cancer, 18, 76, 203, 496, 503, 505, 614, 626n7, 685
capacity: carrying, 164–5, 168; productive, 121, 165, 894–5
care: dental, 1086, **1087**; of the deceased, 387–8, 392–3, 395–6; for elderly (*see* elderly care); family-provided, 497; giving, 121–2, 129, 201–6, 210–13, 660–1, 766, 772–3; institutional, 206, 690, 696, 699, 1039, 1044, 1050, 1059–61; insurance, 136, **147**, 155–6, 160, 201–2, **205**, 207–9, 653n1, 660–1, 678–9, 683–4, 686, 819, 841, 845, 850–1, 853, 891, 944, 1010, 1038–40, 1044, 1058, 1065, 1074–5, 1080, **1081–2**, 1092; level, 209–10, 850, 1060; management, 192, 208, 1059; manager, 155, 201, 208, 210, 212, 1059, 1060; out-of-school hours (OSH care) club, 277, 290–1; preventative, 1061–2, 1086, 1094; provision of, 256, 265, 689, 819, 1062, 1078; socialization of, 661, 1040; visit, 715; and welfare association, 712, 716
career, 18, 37, 75, 122, 166–70, 174, 176, 184, 206, 208, 247, 250, 265, 278, 442, **483**, 542, 553, 583, 649–50, 759, 905, 956–7, 975, 981, 988, 992, 1052, 1117, 1124–5; counsellor, 957; development, 270, 552, 728, 957–8; exchange plazas, 955; interruption, 270, 272
cash benefit, 291, 661, 685, 1059–60, 1084, 1086, **1087**
census, 357, 537, 541 *see also* population census
Central Conference of the Elderly, 656
Central Council for Education, 726, 739, 741, 745
Central Council for Financial Services information, 891
Central Council for Savings Information, 891
Central Council for Savings Promotion, 890–1
Central Social Insurance Medical Council, 1088, **1089**
Central Social Welfare Council, 655
centralism, 5, 63, 99, 676, 794–5, 869, 900, 1087
Centre for the Development of a Society of Longevity, 134–135
Centre for Universal Design, 792
Charter on the Aeing Society, 701
Chiba, 61, 63, **66**, **68–9**, **158**, **303**, 604, 625, **693**, 769, **789**, 1024
child: abuse, 750, 752, 755, 758; allowance, 20, 171, 647, 749, 760, 1041; benefit system, 685; development of, 283, 287–9, **692**; education of, 568, 639, 742–3, 775;

and infant mortality, 6–7, 10–12, 29, 109, 238, 1077; out-of-school-hours (OSH) club, 277, 290–1; Child Welfare Law, 282n2, 283, 290
child-staff ratio, 286, 290, 753
childbearing, 10, 15–16, 54, 170, 256–7, 261–2, 264, 266–7, 277, 642; non-marital, 261, 267
childbirth, 109, 170, 172, 175–6, 262, 265, 277, 544, 743, 757, 760, 972–3, 1034, 1041, 1045, 1128
child-care: arrangement, 277, **278–280**; cost, 277; facility, 123, 171–3, 282–3, 286, 544, 649–51, 749, 751, 753–6, 1044; full-time, 716, 539, 933; service, 20, 174–5, **281**, 283, 285–7, **288**, 291, 648–50, 749, 751–3, 818, 941, 943–5; support, 290, 751, 753–4, 757–8, 1042
child-care centre, 189, 648, 753; with extended hours, 173, 751–2, 1041, **1042**; structural quality of, 281, 283, 288–9
Child Care and Family Care Leave Law, 420
Child Care and Long-term Care Leave Law, 756
Child Care Leave Law, 172
childhood, 345, 496, 528; education, early- 287, 749; health, 109; second, 495, 609; traumatic, 496
childless: couple, 36, 262n2, 355; elderly people, 126, 202, 1056; marriage, 262; women, 8, 393
childrearing, 92, 186, 247, 262, 277, 280, 478, 532, 544, 600, 649, 741n6, 742, 750–6, 758–61, 818, 933–4, 936, 939, 945, 1044; men's, 752–3
children: association for, 536, 707, 716; authorized centres for, 289–90; overprotection of, 742; and poverty, 291, 925; service, 698; shrinking number of, 547; upbringing of, 750
Children and Childrearing Support Plan, 637, 750, 754, 758 *see also* Angel Plans
Children's Future Foundation, 751
China, 33, 82, **83**–4, **85–6**, **90**–1, **93**–4, 98, 100, 107, 146, **299–301**, **304–6**, 329, 415, 555, 579, 635, 639–40, 642, 766–8, 772, 835, **836**, 841n1, 895
Christianity, 102, **400**, 401–2, **403**, **411**, 414
cities, shrinking of, 594, 794
Cities, Towns, and Villages Amalgamation Law, 362, 382
citizen: elderly (*see* elderly); with multiple identities, 308, 312; naturalized, 293–4, 303, 311, 766; new elderly, 160, 507, 528; non-Japanese, 57; participation, 703–4, 792; retired (*see* retiree); voluntary organizations, 690
civil: code, 126, 128–9, 690; liberty commissioner, 711; servant, 107, 111, 243, 564, 672, 685–6, 800, 1123, **1137**
Civil Affairs Bureau, 1069–70
Civil Code Committee, 1069–70
civil society, 635–7, 670, 681, 689, 691, 695, 701–4, 707–8, 710n8, 712, 724, 1040; group, **670**, 708, 1040; organization, 636–7, 681, 695, 701–2, 707–8, 712
class *see* social class
cohabitation, 15–17, 36, 134, 255–7, 260, **261**–2, 266, 271, 478; premarital, 255, 260, 266
cohort, 8–10, 15, 17, 46, 52–5, 66, 71, 158, 260–1, 476, 485–6, 547, 549, 580–1, 583, 596, 626, 645–7, 736–7, 738, 901, 971, **974**–5, 1110; age, 47, 319, 325, **405**, 478, 483, 526, 621, 627, 678, 734, 738, 949, 969, **970–4**, 975, 984, 986; analysis, 477; baby-boom, 12, 157; fertility method, 52; component method, 44–7, 51; elderly, 17, 49, 179n1, 608, 874, 975–6, 979; female, 12, 55, 644, 646, 973; marriage, **261**; typical behaviour of, 580–1; younger, 52, 865, 875, 964, 973, 975, 984, 993, 1110
college, 14, **147**, 170, 180, 182, 189, 293, 539, 542, 549, 551, 553, 556, 603, 649, 725–6, 728–9, 74, 759, **769**, 773, 936, **937**–8, 985; education, 170, 936; graduate, 268–9, 755
commercialisation, 202, 562, 593, 786
communication, 75, 102, 166–7, 181, 186–7, 191, 196, 323, 455, 460, 468–9, 474, **480**, 482, 497, 500, 502, 523, 540, 589, 714, 718, 799, 802, 807, 887, 988, 992
Committee to Improve Systems of Selecting Entrants to Senior High Schools, 739

Committee of Ten Thousand Citizens to Advance the Socialization of Care, 661
community: activities, 185, 541, 702; ageing of whole, 590; building of, **692**, 700, 703; care, 197, 1058–61; centre, **709**, 956; child-care support centres, 290; childrearing, 752, 754–5; elderly participating in, 180; groups, 185, 1040; initiative, 181, 185; life, 361–2, 372; school participating in, 194; service, 182, 703, 813, 1059, 1062; shrinking of, 593, 596; smaller, 704; support, 197, 381, 759
community-based: activities, 1051; care system, 154, 1080; elderly care, 1038; health insurance, 1084, 1092; initiative, 181; practice, 792; service, 752, 1056, 1060; support centre, 1041
Confucian virtues and values, 146, 148, 319–20, 324, 332–3, 337, 434, 493–5, 497, 879, 887, 1050 *see also* filial piety, respect for the elderly
conscription, 102, 350n2
consensus: on decline of fertility, 1041; on educational reform, 744–5; on factors for population decline, 933; on health and welfare, 1040; on migration policy, 296, 765; on reform within community, 659; on social security programme, 858
conservatives, 428, 654, 660
constituency, 677–8
constitution, 9, 28, 236, 400, 418–9, 425–5, 428–34, 436–40, 443–4, 446, 448, 450–1, 453, 532, 647, 654, 667, 681, 744, 756–7
construction industry, 782–3, 874, 901, **950**
"construction state", 781, 784, 793, 796
consumer: behaviour, 819, 999–1000, 1002, 1007; credit, 879, 888, 891, 895; goods, 601, 874, 1008; price index (CPI), 1074, 1098, 1116, 1119, 1125, 1129
consumption, 17, 45, 76, 153, 164–7, 218, 222, 493, 502, 599–601, 604–5, 609, 613, 624, **826**, 828, 830, 874, 881n3, 888, 899, 908–9, 934, 1000, 1003, 1006, **1008**, 1010, 1015, 1123n7, 1133; and diminished domestic demand, 874; inequality, 899, 908–9; pattern, 164, 166, 888; tax, 659, 854, **855**–**856**, 858, **1081**, 1100, 1105, 1112, 1130, **1131**
contraceptive, 10–11, 36, 87, 641–2, 644, 647
conurbation, 67, 69, 590, 862, 872
conviviality, 498, 605
co-residence, 179, 203–4, **205**–6, 209, 212, 218, 220, 230, 255, 263, 265, 270–2, 340–1, 489, 775, 1035, **1090**; intergenerational, 489; with parents, extended, 255, 265, 270; rate of elderly per capita, **1090**
corporations, 208–9, 243, 250, 282n1, 357, 400, 422n16, 437, 690–2, 697, 707n3, 723n1, 753, 757, 795, 799, 804, 810–11, 867, 895, 940n5, 942, 949, 952, 957–60, 968, 981, 986
Council on Fiscal and Economic Reform, 684
Council for Measures for Society with Decreasing Birthrate, 674
Council on Population Problems, 644, 649, 752
Council on Regulatory Reform and Promotion of the Liberalization of the Private Sector, 772
countryside, 66, 244, 296, 328, 358, 369, 388, 555, 602, 605, 737–8, 759, 786, 811, 871, 873, 875
couple: childless, 36, 262n2, 355; crisis in, 533; elderly, 328–9, 355, 582, 924, 1129; fertility of, 54; reproductive behaviour of, 53–4
couple-only: elderly family, 1065; household, 218, **220**, 224, 226, **227**–30, 1040
criminal justice parole system, 702
crude birth rate (CBR), 6, **28**, 34 *see also* birth rate
crude death rate (CDR), 6, **28**, 30, 82 *see also* death rate
cultural: activities, xiv, 335, 535, 542, 590, **696**–7, 728; ageing, 819, 999–1001, 1003, 1005; background, 299, 615; clash, 637; history, 361, 383; production, xi, 321, 727; resources, 589, 601; cultural transmission, 320
culture: local, 20, 372, 375; multi-relational theory of, 297; regional, 588; youth, 193, 1015
curriculum, 184, 376, 381, 613, 636, 721–2, 724, 737, 741, 753, 775n3
Curriculum Council, 741, 745

customer, 424, 589, 594, 1018, 1026–7, 1136; handicapped, 588; older, 488, 624, 807

DALE (Disability Adjusted Life Expectancy), 29, 321
Denmark, **86**, 89, 171, **413**, 769n2, **885**–6, **889**, **1109**
daughter-in-law, 151, 203–4, 206, 210, 212–13, 239, 339, 351, 497, 500, 1055
day care, **147**, 190, 192, 201, 207, 209–13, 256, 376, **483**, 607, **709**, 752–4, 1041, 1058; centre, 277–83, **284**–7, **288**–90, 660; evaluation of centre, 289; services and equity problem among parents, 280
day service, 189–91, 196, 208, **696**, **698**–9, 1038–9
Day of Respect for Old Age, 183, 326, 463, 493, 608, 714 *see also* Respect for the Elderly Day
death: afterlife, 319, 335, 403; average age of oldest, **824**; causes of, 7, 19, 29–30, **31–2**, 33, 47, 205; ease fear of, 506; in Japanese society, 493; meaning of, 319; pollution by, 330; scenario, 492; socialization of, 505; and sociology of dying, 130
death rate, 5–7, 22–7, **28**, 30–32, **33**–4, 92, 110, 655; crude (CDR), 6, **28**, 30, 82
decentralization, 20, 67, 154, 361–21, 367, 685, 795, 866–7
Decentralization Promotion Law, 367
decision making, 58, 137, 146, 168, 441n74, 448, 635, 663, 665, 791, 1067
de-economization, 637, 789
deindustrialization, 789
dementia, 89, 136, 151, 153, 160, 206, 456, 465, **466**–7, **468**–9, 495, 497, 620, 1060, 1061n7, 1065, 1072; rising number of, 466; new word for, **468**
democracy, 308, 435, 668, 672, 682, 785
Democratization, 11, 248, 487–8
demographic: after-effect, 645; demographic ageing, 69, 165, 175, 321, 637, 781, 789, **870**, 872–3, 875, 1033–5, 1038–40, **1042**–3, 1163; behaviour, 50, 218; challenge, xii–xiv, 169, 179, 188, 197, 321, 547, 556, 571, 707,712, 716, 718, 785, 1031; dilemma, 163, 169; disparity, 94; demographic dividend, 13, 821, 825–6, 828–31, **832**–3, 835, **836**, 838; factor, 67, 97, 489, 868, 1043, 1124–5, 1127–8, 1130, 1132; movement, 46; pattern, 164; shift, xi, 213, 356, 361, 547, 549–51, 555, 557–8, 1045; shrinking, 637, 781, 789; stratification, 613; structure, 218, 320, 907; theory, 99; trend, 41, 114, 313, 639–40, 651, 655, 823–5, 1045
demographic transition, xi–xii, 5, 9, 26–7, 30, 38, 50, 468, 640, 793, 821, 825, 833; second, 35, 42, 87, 255, 264, 821
demography, 45, 81, 97–100, 111–14, 321, 571, 600, 640, 643–4, 648, 735, 829, 1118; anthropological, 114; applied, 97, 99, 114; basic, 97; formal, 97, 114; historical, 112–14; mathematical, 114; socioeconomic, 97
dependency, 163–4, 167, 204, 213, 262, 341, 626n7, 662, 742; ratio, **83**, 121, **157**, **163**–4, 166, 168, 819, **836**, 842–4, 849, 1035–7, 1040, 1043
"depth of engagement scale", 188
depopulation, xi, xiii, 63, 66, 123, 149, 163, 296, 320, 357, 364, 366, 374–5, 379, 387–8, 392–4, 592, 599, 636–7, 705, 786, 789, 807, 809, 813, 871
depression, 180, 206, 504
descendants, 76n6, 148, 320, 340, 358, 434–6, 446, 475, 770, 872
"design for all", 571, 577 *see also* universal design
de-socialization, 637, 789
development projects: economic, 375; local, 375; municipal, 375; by Towa-cho, 376
deviant behaviours, 181, 267
Diet, 308, 311, **414**, 427, 567, 574, 656–8, 660, 663, 667–75, 677–9, 681–3, 685–6, 690,726, 756–7, 802, 810, 921, 1003, 1070, 1080, 1123
disability, 167, 210, 321, 334, 446, 497, 573–4, 575–6, 627, 1039, 1099 *see also* handicap
discrimination, anti- 428; against elderly, 50, 125, 136, 150, 180, 321, 418, 423, 427, 445, 457, 984, 1022; by corporations, 437; historical, 307; against illegitimate children, 450–1; based on nationality, 296, 321, 307–8,

418, 425; "reasonable", 418–9, 432–3, 436–7, 442–9, 452–3
discriminatory treatment prohibition, 173
diseases of ageing, 208; chronic and degenerative, 10–11, 18–19, 31, 121, 203, 205, 208, 572, 627, 844, 1094; lifestyle-related, 617, 1082, 1094; sexually transmitted, 759
distrust of government commitment, 1115, 1121, 1126; of public enterprises, 805
diversification: of family, 248; of life choices, 542; employment, **966**
diversity, 154, 231, 293–4, 302–3, 306, 729, 771
divorce, 17, 53–4, 97, 206, 246, 248, 256, 260, 262, 266–7, 271, 535–7, 544, 1034; rate, 15, 17, 36, 218, 248, 265, 536, 537, 541, 544, 1036
domestic: labour (*see* housework); responsibility, 271, 750; violence, 423, 534
double burden: for wives, 37; in pension system, 1104, 1132n14
dual-earner families, 222, 964, 975–6

economic: boom, 590; decline, 771, 869; development, 5, 7, 9, 13, 92, 375, 712, 567, 825, 861, 863, 866, 868, 872, 875, 947, 989, 1037; development project, 375; independence, 161, 255, 267–70, 930, 976; inequality, xiv, 122, 221, 818, 899–200, 909; organization, 755, 765, 772–3; productivity, 32, 167, 823; prosperity; symbol of Japan's, 785; rebuilding in post-war Japan, 653; recession, 217, 225, 553, 768; restructuring, 765; security, 229, 963, 965, 971; stimulus package, 782; thinking, liberal, 811; trajectory, 296
Economic Partnership Agreement (EPA), 772
economic growth, 5, 9, 13, 17, 30, 64, 66–7, 69, 84, 148–9, **150**, 222, 243, 245, 358, 414, 452, 534, 561–2, 583, 654–5, 678, 684–5, 782, 804, 817, 821, 823, 825, 828, **829**, 832, 834, 838, 845–7, **848**, 857–8, 865–6, 891, 894, 943, 945, 981, 1034, 1089, 1102, 1121n7; period of high, 66, 148, 222, 243, 414, 561–2, **829**, 832, 943, 981, 1089; rate, 13, 845–6, **848**, 858
economy: "bubble", 67, 134, 221, 247, 421, 502, 540, 549, 583, 659, 661, 776, 784, 969, 975, **829**, 832, 834, 900–1, 904, 981, 995, 1034; Fordist, 121, 165, 165, 167, 174–5; free-market, 661, 800, 805; "new", 165, 168; post-Fordist, 121, 163, 165–9, 175; regional, 818, 863–4, 868–9, 873–4; service-oriented, 168
Edo period, 64, 73, 76n5, 102, 112, 125–6, 325–7, 332, 334–5, 337–40, 363, 370, 383, 593, 1136, **1137**
education, board of, 363, 365, 376, 381, 721, 723; and career consciousness, 759; compulsory, 11, 14, 102, 547–9, 736, 741, 774; facility, 183; faith heritage, 381; fees, 540, 743; of the heart, 184–5, 639; higher, 14, 18, 272, 539, 542, 549–51, 553, 555–8, 643, 734–5, 740n5, 901, 907, 936; private, 548; system, xiii, 171, 184, 309, 321, 412, 547–51, 555–8, 636, 734, 736n2, 740, 744–5; tertiary, 556, 603; vocational, 603
educational: attainment, 18, 76, 87, 168, 267–9, 271, 580; costs, 755; crisis, 734; differentiation, 557; expenses, 760; institution, 175, 209, 280, **281**, 733, 744; policy, 382, 723, 725, 732–5, 741, 745; reform, 554, 558, 733–6, 740–6
elders, 137, 180, 183–5, 192n12, 329, 336, 338, 346–7, **348**–50, 352, 354, 395, 532, 715, 1058
elderly: abuse of, 423, 1076; bedridden, 89, 192, 347, 354, 461, 497–8, 538, 607, 655, 1010; care-dependent, 492, 843, **844**; childless, 126, 202, 1056; clubs for the, 138, clubs for, 181, 183, 464, 608, 703, 707, 712, 714–16; couples, 355, 582, 924, 1129; dependents, 163–4; dignity of, 489; as homogeneous group, 231, 625; institutionalized, 1056; integration into community networks, 715; labour force participation of, 1108, **1109**; living alone, 183, 195, 207, 209, 220, 228, 230, 348n1, 461, 481, 531, 655, 834, 924–5, 928, 1014, 1056, 1058; mental ability, age-related changes in, 575–6; new, 160, 507, 528; nursing of, 488, **1081**; office for policy on the, 180; and "old people problem", 129, 655; parents, 129, 204, 339,

341, 538, 1035; population, 12, **70**, 91, 151, 164, 166–7, 203, 218, 299, 468, 542, 645, 694, 700, 828–9, 850, 951, 1035, 1111; and poverty, 328, 600, 922–3, 925–6, 928, 1129; elderly relatives, 201, 205, 690, 1038; and "second lives", 609; social inclusion of, 921; and sociology of old people, 128, 130; terms for the, 460–2, **463**–5, 468; voters, 677, 679; wealth owned by the, 833; and wisdom, 148, 329, 460, 493, 507–8; women, 133, 135, 230, 320, 339–40, 355, 458, 495, 531, 537, 586, 605; working, 127, 159, 194, 348, 481, 585, 723, 947, **948**, **950–1**, 952–3, 956, 999, 1108, **1109**

elderly care, xii, 19, 129, 133, 136, 138, 160, 182, 189, 204, 212–13, 248, 281, 329, 331, 492, 495, 497, 538, 606, 636, 645, 656, 658, 679, 689–90, 692, **693**–4, 697, 699, 784, 819, 1033, 1035, 1037–40, 1043–5, 1049, 1055–6, 1078, **1081**, 1086, 1092; service, 208, 941, 1038, 1044

election, 308, 437n65, 439n69, 654, 658, 663–4, 667–74, 676, **677**–81, 684–6, 802–3, 811, 813, 1057; campaign, 659–60, 662; district, 670, 672, 676; general, 677, 795, 810

electoral, 664, 680–1, 799, 803, 812; assistance, 679; process, 667; rules, 686; system, 671, 680, 795

electorate, 670, 808

elite, 107, 295, 550–1, 636, 669, 686–7; culture, 564; school, 737, 1052

employee, non-regular, 965, **970**, 973, 976, 984; pension insurance, 967, 969, **970**, 1119, **1120**–1, 1123,–4, 1126, **1127**, 1130, **1131**–2; middle-aged, 957; regular, 251, 540, 543, 891, 893, 964–5, **967**, 972–3, 975, 999; remuneration of older, 952; white-collar, 243, 953, 955–7, 986, 988, 991–2

Employees' Pension Fund (EPF), **1137–42**, **1147**–1148

Employees' Pension Insurance (EPI), 1098–1100, 1102, **1103**, 1105, 1108–9, 1112, 1117

Employees' Pension System (EPS), 654, **1138**

employers: long-term, 953; as subcontractor, 951; organizations for, 951

employment: appraisal, 987–8, 990–5; and bonus system, 880, 890, 895; and compensation, 20, 880, 890–1, 893, 895, 979, 981, 987–9, 990–2, 994, 1078, 1146; contract, 442n16, 774, 939, 950, 963, 966, **967**, 982, 986–7, 995; deregulation of, 964; female (*see* women in the workforce); of foreigners, 417, 421; gendered, 963; and human resources, 11, 107, 564, 590, 722, 835, 958, 981, 995; insecurity, 907, 965; maternal, 174; M-shaped curve of women's, 256, 277; non-regular, 251, 923, 963–5, **966**–7, 969, **970–3**, 976; of older people, 20, 127, 420, 427, 445, 836, 947–9, 953–5, 957, 959, 960, 984–5, 987, 994–5; opportunities, 75, 867, **870**, 947–8, 953–6, 964, 982, 985, 1125; part-time (*see* part-time); pattern, 174, 204; policy, 751, 964; practices, 169, 650, 752, 936–7, 940, 964, 980, 986; programme, 759, 783; and promotion, 19, 438–40, 444, 487, 532, 539, 543, 987–92; promotion centres for older workers, 1033; protection, 937–9, 964–5, 967, 982; rate, 836, 900, 959, 976, 982, **983**, 1034, 1121n7, 1126; re- 159, 952–5, 987, 995; security, 159, 418, 443, 937–8, 953, 955, 965; self-13, 159, 240, 513, 714, 760, 848, 934–5, 950, 964, 968, 1077, 1084, 1098, 1112; and semi-annual bonus, 890, 1117n3; and skill-grading system, 988–93; stability, 759, 775, 812, 954, 982; structure, 168, 356, 700; system, 19–20, 171, 443, 541, 649–50, 782, 954–5, 957, 980–4, 994, 1136 (*see also* seniority); training, 112, 173, 176, 197, 209, 251, 481, 551–2, 564, 567, 656, 696, 718, 721, 724, 735, 773, 905, 907, 957, 979, 983–7, 994–5, 1026, 1051; *see also* job, occupation

Employment Measures Law, 427, 958–9

Employment Status Survey, 969

end-of-life decision-making, 137

entrepreneurship, 799

environmental, 31, 44–5, 91, 534, **713**, 717, 741, 744, 783–4, 796; protection, 159, **692**, 721
epidemiological profile, 1094; transition, 9, 18, 30–1
equality, economic, 122, 813, 818; educational, 548; gender (*see* gender equality); equality, income, 222, 900; equality rights, xiii, 129, 236, 417, 417n1, 418–9, 423–37, 439–41, 444, 447–54, 743
equity capital, **1147**; intergenerational, 819, 823, 1091, 1105, 1105, 1110, 1116, 1129–30, 1133; issues, 280, 700, 791, 819
ethnicity, 97, 298–9, 308
ethnoscape, 308
eugenics, 107
Eugenics Protection Law, 10, 109
European Union, 625n6, 1044
euthanasia, 504, 507
extension: of life expectancy, 481; of retirement age, 159, 833, 835; of the healthy life span, 620; of compulsory pension enrolment, 1037; of the pension contribution exemption, 1037
extramarital birth, 15, 17n10; fertility, 16

familial transfer, 833
family: branch, 241; breakdown, 535; care, 122, 152, 174, 176, 201–3, **205**,–6, 211, 213, 340, 395, 420, 660–1, 1059; caregiver, **205**, 206–8, 210–13, 661, 1082; constraints, 87; continuity of the, 354; as cooperative living system, 54, 235, 237–8, 242; democratic, 237; dual-earner, 222, 964, 975–6; duties, 758; economic welfare of, 644; education, 743; employee, 239–40, 243; extended, 434, 494, 759; formation, 18, 35, 255–7, 271–2, 758–9; and gender-equal policy, 174; grave, 13, 351, 355–6, 358, 389–92; income, 241, 557, 641, 827, 899, 902–3, **911–12**; labour, 123, 240, 242; life, 146, 175, 246, 291, 357, 543, 585, 752, 754, 757; life course, 256; life cycle, 235, 255, 581–2; and male-based succession, 249; man, 244; as management body, 235, 237; meaning of, 741n6; members, 29, 202–4, 206, 211–13, 215, 229–30, 236, 240, 338, 341, 355, 387, 389, 390, 395, 446, 457, 460, 474, 494, 498, 517, 534, 582, 602, 690, 696, 699, 711, 774–5, 1053; modern, 15, 18, 123, 235–8, 240–5, 248, 251; modernization of the, 236; nuclear, 9, 14, 37, 149, 152, 181, 193, 240, 244–5, 248, 357, 414, 473, 481, 489, 532, 537, 742; nuclearization of, 121–2, 179, 562; obligations, 170; patriarchal, 9, 146, 169, 236, 1052; planning, 126, 149, 639, 643, 646–7, **822**; policy, 87, 169, 172, 174–5, 636–7, 686, 729, 749–55, 757–61, 1033; register, 236, 239, 241, 813, 1069, 1071, 1073; roles, 170, 256, 264, 272; size, 651, **822**, 1162–3; structure, xi, 123, 229, 235, 237, 282–3, 404, 414, 1034, 1039, 1043; succession, 354, 358; support policy, 248, 749; system villages, 353; and tax-financed benefits, 681; types, 73, 235, 242, **244**, **249–50**; urban, 240–1, 641; values, 291, 660, 752
family-friendly, 170, 172, 174, 272, 752, 755, 757
family-work harmonization, 1035, 1040–1
famine, 26, 31, 102, 1161
farmer, 11, 126, 159, 166, 203, 238–9, 296, 335–6, 338, 370, 567, 584, 654, 714, **1058**, 1098
father, 239, **244**, 247, 279, **280**, 333, 335–6, 338–9, 346, 348, 352, 433, 457, 488–9, 495–7, 501, 506, 508, 510, 535–6, 650–1, 750–2, 754–6, 1041
fecundity, 8, 106
female old age, 339; politician, 757
feminists, 36–7, 246, 647, 661, 717n17, 750, 1059
feminization, 167–8
fertility: behaviour, 14, 34, 122, 262n2, 635, 646, 649; below replacement, xiii, 5 ,13, 16–7, 19, 42, 46, 73, 87, 94, 1160; control, 10–11; extra-marital, 16; level, 47, 73, 87, 169, 174; lowest-low, 16, 86–7, 89; marital, 8, 10, 36–7, 54, 73, 75, 175–6, 754, 756; natural, 8; policy, 20, 291, 640, 648, 761, 818, 844–5, 943, 945; projection, 49, **51**–2, **54**, 259n1, 644, **935–6**, 1101, 1118,

1128; regional differences in, 3, 25, 69, 77, 353, 355, 590; scenario, 55, 843; survey, 265–6, 644–5; transition, 9–13; treatment, 757–9
fertility decline, xi, xiii, 4–5, 8, 10, 13, 16–20, 25, 35n7, 36, 44, 58, 73, 87, 91, 122, 163, 165–70, 174–5, 259, 291, 364, 379, 637, 640, 646–51, 707, 716, 718, 749, 760, 817–19, 821, 823, 832, 837, 933, 939, 943, 945, 1034–5, 1040–1, 1043, 1045
fertility rate, 52–4, 87, 169, 179, 383, 639–40, 649–50, 756, 934, 936; age-specific, 35n5, 52–3, 170; annual, 53; attempts to influence, 291, 640, 645, 648, 650–1, 752, 761, 1128; decline of, 34, 36 , 218, 361, 364, 637, 639–41, 646–9, 716, 718, 749, 756, 760, 933–4, 1038, 1041, 1128, 1162; highest total, 84, 86; low, 87, 92, 145, 374, 639, 933, 1044; major obstacles to recovering, 752; nation's, 366; period of virtually constant, 935; projections of, **936**, 1097, 1101; and replacement levels, 12, 15, 16, 19, 35–6, 42, 46, 73, 84, 86–7, 89, 94, 169, 174, 821, 823; societal replacement, below, 36, 87; total (TFR) xii, 8, 15, **34**–5, 43, 51–5, 69, 71, 73, **74**, **83–4**, **86**–7, **88**, 145, **156**, 217, 361, 383, 637, 646, 649, 651, 749, 761, 821, **822**, 933–4, **935**, 1034–5, 1038, 1043, 1097, 1101–2, 1118
feudal: domain system, 363; *ie* system, 236; institution, semi- 802; lord, 334, 1050–1; mode of production, 97; social-class system, 801
filial piety, xiii, 146, 148, 320, 337–8, 434, 495, 497
Filipinos, 298–9, 302
financial: market, 835; reserve, 538, 841; resources, 70, 367–8, 380, 582, 838, 1136; support, 180, **282**, 286, 368, 373, 376, 568, 691, 699, 758, 760, 959, 1038, 1044
financing, 853, 1088, 1188
Finland, 89, **93**, **885**–6, **889**
first-born: daughter, 148, 236, 456, **457**; son, 66, 126, 129, 146, 148, 201, 236, 238, 244, 334, 346, 356–7, **457**, 537, 1055
fiscal: autonomy, 285; balance, primary, 857–8; conservatives, 661; crisis, 783; deficit, 853, **854**, **856**; policy, 922; reform, 684; restraint, 667, 782, 794; sustainability, xiii, 639, 647, 854
Fiscal Investment and Loan Program (FILP), 804, 808
folk tradition, 349, 361–3, 364–8, 370, 372–6, 379–83
foreign language teaching, 742; nurse, 772–3; population, 92, 295, **769**, 773; resident, 71, **299**, 442n14, 439, 450, **769**, 773; spouse, 767; student, 295, 307, 555; women, 55; worker, 21, 149, 296, 309–10, 420, 637, 766–7
foreigner, 64, 295–6, **299–1**, 302, **303–6**, 308–9, 311, 320, 417–9, 421–5, 437–8, 440–1, 446, 449–50, 452–3, 653, 765, 767–8, 771, 773–4, 776
"foster grandchild system", 184
France, **34**, 82, **83**, **85–6**, 87, **90**, 94, **163**, 169, 171, 174, 291, 296, **304**, **413**, 551, 653n1, 771, 776, **783**, 855, **885–7**, **889**, 891, **913**, 947, **948**, 1043, 1067, **1106**
Free Health Service System for the Elderly, 1079 etc
*freeter*, 18, 251, 721, 759
full-time: child care, 539, 716, 933; couple working, 933–4, 938; female, 968; homemaker, 1124; housewife, 14–15, 245–6, 248, 265, 539, 933, 964, 1034; mother working, 283, 650; part-timer, 968–9; parents working, 287, 940; seniors working, 582, 986; teachers, 737–8; temporary work, 168; women, 170, 933; women working, 422, 756, 937

gender: context, 255, 267, 271; convergence, 271, 600, 605–5; differences, 256, 265; division, 18, 174–6, 269; equality, 9, 18, 89, 255, 422, 423n20, 468, 542, 648, 684, **692**, 752, 964, 975, 1041–2, 1044; problems in old age related to, 531; policy reform, family and, 1044; ratio, 701; roles, 75, 175, 202, 255, 321, 423, 497, 532, 534–5, 539, 545, 650, 760; specialization, 265, 268, 270; studies, 744
gender-asymmetric work, 271–2
gender-equal family policy, 174
gender-equal society, 250, 420, 545, 717, 1041

generation: contract, 121, 137, 340; curve, 477; future, 730, 817, 842, 8583, 857–8, 1097, 1103–5, 1107, 1115, 1126, 1131; "*monozukuri*", 684; next, 21, 202, 238, 356, 358, 561, 567, 754–60, 1015; older, 130, 182, 184, 187, 196, 231, 484, 487, 502, 569, 571, 601, 603, 605, 900, 906, 1013, 1026, 1030, 1105, 1107; re-engagement of, 181, 188, 193, 197; young, 228, 627, 1102; younger, 122, 145, 149, 179–80, 188, 196, 201, 203, 218, 220, 228–31, 336, 340, 479, 487, 564, 569, 613, 697, 702–3, 841, 872, 974, 1036, 1112, 1126, 1130
generation-cohort typical behaviour, 580
generational: differences, 526, 483, 1103; disengagement, 188; imbalance, 218; inheritance, 235; transition, 491–2, 501, 503, 590
geriatric: care, 296; facilities, 494
Germany, **34**, 44, 82, **83**–4, **85**, 87, 89, **93**–4, 138, 149, **163**, 169, 171, 174, 179, 291, 296, **304**, **306**, **413**, 531, 580, 617–18, 653n1, 769n2, 771, 776, **783**, **836**, 855, 866–7, 874, **885**–6, **889**, 891, **913**, 947, **948**, 963–5, 1023, 1026, 1030, 1043, 1051, 1060, 1068, **1109**, 1128, 1130n11, 1132
gerontocracy, 146, 148
gerontolinguistics, 475
gerontology, 128, 131, 136–7, 577, 615
gini coefficient, 222, **223**–4, **225**–6, **227**, 899, 904, **911**, **913–14**, 921, 975, 1110, **1111**
"give birth and multiply" (*umeyo fuyaseyo*), 108, 636, 639, 641, 645, 647–8, 750
globalization, 166, 294–5, 308, 310, 312, 583, 608, 735, 744, 804–5, 810, 963
Gold Plan, 153, 191, 207–8, 648, 659–61, 664, 1038, **1039**, 1041, 1057–8, 1080, **1081**; New, 1039, 1057, **1081**
government: agency, 691, 698, 1083; central, 153–4, 157, 159, 284–6, 628–9, 685, 756, 782, 869, 871n3, 875, 1078, 1083–4, **1085**–6, 1088, 1121; expenditures, 628, 749, 851, 857; fund, 107, 555, 812, 855; local, 20, 101, 154, 181, 190, 205, 207–9, 281, 284–6, 289–90, 311, 364, 423, 428, 439, 441, 548, 600, 607, 628n9, 660, **710**–12, 716, 727, 755–6, 758, 761, 781, 791, 800, 808–9, 813, 851, 869n2, 1038, 1040, 1052, 1056, 1058, 1060, 1076, 1086, 1088; performance, 712; policy, 21, 36, 170–1, 420, 421, 436, 439, 452, 669, 689, 712, 750, 761, 838, 941, 1041, 1049, 1063; saving, 891, 895; spending, 657, 659; statistics, 100, 104; subsidies, 281, 849–51, **852**, 1088, 1097, 1099–1101, 1117
governmentality, 727–9
governor, 309, 507, 656, 668, 730, 785
grass-roots movement, 589, 656, 681
gravesite, 320, 388, 390, 392, 396
graveyard, 351, 353, 355, 394–5
Great Britain *see* United Kingdom
Great Hanshin earthquake, 154, 182
Great Heisei Era Amalgamation Initiative, 361–3, 366–8, 370, 379, 382
Great Meiji Era Amalgamation Initiative, 363
Great Showa Era Amalgamation Initiative, 364–5, 373–4
greying: of society, 469, 563, 613; of population, 909; of workforce, 982
gross domestic product (GDP), 13, **83**, 284, 285n6, 617, 653n1, 655, 782, **783**–4, **829**, **832**, 836, **837**, 846–7, **848**, 851, **852**–3, **854**, **856**–7, 1017, 1060, 1077, **1090**, 1092, 1103, 1118, 1119n5, 1120; per capita, **83**, 836, **837**, 846–7; potential, **837**
gross regional product (GRP), 863, **864–5**
guardianship: adults, 1065; law, 1067, 1071–6; statutory, 1066, 1070–3, **1074**; 1066, 1069–73, **1074**

handicap, 37n10, 160, 488, 496, 558, 588, **713**, 792, 808, 1022, 1024, 1028 *see also* disability
health: benefits, 614, 714; concerns, 714; expenditures, 1079, **1085**, 1089, 1092, 1094; facilities, 690, 714, 753; profession, 438, 615, 717; shops, 624
health care, 179, 418, 445, 645, 663, 679, 683–4, 1033, 1038, 1040, 1042, 1044–5, 1050–1, 1055–6, 1059, **1081**–2, 1089, 1092, 1118, 1120, 1161; benefits, 422n14, 655; costs, 423, 600, 850, 1056, 1033; delivery system, 1077, 1086; for the elderly, 1056, 1092; free, 645; institutions,

1086; insurance, 678, 683–4, 859, 1086; projection concerning, 616, 850; reforms in, 658, 682–5, 928, 1042, 1056, 1077, **1082**–3, 1088, 1092–3, 1082; health-care service, 423, 655, 1058, 1077, 1086, 1093–4; system, 562, 662, 683, 686, 757, 790, 819, 1049, 1053, 1077–80, **1082**, 1084–9, 1092–3; *see also* public health insurance

Health Care for the Aged Law, 658

Health Facilities for the Elderly (HFE), 1057–8, 1060–1

health insurance, 616, 656, 662, 679, 682–3, 686, 775n3, 841, 843, 845, 850–1, 853, 855, 1038, 1058, 1060n6, 1061–2, 1077–80, **1081–2**, 1083–4, **1085**–6, **1087**–8, **1089**–92, 1094; employer-based, 679, 1078–80, 1083–4, **1085**, 1091; government-managed, 1078, **1081**, 1083; society-managed, 1083; system, 616, 656, 683, 841, 1077–80, 1083, **1085**, **1089**; *see also* public health

Health Insurance Law, 1077–8, **1081**

Health Service Programme for the Elderly, 1080, **1081**–4, **1085**, 1088, 1092

Health and Welfare Bureau for the Elderly, 655, 1040

healthy ageing, 832, 838; elderly, 154, 833, 835; families, 21 (*Sukoyaka Oyako, 21*), 760

'Healthy Japan, 21' (*Kenkō Nihon, 21*), 620

heterogeneity, 256, 272, 306

highway, 394, 782

*hinoeuma* (Fire horse) year, 15n8, 35n8, 646

history, xiv, 181, 183, 185, 195–6, 236–7, 294, 298, 306, 324, 331, 340, 346, 349–50, 361, 370, 374, 383, 493, 503, 567–8, 583, 587, 604, 635, 644, 651, 662, 730, 739, 750, 757, 800, 804, 821, 855, 892, 1013, 1077, 1081, 1120, 1135

HIV, **33**, 90–1, 673

Hokkaido, 61, 64, 73, 75–6, 293, 475, 481, 592, **693**, 782, 806, 862

home care, 202, 207–9, 459, **696**, 704, **1039**; economics, 182, 184, 187, 743; education, 754; group, **696**–7, 1060; helper, 201, 207–10, 212, **483**, 540, 659, **696**; service provision, 704; visit, 187, 696

homes for the aged, 151, **152**, 192, 459, 697, **1039**, 1056; special (SHA), 151, **152**, 183, 186, 189–92, **1039**, 1056–7, 1060

homemaker, 15, 18, 272, 513, **515**, 520, 751, 1124

homogamy, 224, 269

homogeneity, 221–2, 231, 298, 296, 310–11, 625

Hong Kong, **86**–7, **90**, 625n6, 895

Hosei Institute on Aging, 841

hospice care, 690

hospital, 205, 208–9, 283, 445, 459, 502, 504, 562, 606, 686, 1038, 1040, 1049, 1051–8, 1061–2, **1081–2**, 1086, **1087**–8, **1089**, 1092–4

House of Councillors, 667–8, 671–2, **677**–8, 680, 1070

House of Representatives, 667–8, 671–2, **677**–8, 1070

household: couple-only, 218, **220**, 224, 226, **227**–30, 1040; with elderly, 218–20, **223**–4, 226, **228–9**, 1040; by family type, **250**; head, 126, 146, 201, 218, 224, **225**–6, 235–6, 239, 241, 346, 351, 904, **917–19**, 975; income, 203, 222, 279, 282–3, 885, 899–900, **926**, 964, 975, 1097, 1109; liabilities, 891; multigenerational, 230, 615; non-relatives, **249–50**; nuclear, 14, 75, 187–8, 218, 220; one-person, 218, 220, 222, 229, **244**, **249–50**; register, 99, 102, 113; religion, 401–3, **404**; saving rate, 818, 879–81, **882–3**, 884, **885**–90, 892–6; single, 14, 36, 218, 220, 222, 226, **227–9**, **244**, **249–50**, 414, 481, 531, 582, 902–5, 923–4, 1034, 1040; structure, 218–19, 229, 923; three-generation, 14, 179, 218, **220**, 226, 230, 241, 244, 475, 478, 537, 581, 924, 104; type, 73, 218, **220**, **223**, 226, **227**, 229–30, 903, **918–19**, 975; wealth holdings, 879, 888, 891, 893, 895

housing, 63, 67, 70, 76, 167, 171, 189n6, 244, 296, 357, 462, 475, 481, 561, 592, 607, 656, 751, 755, 758, 784, 790, 796, 834, 873–4, 888, 894, 1012, 1060–1, 1071

housewives, 14–15, 203, 242–8, 265, 291, 339, 498, 509, 533, 535, 539,

552, 603, 716, 933, 964, 1034, 1037–8
housework, 14, 239–43, 246, 250, 255–6, 267–71, 277–8, 532–3, 535, 537, 544, 604, 758, 774
human: capital, 270–2, 291, 867, 900, 905, 907, 982; dignity, 429; lifespan, 477, 489; resource, 11, 107, 564, 590, 772, 819, 835, 906, 937, 955–6, 958, 979–83, 985, 987, 989, 991, 993–5, 1144; rights, 159, 307, 310, 421n12, 428–9, 452, 684, 774
Human Rights Protection Bill, 427
husbands, 15n8, 37, 54, 73, 135, 170–1, 203–4, 230, 236–7, 241–2, 244, 246, 248–9, 251, 255–6, 264–5, 268, 272, 277, 329, 356, 393, 457, 494–7, 500, 505–6, 509, 532–3, 535–6, 539–41, 544, 646, 649, 823, 933–4, 938, 1003, 1036, 1117
hyper-aged society, 16, 18
hyper-ageing: 18–20, 37–8

identity, 293–4, 297, 299, 308, 324, 494, 532, 608, 610, 668, 690, 723, 727, 1050, 1052
*ie* system, 9, 236–8, 241–2, 245–6, 248, 323
immigrant, 21, 71, 124, 294–6, 306–7, 312, 423, 475, 489, 770, 775n4 ; illegal, 21
immigration, 64, 94, 123, 165, 295–6, 298, 307, 309, 421–2, 549, 555, 585, 766–7, **769**–70, 823, 833, 862–3; newcomer, 64, 198, 773; policy, xiii, 21, 57, 295, 637, 765, 773–6; rate, 57, 121; large-scale, 67, 295, 862; and restrictive society, 307
Immigration Control and Refugee Recognition Law, 420, 766
income: average, 173, 541, 582, 902, 905, 1060n6, 1111; discrepancy, **229**; disparities, 280, 838, 868, 922; disposable, 222–3, **227–8**, 229, 231, 625, 629, 891, 925, 1133; distribution, 221, 838, 899, 921, 1097–8, 1107; dividend, 893; equality, 222, 900; growth rate of, 879, 888, 893, 895; of household (*see* household income); inequality, 218–26, 230–1, 291, 818, 900–4, 908–9, 921–2, 975, 1110–12; level, 282, 422n15, 908, 925; low- 224, 230, 678, 681–2, 753, 782; median, 228–9, 279; net, 1137, 1135; per-capita, 13, 19, 81, 223, 832, 847, 1121, **1122**; redistribution, 902, 1110, **1111**; "replacement ratio", 1125; security, 20, 820, 910, 1135, 1140–5, 1148, **1149**; survey, 899; and take-home pay, 1117, 1121–7; tax, 686, 858, 1110, 1112, 1120–1, 1131, 1137, 1139; threat to lifelong, 909; transfer, 908, 952, 1110–12, 1115, 1121; *see also* salary, wage system
independence, 114, 155, 161, 209, 213, 255, 267–70, 447–8, 452n105, 534, 539, 542, 580, 615–16, 625, 722, 924, 930–1, 976, 1052
India, 82, **83**–4, **85**, 91, 94, **304–6**, 502
individual right, 432, 743
individuality, 311, 740, 744
individualization, 37, 235, 414, 734
Indonesia, **85**, 94, **304**, **306**, 767, **836**
industry, 8, 13, 87, 98, 105, 149, 159, 238, 240, 374, 540, 594, 608, 614, 624, 681, 735, 772, 774, 862, 867, 873–5, 789, 901, 944, **950**, 952, 988, 1017, 1087, 1129, 1135n1; agricultural, 239, **950**; automobile, 165, 766, 819, 986, 1017, 1030; construction, 782–3, 874, 901, **950**; manufacturing, 67, 159, 166, 240–41, 296, 540, 768, 862, 868, 874, **950**–1, 986, 992, 1017; service, 127, 166, 296, 540, 768, 874, 936; silver (*see* silver market); tourism, 579–81, 583, 588–90, 592–3, 596
industrialization, 3, 7–8, 11, 13, 37–8, 63, 91, 104, 113, 149, 221, 241, 243, 566, 643, 759, 784, 789, 800
inequality: economic, xiv, 122, 221, 818, 899–200, 909; income, 218–26, 230–1, 291, 818, 900–4, 908–9, 921–2, 975, 1110–12; social, 684–5, 734, 963
infant and child mortality, 6–7, 10–12, 29, 109, 238, 1077
infanticide, 7
infertility, 176, 753, 759
information technology, 156–6, 567, 583, 1010
infrastructure, 70, 589, 596, 618, 637, 718, 781–4, 789–92, 796, 864, 869, **870**–3, 894, 1038, 1051
inheritance, 202, 235–6, 238, 246, 450, 509, 801–2, 908, 1131
initiation, 146, 352, 491, 500, 505

innovation, xi, 38, 42, 100, 165–6, 321, 565–6, 605, 795, 907, 1028
institutionalisation, 114, 154, 212, 236, 246, 260, 327, 506, 690–1, 695, 959, 992, 1041, 1056, 1078
intergenerational: activities, 182–3, 185–8; burden, 1036–7; child care, 186; communication, 191; conflicts, 339, 341, 844; contact, 122, 180, 185, 475, 1115; co-residence, 489; equity, 819, 823, 1091, 1105, 1105, 1110, 1116, 1129–30, 1133; income distribution, 1107; income transfer, 908, 1110; inequality, 1104; initiative, 181–2, 186–7; interaction, 182, 181, 186–8, 190–1, 193, 197; interdependence, 189; mobility into upper class, 221–2; programmes, 181–3, 186–7, 192, 196–7; redistribution, 909; relations, xiii, 134, 188, 265, 319; transfer, 858; volunteer, 187
internationalization, 57, 295, 558, 733, 741, 744
Internet users, 513, 315, **519**–20, 523, 525, 528, 602, 1014
intervention, 207, 338, 426, 629, 635, 651, 750, 761, 869, 1148
intra-regional transfer, 871
investment, 13, 19, 45, 166, 168, 176, 553, 590, 593–4, 596, 606, 684, 723n1, 782, **783**–4, 793–5, 801, 804, 808, 813, 835, 846–7, 873–4, 880, 894–5, 900, 982, 995, 1013, 1129, 1140, **1143**, **1147**, 1149
Ireland, **86**–7, **413**, **885**, 887, **889**
iron triangle, 784–5, 799, 803
Italy, 44, 82, **85**, 87, **90**, **93**–4, **163**, 169, 171, 174, 267, 291, **413**, 769n2, 824, **836**, 854, 884, **885**–6, **889**, 891, **913**, 1043–4, 1100, **1109**

Japan: as diverse, 310; as a dominant party democracy, 668; as an equal society, 221; as group-oriented society, 583; Japan, homogeneous, 221–2, 296, 310; household saving rate of, 818, 879–81, **882–3**, 884, **885**–90, 892–6; Japan and hybridization, 310; as a multicultural co-existence society, 308, 773; as multiethnic, 310; as a "network society", 175; as a "new mass middle-class" society, 221; as a symbiotic society, 295
"Japan as No., 1", **829**
Japan Birth Control League, 643
Japan Business Federation (Nippon Keidanren), 295, 426, 755, 771–2, 805, 984, 1126
Japan Federation of Bar Associations, 753, 757
Japan Federation of Employers' Association, 751, 1136
Japan Geriatrics Society, 128
Japan Gerontological Society, 128
Japan Immigration Policy Institute, 295
Japan Intergenerational Unity Association, 187
Japan Medical Association, 662, 1049, 1055, 1087
Japan Nurses Association, 773
Japan Organization for Employment of the Elderly and Persons with Disabilities, 995
Japan Post, 674, 806, 813
Japan Postal Savings Bank, 674
Japan Productivity Center for Socio-Economic Development, 989
Japan Society for Biomedical Gerontology, 128
Japan Socio-Gerontological Society, 128, 131
Japan-U.S. alliance, 678–9
Japanese Institute for Labour Policy and Training, 983
Japanese Psychogeriatric Society, 128
Japanese Society of Gerodontology, 128
Japanese Trade Union Confederation, 1126
*jitsunen* see age of fruition
job: 3K, 298; cafes, 759; market, 208, 251; mobility, 170; rotation, 937, 981, 985–6, 991; skills, 953, 957–8
*jukunen* see age of maturity
*jus sanguinis*, 769
*jus soli*, 769

*Kaigo Hoken* see Long-term Care Insurance System
Kanagawa, 61n1, 63, **66**, **69**, **158**, **158**, **303**, 464, 680, **693**, 769, **789**
*kanreki* (60th birthday), 126, 325, 491, 499, 510, 563
Keidanren *see* Japan Business Federation
kindergarten, **147**, 182, **278–81**, 283–4, 286–7, 289, 603, 607–8, 723, 725, 743, 790

kinship, 320, 456, **457**, 459–60, 469; fictive terms, 459
knowledge transfer, 100, 319, 987
Korea, xi, 81, **86**–7, 89, 92, **93**, 146, 169, 299, **300–1**, **304–6**, 307, 415, 555, 604, 625n6, 766, 768, 769n2, **783**, **836**, 841n1, **885–6**, **889**, 947, **948**, 1043–4
Korean-Japanese, 308, 438
Koreans, 294, 298–9, 302–8, 766
Kumamoto, 186, 240, **693**, 695, 786

labour: costs, 13, 284, 442, 905, 937, 968, 981, 987, 989–90; demand, 866, 901, 960; division of, xiii, 165, 169, 174–6, 268, 271, 697, 699, 938–9; gendered division of, 201, 237, 752; growth rate of, 847; migration, 635, 771; permanent, 771; productivity, 863, 868, 905; requirements, 295; shortage, 91, 246, 296, 545, 637, 751, 772, 867–8, 960, 986, 1035, 1043; skilled, 168, 302, 769 (*see also* worker, skilled); supply, 19, 262, 818, 835, 847, 863, 866–7, 871, 875, 960, 994; unskilled, 302, 420n10, 424, **768** (*see also* worker, unskilled)
Labour Policy Advisory Council, 957
labour force: ageing, 818–19, 823, 902, 963, 979, 982, 994–5; average age of the, 981; female participation in (*see* women in the workforce); participation, 168–9, **247**, 255–6, 264, 277, 684, 818, 833, 835–7, 866, 936, 939, 947–8, 959–60, 976, 993, 1108, **1109**–1110, 1112, 1134; projected elderly participation in, **837**; projection, 419, 847, 849; shrinking in, xiii, 19, 168, 772, 804, 1101; survey, 105, **245**; *see also* workforce
labour market, 66, 159, 167–8, 170, 174, 176, 208, 246, 251, 256, 262, 268, 277, 291, 422n15, 453, 553–5, 661, 776, 818, 865–7, 900, 906, 934, 937–41, 945, 947, 953, 956–7, 963–4, 967, 971–3, 975, 983, 983, 985–6, 994, 1015, 1037, 1043, 1110, 1125; dualism, 174; mobility, 176; reform in the, 168, 653, 934, 939, 993
Labour Standards Law, 426, 438–9, 443, 773
lack of manpower, 25, 149, 594
land registers, 113; squeeze, 190
language: acquisition, 473–4, 482; ageist, 457–8, 467; change, 321, 469, 473–9, 481–2, 489–90; deterioration, 484; discontinuation, 479; shift, 489; teaching, foreign, 472; youth, 474, 479, 484
Laws: Adult Guardianship Law, 1067, 1071–6; Child Welfare Law, 282n2, 283, 290; Child Care and Long-term Care Leave Law, 756; Cities, Towns, and Villages Amalgamation Law, 362, 382; Decentralization Promotion Law, 367; Defined Benefit Corporate Pension Law, 1139; Defined Contribution Pension Law, 1139; Employment Measures Law, 427, 958–9; Equal Employment Opportunity Law (EEOL), 173, 247, 250, 420, 424, 426–7, 444n81, 542, 964; Eugenics Protection Law, 10, 109; Fundamental Law of Education, 726, 730; Health Care for the Aged Law, 658; Health Insurance Law, 1077–8, **1081**; Immigration Control and Refugee Recognition Law, 420, 766; Labour Standards Law, 426, 438–9, 443, 773; Law Concerning the Stabilization of Employment of Older Persons, 420, 953; Law Governing the Population Census, 104–5; Law for the Prevention of Abuse of the Elderly, 423, 1076; Law to Promote Specified Non-profit Activities (NPO Law), 207, 723, 727, 794; Law Promoting Measures for Supporting Nurturing the Next Generation, 21; Law for the Promotion of Lifelong Learning, 727; Law on Promotion of Measures for Human Rights Protection, 428; Long-term Care Insurance Law, 1038, 1040, 1075; Long-term Care Leave Law, 756; Motherhood Protection Law of Japan, 37n10; National Public Service Mutual Aid Association Law, 1078; Next Generation Childrearing Support Measures Law, 755–8; Pharmaceutical Affairs Law, 644; School Education Law, 726; Statistics Law, 105, 110; Welfare Law for the Aged, 192, 149, 655, 1056, **1081**; *see also* Basic Laws

leadership, 108, 175, 452, 564, 658, 664, 669–70, 673, 675, 677, 679, 681, 795
Lee-Carter model, 49, 55
legislation, 417n1, 427–8, 436, 451, 650, 667, 672–5, 682, 685, 715–16, 754–6, 811, 853, 956, 1039, 1068, 1073, 1125, 1139
legislative: council, 1069–70; majority, 685–686; process, 667, 683
legitimacy, 11, 419, 451, 453, 682, 793, 795
liberalization, 10–11, 37, 643–4, 728–9, 732, 734, 740, 772, 805–6, 811, 870, 963, 1034–5
life: course, 12, 14, 17, 47–9, 58, 122, 135, 165, 171, 175, 197, 225, 243, 251, 256, 264–5, 272, 319, 334, 337, 599, 760, 964, 971–2, 975; cycle, 121, 126, 164–5, 167, 235, 251, 255, 319, 581–2, 823, 829, 889, 892, 938; meaning of, 502, 533; satisfaction, 581–2, 615; table, 45, 48–9, 55, 57
life expectancy, xi, 12, 28, 30, 43, 57–8, 82, **90**, 110, 455, 464, 468, 476–7, 481–2, 488, 491, 538, 563, 735, 828, 837, 841, 1077, 1091, 1094, 1101, 1124, 1148; average, 28–32, 76, 455, 531, 537, 582, 1015; at birth, 6–7, 12, 18–19, 27, **29**, 51, **90**, 822, **1090**; countries highest, **90**; countries with lowest, **90**; disability-adjusted (DALE), 29, 321; extension of, 481; female, 28, 69, 76, 823; gains, xiii, 42, 47, 55, 319, 321; healthy, xii, 20; highest in the world, 49, 76, 134, 822; longest, 29, 1077, 1118; lowest in Japan, 77; projection, 28, **51**, 57, 645
lifelong: education, 184, 735; job, 167; learning, 181, 365, 725, 727, 729, 735; marriage, 255; self-education, 332; sport, 618–9, 625, 628; work, 502
lifestyle, 134–5, 157, 171, 241, 248, 250–1, 270, 293, 308, 334, 357–8, 375, 398, 509, **521**, 526, **529–30**, 542, 561–2, 580, 601, 615–17, 619–22, 625–7, 684, 952, 999, 1003, 1082, **1089**, 1094
lifetime employment, 244, 247, 251, 270, 541, 649–50, 819, 980–4, 987, 994–5, 1136
linguistic encoding of age, 456, 469
literacy, 101, 742
livelihood security, 218, 229–30, 964
living: arrangements, xi, xiii, 136, 230–1; conditions, 27, 32, 76n6, 219–20, 223, 224n2, 230, 341, 581; costs, 582, 766, 1079, 1125; expenses, 158, 241, 271, 841, 892, 925, 929; standard, xi, 32, 37, 122, 175, 251, 263, 758, 866, 888, 899, 909, 925n2, 928–9, **951**, 1091
lobbying activities, 669, 715–16, 718, 773, 781, 794–5, 803–6, 810, 813, 1038
local: authorities, 283, 703, 760, 792, 807; community, 136, 146, 149, 308, 541, 594, 709, 727, 742–3; comprehensive care centres, 1061; culture, 20, 361, 372, 375; festival, 594, **709**; government, 20, 101, 154, 181, 190, 205, 207–9, 281, 284–6, 289–90, 311, 364, 423, 428, 439, 441, 548, 600, 607, 628n9, 660, **710**–12, 716, 727, 755–6, 758, 761, 781, 791, 800, 808–9, 813, 851, 869n2, 1038, 1040, 1052, 1056, 1058, 1060, 1076, 1086, 1088; policy, 1088; residents, 289, 372, 380, 710, 727–8, 784, 803, 809; traditions, 362, 365–6
longevity, 18–19, 89, 154, 159, 202, 204, 208, 325–7, 387, 479, 610, 832–3, 909, 1124; age of mass, 134; cultivation of, 493; society of, 134–5, 153, 213
long-term: economic recession, 217, 225; economic statistics, 880; interest rate, 846–7, 851; unemployment, 963
long-term care incidence rate, 850; patients, 686; system, 160, 661
long-term care insurance (LTCI), 160, 653n1, 661, 678–9, 683–4, 686, 819, 841, 845, 850–1, 853, 891, 944, 1038–40, 1044, 1058–62, 1065, 1080, **1081–2**, 1092; expenditures, 1060, 1062; projection of expenditures, 1060; reform of (*Kaigo Hoken*), 662, 678; system, 155–6, 201, 207–8, 678, 1074–5
Long-term Care Insurance Law, 1038, 1040, 1075
long-term trend: family, 266; income inequality, 904; mortality, 6; and wage gaps, 901
lost knowledge, 952

Low Fertility Measures Plus One Programme, 639, 650, 754, 757–8, 1041
low birth society, 277, 749, 755, 766–61
lump sum grant, 172

*machizukuri* (building of community), **692**, 700, 703
macroeconomic: changes, 874, 1097, 1101; factors, 866; impact, 841; indicator, 845; model, 846; perspective, 817; sector, 845, 851; shocks, 1101; "slide", 853
Malaysia, **304**, **836**
Malthusian transition, 8, 10
manifesto, 663, 671, 684
manufacturing industry, 67, 159, 166, 240–41, 296, 540, 552, 768, 862, 868, 874, **950**–1, 986, 992, 1017
marital: behaviour, 257, 262; dissolution, 257, 260–1; fertility, 8, 10, 16, 36–7, 54, 73, 75, 175–6, 754, 756; stability, 260; status, 45, 54, 97, 103, 246, 968, **970**
market: automobile, 1017, 1023, 1030; capital, 853; clothing, 1011; consumer, 196, 584, 819, 999–1000, 010–11; domestic, 19, 84; financial, 835; food, 1011–12; free- 661, 799, 800, 804–5, 809, 812–14, 870, 875; housing, 1012; income, 923, **1111**; media, 564; senior (*see* silver market); therapeutic, 1014; travel, 579–81, 583–4, 593, 602, 1013
marketing, 41, 46, 571, 584, 599, 602, 624–5, 644, 819, 1018, 1022, 1024, 1026–30
marriage: age at, 8, 15–16, 54, 73n4, 109, 171, 246–7, 257, **258**–9, 481–2, 539, 543, 582, 642, 742; arranged, 245, 260, 532; attitudes towards, 543; behaviour, 15, 17, 534, 73, 75, 267, 270; ceremonies, 328; childless, 262; of convenience, 802; among co-workers, 260; delayed, 270, 751–2, 255; downward mobility after, 171; gender asymmetric, 271; homogamous, 269; hypergamous, 269; international, 307; institution of, 450–1; intentions, 263; lifelong, 255; love, 245–6; market, 255, 68–71; patterns, 255; postponement, 8, 10, 16–17, 169–70, 173, 176; process, 259–60; rates, 75, 218, 255, 257, 260, 263, 268, 938; re- 53–4, 262; squeeze, 258; timing, 54, 257, 266
marriage-facilitating effect, 269
marriage-inhibiting effect, 269
married couple, 10–12, 17, 54, 109, 249, 497
mass: communication, 523; culture, 149, 562, 564; higher education, 551; media, 132, 154, 180, 196, 321, 457, 460, 473, 478, 484, 486, 565; society, 540
Materials from Cabinet Meetings on Monthly Economic Reports, 922
maternal, **33**, 109, 174, 212, 753, 755, 757; care provision, 256; employment, 174
maternity leave, 171–2, 174–5, 272, 933, 939, 1044, 1086
meal delivery, 696, 699
Measures to Cope with a Fewer Number of Children Plus One, 639, 650, 754, 757–8, 1041
media, xiii, 35, 121, 129, 132, 154, 180, 194, 196, 202, 212, 295–7, 319, 321, 361, 415, 423, 453, 457, 460, 462–3, 467, 473, 478–9, 484, 486, 489, 504, 513, 526, 528, 530, 565, 627, 658, 721, 765, 773, 873, 957, 969, 981, 990, 1038–9; complementary, 520; environment, 519; market, 564; use, 519, **522**, 526
medical: association, 209, 662, 1040, 1049, 1055, 1087; costs, 600, 618, 624, 657; equipment, 208, 874; examinations, 656, 808; facilities, 498, 656, 1080, 1088; institutions, 607, 690; school, 1050–2; spending, 662; technology, 167, 874
medical care, 136, 538, 606, 636, 653, 656–8, 664, 686, **852**, 1033, 1049–50, 1053, 1055–6, 1062, **1081**, **1087**; for the aged, 136, 538, 606, 656–7; free, 656–8, 664, 1033, 1062, **1081**
Medical Treatment Fee Reimbursement Scheme, 445
Meiji period, xii, 4–6, 25, 64, 76n5, 98, 100–2, 105, 113, 235, 238, 319, 326, 336–7, 350n2, 363, 466, 561–2, 800–1, 804, 806, 1050–2, **1137**
merger, 362, 379, 381, 564, 668, 671, 678, 942
meritocracy, 498, 548, 557

metropolis, 73, 503, 555, 657, 794, 862, 867
metropolitan areas, 75, 184–5, 190, 285, 287, 592, 642, 704, 721, 782, 818, 863, **864**–5, 867–8, 872–3, 875
metropolitan regions, 14, 61, 63–4, 67–8, 71, 464, **790**–1, 794, 862–3, 865, 867–8, 871, 873
*miai*, 245, 260, 532
middle age, 10, 70, 133–4, 137, 209, 226, 236, 319, 333–4, 308, 459, 485, 493, 502, 534, 536, 601, 605, 622, 624–6, 629, 701, 703–4, 901, 905, 907, 955, 957, 969, 974–5, 982, 1012, 1126
migration, xiv, 14, 25, 35n5, 47–51, 57, 64, 66–73, 82, 92–4, 97, 107, 123, 149, 246, 298, 635, 765, 770–6, 818, 873, 875; behaviour, 47–9, 872; across borders, 25; changes in net, **68**; domestic, 818, 861, 875; foreign, 776; migration gains, net, 864; in- 67 (*see also* immigration); internal, 30, 64, **66**–7, 69, 71, 73; international, 47–8, 51, 57, 64, 71, 92; large-scale, 149; migrant-receiving countries, 94; migrant-sending countries, 82; out- 66–7, 70, 77, 94; policy, xiii, 19, 57, 637, 765, 773, 775; and population maintenance, 770–1; rate, 49, 57, 66, 68, 121, 786; replacement, 296, 833; return, 67; undocumented, 92
Ministry of Construction, 751
Ministry of Economy, Trade and Industry (METI), 772, 776, 862–3, **864**, 874, 1126
Ministry of Education, 183, 191, 552n2, 617–8, 627–8, 733, 741, 751–2, 760
Ministry of Education, Culture, Sports, Science, and Technology (MEXT), 283–4, 291, 618, 724–6
Ministry of Finance (MOF), 100, 654, 658–9, 809
Ministry of Health and Welfare (MHW), 107–10, 112–13, 191, 461, 465n1, 467, 617, 642–3, 645, 649, 654–62, 664, 673, 750–1, 903, 1040, 1078
Ministry of Health, Labour and Welfare (MHLW), 170, 172–3, 224n2, 281, **282**, **284**, 286, 289, 465n1, 609, 648, 650, 662–3, 664n6, 730, 749–50, 754–7, 760–1, 772, 776, 785, 845, 847, 849–50, 891, 948, 854–5, 957, 984, 990, 1118, 1124
Ministry for Home Affairs, 745
Ministry of the Interior's Regional Bureau, 241
Ministry of Internal Affairs and Communications, 102, 294, 469, 801, 1121
Ministry of Justice (MOJ), 302, 427, 637, 765–8, 774–6, 1069–70
Ministry of Labour, 465, 750n2, 751, 958
Ministry of Land, Infrastructure and Transport, 784, 834
Ministry of Public Management, 186, 843
Ministry of Public Management, Home Affairs, Posts and Telecommunications, 186
minorities, 303, 309–11, 418–9, 424, 608; "insider", 303, 311; "outsider", 303
mobilization, 661, 723–4, 725–7, 730, 803, 808, 1038, 1040
modernization, 4–7, 11, 25–7, 30–2, 35n7, 38, 98–100, 104, 113, 236, 350m2, 561, 565, 759
mono-ethnic society, 298, 311
moral, 11, 101, 129, 181–2, 246, 297, 320, 332, 352, 425, 434–5, 496, 627, 726, 741, 744, 910, 943, 1042, 1091, 1145; education, 726, 741, 744; guideposts, grandparents as, 181
morbidity, 31, 97
mortality, xi, xiv, 6–7, 11–12, 19, 25, 27, 29–35, 38, 46–9, **50**–2, **53**, 55, **56**–7, 69, 73, 76, 83, 86, 89, 91, 94, 109, 114, 179, 238, 327, 486, 640, 822–3, 849, 1077; changes in, 30, 38, 114, 823; decline, xi, 6–7, 11–12, 19, 25, 27, 29, 31–3, 46, 91, 179, 640, 822–3; and increase in survival rate, 6, 9; of infant and child, 6–7, 10–12, 29, 109, 238, 1077; projection, 49, **50**, 55; rate, 6, 31, 49, 55, 57, 76, 86, 114, 238, 640, 822, 1077; trend, 6n2, 48, 55
mother: non-working, 20, **279**, 283–4, 291; single, 170, 808, 976, 1044; stay-at-home, 750–2, 754
mother working, 20, 123, 173, **279**, 282–3, 287, 291, 508, 649–50, 751–2; full-time, 283, 650; part-time, 284, 287, 649–50; single, 976

motherhood, 37n10, 169–70, 641, 650, 717
mother-in-law, 210, 213, 240, 339, 498
multicultural communities, 303; society, 21, 308
multiculturalism, 294, 297, 308, 312, 773
multi-ethnic society, 21, 289, 306, 310
multigenerational, 186, 193; household, 152, 230, 615, 1028; participation, 186
municipal: amalgamation, 361, 363, 368, 871; assembly representatives, 685; level, 290, 724; treasury, 374
municipality, 63, 69, 71, 105, 155, 159, 185, **202**, 282, **284**–6, 289–90, 362, 364–5, 290, 362–70, 373, 375–6, 382, 387, 593–4, 623, 627–8, 660, 708n6, 711, 713, 715, 753, 755, 760, 861, 868, 869, **870**–5, 940, 944, 1010, 1058, 1061, **1081**, **1085**
Mutual Aid Associations, 1078, 1083, **1085**
Mutual Aid Insurance (MAI), 1098–9

*Narayama bushi-kō* [The Ballad of Narayama], 129, 147, 329, 492, 498 *see also* Obasuteyama
national: burden, 853, **854**, **856–7**, **1081**; census, 357, 537, 541; election, 668, 679; fertility surveys, 256–7, 260, 262–5, 266; government, 149, 154, 156–7, 690, 692, 716, 740, 757–8, 783, 849, **1085**, **1138**; health-care expenditure, 850; health insurance, **147**, 616, 1038, 1078, 1080, 1083–4, **1085**–6, 1088, **1089**, 1092; household survey, 628, 1040; saving, 894–5; security, 20, 765
National Association of Commissioned Postmasters, 802, 808
National Eugenics Law, 109 DOP: Laws
National Federation of Neighbourhood Associations, 715
National Federation of Regional Women's Organisation, 717–18
National Institute of Population and Social Security Research (NIPSSR), 3, 19, 41–2, 50, 58, 71, 84, 108, 112, 129, 217, 383, 645–6, 649, 785–6, 843, 847, 862, 1118, 1128
National Land Sustainability Plan Act, 791
National Movement for Health Promotion, 617
National Opinion Survey on Land Issues, 834
National Organization for Women (NOW), 708, 717
National Pension Insurance (NPI), 964, 968–9, 1098–9, 1102, 1112, **1122**–3
National Pension System (NPS), 336, 654
National Survey on Family Income and Expenditure, 899, **911**–12, 902
National Survey of Individual Viewing Rates, 513, **514–15**
National Treasury Subsidy System, 364
NEET, 18, 251, 721
neighbourhood activities, 182, 185, 291, 354, 361, 536, 562, 606, 608, 702, 708–9, 742; association (NHA), 185, 380, 539, 636, 701, 707–8, **709–11**, 712, **713**–18, 729, 807
neoliberal, 629, 661, 678, 728–9, 870
Netherlands, 44, 61, 101, 174, 769n2, **836**, **885**, 887, **889**, 967
never-married, 8n4, 16, 54, 255, 257–8, **259**, 263
New Angel Plan *see* Angel Plan
New Elderly Society, 507
New Gold Plan *see* Gold Plan
New Public, 726
Next Generation Childrearing Support Measures Law, 755–8
NHA *see* neighbourhood associations
NHK survey, 398, 479, 484–6
*Nikkeijin*, 6, 299, 775
Nippon Keidanren see Japan Business Federation
Non-Governmental Organization (NGO), 10, 207, 309, 636, 681, 687, 707n3, 767, 770, 785, 808
non-marital, cohabitation, 256; non-marital childbearing, 261, 267
non-profit organization (NPO), 20, 160, 186, 192, 207, 282, 309, 589, 592, 363, 689–91, **692–3**, 694–5, **696**–7, **698**–700, **701**–3, **704**–5, 712, 716, 723, 727–30, 792; geographic distribution of, 699–700; and legal incorporation, 697; participation, 697, 702, 704, 792; providing community contact, 697; organizational capacity of, 699; services, 207
NPO Law, 207, 723, 727, 794

non-profit: sector, 689–92, 697; social welfare organization, 282
norms, 172, 423, 729, 1035; age, 150; cultural, 170, 174, 176; family, 235, 238, 1033; gender, 176, 242, 650, 1033; social, 17, 189; traditional, 176, 235, 726
North America, 26, 81, 109, 221, 246, **304**, 584, 603 *see also* USA
North Korea, 300, 766, 768
Norway, **86**, 89, **90**, **413**, **885**–6, **889**, 936
nurse, 207–9, 211–13, 459, 488, 504, 607, 772–3, 1056, 1058–9, **1081**
nursery, 183, 189–90, 192–3, 283, 818, 933–4, 940–2, 945; school, 933–4, 940–2; services, 818, 934, 940–2, 945
nursing: care, 136, 160, 250, 537–8, 607, 1000, 1010, 1053, **1081**; corners at departments, 751; of elderly people, 488, **1081**; home, 151, 183–4, 186, 189–92, 202, 205, 207–9, 211, 459, 497, 685–6, 1010, **1039**, 1056, 1058, 1061–32
nutrition, 7–8, 32, **33**, 76, 82, 571, 617, 753

Obasuteyama, 147–8, 329, 491, 495, 497–9
obstetric service, 562, 760
occupation, 75–6, 104, 127, 129, 159, 167, 201, 209, 221, 271, 358, 503, 513, 520, 604, 643, 653, 726, 766, 771, 803, 905, 935, 949, 954, 956, 958, 976, 994, 1036–7, 1083, 1121, 1135 *see also* job, employment
oil shock, 222, 243, 246, 534, 657, **1081**
Okinawans, 298, 302, 311, 479, 781
old age, 127–8, 130, 493; active, 341; aesthetics of, 506–7, 610; attitudes towards, 129, 196, 324, 329; clubs (*see* elderly, clubs for the); concept of, 126, 146, 153, 160; decay of, 328; eroticism, 491, 500–1; expressions for, 125, 128, 321, 325, 456, 458, 460–2, 466, 468, 487; groups, 181; images of, 160, 323–4; income security, 820, 1135, 1145, 1148, **1149**; late, 568; life in, 134, 616; lifestyles, 135, 526, **527**, 530; negative perception of ageing and, 180; philosophical discourse, 491–2, 506; population, 663; problem of, 129–30, 132, 655; quality of life in, 494, 506; sociology of, 128, 130, 132; value of, 329, 353, 960; veneration of, 320
oldest deaths, average age of, **824**
old-old age, 19, 180, 626, 645
opinion poll, 25, 127, 204, 399, 467, 482, 484, **485–6**, 490, 661, 689, 760, 1039
opportunity cost, 18, 266, 770–1, 291, 649–51, 818, 905, 933, 936–9, 945
Organization for Economic Cooperation and Development (OECD), 45, 221, 223, 547, 552n1, 555n5, 558, 653n1, 769n2, 782, 822, 835, 884, **885**–6, **889**, 891–2, 922, 951, 982, 993, 1043–4, **1090**
OSH (out-of-school hours) care, 277, 290–1
Others, 294, 302, 307–11, 313
outpatient services, 1093
overpopulation, 37, 66, 106, 113, 148
overstay, 302, 768, 773
overtime, 751, 753, 937; attempt to abolish, 173; compulsory, 170; pay, 988; reduced, 754; shorten, 758

parental leave, 20, 291, 1037, 1041, 1044
parenthood, 179, 526, 716–17
parent-child relationship, 148, 540
parents, 14, 18, 35n8, 76, 124, 126, 129, 146, 148, 203–4, 206, 218, 220, 238, **244**–5, 248, **249**, **250**–1, 255–6, 263, 267, 270, 272, **278–80**, 283, 287, 289, 320, 329, 338–9, 341, 346, 356, 372–3, 393–4, 435, 456, 474, 478, 496–7, 508, 538–40, 544, 548, 582, 648, 708, 718, 740, 742, 752–4, 758–60, 768, 908, 940, 1050; clubs and groups, 716, 752; elderly, 129, 204, 339, 341, 538, 1035; low-income, 753; of the next generation, 754, 758–60; potential, 708; working (full-time), 287, 649–50, 753–5, 940; working shorter hours, 650, 754
parent-teacher-association (PTA), 807
parents-in-law, 532, 537
parliamentary committees, 675
participation rates, 75, 256, 277, 614, 617, 621, 623, 625, 627, 629, 684, 698, 702–3, 835–6, 849, 866, 947, 981, 993, 1108, **1109**
part-time: employment, 170, 251, 444, 965–, **967**, 969, **970**, 976; female,

590, 968; job, 127, 538–9, 1007; labourer, 986; mother working, 284, 287, 649–50; pay, gap in part-time and full-time, 967; re-employment, 952; after retirement, 582; teacher, 182; wage, 169, 968; wife, 240; women working, 173, 262, 422, 444, 540, 543, 756, 931; work, 167–70, 174, 966–7, 973, 1041; work and national pension insurance, 968; worker, 18n12, 168–9, 721, 754, 968–9, 980, 984, 995, 1110
part-timer, full-time, 968–9
party: ballot, 671–2, 681; candidates, 681, 810; congress, 670, 676; elites, 636, 669; leadership, 670, 673, 677, 679; members, 659, 669, 670, 673, 679, 681; policy committees, 669, 683; politics, 668, 672, 677
pastime, 126, 321, 567, 599–601, 605–6, 609–10 *see also* cultural activities
paternalistic: family system, 532; values, 814; employers, 937
patriarchy, 9, 146, 169, 236, 252, 1052
patricide, 433, 435, 440, 451
patriotism, 642, 730
PAYG *see* pension, pay-as-you-go system
pension: adjustment indexication, 1101; basic, 843, 848–9, 930, 994, 1037, 1098–1101, 1105, 1116, 1123–4, 1128–9; benefit, 225, 446, 639, 663, 833, **834**, 849, 880, 890–1, 895, 925, 994, 1036–7, 1097–1112, 1115–18, 1120, 1123, 1128, 1131–5, 1142, **1143**–4, 1148–9; and cash-balance (CB) plans, 1141–2, **1143–4**, 1149; closed-period balancing method, 1101; contribution, 851, 968, 971, 1036–7, 1099, **1100**, 1116–7, 1120–1, **1122**–3, 1126, 1139; corporate, 819–20, 1099, 1135–6, **1137**–9, **1140–3**, 1144–9; and defined benefit (DB) plan, 1140–1, **1142–3**, 1145–6; and defined contribution (DC) plan, 1140–1, **1143**, 1145; eligibility, 953; employment-related, 443, 783, 654, 662, **969**; finance, 662, 819, 1029, 1101; fund, 846–7, 1036, 1107, **1147**–8; *goman'en nenkin*, 657; laws concerning pension, 1139; liability, 819, 1047, 1097, 1101–1105, **1106**–7, 1110, 1112, 1119; insurance, national (NPI), 964, 968–9, 1098–9, 1102, 1112, **1122**–3; and net replacement rate, 1101; and notional-defined contribution (NDC), 820, 1105, 1131–2, **1133**; occupational, 1136–7; old-age benefit, 890–1, 1133; pay-as-you-go system, 841–3, 893, 906, 1036, 1104, 1110, 1115–16, 1129n10, 1132–3; policy, 662, 664, 684, 819; programmes, 645, 685, **829**, 841, 848–9, 1097, 1099–1100, 1102, 1104, 1108, 1112, 1115–16, 1119n5, 1121, 1132; projection, 845–7, 850, 1101, 1125, 1128–9, 1134; reform, 658, 662–3, 682–3, 819, 833, 851, 853, 925, 928, 964, 968, 1033, 1036–7, 1042, 1097–1102, **1103**, 1104–5, **1106**–8, 1112, 1116, **1120**, 1123–6, **1127**–8, 1130, 1135, 1144; and reserve fund, 841; spending, 658; status, 848; pension and sustainability, 819, 1097, 1112, 1132; pension system, xiii, 128, 231, 366, 383, 654, 653–4, 683, 772, 819, 893, 906, 908–9, 952, 1036, 1097–1102, 1005, 1110, 1112, 1115–17, 1119, 1122–5, 1128–30, 1132–3, 1135–6, **1137–8**, 1139, 1142, 1144–6; *see also* public pension
Pension Benefit Guarantee Corporation (PBGC), 1144–5
Pension Subcommittee of Social Security Council, 846
periphery: nation's, 123, 361; rural, 786, 871–2
personnel, xiii, 20, 103, 110, 170, 422n16, 441–2, 444, 449–50, 590, 691, 699, 753, 956, 974–5, 986–7, 989, 991, 1026, 1136
Pharmaceutical Affairs Law, 644
pharmaceuticals, 644, 1077, 1086, 1088
Philippines, 84, **85**, 94, **299–301**, **304–5**, 306, 413, 767–8
Plus One Plans, 639, 650, 754, 757–8, 1041
policy: framework, 155, 749–750, 758, 765, 773, 979, 993–4; guidelines, 181, 636; implementation, 269, 721–2; makers, 92, 97, 154, 164, 175–6, 202, 721, 723, 746, 789, 812, 819, 828, 947, 951–3, 957, 960, 1039–41; making, xiv, 23, 176, 430, 635–6, 653, 664–5, 686, 794, 870, 1049, 1088; measures, 18, 109, 717, 972,

909, 928, 933, 960, 1108, 1126, 1130; option, 21, 817, 821, 832–3, 838, 939, 1116, 1128; proposal, 647, 676, 684–5, 715, 774; reform, 681, 964, 1033, 1042–5; responses, 20, 648, 818, 823, 832, 876; visions, 636, 708, 712, 718

Policy Affairs Research Council (PARC), 669, 675

political: actors, xiv, 635–6, 689; agenda, 106, 110, 161, 291, 616, 635–6, 663, 934; corruption, 673, 795, 804; economy, 101, 373, 795, 799, 804, 811; institutions, 430, 667; power, 667, 1050

political parties: Democratic Party of Japan (DPJ), 663, 668, 670, 676, 677–8, 681–2, 685, 757, 795; Japan Communist Party (JCP), 618, 670, 676, 678, 681–2, 685–6, 717n17; Japan Socialist Party (JSP), 654, 659, 661, 678; Kōmeitō Clean Government Party, 680; Liberal Democratic Party (LPD), 448n96, 567, 636, 654, 656–9, 661–4, 667–76, **677**–86, 756, 784, 794–5, 799, 802–4, 810–12; New Conservative Party, **677**; New Green Breeze Party, **677**; New Kōmei Party, 668, 670, 676, **677**–8, 680–2, 684; Social Democratic Party of Japan (SDPJ), 681, 757

politicians, 35, 132, 323, 507, 636, 654, 656, 658–64, 669, 672–4, 678, 680, **710**, 730, 757, 773, 784, 795, 799, 802–4, 808, 810, 812, 857, 1038, 1130

politics, xi, 110, 123, 297, 310, 333–4, 336, 361, 374, 380, 397, 400, 408, 599, 617–8, 626–9, 635, 653, 660, 667–9, 670, 672, 677–9, 681, 684, 687, 728–9, 734, 784–5, 812; partisan, 660, 664, 785

population: active, 71, 164, 617, 1035; age distribution of the, 823, 900; aged, 25, 83, 164, 728, 786, **788**, **889**–90; aged, 65 and over, 41, 52, **65**, 121–2, 129–30, 135, 145, 156, 164, 217–19, **220**, 224–5, 836–7, 580–1, **591**, 923–4, 926, **927**, 1021, 1035n1, 1043–4, 1056, 1060, 1118; aged, 80 or over, 599; aged over, 100 years old, 476, 824; "bonus", 5, 13, 145, **157**; census, 6n1, 8, 25, 27, 50, 61, 98, 100–5, 107, 110, 113, 135, 145, **158**, **245**, 256–7, 357, 365, 387, 537, 541, 843, 786; change, 5, 20, 26, 35n7, 41, 46–7, 52, 64, **65**, **72**, 97, 362, 364, 473, **787**, 823, **1089**; countries with oldest and youngest, **93**; density, 7n3, 61, **62**, 63, 91, 121, 592, 640; dependent, 92, 145, 163–4, 166; development, xi–xiii, 47, 58, 64, 67, 91, 156, 637, 744, 861–2; distribution, 63–4, 71, 73, 590, 789; dynamics, xiii–xiv, 13, 20–1, 27, 43, 47, 97, 113, 858; effort to increase, 109; elderly, 12, **70**, 91, 151, 164, 166–7, 203, 218, 299, 468, 542, 645, 694, 700, 828–9, 850, 951, 1035, 1111; explosion, 26; foreign, 92, 295, **769**, 773; gain, 64, 869; growth, 3, 5–6, 12, 26–7, 44–6, 86, 102, 105, 121, 145, 243, 388, 635, 644; level, 73, 361, 366; median age of, 12, 19, 92, **93**, 482; momentum, 12, 19; non-working, 20, 279, 283, 291, 585, 826; old-age, 663; onus, 145, 156; policy, 107, 109–11; problems, council on, 644, 649, 752; pyramid, **56**, 146, 636; and ratio of graduate students, 551; register, 113; religious, 400; replacement rate, 645, 760; resident, 50, 53, 862; retired, 218, 589, 599, 1121; senior-citizen, 563; school-leaving, 550; shifts, 69, 127, 356, 412; size, 41, 46, 52, 64, 83–4, 364, 592, 639, 863; spatial concentration of, 61; Stable Population Theory, 44; structure, xiii, 49, 91,219, 531, 505, 589–90, 594, 760, 845, 865, 867–8, 872, 900, 923, 1017; studies, xiv, 4, 44, 98, 108, 110–11; total, 14, 41, 44–6, 51–2, 61, 63, 83, 91–2, 219, 387, 400, 406, 563, 700, 728, 768, 770, 786, **789**, 824, 865, 889, 891–2, 923, 1033, 1043, 1077, 1111, 1118; urban, 69, 121, 124, 243; of working age, 52, 164, 239, 600; world, 44–5, 82, **85**, 874; zero growth of, 12, 644

population ageing, xii, xiv, 9, 12, 81, 91, 122, 150, 152, 165, 217, 319, 321, 323, 456, 469, 473, 475–6, 478–9, 319, 321, 323, 456, 469, 473, 475–6, 478–9, 481–2, 484, 489–90, 817, 819, 821, 823, 828, 832–3, 853, 867, 902,

1033–5, 1037, 1039, 1045, 1097–9, 1110, 1112 *see also* ageing population
population decline, 19–20, 26, 35, 41–2, 44, 71, 81, 83–4, 87, 91–2, 105, 123, 127, 156, 160, 291, 3 –2, 367, 370, 383, 387, 395, 563, 593, 596, 635, 730, 765, 770, 776, 786, 823, 825, 833, 858, 862, 863, 865, 868, **870**–4, 895, 1012, 1035, 1043, 1097, 1108, 1112
population projection, xi, xiv, 3, 19, 30, 41–9, **50–1**, 52, **53**, **56**, 58, 70–1, **72**, **85**–6, 163, 259, 383, **388**, 694–5, 781, 785–6, **787–8**, **790**, 827, **830**, 843, **844**–5, 847–50, 854, 861–5, 892, 1097, 1118, 1128; by, 2055, estimated, 41, **50**–2, **53**, **56**, 383; global, 42; national total, **789**; proportion of elderly, **70**; regional, 42, 45, 781, 786, **789**, 861; by the UN, 42, 84, 94, **163**, 770, 785
post office, 800–2, 806–9, 811–14; commissioned, 800, 802
post-Bubble period, 421, 776, 784, 981, 995
post-retirement, 873, 1008, 1015, **1149**; activities, 600, 606, 701, 703; incomes, 600; life, 600; plans, 702; work, 127, 582
post-war: Japan, 222, 644, 736n2, 784, 803, 821, 823, 825, 828; period, 258, 365–6, 368, 370, 373–4, 399, 556n8, 781, 802–3, 879–81, 887–8, 890, 892–5, 934
postal: insurance, 808–9, 811; life insurance, 678; lobby, 803–6, 810; network, 812–13; privatization, 800, 804–6, 809–13; reform, 674, 799–800, 803, 805, 811–12; savings, 799, 801, 808–9, 811; system, 637, 799–813
Postal Workers' Union (*Zentei*), 802–3
poverty, 231, 291, 328, 538, 600, 818, 921, **922**–3, 925–6, 928, 1129; amongst the elderly, 328, 600, 922–3, 925–6, 928, 1129; rate for children, 291, 925
prefecture: governments, 692; with highest migration increase, **66**
prefectural: election districts, 672; level, 670, 725; organization, 363, 717
pregnancy, 17, 109, 172, 260, **261**, 271, 759, 1044, 1086
prejudice, 307, 340, 423, 430, 702
premarital: cohabitation, 255, 260, 266; pregnancy, 17, 260; sex, 15, 17, 266
pre-modern Japan, 5, 25, 324, 329, 492, 564–5
pre-war, 110, 237–8, 298, 408, 562, 642, 879–80, 884, 887–8, 895
Priority Plan for Social Infrastructure Development, 790, 795
private: finance initiatives, 791, 793, 799; sphere, 235, 237, 737
privatization, 149, 285, 357–8, 637, 674, 678, 799–1001, 803–14, 1104; postal, 637, 674, 678, 799
productivity, 32, 159, 164–7, 175, 462, 575, 684–5, 772, 823, 846, 863, 868, 905–6, 952, 989, 991; total factor (TFP), 846
projection: of birth rate, 765, 1128; of the *Cost and Benefits of Social Security*, 850; of consumption tax rate required in, 2055, estimated, **855–6**; demographic, 49, 646, 754, 936, 1035–6, 1124; of elderly dependency ratio, 844; economic and fiscal, 846; fertility, 49–52, 54, 259n1, **935–6**, 1101, 1118, 1128; fertility rate in, 2055, assumed total, **51**; life expectancy, 28, 645; of life expectancy in, 2055, assumed, **51**, 57; health-care per capita, 850; of health-related expenses, 616; of household saving rate, 818, 892–4; of households with eldery, 1040; labour force, 419, 847, 849; labour force participation among elderly, **837**; of LTCI expenditures, 1060; mortality, 49, **50**; national burden ratio in, 2055, estimated, **854**; of payroll tax rate, 849; pension, 845–7, 850, 1101, 1125, 1128–9, 1134; population (*see* population projection); of public pension contributors and beneficiaries, **1100**–1, 1107, 1124, 1139; social security contributions in, 2055, estimated, **852**; of urban spaces, **790**
pro-natalism, 36, 635, 640, 642, 647, 651, 750, 758, 761, 833
prosumer, 156–7
protests, 408, 459, 663, 757, 784
public: administration, xi, 201, 689, 700, 728–9, 792; affairs, 726, 729, 794; assistance, 655, 921, 925–6, **927**–8, **929**–30, 1049, 1062, 1092; child-care, 934, 1044; corporation, 795, 799,

805–6; debt, 781, 784, 842, 845, 851, 853, 857; expenditure, 628, 842, 854; finance, 841; funds, shrinking, 618; hygiene, 32; infrastructure, 789, 864, 869, **870**–1; interest corporations, 690; investment, 782, 784, 794; involvement, 791–2, 794; long-term care insurance, 160, 819, 891, 944; need, 704, 784; nursing care, 537, 1010; opinion, 138, 151, 204, 398, 400–1, 405, 489, 467, 482, 484, 513, 526, 657, 760, 865, 1034, 1039; policy, 154, 164, 175, 425, 440, 663, 818, 832; servants, 801, 803, 812; social security expenditure, 943; social welfare policies, 704; space, 759, 790, 794; sphere, 237, 239, 241, 1044; sport, 618, 628–9; transfers, 829, 841, 976; welfare, 432, 538, 636, 704, 1056; works, 661, 792–4, 799, 879

public health, 7, 82, 91, 98, 102, 108, 110, 154, 617, 676, 690, 819, 1038; facilities, 690; programmes, 1083

public health insurance, 622, 843, 845, 850, 855, 1077–9, **1081**, **1087**–8, **1089**; benefits, 850; deficits, 662; financing of, 1088; history of, **1081**; system, 1077–9, **1089**

public pension, 636, 653, 679, 819, 843–55, 904, 906, 993–4, 1136, 1079, 1097, 1102–4, 1112, 1135–7, 1145, 1148; benefits, 225, 833, **834**, 880, 890, 895, 994, 1097, 1108–9, 1111, 1135; compulsory, 906, 1037; contributors and beneficiaries, **1100**; plan, 685, 833, 841, 1124, 1127; programme, 848, 1097, 1099, 1104, 1112; projection of contributors and beneficiaries, **1100**–1, 1107, 1124, 1139; reform of, **1106**, 1108, 1135; scheme, **831**, 1045, 1098–9, 1102, 1123–4; sustainability of system, 819, 1097, 1112; system, xiii, 383, 893, 906, 909, 1036, 1097–8, 1100–2, 1110, 1112, 1115–17, 1119, 1123, 1128; value of wealth, 833, 1109; *see also* pension

pupils, 547–8, 568, 613, 636, 736–40, 742, 746

quality of life, 166, 180, 494, 506, 580, 615, 796, 838, 894, 1094; in old age, 494, 506

race, 106, 303, 307, 309, 311, 424, 430, 437n64, 640, 771

racism, 110, 309, 415, 427–8

recreation, 167, 583, 590, 596, 609, 616, 624, 663n5, 698, 790, 809, 1013

reform: administrative, 659, 667, 794–5, 804–6, 811–13; agricultural, 9; care for elderly, 945; child care, 1044; of child welfare system, 1041; educational, 554, 558, 733–6, 740–6; family and gender policy, 1044; in health care, 658, 682–5, 928, 1042, 1056, 1077, **1082**–3, 1088, 1092–3, 1082; in labour market, 168, 653, 934, 939, 993; of long-term care insurance, 662, 678; pension, 658, 662–3, 682–3, 819, 833, 851, 853, 925, 928, 964, 968, 1033, 1036–7, 1042, 1097–1102, **1103**, 1104–5, **1106**–8, 1112, 1116, **1120**, 1123–6, **1127**–8, 1130, 1135, 1144; postal, 674, 799–800, 803, 805, 811–12; social security, 231, 716, 855, 858, 1036, 1043, 1079–80; "Trinity", 284–5, 869–71, 875; welfare, 1033, 1041, 1043, **1081**

refugees, 766, 768

regional: development, 69, 357, 781–2, 784, 789, 794–5, 818, 871, 875–6; disparities, 782, 865; economies, 818, 863–4, 868–9, 873–4; finance, deterioration of, 864; municipalities, 364, 367, 370; public bodies, 757; subsidy system, 366; politics, 617

regional differences: in age structure, 73; in ageing, 590; of diseases, 77; in fertility, 3, 25, 69, 77, 353, 355, 590; in health expenditure, 1094; in marriage behaviour, 75; in migration, 67–**68**; in mortality, 7n3; in number of elderly in accommodation facilities, 591; in passing on traditions, 358; in village societies, 353

Regional Support Fund, 364–7, 375, 379

Regional Support Tax, 365–5

reimbursement, 445, 873, 1060, **1082**–3, 1087, 1092–3

religion, 81, 97, 103, 137, 297, 308, 320, 326, 339, 346, 393, 398, **399–400**, 4012, **403–5**, 407–9, **410**, 412, 414–15, 430, 505, 607, 609, 713, 716, 771

religious movements, 415; organization, 400, **402**, 404, **410**, **413**, 607; service, 347; teacher, **400**
repatriation, 37, 643
replacement rates and levels, 5, 12–13, 16–17, 19, 35–36,42, 46, 73, 84, 86–7, 89, 94, 169, 174, 296, 645, 760, 821, 823, 833, 1163
repopulation, 375–6, 589
reproduction, 27, 36, 109, 557, 750, 933
reproductive: choice, 163, 750, 758; behaviour, 53–4, 122
resident: long-term, 766; newcomer, 64n2, 733; old-comer, 766; (special) permanent, 295, 299, 438, 450, 766, **769**–**70**, 774; population, 50, 53, 103, 790, 862
residential: area, 357, 708; care facilities, 207, 209, 210n5; communities, 380; homes, 607; institution, 201; neighbourhood, 606, 708
resources: cultural, 589, 601; financial, 70, 367–8; human, 11, 107, 564, 590, 722, 835, 958, 981, 995; natural, 562, 589, 678
respect for the elderly, 146, 320, 323–4, 332, 341, 463, 492–3, 504
Respect for the Elderly Day, 183, 326, 463–4, 493, 563, 608, 714 *see also* Day of Respect for Old Age
retiree, 149, 158–9, 336, 645, 669, 703, 842–3, 849, 873, 1000, 1008, 1013–14, 1084, **1106**–7, 1115, 1117, 1133–4, 1140, 1149
retirement: abolition of (mandatory), 159, 337, 986; benefits, 843, 849, 988–9, 1136, **1137**, 1139, 1144, 1146; gradual, 959; house, 146; leisurely, 126, 337; mandatory, 159, 420, 442, 444n82, 445, 564, 835, 838, 955, 984, 994; partial, 167; practices, enforced, 130; shock, 127, 337
retirement age: 127, 145, 158–9, 173, 357, 427, 540, 580, 582, 600, 616, 624, 645, 701, 833, 938, 948–50, 952, 954–5, 959–60, 969, 972, 975, 984–7, 994–5, 1108, 1110, 1142; extension of, 159, 833, 835; fixed, 949; government-regulated compulsory, 158; mandatory, 173, 427, 955, 984–7, 995, 1108; retire before official, 948
returnees, 294, 299, 303
revenues, 63, 208, 367, 628, 657, 659, 661–3, 795, 845, 849, 851, 857, 945, 1100–1, 1104, 1121, 1129
rites of passage, 127, 319, 326, 493
rituals, 124, 436–8, 351–2, 354, 369–70, 372, 388–93, 396
rural: areas, 7n3, 14, 66, 69, 76, 123, 148–9, 159, 181, 244, 246, 320, 361, 363, 365–7, 372, 392, 394–5, 476, 479, 548, 589, 654, 671, 674, 676, 684, 704–5, 753, 782–4, 790, 802, 806, 863, **864**, 871–2, 875; depopulation, 63, 123, 149, 364, 387, 392–3, 599; Japan, 73, 130, 361, 387, 393, 786, 814; municipalities, 382, 387, 628; shrinking, 875

Saitama, 61n1, 63, **66**, **69**–70, 158, **186**, 303, 693, **769**, 789
salary, 243, 442, 548, 801, 807, 906, 1054, 1117, 1121, 1136, 1142
salaryman, 243, **245**, 357, 532, 1034
scandal, 497, 588, 659, 663, 673, 795
school: admission and entrance exams, 738; bullying at, 184; class sizes in, 547, 733, 357; classroom at, 188–11, 194, 290, 555n6, 567–8, 603, 721, 724, 733, 742n7; culture festivals at, 183; consolidation, 381; cram, 739; curriculum, 184, 376, 381, 613, 636, 721–2, 724, 737, 741, 753, 775n3; education, 726, 736n6, 743–4; elementary, 182, 190, 293, 388, **515**, 548, 568, 607, 618, 726, 736–7; elite, 737, 1052; and graduation requirements, 721; as "interaction room", 194–5; junior high, 189n6, 190, 293, 547–8, 607, 726, 728–9, 736–9; middle, 388, 515, 548, 568, 618, 736–7; and "Period for integrated Study", 741, 743; phobia, 184; population, 733, 736; primary, 568, 736–8, 740, 743; professional, 552; public, 190n8, 293, 376, 733; public high, 636, 721–2; rules, 737; state, 737–8; senior high, 183, 478, 548, 726, 736, 738–9, 743, 746, 759; system, 547, 726, 734–5, 738, 741, 745, 768, 775n4; vocational, 554, 556, 1051, 1053
school-community partnership, 184
second childhood, 495, 609

sector: agricultural, 127, 166; manufacturing, 166, 874, 986; primary, 13, 357; private, 152, 156, 167, 285, 365–7, 373, 422, 441, 443, 549, 594, 607, 669, 772, 804, 811, 826, 976, 1077, 1083, 1098, 1117; public, 367–8, 373, 549, 686, 823, 826–7, 845, 857, 874, 934, 940, 845, 857, 874, 934, 940, 976, 1053–5, 1083, 1048–9; secondary, 357, 723; tertiary, 87, 379, 542, 723, 727–9, 868; voluntary, 690–1
self-governing bodies, 368, 871
self-government association, 708
senescence, 330, 333
senility, 137, 320, 333, 460, **461**, 492, 494–6, 510
senior citizens, 134, 145, 160, 181, 207, 375, 494, 500, 507, 510, 563, 566–7, 579, 581–2, 590, 592–3, 596, 607, 616, 618–19, 622–3, 636, 694–5, **696**–9, 701–4, 1034, 1036, 1065, 1145; active, 145, 149–50, 152–4, 156–7, 160–1, 181, 213, 323, 325, 334, 340–1, 481, 507, 510, 625, 601, 603, 607, 609, 615, **622**, 625–6, 704, 872, 947, 950; care of, 494 (*see also* elderly care); centres for, 729; energies of, 701; percentage of, 375, 579, 590, 592–3, 596; population of, 563; and voluntary activities, 181–3, 609, 701
senior market, 579–80, 584, 589 *see also* silver market
seniors, 180, 182, 324–7, 332, 361, 366, 462, 487, **488**, 580–9, 601, 621, 623, 625–7, 701, 712, 714–16, 1011; living conditions of, 219, 580–1; younger, 623; very-old, 160
seniority, 146, 250, 320, 458, 460–1, 487, 800, 905–6, 958–9, 991; concept of, 148; and promotion, 19, 532, 987; as opposed to skill-grading system, 988–92; in social organizations, 456; and pay system, 19–20, 146, 250, 244, 247, 442, 819, 899, 901, 905–6, 934, 937, 940, 980–1, 987–95
service: employment, 168; industry, 127, 166, 296, 540, 768, 874, 936; provision, 207, 655, 686, 689, 691–700, 704, 752, 940
sexual behaviour, 17, 266
sexuality, 246, 499–501, 503, 610
*shakai fukushi hōjin* see social welfare institution
Shimane, **66**, **69–70**, 112, **683**, 786
Shinto, 124, 352, 362, 369, 372, **400**–1, **402–3**, 407, 409, **410**, 141, 713, 716, 1050
Shizuoka, 134, 182, **303**, **693**, 769
*shōshika*, 291, 636, 646, 741, 745, 749, 754–5, 758, 1041 *see also* fertility decline
Shōwa period, 98, 106, 363–4, 561–2
silver, 134, 151–3, 189n6, 462, **463**, 509–10, 588, 603, 623–4, 873, 956, 1023; market, 152, 208, 509–10, 571, 579–81, 584, 588–9, 602–3, 624, 1012
Silver Human Resource Centre, 956, 1033
Singapore, 81, **86**–7, 89, **90**, **93**, **304**, 652n6, **836**, 895, 948
single, 175, 581; aristocratic, 270; elderly (*see* elderly, living alone); household, 14, 36, 226, **227–9**, 414, 481, 531, 582, 902–5, 923–4, 1034, 1040; lifestyle, 171; male, 226, **227–9**, 460; mother, 170, 808, 976, 1044; parent household and families, **249**–250, 267, 760, 940; parasite, 18, 270, 582, 758–9; and personal freedom, 263
social: advocacy, 716; age, indicators of, 126; benefits, 801, 881; breakdown, 152; burden, 683; capital, 707, 712, 714–15, 718; change, 37, 122, 128, 136, 149, 294, 308, 408, 473, 478, 487, 605, 649, 741, 804; development, xii, 89, 108, 112; education, 159, 184, 190n8, 195, 618, **692**; exclusion, 237, 963; function, 606, 814, 1049; gerontology, 128, 131, 136, 324; identity, 723, 727; implications, xiii, 121, 180; inclusion, 790, 921, 931; inequality, 684–5, 734, 963; insecurity, 969; institution, 175, 613, 727; isolation, 759, 930; life, 408, 625, 714, 812, 928, **929**–30; mobility, 37, 149, 222; networks, xiii, 136, 308; norms, 15, 17, 146–7, 189, 1035, 1055; order, 146, 150, 678; organization, 121, 164, 174, 456, 701; participation, 129, 135, 181, **696**, 703–4, 726, 744; problems, 197, 202, 251, 744, 750; programme, 664, 805; reality, 43, 745; relations, 294, 424, 458, 615; rights, 749; service facilities, 699; spending, 657–8, 661, 930;

stability, 795, 806; status, 127, 146, 149, 221, 243, 424–6, 430, 444–5, 801, 803; strata, 8, 221, 323, 325, 613; stratification, 149, 218; studies, 726; support, 180, 699, 758, 1038; values, 329; worker, 136, 495, 807
social ageing, xiii, 121, 125, 127–8, 132, 133, 135, 137–8, 153, 397, 735, 819, 999–1000, 1005, **1006**
social class: bourgeois, 561; higher class, 337; lower, 241–2; mass society without, 221; middle, 221, 243, 534, 1058; new mass middle- 221; and status inconsistency, 221; upper-middle, 501; upper, 37, 561
social insurance, 222, 640, 660–1, 663–4, 756, 774–5, 818, 841–2, 845, 851, 855, 886, 943, 945, 965, 969, 976, 1039, 1082, 1088, **1089**, 1124–5; compulsory, 1039; programmes, 639, 647, 775, 842, 851, 976; sector, 845, 851
social security, xi, xiv, 108, 112, 146, 179, 226, 383, 754, 817, 819–20, 842, 844, 853, 858, 921, 935n2, 943, 975–6, 1033, 1035, 1045, 1109, **1111**, 1118, 1129; benefits, 225, 446, 857, 921, 1118, 1135; budget, 749, 943; contributions, 683, 730, **852**–3, **854**, **856**, 1120–1, 1137; costs, 92, 730; expenditures, 943, 945, 1038n2, 1042, 1079, 1112; policy, 197, 225; reform, 716, 858, 1033; spending, 655; system, xiv, 20, 41, 91, 156, 218, 224n2, 225–6, 230–1, 684, 730, 818, 842–4, 858, 923, 1033, 1043, 1078
social service, xiii, 134, **147**, 149, 151, 153–4, 157, 160, 166, 190, 196–7, 213, 151, 689, 691, 696–9, 701, 722–3, 726–8, 730, 790, 806, 808, 1038, 1056–9
social policy, 27, 108, 122, 138, 153, 175, 654, 658, 662, 668, 685, 963–4, 979, 993–4, 1033, 1042–3, 1045
social welfare, 108, 129–31, 133, 151, 153, 155, 165, 183–4, 190n8, 197, 208, 229, 289, 310, 418, 462, 655, 691–2, 696–7, 704, 714n11, 721–2, 760, 772, 782, 808, 819, 823, 873, 930, 1035, 1040, 1043, 1045, 1056, 1058, 1060; activities, 696; corporations, 691–2, 707n3, 753, 940n5, 942; council, 655, 712, **713**, 715–16; foundations, 694; institutions, 289, 690, 694–7, 1033; non-profit organizations, 282, 287, **693**; policy, 704, 749; programme, 799; reforms, 289, 1033; services, 289, 696, 699, 809, 1072; system, 129, 723, 730, 1043
society: aged (*see* aged society); ageing (*see* ageing society); age-segregated, 180; class, 221; equal, 221; gender-equal, 250, 420, 545, 717, 1041; gender-inegalitarian, 268; group-oriented, 583; immigrant, 295; low birth, 277, 749, 755, 766–61; manufacturing, 238; middle-class, 221; multiethnic, 21, 289, 306, 310; new policy agenda for the declining fertility, 291; post-industrial, 87, 627; traditional, 126; transcultural, 293
socio-economic characteristics, 45, 97, 270–1, 580–1, 781, 1043, 1101
sociology: of ageing, 129–33, 136, 604; of dying, 130; of old age, 128, 130, 132; of religion, 346
soldiers, 37, 247, 639, 643, 647
sons, 148, 179n1, 204, **205**, 210, 212, 221, 236, 238–41, 244, 250, 293, 329, 334, 336–9, 341, 346, 349, 352, 354, 356–7, 392, 456, **457**, 495–7, 494, 509, 537–9, 672, 801, 1055
Sōka Gakkai, **402**, 610, 680–1
Soviet Union, 44, 681
Spanish influenza, 105
Special Committee Report on the Desirable Form of the Public Assistance System, 930
sport, meaning of, 629; ideology, 614; population, 621, **622**; training and fitness, 607, 620–4, 1061
spouse, 66, 202–4, 206–7, 209, 229–30, 245, 249, 251, 260, 271, 347n1, 450, 526, **527**, 535, 537, 600, 604, 643, 702, 767, **769–70**, 774, 848–9, 938, 964, 968, 1003, 1008, 1058, 1073; dependent, 848–9, 964, 968; selection criteria, 265, 268–70; tax exepemtion for, 248
state funding, 248, 367, 1036, 1128–9; institutions, 635, 637; policies, 182, 362, 364, 383, 767
Statistical Yearbook, 101, 104
Statistics Bureau, 102–7, 110–1, 827
stereotype, 154, 293, 307, 312, 430, 440, 492, 702
stigmatization, 136, 154, 192n12, 193, 207, 451, 603, 905

stratification, age, 319 ; demographic, 613; social, 149, 218
subsidy, 281, **282**, 284–6, 290–1, 338, 364–70, 375, 379, 540, 628, 684, 711, 753, 759, 789, 849–51, **852**, 855, 871n3, 873 , 741–2, 944, 950, 955, 1044, 1054, 1077, **1081**, 1083, **1085**, 1088, 1097, 1099–1101, 1117, 1123; government, 281, 849–51, **852**, 1088, 1097, 1099–1101, 1117
suburban areas, 64, 68–71, 158, 594, 603, 606–7, 648, 867
suicide, 63, 135, 354, 497–8, 501, 503–4, 506, 508, 655, 632
Sun Goddess, 369
support centres, 192, 290, 462, 689, 725, 752, **1039**, 1041, **1042**, 1075–6; organization, 372, 773, 803
Survey Concerning the Working Situation of Elder People, 949
Survey on the Japanese National Character, 397–8
Survey on the Poor, 241
Survey on Time Use and Leisure Activities, 584, 629
sustainability: of gross domestic product, 854; of health care, 1082; of infrastructural policy, 783, 791, 794, 796; of public pension, 819, 1097, 1112, 1131, 1149; of social insurance, 639, 647; of social security, 218, 1041; of social services, xiii
System of National Accounts (SNA), 881, **882–3**, 884
Sweden, **34**, 44, 89, **90**, 132, 138, **163**, 171, 174, 180, **229**–30, 267, 296, 650, 653n1, 820, 854, **885**–7, **889**, 936, 947, **948**, 1100, 1105, 1128, 1132
Switzerland, 87, 89, **90**, **93**, 296, **413**, **885**–6, **889**

taboo, 15, 246, 310, 468, 498, 562, 635, 651
Taishō period, 98, 105–6, 238, 498, 561
Taiwan, 86–7, 89, **229**–30, 580, 895, 1043–5
tax: exemption, 248, 808, 890, 1048n4, 1139; policies, 262, 663n5, 749; rate, 804, 842, 849, 855, **856**–7, 943, 1100, 1105; rate increase, 804; revenue, 207–8, 366–7, 657, 661, 663, 795, 918, 842, 851, 853, 857–8, 943, 945, 1100, 1104, 1121, 1129; system, 153, 170, 437
taxation, 3, 9, 686, **1111**, 1137
taxpayer, 154, 647, 784, 1129
tax-qualified pension (TQP), 1136, **1137**, **1140**, **1142**
teachers, 101, 243, 501, 548, 721, 734, 736–8, 740n5, 742–4, 746, 759, 979; age of, 548, 738; association of parents and, 807; elderly people as, 324; female, 543, 605; nursery, 193; part-time, 182; progressive, 743–4; religious, **400**; student-teacher-ratio, 636, 733, 737; union, 734; the young as, 195
teaching methods, 744, 746; profession, 548, 737
technology, 47, 159, 165–7, 202–3, 284, 319, 321, 542, 552, 564–7, 571, 583, 703, 767, 792, 874, 901, 1010, 1014, 1018, 1021–2, 1054–5, 1080, **1081**
telecommuting, 754
Ten-Year Strategy on Health and Welfare for the Aged *see* Gold Plans
Thailand, **85**, **304–6**, 768, **836**
three-generational cohabitation, 478; festival, 185; households, 14, 179, 218, **220**, 226, 230, 241, 244, 475, 478, 537, 581, 924, 1040; sports, 185
Three-Year National Children Plan, 184
Tokyo Metropolitan Government, 438, 441n74, 442–3, 446, 449, 721–2
Tokyo Metropolitan Institute for Gerontology, 131
tolerance, 181, 196, 266–7, 1019
total fertility rate (TFR) *see* fertility rate, total
tourism industry, 579–81, 583, 588–90, 592–3, 596
traditional values, 758–60 *see also* filial piety, respect for the eldery
traffic, 70, 91, 702–3, 711, 791, 796, 873
trainee system 420, 773–4
transculturalism, 293–4, 297–8, 308, 312
transformation, xiii–xiv, 9, 13, 18, 42, **56**, 87, 122, 152, 154, 156, 163–169, 218–19, 293–4, 310, 312, 321, 350–2, 383, 613, 671, 817, 823–5, 828, 832, 837
transmission of culture, 473–4, 478; of folk culture, 320, 561–2;

of know-how; of skills, 321, 565; of tradition, 323
transnational, 294, 297, 308, 311–2
"Trinity" reform, 284–5, 869, 871, 875
trust bank, **1142**; investment, 813; non-profit sector, 690
TV viewing time, 513, **514–15**
*Twilight Years, The*, 131, 151, 331, 491, 495, 566

*ubasute* [granny abandonment] *see* Obasuteyama
UK *see* United Kingdom
UN *see* United Nations
*umeyo fuyaseyo* see "give birth and multiply"
underpopulated area, 63, 871
unemployment, 106–7, 113, 148, 168, 270, 809, 813, 867, 900, 963, 994, 1120; rate, **982–3**, 1121n7, **1126**
union, 533, 656, 676, 684, 686; company, 954, 980; labour, **713**, 900, 934, 939, 945, 984, 1107; teachers' 734; trade, 607, 1126; postal workers' 802–3
United Kingdom, 48, **34**, 82, **83**–4, **85**, 87, 94, 132, **163**, 169, 171, **229**, 302, **304–6**, **413**, 550–1, 553–4, 621, 653n1, 771, 776, **783**, **836**, 855, **885**–6, **889**, 891, 900, 909, **913**, 1043, 1068, 1072–3
United Nations, 42, 45, 81, 84, 89, 94, 155, **163**, 295, 607, 770, 785, 836, 881; United Nations Human Rights Commission Report of Japan, 309; United Nations, population projection by the, 42, 84, 94, **163**, 785
United States, 34, **42**, 44–5, 82, **83**–4, **85–6**, **90**, 92, 94, 105, 132, 137, **156**, 158, **163**, 169, 171–2, 179–80, 191, 221, 229–30, 260–1, 263, 267–9, 291, 293, **299–301**, **304–6**, 404n1, **413**, 431, 431n50, 437n64, 580, 664, 678–9, 714, 725, 739, 751, 768, 771, **783**, **836**, **885**–6, **889**, 891, 894, 899–901, 907, 909, **913**, 948, 1017, 1067–8, 1104, 1144 *see also* North America
universal design, 571, 577, 588, 637, 791–2, **793**–4, 1017, 1022–4, 1030
university: admission, 738; admission rate, 636; cohort, shrinking, 549; "examination hell", 738, 740; private, 549–50, 553, 557–8, 740; and standardized entrance examination tests, 783, 739, 744
unmarried: men, 260, 263–6, 543, 742; mother, 261; people, 218, 220, 540; rate, 752; women, 18, 109, 169, 176, 258, 260, 263–6, 272, 277, 543, 742, 938n3
Upper House, 659, 677–8, 803, 810
urban: agglomeration, 64, 69, 73, 75, 867, 873; areas, 7n3, 8, 14, 68, 71, 148, 158, 173, 303, 306, 366, 478, 555, 561, 593, 602–3, 642, 648, 671, 676, 680, 684–5, 699, 753, 768, 811, 862–3, **864**, 934, 941–2; decline, 637, 781; development, 684, 792, 794; renaissance, 937, 791, 794; space, projection of, **790**–1
urbanization, 7–8, 11, 14, 30, 67, 71, 73, 75, 91, 149, 179, 489, 592, 641, 643, 759, 784, 786
USA *see* United States

values: change, 37, 122, 201, 355, 357, 408, 733, 742, 744, 804, 806, 811, 999, 1001; post-material, 166; traditional, 758–60 (*see also* filial piety, respect for the eldery)
violence against elderly, 496, 685
vital: events, 3, 48–9, 51; statistics, 8n4, 50, 256–7, 260
voluntarism, 691, 721–2; and making of state and society, 726
voluntary groups, 708; organizations, 690–1, 698, 701
volunteer, 20, 136, 160, 167, 182–8, 187, 193–6, 381, 567, 700–1, 715, 727–30; activities, 157, 187, 701–2, 704, 716, 728, 741n6, 807; local, 185, 593, 727; middle-aged, 701; mobilization, 724–6, 730; organization, 372, 691, 697, 699, 703; school programme, 183–4, 194; staff, 636, 705; subjectivity, 636, 723, 727, 729
volunteerism, 183, 247, 723–4, 727, 730; as self-improvement, 247

wage: differentials, 18, 901; dumping, 637; gap, 169, 901, 905; minimum, 900; performance-based wage system, 988–93; seniority-based wage system, 19–20, 146, 250, 244, 247, 442, 819, 899, 901, 905–6, 934, 937, 940, 980–1, 987–95

welfare: associations, 712, 716; commissioners, 711; corporate, 614, 965; era, first year of the, 657, 843; function, social, 229, 808, 810; policy, 498, 704, 749, 940; service, 154, 184, 219, 289, 696, 699, 704, 807, 809, 1056, 1072, 1088, 1094; society, 229, 1043; state, 108, 219, 617, 654, 658, 660–1, 664–5, 1079, **1081**; terminology, 462; vehicle, 1023, 1027–8, **1029**–30
Welfare Law for the Aged, 192, 149, 655, 1056, **1081**
Westernization, 243, 323, 1050
wheelchairs, 184, 723, 1010, 1024, **1025**, 1028–30, 1058
White Paper on Ageing Society, 186
White Paper on Economic and Fiscal Policy, 922
White Paper on the Greying of Society, 563, 728n2
White Paper on Health and Welfare, 655, 752, 1041
White Paper on the Low Birth Society, 757
White Paper on Peoples' Life, 938
White Paper on Welfare and Labour, 152–3, 160
WHO *see* World Health Organization
wives, 14, 37, 54, 73, 89, 126, 201, 204, **205**–6, 230, 236, 239–51, 255–6, 262–5, 268, 329, 336, 339, 348–51, 354–7, 457, 459, 495–7, 500, 502, 505, 509, 532–7, 540–1, 756, 803, 823, 933–4, 938, 964, 1003, 1117, 1124
women: associations for, 707, 713, 716–7; economic resources of, 267, 269, 271; equality rights of, 418, 426, 453; groups for, 642, 647, 717, 750, 1038, 1040; independence of, 161, 255, 267–70, 534, 539, 542, 976; liberation movement by, 245–6; negative view of elderly, 495; in old age (*see* elderly women); and single household, **227–9**, 230; social advancement of, 752
women in the workforce, 14, 20, 121–3, 168–70, 172, 174, 176, 239–41, 243, 246–7, 251, 255, 262, 264–5, 277, 283, 287, 290–1, 419–22, 452, 495, 504, 539–40, 543–5, 558, 590, 684, 669, 683–4, 750–1, 773, 934, 936, 938, 940–1, 965–6, **967**–9, **971–3**, 975–8; full-time, 422, 756, 937; increase of, 419–21, 452; part-time, 173, 262, 422, 444, 540, 543, 590, 756, 931, 968
World Health Organization (WHO), 29, 155, 167
work, ability to, 248, 948; work experience, 262, 728; work incentives, 1115; work and mid-career hiring, 170, 988, 1125; work, part-time *see* part-time work; work sharing, 159, 754; work styles, 170, 754–6; *see also* full-time, overtime, part-time
work-family balance, 269–70, 272, 755, 975
work-life balance, 758, 819
workforce, 98, 165, 167, 169, 172, 176, 246–7, 420–1, 562, 635, 669, 683–4, 686, 751, 818–19, 837, 865, 872, 963, 965, 966n2, 969, 971, 976, 979, 982–3, 985, 991, 994, 1126 (*see also* labour force); auxiliary, 176; ageing, 818–19, 823, 963, 979, 982, 994–5; participation rate, 684; shrinking, 635, 872, 982; *see also* women in the workforce
worker, blue-collar, 773, 988, 991–2; elderly people as non-paid, 723; foreign *see* foreign worker; housing supply for, 357; skilled, 159, 565–6, 767, 771 (*see also* labour, skilled); special skills, 774–5; temporary, 18, 168, 170, 173, 754, 756, 939, 967–9; unskilled, 21, 420, 766, 771, 906 (*see also* labour, unskilled)
working conditions, 426, 773, 802n8, 990; generation, 841, 1101, 1111, 1115, 1133; hours, 240, 426, 753, 937, 958, 968n4; population, 121, 127, 145, 156, 163–4, 166, 218, 356, 172, 585, 596, 663, 782, 866, **948**, 1112, 1127, 1136
working-age population, 13, 20, 52, 91, 164, 239, 600, 770, 826, 865–8, 890, 1036
workplace, 173, 242, 250, 424, 442, 474, 485, 536, 539, 541–3, 565, 574, 752, 754, 756–7, 907, 986, 992, 1044, 1052, 1108, 1110; child-care facilities, 1044; family-friendly, 272, 752
world population, 44–5, 82, **85**, 874
World Population Conference, 106
World War, First, 104, 113; Second, 5, 9–10, 44–5, 82, 91, 99, 103, 105,

110, 113, 126, 128, 146, 148, 202, 222, 298, 361, 397, 434, 473, 475–6, 484, 532, 538, 613, 636, 639, 643, 737, 802, 807, 821, 831, 833, 880, 888, 906, 1050, 1053, 1055, 1078, 1136

xenophobia, 308–9, 1023

Yamagata, 354, 383, **388**, 477–8, **693**, 786
Yamaguchi, **69**, 135, 351–2, 623, **693**, 786
Yokohama, 66, 183, 286, 303, **305**, 588, 621, 697, **709–10**, 714, 806, 1024
young people, 7, 14, 17–8, 66, 69, 146, 148, 156, 218, 225, 245, 251, 307, 331, 336, 349, 375, 381, 415, 476, 478–9, 481, 484, 487, **527**, 543, 605, 649, 721, 725, 731, 741, 754–5, 758–9, 862, 875, 901, 922–3, 982, 1002, 1041, 1125, 1128n9
youth, 12, 17–8, 172, 180–2, 187–8, 251, 328, 333–4, 349, 379, 399, 474, 479, 484, 496, 498–500, 541, 551, 564, 614, 617, 621, **709**, **713**, 758, 772, 1015; "cults" of, 323; culture, 193, 1015; language, 474, 479, 484; problems, 733, 736

*Zainichi*, 299, 306, 773
Zero Waiting for Day Care Program, 753